PSYCHOLOGICAL TESTING

Principles, Applications, and Issues

SIXTH EDITION

Robert M. Kaplan
University of California, Los Angeles

Dennis P. Saccuzzo
San Diego State University

THOMSON

WADSWORTH

Australia • Canada • Mexico • Singapore • Spain • United Kingdom • United States

Psychological Testing: Principles, Applications, and Issues, 6e
Robert M. Kaplan & Dennis P. Saccuzzo

Copyright © 2005 Wadsworth
a division of Thomson Learning Inc.
Thomson Learning ™ is a trademark used herein under license.

ISBN: 81-315-0209-0

First Indian Reprint 2007

Printed & Bound in India by
Sanat Printers, Kundli Haryana

Brief Contents

Part I   *Principles*

CHAPTER 1 Introduction 1
CHAPTER 2 Norms and Basic Statistics for Testing 25
CHAPTER 3 Correlation and Regression 62
CHAPTER 4 Reliability 99
CHAPTER 5 Validity 132
CHAPTER 6 Writing and Evaluating Test Items 157
CHAPTER 7 Test Administration 183

Part II   *Applications*

CHAPTER 8 Interviewing Techniques 201
CHAPTER 9 Theories of Intelligence and the Binet Scales 230
CHAPTER 10 The Wechsler Intelligence Scales: WAIS-III, WISC-IV, and WPPSI-III 252
CHAPTER 11 Other Individual Tests of Ability in Education and Special Education 278
CHAPTER 12 Standardized Tests in Education, Civil Service, and the Military 311
CHAPTER 13 Applications in Clinical and Counseling Settings 347
CHAPTER 14 Projective Personality Tests 390
CHAPTER 15 Tests Based on Psychological Science and the New Age of Computers 421
CHAPTER 16 Testing in Counseling Psychology 452
CHAPTER 17 Testing in Health Psychology and Health Care 475
CHAPTER 18 Testing in Industrial and Business Settings 509

Part III   *Issues*

CHAPTER 19 Test Bias 538
CHAPTER 20 Testing in Forensic Settings 573
CHAPTER 21 Ethics and the Future of Psychological Testing 611

Contents

Part I   *Principles*

CHAPTER 1   Introduction   1

Basic Concepts 6
What a Test Is 6
Types of Tests 7

Overview of the Book 10
Principles of Psychological Testing 10
Applications of Psychological Testing 10
Issues of Psychological Testing 11

Historical Perspective 11
Early Antecedents 12
Charles Darwin and Individual Differences 12
Experimental Psychology and Psychophysical Measurement 13
The Evolution of Intelligence and Standardized Achievement Tests 14
Personality Tests: 1920–1940 17
The Emergence of New Approaches to Personality Testing 20
The Period of Rapid Changes in the Status of Testing 20
The Current Environment 22

Summary 23
Web Activity 24

CHAPTER 2   Norms and Basic Statistics for Testing 25

Why We Need Statistics 26
Scales of Measurement 27
Properties of Scales 27
Types of Scales 29
Permissible Operations 31

Frequency Distributions 31
Percentile Ranks 34
Percentiles 38
Describing Distributions 39
Mean 39
Standard Deviation 40
Z Score 42
Standard Normal Deviation 45
McCall's *T* 50
Quartiles and Deciles 51

Norms 53
Age-Related Norms 54
Tracking 54
Criterion-Referenced Tests 59

Summary 60
Web Activity 61

CHAPTER 3 Correlation and Regression 62

The Scatter Diagram 63
Correlation 65
Regression 66
The Regression Line 66
The Best-Fitting Line 68
Testing the Statistical Significance of a Correlation Coefficient 70
How to Interpret a Regression Plot 75

Other Correlation Coefficients 79
Terms and Issues in the Use of Correlation 80
Residual 80
Standard Error of Estimate 82
Coefficient of Determination 82
Coefficient of Alienation 83
Shrinkage 83
Cross Validation 84
The Correlation-Causation Problem 84
Third Variable Explanation 84
Restricted Range 84

Multivariate Analysis (Optional) 86
General Approach 87
An Example Using Multiple Regression 87
Discriminant Analysis 88
Factor Analysis 89

Summary 92
Appendix 3-1: Calculation of a Regression Equation and a Correlation Coefficient 93
Calculation of a Regression Equation (Data from Table 3-5) 94
Calculation of a Correlation Coefficient (Data from Table 3-5) 96

Web Activity 98

CHAPTER 4 Reliability 99

History and Theory of Reliability 100
Conceptualization of Error 100
Spearman's Early Studies 101
Basics of Test Score Theory 101

The Domain Sampling Model 103

Models of Reliability 105

Sources of Error 106

Time Sampling: The Test–Retest Method 107

Item Sampling: Parallel Forms Method 108

Split-Half Method 109

KR_{20} Formula 111

Coefficient Alpha 113

Reliability of a Difference Score 114

Reliability in Behavioral Observation Studies 117

**Connecting Sources of Error with Reliability
   Assessment Method 119**

Using Reliability Information 120

Standard Errors of Measurement and the Rubber Yardstick 120

How Reliable Is Reliable? 123

What to Do About Low Reliability 124

Summary 128

**Appendix 4-1: Using Coefficient Alpha to Estimate Split-Half
   Reliability When the Variances for the Two Halves of the Test
   Are Unequal 129**

Appendix 4-2: The Calculation of Reliability Using KR_{20} 129

Web Activity 131

CHAPTER 5 Validity 132

Defining Validity 134

Aspects of Validity 134

Face Validity 135

Content-Related Evidence for Validity 135

Criterion-Related Evidence for Validity 137

Construct-Related Evidence for Validity 147

Relationship Between Reliability and Validity 154

Summary 155

Web Activity 156

CHAPTER 6 Writing and Evaluating Test Items 157

Item Writing 158

Item Formats 159

Other Possibilities 167

Item Analysis 168

Item Difficulty 168

Discriminability 170

Pictures of Item Characteristics 172
Linking Uncommon Measures 178
Items for Criterion-Referenced Tests 179
Limitations of Item Analysis 180

Summary 181
Web Activity 182

CHAPTER 7 Test Administration 183

The Examiner and the Subject 184
The Relationship Between Examiner and Test Taker 184
The Race of the Tester 185
Language of Test Taker 188
Training of Test Administrators 188
Expectancy Effects 188
Effects of Reinforcing Responses 190
Computer-Assisted Test Administration 193
Subject Variables 195

Behavioral Assessment Methodology 195
Reactivity 196
Drift 197
Expectancies 197
Deception 198
Statistical Control of Rating Errors 199

Summary 199
Web Activity 200

Part II   *Applications*

CHAPTER 8 Interviewing Techniques 201

The Interview as a Test 205
Reciprocal Nature of Interviewing 206
Principles of Effective Interviewing 207
The Proper Attitudes 207
Responses to Avoid 207
Effective Responses 209
Responses to Keep the Interaction Flowing 210
Measuring Understanding 214

Types of Interviews 216
Evaluation Interview 216
Structured Clinical Interviews 217
Case History Interview 221

Mental Status Examination 222
Developing Interviewing Skills 223

Sources of Error in the Interview 224
Interview Validity 224
Interview Reliability 227

Summary 227
Web Activity 229

CHAPTER 9 Theories of Intelligence and the Binet Scales 230

The Problem of Defining Intelligence 231
Binet's Principles of Test Construction 233
Principle 1: Age Differentiation 233
Principle 2: General Mental Ability 234

Spearman's Model of General Mental Ability 234
Implications of General Mental Intelligence (g) 235
The *gf-gc* Theory of Intelligence 236

The Early Binet Scales 236
The 1905 Binet-Simon Scale 236
The 1908 Scale 237

Terman's Stanford-Binet Intelligence Scale 239
The 1916 Stanford-Binet Intelligence Scale 239
The Intelligence Quotient (IQ) 240
The 1937 Scale 241
The 1960 Stanford-Binet Revision and Deviation IQ (SB-LM) 243

The Modern Binet Scale 244
Model for the Fourth and Fifth Editions of the Binet Scale 244
Characteristics of the 1986 Revision 246
Characteristics of the 2003 Fifth Edition 247
Psychometric Properties of the 2003 Fifth Edition 249
Median Validity 250

Summary 250
Web Activity 251

CHAPTER 10 The Wechsler Intelligence Scales: WAIS-III, WISC-IV, and WPPSI-III 252

The Wechsler Intelligence Scales 254
Point and Performance Scale Concepts 254

From the Wechsler-Bellevue Intelligence Scale to the WAIS-III 256
Scales, Subtests, and Indexes of the WAIS-III 256
The Verbal Subtests 258
Raw Scores, Scaled Scores, and the Verbal IQ 261
The Performance Subtests 262

Performance IQs 264
Full-Scale IQs 264
Index Scores 264

Interpretive Features of the Wechsler Tests 265
Verbal-Performance IQ Comparisons 265
Pattern Analysis 266
Hypothetical Case Studies 266

Psychometric Properties of the Wechsler Adult Scale 268
Standardization 268
Reliability 269
Validity 270

Evaluation of the Wechsler Adult Scales 270
**Downward Extensions of the WAIS-III: The WISC-IV and the
    WPPSI-III 270**
The WISC-IV 271
The WPPSI-III 274

Summary 275
Web Activity 277

CHAPTER 11 Other Individual Tests of Ability in Education and Special Education 278

**Alternative Individual Ability Tests Compared with the Binet
    and Wechsler Scales 279**
Alternatives Compared with One Another 281
Specific Individual Ability Tests 283
Infant Scales 283
Major Tests for Young Children 289
General Individual Ability Tests for Handicapped and
    Special Populations 295

Testing Learning Disabilities 299
Visiographic Tests 303
Creativity: Torrance Tests of Creative Thinking (TTCT) 306
Individual Achievement Tests: Wide Range Achievement
    Test–3 (WRAT-3) 307

Legal Issues in Special Education 308
Schools Are Required by Law to Identify Students with Disabilities 308
Enforcing a Child's Right Under IDEA 308

Summary 309
Web Activity 310

CHAPTER 12 Standardized Tests in Education, Civil Service, and the Military 311

Comparison of Group and Individual Ability Tests 313
Advantages of Individual Tests 313
Advantages of Group Tests 314

Overview of Group Tests 315
Characteristics of Group Tests 315
Selecting Group Tests 315
Using Group Tests 316

Group Tests in the Schools: Kindergarten Through 12th Grade 317
Achievement Tests Versus Aptitude Tests 317
Group Achievement Tests 318
Group Tests of Mental Abilities (Intelligence) 320

College Entrance Tests 323
The Scholastic Assessment Test 323
Cooperative School and College Ability Tests 328
The American College Test 328

Graduate and Professional School Entrance Tests 330
Graduate Record Examination Aptitude Test 330
Miller Analogies Test 336
The Law School Admission Test 337

Nonverbal Group Ability Tests 339
Raven Progressive Matrices 339
Goodenough-Harris Drawing Test 342
IPAT Culture Fair Intelligence Test 343
Standardized Tests Used in the U.S. Civil Service System 344
Standardized Tests in the U.S. Military: The Armed Services Vocational
    Aptitude Battery 344

Summary 345
Web Activity 346

CHAPTER 13 Applications in Clinical and Counseling Settings 347

Strategies of Structured Personality-Test Construction 349
Deductive Strategies 350
Empirical Strategies 351
Criteria Used in Selecting Tests for Discussion 352

The Logical-Content Strategy 353
Woodworth Personal Data Sheet 353
Early Multidimensional Logical-Content Scales 354
Mooney Problem Checklist 354
Criticisms of the Logical-Content Approach 354

The Criterion-Group Strategy 355
Minnesota Multiphasic Personality Inventory 355
California Psychological Inventory–Third Edition 366

The Factor Analytic Strategy 367
Guilford's Pioneer Efforts 368

Cattell's Contribution 368
Problems with the Factor Analytic Strategy 371

The Theoretical Strategy 371

Edwards Personal Preference Schedule 372
Personality Research Form and Jackson Personality Inventory 375
Self-Concept 375

Combination Strategies 378

Positive Personality Measurement and the NEO-PI-R 378
The NEO Personality Inventory (NEO-PI-R) 378

Frequently Used Measures of Positive Personality Traits 382

Rosenberg Self-Esteem Scale 382
General Self-Efficacy Scale 382
Ego Resiliency Scale 382
Dispositional Resilience Scale 383
Hope Scale 383
Life Orientation Test–Revised (LOT-R) 383
Satisfaction with Life Scale 384
Positive and Negative Affect Schedule 385
Coping Intervention for Stressful Situations 385
Core Self-Evaluations 385

Future of Positive Personality Research 386
Summary 387
Web Activity 389

CHAPTER 14 Projective Personality Tests 390

The Projective Hypothesis 392
The Rorschach Inkblot Test 393

Historical Antecedents 393
Stimuli, Administration, and Interpretation 395
Psychometric Properties 401

An Alternative Inkblot Test: The Holtzman 409
The Thematic Apperception Test 410

Stimuli, Administration, and Interpretation 411
Psychometric Properties 414

Alternative Apperception Procedures 415
Nonpictorial Projective Procedures 416

Word Association Test 416
Sentence Completion Tasks 417
Figure Drawing Tests 418

Summary 419
Web Activity 420

CHAPTER 15 Tests Based on Psychological Science and the New Age of Computers 421

Cognitive-Behavioral Assessment Procedures 423
The Rationale for Cognitive-Behavioral Assessment 423
Procedures Based on Operant Conditioning 424
Self-Report Techniques 427
Kanfer and Saslow's Functional Approach 431
The Dysfunctional Attitude Scale 432
Irrational Beliefs Test 433
Cognitive Functional Analysis 434

Psychophysiological Procedures 435
Physiological Variables with Treatment Implications 436
Evaluation of Psychophysiological Techniques 436

Computers and Psychological Testing 437
Computer-Assisted Interview 438
Computer-Administered Tests 439
Computer Diagnosis, Scoring, and Reporting of Results 440
Internet Usage for Psychological Testing 442
The Computerization of Cognitive-Behavioral Assessment 443
Tests Possible Only by Computer 444
Computer-Adaptive Testing 445
Psychophysical and Signal-Detection Procedures 446

Summary 449
Web Activity 450

CHAPTER 16 Testing in Counseling Psychology 452

Measuring Interests 453
The Strong Vocational Interest Blank 454
The Strong-Campbell Interest Inventory 455
The Campbell Interest and Skill Survey 457
The Kuder Occupational Interest Survey 462
The Jackson Vocational Interest Survey 466
The Minnesota Vocational Interest Inventory 466
The Career Assessment Inventory 466
The Self-Directed Search 467
Eliminating Gender Bias in Interest Measurement 468
Aptitudes and Interests 469

Measuring Personal Characteristics for Job Placement 469
Trait Factor Approach: Osipow's Vocational Dimensions 469
The Career Maturity Inventory: Super's Development Theory 470
The California Occupational Preference Survey: Roe's Career-Choice Theory 471
Are There Stable Personality Traits? 472

Summary 473
Web Activity 474

CHAPTER 17 Testing in Health Psychology and Health Care 475

Neuropsychological Assessment 476
Clinical Neuropsychology 476
Developmental Neuropsychology 481
Adult Neuropsychology 484
California Verbal Learning Test 490

Anxiety and Stress Assessment 493
Stress and Anxiety 493
The State-Trait Anxiety Inventory 494
Measures of Test Anxiety 495
Measures of Coping 499
Ecological Momentary Assessment 500
Measures of Social Support 501

Quality-of-Life Assessment 502
What Is Health-Related Quality of Life? 503
Common Methods for Measuring Quality of Life 504

Summary 506
Web Activity 507

CHAPTER 18 Testing in Industrial and Business Settings 509

Personnel Psychology—The Selection of Employees 510
Employment Interview 510

Base Rates and Hit Rates 512
Taylor-Russell Tables 516
Utility Theory and Decision Analysis 521
Incremental Validity 523

**Personnel Psychology from the Employee's Perspective:
    Fitting People to Jobs 525**
The Myers-Briggs Type Indicator 525
Tests for Use in Industry: Wonderlic Personnel Test 526

Measuring Characteristics of the Work Setting 527
The Social-Ecology Approach 528
Classifying Environments 529

Job Analysis 531
Measuring the Person–Situation Interaction 533
Summary 537
Web Activity 537

Part III   Issues

CHAPTER 19 Test Bias 538

Why Is Test Bias Controversial? 539
Test Fairness and the Law 540
The Traditional Defense of Testing 544
Content-Related Evidence for Validity 545
Criterion-Related Sources of Bias 548

Other Approaches to Testing Minority Group Members 553
Ignorance Versus Stupidity 553
The Chitling Test 554
The Black Intelligence Test of Cultural Homogeneity 555
The System of Multicultural Pluralistic Assessment 556

Suggestions for Solutions 560
Ethical Concerns and the Definition of Test Bias 560
Thinking Differently: Finding New Interpretations of Data 563
Developing Different Criteria 565

Changing the Social Environment 568
Summary 571
Web Activity 572

CHAPTER 20 Testing in Forensic Settings 573

Laws Governing the Use of Tests 574
Federal Authorities 574
Specific Laws 583

Major Lawsuits That Have Affected Psychological Testing 585
Early Desegregation Cases 585
Stell v. Savannah-Chatham County Board of Education 587
Hobson v. Hansen 587
Diana v. State Board of Education 588
Larry P. v. Wilson Riles 589
Parents in Action on Special Education v. Hannon 591
Crawford et al. v. Honig et al. 595
Marchall v. Georgia 596
Debra P. v. Turlington 596
Regents of the University of California v. Bakke 598
Golden Rule Insurance Company et al. v. Washburn et al. 599
Adarand Constructors, Inc. v. Pena, Secretary of Transportation et al. 600
Affirmative Action in Higher Education 600
Grutter v. Bollinger and Gratz v. Bollinger 601
Personnel Cases 602
Cases Relevant to the Americans with Disabilities Act 607
A Critical Look at Lawsuits 609

Summary 609
Web Activity 610

CHAPTER 21 Ethics and the Future of Psychological Testing 611

Issues Shaping the Field of Testing 612
Professional Issues 612
Moral Issues 617
Social Issues 621

Current Trends 624
The Proliferation of New Tests 624
Higher Standards, Improved Technology, and Increasing Objectivity 625
Greater Public Awareness and Influence 626
The Computerization of Tests 627
Testing on the Internet 627

Future Trends 628
Future Prospects for Testing Are Promising 628
The Proliferation of New and Improved Tests Will Continue 629
Revolutionary Changes: "Perestroika" in School Testing? 630
Controversy, Disagreement, and Change Will Continue 632
The Integration of Cognitive Science and Computer Science Will Lead
    to Several Innovations in Testing 632

Summary 633
Web Activity 633

APPENDIX 1 Areas of a Standard Normal Distribution 634

APPENDIX 2 Publishers of Major Tests 637

APPENDIX 3 Critical Values of r for $\alpha = .05$ and $\alpha = .01$ (Two-Tailed Test) 641

APPENDIX 4 Critical Values of t 642

APPENDIX 5 Code of Fair Testing Practices in Education 644

Glossary 649

References 655

Name Index 724

Subject Index 734

List of Sample Test Profiles

Figure 9-7	Cover page of the Stanford-Binet Intelligence Scale	245
Figure 12-1	Example of a score report for the Stanford Achievement Test	319
Figure 12-2 & Figure 12-3	Sample items from the verbal and mathematical sections of the Scholastic Aptitude Test	325–326
Figure 12-4	A sample student profile from the ACT	329
Figure 12-5	GRE verbal ability sample items	331
Figure 12-6	GRE quantitative ability sample items	332
Figure 12-7	GRE analytical ability sample items	333
Figure 12-9	MAT sample items	336
Figure 13-2	An MMPI profile sheet	356
Figure 13-3	An MMPI-2 profile sheet	362
Figure 13-4	Jackson Personality Inventory profile sheet	376
Figure 13-5	NEO Personality Inventory profile sheet	379
Table 14-1	Summary of Rorschach Scoring	400
Focused Example 14-2	The danger of basing Rorschach interpretations on insufficient evidence	406–407
	Sentence completion tasks	417
Figure 17-4	Profile of a patient tested with the Luria-Nebraska battery	489
Table 17-4	Some of the questions used in the Test Anxiety Questionnaire	497
Figure 18-2	Sample questions from the Wonderlic	527
Figure 19-8	Sample SOMPA profile	559
Table 20-1	Examples of items from a minimum competence test	597
Table 21-1	Performance testing	631

Preface

Psychology is a broad, exciting field. Psychologists work in settings ranging from schools and clinics to biochemical laboratories and private international companies. Despite this diversity, all psychologists have at least two things in common: They all study behavior, and they all depend to some extent on its measurement. This book concerns a particular type of measurement, psychological tests, which measure characteristics that pertain to all aspects of behavior in human beings.

Psychological Testing is the result of a long-standing partnership between the authors. As active participants in the development and use of psychological tests, we became disheartened because far too many undergraduate college students view psychological testing courses as boring and unrelated to their goals or career interests. In contrast, we view psychological testing as an exciting field. It has a solid place in the history of psychology, yet it is constantly in flux because of challenges, new developments, and controversies. A book on testing should encourage, not dampen, a student's interest. Thus, we provide an overview of the many facets of psychological tests and measurement principles in a style that will appeal to the contemporary college student.

To understand the applications and issues in psychological testing, the student must learn some basic principles, which requires some knowledge of introductory statistics. Therefore, some reviewing and a careful reading of Part I will pave the way for an understanding of the applications of tests discussed in Part II. Part III examines the issues now shaping the future of testing. Such issues include test anxiety, test bias, and the interface between testing and the law. The future of applied psychology may depend on the ability of psychologists to face these challenging issues.

Throughout the book, we present a series of focused discussions and focused examples. These sections illustrate the material in the book through examples or provide a more detailed discussion of a particular issue. We also use technical boxes to demonstrate material such as statistical calculations.

Increased Emphasis on Application

Students today often favor informal discussions and personally relevant examples. Consequently, we decided to use models from various fields and to write in an informal style. However, because testing is a serious and complicated field in which major disagreements exist even among scholars and experts, we have treated the controversial aspects of testing with more formal discussion and detailed referencing.

The first edition of *Psychological Testing: Principles, Applications, and Issues* was published in 1982. In the nearly one-quarter century since the text was first introduced, the world has changed in many ways. For example, personal computers were new in 1982. Most students and professors had never heard of e-mail or the Internet. There were many fewer applications of psychological testing than there are today. On the other hand, principles of psychological testing have remained relatively constant. Thus, newer editions have included improvements and refinements in the Principles chapters. The later chapters on Applications and Issues have evolved considerably.

Not only has the field of psychological testing changed, but so have the authors. One of us (RMK) has spent most of his career as a professor in a school of medicine and is now in a school of public health. The other (DPS) completed law school and works as both a psychology professor and an attorney. While maintaining our central identities as psychologists, we have also had the opportunity to explore cutting-edge practice in medicine, public health, education, and law. The sixth edition goes further than any previous edition in spelling out the applications of psychological testing in a wide variety of applied fields.

In developing the sixth edition, we have organized topics around the application areas. Chapter 11 considers psychological testing in education and special education. Chapter 12 looks at the use of standardized tests in education, civil service, and the military. Chapters 13 and 14 consider the use of psychological tests in clinical and counseling settings.

The age of computers has completely revolutionized psychological testing. We deal with some of these issues in the Principles chapters by discussing computer-adaptive testing and item response theory. In Chapter 15, we discuss new applications of psychological science in the computer age. Chapter 16 discusses the use of psychological testing in the field of counseling psychology and focuses primarily on interest inventories. Chapter 17 explores the rapidly developing fields of psychological assessment in health psychology, medicine, and health care. Chapter 18, which is new to the sixth edition, reviews psychological testing in industry and business settings.

The final chapters on issues in psychological testing retain the previous titles but have been extensively updated to reflect new developments in these areas.

The first edition of *Psychological Testing* was produced on typewriters before word processors were commonly used. At the time, few professors or students had access to private computers. The early editions of the book offered instruction for preparing the submission of statistical analysis to mainframe computers. As recently as the production of the third edition, the Internet was largely unused by university students. Today, nearly all students have ready access to the Internet and World Wide Web, and we now commonly provide references to Web sites. Furthermore, we provide greater discussion of computer-administered tests.

Changes in the Sixth Edition

Producing six editions of *Psychological Testing* over nearly a quarter of a century has been challenging and rewarding. We are honored that hundreds of professors have adopted our text and that it is now used in hundreds of colleges and universities all over the world. However, some professors have suggested that we reorganize the book to facilitate their approach to the class. To accommodate the large variety of approaches, we have tried to keep the chapters independent enough for professors to teach them in whatever order they choose. For example, one approach to the course is to go through the book in the sequence that we present.

Professors who wish to emphasize psychometric issues, however, might assign Chapters 1 through 7, followed by Chapters 19 and 20. Then, they might return to certain chapters from the Applications section. On campuses that require a strong statistics course as a prerequisite, Chapters 2 and 3 might be dropped. Professors who emphasize applications might assign Chapters 1 through 5 and then proceed directly to Part II, with some professors assigning only some of its chapters. Though Chapters 9 through 13 are the ones most likely to be used in a basic course, we have found sufficient interest in Chapters 14 through 18 to retain them. Chapters 17 and 18 represent newer areas into which psychological testing is expanding. Finally, Chapters 19 and 20 were written so that they could be assigned either at the end of the course or near the beginning. For example, some professors prefer to assign Chapters 19 and 20 after Chapter 5.

Supplements Beyond Compare

As with the previous editions, a student workbook is available. Professors have access to an instructor's manual and a bank of electronic test items.

Book Companion Web Site

The Web site contains several components that will be invaluable to instructors. First, a data set consisting of 25 examinees' scores on several measures can be downloaded and used with accompanying reliability and validity exercises. Second, several integrative assignments—including a report on a battery of psychological tests, an evaluation of a mock test manual, and a test critique—and associated grading rubrics will be posted on the Web site. The integrative assignment files and grading rubrics are modifiable, allowing you to make changes so they better fit your specific course objectives.

Student Workbook (ISBN 0-534-63308-0)

More than a traditional study guide, the Student Workbook—written by Katherine Nicolai of Rockhurst University—truly helps students understand the connections between abstract measurement concepts and the development, evaluation, selection, and use of psychological tests in the real world. The Student Workbook contains interesting hands-on exercises and assignments, including case studies to critique, test profiles to interpret, and studies on the psychometric properties of tests to evaluate. Of course, the Student Workbook also contains traditional features such as chapter outlines and practice multiple-choice quizzes. Best of all, the workbook is presented in a three-ring binder in which students can keep other course notes and handouts. Students will discover that the Student Workbook will help them organize their study of Kaplan and Saccuzzo's text and excel on course exams, assignments, and projects!

Instructor's Resource Manual/Test Bank (ISBN: 0-534-63307-2)

The Instructor's Resource Manual (IRM) was written by Katherine Nicolai of Rockhurst University, and the Test Bank by Ira Bernstein and Kimberly McConnell of the University of Texas at Arlington

In an easy-to-use three-ring binder, the IRM contains a bevy of resources, including guides on designing your course, the use of psychological tests in the classroom, the use of student test data to teach measurement, suggested use of class time, and demonstrations, activities, and activity-based lectures. The IRM provides a description of integrative assignments found on the book companion Web site and gives the instructors unique mock projectives and much more. The test bank contains more than 750 multiple-choice questions in addition to many "thought" essay questions.

Acknowledgments

We are highly indebted to the many reviewers and professors who provided feedback on the fourth edition or reviewed drafts of the fifth edition. Special thanks go to reviewers of this edition, including: Virginia Allen, Idaho State University; David Bush, Utah State University; Maureen Hannah, Siena College; Ronald McLaughlin, Juniata College; Michael Mills, Loyola Marymount University; Philip Moberg, University of Akron; Jennifer Neemann, University of Baltimore; Karen Obremski Brandon, University of South Florida; Frederick Oswald, Michigan State University; Stefan Schulenberg, University of Mississippi; Chockalingam Viswesvaran, Florida International University; and Mark Wagner, Wagner College.

The six editions of this book have been developed under five different editors at Wadsworth. The earlier editions benefited from the patient and inspired supervision of Todd Lueders, C. Deborah Laughton, Phil Curson, Marianne Taflinger, and Jim Brace-Thompson. We are pleased that the editor for the third edition, Marianne Taflinger, has returned to help us complete the sixth edition. We are most appreciative of her patience, wisdom, and support in the development of the current edition. Although we have had many editors, we have learned from each of them. We also want to thank Paul Wells, production project manager, Vernon Boes for coordinating the cover, Joohee Lee for permissions, and Jennifer Keever, assistant editor for coordinating supplements. We want to give particular thanks to Kate Nicolai for authoring the exciting new Student Workbook and the much expanded Instructor's Resource Manual.

Special thanks go to Wendy Koen and Nancy E. Johnson. Wendy conducted much of the research for the updating of about half the chapters, drafted several new sections, and attended to numerous details. Nancy also assisted in numerous way, including research, editing, and locating difficult-to-find sources. Without these two individuals, publication of this edition would have been much delayed.

Robert M. Kaplan
Dennis P. Saccuzzo
May 2004

About the Authors

Robert M. Kaplan is the chair of the Department of Health Services and Professor of Medicine at UCLA. Previously, he was professor and chair of the Department of Family and Preventive Medicine at the University of California, San Diego. He is also a past president of several organizations, including the American Psychological Association Division of Health Psychology, Section J of the American Association for the Advancement of Science (Pacific), the International Society for Quality of Life Research, and the Society for Behavioral Medicine. Dr. Kaplan is the editor-in-chief of the *Annals of Behavioral Medicine* and an associate or consulting editor for several other academic journals. Selected additional honors include the APA Division of Health Psychology Annual Award for Outstanding Scientific Contribution in 1987, Distinguished Research Lecturer, 1988, and Health Net Distinguished Lecturer in 1991; University of California 125th Anniversary Award for Most Distinguished Alumnus, University of California, Riverside; American Psychological Association Distinguished Lecturer; and the Distinguished Scientific Contribution Award from the American Association of Medical School Psychologists. His public service contributions include various National Institutes of Health (NIH), Agency for Healthcare Research and Quality, and VA grant review groups, as well as service on the local American Lung Association Board of Directors. He served as co-chair of the Behavioral Committee for the NIH Women's Health Initiative and a member of both the National Health, Lung, and Blood Institute (NHLBI) Behavioral Medicine Task Force and the Institute of Medicine National Academy of Sciences Committee on Health and Behavior. In addition, he is the chair of the Cost/Effectiveness Committee for the NHLBI National Emphysema Treatment Trial (NETT). Dr. Kaplan is the author of 14 books and over 390 publications.

Dennis P. Saccuzzo is a professor of psychology at San Diego State University, an adjunct professor of psychiatry at the University of California, San Diego, and an adjunct professor of law at the California Western School of Law. He has been a scholar and practitioner of psychological testing for over 27 years and has numerous peer-reviewed publications and professional presentations in the field. Dr. Saccuzzo's research has been supported by the National Science Foundation, the National Institutes of Mental Health, the National Institutes of Health, the U.S. Department of Education, the Scottish Rite Foundation, and the U.S. armed services. He is also a California licensed psychologist and a California licensed attorney. He is board certified in clinical psychology by the American Board of Professional Psychology (ABPP). In addition, he is a Diplomate of the American Board of Assessment Psychology, American Board of Forensic Medicine, American Board of Forensic Examiners, and American Board of Psychological Specialties (in forensic psychology). He is a fellow of the American Psychological Association, American Psychological Society, and Western Psychological Association for outstanding and unusual contributions to the field of psychology. Dr. Saccuzzo is the author or co-author of over 250 peer-reviewed papers and publications, including eight textbooks.

CHAPTER 1

Introduction

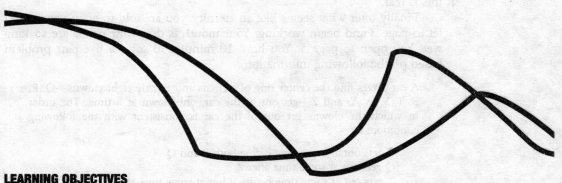

LEARNING OBJECTIVES

When you have completed this chapter, you should be able to:

- Define the basic terms pertaining to psychological and educational tests
- Distinguish between an individual test and a group test
- Define the terms *achievement*, *aptitude*, and *intelligence* and identify a concept that can encompass all three terms
- Distinguish between ability tests and personality tests
- Define the term *structured personality test*
- Explain how structured personality tests differ from projective personality tests
- Explain what a normative or standardization sample is and why such a sample is important
- Identify the major developments in the history of psychological testing
- Explain the relevance of psychological tests in contemporary society

You are sitting at a table. You have just been fingerprinted and have shown a picture ID. You look around and see 40 nervous people. A stern-looking test proctor with a stopwatch passes out booklets. You are warned not to open the booklet until told to do so; you face possible disciplinary action if you disobey. This is not a nightmare or some futuristic fantasy—this is real.

Finally, after what seems like an eternity, you are told to open your booklet to page 3 and begin working. Your mouth is dry; your palms are soaking wet. You open to page 3. You have 10 minutes to solve a five-part problem based on the following information.[1]

A car drives into the center ring of a circus and exactly eight clowns—Q, R, S, T, V, W, Y, and Z—get out of the car, one clown at a time. The order in which the clowns get out of the car is consistent with the following conditions:

V gets out at some time before both Y and Q.
Q gets out at some time after Z.
T gets out at some time before V but at some time after R.
S gets out at some time after V.
R gets out at some time before W.

Question 1. If Q is the fifth clown to get out of the car, then each of the following could be true *except:*

Z is the first clown to get out of the car.
T is the second clown to get out of the car.
V is the third clown to get out of the car.
W is the fourth clown to get out of the car.
Y is the sixth clown to get out of the car.

Not quite sure how to proceed, you look at the next question.

Question 2. If R is the second clown to get out of the car, which of the following must be true?

S gets out of the car at some time before T does.
T gets out of the car at some time before W does.
W gets out of the car at some time before V does.
Y gets out of the car at some time before Q does.
Z gets out of the car at some time before W does.

Your heart beats a little faster and your mind starts to freeze up like an overloaded computer with too little working memory. You glance at your watch and notice that 2 minutes have elapsed and you still don't have your bearings. The person sitting next to you looks a bit faint. Another three rows up someone storms up to the test proctor and complains frantically that he cannot do

---

[1]Used by permission from the Law Schools Admission Test, October 2002. Answer to question one is D, answer to question two is E.

this type of problem. While the proctor struggles to calm this person down, another makes a mad dash for the restroom.

Welcome to the world of competitive, "high stakes," standardized psychological tests in the 21st century. The questions you just faced were actual problems from a past version of the LSAT—the Law School Admission Test. Whether or not a student is admitted into law school in the United States is almost entirely determined by that person's score on the LSAT and undergraduate college grade point average. Thus, one's future can depend to a tremendous extent on a single score from a single test given in a tension-packed morning or afternoon. Similar problems appear on the GRE—the Graduate Record Exam, a test that plays a major role in determining who gets to study at the graduate level in the United States. (Later in this book we shall discuss how to prepare for such tests and what their significance, or predictive validity, is.)

Tests such as the LSAT and GRE are the most difficult modern psychological tests. The scenes we've described are real; some careers do ride on a single test. Perhaps you have already taken the GRE or LSAT. Or perhaps you have not graduated yet but are thinking about applying for an advanced degree or professional program and will soon be facing the GRE, LSAT, or MCAT (Medical College Admission Test). Clearly, it will help you to have a basic understanding of the multitude of psychological tests people are asked to take throughout their lives.

From our birth, tests have a major influence on our lives. When the pediatrician strokes the palms of our hands and the soles of our feet, she is performing a test. When we enter school, tests decide whether we pass or fail classes. Testing may determine if we need special education. There is a movement to have competence tests to determine if students will graduate from high school (Gutloff, 1999; Jacob, 2001; Liu, Spicuzza, & Erickson, 1999; Mehrens, 2000; Shimmel & Langer, 2001). More tests determine which college we may attend. And, of course, when we get into college we face still more tests.

After graduation, those who choose to avoid tests such as the GRE may need to take tests to determine where they will work. In the modern world, a large part of everyone's life and success depends on test results. Indeed, tests even have international significance.

For example, 15-year-old children in 32 nations were given problems such as the following from the Organization for Economic Co-operation and Development (OECD) and the Programme for International Student Assessment (PISA) (Schleicher & Tamassia, 2000):

A result of global warming is that ice of some glaciers is melting.

Twelve years after the ice disappears, tiny plants, called lichen, start to grow on the rocks. Each lichen grows approximately in the shape of a circle.

The relationship between the diameter of the circles and the age of the lichen can be approximated with the formula: $d = 7.0 \times$ the square root of $(t - 12)$ for any t less than or equal to 12, where d represents the diameter of the lichen in millimeters, and t represents the number of years after the ice has disappeared.

FIGURE 1-1

Approximate average scores of 15-year-old students on the PISA mathematical literacy test.

(Statistics used by permission of the OECD and PISA. Figure courtesy of W. J. Koen.)

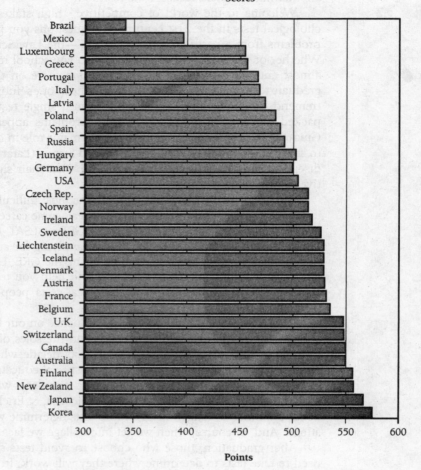

International Mathematical Literacy Scores

Calculate the diameter of the lichen 16 years after the ice disappeared. The complete and correct answer is:

$$d = 7.0 \times \text{the square root of } (16 - 12 \text{ mm})$$
$$d = 7.0 \times \text{the square root of } 4 \text{ mm}$$
$$d = 14 \text{ mm}$$

Eighteen countries ranked above the United States in the percentage of 15-year-olds who had mastered such concepts (see Figure 1-1).

The results were similar for an OECD science literacy test (see Figure 1-2), which had questions such as the following:

A bus is moving along a straight stretch of road. The bus driver, named Ray, has a cup of water resting in a holder on the dashboard. Suddenly Ray has to

FIGURE 1-2

Approximate average scores of 15-year-old students on the PISA scientific literacy test.

(*Statistics used by permission of the OECD and PISA. Figure courtesy of W. J. Koen.*)

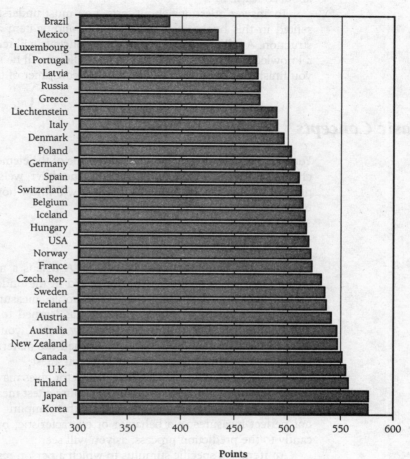

International Scientific Literacy Scores

slam on the brakes. What is most likely to happen to the water in the cup immediately after Ray slams on the brakes?

A. The water will stay horizontal.
B. The water will spill over side 1.
C. The water will spill over side 2.
D. The water will spill but you cannot tell if it will spill over side 1 or side 2.

The correct answer is C.

How useful are tests such as these? Do they measure anything meaningful? How accurate are they? Such questions concern not only every U.S. citizen but also all members of the highly competitive international community. To answer them, you must understand the principles of psychological testing that you are about to learn.

To answer questions about tests, you must understand the concepts presented in this book, such as reliability, validity, item analysis, and test construction. A full understanding of these concepts will require careful study and a knowledge of basic statistics, but your efforts will be richly rewarded. When you finish this book, you will be a better consumer of tests.

Basic Concepts

You are probably already familiar with some of the elementary concepts of psychological testing. For the sake of clarity, however, we shall begin with definitions of the most basic terms so that you will know how they are used in this textbook.

What a Test Is

Everyone has had experience with tests. A **test** is a measurement device or technique used to quantify behavior or aid in the understanding and prediction of behavior. A spelling test, for example, measures how well someone spells or the extent to which someone has learned to spell a specific list of words. At some time during the next few weeks, your instructor will likely want to measure how well you have learned the material in this book. To accomplish this, your instructor may give you a test.

As you well know, the test your instructor gives may not measure your full understanding of the material. This is because a test measures only a sample of behavior, and error is always associated with a sampling process. Test scores are not perfect measures of a behavior or characteristic, but they do add significantly to the prediction process, as you will see.

An **item** is a specific stimulus to which a person responds overtly; this response can be scored or evaluated (for example, classified, graded on a scale, or counted). Because psychological and educational tests are made up of items, the data they produce are explicit and hence subject to scientific inquiry.

In simple terms, items are the specific questions or problems that make up a test. The problems presented at the beginning of this chapter are examples of test items. The overt response would be to fill in or blacken one of the spaces:

A **psychological test** or educational test is a set of items that are designed to measure characteristics of human beings that pertain to behavior. There are many types of behavior. *Overt* behavior is an individual's observable activity. Some psychological tests attempt to measure the extent to which someone might engage in or "emit" a particular overt behavior. Other tests measure how much a person has previously engaged in some overt behavior. Behavior can also be *covert*—that is, it takes place within an individual and cannot be directly observed. For example, your feelings and thoughts are types of covert behavior. Some tests attempt to measure such behavior. Psychological and educational tests thus measure past or current behavior. Some also attempt to predict future behavior, such as success in college or in an advanced degree program.

What does it mean when someone gets 75 items correct on a 100-item test? One thing it means, of course, is that 75% of the items were answered correctly. In many situations, however, knowing the percentage of correct items a person obtained can be misleading. Consider two extreme examples. In one case, out of 100 students who took the exam, 99 had 90% correct or higher, and 1 had 75% correct. In another case, 99 of the 100 students had scores of 25% or lower, while 1 had 75% correct. The meaning of the scores can change dramatically, depending on how a well-defined sample of individuals scores on a test. In the first case, a score of 75% is poor because it is in the bottom of the distribution; in the second case, 75% is actually a top score. To deal with such problems of interpretation, psychologists make use of **scales,** which relate raw scores on test items to some defined theoretical or empirical distribution. Later in the book you will learn about such distributions.

Scores on tests may be related to traits, which are enduring characteristics or tendencies to respond in a certain manner. "Determination," sometimes seen as "stubbornness," is an example of a trait; "shyness" is another. Test scores may also be related to the state, or the specific condition or status, of an individual. A determined individual after many setbacks may, for instance, be in a weakened state and therefore be less inclined than usual to manifest determination. Tests measure many types of behavior.

Types of Tests

Just as there are many types of behavior, so there are many types of tests. Those that can be given to only one person at a time are known as **individual tests** (see Figure 1-3). The examiner or **test administrator** (the person giving the test) gives the test to only one person at a time, the same way that psychotherapists see only one person at a time. A **group test,** by contrast, can be administered to more than one person at a time by a single examiner, such as when an instructor gives everyone in the class a test at the same time.

One can also categorize tests according to the type of behavior they measure. Ability tests contain items that can be scored in terms of speed, accuracy, or both. On an ability test, the faster or the more accurate your responses, the better your scores on a particular characteristic. The more algebra problems you can correctly solve in a given amount of time, the higher you score in ability to solve such problems.

FIGURE 1-3
*An individual test
administration.*
(Ann Chwatsky/
Jeroboam.)

Historically, experts have distinguished among achievement, aptitude, and intelligence as different types of ability. **Achievement** refers to previous learning. A test that measures or evaluates how many words you can spell correctly is called a *spelling achievement test.* **Aptitude,** by contrast, refers to the potential for learning or acquiring a specific skill. A spelling aptitude test measures how many words you might be able to spell given a certain amount of training, education, and experience. Your musical aptitude refers in part to how well you might be able to learn to play a musical instrument given a certain number of lessons. Traditionally distinguished from achievement and aptitude, **intelligence** refers to a person's general potential to solve problems, adapt to changing circumstances, think abstractly, and profit from experience. When we say a person is "smart," we are usually referring to intelligence. When a father scolds his daughter because she has not done as well in school as she can, he most likely believes that she has not used her intelligence (general potential) to achieve (acquire new knowledge).

The distinctions among achievement, aptitude, and intelligence are not always so cut-and-dried because all three are highly interrelated. Attempts to separate prior learning from potential for learning, for example, have not succeeded. In view of the considerable overlap of achievement, aptitude, and intelligence tests, all three concepts are encompassed by the term **human ability.**

There is a clear-cut distinction between ability tests and personality tests. Whereas ability tests are related to capacity or potential, **personality tests** are related to the overt and covert dispositions of the individual—for example, the

FIGURE 1-4
Self-report test items.

	True	False
1. I like heavy metal music.	☐	☐
2. I believe that honesty is the best policy.	☐	☐
3. I am in good health.	☐	☐
4. I am easily fatigued.	☐	☐
5. I sleep well at night.	☐	☐

tendency of a person to show a particular behavior or response in a given situation. Remaining isolated from others, for instance, does not require any special skill or ability, but some people typically prefer or tend to remain thus isolated. Personality tests measure typical behavior.

There are several types of personality tests. In Chapter 13, you will learn about structured, or objective, personality tests. **Structured personality tests** provide a statement, usually of the "self-report" variety, and require the subject to choose between two or more alternative responses such as "True" or "False" (see Figure 1-4).

In contrast to structured personality tests, projective personality tests are unstructured. In a **projective personality test,** either the stimulus (test materials) or the required response—or both—are ambiguous. For example, in the highly controversial Rorschach test, the stimulus is an inkblot. Furthermore, rather than being asked to choose among alternative responses, as in structured personality tests, the individual is asked to provide a spontaneous response. The inkblot is presented to the subject, who is asked, "What might this be?" Projective tests assume that a person's interpretation of an ambiguous stimulus will reflect his or her unique characteristics (see Chapter 14).

See Table 1-1 for a brief overview of ability and personality tests.

Psychological testing refers to all the possible uses, applications, and underlying concepts of psychological and educational tests. The main use of these tests, though, is to evaluate individual differences or variations among individuals. Such tests measure individual differences in ability and personality and

TABLE 1-1
Types of Tests

I. **Ability tests:** Measure skills in terms of speed, accuracy, or both.

   A. **Achievement:** Measures previous learning.

   B. **Aptitude:** Measures potential for acquiring a specific skill.

   C. **Intelligence:** Measures potential to solve problems, adapt to changing circumstances, and profit from experiences.

II. **Personality tests:** Measure typical behavior—traits, temperaments, and dispositions.

   A. **Structured (objective):** Provides a self-report statement to which the person responds "True" or "False," "Yes" or "No."

   B. **Projective:** Provides an ambiguous test stimulus; response requirements are unclear.

assume that the differences shown on the test reflect actual differences among individuals. For instance, individuals who score high on an IQ test are assumed to have a higher degree of intelligence than those who obtain low scores. Thus, the most important purpose of testing is to differentiate among those taking the tests. We shall discuss the idea of individual differences later in this chapter.

Overview of the Book

This book is divided into three parts: *Principles, Applications,* and *Issues*. Together, these parts cover psychological testing from the most basic ideas to the most complex. Basic ideas and events are introduced early and stressed throughout to reinforce what you have just learned. In covering principles, applications, and issues, we intend to provide not only the *who's* of psychological testing but also the *how's* and *why's* of major developments in the field. We also address an important concern of many students—relevance—by examining the diverse uses of tests and the resulting data.

Principles of Psychological Testing

By *principles of psychological testing* we mean the basic concepts and fundamental ideas that underlie all psychological and educational tests. Chapters 2 and 3 present statistical concepts that provide the foundation for understanding tests. Chapters 4 and 5 cover two of the most fundamental concepts in testing: reliability and validity. **Reliability** refers to the accuracy, dependability, consistency, or repeatability of test results. In more technical terms, reliability refers to the degree to which test scores are free of measurement errors. As you will learn, there are many ways a test can be reliable. For example, test results may be reliable over time, which means that when the same test is given twice within any given time interval, the results tend to be the same or highly similar. **Validity** refers to the meaning and usefulness of test results. More specifically, validity refers to the degree to which a certain inference or interpretation based on a test is appropriate. When one asks the question, "What does this psychological test measure?" one is essentially asking "For what inference is this test valid?"

Another principle of psychological testing concerns how a test is created or constructed. In Chapter 6, we present the principles of test construction. The act of giving a test is known as **test administration,** which is the main topic of Chapter 7. Though some tests are easy to administer, others must be administered in a highly specific way. The final chapter of Part I covers the fundamentals of administering a psychological test.

Applications of Psychological Testing

Part II, on applications, provides a detailed analysis of many of the most popular tests and how they are used or applied. It begins with an overview of the essential terms and concepts that relate to the application of tests. Chapter 8 discusses interviewing techniques. An **interview** is a method of gathering information through verbal interaction, such as direct questions. Not only has the interview traditionally served as a major technique of gathering psychological information in general, but also data from interviews provide an important complement to test results.

Chapters 9 and 10 cover individual tests of human ability. In these chapters, you will learn not only about tests but also about the theories of intelligence that underlie them. In Chapter 11, we cover testing in education with an emphasis on special education. In Chapter 12, we present group tests of human ability. Chapter 13 covers structured personality tests, and Chapter 14 covers projective personality tests. In Chapter 15, we discuss the important role of computers in the testing field. We also consider the influence of cognitive psychology, which today is the most prominent of the various schools of thought within psychology (Kellogg, 2003; Leahy & Dowd, 2002; Weinstein & Way, 2003).

These chapters not only provide descriptive information but also delve into the ideas underlying the various tests. Chapter 16 reviews the relatively new area of medical testing for brain damage and health status. It also covers important recent advancements in developmental neuropsychology. Chapter 17 examines interest tests, which measure behavior relevant to such factors as occupational preferences. Finally, Chapter 18 covers tests for industrial and organizational psychology and business.

Issues of Psychological Testing

Many social and theoretical issues, such as the controversial topic of racial differences in ability, accompany testing. Part III covers many of these issues. As a compromise between breadth and depth of coverage, we focus on a comprehensive discussion of those issues that have particular importance in the current professional, social, and political environment.

Chapter 19 examines test bias, one of the most volatile issues in the field today (Fox, 1999; Geisinger, 2003; Reynolds & Ramsay, 2003 Ryan & DeMark, 2002). Because psychological tests have been accused of being discriminatory or biased against certain groups, this chapter takes a careful look at both sides of the argument. Because of charges of bias and other problems, psychological testing is increasingly coming under the scrutiny of the law (Phillips, 2002; Saccuzzo, 1999). Chapter 20 examines test bias as related to legal issues and discusses testing in forensic settings. Chapter 21 presents a general overview of other major issues currently shaping the future of psychological testing in the United States with an emphasis on ethics. From our review of the issues, we also speculate on what the future holds for psychological testing.

Historical Perspective

We shall now briefly provide the historical context of psychological testing. This discussion will touch on some of the material presented earlier in this chapter.

Early Antecedents

Most of the major developments in testing have occurred over the last century, many of them in the United States. The origins of testing, however, are neither recent nor American. Evidence suggests that the Chinese had a relatively sophisticated civil service testing program more than 4000 years ago (DuBois, 1970, 1972). Every third year in China, oral examinations were given to help determine work evaluations and promotion decisions.

By the Han Dynasty (206 B.C.E. to 220 C.E.), the use of **test batteries** (two or more tests used in conjunction) was quite common. These early tests related to such diverse topics as civil law, military affairs, agriculture, revenue, and geography. Tests had become quite well developed by the Ming Dynasty (1368–1644 C.E.). During this period, a national multistage testing program involved local and regional testing centers equipped with special testing booths. Those who did well on the tests at the local level went on to provincial capitals for more extensive essay examinations. After this second testing, those with the highest test scores went on to the nation's capital for a final round. Only those who passed this third set of tests were eligible for public office.

The Western world most likely learned about testing programs through the Chinese. Reports by British missionaries and diplomats encouraged the English East India Company in 1832 to copy the Chinese system as a method of selecting employees for overseas duty. Because testing programs worked well for the company, the British government adopted a similar system of testing for its civil service in 1855. After the British endorsement of a civil service testing system, the French and German governments followed suit. In 1883, the U.S. government established the American Civil Service Commission, which developed and administered competitive examinations for certain government jobs. The impetus of the testing movement in the Western world grew rapidly at that time (Wiggins, 1973).

Charles Darwin and Individual Differences

Perhaps the most basic concept underlying psychological and educational testing pertains to individual differences. No two snowflakes are identical, no two fingerprints the same. Similarly, no two people are exactly alike in ability and typical behavior. As we have noted, tests are specifically designed to measure these individual differences in ability and personality among people.

Although human beings realized long ago that individuals differ, developing tools for measuring such differences was no easy matter. To develop a measuring device, we must understand what we want to measure. An important step toward understanding individual differences came with the publication of Charles Darwin's highly influential book, *The Origin of Species,* in 1859. According to Darwin's theory, higher forms of life evolved partially because of differences among individual forms of life within a species. Given that individual members of a species differ, some possess characteristics that are more adaptive or successful in a given environment than are those of other members. Dar-

FIGURE 1-5
*Sir Francis
Galton.*
(*From the National
Library of Medicine.*)

win also believed that those with the best or most adaptive characteristics survive at the expense of those who are less fit and that the survivors pass their characteristics on to the next generation. Through this process, he argued, life has evolved to its currently complex and intelligent levels.

Sir Francis Galton, a relative of Darwin's, soon began applying Darwin's theories to the study of human beings (see Figure 1-5). Given the concepts of survival of the fittest and individual differences, Galton set out to show that some people possessed characteristics that made them more fit than others, a theory he articulated in his book *Hereditary Genius,* published in 1869. Galton (1883) subsequently began a series of experimental studies to document the validity of his position. He concentrated on demonstrating that individual differences exist in human sensory and motor functioning, such as reaction time, visual acuity, and physical strength. In doing so, Galton initiated a search for knowledge concerning human individual differences, which is now one of the most important domains of scientific psychology.

Galton's work was extended by the U.S. psychologist James McKeen Cattell, who coined the term *mental test* (Cattell, 1890). Cattell's doctoral dissertation was based on Galton's work on individual differences in reaction time. As such, Cattell perpetuated and stimulated the forces that ultimately led to the development of modern tests.

Experimental Psychology and Psychophysical Measurement

A second major foundation of testing can be found in experimental psychology and early attempts to unlock the mysteries of human consciousness through the scientific method. Before psychology was practiced as a science, mathematical models of the mind were developed, in particular those of J. E. Herbart. Herbart eventually used these models as the basis for educational theories that strongly influenced 19th-century educational practices. Following Herbart, E. H. Weber attempted to demonstrate the existence of a psychological threshold, the minimum stimulus necessary to activate a sensory system. Then, following Weber, G. T. Fechner devised the law that the strength of a sensation grows as the logarithm of the stimulus intensity.

Wilhelm Wundt, who set up a laboratory at the University of Leipzig in 1879, is credited with founding the science of psychology, following in the tradition of Weber and Fechner (Hearst, 1979). Wundt was succeeded by E. B. Titchner, whose student, G. Whipple, recruited L. L. Thurstone. Whipple provided the basis for immense changes in the field of testing by conducting a seminar at the Carnegie Institute in 1919 attended by Thurstone, E. Strong, and other early prominent U.S. psychologists. From this seminar came the Carnegie Interest Inventory and later the Strong Vocational Interest Blank. Later in this book we discuss in greater detail the work of these pioneers and the tests they helped to develop.

Thus, psychological testing developed from at least two lines of inquiry: one based on the work of Darwin, Galton, and Cattell on the measurement of individual differences, and the other (more theoretically relevant and probably stronger) based on the work of the German psychophysicists Herbart, Weber, Fechner, and Wundt. Experimental psychology developed from the latter. From this work also came the idea that testing, like an experiment, requires rigorous experimental control. Such control, as you will see, comes from administering tests under highly standardized conditions.

The efforts of these researchers, however necessary, did not by themselves lead to the creation of modern psychological tests. Such tests also arose in response to important needs such as classifying and identifying the mentally and emotionally handicapped. One of the earliest tests resembling current procedures, the Seguin Form Board Test (Seguin, 1866/1907), was developed in an effort to educate and evaluate the mentally disabled. Similarly, Kraepelin (1912) devised a series of examinations for evaluating emotionally impaired people.

An important breakthrough in the creation of modern tests came at the turn of the 20th century. The French minister of public instruction appointed a commission to study ways of identifying intellectually subnormal individuals in order to provide them with appropriate educational experiences. One member of that commission was Alfred Binet. Working in conjunction with the French physician T. Simon, Binet developed the first major general intelligence test. Binet's early effort launched the first systematic attempt to evaluate individual differences in human intelligence (see Chapter 9).

The Evolution of Intelligence and Standardized Achievement Tests

The history and evolution of Binet's intelligence test are instructive. The first version of the test, known as the Binet-Simon Scale, was published in 1905. This instrument contained 30 items of increasing difficulty and was designed to identify intellectually subnormal individuals. Like all well-constructed tests, the Binet-Simon Scale of 1905 was augmented by a comparison or standardization sample. Binet's standardization sample consisted of 50 children who had been given the test under *standard conditions*—that is, with precisely the same instructions and format. In obtaining this standardization sample, the authors of the Binet test had norms with which they could compare the results from any new subject. Without such norms, the meaning of scores would have been difficult, if not impossible, to evaluate. However, by knowing such things as the average number of correct responses found in the standardization sample, one could at least state whether a new subject was below or above it.

It is easy to understand the importance of a standardization sample. However, the importance of obtaining a standardization sample that represents the population for which a test will be used has sometimes been ignored or overlooked by test users (Malreaux, 1999). For example, if a standardization sample consists of 50 white men from wealthy families, then one cannot easily or fairly evaluate the score of an African American girl from a poverty-stricken family. Nevertheless, comparisons of this kind are sometimes made. Clearly, it is not appropriate to compare an individual with a group that does not have the same characteristics as the individual (Garcia & Fleming, 1998).

Binet was aware of the importance of a standardization sample. Further development of the Binet test involved attempts to increase the size and representativeness of the standardization sample. A **representative sample** is one that comprises individuals similar to those for whom the test is to be used. When the test is used for the general population, a representative sample must reflect all segments of the population in proportion to their actual numbers.

By 1908, the Binet-Simon Scale had been substantially improved. It was revised to include nearly twice as many items as the 1905 scale. Even more significantly, the size of the standardization sample was increased to more than 200. The 1908 Binet-Simon Scale also determined a child's **mental age,** thereby introducing a historically significant concept. In simplified terms, you might think of mental age as a measurement of a child's performance on the test relative to other children of that particular age group. If a child's test performance equals that of the average 8-year-old, for example, then his or her mental age is 8. In other words, in terms of the abilities measured by the test, this child can be viewed as having a similar level of ability as the average 8-year-old. The chronological age of the child may be 4 or 12, but in terms of test performance, the child functions at the same level as the average 8-year-old. The mental age concept was one of the most important contributions of the revised 1908 Binet-Simon Scale.

In 1911, the Binet-Simon Scale received a minor revision. By this time, the idea of intelligence testing had swept across the world. By 1916, L. M. Terman of Stanford University had revised the Binet test for use in the United States. Terman's revision, known as the Stanford-Binet Intelligence Scale (Terman, 1916), was the only American version of the Binet test that flourished. It also characterizes one of the most important trends in testing—the drive toward better tests.

Terman's 1916 revision of the Binet-Simon Scale contained many improvements. The standardization sample was increased to include 1000 people, original items were revised, and many new items were added. Terman's 1916 Stanford-Binet Intelligence Scale added respectability and momentum to the newly developing testing movement.

World War I. The testing movement grew enormously in the United States because of the demand for a quick, efficient way of evaluating the emotional and intellectual functioning of thousands of military recruits in World War I. The war created a demand for large-scale group testing because relatively few trained personnel could evaluate the huge influx of military recruits. However, the Binet test was an individual test.

Shortly after the United States became actively involved in World War I, the army requested the assistance of Robert Yerkes, who was then the president of the American Psychological Association (see Yerkes, 1921). Yerkes headed a committee of distinguished psychologists who soon developed two structured group tests of human abilities: the Army Alpha and the Army Beta. The Army Alpha required reading ability, whereas the Army Beta measured the intelligence of illiterate adults.

World War I fueled the widespread development of group tests. About this time, the scope of testing also broadened to include tests of achievement, aptitude, interest, and personality. Because achievement, aptitude, and intelligence tests overlapped considerably, the distinctions proved to be more illusory than real. Even so, the 1916 Stanford-Binet Intelligence Scale had appeared at a time of strong demand and high optimism for the potential of measuring human behavior through tests. World War I and the creation of group tests had then added momentum to the testing movement. Shortly after the appearance of the 1916 Stanford-Binet Intelligence Scale and the Army Alpha test, schools, colleges, and industry began using tests. It appeared to many that this new phenomenon, the psychological test, held the key to solving the problems emerging from the rapid growth of population and technology.

Achievement tests. Among the most important developments following World War I was the development of standardized achievement tests. In contrast to essay tests, standardized achievement tests provide multiple-choice questions that are standardized on a large sample to produce norms against which the results of new examinees can be compared.

Standardized achievement tests caught on quickly because of the relative ease of administration and scoring and the lack of subjectivity or favoritism that can occur in essay or other written tests. In school settings, standardized achievement tests allowed one to maintain identical testing conditions and scoring standards for a large number of children. Such tests also allowed a broader coverage of content and were less expensive and more efficient than essays. In 1923, the development of standardized achievement tests culminated in the publication of the Stanford Achievement Test by T. L. Kelley, G. M. Ruch, and L. M. Terman.

By the 1930s, it was widely held that the objectivity and reliability of these new standardized tests made them superior to essay tests. Their use proliferated widely. It is interesting, as we shall discuss later in the book, that teachers of today appear to have come full circle. Currently, many people favor written tests and work samples (portfolios) over standardized achievement tests as the best way to evaluate children (Boerum, 2000; Harris, 2002; Muir & Tracy, 1999; Potter, 1999; Russo & Warren, 1999).

Rising to the challenge. For every movement there is a countermovement, and the testing movement in the United States in the 1930s was no exception. Critics soon became vocal enough to dampen enthusiasm and to make even the most optimistic advocates of tests defensive. Researchers, who demanded nothing short of the highest standards, noted the limitations and weaknesses of existing tests. Not even the Stanford-Binet, a landmark in the testing field, was safe from criticism. Although tests were used between the two world wars and many new tests were developed, their accuracy and utility remained under heavy fire.

Near the end of the 1930s, developers began to reestablish the respectability of tests. New, improved tests reflected the knowledge and experience of the previous two decades. By 1937, the Stanford-Binet had been revised again. Among the many improvements was the inclusion of a standardization sample of more than 3000 individuals. A mere 2 years after the 1937 revision of the Stanford-Binet test, David Wechsler published the first version of the Wechsler intelligence scales (see Chapter 10), the Wechsler-Bellevue Intelligence Scale (W-B) (Wechsler, 1939). The Wechsler-Bellevue scale contained several interesting innovations in intelligence testing. Unlike the Stanford-Binet test, which produced only a single score (the so-called IQ, or intelligence quotient), Wechsler's test yielded several scores, permitting an analysis of an individual's pattern or combination of abilities.

Among the various scores produced by the Wechsler test was the performance IQ. Performance tests do not require a verbal response; one can use them to evaluate intelligence in people who have few verbal or language skills. The Stanford-Binet test had long been criticized because of its emphasis on language and verbal skills, making it inappropriate for many individuals, such as those who cannot speak or who cannot read. In addition, few people believed that language or verbal skills play an exclusive role in human intelligence. Wechsler's inclusion of a nonverbal scale thus helped overcome some of the practical and theoretical weaknesses of the Binet test. In 1986, the Binet test was drastically revised to include performance subtests. More recently, it was overhauled again in 2003, as we shall see in Chapter 9. (Other important concepts in intelligence testing will be formally defined in Chapter 10, which covers the various forms of the Wechsler intelligence scales.)

Personality Tests: 1920–1940

Just before and after World War II, personality tests began to blossom. Whereas intelligence tests measured ability or potential, personality tests measured presumably stable characteristics or traits that theoretically underlie behavior.

FIGURE 1-6
*The Woodworth
Personal Data
Sheet represented
an attempt to
standardize the
psychiatric
interview. It
contains questions
such as those
shown here.*

	Yes	No
1. I wet the bed.	☐	☐
2. I drink a quart of whiskey each day.	☐	☐
3. I am afraid of closed spaces.	☑	☐
4. I believe I am being followed.	☐	☐
5. People are out to get me.	☐	☐
6. Sometimes I see or hear things that other people do not hear or see.	☐	☐

Traits are relatively enduring dispositions (tendencies to act, think, or feel in a certain manner in any given circumstance) that distinguish one individual from another. For example, we say that some people are optimistic and some pessimistic. Optimistic people tend to remain so regardless of whether or not things are going well. A pessimist, by contrast, tends to look at the negative side of things. Optimism and pessimism can thus be viewed as traits. One of the basic goals of traditional personality tests is to measure traits. As you will learn, however, the notion of traits has important limitations.

The earliest personality tests were structured paper-and-pencil group tests. These tests provided multiple-choice and true–false questions that could be administered to a large group. Because it provides a high degree of structure—that is, a definite stimulus and specific alternative responses that can be unequivocally scored—this sort of test is a type of structured personality test. The first structured personality test, the Woodworth Personal Data Sheet, was developed during World War I and was published in final form just after the war (see Figure 1-6).

As indicated earlier, the motivation underlying the development of the first personality test was the need to screen military recruits. History indicates that tests such as the Binet and the Woodworth were created by necessity to meet unique challenges. Like the early ability tests, however, the first structured personality test was simple by today's standards. Interpretation of the Woodworth test depended on the now-discredited assumption that the content of an item could be accepted at face value. If the person marked "False" for the statement "I wet the bed," then it was assumed that he or she did not "wet the bed." As logical as this assumption seems, experience has shown that it is often false. In addition to being dishonest, the person responding to the question may not interpret the meaning of "wet the bed" the same way as the test administrator does. (Other problems with tests such as the Woodworth are discussed in Chapter 13.)

The introduction of the Woodworth test was enthusiastically followed by the creation of a variety of structured personality tests, all of which assumed that a subject's response could be taken at face value. However, researchers

FIGURE 1-7

*Card 1 of the
Rorschach inkblot
test, a projective
personality test.
Such tests provide
an ambiguous
stimulus to which
a subject is asked
to make some
response.*

scrutinized, analyzed, and criticized the early structured personality tests, just as they had done with the ability tests. Indeed, the criticism of tests that relied on face value alone became so intense that structured personality tests were nearly driven out of existence. The development of new tests based on more modern concepts followed, revitalizing the use of structured personality tests. Thus, after an initial surge of interest and optimism during most of the 1920s, structured personality tests declined by the late 1930s and early 1940s. Following World War II, however, personality tests based on fewer or different assumptions were introduced, thereby rescuing the structured personality test.

During the brief but dramatic rise and fall of the first structured personality tests, interest in projective tests began to grow. In contrast to structured personality tests, which in general provide a relatively unambiguous test stimulus and specific alternative responses, projective personality tests provide an ambiguous stimulus and unclear response requirements. Furthermore, the scoring of projective tests is often subjective.

Unlike the early structured personality tests, interest in the projective Rorschach inkblot test grew slowly (see Figure 1-7). The Rorschach test was first published by Herman Rorschach of Switzerland in 1921. However, several years passed before the Rorschach came to the United States, where David Levy introduced it. The first Rorschach doctoral dissertation written in a U.S. university was not completed until 1932, when Sam Beck, Levy's student, decided to investigate the properties of the Rorschach test scientifically. Although initial interest in the Rorschach test was lukewarm at best, its popularity grew rapidly after Beck's work, despite suspicion, doubt, and criticism from the scientific community. Today, however, the Rorschach is under a dark cloud (see Chapter 14).

Adding to the momentum for the acceptance and use of projective tests was the development of the Thematic Apperception Test (TAT) by Henry Murray and Christina Morgan in 1935. Whereas the Rorschach test contained completely ambiguous inkblot stimuli, the TAT was more structured. Its stimuli consisted of ambiguous pictures depicting a variety of scenes and situations, such as a boy sitting in front of a table with a violin on it. Unlike the Rorschach test, which asked the subject to explain what the inkblot might be, the TAT required the subject to make up a story about the ambiguous scene. The TAT purported to measure human needs and thus to ascertain individual differences in motivation.

The Emergence of New Approaches to Personality Testing

The popularity of the two most important projective personality tests, the Rorschach and TAT, grew rapidly by the late 1930s and early 1940s, perhaps because of disillusionment with structured personality tests (Dahlstrom, 1969a). However, as we shall see in Chapter 14, projective tests, particularly the Rorschach, have not withstood a vigorous examination of their psychometric properties (Wood, Nezworski, Lilienfeld, & Garb, 2003).

In 1943, the Minnesota Multiphasic Personality Inventory (MMPI) began a new era for structured personality tests. The idea behind the MMPI—to use empirical methods to determine the meaning of a test response—helped revolutionize structured personality tests. The problem with early structured personality tests such as the Woodworth was that they made far too many assumptions that subsequent scientific investigations failed to substantiate. The authors of the MMPI, by contrast, argued that the meaning of a test response could be determined only by empirical research. The MMPI, along with its updated companion the MMPI-2 (Butcher, 1989, 1990), is currently the most widely used and referenced personality test. Its emphasis on the need for empirical data has stimulated the development of tens of thousands of studies.

Just about the time the MMPI appeared, personality tests based on the statistical procedure called *factor analysis* began to emerge. **Factor analysis** is a method of finding the minimum number of dimensions (characteristics, attributes), called *factors,* to account for a large number of variables. We may say a person is outgoing, is gregarious, seeks company, is talkative, and enjoys relating to others. However, these descriptions contain a certain amount of redundancy. A factor analysis can identify how much they overlap and whether they can all be accounted for or subsumed under a single dimension (or factor) such as extroversion.

In the early 1940s, J. R Guilford made the first serious attempt to use factor analytic techniques in the development of a structured personality test. By the end of that decade, R. B. Cattell had introduced the Sixteen Personality Factor Questionnaire (16PF); despite its declining popularity, it remains one of the most well-constructed structured personality tests and an important example of a test developed with the aid of factor analysis. Today, factor analysis is a tool used in the design or validation of just about all major tests. (Factor analytic personality tests will be discussed in Chapter 13.) See Table 1-2 for a brief overview of personality tests.

The Period of Rapid Changes in the Status of Testing

The 1940s saw not only the emergence of a whole new technology in psychological testing but also the growth of applied aspects of psychology. The role and significance of tests used in World War I were reaffirmed in World War II.

TABLE 1-2
*Summary of
Personality Tests*

Woodworth Personal Data Sheet: An early structured personality test that assumed that a test response can be taken at face value.

The Rorschach Inkblot Test: A highly controversial projective test that provided an ambiguous stimulus (an inkblot) and asked the subject what it might be.

The Thematic Apperception Test (TAT): A projective test that provided ambiguous pictures and asked subjects to make up a story.

The Minnesota Multiphasic Personality Inventory (MMPI): A structured personality test that made no assumptions about the meaning of a test response. Such meaning was to be determined by empirical research.

The California Psychological Inventory (CPI): A structured personality test developed according to the same principles as the MMPI.

The Sixteen Personality Factor Questionnaire (16PF): A structured personality test based on the statistical procedure of factor analysis.

By this time, the U.S. government had begun to encourage the continued development of applied psychological technology. As a result, considerable federal funding provided paid, supervised training for clinically oriented psychologists. By 1949, formal university training standards had been developed and accepted, and clinical psychology was born. Other applied branches of psychology—such as industrial, counseling, educational, and school psychology—soon began to blossom.

One of the major functions of the applied psychologist was providing psychological testing. The Shakow, Hilgard, Kelly, Sanford, and Shaffer (1947) report, which was the foundation of the formal training standards in clinical psychology, specified that psychological testing was a unique function of the clinical psychologist and recommended that testing methods be taught only to doctoral psychology students. A position paper of the American Psychological Association published 7 years later (APA, 1954) affirmed that the domain of the clinical psychologist included testing. It formally declared, however, that the psychologist would conduct psychotherapy only in "true" collaboration with physicians. Thus, psychologists could conduct testing independently, but not psychotherapy. Indeed, as long as psychologists assumed the role of testers, they played a complementary but often secondary role vis-à-vis medical practitioners. Though the medical profession could have hindered the emergence of clinical psychology, it did not, because as tester the psychologist aided the physician. Therefore, in the late 1940s and early 1950s, testing was the major function of the clinical psychologist (Shaffer, 1953).

For better or worse, depending on one's perspective, the government's efforts to stimulate the development of applied aspects of psychology, especially clinical psychology, were extremely successful. Hundreds of highly talented and creative young people were attracted to clinical and other applied areas of psychology. These individuals, who would use tests and other psychological techniques to solve practical human problems, were uniquely trained as practitioners of the principles, empirical foundations, and applications of the science of psychology.

Armed with powerful knowledge from scientific psychology, many of these early clinical practitioners must have felt frustrated by their relationship to physicians (see Saccuzzo & Kaplan, 1984). Unable to engage independently in the practice of psychotherapy, some psychologists felt like technicians serving the medical profession. The highly talented group of post–World War II psychologists quickly began to reject this secondary role. Further, because many psychologists associated tests with this secondary relationship, they rejected testing (Lewandowski & Saccuzzo, 1976). At the same time, the potentially intrusive nature of tests and fears of misuse began to create public suspicion, distrust, and contempt for tests. Attacks on testing came from within and without the profession. These attacks intensified and multiplied so fast that many psychologists jettisoned all ties to the traditional tests developed during the first half of the 20th century. Testing therefore underwent another sharp decline in status in the late 1950s that persisted into the 1970s (see Holt, 1967).

The Current Environment

During the 1980s, 1990s, and 2000s several major branches of applied psychology emerged and flourished: neuropsychology, health psychology, forensic psychology, and child psychology. Because each of these important areas of psychology makes extensive use of psychological tests, psychological testing again grew in status and use. Neuropsychologists use tests in hospitals and other clinical settings to assess brain injury. Health psychologists use tests and surveys in a variety of medical settings. Forensic psychologists use tests in the legal system to assess mental state as it relates to an insanity defense, competency to stand trial or to be executed, and emotional damages. Child psychologists use tests to assess childhood disorders. As in the past, psychological testing in the first decade of the 21st century remains one of the most important yet controversial topics in psychology.

As a student, no matter what your occupational or professional goals, you will find the material in this text invaluable. If you are among those who are interested in using psychological techniques in an applied setting, then this information will be particularly significant. From the roots of psychology to the present, psychological tests have remained among the most important instruments of the psychologist in general and of those who apply psychology in particular.

Testing is indeed one of the essential elements of psychology. Though not all psychologists use tests and some psychologists are opposed to them, all areas of psychology depend on knowledge gained in research studies that rely on measurements. The meaning and dependability of these measurements are essential to psychological research. To study any area of human behavior effectively, one must understand the basic principles of measurement.

In today's complex society, the relevance of the principles, applications, and issues of psychological testing extends far beyond the field of psychology. Even if you do not plan to become a psychologist, you will likely encounter psychological tests. Attorneys, physicians, social workers, business managers, educators, and many other professionals must frequently deal with reports based on such tests. Even as a parent, you are likely to encounter tests (taken by your children). To interpret such information adequately, you need the information presented in this book.

The more you know about psychological tests, the more confident you can be in your encounters with them. Given the attacks on tests and threats to prohibit or greatly limit their use, you have a responsibility to yourself and to society to know as much as you can about psychological tests. The future of testing may well depend on you and people like you. A thorough knowledge of testing will allow you to base your decisions on facts and to ensure that tests are used for the most beneficial and constructive purposes.

Tests have probably never been as important as they are today. For example, consider just one type of testing—academic aptitude. Every year more than 2.5 million students take tests that are designed to measure academic progress or suitability, and the testing process begins early in students' lives. Some presecondary schools require certain tests, and thousands of children take them each year. When these students become adolescents and want to get into college preparatory schools, tens of thousands will take a screening examination. Few students who want to go to a 4-year college can avoid taking a college entrance test. The SAT alone is given to some 2 million high-school students each year. Another 100,000 high-school seniors take other tests in order to gain advanced placement in college.

These figures do not include the 75,000 people who take a special test for admission to business school or the 148,000 who take a Law School Admission Test—or tests for graduate school, medical school, dental school, the military, professional licenses, and others. In fact, the Educational Testing Service alone administers more than 11 million tests annually in 181 countries (Gonzalez, 2001). As sources of information about human characteristics, the results of these tests affect critical life decisions.

SUMMARY

The history of psychological testing in the United States has been brief but intense. Although these sorts of tests have long been available, psychological testing is very much a product of modern society with its unprecedented technology and population growth and unique problems. Conversely, by helping to solve the challenges posed by modern developments, tests have played an important role in recent U.S. and world history. You should realize, however, that despite advances in the theory and technique of psychological testing, many unsolved technical problems and hotly debated social, political, and economic issues remain. Nevertheless, the prevalence of tests despite strong opposition indicates that, although they are far from perfect, psychological tests must fulfill some important need in the decision-making processes permeating all facets of society. Because decisions must be made, such tests will probably flourish until a better or more objective way of making decisions emerges.

Modern history shows that psychological tests have evolved in a complicated environment in which hostile and friendly forces have produced a balance characterized by innovation and a continuous quest for better methods. One interesting thing about tests is that people never seem to remain neutral about them. If you are not in favor of tests, then we ask that you maintain a flexible, open mind while studying them. Our goal is to give you enough information to assess psychological tests intelligently throughout your life.

WEB ACTIVITY

For some interesting and relevant Web sites, you might want to check the following:

www.aclu.org/FreeSpeech/FreeSpeechMain.cfm
Officials silence critic of high-stakes testing

www.apa.org/pi/psych.html
Psychological testing of language minority and culturally different children

www.apa.org/science/fairtestcode.html
Code of fair testing practices in education

www.bccla.org/positions/privacy/87psytest.html
Privacy in psychological testing

www.romingerlegal.com/expert/
Psychological assessment by expert witnesses in legal cases

CHAPTER 2

Norms and Basic Statistics for Testing

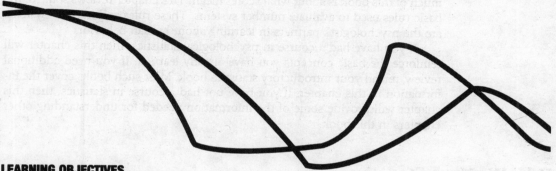

LEARNING OBJECTIVES

When you have completed this chapter, you should be able to:

☐ Discuss three properties of scales of measurement

☐ Determine why properties of scales are important in the field of measurement

☐ Tell why methods are available for displaying distributions of scores

☐ Describe the mean and the standard deviation

☐ Define a Z score and explain how it is used

☐ Relate the concepts of mean, standard deviation, and Z score to the concept of a standard normal distribution

☐ Define quartiles, deciles, and stanines and explain how they are used

☐ Tell how norms are created

☐ Relate the notion of tracking to the establishment of norms

W̲e all use numbers as a basic way of communicating: Our money system requires us to understand and manipulate numbers, we estimate how long it will take to do things, we count, we express evaluations on scales, and so on. Think about how many times you use numbers in an average day. There is no way to avoid them.

One advantage of number systems is that they allow us to manipulate information. Through sets of well-defined rules, we can use numbers to learn more about the world. *Tests* are devices used to translate observations into numbers. Because the outcome of a test is almost always represented as a score, much of this book is about what scores mean. This chapter reviews some of the basic rules used to evaluate number systems. These rules and number systems are the psychologist's partners in learning about human behavior.

If you have had a course in psychological statistics, then this chapter will reinforce the basic concepts you have already learned. If you need additional review, reread your introductory statistics book. Most such books cover the information in this chapter. If you have not had a course in statistics, then this chapter will provide some of the information needed for understanding other chapters in this book.

Why We Need Statistics

Through its commitment to the scientific method, modern psychology has advanced beyond centuries of speculation about human nature. Scientific study requires systematic observations and an estimation of the extent to which observations could have been influenced by chance alone (Collett, 2003). Statistical methods serve two important purposes in the quest for scientific understanding.

First, statistics are used for purposes of description. Numbers provide convenient summaries and allow us to evaluate some observations relative to others (Cohen & Lea, 2004; Pagano, 2004). For example, if you get a score of 54 on a psychology examination, you probably want to know what the 54 means. Is it lower than the average score, or is it about the same? Knowing the answer can make the feedback you get from your examination more meaningful. If you discover that the 54 puts you in the top 5% of the class, then you might assume you have a good chance for an A. If it puts you in the bottom 5%, then you will feel differently.

Second, we can use statistics to make **inferences**, which are logical deductions about events that cannot be observed directly. For example, you do not know how many people watched a particular television movie unless you ask everyone. However, by using scientific sample surveys, you can infer the percentage of people who saw the film. Data gathering and analysis might be considered analogous to criminal investigation and prosecution (Nathanson, Higgins, Giglio, Munshi, & Steingrub, 2003; Tukey, 1977). First comes the detective work of gathering and displaying clues, or what the statistician John Tukey calls *exploratory data analysis.* Then comes a period of *confirmatory data* *analysis,* when the clues are evaluated against rigid statistical rules. This latter phase is like the work done by judges and juries.

Some students have an aversion to numbers and anything mathematical. If you find yourself among them, you are not alone. Not only students but also professional psychologists can feel uneasy about statistics. However, statistics and the basic principles of measurement lie at the center of the modern science of psychology. Scientific statements are usually based on careful study, and such systematic study requires some numerical analysis.

This chapter will review both descriptive and inferential statistics. **Descriptive statistics** are methods used to provide a concise description of a collection of quantitative information. **Inferential statistics** are methods used to make inferences from observations of a small group of people known as a *sample* to a larger group of individuals known as a *population.* Typically, the psychologist wants to make statements about the larger group but cannot possibly make all the necessary observations. Instead, he or she observes a relatively small group of subjects (sample) and uses inferential statistics to estimate the characteristics of the larger group.

Scales of Measurement

One may define *measurement* as the application of rules for assigning numbers to objects. The rules are the specific procedures used to transform qualities of attributes into numbers (Camilli, Cizek, & Lugg, 2001; Nunnally & Bernstein, 1994; Yanai, 2003). For example, to rate the quality of wines, wine tasters must use a specific set of rules. They might rate the wine on a 10-point scale where 1 means extremely bad and 10 means extremely good. For a taster to assign the numbers, the system of rules must be clearly defined. The basic feature of these types of systems is the scale of measurement. For example, to measure the height of your classmates, you might use the scale of inches; to measure their weight, you might use the scale of pounds.

There are numerous systems by which we assign numbers in psychology. Indeed, the study of measurement systems is what this book is about. Before we consider any specific scale of measurement, however, we should consider the general properties of measurement scales.

Properties of Scales

Three important properties make scales of measurement different from one another: magnitude, equal intervals, and an absolute 0.

Magnitude. Magnitude is the property of "moreness." A scale has the property of magnitude if we can say that a particular instance of the attribute represents more, less, or equal amounts of the given quantity than does another instance (Aron & Aron, 2003; Hurlburt, 2003; McCall, 2001). On a scale of height, for example, if we can say that John is taller than Fred, then the scale has the property of magnitude. A scale that does not have this property arises, for example, when a gym coach assigns identification numbers to teams in a league (team 1, team 2, and so forth). Because the numbers only label the teams, they do not have the property of magnitude. If the coach were to rank the teams by the number of games they have won, then the new numbering system (games won) would have the property of magnitude.

Equal intervals. The concept of equal intervals is a little more complex than that of magnitude. A scale has the property of equal intervals if the difference between two points at any place on the scale has the same meaning as the difference between two other points that differ by the same number of scale units. For example, the difference between inch 2 and inch 4 on a ruler represents the same quantity as the difference between inch 10 and inch 12: exactly 2 inches.

As simple as this concept seems, a psychological test rarely has the property of equal intervals. For example, the difference between IQs of 45 and 50 does not mean the same thing as the difference between IQs of 105 and 110. Although each of these differences is 5 points ($50 - 45 = 5$ and $110 - 105 = 5$), the 5 points at the first level do not mean the same thing as 5 points at the second. We know that IQ predicts classroom performance. However, the difference in classroom performance associated with differences between IQ scores of 45 and 50 is not the same as the differences in classroom performance associated with IQ score differences of 105 and 110. In later chapters we will discuss this problem in more detail.

When a scale has the property of *equal intervals*, the relationship between the measured units and some outcome can be described by a straight line or a linear equation in the form $Y = a + bX$. This equation shows that an increase in equal units on a given scale reflects equal increases in the meaningful correlates of units. For example, Figure 2-1 shows the hypothetical relationship between scores on a test of manual dexterity and ratings of artwork. Notice that the relationship is not a straight line. By examining the points on the figure, you can see that at first the relationship is nearly linear: Increases in manual dexterity are associated with increases in ratings of artwork. Then the relationship becomes nonlinear. The figure shows that after a manual dexterity score of approximately 5, increases in dexterity produce relatively smaller increases in quality of artwork.

Absolute 0. An absolute 0 is obtained when nothing of the property being measured exists. For example, if you are measuring heart rate and observe that your patient has a rate of 0 and has died, then you would conclude that there is no heart rate at all. For many psychological qualities, it is extremely difficult, if not impossible, to define an absolute 0 point. For example, if one measures shyness on a scale from 0 through 10, then it is hard to define what it means for a person to have absolutely no shyness (McCall, 2001).

FIGURE 2-1
*Hypothetical
relationship
between ratings of
artwork and
manual dexterity.
In some ranges of
the scale, the
relationship is
more direct than
it is in others.*

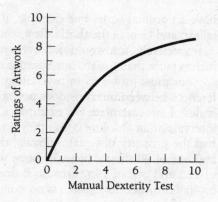

Types of Scales

Table 2-1 defines four scales of measurement based on the properties we have just discussed. You can see that a nominal scale does not have the property of magnitude, equal intervals, or an absolute 0. **Nominal scales** are really not scales at all; their only purpose is to name objects. For example, the numbers on the backs of football players' uniforms are nominal. Nominal scales are used when the information is qualitative rather than quantitative. Social science researchers commonly label groups in sample surveys with numbers (such as 1 = African American, 2 = white, and 3 = Mexican American). When these numbers have been attached to categories, most statistical procedures are not meaningful. On the scale for ethnic groups, for instance, what would a mean of 1.87 signify? This is not to say that the sophisticated statistical analysis of nominal data is impossible. Indeed, several new and exciting developments in data analysis allow extensive and detailed use of nominal data (Chen, 2002; Miller, Scurfield, Drga, Galvin, & Whitmore, 2002; Stout, 2002).

A scale with the property of magnitude but not equal intervals or an absolute 0 is an **ordinal scale**. This scale allows you to rank individuals or objects but not to say anything about the meaning of the differences between the ranks. If you were to rank the members of your class by height, then you would

TABLE 2-1
*Scales of
Measurement and
Their Properties*

| Type of scale | Property | | |
	Magnitude	Equal intervals	Absolute 0
Nominal	No	No	No
Ordinal	Yes	No	No
Interval	Yes	Yes	No
Ratio	Yes	Yes	Yes

have an ordinal scale. For example, if Fred was the tallest, Susan the second tallest, and George the third tallest, you would assign them the ranks 1, 2, and 3, respectively. You would not give any consideration to the fact that Fred is 8 inches taller than Susan, but Susan is only 2 inches taller than George.

For most problems in psychology, the precision to measure the exact differences between intervals does not exist. So, most often one must use ordinal scales of measurement. For example, IQ tests do not have the property of equal intervals or an absolute 0, but they do have the property of magnitude. If they had the property of equal intervals, then the difference between an IQ of 70 and one of 90 should have the same meaning as the difference between an IQ of 125 and one of 145. Because it does not, the scale can only be considered ordinal. Furthermore, there is no point on the scale that represents no intelligence at all—that is, the scale does not have an absolute 0.

When a scale has the properties of magnitude and equal intervals but not absolute 0, we refer to it as an **interval scale.** The most common example of an interval scale is the measurement of temperature in degrees Fahrenheit. This temperature scale clearly has the property of magnitude, because 35°F is warmer than 32°F, 65°F is warmer than 64°F, and so on. Also, the difference between 90°F and 80°F is equal to a similar difference of 10 degrees at any point on the scale. However, on the Fahrenheit scale, temperature does not have the property of absolute 0. If it did, then the 0 point would be more meaningful. As it is, 0 on the Fahrenheit scale does not have a particular meaning. Water freezes at 32°F and boils at 212°F. Because the scale does not have an absolute 0, we cannot make statements in terms of ratios. A temperature of 22°F is not twice as hot as 11°F, and 70°F is not twice as hot as 35°F.

The Celsius scale of temperature is also an interval rather than a ratio scale. Although 0 represents freezing on the Celsius scale, it is not an absolute 0. Remember that an absolute 0 is a point at which nothing of the property being measured exists. Even on the Celsius scale of temperature, there is still plenty of room on the thermometer below 0. When the temperature goes below freezing, some aspect of heat is still being measured.

A scale that has all three properties (magnitude, equal intervals, and an absolute 0) is called a **ratio scale.** To continue our example, a ratio scale of temperature would have the properties of the Fahrenheit and Celsius scales but also include a meaningful 0 point. There is a point at which all molecular activity ceases, a point of absolute 0 on a temperature scale. Because the Kelvin scale is based on the absolute 0 point, it is a ratio scale: 22°K is twice as cold as 44°K. Examples of ratio scales also appear in the numbers we see on a regular basis. For example, consider the number of yards gained by running backs on football teams. Zero yards actually means that the player has gained no yards at all. If one player has gained 1000 yards and another has gained only 500, then we can say that the first athlete has gained twice as many yards as the second.

Another example is the speed of travel. For instance, 0 miles per hour (mph) is the point at which there is no speed at all. If you are driving onto a highway at 30 mph and increase your speed to 60 when you merge, then you have doubled your speed.

Permissible Operations

Level of measurement is important because it defines which mathematical operations we can apply to numerical data. For nominal data, each observation can be placed in only one mutually exclusive category. For example, you are a member of only one gender. One can use nominal data to create frequency distributions (see the next section), but no mathematical manipulations of the data are permissible. Ordinal measurements can be manipulated using arithmetic; however, the result is often difficult to interpret because it reflects neither the magnitudes of the manipulated observations nor the true amounts of the property that have been measured. For example, if the heights of 15 children are rank ordered, knowing a given child's rank does not reveal how tall he or she stands. Averages of these ranks are equally uninformative about height.

With interval data, one can apply any arithmetic operation to the differences between scores. The results can be interpreted in relation to the magnitudes of the underlying property. However, interval data cannot be used to make statements about ratios. For example, if IQ is measured on an interval scale, one cannot say that an IQ of 160 is twice as high as an IQ of 80. This mathematical operation is reserved for ratio scales, for which any mathematical operation is permissible.

Frequency Distributions

A single test score means more if one relates it to other test scores. A *distribution* of scores summarizes the scores for a group of individuals. In testing, there are many ways to record a distribution of scores.

The **frequency distribution** displays scores on a variable or a measure to reflect how frequently each value was obtained. With a frequency distribution, one defines all the possible scores and determines how many people obtained each of those scores. Usually, scores are arranged on the horizontal axis from the lowest to the highest value. The vertical axis reflects how many times each of the values on the horizontal axis was observed. For most distributions of test scores, the frequency distribution is bell-shaped, with the greatest frequency of scores toward the center of the distribution and decreasing scores as the values become greater or less than the value in the center of the distribution.

Figure 2-2 shows a frequency distribution of 1000 observations that takes on values between 61 and 90. Notice that the most frequent observations fall toward the center of the distribution, around 75 and 76. As you look toward the extremes of the distribution, you will find a systematic decline in the frequency with which the scores occur. For example, the score of 71 is observed less frequently than 72, which is observed less frequently than 73, and so on. Similarly, 78 is observed more frequently than 79, which is noted more often than 80, and so forth.

Though this neat symmetric relationship does not characterize all sets of scores, it occurs frequently enough in practice for us to devote special attention

FIGURE 2-2
*Frequency
distribution
approximating
a normal
distribution
of 1000
observations.*

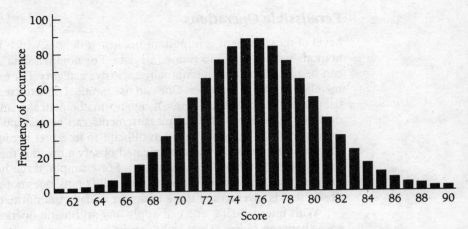

to it. In the section on the normal distribution, we explain this concept in greater detail.

Table 2-2 lists the rainfall amounts in San Diego, California, between 1970 and 2003. Figure 2-3 is a histogram based on the observations. The distribution is slightly skewed, or asymmetrical. We say that Figure 2-3 has a *positive* skew because the tail goes off toward the higher or positive side of the X axis. There is a slight skew in Figures 2-3 and 2-4, but the asymmetry in these figures is relatively hard to detect. Figure 2-5 gives an example of a distribution that is clearly skewed. The figure summarizes annual household income in the United States in 2002. Very few people make high incomes, while the great bulk of the population is bunched toward the low end of the income distribution. Of particular interest is that this figure only includes household incomes less than $100,000. For household incomes greater than $100,000, the government only reports incomes using class intervals of $50,000. In 2002, about 14% of the U.S. households had incomes greater than $100,000. Since some households have extremely high incomes, you can imagine that the tail of this distribution would go very far to the right. Thus, income is an example of a variable that has positive skew.

One can also present this same set of data as a frequency polygon (see Figure 2-4). Here the amount of rainfall is placed on the graph as a point that represents the frequencies with which each interval occurs. Lines are then drawn to connect these points.

Whenever you draw a frequency distribution or a frequency polygon, you must decide on the width of the class interval. The **class interval** for inches of rainfall is the unit on the horizontal axis. For example, in Figures 2-3 and 2-4, the class interval is 3 inches—that is, the demarcations along the X axis increase in 3-inch intervals. This interval is used here for convenience; the choice of 3 inches is otherwise arbitrary.

TABLE 2-2

Inches of Rainfall in San Diego, 1970–2003

Year	Inches
1970	6.48
1971	8.20
1972	6.24
1973	11.16
1974	6.68
1975	10.80
1976	9.24
1977	9.32
1978	17.56
1979	15.52
1980	15.72
1981	7.48
1982	12.04
1983	18.76
1984	5.44
1985	9.76
1986	15.20
1987	9.44
1988	12.64
1989	5.96
1990	7.76
1991	12.20
1992	12.48
1993	18.23
1994	9.92
1995	17.08
1996	5.91
1997	7.75
1998	16.9
1999	6.49
2000	6.92
2001	8.52
2002	4.23
2003	7.97
Sum	356
Mean	10.47
Variance	17.58
Standard deviation	4.19
N	34

Data for year 2003 are estimates based on projections at the time the book went to press.

Full data going back to 1850 can be found at http://cdec.water.ca.gov/cgi-progs/queryMonthly?SDG&d=29-Aug-2001+11:15&span=2years.

FIGURE 2-3

Histogram for San Diego rainfall, 1970–2003.

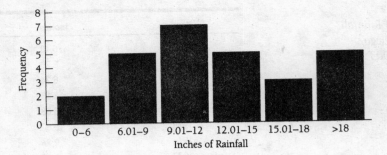

FIGURE 2-4

Frequency polygon for rainfall in San Diego, 1970–2003.

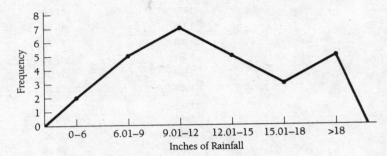

FIGURE 2-5

Household income up to $100,000 in the United States for 2002. This is an example of positive skew.

(Data from the United States Department of Labor Statistics and the Bureau the Census. http://ferret.bls. census.gov/macro/ 032003/hhinc/ new06_000.htm.)

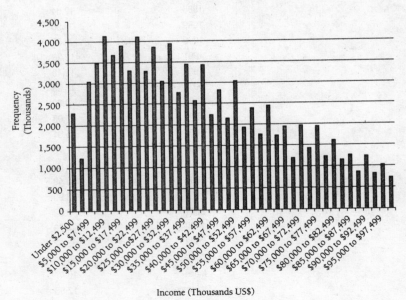

Percentile Ranks

Percentile ranks replace simple ranks when we want to adjust for the number of scores in a group. A **percentile rank** answers the question "What percent of the scores fall below a particular score (X_i)?" To calculate a percentile rank, you need only follow these simple steps: (1) Determine how many cases fall below the score of interest, (2) Determine how many cases are in the group, (3) Divide the number of cases below the score of interest (Step 1) by the total number of cases in the group (Step 2), and (4) Multiply the result of Step 3 by 100. The formula is

$$P_r = \frac{B}{N} \times 100 = \text{percentile rank of } X_1$$

where

P_r = percentile rank

X_i = the score of interest

B = the number of scores below X_i

N = the total number of scores

This means that you form a ratio of the number of cases below the score of interest and the total number of scores. Because there will always be either the same or fewer cases in the numerator (top half) of the equation than there are in the denominator (bottom half), this ratio will always be less than or equal to 1. To get rid of the decimal points, you multiply by 100.

As an example, consider the runner who finishes 62nd out of 63 racers in a gym class. To obtain the percentile rank, divide 1 (the number of people who finish behind the person of interest) by 63 (the number of scores in the group). This gives you 63, or .016. Then multiply this result by 100 to obtain the percentile rank, which is 1.6. This rank tells you the runner is below the 2nd percentile.

Now consider the Bay to Breakers race, which attracts 50,000 runners to San Francisco. If you had finished 62nd out of 50,000, then the number of people who were behind you would be 49,938. Dividing this by the number of entrants gives .9988. When you multiply by 100, you get a percentile rank of 99.88. This tells you that finishing 62nd in the Bay to Breakers race is exceptionally good because it places you in the 99.88th percentile.

Technical Box 2-1 presents the calculation of percentile ranks of the infant mortality rates of selected countries as reported by the World Health Organization in 2003. Infant mortality is defined as the number of babies out of 1000 who are born alive but die before their first birthday. Before proceeding, we should point out that the meaning of this calculation depends on which countries are used in the comparison.

In this example, the calculation of the percentile rank is broken into five steps and uses the raw data in the table. In Step 1, we arrange the data points in descending order. Sweden has the lowest infant mortality rate (2.4), Japan is next (3.4), and Zambia has the highest rate (168.1).

In Step 2, we determine the number of cases with worse rates than that of the case of interest. In this example, the case of interest is the United States. Therefore, we count the number of cases with a worse rate than that of the United States. Ten countries—Colombia, Saudi Arabia, Turkey, China, Morocco, Bolivia, Laos, Zambia, Ethiopia, and Mozambique—have infant mortality rates greater than 7.58.

TECHNICAL BOX 2-1

Infant Mortality in Selected Countries, 2003

Country	Infant Mortality per 1000 Live Births
Australia	5
Bolivia	66.4
Colombia	20.4
China	37.9
Ethiopia	142.6
France	4.5
Israel	6.1
Italy	4.8
Japan	3.4
Laos	105.8
Morocco	56.3
Mozambique	148.6
Saudia Arabia	23.7
Spain	3.9
Sweden	2.4
Turkey	34.3
United States	7.5
Zambia	168.1
Mean	46.76
SD	56.29

To calculate the percentile rank of infant mortality in the United States in comparison to that in selected countries, use the following formula:

$$P_r = \frac{B}{N} \times 100$$

where

P_r = the percentile rank

B = the number of cases with worse rates than the case of interest

N = the total number of cases

Country	Infant Mortality per 1000 Live Births
Sweden	2.4
Japan	3.4
Spain	3.9
France	4.5
Italy	4.8
Australia	5
Israel	6.1
United States	7.5
Colombia	20.4
Saudia Arabia	23.7
Turkey	34.3
China	37.9
Morocco	56.3
Bolivia	66.4
Laos	105.8
Ethiopia	142.6
Mozambique	148.6
Zambia	168.1

Steps

1. Arrange data in ascending order—that is, the lowest score first, the second lowest score second, and so on.

$$N = 18, \text{ mean} = 46.76, \text{ standard deviation} = 56.29$$

2. Determine the number of cases with worse rates than the score of interest. There are 10 countries in this sample with infant mortality rates greater than that in the United States.

3. Determine the number of cases in the sample (18).

4. Divide the number of scores worse than the score of interest (Step 2) by the total number of scores (Step 3):

$$\frac{10}{18} = .56$$

5. Multiply by 100:

$$.56 \times 100 = 56\text{th percentile rank}$$

In Step 3, we determine the total number of cases (18).

In Step 4, we divide the number of scores worse than the score of interest by the total number of scores:

$$\frac{10}{18} = .56$$

Technically, the percentile rank is a percentage. Step 4 gives a proportion. Therefore, in Step 5 you transform this into a whole number by multiplying by 100:

$$.56 \times 100 = 56$$

Thus, the United States is in the 56th percentile.

The percentile rank depends absolutely on the cases used for comparison. In this example, you calculated that the United States is in the 56th percentile for infant mortality within this group of countries. If all countries in the world had been included, then the ranking of the United States might have been different.

Using this procedure, try to calculate the percentile rank for Bolivia. The calculation is the same except that there are four countries with worse rates than Bolivia (as opposed to 10 worse than the United States). Thus, the percentile rank for Bolivia is

$$\frac{4}{18} = .22 \times 100 = 22$$

or the 22nd percentile. Now try France. You should get a percentile rank of 78.

Percentiles

Percentiles are the specific scores or points within a distribution. Percentiles divide the total frequency for a set of observations into hundredths. Instead of indicating what percentage of scores fall below a particular score, as percentile ranks do, percentiles indicate the particular score, below which a defined percentage of scores falls.

Try to calculate the percentile and percentile rank for some of the data in Technical Box 2-1. As an example, look at Italy. The infant mortality rate in Italy is 4.8/1000. When calculating the percentile rank, you exclude the score of interest and count those below (in other words, Italy is not included in the count). There are 13 countries in this sample with infant mortality rates worse than Italy's. To calculate the percentile rank, divide this number of countries by the total number of cases and multiply by 100:

$$P_r = \frac{B}{N} \times 100 = \frac{13}{18} \times 100 = .72 \times 100 = 72$$

Thus, Italy is in the 72nd percentile rank, or the 72nd percentile in this example is 4.8/1000 or 4.8 deaths per 1000 live births.

Now take the example of Israel. The calculation of percentile rank requires looking at the number of cases below the case of interest. In this example, 11 countries in this group have infant mortality rates worse than Israel's. Thus, the percentile rank for Israel is $11/18 \times 100 = 61$. The 61st percentile corresponds with the point or score of 6.1 (6.1/1000 live births).

In summary, the percentile and the percentile rank are similar. The percentile gives the point in a distribution below which a specified percentage of cases fall (4.8/1000 for Italy). The percentile is in raw score units. The percentile rank gives the percentage of cases below the percentile; in this example, the percentile rank is 72.

When reporting percentiles and percentile ranks, you must carefully specify the population you are working with. Remember that a percentile rank is a measure of relative performance. When interpreting a percentile rank, you should always ask the question "Relative to what?" Suppose, for instance, that you finished in the 17th percentile in a swimming race (or fifth in a heat of six competitors). Does this mean that you are a slow swimmer? Not necessarily. It may be that this was a heat in the Olympic games, and the participants were the fastest swimmers in the world. An Olympic swimmer competing against a random sample of all people in the world would probably finish in the 99.99th percentile. The example for infant mortality rates depends on which countries in the world were selected for comparison. The United States actually does quite poorly when compared with European countries. However, the U.S. infant mortality rate looks much better compared with countries in the developing world.

Describing Distributions

Mean

Statistics are used to summarize data. If you consider a set of scores, the mass of information may be too much to interpret all at once. That is why we need numerical conveniences to help summarize the information. An example of a set of scores that can be summarized is shown in Table 2-2 (see page 33), amounts of rainfall in San Diego. We signify the variable as X. A *variable* is a score that can have different values. The amount of rain is a variable because different amounts of rain fell in different years.

The arithmetic average score in a distribution is called the **mean**. To calculate the mean, we total the scores and divide the sum by the number of cases, or N. The capital Greek letter sigma (Σ) means summation. Thus, the formula for the mean, which we signify as $\bar{X}$, is

$$\bar{X} = \frac{\Sigma X}{N}$$

In words, this formula says to total the scores and divide the sum by the number of cases. Using the information in Table 2-2, we find the mean by following these steps:

1. Obtain ΣX, or the sum of the scores: $6.48 + 8.20 + 6.24 + 11.16 + 6.68 + \cdots + 7.97 = 356.00$
2. Find N, or the number of scores:

$$N = 34$$

3. Divide ΣX by N: $356/34 = 10.47$

Technical Box 2-2 summarizes common symbols used in basic statistics.

Standard Deviation

The standard deviation is an approximation of the average deviation around the mean. The standard deviation for the amount of rainfall in San Diego is 4.19. To understand rainfall in San Diego, you need to consider at least two dimensions: first, the amount of rain that falls in a particular year; second, the degree of variation from year to year in the amount of rain that falls. The calculation suggests that, on the average, the variation around the mean is approximately 4.19 inches.

However informative, knowing the mean of a group of scores does not give you that much information. As an illustration, look at the following sets of numbers.

Set 1	Set 2	Set 3
4	5	8
4	5	8
4	4	6
4	4	2
4	3	0
4	3	0

TECHNICAL BOX 2-2

Common Symbols

You need to understand and recognize the symbols used throughout this book. $\bar{X}$ is the mean; it is pronounced "X bar." Σ is the summation sign. It means sum, or add, scores together and is the capital Greek letter sigma. X is a variable that takes on different values. Each value of X_i represents a raw score, also called an *obtained score*.

Calculate the mean of the first set. You should get 4. What is the mean of the second set? If you calculate correctly, you should get 4 again. Next find the mean for Set 3. It is also 4. The three distributions of scores appear quite different but have the same mean, so it is important to consider other characteristics of the distribution of scores besides the mean. The difference between the three sets lies in *variability*. There is no variability in Set 1, a small amount in Set 2, and a lot in Set 3.

Measuring this variation is similar to finding the average deviation around the mean. One way to measure variability is to subtract the mean from each score $(X - \bar{X})$ and then total the deviations. Statisticians often signify this with a lowercase x, as in $x = (X - \bar{X})$. Try this for the data in Table 2-2. Did you get 0? You should have, and this is not an unusual example. In fact, the sum of the deviations around the mean will always equal 0. However, you do have an alternative: You can square all the deviations around the mean in order to get rid of any negative signs. Then you can obtain the average squared deviation around the mean, known as the **variance**. The formula for the variance is

$$\sigma^2 = \frac{\Sigma(X - \bar{X})^2}{N}$$

where $(X - \bar{X})$ is the deviation of a score from the mean. The symbol σ is the lowercase Greek sigma; σ^2 is used as a standard description of the variance.

Though the variance is a useful statistic commonly used in data analysis, it shows the variable in squared deviations around the mean rather than in deviations around the mean. In other words, the variance is the average squared deviation around the mean. To get it back into the units that will make sense to us, we need to take the square root of the variance. The square root of the variance is the standard deviation (σ), and it is represented by the following formula

$$\sigma^2 = \sqrt{\frac{\Sigma(X - \bar{X})^2}{N}}$$

The **standard deviation** is thus the square root of the average squared deviation around the mean. Although the standard deviation is not an average deviation, it gives a useful approximation of how much a typical score is above or below the average score.

Because of their mathematical properties, the variance and the standard deviation have many advantages. For example, knowing the standard deviation of a normally distributed batch of data allows us to make precise statements about the distribution. The formulas just presented are for computing the variance and the standard deviation of a population. That is why we use the lowercase Greek sigma (σ and σ^2). Technical Box 2-3 summarizes when you should use Greek and Roman letters. Most often we use the standard deviation for a sample to estimate the standard deviation for a population. When we talk about a sample, we replace the Greek σ with a Roman letter S. Also, we divide

TECHNICAL BOX 2-3

Terms and Symbols Used to Describe Populations and Samples

	Population	Sample
Definition	All elements with the same definition	A subset of the population, usually drawn to represent it in an unbiased fashion
Descriptive characteristics	Parameters	Statistics
Symbols used to describe	Greek	Roman
Symbol for mean	μ	$\bar{X}$
Symbol for standard deviation	σ	S

by $N - 1$ rather than N to recognize that S of a sample is only an estimate of the variance of the population.

$$S = \sqrt{\frac{\Sigma(X - \bar{X})^2}{N - 1}}$$

In calculating the standard deviation, it is often easier to use the raw score equivalent formula, which is

$$S = \sqrt{\frac{\Sigma X^2 - \frac{(\Sigma X)^2}{N}}{N - 1}}$$

This calculation can also be done automatically by some minicalculators.

In reading the formula, you may be confused by a few points. In particular, be careful not to confuse ΣX^2 and $(\Sigma X)^2$. To get ΣX^2, each individual score is squared and the values are summed. For the scores 3, 5, 7, and 8, ΣX^2 would be $3^2 + 5^2 + 7^2 + 8^2 = 9 + 25 + 49 + 64 = 147$. To obtain $(\Sigma X)^2$, the scores are first summed and the total is squared. Using the example, $(\Sigma X)^2 = (3 + 5 + 7 + 8)^2 = 23^2 = 529$.

Z Score

One problem with means and standard deviations is that they do not convey enough information for us to make meaningful assessments or accurate interpretations of data. Other metrics are designed for more exact interpretations. The Z score transforms data into standardized units that are easier to interpret.

A Z score is the difference between a score and the mean, divided by the standard deviation:

$$Z = \frac{X - \bar{X}}{S}$$

In other words, a Z score is the deviation of a score X from the mean $\bar{X}$ in standard deviation units. If a score is equal to the mean, then its Z score is 0. For example, suppose the score and the mean are both 6; then $6 - 6 = 0$. Zero divided by anything is still 0. If the score is greater than the mean, then the Z score is positive; if the score is less than the mean, then the Z score is negative.

Let's try an example. Suppose that $X = 6$, the mean $\bar{X} = 3$, and the standard deviation $S = 3$. Plugging these values into the formula, we get

$$Z = \frac{6 - 3}{3} = \frac{3}{3} = 1$$

Let's try another example. Suppose $X = 4$, $\bar{X} = 5.75$, and $S = 2.11$. What is the Z score? It is $-.83$:

$$Z = \frac{4 - 5.74}{2.11} = \frac{-1.74}{2.11} = -.82$$

This means that the score we observed (4) is .83 standard deviation below the average score, or that the score is below the mean but its difference from the mean is slightly less than the average deviation.

Example of depression in medical students: Center for Epidemiologic Studies Depression Scale (CES-D). The CES-D is a general measure of depression that has been used extensively in epidemiological studies. The scale includes 20 items and taps dimensions of depressed mood, hopelessness, appetite loss, sleep disturbance, and energy level. Each year, students at the University of California, San Diego, School of Medicine are asked to report how often they experienced a particular symptom during the first week of school on a 4-point scale ranging from rarely or none of the time [0 to 1 days (0)] to most or all of the time [5 to 7 days (3)]. Items 4, 8, 12, and 16 on the CES-D are reverse scored. For these items, 0 is scored as 3, 1 is scored as 2, 2 as 1, and 3 as 0. The CES-D score is obtained by summing the circled numbers. Scores on the CES-D range from 0 to 60, with scores greater than 16 indicating clinically significant levels of depressive symptomatology in adults.

Feel free to take the CES-D measure yourself. Calculate your score by summing the numbers you have circled. However, you must first reverse the scores on items 4, 8, 12, and 16. As you will see in Chapter 5, the CES-D does not have high validity for determining clinical depression. If your score is less than 16, the evidence suggests that you are not clinically depressed. If your score is high, it raises suspicions about depression—though this does not mean you have a problem. (Of course, you may want to talk with your college counselor if you are feeling depressed.)

Center for Epidemiologic Studies Depression Scale (CES-D)

Instructions: Circle the number for each statement that best describes how often you felt or behaved this way DURING THE PAST WEEK.

		Rarely or none of the time (less than 1 day)	Some or a little of the time (1–2 days)	Occasionally or a moderate amount of the time (3–4 days)	Most or all of the time (5–7 days)
	1. I was bothered by things that usually don't bother me.	0	1	2	3
	2. I did not feel like eating.	0	1	2	3
	3. I felt that I could not shake off the blues even with help from my family or friends.	0	1	2	3
R	4. I felt that I was just as good as other people.	0	1	2	3
	5. I had trouble keeping my mind on what I was doing.	0	1	2	3
	6. I felt depressed.	0	1	2	3
	7. I felt that everything I did was an effort.	0	1	2	3
R	8. I felt hopeful about the future.	0	1	2	3
	9. I thought my life had been a failure.	0	1	2	3
	10. I felt fearful.	0	1	2	3
	11. My sleep was restless.	0	1	2	3
R	12. I was happy.	0	1	2	3
	13. I talked less than usual.	0	1	2	3
	14. I felt lonely.	0	1	2	3
	15. People were unfriendly.	0	1	2	3
R	16. I enjoyed life.	0	1	2	3
	17. I had crying spells.	0	1	2	3
	18. I felt sad.	0	1	2	3
	19. I felt that people disliked me.	0	1	2	3
	20. I could not get "going."	0	1	2	3

Table 2-3 shows CES-D scores for a selected sample of medical students. You can use these data to practice calculating means, standard deviations, and Z scores.

In creating the frequency distribution for the CES-D scores of medical students we used an arbitrary class interval of 5.

TABLE 2-3

The Calculation of Mean, Standard Deviation, and Z Scores for CES-D Scores

Name	Test score (X)	X^2	Z score
John	14	196	.42
Carla	10	100	−.15
Fred	8	64	−.44
Monica	8	64	−.44
Eng	26	676	2.13
Fritz	0	0	−1.58
Mary	14	196	.42
Susan	3	9	−1.15
Debbie	9	81	−.29
Elizabeth	10	100	−.15
Sarah	7	49	−.58
Marcel	12	144	.14
Robin	10	100	−.15
Mike	25	625	1.99
Carl	9	81	−.29
Phyllis	12	144	.14
Jennie	23	529	1.70
Richard	7	49	−.58
Tyler	13	169	.28
Frank	1	1	−1.43
	$\Sigma X = 221$	$\Sigma X^2 = 3377$	

$$\bar{X} = \frac{\Sigma X}{N} = \frac{221}{20} = 11.05$$

$$S = \sqrt{\frac{\Sigma X^2 - \frac{(\Sigma X)^2}{N}}{N-1}} = \sqrt{\frac{3377 - \frac{(221)^2}{20}}{20-1}} = 7.01$$

Monica's Z score $= \dfrac{X - \bar{X}}{S} = \dfrac{8 - 11.05}{7.01} = -.44$

Marcel's Z score $= \dfrac{X - \bar{X}}{S} = \dfrac{12 - 11.05}{7.01} = .14$

Jennie's Z score $= \dfrac{X - \bar{X}}{S} = \dfrac{23 - 11.05}{7.01} = 1.70$

Standard Normal Deviation

Now we consider the standard normal distribution because it is central to statistics and psychological testing. First, though, you should participate in a short exercise. Take any coin and flip it 10 times. Now repeat this exercise of 10 coin flips 25 times. Record the number of heads you observe in each group of 10 flips. When you are done, make a frequency distribution showing how many times you observed 1 head in your 10 flips, 2 heads, 3 heads, and so on.

Your frequency distribution might look like the example shown in Figure 2-6. The most frequently observed events are approximately equal numbers of

FIGURE 2-6

Frequency distribution of the number of heads in 25 sets of 10 flips.

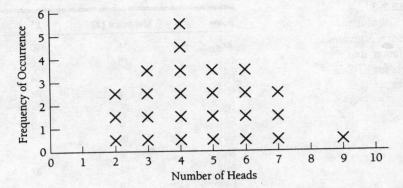

heads and tails. Toward the extremes of 10 heads and 0 tails or 10 tails and 0 heads, events are observed with decreasing frequency. For example, there were no occasions in which fewer than 2 heads were observed and only one occasion in which more than 8 heads were observed. This is what we would expect from the laws of probability. On the average, we would expect half of the flips to show heads and half to show tails if heads and tails are equally probable events. Although observing a long string of heads or tails is possible, it is improbable. In other words, we sometimes see the coin come up heads in 9 out of 10 flips. The likelihood that this will happen, however, is quite small.

Figure 2-7 shows the theoretical distribution of heads in an infinite number of flips of the coin. This figure might look a little like the distribution from your coin-flipping exercise or the distribution shown in Figure 2-6. Actually, this is a normal distribution, or what is known as a *symmetrical binomial probability distribution*.

On most occasions, we refer to units on the X (or horizontal) axis of the normal distribution in Z score units. Any variable transformed into Z score units takes on special properties. First, Z scores have a mean of 0 and a standard deviation of 1.0. If you think about this for a minute, you should be able

FIGURE 2-7

The theoretical distribution of the number of heads in an infinite number of coin flips.

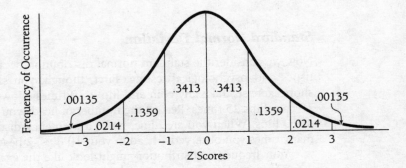

to figure out why this is true. Recall that the sum of the deviations around the mean is always equal to 0. The numerator of the Z score equation is the deviation around the mean, while the denominator is a constant. Thus, the mean of Z scores can be expressed as

$$\frac{\Sigma(X - \bar{X})/S}{N} \quad \text{or} \quad \frac{\Sigma Z}{N}$$

Because $\Sigma(X - \bar{X})$ will always equal 0, the mean of Z scores will always be 0. In Figure 2-7, the standardized, or Z score, units are marked on the X axis. The numbers under the curve are the proportions of cases (in decimal form) that we would expect to observe in each area. Multiplying these proportions by 100 yields percentages. For example, we see that 34.13% or .3413 of the cases fall between the mean and one standard deviation above the mean. Do not forget that 50% of the cases fall below the mean. Putting these two bits of information together, we can conclude that if a score is one standard deviation above the mean, then it is at about the 84th percentile rank (50 + 34.13 = 84.13 to be exact). A score that is one standard deviation below the mean would be about the 16th percentile rank (50 − 34.13 = 15.87). Thus, you can use what you have learned about means, standard deviations, Z scores, and the normal curve to transform raw scores, which have little meaning, into percentile scores, which are easier to interpret. These methods can be used only when the distribution of scores is normal or approximately normal. Methods for nonnormal distributions are discussed in most statistics books under "nonparametric statistics."

Percentiles and Z scores. These percentile ranks are the percentage of scores that fall below the observed Z score. For example, the Z score 21.6 is associated with the percentile rank of 5.48. The Z score 1.0 (third column) is associated with the percentile rank of 84.13.

Part I of Appendix 1 is a simplified version of Part II, which you need for more advanced use of Z scores. Part II gives the areas between the mean and various Z scores. Standard scored values are listed in the "Z" column. To find the proportion of the distribution between the mean of the distribution and a given Z score, you must locate the entry indicated by a specific Z score. Z scores are carried to a second decimal place in the columns that go across the table. First, consider the second column of the table because it is similar to Part I of Appendix 1. Take the Z score of 1.0. The second column is labeled .00, which means that the second decimal place is also 0. The number listed in the table is .3413. Because this is a positive number, it is above the mean. Because the area below the mean is .5, the total area below a Z score of 1.0 is .5 + .3413 = .8413. To make this into a percentile (as shown in Part I of the appendix), multiply by 100 to get 84.13. Now try the example of a Z score of 1.64. To locate this value, find 1.6 in the first column. Then move your hand across the row until you get to the number below the heading .04. The number is .4495. Again, this is a positive Z score, so you must add the observed proportion to the .5 that falls below the mean. The proportion below 1.64 is .9495. Stated another way, 94.95% of the cases fall below a Z score of 1.64. Now try to find the percentile rank of cases that fall below a Z score of 1.10. If you are using the table correctly, you should obtain 86.43.

Now try −.75. Because this is a negative Z score, the percentage of cases falling below the mean should be less than 50. But there are no negative values in Part II of Appendix 1. For a negative Z score, there are several ways to obtain the appropriate area under the curve. The tables in Appendix 1 give the area from the mean to the Z score. For a Z score of −.75, the area between the mean and the Z score is .2734. You can find this by entering the table in the row labeled .7 and then moving across the row until you get to the figure in that row below the heading .05. There you should find the number .2734. We know that .5 of the cases fall below the mean. Thus, for a negative Z score, we can obtain the proportion of cases falling below the score by subtracting .2734, the tabled value listed in the appendix, from .5. In this case, the result is

$$.5 - .2734 = .2266$$

Because finding the percentile ranks associated with negative Z scores can be tricky, you might want to use Part I of Appendix 1 to see if you are in the right ballpark. This table gives both negative and positive Z scores but does not give the detail associated with the second decimal place. Look up −.7 in Part I. The percentile rank is 24.20. Now consider a Z score of −.8. That percentile rank is 21.19. Thus, you know that a Z score of −.75 should be associated with a percentile rank between 21.19 and 24.20. In fact, we have calculated that the actual percentile rank is 22.66.

Practice with Appendix 1 until you are confident you understand how it works. Do not hesitate to ask your professor or teaching assistant if you are confused. This is an important concept that you will need throughout the rest of the book.

Look at one more example from Table 2-2 (rainfall in San Diego, page 33). California had a dry year in 1999. The newscasters frequently commented that this was highly unusual. They described it as the "La Niña" effect, and some even claimed that it signaled global warming. The question is whether or not the amount of rainfall received in 1999 was unusual given what we know about rainfall in general. To evaluate this, calculate the Z score for rainfall. According to Table 2-2, there were 6.49 inches of rainfall in 1999. The mean for rainfall is 10.47 inches and the standard deviation is 4.19. Thus, the Z score is

$$\frac{6.49 - 10.47}{4.19} = -0.95$$

Next determine where a Z score of −0.95 falls within the Z distribution. According to Appendix 1, a Z score of −0.95 is equal to the 17.11th percentile (50 − 32.89). Thus, the low rainfall year in 1999 was unusual—given all years, it was in about the 17th percentile. However, it was not *that* unusual. You can estimate that there would be less rainfall in approximately 17% of all years.

You can also turn the process around. Instead of using Z scores to find the percentile ranks, you can use the percentile ranks to find the corresponding Z scores. To do this, look in Part II of Appendix 1 under percentiles and find the corresponding Z score. For example, suppose you wish to find the Z score associated with the 90th percentile. When you enter Part II of Appendix 1, look for the value closest to the 90th percentile. This can be a little tricky because of the way the table is structured. Because the 90th percentile is associated with a positive Z score, you are actually looking for the area above the 50th percentile. So you should look for the entry closest to .4000 (.5000 + .4000 = .9000). The closest value to .4000 is .3997, which is found in the row labeled 1.2 and the column labeled .08. This tells you that a person who obtains a Z score of 1.28 is at approximately the 90th percentile in the distribution.

Now return to the example of CES-D scores for medical students (Table 2-3). Monica had a Z score on the CES-D of −.44. Using Appendix 1, you can see that she was in the 33rd percentile (obtained as .50 − .1700 = .33 × 100 = 33). Marcel, with his Z score of .14, was in the 56th percentile; and Jennie, with a Z score of 1.70, was in the 96th percentile. You might have few worries about Monica and Marcel. However, it appears that Jennie is more depressed than 96% of her classmates and may need to talk to someone.

An example close to home. One of the difficulties in grading students is that performance is usually rated in terms of raw scores, such as the number of items a person correctly answers on an examination. You are probably familiar with the experience of having a test returned to you with some number that makes little sense to you. For instance, the professor comes into class and hands you your test with a 72 on it. You must then wait patiently while he or she draws the distribution on the board and tries to put your 72 into some category that you understand, such as B+.

An alternative way of doing things would be to give you a Z score as feedback on your performance. To do this, your professor would subtract the average score (mean) from your score and divide by the standard deviation. If your Z score was positive, you would immediately know that your score was above average; if it was negative, you would know your performance was below average.

Suppose your professor tells you in advance that you will be graded on a curve according to the following rigid criteria. If you are in the top 15% of the class, you will get an A (85th percentile or above); between the 60th and the 84th percentiles, a B; between the 20th and the 59th percentiles, a C; between the 6th and the 19th percentiles, a D; and in the 5th percentile or below, an F. Using Appendix 1, you should be able to find the Z scores associated with each of these cutoff points for normal distributions of scores. Try it on your own and then consult Table 2-4 to see if you are correct. Looking at Table 2-4, you should be able to determine what your grade would be in this class on the basis of your Z score. If your Z score is 1.04 or greater, you would receive an A; if it were greater than .25 but less than 1.04, you would get a B; and so on. This system assumes that the scores are distributed normally.

TABLE 2-4
Z Score Cutoffs for a Grading System

Grade	Percentiles	Z score cutoff
A	85–100	1.04
B	60–84	.25
C	20–59	−.84
D	6–19	−1.56
F	0–5	< −1.56

Now try an example that puts a few of these concepts together. Suppose you get a 60 on a social psychology examination. You learned in class that the mean for the test was 55.70 and that the standard deviation was 6.08. If your professor uses the grading system that was just described, what would your grade be?

To solve this problem, first find your Z score. Recall the formula for a Z score:

$$Z = \frac{X - \bar{X}}{S}$$

So your Z score would be

$$Z = \frac{60 - 55.70}{6.08} = \frac{4.30}{6.08} = .707$$

Looking at Table 2-4, you see that .707 is greater than .25 (the cutoff for a B) but less than 1.04 (the cutoff for an A). Now find your exact standing in the class. To do this, look again at Appendix 1. Because the table gives Z scores only to the second decimal, round .707 to .71. You will find that 76.11% of the scores fall below a Z score of .71. This means that you would be in approximately the 76th percentile, or you would have performed better on this examination than approximately 76 out of every 100 students.

McCall's T

There are many other systems by which one can transform raw scores to give them more intuitive meaning. One system was established in 1939 by W. A. McCall, who originally intended to develop a system to derive equal units on mental quantities. He suggested that a random sample of 12-year-olds be tested and that the distribution of their scores be obtained. Then percentile equivalents were to be assigned to each raw score, showing the percentile rank in the group for the people who had obtained that raw score. After this had been accomplished, the mean of the distribution would be set at 50 to correspond with the 50th percentile. In McCall's system, called **McCall's T**, the standard deviation was set at 10.

In effect, McCall generated a system that is exactly the same as standard scores (Z scores), except that the mean in McCall's system is 50 rather than 0 and the standard deviation is 10 rather than 1. Indeed, a Z score can be transformed to a **T score** by applying the linear transformation

$$T = 10Z + 50$$

You can thus get from a Z score to McCall's T by multiplying the Z score by 10 and adding 50. It should be noted that McCall did not originally intend to create an alternative to the Z score. He wanted to obtain one set of scores that could then be applied to other situations without standardizing the entire set of numbers.

There is nothing magical about the mean of 50 and the standard deviation of 10. It is a simple matter to create systems such as standard scores with any mean and standard deviation you like. If you want to say that you got a score 1000 points higher than a person who was one standard deviation below you, then you could devise a system with a mean of 100,000 and a standard deviation of 1000. If you had calculated Z scores for this distribution, then you would obtain this with the transformation

$$NS \text{ (for new score)} = 1000Z + 100,000$$

In fact, you can create any system you desire. To do so, just multiply the Z score by whatever you would like the standard deviation of your distribution to be and then add the number you would like the mean of your new distribution to be.

An example of a test developed using standardized scores is the Scholastic Aptitude Test (SAT). When this test was created in 1941, the developers decided to make the mean score 500 and the standard deviation 100. Thus, they multiplied the Z scores for those who took the test by 100 and added 500. For a long time, the basic scoring system was used and the 1941 norms were applied. In other words, if the average score of test takers was below the 1941 reference point, the mean for any year could be less than or more than 500. However, in 1995, the test was changed so that the mean each year would be 500 and the standard deviation would be 100. In other words, the test is recalibrated each year. However, drifts continue. For example, in 2002 the average scores on the SAT were 504 verbal and 516 math (data from www.college board.com/about/newsat).

It is important to make the distinction between standardization and normalization. McCall's T and the other methods described in this section standardize scores by applying a linear transformation. These transformations do not change the characteristics of the distributions. If a distribution of scores is skewed before the transformation is applied, it will also be skewed after the transformation has been used. In other words, transformations standardize but do not normalize.

Quartiles and Deciles

The terms *quartiles* and *deciles* are frequently used when tests and test results are discussed. The two terms refer to divisions of the percentile scale into groups. The quartile system divides the percentage scale into four groups, whereas the decile system divides the scale into 10 groups.

Quartiles are points that divide the frequency distribution into equal fourths. The first quartile is the 25th percentile; the second quartile is the **median,** or 50th, percentile; and the third quartile is the 75th percentile. These are abbreviated Q1, Q2, and Q3, respectively. One-fourth of the cases will fall below Q1, one-half will fall below Q2, and three-fourths will fall below Q3. The interquartile range is the interval of scores bounded by the 25th and 75th percentiles. In other words, the **interquartile range** is bounded by the range of scores that represents the middle 50% of the distribution.

Deciles are similar to quartiles except that they use points that mark 10% rather than 25% intervals. Thus, the top decile, or D9, is the point below which 90% of the cases fall. The next decile (D8) marks the 80th percentile, and so forth.

Another system developed in the U.S. Air Force during World War II is known as the **stanine system.** This system converts any set of scores into a transformed scale, which ranges from 1 to 9. Actually the term *stanine* comes from "standard nine." The scale is standardized to have a mean of 5 and a standard deviation of approximately 2. It has been suggested that stanines had computational advantages because they required only one column on a computer card (Anastasi & Urbina, 1997). Because computer cards are no longer used, this advantage is now questionable.

Table 2-5 shows how percentile scores are converted into stanines. As you can see, for every 100 scores, the lowest 4 (or bottom 4% of the cases) fall into the first stanine. The next 7 (or 7% of the cases) fall into the second stanine, and so on. Finally, the top 4 cases fall into the top stanine. Using what you have learned about Z scores and the standard normal distribution, you should be able to figure out the stanine for a score if you know the mean and the standard deviation of the distribution that the score comes from. For example, suppose that Igor received a 48 on his normally distributed chemistry midterm. The mean in Igor's class was 42.6, and the standard deviation was 3.6. First you must find Igor's Z score. Do this by using the formula

$$Z = \frac{X - \bar{X}}{S} \quad \text{so} \quad Z = \frac{48 - 42.6}{3.6} = 1.5$$

Now you need to transform Igor's Z score into his percentile rank. To do this, use Appendix 1. Part I shows that a Z score of 1.5 is in approximately the 93rd percentile. Thus, it falls into the 8th stanine.

Actually, you would rarely go through all these steps to find a stanine. There are easier ways of doing this, including computer programs that do it automatically. However, working out stanines the long way will help you become familiar with a variety of concepts covered in this chapter, including standard scores, means, standard deviations, and percentiles. First, review the five steps to go from raw scores to stanines:

1. Find the mean of the raw scores.
2. Find the standard deviation of the raw scores.
3. Change the raw scores to Z scores.

TABLE 2-5

Transformation of Percentile Scores into Stanines

Percentage of cases	Percentiles	Stanines
4	1–4	1 Top 4 percent
7	5–11	2
12	12–23	3
17	24–40	4
20	41–60	5
17	61–77	6
12	78–89	7
7	90–96	8
4	97–100	9 Bottom 4 percent

4. Change the Z scores to percentiles (using Appendix 1).

5. Use Table 2-5 to convert percentiles into stanines.

An alternative method is to calculate the percentile rank for each score and use Table 2-5 to obtain the stanines. Remember: In practice, you would probably use a computer program to obtain the stanines. Although stanines are not used much in the modern computer era, you can still find them in popular educational tests such as the Stanford Achievement Test.

Norms

Norms refer to the performances by defined groups on particular tests. There are many ways to express norms, and we have discussed some of these under the headings of Z scores, percentiles, and means. The norms for a test are based on the distribution of scores obtained by some defined sample of individuals. The mean is a norm, and the 50th percentile is a norm. Norms are used to give information about performance relative to what has been observed in a standardization sample.

Much has been written about norms and their inadequacies. In later chapters, we shall discuss this material in relation to particular tests. We cover only the highlights here. Whenever you see a norm for a test, you should ask how it was established. Norms are obtained by administering the test to a sample of people and obtaining the distribution of scores for that group.

For example, say you develop a measure of anxiety associated with taking tests in college. After establishing some psychometric properties for the test, you administer the test to normative groups of college students. The scores of these groups of students might then serve as the norms. Say that, for the normative groups of students, the average score is 19. When your friend Alice comes to take the test and obtains a score of 24, the psychologist using the test might conclude that Alice is above average in test anxiety.

The SAT, as indicated earlier, has norms. The test was administered to millions of high-school seniors from all over the United States. With distributions of scores for this normative group, one could obtain a distribution to provide meaning for particular categories of scores. For example, in the 1941 national sample, a person who scored 650 on the verbal portion of the SAT was at the 93rd percentile of high-school seniors. However, if you took the test before 1995 and scored 650, it did not mean that you were in the 93rd percentile of the people who took the test when you did. Rather, it meant that you would have been at the 93rd percentile if you had been in the group the test had been standardized on. However, if the normative group was a representative sample of the group to which you belonged (and there is every reason to believe it was), then you could reasonably assume that you were in approximately the 93rd percentile of your own group.[1] After 1995, an SAT score of 650 would place you in the 93rd percentile of the people who took the test during the year you completed it. Some controversies surrounding norms are discussed in Technical Box 2-4.

In Chapters 9 and 10 we will review intelligence tests. Most intelligence tests are transformed to have a mean of 100 and a standard deviation of 15. Thus, an IQ score of 115 is one standard deviation above the mean and an IQ score of 130 is two standard deviations above the mean. Using the information we have reviewed, you can determine an IQ score of 115 is approximately in the 84th percentile, while an IQ score of 85 is approximately in the 16th percentile. Only some 0.13 percent of the population obtains an IQ score of 145, which is three standard deviations above the mean. Figure 2-8 shows the standard normal distribution with the Z scores, T scores, IQ scores, and stanines. Examining the figure, locate the point that is one standard deviation above the mean. That point is associated with a Z score of 1.0, a T score of 60, an IQ score of 115, and the seventh stanine. Using the figure, try to find the score on each scale for an observation that falls two standard deviations below the mean. You should get a Z score of -2.0, a T score of 30, an IQ score of 64, and a stanine of 1.

Age-Related Norms

Certain tests have different normative groups for particular age groups. Most IQ tests are of this sort. When the Stanford-Binet IQ test was originally created, distributions of the performance of random samples of children were obtained for various age groups. When applying an IQ test, the tester's task is to determine the mental age of the person being tested. This is accomplished through various exercises that help locate the age-level norm at which a child is performing.

Tracking

One of the most common uses of age-related norms is for growth charts used by pediatricians. Consider the question "Is my son tall or short?" The answer will usually depend on a comparison of your son to other boys of the same age.

---

[1]Based on the *American Testing Program Guide for 1989–1991*, College Board of the Educational Testing Service, Princeton, New Jersey.

TECHNICAL BOX 2-4

Within-Group Norming Controversy

One of the most troubling issues in psychological testing is that different racial and ethnic groups do not have the same average level of performance on many tests (see Chapter 19). When tests are used to select employees, a higher percentage of majority applicants are typically selected than their representation in the general population would indicate. For example, employers who use general aptitude tests consistently overselect white applicants and underselect African Americans and Latinos or Latinas. *Overselection* is defined as selecting a higher percentage from a particular group than would be expected on the basis of the representation of that group in the applicant pool. If 60% of the applicants are white and 75% of those hired are white, then overselection has occurred.

The U.S. Department of Labor uses the General Aptitude Test Battery (GATB) to refer job applicants to employers. At one point, however, studies demonstrated that the GATB adversely affected the hiring of African Americans and Latinos and Latinas. To remedy this problem, a few years ago the department created separate norms for different groups. In other words, to obtain a standardized score, each applicant was compared only with members of his or her own racial or ethnic group. As a result, overselection based on test scores was eliminated. However, this provoked other problems. For example, consider two applicants, one white and one African American, who are in the 70th percentile on the GATB. Although they have the same score, they are compared with different normative groups. The raw score for the white applicant would be 327, while that for the African American would be 283 (Brown, 1994). This was seen as a problem because an African American applicant might be selected for a job even though she had a lower raw score, or got fewer items correct, than did a white applicant.

The problem of within-group norming is highlighted by opposing opinions from different prestigious groups. The National Academy of Sciences, the most elite group of scholars in the United States, reviewed the issue and concluded that separate norms were appropriate. Specifically, they argued that minority workers at a given level of expected job performance are less likely to be hired than are majority group members. The use of separate norms was therefore required in order to avoid adverse impact in hiring decisions (Gottfredson, 1994; Hartigan & Wigdor, 1989).

In contrast to this conclusion, legislation has led to different policies. Section 106 of the Civil Rights Act of 1991 made it illegal to use separate norms. The act states that it is unlawful for employers

> in connection with the selection or referral of applicants or candidates for employment or promotion to adjust the scores of, use different cut-offs for, or otherwise alter the results of employment-related tests on the basis of race, color, religion, sex, or national origin.

Employers may have a variety of different objectives when making employment decisions. One goal may be to enhance the ethnic and racial diversity of their workforce. Another goal may be to hire those with the best individual profiles. Often these goals compete. The law may now prohibit employers from attempting to balance these competing objectives (Sackett & Wilk, 1994).

FIGURE 2-8

Tracking chart for boys' physical growth from birth to 36 months.

(Adapted from the National Center for Health Statistics: NCHS Growth Charts, Health Resources Administration, Rockville, MD, June 1976.)

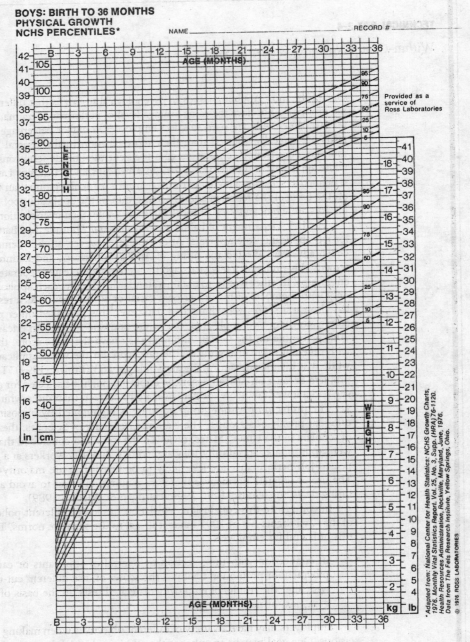

BOYS: BIRTH TO 36 MONTHS
PHYSICAL GROWTH
NCHS PERCENTILES*

NAME_____   RECORD #_____

Provided as a service of Ross Laboratories

* Adapted from: National Center for Health Statistics: NCHS Growth Charts, 1976. Monthly Vital Statistics Report, Vol. 25, No. 3, Supp. (HRA) 76–1120. Health Resources Administration, Rockville, Maryland, June, 1976. Data from The Fels Research Institute, Yellow Springs, Ohio.

© 1976 ROSS LABORATORIES

Your son would be quite tall if he were 5 feet at age 8 but quite short if he were only 5 feet at age 18. Thus, the comparison is usually with people of the same age.

Beyond this rather obvious type of age-related comparison, child experts have discovered that children at the same age level tend to go through differ-

FIGURE 2-9

Tracking chart for girls' physical growth from birth to 36 months.

(Adapted from the National Center for Health Statistics: NCHS Growth Charts, Health Resources Administration, Rockville, MD, June 1976.)

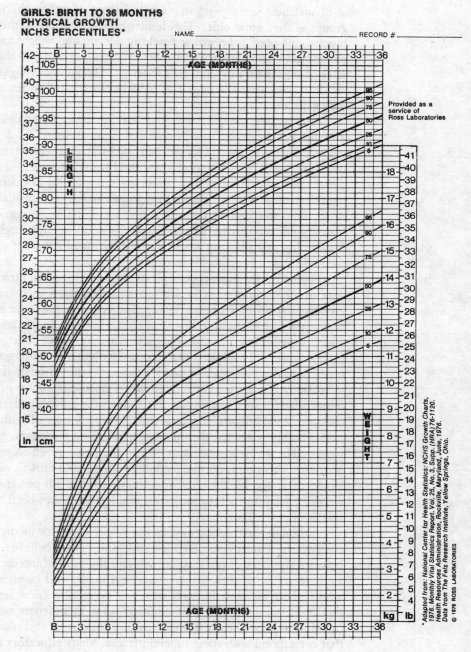

GIRLS: BIRTH TO 36 MONTHS
PHYSICAL GROWTH
NCHS PERCENTILES*

NAME _____   RECORD # _____

Provided as a service of Ross Laboratories

*Adapted from: National Center for Health Statistics: NCHS Growth Charts, 1976. Monthly Vital Statistics Report. Vol. 25, No. 3, Supp. (HRA) 76-1120. Health Resources Administration, Rockville, Maryland, June, 1976. Data from The Fels Research Institute, Yellow Springs, Ohio.

© 1976 ROSS LABORATORIES

ent growth patterns. Children who are small as infants often remain small and continue to grow at a slower pace than do others. Pediatricians must therefore know more than a child's age; they must also know the child's percentile within a given age group. For a variety of physical characteristics, children tend to stay at about their same percentile level, relative to other children in their age group, as they grow older. This tendency to stay at about the same level relative to one's peers is known as **tracking.** Height and weight are good examples of physical characteristics that track. Figures 2-8 and 2-9 show the expected rates of growth for boys and girls in terms of height and weight. Notice that the children who were the largest as babies are expected to remain the largest as they get older.

Pediatricians use the charts to determine the expected course of growth for a child. For example, if a 3-month-old boy weighed 13.2 pounds (6 kilograms), the doctor would locate the child on the center line on the bottom half of Figure 2-8. By age 36 months, the child would be expected to weigh just under 33 pounds. The tracking charts are quite useful to doctors because they help determine whether the child is going through an unusual growth pattern. A boy who weighed 13 pounds at age 3 months might come under scrutiny if at age 36 months he weighed only 28 pounds. This might be normal for 3-year-olds in a different track, but the doctor might want to determine why the child did not stay in his track.

Figure 2-10 shows an example of a child going off her track. There is some concern that children who are fed a fat-restricted diet experience stunted growth (Kaplan & Toshima, 1992). The consequences of a slightly restricted vegetarian diet are mild if they exist at all. However, highly restricted diets may affect growth. For instance, Pugliese, Lifshitz, Grad, Fort, and Marks-Katz (1983) studied 24 adolescents who had voluntarily undergone severe caloric restrictions because they wanted to lose weight. Though they did not have anorexia nervosa, they consumed only a small percentage of the calories recommended for their age. Figure 2-10 shows the growth pattern for one of these children. As the figure suggests, the child grew normally until age 9. At that point, highly restricted dieting began. Within a few years, growth was interrupted. The arrow in the figure shows the point at which psychotherapy began. After this point, normal feeding resumed, and growth started once again. However, at age 18, the child was still below the 5th percentile in height and weight. Given normal tracking, this child should have been between the 25th and 50th percentiles.

Although the tracking system has worked well for medicine, it has stirred considerable controversy in education. Some people believe there is an analogy between the rates of physical growth and the rates of intellectual growth: Just as there are some slow growers who eventually will be shorter than average adults, there are slow learners who will eventually know less as adults. Furthermore, some suggest that children learn at different rates. Children are therefore separated early in their educational careers and placed in classrooms that correspond with these different tracks. Many educators have attacked the tracking system because it discriminates against some children. Because people use psychological tests to place children in these tracks, some tests have come under severe scrutiny and attack. We shall return to this controversy in Chapters 19 and 20.

FIGURE 2-10
Growth in the case of severe dietary restriction. The scales represent percentile standards for height and weight, and the plotted values are for the clinical case.

(From Pugliese et al., 1983, p. 514; reprinted by permission of The New England Journal of Medicine, 309, 513–518, 1983.)

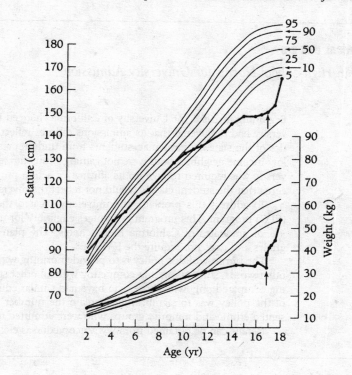

Criterion-Referenced Tests

The purpose of establishing norms for a test is to determine how a test taker compares with others. A **norm-referenced test** compares each person with a norm. Many critics have objected that this use of tests forces competition among people. Young children exposed to many norm-referenced tests in elementary school can get caught up in a never-ending battle to perform better than average. In addition to ranking people according to performance, however, tests can play an important role in identifying problems and suggesting new directions for individualized programs of instruction. During the last two decades, interest has grown in tests that are applied to determine whether students know specific information. These tests do not compare students with one another; they compare each student's performance with a criterion or an expected level of performance (Hartman & Looney, 2003; Wiberg, 2003).

A **criterion-referenced test** describes the specific types of skills, tasks, or knowledge that the test taker can demonstrate such as mathematical skills. The results of such a test might demonstrate that a particular child can add, subtract, and multiply but has difficulty with both long and short division. The results of the test would not be used to make comparisons between the child and other members of his or her class. Instead, they would be employed to design an individualized program of instruction that focuses on division. Thus, the

TECHNICAL BOX 2-5

Within High-School Norms for University Admission

Beginning in 2002, the University of California changed its admissions policy. The university had discovered that its admissions did not reflect the demographic characteristics of the state. In particular, students from underrepresented groups and those from low-income neighborhoods were not gaining admission to the university. When the university was required to give up its affirmative action program, there were serious concerns that the student classes would not reflect the diversity of the state of California.

To address this problem, the university created the Eligibility in Local Context (ELC) program. This program guarantees eligibility for university admission to the top 4% of graduates of California high schools. The plan focuses only on high-school grades and does not require the SAT test.

The purpose of this policy is to provide norming within particular high schools. In other words, students are not competing with all other students in the state but are being compared only with those who have had similar educational exposures. The effect of the policy was to significantly increase the number of students from underrepresented ethnic and minority groups who were admitted to the university.

Details can be obtained from www.ucop.edu/sas/elc.

criterion-referenced testing movement emphasizes the diagnostic use of tests—that is, using them to identify problems that can be remedied.

SUMMARY

In this chapter, we discussed some basic rules for translating observations of human activities into numbers. The use of number systems is important for precision in all scientific exercises. Measures of psychological processes are represented by one of four types of scales. A *nominal scale* simply assigns numbers to categories. This type of scale has none of the properties of a numbered scale. An *ordinal scale* has the property of magnitude and allows us to rank objects, but it does not have the property of equal intervals or an absolute 0. An *interval scale* can describe the distances between objects because it has the property of equal intervals in addition to the property of magnitude. A *ratio scale* has an absolute 0 in addition to equal intervals and magnitude. Any mathematical operation on a ratio scale is permissible.

To make sense out of test scores, we have to examine the score of an individual relative to the scores of others. To do this requires creating a distribution of test scores. There are several ways to display the distribution of scores, including frequency distributions and frequency polygons. We also need statistics to describe the distribution. The *mean* is the average score, the *variance* is the averaged squared deviation around the mean, and the *standard deviation* is the square root of the variance. Using these statistics, we can tell a lot about a particular score by relating it to characteristics of a well-known probability distribution known as the standard normal distribution.

Norms are used to relate a score to a particular distribution for a subgroup of a population. For example, norms are used to describe where a child is on some measure relative to other children of the same age. In contrast, *criterion-referenced tests* are used to document specific skills rather than to compare people.

In summary, this chapter reviewed basic statistical methods for describing scores on one variable. In Chapter 3, we shall discuss statistical methods for showing the relationship between two or more variables.

WEB ACTIVITY

For interesting and relevant Web sites, check the following:

www.aaamath.com/B/sta518x2.htm
Gives simple examples and definitions for calculation of the mean

www.mathgoodies.com/lessons/toc_vol8.shtm
Offers definitions and examples for basic statistical concepts

www.robertniles.com/stats/stdev.shtml
Summary of the concepts of standard deviation and variability

davidmlane.com/hyperstat/A16252.html
Formulae for standard deviation and variance

CHAPTER 3

Correlation and Regression

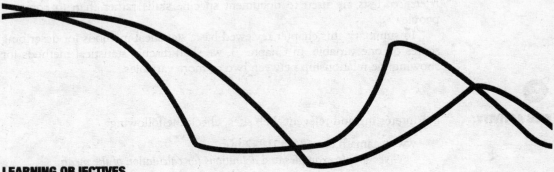

LEARNING OBJECTIVES

When you have completed this chapter[1], you should be able to:

☐ Express the extent to which two measures are associated

☐ Explain what a scatter diagram is and how it is used

☐ Define a positive correlation and a negative correlation

☐ Discuss some of the differences between correlation and regression

☐ Tell how a regression line describes the relationship between two variables

☐ Discuss under which circumstances you would use the point biserial correlation, the phi coefficient, and the tetrachoric correlation

☐ Outline the procedure you would use to predict one score from the linear combination of several scores

☐ Explain factor analysis and how it is used

---

[1]Portions of this chapter are taken from *Basic Statistics for the Behavioral Sciences* by Robert M. Kaplan (Newton, MA: Allyn & Bacon, 1987).

A banner headline in an issue of the *National Enquirer* read, "FOOD CAUSES MOST MARRIAGE PROBLEMS." The article talked about "Startling Results of Studies by Doctors and Marriage Counselors." Before we are willing to accept the magazine's conclusion, we must ask many questions. Did the *National Enquirer* report enough data for us to evaluate the hypothesis? Do we feel comfortable concluding that an association between diet and divorce has been established?

There were many problems with the *National Enquirer* report. The observation was based on the clinical experiences of some health practitioners who found that many couples who came in for counseling had poor diets. One major oversight was that there was no control group of people who were not having marriage problems. We do not know from the study whether couples with problems have poor diets more often than do people in general. Another problem is that neither diet nor marital happiness was measured in a systematic way. Thus, we are left with subjective opinions about the levels of these variables. Finally, we do not know the direction of the causation: Does poor diet cause unhappiness, or does unhappiness cause poor diet? Another possibility is that some other problem (such as stress) may cause both poor diet and unhappiness. So it turns out that the article was not based on any systematic study. It merely cited the opinions of some physicians and marriage counselors who felt that high levels of blood sugar are related to low energy levels, which in turn cause marital unhappiness.

This chapter focuses on one of the many issues raised in the report—the level of association between variables. The *Enquirer* tells us that diet and unhappiness are associated, but not to what extent. Is the association greater than we would expect by chance? Is it a strong or is it a weak association?

Lots of things seem to be related. For example, long-term stress is associated with heart disease, training is associated with good performance in athletics, overeating is associated with indigestion. People often observe associations between events. For some events, the association is obvious. For example, the angle of the sun in the sky and the time of day are associated in a predictable way. This is because time was originally defined by the angle of the sun in the sky. Other associations are less obvious, such as the association between performing well on the SAT and obtaining good grades in college.

Sometimes, we do not know whether events are meaningfully associated with one another. If we do conclude that events are fundamentally associated, then we need to determine a precise index of the degree. This chapter discusses statistical procedures that allow us to make precise estimates of the degree to which variables are associated. These methods are quite important; we shall refer to them frequently in the remainder of this book. The indexes of association used most frequently in testing are *correlation, regression,* and *multiple regression.*

The Scatter Diagram

Before discussing the measures of association, we shall look at visual displays of the relationships between variables. In Chapter 2, we concentrated on univariate distributions of scores, which involve only one variable for each

FIGURE 3-1

*A scatter
diagram. The
circled point
shows a person
who had a score
of 21 on X and
14 on Y.*

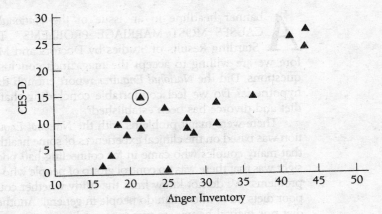

individual under study. This chapter considers statistical methods for studying *bivariate distributions*, which have two scores for each individual. For example, when we study the relationship between test scores and classroom performance, we are dealing with a bivariate distribution. Each person has a score on the test and a score for classroom performance. We must examine the scores of all the individuals to know whether these two variables are associated.

The American Psychological Association's Task Force on Statistical Inference has suggested that visual inspection of data is an important step in data analysis (Wilkinson, 1999). A **scatter diagram** is a picture of the relationship between two variables. An example of a scatter diagram is shown in Figure 3-1, which relates scores on a measure of anger for medical students to scores on the CES-D. The axes in the figure represent the scales for two variables. Values of X for the anger inventory are shown on the horizontal axis, and values of Y for the CES-D are on the vertical axis. Each point on the scatter diagram shows where a particular individual scored on both X and Y. For example, one person had a score of 14 on the CES-D and a score of 21 on the anger inventory. This point is circled in the figure. You can locate it by finding 21 on the X axis and then going straight up to the level of 14 on the Y axis. Each point indicates the scores for X and Y for one individual. As you can see, the figure presents a lot of information. Each point represents the performance of one person who has been assessed on two measures.

The next sections present methods for summarizing the information in a scatter diagram by finding the straight line that comes closest to more points than any other line. One important reason for examining the scatter diagram is that the relationships between X and Y are not always best described by a straight line. For example, Figure 3-2 shows the hypothetical relationship between levels of antidepressant medication in the blood of depressed patients and the number of symptoms they report. However, the relationship is systematic. Patients who have too little or too much medication experience more symptoms than do those who get an intermediate amount. The methods of lin-

FIGURE 3-2

*A scatter diagram
showing a
nonlinear
relationship.*

*(From R. M. Kaplan &
Grant, 2000.)*

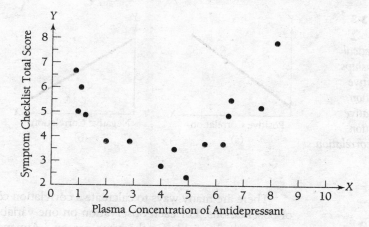

ear correlation or linear regression to be presented in this chapter are not appropriate for describing nonlinear relationships such as this.

Correlation

In correlational analysis, we ask whether two variables covary. In other words, does Y get larger as X gets larger? For example, does the patient feel dizzier when the doctor increases the dose of a drug? Do people get more diseases when they are under more stress? Correlational analysis is designed primarily to examine linear relationships between variables. Although one can use correlational techniques to study nonlinear relationships, doing so lies beyond the scope of this book.[2]

A **correlation coefficient** is a mathematical index that describes the direction and magnitude of a relationship. Figure 3-3 shows three different types of relationships between variables. Part (a) of the figure demonstrates a *positive correlation*. This means that high scores on Y are associated with high scores on X, and low scores on Y correspond to low scores on X. Part (b) shows *negative correlation*. When there is a negative correlation, higher scores on X are associated with lower scores on X, and lower scores on Y are associated with higher scores on X. This might describe the relationship between barbiturate use and amount of activity: the higher the drug dose, the less active the patients are. Part (c) of Figure 3-3 shows no correlation, or a situation in which the variables are not related. Here, scores on X do not give us information about scores on Y. An example of this sort of relationship is the lack of correlation between shoe size and IQ.

---

[2]Readers who are interested in studying nonlinear relationships should review Pedhazur (1997).

FIGURE 3-3

Three hypothetical relationships: (a) positive correlation, (b) negative correlation, (c) no correlation.

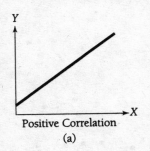

Positive Correlation
(a)

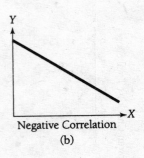

Negative Correlation
(b)

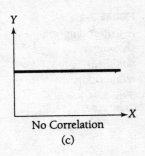

No Correlation
(c)

There are many ways to calculate a correlation coefficient. All involve pairs of observations: For each observation on one variable, there is an observation on one other variable for the same person.[3] Appendix 3-1 (at the end of this chapter) offers an example of the calculation of a correlation. All methods of calculating a correlation coefficient are mathematically equivalent. Before we present methods for calculating the correlation coefficient, however, we shall discuss regression, the method on which correlation is based.

Regression

The Regression Line

We use correlation to assess the magnitude and direction of a relationship. A related technique, known as *regression,* is used to make predictions about scores on one variable from knowledge of scores on another variable. These predictions are obtained from the **regression line,** which is defined as the best-fitting straight line through a set of points in a scatter diagram. It is found by using the *principle of least squares,* which minimizes the squared deviation around the regression line. Let us explain.

The mean is the point of least squares for any single variable. This means that the sum of the squared deviations around the mean will be less than it is around any value other than the mean. For example, consider the scores 5, 4, 3, 2, and 1. The mean is $\Sigma X/N = 15/5 = 3$. The squared deviation of each score around the mean can be found. For the score 5, the squared deviation is $(5 - 3)^2 = 4$. For the score 4, it is $(4 - 3)^2 = 1$. The score 3 is equal to the mean, so the squared deviation around the mean will be $(3 - 3)^2 = 0$. By definition, the mean will always be the point of least squares.

The regression line is the running mean or the line of least squares in two dimensions or in the space created by two variables. Consider the situation

---

[3]The pairs of scores do not always need to be for a person. They might also be for a group, an institution, a team, and so on.

shown in the scatter diagram in Figure 3-1. For each level of X (or point on the X scale), there is a distribution of scores on Y. In other words, we could find a mean of Y when X is 3, another mean of Y when X is 4, and so on. The least squares method in regression finds the straight line that comes as close to as many of these Y means as possible. In other words, it is the line for which the squared deviations around the line are at a minimum.

Before we get to the regression equation, we must define some of the terms it includes. The term on the left of the equation is Y. This is the predicted value of Y. When we create the equation, we use observed values of Y and X. The equation is the result of the least squares procedure and shows the best linear relationship between X and Y. When the equation is available, we can take a score on X and plug it into the formula. What results is a predicted value of Y, or Y'.

The most important term in the equation is the *regression coefficient,* or *b*, which is the slope of the regression line. The regression coefficient can be expressed as the ratio of the sum of squares for the covariance to the sum of squares for X. *Sum of squares* is defined as the sum of the squared deviations around the mean. For X, this is the sum of the squared deviations around the X variable. *Covariance* is used to express how much two measures covary, or vary together. To understand covariance, let's look at the extreme case of the relationship between two identical sets of scores. In this case, there will be a perfect association. We know that we can create a new score that exactly repeats the scores on any one variable. If we created this new twin variable, then it would covary perfectly with the original variable. Regression analysis attempts to determine how similar the variance between two variables is by dividing the covariance by the average variance of each variable. The covariance is calculated from the cross products, or products of variations around each mean. Symbolically, this is

$$\Sigma XY = \Sigma(X - \bar{X})(Y - \bar{Y})$$

The regression coefficient or slope is:

$$b = \frac{N(\Sigma XY) - (\Sigma X)(\Sigma Y)}{N\Sigma X^2 - (\Sigma X)^2}$$

The *slope* describes how much change is expected in Y each time X increases by one unit. For example, Figure 3-4 shows a regression line with a slope of .67. In this figure, the difference between 1 and 2 in units of X is associated with an expected difference of .67 in units of Y (for $X = 1$, $Y = 2.67$ and for $X = 2$, $Y = 3.34$; $3.34 - 2.67 = .67$). The regression coefficient is sometimes expressed in different notation. For example, the Greek β is often used for a population estimate of the regression coefficient.

The **intercept**, *a*, is the value of Y when X is 0. In other words, it is the point at which the regression line crosses the Y axis. This is shown in Figure 3-4. It is easy to find the intercept when we know the regression coefficient. The intercept is found by using the following formula:

$$a = Y - bX$$

FIGURE 3-4

The regression equation. The slope is the change in Y per unit change in X. The intercept is value of Y when X is 0.

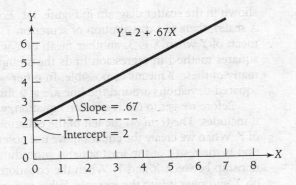

The Best-Fitting Line

Correlational methods require finding the best-fitting line through a series of data points. In Figure 3-4, a regression line is shown that is based on a series of observations for particular individuals. Each individual had actually obtained a score on X and on Y. Take the example of someone who obtained a score of 4 on X and 6 on Y. The regression equation gives a predicted value for Y, denoted as Y'. Using the regression equation, we can calculate Y' for this person. It is

$$Y' = 2 + .67X$$

so

$$Y' = 2 + .67(4)$$
$$= 4.68$$

The actual and predicted scores on Y are rarely exactly the same. Suppose that the person actually received a score of 4 on Y and that the regression equation predicted that he or she would have a score of 4.68 on Y. The difference between the observed and predicted score (Y − Y') is called the **residual**. The best-fitting line keeps residuals to a minimum. In other words, it minimizes the deviation between observed and predicted Y scores. Because residuals can be positive or negative and will cancel to 0 if averaged, the best-fitting line is most appropriately found by squaring each residual. Thus, the best-fitting line is obtained by keeping these squared residuals as small as possible. This is known as the *principle of least squares*. Formally, it is stated as

$$\Sigma(Y - Y')^2 \quad \text{is at a minimum}$$

An example showing how to calculate a regression equation is given in Appendix 3-1. Whether or not you become proficient at calculating regression equations, you should learn to interpret them in order to be a good consumer of research information.

TABLE 3-1

Relationship of Cigarette Price and Consumption

	Country	Average cigarettes/year	Price per pack ($)
1.	Belgium	1990	1.54
2.	Czechoslovakia	2520	1.90
3.	Denmark	2110	3.60
4.	Finland	1720	2.50
5.	France	2400	0.80
6.	GFR	2380	2.90
7.	GDR	2340	1.78
8.	Greece	3640	0.48
9.	Hungary	3260	0.36
10.	Iceland	3100	3.51
11.	Ireland	2560	2.77
12.	Italy	2460	1.21
13.	Netherlands	1690	1.65
14.	Norway	710	4.17
15.	Portugal	1730	0.72
16.	Romania	2110	0.37
17.	Spain	2740	0.55
18.	Sweden	1660	2.30
19.	Switzerland	2960	1.84
20.	Turkey	3000	0.54
21.	USSR	2170	0.80
22.	UK	2120	2.45

Table 3-1 and Figure 3-5 present an example of a regression problem. The data come from international studies on the relationship between price per pack of cigarettes and the number of cigarettes consumed per capita. There is considerable variability in the price per pack of cigarettes among European countries. The differences between countries is primarily defined by the level of taxation. Some countries, such as Norway, have high taxes on tobacco; therefore, the price per pack for cigarettes is much higher. Figure 3-5 shows the scatter diagram as it relates price to number of cigarettes consumed.

Although the relationship is not strong, there is a negative trend, which is defined by the regression equation. The intercept in this equation is 2764.6. This means the line intersects the Y axis at 2764.6. The intercept provides an estimate of the number of cigarettes that would be consumed if cigarettes were free. The regression coefficient for this model is $b = -243.99$ and tells how much cigarette consumption should decline for each dollar that is added to the price of a pack of cigarettes. In other words, this equation suggests that, on average, people will smoke 244 fewer cigarettes per year for each dollar added to the price of cigarettes. Thus, according to this simple model, adding a $2 tax to cigarettes would decrease consumption on average by approximately 488 cigarettes per year (Kaplan et al., 1995).

FIGURE 3-5
Scatter diagram relating price to number of cigarettes consumed.

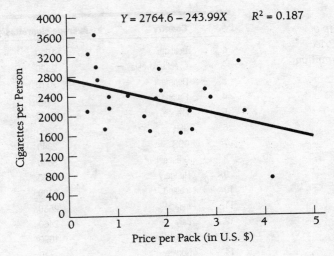

Correlation is a special case of regression in which the scores for both variables are in standardized, or Z, units. Having the scores in Z units is a nice convenience because it eliminates the need to find the intercept. In correlation, the intercept is always 0. Furthermore, the slope in correlation is easier to interpret because it is in a standardized unit. An example of how to calculate a correlation coefficient is given in Appendix 3-1. In calculating the correlation coefficient, we can bypass the step of changing all the scores into Z units. This gets done as part of the calculation process. You may notice that Steps 1–13 are identical for calculating regression and correlation (Appendix 3-1). Technical Box 3-1 gives a theoretical discussion of correlation and regression.

The **Pearson product moment correlation** coefficient is a ratio used to determine the degree of variation in one variable that can be estimated from knowledge about variation in the other variable. The correlation coefficient can take on any value from −1.0 to 1.0.

Table 3-2 gives the raw data for CES-D scores (X) and anger inventory scores (Y) for medical students. Try to find the regression of anger on CES-D and the correlation between these two measures. The correct answer is $r = 0.82$.

As you will see from Appendix 3-1, calculations of the correlation coefficient and the regression can be long and difficult. You may be able to avoid the many computational steps by using a calculator. Many inexpensive pocket calculators automatically perform correlation and regression. When you buy a calculator, choose one with these functions.

Testing the Statistical Significance of a Correlation Coefficient

One of the most important questions in evaluating a correlation is whether it is larger than we would expect by chance. The correlation between two randomly created variables will not always be 0.0. By chance alone, it is possible

TECHNICAL BOX 3-1

A More Theoretical Discussion of Correlation and Regression

The difference between correlation and regression is analogous to the difference between standardized scores and raw scores. In correlation, we look at the relationship between variables when each one is transformed into standardized scores. In Chapter 2, standardized scores (Z scores) were defined as $(X - \bar{X})/S$. In correlation, both variables are in Z scores, so they both have a mean of 0. In other words, the mean for the two variables will always be the same. As a result of this convenience, the intercept will always be 0 (when X is 0, Y is also 0) and will drop out of the equation. The resulting equation for translating X into Y then becomes $Y = rX$. The correlation coefficient (r) is equal to the regression coefficient when both X and Y are measured in standardized units. In other words, the predicted value of Y equals X times the correlation between X and Y. If the correlation between X and Y is .80 and the standardized (Z) score for the X variable is 1.0, then the predicted value of Y will be .80. Unless there is a perfect correlation (1.0 or −1.0), scores on Y will be predicted to be closer to the Y mean than scores on X will be to the X mean. A correlation of .80 means that the prediction for Y is 80% as far from the mean as is the observation for X. A correlation of .50 means that the predicted distance between the mean of Y and the predicted Y is half of the distance between the associated X and the mean of X. For example, if the Z score for X is 1.0, then X is one unit above the mean of X. If the correlation is .50, then we predict that Y will have a Z score of .50.

One benefit of using the correlation coefficient is that it has a reciprocal nature. The correlation between X and Y will always be the same as the correlation between Y and X. For example, if the correlation between drug dose and activity is .68, the correlation between activity and drug dose is .68.

On the other hand, regression does not have this property. Regression is used to transform scores on one variable into estimated scores on the other. We often use regression to predict raw scores on Y on the basis of raw scores on X. For instance, we might seek an equation to predict a student's grade point average (GPA) on the basis of his or her SAT score. Because regression uses the raw units of the variables, the reciprocal property does not hold. The coefficient that describes the regression of X on Y is usually not the same as the coefficient that describes the regression of Y on X.

The term *regression* was first used in 1885 by an extraordinary British intellectual named Sir Francis Galton. Fond of describing social and political changes that occur over successive generations, Galton noted that extraordinarily tall men tended to have sons who were a little shorter than they and that unusually small men tended to have sons closer to the average height (but still shorter than average). Over time, individuals with all sorts of unusual characteristics tended to produce offspring who were closer to the average. Galton thought of this as a regression toward mediocrity, an idea that became the basis for a statistical procedure that described how scores tend to regress toward the mean. If a person is extreme on X, then regression predicts that he or she will be less extreme on Y. Karl Pearson developed the first statistical models of correlation and regression in the late 19th century.

Continued

Continued

Statistical Definition of Regression

Regression analysis shows how change in one variable is related to change in another variable. In psychological testing, we often use regression to determine whether changes in test scores are related to changes in performance. Do people who score higher on tests of manual dexterity perform better in dental school? Can IQ scores measured during high school predict monetary income 20 years later? Regression analysis and related correlational methods reveal the degree to which these variables are linearly related. In addition, they offer an equation that estimates scores on a criterion (such as dental-school grades) on the basis of scores on a predictor (such as manual dexterity).

In Chapter 2, we introduced the concept of variance. You might remember that *variance* was defined as the average squared deviation around the mean. We used the term *sum of squares* for the sum of squared deviations around the mean. Symbolically, this is

$$\Sigma(X - \bar{X})^2$$

The variance is the sum of squares divided by $N - 1$. The formula for this is

$$S_X^2 = \frac{\Sigma(X - \bar{X})^2}{N - 1}$$

We also gave some formulas for the variance of raw scores. The variance of X can be calculated from raw scores using the formula

$$S_X^2 = \frac{\Sigma X^2 - \frac{(\Sigma X)^2}{N}}{N - 1}$$

If there is another variable, Y, then we can calculate the variance using a similar formula:

$$S_Y^2 = \frac{\Sigma Y^2 - \frac{(\Sigma Y)^2}{N}}{N - 1}$$

To calculate regression, we need a term for the covariance. To calculate the covariance, we need to find the sum of cross products, which is defined as

$$\Sigma XY = \Sigma(X - \bar{X})(Y - \bar{Y})$$

and the raw score formula, which is often used for calculation, is

$$\Sigma XY - \frac{(\Sigma X)(\Sigma Y)}{N}$$

The covariance is the sum of cross products divided by $N - 1$.

Now look at the similarity of the formula for the covariance and the formula for the variance:

$$S_{XY}^2 = \frac{\Sigma XY - \dfrac{(\Sigma X)(\Sigma Y)}{N}}{N-1}$$

$$S_X^2 = \frac{\Sigma X^2 - \dfrac{(\Sigma X)^2}{N}}{N-1}$$

Try substituting X for Y in the formula for the covariance. You should get

$$\frac{\Sigma XX - \dfrac{(\Sigma X)(\Sigma X)}{N}}{N-1}$$

If you replace ΣXX with ΣX^2 and $(\Sigma X)(\Sigma X)$ with $(\Sigma X)^2$, you will see the relationship between variance and covariance:

$$\frac{\Sigma X^2 - \dfrac{(\Sigma X)^2}{N}}{N-1}$$

In regression analysis, we examine the ratio of the covariance to the average of the variances for the two separate measures. This gives us an estimate of how much variance in one variable we can determine by knowing about the variation in the other variable.

to observe a correlation higher or lower than 0.0. However, the expected value the correlation averaged over many randomly created data sets is 0.0, and we can estimate the probability that correlations of various magnitudes occurred by chance alone. We begin with the null hypothesis that there is no relationship between variables. The null hypothesis is rejected if there is evidence that the association between two variables is significantly different from 0. Correlation coefficients can be tested for statistical significance using the t distribution. The t distribution is not a single distribution (such as the Z distribution) but a family of distributions, each with its own degrees of freedom. The *degrees of freedom (df)* are defined as the sample size minus one, or $N-1$. The formula for calculating the t value is

$$t = r\sqrt{\frac{N-2}{1-r^2}}$$

TABLE 3-2
CES-D
Correlation
Example

X, anger inventory	Y, CES-D	X^2	Y^2	XY	Predicted	Residual
21	14	441	196	294	7.31	6.69
21	10	441	100	210	7.31	2.69
21	8	441	64	168	7.31	.69
27	8	729	64	216	11.35	−3.35
43	26	1849	676	1118	22.14	3.86
24	0	576	0	0	9.33	−9.33
36	14	1296	196	504	17.42	−3.42
17	3	289	9	51	4.61	1.61
31	9	961	81	279	14.05	−5.05
19	10	361	100	190	5.96	4.04
19	7	361	49	133	5.96	1.04
24	12	576	144	288	9.33	2.67
27	10	729	100	270	11.35	−1.35
41	25	1681	625	1025	20.79	4.21
18	9	324	81	162	5.29	3.71
24	12	576	144	288	9.33	2.67
43	23	1849	529	989	22.14	.86
28	7	784	49	196	12.03	−5.03
31	13	961	169	403	14.05	−1.05
16	1	256	1	16	3.94	−2.94

See Appendix 3-1 for definitions of steps.

Step 1: $N = 20$

Step 2: $\Sigma X = 531$

Step 3: $\Sigma Y = 221$

Step 4: $\Sigma X^2 = 15,481$

Step 5: $\Sigma Y^2 = 3377$

Step 6: $\Sigma XY = 6800$

Step 7: 281,961

Step 8: 48,841

Steps 9, 10, 11: 20(6800) − (531)(221) = 18,649

Steps 12, 13: 20(15,481) − (531)(531) = 27,659

Step 14: $b = .67$

Step 15: $\bar{X} = 26.55$

Step 16: $\bar{Y} = 11.05$

Steps 17, 18: $a = 6.85$

Step 19: CES-D = −6.85 + .67(anger)

For correlation:

Step 16: 22,741.93

Step 17 correlation: .82

The significance of the *t* value—here, $df = N - 2$ and *N* is the number of pairs—can then be obtained by using Appendix 4.

Let's take one example of a correlation of .37 based on 50 pairs of observations. Using the formula, we obtain

$$t = .37 \sqrt{\frac{48}{.86}}$$

$$= .37(7.47)$$

$$= 2.76$$

Suppose we had stated the null hypothesis that the population association between these two variables is 0. Test statistics are used to estimate whether the observed correlation based on samples is significantly different from 0. This would be tested against the alternative hypothesis that the association between the two measures is significantly different from 0 in a **two-tailed test**. A significance level of .05 is used. Formally, then, the hypothesis and alternative hypothesis are

$$H_0: r = 0$$
$$H_1: r \neq 0$$

Using the formula, we obtain a *t* value of 2.76 with 48 degrees of freedom. According to Appendix 4, this *t* value is sufficient to reject the null hypothesis. Thus, we conclude that the association between these two variables was not the result of chance.

There are also statistical tables that give the critical values for *r*. One of these tables is included as Appendix 3. The table lists critical values of *r* for both the .05 and the .01 alpha levels according to degrees of freedom. For the correlation coefficient, $df = N - 2$. Suppose, for example, that you want to determine whether a correlation coefficient of .45 is statistically significant for a sample of 20 subjects. The degrees of freedom would be 18 ($20 - 2 = 18$). According to Appendix 3, the critical value for the .05 level is .444 with 18 *df*. Because .45 exceeds .444, you would conclude that the chances of finding a correlation as large as the one observed by chance alone would be less than 5 in 100. However, the observed correlation is less than the criterion value for the .01 level (that would require .561 with 18 *df*).

How to Interpret a Regression Plot

Regression plots are pictures that show the relationship between variables. A common use of correlation is to determine the **criterion validity evidence** for a test, or the relationship between a test score and some well-defined criterion. The association between a test of job aptitude and the criterion of actual performance on the job is an example of criterion validity evidence. The problems dealt with in studies of criterion validity evidence require one to predict some criterion score on the basis of a predictor or test score. Suppose that you want to build a test to predict how enjoyable someone will turn out to be as a date.

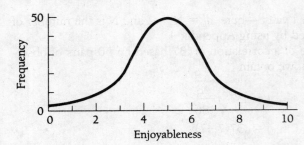

FIGURE 3-6
Hypothetical distribution of the enjoyableness of dates. Few dates are extremely enjoyable or extremely unenjoyable. The greatest number fall near the middle.

If you selected your dates randomly and with no information about them in advance, then you might be best off just using normative information.

You might expect the distribution of enjoyableness of dates to be normal. In other words, some people are absolutely no fun for you to go out with, others are exceptionally enjoyable, and the great majority are somewhere between these two extremes. Figure 3-6 shows what a frequency distribution of enjoyableness of dates might look like. As you can see, the highest point, which shows where dates are most frequently classified, is the location of the average date.

If you had no other way of predicting how much you would like your dates, the safest prediction would be to pick this middle level of enjoyableness because it is the one observed most frequently. This is called *normative* because it uses information gained from representative groups. Knowing nothing else about an individual, you can make an educated guess that a person will be average in enjoyableness because past experience has demonstrated that the mean, or average, score is also the one observed most frequently. In other words, knowing about the average date gives you some information about what to expect from a particular date. But it is doubtful that you would really want to choose dates this way. You probably would rather use other information such as educational background, attitudes, and hobbies to predict a good date.

Most of us, in fact, use some system to help us make important personal choices. The systems we come up with, however, are never perfect, but they are better than using normative information alone. In regression studies, researchers develop equations that help them describe more precisely where tests fall between being perfect predictors and being no better than just using the normative information. This is done by graphing the relationship between test scores and the criterion. Then a mathematical procedure is used to find the straight line that comes as close to as many of the points as possible. (You may want to review this chapter's earlier section on the regression line.)

Figure 3-7 shows the points on hypothetical scales of dating desirability and the enjoyableness of dates. The line through the points is the one that minimizes the squared distance between the line and the data points. In other words, the line is the one straight line that summarizes more about the relationship between dating desirability and enjoyableness than does any other straight line.

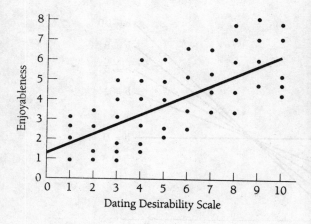

FIGURE 3-7

Hypothetical relationship between dating desirability and the enjoyableness of dates. Each point summarizes the dating desirability score and the enjoyableness rating for a single subject. The line was derived from a mathematical procedure to come as close to as many points as possible.

Figure 3-8 shows the hypothetical relationship between a test score and a criterion. Using this figure, you should be able to find the predicted value on the criterion variable by knowing the score on the test or the predictor. Here is how you read the graph. First, pick a particular score on the test—say, 8. Find 8 on the axis of the graph labeled "Test Score." Now draw a line straight up until you hit the slanted line on the graph. This is the regression line. Now make a 90° left turn and draw another line until it hits the other axis, which is labeled "Criterion Score." The dashed line in Figure 3-8 shows the course you should take. Now read the number on the criterion axis where your line has stopped. On the basis of information you gained by using the test, you would thus expect to obtain 7.4 as the criterion variable.

Notice that the line in Figure 3-8 is not at a 45° angle and that the two variables are measured in the same units. If it were at a 45° angle, then the test would be a perfect (or close to perfect) forecaster of the criterion. However, this is almost never the case in practice. Now do the same exercise you did for the

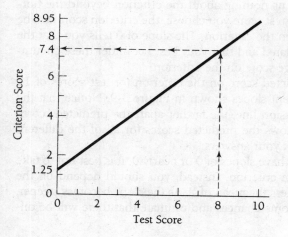

FIGURE 3-8

Predicted relationship between a test score and a criterion. The dotted line shows how you should have obtained a predicted criterion score of 7.4 from the test score of 8.

FIGURE 3-9

Regression lines with different standardized slopes.

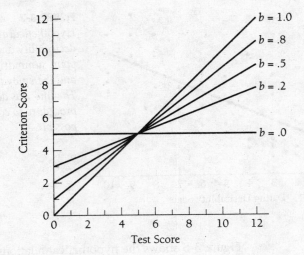

test score of 8 with test scores from the extremes of the distributions. Try the scores 0 and 10. You will find that the score of 10 for the test gives a criterion score of 8.95, and the test score of 0 gives a criterion score of 1.25. Notice how far apart 0 and 10 are on the test. Now look at how far apart 1.25 and 8.95 are on the criterion. You can see that using the test as a predictor is not as good as perfect prediction, but it is still better than using the normative information. If you had used only the normative information, you would have predicted that all scores would be the average score on the criterion. If there were perfect prediction, then the distance between 1.25 and 8.95 on the criterion would be the same as the distance between 0 and 10 on the test.

Figure 3-9 shows a variety of different regression slopes. Notice that the higher the standardized regression coefficient (*b*), the steeper the line. Now look at the regression line with a slope of 0. It is parallel to the "Test Score" axis and perpendicular to the "Criterion Score" axis. A regression line such as this shows that the test score tells us nothing about the criterion beyond the normative information. Whatever test score you choose, the criterion score will be the same—the average score on the criterion. The slope of 0 tells you that the test and the criterion are unrelated and that your best bet under these circumstances is to predict the average score on the criterion.

Now try to find the predicted score on the criterion for test scores of 11 and 3 for several of the different slopes shown in Figure 3-9. Notice that the steeper the slope of the regression line, the farther apart the predicted scores on the criterion. Table 3-3 shows the predicted scores for all of the different slopes. You can use it to check your answers.

When the regression lines have slopes of 0 or nearly 0, it is best not to take any chances in forecasting the criterion. Instead, you should depend on the normative information and guess the mean of *Y*. As the slope becomes steeper, it makes more sense to take some chances and estimate that there will be differences in criterion scores.

TABLE 3-3

Expected Criterion Scores for Two Test Scores when Predicted from Regression Lines with Different Slopes

Test score	Slope	Predicted criterion score
11	1.0	11.00
3	1.0	3.00
11	.8	9.90
3	.8	3.50
11	.5	8.25
3	.5	4.25
11	.2	6.60
3	.2	5.00
11	.0	5.50
3	.0	5.50

Figure 3-9 is also instructive regarding psychological tests. For example, if SAT scores have a slope of .5 for predicting grades in college, this means that the relationship between the SAT and performance is defined by the "$b = .5$" line. Using this sort of information, college administrators can infer that SAT scores may predict differences in college performance. However, because the slope is not steep, those predictions are not far from what they would get if they used the normative information.

Other Correlation Coefficients

The Pearson product moment correlation is only one of many types of correlation coefficients. It is the most commonly used because most often we want to find the correlation between two continuous variables. Continuous variables such as height, weight, and intelligence can take on any values over a range of values. But sometimes we want to find the correlations between variables scaled in other ways.

Spearman's rho is a method of correlation for finding the association between two sets of ranks. The rho coefficient (ρ) is easy to calculate and is often used when the individuals in a sample can be ranked on two variables but their actual scores are not known or have a normal distribution.

One whole family of correlation coefficients involve dichotomous variables. Dichotomous variables have only two levels. Examples are yes–no, correct–incorrect, and male–female. Some dichotomous variables are called *true dichotomous* because they naturally form two categories. For example, gender is a true dichotomous variable. Other dichotomous variables are called *artificially dichotomous* because they reflect an underlying continuous scale forced into a dichotomy. Passing or failing a bar examination is an example of such an artificial dichotomy; although many scores can be obtained, the examiners consider only pass and fail. The types of correlation coefficients used to find the

TABLE 3-4
*Appropriate
Correlation
Coefficients for
Relationships
Between
Dichotomous
and Continuous
Variables**

	Variable X		
Variable Y	**Continuous**	**Artificial dichotomous**	**True dichotomous**
Continuous	Pearson *r*	Biserial *r*	Point biserial *r*
Artificial dichotomous	Biserial *r*	Tetrachoric *r*	Phi
True dichotomous	Point biserial *r*	Phi	Phi

*The entries in the table suggest which type of correlation coefficient is appropriate given the characteristics of the two variables. For example, if variable Y is continuous and variable X is true dichotomous, you would use the point biserial correlation.

relationship between dichotomous and continuous variables are shown in Table 3-4.

The **biserial correlation** expresses the relationship between a continuous variable and an artificial dichotomous variable. For example, the biserial correlation might be used to assess the relationship between passing or failing the bar examination (artificial dichotomous variable) and grade point average (GPA) in law school (continuous variable). If the dichotomous variable had been "true" (such as gender), then we would use the *point biserial correlation*. For instance, the point biserial correlation would be used to find the relationship between gender and GPA. When both variables are dichotomous and at least one of the dichotomies is "true," then the association between them can be estimated using the *phi coefficient*. For example, the relationship between passing or failing the bar examination and gender could be estimated using the phi coefficient. If both dichotomous variables are artificial, we might use a special correlation coefficient known as the *tetrachoric correlation*. Among these special correlation coefficients, the point biserial, phi, and Spearman's rho coefficients are probably used most often. The formulas for calculating these correlations are given in Technical Box 3-2.

Terms and Issues in the Use of Correlation

When you use correlation or read studies that report correlational analysis, you will need to know the terminology. Some of the terms and issues you should be familiar with are *residual, standard error of estimate, coefficient of determination, coefficient of alienation, shrinkage, cross validation, correlation-causation problem,* and *third variable.* Brief discussions of these terms and concepts follow.

Residual

A regression equation gives a predicted value of Y' for each value of X. In addition to these predicted values, there are observed values of Y. The difference between the predicted and the observed values is called the **residual**. Symbolically, the residual is defined as $Y - Y'$.

TECHNICAL BOX 3-2

Formulas for Spearman's Rho, the Point Biserial Correlation, and the Phi Coefficient

$$\text{Spearman's rho formula: } \rho = 1 - \frac{6\,\Sigma d_i^2}{N^3 - 3}$$

where ρ = Spearman's rho coefficient

d_i = a subject's rank order on variable 2 minus his or her rank order on variable 1

N = the number of paired ranks

When used: To find the association between pairs of observations, each expressed in ranks.

$$\text{Point biserial correlation formula: } r_{\text{pbis}} = \left[\frac{\overline{Y}_1 - \overline{Y}}{S_y}\right]\sqrt{\frac{P_x}{1 - P_x}}$$

where r_{pbis} = the point biserial correlation coefficient

X = a true dichotomous (two-choice) variable

Y = a continuous (multilevel) variable

Y_1 = the mean of Y for subjects having a "plus" score on X

P = the mean of Y for all subjects

S_y = the standard deviation for Y scores

P_x = the proportion of subjects giving a "plus" score on X

When used: To find the association between a dichotomous (two-choice) variable and a continuous variable. For the true dichotomous variable, one of the two choices is arbitrarily designated as a "plus" response.

$$\text{Phi coefficient formula: } \phi = \frac{P_c - P_x P_y}{P_x(1 - P_x)P_y(1 - P_y)}$$

where ϕ = the phi coefficient

P_c = the proportion in the "plus" category for both variables

P_x = the proportion in the "plus" category for the first variable

P_y = the proportion in the "plus" category for the second variable

When used: To find the association between two dichotomous (two-category) variables. A dichotomous variable might be yes/no or on/off. In each case, one of the two choices is arbitrarily chosen as a "plus" response. When you use phi, one of the variables must be "true" dichotomy (if both were "artificial," the tetrachoric correlation would be more appropriate).

Consider the example of the CES-D. Earlier we calculated the regression equation that predicted CES-D scores from scores on the anger inventory. The equation suggested that predicted CES-D = −6.85 + .67 × anger score. Let's take the example of a person who had an anger score of 19 and an observed CES-D score of 7. The predicted CES-D score is

$$-6.85 + (.67 \times 19) = 5.88$$

In other words, the person had an observed score of 7 and a predicted score of 5.88. The residual is[4]

$$7 - 5.88 = 1.12$$

In regression analysis, the residuals have certain properties. One important property is that the sum of the residuals always equals 0 $[\Sigma(Y - Y') = 0]$. In addition, the sum of the squared residuals is the smallest value according to the principle of least squares $[\Sigma(Y - Y')^2 = \text{smallest value}]$.

Standard Error of Estimate

Once we have obtained the residuals, we can find their standard deviation. However, in creating the regression equation, we have found two constants (*a* and *b*). Thus, we must use two degrees of freedom rather than one, as is usually the case in finding the standard deviation. The standard deviation of the residuals is known as the **standard error of estimate**, which is defined as

$$S_{yx} = \sqrt{\frac{\Sigma(Y - Y')^2}{N - 2}}$$

The standard error of estimate is a measure of the accuracy of prediction. Prediction is most accurate when the standard error of estimate is relatively small. As it becomes larger, the prediction becomes less accurate.

Coefficient of Determination

The correlation coefficient squared is known as the **coefficient of determination**. This value tells us the proportion of the total variation in scores on Y that we know as a function of information about X. For example, if the correlation between the SAT score and performance in the first year of college is .40, then the coefficient of determination is .16. The calculation is simply $.40^2 = .16$. This means that we can explain 16% of the variation in first-year college performance by knowing SAT scores. In the CES-D and anger example, the correlation is .82. Therefore, the coefficient of determination is .67 (calculated as $.82^2 = .67$), suggesting that 67% of the variance in CES-D can be accounted for by the anger score.

---

[4]*Note:* There is a small discrepancy between 1.12 and the 1.04 for the example in Table 3-2. The difference is the result of rounding error.

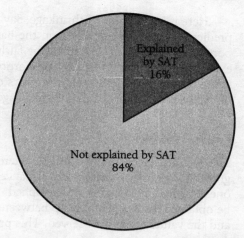

FIGURE 3-10   *Proportion of variance in first-year college performance explained by SAT score. Despite a significant relationship between SAT and college performance (r = .40), the coefficient of determination shows that only 16% of college performance is explained by SAT scores. The coefficient of alienation is .92, suggesting that most of the variance in college performance is not explained by SAT scores.*

Coefficient of Alienation

The **coefficient of alienation** is a measure of nonassociation between two variables. This is calculated as $\sqrt{1 - r^2}$, where r^2 is the coefficient of determination. For the SAT example, the coefficient of alienation is $\sqrt{1 - .16} = \sqrt{.84} = .92$. This means that there is a high degree of nonassociation between SAT scores and college performance. In the CES-D and anger example, the coefficient of alienation is $\sqrt{1 - .67} = .57$. Figure 3-10 shows the coefficient of determination and the coefficient of alienation represented in a pie chart.

Shrinkage

Many times a regression equation is created on one group of subjects and then used to predict the performance of another group. One problem with regression analysis is that it takes advantage of chance relationships within a particular sample of subjects. Thus, there is a tendency to overestimate the relationship, particularly if the sample of subjects is small. **Shrinkage** is the amount of decrease observed when a regression equation is created for one population and then applied to another. Formulas are available to estimate the amount of shrinkage to expect given the characteristics of variance, covariance, and sample size (Brennan, 1994; Camilli, 1999; Jaccard & Wan, 1995; Longford, 1997; Lord, 1950; McNemar, 1969).

Here is an example of shrinkage. Say a regression equation is developed to predict first-year college GPAs on the basis of SAT scores. Although the proportion of variance in GPA might be fairly high for the original group, we can expect to account for a smaller proportion of the variance when the equation is used to predict GPA in the next year's class. This decrease in the proportion of variance accounted for is the shrinkage.

Cross Validation

The best way to ensure that proper references are being made is to use the regression equation to predict performance in a group of subjects other than the ones to which the equation was applied. Then a standard error of estimate can be obtained for the relationship between the values predicted by the equation and the values actually observed. This process is known as **cross validation.**

The Correlation-Causation Problem

Just because two variables are correlated does not necessarily imply that one has caused the other (see Focused Example 3-1). For example, a correlation between aggressive behavior and the number of hours spent viewing television does not mean that excessive viewing of television causes aggression. This relationship could mean that an aggressive child might prefer to watch a lot of television. There are many examples of misinterpretation of correlations. We know, for example, that physically active elderly people live longer than do those who are sedentary. However, we do not know if physical activity causes long life or if healthier people are more likely to be physically active. Usually, experiments are required to determine whether manipulation of one variable causes changes in another variable. A correlation alone does not prove causality, although it might lead to other research that is designed to establish the causal relationships between variables.

Third Variable Explanation

There are other possible explanations for the observed relationship between television viewing and aggressive behavior. One is that some third variable, such as poor social adjustment, causes both. Thus, the apparent relationship between viewing and aggression actually might be the result of some variable not included in the analysis. In the example of the relationship between physical activity and life expectancy, chronic disease may cause both sedentary lifestyle and shortened life expectancy. We usually refer to this external influence as a **third variable.**

Restricted Range

Correlation and regression use variability on one variable to explain variability on a second variable. In this chapter, we use many different examples such as the relationship between smoking and the price of a pack of cigarettes, the re-

Focused Example 3-1

THE DANGER OF INFERRING CAUSATION FROM CORRELATION

A newspaper article once rated 130 job categories for stressfulness by examining Tennessee hospital and death records for evidence of stress-related diseases such as heart attacks, ulcers, arthritis, and mental disorders. The 12 highest and the 12 lowest jobs are listed in the table to the right.

The article advises readers to avoid the "most stressful" job categories. The evidence, however, may not warrant the advice offered in the article. Although certain diseases may be associated with particular occupations, holding these jobs does not necessarily cause the illnesses. Other explanations abound. For example, people with a propensity for heart attacks and ulcers might tend to select jobs as unskilled laborers or secretaries. Thus, the direction of causation might be that a health condition causes job selection rather than the reverse. Another possibility involves a third variable, some other factor that causes the apparent relationship between job and health. For example, a certain income level might cause both stress and illness. Finally, wealthy people tend to have better health than poor people. Impoverished conditions may cause a person to accept certain jobs and also to have more diseases.

These three possible explanations are diagrammed in the right-hand column. An arrow indicates a causal connection. In this example we are not ruling out the possibility that jobs cause illness. In fact, it is quite plausible. However, because the nature of the evidence is correlational, we cannot say with certainty that job causes illness.

Most Stressful	Least Stressful
1. Unskilled laborer	1. Clothing sewer
2. Secretary	2. Garment checker
3. Assembly-line inspector	3. Stock clerk
4. Clinical lab technician	4. Skilled craftsperson
5. Office manager	5. Housekeeper
6. Foreperson	6. Farm laborer
7. Manager/administrator	7. Heavy-equipment operator
8. Waiter	8. Freight handler
9. Factory machine operator	9. Child-care worker
10. Farm owner	10. Factory package wrapper
11. Miner	11. College professor
12. House painter	12. Personnel worker

$Job \rightarrow Illness$ $Illness \rightarrow Job$ *Economic Status*

$\downarrow \quad \downarrow$

Job   Illness

Job causes illness

Tendency toward illness causes people to choose certain jobs

Economic status (third variable) causes job selection and illness

lationship between anger and depression, and the relationship between dating desirability and satisfaction. In each of these cases, there was meaningful variability on each of the two variables under study. However, there are circumstances in which the ranges of variability are restricted. Imagine, for example, that you were attempting to study the relationship between scores on the GRE quantitative test and performance during the first year of graduate school in the math department of an elite Ivy League university. No students had been admitted to the program with GRE verbal scores less than 700. Further, most

FIGURE 3-11

Hypothetical relationship between GRE-Q and GPA for all students and for students in elite program.

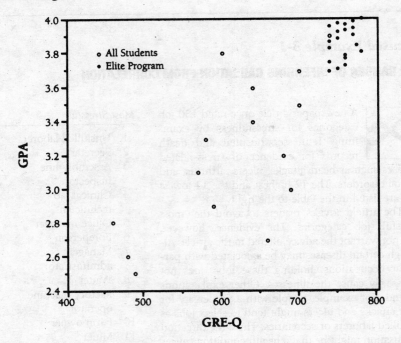

grades given in the graduate school were A's. Under these circumstances, it might be extremely difficult to demonstrate a relationship even though a true underlying relationship may exist.

This is illustrated in Figure 3-11. The squares in the hypothetical example represent the relationship between SAT quantitative and graduate school GPA across all potential students. For all students, the correlation is 0.53. The triangles in the figure show the same relationship for the elite group of students under consideration. Because the elite students do not vary much on GRE quantitative, it is difficult to observe significant correlation between GRE quantitative (GRE-Q) and any other variable. In this example, the correlation is 0.08. This is called the **restricted range problem**. Correlation requires variability. If the variability is restricted, then significant correlations are difficult to find.

Multivariate Analysis (Optional)

Multivariate analysis considers the relationship among combinations of three or more variables. For example, the prediction of success in the first year of college from the linear combination of SAT verbal and math scores is a problem for multivariate analysis. However, because the field of multivariate analysis requires an understanding of linear and matrix algebra, a detailed discussion of it lies beyond the scope of this book.

On the other hand, you should have at least a general idea of what the different common testing methods entail. This section will familiarize you with some of the multivariate analysis terminology. It will also help you identify the situations in which some of the different multivariate methods are used. Several references are available in case you would like to learn more about the technical details (Cliff, 1987; Grim & Yarnold, 1995; Tabachnick & Fidell, 1996).

General Approach

The correlational techniques presented to this point describe the relationship between only two variables such as stress and illness. To understand more fully the causes of illness, we need to consider many potential factors besides stress. Multivariate analysis allows us to study the relationship between many predictors and one outcome, as well as the relationship among the predictors.

Multivariate methods differ in the number and kind of predictor variables they use. All of these methods transform groups of variables into linear combinations. A *linear combination* of variables is a weighted composite of the original variables. The weighting system combines the variables in order to achieve some goal. Multivariate techniques differ according to the goal they are trying to achieve.

A linear combination of variables looks like this:

$$Y' = a + b_1X_1 + b_2X_2 + b_3X_3 + \ldots + b_kX_k$$

where Y' is the predicted value of Y, a is a constant, X_1 to X_k are variables and there are k such variables, and the b's are regression coefficients. If you feel anxious about such a complex-looking equation, there is no need to panic. Actually, this equation describes something similar to what was presented in the section on regression. The difference is that instead of relating Y to X, we are now dealing with a linear combination of X's. The whole right side of the equation creates a new composite variable by transforming a set of predictor variables.

An Example Using Multiple Regression

Suppose we want to predict success in law school from three variables: undergraduate GPA, rating by former professors, and age. This type of multivariate analysis is called **multiple regression**, and the goal of the analysis is to find the linear combination of the three variables that provides the best prediction of law school success. We find the correlation between the criterion (law school GPA) and some composite of the predictors (undergraduate GPA plus professor rating plus age). The combination of the three predictors, however, is not just the sum of the three scores. Instead, we program the computer to find a specific way of adding the predictors that will make the correlation between the composite and the criterion as high as possible. A weighted composite might look something like this:

law school GPA = .80(Z scores of undergraduate GPA)
+ .24(Z scores of professor ratings)
+ .03(Z scores of age)

This example suggests that undergraduate GPA is given more weight in the prediction of law school GPA than are the other variables. The undergraduate GPA is multiplied by .80, whereas the other variables are multiplied by much smaller coefficients. Age is multiplied by only .03, which is almost no contribution. This is because .03 times any Z score for age will give a number that is nearly 0; in effect, we would be adding 0 to the composite.

The reason for using Z scores for the three predictors is that the coefficients in the linear composite are greatly affected by the range of values taken on by the variables. GPA is measured on a scale from 0 to 4.0, whereas the range in age might be 21 to 70. To compare the coefficients to one another, we need to transform all the variables into similar units. This is accomplished by using Z scores (see Chapter 2). When the variables are expressed in Z units, the coefficients, or weights for the variables, are known as *standardized regression coefficients* (sometimes called B's or betas). There are also some cases in which we would want to use the variables' original units. For example, we sometimes want to find an equation we can use to estimate someone's predicted level of success on the basis of personal characteristics, and we do not want to bother changing these characteristics into Z units. When we do this, the weights in the model are called *raw regression coefficients* (sometimes called b's).

Before moving on, we should caution you about interpreting regression coefficients. Besides reflecting the relationship between a particular variable and the criterion, the coefficients are affected by the relationship among the predictor variables. Be careful when the predictor variables are highly correlated with one another. Two predictor variables that are highly correlated with the criterion will not both have large regression coefficients if they are highly correlated with each other as well. For example, suppose that undergraduate GPA and the professors' rating are both highly correlated with law school GPA. However, these two predictors also are highly correlated with each other. In effect, the two measures seem to be of the same thing (which would not be surprising, because the professors assigned the grades). As such, professors' rating may get a lower regression coefficient because some of its predictive power is already taken into consideration through its association with undergraduate GPA. We can only interpret regression coefficients confidently when the predictor variables do not overlap and are uncorrelated. They may do so when the predictors are uncorrelated.

Discriminant Analysis

Multiple regression is appropriate when the criterion variable is continuous (not nominal). However, there are many cases in testing where the criterion is a set of categories. For example, we often want to know the linear combination of variables that differentiates passing from failing. When the task is to find the linear combination of variables that provides a maximum discrimination between categories, the appropriate multivariate method is **discriminant analysis.** An example of discriminant analysis involves attempts to determine whether a set of measures predicts success or failure on a particular performance evaluation.

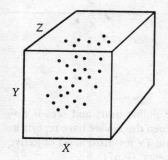

FIGURE 3-12

A three-dimensional scatter plot might be represented by this box. In addition to plotting points on the X and Y axes, we must locate them in relation to a third Z axis.

Sometimes we want to determine the categorization in more than two categories. To accomplish this we use multiple discriminant analysis.

Discriminant analysis has many advantages in the field of test construction. One approach to test construction is to identify two groups of people who represent two distinct categories of some trait. For example, say that two groups of children are classified as "language disabled" and "normal." After a variety of items are presented, discriminant analysis is used to find the linear combination of items that best accounts for differences between the two groups. With this information, researchers could develop new tests to help diagnose language impairment. This information might also provide insight into the nature of the problem and eventually lead to better treatments.

Factor Analysis

Discriminant analysis and multiple regression analysis find linear combinations of variables that maximize the prediction of some criterion. Factor analysis is used to study the interrelationships among a set of variables without reference to a criterion. You might think of factor analysis as a data-reduction technique. When we have responses to a large number of items or a large number of tests, we often want to reduce all this information to more manageable chunks. In Figure 3-1, we presented a two-dimensional scatter diagram. The task in correlation is to find the best-fitting line through the space created by these two dimensions. As we add more variables in multivariate analysis, we increase the number of dimensions. For example, a three-dimensional plot is shown in Figure 3-12. You can use your imagination to visualize what a larger set of dimensions would look like. Some people claim they can visualize more than three dimensions, while others feel they cannot. In any case, consider that points are plotted in the domain created by a given dimension.

In factor analysis, we first create a matrix that shows the correlation between every variable and every other variable. Then we find the linear combinations, or *principal components*, of the variables that describe as many of the interrelationships among the variables as possible. We can find as many principal components as there are variables. However, each principal component is extracted according to mathematical rules that make it independent of or uncorrelated with the other principal components. The first component will be

Focused Example 3-2

THE FACTORS OF TRUST

Rotter (1967) described a scale for the measurement of interpersonal trust. *Trust* was defined as "an expectancy held by an individual or a group that the word, promise, verbal or written statement of another individual or group can be relied upon" (p. 651). However, after the publication of the original trust article, several authors reported that trust seems to be composed of several independent factors (Chun & Campbell, 1974; R. M. Kaplan, 1973; T. L. Wright & Tedeschi, 1975). In each case, the items were given to a large group of people, and the results were subjected to factor analysis. This procedure reduces the many items down to a smaller number of *factors,* or linear combinations of the original items. Then *item loadings,* or the correlations of the original items with the factors, are studied in order to name the factors. The table that follows shows the loadings of the items on three of the factors (R. M. Kaplan, 1973).

Once they have obtained the factor loadings, researchers must attempt to name the factors by examining which items load highly on them. In this case, an item was used to help interpret a factor if its item loading on the factor was greater than .35 or less than −.35. Three factors of trust were found.

Factor I: Institutional trust. This represented trust toward major social agents in society. It included items regarding the competence of politicians, such as "This country has a dark future unless we can attract better people into politics" (−.67). Many of the items conveyed the idea of misrepresentation of public events by either the government or the mass media. For example, some items with high loadings were "Most people would be horrified if they knew how much news the public hears and sees is distorted" (−.69) and "Even though we have reports in newspapers, radio, and TV, it is hard to get objective accounts of public events" (−.67).

Factor II: Sincerity. Items loading highly on sincerity tended to focus on the perceived sincerity of others. These items included "Most idealists are sincere and usually practice what they preach" (.62) and "Most people answer public opinion polls honestly" (.58). Nearly all the items with high loadings on the second factor began with the word "most." Because of this loose wording, it would be possible for people to agree with the items because they believe in the sincerity of most people in a given group but still feel little trust for the group because of a few "rotten eggs." Thus, a woman could believe most car repairers are sincere but still service her car herself because she fears being overcharged.

Factor III: Caution. This contained items that expressed fear that some people will take advantage of others, such as "In dealing with strangers, one is better off being cautious until they have provided evidence that they are trustworthy" (.74) and "In these competitive times you have to be alert or someone is likely to take advantage of you" (.53). Note that caution appears to be independent of perceived sincerity.

The data imply that generalized trust may be composed of several dimensions. It also implies that focusing on specific components of trust rather than the generalized case will likely help researchers the most in using this trust scale.

Focused Example adapted from Rotter (1967); table taken from R. M. Kaplan (1973).

the most successful in describing the variation among the variables, with each succeeding component somewhat less successful. Thus, we often decide to examine only a few components that account for larger proportions of the variation. Technically, principal components analysis and true factor analysis differ in how the correlation matrix is created. Even so, principal components are often called *factors.*

Item number	Item	Loading factor		
		I	II	III
A. Items with high loadings on institutional factor				
4.	This country has a dark future unless we can attract better people into politics.	−.67	−.12	−.06
5.	Fear of social disgrace or punishment rather than conscience prevents most people from breaking the law.	−.54	.02	−.06
13.	The United Nations will never be an effective force in keeping world peace.	−.41	.09	−.21
16.	The judiciary is a place where we can all get unbiased treatment.	.37	.23	.00
19.	Most people would be horrified if they knew how much news the public hears and sees is distorted.	−.69	.18	.28
21.	Most elected public officials are really sincere in their campaign promises.	.44	.17	−.02
24.	Even though we have reports in newspapers, radio, and TV, it is hard to get objective accounts of public events.	−.67	−.08	.00
28.	If we really knew what was going on in international politics, the public would have more reason to be more frightened than it now seems to be.	−.49	.01	.24
33.	Many major national sports contests are fixed in one way or another.	−.55	−.04	.28
B. Items with high loadings on sincerity factor				
1.	Hypocrisy is on the increase in our society.	.09	−.52	.08
12.	Most students in school would not cheat even if they were sure of getting away with it.	.29	.45	.07
27.	Most experts can be relied upon to tell the truth about the limits of their knowledge.	.20	.66	.20
34.	Most idealists are sincere and usually practice what they preach.	.12	.62	−.20
38.	Most repair persons will not overcharge even if they think you are ignorant of their specialty.	.11	.48	−.35
44.	Most people answer public opinion polls honestly.	.04	.58	.16
C. Items with high loadings on caution factor				
2.	In dealing with strangers, one is better off being cautious until they have provided evidence that they are trustworthy.	−.22	−.03	.74
7.	Using the honor system of *not* having a teacher present during examinations would probably result in increased cheating.	.13	.08	.45
32.	In these competitive times you have to be alert or someone is likely to take advantage of you.	−.12	−.01	.53
42.	A large share of the accident claims filed against insurance companies are phony.	−.07	−.14	.57

Once the linear combinations or principal components have been found, we can find the correlation between the original items and the factors. These correlations are called *factor loadings*. The expression "item 7 loaded highly on factor I" means there is a high correlation between item 7 and the first principal component. By examining which variables load highly on each factor, we can start interpreting the meanings of the factors. Focused Example 3-2 shows how the meanings of various factors in a scale on interpersonal trust are evaluated.

Factor analysis is a complex and technical method with many options the user must learn about. For example, users frequently use methods that help them get a clearer picture of the meaning of the components by transforming the variables in a way that pushes the factor loadings toward the high or the low extreme. Because these transformational methods involve rotating the axes in the space created by the factors, they are called *methods of rotation*. Researchers have many options for transforming variables. They can choose among several methods of rotation, and they can explore the many characteristics of the matrix originally used in their analyses. If you are interested, several books discuss factor analysis methods in great detail (Bartholomew & Knott, 1999; Bryant & Yarnold, 1995; Kline, 1994; Loehlin, 1998).

SUMMARY

This chapter began with a discussion of a claim made in the *National Enquirer* that poor diet causes marital problems. Actually, there was no specific evidence that diet causes the problems—only that diet and marital difficulties are associated. However, the *Enquirer* failed to specify the exact strength of the association. The rest of the chapter was designed to help you be more specific than the *Enquirer* by learning to specify associations with precise mathematical indexes known as *correlation coefficients*.

First, we presented pictures of the association between two variables; these pictures are called *scatter diagrams*. Second, we presented a method for finding a linear equation to describe the relationship between two variables. This regression method uses the data in raw units. The results of regression analysis are two constants: a *slope* describes the degree of relatedness between the variables, and an *intercept* gives the value of the Y variable when the X variable is 0. When both of the variables are in standardized or Z units, the intercept is always 0 and drops out of the equation. In this unique situation, we solve for only one constant, which is r, or the *correlation coefficient*.

When using correlational methods, we must take many things into consideration. For example, correlation does not mean the same thing as causation. In the case of the *National Enquirer* article, the observed correlation between diet and problems in marriage may mean that diet causes the personal difficulties. However, it may also mean that marriage problems cause poor eating habits or that some *third variable* causes both diet habits and marital problems. In addition to the difficulties associated with causation, we must always consider the strength of the correlational relationship. The *coefficient of determination* describes the percentage of variation in one variable that is known on the basis of its association with another variable. The *coefficient of alienation* is an index of what is not known from information about the other variable.

A *regression line* is the best-fitting straight line through a set of points in a scatter diagram. The regression line is described by a mathematical index known as the regression equation. The *regression coefficient* is the ratio of covariance to variance and is also known as the slope of the regression line. The regression coefficient describes how much change is expected in the *Y* variable each time the *X* variable increases by one unit. Other concepts discussed were the *intercept,* the *residual* (the difference between the predicted value given by a regression equation and the observed value), and the *standard error of estimate* (the standard deviation of the residuals obtained from the regression equation).

The field of *multivariate analysis* involves a complicated but important set of methods for studying the relationships among many variables. *Multiple regression* is a multivariate method for studying the relationship between one criterion variable and two or more predictor variables. A similar method known as *discriminant analysis* is used to study the relationship between a categorical criterion and two or more predictors. *Factor analysis* is another multivariate method for reducing a large set of variables down to a smaller set of composite variables.

Correlational methods are the most commonly used statistical techniques in the testing field. The concepts presented in this overview will be referred to throughout the rest of this book.

Appendix 3-1: Calculation of a Regression Equation and a Correlation Coefficient

In this appendix, we consider the relationship between team performance and payroll for teams in baseball's American League. Data used here are from the 2003 season and available on the Internet at www.espn.com. The 2003 season was of particular interest to baseball fans because the World Series paired the New York Yankees with a payroll of more than $180 million versus the Florida Marlins with a payroll of a mere $63 million. The Marlins won the Series, raising the question of whether there is a relationship between expenditure and performance of professional baseball teams.

In this example, payroll for American League teams is measured in millions of dollars spent per team, whereas performance is measured by the number of games won. The data are shown in Table 3-5 and summarized in Figure 3-13. Each dot in the figure represents one team. In 2003, there was a positive relationship between payroll and performance. In other words, teams with higher payrolls had better performance. As Figure 3-13 indicates, each increase in expenditure is associated with an increase in performance. The regression coefficient (0.207) suggests that for each million dollars spent, the team's performance increases by an average of .207 games per season. In other words, an owner must spend about $5 million to win a game. Overall, the relationship is significant, and the best explanation is that there is an association between payroll and performance.

TABLE 3-5

Games Won and Average Salaries for Teams in Baseball's American League

Club	Payroll (in millions) (X)	Games won (Y)	X²	Y²	XY
New York Yankees	180.322	101	32,516.169	10,201	18,212.563
Texas	106.278	71	11,294.988	5041	7,545.729
Boston	104.874	95	10,998.473	9025	9,962.993
Seattle	92.268	93	8,513.395	8649	8,580.930
Anaheim	83.235	77	6,928.082	5929	6,409.103
Baltimore	75.502	71	5,700.575	5041	5,360.653
Chicago White Sox	71.336	86	5,088.829	7396	6,134.898
Minnesota	65.319	90	4,266.569	8100	5,878.708
Toronto	61.176	86	3,742.459	7396	5,261.105
Detroit	59.007	43	3,481.819	1849	2,537.298
Cleveland	58.109	68	3,376.635	4624	3,951.400
Oakland	56.597	96	3,203.185	9216	5,433.282
Kansas City	48.475	83	2,349.857	6889	4,023.452
Tampa Bay	31.661	63	1,002.394	3969	1,994.618
SUM	1094.158	1123	102,463.429	93,325	91,286.732

Summary

ΣX	1094.16	$b = .208$	
ΣY	1123	$a = 63.98$	
ΣXY	91,286.73	$r = 0.475$	
ΣX^2	102,463.43		
ΣY^2	93,325		
N	14		
$\bar{X}$	78.14		
$\bar{Y}$	80.21		

Calculation of a Regression Equation (Data from Table 3-5)

Formulas:
$$b = \frac{N(\Sigma XY) - (\Sigma Y)(\Sigma Y)}{N\Sigma X^2 - (\Sigma X)^2}$$

$$a = \bar{Y} - b\bar{X}$$

Steps

1. Find N by counting the number of pairs of observations. $N = 14$
2. Find ΣX by summing the X scores.

$$180.32 + 106.28 + 104.87 + \ldots + 31.66 = 1094.16$$

3. Find ΣY by summing the Y scores.

$$101 + 71 + 95 + \ldots + 63 = 1123$$

FIGURE 3-13
Payroll (in $million) versus performance (games won) by American League teams in 2003.
(Data from www.espn.com.)

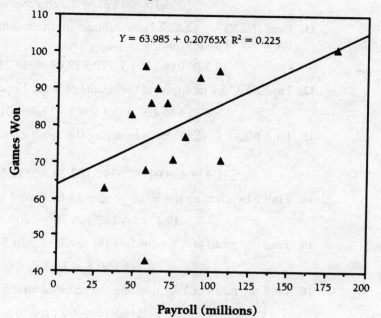

Payroll vs. games won American League 2003
(data from www.espn.com)

$Y = 63.985 + 0.20765X$ $R^2 = 0.225$

4. Find ΣX^2. Square each X score and then sum them.

$$(180.32)^2 + (106.28)^2 + (104.87)^2 + \ldots + (31.66)^2$$
$$= 102,463.43$$

5. Find ΣY^2. Square each Y score and then sum them.

$$(101)^2 + (71)^2 + (95)^2 + \ldots + (63)^2 = 93,325$$

6. Find ΣXY. For each pair of observations multiply X by Y. Then sum the products.

$$(180.32 \times 101) + (106.28 \times 71) + (104.87 \times 95) + \ldots + (31.66 \times 63)$$
$$= 18,212.56 + 7545.73 + 9962.99 + \ldots + 1994.62$$
$$= 91,286.73$$

7. Find $(\Sigma X)^2$ by squaring the results of Step 2.

$$(1094.16)^2 = 1,197,182.23$$

8. Find $(\Sigma Y)^2$ by squaring the results of Step 3.

$$(1123)^2 = 1,261,129$$

9. Find $N\Sigma XY$ by multiplying the results of Step 1 by Step 6.

$$14 \times 91,286.73 = 1,278,014.25$$

10. Find $(\Sigma X)(\Sigma Y)$ by multiplying the results of Steps 2 and 3.

$$1094.16 \times 1123 = 1,228,739.69$$

11. Find $(N\Sigma XY) - (\Sigma X)(\Sigma Y)$ by subtracting the results of Step 10 from the result of Step 9.

$$1,278,014.22 - 1,228,739.69 = 49,274.56$$

12. Find $N\Sigma X^2$ by multiplying the results of Steps 1 and 4.

$$14 \times 102,463.43 = 1,434,488.01$$

13. Find $N\Sigma X^2 - (\Sigma X)^2$ by subtracting the result of Step 7 from that of Step 12.

$$1,434,488.01 - 1,197,182.23 = 237,305.78$$

14. Find b by dividing the result of Step 11 by that of Step 13.

$$49,272.56/237,305.78 = .208$$

15. Find the mean of X by dividing the result of Step 2 by that of Step 1.

$$1094.16/14 = 78.14$$

16. Find the mean of Y by dividing the result of Step 3 by that of Step 1.

$$1123/14 = 80.21$$

17. Find $b\bar{X}$ by multiplying the results of Steps 14 and 15.

$$.208 \times 78.14 = 16.23$$

18. Find a by subtracting the results of Step 17 from Step 16.

$$80.21 - 16.23 = 63.98$$

19. The resultant regression equation is

$$Y = a + bX$$
$$Y = 63.98 + .208(X)$$

Calculation of a Correlation Coefficient (Data from Table 3-5)

Formula: $r = \dfrac{N\Sigma XY - (\Sigma X)(\Sigma Y)}{\sqrt{[N\Sigma X^2 - (\Sigma X)^2][N\Sigma Y^2 - (\Sigma Y)^2}}$

1. Find N by counting the number of pairs of observations. $N = 14$
2. Find ΣX by summing the X scores.

$$180.32 + 106.28 + 104.87 + \ldots + 31.66 = 1094.16$$

3. Find ΣY by summing the Y scores.

$$101 + 71 + 95 + \ldots + 63 = 1123$$

4. Find ΣX^2. Square each X score and then sum them.

$$(180.32)^2 + (106.28)^2 + (104.87)^2 + \ldots + (31.66)^2 = 102,463.43$$

5. Find ΣY^2. Square each Y score and then sum them.

$$(101)^2 + (71)^2 + (95)^2 + \ldots + (63)^2 = 93,325$$

6. Find ΣXY. For each pair of observations multiply X by Y. Then sum the products.

$$(180.32 \times 101) + (106.28 \times 71) + (104.87 \times 95) + \ldots + (31.66 \times 63)$$
$$= 18,212.56 + 7545.73 + 9962.99 + \ldots + 1994.62$$
$$= 91,286.73$$

7. Find $(\Sigma X)^2$ by squaring the results of Step 2.

$$(1094.16)^2 = 1,197,182.23$$

8. Find $(\Sigma Y)^2$ by squaring the results of Step 3.

$$(1123)^2 = 1,261,129$$

9. Find $N\Sigma XY$ by multiplying the results of Step 1 by Step 6.

$$14 \times 91,286.73 = 1,278,014.25$$

10. Find $(\Sigma X)(\Sigma Y)$ by multiplying the results of Steps 2 and 3.

$$1094.16 \times 1123 = 1,228,739.69$$

11. Find $(N\Sigma XY) - (\Sigma X)(\Sigma Y)$ by subtracting the results of Step 10 from the result of Step 9.

$$1,278,014.22 - 1,228,739.69 = 49,274.56$$

12. Find $N\Sigma X^2$ by multiplying the results of Steps 1 and 4.

$$14 \times 102,463.43 = 1,434,488.01$$

13. Find $N\Sigma X^2 - (\Sigma X)^2$ by subtracting the result of Step 7 from that of Step 12.

$$1,434,488.01 - 1,197,182.23 = 237,305.78$$

14. Find $N\Sigma Y^2$ by multiplying the results of Steps 1 and 5.

$$14 \times 9325 = 1,306,550$$

15. Find $N\Sigma Y^2 - (\Sigma Y)^2$ by subtracting the result of Step 8 from that of Step 14.

$$1,306,550 - 1,261,129 = 45,421$$

16. Find $\sqrt{[N\Sigma X^2 - (\Sigma X)^2][N\Sigma Y^2 - (\Sigma Y)^2]}$ by multiplying the results of Steps 13 and 15 and taking the square root of the product.

$$\sqrt{237,305.78 \times 45421} = 103,820.35$$

17. Find $r = \dfrac{N\Sigma XY - (\Sigma X)(\Sigma Y)}{\sqrt{[N\Sigma X^2 - (\Sigma X)^2][N\Sigma Y^2 - (\Sigma Y)^2]}}$ by dividing the result of Step 11 by that of Step 16.

$$49{,}274.56/103{,}820.35$$
$$r = 0.475$$

WEB ACTIVITY For interesting and relevant Web sites, check the following:

www.scit.wlv.ac.uk/~cm1912/cwp27.html
  Example of calculation of correlation and regression

bmj.bmjjournals.com/collections/statsbk/11.shtml
  A simple general overview of correlation and regression

noppa5.pc.helsinki.fi/koe/corr/cor7.html
  Offers visual examples of the relationship between scatter diagrams and correlations

www.mega.nu:8080/ampp/rummel/uc.htm#S4.1
  A more detailed, but intuitive overview of correlation and regression

Reliability

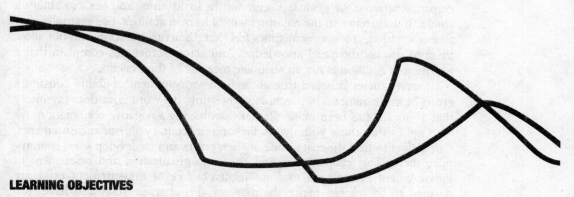

LEARNING OBJECTIVES

When you have completed this chapter, you should be able to:

☐ Tell what measurement error is and how it interferes with scientific studies in psychology

☐ Know that reliability is the ratio of true variability to observed variability and explain what this tells us about a test with a reliability of .30, .60, or .90

☐ Describe how test–retest reliability is assessed

☐ Explain the difference between test–retest reliability estimates and split-half reliability estimates

☐ Discuss how the split-half method underestimates the reliability of a short test and what can be done to correct this problem

☐ Know the easiest way to find average reliability

☐ Define *coefficient alpha* and tell how it differs from other methods of estimating reliability

☐ Discuss how high a reliability coefficient must be before you would be willing to say the test is "reliable enough"

☐ Explain what can be done to increase the reliability of a test

☐ Tell how the reliability of behavioral observations is assessed

In the gymnastics competition at an international meet, a young Romanian woman received an 8.9 for the first portion of her routine. As she reappeared for the second portion, the television commentator said, "The 8.9 rating for her first routine does not accurately represent her ability. This young woman is clearly a 9.5 performer." With this remark, the commentator indicated a discrepancy between the gymnast's score for the first routine and her true ability, a common occurrence in the measurement of human abilities. For example, after an examination, students sometimes feel that the actual questions did not allow them to display their real knowledge. And actors sometimes complain that a five-minute audition is not an adequate measure of their talents.

Discrepancies between true ability and measurement of ability constitute errors of measurement. In psychological testing, the word *error* does not imply that a mistake has been made. Rather than having a negative connotation, *error* implies that there will always be some inaccuracy in our measurements. Our task is to find the magnitude of such errors and to develop ways to minimize them. This chapter discusses the conceptualization and assessment of measurement error. Tests that are relatively free of measurement error are deemed to be *reliable,* hence the name of this chapter. Tests that have "too much" measurement error are considered unreliable. We shall see the ways we can determine "how much is too much" in these cases.

History and Theory of Reliability

Conceptualization of Error

Students who major in physical science have chosen to study phenomena that are relatively easy to measure with precision. If you want to measure the width of this book, for example, you need only apply a ruler and record the number of inches or centimeters.

In psychology, many things make the measurement task more difficult. First, researchers are rarely interested in measuring simple qualities such as width. Instead, they usually pursue complex traits such as intelligence or aggressiveness, which one can neither see nor touch. Further, with no rigid yardsticks available to measure such characteristics, testers must use "rubber yardsticks"; these may stretch to overestimate some measurements and shrink to underestimate others (Mislevy, 2002; Nunnally & Bernstein, 1994). Psychologists must assess their measuring instruments to determine how much "rubber" is in them. A psychologist who is attempting to understand human behavior on the basis of unreliable tests is like a carpenter trying to build a house with a rubber measuring tape that never records the same length for the same piece of board.

As you will learn from this chapter, the theory of measurement error is well developed within psychology. This is not to say that measurement error is unique to psychology. In fact, serious measurement error occurs in most physical, social, and biological sciences. For example, measures of the gross national product (economics) and blood pressure (medicine) are known to be less reliable than well-constructed psychological tests. However, the concern with reliability has been a particular obsession for psychologists and p[...] of the advanced scientific status of the field (Shavelson & Ruiz-[...]

Spearman's Early Studies

Psychology owes the advanced development of reliability assessment to the early work of the British psychologist Charles Spearman. In 1733, Abraham De Moivre introduced the basic notion of sampling error (Stanley, 1971); and in 1896, Karl Pearson developed the product moment correlation (see Chapter 3 and Pearson, 1901). Reliability theory puts these two concepts together in the context of measurement. A contemporary of Pearson, Spearman actually worked out most of the basics of contemporary reliability theory and published his work in a 1904 article entitled "The Proof and Measurement of Association between Two Things." Because the *British Journal of Psychology* did not begin until 1907, Spearman published his work in the *American Journal of Psychology*. Spearman's work quickly became known in the United States. The article came to the attention of measurement pioneer Edward L. Thorndike, who was then writing the first edition of *An Introduction to the Theory of Mental and Social Measurements* (1904).

Thorndike's book is remarkably sophisticated, even by contemporary standards. Since 1904, many developments on both sides of the Atlantic ocean have led to further refinements in the assessment of reliability. Most important among these is a 1937 article by Kuder and Richardson, in which several new reliability coefficients were introduced. Later, Cronbach and his colleagues (Cronbach, 1989, 1995) made a major advance by developing methods for evaluating many sources of error in behavioral research. Reliability theory continues to evolve. In recent years, sophisticated mathematical models have been developed to quantify "latent" variables based on multiple measures (Bartholomew & Knott, 1999; Bentler, 1990, 1991, 1994). More recently, item response theory (IRT) has taken advantage of computer technology to advance psychological measurement significantly (Drasgow & Olson-Buchanan, 1999; McDonald, 1999; Michell, 1999). However, IRT is built on many of the ideas Spearman introduced a century ago.

Basics of Test Score Theory

Classical test score theory assumes that each person has a true score that would be obtained if there were no errors in measurement. However, because measuring instruments are imperfect, the score observed for each person almost always differs from the person's true ability or characteristic. The difference between the true score and the observed score results from measurement error. In symbolic representation, the observed score (X) has two components; a true score (T) and an error component (E):

$$X \quad = \quad T \quad + \quad E$$

Observed score   True score   Error

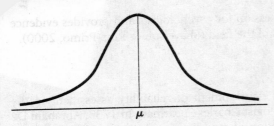

FIGURE 4-1
Distribution of observed scores for repeated testing of the same person. The mean of the distribution is the estimated true score, and the dispersion represents the distribution of random errors.

Or we can say that the difference between the score we obtain and the score we are really interested in equals the error of measurement:

$$X - T = E$$

A major assumption in classical test theory is that errors of measurement are random. Although systematic errors are acknowledged in most measurement problems, they are less likely than other errors to force an investigator to make the wrong conclusions. A carpenter who always misreads a tape measure by 2 inches (or makes a systematic error of 2 inches) would still be able to cut boards the same length. Using the rubber-yardstick analogy, we would say that this carpenter works with a ruler that is always 2 inches too long. Classical test theory, however, deals with rubber-yardstick problems in which the ruler stretches and contracts at random.

Using a rubber yardstick, we would not get the same score on each measurement. Instead, we would get a distribution of scores like that shown in Figure 4-1. Basic sampling theory tells us that the distribution of random errors is bell-shaped. Thus, the center of the distribution should represent the true score, and the dispersion around the mean of the distribution should display the distribution of sampling errors. Though any one application of the rubber yardstick may or may not tell us the true score, we can estimate the true score by finding the mean of the observations from repeated applications.

Figure 4-2 shows three different distributions. In the far left distribution, there is a great dispersion around the true score. In this case, you might not want to depend on a single observation because it might fall far from the true score. The far-right distribution displays a tiny dispersion around the true score. In this case, most of the observations are extremely close to the true score so that drawing conclusions on the basis of fewer observations will likely produce fewer errors than it will for the far-left curve.

The dispersions around the true score in Figures 4-1 and 4-2 tell us how much error there is in the measure. Classical test theory assumes that the true score for an individual will not change with repeated applications of the same test. Because of random error, however, repeated applications of the same test can produce different scores. Random error is responsible for the distribution of scores shown in Figures 4-1 and 4-2. Theoretically, the standard deviation of the distribution of errors for each person tells us about the magnitude of measurement error. Because we usually assume that the distribution of random

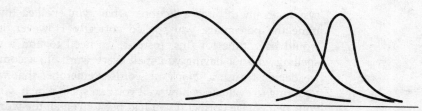

FIGURE 4-2   *Three distributions of observed scores. The far-left distribution reflects the greatest error, and the far-right distribution reflects the least.*

errors will be the same for all people, classical test theory uses the standard deviation of errors as the basic measure of error. Usually this is called the **standard error of measurement:**

$$\sigma_{meas}$$

The rubber-yardstick analogy may help you understand this concept. Suppose you have a table that is 30 inches high. You measure the height of the table several times using a steel yardstick and keep coming up with the same height: 30 inches. Next you try to measure the table with the rubber yardstick. The first time you try, the stick has stretched, and you record 28 inches. The next time, you discover the stick has shrunk, and it gives you 32 inches. Now you are in trouble, because repeated applications of the yardstick do not always give you the same information about the height of the table.

There is one way out of this situation. Assuming that the yardstick stretches and shrinks randomly, you can say that the distribution of scores given by the yardstick will be normal. Most scores will be close to the actual or true score. Scores that greatly differ from the true score will occur less frequently—that is, you will rarely observe a score as low as 5 inches or as high as 53 inches. The mean of the distribution of scores from repeated applications of the rubber yardstick will be an estimate of the table's true height. The standard deviation will be the standard error of measurement. Remember from Chapter 3 that the standard deviation tells us something about the average deviation around the mean. The standard error of measurement tells us, on the average, how much a score varies from the true score. In practice, the standard deviation of the observed score and the reliability of the test are used to estimate the standard error of measurement.

The Domain Sampling Model

The domain sampling model is another central concept in classical test theory. This model considers the problems created by using a limited number of items to represent a larger and more complicated construct. For example, suppose we want to evaluate your spelling ability. The best technique would be to go systematically through a dictionary, have you spell each word, and then determine the percentage you spelled correctly. However, it is unlikely that we would have time for this. Instead, we need to find a way to evaluate your spelling without having you spell every word. To accomplish this evaluation, we decide to use a *sample* of words. Remember that what we are really attempting to evaluate is how well you can spell, which would be determined by your percentage correct if you had been given all the words in the English language. This percentage would be your "true score." Our task in reliability analysis is to estimate how much error we would make by using the score from the shorter test as an estimate of your true ability.

This model conceptualizes reliability as the ratio of the variance of the observed score on the shorter test and the variance of the long-run true score. The measurement considered in the domain sampling model is the error introduced by using a sample of items (or words in this case) rather than the entire domain.[1] As the sample gets larger, it represents the domain more and more accurately. As a result, the greater the number of items, the higher the reliability. A later section of this chapter shows how a larger number of items increases test reliability.

When tests are constructed, each item is a sample of the ability or behavior to be measured. Long tests have many such samples, and short tests have few. However, each item should equally represent the studied ability. When testing your spelling ability, for example, we could use 5 words, 100 words, or 5000 words.

Reliability can be estimated from the correlation of the observed test score with the true score.[2] This would be easy to find if one could obtain true scores. However, finding the true scores is not practical and is rarely possible. In the spelling example, finding the true score would involve testing people on all of the words in the English language.

Because true scores are not available, our only alternative is to estimate what they would be. Given that items are randomly drawn from a given domain, each test or group of items should yield an unbiased estimate of the true score. Because of sampling error, however, different random samples of items might give different estimates of the true score. The distribution of these estimates should be random and normally distributed. If we create many tests by sampling from the same domain, then we should get a normal distribution of unbiased estimates of the true score. To estimate reliability, we can create many randomly parallel tests by drawing repeated random samples of items from the same domain. In the spelling example, we would draw several different lists of

---

[1]The term *domain* is used to describe an extremely large collection of items. Some authors prefer the term *universe* or *population* to describe the same concept (Nunnally & Bernstein, 1994).

[2]As M. J. Allen and Yen (1979) point out, there are at least six alternative interpretations of the reliability coefficient. The interpretation we offer here is the one most commonly used.

TECHNICAL BOX 4-1

The Unbiased Estimate of Reliability

Theorists have demonstrated mathematically that an unbiased estimate of a test's reliability is given by the square root of the average correlation between a test and all other randomly parallel tests from the domain. Symbolically,

$$r_{1t} = \sqrt{\bar{r}_{1j}}$$

where

   1 = scores on test 1
   t = the true score for the ability of interest
   r_{1j} = the average correlation between test 1 and all other randomly parallel tests

As you learned in Chapter 3, product moment correlation coefficients always take on values between -1 and 1. When we estimate reliability, the correlation will always be positive. When a number is less than 1.0, its square root will always be larger than itself. Thus, the correlation between two randomly parallel tests will be smaller than the estimated correlation between one of the tests and the true score according to the formula. For example, if the correlation between two randomly parallel tests is .64, the estimated reliability of the test will be $\sqrt{.64}$ = .80. This is built into the estimation of reliability because it would be impossible for a test to correlate more highly with any other test than it would correlate with its own true score. Thus, the correlation between two randomly parallel tests would be expected to be less than the correlation of either test with the true score.

words randomly from the dictionary and consider each of these samples to be an unbiased test of spelling ability. Then we would find the correlation between each of these tests and each of the other tests. The correlations then would be averaged.[3] Technical Box 4-1 considers one of the technical issues in estimating true reliability.

Models of Reliability

Federal government guidelines require that a test be reliable before one can use it to make employment or educational placement decisions (Heubert & Hauser, 1999). In this section, we hope to justify the need for high standards

---

[3]Technically, it is inappropriate to average correlation coefficients. The appropriate method is to use Fisher's r to Z' transformation to convert the correlations into approximate Z scores. Then the Z' scores are averaged, and the mean Z' is transformed back into a correlation (Silver & Dunlap, 1987).

of reliability. Most reliability coefficients are correlations; however, it is sometimes more useful to define reliability as its mathematically equivalent ratio. The reliability coefficient is the ratio of the variance of the true scores on a test to the variance of the observed scores:

$$r = \frac{\sigma_T^2}{\sigma_X^2}$$

where

r = the theoretical reliability of the test

σ_T^2 = the variance of the true scores

σ_X^2 = the variance of the observed scores

We have used the Greek σ^2 instead of S^2 to symbolize the variance because the equation describes theoretical values in a population rather than those actually obtained from a sample. The ratio of true score variance to observed score variance can be thought of as a percentage. In this case, it is the percentage of the observed variation (σ_X^2) that is attributable to variation in the true score. If we subtract this ratio from 1.0, then we will have the percentage of variation attributable to random error. $\sigma_T^2 + \sigma_E^2$ could also be used as the denominator because $\sigma_X^2 = \sigma_T^2 + \sigma_E^2$.

Suppose you are given a test that will be used to select people for a particular job, and the reliability of the test is .40. When the employer gets the test back and begins comparing applicants, 40% of the variation or difference among the people will be explained by real differences among people, and 60% must be ascribed to random or chance factors. Now you can see why the government needs to insist on high standards of reliability.

Sources of Error

An observed score may differ from a true score for many reasons. There may be situational factors such as loud noises in the room while the test is being administered. The room may be too hot or too cold. Some of the test takers may have a cold or be feeling depressed. Also, the items on the test might not be representative of the domain. For example, suppose you could spell 96% of the words in the English language correctly but the 20-item spelling test you took included 5 items (20%) that you could not spell.

Test reliability is usually estimated in one of three ways. In the *test–retest method,* we consider the consistency of the test results when the test is administered on different occasions. Using the method of *parallel forms,* we evaluate the test across different forms of the test. With the method of *internal consistency,* we examine how people perform on similar subsets of items selected from the same form of the measure. Each approach is based on a different source of variability. We shall consider each method separately.

Time Sampling: The Test–Retest Method

Test–retest reliability estimates are used to evaluate the error associated with administering a test at two different times. This type of analysis is of value only when we measure "traits" or characteristics that do not change over time. For instance, we usually assume that an intelligence test measures a consistent general ability. As such, if an IQ test administered at two points in time produces different scores, then we might conclude that the lack of correspondence is the result of random measurement error. Usually we do not assume that a person got more or less intelligent in the time between tests.

Tests that measure some constantly changing characteristic are not appropriate for test–retest evaluation. For example, the value of the Rorschach inkblot test seems to be to tell the clinician how the client is functioning at a particular time. Thus, differences between Rorschach scores at two times could reflect one of two things: (1) a change in the true score being measured or (2) measurement error. Clearly the test–retest method applies only to measures of stable traits.

Test–retest reliability is relatively easy to evaluate: Just administer the same test on two well-specified occasions and then find the correlation between scores from the two administrations using the methods presented in Chapter 3.

However, you need to consider many other details besides the methods for calculating the test–retest reliability coefficient. Understanding and using the information gained from these mechanical exercises requires careful thought. One thing you should always consider is the possibility of a *carryover effect*. This effect occurs when the first testing session influences scores from the second session. For example, test takers sometimes remember their answers from the first time they took the test. Suppose we ask someone the trivia question "Who was the next-door neighbor in the television program *Home Improvement?*" Then we ask the same question two days later. Some of the test takers might have watched the show in the meantime and found out they were wrong the first time. When there are carryover effects, the test–retest correlation usually overestimates the true reliability.

Carryover problems are of concern only when the changes over time are random. In cases where the changes are systematic, carryover effects do not harm the reliability. An example of a systematic carryover is when everyone's score improves exactly 5 points. In this case, no new variability occurs. Random carryover effects occur when the changes are not predictable from earlier scores or when something affects some but not all test takers. If something affects all the test takers equally, then the results are uniformly affected and no net error occurs.

Practice effects are one important type of carryover effect. Some skills improve with practice. When a test is given a second time, test takers score better because they have sharpened their skills by having taken the test the first time. Asking people trivia questions about old movies might stimulate them to think more about the movies or may actually give them some of the information. Practice can also affect tests of manual dexterity: Experience taking the test can improve dexterity skills. As a result, scores on the second administration are usually higher than they were on the first. Practice may affect test takers in different ways, so the changes are not constant across a group.

Because of these problems, the time interval between testing sessions must be selected and evaluated carefully. If the two administrations of the test are close in time, there is a relatively great risk of carryover and practice effects. However, as the time between testing sessions increases, many other factors can intervene to affect scores. For example, if a test is given to children at ages 4 and 5, and the scores from the two administrations of the test correlate at .43, then we must deal with many possible explanations. The low correlation might mean that (1) the test has poor reliability, (2) children change on this characteristic between ages 4 and 5, or (3) some combination of low reliability and change in the children is responsible for the .43 correlation. Further, most test–retest evaluations do not indicate a most likely choice among alternative explanations.

When you find a test–retest correlation in a test manual, you should pay careful attention to the interval between the two testing sessions. A well-evaluated test will have many retest correlations associated with different time intervals between testing sessions. Most often you want to be assured that the test is reliable over the time interval of your own study. You also should consider what events occurred between the original testing and the retest. For example, activities such as reading a book, participating in a course of study, or watching a TV documentary can alter the test–retest reliability estimate.

Of course, sometimes poor test–retest correlations do not mean that a test is unreliable. Instead, they suggest that the characteristic under study has changed. One of the problems with classical test theory is that it assumes that behavioral dispositions are constant over time. For example, if you are an aggressive person, it is assumed that you will be aggressive all the time. However, some authors have suggested that important behavioral characteristics, such as motivation, fluctuate over time. In fact, important variables such as health status are expected to vary (Jones & Kaplan, 2003; Kaplan, 2002; Patrick, Bushnell, & Rothman, 2004). In classical test theory, these variations are assumed to be errors. Because advanced theories of motivation actually predict these variations, test theorists have been challenged to develop models to account for systematic variations (Atkinson, 1981; Langenbucher et al., 2004; McClelland, 1994; Pattishall, 1992; Yanai, 2003).

Item Sampling: Parallel Forms Method

Building a reliable test also involves making sure that the test scores do not represent any one particular set of items or a subset of items from the entire domain. For example, if you are developing a test of spelling ability, then you would include a particular subset of words from the dictionary in the test. But, as we saw earlier, a test taker may get a score different from the ideal precisely because of the items you have chosen. One form of reliability analysis is to determine the error variance that is attributable to the selection of one particular set of items.

Parallel forms reliability compares two equivalent forms of a test that measure the same attribute. The two forms use different items; however, the rules used to select items of a particular difficulty level are the same.

When two forms of the test are available, one can compare performance on one form versus the other. Some textbooks refer to this process as *equivalent forms reliability,* whereas others call it simply *parallel forms.* Sometimes the two forms are administered to the same group of people on the same day. The Pearson product moment correlation coefficient (see Chapter 3) is used as an estimate of the reliability. When both forms of the test are given on the same day, the only sources of variation are random error and the difference between the forms of the test. (The order of administration is usually counterbalanced to avoid practice effects.) Sometimes the two forms of the test are given at different times. In these cases, error associated with time sampling is also included in the estimate of reliability.

The method of parallel forms provides one of the most rigorous assessments of reliability commonly in use. Unfortunately, the use of parallel forms occurs in practice less often than is desirable. Often test developers find it burdensome to develop two forms of the same test, and practical constraints make it difficult to retest the same group of individuals. Instead, many test developers prefer to base their estimate of reliability on a single form of a test.

In practice, psychologists do not always have two forms of a test. More often they have only one test form and must estimate the reliability for this single group of items. You can assess the different sources of variation within a single test in many ways. One method is to evaluate the internal consistency of the test by dividing it into subcomponents.

Split-Half Method

In split-half reliability, a test is given and divided into halves that are scored separately. The results of one half of the test are then compared with the results of the other. The two halves of the test can be created in a variety of ways. If the test is long, the best method is to divide the items randomly into two halves. For ease in computing scores for the different halves, however, some people prefer to calculate a score for the first half of the items and another score for the second half. Although convenient, this method can cause problems when items on the second half of the test are more difficult than items on the first half. If the items get progressively more difficult, then you might be better advised to use the *odd–even system,* whereby one subscore is obtained for the odd-numbered items in the test and another for the even-numbered items.

To estimate the reliability of the test, you could find the correlation between the two halves. However, this would be an underestimate because each subtest is only half as long as the full test. As we discussed earlier, test scores gain reliability as the number of items increases. An estimate of reliability based on two half-tests would be deflated because each half would be less reliable than the whole test. The correlation between the two halves of the test would be a reasonable estimate of the reliability of half the test. To correct for half-length, you can apply the *Spearman-Brown formula,* which allows you to estimate what the correlation between the two halves would have been if each half had been the length of the whole test:

$$r = \frac{2r}{1 + r}$$

where r is the estimated correlation between the two halves of the test if each had had the total number of items, and r is the correlation between the two halves of the test. (There are different forms of the estimation formula, as you will see later in the chapter.) For example, when the CES-D (which was described in Chapter 3) is divided into two equal parts, the correlation between the two halves of the test (for medical students) is .78. According to the formula, the estimated reliability would be

$$r = \frac{2(.78)}{1 + .78} = \frac{1.56}{1.78} = .876$$

Using the Spearman-Brown formula increases the estimate of reliability. The left-hand column in Table 4-1 shows several estimates of reliability that are not corrected using the Spearman-Brown procedure. The middle column shows the same values after they have been corrected. The right-hand column shows the amount of change the correction introduces. As you can see, the Spearman-Brown procedure has a substantial effect, particularly in the middle ranges.

Using the Spearman-Brown correction is not always advisable. For instance, when the two halves of a test have unequal variances, Cronbach's (1951) coefficient alpha (a) can be used. This general reliability coefficient provides the lowest estimate of reliability that one can expect. If alpha is high, then you might assume that the reliability of the test is acceptable because the lowest boundary of reliability is still high; the reliability will not drop below alpha. A low alpha level, on the other hand, gives you less information. Because the alpha coefficient marks only the lower bound for the reliability, the actual reliability may still be high. Thus, if the variances for the two halves of the test are unequal, coefficient alpha can confirm that a test has substantial reliability;

TABLE 4-1
Estimates of Split-Half Reliability Before and After Correction for Half-Length Using the Spearman-Brown Formula

Before correction	After correction	Amount of change
.05	.09	.04
.15	.26	.11
.25	.40	.15
.35	.52	.17
.45	.62	.17
.55	.71	.16
.65	.79	.14
.75	.86	.11
.85	.92	.07
.95	.97	.02

however, it cannot tell you that a test is unreliable. (Appendix 4-1 provides an example.) The formula for coefficient alpha is

$$\alpha = \frac{2[\sigma_x^2 - (\sigma_{y1}^2 \sigma_{y2}^2)]}{\sigma_x^2}$$

where

α = the coefficient alpha for estimating split-half reliability

σ_x^2 = the variance for scores on the whole test

$\sigma_{y1}^2 \sigma_{y2}^2$ = the variances for the two separate halves of the test

When the variances for the two halves of the test are equal, the Spearman-Brown coefficient and coefficient alpha give the same results. Under other specific circumstances, both procedures may underestimate the true reliability (see Allen & Yen, 1979).

KR_{20} *Formula*

In addition to the split-half technique, there are many other methods for estimating the internal consistency of a test. Many years ago, Kuder and Richardson (1937) greatly advanced reliability assessment by developing methods for evaluating reliability within a single test administration.

Their approach does not depend on some arbitrary splitting of the test into halves. Decisions about how to split tests into halves cause many potential problems for split-half reliability. The two halves may have different variances. The split-half method also requires that each half be scored separately, possibly creating additional work. The Kuder-Richardson technique avoids these problems because it simultaneously considers all possible ways of splitting the items.

The formula for calculating the reliability of a test in which the items are dichotomous, scored 0 or 1 (usually for right or wrong), is known as the **Kuder-Richardson 20**, or KR_{20} or $KR\ 20$. The formula came to be labeled this way because it was the 20th formula presented in the famous article by Kuder and Richardson.

The formula is

$$KR_{20} = r = \frac{N}{N-1}\left(\frac{S^2 - \Sigma pq}{S^2}\right)$$

where

KR_{20} = the reliability estimate (r)

N = the number of items on the test

S^2 = the variance of the total test score

p = the proportion of people getting each item correct (this is found separately for each item)

q = the proportion of people getting each item incorrect. For each item, q equals $1 - p$.

Σpq = the sum of the products of p times q for each item on the test

Studying the components of the formula may give you a better understanding of how it works. First, you will recognize the term S^2 from Chapter 2. This is the variance of the test scores. The variance appears twice in the formula: once on the top of the right portion in the equation and once on the bottom of the right portion. The other term in the right portion is Σpq. This is the sum of the product of the proportion of people passing each item times the proportion of people failing each item. The product pq is the variance for an individual item. Thus Σpq is the sum of the individual item variances.

Think about conditions that would make the term on the right side of the equation either large or small. First, consider the situation in which the variance (S^2) is equal to the sum of the variances of the individual items. Symbolically, this would be $S^2 = \Sigma pq$. In this case, the right-hand term in the formula would be 0 and, as a result, the estimate of reliability would be 0. This tells us that to have nonzero reliability, the variance for the total test score must be greater than the sum of the variances for the individual items. This will happen only when the items are measuring the same trait. The total test score variance is the sum of the item variances and the covariances between items (Crocker & Algina, 1986).

The only situation that will make the sum of the item variance less than the total test score variance is when there is covariance between the items. Covariance occurs when the items are correlated with each other. The greater the covariance, the smaller the Σpq term will be. When the items covary, they can be assumed to measure the same general trait, and the reliability for the test will be high. As Σpq approaches 0, the right side of the equation approaches 1.0. The other factor in the formula is an adjustment for the number of items in the test. This will allow an adjustment for the greater error associated with shorter tests. (Appendix 4-2 provides an example.)

In addition to the KR_{20}, Kuder and Richardson presented Formula 21, or KR_{21}, a special case of the reliability formula that does not require the calculation of the p's and q's for every item. Instead, the KR_{21} uses an approximation of the sum of the pq products—the mean test score. The KR_{21} procedure rests on several important assumptions. The most important is that all the items are of equal difficulty, or that the average difficulty level is 50%. *Difficulty* is defined as the percentage of test takers who pass the item. In practice, these assumptions are rarely met, and it is usually found that the KR_{21} formula underestimates the split-half reliability:

$$KR_{21} = \frac{N}{N-1}\left[1 - \frac{\bar{X}\left(1 - \frac{\bar{X}}{N}\right)}{S^2}\right]$$

where all terms are as previously defined.

Mathematical proofs have demonstrated that the KR_{20} formula gives the same estimate of reliability that you would get if you took the mean of the split-half reliability estimates obtained by dividing the test in all possible ways (Cronbach, 1951). You can see that because the Kuder-Richardson procedure is general, it is usually more valuable than a split-half estimate of internal consistency.

Coefficient Alpha

The KR_{20} formula is not appropriate for evaluating internal consistency in some cases. The KR_{20} formula requires that you find the proportion of people who got each item "correct." There are many types of tests, though, for which there are no right or wrong answers, such as many personality and attitude scales. For example, on an attitude questionnaire, you might be presented with a statement such as "I believe extramarital sexual intercourse is immoral." You must indicate whether you *strongly disagree, disagree, are neutral, agree,* or *strongly agree.* None of these choices is incorrect, and none is correct. Rather, your response indicates where you stand on the continuum between agreement and disagreement. To use the Kuder-Richardson method with this sort of item, Cronbach developed a formula that estimates the internal consistency of tests in which the items are not scored as 0 or 1 (right or wrong). In doing so, Cronbach developed a more general reliability estimate, which he called **coefficient alpha,** or α. The formula for coefficient alpha is[4]

$$r = \alpha = \left(\frac{N}{N-1}\right)\left(\frac{S^2 - \Sigma S_i^2}{S^2}\right)$$

As you may notice, this looks quite similar to the KR_{20} formula. The only difference is that Σpq has been replaced by ΣS_i^2. This new term, S_i^2, is for the variance of the individual items (i). The summation sign informs us that we are to sum the individual item variances. S^2 is for the variance of the total test score. The only real difference is the way the variance of the items is expressed. Actually, coefficient alpha is a more general reliability coefficient than KR_{20} because S_i^2 can describe the variance of items whether or not they are in a right–wrong format. Thus, coefficient alpha is the most general method of finding estimates of reliability through internal consistency.

All of the measures of internal consistency evaluate the extent to which the different items on a test measure the same ability or trait. They will all give low estimates of reliability if the test is designed to measure several traits. Using the domain sampling model, we define a domain that represents a single trait or characteristic, and each item is an individual sample of this general characteristic. When the items do not measure the same characteristic, the test will not be internally consistent.

Factor analysis is one popular method for dealing with the situation in which a test apparently measures several different characteristics (see Chapter 3). This can be used to divide the items into subgroups, each internally consistent; however, the subgroups of items will not be related to one another. Factor analysis can help a test constructor build a test that has submeasures for several different traits. When factor analysis is used correctly, these subtests will be internally consistent (highly reliable) and independent of one another. For

---

[4]Although this formula appears different from the formula for coefficient alpha from the section "Split-Half Method," the equations are mathematically equivalent.

example, you might use factor analysis to divide a group of items on interpersonal communication into two subgroups, perhaps assertiveness items and self-esteem items. The reliability of the self-esteem and the assertiveness subscales might be quite high; however, the correlation between assertiveness and self-esteem scores could be quite low. The nature of the factor analysis method ensures these characteristics. Thus, factor analysis is of great value in the process of test construction.

Reliability of a Difference Score

Some applications of psychological testing require a *difference score,* which is created by subtracting one test score from another. This might be the difference between performances at two points in time—for example, when you test a group of children before and after they have experienced a special training program. Or it may be the difference between measures of two different abilities, such as whether a child is doing better in reading than in math. Whenever comparisons between two different attributes are being made, one must make the comparison in Z, or standardized, units (see Chapter 2).

Difference scores create a host of problems that make them more difficult to work with than single scores. To understand the problems, you must refer back to the definition of an observed score as composed of both true score (T) and error (E). In a difference score, E is expected to be larger than either the observed score or T because E absorbs error from both of the scores used to create the difference score. Furthermore, T might be expected to be smaller than E because whatever is common to both measures is canceled out when the difference score is created. As a result of these two factors, the reliability of a difference score is expected to be lower than the reliability of either score on which it is based. If two tests measure exactly the same trait, then the score representing the difference between them is expected to have a reliability of 0.

As we have previously mentioned, it is most convenient to find difference scores by first creating Z scores for each measure and then finding the difference between them (score 2 − score 1). The reliability of scores that represent the difference between two standard scores (or Z scores) is given by the formula

$$r = \frac{\frac{1}{2}(r_{11} + r_{22}) - r_{12}}{1 - r_{12}}$$

where

r_{11} = the reliability of the first measure
r_{22} = the reliability of the second measure
r_{12} = the correlation between the first and the second measures

Using this formula, you can calculate the reliability of a difference score for any two tests for which the reliabilities and the correlation between them are known. For example, suppose that the correlation between two measures is .70

and the reliabilities of the two measures are .90 and .70, respectively. The reliability of the difference between these two measures is

$$r = \frac{\frac{1}{2}(.90 + .70) - .70}{1 - .70}$$

$$= \frac{.10}{.30}$$

$$= .33$$

As this example demonstrates, the reliability of the difference score between tests with reliabilities as high as .90 and .70 is only .33. The situation in which the reliability of the difference score is lower than the average reliabilities of the two initial measures is not unusual. In fact, it occurs in all cases except when the correlation between the two tests is 0.

The low reliability of a difference score should concern the practicing psychologist and education researcher. Because of their poor reliabilities, difference scores cannot be depended on for interpreting patterns.

For example, it may be difficult to draw the conclusion that a patient is more depressed than schizophrenic on the basis of an MMPI profile that shows a lower depression than schizophrenia score. Any differences between these two scales must be interpreted cautiously because the reliability of the score that represents the difference between the two scales can be expected to be low. The difficulties associated with using difference scores have been well studied. In a widely cited article, Cronbach and Furby (1970) demonstrated that there are many pitfalls associated with using difference scores to measure change. For example, it appears impossible to make a meaningful interpretation of the difference between scores on the same children that are taken at the beginning and at the end of a school year. Measuring the "change" that occurred during that school year requires the use of sophisticated experimental designs in which children are randomly assigned to experimental and control conditions.

Although reliability estimates are often interpreted for individuals, estimates of reliability are usually based on observations of populations, not observations of the same individual. One distinction is between reliability and information. Low reliability implies that comparing gain scores in a population may be problematic. For example, average improvements by schools on a statewide achievement test may be untrustworthy if the test has low reliability. Low information suggests that we cannot trust *gain-score* information about a particular person. This might occur if the test taker was sick on one of the days a test was administered, but not the other. However, low reliability of a change score for a population does not necessarily mean that gains for individual people are not meaningful (Mellenbergh, 1999). An improvement for an individual student might offer important information even though the test may have low reliability for the population.

Although reliability is often difficult to calculate, computer programs that do much of the work are now available. Technical Box 4-2 describes estimates of reliability using the SPSS program (Coakes & Steed, 1999; Sweet, 1999).

TECHNICAL BOX 4-2

Although calculating reliability is difficult to do by hand, a computer does it quite easily and efficiently. One of the most common statistical programs for calculating reliability is part of the Statistical Package for the Social Sciences (SPSS, 1995). The SPSS program calculates several different types of reliability. A summary of an analysis performed by SPSS is given here. The data for this analysis come from the CES-D example. However, instead of using the subsample of 20 medical students that we did in Chapter 3, we used an entire class of 117 medical students.

The first column in the table gives the item number. The second column lists the mean of the CES-D if an item was deleted. Unfortunately, the program is unable to make the adjustment for the CES-D, in which 20 points are subtracted from each score. This adjustment has no impact on the statistical properties of the CES-D (i.e., it does not affect the correlation with other variables); however, it does affect the mean. The table tells us that if the first item of the CES-D was eliminated, the mean score for the CES-D would be 28.5983; with the 20-point adjustment, the mean is 8.5983.

The second column in the table shows that the mean CES-D score is relatively unaffected by the elimination of any particular item. The third column in the table gives the scale variance if the item was deleted. We shall not attempt to interpret that in this exercise. The fourth column gives the corrected item–total correlation. This column describes the correlation between any particular item and the total test score minus the item. Notice that the item–test correlation for item 2 is relatively low (.1689), meaning that item 2 is a relatively poor item because it is unrelated to the total test score. Item 2 is "I did not feel like eating: my appetite was poor." Item 18, on the other hand, had a high correlation with the total score. Item 18 is "I enjoy life," and it was scored in the reverse direction. This item is conceptually close to the total score of the CES-D.

The column labeled "Squared Multiple Correlation" gives the proportion of variance in each item that can be explained by the other items. For example, about 35% of the variance in item 1 (.3520) can be explained by its relationship to the other items on the scale. For item 20, about 51% of the variance (.5096) can be explained through its associations with other items. These values are obtained by performing a multiple regression analysis in which each item is predicted from the combination of all the other items.

The final column in the table is the alpha for the total test if the particular item was deleted. As the numbers suggest, the alpha for the scale remains approximately the same if any single item is left out.

The computer summary also provides summary statistics for different methods of calculating reliabilities. It gives the alpha coefficient and a more complex standardized-item alpha. The program is also capable of calculating different types of reliability. For example, the program was asked to calculate the split-half reliability. The printout shows that the correlation between the two halves of the test is .7807. The Spearman-Brown correction adjusts this reliability to .8768. Another method of split-half reliability that performs the correction automatically is called the *Guttman split-half method,* which gives a reliability of .8760. This program also calculates the alpha coefficient for the first and the second halves of the tests separately.

```
                 RELIABILITY  ANALYSIS  -  SCALE  (CES-D)
   ITEM-TOTAL STATISTICS

             SCALE        SCALE      CORRECTED
             MEAN        VARIANCE     ITEM-                 SQUARED      ALPHA
             IF ITEM     IF ITEM     TOTAL                 MULTIPLE     IF ITEM
             DELETED*    DELETED     CORRELATION           CORRELATION
      DELETED

   1         28.5983     48.3286      .4884                .3520        .8671
   2         28.9145     51.9237      .1689                .2528        .8773
   3         28.7521     48.0329      .5290                .4813        .8655
   4         28.8547     49.0908      .3800                .3736        .8715
   5         28.4957     48.9073      .3793                .2736        .8718
   6         28.4872     46.1830      .7330                .6876        .8577
   7         28.6581     47.9338      .5768                .5180        .8639
   8         28.8974     49.2825      .5321                .4468        .8661
   9         29.1368     52.3604      .2585                .2270        .8734
   10        28.6325     49.4241      .3896                .3216        .8707
   11        28.6752     50.4626      .2880                .2533        .8743
   12        28.6496     47.6089      .6275                .5927        .8622
   13        28.6325     49.4586      .3781                .3367        .8712
   14        28.2991     46.5735      .5958                .5930        .8628
   15        28.8205     49.7175      .4466                .3494        .8685
   16        28.7778     47.7605      .6068                .5635        .8629
   17        28.9145     50.8375      .3372                .2737        .8717
   18        28.6154     47.5663      .6525                .5671        .8615
   19        28.8718     49.5610      .5209                .4631        .8666
   20        28.7009     48.1080      .6074                .5096        .8632

   Alpha Method

   RELIABILITY COEFFICIENTS    20 ITEMS

   ALPHA =   .8734  STANDARDIZED ITEM ALPHA =  .8739

   Split-Half Method

   RELIABILITY COEFFICIENTS    20 ITEMS

   CORRELATION BETWEEN FORMS = .7807    EQUAL LENGTH SPEARMAN-BROWN =      .8768

   GUTTMAN SPLIT-HALF =         .8760   UNEQUAL-LENGTH SPEARMAN-BROWN =    .8768

   ALPHA FOR PART 1 = .7424    ALPHA FOR PART 2 =        .8031

   10 ITEMS IN PART 1          10 ITEMS IN PART 2

   *NOTE—The CES-D uses a correction in which 20 is subtracted from each score.
   This correction is not reflected in the computer program. So, for example, the
   mean if item 1 was deleted would be 8.5983, not 28.5983.
```

Reliability in Behavioral Observation Studies

Psychologists with behavioral orientations usually prefer not to use psychological tests. Instead, they favor the direct observation of behavior. To measure aggression, for example, they would record the number of times a child hits or kicks another child. Observers would tabulate the number of observable responses in each category. Thus, there would be one score for "hits," another for "kicks," and so on.

Some people feel that behavioral observation systems are so simple that they have no psychometric problems, but they have many sources of error. Because psychologists cannot always monitor behavior continuously, they often take samples of behavior at certain time intervals. Under these circumstances, sampling error must be considered (C. Kaplan, 1993).

Sources of error introduced by time sampling are similar to those with sampling items from a large domain. When each time sample is thought of as an "item," these problems can be handled using sampling theory and methods such as alpha reliability.

In practice, behavioral observation systems are frequently unreliable because of discrepancies between true scores and the scores recorded by the observer. For example, an observer might miss one or two times a child hits or kicks; another observer might catch them all. The problem of error associated with different observers presents unique difficulties. To assess these problems, one needs to estimate the reliability of the observers (Cordes, 1994). These reliability estimates have various names, including *interrrater, interscorer, interobserver,* or *interjudge reliability.* All of the terms consider the consistency among different judges who are evaluating the same behavior. There are at least three different ways to do this. The most common method is to record the percentage of times that two or more observers agree. Unfortunately, this method is not the best one, for at least two reasons. First, this percentage does not consider the level of agreement that would be expected by chance alone. For instance, if two observers are recording whether a particular behavior either occurred or did not occur, then they would have a 50% likelihood of agreeing by chance alone. A method for assessing such reliability should include an adjustment for chance agreement. Second, percentages should not be mathematically manipulated. For example, it is not technically appropriate to average percentages. Indexes such as Z scores are manipulable and thus better suited to the task of reliability assessment.

The *kappa statistic* is the best method for assessing the level of agreement among several observers. The kappa statistic was introduced by J. Cohen (1960) as a measure of agreement between two judges who each rate a set of objects using nominal scales. Fleiss (1971) extended the method to consider the agreement between any number of observers. *Kappa* indicates the actual agreement as a proportion of the potential agreement following correction for chance agreement. Values of kappa may vary between 1 (perfect agreement) and −1 (less agreement than can be expected on the basis of chance alone). A value greater than .75 generally indicates "excellent" agreement, a value between .40 and .75 indicates "fair to good" ("satisfactory") agreement, and a value less than .40 indicates "poor" agreement (Fleiss, 1981). The calculation of kappa is beyond the scope of this presentation, but interested readers can find the procedures in Fleiss (1971) and Shrout, Spitzer, and Fleiss (1987). Discussion of the interpretation of low kappas is offered in Feinstein and Cicchetti (1990). An approximation of the coefficient for the agreement between two observers is also given by the phi coefficient, which was discussed in Chapter 3.

Studies of agreement are common in behavioral and medical sciences. In one example, researchers used two methods for learning about sexual history. One method asked questions at two different points in time, while the other asked about current behavior and required the subject to recollect behavior at a previous point in time. In an evaluation of 962 heterosexual men and women, the kappa for reporting condom use (as reported by the same people using the two methods) was only moderate (kappa = 0.38) Among heterosexual men, the two methods showed poor agreement for reporting the number of sexual partners (kappa = −0.14) (Stone, Catania, & Binson, 1999).

Although studies of interrater reliability have become common, the validity of behavioral ratings has received relatively little study (Harwell, 1999).

Connecting Sources of Error with Reliability Assessment Method

Table 4-2 relates sources of measurement error to the methods used to assess reliability. Remember that *reliability* is a generic term. Psychologists use different methods of reliability assessment to describe different sources of measurement error, and each has a different meaning. As Table 4-2 suggests, one source of measurement error is *time sampling*. The same test given at different points in time may produce different scores, even if given to the same test takers. This source of error is typically assessed using the test–retest method. Another source of error is *item sampling*. The same construct or attribute may be assessed using a wide pool of items. For example, no one item is used to assess human intelligence, yet different items used to measure this general construct may not always give the same reflection of the true ability. This sort of error is assessed using alternate forms, or parallel forms reliability. Typically, the correlation between two forms of a test is created by randomly sampling a large pool

TABLE 4-2 *Sources of Measurement Error and Methods of Reliability Assessment*

Source of error	Example	Method	How assessed
Time sampling	Same test given at two points in time (item sampling)	Test–retest	Correlation between scores obtained on the two occasions
Item sampling	Different items used to assess the same attribute	Alternate forms or parallel forms	Correlation between equivalent forms of the test that have different items
Internal consistency	Consistency of items within the same test	1. Split-half	1. Corrected correlation between two halves of the test
		2. KR_{20}	2. See Appendix 4-1
		3. Alpha	3. See Appendix 4-2
Observer differences	Different observers recording	Kappa statistic	See Fleiss (1981)

of items believed to assess a particular construct. This correlation is used as an estimate of this type of reliability.

The *internal consistency* of a test refers to the intercorrelations among items within the same test. If the test is designed to measure a single construct and all items are equally good candidates to measure that attribute, then there should be a high correspondence among the items. This internal consistency is evaluated using split-half reliability, the KR_{20} method, or coefficient alpha. Another source of measurement error occurs when different observers record the same behavior. Even though they have the same instructions, different judges observing the same event may record different numbers. To determine the extent of this type of error, researchers can use an adjusted index of agreement such as the kappa statistic.

As you can see, the term *reliability* refers to several methods that are used to assess different sources of error. Sometimes different sources of error occur in the same situation—for example, error associated with item sampling and additional error linked to time sampling. When evaluating reliability information, you should take into consideration all potential sources of error. Interrater agreement can be a problem in basic medical as well as behavioral studies (see Focused Example 4-1). A summary of the standards for reporting information about reliability is presented in Focused Example 4-2.

Using Reliability Information

Now that you have learned about reliability theory and methods, you will benefit from reviewing some practical aspects of reliability assessment. Different situations call for different levels of reliability.

Standard Errors of Measurement and the Rubber Yardstick

Earlier in this chapter, we used the rubber yardstick to introduce the concept of the standard error of measurement. Remember that psychologists working with unreliable tests are like carpenters working with rubber yardsticks that stretch or contract and misrepresent the true length of a board. However, as all rubber yardsticks are not equally inaccurate, all psychological tests are not equally inaccurate. The standard error of measurement allows us to estimate the degree to which a test provides inaccurate readings; that is, it tells us how much "rubber" there is in a measurement. The larger the standard error of measurement, the less certain we can be about the accuracy with which an attribute is measured. Conversely, a small standard error of measurement tells us that an individual score is probably close to the measured value. Some textbooks refer to the standard error of measurement as the standard error of a score. To calculate the standard error of measurement, we need to use the standard deviation and the reliability coefficient. The formula for this calculation is

$$S_m = S\sqrt{1 - r}$$

Focused Example 4-1

INTERRATER AGREEMENT IN PATHOLOGY

Psychologists have always been self-critical about the less-than-perfect reliability rates in behavioral studies. They assume that agreement must be higher in other fields, particularly when there is an opportunity for more careful study. For example, we would expect high interrater agreement among pathologists who study tissue under a microscope. However, many studies suggest that agreement among pathologists who study the same specimens is often no better than among behavioral scientists who observe the activities of the same individuals. For example, one study evaluated the reliability of pathologist-assessed ductile carcinoma in situ (DCIS). Six pathologist subjects were given written guidelines and examples of each of the problems they were looking for. Following this training, these experienced pathologists were given 24 high-quality slides of breast tissue. There was considerable variability in the propensity to see DCIS: One pathologist saw cancer in 12% of the slides, while another saw DCIS in 33% of the same slides.

Figure 4-3 summarizes the results for 10 slides where at least one pathologist saw DCIS. The columns represent women, and the rows represent pathologists. Hatched squares indicate that the pathologist saw DCIS; open squares indicate that DCIS was not seen. No two pathologists had the same pattern of identification. One pathologist saw cancer in eight of the 10 cases, while another saw DCIS in only three. One case was diagnosed by only one pathologist, and only two cases were seen by all six. These variations in diagnostic patterns imply that patients with the same problem, going to different doctors, may get different diagnoses (Welch, 2004).

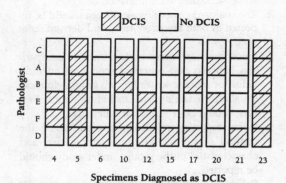

FIGURE 4-3 *Interobserver agreement among six pathologists on DCIS for 10 cases.*

(Welch, H. G., and Black W. C. Using autopsy series to estimate the disease "reservoir" for ductal carcinoma in situ of the breast: How much breast cancer can we find? Ann Intern Med. Dec. 1 1997; 127(11): 1023–1028.)

where

S_m = the standard error for the measurement

S = the standard deviation of the scores

r = the reliability coefficient

For example, suppose that an IQ test has a mean of 100 for a particular sample, with a standard deviation of 14. You are particularly interested in a person with a score of 106. The reliability of the test is .89. Plugging these values into the formula, you find

$$S_m = 14\sqrt{1 - .89} = 4.64$$

Focused Example 4-2

SUMMARY OF GUIDELINES FOR RELIABILITY

 The American Psychological Association, American Educational Research Association, and National Council on Measurement in Education (1999) suggest 20 standards for reliability.* Here is a summary of these standards:

1. Estimates of reliabilities and standard errors of measurement should be provided for each total score, subscore, or combination of scores.
2. The standard error of measurement should be reported in both raw score units and derived score units.
3. Sometimes test interpretation involves comparison between two observed scores for an individual or average scores for two groups. In these situations, reliability data, including standard errors, should be reported for differences.
4. When reporting reliability, information on the method of subject selection, sample size, and characteristics of the groups under study should be reported.
5. Reliability coefficients and standard errors, typically derived using a particular technique, should

not be used interchangeably with estimates obtained using other methods.
6. If reliability coefficients are adjusted for a restricted range, these adjustments must be reported.
7. If a test has multiple factors or measures multiple traits simultaneously, this multifactorial structure must be recognized in the reports of reliability.
8. Those who take the test must be told if the rate of work may affect their performance.
9. For tests that are timed, reliability estimates should be obtained using alternate form or test–retest methods that adjust for the amount of time subjects have to complete the test.
10. Judges can make subjective errors in rating behavior. When subjective errors are possible, an interrater consistency evaluation should consider within-examinee comparisons as well as between rater reliability.
11. Whenever feasible, test publishers should provide reliability evidence for major subpopulations. For example, they should provide separate

---

Researchers use standard errors of measurement to create confidence intervals around specific observed scores. You may want to review the concept of a confidence interval in your introductory statistics textbook. Briefly, we never know whether an observed score is the "true" score. However, we can form intervals around an observed score and use statistical procedures to estimate the probability that the true score falls within a certain interval. Common intervals used in testing are the 68% interval, the 95% interval, and the 99% interval. These intervals are created using Z scores (see Chapter 2).

Let's suppose we wish to create the 95% confidence interval for this specific IQ test. The 95% confidence interval is associated with the Z score of 1.96. The upper bound of the confidence interval is equal to the mean plus $1.96(S_m)$, or, in this example,

$$106 + 1.96(4.64) = 115.09$$

The lower bound of the interval is equal to the mean minus

$$1.96 \times S_m$$

reliability estimates for white, African-American, Asian-American, and Hispanic groups.

12. If a test is applied to different grade levels or different age groups and separate norms are provided for each group, reliability data should be provided for each age or population group separately.

13. Sometimes national tests are applied in local areas. Whenever possible, reliability data should be evaluated and reported at the local level.

14. Conditional standard errors of measurement should be reported. This means that if the test divides examinees into specific subgroups, the standard error of measurement for each of these subgroups should be considered.

15. If a test is used to divide examinees into categories, estimates should be reported for the percentage of people who would be placed in the same category if the test were administered on two separate occasions.

16. Sometimes different examinees complete tests with different items. The items might be randomly selected from some larger pool of items (as is often the case using item response theory). Under these circumstances, reliability should be estimated on the basis of successive administrations

of the test under conditions similar to those under which the test is typically administered.

17. Some tests are available in both long and short versions. Under these circumstances, reliability should be reported for each version of the test.

18. If variations are allowed in the procedures for test administration, separate reliability estimates should be provided under each of the major variations.

19. When average scores for groups are used to evaluate programs, the groups tested should be considered samples from a larger population. The standard error of the group mean should be reported.

20. Sometimes, program evaluation administrators give small subsets of items to many subsamples of examinees. Then the data are aggregated to estimate performance for the group. When these procedures are used, the reliability analysis must take the sampling scheme into consideration.

---

*Standards not applicable to basic psychometrics are not listed here.

Adapted from American Educational Research Association et al. (1999, pp. 31–36).

So, in this example, the lower bound would be

$$106 - 1.96(4.64) = 96.91$$

Although we do not know the true score for a person who received the score of 106, we can be 95% confident that the true score falls between 96.9 and 115.1. As you can see, however, the scores of 96 and 115 on an IQ test (see Chapters 11 and 12) are quite different. Tests with more measurement error include more "rubber." In other words, the larger the standard error of measurement, the larger the confidence interval. When confidence intervals are especially wide, our ability to make precise statements is greatly diminished.

How Reliable Is Reliable?

People often ask how high a reliability coefficient must be before it is "high enough." The answer depends on the use of the test. It has been suggested that reliability estimates in the range of .70 and .80 are good enough for most purposes in basic research. In many studies, researchers attempt to gain only approximate estimates of how two variables are related. For research, it may be appropriate to estimate what the correlation between two variables would have been if the measures had been more reliable. Promising results can justify spending extra time and money to make the research instruments more reliable. Some people have argued that it would be a waste of time and effort to refine research instruments beyond a reliability of .90. Although the higher reliability is desirable, it may not be worth the added burden and costs (Nunnally & Bernstein, 1994). A report from the National Academy of Sciences notes that extremely high reliability might be expected for tests that are highly focused. For example, a test of skill at using the multiplication tables for one-digit numbers would be expected to have an especially high reliability. Tests of complex constructs, such as creativity, might be expected to be less reliable (Heubert & Hauser, 1999).

In clinical settings, high reliability is extremely important. When tests are used to make important decisions about someone's future, evaluators must be certain to minimize any error in classification. Thus, a test with a reliability of .90 might not be good enough. For a test used to make a decision that affects some person's future, evaluators should attempt to find a test with a reliability greater than .95.

Perhaps the most useful index of reliability for the interpretation of individual scores is the standard error of measurement. This index is used to create an interval around an observed score. The wider the interval, the lower the reliability of the score. Using the standard error of measurement, we can say that we are 95% confident that a person's true score falls between two values.

What to Do About Low Reliability

Often, test constructors want their tests to be used in applied settings, but analysis reveals inadequate test reliability. Fortunately, psychometric theory offers some options. Two common approaches are to increase the length of the test and to throw out items that run down the reliability. Another procedure is to estimate what the true correlation would have been if the test did not have measurement error.

Increase the number of items. According to the domain sampling model, each item in a test is an independent sample of the trait or ability being measured. The larger the sample, the more likely that the test will represent the true characteristic. In the domain sampling model, the reliability of a test increases as the number of items increases.

A medical example will clarify why longer tests are more reliable. Suppose that you go to the doctor with indigestion. You want the doctor to make a reliable judgment about what is causing it. How comfortable would you feel if the doctor asked only one question before making a diagnosis? You would probably feel more comfortable if the doctor asked many questions. In general, people feel that the more information a doctor obtains by asking questions and performing tests, the more reliable the diagnosis will be. This same principle applies to psychological tests.

A decision to increase the number of items in a test might engender a long and costly process. With new items added, the test must be reevaluated; it may turn out to fall below an acceptable level of reliability. In addition, adding new items can be costly and can make a test so long that few people would be able to sit through it. Fortunately, by applying the Spearman-Brown prophecy formula, one can estimate how many items will have to be added in order to bring a test to an acceptable level of reliability.

The prophecy formula for estimating how long a test must be to achieve a desired level of reliability is another case of the general Spearman-Brown method for estimating reliability. Algebraic manipulations of the general formula allow one to solve it for the length needed for any desired level of reliability:

$$N = \frac{r_d(1 - r_o)}{r_o(1 - r_d)}$$

where

N = the number of tests of the current version's length that would be needed to have a test of the desired level of reliability

r_d = the desired level of reliability

r_o = the observed level of reliability based on the current version of the test

Consider the example of the 20-item CES-D test that had a reliability for medical students of .87. We would like to raise the reliability to .95. Putting these numbers into the prophecy formula, we get

$$N = \frac{.95(1 - .87)}{.87(1 - .95)} = \frac{.124}{.044} = 2.82$$

These calculations tell us that we would need 2.82 tests of the same length as the current 20-item test to bring the reliability up to the desired level. To find the number of items required, we must multiply the number of items on the current test by N from the preceding formula. In the example, this would give 20 × 2.82 = 56.4. So the test would have to be expanded from 20 to approximately 56 items to achieve the desired reliability, assuming that the added items come from the same pool as the original items and that they have the same psychometric properties.

The decision to expand a test from 20 to 56 items must depend on economic and practical considerations. The test developer must first ask whether the increase in reliability is worth the extra time, effort, and expense required to achieve this goal. If the test is to be used for personnel decisions, then it may be dangerous to ignore any enhancement of the test's reliability. On the other hand, if the test is to be used only to see if two variables are associated, the expense of extending it may not be worth the effort and cost.

When the prophecy formula is used, certain assumptions are made that may or may not be valid. One of these assumptions is that the probability of error in items added to the test is the same as the probability of error for the original items in the test. However, adding many items may bring about new sources of error, such as the fatigue associated with taking an extremely long test.

As an example of a situation in which increasing the reliability of a test may not be worthwhile, consider a 40-item test with a reliability of .50. We would like to bring the reliability up to .90. Using the prophecy formula, we get

$$N = \frac{.90(1 - .50)}{.50(1 - .90)} = \frac{.90(.50)}{.50(.10)} = \frac{.45}{.05} = 9$$

These figures tell us that the test would have to be nine times its present length to have a projected reliability of .90. This is calculated as $9 \times 40 = 360$ items long. Creating a test that long would be prohibitively expensive, and validating it would require a considerable investment of time for both test constructors and test takers. Also, new sources of error might arise that were not present in the shorter measure. For example, many errors may occur on the longer test simply because people get tired and bored during the long process of answering 360 questions. There is no way to take these factors into account by using the prophecy formula.

Factor and item analysis. The reliability of a test depends on the extent to which all of the items measure one common characteristic. Although psychologists set out to design test items that are consistent, often some items do not measure the given construct. Leaving these items in the test reduces its reliability. To ensure that the items measure the same thing, two approaches are suggested. One is to perform factor analysis (see Chapter 3 and Bartholomew & Knott, 1999; Loehlin, 1998; Tabachnick & Fidell, 1996). Tests are most reliable if they are *unidimensional*. This means that one factor should account for considerably more of the variance than any other factor. Items that do not load on this factor might be best omitted.

Another approach is to examine the correlation between each item and the total score for the test. This form of item analysis (see Chapter 6) is often called **discriminability analysis.** When the correlation between the performance on a single item and the total test score is low, the item is probably measuring something different from the other items on the test. It also might mean that the item is so easy or so hard that people do not differ in their response to it. In either case, the low correlation indicates that the item drags down the estimate of reliability and should be excluded.

Correction for attenuation. Low reliability is a real problem in psychological research and practice because it reduces the chances of finding significant correlations between measures. If a test is unreliable, information obtained with it is of little or no value. Thus, we say that potential correlations are attenuated, or diminished, by measurement error.

Fortunately, measurement theory does allow one to estimate what the correlation between two measures would have been if they had not been measured with error. These methods "correct" for the attenuation in the correlations caused by the measurement error. To use the methods, one needs to know only the reliabilities of two tests and the correlation between them. The **correction for attenuation** is

$$\hat{r}_{12} = \frac{r_{12}}{\sqrt{r_{11}r_{22}}}$$

where

$\hat{r}_{12}$ = the estimated true correlation between tests 1 and 2

r_{12} = the observed correlation between tests 1 and 2

r_{11} = the reliability of test 1

r_{22} = the reliability of test 2

Suppose, for example, that the correlation between the CES-D and ratings of clinical skill was .34; the reliabilities of the tests were .87 and .70 for the CES-D and the clinical skill tests, respectively. The estimated true correlation between depression and clinical skill would be

$$\frac{.34}{\sqrt{(.87)(.70)}} = \frac{.34}{\sqrt{.609}} = \frac{.34}{.78} = .44$$

As the example shows, the estimated correlation increases from .34 to .44 when the correction is used.

Sometimes one measure meets an acceptable standard of reliability but the other one does not. In this case, we would want to correct for the attenuation caused only by the one unreliable test. To do this, we use the formula

$$\hat{r}_{12} = \frac{r_{12}}{\sqrt{r_{11}}}$$

where

$\hat{r}_{12}$ = the estimated true correlation

r_{12} = the observed correlation

r_{11} = the reliability of the variable that does not meet our standard of reliability

For example, suppose we want to estimate the correlation between the CES-D score and GPA in medical school. The reliability of the CES-D test is .75, which is not quite as good as we would like, but medical school GPA is assumed to be measured without error. Using the fallible CES-D depression test, we observe the correlation to be .53. Plugging these numbers into the formula, we get

$$\frac{.53}{\sqrt{.75}} = \frac{.53}{.87} = .61$$

This informs us that correcting for the attenuation caused by the CES-D test would increase our observed correlation from .53 to .61.

SUMMARY

Measurement error is common in all fields of science. Psychological and educational specialists, however, have devoted a great deal of time and study to measurement error and its effects. Tests that are relatively free of measurement error are considered to be reliable, and tests that contain relatively large measurement error are considered unreliable. In the early part of the 20th century, Charles Spearman worked out the basics of contemporary theories and methods of reliability. Test score and reliability theories have gone through continual refinements.

When we evaluate *reliability,* we must first specify the source of measurement error we are trying to evaluate. If we are concerned about errors that result from tests being given at different times, then we might consider the *test–retest method* in which test scores obtained at two different points in time are correlated. On other occasions, we may be concerned about errors that arise because we have selected a small sample of items to represent a larger conceptual domain. To evaluate this type of measurement error, we could use a method that assesses the internal consistency of the test such as the *split-half method.* The KR_{20} method and *alpha coefficient* are other methods for estimating the internal consistency of a test.

The standard of reliability for a test depends on the situation in which the test will be used. In some research settings, bringing a test up to an exceptionally high level of reliability may not be worth the extra time and money. On the other hand, strict standards for reliability are required for a test used to make decisions that will affect people's lives. When a test has unacceptably low reliability, the test constructor might wish to boost the reliability by increasing the test length or by using factor analysis to divide the test into homogeneous subgroups of items. In research settings, we can sometimes deal with the problem of low reliability by estimating what the correlation between tests would have been if there had been no measurement error. This procedure is called *correction for attenuation.*

Recently, interest has increased in evaluating the reliability of behavioral observations. The percentage of items on which observers agree is not the best index of reliability for these studies because it does not take into consideration how much agreement is to be expected by chance alone. Correlation-like indexes such as kappa or phi are better suited to estimate reliability in these behavioral studies.

Reliability is one of the basic foundations of behavioral research. If a test is not reliable, then one cannot demonstrate that it has any meaning. In the next chapter, we focus on how the meaning of tests is defined.

Appendix 4-1: Using Coefficient Alpha to Estimate Split-Half Reliability When the Variances for the Two Halves of the Test Are Unequal

Formula: $$\alpha = \frac{2[S_x^2 - (S_{y1}^2 + S_{y2}^2)]}{S_x^2}$$

Data: $S_x^2 = 11.5$

$S_{y1}^2 = 4.5$

$S_{y2}^2 = 3.2$

Steps

1. Find the variance for the whole test.

$$S_x^2 = 11.5$$

2. Add the variances for the two halves of the test.

$$S_{y1}^2 = 4.5 \quad S_{y2}^2 = 3.2 \quad 4.5 + 3.2 = 7.7$$

3. Find $S_x^2 - (S_{y1}^2 + S_{y2}^2)$ by subtracting the result of Step 2 from that of Step 1.

$$11.5 - 7.7 = 3.8$$

4. Find $2[S_x^2 - (S_{y1}^2 + S_{y2}^2)]$ by multiplying the result of Step 3 times 2.

$$2(3.8) = 7.6$$

5. Find alpha by dividing the result of Step 4 by that of Step 1.

$$\frac{7.6}{11.5} = .66$$

Appendix 4-2: The Calculation of Reliability Using KR₂₀

Formula: $$KR_{20} = \frac{N}{N-1}\left(\frac{S^2 - \Sigma pq}{S^2}\right)$$

Data: NS = number of test takers = 50

N = number of items = 6

S^2 = variance (Step 6) = 2.8

Item	Number of Test Takers Responding Correctly	p (from Step 2)	q (from Step 3)	pq (from Step 4)
1	12	.24	.76	.18
2	41	.82	.18	.15
3	18	.36	.64	.23
4	29	.58	.42	.24
5	30	.60	.40	.24
6	47	.94	.06	.06
				$\Sigma pq = 1.10$ (from Step 5)

Steps

1. Determine the number of test takers *NS*.

$$NS = 50$$

2. Find p by dividing the number of people responding correctly to each item by the number of people taking the test (Step 1). This is the level of difficulty.

$$\frac{12}{50} = .24 \quad \frac{41}{50} = .82 \cdots$$

3. Find q for each item by subtracting p (the result of Step 2) from 1.0. This gives the proportion responding incorrectly to each item.

$$1.0 - .24 = .76 \quad 1.0 - .82 = .18 \cdots$$

4. Find pq for each item by multiplying the results of Steps 2 and 3.

$$(.24)(.76) = .18 \quad (.82)(.18) = .15 \cdots$$

5. Find Σpq by summing the results of Step 4 over the N items.

$$.18 + .15 + .23 + .24 + .24 + .06 = 1.1$$

6. Find S^2, which is the variance for the test sources. To do this, you need the scores for each individual in the group. The formula for the variance is

$$S^2 = \frac{\Sigma X^2 - \left[\dfrac{(\Sigma X)^2}{NS}\right]}{NS - 1}$$

In this example $S^2 = 2.8$.

7. Find $S^2 - \Sigma pq$ by subtracting the result of Step 5 from that of Step 6.

$$2.8 - 1.1 = 1.7$$

8. Find $(S^2 - \Sigma pq)/S^2$ by dividing the result of Step 7 by that of Step 6.

$$\frac{1.7}{2.8} = .607$$

9. Find N or the number of items.

$$N = 6$$

10. Find $N/(N - 1)$ by dividing the result of Step 9 by Step 9 minus 1.

$$\frac{6}{5} = 1.2$$

11. Find KR_{20} by multiplying the results of Steps 8 and 10.

$$(1.2)(.607) = .73$$

WEB ACTIVITY

For interesting and relevant Web sites, check the following:

trochim.human.cornell.edu/kb/truescor.htm
A simple explanation of true score theory

trochim.human.cornell.edu/kb/reliable.htm
Explanation of reliability theory

seamonkey.ed.asu.edu/~alex/teaching/assessment/reliability.html
Overview of types of reliability

web.uccs.edu/lbecker/Psy590/relval_I.htm#II.
%20Scale%20Development%20Issues
Discussion of reliability in relation to scale construction

CHAPTER 5

Validity

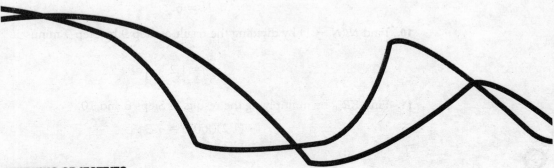

LEARNING OBJECTIVES

When you have completed this chapter, you should be able to:

- [ ] Determine the relationship between establishing test validity and using the scientific method

- [ ] Explain why it is inappropriate to refer to so-called face validity as real evidence of validity

- [ ] List the categories of validity evidence recognized in the booklet *Standards for Educational and Psychological Testing*

- [ ] Tell how the strategy for establishing content validity evidence differs from the strategy used to obtain other types of validity evidence

- [ ] Discuss the difference between predictive and concurrent criterion validity evidence

- [ ] Relate the concept of the coefficient of determination (from Chapter 3) to the interpretation of the validity coefficient in criterion validity evidence

- [ ] Tell how to interpret the results of a test that, for example, had a validity coefficient of .35 for predicting success on a particular job

- [ ] List some of the issues to consider when you interpret a validity coefficient

- [ ] Know how to evaluate evidence for construct validity

- [ ] Select a hypothetical construct and describe how you would go about developing a measure for it

The case of Willie Griggs was argued before the U.S. Supreme Court in October 1970. Griggs and 12 other black laborers were employees of the Dan River Steam Station of the Duke Power Company in Draper, North Carolina. The company classified Griggs and the other complainants as laborers whose primary work assignment was sweeping and cleaning. The men would have preferred promotion to the next higher classification level of coal handler. However, the company required a passing score on a general intelligence test for that promotion. Of the 95 employees at the power station, 14 were black. Among the 14 black workers, 13 were assigned to sweeping and cleaning duties. The main obstacle for the men who wanted to move up in the company was their performance on the test.

Because the test appeared to render ineligible a much higher proportion of black employees than white ones, the power company was sued for engaging in discriminatory employment practice. The lawsuit centered on the meaning of the test scores. The power company managers argued that using the test "would improve the overall quality of the work force." They suggested that they did not intend to discriminate on the basis of race and that the test only helped them find the most capable employees (*Griggs v. Duke Power,* 1971).

In court, the power company was required to show why the test had meaning for the particular jobs within its establishment. In other words, the company had to prove that the test had a specific meaning for particular jobs such as laborer or coal handler. On hearing the arguments, the Supreme Court ruled that the tests served as "built-in head winds" for minority groups and had no meaning for the purpose of hiring or promoting workers to the classification of coal handler. In other words, the test did not measure specific job capabilities. The decision has been reaffirmed and eventually became the basis of the Civil Rights Bill of 1991.

As a result of the *Griggs v. Duke Power* decision, employers must provide evidence that a test used for the selection or promotion of employees has a specific meaning. In the field of testing, we refer to this meaning as *validity*. The meaning of a test is defined by specific evidence acquired by specific methods. Not only must there be evidence that a test has meaning in general, but also there must be evidence that it has validity for the particular situation it which it is applied. This evidence—not the word of a psychologist—is what establishes the meaning of a test. As in a legal court proceeding, a psychologist must obey specific rules of evidence in establishing that a test has a particular meaning for a specific purpose. This chapter reviews the rules of evidence that people use the most. Court cases similar to the one involving Willie Griggs will be discussed in Chapter 20.

Obtaining data in validity studies is like gathering evidence for a court trial. For instance, psychologists always begin by assuming that there is no reason to believe a measure is valid. Evidence for validity comes from showing the association between the test and other variables. The rules strictly forbid saying there is a relationship without showing some proof, which is similar to the legal notion of innocent until proven guilty. Proof of guilt must be persuasive. In a similar manner, one must have convincing proof that there is a relationship between two variables before one justifiably touts the connection.

Psychologists and other professionals continually attempt to convince the public that their discipline is meaningful. Regarding psychological tests, certain segments of the public may have become too trusting. After you read this chapter, we hope that you can determine when test results are meaningful and when they are questionable.

Defining Validity

Validity can be defined as the agreement between a test score or measure and the quality it is believed to measure. Validity is sometimes defined as the answer to the question, "Does the test measure what it is supposed to measure?" To address this question, we use systematic studies to determine whether the conclusions from test results are justified by evidence. Throughout the 20th century, psychologists created many subcategories of validity. Definitions of validity blossomed, making it hard to determine whether psychologists who referred to different types of validity were really talking about different things. Though validity defined the meaning of tests and measures, the term itself was beginning to lose its meaning. In 1985, a joint committee of the American Educational Research Association (AERA), the American Psychological Association (APA), and the National Council on Measurement in Education (NCME) published a booklet entitled *Standards for Educational and Psychological Testing*. These standards were revised in 1999. We shall refer to the standards frequently because they provide a sensible set of psychological test guidelines that have won approval by major professional groups.

In their original work, the joint committee set aside numerous possible definitions of validity by suggesting the following: Validity is the evidence for inferences made about a test score. There are three types of evidence: (1) construct-related, (2) criterion-related, and (3) content-related. People have many other names for different aspects of validity, but most aspects can be seen in terms of these categories.

The most recent standards emphasize that validity is a unitary concept that represents all of the evidence that supports the intended interpretation of a measure. The consensus document cautions against separating validity into subcategories such as content validity, predictive validity, and criterion validity. Though categories for grouping different types of validity are convenient, the use of categories does not imply that there are distinct forms of validity. Sometimes psychologists have been overly rigorous about making distinctions among categories when, indeed, the categories overlap (Anastasi, 1995; Messick, 1998b).

Aspects of Validity

In this section, we discuss the three aspects of validity suggested by the joint committee. First, however, we address what some call *face validity*. The joint committee refused to recognize face validity as a legitimate category because it is not technically a form of validity. The term needs to be mentioned because it is commonly used in the testing literature.

Face Validity

Face validity is the mere appearance that a measure has validity. We often say a test has face validity if the items seem to be reasonably related to the perceived purpose of the test. For example, a scale to measure anxiety might include items such as "My stomach gets upset when I think about taking tests" and "My heart starts pounding fast whenever I think about all of the things I need to get done." On the basis of positive responses to these items, can we conclude that the person is anxious? Remember that validity requires evidence in order to justify conclusions. In this case, we can only conclude that the person answers these two items in a particular way. If we want to conclude that the person has a problem with anxiety, then we need systematic evidence that shows how responses to these items relate to the psychological condition of anxiety. Face validity is really not validity at all because it does not offer evidence to support conclusions drawn from test scores.

We are not suggesting that face validity is unimportant. In many settings, it is crucial to have a test that "looks like" it is valid. These appearances can help motivate test takers because they can see that the test is relevant. For example, suppose you developed a test to screen applicants for a training program in accounting. Items that ask about balance sheets and ledgers might make applicants more motivated than items about fuel consumption. However, both types of items might be testing the same arithmetic reasoning skill.

Content-Related Evidence for Validity

How many times have you studied for an examination and known almost everything only to find that the professor has come up with some strange items that do not represent the content of the course? If this has happened, you may have encountered a test with poor content-related evidence for validity. Content-related evidence for validity of a test or measure considers the adequacy of representation of the conceptual domain the test is designed to cover. For example, if you are being tested on the first six chapters of this book, then content-related evidence of validity is provided by the correspondence between the items on the test and the information in the chapters.

Traditionally, **content validity evidence** has been of greatest concern in educational testing. The score on your history test should represent your comprehension of the history you are expected to know. Many factors can limit performance on history tests, however, making the professor's inferences about your knowledge less valid. These factors could include characteristics of the items (such as vocabulary words that some students do not understand) and the sampling of items (such as items on World War I in a test on ancient Chinese culture).

Because the boundaries between content and other types of evidence for validity are not clearly defined, we no longer think of content validity evidence as something separate from other types of validity evidence (Anastasi, 1993,

1995; Cronbach, 1989, 1995; Landy, 1986; Lawshe, 1985; Messick, 1994, 1998a, 1998b; Tenopyr, 1993; Zumbo, 1998). However, content validity evidence offers some unique features. For example, it is the only type of evidence besides face validity that is logical rather than statistical.

In looking for content validity evidence, we attempt to determine whether a test has been constructed adequately. (See Focused Example 5-1.) For example, we ask whether the items are a fair sample of the total potential content. Establishing content validity evidence for a test requires good logic, intuitive skills, and perseverance. The content of the items must be carefully evaluated. For example, test developers must consider the wording of the items and the appropriateness of the reading level (Messick, 1998a, 1998b). Determination of content validity evidence is often made by expert judgment. There are several methods for aggregating judgments into an index of content representation. Typically, multiple judges rate each item in terms of its match or relevance to the content (Rubio, Berg-Weger, Tebb, Lee, & Rauch, 2003). Statistical methods such as factor analysis have also been used to determine whether items fit into conceptual domains (Sireci, 1998).

Two new concepts that are relevant to content validity evidence were emphasized in the latest version of the standards for educational and psychological tests (AERA, APA, & NCME, 1999): construct underrepresentation and construct-irrelevant variance. *Construct underrepresentation* describes the failure to capture important components of a construct. For example, if a test of mathematical knowledge included algebra but not geometry, the validity of the test would be threatened by construct underrepresentation. *Construct-irrelevant variance* occurs when scores are influenced by factors irrelevant to the construct. For example, a test of intelligence might be influenced by reading comprehension, test anxiety, or illness.

Often, test scores reflect many factors besides what the test supposedly measures. For example, many students do poorly on tests because of anxiety or reading problems. A slow reader may get a low score on an examination because he or she did not have adequate time to read through all of the questions.

Focused Example 5-1

CHALLENGING THE PROFESSOR

Most professors have had the content validity evidence of their tests challenged at some time or other. A student may complain, "Your test did not give me an opportunity to demonstrate what I know" or "You assigned Chapters 1 through 5, but nearly all of the items came from Chapters 1 and 2—how can you evaluate whether we know anything about the other material we were supposed to read?" In the process of creating good and fair tests, professors should continually face this sort of questioning and attempt to create tests that will not evoke legitimate criticism. Good judgment is always required in test development: We can never get around the need for careful planning (Cureton, Cronbach, Meehl, Ebel, et al., 1996; Ebel, 1977).

Only by taking such factors into account can we make accurate generalizations about what the test score really means. Chapter 8 will present a more detailed discussion of this problem.

Criterion-Related Evidence for Validity

Folklore includes stories about fortune tellers who can look into crystal balls and see the future. Most people in our society do not believe that anyone can actually do this. When we want to know how well someone will do on a job, which students we should select for our graduate program, or who is most likely to get a serious disease, we often depend on psychological testing to forecast behavior and inclinations.

Criterion validity evidence tells us just how well a test corresponds with a particular criterion. Such evidence is provided by high correlations between a test and a well-defined criterion measure. A criterion is the standard against which the test is compared. For example, a test might be used to predict which engaged couples will have successful marriages and which ones will get divorced. Marital success is the criterion, but it cannot be known at the time the couples take the premarital test. The reason for gathering criterion validity evidence is that the test or measure is to serve as a "stand-in" for the measure we are really interested in. In the marital example, the premarital test serves as a stand-in for estimating future marital happiness.

Predictive and concurrent evidence. The forecasting function of tests is actually a type or form of criterion validity evidence known as **predictive validity evidence.** For example, the SAT serves as predictive validity evidence as a college admissions test if it accurately forecasts how well high-school students will do in their college studies. The SAT, including its quantitative and verbal subtests, is the *predictor variable,* and the college grade point average (GPA) is the *criterion.* The purpose of the test is to predict the likelihood of succeeding on the criterion—that is, achieving a high GPA in college. A valid test for this purpose would greatly help college admissions committees because they would have some idea about which students would most likely succeed. Unfortunately, many tests do not have exceptional prediction records, and we must search continually for better ways to predict outcomes.

Another type of evidence for criterion validity is concurrent. Concurrent-related evidence for validity comes from assessments of the simultaneous relationship between the test and the criterion—such as between a learning disability test and school performance. Here the measures and criterion measures are taken at the same time because the test is designed to explain why the person is now having difficulty in school. The test may give diagnostic information that can help guide the development of individualized learning programs. Concurrent evidence for validity applies when the test and the criterion can be measured at the same time.

Job samples provide a good example of the use of **concurrent validity evidence** (Triandis, Dunnette, & Hough, 1994; Van Scotter, Motowidlo, & Cross, 2000). Industrial psychologists often have to select employees on the basis of limited information. One method is to test potential employees on a sample of behaviors that represent the tasks to be required of them. For example, Campion (1972) found that the most effective ways to select maintenance mechanics was to obtain samples of their mechanical work. Because these samples were shown to correlate well with performance on the job, the samples alone could be used for the selection and screening of applicants. Impressive results support the use of work samples for selecting employees in a variety of areas, including motor skills (Asher & Sciarrino, 1974) and work in the petroleum industry (Dunnette, 1972). However, samples seem to be more meaningful for

Focused Example 5-2

VALIDATION OF A SELF-REPORT MEASURE OF DEPRESSION

In Chapters 2, 3, and 4, we offered some data on depression based on the Center for Epidemiologic Studies Depression Scale (CES-D). The CES-D is a general measure of depressive symptoms that has been used extensively in epidemiologic studies (M. M. Weissman et al., 1977). Recall that the scale includes 20 items and taps dimensions of depressed mood, feelings of guilt and worthlessness, appetite loss, sleep disturbance, and energy level. These items are assumed to represent all the major components of depressive symptomatology. Sixteen of the items are worded negatively, whereas the other four are worded positively to avoid the possibility of patterned responses. The respondents are asked to report how often they experienced a particular "symptom" during the past week on a 4-point scale: 0 (rarely or none of the time—less than 1 day), 1 (some or a little of the time—1 to 2 days), 2 (occasionally or a moderate amount of the time—3 or 4 days), and 3 (most or all of the time—5 to 7 days). The responses to the four positive items are reverse scored. Scores on the CES-D scale can range from 0 to 60, with scores greater than 18 suggesting clinically significant levels of depression.

Validity studies have demonstrated that the CES-D is highly correlated with other measures of depression. For example, one validity study demonstrated significant correlations with the more complete Beck Depression Inventory. The CES-D, however, was designed for studies of nonpsychiatric

populations (Gottlib & Cine, 1989). A series of studies have demonstrated that the CES-D is associated with clinical diagnoses of depression; however, the CES-D is a better screening instrument than diagnostic tool. Lewinsohn and Teri (1982) demonstrated that scores of less than 16 on the CES-D were highly associated with clinical judgments of nondepression. Conversely, scores of 17 or greater had only a moderate association with psychiatric diagnoses of depression.

Because the CES-D has only moderate evidence of validity for the evaluation of clinical depression, one needs more-complex methods for such evaluations. It has been suggested that as much as 3% of the population experiences major depressive problems at any given time. The American Psychiatric Association, in the fourth edition of its *Diagnostic and Statistical Manual of Mental Disorders,* (DSM-IV) (1995), suggests that the diagnosis of major depressive disorder involves three components:

1. A clinician identifies a series of specific symptoms.
2. The symptoms persist for at least 2 weeks.
3. The diagnosis is not ruled out for another reason.

A diagnosis of depression thus requires the active involvement of a trained psychiatrist or psychologist. Most measures of depression do not provide enough information for anyone to make such a complex judgment.

blue-collar trades or jobs that require the manipulation of objects. They may not be equally meaningful for all jobs (Callinan & Robertson, 2000).

According to current standards for equal employment opportunity, employers must demonstrate that tasks used to test potential new employees relate to actual job performance. Thompson and Thompson (1982) reviewed 26 federal court decisions in which the validity of tests used to screen employees were challenged. The judgments in the various cases show that the job-related test must focus on tasks, should be in a written form, and must include several data sources with large samples. In other words, the courts require good

---

M. Zimmerman and Coryell (1987) have offered a 22-item self-report scale that can be used to diagnose major depressive disorder. They suggest that the scale may give an accurate estimate of the prevalence of these problems in the general population. Thus, researchers can estimate the proportion of the general population that suffers from depression but not incur the expense of having a psychiatrist or psychologist interview large samples. Zimmerman and Coryell call their measure the Inventory to Diagnose Depression (IDD). The IDD includes 22 items. For each item, the person records a score of 0 (which represents no disturbance) through 4 (which indicates that the symptom is present). The numbers 1, 2, and 3 suggest different gradations of the symptom. For example, the IDD item about insomnia includes the following choices:

0 = I am not sleeping less than usual.

1 = I occasionally have slight difficulty sleeping.

2 = I clearly don't sleep as well as usual.

3 = I sleep about half my normal amount of time.

4 = I sleep less than 2 hours per night.

The IDD also considers whether the symptoms have been present for less than or more than two weeks. Some of the depressive symptoms considered by the IDD are decreased energy, decreased interest in sex, guilt, weight gain, anxiety, irritability, and weight loss.

Although the IDD seems to measure the concept of depression (face validity), systematic evidence obtained in validity studies is required. In other words, we need to ask, "What is the evidence that self-reports on this scale actually measure depression?"

The first step in establishing the validity of the IDD is to demonstrate that it is related to other measures designed to assess depression. For example, studies have shown it to be significantly correlated with the Hamilton Rating Scale for Depression in 234 adults ($r = .80$), the Beck Depression Inventory in 234 adults ($r = .87$), and the Carroll Depression Scale in 105 adults ($r = .81$). In addition, reports of the experience of specific symptoms on the IDD were systematically related to clinicians' judgments of individual symptoms for the same patients.

In another study, first-degree relatives of patients with psychiatric disorders were interviewed using a highly structured system known as the *diagnostic interview schedule*. The system uses a computer program to generate diagnoses for specific disorders. In 97.2% of the 394 cases, the IDD gave the same diagnostic classification of depression as did the more complex interview. Though the detailed interview identified some cases not detected by the IDD, the estimates of the rates of major depression assessed with the IDD came quite close to those found in major studies of the general population.

There are many other measures of depression besides the IDD. However, most of these are not designed to make the specific diagnosis of major depressive disorder. Discriminant evidence for validity demonstrates the advantage of the IDD over other approaches. In particular, other measures do not feed directly into the DSM-IV classification system.

scientific evidence that a test used to screen employees is valid in terms of how job candidates will perform if employed (Zedeck & Cascio, 1984). Focused Example 5-2 describes the process of validating a measure of depression.

Another use of concurrent validity evidence occurs when a person does not know how he or she will respond to the criterion measure. For example, suppose you do not know what occupation you want to enter. In each occupation, some people are happy and others are less satisfied. The Strong-Campbell Interest Inventory (SCII) uses as criteria patterns of interest among people who are satisfied with their careers (Campbell, 1977). Then the patterns of interest for people taking the tests before they have chosen an occupation are matched to patterns of interest among people who are happy in various occupations.

Validity coefficient. The relationship between a test and a criterion is usually expressed as a correlation called a *validity coefficient*. This coefficient tells the extent to which the test is valid for making statements about the criterion.

There are no hard-and-fast rules about how large a validity coefficient must be to be meaningful. In practice, one rarely sees a validity coefficient larger than

---

Focused Example 5-3

THE TESTING INDUSTRY AND THE PUBLIC

Aptitude testing has become a major industry. All college-bound high-school students must take the SAT or the ACT (American College Test). Often these tests are taken several times. In addition, students often take subject area tests (SAT-II) and enroll in preparation courses, such as the Princeton Review or the Stanley Kaplan preparation class.

Concern about the power of the testing industry is not new. Ralph Nader, an aggressive attorney and consumer advocate, earned a solid reputation over the years for his attacks on giant corporations, including automobile manufacturers and food producers. Nader "exposed" the misdeeds of corporations to the public. Early in 1980, Nader released the results of his 6-year investigation of the Educational Testing Service (ETS)—the largest test producer in the United States. At a press conference he exclaimed, "What this report makes clear is that ETS's claims to measure aptitude and predict success are false and unsubstantiated and can be described as a specialized kind of fraud" (R. M. Kaplan, 1982).

What Nader disputed was the use of ETS tests such as the SAT and Graduate Record Examination (GRE) as evidence for predictive validity. The data used by Nader and his team of researchers were no different from those used by ETS officials; however, the way Nader chose to interpret the data was markedly different. ETS has consistently reported that the SAT, for example, accounts for a small but significant percentage of the variance in first-year college grade point averages. Nader did not interpret the results in the typical terms of percentage of variance. Instead, he reported the percentage of cases the test successfully predicted according to his own criteria. On the basis of this approach, he concluded that the test predicted successfully in only 12% of the cases; however, Nader's calculations were not based on an appropriate statistical model (Kaplan, 1982, 1985). On the basis of his interpretation, Nader suggested that there should be more regulation of the testing industry. Referring to ETS, he explained, "They have assumed a rare kind of corporate power, the power to change the way people think about their own potential, and

.60, and validity coefficients in the range of .30 to .40 are commonly considered high. A coefficient is statistically significant if the chances of obtaining its value by chance alone are quite small: usually less than 5 in 100. For example, suppose that the SAT had a validity coefficient of .40 for predicting GPA at a particular west coast university. Because this coefficient is likely to be statistically significant, we can say that the SAT score tells us more about how well people will do in college than we would know by chance.

College students differ in their academic performance for many reasons. You probably could easily list a dozen. Because there are so many factors that contribute to college performance, it would be too much to expect the SAT to explain all of the variation. The question we must ask is "How *much* of the variation in college performance will we be able to predict on the basis of SAT scores?"

The validity coefficient squared is the percentage of variation in the criterion that we can expect to know in advance because of our knowledge of the test scores. Thus, we will know .40 squared, or 16%, of the variation in college performance because of the information we have from the SAT test. This is the coefficient of determination that was discussed in Chapter 2. The remainder of

through the passive acceptance of their test scores by admissions officers, to decide who will be granted and who will be denied access to education and career opportunities" [from *APA Monitor,* 1980, *11*(2), 1–7].

Though Nader uncovered an important problem, it is not certain that the Educational Testing Service deserves all of the blame. ETS puts out its own guidelines for the use of the SAT and other tests. Designed to be read by college admissions officers, these booklets clearly acknowledge the limitations of the tests. For example, college administrators are told that the test accounts for a small but significant percentage of the variation in college performance, and they are advised to look at other criteria in addition to test scores. Thus, much of the problem lies with admissions committees and with college administrators who passively accept SAT scores as the ultimate predictor of college performance. However, the Nader report started the process of questioning the value of testing. Personnel testing is now more closely regulated (Tenopyr, 1998), and some people have seriously questioned aptitude testing.

In 1997 President Bill Clinton proposed to create voluntary national tests in reading and mathematics. The Clinton proposal aroused considerable debate about the value of tests. As a result, the administra-

tion and Congress asked the National Research Council of the prestigious National Academy of Sciences to study test use. In 1999, the committee released a report entitled *High Stakes: Testing for Tracking, Promotion, and Graduation.* Although generally supportive of testing, the report raised some of the same issues originally surfaced by Nader. In particular, the National Academy expressed concern that test results are commonly misinterpreted and that misunderstanding of test results can damage individuals (Heubert & Hauser, 1999).

In response to these criticisms, a new SAT will be released in 2005 for the entering college classes of 2006. The SAT verbal section will be replaced by a new test called *Critical Reading.* The SAT will no longer use analogies and instead will focus on reading short passages. A new writing section will also be added to the test. It will include both multiple-choice questions on grammar as well as a written essay. Further, the SAT math section will be completely revised. Previously, the SAT math section covered only geometry and algebra I. Because so many more high school students take advanced math, the new math section will cover three years of high school math and will include material covered in algebra II.

the variation in college performance is actually the greater proportion: 84% of the total variation is still unexplained. In other words, when students arrive at college, most of the reasons they perform differently will be a mystery to college administrators and professors. (See Focused Examples 5-3 and 5-4.) In many circumstances, using a test is not worth the effort because it contributes only a few percentage points to the understanding of variation in a criterion. However, low validity coefficients (.30 to .40) can sometimes be especially useful even though they may explain only 10% of the variation in the criterion. For example, Dunnette (1967) demonstrated how a simple questionnaire used for military screening could save taxpayers millions of dollars every month even though the validity was not remarkably high. Landy, Farr, and Jacobs (1982) found that a performance evaluation and feedback system for computer programmers with a validity of .30 could translate into increased earnings of $5.3 million in one year. In some circumstances, though, a validity coefficient of .30 or .40 means almost nothing. In Chapter 7, we show how validity coefficients are translated into specific decision models and how industrial psychologists use information about test validity to save money (Landy, 2003; Landy & Shankster, 1994). Focused Example 5-5 discusses the validity of tests used in the medical field.

Evaluating validity coefficients. To be an informed consumer of testing information, you should learn to review carefully any information offered by a test developer. Because not all validity coefficients of .40 have the same meaning, you

---

Focused Example 5-4

WHY THE UNIVERSITY OF CALIFORNIA REJECTED THE SAT-1

In 2001 Richard Atkinson, a psychologist and president of the University of California (UC) system, proposed that the statewide university no longer require the Scholastic Aptitude Test-1 for freshman admission. This made the University of California the first major university system to reject the use of the SAT-I. The decision was based on a major study of 78,000 first-time UC freshmen. The study compared the SAT-1 with the SAT-II. The SAT-I is the traditional test that evaluates reasoning ability, while the SAT-2 is an achievement test that evaluates student knowledge in particular areas.

The study found that the SAT-II achievement tests were consistently better predictors of grades during the freshman year than was the SAT-1. In fact, controlling for SAT-II and high-school grades, the SAT-I contributes little or nothing to the prediction of first-year grades in the university. Furthermore, the study found that SAT-I scores were more sensitive to the socioeconomic background of students than were SAT-II scores. When compared against students with similar socioeconomic backgrounds, the SAT-I was unable to predict college performance. However, even after statistically controlling for socioeconomic background, the SAT-II remained a good predictor.

For copy of this study, see www.ucop.edu/sas/research/research andplanning/.

Focused Example 5-5

THE CHOLESTEROL TEST: PREDICTIVE VALIDITY EVIDENCE

 The concept of predictive validity evidence applies to medical tests as well as to psychological measures. A major issue in contemporary public health is the relationship between cholesterol levels and death from heart disease. Systematic studies have demonstrated that high levels of cholesterol in the blood can help predict early death from heart disease and stroke. To learn more about these problems, physicians take blood samples to examine cholesterol levels. To evaluate this information, they must consider the relationship between the test (blood cholesterol level) and the criterion (premature death). Although this relationship has been established in many studies, the level of association is actually quite low. Some studies show the relationship to fall near .1, or to account for about 1% of the variance in mortality.

Furthermore, those with high levels of blood cholesterol are advised to eat foods low in saturated fats and cholesterol. However, some systematic studies have failed to find strong, statistically significant relationships between these dietary habits and mortality rates (Stallones, 1983). These low validity coefficients suggest that these measures tell us little about what can be predicted for a particular individual. However, heart disease is a profoundly serious problem for the general population. Each year, more than 600,000 Americans die of these problems. Thus, even weak associations help explain a significant number of cases. As a society, if we reduce blood cholesterol levels, there will be a significant reduction in the number of deaths associated with cholesterol. The low correlation between cholesterol tests and heart disease suggests that we cannot say precisely which specific individuals will benefit. However, the small but significant statistical relationship tells us that there is some important predictive value in cholesterol tests (Golomb, Stattin, & Mednick, 2000; R. M. Kaplan & Golomb, 2001; Landy, 2003; Murphy, 2003b; Sackett, 2003).

should watch for several things in evaluating such information. We will cover some of these issues here and go into more depth in Chapter 7.

In its booklet *Standards for Educational and Psychological Testing,* the joint committee of the American Educational Research Association, the American Psychological Association, and the National Council on Measurement in Education (1999) lists several issues of concern when interpreting validity coefficients. Here are some of its recommendations.

Look for changes in the cause of relationships. Be aware that the conditions of a validity study are never exactly reproduced. For example, if you take the GRE to gain admission to graduate school, the conditions under which you take the test may not be exactly the same as those in the studies that established the validity of the GRE. Many things may differ, including the way grades are assigned in graduate school and the population taking the test.

The logic of criterion validation presumes that the causes of the relationship between the test and the criterion will still exist when the test is in use. Though this presumption is true for the most part, there may be circumstances under which the relationship changes. For example, a test might be used and shown to be valid for selecting supervisors in industry; however, the validity study may have been done at a time when all the employees were men, making the test valid for selecting supervisors for male employees. If the company hires female employees, then the test may no longer be valid for selecting supervisors because it may not consider the abilities necessary to supervise a sexually mixed group of employees.

What does the criterion mean? Criterion-related validity studies mean nothing at all unless the criterion is valid and reliable. Some test constructors attempt to correlate their tests with other tests that have unknown validity. A meaningless group of items that correlates well with another meaningless group remains meaningless.

For applied research, the criterion should relate specifically to the use of the test. Because the SAT attempts to predict performance in college, the appropriate criterion is grade point average, a measure of college performance. Any other inferences made on the basis of the SAT require additional evidence. For example, if you want to say that the SAT tells you something about adaptability, then you must obtain evidence on the relationship between the SAT and a separate measure of adaptability.

Review the subject population in the validity study. Another reason to be cautious of validity coefficients is that the validity study might have been done on a population that does not represent the group to which inferences will be made. For example, some researchers have debated whether validity coefficients for intelligence and personnel tests that are based primarily on white samples are accurate when used to test African American students (Educational Testing Service, 1991; Gottfredson, 1994; Herrnstein & Murray, 1994; Landy, 2003; Murphy, 2003b; Oakland & Parmelee, 1985; Sackett & Wilk, 1994; Sackett, 2003; Sattler, 1992). We review this problem in detail in Chapter 19.

In industrial settings, attrition can seriously jeopardize validity studies. Those who do poorly on the job either drop out or get fired and thus cannot be studied when it comes time to do the job assessment. If there was a group that did well on the test but failed on the job, then it might not be represented and could be systematically eliminated from the study because the workers were already off the job by the time the assessment came around.

Be sure the sample size was adequate. Another problem to look for is a validity coefficient that is based on a small number of cases. Sometimes a proper validity study cannot be done because there are too few people to study. A common practice is to do a small validity study with the people available. Unfortunately, such a study can be quite misleading. You cannot depend on a correlation obtained from a small sample, particularly for multiple correlation and multiple regression. The smaller the sample, the more likely chance variation in the data will affect the correlation. Thus, a validity coefficient based on a small sample tends to be artificially inflated.

A good validity study will present some evidence for cross validation. A cross validation study assesses how well the test actually forecasts performance for an independent group of subjects.[1] In other words, the initial validity study assesses the relationship between the test and the criterion, whereas the cross validation study checks how well this relationship holds for an independent group of subjects. The larger the sample size in the initial study, the better the likelihood that the relationship will cross validate.

Never confuse the criterion with the predictor. In at least one university, students are required to meet a certain cutoff score on the GRE before they can be admitted to a graduate program. Occasionally, the department admits a student who did not get the cutoff score, but it still requires the student to meet the minimum GRE score before it confers a degree. The logic behind this policy represents a clear misunderstanding of the test and its purpose.

In this case, the GRE is the predictor, and success in graduate school is the criterion. The only reason for using the test in the first place is to help select students who have the highest probability of success in the program. By completing the program, the students have already succeeded on the criterion (success in the program). Before the university would acknowledge that the students indeed had succeeded, the students had to go back and demonstrate that they would have been predicted to do well on the criterion. This reflects a clear confusion between predictor and criterion. Further, most of the students provisionally admitted because of low GRE scores succeeded by completing the program.

Check for restricted range on both predictor and criterion. A variable has a "restricted range" if all scores for that variable fall very close together. For example, the grade point averages of graduate students in Ph.D. programs tend to fall within a limited range of the scale—usually above 3.5 on a 4-point scale. The problem this creates is that correlation depends on variability. If all the people in your class have a GPA of 4.0, then you cannot predict variability in graduate-school GPA. Correlation requires that there be variability in both the predictor and the criterion.

One major problem with the GRE is that it does not correlate well with graduate-school grade point averages. More than 25 years ago, R. E. Ingram (1980) did a detailed review of studies on the value of the GRE as a predictor of success in graduate school. He found that among all the published studies, the verbal portion of the GRE significantly predicted graduate-school GPA in only 25% of the studies and the quantitative portion predicted this same criterion in only 12.5% of the studies. Sternberg and Williams (1997) did a detailed study of predictors of success among Yale psychology graduate students. They

---

[1]Correct cross validation methodology requires that the raw score weights from the original sample be applied to the validation sample. The use of standard score or standardized weights is not appropriate because the means and standard deviations for the validation sample may differ from those in the original sample (Dorans & Drasgow, 1980).

found that GRE verbal scores were weakly correlated with GPA at Yale ($r = 0.17$) but that GRE quantitative scores were not significant predictors of graduate-school performance. Further GRE scores were not significantly related to faculty ratings of analytical skills, creativity, practicality, research skills, teaching skills, or the quality of doctoral dissertations. The Educational Testing Service now disputes these findings. However, according to its documents, the average correlation between GRE verbal and first-year psychology graduate-school GPA is .28. The correlation between GRE quantitative and first-year grade point average is .29. The validity coefficient for the analytic portion of the GRE is .38 (*GRE Guide*, 2003). Of course, GPA is not the best criterion for college success. However, other measures, such as career success, are rarely available.

There are at least three explanations for the failure of the GRE to predict graduate-school performance. First, the GRE may not be a valid test for selecting graduate students. Second, those students who are admitted to graduate school represent such a restricted range of ability that it is not possible to find significant correlations. Students with low GRE scores are usually not admitted to graduate school and, therefore, are not considered in validity studies. Third, grades in graduate school often represent a restricted range. Once admitted, students in graduate programs usually receive A's and B's. A grade of C is usually considered a failing grade. Although the restricted-range problem cannot be ruled out, many studies do show substantial variability in GRE scores and in graduate-school grades. Even in the study of the prestigious Yale program, GRE verbal scores ranged from 250 to 800 (mean = 653) and GRE quantitative scores ranged from 320 to 840 (mean = 672). Ratings by professors had substantial variability (Sternberg & Williams, 1997).

In addition to graduate schools, most schools of veterinary medicine use the GRE. Because veterinary schools are larger than most graduate programs, estimating veterinary school success from the GRE provides a good opportunity for study. There are 27 schools of veterinary medicine in the United States. One study obtained data from approximately 1400 students who had applied to 16 schools. The study suggested that undergraduate GPA is the best predictor of grades in veterinary school ($r = .53$). The correlation for the GRE-V verbal was 0.41; the correlation for the quantitative portion of the GRE (GRE-Q) was 0.47; and the correlation for the analytic section (GRE-A) was 0.45. The authors of the study corrected for the restricted range and measurement error in the GRE. As would be expected, these validity coefficients increase with these corrections (Powers, 2001). However, not all reviewers believe that correction is appropriate. In summary, even the best evidence suggests that GRE accounts for only one-fifth of the variation in veterinary school success ($0.47^2 = 0.22$).

Review evidence for validity generalization. Criterion-related validity evidence obtained in one situation may not be generalized to other similar situations. *Generalizability* refers to the evidence that the findings obtained in one situation can be generalized—that is, applied to other situations. This is an issue of empirical study rather than judgment. In other words, we must prove that the results obtained in a validity study are not specific to the original situation. There are many reasons why results may not be generalized. For example, there may be differences in the way the predictor construct is measured or in the type of job or curriculum involved—in the actual criterion measure—between the groups of people who take the test; there may also be differences in the time period—year or month—when the test is administered. Because of these problems, we cannot always be certain that the validity coefficient reported by a test developer will be the same for our particular situation. An employer, for example, might use a work-sample test based on information reported in the manual, yet the situation in which he or she uses the test may differ from the situations of the original validation studies. When using the test, the employer might be using different demographic groups or different criterion measures or else predicting performance on a similar but different task. Generalizations from the original validity studies to these other situations should be made only on the basis of new evidence.

Consider differential prediction. Predictive relationships may not be the same for all demographic groups. The validity for men could differ in some circumstances from the validity for women. Or the validity of the test may be questionable because it is used for a group whose native language is not English, even though the test was validated for those who spoke only English. Under these circumstances, separate validity studies for different groups may be necessary. This issue will be discussed in more detail in Chapter 19.

Although criterion-related validity evidence is common in psychological and educational research, it simply does not apply in some instances. By definition, the criterion must be the most accurate measure of the phenomenon if it is to serve as the "gold standard." If a criterion exists, then only greater practicality or less expense justifies the use of concurrent measures as proxies or substitutes for the criterion. If the criterion is not a superior measure, then failure of correspondence by any new measure may reveal a defect in the criterion itself. For example, studies on the validity of measures of general health have been hindered because a clear criterion of health has never been defined (R. M. Kaplan, 2002). The development of a health index helped define the meaning of the term *health*. Often work on a psychological test involves the simultaneous development of a concept and the instrumentation to measure the concept. This cannot be accomplished by criterion-related validity studies. Instead, we need a more involved approach that involves construct-related evidence for validity.

Construct-Related Evidence for Validity

Before 1950, most social scientists considered only criterion and content evidence for validity. By the mid-1950s, investigators concluded that no clear criteria existed for most of the social and psychological characteristics they wanted to measure. Developing a measure of intelligence, for example, was difficult because no one could say for certain what intelligence was. Studies of criterion validity evidence would require that a specific criterion of intelligence be established against which tests could be compared. However, there was no criterion for intelligence because it is a hypothetical construct. A *construct* is defined as something built by mental synthesis. As a construct, intelligence does not exist as a separate thing we can touch or feel, so it cannot be used as an objective criterion.

Focused Example 5-6

THE MEANING OF LOVE

 An interesting example of construct validity evidence comes from the work of Zick Rubin (1970, 1973), who noted that love has been one of the most discussed issues of all time. Throughout history, men and women have written and sung about love more than any other topic. The index to Bartlett's *Familiar Quotations* shows that references to love are second only to citations to "man" (with "love" cited 769 times and "man" cited 843 times). All this preoccupation with love, however, has not led to a better understanding of its true meaning. Perhaps it is something we can feel but not necessarily understand well enough to describe in a definite way.

In the mid-1970s, there was a famous trial in Los Angeles in which singer Michelle Triola Marvin sued actor Lee Marvin for half the earnings he gained while the couple lived together. A major issue in the trial was the couple's unmarried status during the period in which the earnings occurred. During the trial, Lee's attorney questioned the actor about the extent to which he loved Michelle while they lived together. If he had been asked his height, he could have used the scale of inches. But love? How could he put that into a number? The actor instead resorted to a gas-tank analogy. He said his love for the singer was like when you are driving your car and you look over at your gas gauge and find it "about half full." That is about how much he loved Michelle—about half a tank. If there had been a measure of love, he would not have needed to use such a vague analogy (Rubin, 1979).

In developing his love scale, Rubin first had to create a list of items that represented all the different things people might call love. This was not an easy task because we all have different ideals. To create a measure of love, Rubin had to condense conventional wisdom about loving and liking into sets of statements to which people could respond on a scale. He eventually developed statements that subjects could agree or disagree with on a 5-point scale (where 1 is for strong disagreement and 5 is for strong agreement).

Collecting a set of items for construct validation is not easy because we never know which items eventually will be relevant to the construct we are attempting to measure. Building the love scale was particularly difficult in this regard. To prepare his measure, Rubin read extensively about love. Elizabeth Barrett Browning wrote, "How do I love thee? Let me count the ways." Indeed, after reading the many diverse views of love, Rubin hardly knew where to begin counting. However, because this was a study in construct validity evidence, it was important that Rubin consider counting. Construct validity evidence requires that there be content validity evidence. Content validity evidence in turn requires that the items fully represent the domain of inference (in this case, love). All the ways that love is defined by different people must be included in this collection.

Rubin began his study with his sets of statements that people could respond to on a scale ranging from disagreement to agreement. Some of the items were intended to measure love, whereas others were supposed to tap liking. Next he gave the

Contemporary psychologists often want to measure intelligence, love, curiosity, or mental health. None of these constructs are clearly defined, and there is no established criterion against which psychologists can compare the accuracy of their tests. These are the truly challenging problems in measurement.

Construct validity evidence is established through a series of activities in which a researcher simultaneously defines some construct and develops the

---

pool of items to 198 students from the University of Michigan. Each item had a blank in which a name could be filled in. The students responded to the questions twice, one time filling in the name of their lover and another time filling in the name of a friend. Then the items were subjected to factor analysis. Recall from Chapter 3 that this is a method for reducing a large number of items or variables into smaller and more manageable composites of items called *factors*.

In the love scale, three factors were obtained: attachment, caring, and intimacy. The items on the attachment scale emphasized desire to be with the loved person or to seek him or her out if lonely. The caring scale included items about empathy and concern for the loved person's welfare. The intimacy scale considered exclusive aspects of the relationship—for example, the willingness to confide in him or her about intimate personal problems. The items on the liking scale focused on favorable aspects of the other person along such dimensions as adjustment, maturity, good judgment, and intelligence.

The data from these scales were subjected to several statistical procedures that helped discriminate between the responses of lovers and friends and eventually led to the establishment of two measures: a love scale and a liking scale. With these measures of liking and loving in hand, Rubin next had to determine whether they were really measuring what they were supposed to measure. One study using the test with dating couples suggested that loving and liking were not necessarily related. There was a modest relationship between scores on the two scales, which was weaker for women than for men. This suggested, especially for women, that we can love someone we do not particularly like.

Several things indicated that the love scale really was measuring "love." For example, men and women scored higher on the love scale when they filled in the names of their lovers than when they filled in the name of a same-sex friend (all were assumed to be heterosexual). There also was a substantial correlation between love-scale scores and estimates of the likelihood of marriage. The greater the love score, the more probable marriage was considered to be.

Finally, some of the dating couples were separated into groups of "strong love" (high love scores) and "weak love" (low love scores). From behind a one-way mirror, the researchers noted how much eye contact the lovers had with each other. Strong lovers spent more time simply gazing into each other's eyes than did weak lovers. When paired with a strong opposite-sex lover from another couple, strong lovers made no more mutual eye contact than did weak lovers.

In summary, Rubin began his study of love with neither a clear definition of love nor a method of measuring it. Through a series of structured exercises, he gradually came to have a better grasp of the construct. For example, he discovered that lovers mark some items differently than do couples who are just friends. He also discovered that "love" may have at least three independent components. Once the basic scale was developed, each new application defined a new meaning. For instance, one study showed that the scale predicts how much time lovers will spend gazing into each other's eyes. Thus, in future applications of the love scale, we would expect couples who score as strong lovers (for one another) to spend much time in mutual gazing.

instrumentation to measure it. This process is required when "no criterion or universe of content is accepted as entirely adequate to define the quality to be measured" (Cronbach & Meehl, 1955, p. 282; Sackett, 2003). Construct validation involves assembling evidence about what a test means. This is done by showing the relationship between a test and other tests and measures. Each time a relationship is demonstrated, one additional bit of meaning can be attached to the test. Over a series of studies, the meaning of the test gradually begins to take shape. The gathering of construct validity evidence is an ongoing process that is similar to amassing support for a complex scientific theory. Although no single set of observations provides crucial or critical evidence, many observations over time gradually clarify what the test means. An example of construct validity evidence is given in Focused Example 5-6.

Years ago, D. T. Campbell and Fiske (1959) introduced an important set of logical considerations for establishing evidence of construct validity. They distinguished between two types of evidence essential for a meaningful test: convergent and discriminant. To argue that a test has meaning, a test constructor must be armed with as much of these two types of evidence as possible.

Convergent evidence. When a measure correlates well with other tests believed to measure the same construct, **convergent evidence** for validity is obtained. This sort of evidence shows that measures of the same construct *converge*, or narrow in, on the same thing. In many ways, convergent evidence that is also construct validity evidence is like criterion validity evidence. In each case, scores on the test are related to scores on some other measure. In the case of convergent evidence for construct-related validity, however, there is no criterion to define what we are attempting to measure. Criterion-related evidence for validity is fine for situations in which we are attempting to predict performance on a particular variable, such as success in graduate school. Here the task is well defined, and all we need to do is find the items that are good predictors of this graduate-school criterion. Because there is no well-defined criterion in construct-related validity, the meaning of the test comes to be defined by the variables it can be shown to be associated with.

An example of the need to obtain construct validation evidence comes from studies that attempt to define and measure the construct "health," a complex concept. Because of this complexity, no single measure can serve as the criterion against which a measure of health can be assessed. This situation requires establishment of evidence for construct validity. Some of the construct validation studies were used to demonstrate the convergent validity evidence for the measure of health that the authors called a *health index*.

Convergent evidence is obtained in one of two ways. In the first, we show that a test measures the same things as other tests used for the same purpose. In the second, we demonstrate specific relationships that we can expect if the test is really doing its job. The studies on the health index included both types of evidence. In demonstrating the meaning of the health index, the authors continually asked themselves, "If we were really measuring health, which relationships would we expect to observe between the health index and other measures?" The simplest relationship, between health index scores and the way people rate their own health status, was strong and clearly showed that the index captured some of the same information that individuals used to evaluate their own health. However, a good measure must go beyond this simple bit of validity evidence because self-ratings are unreliable. If they were not, then we would use self-perceived health status itself as the index of health and not bother to develop another health index.

In construct validity evidence, no single variable can serve as the criterion. In the case of the health index, other studies were used to show a variety of other relationships. For example, people who scored as less healthy on the health index also tended to report more symptoms and chronic medical conditions. The authors also hypothesized that health status would be related to age, and they observed that these two variables were indeed systematically related: Older people in the sample tended to have a lower health status than did younger people.

The researchers also evaluated specific hypotheses based on certain theoretical notions about the construct. In the health index studies, the authors reasoned that "if the index really measures health, then we would expect that people who score low on the measure will visit doctors more often." A study confirming that those scoring lower on health status visited doctors more often provided evidence for one more inference. Also, certain groups (such as disabled people) should have lower average scores on the index than do other groups (such as nondisabled people). Again, a study confirmed this hypothesis (Kaplan, Ganiats, Sieber, & Anderson, 1998).

In another series of studies, investigators argued that a health index should correlate with specific physiological measures representing disease states. In one study, for example, patients with chronic lung diseases took measures of lung function. These measures were more strongly correlated with the general health index than they were with a variety of other physiological and social variables (R. M. Kaplan & Ries, 1996). Other studies demonstrated that the measures were related to clinical indicators of arthritis, Alzheimer's disease, depression, schizophrenia, and other conditions. If a health index really measures health, then treatments designed to improve health should be reflected by changes in the measure. In one study, patients with arthritis underwent a new treatment believed to remedy their condition. The general health index demonstrated the significant improvements caused by the treatment (Bombardier, Ware, Russell, et al., 1986). Other studies showed the measure was related to improvements in conditions such as Alzheimer's disease (Kerner, Patterson, Grant, & Kaplan, 1998), schizophrenia (T. Patterson et al., 1996), arthritis (Groessl, Kaplan, & Cronan, 2003), diseases of the veins (Kaplan, Criqui, Denenberg, Bergan, & Fronek, 2003), depression (Pyne et al., 2003), and several other conditions (R. M. Kaplan, 2002).

A series of studies thus expanded the number of meanings that could be given to the health index. Yet, convergent validity evidence does not constitute all of the evidence necessary to argue for the meaning of a psychological test or measure. In this case, we also must have discriminant evidence (see Focused Example 5-7).

Focused Example 5-7

CONSTRUCT VALIDITY OF THE WOMEN'S HEALTH INITIATIVE INSOMNIA RATING SCALE

A brief measure known as the Women's Health Initiative Insomnia Rating Scale (WHIIRS) was administered to 67,999 postmenopausal women. The study also measured a wide variety of other variables.

Validity of the WHIIRS is defined by its associations with other measures. Some of the validity coefficients are shown in Figure 5-1. In the figure, three of these validity coefficients are negative. For example, higher scores on insomnia that represents poor sleep are associated with low levels of emotional well-being, energy, and general health. The researchers did not expect emotional expression to be associated with sleep. Indeed, they observed little correlation between emotional expression and the WHIIRS. The WHIIRS was positively correlated with hot flashes and sleep duration. This suggests that women with high scores on insomnia experienced more hot flashes at night and slept fewer hours. Overall, these findings support the validity of the WHIIRS (Levine et al., 2003).

FIGURE 5-1
Validity correlations for WHIIRS.

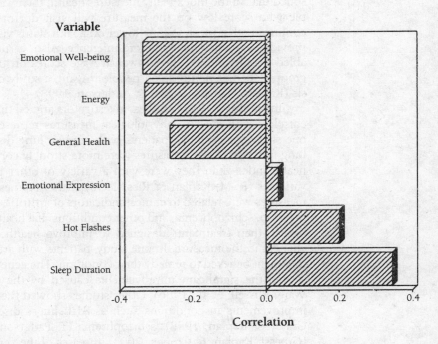

Discriminant evidence. Scientists often confront other scientists with difficult questions such as "Why should we believe your theory if we already have a theory that seems to say the same thing?" An eager scientist may answer this question by arguing that his or her theory is distinctive and better. In testing, psychologists face a similar challenge. Why should they create a new test if there is already one available to do the job? Thus, one type of evidence a person needs in test validation is proof that the test measures something unique. For example, if a health index measures the same thing that self-ratings of health, symptoms, and chronic medical conditions measure, then why do we need it in addition to all these other measures? The answer is that the index taps something other than the tests used in the convergent evidence studies. This demonstration of uniqueness is called **discriminant evidence,** or what some call *divergent validation*. To demonstrate discriminant evidence for validity, a test should have low correlations with measures of unrelated constructs, or evidence for what the test does not measure.

By providing evidence that a test measures something different from other tests, we also provide evidence that we are measuring a unique construct. Discriminant evidence indicates that the measure does not represent a construct other than the one for which it was devised.

As this discussion implies, construct-related validity evidence actually subsumes all the activities used in other types of validity evidence studies. In construct-related validation, for example, content-related validation is an essential step. Furthermore, convergent and discriminant studies actually correlate the tests with many different criteria. For example, a measure of health status might be validated by showing correlations with symptoms, doctor visits, or physiological variables. Assembling construct-related evidence for validity requires validation against many criteria. Until quite recently, textbooks divided validity into different types. However, this was often confusing because there is a similarity between what was called *construct-* and *criterion-related validity*. Many psychologists now believe that construct-related evidence for validity actually is the only major type of validity that need concern us. Validity is defined by evidence and other categories (such as criterion-related and convergent) that might be thought of as subcategories of validity evidence (Anastasi & Urbina, 1997; Heubert & Hauser, 1999; Landy, 2003; Messick, 1998a, 1998b, 1999; Murphy, 2003a, 2003b; Rothstein, 2003; Sackett, 2003; Schmidt & Hunter, 2003). According to the testing pioneer Lee Cronbach, it may not be appropriate to continue to divide validity into three parts: "All validation is one, and in a sense all is construct validation" (1980, p. 99). Recall that the 1999 edition of *Standards for Educational and Psychological Testing* no longer recognizes different categories of validity. Instead, it recognizes different categories of evidence for validity.

Criterion-referenced tests. The procedures for establishing the validity of a criterion-referenced test resemble those for studying the validity of any other test. As you may recall from Chapter 2, criterion-referenced tests have items that are designed to match certain specific instructional objectives. For example, if the objective of some educational program is for children to be able to list 75% of the countries in Europe, then the criterion-referenced test could ask that the countries be listed. Children who listed 75% of the countries would pass the test. They would be evaluated against this specific criterion rather than on the basis of how they perform relative to other students. Validity studies for the criterion-referenced tests would compare scores on the test to scores on other measures that are believed to be related to the test. Specific procedures for evaluating the validity of a criterion-referenced test have been discussed in more technical articles (see Forsyth, 1991; Hambleton, 1994; Popham, 1994). The idea of comparing an individual with him- or herself rather than to the norms of a group remains appealing (Freeman & Miller, 2001).

Relationship Between Reliability and Validity

Attempting to define the validity of a test will be futile if the test is not reliable. Theoretically, a test should not correlate more highly with any other variable than it correlates with itself. The maximum validity coefficient (r_{12max}) between two variables is equal to the square root of the product of their reliabilities, or $r_{12max} = \sqrt{r_{11}r_{22}}$, where r_{11} and r_{22} are the reliabilities for the two variables.

Because validity coefficients are not usually expected to be exceptionally high, a modest correlation between the true scores on two traits may be missed if the test for each of the traits is not highly reliable. Table 5-1 shows the maximum validity you can expect to find given various levels of reliability for two

TABLE 5-1
*How Reliability
Affects Validity**

Reliability of test	Reliability of criterion	Maximum validity (correlation)
1.0	1.0	1.00
.8	1.0	.89
.6	1.0	.77
.4	1.0	.63
.2	1.0	.45
.0	1.0	.00
1.0	.5	.71
.8	.5	.63
.6	.5	.55
.4	.5	.45
.2	.5	.32
.0	.5	.00
1.0	.0	.00
.8	.0	.00
.6	.0	.00
.4	.0	.00
.2	.0	.00
.0	.0	.00

* The first column shows the reliability of the test. The second column displays the reliability of the validity criterion. The numbers in the third column are the maximum theoretical correlations between tests, given the reliability of the measures.

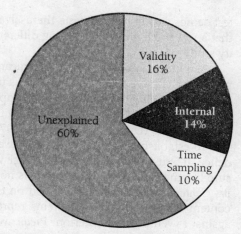

FIGURE 5-2   *Division of total variation on a performance measure as a function of validity and reliability. Many sources of variation are reflected in a test score. Most of the variance in scores remains unexplained (60%). Internal error (14%) and time-sampling error (10%) are two types of reliability that reduce the validity of the test. Validity accounts for approximately 16% of the total variance in this example.*

tests. Sometimes we cannot demonstrate that a reliable test has meaning. In other words, we can have reliability without validity. However, it is logically impossible to demonstrate that an unreliable test is valid.

Reliability and validity are related concepts. Figure 5-2 divides the total variation of a test score into different parts. The example used is a test with a validity coefficient of .40. If we consider the total variability on some measure, such as college performance, approximately 16% of the variation might be explained by performance on a predictor test. There is also variation in the score, part of which is explained by measurement error. As noted in Chapter 4, this error might be related to time sampling, internal consistency, item sampling, and so forth. The figure hypothetically shows these relationships. Finally, some of the variability is "unexplained" or explained by factors of which we are unaware.

SUMMARY   *Validity* is a basic idea in measurement and in the science of psychology. Although we have emphasized the validity of psychological tests, the ideas we discussed apply equally to all measures. To make any inference, a good scientist must have substantiating data.

Once a test is "validated," many psychologists mistakenly think it can be used to support many different inferences. Actually, there should be as many validity studies as there are inferences about the scores (Cronbach, 1995). Validity really refers to evidence supporting what can be said on the basis of the test scores and not to the tests themselves (Landy, 2003). Any time we claim that a test score means something different from before, we need a new validity study.

Acquiring evidence about the meaning of tests should be an ongoing process. The more a test or a measure is used, the more we learn about what it means. According to two well-known applied psychologists, "Test users should never feel that they know enough about the behavioral meaning of their selection methods" (Dunnette & Borman, 1979, p. 484).

To establish the validity of a test, we need to gather several types of evidence. It is usually valuable to have *face validity,* or the appearance that a measure has meaning, even though this is not a formally recognized type of validity. *Content validity evidence* is based on the correspondence between the item content and the domain the items represent. Sometimes tests are evaluated against a well-defined criterion. *Predictive validity evidence* comes from studies that use a test to forecast performance on a criterion that is measured at some point in the future. *Concurrent validity evidence* is obtained from correlations between the test and a criterion when both are measured at the same point in time. *Construct validity evidence* is used when a specific criterion is not well defined. *Convergent evidence* comes from correlations between the test and other variables that are hypothetically related to the construct. *Discriminant evidence* shows that the measure does not include superfluous items and that the test measures something distinct from other tests. Reliability and validity are related because it is difficult to obtain evidence for validity unless a measure has reasonable validity. On the other hand, a measure can have high reliability without supporting evidence for its validity. Validity is central to the understanding of psychological tests and measures. We shall refer to validity in all of the remaining chapters.

WEB ACTIVITY   For interesting and relevant Web sites, check the following:

www.fairtest.org/facts/satvalidity.html
Critical review of the validity of the SAT-I

www-hoover.stanford.edu/pubaffairs/Releases/2003/08/ednext.html
Review of test validity from conservative political perspective

psychclassics.yorku.ca/Cronbach/construct
Provides access to the classic article by Cronbach and Meehl (1955) on construct validity

www.employment-testing.com/validity.htm
Reviews validity in relation to employment testing

CHAPTER 6

Writing and Evaluating Test Items

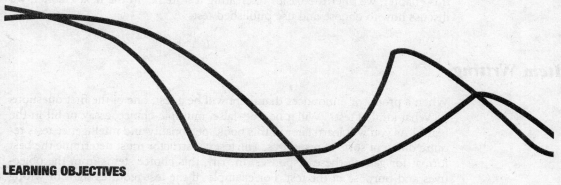

LEARNING OBJECTIVES

When you have completed this chapter, you should be able to:

- Describe two types of item formats commonly used in objective classroom examinations

- Know whether or not you should guess on a multiple-choice examination when you are not sure of the correct answer

- Explain the types of measurement problems the Likert format is used for

- Discuss what sorts of problems you might encounter if you used a 10-point category scale to rate the abilities of a group of similar individuals

- Set the level of item difficulty needed for a test that discriminates well among individuals

- Describe the process of assessing item discriminability

- Define an item characteristic curve and tell how it is used

- Draw an item characteristic curve for an item that discriminates well at high but not low levels of performance

- Explain how item characteristic curves can be used to find items that are unfair to students who overstudied

- Discuss some of the limitations of item analysis for tests that are designed to find specific learning problems

At this point in your studies, you have had much experience taking tests. Most of these have been classroom exercises; however, you have also been exposed to standardized tests such as the SAT or the Iowa Test of Basic Skills.

As a seasoned test taker, you also may have become an experienced test critic. After taking a test, most students are willing to judge whether it was a fair or good test. When you feel that you have taken a bad test, you might ask yourself how it could have been better. As an exercise, you might consider creating a fair test of the material covered in the first five chapters of this book. In this chapter, we offer the basics of creating test items. In the next chapter, we discuss how to choose and use published tests.

Item Writing

When a professor announces that there will be a test, one of the first questions is "What kind of test?" Will it be true–false, multiple-choice, essay, or fill-in-the blank? As you will learn later in this book, personality and intelligence tests require different sorts of responses. The test constructor must determine the best format for getting these responses. In part, this choice stems from the objectives and purpose of the test. For example, if the test requires right or wrong answers, then the task will usually be true–false, multiple-choice, matching, or essay.

Writing test items can be difficult. DeVellis (1991) provided several simple guidelines for item writing. Here are six of them:

1. Define clearly what you want to measure. To do this, use substantive theory as a guide and try to make items as specific as possible.
2. Generate an item pool. Theoretically, all items are randomly chosen from a universe of item content. In practice, however, care in selecting and developing items is valuable. Avoid redundant items. In the initial phases, you may want to write three or four items for each one that will eventually be used on the test or scale.
3. Avoid exceptionally long items, which are rarely good.
4. Keep the level of reading difficulty appropriate for those who will complete the scale.
5. Avoid "double-barreled" items that convey two or more ideas at the same time. For example, consider an item that asks the respondent to agree or disagree with the statement, "I vote Democratic because I support social programs." There are two different statements with which the person could agree: "I vote Democratic" and "I support social programs."
6. Consider mixing positively and negatively worded items. Sometimes, respondents develop the "acquiescence response set." This means that the respondents will tend to agree with most items. To avoid this bias, you can include items that are worded in the opposite direction. For example, in asking about depression, the CES-D (see Chapter 2) uses

mostly negatively worded items (such as "I felt depressed"). However, the CES-D also includes items worded in the opposite direction ("I felt hopeful about the future").

Times change, and tests may have a half-life (Chan, Drasgow, & Sawin, 1999). When writing items, you need to be sensitive to ethnic and cultural differences. For example, items on the CES-D concerning appetite, hopefulness, and social interactions may have a different meaning for African American than for white respondents (Foley, Reed, Mutran, & DeVellis, 2002). It is also important to recognize that tests may become obsolete. In one study, the reliability of items in the Armed Services Vocational Aptitude Battery was studied over a 16-year period. Approximately 12% of the items became less reliable over this time. Items that retained their reliability were more likely to focus on skills, while those that lost reliability focused on more abstract concepts.

Item Formats

The type of test you have probably experienced most in the classroom is one in which you receive credit for a specific response, or selection of the single "correct" alternative for each test item. True–false and multiple-choice examinations use this system. Similar formats are used for many other purposes such as evaluating attitudes, determining knowledge about traffic laws, or deciding whether someone has characteristics that are associated with a particular health condition. The simplest test of this type uses a dichotomous format.

The dichotomous format. The **dichotomous format** offers two alternatives for each item. Usually a point is given for the selection of one of the alternatives. The most common example of this format is the true–false examination. This test presents students with a series of statements. The student's task is to determine which statements are true and which are false. There are many virtues of the true–false test, including ease of construction and ease of scoring, but the method has also become popular because a teacher can easily construct a test by copying lines out of a textbook. The lines that are copied verbatim are designated as "true." Other statements are altered so that they are no longer true.

The advantages of true–false items include their obvious simplicity, ease of administration, and quick scoring. Another attractive feature is that the true–false items require absolute judgment. The test taker must declare one of the two alternatives. However, there are also disadvantages. For example, true–false items encourage students to memorize material, making it possible for students to perform well on a test that covers materials they do not really understand. Furthermore, "truth" often comes in shades of gray, and true–false tests do not allow test takers the opportunity to show they understand this complexity. Also, the mere chance of getting any item correct is 50%. Thus, to be reliable, a true–false test must include many items. Overall, dichotomous items tend to be less reliable, and therefore less precise than some of the other item formats.

The dichotomous format does not appear only as true–false on educational tests. Many personality tests require responses in a true–false or some other two-choice format, such as yes–no. Personality test constructors often prefer this type of format because it requires absolute judgment. For example, in response to an item such as "I often worry about my sexual performance," people cannot be ambivalent—they must respond "True" or "False." Dichotomous items have many advantages for personality tests with many subscales. One is that they make the scoring of the subscales easy. All that a tester needs to do is count the number of items a person endorses from each subscale.

Although the true–false format is popular in educational tests, it is not used as frequently as the multiple-choice test, which represents the polytomous format.

The polytomous format. The **polytomous format** (sometimes called *polychotomous*) resembles the dichotomous format except that each item has more than two alternatives. Typically, a point is given for the selection of one of the alternatives, and no point is given for selecting any other choice. Because it is a popular method of measuring academic performance in large classes, the multiple-choice examination is the polytomous format you have likely encountered most often. Multiple-choice tests are easy to score, and the probability of obtaining a correct response by chance is lower than it is for true–false items. A major advantage of this format is that it takes little time for test takers to respond to a particular item because they do not have to write. Thus, the test can cover a large amount of information in a relatively short time.

When taking a multiple-choice examination, you must determine which of several alternatives is "correct." Incorrect choices are called **distractors**. As we shall demonstrate in the section on item analysis, the choice of distractors is critically important.

Because most students are familiar with multiple-choice tests and related formats such as matching, there is no need to elaborate on their description. However, it is worthwhile to consider some of the issues in the construction and scoring of multiple-choice tests.

First, how many distractors should a test have? Psychometric theory suggests that adding more distractors should increase the reliability of the items. However, in practice, adding distractors may not actually increase the reliability because it is difficult to find good ones. The reliability of an item is not enhanced by distractors that no one would ever select. Studies have shown that it is rare to find items for which more than three or four distractors operate efficiently. Ineffective distractors actually may hurt the reliability of the test because they are time-consuming to read and can limit the number of good items that can be included in a test. A review of the problems associated with selecting distractors suggests that it is usually best to develop three or four good distractors for each item (Anastasi & Urbina, 1997). Well-chosen distractors are an essential ingredient of good items.

Sometimes psychometric analysis can pave the way for simpler tests. For example, most multiple-choice tests have followed the suggestion of four or five alternatives. However, this traditional practice may not be the best use of resources. In one evaluation of tests for entry-level police officers, applicants completed a test battery with either five alternative multiple-choice items or three alternative items. Psychometric analysis showed that the validity and reliability were about equal for the two types of tests. This result suggests that three alternative multiple-choice items may be better than five alternative items because they retain the psychometric value but take less time to develop and administer (Sidick, Barrett, & Doverspike, 1994).

Poorly written distractors can adversely affect the quality of the test. Sometimes a test maker will throw in "cute" distractors that are extremely unlikely to be chosen. If distractors are too easy, then a poorly prepared test taker has a high chance of guessing the correct answer. As a result, the test will have lower reliability and validity.

Another issue concerns the scoring of multiple-choice examinations. Suppose you bring your roommate to your sociology test, and he or she fills out an answer sheet without reading the items. Will your roommate get any items correct? The answer is yes—by chance alone. If each test item has four choices, the test taker would be expected to get 25% of the total number of items correct. If the test items had three choices, then a 33.33% rate of success would be expected. Because test takers get some "correct" answers simply by guessing, a correction for guessing is sometimes used. The formula to correct for guessing on a test is

$$\text{corrected score} = R - \frac{W}{n-1}$$

where

$$R = \text{the number of right responses}$$
$$W = \text{the number of wrong responses}$$
$$n = \text{the number of choices for each item}$$

Omitted responses are not included; they provide neither credit nor penalty. The expression $W/n - 1$ is an estimate of how many items the test taker is expected to get right by chance. For example, suppose that your roommate randomly filled out the answer sheet to your sociology test. The test had 100 items, each with four choices. By chance, her expected score would be 25 correct. Let's assume that she got exactly that, though in practice this may not occur, because 25 is the *average* random score. The expected score corrected for guessing would be

$$R - \frac{W}{n-1} = 25 - \frac{75}{4-1} = 25 - \frac{75}{3} = 25 - 25 = 0$$

In other words, when the correction for guessing is applied, the expected score is 0.

A question that students frequently ask is "Should I guess on multiple-choice items when I don't know the answer?" The answer depends on how the test will be scored. If a correction for guessing is not used, then the best advice is "guess away." By guessing, you have a chance of getting the item correct. You do not have this chance if you do not guess. However, if a correction for guessing is used, then random guessing will do you no good. Some speeded tests are scored so that the correction for the guessing formula includes only the items that were attempted—that is, those that were not attempted are not counted either right or wrong. In this case, random guessing and leaving the items blank have the same expected effect.

How about cases where you do not know the right answer but can eliminate one or two of the alternatives? How many times have you narrowed your answer down to two alternatives but could not figure out which of the two was correct? In this case, we advise you to guess. The correction formula assumes that you are equally likely to respond to each of the four categories. For a four-choice item, it would estimate your chance of getting the item correct by chance alone to be 1 in 4. However, if you can eliminate two alternatives, then the chances are actually 1 in 2. This gives you a slight advantage over the correction formula.

Research has shown that students are more likely to guess when they anticipate a low grade on a test than when they are more confident (Bereby-Meyer, Meyer, & Flascher, 2002). Recently, new mathematical methods have been introduced to summarize information in multiple-choice tests and dichotomous-item tests (Huibregtse, Admiraal, & Meara, 2002). These methods summarize the mean, the reliability as calculated from the binomial distribution, and a guessing threshold. The *guessing threshold* describes the chances that a low-ability test taker will obtain each score. These newer methods are highly technical and are beyond the scope of this book. In summary, the techniques are derived from the first three moments of the test score distribution. Mathematically inclined readers who are interested in the methods should consult Carlin and Rubin (1991).

As you have seen, true–false and multiple-choice formats are common to educational and achievement tests. Similar formats are found on personality tests. For example, frequently used personality inventories such as the Minnesota Multiphasic Personality Inventory (MMPI) or the California Psychological Inventory (CPI) present subjects with a long list of statements to which one responds either "True" or "False" (see Chapter 15).

Other personality and attitude measures do not judge any response as "right" or "wrong." Rather, they attempt to quantify characteristics of the response. These formats include the Likert format, the category scale, and the Q-sort. Some of these formats will be discussed in more detail in Chapter 15.

Another format, the essay, is commonly used in classroom evaluation, and the Educational Testing Service now uses a writing sample as a component of its testing programs. Essay exams can be evaluated using the same principles used for structured tests. For example, the validity of the test can be established through correlations with other tests. The reliability of the scoring procedure should be assessed by determining the association between two scores provided by independent scorers. In practice, however, the psychometric properties of essay exams are rarely evaluated.

The Likert format. One popular format for attitude and personality scales requires that a respondent indicate the degree of agreement with a particular attitudinal question. This technique is called the **Likert format** because it was used as part of Likert's (1932) method of attitude scale construction. A scale using the Likert format consists of items such as "I am afraid of heights." Instead of asking for a yes–no reply, five alternatives are offered: *strongly disagree, disagree, neutral, agree,* and *strongly agree*. Examples of Likert scale items are given in Table 6-1. In some applications, six options are used to avoid allowing the respondent to be neutral. The six responses might be *strongly disagree, moderately disagree, mildly disagree, mildly agree, moderately agree,* and *strongly agree*. Scoring requires that any negatively worded items be reverse scored and the responses are then summed. This format is especially popular in measurements of attitude. For example, it allows researchers to determine how much people endorse statements such as "The government should not regulate private business."

Because responses in a Likert format can be subjected to factor analysis, test developers can find groups of items that go together. The Likert format is often used to create Likert scales (Clark & Watson, 1998). The scales require assessment of item discriminability, a concept that we address later in the chapter. A variety of technical approaches to Likert scale development are available (Ferrando, 1999). Some research favors the validity of forced-choice formats over the traditional Likert format (Roberts, Laughlin, & Wendel, 1999). Some recent studies have demonstrated that the Likert format is superior to methods such as the visual analogue scale for measuring complex coping responses (Flynn,

TABLE 6-1

Examples of Likert Scale Items

Following is a list of statements. Please indicate how strongly you agree or disagree by circling your answer to the right of the statement.

Five-choice format with neutral point

Some politicians can be trusted	Strongly disagree	Somewhat disagree	Neither agree nor disagree	Somewhat agree	Strongly agree
I am confident that I will achieve my life goals	Strongly disagree	Somewhat disagree	Neither agree nor disagree	Somewhat agree	Strongly agree
I am comfortable talking to my parents about personal problems	Strongly disagree	Somewhat disagree	Neither agree nor disagree	Somewhat agree	Strongly agree

Alternative set of choices: strongly disagree, disagree, undecided, agree, strongly agree

Six-choice format without neutral point

Some politicians can be trusted	Strongly disagree	Moderately disagree	Mildly disagree	Mildly agree	Moderately agree	Strongly agree
I am confident that I will achieve my life goals	Strongly disagree	Moderately disagree	Mildly disagree	Mildly agree	Moderately agree	Strongly agree
I am comfortable talking to my parents about personal problems	Strongly disagree	Moderately disagree	Mildly disagree	Mildly agree	Moderately agree	Strongly agree

Alternative set of choices: strongly disagree, disagree, lean toward disagree, lean toward agree, agree, strongly agree

Schaik, & van Wersch, 2004). Nevertheless, the Likert format is familiar and easy to use. It is likely to remain popular in personality and attitude tests.

The category format. A technique that is similar to the Likert format but that uses an even greater number of choices is the **category format.** Most people are familiar with 10-point rating systems because we are regularly asked questions such as "On a scale from 1 to 10, with 1 as the lowest and 10 as the highest, how would you rate your new boyfriend in terms of attractiveness?" Doctors often ask their patients to rate their pain on a scale from 1 to 10 where 1 is little or no pain and 10 is intolerable pain. A category scale need not have exactly 10 points; it can have either more or fewer categories.

Although the 10-point scale is common in psychological research and everyday conversation, controversy exists regarding when and how it should be used. We recently encountered a college basketball coach who rates the

---

Focused Example 6-1

THE EFFECT OF CONTEXT ON VALUE RATINGS

The numbers we assign when using rating scales are sometimes influenced by the context or the background against which objects are rated. In one experiment, college students were asked to rate how immoral they believed certain acts to be. The students were divided into two groups. One group rated the items that typically represented "mild" actions (List 1) with items ranging from keeping a dime found in a phone booth to avoiding criticism by contributing money to a cause you don't believe in. The other group rated items that typically represented more severe actions (List 2). These ranged from failure to repay money borrowed from friends to murdering your mother. The numbers on the right represent average ratings by a large number of college students. The six items included on both lists are marked with asterisks. These items are judged more leniently when included in List 2 than when included in List 1. This experiment shows that the numbers we assign when using rating scales are affected by context (Parducci, 1968).

List 1

Registering in a hotel under a false name.	1.68
Bawling out servants publicly.*	2.64

Contributing money to a cause in which you do not believe in order to escape criticism.	3.03
Keeping a dime you find in a telephone booth.	1.08
Publishing under your own name an investigation originated and carried out without remuneration by a graduate student working under you.*	3.95
Failing to pay your bus fare when the conductor overlooks you.	2.36
Playing poker on Sunday.	1.17
Failing to put back in the water lobsters shorter than the legal limit.*	2.22
Cheating at solitaire.	1.53
Fishing without a license.	2.27
Habitually borrowing small sums of money from friends and failing to return them.*	2.93
Stealing towels from a hotel.	2.58
Stealing a loaf of bread from a store when you are starving.	1.79
Poisoning a neighbor's dog whose barking bothers you.*	4.19

quality of high-school prospects on a 10-point rating scale. It is assumed that this rating provides a reliable estimate of the players' abilities. However, experiments have shown that responses to items on 10-point scales are affected by the groupings of the people or things being rated. For example, if coaches are asked to rate the abilities of a group of 20 talented players, they may tend to make fine distinctions among them so as to use most or all of the categories on the 10-point scale. A particular player rated as a 6 when he was on a team with many outstanding players might be rated as a 9 if he were judged with a group of poorly coordinated players (Parducci, 1968, 1995). We know from a variety of studies that people will change ratings depending on context (Norman, 2003). When given a group of objects to rate, subjects have a tendency to spread their responses evenly across the 10 categories (Stevens, 1966). See Focused Example 6-1 for more on the effect of context on value ratings.

Lying about your whereabouts to protect a friend's reputation.	1.60	Failing to put back in the water lobsters that are shorter than the legal limit.*	1.82
Wearing shorts on the street where it is illegal.	1.59	Having sexual relations with a sibling (brother or sister).	3.72
Pocketing the tip the previous customer left for the waitress.*	3.32	Putting your deformed child in the circus.	3.81
Getting your own way by playing on people's sympathies.	2.90	Habitually borrowing small sums of money from friends and failing to return them.*	2.37
		Having incestuous relations with your parent.	3.88

List 2

Using guns on striking workers.	3.82	Murdering your mother without justification or provocation.	4.79
Bawling out servants publicly.*	2.39	Poisoning a neighbor's dog whose barking bothers you.*	3.65
Stealing ten dollars from an impecunious acquaintance.	3.79	Testifying falsely against someone for pay.	4.07
Selling to a hospital milk from diseased cattle.	4.51	Teaching adolescents to become dope addicts.	4.51
Publishing under your own name an investigation originated and carried out without remuneration by a graduate student working under you.*	3.47	Pocketing the tip the previous customer left for the waitress.*	2.46
Spreading rumors that an acquaintance is a sexual pervert.	3.91	Sending another person to take a civil service exam for you.	3.39
Having a sane person committed to a mental hospital in order to get rid of him.	4.46		

*Items followed by an asterisk appear on both lists.
From Parducci (1968).

Experiments have shown that this problem can be avoided if the endpoints of the scale are clearly defined and the subjects are frequently reminded of the definitions of the endpoints. For example, instead of asking coaches to rate the ability of basketball players on a 10-point scale, testers might show them films that depict the performance of a player rated as 10 and other films showing what the rating of 1 means. Under these circumstances, the subjects are less likely to offer a response that is affected by other stimuli in the group (R. M. Kaplan & Ernst, 1983).

People often ask, "Why use a 10-point scale instead of a 13-point or a 43-point scale?" This question has generated considerable study. More than 80 years ago, researchers argued that the optimal number of points is 7 (Symonds, 1924), whereas others have suggested that the optimal number of categories should be three times this number (Champney & Marshall, 1939). As is often the case, the number of categories required depends on the fineness of the discrimination that subjects are willing to make. If the subjects are unconcerned about a given topic, then they will not make fine discriminations about it, and a scale with a few categories will do about as well as a scale with many. However, when people are highly involved with some issue, they will tend to respond best to a greater number of categories. For most rating tasks, however, a 10-point scale seems to provide enough discrimination. N. H. Anderson (1991) has found that a 10-point scale provides substantial discrimination among objects for a wide variety of stimuli. Some evidence suggests that increasing the number of response categories may not increase reliability and validity. In fact, increasing the number of choices beyond nine or so can reduce reliability because responses may be more likely to include an element of randomness when there are so many alternatives that respondents cannot clearly discriminate between the fine-grained choices (Clark & Watson, 1998).

An approach related to category scales is the *visual analogue* scale. Using this method, the respondent is given a 100-centimeter line and asked to place a mark between two well-defined endpoints. The scales are scored according to the measured distance from the first endpoint to the mark (see Figure 6-1). Visual analogue scales are popular for measuring self-rated health. However, they are not used often for multi-item scales, because scoring is time-consuming (Clark & Watson 1998). Methods are available for creating confidence intervals around item means for rating scales (Penfield, 2003b).

Checklists and Q-sorts. One format common in personality measurement is the adjective checklist (Gough, 1960). With this method, a subject receives a long list of adjectives and indicates whether each one is characteristic of him- or herself. Adjective checklists can be used for describing either oneself or someone else. For example, in one study at the University of California at Berkeley, raters checked the traits they thought characterized a group of 40 graduate students. Half of these students had been designated by their instructors as exceptional in originality, and the other half low in originality. The results demonstrated that the adjectives chosen to describe members of these two groups differed. The highly original students were described most often by the traits *adventur-*

FIGURE 6-1   *The 100-mm visual analogue scale. The subject has rated her pain 63 mm from the base of no pain at all. On a scale ranging from 0 to 100, this level of pain is scored as 63.*

ous, alert, curious, quiet, imaginative, and *fair-minded.* In contrast, the low-originality students were seen as *confused, conventional, defensive, polished, prejudiced,* and *suggestible.*

The adjective checklist requires subjects either to endorse such adjectives or not, thus allowing only two choices for each item. A similar technique known as the *Q-sort* increases the number of categories. The Q-sort can be used to describe oneself or to provide ratings of others (Stephenson, 1953). With this technique, a subject is given statements and asked to sort them into nine piles. For example, Block (1961) gave observers 100 statements about personal characteristics. The statements were sorted into piles that indicated the degree to which they appeared to describe a given person accurately. If you were using this method, you might be asked to rate your roommate. You would receive a set of 100 cards, each with a statement on it such as the following:

Has a wide range of interests.

Is productive; gets things done.

Is self-dramatizing; is histrionic.

Is overreactive to minor frustrations; is irritable.

Seeks reassurance from others.

Appears to have a high degree of intellectual capacity.

Is basically anxious.

If a statement really hit home, you would place it in pile 9. Those that were not at all descriptive would be placed in pile 1. Most of the cards are usually placed in piles 4, 5, and 6. The frequency of items placed in each of the categories usually looks like a bell-shaped curve (see Figure 6-2). The items that end up in the extreme categories usually say something interesting about the person.

Other Possibilities

We have discussed only a few of many item formats. The forced-choice (such as multiple-choice and Q-sort) and Likert formats are clearly the most popular in contemporary tests and measures. Other formats have become less popular in recent years. For example, checklists have fallen out of favor because they are more prone to error than are formats that require responses to every item. If you are interested in learning more about item writing and item formats, then you might check some general references (Clark & Watson, 1998).

FIGURE 6-2
The California Q-sort. The numbers of items distributed in the nine piles of the California Q-sort approach a normal distribution.

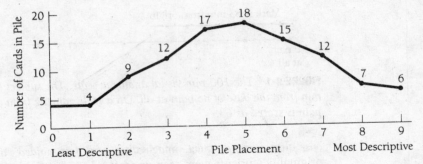

Unfortunately, there is no simple recipe for item writing. Several people have studied the issue carefully and have contributed many useful suggestions (see DeVellis, 1991). If you need to write test items, you should consult these sources. However, writing good items remains an art rather than a science. There is no substitute for using precise language, knowing the subject matter, being familiar with the level of examinees, and using your imagination (Wesman, 1971). Once the items are written and have been administered, you can use item-analysis techniques to evaluate them.

Item Analysis

A good test has good items. But what are good items? How many times have you been in a class in which students launched a full-scale battle over particular items in a multiple-choice test? Tests with good items are hard to create. Good test making requires careful attention to the principles of test construction. **Item analysis,** a general term for a set of methods used to evaluate test items, is one of the most important aspects of test construction. The basic methods involve assessment of item difficulty and item discriminability.

Item Difficulty

For a test that measures achievement or ability, **item difficulty** is defined by the number of people who get a particular item correct. For example, if 84% of the people taking a particular test get item 24 correct, then the difficulty level for that item is .84. Some people have suggested that these proportions do not really indicate item "difficulty" but item "easiness." The higher the proportion of people who get the item correct, the easier the item (Allen & Yen, 1979).

How hard should items be in a good test? This depends on the uses of the test and the types of items. The first thing a test constructor needs to determine is the probability that an item could be answered correctly by chance alone. A true–false item could be answered correctly half the time if people just guessed randomly. Thus, a true–false item with a difficulty level of .50 would not be a good item. A multiple-choice item with four alternatives could be answered correctly 25% of the time. Therefore, we would require difficulty greater than 25% for an item to be reasonable in this context. Other obvious limits are the extremes of the scale. An item that is answered correctly by 100% of the respondents offers little value because it does not discriminate among individuals.

The optimum difficulty level for items is usually about halfway between 100% of the respondents getting the item correct and the level of success expected by chance alone. Thus, the optimum difficulty level for a four-choice item is approximately .625. To arrive at this value, we take the 100% success level (1.00) and subtract from it the chance performance level (.25). Then we divide the result by 2 to find the halfway point and add this value to the expected chance level. The steps are outlined here.

Step 1. Find half of the difference between 100% success and chance performance.

$$\frac{100. - .25}{2} = \frac{.75}{2} = .375$$

Step 2. Add this value to the probability of performing correctly by chance.

Chance
performance
$\cdot \downarrow$
$.375 + .25 = .625$
$\swarrow \qquad \searrow$

Midway   Optimum item
point   difficulty

A simpler method for obtaining the same result is to add 1.00 to chance performance and divide by 2.0. For this example, the result would be

$$\frac{.25 + 1.0}{2.00} = .625$$

In most tests, the items should have a variety of difficulty levels because a good test discriminates at many levels. For example, a professor who wants to determine how much his or her students have studied might like to discriminate between students who have not studied at all and those who have studied just a little, or between those who have studied just a little and those who have studied a fair amount, or perhaps between those students who have studied more than average and those who have worked and studied exceptionally hard. In other words, the professor needs to make many discriminations. To accomplish this, he or she requires items at many different levels of difficulty.

For most tests, items in the difficulty range of .30 to .70 tend to maximize information about the differences among individuals. However, some tests require a concentration of more-difficult items. For example, if a test is to be used to select medical students and only a small number of qualified applicants can be accepted, then a test with especially difficult items will make fine discriminations in a way that a test with a broader range of difficulty would not. Conversely, a test used to select students for educable mentally challenged classes should have a greater concentration of easier items to make fine discriminations among individuals who ordinarily do not perform well on tests (Allen & Yen, 1979). In constructing a good test, one must also consider human factors. For example, though items answered correctly by all students will have poor psychometric qualities, they may help the morale of the students who take the test. A few easier items may help keep test anxiety in check, which in turn adds to the reliability of the test. Although we have discussed item analysis in relation to achievement tests, the same methods can be used to evaluate other measures. For example, instead of considering an item as right or wrong, one could set it up to indicate whether it is or is not associated with a particular diagnosis, group membership, and so forth.

Item difficulty is only one way to evaluate test items. Another way is to examine the relationship between performance on particular items and performance on the whole test. This is known as discriminability.

Discriminability

In the previous section, we discussed the analysis of item difficulty, which determines the proportion of people who succeed on a particular item. Another way to examine the value of items is to ask, "Who gets this item correct?" Assessment of **item discriminability** determines whether the people who have done well on particular items have also done well on the whole test. One can evaluate the discriminability of test items in many ways.

The extreme group method. This method compares people who have done well with those who have done poorly on a test. For example, you might find the students with test scores in the top third and those in the bottom third of the class. Then you would find the proportions of people in each group who got each item correct. The difference between these proportions is called the *discrimination index*. Technical Box 6-1 demonstrates this method.

The point biserial method. Another way to examine the discriminability of items is to find the correlation between performance on the item and performance on the total test. You might remember from Chapter 3 that the correlation between a dichotomous (two-category) variable and a continuous variable is called a *point biserial correlation*. The point biserial correlation between an item and a total test score is

$$r_{\text{pbis}} = \left[\frac{\bar{Y}_1 - \bar{Y}}{S_y} \right] \sqrt{\frac{P_x}{1 - P_x}}$$

TECHNICAL BOX 6-1

Finding the Item Discrimination Index by Using the Extreme Group Method

Step 1. Identify a group of students who have done well on the test—for example, those in the 67th percentile and above. Also identify a group that has done poorly—for example, those in the 33rd percentile and below.

Step 2. Find the proportion of students in the high group and the proportion of students in the low group who got each item correct.

Step 3. For each item, subtract the proportion of correct responses for the low group from the proportion of correct responses for the high group. This gives the item discrimination index (d_i).

Example

Item Number	Proportion Correct for Students in the Top Third of Class (P_t)	Proportion Correct for Students in the Bottom Third of Class (P_b)	Discriminability Index $(d_i = P_t - P_b)$
1	.89	.34	.55
2	.76	.36	.40
3	.97	.45	.52
4	.98	.95	.03
5	.56	.74	−.18

In this example, items 1, 2, and 3 appear to discriminate reasonably well. Item 4 does not discriminate well because the level of success is high for both groups; it must be too easy. Item 5 appears to be a bad item because it is a "negative discriminator." This sometimes happens on multiple-choice examinations when overprepared students find some reason to disqualify the response keyed as "correct."

where

r_{pbis} = the point biserial correlation or index of discriminability

$\overline{Y}_1$ = the mean score on the test for those who got item 1 correct

$\overline{Y}$ = the mean score on the test for all persons

S_y = the standard deviation of the exam scores for all persons

P_x = the proportion of persons getting the item correct (Allen & Yen, 1979)

For example, suppose that 58% of the students in a psychology class gave the correct response to item 15 on their midterm exam. The mean score on the whole test for these students who got item 15 correct was 57.6, and the mean score for the entire class was 54.3. The standard deviation on the test was 9.7.

To calculate the discriminability of item 15 by the point biserial method, you would enter this information into the formula:

$$\left(\frac{57.6 - 54.3}{9.7}\right)\sqrt{\frac{.58}{.42}} = .34 \times \sqrt{1.38} = (.34)(1.17) = .40$$

In other words, the correlation between succeeding on item 15 and total test performance is .40.

On tests with only a few items, using the point biserial correlation is problematic because performance on the item contributes to the total test score. For example, if a test has six items, there is bound to be a positive correlation between getting a particular item correct and the total test score because one-sixth of the total score is performance on that item. To compensate for this problem, it is sometimes advisable to exclude the item from the total test score. For the six-item test, we might look at the point biserial correlation between passing item 1 and the test score derived from items 2 through 6.

The point biserial correlation (r_{pbis}) between an item and the total test score is evaluated in much the same way as the extreme group discriminability index. If this value is negative or low, then the item should be eliminated from the test. The closer the value of the index is to 1.0, the better the item. Note that the easiest items, such as those answered correctly by 90% or more, usually do not appear to be good items on the discriminability index. If 90% of test takers get an item correct, then there is too little variability in performance for there to be a substantial correlation with the total test score. Similarly, if items are so hard that they are answered correctly by 10% or fewer of the test takers, then there is too little room so show a correlation between the items and the total test score.

Pictures of Item Characteristics

A valuable way to learn about items is to graph their characteristics, which you can do with the **item characteristic curve.** For particular items, one can prepare a graph in which the total test score is plotted on the horizontal (X) axis and the proportion of examinees who get the items correct is plotted on the vertical (Y) axis. The total test score is used as an estimate of the amount of a "trait" possessed by individuals. Because we can never measure traits directly, the total test score is the best approximation we have. Thus, the relationship between performance on the item and performance on the test gives some information about how well the item is tapping the information we want.

Drawing the item characteristic curve. To draw the item characteristic curve, we need to define discrete categories of test performance. If the test has been given to many people, we might choose to make each test score a single category (65, 66, 67, and so on). However, if the test has been given to a smaller group, then we might use a smaller number of class intervals (such as 66–68, 69–71). When only a small number of people took the test, some scores would not be observed and would appear as gaps on the graph. Using fewer class intervals allows the curve to take on a smoother appearance. Once you have arrived at these categories, you need to determine what proportion of the people within each category got each item correct. For example, you must determine what proportion of the people with a total test score of 65 got item 34 correct, what proportion of the people with a total test score of 66 got item 34 correct, and so on. Once you have this series of breakdowns, you can create a plot of the proportions of correct responses to an item by total test scores. Examples of these graphs are shown in Figures 6-3 through 6-7.

Figure 6-3 shows the item characteristic curve for a "good" test item. The gradual positive slope of the line demonstrates that the proportion of people who pass the item gradually increases as test scores increase. This means that the item successfully discriminates at all levels of test performance. The curve shown in Figure 6-4 illustrates an item that discriminates especially well among people at the lower level of performance. However, because all of the

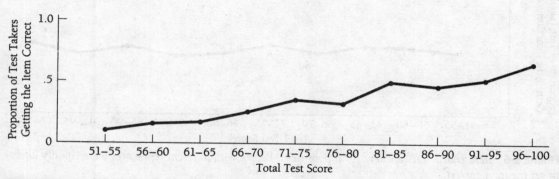

FIGURE 6-3   *Item characteristic curve for a "good" test item. The proportion of test takers who get the item correct increases as a function of the total test score.*

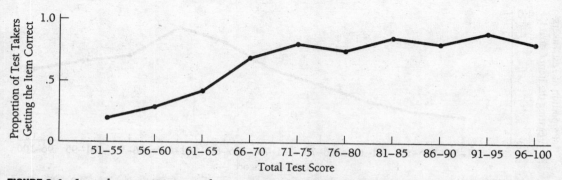

FIGURE 6-4   *Item characteristic curve for a test item that discriminates well at low levels of performance but not at higher levels.*

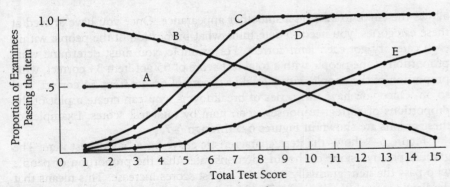

FIGURE 6-5 *Item characteristic curves for several items.*

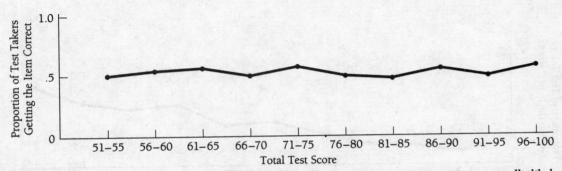

FIGURE 6-6 *Item characteristic curve for a poor item. People with different test scores were equally likely to get the item correct.*

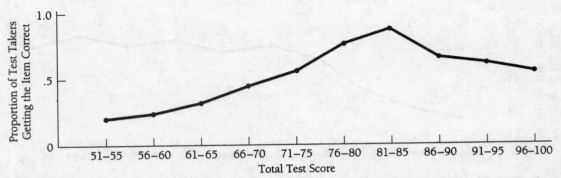

FIGURE 6-7 *Another example of a problem item. Sometimes test takers who "know too much" will rule out the alternative designated as correct.*

people who scored above average on the test got this item correct, it did not provide much discrimination in the higher ranges of performance.

Figure 6-5 shows a variety of item characteristic curves. Ranges in which the curve changes suggest that the item is sensitive, while flat ranges suggest areas of low sensitivity. The items are each sensitive in a particular range. Figures 6-6 and 6-7 show item characteristic curves for poor items. The flat curve in Figure 6-6 indicates that test takers at all levels of ability were equally likely to get the item correct. Figure 6-7 demonstrates a particularly troublesome problem. The item characteristic curve gradually rises, showing that the item is sensitive to most levels of performance. Then it turns down for people at the highest levels of performance, suggesting that those with the best overall performance on the test did not have the best chances of getting the item correct. This can happen on multiple-choice examinations when one of the alternatives is "none of the above." Students who are exceptionally knowledgeable in the subject area can sometimes rule out all the choices even though one of the alternatives has actually been designated as correct.

Another convenient picture of item characteristics is shown in Figure 6-8. This graph plots the item numbers within the space created by difficulty on one axis and discriminability (in this case, point biserial correlation between item passage and test score) on the other axis. Item 12 has been circled on the graph so that you can identify it. Of all respondents, 46% got this item correct, and its discriminability level is .60. Thus, item 12 on the graph is aligned with 46 on the difficulty axis and .60 on the discriminability axis. Earlier in the discussion we noted that "good" items usually fall within a difficulty range of 30% and 70%. In Figure 6-8, the shaded region bound by the dotted lines represents the region in which acceptable levels of difficulty and discriminability are achieved. Thus, items for the final version of the test should be selected from this area.

In summary, item analysis breaks the general rule that increasing the number of items makes a test more reliable. When bad items are eliminated, the effects of chance responding can be eliminated and the test can become more efficient, reliable, and valid. In the next section, we will consider item response theory, which is a modern method to improve test efficiency even further.

Item response theory. New approaches to item analysis have generated a new model of psychological testing (Yanai, 2003). According to classical test theory, a score is derived from the sum of an individual's responses to various items, which are sampled from a larger domain that represents a specific trait or ability. Newer approaches to testing based on item analysis consider the chances of getting particular items right or wrong. These approaches, now known as *item response theory* (IRT), make extensive use of item analysis (Holland & Hoskens, 2003). According to these approaches, each item on a test has its own item characteristic curve that describes the probability of getting each particular item right or wrong given the ability level of each test taker. With the computer, items can be sampled, and the specific range of items where the test taker begins to have difficulty can be identified (Bolt, 2003; Schmidt & Embretson, 2003). In this way, testers can make an ability judgment without subjecting the

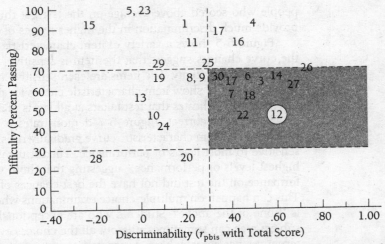

FIGURE 6-8 *Items from a 30-item test are plotted on a graph with discriminability on one axis and difficulty on the other. Each number on the graph represents a test item: 1 is for item 1 and so on. The shaded area represents items above a discriminability level of .30 and between 30% and 70% in difficulty level. These items would be the best candidates to include in the final version of the test. Item 12 (circled) was passed by 46% of the respondents and was correlated .60 with total test score, so it should be retained.*

test taker to all of the test items. Computer programs are now available to teach the complex theory underlying IRT (Penfield, 2003a).

The implications of IRT are profound. In fact, some people believe that IRT was the most important development in psychological testing in the second half of the 20th century. This theory has many technical advantages. It builds on traditional models of item analysis and can provide information on item functioning, the value of specific items, and the reliability of a scale (Hayes, 2000). Perhaps the most important message for the test taker is that his or her score is no longer defined by the total number of items correct, but instead by the level of difficulty of items that he or she can answer correctly.

There are various approaches to the construction of tests using IRT. Some of the approaches use the two dimensions shown in Figure 6-8: difficulty and discriminability. Other approaches add a third dimension for the probability that test takers with the lowest levels of ability will get a correct response. Still other approaches use only the difficulty parameter. All of the approaches grade items in relation to the probability that those who do well or poorly on the exam will have different levels of performance. One can average item characteristic curves to create a test characteristic curve that gives the proportion of responses expected to be correct for each level of ability (Guion & Ironson, 1983).

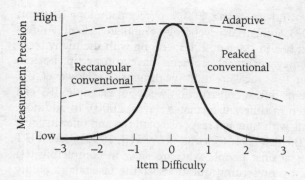

FIGURE 6-9
Measurement precision as a function of trail level for adaptive, peaked, and rectangular conventional tests. Adaptive tests based on item response theory (IRT) have higher precision across the range of ability levels.
(From Weiss, 1985.)

Perhaps the most attractive advantage of tests based on IRT is that one can easily adapt them for computer administration. The computer can rapidly identify the specific items that are required to assess a particular ability level. With this approach, test takers do not have to suffer the embarrassment of attempting multiple items beyond their ability. Conversely, they do not need to waste their time and effort on items far below their capability. In addition, each test taker may get different items to answer, greatly reducing the chances of cheating. It has been suggested that computer-adaptive testing will increase efficiency by 50% or more by reducing the amount of time each test taker spends responding to items (Schmidt & Embretson, 2003).

Figure 6-9 shows the measurement precision associated with conventional and computer-adaptive tests. Most conventional tests have the majority of their items at or near an average level of difficulty; this is represented by the "peaked conventional" portion of the figure. Though the precision of the test is best for those at average ability levels, those with the lowest or highest ability levels are not well assessed by this type of test. An alternative approach, labeled "rectangular conventional" in Figure 6-9, requires that test items be selected to create a wide range in level of difficulty. These items are pretested and selected to cover evenly the span from easiest to most difficult. The problem with this approach is that only a few items of the test are appropriate for individuals at each ability level; that is, many test takers spend much of their time responding to items either considerably below their ability level or too difficult to solve. As a result, measurement precision is constant across the range of test-taker abilities but relatively low for all people, as shown in Figure 6-9.

The supporters of IRT believe that the solution to this problem lies in computer-adaptive testing. The computer samples items and determines the range of ability that best represents each test taker. Then testing time is spent focusing on the specific range that challenges the respondent—specifically, items that have a 50% probability of a correct response (assuming no guessing) for each individual. This results in a measurement instrument of equally high precision for all test takers.

IRT is now widely used in many areas of applied research, and there are specialized applications for specific problems such as the measurement of self-efficacy (Smith, Wakely, De Kruif, & Swartz, 2003), psychopathology (Nugent, 2003; Reise & Waller, 2003), industrial psychology (Schneider, Goff, Anderson, & Borman, 2003), and health (Meijer, 2003). Along with the many technical developments in IRT, new technical problems have sprung up. For example, difficulties arise when tests measure multiple dimensions. However, IRT addresses traditional problems in test construction well. For example, IRT can handle items that are written in different formats (Hayes, 2000). In addition, IRT can identify respondents with unusual response patterns and offer insights into cognitive processes of the test taker (Sijtsma & Verweij, 1999). Use of IRT may also reduce the biases against people who are slow in completing test problems. In other words, by presenting questions at the test taker's ability level, IRT and computer adaptive testing allow the defined time spent on taking the test to be used most efficiently by test takers (van der Linden, Scrams, & Schnipke, 1999).

Many critics have asserted that computer-adaptive testing using item response theory is not feasible. However, a variety of computer-adaptive tests are available, and enthusiasm for this approach has grown (Weiss, 1985). Computers have now been used in many different aspects of psychological testing for two decades (Fowler, 1985).

External criteria. Item analysis has been persistently plagued by researchers' continued dependence on *internal criteria,* or total test score, for evaluating items. The examples we have just given demonstrate how to compare performance on an item with performance on the total test. You can use similar procedures to compare performance on an item with performance on an external criterion. For example, if you were building a test to select airplane pilots, you might want to evaluate how well the individual items predict success in pilot training or flying performance. The advantages of using external rather than internal criteria against which to validate items were outlined by Guttman (1950) more than 55 years ago. Nevertheless, external criteria are rarely used in practice (Linn, 1994a, 1994b).

Linking Uncommon Measures

One challenge in test applications is how to determine linkages between two different measures. There are many cases in which linkages are needed. For example, the SAT uses different items each time it is administered. Interpretation of the test results for students who took the test at different times requires that scores on each administration have the same meaning, even though the tests include different items—that is, we assume that a score of 600 means the same thing for two students even though the two students completed different tests. Attempts to link scores on a test such as the SAT with those of an equivalent test, such as the American College Test (ACT), pose a more difficult problem. Often these linkages are achieved through statistical formulas. This is analogous to converting a temperature from Celsius to Fahrenheit. Between tests, however, such conversions are not so straightforward. For instance, public schools often give reading and mathematics tests. Although researchers can create a formula that will link mathematics scores to reading scores, it makes little sense to try to interpret mathematical ability in terms of reading skill.

Problems in test linkages became important in the late 1990s when the National Assessment of Educational Progress (NAEP) program was proposed. As part of the program, different students will most likely take different tests and be compared on these "uncommon measures." The National Research Council of the National Academy of Sciences was asked if it was feasible to develop equivalency measures that would allow commercial and state test developers to link their measures together. After a detailed study, the committee concluded that it was not feasible to compare the wide array of commercial and state achievement tests to one another. Further, they concluded that developing transformation methods for individual scores should not be done (Feuer et al., 1999).

Items for Criterion-Referenced Tests

In Chapter 2, we briefly mentioned criterion-referenced testing. The traditional use of tests requires that we determine how well someone has done on a test by comparing the person's performance to that of others. For example, the meaning of Jeff's 67 on a geography test is interpreted by his percentile rank in the geography class. Another way of evaluating Jeff's performance is to ask how much he learned in comparison to how much he "should have" learned. Jeff is no longer in competition with everyone else. Instead, we have defined what Jeff must do to be considered knowledgeable about a certain unit. How much Jeff knows rather than whether or not he knows more than someone else determines his grade.

A *criterion-referenced test* compares performance with some clearly defined criterion for learning. This approach is popular in individualized instruction programs. For each student, a set of objectives is defined that state exactly what the student should be able to do after an educational experience. For example, an objective for a junior-high algebra student might be to solve linear equations with two unknowns. The criterion-referenced test would be used to determine whether this objective had been achieved. After demonstrating this knowledge, the student could move ahead to another objective. Many educators regard criterion-referenced tests as diagnostic instruments. When a student does poorly on some items, the teacher knows that the individualized education program needs more focus in a particular area.

The first step in developing criterion-referenced tests involves clearly specifying the objectives by writing clear and precise statements about what the learning program is attempting to achieve. These statements are usually stated in terms of something the student will be able to do. For example, a unit in high-school civics might aim at getting students to understand the operation of municipal government. Test items that assess the attainment of this objective might ask about the taxation powers of local governments, the relation of municipal to state government, and so on.

FIGURE 6-10
Frequency polygon used to evaluate a criterion-referenced test.

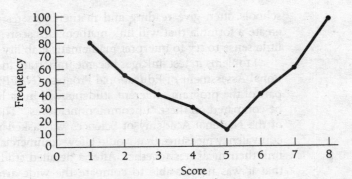

To evaluate the items in the criterion-referenced test, one should give the test to two groups of students—one that has been exposed to the learning unit and one that has not. Figure 6-10 shows what the distribution of scores would look like. The frequency polygon looks like a V. The scores on the left side of the V are probably those from students who have not experienced the unit. Scores on the right represent those who have been exposed to the unit. The bottom of the V is the *antimode,* or the least frequent score. This point divides those who have been exposed to the unit from those who have not been exposed and is usually taken as the *cutting score* or *point,* or what marks the point of decision. When people get scores higher than the antimode, we assume that they have met the objective of the test. When they get lower scores, we assume they have not. In Figure 6-10 the cutting score is 5.

Criterion-referenced tests offer many advantages to newer educational approaches. For example, in computer-assisted instruction, each student works at his or her own pace on an individualized program of instruction, after which a criterion-referenced test is used to evaluate progress. Students who pass the test can move on to the next unit. Students who do not pass can repeat some of the instruction until they pass.

Similarly, the Internet has provided abundant opportunities for "distance learning" (Black, 2003). Using the Internet, students can gain educational experiences interactively. As more college courses come online, there will be a variety of challenges for evaluation and student assessment.

Limitations of Item Analysis

The growing interest in criterion-referenced tests has posed new questions about the adequacy of item-analysis procedures. The main problem is this: Though statistical methods for item analysis tell the test constructor which items do a good job of separating students, they do not help the students learn. Young children do not care as much about how many items they missed as they do about what they are doing wrong (Davis, 1979). Many times children make specific errors and will continue to make them until they discover why they are making them.

For example, an achievement test might ask a fourth-grade student to add .40 and .30. One of the multiple-choice alternatives would be .07 because item analysis had demonstrated that this was a good distractor. The child who selected .07 would not receive a point on the item and also might continue to make similar errors. Although the data are available to give the child feedback on the "bug" in his or her thinking, nothing in the testing procedure initiates this guidance (Linn, 1994a). One study that involved 1300 fourth, fifth, and sixth graders found that 40% of the children made the same type of error when given problems of a particular kind (Brown & Burton, 1978). Some researchers in educational measurement now appear to be moving toward testing programs that diagnose as well as assess (Linn, 1994a, 1994b; Linn & Burton, 1994). Tests can have different purposes. In the past, many have placed too much emphasis on ranking students and not enough on discovering specific weaknesses or gaps in knowledge. There are other disadvantages of criterion-referenced tests. One that has caused considerable concern is that teachers "teach to the test." For example, they may concentrate on skills that are easy to test while ignoring more important skills such as critical thinking, judgment, reading comprehension, and self-expression.

SUMMARY

There is an art and a science to test construction. Writing good items is a complex and demanding task. In the first step, developers decide what sort of information they are trying to obtain. If they want to know whether or not test takers know "the right information," developers may use true–false items—that is, a *dichotomous format*. They may also use for the same purpose multiple-choice items, a *polytomous format*, in which a correct choice must be selected among several alternatives. With these types of formats, the test constructor must always consider the probability that someone will get an answer correct by chance.

Many formats are available for tests that do not have right or wrong answers. The *Likert format* is popular for attitude scales. In this format, respondents check on a 5-point scale the degree to which they agree or disagree with the given statements. Similarly, in the category-scaling method, ratings are obtained on a scale with defined endpoints. The familiar 10-point scale is an example of a category scale. Unfortunately, category scales are subject to some bias when the endpoints are not clearly defined. Checklists and Q-sorts are among the many item formats used in personality research. These methods require people to make judgments about whether or not certain items describe themselves or others.

Once developers have created test items, they can administer them to groups of individuals and systematically assess the values of the items. One method of item analysis requires evaluation of item difficulty, which is usually assessed by examining the number of people who get each item correct. In addition to difficulty analysis, test constructors usually examine the correlation between getting any item correct and the total test score. This correlation is used as an index of *discriminability*.

Another way to learn about the value of items is to draw a picture of the *item characteristic curve.* For example, the proportion of people who get an item correct can be plotted as a function of the total test score. The best items are those for which the probability of getting the item correct is highest among those with the highest test scores.

The most important contemporary development in psychological testing is *item response theory* (IRT). In this method, a computer identifies the specific items that characterize the skill level of a particular test taker. The test is tailored to that individual. This method allows more precision and less burden on the test taker. Although all test takers may be scored on the same dimensions, the actual items they complete are likely to differ.

Criterion-referenced tests require a different approach to test construction. With such tests, a person's knowledge is evaluated against what he or she is expected to know rather than against what others know. To evaluate items in criterion-referenced tests, one compares the performance of those who would be expected to know the material with the performance of others who would not be expected to have learned the information.

WEB ACTIVITY

For some interesting and relevant Web sites, you might want to check the following:

> www.delweg.com/dpwessay/tests.htm
> *A discussion of factors to consider when constructing test questions*

> www.psychologicaltesting.com/test_construction
> *A list of practical suggestions for test construction*

> www.uts.psu.edu/Test_construction_frame.htm
> *A more technical discussion of test construction and psychometric analysis*

> trochim.human.cornell.edu/kb/scallik.htm
> *A good review of scale construction*

CHAPTER 7

Test Administration

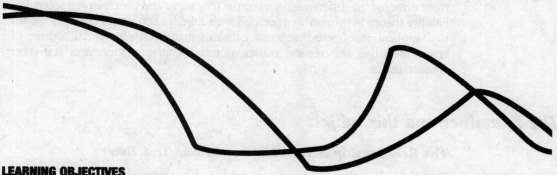

LEARNING OBJECTIVES

When you have completed this chapter, you should be able to:

☐ Know whether the majority of the research evidence shows that white examiners impede the intelligence test performance of African American children

☐ Discuss how the relationship between the examiner and the test taker can affect test scores

☐ Explain how an expectancy effect might affect a test score

☐ Examine the relationship between test performance and reinforcing particular responses

☐ Outline some of the advantages of computer-assisted test administration

☐ List what characteristics of the state of the subject should be considered when a test score is evaluated

☐ Know what problems you would need to consider in training your observers if you were in charge of a behavioral observation study

*I*n the last six chapters, we discussed many topics related to test construction. Before we move on to applications of the tests, one final methodological issue needs to be covered: the administration of tests.

Many factors influence test scores. We have a tendency to think that an observed score really represents the true ability or trait we are trying to measure. In Chapter 4, we reviewed the concept of reliability and introduced measurement error, or the difference between the true score and the observed score. Reliability theory is primarily concerned with random sources of error. In the actual application of tests, we must consider many other potential sources of error, including the testing situation, tester characteristics, and test-taker characteristics.

The Examiner and the Subject

The Relationship Between Examiner and Test Taker

Both the behavior of the examiner and his or her relationship to the test taker can affect test scores. In one older study, first- through seventh-grade children were given the Wechsler Intelligence Scale for Children (or WISC; see Chapter 10) under one of two conditions. Half of the children were given the test under an enhanced rapport condition in which the examiner used friendly conversation and verbal reinforcement during the test administration. The other children took the test under a neutral rapport condition in which the examiner neither initiated conversation nor used reinforcement (Feldman & Sullivan, 1960). The examiner's rapport had little effect on the scores of the younger children (through third grade). However, average IQ scores for the fifth-grade through ninth-grade students were higher for those who had received the test under the enhanced rapport condition (mean IQ = 122) than for those with a neutral administrator (mean IQ = 109). This difference (122 − 109) is almost a full standard deviation.

Another study compared scores obtained by examiners who made approving comments (such as "good" or "fine") with scores obtained by examiners who used disapproving comments ("I thought you could do better than that") or neutral comments. Children who took the test under a disapproving examiner received lower scores than did children exposed to a neutral or an approving examiner (Witmer, Bernstein, & Dunham, 1971). For younger children, a familiar examiner may make a difference. In one study, 137 children took a reading test, half with a familiar proctor, half with an unfamiliar proctor. Reading scores were significantly lower when the proctor was unfamiliar (DeRosa & Patalano, 1991).

In a quantitative review of the literature, Fuchs and Fuchs (1986) considered 22 different studies that involved 1489 children. Averaging across the studies, they found that test performance was approximately .28 standard deviation (roughly 4 IQ points) higher when the examiner was familiar with the test taker than when not. In those studies that involved children from lower socioeconomic classes, familiarity accounted for approximately 7.6 IQ points. The review raises important concerns because it demonstrates that familiarity with the test taker, and perhaps preexisting notions about the test taker's ability, can either positively or negatively bias test results.

Other assessment situations have shown substantial interviewer effects (Bergstrom & Lunz, 1999; Campbell, Rohlman, Storzbach, & Binder, 1999; Hanson, Borman, Mogilka, Manning, & Hedge, 1999). For example, in attitudinal surveys, respondents may give the response that they perceive to be expected by the interviewer. When interviewed by telephone, for example, respondents might take their cues from the sex and age of the interviewer. A substantial number of studies have documented the effects of having a live interviewer versus self-completion of the questionnaires. For example, people tend to disclose more information in a self-report format than they do to an interviewer (Moun, 1998). In addition, people report more symptoms and health problems in a mailed questionnaire than they do in a face-to-face interview (McHorney, 1999). Several studies have shown that computer administration is at least as reliable as traditional test administration (Bergstrom & Lunz, 1999; Campbell, Rohlman, Storzbach, & Binder, 1999). Focused Example 7-1 shows how the type of test administration might affect estimates for the rates of psychiatric disability.

In most testing situations, examiners should be aware that their rapport with test takers can influence the results. They should also keep in mind that rapport might be influenced by subtle processes such as the level of performance expected by the examiner.

The Race of the Tester

Because of concern about bias, the effects of the tester's race have generated considerable attention. Some groups feel that their children should not be tested by anyone except a member of their own race. For example, some people claim that African American children receive lower test scores when tested by white examiners than by examiners of their own race. Although the effects of racial bias in test administration are discussed frequently, relatively few experimental studies have examined the exact impact of these effects. Sattler reviewed such effects on several occasions (Sattler, 2002, 2004). After careful consideration of the problem and occasional reanalysis of the data, Sattler concluded that there is little evidence that the race of the examiner significantly affects intelligence test scores.

The most common finding in studies of this type is that the race of the examiner has nonsignificant effects on test performance for both African American and white children. Most of these studies were conducted many years ago, and interest in these research topics seems to have died. The early results occurred for both the Stanford-Binet scale and the Peabody Picture Vocabulary Test (Costello & Dickie, 1970; Miller & Phillips, 1966). A similar study with older children (African American sixth graders) failed to show differences between the children when they were given the Stanford-Binet by an African American examiner and by a white one (Caldwell & Knight, 1970).

Focused Example 7-1

HOW TEST ADMINISTRATION AFFECTS RATES OF REPORTING SYMPTOMS OF ANXIETY AND DEPRESSION

It is commonly believed that a well-trained and empathetic interviewer can elicit more symptoms of anxiety and depression than can a telephone interviewer or a mail survey. Two large public health surveys in Norway evaluated these beliefs. Scales that measured symptoms of anxiety and depression were administered to 13,850 Norwegian adults. In one portion of the study, the questions were administered either face-to-face or by telephone. The interviewer's age and gender were systematically varied. In another portion of the study, information was reported in a mailed-out, self-administered questionnaire.

The results of the study demonstrated that the self-administered questionnaires identified two to three times as many probable cases of psychological distress as did the personally interviewed cases. The study also attempted to identify which respondents

of the two groups would be more likely to report psychological symptoms. Rates of anxiety and depression were significantly lower for young and well-educated adults who completed face-to-face interviews than for young and well-educated adults who completed the self-report questionnaire. The age and gender of the interviewer did not appear to have strong effects, with one exception: Fewer symptoms were reported when the interviewer was young and male (Moun, 1998). Figure 7-1 shows the effects of administration for the more highly educated subjects in the study. Mailed-in administration had a particularly strong effect on the younger subjects. Researchers use data on anxiety and depression to estimate the likelihood that the person will receive a psychiatric diagnosis. For the younger subjects, these diagnoses would be more common if the questions were self-administered.

FIGURE 7-1

Effects of mode of interviewing and age on percentage of probable psychiatric cases.

(Data adapted from Moun, 1998.)

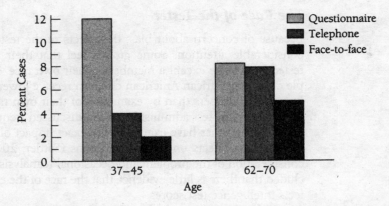

This same result also has been obtained for group intelligence tests. Scores of African American and white fourth, fifth, and sixth graders were not found to be significantly influenced by having a trained African American or white examiner give the Lorge-Thorndike Group Intelligence Test (Lipsitz, 1969). Only a few studies have shown an effect attributed to the race of the examiner; in fact, these effects have been found in only 4 of 29 studies (Sattler, 1979a). Sattler and Gwynne (1982) have referred to the belief that white examiners impede the test performance of African American children as a myth widely held but unsupported by scientific studies.

One reason why so few studies show effects of the examiner's race on the results of IQ tests is that the procedures for properly administering an IQ test are so specific. Anyone who gives the test should do so according to a strict procedure. In other words, well-trained African American and white test administrators should act almost identically. Deviation from this procedure might produce differences in performance associated with the race of the examiner. For example, in the next sections we show how subtle nonverbal cues can affect test scores. Even though most standardized tests require a strict administration procedure, the examiner can still communicate a hostile or a friendly atmosphere, a hurried or a relaxed manner, or an inquisitorial or a therapeutic role. Rather than race, these effects may reflect individual or cultural differences.

Sattler (1973b, 1973c) has shown that the race of the examiner affects test scores in some situations. Examiner effects tend to increase when examiners are given more discretion about the use of the tests. In one study in which a small effect of the examiner's race was found, the examiners were paraprofessionals rather than psychologists. The white examiners obtained higher scores from white than from African American children, whereas scores for both groups of children were comparable when tested by African American examiners (Abramson, 1969).

There may be some biases in the way items are presented. One study compared African American and white preschool children on the Preschool Language Assessment Instrument. All children completed the test in two formats during two sessions that were separated by two weeks. In one session, the administration was standard; in the other, the administrators were allowed a greater use of context and themes in explaining the test. The African American children obtained higher test scores when the items were administered in the thematic mode. In particular, the researchers noted a significant increase in performance on the more complex and difficult items (Fagundes, Haynes, Haak, & Moran, 1998). Another study hypothesized that African American children may score lower on IQ tests because they have poorer reading skills. In one experiment, some children read the items on the Otis-Lennon School Ability Test (OLSAT), while a second group read while listening to an audio-taped version. Fourth- and fifth-grade African American students who had heard the audiotape scored significantly higher on the test (Warner-Benson, 2001). Although standardization is required, variations from the standard might reveal some unnoticed skills in disadvantaged test takers. Studies of these problems might lead to the development of better tests.

Even so, after a detailed review of the literature, Sattler (1988) concluded that the effects of administrators' race are negligible. Even though race effects in test administration may be relatively small, efforts must be made to reduce all potential bias. The new versions of the Wechsler (see Chapter 10) have introduced greater standardization and procedures for fair test administration (Bridgeman & Schmitt, 1997; Frisby, 1998; Lindsey, 1998).

Language of Test Taker

Some of the new standards concern testing individuals with different linguistic backgrounds. The standards emphasize that some tests are inappropriate for people whose knowledge of the language is questionable. For example, the validity and reliability of tests for those who do not speak English is suspect. Translating tests is difficult, and it cannot be assumed that the validity and reliability of the translation are comparable to the English version. Concern about the internal validity of research studies often compromises external validity (Okazaki & Sue, 2003; Sue, 2003). External validity concerns the use of research findings in groups other than those who participated in the original validation studies. The standard is that, for test takers who are proficient in two or more languages, the test should be given in the language that the test takers feel is their best. Evidence for test comparability across languages should be available. Furthermore, interpreters should be used only with great caution because test interpreters can introduce bias into the testing situation (American Educational Research Association, American Psychological Association, & National Council on Measurement in Education, 1999).

Training of Test Administrators

Different assessment procedures require different levels of training. Many behavioral assessment procedures require training and evaluation but not a formal degree or diploma. Psychiatric diagnosis is sometimes obtained using the Structured Clinical Interview for DSM-IV (SCID) (Spitzer et al., 1997). Typical SCID users are licensed psychiatrists or psychologists with additional training on the test. There are no standardized protocols for training people to administer complicated tests such as the Wechsler Adult Intelligence Scale–Revised (WAIS-R; see Chapter 10), although these tests are usually administered by licensed psychologists. Many training programs have students complete only four practice administrations of the WAIS-R. In a study of 22 graduate students, there were numerous errors in scoring the test, with no improvement over five practice administrations. The error rate went down only after approximately 10 administrations, suggesting that students need at least 10 practice sessions to begin gaining competence with the WAIS-R (Patterson, Slate, Jones, & Steger, 1995). The reliability of DSM classifications for conditions such as pathological gambling are acceptable but far from perfect (Stinchfield, 2003).

Expectancy Effects

A well-known line of research in psychology has shown that data sometimes can be affected by what an experimenter expects to find. Robert Rosenthal and his colleagues at Harvard University conducted many experiments on such **expectancy effects**, often called **Rosenthal effects** (Rosenthal, 2002a). In a typical experiment, Rosenthal employed a large number of student experimenters to help collect data on a task such as rating human faces for success or failure. Half of the student experimenters were led to believe that the average response would fall toward the success side of the scale, and the other half were told that the average response would fall on the failure side. The results of these experiments have consistently demonstrated that the subjects actually provide data that confirm the experimenter's expectancies. However, the magnitude of the effects is small—approximately a 1-point difference on a 20-point scale (Rosenthal, 1966).

The experimenter's influence is not limited to human subjects. Other experiments have demonstrated that rats who are expected to be "maze bright" will learn to run through a maze more quickly than will rats that are expected to be "maze dull." In reality all of the rats were from the same litter and they were randomly assigned to be labeled as maze bright or maze dull (Rosenthal & Fode, 1963).

Several authors have challenged the Rosenthal experiments, claiming that they are based on unsound statistical procedures or faulty design (Barber & Silver, 1968; Elashoff & Snow, 1971; Thorndike, 1968). Rosenthal has acknowledged some problems in his early work and has greatly improved his own skills as a methodologist (Rosenthal & Rosnow, 1991). Other questions have been raised about the expectancy effect. For example, in one study from Israel, women supervisors were told that some women officer cadets offered exceptional potential. This selection was made randomly instead of on the basis of any evidence. The study failed to show any expectancy effect. In a follow-up study, expectancy information was given to men and women who were leaders with regard to men and women who were subjects. The results replicated the effect of expectancy for men when they were supervised by men and for women when they were led by men but failed to replicate the results when women were led by women (Dvir, Eden, & Banjo, 1995). A review of many studies suggests that an expectancy effect exists in some but not all situations.

Expectancies shape our judgments in many important ways (Kirsch, 1999). One of the most important responsibilities for faculty in research-oriented universities is to apply for grant funding. Grant reviewers are supposed to judge the quality of proposals independently of the reputation of the applicant. However, studies suggest that reviewers' expectancies about the investigators do influence their judgment (Marsh & Bazeley, 1999).

Two aspects of the expectancy effect relate to the use of standardized tests. First, the expectancy effects observed in Rosenthal's experiments were obtained when all of the experimenters followed a standardized script. Although gross forms of bias are possible, Rosenthal argued that the expectancy effect results from subtle nonverbal communication between the experimenter and the subject. The experimenter may not even be aware of his or her role in the process. Second, the expectancy effect has a small and subtle effect on scores and occurs in some situations but not in others (Rosenthal, 2002b). Determining whether expectancy influences test scores requires careful studies on the particular tests that are being used.

The expectancy effect can impact intelligence testing in many ways, such as scoring. In a series of experiments, graduate students with some training in intelligence testing were asked to score ambiguous responses from intelligence tests. Sometimes they were told that the responses had been given by "bright" people, and other times they were told the responses were from "dull" people. The students tended to give more credit to responses purportedly from bright test takers (Sattler, Hillix, & Neher, 1970; Sattler & Winget, 1970). Other studies have demonstrated that the expectancy effect can occur even if the responses are not ambiguous (Sattler, 1998).

A variety of interpersonal and cognitive process variables have been shown to affect our judgment of others (Arkes, 1991). These biases may also affect test scoring. For example, Donahue and Sattler (1971) demonstrated that students who scored the WAIS would most likely give credit for selected items to examinees they liked or perceived to be warm. Thus, examiners must remain aware that their relationships with examinees can affect their objectivity when they score certain types of tests.

Studies of expectancies in test administrators (who give rather than merely score tests) have yielded somewhat inconsistent results. Some have shown a significant effect (Hersh, 1971; Larrabee & Kleinsaser, 1967; Schroeder & Kleinsaser, 1972), whereas others have not demonstrated an expectancy effect (Dangel, 1970; Ekren, 1962; Gillingham, 1970; Saunders & Vitro, 1971).

Many studies have attempted to find subtle variables that affect test responses. For example, Rappaport and McAnulty (1985) presented tape-recorded responses to people scoring IQ tests. Though the children on the recording gave the same response with or without an accent, no difference between these two conditions surfaced.

In reviewing these studies, Sattler (1988) noted that those that showed an expectancy effect tended to have an administrator test only two children (one under a high and one under a low expectancy condition). The studies that did not find an expectancy effect tended to have more subjects tested by each test administrator. The studies that used more samples of each tester's behavior should produce more reliable estimates of the expectancy effect; therefore, the studies that failed to show an expectancy effect may be more credible than those that showed it.

In spite of these inconsistent results, you should pay careful attention to the potentially biasing effect of expectancy. Even Rosenthal's harshest critics do not deny the possibility of this effect. Thus, it is always important to do as much as you can to eliminate this possibility.

Effects of Reinforcing Responses

Because reinforcement affects behavior, testers should always administer tests under controlled conditions. Sattler and Theye (1967) reviewed the literature on procedural and situational variables in testing and found that an inconsistent use of feedback can damage the reliability and validity of test scores.

Several studies have shown that reward can significantly affect test performance. For example, incentives can help improve performance on IQ tests for specific subgroups of children. In one study, 6- to 13-year-olds received tokens they could exchange for money each time they gave a correct response on the WISC verbal scale. This incentive improved the performance of lower-class white children but not for middle-class children or lower-class African American children (Sweet, 1970).

Many studies have shown that children will work quite hard to obtain praise such as "You are doing well" (Eisenberger & Cameron, 1998). Several studies have shown that the effects of praise are about as strong as the effects of money or candy (Merrell, 1999). The results of these studies, however, are sometimes complicated. For instance, one study found that girls increased their accuracy on the WISC block design subtest when given any type of reinforcement for a correct response. Boys increased their accuracy only when given chips that could be exchanged for money. However, girls decreased in speed when given reinforcement, and boys increased in speed only when given verbal praise (Bergan, McManis, & Melchert, 1971).

Some evidence suggests that African American children do not respond as well to verbal reinforcement as they do to tangible rewards such as money or candy (Schultz & Sherman, 1976). However, Terrell and his colleagues suggested that this is because the verbal reinforcement given to the African American children is often not culturally relevant (Terrell, Taylor, & Terrell, 1978). To demonstrate their point, they administered the WISC-R intelligence test to lower-income African-American second graders and gave one of four types of feedback for each correct response. One-quarter of the children received no feedback at all about whether or not they had made a correct response. One group received verbal praise; another group, candy. The final group was given culturally relevant verbal praise. For example, after each correct response, the African American test administrator remarked "Nice job, Blood" or "Nice job, little Brother." Culturally relevant feedback boosted IQ a remarkable 17.6 points, whereas other feedback had minimal effect (about 3 points). Tangible rewards boosted performance approximately 11 points. This result is most unusual in light of several previous studies that show only minor reinforcement effects. Certainly, the effects of culturally relevant rewards deserve more attention (Frisby, 1998; Frumkin, 1997; Lindsey, 1998).

Some of the most potent effects of reinforcement arise in attitudinal studies. In survey research, the answer given by a respondent is not necessarily right or wrong but rather an expression of how someone feels about something. Repeated studies have demonstrated that the way an interviewer responds affects the content of responses in interview studies (Cannell & Henson, 1974). In one of the most interesting of these, respondents in a household survey were asked if they suffered from certain physical symptoms. For half of the subjects, the interviewer gave an approving nod each time a symptom was reported. For the other half, the interviewer remained expressionless. The number of symptoms reported increased significantly with such approval. In a similar study, two symptoms that no one should report were added to the list: "Are your intestines too long?" and "Do the ends of your hair itch?" More people reported these symptoms if they had been reinforced for reporting other symptoms than if they had not.

Reinforcement and feedback guide the examinee toward a preferred response. Another way to demonstrate the potency of reinforcement involves misguiding the subject. A variety of studies have demonstrated that random reinforcement destroys the accuracy of performance and decreases the motivation to respond (Eisenberger & Cameron, 1998). Consider how you might feel if the grades you received were totally random. The effects of random feedback are rather severe, causing depression, low motivation for responding, and inability to solve problems. This condition is known as *learned helplessness* (Abramson, Alloy, & Metalsky, 1995).

The potency of reinforcement requires that test administrators exert strict control over the use of feedback (see Technical Box 7-1). Because different test takers make different responses, one cannot ensure that the advantages resulting from reinforcement will be the same for all people. As a result, most test manuals and interviewer guides insist that no feedback be given.

Testing also requires standardized conditions because situational variables can affect test scores. The book *Standards for Educational and Psychological Testing*, published by the American Psychological Association and other professional groups (AERA, APA, & NCME, 1999), emphasizes that a test manual should clearly spell out the directions for administration. These directions should be sufficiently detailed to be duplicated in all situations in which the test is given. A good test manual gives the test examiner instructions that in-

---

TECHNICAL BOX 7-1

The Incentive Scoreboard

As noted in the text, because most psychologists agree that reinforcement can affect test performance, methods are usually implemented to standardize reinforcement during testing procedures. However, as in most areas of psychology, there is some inconsistency in the literature. Sattler (1988) reviewed 34 studies that evaluated the effect of incentives, which included praise, candy, money, social reinforcement, and tokens. The subjects in these experiments included normal and handicapped children of various ethnic groups. By tallying the results of these studies, Sattler observed that 14 studies found that incentives or feedback did not affect performance, 13 studies found mixed results, and 7 studies found clear evidence that reinforcement either improved or hindered performance.

There appeared to be no clear and consistent difference between the studies that showed a positive effect and those that showed a negative effect of token and social reinforcement. One issue raised by research on incentive effects concerns what the results imply for test interpretation. For example, if a child's IQ score of 110 can be boosted to 120 with reinforcement for correct responses, does this mean the child is likely to do well in school? The validity of the test is based on a standardized administration procedure, so it is not clear that enhancing IQ scores with reinforcement would enhance the validity of the test.

clude the exact words to be read to the test takers. It also includes questions that testers will likely ask and instructions on how administrators should answer them.

Inexperienced test administrators often do not fully appreciate the importance of standardization in administration. Whether they give a test or supervise others who do, they must consider that the test may not remain reliable or valid if they deviate from the specified instructions.

A few occasions do require deviation from standardized testing procedures. Sattler (1988) acknowledges that the blind need special considerations, and Edelstein and Kalish (1999) discuss the testing needs of the aged. However, many widely used tests have now developed special standardized methods for testing particular populations. To ensure that tests are given under standardized conditions, some examiners prefer to give instructions through a tape recorder. Others have opted for computer-assisted test administration.

Computer-Assisted Test Administration

Computer technology affects many fields, including testing and test administration. Today, virtually all educational institutions and a growing number of households enjoy access to the Internet. This easy access has caused test administration on computers to blossom.

Interactive testing involves the presentation of test items on a computer terminal or personal computer and the automatic recording of test responses. The computer can also be programmed to instruct the test taker and to provide instruction when parts of the testing procedure are not clear. As early as 1970, Cronbach recognized the value of computers as test administrators. Here are some of the advantages that computers offer:

- excellence of standardization,
- individually tailored sequential administration,
- precision of timing responses,
- release of human testers for other duties,
- patience (test taker not rushed), and
- control of bias.

Since the publication of the first edition of this book in 1982, computer technology has bloomed in testing. Today, many of the major psychological tests are available for use on a personal computer. Furthermore, the computer is playing an increasingly important role in test administration. Some people, though, feel uneasy interacting with computers, or suffer from "keyboard phobia."

Newer technologies use bar codes or other procedures to reduce resistance to computers (Pfister, 1995). The computer offers many advantages in test administration, scoring, and interpretation (Britton & Tidwell, 1995), including ease of application of complicated psychometric issues and the integration of testing and cognitive psychology (DiBello, Stout, & Roussos, 1995).

Computer-assisted test administration does not necessarily depend on a structured order of test items. Indeed, one advantage of this approach is that the items can be given in any order or in a unique random order for every test taker. Computers are objective and cost-effective. Furthermore, they allow more experimental control than do other methods of administration. For example, if you want a precise limit on the amount of time any one item can be studied, the computer can easily be programmed to flash the items on the screen for specific durations. The computer-assisted method also prevents test takers from looking ahead at other sections of the test or going back to sections already completed (Groth-Marnat & Shumaker, 1989; Lautenschlager & Flaherty, 1990). Comparisons of test scores have not tended to show large differences between computer-assisted and paper-and-pencil tests (Ward et al., 1989), yet the computer method ensures standardization and control and also reduces scoring errors. It was once thought that people would rebel against interactions with machines. However, evidence suggests that test takers actually find interactions with computers more enjoyable than paper-and-pencil tests (Rosenfeld, Doherty, Vicino, Kantor, et al., 1989).

One of the most interesting findings concerns the use of computers to obtain sensitive information. In one study, 162 college students were assessed on the MMPI and questionnaires that concerned drinking and other personal information. The information was obtained in one of three ways: computer, questionnaire, or interview. The results suggested that students were less likely to disclose socially undesirable information during a personal interview than on a computer. In fact, students may be more honest when tested by a computer than by a person. Furthermore, students had the most positive experience with the computer (Locke & Gilbert, 1995).

There has been a substantial increase in the number of studies devoted to computer-administered testing. Most studies show that computer administration is at least as reliable as traditional assessment (Handel, Ben-Porath, & Matt, 1999; Schulenberg & Yutrzenka, 1999). Computer assessment has been applied in a variety of areas including the administration of the MMPI (Handel et al., 1999), personnel selection (Hanson, Borman, Mogilka, et al., 1999), and cognitive process (Senior, Phillips, Barns, & David, 1999). As more and more types of tests are prepared for computer administration, independent reliability and validity studies will be needed. Evidence that shows the equivalence between traditionally administered and computer-administrated tests for personnel selection does not necessarily mean that the same equivalence will apply to tests on depression (Schulenberg & Yutrzenka, 1999).

Not all observers endorse the rapid development of computerized test administration. For example, J. D. Matarazzo (1986) suggested that computer-generated test reports in the hands of an inexperienced psychologist cannot replace clinical judgment. In such cases, computerized reports may actually cause harm if misinterpreted. Other problems include computerized scoring routines that have errors or are poorly validated; such problems are often difficult to detect within the software. Hartman (1986b) accurately predicted an increase over the last fifteen years in consumer liability cases involving software products. Groth-Marnat and Schumaker (1989) outlined several problems caused by faulty computerized testing systems. For example, some programs have untested claims of validity, and computerized reports might be based on an obsolete database. A clinical psychologist who lets the computer do too much of the thinking may misinterpret test responses. With the growth in computerized testing, the industry may need new guidelines.

Subject Variables

A final variable that may be a serious source of error is the state of the subject. Motivation and anxiety can greatly affect test scores. For example, many college students suffer from a serious debilitating condition known as **test anxiety.** Such students often have difficulty focusing attention on the test items and are distracted by other thoughts such as "I am not doing well" or "I am running out of time" (Sapp, 1999). Test anxiety appears to have three components: worry, emotionality, and lack of self-confidence (Oostdam & Meijer, 2003).

It may seem obvious that illness affects test scores. When you have a cold or the flu, you might not perform as well as when you are feeling well. Many variations in health status affect performance in behavior and in thinking (Kaplan, 2004). In fact, medical drugs are now evaluated according to their effects on the cognitive process (Spilker, 1996). Some populations need special consideration. For example, the elderly may do better with individual testing sessions, even for tests that can be administered to groups (Martin, Poon, Clayton, et al., 1994). The measurement of the effects of health status on functioning also will be discussed in more detail in Chapter 17.

Some researchers have debated whether normal hormonal variations affect test performance. For instance, healthy women experience variations in their perceptual and motor performance as a function of menstrual cycle. In the middle of each monthly cycle, women may perform better on tests of speeded motor coordination than they would during menstruation. However, these same women may perform more poorly on tests of perceptual and spatial abilities during midcycle than during menses (Hampson & Kimura, 1988). Studies by Kimura (1999) suggest that men also vary in test performance as a function of variations in sex hormones.

Behavioral Assessment Methodology

Measurement goes beyond the application of psychological tests. Many assessment procedures involve the observation of behavior. For example, personnel psychologists often obtain work samples to estimate job performance. These samples require the performance of tasks in environments similar to the actual work setting. During this performance, psychologists make systematic observations of behavior. Some applied psychologists believe that work samples provide the most valid indication of actual work performance (Green & Wing, 1988). Cognitive ability tends not to be the best predictor of work performance. Studies in the military show that work-sample performance is well predicted instead by knowledge about the job and job experience (Wagner, 1997).

The Individuals with Disabilities Education Act (IDEA) Amendments mandate the use of functional behavioral assessment (FBA) for disabled students. However, one review of the literature showed that FBA was used in combination with school-based intervention (Gresham, McIntyre, Olson-Tinker, Dolstra, McLaughlin, & Van, 2004). Improving methods of behavioral observation has long been recognized as important in clinical psychology (Bellack, 1998; Hersen, Kazdin, & Bellack, 1991; Tryon, 1991). Many new problems, though, have accompanied the increasing use of behavioral observation methods. As you have seen in this chapter, minor variations in standard test-administration procedures can affect test scores. However, testers can overcome most of these problems by adhering closely to standard administration procedures. In behavioral observation studies, the observer plays a more active role in recording the data and, therefore, is much more likely to make errors. Some of the problems include reactivity, drift, and expectancies (Kazdin, 2004). Those who are interested in more detailed information about behavioral assessment might be interested in a comprehensive Web site: mfba.net/index.

Reactivity

The reliability of observers in behavioral observation studies is usually assessed in selected sessions during which an experimenter "observes the observers." In other words, someone looks over the observer's shoulder to determine whether he or she is recording properly. Studies have shown that reliability and accuracy are highest when someone is checking on the observers. This increase in reliability is called **reactivity** because it is a reaction to being checked. In one study, observers rated behavior recorded on a videotape under one of two conditions. First, the observers were told that their ratings would be checked against a standard for accuracy. Later, the observers were told there was no standard. In both cases, there actually was a standard against which the accuracy of each was checked. The data demonstrated that accuracy dropped by 25% when the observers were led to believe their observations would not be evaluated (Reid, 1970). Indeed, many studies have demonstrated that accuracy and interrater agreement decrease when observers believe their work is not being checked (Harris & Lahey, 1982; Kent, Kanowitz, O'Leary, & Cheiken, 1977; Taplin & Reid, 1973).

To deal with this problem, some experimenters resort to covert operations. For example, the experimenter might randomly check on the performance of the observers without their knowledge. In general, you should always use caution in interpreting reports on interrater reliability. Often the estimate of rater reliability is based on assessment during training. When observers are not observed (when they are actually collecting data), then their accuracy will likely have dropped.

Drift

When trained in behavioral observation methods, observers receive extensive feedback and coaching. After they leave the training sessions, though, observers have a tendency to **drift** away from the strict rules they followed in training and to adopt idiosyncratic definitions of behavior (O'Leary & Kent, 1973; Reid & DeMaster, 1972). One of the most common problems, the *contrast effect,* is the tendency to rate the same behavior differently when observations are repeated in the same context. Standards may also shift, resulting in biased ratings of behavior. This bias can affect performance ratings or ratings of potential employees in interviews (Maurer & Alexander, 1991). Sometimes when many observers work together on the same job, they seem to drift as a group away from the original definitions of the behavior (O'Leary & Kent, 1973). Observer drift and contrast effects suggest that observers should be periodically retrained. They should also participate in frequent meetings to discuss methods. As important as these issues are for scientific studies of behavior, details are rarely reported in the scientific literature. In one review of 63 clinical trials on depression published between 1996 and 2000, only 11 studies (17%) even reported the number of raters. Only about 10% of reports of major clinical studies documented rater training. Further, only three of the 63 articles provided information on rater drift (Mulsant, Kastango, Rosen, Stone, Mazumdar, & Pollock, 2002).

Expectancies

As noted earlier, Rosenthal has accumulated evidence that the expectancies of experimenters can affect the results of behavioral experiments. Some of the Rosenthal experiments show the effects of such expectancies, whereas others do not. Similarly, some studies show that administrator expectancies can affect scores on individual IQ tests, whereas other studies do not (Sattler, 1988).

The same sort of inconsistent picture appears in the literature on behavioral observation. Some studies have shown that behavioral observers will notice the behavior they expect (Azrin, Holz, Ulrich, & Goldiamond, 1961; Scott, Burton, & Yarrow, 1967). On the other hand, some thorough studies do not support an expectancy effect (Kent et al., 1974; Redfield & Paul, 1976). Expectancies more consistently cause bias in the behavioral observation when observers receive reinforcement for recording a particular behavior than when they do not (O'Leary, Kent, & Kanowitz, 1975).

The impact of expectancy is subtle. It probably has some minor biasing effect on behavioral data. The finding that expectancy bias occurs significantly in some studies but not others is consistent with the notion that expectancy produces a minor but potentially damaging effect. To avoid this sort of bias, observers should not know what behavior to expect.

Deception

Most people feel confident that they can accurately judge other people. For example, we often feel we can figure out whether someone else is lying. Different people use different cues in their attempts to catch a liar. When President Bill Clinton was accused of having an affair with a White House intern, he initially went on television and denied it. Most observers were convinced that he was telling the truth. However, physical evidence later proved that, indeed, the president had not been truthful, though he claimed he had not *technically* lied.

Systematic studies show that most people do a remarkably poor job in detecting a liar. Many of these studies use videotapes in which someone is either lying or telling the truth. Not only do average people detect deception poorly but also so do people in professions that obligate them to detect these problems. For example, one study evaluated agents from the U.S. Secret Service, Central Intelligence Agency (CIA), and Federal Bureau of Investigation (FBI), as well as employees of the National Security Agency and of the Drug Enforcement Agency, police officers, judges, and psychiatrists. Evaluation of the data suggested that only Secret Service agents performed better than chance in spotting deception (Ekman & O'Sullivan, 1991).

The detection of lying and honesty has become a major industry (Ekman, 2003). For example, despite substantial evidence questioning their value, lie detector tests are commonly given. In addition, a new industry of "psychological services" has created commercial tests to evaluate the honesty and integrity of prospective employees. One current controversy concerns the use of tests to predict the integrity of employees. These tests supposedly estimate who would likely steal cash or merchandise. Several groups have reviewed the issue of integrity tests. The U.S. Congress's Office of Technology Assessment did so to decide whether preemployment integrity tests should be banned. Lie detectors are prohibited under the Employee Polygraph Protection Act of 1988. Although integrity tests are widely used, their validity is questionable. For example, the correlation between scores on honesty tests and documented thefts is approximately .13. In other words, the tests account for barely more than 1% of the variance in actual thefts. The Office of Technology Assessment estimated that, among those who fail the test, 95.6% would be false positives or incorrectly labeled as dishonest. Projected to a national scale, this would mean that more than 1 million U.S. workers would be falsely accused of being dishonest each year (Rieke & Guastello, 1995). In an important statement on this topic, Camara and Schneider (1994) suggested that the use of integrity tests did not meet the APA's ethical principles of psychologists and its Code of Conduct.

In rebuttal, Ones, Chockalingam, and Schmidt (1995) argued that integrity tests are valid and useful for employment decisions. They compiled more than 650 criterion-related validity coefficients using a meta-analysis concerning a half million participants. The review suggested that integrity tests, on average, are good predictors of overall supervisor ratings of job performance. The mean validity coefficient was .41. In addition, integrity tests were also correlated with measures of counterproductive behavior. Ones et al. argued then that integrity tests measure a broad construct relevant to job performance instead of providing a narrow measure of honesty. Clearly, continuing scrutiny of integrity tests is important (Lilienfeld, Alliger, & Mitchell, 1995).

Statistical Control of Rating Errors

Many efforts to improve the accuracy of raters have produced discouraging results. Attempts to increase rater reliability through extended training have been particularly frustrating for many researchers and applied psychologists because training is expensive and time-consuming. The *halo effect* is the tendency to ascribe positive attributes independently of the observed behavior. Some psychologists have argued that this effect can be controlled through *partial correlation* in which the correlation between two variables is found while variability in a third variable is controlled.

For example, one study evaluated 537 supervisory ratings of middle-level managers. Each manager was rated on 15 specific attributes and overall performance rating. Then the variance associated with the overall performance rating was separated from the other ratings. By using this method, the variance attributable to the halo effect was reduced and the discriminant validity of the method for rating performance was improved (Landy, Vance, Barnes-Farrell, & Steele, 1980). Rater characteristics may play an important role in the accuracy of evaluations. Greater cognitive abilities, higher spatial aptitudes, and critical abilities are all associated with greater accuracy. However, we need more research on factors associated with rater accuracy because accurate performance evaluations provide the basis for employee selection and advancement (Borman & Hallman, 1991).

SUMMARY

Standardized test administration procedures are necessary for valid results. Extensive research in social psychology has clearly demonstrated that situational factors can affect scores on mental and behavioral tasks. These effects, however, can be subtle and may not be observed in all studies. For example, a few studies have shown that the race of the examiner affects scores on standardized intelligence tests; however, the majority of the studies do not confirm this. Similarly, the examiner's rapport and expectancies may influence scores on some but not all occasions. Direct reinforcement of specific responses does have an acknowledged impact and therefore should not be given in most testing situations.

Interest has increased in computer-assisted test administration because it may reduce examiner bias. Computers can administer and score most tests with great precision and with minimum bias. This mode of test administration is expected to become more common in the near future. Other issues relevant to test administration are provided in recent overviews of personality testing (Beutler & Berren, 1995; Hurt, Reznikoff, & Clarkin, 1995).

The state of the subject also affects test scores. For example, some students suffer from debilitating *test anxiety,* which seriously interferes with performance.

Behavioral observation raises some of the same problems faced in test administration. In such observation, an observer records the responses of others, whereas in traditional test taking the subject records his or her own behavior. A common problem in behavioral observation is *reactivity* in which the observer is most accurate only when he or she thinks someone is checking the work. A second problem is *drift* in which observers gradually come to ignore the procedure they were taught and adopt their own observation method. A third problem is *expectancy,* or the tendency for observations to be affected by what the observer expects to observe (the *Rosenthal effect*). Though the magnitude of these effects is probably small, the potential bias they introduce is serious enough to make taking precautions a recommended practice.

WEB ACTIVITY

For interesting and relevant Web sites, check the following:

www.mfba.net
Offers an overview of multimodal functional behavioral assessment

www.state.nj.us/njded/specialed
This State of New Jersey Web site describes procedures for test administration to accommodate people with disabilities

www.psichi.org/pubs
Summary of studies on the Rosenthal effect

CHAPTER 8

Interviewing Techniques

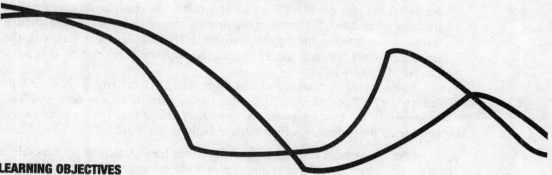

LEARNING OBJECTIVES

When you have completed this chapter, you should be able to:

☐ Explain the difference between a structured and an unstructured interview

☐ Discuss the importance of setting the proper tone for an interview

☐ Describe the role of the interviewer's attitude in the interviewing process

☐ Identify some of the characteristics of effective interviewing

☐ List which types of statements tend to keep the interaction flowing or to elicit self-exploration in the interviewee

☐ Explain the effects of empathy statements on interviewee responses

☐ Identify the various sources of error in the interview

☐ Appreciate the role of cultural, ethnic, and socioeconomic factors in the interview process

☐ Explain how interview skills are acquired and developed

aria was being considered for a high-level public relations position with the computer firm for which she worked. The job duties would require her to interact with a wide variety of people, ranging from heads of state and corporation presidents to rank-and-file employees and union officials. In addition, the position would involve making formal policy statements for news media. Any poorly phrased statement or inappropriate reaction on her part could result in adverse publicity, which could cost the firm millions of dollars. The application process therefore involved an elaborate testing procedure, including two lengthy interviews. The first was with the firm's personnel selection officer, the second with the firm's clinical psychologist (see Figure 8-1).

Knowing the importance of first impressions (Dougherty, Turban, & Callender, 1994; Roeckelein, 2002), Maria took care to appear neat and well groomed. In her first interview, the personnel officer read from a form as she conducted the interview, which went something like this:

Officer: I've read your application form and have gone over your qualifications. Would you now please outline your educational experiences, beginning with high school?

Maria: I graduated from high school in June 1990 with a major in history and social studies. I began attending college in September 1990. I graduated in June 1995 with a major in psychology and minor in business management. I then entered the university's graduate program in business. I obtained my master's degree in business administration in 1997.

Officer: What is your work history? Begin with your first full-time employment.

Maria described her work history. The personnel officer then continued a series of questions, which Maria systematically answered. The questions went something like this:

How do your education and experience relate to the job for which you are applying?

What educational experiences have you had that might help you function in the job for which you are applying?

What employment experiences have you had that might help you function in the job for which you are applying?

Identify any deficiencies in your educational and work experiences.

What educational and work experiences have you had that might impair your ability to function in the job for which you are applying?

The interview continued in a similar manner. With each question, the personnel officer attempted to relate Maria's educational and work experiences to the particular job duties she hoped to assume. For her final question, the personnel officer asked, "Why do you believe you would make a good candidate for this position?"

Maria felt good about her interview with the personnel officer. She thought the questions were clear and straightforward, and she was pleased by her an-

FIGURE 8-1

An interview.

(© Steven
Lunetta/PhotoEdit)

swers. The next day she appeared for her interview with the clinical psychologist. Unlike the personnel officer, the psychologist conducted the interview without using written interview questions. This second interview, quite different from the first, went something like this:

Psychologist:	Maria, why don't you tell me a little bit about yourself.
Maria:	Where do you want me to begin?
Psychologist:	Oh, it doesn't matter. Just tell me about yourself.
Maria:	I graduated from high school in June of 1990. I majored in history and social studies.
Psychologist:	Yes, I see.
Maria:	I then attended college and finally finished graduate school in 1997. My master's degree should help me to assume the duties of the new position.
Psychologist:	You feel that your master's degree is a useful asset in your application.
Maria:	Yes, my graduate experiences taught me how to work with others.
Psychologist:	With these graduate experiences, you learned the art of working with other people.
Maria:	Well, I guess I didn't learn it all in graduate school. I've always managed to get along well with others.
Psychologist:	As far as you can tell, you work pretty well with people.

Maria:	That's right. As the oldest of four children, I've always had the responsibility for supervising others. You know what I mean?
Psychologist:	Being the oldest, you were given extra responsibilities as a child.
Maria:	Not that I resented it. Well, maybe sometimes. It's just that I never had much time for myself.
Psychologist:	And having time for yourself is important to you.
Maria:	Yes, of course it is. I guess everybody needs some time alone.
Psychologist:	As a person who deals with others all day long, you must treasure those few moments you have to yourself.
Maria:	I really do. Whenever I get a chance I like to drive up to the lake all by myself and just think.
Psychologist:	Those moments are precious to you.

The interview continued like this for about an hour. After it was over, Maria wasn't sure how she had done. Think about the two interviews. In what ways were they alike? How did they differ? As you contemplate your answers, you will soon realize that there is more than one type of interview and that interviews can differ considerably.

The first interview with the personnel officer was highly structured. The interviewer read from a printed set of questions, using a standardized interview. Thus, all applicants for the position were asked the same questions in the same sequence. By contrast, the second was an unstructured interview and therefore unstandardized. The clinical psychologist didn't appear to have any specific or particular questions in mind, and the sequence of questions followed from Maria's statements. Each applicant, no doubt, would be asked different questions, depending on his or her responses.

Can you identify other differences between the two interviews? The first was narrow and restricted. It focused on two specific areas: Maria's education and her work experiences. The second was broad and unrestricted. Although the interview clearly focused on Maria herself, it touched on a variety of areas. The first interview was *directive*. The personnel officer directed, guided, and controlled the course of the interview. The second interview was *nondirective*. The clinical psychologist let Maria determine the direction of the interview. When Maria talked about her master's degree, the psychologist discussed it. When Maria talked about being the oldest of four children, this became the focus of the psychologist's response. Further, unlike the personnel officer, the psychologist rarely asked questions. Instead, the psychologist tended to comment or reflect on Maria's previous statement. Last, but perhaps most important, Maria's interview with the personnel officer can best be described as an employment interview, also called a *selection interview;* it was designed to elicit information pertaining to Maria's qualifications and capabilities for particular employment duties (employment interviews are discussed in greater detail in Chapter 18). The second interview, on the other hand, was a diagnostic interview, centered on Maria's emotional functioning rather than her qualifications—that is, the clinical psychologist was interested in uncovering those feelings, thoughts, and attitudes that might impede or facilitate Maria's competence.

The Interview as a Test

In many respects, an interview resembles a test (see Table 8-1). Like any psychological or educational test, an interview is a method for gathering data or information about an individual. This information is then used to describe the individual, make future predictions, or both. Like tests, interviews can be evaluated in terms of standard psychometric qualities such as reliability and validity. Furthermore, there are several types of interview procedures; each is chosen according to the type of information sought and the interviewer's goals.

Like any test, the interview involves the interaction of two or more people. Some interviews proceed like individually administered tests, with the interviewer interacting with a single individual at a time. In others, such as the family interview, a single interviewer works with two or more individuals at the same time, as in a group test. Like all tests, an interview has a defined purpose. Furthermore, just as the person who gives a test must take responsibility for the test-administration process, so the interviewer must assume responsibility for the conduct of the interview.

Many tests, such as the Thematic Apperception Test (TAT), cannot be properly used without adequate interview data. The interview, on the other hand, is often the only or most important source of data. The interview remains one of the most prevalent selection devices for employment (Posthuma, Morgeson, & Campion, 2002). Good interviewing skills may be one of the most important tools for functioning in today's society. Furthermore, interviewing is the chief method of collecting data in clinical psychiatry (Allen & Smith, 1993; Groth-Marnat, 2003; Shaffer, 1994). It is also used in all health-related professions, including general medicine and nursing (Eggly, 2002). Interviewing is an essential testing tool in subspecialties such as clinical, industrial, counseling, school, and correctional psychology.

A wide variety of other professions depend on interviewing. Indeed, interview skills are important in most professions that involve people: social workers, vocational and guidance counselors, and marriage and family counselors;

TABLE 8-1

Similarities Between an Interview and a Test

Method for gathering data
Used to make predictions
Evaluated in terms of reliability
Evaluated in terms of validity
Group or individual
Structured or unstructured

parole boards; researchers; businesspeople (to evaluate employees as well as potential clients); courtroom attorneys; contractors or architects (to determine exactly what their customers want them to do)—the list goes on and on. Interviewing also plays a role in our nonprofessional lives, such as when a parent questions a group of children to find out whose soccer ball broke the window. To begin new relationships on a positive note, one must possess a degree of interviewing skill. Given such a broad application, no introductory text on psychological tests could be complete without reference to the interview.

Reciprocal Nature of Interviewing

Although there are many types and purposes of interviews, all share certain factors. First, all interviews involve mutual interaction whereby the participants are interdependent—that is, they influence each other (Breggin, 2002; Ridge, Campbell, & Martin 2002). A study by Akehurst and Vrij (1999) illustrates the transactional or reciprocal nature of the interview process. Criminal suspects were observed while being interrogated. The researchers found that if one of the participants in the interview increased his or her activity level, then the activity of the other participant also increased. Similarly, a reduction in activity by one triggered a reduction in the other. The researchers concluded that the participants in an interview profoundly affect each other. Unfortunately for the suspects, a second experiment demonstrated that increased activity on the part of the suspect was related to increased suspiciousness on the part of the interrogator. Results revealed that highly active interrogators increased activity in the suspects, which, in turn, increased the interrogators' suspiciousness (Akehurst & Vrij, 1999).

Interview participants also affect each other's mood. In a classic study, Heller (1971) found that when professional actors responded with anger to highly trained, experienced interviewers, the interviewers became angry themselves and showed anger toward the actors. In this phenomenon, called *social facilitation*, we tend to act like the models around us. If the interviewer is tense, anxious, defensive, and aloof, then the interviewee tends to respond in kind. Thus, if the interviewer wishes to create conditions of openness, warmth, acceptance, comfort, calmness, and support, then he or she must exhibit these qualities.

Because the participants in an interview influence each other, the good interviewer knows how to provide a relaxed and safe atmosphere through social facilitation. However, although both parties influence each other, the good interviewer remains in control and sets the tone. If he or she reacts to the interviewee's tension and anxiety with more tension and anxiety, then these feelings will mount. By remaining relaxed, confident, and self-assured, the interviewer has a calming effect on the interviewee. Even potentially violent prison inmates or disturbed psychotic people can become manageable when the interviewer sets the proper tone. Clearly, social facilitation is one of the most important concepts underlying the interview process.

Principles of Effective Interviewing

Naturally, specific interviewing techniques and approaches vary, depending on such factors as the type of interview (e.g., employment versus diagnostic) and the goals of the interviewer (e.g., description versus prediction). Thus, there are no set rules that apply to all interviewing situations. However, some principles facilitate the conduct of almost any interview. Knowing these principles will not only increase your understanding of the factors and processes that underlie the interview but also help you acquire interview skills of your own.

The Proper Attitudes

Good interviewing is actually more a matter of attitude than skill (Duan & Kivlighan, 2002; Tyler, 1969). Experiments in social psychology have shown that *interpersonal influence* (the degree to which one person can influence another) is related to *interpersonal attraction* (the degree to which people share a feeling of understanding, mutual respect, similarity, and the like) (Dillard & Marshall, 2003; Green & Kenrick, 1994; Hensley, 1994). Attitudes related to good interviewing skills include warmth, genuineness, acceptance, understanding, openness, honesty, and fairness. For example, Saccuzzo (1975) studied the initial psychotherapeutic interviews of first-year clinical psychology graduate students. Patients and therapists both responded to a questionnaire. Their task was to rate the quality of the interview and indicate the topics, concerns, problems, and feelings of the patient as well as the feelings of the therapist.

The most important factor in the patients' evaluation was their perception of the interviewer's feelings. The session received a good evaluation by both participants when the patient saw the interviewer as warm, open, concerned, involved, committed, and interested, regardless of subject matter or the type or severity of the problem. On the other hand, independent of all other factors, when the interviewer was seen as cold, defensive, uninterested, uninvolved, aloof, and bored, the session was rated poorly. To appear effective and establish rapport, the interviewer must display the proper attitudes.

Responses to Avoid

In a "stress interview," the interviewer may deliberately induce discomfort or anxiety in the interviewee. As a rule, however, making interviewees feel uncomfortable tends to place them on guard, and guarded or anxious interviewees tend to reveal little information about themselves. However, one purpose of the stress interview is to determine how well an individual functions in adversity and the types of responses that interviewers should avoid. If the goal is to elicit as much information as possible or to receive a good rating from the interviewee, then interviewers should avoid certain responses, including judgmental or evaluative statements, probing statements, hostility, and false reassurance.

Judgmental or evaluative statements are particularly likely to inhibit the interviewee. Being *judgmental* means evaluating the thoughts, feelings, or actions of another. When we use such terms as *good, bad, excellent, terrible, disgusting, disgraceful,* and *stupid,* we make evaluative statements. By judging others, we put them on guard because we communicate the message "I don't approve of this aspect of you." Such judgments also inhibit others' ease in revealing important information. Thus, unless the goal of the interview is to determine how a person responds to being evaluated, evaluative or judgmental statements should usually be avoided.

Most interviewers should also avoid probing statements. These demand more information than the interviewee wishes to provide voluntarily. The most common way to phrase a probing statement is to ask a question that begins with "Why?" Asking "Why?" tends to place others on the defensive. When we ask "Why?" as in "Why did you stay out so late?" we are demanding that the person explain his or her behavior. Such a demand has an obvious judgmental quality. Furthermore, in probing we may induce the interviewee to reveal something that he or she is not yet ready to reveal. If this happens, the interviewee will probably feel anxious and thus not well disposed to revealing additional information.

In some circumstances, probes are appropriate and necessary. With children or individuals with mental retardation, for instance, one often needs to ask questions to elicit meaningful information (Devoe & Faller, 2002). Highly anxious or withdrawn individuals may also need a probe to get beyond a superficial interchange. In such circumstances, one must use the probe wisely, avoiding "Why?" statements and replacing them with "Tell me" or "How?" statements, as illustrated in Table 8-2.

The hostile statement directs anger toward the interviewee. Clearly, one should avoid such responses unless one has a specific purpose, such as determining how an interviewee responds to anger.

The reassuring statement attempts to comfort or support the interviewee: "Don't worry. Everything will be all right." Though reassurance is sometimes appropriate, you should almost always avoid false reassurance. For example,

TABLE 8-2
Effective Probing Statements

Poor	Better
Why did you yell at him?	1. Tell me more about what happened.
	2. How did you happen to yell at him?
	3. What led up to the situation?
Why did you say that?	1. Can you tell me what you mean?
	2. I'm not sure I understand.
	3. How did you happen to say that?
Why can't you sleep?	1. Tell me more about your sleeping problem.
	2. Can you identify what prevents you from sleeping?
	3. How is it that you are unable to sleep?

FIGURE 8-2
Responses to avoid in an unstructured interview.

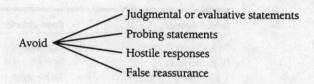

imagine a friend of yours flunks out of college, loses her job, and gets kicked out of her home by her parents. You are lying to this person when you say, "Don't worry; no problem; it's okay." This false reassurance does nothing to help your friend except perhaps make her realize that you are not going to help her. What has happened to your friend is terrible and will require specific action on her part to prevent even more disastrous developments. Naturally, you should not overwhelm your friend with all the facts at once, but she needs to come to grips with the situation in manageable doses before taking the necessary steps to constructively solve the problem. The person who gives false reassurance usually knows he or she is doing it, as does the person who receives it (see Figure 8-2).

Effective Responses

Knowing what types of responses to avoid, how does one go about conducting an effective interview? One major principle of effective interviewing is keeping the interaction flowing. The interview is a two-way process; first one person speaks, then the other, and so on. Furthermore, the interviewer usually exerts a minimum amount of effort to keep the interaction flowing. As long as the interviewee's verbalizations relate to the purpose of the interview, the interviewer listens with interest by maintaining face-to-face contact.

Except in structured interviews or for a particular purpose, one can effectively initiate the interview process by using an open-ended question. This is one that usually cannot be answered specifically, as opposed to a closed-ended question, which can. Examples of open-ended questions are "Tell me a little bit about yourself," "Tell me about what interests you," and "What is it that brings you here to see me?" Examples of closed-ended questions are "Do you like sports?" "Are you married?" and "How old are you?"

A closed-ended question brings the interview to a dead halt, thus violating the principle of keeping the interaction flowing. In the example at the beginning of this chapter, even the personnel officer's opening statement—"Would you please outline your educational experiences"—was sufficiently open-ended to permit a variety of responses, depending on the interviewee. Where one individual might provide every minute detail of his or her education, a second might simply include major events. The clinical psychologist's opening statement—"Why don't you tell me a little bit about yourself?"—was even more open-ended. Maria could have replied with just about anything.

Open-ended questions give the interviewee wide latitude in choosing the topics that he or she feels are important. Except for highly specific structured

TABLE 8-3
Open- and Closed-Ended Questions

Closed-ended	Open-ended
Do you like sports cars?	What kinds of cars do you like?
Do you like baseball?	What kinds of recreational activities do you prefer?
Are you having a problem?	Tell me about your problems.
Is your father strict?	Describe your father.
Would you like to vacation in Hawaii?	What are your favorite vacation spots?

interviews, we usually can learn a lot more about people when they tell us what they think is important than when we try to guess by asking a series of closed-ended questions. The open-ended question requires the interviewee to produce something spontaneously; the closed-ended question to recall something. Table 8-3 presents some closed-ended questions along with corresponding open-ended ones.

Conducting an interview requires flexibility. If not structured, most interviews cannot be conducted in precisely the same way. In therapeutic or diagnostic interviews, interviewers usually follow only general guidelines in conducting the interview. Their goal is to get to know the interviewees as well as possible to understand them and predict their behavior.

Responses to Keep the Interaction Flowing

After asking the open-ended question, the interviewer as a rule lets the interviewee respond without interruption; that is, the interviewer remains quiet and listens. Unless the interview is structured, once the interviewee's response dies down, the interviewer usually responds in a way that will keep the interaction flowing. (See Table 8-4 for a summary of responses that do this.) He or she should use minimum effort to maintain the flow, such as using a transitional phrase such as "Yes," "And," or "I see." These phrases imply that the interviewee should continue on the same topic. In Maria's interview with the clinical psychologist, for example, Maria stated, "I graduated from high school in June 1990. I majored in history and social studies." The clinical psychologist simply responded with the transition, "Yes, I see." Maria then elaborated.

TABLE 8-4
Responses to Keep the Interaction Flowing

Response	Definition or example
Transitional phrase	"Yes," "I see," "Go on"
Verbatim playback	Repeats interviewee's exact words
Paraphrasing and restatement	Repeats interviewee's response using different words
Summarizing	Pulls together the meaning of several responses
Clarification response	Clarifies the interviewee's response
Empathy and understanding	Communicates understanding

Sometimes the transitional phrase fails to have the desired effect. When this occurs, the interviewer should make a response relevant to what has just been communicated. In other words, the interview is thematic; it does not jump from one unrelated topic to another as it might if the interviewer asked a series of set questions. The theme in Maria's interview with the clinical psychologist was Maria. Although the topics changed from Maria's education to her feelings about being the oldest of four, Maria herself remained the central focus. The psychologist accomplished this by making statements relevant to what Maria was saying.

To make such a response, the interviewer may use any of the following types of statements: verbatim playback, paraphrasing, restatement, summarizing, clarifying, and understanding. You can view these statements on a continuum ranging from being totally interchangeable with the interviewee's response to adding to or going beyond it.

In a *verbatim playback,* the interviewer simply repeats the interviewee's last response. For example, in his interview with the clinical psychologist, Maria stated, "I majored in history and social studies." The psychologist replied with the transitional phrase "Yes, I see." A verbatim playback, "You majored in history and social studies," would have been equally effective. In either case, Maria most likely would continue to elaborate on her previous response. Thus, like the transitional phrase, the verbatim playback generally leads to an elaboration of the interviewee's previous response.

Paraphrasing and *restatement* responses are also interchangeable with the interviewee's response. A paraphrase tends to be more similar to the interviewee's response than a restatement, but both capture the meaning of the interviewee's response. When Maria said, "My master's degree should help me assume the duties of the new position," the psychologist replied, "You feel that your master's degree is a useful asset in your application"—a restatement. A paraphrase might have taken the form "You feel that your master's degree will be an important aid in taking on the responsibilities of the new position." In his restatement, the psychologist introduced "useful asset" to restate Maria's attitude toward her master's degree. The paraphrase, on the other hand, simply substituted "important aid" for "help" and "taking on the responsibilities" for "assuming the duties." Neither statement added anything to Maria's. Both, however, communicated to Maria that the interviewer was listening, and made it easy for Maria to elaborate.

Summarizing and *clarification* statements go just beyond the interviewee's response. In summarizing, the interviewer pulls together the meaning of several interviewee responses. To Maria's last statement in the example, the psychologist could have replied with the summarizing statement "As a youth you never had much time to yourself because you were responsible for taking care of the three younger children. Today you enjoy those few moments you have to be alone. Whenever you get a chance to be alone you drive to the lake all by yourself and just think." Notice that this summarizing statement involves verbatim playback, paraphrasing, and restating. With these three types of statements, the psychologist summarizes an entire sequence of responses.

The clarification statement, as its name implies, serves to clarify the interviewee's response. When Maria stated "Not that I resented it. Well, maybe sometimes. It's just that I never had much time for myself," the psychologist attempted to clarify what Maria was trying to say. It was not that Maria resented the extra responsibilities; rather, she simply wanted some time to be alone. Thus, the psychologist clarified Maria's statement by saying, "And having time for yourself is important to you."

Like summarizing, paraphrasing, restatement, and verbatim playback, the clarification statement remains close to the meaning of the interviewee's response. Each of these interviewer responses communicates a degree of understanding. At the lowest level, the verbatim playback communicates that the interviewer at least heard the communication. The restatement, paraphrase, and summarizing responses go a bit further by communicating that the interviewer has a good idea of what the interviewee is trying to communicate. And clarification shows yet further comprehension.

Even more powerful is the empathy or understanding response. This response communicates that the interviewer understands how the interviewee *feels.* When the psychologist stated, "These moments are precious to you," he did not simply paraphrase or restate. Instead, he communicated that he understood how Maria felt about having time to herself.

Many students find it difficult to see the value of statements that stay close to the interviewee's response. Some students consider such statements artificial and weak because of their noncommittal quality. However, the rationale for such responses is based on the well-known and well-documented finding that when we show people we understand, they will talk about or explore themselves at ever deeper levels (Maj, Gaebel, Lopez-Ibor, & Sartorius, 2002; Rogers, 1980; Walker, 2001). Accurate empathy elicits self-exploration. Consider the following example:

Psychologist:	What's been happening today, Kerry? *(open-ended question)*
Kerry:	My physics teacher yelled at me in front of the whole class.
Psychologist:	That's embarrassing. *(understanding)*
Kerry:	Not only that, she seems to pick on me all the time.
Psychologist:	That must make you angry. *(understanding)*
Kerry:	Yeah, I guess so. It seems like she's always finding fault with my work. No matter what I do, she just doesn't like it.
Psychologist:	That is really frustrating, Kerry. You just can't seem to please her. *(understanding)*
Kerry:	The other day we had an exam and I got an F. I checked my answers with Hector, and mine were the same as his. Yet I got an F and Hector got a B.
Psychologist:	Hey, that doesn't seem fair. *(clarification and understanding)*
Kerry:	You bet it isn't fair. But when I tried to talk to her about it, she refused to listen.

Psychologist:	That's scary. (*understanding*)
Kerry:	It sure is. If I get one more F, I'll be kicked out of school.
Psychologist:	This is really serious. (*clarification*)
Kerry:	Yeah, If I got kicked out of school, I couldn't face my parents or friends.
Psychologist:	This whole thing has got you really upset (*understanding*).

Certainly, the psychologist's responses are not the only ones that would work. However, note how the psychologist, in providing a series of understanding responses, "uncovered" the real source of Kerry's anguish. The feelings Kerry expressed moved from embarrassment to anger to fear of being kicked out of school and finally to fear of how his friends and family would view his failure.

Let's consider four other responses that the psychologist could have made to Kerry's initial statement, "My physics teacher yelled at me in front of the whole class."

1. "Why did she do that?" With this probing statement, Kerry has to defend himself or explain why it happened. He has to go over the circumstances that preceded the incident, actually leading away from Kerry's real feelings and concerns.

2. "Why did you let her do that to you? That wasn't very smart of you." This evaluative statement places Kerry on the defensive, criticizes him, and possibly hurts his feelings. Given this type of reaction from the psychologist, Kerry will not feel safe exploring his real feelings.

3. "That woman is always yelling at somebody. You should report her to the dean." With this off-the-cuff advice, the psychologist again removes himself from Kerry's real concerns. The two might spend the rest of their time together weighing the pros and cons of reporting Kerry's physics teacher. Still worse, Kerry might impulsively follow the advice and get into real trouble if he cannot substantiate his claims.

4. "Don't worry. That physics teacher yells at everyone. It doesn't mean a thing." With this false reassurance, Kerry is no longer free to express his real concern. The psychologist has already dismissed the whole matter as insignificant.

In short, understanding responses that stay close to the content and underlying feeling provided by interviewees permit them to explore their situations more and more fully. Effective unstructured interviewing serves to uncover information from the interviewee. One good way to accomplish this involves what we call *understanding statements*. To establish a positive atmosphere, interviewers begin with an open-ended question followed by understanding statements that capture the meaning and feeling of the interviewee's communication. See Figure 8-3 for an exercise in keeping the interaction flowing.

FIGURE 8-3
Exercise in keeping the interaction flowing.

Directions: Below is a list of statements, each followed by two possible replies. Select the one that would tend to keep the interaction flowing.

1. I hate school.
   ☐ a. It sounds like you're fed up with school.
   ☐ b. What's wrong with school?

2. My dad is a jerk.
   ☐ a. Why don't you just tell him to "chill out"?
   ☐ b. You're angry with your dad.

3. Most people are liars.
   ☐ a. Don't be so negative.
   ☐ b. You feel that most people can't be trusted.

4. We were ahead until the last minute of the game.
   ☐ a. That's disappointing.
   ☐ b. Why didn't you win?

5. She stood me up again.
   ☐ a. If I were you, I wouldn't ask her out again.
   ☐ b. It hurts to be treated like that.

6. I hope I passed the test.
   ☐ a. You're worried about how you did on the test.
   ☐ b. Don't worry. I'm sure you passed.

Answers: 1. a; 2. b; 3. b; 4. a; 5. b; 6. a

Notes:
1b is a probing statement.
2a is advice.
3a is advice.
4b is a probing statement.
5a is advice.
6b is false reassurance.

Measuring Understanding

We can further appreciate understanding statements by analyzing measures of understanding. Attempts to measure understanding or empathy originated with Carl Rogers's seminal research into the effects of client-centered therapy (Rogers, 1959a, 1959b; Walker, Rablen, & Rogers, 1960). It culminated in a 5-point scoring system (Truax & Carkhuff, 1967, pp. 46–58) that has since been revised (Carkhuff & Berenson, 1967). Each level in this system represents a degree of empathy. The levels range from a response that bears little or no relationship to the previous statement to a response that captures the precise meaning and feeling of the statement. The highest degrees of empathy, levels four and five, are relevant primarily for therapeutic interviews. Level three represents various degrees of true empathy or understanding and may be used in all types of unstructured or semistructured (that is, partially structured) interviews. The lowest levels, one and two, have no place in a professional interview and should be avoided. Low-level responses, however, occur frequently in everyday conversations. We discuss these levels to illustrate one way to measure understanding.

Level-one responses. Level-one responses bear little or no relationship to the interviewee's response. A level-one conversation might proceed as follows:

Sarah: Victor, look at my new dress.

Victor: I sure hope it doesn't rain today.

Sarah: See, it's red with blue stripes.

Victor: If it rains, my baseball game might get canceled.

Sarah: I really love this dress, it's my favorite.

Victor: It's sure going to tick me off if that game gets canceled.

The two are really talking only to themselves.

Level-two responses. The level-two response communicates a superficial awareness of the meaning of a statement. The individual who makes a level-two response never quite goes beyond his or her own limited perspective. Level-two responses impede the flow of communication. For example,

Sarah: Boy, I feel good. I just got a beautiful new dress.

Victor: I feel bad. It's probably going to rain.

Sarah: I'll wear this dress to your baseball game.

Victor: If it rains, there won't be a game.

Here the conversation is related, but only superficially. Neither person really responds to what is going on with the other.

Level-three responses. A level-three response is interchangeable with the interviewee's statement. According to Carkhuff and Berenson (1967), level three is the minimum level of responding that can help the interviewee. Paraphrasing, verbatim playback, clarification statements, and restatements are all examples of level-three responses.

Level-four and level-five responses. Level-four and level-five responses not only provide accurate empathy but also go beyond the statement given. In a level-four response, the interviewer adds "noticeably" to the interviewee's response.

In a level-five response, the interviewer adds "significantly" to it (Carkhuff & Berenson, 1967). We recommend that beginning interviewers learn to respond at level three before going on to the more advanced levels. In the example with Sarah and Victor, a level-four interchange might proceed as follows:

Sarah: I just got a new dress.

Victor: You feel happy because you like new clothes.

Sarah: This one is beautiful; it has red and blue stripes.

Victor: You really love that new dress. It is a nice addition to your wardrobe.

Active listening. An impressive array of research has accumulated to document the power of the understanding response (Laub, 2002; Norcross & Beutler, 1997; Rogers, 1980; Truax & Mitchell, 1971). This type of responding, sometimes called *active listening,* is the foundation of good interviewing skills for many different types of interviews.

Types of Interviews

The previously discussed guides provide a general format for conducting an interview. The specifics vary, however, depending on the interviewer's goal, purpose, and theoretical orientation. We shall distinguish here among four types of interviews: the evaluation interview, the structured clinical interview, the case history interview, and the mental status examination. (For information on the employment or selection interview, see Chapter 18.)

Evaluation Interview

Maloney and Ward's (1976) conception of an evaluation interview provides guides that are similar to those presented in this chapter. This similarity is not surprising because both methods stem from the research-based principle that accurate understanding leads to self-exploration (Breggin, Breggin, & Bemak, 2002). Thus, Maloney and Ward recommend beginning with an open-ended question, with the interviewer "listening, facilitating, and clarifying" during the initial phases of the interview. In addition, they recommend that the powerful tool of confrontation be included in the process.

Though confrontation is usually most appropriate in therapeutic interviews, all experienced interviewers should have this technique at their disposal. A confrontation is a statement that points out a discrepancy or inconsistency. Carkhuff (1969) distinguished among three types: (1) a discrepancy between what the person is and what he or she wants to become, (2) a discrepancy between what the person says about him- or herself and what he or she does, and (3) a discrepancy between the person's perception of him- or herself and the interviewer's experience of the person.

Confrontation may induce anxiety by bringing conflicts or inconsistencies into a person's awareness when he or she is not ready to handle them. We therefore strongly recommend that the beginning student leave confrontation for the more experienced practitioner.

Direct questions can be used toward the end of the interview to fill in any needed details or gaps in the interviewer's knowledge. For unstructured or semistructured interviews, we advocate the use of direct questions whenever (1) the data can be obtained in no other way, (2) time is limited and the interviewer needs specific information, or (3) the interviewee cannot or will not cooperate with the interviewer. The open-ended, facilitative technique does not work well for nonverbal, intellectually limited, and uncooperative subjects (Dattilo, Hoge, & Malley, 1996; Othmer & Othmer, 2002). It also doesn't work well with children, who require direct questioning and careful observation (Devoe & Faller, 2002; Hershkowitz, 2002; Shaffer, 1994). With these subjects, it is exceedingly difficult to get the interview off the ground. Thus, direct questioning becomes necessary.

Structured Clinical Interviews

Over the past two decades, structured clinical interviews have proliferated (Costello, Moss, Prosser, & Hatton, 1997; Craig, 2003; Grillis & Ollendick, 2002; Segal, 1997; Summerfeldt & Antony, 2002). Recall that structured interviews provide a specific set of questions presented in a particular order. In addition, there is usually a carefully specified set of rules for probing so that, as in a standardized test, all interviewees are handled in the same manner. Structured interviews lend themselves to scoring procedures from which norms can be developed and applied. Typically, cutoff scores are used so that a particular score indicates the presence or absence of a given condition.

The development of structured clinical interviews followed the evolution of the *Diagnostic and Statistical Manual of Mental Disorders* (DSM). First published in 1952 and revised in 1968, 1980, 1987, and 1994, the DSM attempts to classify mental disorders into specific, definable categories. Before the 1980 DSM-III however, mental disorders were poorly defined. The result was a markedly low reliability in psychiatric diagnosis.

The DSM-III and subsequent editions (DSM-IV and DSM-IV-TR) attempted to overcome this lack of reliability by providing a specific set of criteria for each category of mental disorder. As an example, Table 8-5 shows the diagnostic criteria for an obsessive–compulsive disorder from the DSM-IV (American Psychiatric Association, 1994).

With specifiable criteria for mental disorders, one could develop a specific set of questions to determine whether or not a person met the criteria. For example, Spitzer and colleagues developed a comprehensive interview specifically for making diagnoses from the DSM-III-R called the Structured Clinical Interview for the DSM-III-R, or the SCID (Spitzer, Williams, Gibbon, & First, 1990a). Table 8-6 provides an example of the SCID used to diagnose obsessive–compulsive disorder. Notice that the interview formula is quite specific, allows for a specific scoring system, and makes clear-cut provisions for unclear responses.

TABLE 8-5

Diagnostic Criteria for an Obsessive–Compulsive Disorder

A. Either obsessions or compulsions

Obsessions

1. Recurrent and persistent thoughts, impulses, or images that are experienced as intrusive and inappropriate and that cause marked anxiety or distress.
2. The thoughts, impulses, or images are not simply excessive worries about real-life problems.
3. The person attempts to ignore or suppress such thoughts, impulses, or images or to neutralize them with some other thought or action.
4. The person recognizes that the obsessions, impulses, or images are the product of his or her own mind.

Compulsions

1. Repetitive behaviors (e.g., hand washing, ordering, checking) or mental acts (e.g., praying, counting, repeating words silently) that the person feels driven to perform in response to an obsession, or according to rules that must be applied rigidly.
2. The behavior or mental acts are aimed at preventing or reducing distress or preventing some dreaded event or situation; however, these behaviors or mental acts either are not connected in a realistic way with what they are designed to neutralize or prevent or are clearly excessive.

From *Diagnostic and Statistical Manual of Mental Disorders,* Fourth Edition, Revised (DSM-IV). Washington, DC: American Psychiatric Association, 1994.

Today, there are countless structured interviews for just about every imaginable problem. Interviews are available to:

- assess disorders in children such as the Diagnostic Interview Schedule for Children and various revisions (or DISC, DISC-R, DISC-2) (Hodges, 1994; Shaffer, 1994), DISCO-9 (Leekham, Libby, Wing, Gould, & Taylor, 2002), and the Child Assessment Schedule (CAS) (Allen, 1994);

- assess personality disorders such as the Structured Clinical Interview for DSM-III-R-Personality Disorders, or SCID-II (Spitzer, Williams, Gibbon, & First, 1990b); and

- do preliminary screening of mental illness in jails through the Referral Decision Scale, or RDS (Teplin & Schwartz, 1989).

There are also:

- the Structured Clinical Interview for Separation Anxiety Symptoms (Cyranowski et al., 2002), which is used for both children and adults;

- the Edinburgh Postnatal Depression Scale (EPDS) (Garcia-Esteve, Ascaso, Ojuel, & Navarro, 2003);

- the Diagnostic Interview Schedule;

- the Anxiety Disorders Interview Schedule for DSM-IV; and

- the Structured Clinical Interview for DSM-IV Axis-I Disorders (Summerfeldt & Antony, 2002).

As we have emphasized, structured interviews offer reliability but sacrifice flexibility. They can especially help researchers document and define a specific group. For example, if you plan to study obsessive–compulsive disorder, then

TABLE 8-6
SCID 9/1/89 Version Obsessive–Compulsive Disorder Anxiety Disorders

Obsessive–compulsive disorder	Obsessive–compulsive disorder criteria				
	A. Either obsessions or compulsions:				
Now I would like to ask you if you have ever been bothered by thoughts that didn't make any sense and kept coming back to you even when you tried not to have them? (What were they?)	Obsessions: (1), (2), (3), and (4):	?	1	2	3
	(1) Recurrent and persistent ideas, thoughts, impulses, or images that are experienced, at least initially, as intrusive and senseless, e.g., a parent's having repeated impulses to hurt a loved child, a religious person's having recurrent blasphemous thoughts				
(What about awful thoughts, like actually hurting someone even though you didn't want to, or being contaminated by germs or dirt?)	NOTE: DO NOT INCLUDE BROODING ABOUT PROBLEMS (SUCH AS HAVING A PANIC ATTACK) OR ANXIOUS RUMINATIONS ABOUT REALISTIC DANGERS.				
When you had these thoughts, did you try hard to get them out of your head? (What would you try to do?)	(2) The person attempts to ignore or suppress such thoughts or to neutralize them with some other thoughts or action	?	1	2	3
IF UNCLEAR: Where did you think these thoughts were coming from?	(3) The person recognizes that the obsessions are the product of his or her own mind, not imposed from without (as in thought insertion)	?	1	2	3
	(4) If another Axis I disorder is present, the content of the obsession is unrelated to it, i.e., the ideas, thoughts, impulses, or images are not about food in the presence of an Eating Disorder, about drugs in the presence of a Psychoactive Substance Use Disorder, or guilty thoughts in the presence of a Major Depression	?	1	2	3
					OBSES-SIONS
	DESCRIBE:				
Was there ever anything that you had to do over and over again and couldn't resist doing, like washing your hands again and again, or checking something several times to make sure you'd done it right?	Compulsions: (1), (2), and (3):	?	1	2	3
	(1) Repetitive, purposeful, and intentional behaviors that are performed in response to an obsession, or according to certain rules, or in a stereotyped fashion				
IF YES: What did you have to do? (What were you afraid would happen if you didn't do it?) (How many times did you have to _____? How much time did you spend each day _____?)	(2) The behavior is designed to neutralize or prevent discomfort or some dreaded event or situation; however, either the activity is not connected in a realistic way with what it is designed to neutralize or prevent, or it is clearly excessive	?	1	2	3
IF UNCLEAR: Do you think that you (DO COMPULSIVE BEHAVIOR) more than you should? (Do you think [COMPULSION] makes sense?)	(3) The person recognizes that the behavior is excessive or unreasonable (this may no longer be true for people whose obsessions have evolved into overvalued ideas)	?	1	2	3

Continued

TABLE 8-6

Continued

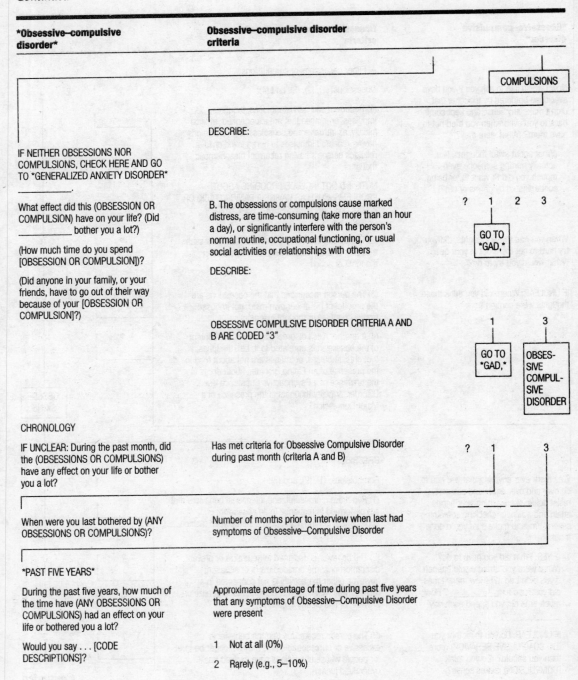

Obsessive–compulsive disorder	Obsessive–compulsive disorder criteria	

COMPULSIONS

DESCRIBE:

IF NEITHER OBSESSIONS NOR COMPULSIONS, CHECK HERE AND GO TO *GENERALIZED ANXIETY DISORDER* _____.

What effect did this (OBSESSION OR COMPULSION) have on your life? (Did _____ bother you a lot?)

(How much time do you spend [OBSESSION OR COMPULSION])?

(Did anyone in your family, or your friends, have to go out of their way because of your [OBSESSION OR COMPULSION]?)

B. The obsessions or compulsions cause marked distress, are time-consuming (take more than an hour a day), or significantly interfere with the person's normal routine, occupational functioning, or usual social activities or relationships with others

DESCRIBE:

    ?   1   2   3

GO TO *GAD,*

OBSESSIVE COMPULSIVE DISORDER CRITERIA A AND B ARE CODED "3"

    1   3

GO TO *GAD,*

OBSES- SIVE COMPUL- SIVE DISORDER

CHRONOLOGY

IF UNCLEAR: During the past month, did the (OBSESSIONS OR COMPULSIONS) have any effect on your life or bother you a lot?

Has met criteria for Obsessive Compulsive Disorder during past month (criteria A and B)

    ?   1   3

When were you last bothered by (ANY OBSESSIONS OR COMPULSIONS)?

Number of months prior to interview when last had symptoms of Obsessive–Compulsive Disorder

PAST FIVE YEARS

During the past five years, how much of the time have (ANY OBSESSIONS OR COMPULSIONS) had an effect on your life or bothered you a lot?

Would you say . . . [CODE DESCRIPTIONS]?

Approximate percentage of time during past five years that any symptoms of Obsessive–Compulsive Disorder were present

1   Not at all (0%)

2   Rarely (e.g., 5–10%)

	3 A significant minority of the time (e.g., 20–30%)
	4 About half the time
	5 A significant majority of the time (e.g., 70–80%)
	6 Almost all the time (e.g., 90–100%)
	7 Unknown
How old were you when the (OBSESSIONS OR COMPULSIONS) first had any effect on your life or bothered you a lot?	Age at onset of Obsessive–Compulsive Disorder (criteria A and B) (CODE 99 IF UNKNOWN) ___ ___

? = inadequate information   1 = absent or false   2 = subthreshold   3 = threshold or true

you need subjects who fall into this category, and there is no better way to document such subjects than to conduct a structured clinical interview. Of course, if you don't know what you're looking for, a structured interview that covers more than 20 diagnoses could become quite a lengthy task. Such interviews require the cooperation of the interviewee, which is not always easy to obtain when the interviewee is a disturbed mental patient or in acute distress.

A major limitation of the structured interview is that it relies exclusively on the respondent. It assumes that the respondent is honest and capable of accurate self-observation and that the respondent will provide frank, candid answers, even to embarrassing questions. As we discuss in Chapter 13, such assumptions cannot always be considered valid. Particularly in forensic settings, one often should not accept the validity of an interviewee's response at face value. After all, if a person facing a death sentence pleads insanity, then we may be wise not to believe the response "Yes, I hear voices all the time." In a less dramatic situation, an interviewee may simply be trying to impress the interviewer or dramatize his or her plight by endorsing symptoms that are not really present. Thus, although structured interviews may be a valuable source of information, you should interpret the results from such procedures cautiously.

Case History Interview

An interview that begins with an open-ended question followed by level-three and perhaps level-four responses can yield a wealth of data about an individual. The interviewer obtains an in-depth description of those factors most important to the interviewee. However, case history data may or may not be revealed, depending on their relevance to central issues in the interviewee's life. To obtain a complete case history—that is, a biographical sketch—one often needs to ask specific questions. Case history data may include a chronology of major events in the person's life, a work history, a medical history, and a family history. A family history should include a complete listing of the ages and genders of each member of the immediate family. One should also note whether any family members—including parents, grandparents, uncles, aunts, and siblings—have had difficulties similar to those of the interviewee. Many conditions occur more frequently in families than in the general population (Allen, 1994; Fairburn & Harrison, 2003; Rush, 2003).

In obtaining a case history, the interviewer often takes a developmental approach, examining an individual's entire life, beginning with infancy or the point at which the given type of history is first relevant. For example, the interviewer may say, "Tell me about your work record, beginning with your first paid job." After the work history is clarified, another category such as medical history can be explored.

The purpose of obtaining a case history is to understand individuals' backgrounds so that one can accurately interpret individual test scores. Toward this end, one should attempt to uncover information pertaining to religious preference, premarital and marital experiences, hobbies, education, accomplishments, and habits. Lifestyle information such as smoking behavior, use of alcohol, exercise patterns, and current stressors can also be useful. If a child is the focus of the interview, then information about the parent as well as the child should be obtained (Kefyalew, 1996).

Case history interviews are relatively easy to present on a computer rather than in person (Harlow, Boulmetis, Clark, & Willis, 2003; Nurius, 1990; Turner, Ku, Rogers, Lindberg, & Pleck, 1998). Naturally, such interviews are highly structured. They do, however, possess some flexibility through structured branching in which algorithms make questions contingent on an examinee's responses. For example, the interviewee may be asked, "Do you smoke?" If the answer is "no," then the program goes to the next main question. If the answer is "yes," however, the questioning branches into other questions about smoking, such as "How many cigarettes do you smoke per day?" "How long have you been smoking?" and "Have you ever tried to quit?" Still another branch may relate to previous efforts to quit, such as "How many times have you tried to quit?" See Table 8-7 for an example of part of a branching algorithm.

Computerized interviews have the advantage of nearly perfect interviewer reliability. However, unlike a human interviewer, the computer cannot respond to facial expressions and similar nonverbal cues, so in some situations valuable information is lost.

Mental Status Examination

An important tool in psychiatric and neurological examinations, the mental status examination is used primarily to diagnose psychosis, brain damage, and other major mental health problems. Its purpose is to evaluate a person suspected of having neurological or emotional problems in terms of variables known to be related to these problems.

The areas covered in the mental status examination include the person's appearance, attitudes, and general behavior. The interviewer is also alert to the interviewee's emotions. For example, is there one dominant emotion that fluctuates little? Is there an absence of emotion (that is, a flat affect)? Are the emotions appropriate? Do the emotions fluctuate widely? The person's thought

TABLE 8-7

*Part of a
Branching
Algorithm for a
Computerized
Interview*

1. Have you ever used tobacco?
   If No, go to 2.
   If Yes, answer *a–d.*
   a. At what age did you first start smoking?
   b. About how many cigarettes did you smoke on the average?
   c. Have you ever tried to quit?
      If No, go to *d.*
      If Yes, answer *i–iii.*
      i. When was the first time you tried to quit?
      ii. To what extent were you able to reduce the number of cigarettes you smoked each day?
      iii. How many times have you tried to quit?
   d. Identify any stressors that seem to cause you to smoke more.
2. Have you ever used alcohol?
   If No, go to 3.
   If Yes, answer *a–e.*

processes are also evaluated. Intelligence can be evaluated by such factors as speed and accuracy of thinking, richness of thought content, memory, judgment, and ability to interpret proverbs. Especially important in the assessment of schizophrenia, a major form of psychosis that involves loss of contact with reality, is the quality of the person's thought processes. This can be assessed through an analysis of thought content. For example, is there anything unusual or peculiar about the person's thoughts? Is the person preoccupied with any particular idea? Are the person's ideas realistic?

Other important areas evaluated in the mental status examination include the person's ability to direct and deploy attention. Is the person distracted? Can he or she stick to a task as long as needed to complete it? Sensory factors also are considered. Is the person seeing things that are not there? What is the accuracy of the person's perceptions? Several guides for conducting mental status exams are available (see, for example, Levitas, Hurley, & Pary, 2002; Sattler, 1998).

Keep in mind that to make proper use of the mental status examination, you must have a broad understanding of the major mental disorders and the various forms of brain damage. There is no room for amateurs or self-appointed practitioners when a mental status examination is needed. However, knowledge of those areas covered in the mental status examination can be useful to interviewers who are interested in knowing the important variables in observing and evaluating another human being.

Developing Interviewing Skills

A continuing controversy in the field of interviewing concerns whether or not interviewing skills can be learned. The general consensus is that people can acquire them (Boegels, van der Vleuten, Blok, & Kreutzkamp, 1996; Latham, 1987; Posthuma, Morgeson, & Campion, 2002; Prinstein, 2004). The first step in doing so is to become familiar with research and theory on the interview in order to understand the principles and underlying variables in the interview.

A second step in learning such skills is supervised practice. Experience truly is the best teacher. No amount of book learning can compare with having one's taped interview analyzed by an expert. Maurer, Solamon, and Troxtel (2001) found that applicants who received coaching performed better in an interview than applicants who did not.

As a third step, one must make a conscious effort to apply the principles involved in good interviewing such as guidelines for keeping the interaction flowing. This application includes constant self-evaluation—for example, continually asking oneself questions such as "What does this person mean? Am I communicating that I understand? Is the person exploring at deeper levels? What is being communicated nonverbally?"

The initial phase of learning any new skill seems to involve attending to a hundred things at once—an impossible task. However, with persistent effort, people eventually respond appropriately by habit. Thus, experienced interviewers automatically attend to the person's appearance, nonverbal communications, emotional tone, and so on. They do so not because they are endowed with special abilities, but because they have trained themselves to do so.

Sources of Error in the Interview

To make appropriate use of the interview, people must develop an awareness of the various sources of error or potential bias in data from interviews. Then they can try to compensate for these negative effects. Furthermore, this knowledge allows one to develop a better awareness of the limitations inherent in judging human beings on the basis of the interview.

Interview Validity

Many sources of interview error come from the extreme difficulty we have in making accurate, logical observations and judgments (Cesare, 1996; Schuler, 1993). Suppose, for example, in his first day of teaching a fifth-grade class, a teacher observes that one child follows all of the rules and directions, but a second child just cannot seem to stay out of trouble. If that teacher is not careful, then he might develop a bias. He might see the first child as good even if she breaks the rules for several weeks in a row. On the other hand, he might see the second child as bad even if she follows the rules for the rest of the school term. Similarly, a child may turn in a paper replete with grammatical and spelling errors. This child may have just had a bad day. However, even if his or her next paper is relatively free of errors, the teacher will have a tendency to look for them and to view the child as weak in grammar. Furthermore, the teacher may see the child as weak in other areas just on the basis of his early impression of the child's grammatical skills.

Long ago, E. L. Thorndike (1920) labeled this tendency to judge specific traits on the basis of a general impression the *halo effect*. Thorndike became aware of this effect when he noticed that ratings of behavioral tendencies (traits) based on interview data tended to correlate more highly than reasonably expected.

People apparently tend to generalize judgments from a single limited experience (Huffcutt, Roth, & McDaniel, 1996; Li, Wang, & Zhang, 2002). In the interview, halo effects occur when the interviewer forms a favorable or unfavorable early impression. The early impression then biases the remainder of the judgment process (Howard & Ferris, 1996). Thus, with an early favorable impression or positive halo, the interviewer will have difficulty seeing the negatives. Similarly, with an early negative halo, the interviewer will have difficulty seeing the positives. In short, halo effects impair objectivity and must be consciously avoided.

Similarly, people tend to judge on the basis of one outstanding characteristic. Hollingworth (1922) first called this error *general standoutishness*. One prominent characteristic can bias the interviewer's judgments and prevent an objective evaluation. In an early classic paper, Burtt (1926) noted the tendency of interviewers to make unwarranted inferences from personal appearance. A well-groomed, attractive individual might be rated higher in intelligence than would a poorly groomed, unattractive individual, even if the latter was actually more intelligent than the former. Results from a 2001 study (Strauss, Miles, & Levesque) showed that less attractive applicants were more favorably rated when interviewed by telephone than in person. This supports the widely recognized concept that physical appearance can play a major role in how a job applicant is perceived and rated (Huffcutt, Roth, & McDaniel, 1996; Reed, 2000). It is important to note, however, that appearance factors that contribute most to the decision-making process are factors that are controllable by the applicant, such as grooming and weight. When it appears that applicants have attempted to manage the controllable factors, they are viewed more favorably, even if they are viewed as unattractive (Posthuma, Morgeson, & Campion, 2002). Another potential source of error in the interview can be found in cross-ethnic, cross-cultural, and cross-class interviewing (Fish, 2001; Sattler, 1977, 1998). In the international business community, ignorance of cultural differences is becoming increasingly apparent. Japanese and Arabs consider direct eye contact a sign of aggression. The Japanese person avoids eye contact as a sign of deference and respect. In the middle-class United States, by contrast, direct eye contact is expected as a sign of honesty and sincerity. Unless we understand and take cultural differences into account, we can easily send the wrong message or misinterpret others' intentions. The misunderstanding of cultural differences within the United States also leads to interviewer bias. For example, whereas middle-class whites generally look at a speaker while listening, many African Americans tend to look away while listening. These differences in style may lead a white interviewer to believe she is not being listened to or an African American to feel as if he is being unduly scrutinized (Sattler, 1988, p. 461). Although reviews of the literature (Nevo & Jager, 1993; Ralston,

TABLE 8-8

*Suggestions
for Handling
Cross-Ethnic,
Cross-Cultural,
and Cross-Class
Interviews*

- **Increase cultural awareness**
  Try to become sensitive to cultural, social class, and ethnic differences. Study the culture, language, and traditions of groups you are likely to have contact with as an interviewer.

- **Know yourself**
  Examine your own stereotypes and prejudices. What are your preconceived notions about individuals from races, cultures, and socioeconomic groups other than your own?

- **Be flexible**
  Try to suspend your preconceived notions. Be willing to accept a perspective other than your own.

- **Look beyond yourself**
  Try to appreciate the interviewee's perspective. Put yourself in the interviewee's shoes. Look for ways to circumvent potential difficulties.

Based on Sattler (1988, p. 462).

1988) have failed to provide a framework from which to understand bias in the personnel selection process, Sattler (1988) has offered several suggestions for handling cross-ethnic, cross-cultural, and cross-class interviews. Table 8-8 summarizes some of these suggestions.

Sources of error such as cultural distortions can reduce the validity of interview data. Recall that validity tells us about the meaning of test scores. Errors that reduce the objectivity of the interviewer produce inaccurate judgments, thus biasing the validity of the evaluation. These tendencies perhaps explain why the predictive validity of interview data varies so widely. R. Wagner (1949), for example, reported studies that attempted to correlate judgments from interview data with such factors as grades, intelligence, and performance on standardized tests. The correlations ranged from .09 to .94, with a median of .19. Studies reviewed by Ulrich and Trumbo (1965) revealed a similar range of predictive validity coefficients, with correlations as low as −.05 and as high as .72 when ratings based on interview data were correlated with a variety of indexes such as job performance. Others have reported similar findings (Arvey & Campion, 1982; Carlson, Thayer, Mayfield, & Peterson, 1971). Other reviews have suggested higher and more consistent coefficients especially when specific characteristics such as cognitive ability are being assessed. In a meta-analytic review of 49 studies, for example, Huffcutt, Roth, and McDaniel (1996) found that .4 provided a good estimate of the relationship between test scores and interview ratings of cognitive abilities.

Although one can question the validity of interview data, the interview does provide a wealth of unique data. The safest approach is to consider interview data as tentative: a hypothesis or a set of hypotheses to be confirmed by other sources of data. Interview data may have dubious value without the support of more standardized procedures. Results from standardized tests, on the other hand, are often meaningless if not placed in the context of case history or other interview data. The two go together, each complementing the other, each essential in the process of evaluating human beings.

Interview Reliability

Recall that reliability refers to the stability, dependability, or consistency of test results. For interview data, the critical questions about reliability have centered on inter-interviewer agreement (agreement between two or more interviewers). As with the validity studies, reliability coefficients for inter-interviewer agreement vary widely. For example, in R. Wagner's (1949) classic study, reliability coefficients ranged from .23 to .97 (median .57) for ratings of traits. The range of coefficients for ratings of overall ability was even wider ($-.20$ to .85; median .53). Ulrich and Trumbo's (1965) widely cited review reported similar findings.

Again, reliability runs twice as high for structured as for unstructured interviews (Harris, 1989; Schwab-Stone, Fallon, Briggs, & Crowther, 1994). E. C. Webster (1964) argued that one reason for fluctuations in interview reliability is that different interviewers look for different things, an argument echoed by others (Harasym, Woloschuk, Mandin, & Brundin-Mather, 1996; Zedeck, Tziner, & Middlestadt, 1983). Thus, whereas one interviewer might focus on strengths, another might focus on weaknesses. The two interviewers would disagree because their judgments are based on different aspects of the individual. To enhance interrater reliability in interviewer behavior, Callender and Dougherty (1983) recommended that interviewers be trained to evaluate highly specific dimensions; such an approach has merit (Dougherty, Ebert, & Callender, 1986; Dreher, Ash, & Hancock, 1988).

As we have noted, agreement among interviewers varies for different types of interviews. The research suggests that a highly structured interview in which specific questions are asked in a specific order can produce highly stable results (Huffcutt, Conway, Roth, & Stone, 2001). For example, if we ask a person his or her name, date of birth, and parents' names, as well as the addresses of all residences within a particular time span, and then ask the same questions a year later, results should be nearly identical. Reliability would be limited only by the memory and honesty of the interviewee and the clerical capabilities of the interviewer. Although extreme, this example should make it clear that highly structured interviews should produce fairly dependable results. The problem is that such structure can limit the content of the interview, thus defeating the purpose of providing a broad range of data.

Unstructured or semistructured interviews frequently provide data that other sources cannot provide. However, the dependability of such results is clearly limited. The same question may not be asked twice, or it may be asked in different ways. Thus, interviewers readily acknowledge the limited reliability of interview data.

SUMMARY

In a *structured interview*, the interviewer asks a specific set of questions. In the structured *standardized* interview, these questions are printed. The interviewer reads the questions in a specific order or sequence. In the *unstructured interview*, there are no specific questions or guidelines for the interviewer to follow. Thus, each unstructured interview is unique. Such interviews provide considerable flexibility at the expense of data stability.

An interview is an *interactive* process. The participants (interviewer and interviewee) influence each other. The tendency for people to behave like the models around them is called *social facilitation*. Good interviewers thus can set a good tone in an interview by maintaining a warm, open, confident atmosphere.

Good interviewing involves developing the proper *attitudes* and displaying them during the interview. Interviewees give positive evaluations to interviewers when the interviewer is seen as warm, genuine, accepting, understanding, open, committed, and involved. Poor evaluations result when interviewers exhibit the opposite attitudes and feelings.

The process of interviewing involves facilitating the flow of communication. An interviewer should avoid statements that are *judgmental* or *evaluative*, *probing, hostile*, or *reassuring*. An unstructured interview should begin with an *open-ended question*—that is, one that cannot be answered briefly. The process of interviewing then involves facilitating the flow of communication. *Closed-ended questions*, which can be answered with a "yes" or "no" or a specific response, usually bring the interview to a halt and typically should be reserved for instances where less directive procedures fail to produce the desired information. Further, transitional phrases such as "I see" help keep the interview flowing. Statements that communicate understanding or are interchangeable with the interviewee's responses tend to elicit self-exploration at increasingly deeper levels. These interviewer responses include *verbatim playback, paraphrasing, restatement, summarizing, clarification*, and *understanding*. *Confrontation* is another response that experienced interviewers use for specific purposes, but it is not recommended as a general strategy.

Efforts to assess the quality of understanding or empathetic statements have led to a 5-point scale system developed by Rogers, Truax, Carkhuff, and co-workers. Understanding statements are extremely powerful in helping the interviewee uncover and explore underlying feelings. Types of interviews include the *evaluation or assessment interview*, the *structured clinical interview*, the *case history interview*, the *mental status examination*, and the *employment interview*.

There are two primary sources of error in the interview: those pertaining to the *validity* or meaning of data and those pertaining to its dependability or *reliability*. Tendencies to draw general conclusions about an individual that are based on just the data of a first impression limit the meaning and accuracy of interview data. Such tendencies have been labeled *the halo effect* and *standoutishness*. Cultural misunderstandings can also bias interview data and lead to inaccurate conclusions. Furthermore, predictive validity coefficients for interview data vary widely. The reliability of interview data has been measured primarily in terms of agreement among interviewers on variables, such as intelligence and traits. The more structured the interview, the more the interviewers agree. Thus, like predictive validity coefficients, reliability coefficients for interview data vary widely. Training tends to enhance reliability.

One develops interviewing skills through knowledge about good interviewing behavior and principles, supervised practice, and a conscious effort to form the right habits. However, the interview is fallible. Interview data can best be seen as the complement of other data sources.

WEB ACTIVITY

For interesting and relevant Web sites, check the following:

http://www.britannica.com/eb/article?eu=115066&tocid=0&query=personality%20assessment&ct=
   Encyclopaedia Britannica on personality assessment

http://psycprints.ecs.soton.ac.uk/archive/00000533/
   A clarification of the importance of comparison groups and accuracy rates with the cognitive interview

http://cpmcnet.columbia.edu/dept/scid/
   Describes the SCID-I and SCID-II

www.mentalhealth.com/dxq/p2q-md01.html
   Internet Mental Health on detecting depressive symptoms with a clinical interview

CHAPTER 9

Theories of Intelligence and the Binet Scales

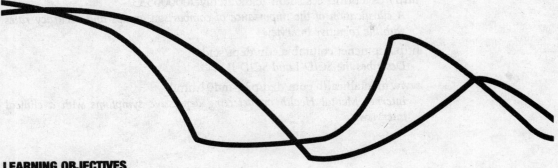

LEARNING OBJECTIVES

When you have completed this chapter, you should be able to:

- Explain how Binet and other psychologists have defined intelligence
- Compare Spearman's g with contemporary gf-gc theory
- Identify Binet's two guiding principles of test construction
- Describe the concept of age differentiation
- Describe the concept of mental age (MA)
- Describe the intelligence quotient (IQ) concept
- Define deviation IQ
- Discuss the various editions of the Stanford-Binet Intelligence Scale

Three 8-year-old children, Fred, Maria, and Roberto, were being evaluated for a special program for the gifted in a magnet school. Those who qualified would be placed in a special accelerated program in which the student–teacher ratio was 15 to 1 rather than the usual 25 to 1. The gifted program also had special funds for enrichment programs such as field trips and hands-on exposure to computers. To qualify, a child had to score three standard deviations above the mean on the Stanford-Binet Intelligence Scale (fifth edition) (Roid, 2003 a, b, c,).

Because the Stanford-Binet is standardized, all three children were exposed to the same conditions. The test began with a set of vocabulary items.

Only Maria scored high enough on the test to be placed in the gifted program. Given that all children were exposed to the same test conditions, can we rest assured that the procedure was fair and that Maria was indeed the most intelligent of the three? As critical thinkers, we of course cannot give an unqualified "Yes" to the question. We need much more information.

The Problem of Defining Intelligence

To say that one person is more intelligent than a second, we must be prepared to define *intelligence*. Unfortunately, of all the major concepts in the field of testing, intelligence is among the most elusive.

Alfred Binet, one of the original authors of the test that bears his name, defined intelligence as "the tendency to take and maintain a definite direction; the capacity to make adaptations for the purpose of attaining a desired end, and the power of autocriticism" (cited in Terman, 1916, p. 45). Spearman (1923), by contrast, defined intelligence as the ability to educe either relations or correlates. According to Freeman (1955), intelligence is "adjustment or adaptation of the individual to his total environment," "the ability to learn," and "the ability to carry on abstract thinking" (pp. 60–61). And Das (1973) defined intelligence as "the ability to plan and structure one's behavior with an end in view" (p. 27). H. Gardner (1983) defined intelligence in terms of the ability "to resolve genuine problems or difficulties as they are encountered" (p. 60), while Sternberg (1986, 1988) defined intelligence in terms of "mental activities involved in purposive adaptation to, shaping of, and selection of real-world environments relevant to one's life" (1986, p. 33). For Anderson (2001), intelligence is two-dimensional and based on individual differences in information-processing speed and executive functioning influenced largely by inhibitory processes.

Such definitions reflect the more general trends and theories that researchers follow. T. R. Taylor (1994) identified three independent research traditions that have been employed to study the nature of human intelligence: the psychometric, the information-processing, and the cognitive approaches. The *psychometric approach* examines the elemental structure of a test (Barenbaum & Winter, 2003; Taylor, 1994). Following the psychometric approach, we examine the properties of a test through an evaluation of its correlates and underlying dimensions (Larson, Parks, Harper, & Heath, 2001). In the *information-processing* approach, we examine the processes that underlie how we learn and solve problems (Sousa, 2001). Finally, the cognitive tradition focuses on how humans adapt to real-world demands (Bourmenskaya, 2002; Ruisel, 2001). Of the three approaches, the psychometric is the oldest (McGrew & Flanagan, 1998) and will be the focus of this chapter. (The information-processing and cognitive approaches will be discussed more thoroughly in Chapter 15.) As you will see, Binet's approach is based heavily on the psychometric tradition.

Returning to our example, how can we begin to judge whether the Binet test allowed testers to judge the three children fairly? A test such as the Binet that examines one's ability to define words and identify numerical sequences certainly does not meet the standards of all or even most definitions of intelligence. Even if we assume that the Stanford-Binet scale is a valid measure of intelligence, can we safely say that the evaluation procedure for Fred, Maria, and Roberto was fair?

Again, we cannot answer unequivocally. Roberto, a Mexican American, had Spanish-speaking parents, neither of whom finished high school. His father spent most of his life working as a tomato picker. Fred, an African American, came from a family of five children. As with Roberto, neither of Fred's parents completed high school. Although Fred's father worked long hard hours as a machine operator on an assembly line, the family was poor. Maria's parents, by contrast, had a combined income of $300,000 per year and were well educated. Her mother was a clinical psychologist, her father an attorney.

There is a correlation between socioeconomic background and scores on all standardized intelligence tests (Bornstein, Hahn, Suwalsky, & Haynes, 2003; Molfese, Modglin, & Molfese, 2003), including Stanford-Binet (Sangwan, 2001). Thus, many people have charged that intelligence tests are biased, especially against ethnic minorities and the poor (Hays, 2001; Miele, 2002). Ironically, intelligence tests were initially developed to eliminate subjectivity in the evaluation of children's ability. And it should be noted that among standardized tests, the Stanford-Binet fifth edition is among the best in providing appropriate cautions for test users.

For many people, the topic of intelligence testing arouses strong feelings and sometimes strong personal biases, even among experts (Reynolds & Ramsay, 2003; Snyderman & Rothman, 1987). Proponents hold that properly used intelligence tests provide an objective standard of competence and potential (Gregory, 1999; Greisinger, 2003; Jackson, 1980). Critics charge that intelligence tests are not only biased against certain racial and economic groups (Jones, 2003; Suzuki & Valencia, 1997) but also used by those in power to maintain the status quo (Gould, 1981; Owen, 1985). In fact, intelligence tests have been under attack almost from their inception.

Formal intelligence testing began with the decision of a French minister of public instruction around the turn of the 20th century. Some people today might criticize the minister's decision to create a procedure for identifying intellectually limited individuals so they could be removed from the regular classroom and receive special educational experiences. This decision provided the force behind the development of modern intelligence tests and the heated controversy now associated with them.

In 1904, the French minister officially appointed a commission, to which he gave a definite assignment: to recommend a procedure for identifying so-called subnormal (intellectually limited) children. One member of this commission, Alfred Binet, had demonstrated his qualifications for the job by his earlier research on human abilities (Binet, 1890a, 1890b). The task of the commission was indeed formidable. No one doubted that human beings were capable of incredible accomplishments, which obviously reflected intelligence. Nor was there much doubt that differences existed among individuals in their level of intelligence. But how was one to define intelligence?

Binet and his colleagues had few guideposts. A study by Wissler (1901) indicated that simple functions such as reaction time and sensory acuity failed to discriminate well among individuals of high and low scholastic ability. Therefore, Binet looked for complex processes in his struggle to understand human intelligence. However, unlike today, there were few available definitions of intelligence. Binet's first problem was to decide what he wanted to measure—that is, to define intelligence. Beginning with this definition, Binet and his colleagues developed the world's first intelligence test.

Binet's Principles of Test Construction

As you have seen, Binet defined intelligence as the capacity (1) to find and maintain a definite direction or purpose, (2) to make necessary adaptations—that is, strategy adjustments—to achieve that purpose, and (3) to engage in self-criticism so that necessary adjustments in strategy can be made. In choosing a definition, Binet took the necessary first step in developing a measure of intelligence.

However, he still faced the problem of deciding exactly what he wanted to measure. Because Binet believed that intelligence expressed itself through the judgmental, attentional, and reasoning facilities of the individual (Binet & Simon, 1905), he decided to concentrate on finding tasks related to these three facilities.

In developing tasks to measure judgment, attention, and reasoning, Binet used trial and error as well as experimentation and hypothesis-testing procedures. He was guided by two major concepts that to this day underlie not only the Binet scale but also major modern theories of intelligence: age differentiation and general mental ability. These principles, which perhaps represent Binet's most profound contribution to the study of human intelligence, provided the foundation for subsequent generations of human ability tests.

Principle 1: Age Differentiation

Age differentiation refers to the simple fact that one can differentiate older children from younger children by the former's greater capabilities. For example, whereas most 9-year-olds can tell that a quarter is worth more than a dime, a dime is worth more than a nickel, and so on, most 4-year-olds cannot. In employing the principle of age differentiation, Binet searched for tasks that could be completed by between 66.67% and 75% of the children of a particular age group and also by a smaller proportion of younger children but a larger proportion of older ones. Thus, Binet eventually assembled a set of tasks that an increasing proportion of children could complete as a function of increases in age.

Using these tasks, he could estimate the mental ability of a child in terms of his or her completion of the tasks designed for the average child of a particular age, regardless of the child's actual or chronological age. A particular 5-year-old child might be able to complete tasks that the average 8-year-old could complete. On the other hand, another 5-year-old might not be capable of completing even those tasks that the average 3-year-old could complete. With the principle of age differentiation, one could determine the equivalent age capabilities of a child independent of his or her chronological age. This equivalent age capability was eventually called *mental age*. If a 6-year-old completed tasks that were appropriate for the average 9-year-old, then the 6-year-old had demonstrated that he or she had capabilities equivalent to those of the average 9-year-old, or a mental age of 9. Today, psychologists use the more sophisticated technique of item response theory (see Chapter 6) to accomplish the goal of evaluating age equivalent capabilities (Bolt, 2003; Glas & Meijer, 2003; Roid, 2003a).

Principle 2: General Mental Ability

Binet was also guided in his selection of tasks by his decision to measure only the total product of the various separate and distinct elements of intelligence, that is, *general mental ability*. With this concept, Binet freed himself from the burden of identifying each element or independent aspect of intelligence. He also was freed from finding the relation of each element to the whole. Binet's decision to measure general mental ability was based, in part, on practical considerations. He could restrict the search for tasks to anything related to the total or the final product of intelligence. He could judge the value of any particular task in terms of its correlation with the combined result (total score) of all other tasks. Tasks with low correlations could be eliminated, and tasks with high correlations retained. The notion of general mental ability is critical to understanding modern conceptions of human intelligence as well as the various editions of the Binet from the first through the present modern fifth edition.

Spearman's Model of General Mental Ability

Binet was not alone in his conception of general mental ability. Before Binet, this notion was propounded by F. Galton (1869) in his classic work, *Hereditary Genius: An Inquiry into Its Laws and Consequences* (see Chapter 1). Independently of Binet, in Great Britain, Charles Spearman (1904, 1927) advanced the

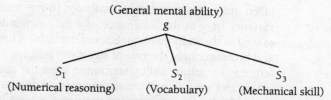

FIGURE 9-1 *Spearman's model of intelligence. According to the model, intelligence can be viewed in terms of one general underlying factor (g) and a large number of specific factors* (S₁, S₂, . . . Sₙ). *Thus, intelligence can be viewed in terms of g (general mental ability) and S (specific factors). Spearman's theory was consistent with Binet's approach to constructing the first intelligence test.*

notion of a general mental ability factor underlying all intelligent behavior (see Thorndike, 1990a, 1990b). According to Spearman's theory, intelligence consists of one general factor (g) plus a large number of specific factors (see Figure 9-1). Spearman's notion of general mental ability, which he referred to as *psychometric g* (or simply *g*), was based on the well-documented phenomenon that when a set of diverse ability tests are administered to large unbiased samples of the population, almost all of the correlations are positive. This phenomenon is called *positive manifold,* which according to Spearman resulted from the fact that all tests, no matter how diverse, are influenced by *g*. For Spearman, *g* could best be conceptualized in terms of mental energy.

To understand how a single general factor can underlie all intelligent behavior, consider the analogy of a central power station for a large metropolitan city. The same station provides the power for lights of all sizes and types. Although some lights may be brighter or better than others, all depend on power from the central power source. Reducing the output from the central source affects all of the lights.

To support the notion of *g*, Spearman developed a statistical technique called *factor analysis*. Factor analysis is a method for reducing a set of variables or scores to a smaller number of hypothetical variables called *factors*. Through factor analysis, one can determine how much variance a set of tests or scores has in common (Abbott, Amtmann, & Munson, 2003; Lorenzo-Seva, 2003; Timmerman & Kiers, 2003). This common variance represents the *g* factor. The *g* in a factor analysis of any set of mental ability tasks can be represented in the first unrotated factor in a principal components analysis (Saccuzzo, Johnson, & Guertin, 1994). Spearman found that, as a general rule, approximately half of the variance in a set of diverse mental-ability tests is represented in the *g* factor.

Implications of General Mental Intelligence (g)

The concept of general intelligence implies that a person's intelligence can best be represented by a single score, *g*, that presumably reflects the shared variance underlying performance on a diverse set of tests. True, performance on any given individual task can be attributed to *g* as well as to some specific or unique variance (just as the luminance of a light depends on the central power source as well as the individual qualities of the light). However, if the set of tasks is large and broad enough, the role of any given task can be reduced to a minimum. Differences in unique ability stemming from the specific task tend to cancel each other, and overall performance comes to depend most heavily on the general factor. Such reasoning guided the development of the Binet scale as well as all its subsequent revisions through the most current fifth edition (Roid, 2003a).

The gf-gc Theory of Intelligence

Recent theories of intelligence have suggested that human intelligence can best be conceptualized in terms of multiple intelligences rather than a single score (Furnham & Petrides, 2003; McGrew & Flanagan, 1998; Riggio, Murphy, & Pirozzolo, 2002). One such theory is called the *gf-gc* theory (Horn & Noll, 1997).

According to *gf-gc* theory, there are two basic types of intelligence: fluid (*gf*) and crystallized (*gc*). Fluid intelligence can best be thought of as those abilities that allow us to reason, think, and acquire new knowledge (Kane & Engle, 2002; Primi, 2002; Stankov, 2003). Crystallized intelligence, by contrast, represents the knowledge and understanding that we have acquired (Bates & Shieles, 2003; Vigil-Colet & Codorniu-Raga, 2002). You might think of this distinction in terms of the abilities that allow us to learn and acquire information (fluid) and the actual learning that has occurred (crystallized).

The Binet began with the notion of a single intelligence, *g*. As the test progressed to its modern form, it has implicitly adopted a model of intelligence that acknowledges these two forms of intelligence. Thus, the evolution of the Binet has in many ways reflected and paralleled the evolution of modern psychometric theory and approaches to intelligence.

The Early Binet Scales

Using the principles of age differentiation and general mental ability, Binet and another appointee of the French minister of public instruction, T. Simon, collaborated to develop the first version of what would eventually be called the Stanford-Binet Intelligence Scale. The first version, the 1905 Binet-Simon scale, was quite limited compared with current applications of intelligence tests. Its purpose was restricted to identifying mentally disabled children in the Paris school system.

The 1905 Binet-Simon Scale

The 1905 Binet-Simon scale was an individual intelligence test consisting of 30 items presented in an increasing order of difficulty. Item 4, for example, tested the subject's ability to recognize food (for example, to discriminate between

FIGURE 9-2
Schematic summary of the evolution of the 1905 Binet scale.

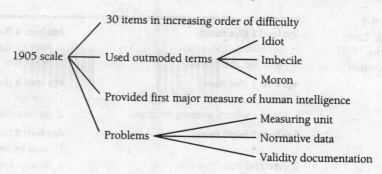

chocolate and wood). Item 14 required subjects to define familiar objects such as a fork. The most difficult item, 30, required subjects to define and distinguish between paired abstract terms (for example, *sad* and *bored*). Binet proposed that item 9, which required subjects to name designated objects in a picture, was the approximate limit of the average 3-year-old.

In Binet's time, three levels of intellectual deficiency were designated by terms no longer in use today because of the derogatory connotations they have acquired. *Idiot* described the most severe form of intellectual impairment, *imbecile* moderate levels of impairment, and *moron* the mildest level of impairment. Binet believed that the ability to follow simple directions and imitate simple gestures (item 6 on the 1905 scale) was the upper limit of adult idiots. The ability to identify parts of the body or simple objects (item 8) would rule out the most severe intellectual impairment in an adult. The upper limit for adult imbeciles was item 16, which required the subject to state the differences between two common objects such as wood and glass.

The collection of 30 tasks of increasing difficulty in the Binet-Simon scale provided the first major measure of human intelligence. Binet had solved two major problems of test construction: He determined exactly what he wanted to measure, and he developed items for this purpose. He fell short, however, in several other areas. The 1905 Binet-Simon scale lacked an adequate measuring unit to express results; it also lacked adequate normative data and evidence to support its validity. The classifications Binet used (idiot, imbecile, and moron) can hardly be considered sufficient for expressing results and, as Binet himself knew, little had been done to document the scale's validity. Furthermore, norms for the 1905 scale were based on only 50 children who had been considered normal based on average school performance (see Figure 9-2).

The 1908 Scale

In the 1908 scale, Binet and Simon retained the principle of age differentiation. Indeed, the 1908 scale was an **age scale,** which means items were grouped according to age level rather than simply one set of items of increasing difficulty, as in the 1905 scale (see Table 9-1). The age scale provided a model for innumerable tests still used in educational and clinical settings. However, the age scale format also presented several challenges and, as we will see, is used in

TABLE 9-1

Sample Items from the 1908 Binet-Simon Scale

Age level 3 (five items)
1. Point to various parts of face.
2. Repeat two digits forward.

Age level 5 (five items)
1. Copy a square.
2. Repeat a sentence containing ten syllables.

Age level 7 (eight items)
1. Copy a diamond.
2. Repeat five digits forward.

Age level 9 (six items)
1. Recall six items from a passage.
2. Recite the days of the week.

Age level 11 (five items)
1. Define abstract words (for example, justice).
2. Determine what is wrong with absurd statements.

Age level 13 (three items)
1. State the differences between pairs of abstract terms.

Age level 4 (four items)
1. Name familiar objects.
2. Repeat three digits forward.

Age level 6 (seven items)
1. State age.
2. Repeat a sentence containing 16 syllables.

Age level 8 (six items)
1. Recall two items from a passage.
2. State the differences between two objects.

Age level 10 (five items)
1. Given three common words, construct a sentence.
2. Recite the months of the year in order.

Age level 12 (five items)
1. Repeat seven digits forward.
2. Provide the meaning of pictures.

---

only a modified or "hybrid" fashion in the 2003 fifth edition. When items are grouped according to age level, comparing a child's performance on different kinds of tasks is difficult, if not impossible, unless items are exquisitely balanced as in the 2003 Binet. For example, does the child perform exceptionally well on one type of item? The current edition has a procedure that allows test users to combine all verbal items into a single scale and all nonverbal items into a single scale to overcome such problems with the age scale format.

Despite its limitations, the 1908 Binet scale clearly reflected improvement over the 1905 scale. However, Binet had done little to meet one persistent criticism: The scale produced only one score, almost exclusively related to verbal, language, and reading ability. Binet claimed that a single score was consistent with the notion of general mental ability and therefore appropriate. Unfortunately, Binet made little effort to diversify the range of abilities tapped. As a result, the scale remained heavily weighted on language, reading, and verbal skills at the expense of other factors such as the integration of visual and motor functioning (for example, eye–hand coordination). Not until the 1986 revision were these problems seriously addressed, and in the 2003 revision major efforts were made to provide a wide diversity of scores as well as a balance of verbal and nonverbal items.

Perhaps the main improvement in the 1908 scale was the introduction of the concept of mental age. Here Binet attempted to solve the problem of expressing the results in adequate units. A subject's mental age was based on his or her performance compared with the average performance of individuals in

FIGURE 9-3
Schematic summary of the evolution of the 1908 Binet scale.

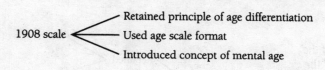

a specific chronological age group. In simple terms, if a 6-year-old can perform the tasks that can be done by two-thirds to three-fourths of the representative group of 8-year-old children, then this child has a mental age of 8. A 10-year-old who can do no more than pass items that two-thirds to three-fourths of the representative group of 5-year-olds can pass is said to have a mental age of 5.

To summarize, the 1908 Binet-Simon scale introduced two major concepts: the age scale format and the concept of mental age. However, even though the mental age concept was eventually abandoned and the age scale format modified, these two concepts found widespread use and application in a host of new tests that are still in use today (see Figure 9-3).

Terman's Stanford-Binet Intelligence Scale

Though Binet and Simon again revised their intelligence scale in 1911, this third version contained only minor improvements. By this time, the potential utility of the Binet-Simon scale had been recognized throughout Europe and in the United States. For example, in the United States, H. H. Goddard published a translation of the 1905 Binet-Simon scale in 1908, and the 1908 scale in 1911 (Herrnstein, 1981). Other U.S. developers subsequently published many versions of the scale. However, it was the 1916 Stanford-Binet version, developed under the direction of L. M. Terman, that flourished and served for quite some time as the dominant intelligence scale for the world.

In this section, we continue our look at the evolution of the Binet scale and its relation to theories of intelligence. First, we examine Terman's 1916 version of the scale and see how he related the concepts of mental age and intelligence quotient (IQ). Then we look at the 1937 and 1960 revisions before we move on to the modern versions of the Binet. Each version illustrates important test concepts as well as the evolution of intelligence tests throughout the world.

The 1916 Stanford-Binet Intelligence Scale

In developing the 1916 Stanford-Binet version, Terman relied heavily on Binet's earlier work. The principles of age differentiation, general mental ability, and the age scale were retained. The mental age concept also was retained (see Figure 9-4).

Terman's 1916 revision increased the size of the standardization sample. Unfortunately, the entire standardization sample of the 1916 revision consisted

FIGURE 9-4
Schematic summary of the evolution of the 1916 Binet scale.

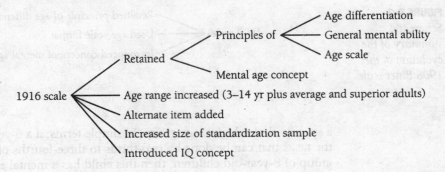

exclusively of white native-Californian children. Thus, although the standardization sample was markedly increased, it was far from representative. In fact, given that even geographic location may affect test performance, this sample cannot even be considered to represent white native-born Americans. Nevertheless, the increased sample size clearly marked an improvement over the meager 50 and 203 individuals of the 1905 and 1908 Binet-Simon versions.

The Intelligence Quotient (IQ)

The 1916 scale provided the first significant application of the now outdated **intelligence quotient (IQ)** concept. This particular IQ concept, recommended by Stern (1912), used a subject's mental age in conjunction with his or her chronological age to obtain a ratio score. This ratio score presumably reflected the subject's rate of mental development. Table 9-2 illustrates how IQ is determined.

In calculating IQ, the first step is to determine the subject's chronological age. To obtain this, we need only know his or her birthday. In the second step, the subject's mental age is determined by his or her score on the scale. Finally, to obtain the IQ, the chronological age (CA) is divided into the mental age (MA) and the result multiplied by 100 to eliminate fractions: IQ = MA/CA × 100.

As you can see in Table 9-2, when MA is less than CA, the IQ is below 100. In this case, the subject was said to have slower-than-average mental development. When MA exceeded CA, the subject was said to have faster-than-average mental development.

The IQ score altered the nature of the measuring unit used to express the results. However, the method may have actually been a step backward; the MA/CA method of calculating IQ scores was ultimately abandoned in all major tests. The 1916 scale had a maximum possible mental age of 19.5 years; that is, if every group of items was passed, this score would result. Given this limitation, anyone older than 19.5 would have an IQ of less than 100 even if all items were passed. Therefore, a maximum limit on the chronological age had to be set. Because back in 1916 people believed that mental age

TABLE 9-2
*The Intelligence
Quotient Concept*

Child 1:

Chronological age (CA): 6 years

Mental age (MA): 6 years

$$IQ = \frac{MA}{CA} \times 100 = \frac{6}{6} \times 100 = 100$$

Child 2:

Chronological age (CA): 6 years

Mental age (MA): 3 years

$$IQ = \frac{MA}{CA} \times 100 = \frac{3}{6} \times 100 = 50$$

Child 3:

CA = 6; MA = 12; IQ = 200

Adult 1:

CA = 50; MA = 16

$$IQ = \frac{16^*}{16} \times 100 = 100$$

← (the maximum CA)

ceased to improve after 16 years of age, 16 was used as the maximum chronological age.

The 1937 Scale

The 1937 scale extended the age range down to the 2-year-old level. Also, by adding new tasks, developers increased the maximum possible mental age to 22 years, 10 months. Scoring standards and instructions were improved to reduce ambiguities, enhance the standardization of administration, and increase interscorer reliability. Furthermore, several performance items, which required the subject to do things such as copy designs, were added to decrease the scale's emphasis on verbal skills. However, only some 25% of the items were nonverbal, so the test was not balanced between the two types of items (Becker, 2003).

The standardization sample was markedly improved. Whereas the 1916 norms were restricted to Californians, the new subjects for the 1937 Stanford-Binet standardization sample came from 11 U.S. states representing a variety of regions. Subjects were selected according to their fathers' occupations. In addition, the standardization sample was substantially increased. Unfortunately, the sample included only whites and more urban subjects than rural ones. Nevertheless, this improved sample represented a desirable trend. The 3184 individuals included in the 1937 standardization sample represented more than a threefold increase from the 1916 scale and was more than 63 times larger than the original sample of the 1905 scale.

Perhaps the most important improvement in the 1937 version was the inclusion of an alternate equivalent form. Forms L and M were designed to be

FIGURE 9-5

Schematic summary of the evolution of the 1937 Binet scale.

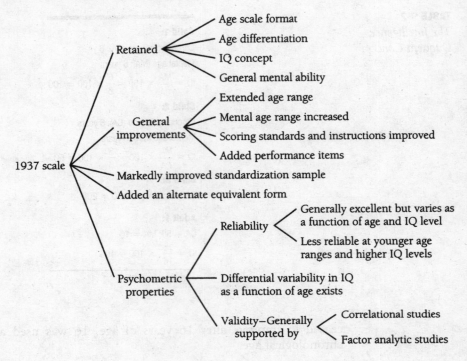

equivalent in terms of both difficulty and content. With two such forms, the psychometric properties of the scale could be readily examined (see Figure 9-5).

Problems with the 1937 scale. A major problem with the 1937 scale was that its reliability coefficients were higher for older subjects than for younger ones. Thus, results for the latter were not as stable as those for the former. Reliability figures also varied as a function of IQ level, with higher reliabilities in the lower IQ ranges (that is, less than 70) and poorer ones in the higher ranges. The lowest reliabilities occurred in the youngest age groups in the highest IQ ranges. These findings apply generally to all modern intelligence tests: Scores are most unstable for young children in high IQ ranges.

Along with the differing reliabilities, each age group in the standardization sample produced a unique standard deviation of IQ scores. This differential variability in IQ scores as a function of age created the single most important problem in the 1937 scale. More specifically, despite the great care taken in selecting the standardization sample, different age groups showed significant differences in the standard deviation of IQ scores. For example, the standard deviation in the IQ scores at age 6 was approximately 12.5. The standard deviations at ages 2.5 and 12, on the other hand, were 20.6 and 20.0, respectively. Because of these discrepancies, IQs at one age level were not equivalent to IQs at another. This concept is explored further in Focused Example 9-1.

Focused Example 9-1

DIFFERENTIAL VARIABILITY IN IQ SCORES

Recall our discussion of standard deviations and percentiles in Chapter 2. A score that is two standard deviations above the mean is approximately at the 98th percentile. Therefore, if the mean IQ is 100, a 6-year-old, where the standard deviation is 12.5, would need an IQ of 125 to be two standard deviations above the mean, or the 98th percentile. However, at 12 years of age, where the standard deviation is 20, the same child would need an IQ of 140 to be two standard deviations above the mean and in the 98th percentile. Say a child at age 6 with an IQ of 125 also obtained an IQ of 125 at age 12. He or she would then be only 1.25 standard deviations above the mean (because the standard deviation at age 12 is 20) and thus at only about the 89th percentile. You can see that in the 1937 scale, an IQ at one age range was not comparable to an IQ at another age range in terms of percentiles.

The 1960 Stanford-Binet Revision and Deviation IQ (SB-LM)

The developers of the 1960 revision (SB-LM) tried to create a single instrument by selecting the best from the two forms of the 1937 scale. Tasks that showed an increase in the percentage passing with an increase in age—a main criterion and guiding principle for the construction of the Binet scale—received the highest priority, as did tasks that correlated highly with scores as a whole—a second guiding principle of the Binet scale. In addition, instructions for scoring and test administration were improved, and IQ tables were extended from age 16 to 18. Perhaps most important, the problem of differential variation in IQs was solved by the deviation IQ concept.

As used in the Stanford-Binet scale, the *deviation IQ* was simply a standard score with a mean of 100 and a standard deviation of 16 (today the standard deviation is set at 15). With the mean set at 100 and assigned to scores at the 50th percentile, the deviation IQ was ascertained by evaluating the standard deviation of mental age for a representative sample at each age level. New IQ tables were then constructed that corrected for differences in variability at the various age levels. By correcting for these differences in variability, one could compare the IQs of one age level with that of another. Thus, scores could be interpreted in terms of standard deviations and percentiles with the assurance that IQ scores for every age group corresponded to the same percentile. Today, the deviation IQ method is considered the most precise way of expressing the results of an intelligence test (see Figure 9-6).

The 1960s revision did not include a new normative sample or restandardization. However, by 1972, a new standardization group consisting of a representative sample of 2100 children (approximately 100 at each Stanford-Binet age level) had been obtained for use with the 1960 revision (Thorndike, 1973). Unlike all previous norms, the 1972 norms included nonwhites. For

FIGURE 9-6
Schematic summary of the evolution of the 1960 Binet scale.

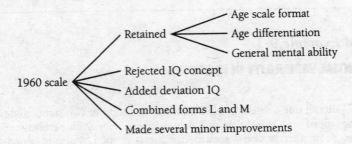

many, however, the general improvements in the 1960 revision, even with the new 1972 norms, did not suffice. In 1986, a new and drastically revised version of the Binet scale was published (Thorndike, Hagen, & Sattler, 1986). Then, in 2003, there was another major revision in which many of the concepts added to the 1986 edition were abandoned in favor of concepts used in the 1960 (SB-LM) version. The changes in 1986, and the possible reasons for the return to the older 1960 model are instructive.

The Modern Binet Scale

Our discussion of the evolution of the Binet scale has illustrated many of the concepts that have dominated intelligence testing from its inception to the present. The fourth and fifth editions of the Stanford-Binet scale continue this tradition of innovation and incorporation of central psychometric and theoretical concepts. In this section, we examine the fourth and fifth edition of the scale, which its authors developed in response to cultural and social changes and new research in cognitive psychology. First, we consider the basic model that guided this development and briefly discuss the features common to both editions. Next, we compare these latest editions to their predecessors. We begin with a brief look at how the fourth edition was changed. Then we consider the 2003 edition in greater detail—the various subtests, summary scores, and procedures. We also examine the scale's psychometric properties. Finally, we examine the modern 2003 edition of the Binet in light of a relatively new theory of intelligence.

Characteristics of the 1986 Revision

The 1986 revision attempted to retain all of the strengths of the earlier revisions while eliminating the weaknesses. This was no easy task; nor was it a complete success as indicated by the backtracking that occurred in the fifth edition. To continue to provide a measure of general mental ability, the authors of the 1986 revision decided to retain the wide variety of content and task characteristics of earlier versions. However, to avoid having this wide content unevenly distributed across age groups, the age scale format was entirely eliminated. In place of the age scale, items with the same content were placed together into any one of 15 separate tests to create point scales. For example, all vocabulary items were placed together in one test; all matrix items placed together in a second.

The more modern 2003 fifth edition provided a more standardized hierarchical model with five factors, as illustrated in Figure 9.8. At the top of the hierarchy is general intelligence, just as in the 1986 edition. However, there are now five rather than four main factors. Each factor, in turn, has an equally weighted nonverbal and verbal measure. Figure 9.9 indicates the types of activities used to measure the various factors.

Placing together items of similar content in a point scale permits the calculation of specific scores for each of the 15 tests. Thus, in addition to an overall score that presumably reflects g, one can obtain scores related to each specific content area. The drawback is less variety to the items. In addition, each of the specific 15 tests were grouped into one of four content areas or factors. Figure 9-10 summarizes the characteristics of the 1986 fourth edition.

FIGURE 9-8

Three-level hierarchical model of the 2003 fifth edition.

(Adapted from Figure 2.1, p. 24 in G. H. Roid, 2003b.)

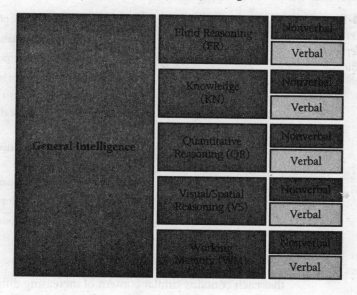

Characteristics of the 2003 Fifth Edition

The fifth edition represents an elegant integration of the age scale and point scale formats. First, the nonverbal and verbal scales are equally weighted. The examination begins with one of two routing measures (subtests): one nonverbal, one verbal. The routing tests are organized in a point scale, which means

FIGURE 9-9

Verbal and nonverbal tasks on 2003 fifth edition.

(Adapted from Figure 2.1, p. 24 in G. H. Roid, 2003b.)

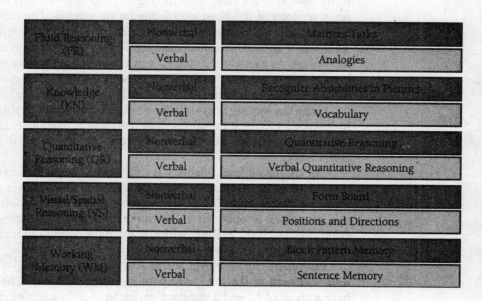

FIGURE 9-10
Characteristics of the modern (1986) Binet.

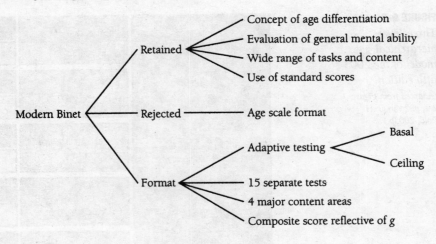

that each contains similar content of increasing difficulty. For example, the verbal routing test consists of a set of vocabulary items of increasing difficulty.

The purpose of the routing tests is to estimate the examinee's level of ability. The nonverbal routing test is used to estimate nonverbal ability; the verbal routing test to estimate verbal ability. The remaining eight subtests are arranged in an age scale format. This means that tasks of differing content are grouped together on the basis of difficulty. For example, an age scale–based subtest might have a mixture of different types of verbal and nonverbal tasks, with the tasks grouped according to the typical age at which individuals are able to correctly complete the task. This mixing of tasks was the procedure used in all prior versions of the Binet except the fourth edition. The difference with the 2003 fifth edition is that because of the equal weighting of verbal and nonverbal items, it is possible to summarize an examinee's score on all items of similar content. As a result, the fifth edition retains the advantage of the point scale by allowing examiners to summarize scores within any given content area while also using a mixture of tasks to maintain an examinee's interest.

Using the routing tests to estimate ability, the examiner then goes to an age scale–based subtest at the appropriate level for the examinee. In that way, items that are too easy are skipped to save time and provide for a more efficient examination.

The estimated level of ability is called the *start point*. However, if a certain number of early items are missed, then the examiner moves to a lower (and therefore easier) level. The level at which a minimum criterion number of correct responses is obtained is known as the **basal**. Testing continues until examinees reach the **ceiling**, which is a certain number of incorrect responses that indicate the items are too difficult.

Examiners can complete scaled scores for each of the five nonverbal subtests and each of the five corresponding verbal subtests. These scaled scores have a mean of 10 and a standard deviation of 3. In addition, a standard score

FIGURE 9-11
Characteristics of the 2003 fifth edition.

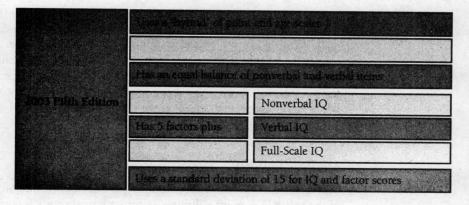

FIGURE 9-11
Characteristics of the 2003 fifth edition.

with a mean of 100 and a standard deviation of 15 is computed for nonverbal IQ, verbal IQ, full-scale IQ, and each of the five factors: fluid reasoning, knowledge, quantitative reasoning, visual-spatial processing, and working memory. Nonverbal and verbal IQ scores are based on summing the five nonverbal and five verbal subtests. The full-scale IQ is based on all 10. The standard scores for each of the five factors are based on summing the nonverbal and corresponding verbal subtest for each respective factor. Figure 9-11 summarizes the characteristics of the 2003 fifth edition.

Psychometric Properties of the 2003 Fifth Edition

The 2003 fifth edition was constructed with exceptional diligence. It continues the tradition of its predecessors in providing a state-of-the-art model for intelligence tests in terms of its psychometric standards and construction.

The awkward standard deviation of 16 for major indexes was finally abandoned if favor of the more common standard deviation of 15. Several new subtests were added, while those that were retained were updated with new artwork, toys, and better items. A major goal of the fifth edition is to tap the extremes in intelligence—the major historical strength of the Binet that had been essentially lost in the fourth edition. The age range touted by the fifth edition spans from 2 to 85+ years of age.

Norms were based on a representative sample of 4800 individuals from age 2 through 85+, stratified by gender, ethnicity, region, and education according to the 2001 census. To augment the standardization sample, 3000 additional individuals were included, encompassing various subpopulations such as gifted, mentally retarded, ADHD, and those with speech, language, and hearing problems. The range of possible scores runs from a low of 40 to a high of 160, reestablishing the Binet as one of the most appropriate tests for evaluating extremes in intelligence.

Overall, the reliability of the fifth edition is quite good. Coefficients for the full-scale IQ are either .97 or .98 for each of the 23 age ranges reported in the manual. Average reliabilities for the three IQ scores are .98 (full-scale IQ), .95 (nonverbal IQ), and .96 (verbal IQ). Coefficients for the five-factor index scores range from .90 to .92. Coefficients for verbal and nonverbal subtests are comparable and consistently in the high .8's. Test–retest coefficients are likewise excellent, with a range from the high .7's to the low .9's, depending on age and testing interval. Interscorer agreement was made high by eliminating items where such agreement was low, with an overall median of .9 reported in the technical manual (Roid, 2003c).

Median Validity

The technical manual reports four types of evidence that support the validity of the test: (1) content validity, (2) construct validity, (3) empirical item analysis, and (4) considerable criterion-related evidence of validity. Full-scale IQs for the fifth edition correlate in the low to mid .8's, with established measures including the Wechsler scales, which are discussed in the next chapter.

As of 2004, only one year after the date the test was released, no research studies were reported on the fifth edition. However, given its sound construction and many uses, we expect considerable research to report in our next revision of this text.

SUMMARY

Binet defined *intelligence* as the capacity (1) to find and maintain a definite direction or purpose, (2) to make necessary adaptations—that is, strategy adjustments—to achieve that purpose, and (3) to engage in self-criticism so that necessary adjustments in strategy can be made.

Binet's two principles of test construction were age differentiation and general mental ability. *Age differentiation* refers to the fact that with increasing age, children develop their abilities. Thus, older children have greater abilities than do younger ones. Spearman developed his own theory of general mental ability, or *g*, based on the idea that a single general factor underlies all intelligence. Modern theorists have taken this concept further in *gf-gc* theory, in which there are two basic types of intelligence: fluid (*gf*) and crystallized (*gc*).

Mental age is a unit of measurement for expressing the results of intelligence tests. The concept was introduced in the second revision of the Binet scale in 1908. A subject's mental age is based on his or her performance compared with the average performance of individuals in a specific chronological age group. For example, if a 6-year-old child can perform tasks that the average 8-year-old can do, then the 6-year-old child is said to have a mental age of 8.

Like mental age, the *intelligence quotient* (IQ) is a unit of measure for expressing the results of intelligence tests. Introduced in the Terman 1916 Stanford-Binet revision of the Binet scale, the IQ is a ratio score. Specifically, the IQ is the ratio of a subject's mental age (as determined by his or her performance on the intelligence scale) and chronological age. This ratio is then multiplied by 100 to eliminate fractions.

The *deviation IQ*, as it is now used in the Stanford-Binet Scale (fifth edition), is a standard score with a mean of 100 and a standard deviation of 15. Older versions had a standard deviation of 16.

The most recent revision of the Binet scale, the fifth edition, was released in 2003. This edition combines the age and point scale methods of test construction.

WEB ACTIVITY

For interesting and relevant Web sites, check the following:

http://cresst96.cse.ucla.edu/products/overheads/aera1999/aera%20glaser.pdf
Intelligence testing theories debated

http://otec.uoregon.edu/intelligence.htm
Three theories of intelligence explained

www.indiana.edu/%7Eintell/binet.shtml
Biography of Alfred Binet

www.indiana.edu/~intell/
Theory and history of intelligence tests

www.radcliffe.edu/documents/murray/0882StudyDescription.pdf
Murray Research Center

www.press.uchicago.edu/Complete/Series/T-CP.html
Classics in psychology

CHAPTER 10

The Wechsler Intelligence Scales: WAIS-III, WISC-IV, and WPPSI-III

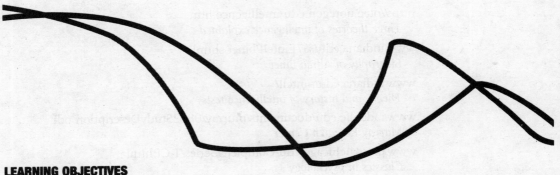

LEARNING OBJECTIVES

When you have completed this chapter, you should be able to:

☐ Identify the major motivation for the development of the Wechsler scales

☐ Briefly describe the point and performance scale concepts

☐ Distinguish between verbal and performance subtests

☐ Explain how IQ scores are determined on the Wechsler scales

☐ Describe the reliability of the Wechsler scales

☐ Describe the validity of the Wechsler scales

☐ Identify some of the major advantages and disadvantages of the Wechsler scales

☐ Describe the advances in testing reflected in the WISC-IV and WPPSI-III

Susan's family has just moved from a small rural town to a large city on the East Coast. At age 9, she remains shy around strangers and lacks confidence. Her attempt to adjust to a new school has been disastrous. Because she started in the middle of the school term, all of the other children seem way ahead of her; she feels hopelessly behind. To make matters worse, she has an unusually strong fear of failure. Rather than make an error, she remains silent even if she knows an answer. With all of her negative experiences in the new school, she begins to develop a poor attitude toward school tasks and therefore avoids them. Eventually, her teacher refers her to the school psychologist for testing. To Susan, this referral is the school's way of punishing her for not doing her homework. Fearful, upset, and angry, she makes up her mind not to cooperate with the psychologist.

When the time finally comes for her appointment, Susan begins to cry. The principal is called in to accompany her to the psychologist's office. Although she appears to calm down, Susan remains fearful and anxious. Finally, the psychologist decides to begin the testing. He starts with a relatively simple task that requires Susan to repeat digits. The psychologist states, "I want you to repeat some numbers that I'm going to say to you. Please say them as I do." He begins the first set of digits and states in a soft, clear voice, "Six, one, three." Susan does not even respond. She has been staring blankly at the walls and has not heard what the psychologist has said. The psychologist attracts her attention and says, "Now say what I say: four, two, seven." This time Susan hears him but again remains silent.

Now think for a moment. How many different factors are involved in the psychologist's ostensibly simple request to repeat three digits forward? To comply with this request, Susan has to direct her attention to the words of the psychologist, possess adequate hearing, and understand the instructions. She also has to cooperate, make an effort, and be capable of repeating what she has heard. Certainly her familiarity with numerals—that is, her previous learning and experience—can influence her performance. If the children in her new school have had more exposure to numerals than she has, then they might have an advantage over her in this regard. Furthermore, her lack of confidence, negative attitude toward school, fear of failure, and shyness have all played a role in her performance. A more confident, less fearful child with positive attitudes toward school would have a clear advantage over Susan. Thus, in addition to memory and other indicators of intelligence, many nonintellective factors (for example, attitude, experience, and emotional functioning) play an extremely important role in a person's ability to perform a task even as "simple" as repeating three digits forward.

Though both Binet and Terman considered the influence of nonintellective factors on results from intelligence tests, David Wechsler, author of the Wechsler scales, has been perhaps one of the most influential advocates of the role of nonintellective factors in these tests. Throughout his career, Wechsler emphasized that factors other than intellectual ability are involved in intelligent behavior. Today, there are three Wechsler intelligence tests, the Wechsler Adult Intelligence Scale, Third Edition (WAIS-III), the Wechsler Intelligence Scale for

Children, Fourth Edition (WISC-IV), and the Wechsler Preschool and Primary Scale of Intelligence, Third Edition (WPPSI-III).

The Wechsler Intelligence Scales

The role of nonintellective factors is apparent in the Wechsler intelligence scales. Just two years after the Binet scale's monumental 1937 revision, the Wechsler-Bellevue Intelligence Scale challenged its supremacy as a measure of human intelligence. With so many different and varied abilities associated with intelligence, Wechsler objected to the single score offered by the 1937 Binet scale. In addition, although Wechsler's test did not directly measure nonintellective factors, it took these factors into careful account in its underlying theory. In constructing his own intelligence test, Wechsler deviated considerably from many of the Binet scale's central concepts.

Wechsler (1939) capitalized on the inappropriateness of the 1937 Binet scale as a measure of the intelligence of adults. Because the Binet scale items were selected for use with children, Wechsler concluded that these items lacked validity when answered by adults. Further, examiner–subject rapport was often impaired when adults were tested with the Binet scale. Wechsler (1939) also correctly noted that the Binet scale's emphasis on speed, with timed tasks scattered throughout the scale, tended to unduly handicap older adults. Furthermore, mental age norms clearly did not apply to adults. Finally, Wechsler criticized the then-existing Binet scale because it did not consider that intellectual performance could deteriorate as a person grew older. (As noted in Chapter 9, the modern 2003 Binet scale has addressed these and many other criticisms of its earlier predecessors.)

Point and Performance Scale Concepts

Many of the differences between the Wechsler and the original Binet scales were profound. Two of the most critical differences were (1) Wechsler's use of the point scale concept rather than an age scale and (2) Wechsler's inclusion of a performance scale.

The point scale concept. Recall that from 1908 to 1972, the Binet scale grouped items by age level. Each age level included a group of tasks that could be passed by two-thirds to three-fourths of the individuals at that age level. In an age scale format, the arrangement of items has nothing to do with their content. At a particular year level, there might be one task related to memory, a second to reasoning, and a third to skill in using numerical data. Another level might also include a task related to memory but then include other tasks related to concentration or language skills. Thus, various types of content are scattered throughout the scale. Furthermore, on the earlier Binet scale, subjects did not receive a specific amount of points or credit for each task completed. For example, if a Binet scale subject is required to pass three out of four tasks in or-

FIGURE 10-1
*Advantages of
Wechsler's scale.*

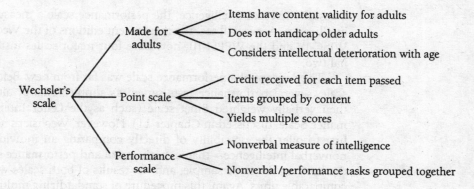

der to receive credit for a particular test, then passing only two tasks would produce no credit at all for that test.

In a point scale, credits or points are assigned to each item. An individual receives a specific amount of credit for each item passed. The point scale offers an inherent advantage. This scale makes it easy to group items of a particular content together, which is exactly what Wechsler did. The effect of such groupings appeared so powerful that a similar concept was used in the 1986 Binet scale. By arranging items according to content and assigning a specific number of points to each item, Wechsler constructed an intelligence test that yielded not only a total overall score but also scores for each content area. Thus, the point scale concept allowed Wechsler to devise a test that permitted an analysis of the individual's ability in a variety of content areas (for example, judgment, vocabulary, and range of general knowledge). Today, Wechsler's concept is the standard. Even the latest 2003 version of the Binet allows examiners to group all items of similar content into a single subtest or scale.

The performance scale concept. The early Binet scale had been persistently and consistently criticized for its emphasis on language and verbal skills. To deal with this problem, Wechsler included an entire scale that provided a measure of nonverbal intelligence: a performance scale. Thus, in addition to measuring intelligence in adults and yielding separate scores, Wechsler's approach offered a third major advantage over the early Binet scales. The performance scale consisted of tasks that require a subject to do something (for example, copy symbols or point to a missing detail) rather than merely answer questions (see Figure 10-1).

Although the early Binet scales contained some performance tasks, these tended to be concentrated at the younger age levels. Furthermore, the results of a subject's response to a performance task on the Binet scale were extremely difficult to separate from the results for verbal tasks, as can be done today. Thus, one could not determine the precise extent to which a subject's response to a performance task increased or decreased the total score. The Wechsler scale, however, included two separate scales. The verbal scale provided a measure of verbal intelligence, the performance scale a measure of nonverbal intelligence. As we will see, the most recent editions of the Wechsler scales, the WISC-IV and the WPPSI-III, now have four major scales instead of the original two.

The concept of a performance scale was far from new. Before the Wechsler scale, several performance tests served as supplements or alternatives to the then verbally weighted Binet scale (such as the Leiter International Performance Scale, discussed in Chapter 11). However, Wechsler's new scale was the first to offer the possibility of directly comparing an individual's verbal and nonverbal intelligence—that is, both verbal and performance scales were standardized on the same sample, and the results of both scales were expressed in comparable units. Again, this procedure of standardizing multiple scales on the same sample has been the standard in modern testing.

A performance scale attempts to overcome biases caused by language, culture, and education. Furthermore, if verbal tasks provide a useful context in which to observe problem solving, then tasks that require the subject to do something physical, such as pointing, can offer an even richer and more varied context. Indeed, performance tasks tend to require a longer interval of sustained effort, concentration, and attention than most verbal tasks. Therefore, they not only measure intelligence but also provide the clinician with a rich opportunity to observe behavior in a standard setting.

From the Wechsler-Bellevue Intelligence Scale to the WAIS-III

Despite his conceptual improvements, Wechsler's first effort to measure adult intelligence, the Wechsler-Bellevue scale (Wechsler, 1939), was poorly standardized. Its normative sample consisted of a nonrepresentative sample of 1081 whites from the eastern United States (primarily New York residents). By 1955, however, Wechsler had revised the Wechsler-Bellevue scale into its modern form, the Wechsler Adult Intelligence Scale (WAIS), which was revised in 1981 (the WAIS-R) and again in 1997 (the WAIS-III). Most likely the test will soon be again revised. If so, it will no doubt follow the innovations and changes that were more recently introduced in the WPPSI-III (Wechsler, 2002) and WISC-IV (Wechsler, 2003), the latest versions of the scales for children. These newer scales will be discussed in greater detail later in the chapter.

Scales, Subtests, and Indexes of the WAIS-III

Like Binet, Wechsler defined intelligence as the capacity to act purposefully and to adapt to the environment. In his words, intelligence is "the aggregate or global capacity of the individual to act purposefully, to think rationally and to deal effectively with his environment" (1958, p. 7). Wechsler believed that in-

TABLE 10-1
Wechsler Subtests

Subtest	Major function measured
Verbal Scales	
Vocabulary	Vocabulary level
Similarities	Abstract thinking
Arithmetic	Concentration
Digit span	Immediate memory, anxiety
Information	Range of knowledge
Comprehension	Judgment
Letter–number sequencing	Freedom from distractibility
Performance scales	
Picture completion	Alertness to details
Digit symbol–coding	Visual–motor functioning
Block design	Nonverbal reasoning
Matrix reasoning	Inductive reasoning
Picture arrangement	Planning ability
Symbol search	Information-processing speed
Object assembly	Analysis of part–whole relationships

telligence comprised specific elements that one could individually define and measure; however, these elements were interrelated—that is, not entirely independent. This is why he used the terms *global* and *aggregate*. Wechsler's definition implies that intelligence comprises several specific interrelated functions or elements and that general intelligence results from the interplay of these elements. Theoretically, by measuring each of the elements, one can measure general intelligence by summing the individual's capacities on each element. Thus, Wechsler tried to measure separate abilities, which Binet had avoided in adopting the concept of general mental ability.

In the WAIS-III and the latest editions of the Wechsler scales (WISC-IV and WPPSI-III), Wechsler's basic approach is maintained. First, there are individual subtests, each of which is related to a basic underlying skill or ability (see Table 10-1). For example, the information subtest measures one's range of knowledge. Each of the various subtests is also part of a more comprehensive scale. On the WAIS-III, the verbal scale simply consists of all of the subtests that require a verbal response; the performance scale consists of those subtests that require the individual to respond by performing, such as pointing to a missing detail. The full-scale IQ is then based on the summed scores of the more comprehensive scales.

The latest wrinkle in the adult test (WAIS-III) can be found in its index approach. An *index* is created where two or more subtests are related to a basic underlying skill. Figure 10-2 shows the WAIS-III's four indexes and their corresponding subtests.

FIGURE 10-2
*Schematic
overview of
WAIS-III index
scores.*

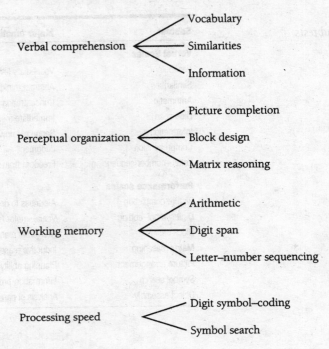

The Verbal Subtests

The seven verbal subtests of the WAIS-III are (1) vocabulary, (2) similarities, (3) arithmetic, (4) digit span, (5) information, (6) comprehension, and (7) letter–number sequencing. Each of these is briefly discussed as follows. In describing these and all other tests in this book, our examples are not those actually used in the test itself unless express permission has been obtained. Our goal is merely to illustrate the type of content to give readers a better understanding of how the actual test works.

The vocabulary subtest. The ability to define words is not only one of the best single measures of intelligence but also the most stable. Vocabulary tests appear on nearly every individual test that involves verbal intelligence. The relative stability of the vocabulary scale is one of its most important features. If an individual has shown *deterioration* (that is, lowered performance compared with a previously higher level) because of emotional factors or brain damage, for example, vocabulary is one of the last subtests to be affected. For example, the poor concentration of schizophrenic people lowers their performance on arithmetic or digit span tasks long before vocabulary is affected (Bryson, Greig, Lysaker, & Bell, 2002). Also, whereas mild concentration difficulties lower optimal performance on arithmetic and digit span tasks, such difficulties generally do not affect vocabulary until they become quite severe. Because the vocabulary subtest provides a relatively stable estimate of general verbal intelligence, one can use it to evaluate baseline or premorbid intelligence (that is, what a person's intellectual capacity probably was prior to an emotional illness, brain injury, or trauma).

The similarities subtest. The similarities subtest consists of some 15 paired items of increasing difficulty. The subject must identify the similarity between the items in each pair. The examiner asks, for example, "In what way are bread and water alike?" Many of the early, easier items are so well known that responses simply reflect previously learned associations (Kaufman, 1990). However, the more difficult items might be something like, "In what way are an ant and a rose alike?" Some items definitely require the subject to think abstractly. This subtest measures the subject's ability to see the similarity between apparently dissimilar objects or things.

The character of a person's thought processes can be seen in many cases. For example, schizophrenic people tend to give *idiosyncratic* concepts, or concepts that have meaning only to them. Such a response to the bread and water item might be "Both are used for torture." Such a response has meaning only to the schizophrenic person.

The arithmetic subtest. The arithmetic subtest contains approximately 15 relatively simple problems. The ninth most difficult item is as easy as this: "A person with $28.00 spends $.50. How much does he have left?" Obviously, you need not be a mathematician to figure this one out; however, you must be able to retain the figures in memory while manipulating them. In a few cases, such as in mentally handicapped or educationally deprived subjects, arithmetic skills can play a significant role. Generally, however, concentration, motivation, and memory are the main factors underlying performance. Figure 10-3 illustrates some of the intellective and nonintellective components of the arithmetic subtest as revealed by factor analytic and logical analyses.

The digit span subtest. The digit span subtest requires the subject to repeat digits, given at the rate of one per second, forward and backward. In terms of intellective factors, the digit span subtest measures short-term auditory memory. As with other Wechsler subtests, however, nonintellective factors (for example, attention) often influence the results (Hale, Hoeppner, & Fiorello, 2002). For example, anxiety in the test situation may impair performance on the digit span subtest (Gregory, 1999).

The information subtest. College students typically find the information subtest relatively easy and fun. As in all Wechsler subtests, items appear in order of increasing difficulty. Item 6 asks something like "Name two people who have been generals in the U.S. army. "How many members are there in the U.S. Congress?" Like all Wechsler subtests, the information subtest involves both intellective and nonintellective components, including several abilities to comprehend instructions, follow directions, and provide a response. Although purportedly a measure of the subject's range of knowledge, nonintellective factors such as curiosity and interest in the acquisition of knowledge tend to influence test scores. The subtest is also linked to alertness to the environment

FIGURE 10-3
Arithmetic subtest: intellective and nonintellective components.

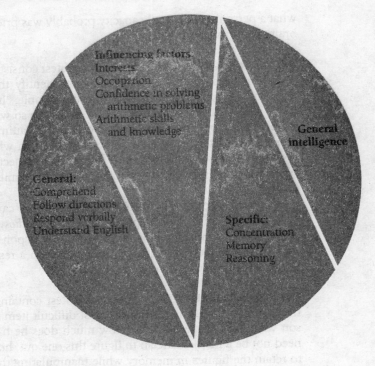

Influencing factors
Interests
Occupation
Confidence in solving
    arithmetic problems
Arithmetic skills
    and knowledge

General intelligence

General:
Comprehend
Follow directions
Respond verbally
Understand English

Specific:
Concentration
Memory
Reasoning

and alertness to cultural opportunities (Gregory, 1999; Kaufman, 1990). Figure 10-4 illustrates how one can parcel a score on the information subtest.

The comprehension subtest. The comprehension subtest has three types of questions. The first asks the subject what should be done in a given situation, as in "What should you do if you find an injured person lying in the street?" The second type of question asks the subject to provide a logical explanation for some rule or phenomenon, as in "Why do we bury the dead?" The third type asks the subject to define proverbs such as "A journey of 1000 miles begins with the first step." Generally, the comprehension subtest measures judgment in everyday practical situations, or common sense. Emotional difficulties frequently reveal themselves on this subtest and lower the person's score (Goldstein, Minshew, Allen, & Seaton, 2002). For example, to the question concerning what to do if you find an injured person, a psychopathic individual might respond, "Tell them I didn't do it." A phobic neurotic might respond, "Make sure I don't get any blood on myself." A schizophrenic might say, "Run!" In each case, the person's emotional disturbance interferes with his or her judgment and results in an inappropriate response.

The letter–number sequencing subtest. The letter–number sequencing task is one of three of the newest WAIS-III subtests. (The other two are matrix reasoning and symbol search, which are performance subtests.) This test is supplemen-

FIGURE 10-4
Information subtest: intellective and nonintellective components. (Based on factor analytic and logical analyses of intellective and nonintellective components in the information subtest.)

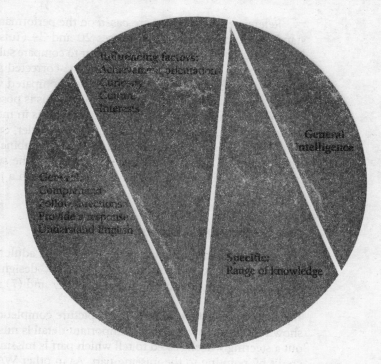

Influencing factors:
Achievement orientation
Curiosity
Cultural
Interests

General
Intelligence

General
Competence:
Follow directions
Provide a response
Understand English

Specific:
Range of knowledge

tary; it is not required to obtain a verbal IQ score, but it may be used as a supplement for additional information about the person's intellectual functioning (Phares & Trull, 2000). It is made up of seven items in which the individual is asked to reorder lists of numbers and letters. For example, Z, 3, B, 1, 2, A, would be reordered as 1, 2, 3, A, B, Z. This subtest is related to working memory and attention (Gregory, 1999; Phares & Trull, 2000).

Raw Scores, Scaled Scores, and the Verbal IQ

Together, the verbal subtests of the WAIS-III make up the verbal scale. Each subtest produces a raw score—that is, a total number of points—and has a different maximum total.

To allow testers to compare scores on individual subtests, raw scores can be converted to standard or scaled scores with a mean of 10 and a standard deviation of 3. Two sets of norms have been derived for this conversion: age-adjusted and reference-group norms.

Age-adjusted norms were created by preparing a normalized cumulative frequency distribution of raw scores for each age group (Tulsky, Zhu, & Ledbetter, 1997, p. 39). Thus, corrections for age-related differences in performance were made at the subtest level. Minor irregularities within and between ages were then smoothed.

Reference-group norms are based on the performance of participants in the standardization sample between ages 20 and 34 (Tulsky et al., 1997, p. 42). Reference-group norms allow the test user to compare subjects at the subtest level.

To obtain the verbal IQ (VIQ), the age-corrected scaled scores of the verbal subtests are summed. This sum is then compared with the standardization sample based on the combined age groups. This is possible because analysis of variance has failed to reveal significant variations in mean scores for the different age groups for scales and indexes (Ryan, Sattler, & Lopez, 2000; Tulsky et al., 1997). Thus, the test constructors could combine the age groups to construct tables of IQ (and index scores) based on the sum of the age-corrected scaled scores. The verbal IQ is a deviation IQ with a mean of 100 and a standard deviation of 15.

The Performance Subtests

The seven performance subtests of the Wechsler adult tests are (1) picture completion, (2) digit symbol–coding, (3) block design, (4) matrix reasoning, (5) picture arrangement, (6) object assembly, and (7) symbol search.

The picture completion subtest. In the picture completion subtest, the subject is shown a picture in which some important detail is missing, such as a car without a steering wheel. Asked to tell which part is missing, the subject can obtain credit by pointing to the missing part. As in other WAIS-III performance subtests, picture completion is timed. As simple to administer as this task seems, an experienced examiner is crucial. For example, if the subject points to a detail in a picture, the examiner must be able to see that the right detail has been identified. What if the subject points a little to the left of the target? Only experience can show how to deal with such ambiguities. An experienced examiner also knows when to move on to the next task before the subject becomes discouraged. In other words, the examiner knows when the subject's struggling is a sign that he or she does not know the answer rather than a sign of working toward an answer—a sometimes difficult distinction.

The digit symbol–coding subtest. The digit symbol–coding subtest requires the subject to copy symbols. In the upper part of the standard WAIS-III response form, the numbers 1 through 9 are each paired with a symbol (see Figure 10-5). After completing a short practice sample, the subject has 120 seconds to copy as many symbols as possible. The subtest measures such factors as ability to learn an unfamiliar task, visual–motor dexterity, degree of persistence, and speed of performance (Gregory, 1999; Kaufman, 1990). Naturally, the subject must have adequate visual acuity and appropriate motor capabilities to complete this subtest successfully, and factors that affect these capabilities, such as age, may affect test results (Kreiner & Ryan, 2001).

The block design subtest. Block design tasks have long been included in nonverbal measures of intelligence (Arthur, 1930; Kohs, 1923). Materials for the design subtest include nine variously colored blocks. The materials also in-

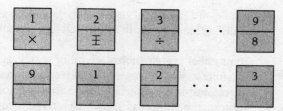

FIGURE 10-5   *Digit symbol–coding: an illustrative example. The top row contains divided boxes with a number in the upper half and a mark underneath. The bottom row contains divided boxes with numbers on top but no marks. The subject must supply the appropriate mark in the lower half of the bottom row.*

clude a booklet with pictures of the blocks arranged according to a specific geometric design or configuration. The subject must arrange the blocks to reproduce increasingly difficult designs. This subtest requires the subject to reason, analyze spatial relationships, and integrate visual and motor functions. The input information (that is, pictures of designs) is visual, but the response (output) is motor. The subtest provides an excellent measure of nonverbal concept formation, abstract thinking (Rapaport, Gill, & Schafer, 1968), and neurocognitive impairment (Lysaker, Clements, Wright, Evans, & Marks, 2001; Paul, Cohen, Moser, Ott, Zawacki, & Gordon, 2001).

The matrix reasoning subtest. As indicated in the previous chapter, modern theories of intelligence emphasize its multidimensional quality (Flanagan, McGrew, & Ortiz, 2000; McGrew & Flanagan, 1998). The matrix reasoning subtest was included in the WAIS-III in an effort to enhance the assessment of fluid intelligence, which involves our ability to reason. In the matrix reasoning subtest, the subject is presented with nonverbal, figural stimuli. The task is to identify a pattern or relationship between the stimuli. In addition to its role in measuring fluid intelligence, this subtest is a good measure of information-processing and abstract-reasoning skills (Phares & Trull, 2000).

The picture arrangement subtest. The picture arrangement subtest also requires the subject to notice relevant details. The subject must also be able to plan adequately and notice cause-and-effect relationships (Gregory, 1999; Kaufman, 1990). The subtest consists of approximately 11 items, each of which contains a series of related pictures similar to those found in most comic strips. The subject must put the misarranged pictures in the right order to tell a story. Because the individual must find the logical sequence of events, the subtest taps nonverbal reasoning ability. Because some of the items involve social or interpersonal content, some say the subtest also taps the ability to interpret social situations accurately (Sattler, 1982; Segal, Westen, Lohr, & Silk, 1993).

The object assembly subtest. Object assembly consists of puzzles (cut-up objects) that the subject is asked to put together as quickly as possible. This subtest measures the subject's ability to see relationships between the part and the whole and involves "visual analysis and its coordination with simple assembly skills" (Phares & Trull, 2000). Object assembly is optional on the WAIS-III.

The symbol search subtest. Symbol search is another new and optional WAIS-III subtest, which was added in recognition of the role of speed of information processing in intelligence (see Saccuzzo, Johnson, & Guertin, 1994). In this subtest, the subject is shown two target geometric figures. The task is then to search from among a set of five additional search figures and determine whether the target appears in the search group. There are 60 items, for which the subject is given 120 seconds. Presumably, the faster a subject performs this task, the faster his or her information-processing speed will be. There is some question whether this subtest is measuring cognitive processing or elementary motor operations (Crowe, Benedict, Enrico, Mancuso, Matthews, & Wallace, 1999). Chapter 15 discusses other measures of information-processing speed.

Performance IQs

As with the verbal subtests, the raw scores for each of the five performance subtests are converted to scaled scores. The mean and standard deviation are the same as for the verbal subtests—10 and 3, respectively. The performance IQ (PIQ) is obtained by summing the age-corrected scaled scores on the performance subtests and comparing this score with the standardization sample. Like the verbal IQ, the performance IQ is a deviation IQ with a mean of 100 and a standard deviation of 15.

Full-Scale IQs

The full-scale IQ (FSIQ) follows the same principles of the verbal and performance IQs. It is obtained by summing the age-corrected scaled scores of the verbal subtests with the performance subtests and comparing the subject to the standardization sample. Again, a deviation IQ with a mean of 100 and a standard deviation of 15 is obtained.

Index Scores

In addition to the verbal, performance, and full-scale IQs, the WAIS-III affords the examiner the opportunity to compute index scores. As indicated in Figure 10-2, there are four such scores: verbal comprehension, perceptual organization, working memory, and processing speed. As indicated, these indexes are consistent with modern notions of the multidimensional nature of human intelligence.

As a measure of acquired knowledge and verbal reasoning, the verbal comprehension index might best be thought of as a measure of crystallized intelligence. According to the technical manual, this index is a "more refined," "purer" measure of verbal comprehension than is the verbal IQ because it excludes the arithmetic and digit span subtests, which have attentional or working memory components (Tulsky et al., 1997, p. 186).

The perceptual organization index, consisting of picture completion, block design, and matrix reasoning (see Figure 10-2), is believed to be a measure of fluid intelligence. Other factors that influence one's performance on this group of tests are attentiveness to details and visual motor integration (Tulsky et al., 1997).

The notion of working memory is perhaps one of the most important innovations on the WAIS-III. *Working memory* refers to the information that we actively hold in our minds, in contrast to our stored knowledge, or long-term memory. Consider the following question: "If you have $10.00 and give $4.50 to your brother and spend 75¢ on candy, how much do you have left? To answer this question, you must mentally hold $10.00 in your head, subtract $4.50, and then hold that result while you subtract 75¢. It is your working memory that allows you to do this.

Finally, the processing speed index attempts to measure how quickly your mind works. For example, while one person may require 20 seconds to solve the given problem, another may require only 5 seconds.

Interpretive Features of the Wechsler Tests

The WAIS-III provides a rich source of data that often furnishes significant cues for diagnosing various conditions. The comparison of verbal and performance IQs, evaluation of index scores, and analysis of the pattern of subtest scores may be helpful, for example, in evaluating brain damage and disordered states (Devanand et al., 2003; Gregory, 1999; Martin et al., 2002; Phares & Trull, 2000).

Verbal-Performance IQ Comparisons

In providing a measure of nonverbal intelligence in conjunction with a verbal IQ, the WAIS-III offers an extremely useful opportunity not offered by the early Binet scales. First, the WAIS-III performance IQ aids in the interpretation of the verbal IQ (Sattler, 1988). Assume, for example, that a subject obtains a verbal IQ in the low ranges (such as VIQ = 60). If the performance IQ is also approximately 60, then the verbal IQ has been confirmed, and we have a good indication that the individual is, in fact, intellectually retarded. Remember, however, that a diagnosis of mental retardation should not be made on the basis of IQ alone. The individual must show significant deficits in adaptive functioning as well as a full-scale IQ below 70. What if the performance IQ exceeds 100, but the verbal IQ is 55? In this case, the individual is at least average in his or her nonverbal skills but three standard deviations below the mean in the verbal area. Even though the full-scale IQ might still fall within the retarded range, it is quite unlikely that such a person is mentally retarded. Instead, language, cultural, or educational factors might account for the differences in the two IQs.

In one study of verbal versus performance IQs, Saccuzzo, Johnson, and Russell (1992) examined approximately 5000 gifted children from four ethnic backgrounds: African American, Caucasian, Filipino, and Hispanic. Results showed that even though all children had IQs of 125 or greater, the nature of the verbal-performance discrepancy, if any, depended on ethnic background. The African American and Caucasian groups had higher verbal than performance IQs. The reverse was found for the Filipinos, who had significantly higher performance IQs. No differences were found between the verbal and performance IQs for the Hispanics. Results such as these indicate that it is not appropriate to make sweeping generalizations about the meaning of verbal and performance IQ discrepancies. Indeed, the VIQ–PIQ distinction has been abandoned in the WISC-IV (Wechsler, 2003) and WPPSI-III (Wechsler 2002), the two latest versions of the Wechsler tests. When considering any test result, we must take ethnic background and multiple sources of information into account.

Pattern Analysis

The separate subtest scores of the WAIS-III and other Wechsler tests offer an opportunity for *pattern analysis*. In such analysis, one evaluates relatively large differences between subtest scaled scores. Wechsler (1958) reasoned that different types of emotional problems might have differential effects on the subtests and cause unique score patterns. For example, hysterics (people with conversion disorders) use denial and repression—that is, they put things out of awareness as a defense mechanism. Therefore, they should show lapses in their long-term store of knowledge, which might produce a relatively low score on the information subtest. Schizophrenia involves poor concentration and impaired judgment, which might turn up as relatively low scores on arithmetic and comprehension. Wechsler (1958) provided a host of patterns tentatively proposed as diagnostically significant.

Following Wechsler's (1958) proposed patterns, many investigators empirically studied the potential validity of pattern analysis. As is the case in many fields of psychology, results were inconclusive and contradictory.

Years of investigation have revealed that analysis of patterns must be done cautiously. At best, such analysis should be used to generate hypotheses. Such hypotheses must then be either corroborated or refuted by other sources of data, such as historical information, medical records, family interviews, and direct observation (Gregory, 1999; Tulsky et al., 1997). The next section presents two hypothetical case studies to illustrate how hypotheses might be generated from WAIS-III data.

Hypothetical Case Studies

A drop in grades. Consider the following example of a 16-year-old high-school junior who has a D average although he previously had a stable B average. Standard achievement tests found his reading and arithmetic grades appropriate. Table 10-2 shows his age-corrected scaled scores on the WAIS-III (remember, the mean is 10 and the standard deviation is 3).

The previously stable B average indicates that this individual is probably of at least average intelligence. The rapid decline in his grades, however, suggests

TABLE 10-2
Hypothetical Scaled Scores for a High-School Junior

Verbal scales	Performance scales
Vocabulary: 11	Picture completion: 10
Similarities: 11	Digit symbol–coding: 4
Arithmetic: 7	Block design: 5
Digit span: 5	Matrix reasoning: 6
Information: 11	Picture arrangement: 11
Comprehension: 9	
Scaled score sum: 54	Scaled score sum: 36
Verbal IQ: 104	Performance IQ: 83
Full-scale IQ: 93	

some dramatic change or shift in functioning. His scaled score of 11 on vocabulary is above the mean. Because vocabulary is a relatively stable measure of IQ, the scaled score of 11 also indicates this individual's IQ of 93 is most likely an underestimate of his intelligence. Assuming that this individual's typical scaled score performance would be approximately 11, as reflected in his scaled score on vocabulary and confirmed by his scaled scores on information and similarities, we find evidence for deterioration in his judgment (comprehension), concentration (arithmetic), and immediate memory (digit span) in the verbal areas. We also find deterioration in his visual–motor speed and integration (digit symbol–coding), nonverbal reasoning (block design), and fluid intelligence (matrix reasoning) in the performance areas.

With no evidence to the contrary, the clinician would strongly suspect that the subject's shift in grades may be the result of a brain injury or tumor, because these impair performance on all the subtests in which the subject has shown evidence of deterioration (e.g., Lincoln, Crosson, Bauer, & Cooper, 1994; Ryan, Paolo, & Van Fleet, 1994). However, the clinician would consider other possibilities as well. Environmental or situational factors could lead to impairment on the various WAIS-III subtests. For example, because the subject may have become involved with drugs, this possibility must be examined. Furthermore, schizophrenia may cause similar decrements in performance. Therefore, signs of peculiar behavior or other symptoms of schizophrenia should be ruled out by an interview and other tests. Ruling out situational, environmental, and schizophrenic factors, the examiner might interview to determine whether the subject has suffered a recent blow to the head. If these possibilities prove to be negative, then the subject should be immediately referred for a neurological examination. As you no doubt have observed, this analysis resulted in several speculations, and the clinician exercised the usual caution in using the results.

A slow learner. Table 10-3 shows the hypothetical age-corrected scaled scores of a 16-year-old girl with chronic school problems. Identified as a slow learner in the earlier grades, she reads far below her grade level.

TABLE 10-3
*Hypothetical
Scaled Scores for
a Slow Learner*

Verbal scales	Performance scales
Vocabulary: 8	Picture completion: 11
Similarities: 11	Digit symbol–coding: 12
Arithmetic: 4	Block design: 13
Digit span: 10	Matrix reasoning: 12
Information: 3	Picture arrangement: 10
Comprehension: 7	
Scaled score sum: 43	Scaled score sum: 58
Verbal IQ: 89	Performance IQ: 112
Full-scale IQ: 99	

The subject is nearly one standard deviation above the mean in her performance IQ; all her subtests in the performance area are at or greater than the mean. Clearly, she does not lack intellectual potential. Thus, her verbal IQ of 89 most likely underestimates her intellectual capacity. Furthermore, she obtains an above-average score on similarities, a noneducationally related measure of abstract thinking skills. Her major weaknesses arise in the subtests related to academic achievement, information, and arithmetic. In addition, she shows some impairment in her judgment. Her verbal IQ thus appears to be lowered because of her lack of motivation for academic achievement and her poor judgment. Her pattern of subtest scores is one typically found in poor readers and delinquents.

In considering these illustrations, remember that the validity of pattern analysis is still questionable. Saccuzzo and Lewandowski (1976) found a pattern for acting-out behavior that Wickham later substantiated (1978). However, evidence supporting the validity of most patterns, for reasons we shall discuss more fully, is still questionable (Alexander, Prohovnik, Stem, & Mayeux, 1994; Lipsitz, Dworkin, & Erlenmeyer-Kimling, 1993). Our illustrations are designed to give you a flavor of the approach taken by many practicing psychologists. Most real-life examples are nowhere nearly as clear-cut as our hypothetical ones.

Psychometric Properties of the Wechsler Adult Scale

Standardization

The WAIS-III standardization sample consisted of 2450 adults divided into 13 age groups from 16–17 through 85–89 (Tulsky et al., 1997, p. 19). The sample was stratified according to gender, race, education, and geographic region based on 1995 census data.

Reliability

The impressive reliability coefficients for the WAIS-III attest to the internal and temporal reliability of the verbal, performance, and full-scale IQs. When the split-half method is used for all subtests except speeded tests (digit symbol–coding and symbol search), the average coefficients across age levels are .98 for the full-scale IQ, .97 for the verbal IQ, and .94 for the performance IQ (Tulsky et al., 1997, p. 50). Test–retest coefficients reported in the manual are only slightly lower (.95, .94, and .88 for FSIQ, VIQ, and PIQ, respectively).

The technical manual reports an overall standard error of measurement of 2.29 for the full-scale IQ, 2.50 for the verbal IQ, and 3.75 for the performance IQ (Tulsky et al., 1997, p. 54). As you may recall from our discussion of correlation and reliability (see Chapter 4), all tests possess a certain degree of measurement error. The standard error of measurement (SEM) is the standard deviation of the distribution of error scores. According to classical test theory, an error score is the difference between the score actually obtained by giving the test and the score that would be obtained if the measuring instrument were perfect. In practice, the SEM is based on the reliability coefficient, given by the formula

$$SEM = SD \sqrt{1 - r_{xx}}$$

where SD is the standard deviation of the test scores and r_{xx} is the reliability coefficient. In practice, the SEM can be used to form a confidence interval within which an individual's true score is likely to fall. More specifically, we can determine the probability that an individual's true score will fall within a certain range a given percentage of the time. To be roughly at the 68% level, an obtained score must fall within the range of one SEM. The 95% confidence interval is approximately two SEMs.

Using this information, we can see that the smaller SEM for the verbal and full-scale IQs means that we can have considerably more confidence that an obtained score represents an individual's true score than we can for the performance IQ. Thus, given a full-scale IQ of 110, we can assume that 95% of the time the subject's true score would fall at ± 4.58 (two SEMs) of the true score. In other words, 95% of subjects with a score of 110 have a true score between 105.42 and 114.58, and only 5% do not.

Test–retest reliability coefficients for the various subtests have tended to vary widely. For data presented in the technical manual, coefficients for most subtests tend to run in the low .70's and .80's. However, some are in the .60's. These relatively low coefficients again indicate the potential hazards of pattern analysis. Unstable subtests would produce unstable patterns, thus limiting the potential validity of pattern interpretation.

Perhaps you can now understand why the validity of pattern analysis is questionable and difficult to document. The dependability of pattern analysis rests on subtest intercorrelation as well as the separate reliabilities of the subtests. As the subtest intercorrelations increase and the reliabilities of individual subtests decrease, pattern analysis becomes increasingly dubious (Saccuzzo, Braff, Shine, & Lewandowski, 1981).

Validity

The validity of the WAIS-III rests primarily on its correlation with the earlier WAIS-R and with its correlation with the earlier children's version (the WISC-III), where the ages overlap. As might be expected, correlations between the WAIS-III and the other tests run higher for the full-scale, verbal, and performance IQs than for the individual subtests. The WAIS-III verbal, performance, and full-scale IQs correlate .94, .86, and .93, respectively, with the corresponding measures on the third edition of the WISC. Correlations with the various major composites of the WISC-IV (Wechsler, 2003) run lower, with a range from .73 to .89 (see Wechsler, 2003, p. 68).

Evaluation of the Wechsler Adult Scales

The Wechsler adult scale is extensively used as a measure of adult intelligence. This scale is well constructed and its primary measures—the verbal, performance, and full-scale IQs—are highly reliable. As with all modern tests, including the 2003 Binet, the reliability of the individual subtests is lower and therefore makes analysis of subtest patterns dubious, if not hazardous, for the purpose of making decisions about individuals. Yet making such conclusions is commonplace. As we have noted, though such analysis may be useful for generating hypotheses, it calls for extreme caution.

The strong correlation between the WAIS-III and WAIS-R is a somewhat mixed blessing. Clearly, the WAIS-III is much the same test as the older WAIS-R, which itself is highly related to the original Wechsler-Bellevue of 1939. Thus, the WAIS-III continues to rely heavily on the theories and data of the 1920s and 1930s. As with the modern Binet, it incorporates modern multidimensional theories of intelligence in its measures of fluid intelligence and processing speed. It does not, however, allow for multiple intelligences, an important concept. According to one modern theory, there are at least seven distinct and independent intelligences—linguistic, body-kinesthetic, spatial, logical-mathematical, musical, intrapersonal, and interpersonal (Gardner, 1983; Sarouphim, 2002). The classical view of intelligence reflected in the WAIS-III leaves little room for such ideas. As indicated, the latest versions of the Wechsler, the WISC-IV, and the WPPSI-III have been more innovative, which suggests there may soon be a WAIS-IV.

Downward Extensions of the WAIS-III: The WISC-IV and the WPPSI-III

Many of the basic ideas of the WAIS-III apply to its downward extension, the WISC-IV, first published in 1949, revised in 1974 and 1991, and most recently revised in 2003. The WISC-IV measures intelligence from ages 6 through 16 years, 11 months. Many basic ideas of the WAIS-III also apply to the Wechsler Preschool and Primary Scale of Intelligence, Third Edition (WPPSI-III). The WPPSI-III, first published in 1967, revised in 1989 and again in 2003, measures intelligence in children from 2.5 to 7 years, 3 months. Because you already know the basic ideas that apply to all Wechsler scales, we present here only the major distinguishing features of the WISC-IV and the WPPSI-III.

The WISC-IV

The Wechsler Intelligence Scale for Children, Fourth Edition (WISC-IV) is the latest version of this scale to measure global intelligence and, in an attempt to mirror advances in the understanding of intellectual properties, the WISC-IV measures indexes of the specific cognitive abilities, processing speed, and working memory (Wechsler, 2003). The original form of the WISC was based on Form 11 of the Wechsler-Bellevue scale, which provided a point scale measure of intelligence for children between the ages of 6 years and 16 years, 11 months. The WISC-IV contains 15 subtests, 10 of which were retained from the earlier WISC-III and five entirely new ones. Three subtests used in earlier versions—picture arrangement, object assembly, and mazes, were entirely deleted. As indicated, the WISC-IV abandoned the VIQ–PIQ dichotomy. In place of these scales are four major indexes, which can be summed to arrive at a full-scale IQ.

Within the WISC-IV verbal comprehension index are comprehension, similarities, and vocabulary subtests. Information and word reasoning are supplementary subtests. Within the WISC-IV perceptual reasoning index are the subtests block design, picture concepts, and matrix reasoning. The supplementary test is a picture completion task.

The processing speed index comprises a coding subtest and a symbol search subtest that consists of paired groups of symbols. In this latter subtest, each pair contains a target group and a search group, just as in the comparable WAIS-III subtest. The child scans the two groups and indicates whether or not a target symbol appears in the search group. A cancellation subtest is supplementary to the processing speed index.

Finally, the working memory index consists of digit span, letter–number sequencing, and a supplemental arithmetic subtest. These subtests, with the exception of symbol search and the deleted mazes, parallel the corresponding WAIS-III subtests in content and functions measured. Items are arranged in order of difficulty and are grouped by content.

The WISC-IV is a major improvement from the earlier WISC-III and, as indicated, has introduced important innovations from earlier versions of the Wechsler scales. As with the 2003 Binet, the modern WISC-IV (also published in 2003) has updated its theoretical underpinnings. In addition to the important concept of fluid reasoning, there is an emphasis on the modern cognitive psychology concepts of working memory and processing speed. To add to its clinical utility, the test manual provides numerous studies of special groups, and the WISC-IV is linked to an achievement test (the Wechsler Individual

Achievement Test, or WIAT-II), which is also published by the Psychological Corporation (2001).

Through the use of teaching items that are not scored, it is possible to reduce errors attributed to a child's lack of understanding. The administration procedures also include many queries and prompts that examiners can use to elicit a maximum performance. Although the use of prompts dates back to early versions of the Binet, the WISC-IV appears to provide examiners with more latitude to encourage a child to perform as well as possible.

Item bias. One of the most important innovations in the WISC-IV is the use of empirical data to identify item biases. Heretofore the primary, and in our opinion, inadequate and insufficient, method of examining for item bias was to use trained judges to examine item content. Although the WISC-IV retains this approach, the use of item analysis and other statistical procedures to determine which items may be biased adds an important and necessary dimension in the elimination of bias. The major reason that empirical approaches are needed is that expert judgments simply do not eliminate differential performance as a function of gender, race, ethnicity, and socioeconomic status. Even if a test has been thoroughly and extensively screened by experts to eliminate content that might be biased, bias nevertheless remains in terms of the number of items passed as a function of gender, race, ethnicity, and socioeconomic status. The WISC-IV has not eliminated item bias, but the use of empirical techniques is a major step in the right direction.

Publishers of other tests discussed throughout this book would do well to follow this lead, which hopefully will soon become the standard. For example, it is widely known that men do better than women on multiple-choice tests, which are widely used in high-stakes testing. This bias is not eliminated by making the content gender-neutral or by using as many references to women as men. The use of empirical methods and sophisticated statistical procedures, as has been done with the WISC-IV, offers the best hope of someday devising a test that accurately measures ability without gender, ethnic, racial, or socioeconomic bias.

Standardization of the WISC-IV. The WISC-IV standardization sample consisted of 2200 children selected to represent the March 2000 U.S. census. The sample was stratified using age, gender, race (African American, Hispanic, white, other), geographic region, parental occupation, and geographic location as variables. As with its predecessor, the WISC-III, the sample contained 100 boys and 100 girls at each age from 6 through 16 years (see Figure 10-6).

Raw scores and scaled scores. In the WISC-IV, scaled scores are calculated from raw scores on the basis of norms at each age level, just as in the WAIS-III. The mean scaled score is also set at 10 and the standard deviation at 3. Scaled scores are summed for the four indexes and full-scale IQs. These totals are then compared against a single table of standard scores with a mean of 100 and a standard deviation of 15 for each of the indexes and full-scale IQ.

Characteristics of the Standardization Sample

Percentage of the population based on the 1980 U.S. Census.

Percentage in the WISC-III norm sample.

These graphs show demographic characteristics of the WISC-III norm sample compared with those of the U.S. population. The total number sampled was 2,200 children between ages 6 and 16, with equal numbers of males and females.

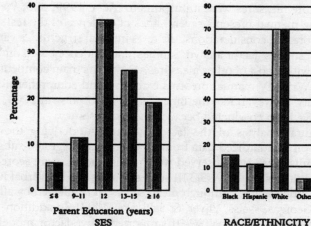

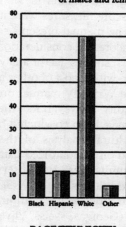

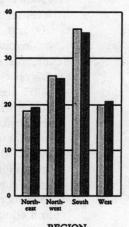

FIGURE 10-6   *Characteristics of the WISC-III standardization sample.*

(From Wechsler Intelligence Scale for Children, 1989, Copyright © 1989 The Psychological Corporation. Reprinted by permission.)

Interpretation. Interpretation of the WISC-IV also parallels that of the WAIS-III. The basic approach involves evaluating each of the four major indexes to examine for deficits in any given area and evaluate the validity of the full-scale IQ. To the extent that large discrepancies exist in the indexes, the validity of the full-scale IQ falls into question. The next step would be to consider the underlying functions measured by each of the subtests and again determine whether large discrepancies exist between one subtest and another, or between one subtest and the overall mean of the subtests. As a simple example, if all subtests are roughly average except for an extremely low score on working memory, the clinician would hypothesize a specific deficit in working memory.

Reliability of the WISC-IV. When the WISC-IV was revised in 2003, developers intended to maintain the strong psychometric properties of its predecessors, which they largely did. The procedure for calculating reliability coefficients for the WISC-IV was analogous to that used for the WISC-III and WAIS-III. Split-half reliabilities for the WISC-IV's composites range from .88 for processing speed to .97 for the full-scale IQ (Wechsler, 2003, p. 35). Naturally, reliabilities for individual subtests run lower, as in all forms of tests.

As usual, test–retest reliability coefficients run a bit below those obtained using the split-half method. As with the Binet scales and other tests, reliability coefficients are poorest for the youngest groups at the highest levels of ability.

WISC-IV validity. In providing evidence of its validity, the WISC-IV manual relies on the modern trend that rejects the distinction between various types of validity and instead examines all of the relevant evidence that indicates whether a test score measures what it purports to (Aera, 1999, p. 5; Wechsler, 2003, p. 47). The manual presents several lines of evidence of the test's validity, involving theoretical considerations, the test's internal structure, a variety of intercorrelational studies, factor analytic studies, and evidence based on WISC-IV's relationship with a host of other measures. As with its main competitor, the 2003 Binet, the WISC-IV manual presents extensive and comprehensive support for its validity. However, like the Binet, as we go to press in 2004, no external studies have been conducted because the test is so new.

A cross-cultural analysis of the factor structure underlying the earlier WISC-III, based on standardized data from 16 countries, suggested substantial cross-cultural similarities. Also observed were no significant mean score differences across the cultures on the WISC-III subtests, full-scale IQ, verbal IQ, performance IQ, or index scores, although mean scores were affected by affluence and education (Georgas, Weiss, Vijver, & Sakloske, 2003). In addition, a confirmatory factor analysis of the WISC-III supported a five-factor model of intelligence including verbal comprehension, constructional praxis, visual reasoning, freedom from distractibility, and processing speed (Burton, Sepehri, Hecht, VandenBroek, Ryan, & Drabman, 2001). As a general rule, experimental findings from a more recent version of the test tend to apply to the more updated version. Future research will help determine whether this principle holds for the WISC-IV.

The WPPSI-III

In 1967, Wechsler published a scale for children 4 to 6 years of age, the Wechsler Preschool and Primary Scale of Intelligence (WPPSI). In its revised (1989) version, the WPPSI-R paralleled the WAIS-III and WISC-III in format, method of determining reliabilities, and subtests. Only two unique subtests are included: (1) animal pegs, an optional test that is timed and requires the child to place a colored cylinder into an appropriate hole in front of the picture of an animal; and (2) sentences, an optional test of immediate recall in which the child is asked to repeat sentences presented orally by the examiner.

The latest version, the WPPSI-III, was substantially revised. It contains most of the new features of the WISC-IV, including five composites, but did not delete the VIQ or PIQ. The WPPSI-III was also restructured to lower the age range. It can now be used for children as young as 2 years, 6 months, and has a special set of subtests specifically for the age range of 2½ to 3 years, 11 months. To support legislation that recommends multiple assessments for identification of children in need of special educational services, WPPSI-III was made compatible with the Adaptive Behavior Assessment System, the WIAT-II, and the Differential Abilities Scale. Seven new subtests were added to enhance the measurement of fluid reasoning, processing speed, and receptive, expressive vocabulary. Clinical studies were conducted with children with mental retardation, developmental delay, giftedness, autism, attention deficit hyperactivity disorder, and language disorder. These validity studies foster a better understanding of the relative performance of clinical and nonclinical groups.

In addition to the extended age range and a special set of core tests for the youngest children, the WPPSI-III includes updated norms stratified as in the WISC-IV and based on the October 2000 census. New subtests were added along with the two additional composites (processing speed quotient, or PSQ; and general language composite, or GLC). Along with the verbal, performance, and full-scale composites, these new composites provide a new dimension to evaluate young children.

Reminiscent of the 2003 Binet, with its routing procedure, the WWPSI-III has age-specific starting points for each of the various subtests. It also has reversal rules in case a child misses an item at the starting point, as well as discontinuation rules to prevent frustration and reduce total testing time. As with the WISC-IV, there are practice items that are not scored as well as wide scope for an examinee to make use of prompts and queries. In addition, an examiner may repeat an item as often as requested.

The WPPSI-III also uses empirical methods to evaluate test bias, which, as indicated, is a welcome and long-needed development in the testing field. As with the 2003 Binet, instructions were modified to make them easier for young children, and materials were revised to make them more interesting. Reliability coefficients are comparable to those of the WISC-IV, and the test manual provides impressive evidence of validity.

As with the WISC-IV, as we go to press it is too early to report the results of any research studies evaluating the WPPSI-III. With analyses already in progress (Institute for Applied Psychometrics, 2003), anticipated widespread use of the WPPSI-III in countries other than the United States such as Australia, the United Kingdom, and Canada (Psychological Corporation, 2003), and the popularity of the latest version of the test (Lichtenberger & Kaufman, 2003), it is certain that the WPPSI-III will be well researched and will add a wealth of information to our understanding of theories of intelligence.

SUMMARY

Motivation for the development of the Wechsler scales began with the search for a more appropriate measure of adult intelligence than that provided by the 1937 Binet scale. The first product of this effort was the Wechsler-Bellevue scale.

In a *point scale,* a specific number of credits or points is assigned to each item. A *performance scale* measures nonverbal intelligence, as opposed to a *verbal scale,* which measures verbal intelligence. On a performance scale, the subject is required to do something other than merely answer questions.

The seven standard verbal subtests of the WAIS-III and the functions they purportedly measure are as follows:

1. Vocabulary: vocabulary level
2. Similarities: abstract thinking
3. Arithmetic: concentration
4. Digit span: immediate memory, anxiety
5. Information: range of knowledge
6. Comprehension: judgment
7. Letter–number sequencing: freedom of distractibility

The seven performance subtests of the WAIS-III and the functions they purportedly measure are as follows:

1. Picture completion: alertness to details
2. Digit symbol–coding: visual–motor functioning
3. Block design: nonverbal reasoning
4. Matrix reasoning: inductive reasoning
5. Picture arrangement: planning ability
6. Object assembly: analysis of part–whole relationships
7. Symbol search: information-processing speed

Three IQ scores can be obtained from the WAIS-III: verbal IQ, performance IQ, and full-scale IQ. The verbal and performance IQs are obtained by (1) converting the raw score of each subtest to a *scaled score*, or an age-corrected standard score of 10 with a standard deviation of 3; (2) adding the verbal subtest scores and then the performance subtest scores to obtain a separate summary score for each; and (3) converting these two scaled scores to IQs by using a table that converts them to a standard score with a mean of 100 and a standard deviation of 15. To obtain the full-scale IQ, (1) add the scaled scores for the verbal and performance IQs, and then (2) convert this figure to an IQ by using the table of norms, which converts it to a standard score (mean 100; SD = 15).

The reliability coefficients of the WAIS-III are excellent for verbal, performance, and full-scale IQs, in terms of both temporal stability and internal consistency. Reliabilities for the individual subtests, however, vary widely. Evidence for the validity of the WAIS-III comes from its high correlation with its earlier predecessor, the WAIS-R, from its high correlation with the WISC-III, and from a variety of sources.

The WISC-IV is a downward extension of the WAIS-III for measuring children's intelligence. First published in 1949, the WISC was revised in 1974, 1991, and most recently in 2003. It contains many significant changes from earlier versions as well as several important innovations, including empirical testing of item bias.

The WPPSI-III is a downward extension of the WISC-IV for measuring intelligence in the youngest children (2.5 years to 7 years, 3 months). It was first published in 1967 and revised in 1989 and again in 2002. Its changes and innovations parallel those found in the WISC-IV.

WEB ACTIVITY

For interesting and relevant Web sites, check the following:

http://www.dpa.state.ky.us/library/advocate/sept99/Waisnot.html
  Article: "WAIS" not, want not: A jurisprudent therapy approach to innovations in forensic assessment of intellectual functioning

www.a-gifted-child.com/evaluations.html
  Intelligence testing and the gifted child

www.gifteddevelopment.com/SBLM%20Media/Problems.pdf
  Problems in the assessment of gifted children

www.tased.edu.au/tasonline/tag/aaegt7/mccann.htm
  The creativity–IQ interface

CHAPTER 11

Other Individual Tests of Ability in Education and Special Education

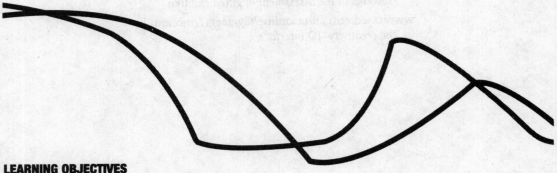

LEARNING OBJECTIVES

When you have completed this chapter, you should be able to:

- [ ] Identify the advantages and disadvantages of the alternative individual ability tests compared with the Binet and Wechsler scales

- [ ] List six differences among the alternative individual ability tests

- [ ] Discuss the strengths and weaknesses of the Bayley Scales of Infant Development compared with other measures of infant intelligence

- [ ] Identify some of the purposes of the Columbia Mental Maturity Scale

- [ ] Explain the main theory behind tests of learning disability

- [ ] Explain the main idea behind testing for brain damage

- [ ] List three possible reasons for errors on the Bender Visual Motor Gestalt Test

- [ ] Describe the general reaction among reviewers to the Torrance Tests of Creative Thinking

- [ ] Identify problems of the Wide Range Achievement Test

- [ ] Describe the legal responsibilities of schools and rights of parents in special education assessment

*I*n Long Beach California, a student was being evaluated for a learning disability. At issue was whether the student qualified for special education. The evaluation used a variety of tests but did not use the Binet or Wechsler test. The student was found not eligible. The parents challenged the evaluation, claiming the district was required to use a standardized IQ test like the Binet or Wechsler in its evaluation. Siding with the school district, the 9th U.S. Circuit Court of Appeals held that the district was not required to use a traditional standardized test such as the Binet or Wechsler in its evaluation of the student (*Ford and Ford v. Long Beach Unified School District,* 37 IDELR I, 9th Circuit 2002). As noted in the *Special Educator 2003 Desk Book* (Norlin, 2003), an important reference book in special education that summarizes recent court decisions in the field, tests must be considered valid for a particular student or they cannot be used. In this case, the Binet and Wechsler apparently did not meet this standard in the court's view.

For assessing general intelligence in relatively normal individuals or to obtain baseline information, the Binet and Wechsler scales are exceptionally good instruments. However, both scales have their limitations and are not valid for all individuals. For instance, the standardization samples do not include individuals with sensory, physical, or language handicaps.

How, then, can one fairly evaluate the performance on the Binet scale of someone who has been blind for life? What about individuals who cannot speak?

Clearly, numerous circumstances arise where a score on the major scales would be either impossible to obtain or seriously biased against the individual. Thus, several individual tests have been created to meet special problems, measure specific abilities, or address the limitations of the Binet and Wechsler scales. Such tests are widely used in education and, in particular, in the important field of special education.

There is quite an array of individual ability tests. Because many were designed to supplement or to provide an alternative to the Binet and Wechsler scales, we begin this chapter by comparing the general features of these tests with those of the Binet and Wechsler scales. We move on to compare the alternative tests to each other, and then we discuss them one at a time. Finally, we devote a special section to learning disabilities and the legal rights of students eligible for special education.

Alternative Individual Ability Tests Compared with the Binet and Wechsler Scales

The tests discussed in this section were developed more recently and are newer and less well established than the Binet and Wechsler scales; however, this does not sufficiently explain why no other individual test is used as much as these two major scales. Despite the limitations of the Binet and Wechsler scales, none of the alternatives is clearly superior from a psychometric standpoint. Although a few of the most recently revised tests are quite good, some of the alternative tests are weaker in terms of the representativeness or quality of the standardization sample. Some are less stable, and most are more limited in their documented validity. Some have inadequacies in the test manual, such as unclear or poorly standardized administration instructions, and others provide insufficient information about psychometric adequacy, appropriate uses, and limitations. Indeed, a few of the alternatives compare poorly on all counts. Except for some specific advantages, perhaps none of the alternatives can be considered better than the two major scales when one considers all relevant factors, except for individuals with special needs.

Though usually weaker in psychometric properties, many of the alternatives to the major scales do not rely on a verbal response as much as the Binet and Wechsler verbal scales do. Many require the subject only to point or to make any response indicating "Yes" or "No" and thus do not depend as much on the complex integration of visual and motor functioning. Like the Wechsler scales, most of the alternatives contain a performance scale or subscale. Indeed, the dearth of performance tasks in the early Binet scales helped to stimulate the development of many alternative individual tests of ability.

In providing a performance component (many alternatives are exclusively performance scales), alternatives to the Binet and Wechsler have particular relevance for special populations. Some were designed for special populations, such as individuals with sensory limitations (for example, deaf people) or physical limitations (for example, people who are paralyzed or partially paralyzed). Others were designed to evaluate those with language limitations, such as culturally deprived people, certain brain-damaged individuals, and foreign born or non–English-speaking individuals. Still others were designed to assess learning disabilities.

Because the tests were designed for special populations or purposes, the existence of alternatives is justifiable. However, their specificity often limits the range of functions or abilities that they can measure. Thus, one may consider the greater specificity of some alternatives as a weakness as well as a strength. Although the alternatives may be much more suitable for special populations than the major scales would be, an IQ score based on one of the alternatives, with rare exception, cannot be compared directly with a score from one of the major scales. However, the alternatives are often useful as a supplement for results obtained with one of the major scales, such as for screening purposes, for follow-up or reevaluations, or when insufficient time is available to administer one of the major scales. In addition, when several such tests are used in conjunction, limitations in one can be reduced or overcome by a particular strength in another. For example, in the case cited at the beginning of this chapter, the evaluation used six alternative measures, and this was considered acceptable (Norlin, 2003).

Because they are designed for special populations, some alternatives can be administered totally without verbal instructions (for example, through pantomime or chalkboard instructions) (Naglieri & Ford, 2003). Furthermore, most are less related than the Binet and Wechsler scales to reading ability, and

TABLE 11-1

Comparison of General Features of Alternatives with the Wechsler and Binet Scales

Disadvantages of alternatives
Weaker standardization sample
Less stable
Less documentation on validity
Limitations in test manual
Not as psychometrically sound
IQ scores not interchangeable with Binet or Wechsler

Advantages of alternatives
Can be used for specific populations and special purposes:
Sensory limitations
Physical limitations
Language limitations
Culturally deprived people
Foreign-born individuals
Non–English-speaking people
Not as reliant on verbal responses
Not as dependent on complex visual–motor integration
Useful for screening, supplement, and reevaluations
Can be administered nonverbally
Less variability because of scholastic achievement

a few are almost totally independent of reading ability. As a consequence, the scores from many alternatives contain less variability because of scholastic achievement than either the Binet or the Wechsler scale, both of which correlate strongly with scholastic achievement.

See Table 11-1 for a summary of alternative tests versus the major scales.

Alternatives Compared with One Another

To construct and publish a useful test, we must develop a better method than is currently available. We may develop a test to measure some factor not tapped by any existing measure or provide a test for a particular group for whom existing procedures have not worked. If a new test offers no specific advantages, most examiners will probably stay with a more established test. Therefore, most alternatives tend to differ from one another in some important way. Alternatives to the major scales that do no more than attempt to measure abilities in the same way, only better, have met with little success.

In comparing tests used in education and special education other than the Binet and Wechsler scales, we find that some apply to only the youngest children, others to older children and adolescents, and still others to both children and adults. Thus, some of the alternatives to the major scales differ in their targeted age ranges. A second important difference concerns what is measured. Some of the alternatives attempt to measure language or vocabulary skills through nonverbal techniques, some to measure nonverbal or nonlanguage intelligence, and others to measure perceptual or motor skills. Alternatives also differ in the type of score they produce. Some give only a single score, as in the early Binet scales, whereas others produce several scores—for example, the modern Binet of 2003 and the Wechsler scales. The alternatives differ also in the type of response required of subjects. Some present the items in a multiple-choice format, requiring that the subject choose or point to a correct alternative; others simply require the subject to indicate "Yes" or "No" by whatever means possible.

Other important differences mark the alternative individual tests of human ability. Some require simple motor skills, whereas others demand relatively complex motor behavior. A few sample a wide range of abilities, but most focus on a narrow range. Still another difference concerns the target population, which may include deaf, blind, physically handicapped, learning disabled, language-impaired, or foreign-born people. Furthermore, some provide timed tasks; others do not. Some claim to have significance for personality and clinical diagnoses; others are exclusively related to an ability.

Another difference is the amount of examiner skill and experience necessary for administration. Whereas some tests require as much skill and experience as the Binet or Wechsler scales do, others require only minimal examiner skill and could probably be administered by a trained paraprofessional under supervision. To avoid confusing the various tests in this chapter, you should compare the various alternatives with the Binet and Wechsler scales; you should also compare them with each other in terms of their main distinguishing features, as summarized in Table 11-2.

TABLE 11-2 *Summary of Differences Among Individual Ability Tests Other Than the Binet and Wechsler Scales*	**Difference**	**Definition or example**
	Age range	Different tests are designed for specific age groups
	What is measured	Verbal intelligence, nonverbal intelligence, and so on
	Type of score	Single score versus multiple scores
	Type of skill required	Simple motor, complex motor, and so on
	Range of abilities sampled	Single specific ability versus a wide range of abilities
	Target population	Deaf, blind, learning disabled, and so on
	Timing	Some are timed; others are not
	Personality versus ability	Some relevant for personality and clinical diagnoses, others for ability
	Examiner skill and experience	Some require far less examiner skill and experience to administer and interpret than others

Specific Individual Ability Tests

The earliest individual ability tests were typically designed for specific purposes or populations. One of the first, the Seguin Form Board Test (Seguin, 1907) first published in the 1800s, actually preceded the Binet. This test, of the performance variety, produced only a single score. It consisted of a simple form board with objects of various shapes placed in appropriately shaped holes (such as squares or circles). The Seguin Form Board Test was used primarily to evaluate mentally retarded adults and emphasized speed of performance. A version of this test is still available. Quite a while after the development of the Seguin test, the Healy-Fernald Test (1911) was developed as an exclusively nonverbal test for adolescent delinquents. Although it produced only a single score, the Healy-Fernald Test provided several types of tasks, rather than just one as in the Seguin Form Board Test, and there was less emphasis on speed. Then Knox (1914) developed a battery of performance tests for non–English-speaking adult immigrants to the United States. The test was one of the first that could be administered without language. Speed was not emphasized.

In sum, early individual ability tests other than the Binet scale were designed for specific populations, produced a single score, and had nonverbal performance scales. The emphasis on speed gradually decreased from the earliest to the more recent tests. These early procedures demonstrated the feasibility of constructing individual nonverbal performance tests that could provide an alternative to the then verbally dependent Binet scale. They could be administered without visual instructions and used with children as well as adults.

Infant Scales

An important category of individual tests of ability attempts to measure intelligence in infants and young children. Generally, there is not much point to estimating the IQ of an infant or preschool toddler. However, where mental retardation or developmental delays are suspected, these tests can supplement observation, genetic testing, and other medical procedures. Thus, our discussion of educational tests begins with tests that can be used well before the child enters the school system.

Brazelton Neonatal Assessment Scale (BNAS). The BNAS is an individual test for infants between 3 days and 4 weeks of age (Botet & Rosales, 1996; Brazelton, 1973, 1984). It purportedly provides an index of a newborn's competence. Developed by a Harvard pediatrician, the Brazelton scale produces 47 scores: 27 behavioral items and 20 elicited responses. These scores are obtained in a variety of areas, including the neurological, social, and behavioral aspects of a newborn's functioning. Factors such as reflexes, responses to stress, startle reactions, cuddliness, motor maturity, ability to habituate to sensory stimuli, and hand–mouth coordination are all assessed. Reviews of the Brazelton scale have been favorable (Majnemer & Mazer, 1998). As Sostek (1978) stated, the Brazelton has "the greatest breadth of the available neonatal examinations" (p. 208). The Brazelton also has a considerable research base (e.g., Gauvain, 1994; see also Britt & Myers, 1994a, 1994b; Field, 1993; Kappelman, 1993).

The Brazelton scale has found wide use as a research tool and as a diagnostic tool for special purposes (Majnemer & Mazer, 1998). For example, the scale has been used to assess the characteristics of drug-addicted neonates (Strauss, Lessen-Firestone, Starr, & Ostrea, 1975) and to evaluate the effects of low birth weight on premature infants (Medoff-Cooper, McGrath, & Bilker, 2000). Researchers have used it to study the effects of cocaine use in pregnancy (Morrow et al., 2001), prenatal alcohol exposure (Coles, Smith, & Falek, 1987), prenatal maternal mood (Field, Diego, Hernandez-Reif, Schanberg, & Kuhn, 2002), prenatal maternal dopamine levels (Field et al., 2001), and environmental agents (Tronick, 1987). Others have used the scale to study parent–infant attachment (Beal, 1991), gender differences in newborns (Lundqvist & Sabel, 2000), and high-risk neonates (Emory, Tynan, & Dave, 1989). Reviews of the relevant literature have been highly enthusiastic (Gauvain, 1994; Majnemer & Mazer, 1998).

Despite the enthusiasm for the scale, it has several significant drawbacks. No norms are available. Thus, although examiners and researchers can state that one infant scored higher than another in a particular area, there is no standard sample against which to compare test results. In addition, more research is needed concerning the meaning and implication of scores. The scale purportedly helps one assess the infant's role in the mother–infant social relationship (Britt & Myers, 1994b), and high scores presumably imply high levels of intelligence (Brazelton, 1993). Like most infant intelligence measures, however, the Brazelton scale has poorly documented predictive and construct validity. The scale has not been shown to be of value in predicting later intelligence (Tronick & Brazelton, 1975). Furthermore, despite relatively good interrater reliability for trained examiners, with coefficients ranging from .85 to .90 (Sostek, 1978), the test–retest reliability (that is, reliability over time) leaves much to be desired. As for all measures of intelligence when development is rapid and uneven, test–retest reliability coefficients for the Brazelton scale are typically poor and unstable for subjects younger than 8 years of age (see Figure 11-1).

In conclusion, although the Brazelton scale may offer much as a research tool and a supplement to medical testing procedures, as an individual test of infant intelligence it leaves much to be desired. Its lack of norms is a serious shortcoming, and its failure to predict future intelligence leaves us wondering what the scale is really measuring. In fairness to the Brazelton, the scale is extremely well constructed. Moreover, as you will see, *all* infant ability tests based on sensorimotor functioning have proven ineffective in predicting later intelligence except in the lowest ranges (Fagan, 1985).

Gesell Developmental Schedules (GDS). The Gesell Developmental Schedules (also known as the Gesell Maturity Scale, the Gesell Norms of Development, and the Yale Tests of Child Development) are one of the oldest and most es-

FIGURE 11-1
*Schematic
summary of the
Brazelton
Neonatal
Assessment Scale.*

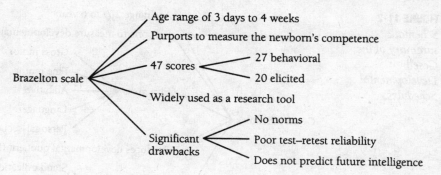

tablished infant intelligence measures. First published in 1925 (Gesell, 1925), the Gesell scale has been subjected to extensive research and refinement (Banerji, 1992a; Gesell, 1925; Rodger, 1994; Williamson, Wilson, Lifschitz, & Thurbers, 1990). One of the leading infant intelligence measures from the 1930s through the 1960s, the Gesell scale continues to be used by those interested in assessing infant intelligence (Banerji, 1992b; Bernheimer & Keogh, 1988) and assessing infants with autism (Yurong, Dun, & Xiurong, 2001). However, because the Gesell scale suffers from several psychometric weaknesses, interest in and use of the scale has fallen despite revisions and improvements.

The Gesell Developmental Schedules claim to provide an appraisal of the developmental status of children from 21.2 months to 6 years of age. The original scale is based on normative data from a carefully conducted longitudinal study of early human development (Gesell et al., 1940). The idea behind procedures based on developmental data is that human development unfolds in stages or in sequences over time. Gesell and colleagues obtained normative data concerning these various stages in maturation. With data on when specific developmental milestones manifest themselves (for example, when the infant first rolls from back to stomach unassisted, when the child first utters words, or when the child learns to walk), one can compare the rate of development of any infant or young child with established norms. If the child shows behavior or responses that are associated with a more mature level of development than is typically found for his or her chronological age, then one can assume that the child is ahead in development compared with others of the same age. Accelerated development can be related to high intelligence.

In the Gesell scale, an individual's **developmental quotient (DQ)** is determined according to a test score, which is evaluated by assessing the presence or absence of behavior associated with maturation. The DQ concept parallels the mental age (MA) concept. Thus, the Gesell produces an intelligence quotient (IQ) score similar to that of the Binet scale. The formula for IQ in the Gesell scale is as follows:

$$IQ = \frac{\text{Developmental Quotient}}{\text{Chronological Age}} \times 100$$

FIGURE 11-2
Schematic summary of the Gesell Developmental Schedules.

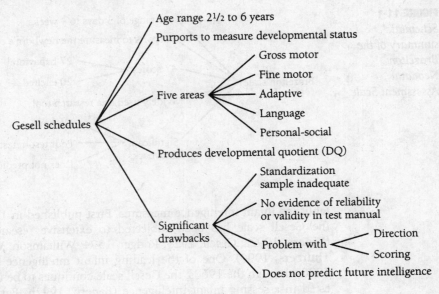

or more simply,

$$IQ = \frac{DQ}{CA} \times 100$$

Despite years of extensive use and updating, the Gesell scale continues to fall short of acceptable psychometric standards. The standardization sample is not representative of the population. As with most infant tests, evidence of reliability or validity are poorly documented. The test directions are sometimes vague, and the scoring procedures are questionable (Naglieri, 1985). As with all sensorimotor infant tests, the Gesell does not predict later intelligence except at the low end of scores (see Figure 11-2). Thus, its main value is in obtaining an early estimate or possible mental retardation.

In conclusion, Gesell's concept of empirically determining developmental sequence norms in evaluating infants and young children is logical and promising. When first constructed, the Gesell scale was nothing short of a breakthrough in infant ability testing. The use of a nonrepresentative sample in its initial development, furthermore, was not at all unusual. However, the Gesell scale continues to fall short of today's more rigorous standards for standardization samples. By providing a standard format for observing behavior, the Gesell scale may be of value to the highly trained and experienced examiner. Even so, the available empirical data indicate that it is not highly accurate for predictive purposes except at the low ranges. The scale does appear to help uncover subtle deficits in infants (Williamson et al., 1990).

Bayley Scales of Infant Development–Second Edition (BSID-II). Like the Gesell scale, the Bayley Scales of Infant Development base assessments on normative maturational developmental data. Originally published only four years before

FIGURE 11-3
Bayley Scales of Infant Development.
(Courtesy of The Psychological Corporation.)

the Brazelton scale, the Bayley scales were the product of 40 years of study (Bayley, 1969; Kimble & Wertheimer, 2003). Revised in 1994, the BSID-II, or Bayley-II, was designed for infants between 1 and 42 months of age; it produces two main scores (mental and motor) and numerous ratings of behavior. To assess mental functions, the Bayley-II uses measures such as the infant's response to a bell, the ability to follow an object with the eyes, and, in older infants, the ability to follow oral instructions. The heart of the Bayley-II is the motor scale because it assumes that later mental functions depend on motor development (Flanagan & Alfonso, 1995) (see Figure 11-3).

Unlike the Gesell and Brazelton scales, the Bayley-II scales have an excellent standardization. With a large normative sample of infants between 1 and 42 months of age divided into subgroups by gender, race, socioeconomic status, rural versus urban area, and geographic region, the Bayley-II is currently the best standardized test of its kind available.

As in the first through fourth editions of the Stanford-Binet, raw scores on the Bayley-II are converted to standard scores with a mean of 100 and a standard deviation of 16. Given the care and effort put into its development, the generally positive reviews of the Bayley-II come as no surprise (Nellis & Gridley, 1994; Pomerlau, Leahey, & Malcuit, 1994). In addition to its exemplary standardization, the median split-half reliability coefficients are approximately .88 for the mental scale and .84 for the motor scale, with ranges from the low .80's to the low .90's for the mental scales and ranges from the high .60's to the low .90's for the motor scales. As might be expected, the psychometric properties of the Bayley-II are weakest in the youngest age ranges (Flanagan & Alfonso, 1995). This weakness is problematic because Bayley-II scores are

FIGURE 11-4
Schematic summary of the Bayley Scales of Infant Development.

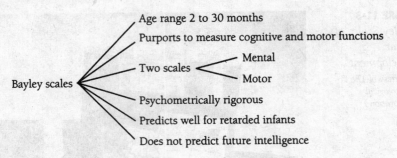

Bayley scales
- Age range 2 to 30 months
- Purports to measure cognitive and motor functions
- Two scales
  - Mental
  - Motor
- Psychometrically rigorous
- Predicts well for retarded infants
- Does not predict future intelligence

often used to determine whether children receive state-funded early intervention (Ross & Lawson, 1997).

Research interest in the Bayley scales continues to grow (Macias, Saylor, Greer, Charles, Bell, & Katikaneni, 1998; Raggio, Massingale, & Bass, 1994). Nevertheless, more validity studies are needed. In terms of construct validity, scores on the performance scale increase with increasing chronological age. However, the bulk of available research casts considerable doubt on the assumption of a relationship between motor behavior and later mental functions. In its favor, the Bayley does predict mental retardation (Niccols & Lachman, 2002; Self & Horowitz, 1979). Infants who score two standard deviations below the mean have a high probability of testing in the retarded ranges later in life (DeWitt, Schreck, & Mulick, 1998; Goldstein, Fogle, Wieber, & O'Shea, 1995). However, for infants who score within the normal ranges, there is no more than low correlation between Bayley scores and those obtained from standard intelligence tests such as the WISC-III and Binet scale (Flanagan & Alfonso, 1995). Like the Brazelton, the Bayley-II is widely used in research (DeWitt et al., 1998; Macias et al., 1998). A major research use is to assess infants of drug-using mothers (e.g., Moe, 2002), premature infants (Kleberg, Westrup, Stjernqvist, & Lagercrantz, 2002; Ratliff-Shaub et al., 2001; Stoelhorst et al., 2003), infants whose mothers suffer from postpartum depression (Righetti-Veltema, Bousquet, & Manzano, 2003), HIV-positive infants (Llorente et al., 2003), and other at-risk infants (Lai, Guo, Guo, & Hsu, 2001; Leslie, Gordon, Ganger, & Gist, 2002) (see Figure 11-4).

In conclusion, the Bayley-II is probably the most psychometrically sound test of its kind (Flanagan & Alfonso, 1995). The question remains as to whether tests of this type can predict future intelligence. Available research indicates that although the Bayley-II may be a good predictor for handicapped populations, it does not predict well within the normal ranges.

Cattell Infant Intelligence Scale (CIIS). Another noteworthy infant ability test is the Cattell Infant Intelligence Scale (CIIS), which is also based on normative developmental data. Designed as a downward extension of the Stanford-Binet scale for infants and preschoolers between 2 and 30 months of age, the Cattell scale purports to measure intelligence in infants and young children. Patterned after the 1937 Binet in an age scale format, the Cattell scale contains five test

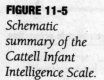

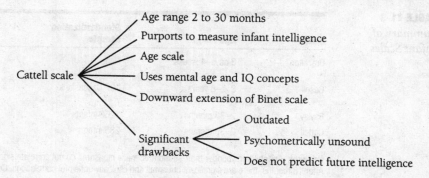

Cattell scale
- Age range 2 to 30 months
- Purports to measure infant intelligence
- Age scale
- Uses mental age and IQ concepts
- Downward extension of Binet scale
- Significant drawbacks
  - Outdated
  - Psychometrically unsound
  - Does not predict future intelligence

items for each month between 2 and 12 months of age and five items for each two-month interval between 12 and 36 months of age. The items are similar to those on other infant tests such as the Gesell scale. Tasks for infants include attending to a voice and following objects with his or her eyes. Tasks for young children involve using a form board and manipulating common objects. The ability to follow oral instructions becomes more and more important as age increases.

Today, the Cattell is rarely used. It was copyrighted nearly three decades before the original Bayley scale and has not been revised. Normative data for the Cattell scale compare unfavorably with those for the original Bayley scales, and even worse with the Bayley-II in several respects. In addition to being outdated and more than four times smaller, the Cattell scale sample is based primarily on children of parents from the lower and middle classes and therefore does not represent the general population.

In one of the few recently published studies comparing the Cattell scale with the Bayley, scores derived from the Bayley predicted Stanford-Binet IQs better than the Cattell scores did (Atkinson, 1990) (see Figure 11-5).

In sum, the Cattell scale has remained relatively unchanged for more than 60 years. It is psychometrically unsatisfactory. Reliability coefficients vary widely, with many being less than acceptable (see Hooper, Conner, & Umansky, 1986). Moreover, what the scale measures is unclear; it does not predict future intelligence for infants in the normal ranges. Its use in clinical settings is highly suspect, and it is presented here only for historical value.

See Table 11-3 for a summary of the properties of infant scales.

Major Tests for Young Children

In this section, we discuss two major individual tests specifically developed to evaluate intelligence in young children: the McCarthy Scales of Children's Abilities (MSCA) and the Kaufman Assessment Battery for Children (K-ABC).

McCarthy Scales of Children's Abilities (MSCA). A product of the early 1970s, the McCarthy Scales of Children's Abilities (MSCA) measure ability in children between 2½ and 8½ years old. Overall, the McCarthy scales comprise a

TABLE 11-3
Summary of Infant Scales

Scale	Age range	Standardization sample	Psychometric properties
Brazelton	3 days–4 weeks	None	Good interrater reliability, poor test–retest reliability
Gesell	2½–6 years	107 Caucasians	Little evidence, some support for construct validity
Bayley	2–30 months	1262 infants	Very good split-half reliability
Cattell	2–30 months	285 infants	Little evidence, some support for construct validity

General: For children younger than 18 months, these measures do not correlate significantly with IQ later in life. After 18 months, there are significant but small and clinically unhelpful correlations. Correlations tend to increase with the age of the infant at the time of testing.

Major alternative: Tests of memory, particularly visual memory and abstraction. Such tests do correlate with IQs in later life, even for infants tested in the first few days after birth.

carefully constructed individual test of human ability. In fact, were it not for its relatively meager validity data, the McCarthy might well have reached the status of the Wechsler scale (WPPSI-III), which overlaps with the McCarthy's age range. Indeed, the McCarthy scales seem to offer some advantages over the WPPSI-III and even the Binet for the 2½- to 8½-year age range. Unfortunately, because McCarthy died before the test was published, the task of strengthening the McCarthy scales falls to interested researchers (see Figure 11-6).

FIGURE 11-6
McCarthy Scales of Children's Abilities.

FIGURE 11-7
*Schematic
overview of the
general cognitive
index of the
McCarthy scales.*

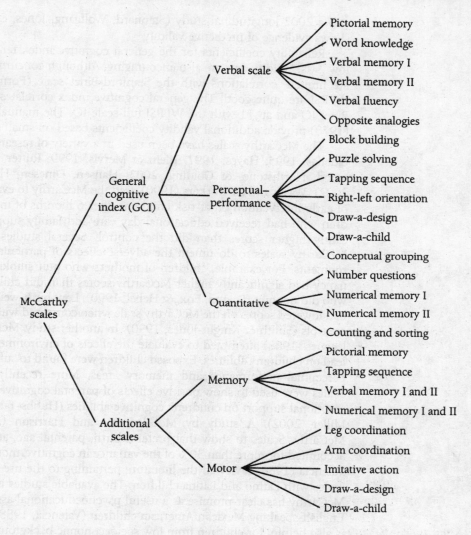

On the positive side, the McCarthy produces a pattern of scores as well as a variety of composite scores. Its battery of 18 tests samples a wide variety of functions long held to be related to human intelligence. Of the 18 scales, 15 are combined into a composite score known as the **general cognitive index (GCI),** a standard score with a mean of 100 and a standard deviation of 16. Presumably, the index reflects how well the child has integrated prior learning experiences and adapted them to the demands of the scales. The concept of combining various subtests to form composite scores is an important idea in testing, and it is one of the main features of the 2003 fifth edition of the Stanford-Binet (see Figure 11-7).

The psychometric properties of the McCarthy scales are relatively good. Picone, Regine, and Ribaudo (2001) have shown evidence of factorial validity, and a 2002 longitudinal study (Stannard, Wolfgang, Jones, & Phelps, 2001) shows evidence of predictive validity.

Reliability coefficients for the general cognitive index tend to run in the low .90's. Validity data are also encouraging. Although concurrent validity data are limited, correlations with the Stanford-Binet scale (Form L-M) and the WPPSI are quite good. The general cognitive index correlates at .81 with the Binet IQ and at .71 with the WPPSI full-scale IQ. The manual and T. V. Hunt (1978) provide additional validity coefficients based on small samples.

The McCarthy scales have been used in a variety of research studies (Cortadellas, 1995; Hayes, 1997; Klein & Mervis, 1999; Rutter, Thorpe, Greenwood, Northstone, & Golding, 2003; Hansen, Dinesen, Hoff, & Greisen, 2002). Wasik and co-workers (1990) used the McCarthy to evaluate the effects of early intervention on at-risk children. After 6 months of intervention, children who had received educational day care and family support had significantly higher scores than did the control. Several studies have used the McCarthy scales to document the adverse effects of particular prenatal environments. For example, children of mothers who quit smoking during pregnancy had significantly higher McCarthy scores than did children of mothers who did not quit (Sexton, Fox, & Hebel, 1990). Low-birth-weight children also had lowered scores on the McCarthy scale when compared with normal-weight controls (Smith & Knight-Jones, 1990). In another study, McMichael and colleagues (1988) attempted to evaluate the effects of environmental exposure to lead on children's abilities. Exposed children were found to suffer deficits in the perceptual–performance and memory areas. More recently, the McCarthy Scales were used to show positive effects of parental cognitive stimulation and emotional support on children's cognitive abilities (Hubbs-Tait, Culp, Culp, & Miller, 2002). A study by McGill-Evans and Harrison (2001) used the McCarthy Scales to show that preterm birth, parental age, and infant gender accounted for more than 30% of the variance in cognitive-motor skills. Finally, Valencia (1988) reviewed the literature pertaining to the use of the McCarthy scales with Latino and Latina children. The available studies indicated that the McCarthy has clear promise as a useful psychoeducational assessment tool for English-speaking Mexican American children (Valencia, 1988). The McCarthy is also helpful for children from low socioeconomic backgrounds (Cortadellas, 1995).

In sum, the McCarthy scale is psychometrically sound. The available studies support its validity and its promise as an assessment tool for Mexican American children is encouraging.

Kaufman Assessment Battery for Children, Second Edition (KABC-II). Originally a product of the early 1980s, the modern 2004 version of the Kaufman Assessment Battery for Children (KABC-II) is an individual ability test for children between 3 and 18 years of age. The KABC-II consists of 18 subtests combined into five global scales called sequential processing, simultaneous processing, learning, planning, and knowledge.

According to the stated purposes and intentions in its test manuals, the KABC-II is quite ambitious (Kaufman & Kaufman, 1983a, 1983b, 2004a). It is intended for psychological, clinical, minority-group, preschool, and neuropsychological assessment as well as research. The test also purports to enable the psychoeducational evaluation of learning disabled and other exceptional children and educational planning and placement. Before we examine the extent to which the K-ABC succeeds in meeting such lofty goals, we shall look at some of its underlying concepts.

Theoretically, the KABC is based on several approaches (see Kaufman, 1984; Kaufman & Kaufman, 2004a), including the neuropsychological model of brain functioning of renowned Russian neuroscientist Aleksander Luria (1966); the theory of split brain functioning of U.S. Nobelist Roger Sperry (1968); and the theories of information processing, most notably that of cognitive scientist Ulric Neisser (1967). In the work of these and other scientists, the Kaufmans noted a major distinction between two types of higher brain processes, which they referred to as the *sequential–simultaneous distinction* (Kaufman, 1984). *Sequential processing* refers to a child's ability "to solve problems by mentally arranging input in sequential or serial order." Examples of sequential processing are number and word-order recall. Presented one at a time, items must be dealt with sequentially, rather than all at once. In contrast, simultaneous processing takes place in parallel. It refers to a child's ability to "synthesize information (from mental wholes) in order to solve a problem" (Kaufman, & Kaufman, 1985, p. 250).

The sequential–simultaneous distinction of the K-ABC is one of the test's most distinguishing characteristics (Reynolds & Kamphaus, 1997). The KABC-II does not claim to provide a pure measure of either sequential or simultaneous processing. Instead, the test developers selected tasks that, from a rational analysis, appeared to distinguish one type of processing from the other. A major intent of providing separate measures of simultaneous and sequential processing is to identify the child's unique strengths and problem-solving strategies. Such information can presumably help others develop educational and remedial intervention strategies for a child.

The KABC-II was conformed with the Kaufman Test of Educational Achievement, Second Edition (KTEA-II), which provides an achievement score. Offering independent and comparable scores for both intelligence and achievement in the same test is a major advantage. In addition, the KABC-II has a nonverbal measure of ability that is specifically designed to be as fair as possible to children who are linguistically different or handicapped.

The KABC-II and its counterpart the KTEA-II are well constructed and psychometrically sound. Raw scores for each of the 18 subtests can be converted to standard scores with a mean of 10 (SD = 3). The global scales can be converted to standard scores (mean = 100, SD = 15), percentiles, and age-equivalent norms.

Validity data reported in the original K-ABC test manual has received considerable attention. Factor analytic studies support its sequential–simultaneous and mental processing achievement distinctions (Meesters, van Gastel, Ghys, & Merckelbach, 1998). The K-ABC intelligence estimates also tend to show smaller (approximately 8 points) differences between African Americans and whites than either the Wechsler or Binet scales, in which whites typically score some 15 points higher than African Americans (see Jensen, 1985). Thus, the K-ABC tends to be less biased against African Americans (Fan, Willson, & Reynolds, 1995; Lamp & Krohn, 2001). However, the K-ABC also tends to underestimate the scores of gifted children (compared with the Binet Form L-M and the WISC-R), so its validity for evaluating giftedness is questionable (McCallum, Karnes, & Oehler-Stinnett, 1985). Moreover, at least one group of researchers has found K-ABC items biased against Mexican Americans (Valencia, Rankin, & Livingston, 1995). As of this writing, no data are available on the KABC-II's validity beyond that reported in the manual, so much work needs to be done.

Since its original publication in April 1983, the K-ABC has generated considerable interest. Reactions have varied widely. On the positive side, Kaufman and Kaufman (1985, p. 268) point to its strong theoretical orientation, separate intelligence and achievement scales, separate nonverbal scale, limited oral instructions, limited verbal responding, colorful and interesting items, inclusion of sociocultural norms, and empirical documentation of smaller differences between African Americans and whites (Lamp & Krohn, 2001), Latinos or Latinas and whites, and Native Americans and whites on the K-ABC compared with other tests. These strengths are acknowledged by independent reviewers (Aiken, 1987; Anastasi, 1984), and the KABC-II has smoothed many of the edges of the original K-ABC.

Despite these strengths, criticism have been harsh (Williams, Voelker, & Ricciardi, 1995). According to Jensen (1984), one can attribute the smaller differences between whites and minorities on the K-ABC to its poorer predictive validity for school achievement and its less effective measurement of general intelligence compared with the Binet and Wechsler scales. Other critics point to the K-ABC's imperfect match with its theoretical foundation and disproportionate contribution of the simultaneous and mental processing composites (Bracken, 1985). Moreover, the neuropsychological model that underlies the sequential–simultaneous distinction is at best poorly supported and at worst inaccurate and outmoded (Herbert, 1982). None of these criticisms appear to have been clearly addressed by the newer KABC-II.

Perhaps the most severe criticism of the K-ABC has come from Sternberg (1984), who charged that the K-ABC manual misrepresents the support for the theory underlying the K-ABC. He also maintained that the test suffers from a noncorrespondence between its definition and its measurement of intelligence. This criticism continues to be voiced and empirically supported by Cahan and Noyman (2001). Furthermore, Sternberg found that empirical support for the theory underlying the K-ABC is questionable. And, like Jensen (1984), he noted an overemphasis on rote learning at the expense of ability to learn.

Although the criticisms of the K-ABC are largely valid and generally apply to the newer KABC-II, it is important to see them in context. First, many of these criticisms, such as lack of correspondence between definition and measurement of intelligence, also apply to the test's major competitors. Even the best available instruments have shortcomings and limitations. Although the underlying theory of the test has yet to be fully established, the test at least *has* a theoretical structure. Indeed, the KABC-II is perhaps the best alternative or supplement for specific questions and educational assessment to date and no doubt will continue to be an important assessment tool for some time to come.

General Individual Ability Tests for Handicapped and Special Populations

Many alternative tests are specifically designed to provide a more valid measure of intellectual functioning for cases in which the Binet and Wechsler may be biased or inappropriate. Each of these general individual ability tests for handicapped and special populations contains unique strengths and limitations.

Columbia Mental Maturity Scale–Third Edition (CMMS). A variety of sensory and physical limitations often make a valid administration of the Binet, Wechsler, or even many of the major alternative scales (such as the McCarthy) quite impossible. Therefore, for children who experience physical limitations (such as cerebral palsy), speech impairments, language limitations, or hearing loss, instruments are needed that do not create negative bias. One attempt at such an instrument is the Columbia Mental Maturity Scale–Third Edition (CMMS), which purports to evaluate ability in normal and variously handicapped children from 3 through 12 years of age. When used for individuals with special needs, the test often provides a more suitable measure of intelligence than do the more established scales (Kamhi, Minor, & Mauer, 1990).

The Columbia scale requires neither a verbal response nor fine motor skills. Presented as a measure of general reasoning ability, the scale requires the subject to discriminate similarities and differences by indicating which drawing does not belong on a 6-by-9-inch card containing three to five drawings, depending on the level of difficulty. The task, then, is multiple-choice.

The Columbia scale contains 92 different cards grouped into eight overlapping levels, or scales, according to chronological age. Testing begins at a scale appropriate for the child's age. Advantages of the Columbia scale include its relative independence of reading skills, the ease of its administration and scoring, and the clarity of its test manual. Because subjects are not timed, pressure is minimal.

Though somewhat outdated, the standardization sample is impressive. It consists of 2600 children divided into 13 levels from 3 years, 6 months to 9 years, 11 months. Each level contains 200 children. The sample is stratified according to the U.S. population in terms of variables that include gender, race, geographic region, and parental occupation.

The scale's manual contains data on both split-half and test–retest reliability for some age groups in the standardization sample. The scale is consistent internally as well as over short intervals of time. Coefficients range between .85 and .90 for both split-half and test–retest reliabilities.

The Columbia scale is highly vulnerable to random error. A young child can obtain a score of 82 simply on chance alone, and a score in the average ranges can be obtained with just a few lucky guesses (Kaufman, 1978).

Theoretically, if 100 apes were administered the lower levels of the Columbia scale, an alarming number might obtain scores in the average ranges for human beings.

In conclusion, the Columbia scale is a reliable instrument that is useful in assessing ability in many people with sensory, physical, or language handicaps. Because of its multiple-choice nature, however, and consequent vulnerability to chance variance, one should use results with caution. When used with subjects for whom the major scales would be appropriate, the Columbia scale might best be seen as a screening device. Although its standardization sample is somewhat outdated, the Columbia scale can be used to test a variety of special populations for whom the Wechsler, Binet, and other scales are inappropriate. Even for these populations, however, the Columbia scale might be best used in conjunction with whatever Wechsler or K-ABC subtests can be given. If the child can point, for example, then Wechsler's picture completion subtest can be given in conjunction with the Columbia scale as an additional check on the accuracy of the results. If the child is physically handicapped but can speak, then some of the Wechsler verbal subtests can be used to support results.

Peabody Picture Vocabulary Test–Third Edition (PPVT-III). Similar to the Columbia scale in several respects, the Peabody Picture Vocabulary Test–Third Edition (PPVT-III) was originally developed by L. M. Dunn and I. M. Dunn (1981). The most recent revision was published in 1997. Although the age range of 2½ through 90 years is considerably wider than the range of the Columbia scale, both are multiple-choice tests that require a subject to indicate only "Yes" or "No" in some manner. Primarily for the physically or language handicapped, the PPVT-III is not usually used with the deaf, because the instructions are administered aloud. Nonetheless, the test has been used in research with the deaf to evaluate their ability to define words (Krinsky, 1990).

The test purports to measure hearing or receptive (hearing) vocabulary, presumably providing a nonverbal estimate of verbal intelligence (Dunn & Dunn, 1997). One can use it as a screening instrument or as a supplement to other measures in evaluating learning problems (Camaioni, Ercolani, Penge, Riccio, & Bernabei, 2001), linguistic problems (Bayles, 1990), and many other special problems (Fielding-Barnsley & Purdie, 2003; Marchman, Saccuman, & Wulfeck, 2004; Ment et al., 2003; Wagner, 1994). Though untimed, the PPVT-III can be administered in 15 minutes or less, and it requires no reading ability. Two forms (IIIA and IIIB) are available. Each form has 204 plates, with each plate presenting four numbered pictures. The subject must indicate which of the four pictures best relates to a word read aloud by the examiner. Items are arranged in increasing order of difficulty, and the administrator must determine a basal and ceiling performance, as in the modern Binet scale. The number of incorrect responses is subtracted from the ceiling to produce a total score. This score can then be converted to a standard score (mean = 100, SD = 15), percentile rank, stanine, or age-equivalent score.

The PPVT-III purports a split-half internal consistency of .86 to .97, alternate form reliability from .88 to .94, and retest reliability of .91 to .94. Its validity has been reported as good, with respectable correlations with the WISC-III VIQ at .91.

The PPVT-R tends to underestimate Wechsler or Binet IQs for retarded children (Prout & Sheldon, 1984) and gifted children (Hayes & Martin, 1986). Research has supported its use for certain adults, such as those with developmental handicaps (Groenweg, Conway, & Stan, 1986). However, the manual advises caution when using the test with adults. Moreover, even where its use is supported, the Peabody test tends to underestimate IQ score (Bell, Lassiter, Matthews, & Hutchinson, 2001; Campbell, Bell, & Keith, 2001; Washington & Craig, 1999). Because it evaluates only receptive vocabulary and not problem solving, abstract thinking, and other functions tapped by the major IQ tests, the PPVT-R should never be used as a substitute for a Wechsler or Binet IQ. Indeed, researchers have repeatedly noted that the PPVT-R cannot be used as a substitute for a major intelligence test (Hodapp & Hass, 1997; Ingram, Caroselli, Robinson, Hetzel, Reed, & Masel, 1998). Nevertheless, much care went into the latest revision, and the test meets today's rigorous psychometric standards. The authors were careful to indicate the limitations of the test as well as its appropriate uses. These include, "establishing and restoring rapport," "testing preschool children," "screening for verbal ability," "screening for giftedness and mental retardation," and "measuring English language proficiency" (Dunn & Dunn, 1997).

In conclusion, the modern Peabody test can be an important component in a test battery or used as a screening devise. It is easy to administer and is useful for a variety of groups. However, its tendency to underestimate IQ scores, in conjunction with the problems inherent in the multiple-choice format, indicate that the Peabody test cannot be used in place of the Binet and Wechsler scales. One should use it for general screening purposes and to evaluate receptive vocabulary, and use it according to the careful instructions specified in the test manual.

Leiter International Performance Scale–Revised (LIPS-R). Whereas the Columbia and Peabody tests measure verbal aspects of intelligence, the Leiter International Performance Scale–Revised (LIPS-R) is strictly a performance scale. It aims at providing a nonverbal alternative to the Stanford-Binet scale for the age range of 2 to 18 years (see Figure 11-8). First developed in the 1930s, and revised most recently in 1997, the Leiter scale has undergone a recent decrease in interest among researchers, although one finds it frequently used in clinical settings. The Leiter scale purports to provide a nonverbal measure of general intelligence by sampling a wide variety of functions from memory to nonverbal reasoning. One can administer it without using language, and it requires no verbal response from subjects.

Presumably, one can apply it to a large range of disabled individuals, particularly the deaf and language-disabled. Like the Peabody test and the Columbia scale, the revised Leiter scale is untimed. Patterned after the old Binet scale, the various tasks of the Leiter scale are arranged in an age scale format at yearly intervals from 2 through 18. The revised Leiter has considerable utility

FIGURE 11-8
*Leiter
International
Performance
Scale.*
*(Courtesy of Stoelting
Co.)*

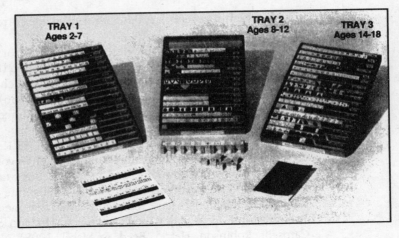

for subjects who cannot or will not provide a verbal response (Bay, 1998; Bos, 1996). The Leiter scale's validity documentation is extremely good, with a range of criterion validity coefficients from .52 to .92 (median = .83). However, there is some evidence that Leiter IQ scores for Latinos and Latinas are significantly higher than corresponding IQs from the Wechsler scales (Lewis & Lorentz, 1994).

The Leiter scale merits consideration as an aid to clinical diagnosis in disabled children (Bradley-Johnson, 2001; Tsatsanis, Dartnall, Cicchetti, Sparrow, Klin, & Volkmar, 2003). However, the test user must exercise caution in interpreting Leiter test results because the meaning of test scores requires more research (Lewis & Lorentz, 1994). With further revisions of the test, researchers in the 21st century may more thoroughly investigate the Leiter's properties and potential.

Porteus Maze Test (PMT). The Porteus Maze Test (PMT) is a popular but poorly standardized nonverbal performance measure of intelligence. Since it was first published around the time of World War I, it has served as an important individual ability test (Krikorian & Bartok, 1998). As its name implies, the Porteus Maze Test consists of maze problems. Like the Leiter scale, the Porteus test can be administered without verbal instruction and thus can be used for a variety of special populations (Levin, Song, Ewing-Cobbs, & Roberson, 2001; Stevens, Kaplan, & Hesselbrock, 2003).

The Porteus test has no manual. Further, its standardization sample is quite old (Doctor, 1972). Despite its problems, the Porteus test meets an important need in providing a measure of ability for many groups to whom the Binet and Wechsler scales do not apply. Like many similar tests, a restandardization would greatly improve the quality of the Porteus.

In sum, the widespread use and interest in tests such as the Peabody, Leiter, and Porteus clearly indicate the need for strictly nonverbal or performance measures of intelligence, especially for the handicapped. Therefore, it is unfortunate that so many of the available instruments need restandardization and additional reliability or validity documentation.

Testing Learning Disabilities

One of the most important areas in education involves the study of specific learning disabilities. A major concept in this field is that a child average in intelligence may fail in school because of a specific deficit or disability that prevents learning. Thus, a learning disability has traditionally been defined in terms of a significant difference between IQ and achievement. In most states, this definition is operationalized in terms of a 1½ to 2 standard deviation difference between a score on an IQ test and one on an achievement test.

A learning disability is just one of the many types of disabilities that may entitle a child to receive special education services under the Individuals with Disabilities Education Act (IDEA) (20 U.S.C. 1400 et seq.) and its state law counterparts. Federal law entitles every eligible child with a disability to a free appropriate public education. To qualify for special education services under IDEA and its state law counterparts, a child must not only have a disability but also have his or her educational performance adversely affected by the disability. Thus, the beginning point for evaluating a learning disability is a problem in how a child is performing in school.

School problems may be the result of any one or a combination of many factors including very low potential (intelligence), emotional upset resulting from such factors as divorce, parental separation, bereavement, drug intoxication, and a host of others. It is only when there is a severe discrepancy between a child's potential to achieve and actual school achievement that a child becomes eligible for special education services on the basis of a "specific learning disability" under federal and most state law counterparts.

Identifying a learning disability is a complex process, and parents are advised to seek professional help. A good resource for parents and teachers is a book written by Barbara Z. Novick and Maureen M. Arnold called *Why is My Child Having Trouble at School?* (Tarcher, 1995). These authors identify several "signs of a learning problem," including:

disorganization—for example, sloppy homework or papers crumpled or out of place;

careless effort—for example, misreads instructions or mishears directions;

forgetfulness—for example, the child's best excuse is "I forgot";

refusal to do schoolwork or homework—for example, turns in work half finished or needs somebody closely supervising in order to complete assignments;

slow performance—for example, takes far more than the expected time to complete an assignment;

poor attention—for example, mind seems to wander or frequently does not know what she or he is supposed to be doing; and

moodiness—for example, child shows anger, sadness, or irritability when asked to complete a school or home assignment.

FIGURE 11-9
*Three-stage
information-
processing model.*

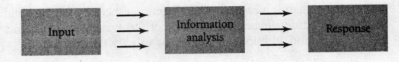

Illinois Test of Psycholinguistic Abilities (ITPA). Of the major tests designed specifically to assess learning disabilities, none more illustrates the theory of learning disabilities and has generated more interest than the controversial Illinois Test of Psycholinguistic Abilities (ITPA). Based on modern concepts of human information processing, the ITPA assumes that failure to respond correctly to a stimulus can result not only from a defective output (response) system but also from a defective input or information-processing system. This test assumes that a human response to an outside stimulus can be viewed in terms of discrete stages or processes. In stage 1, the senses receive input, or incoming environmental information. Thus, the information must first be received by the senses before it can be analyzed. During stage 2, this information is analyzed or processed. Finally, having processed the information, the individual must make a response—stage 3 (see Figure 11-9).

Assuming that a learning disability can occur at any level of processing, the Illinois test theorizes that the child may be impaired in one or more specific sensory modalities. Input may be visual, auditory, or tactile. The Illinois test provides three subtests that measure the individual's ability to receive visual, auditory, or tactile input independently of processing and output factors.

Three additional subtests provide independent measures of processing in each of these three modalities, and other subtests provide independent measures of motor and verbal output (see Table 11-4).

By providing relatively independent measures for each of these areas, the Illinois test purports to help isolate the specific site of a learning disability. For example, a child may receive age-appropriate scores for all three input and all three processing subtests but may have an unusually low score on motor (but not verbal) output. This result would indicate that, although the child can receive and process information as well as others do, he or she has trouble in motor output. The treatment can therefore focus on enhancing motor skills. Similarly, if the problem involves auditory processing, then this area becomes the focus.

Designed for use with children ages 2 through 10, the Illinois test has found widespread use and interest among educators, psychologists, learning disability specialists, and researchers (Andersson, 1996; Klausen, Moller, Holmefjord, Reiseaeter, & Asbjornsen, 2000; Ottem, 2002a, 2002b). This popularity, however, does not come from its psychometric qualities. Not only is the Illinois test one of the most difficult individual ability tests to administer, but also the manual presents no reliability or validity data. Although normative data are provided, the exact nature of the normative sample is difficult to ascertain from the manual—a problem that has been severely criticized (Bell, 1990). In fact, the Illinois test has been criticized on many grounds, including

TABLE 11-4

Description of Illinois Test of Psycholinguistic Abilities (ITPA) Subtests

Subtest	Description
Auditory Reception	Measures ability to understand spoken words. Example: "Do chairs eat?"
Visual Reception	Measures ability to gain meaning from familiar pictures. Example: Matching picture stimulus with picture from same category.
Auditory Association	Measures ability to relate concepts presented orally. Example: Verbal-analogies test (e.g., "Grass is green, sugar is _____.").
Visual Association	Measures ability to relate concepts presented visually. Example: Relating a pictorial stimulus to its conceptual counterpart (e.g., bone goes with dog).
Verbal Expression	Measures ability to express concepts verbally. Example: Describing common objects verbally.
Manual Expression	Measures ability to demonstrate knowledge of the use of objects pictured. Example: Express an idea with gestures (e.g., "Show me what to do with a hammer.").
Grammatic Closure	Measures ability to use proper grammatical forms to complete statement. Example: "Here is a dog. Here are two _____."
Visual Closure	Measures ability to identify common objects from an incomplete visual presentation. Example: Locating specific objects in a scene filled with distracting stimuli.
Auditory Sequential Memory	Measures ability to reproduce orally a sequence of digits from memory. Example: Repeating digits.
Visual Sequential Memory	Measures ability to reproduce sequences of geometrical forms from memory. Example: Placing geometric shapes in proper sequence from memory.
Auditory Closure	Measures ability to complete a word when only fragments of it are orally presented. Example: "Listen. Tell me who I am talking about. DA/ Y. Who is that?"
Sound Blending	Measures ability to synthesize into words syllables spoken at half-second intervals. Example: "What word is D—OG?"

Note: The two supplementary subtests are Auditory Closure and Sound Blending.
From Illinois Test of Psycholinguistic Abilities (ITPA) Subtests, 1988, Copyright © 1988 Jerome N. Sattler Publishers, Inc. Reprinted by permission of the publisher.

inadequate validity, excessively low reliabilities for individual subtests, and failure to provide normalized standard scores. Moreover, because it was normed on middle-class children and contains culturally loaded content, the ITPA is not appropriate for use with lower-class children or disadvantaged minority groups. It is widely held that the test should not be used to assess learning disabilities. As with a few other tests, we present the ITPA here because it illustrates important concepts. It is not recommended for clinical use.

Woodcock-Johnson III. A much better test for evaluating learning disabilities is the Woodcock-Johnson III (Woodcock, McGrew, & Mather, 2001). The Woodcock-Johnson III was designed as a broad-range individually administered test to be used in educational settings. It assesses general intellectual ability (g), specific cognitive abilities, scholastic aptitude, oral language, and achievement (Schrank, McGrew, & Woodcock, 2001). The 2001 version of the Woodcock-Johnson was created based on the Cattell-Horn-Carroll (CHC) three-stratum theory of intelligence, comprising 69 narrow abilities (stratum 1) and grouped into broad categories of cognitive ability (stratum 2). Stratum 3 of the CHC model is the factor of g (general intelligence) (Schrank et al., 2001). Basically, the CHC theory was used as a blueprint in the creation of Woodcock-Johnson III, and in turn, the test is a measurement model of CHC theory (Schrank et al., 2001, p. 3).

By comparing a child's score on cognitive ability with his or her score on achievement, one can evaluate possible learning problems (Mather & Schrank, 2001; Schrank, Flanagan, Woodcock, & Mascolo, 2002). Because both the cognitive abilities battery and the achievement battery of the Woodcock-Johnson III were normed together, they provide for evaluating the presence of discrepancies without the errors associated with comparing results based on separately normed tests (Mather & Schrank, 2001). Co-normed batteries have also enabled the creators of the Woodcock-Johnson III to incorporate specific regression coefficients between all predictor and criterion variables for each age and population group. This allows evaluators to calculate the presence and significance of both intra-ability discrepancies (such as a discrepancy between an individual test taker's scores on processing speed and fluid reasoning) and ability–achievement discrepancies (such as a high score on the cognitive abilities battery and a low score on the achievement battery). Such discrepancies are defined in terms of a major discrepancy (usually 1.5 to 2 standard deviations) between cognitive ability (intelligence) and achievement. If a child is at the mean for cognitive ability (i.e., 50th percentile) and is two standard deviations below the mean in achievement (i.e., 2.2 percentile rank), evaluators would suspect a learning disability and call for further evaluation. The Woodcock-Johnson III also allows an evaluator to pinpoint specific deficits in cognitive ability. For instance, in evaluating a child who is struggling to keep up with the class in reading and has scored one standard deviation above the mean on the cognitive ability battery, it would be beneficial to discover that the child's results on the processing speed subtest were slightly below average. In this way, diagnosis of learning disabilities using the Woodcock-Johnson III can precisely isolate specific areas of concern, provide accurate diagnoses, and even suggest avenues of intervention.

The Woodcock-Johnson III's cognitive ability standard battery includes 10 tests such as verbal comprehension, visual–auditory learning, spatial relations, and visual matching. The extended battery for cognitive abilities, also made up of 10 subtests, includes tests such as picture recognition, decision speed, and memory for words. The 12 tests of the achievement standard battery cover letter and word identification, reading fluency and comprehension, math fluency, and language development. The remaining 10 tests make up the extended battery of achievement and cover items such as punctuation, reading vocabulary, and quantitative concepts. Scores can be converted to percentile ranks. These ranks, in turn, can be converted to a standard score with a mean of 100 and a standard deviation of 15.

The Woodcock-Johnson III has relatively good psychometric properties. The standardization sample included more than 8818 people representative of the U.S. population in terms of gender, race, occupational status, geographic region, and urban versus rural status. Thirty-eight of the 42 median test reliabilities reported by Schrank et al. (2001) have split-half reliabilities in the .80's and .90's.

In addition, construct validity for the test was evidenced by confirmatory factor analysis (Schrank et al., 2001, p. 17). Virtually every test from the cognitive abilities battery individually loaded solely on a single factor, indicating that the cognitive subtests minimize the influence of variance resulting from construct irrelevance. This is contrasted with the factorial complexity of the achievement battery, suggesting the influence of factors other than g.

Also supporting the interpretation that general intellectual ability is measured by the cognitive abilities battery, McGrew and Woodcock (2001) report correlations of .67 to .76 of the Woodcock-Johnson III with composite or full-scale scores from the Differential Abilities Scale (DAS) (Elliott, 1990), the Wechsler Intelligence Scale for Children–III (WISC-III) (Wechsler, 1991b), the Wechsler Preschool and Primary Scale of Intelligence–Revised (WPPSI-R) (Wechsler, 1989), the Stanford-Binet Intelligence Scale–Fourth Edition (SB-IV) (Thorndike, Hagen, & Sattler, 1986), and the Kaufman Adolescent and Adult Intelligence Test (KAIT) (Kaufman & Kaufman, 1993).

Moreover, Woodcock-Johnson III tests that measure select CHC cognitive abilities were shown to be significantly related to mathematics achievement (Floyd, Evans, & McGrew, 2003) and components of reading achievement (Evans, Floyd, McGrew, & Leforgee, 2002) and has shown potential for classifying exceptional students (Rizza, McIntosh, & McCunn, 2001).

The field of learning disability assessment is relatively new, and so are tests in this area. As a result, with the possible exception of the K-ABC, new tests of learning disability are in the same stage as early intelligence instruments. When judged by modern standards for individual ability tests, especially those that purportedly measure intelligence, these tests compare unfavorably in many respects.

For learning disability tests, three conclusions seem warranted. First, test constructors should attempt to respond to the same criticisms that led to changes in the Binet and Wechsler scales and ultimately to the development of the K-ABC. Second, much more empirical and theoretical research is needed (Flanagan & McGrew, 1998). Finally, users of learning disabilities tests should take great pains to understand the weaknesses of these procedures and not overinterpret results (Shull-Senn, Weatherly, Morgan, & Bradley-Johnson, 1995). The ITPA should not be used to make decisions that might affect the future of a child. The Woodcock-Johnson is much more suitable but should be used carefully. Later in the chapter we will discuss the legal rights of learning disabled students and others who may qualify for special education services.

Visiographic Tests

Visiographic tests require a subject to copy various designs. Such tests are used in education and have achieved a central position in neuropsychological testing because of their sensitivity to many different kinds of brain damage (Jacobson, Delis, & Bondi, 2002). In this section, we briefly describe three such tests and then, in Chapter 18, discuss neuropsychological testing in greater detail.

Benton Visual Retention Test (BVRT). Tests for brain damage are based on the concept of *psychological deficit,* in which a poor performance on a specific task is

FIGURE 11-10
*Designs similar to
those on the
Benton Visual
Retention Test.*

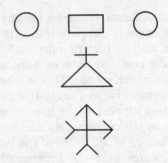

related to or caused by some underlying deficit. By knowing the underlying function or ability measured by a specific psychological test, the test examiner can relate a poor performance on that test to this underlying function (Downey, Elkin, Ehrhardt, Meyer-Bahlburg, Bell, & Morishima, 1991). Such is the idea behind the Benton Visual Retention Test (BVRT), which assumes that brain damage easily impairs visual memory ability. Thus, a deficit on a visual memory task is consistent with possible brain damage or brain diseases such as Alzheimer's (Yan, Yang, & Wang, 2001).

Designed for individuals ages 8 and older, the Benton test consists of geometric designs briefly presented and then removed (see Figure 11-10). The subject must then reproduce the designs from memory. The responses are scored according to criteria in the manual. The subject loses points for mistakes and omissions and gains points for correct or partially correct responses. Norms are then available to evaluate scores. As the number of errors increases, the subject approaches the organic (brain-damaged) range. Errors are also associated with normal aging (Resnick, Trotman, Kawas, & Zonderman, 1995), learning disabilities (Snow, 1998), and schizophrenia (Rollnick et al., 2002; Silver & Shlomo, 2001).

Bender Visual Motor Gestalt Test (BVMGT). Also used in the assessment of brain damage, the Bender Visual Motor Gestalt Test (BVMGT) has a variety of uses and is one of the most popular individual tests. It consists of nine geometric figures (such as a circle and a diamond) that the subject is simply asked to copy (see Figure 11-11). With specific errors identified for each design, the Bender test is scored according to the number of errors the subject makes (Bolen, Hewett, Hall, & Mitchell, 1992; Xu, Fu, & Zhang, 1996). Developmental norms are available that describe the number of errors associated with children ages 5 through 8 (see Koppitz, 1964). By age 9, any child of normal intelligence can copy the figures with only one or two errors. Therefore, anyone older than 9 who cannot copy the figures may suffer from some type of deficit.

Research on the Bender test has shown that errors can occur for people whose mental age is less than 9 (for example, because of low intelligence), those with brain damage (Bobic, Pavicevic, & Gomzi, 2000), those with nonverbal learning disabilities (Jing, Deqing, & Longhui, 2001), and those with emotional problems (Dixon, 1998; Shapiro & Simpson, 1994). Errors associ-

FIGURE 11-11

The figures of the Bender Visual Motor Gestalt Test.

(From the Bender Visual Motor Gestalt Test by L. Bender, 1962. Reprinted by permission from the publisher.)

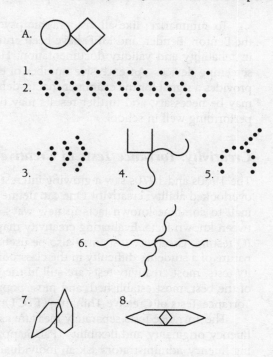

ated with brain damage have been identified, and a variety of scoring systems for brain damage are available. However, the reliability of such systems has been questioned (Fuller & Vance, 1995; Lubin & Sands, 1992; Wagner & Flamos, 1988). Nevertheless, the Bender ranks among the top 10 most widely used assessment instruments (Piotrowski, 1995).

Memory-for-Designs (MFD) Test. Another simple drawing test that involves perceptual–motor coordination is the Memory-for-Designs (MFD) Test. Requiring only a 10-minute administration, the Memory-for-Designs Test can be used for individuals 8½ to 60 years of age. Empirical data have tended to support its use as an indicator of brain injury and brain disease (Strauss & Brandt, 1990; Teng et al., 1989). As in the Benton test, the subject attempts to draw a briefly presented design from memory. Drawings are scored from 0 to 3, depending on how they compare with representative drawings from normal controls and people with varying degrees of brain injury. A raw score total based on all 15 drawings can then be corrected for age and intelligence by reference to a table. This corrected score can then be evaluated against a relatively large (825) normative sample.

Reported split-half reliability indexes are quite good (.92), and test–retest indexes range from .81 to .90 (Graham & Kendall, 1960). Like so many psychological tests, the MFD needs additional validity documentation. Available studies have been quite supportive (Goldstein, Canavan, & Polkey, 1988; Mandes & Gessner, 1988).

To summarize, like all visiographic psychological tests used in isolation, the Benton, Bender, and MFD have been criticized because of their limitations in reliability and validity documentation. However, all three can be used as screening devices. An excessive number of errors on any of these procedures provides a signal for the examiner that in-depth testing or a medical evaluation may be necessary, and further results may help explain why a student is not performing well in school.

Creativity: Torrance Tests of Creative Thinking (TTCT)

The 1960s and 1970s saw a growing interest in the assessment of a previously overlooked ability: creativity. One can define *creativity* as the ability to be original, to combine known facts in new ways, or to find new relationships between known facts. Evaluating creativity may provide a possible alternative to IQ testing. Creativity tests may also be useful in a battery to help explain the nature of a student's difficulty in the classroom. However, like learning disability tests, most creativity tests are still in the early stages of development. One of the best, most established, and most popular of these creativity tests is the Torrance Tests of Creative Thinking (TTCT).

The Torrance tests separately measure aspects of creative thinking such as fluency, originality, and flexibility (Palaniappan & Torrance, 2001). In measuring fluency, administrators ask an individual to think of as many different solutions to a problem as possible. The more distinct solutions a person can find, the greater his or her fluency. To evaluate originality, a test maker attempts to evaluate how new or unusual a person's solutions to problems are. Finally, flexibility is measured in terms of an individual's ability to shift directions or try a new approach to problem solving. For example, if the way you study for exams has not met your goals, then you would show flexibility if you tried a new approach. For example, instead of spending all your time passively rereading, you might try the recall method in which you spend half your study time trying to recall and synthesize what you have learned.

Like individual ability tests for the handicapped and tests of learning disability, the TTCT does not meet the Binet and Wechsler scales in terms of standardization, reliability, and validity. Reliability studies have varied widely (for example, correlations of .35 to .73 for a 3-year period), and validity studies have tended to be varied as well as inconclusive (Hattie, 1980). Unlike some creativity tests, the TTCT was conservatively presented as a research tool, but little has been done to prevent it from being applied in educational settings. Caution is indicated. On the positive side, several research studies have supported the utility of the Torrance tests as an unbiased indicator of giftedness (Torrance, 1970, 1977; see also Chan, 2000).

Factor analytic studies have suggested that the various types of creative thinking (fluency, flexibility, originality) tend to load on a single, general factor (Clapham, 1998). However, far more work is needed; today, human creativity surprisingly remains a largely unexplained field.

In sum, the Torrance tests are typical of creativity tests. Applied practitioners demand such a tool for their work. Though inconsistent, available data reflect the tests' merit and fine potential. As with so many other tests, however, more work is needed. One should view results from creativity tests as tentative, and to be used only in conjunction with other tests.

Individual Achievement Tests: Wide Range Achievement Test–3 (WRAT-3)

We have discussed the widely made distinction between intelligence and achievement. As you know, intelligence tests measure potential ability, whereas achievement tests measure what the person has actually acquired or done with that potential. Although scores from intelligence tests and achievement tests often overlap, discrepancies sometimes arise between the two, for instance, when a person of average potential has not made full use of that potential. Such a person would tend to score higher on a general ability test than on a specific achievement test, especially if the general ability test minimizes the effects of learning and the achievement test is highly specific. Similarly, a person may score average on a general intelligence test but, because of a high level of interest, motivation, or special training, score above average on achievement. Thus, despite the overlap of intelligence and ability tests, comparing their data can sometimes be extremely revealing. Indeed, as we indicated, discrepancies between IQ and achievement have traditionally been the main defining feature of a learning disability.

Most achievement tests are group tests, which will be discussed in the next chapter. Among the most widely used individual achievement tests is the Wide Range Achievement Test–3 (WRAT-3), which purportedly permits an estimate of grade-level functioning in reading, spelling, and arithmetic (Kareken, Gur, & Saykin, 1995; Snelbaker, Wilkinson, Robertson, & Glutting, 2001). It can be used for children ages 5 and older and has two levels for each of the three achievement areas.

The WRAT-3 is easy to administer. It also is highly popular. Despite the test's research and clinical uses, however, it has many problems (Johnstone, Holland, & Larimore, 2000).

The earlier WRAT-R had been severely criticized for its inaccuracy in evaluating grade-level reading ability. The test merely required participants to pronounce words from a list. The 1993 version retained this format, which led one reviewer to conclude that "on no grounds can this be considered a test of reading" (Mabry, 1995, p. 1108). Because the basic concept of the test has not changed for nearly 60 years, it is "already outdated" (Mabry, 1995, p. 1109).

The problems with the WRAT-3 underscore our repeated warning for caution in the use of test results. All test users should learn as much as they can about the tests they use. Statements from the test publishers or distributors of tests, and even statements in the test manuals, must always be carefully examined. Nevertheless, in evaluating learning disabilities, many educators continue to rely on the WRAT-3. As a screening tool, such use may be justified, but the test should never be used in place of a comprehensive assessment to evaluate reading level. In our final section, we turn to some of the legal issues involved in using educational tests in assessing for special education.

Legal Issues in Special Education

Schools Are Required by Law to Identify Students with Disabilities

It is important to emphasize that the diagnosis of a learning disability requires an experienced professional. In addition, problem school performance may be the result of a disability other than learning. Moreover, special education services are the responsibility of the educational agency for each state, which delegates this responsibility to the child's local school district. Thus, it is the local school district that is responsible for identifying children in need of special education services, and providing them a free appropriate public education [20 U.S.C. 1400 (d)]. Unfortunately, some local school districts are unwilling or unable to fulfill their responsibilities, requiring the parent to enforce the child's rights.

Enforcing a Child's Right Under IDEA

In enforcing a child's rights, a parent needs to be familiar with the laws and regulations that pertain to assessment, issues of notice, the individual education program (IEP), and due process. It is important to realize, however, that all the law requires the school to provide is "a free and appropriate" public education. The U.S. Supreme Court has interpreted this to mean education appropriate for the child's needs, but not necessarily the best available public education (*Board of Education v. Rowley*, 1982).

Assessment. Assessment is the process the school uses to determine whether a child is entitled to special education services. It typically involves the administration of tests as well as observation and evaluation of input from parents and teachers. Under federal law, the school has an obligation to find children who need assessment [20 U.S.C. 1412 (a) (3)]. When a school identifies such a child, it is required to obtain the written consent of the parent to conduct the assessment.

Parents who believe their child is in need of an assessment should make a written, dated request. The school then has 15 days to provide an assessment plan; and the parents then have 15 days to respond to or approve the plan.

Federal law places restrictions on which tests may be used (tests must be validated for the purpose used) and who can conduct the assessment. The assessor must be knowledgeable about the suspected disability [20 U.S.C. 1414 (b) (3) (B)].

Assessment Report. The results of the assessment should be a report that indicates the basis for any determination of whether the child is eligible for special education services. Where there is a learning disability, the report must also indicate if there is a discrepancy between potential to achieve (intelligence) and actual achievement that cannot be corrected without special education services.

Notice. As indicated, the request for an assessment must be in writing. Often, months are wasted because a parent made the request over the telephone. When push comes to shove, some school districts will comply only with the "letter of the law." If the request is not in writing, the school can choose to ignore it.

Independent Assessment. Parents who disagree with an assessment have the option of obtaining an independent assessment. Although federal law does not specifically require parents to notify the school prior to obtaining such an assessment, a parent is far less likely to prevail in any efforts for reimbursement where such notice has not been given because the school can claim that it would have administered additional tests. Parents who disagree with an assessment should strongly consider seeking legal advice.

The Individual Education Program (IEP). An IEP provides written documentation of the child's special education needs. The initial IEP meeting must occur within 50 calendar days of the school's receipt of a written consent to assessment. The end of the school year and vacation days may extend this time limit. Moreover, some school districts are lax in meeting this requirement. Federal and considerable case law ensure the parents' right to input at an IEP meeting [20 U.S.C. 1414 (d) (1) (B) (i)].

Due Process. Federal law guarantees parents of disabled children due process rights, such as the right to notice prior to assessment, placement in special education, and changes in placement. Parents who have a dispute regarding the contents or implementation of an IEP also have a right to a due process hearing.

Due process hearings must be requested in writing through the state educational agency. In California, for example, there is a Special Education Hearing Office. To protect parents, such hearings usually have strict timelines. In California, for example, once a due process hearing request is made, a final determination must be made within 45 days [C.F.R. 300.512 (a); Cal. Ed. Code 56502 (a)].

Timelines are double-edged. Parents or their representatives must be prepared to present their case to a hearing officer who will pass judgment after hearing all evidence. Being "in the right" is not good enough. The hearing officer will decide the case based on the evidence presented and the relevant case and statutory law. Prior to instituting a due process hearing, parents are strongly advised to seek legal advise.

SUMMARY

The number of individual ability tests is almost overwhelming. Most of these tests serve highly specific purposes, and their strength lies in their specificity. Table 11-2 summarizes the major differences among the various individual tests of ability. Of the infant and preschool scales, the Bayley Scales of Infant Development are the most psychometrically sound. The McCarthy Scales of

Children's Abilities appear to be promising tests for measuring intelligence in young children, but more work is needed. The KABC-II is a relatively new test of considerable value, but it has been strongly criticized. Overall, general ability tests for handicapped and special populations should be used cautiously. Among ability tests for the handicapped, the Columbia Mental Maturity Scale–Third Edition is one of the most promising.

Learning disability tests are based on information-processing theory. Because these tests are relatively new, one should view their results with caution. Like creativity tests, these tests have a long way to go to reach the standards of the Binet and Wechsler scales. Drawing tests such as the Bender, the Benton, and the Memory-for-Designs are all excellent and economical screening devices for brain damage. These tests attempt to measure an ability related to brain functioning. The Bender Visual Motor Gestalt Test, in addition to being a screening device for brain damage, can be used to measure intellectual and emotional functioning.

Although achievement and intelligence tests often overlap, a comparison of the two can be useful. A major individual achievement test, the Wide Range Achievement Test–3, can lead to incorrect conclusions because of several serious problems. Diagnosis of learning disabilities is a complex process. School districts have numerous responsibilities, and federal, state, and case law afford parents many rights.

WEB ACTIVITY   For interesting and relevant Web sites, check the following:

http://searcheric.org/scripts/seget2.asp?want=http://searcheric.org/ericdb/ED415591.htm
Testing students with disabilities

www.academyprojects.org/
Legal, ethical, and professional issues in psychoanalysis and psychotherapy

www.apa.org/science/testing.html
APA science directorate: Testing and assessment

www.nldontheweb.org/loring-meador.htm
Neuropsychology for neurologists

www.widerange.com/wrat3.html
Wide Range Achievement Test 3 (WRAT 3)

www.cps.nova.edu/~cpphelp/BVRT.html
Benton Visual Retention Test (BVRT)—5th edition

http://www.riverpub.com/products/clinicalindex.html
Woodcock-Johnson Psycho-Educational Battery—Revised (WJ-R)

CHAPTER 12

Standardized Tests in Education, Civil Service, and the Military

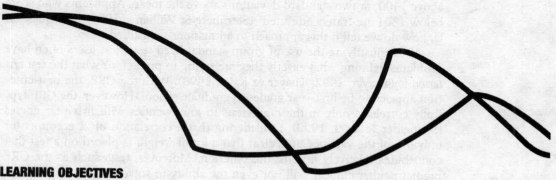

LEARNING OBJECTIVES

When you have completed this chapter, you should be able to:

☐ Compare group and individual ability tests

☐ Identify the major characteristics of group tests

☐ List four general rules for using results from group ability tests

☐ Evaluate the adequacy of the group ability tests used in kindergarten through 12th grade

☐ Identify and evaluate two major group ability tests for college entrance

☐ Identify and evaluate two major group ability tests for graduate-school entrance

☐ Identify some of the advantages of the Goodenough-Harris Drawing Test

☐ Identify some group ability tests widely used in business and industry

You no doubt have experienced taking a standardized group test. Such tests are given in kindergarten through 12th grade. Most colleges require standardized group entrance exams.

One test that has been the bane of many psychology and education majors is the Graduate Record Examination (GRE). The GRE is one of the most widely used tests for admission into postgraduate programs. If you plan to go on to graduate school, you will probably face the GRE. The extent to which graduate programs rely on the GRE can best be summed up by Sternberg and Williams (1997). Applications for admission into the Ph.D. program of one major research university are sorted on arrival into one of four boxes: below 1200, 1200–1300, 1301–1400, and above 1400, where the mean is 1000 and the standard deviation is 200. The first applications to be read are from the box above 1400, or two standard deviations above the mean. Applicants who score below 1301 are "rarely admitted" (Sternberg & Williams, 1997). The question is, how do we tell if this approach to admissions is justified?

When justifying the use of group standardized tests, test users often have problems defining what exactly they are trying to predict, or what the test *criterion* is (Thayer, 1992; Thayer & Kalat, 1998). With the GRE, the best criterion appears to be first-year grades in graduate school. However, the GRE typically correlates only in the high teens to low twenties with first-year grades (Schneider & Briel, 1990). Considering that a correlation of .2 accounts for only 4% of the variance, it is clear that a lot of weight is placed on a test that contributes relatively little to the criterion. Moreover, tests such as the GRE predict neither clinical skill nor even the ability to solve real-world problems (see Neisser et al., 1996).

To investigate the criterion problem, Saccuzzo and Johnson (2000) examined scores on the Law School Admission Test (LSAT) as they related to first-time bar pass rates. The LSAT was found to correlate from .063 to .146 with bar pass rates, depending on the sample. Strikingly, a student's cumulative law school GPA correlated between .591 and .587 with bar pass rates. Using multiple regression analysis, the researchers found that cumulative law school GPA accounted for 35.2% of the variation in bar pass rate, but the LSAT accounted for only an additional 2.3% of the variance. The implication was clear. Although the test did contribute to prediction, its weight was miniscule compared to actual performance as measured by a student's law school grade point average.

In this chapter, we continue our discussion of testing in education, evaluating many of the group tests used on a daily basis in schools, colleges, and graduate and professional schools. We also examine standardized tests used in the United States civil service and military. Tests used in business and industry are discussed in Chapter 17. As you encounter these tests, keep in mind that even though they do add accuracy in the selection process, the amount of variability they account for is relatively small. If the test correlates with a criterion at the .4 level, then it accounts for 16% of the variability in that criterion, with the other 84% resulting from unknown factors and errors. Before discussing specific tests, we compare group and individual tests and also reexamine the distinctions among achievement, aptitude, and intelligence.

Comparison of Group and Individual Ability Tests

Individual tests (as discussed in Chapters 9, 10, and 11) require a single examiner for a single subject. The examiner provides the instructions according to a standardized procedure stated in the test manual. The subject responds, and the examiner records the response verbatim. The examiner then evaluates and scores the subject's responses. This scoring process usually involves considerable skill. In contrast, a single examiner can administer group tests to more than one person at the same time. The examiner may read the instructions and impose time limits. Subjects record their own responses, which are usually choices between two or more alternatives. Scoring is usually objective and requires no skill on the part of the examiner, who simply adds the number of correct responses and in some cases subtracts a certain percentage for incorrect responses.

Further, in most individual tests, the examiner takes responsibility for eliciting a maximum performance. If a problem exists that might inhibit a maximum performance—for example, if a subject is frightened, nervous, uncooperative, or unmotivated—the examiner takes action to address this problem. For example, the examiner may encourage guessing by saying in a warm, friendly, supportive tone, "Sure you know that; just guess." On the other hand, those who use the results of group tests must *assume* that the subject was cooperative and motivated. Subjects are not praised for responding, as they may be on individual tests, and there are no safeguards to prevent a person from receiving a low score for reasons other than low ability—such as lack of motivation, lack of cooperation, or emotional upset. As a result, low scores on group tests are often difficult to interpret. With high scores, and especially high scores, one can logically assume that the subject was motivated and has mental abilities commensurate with the obtained score. Low scores, however, may have resulted from low ability, lack of interest, inadequate motivation, clerical errors in recording responses, or a host of other factors. Table 12-1 compares individual and group tests.

Advantages of Individual Tests

Individual tests can provide a wealth of information about a subject beyond the test score. In these tests, the instructions and methods of administration are as identical as possible, so subjects take an individual test in typically the same circumstances. Therefore, differences observed in behavior and attitudes most likely reflect differences in the individuals taking the test. One person may respond quickly and enthusiastically when correct but become hesitant or withdrawn following failure. Another person may react to failure by trying harder and may actually do better in the face of frustration and failure.

After examiners have gained experience with an individual test and know how to use it properly, they can observe different reactions from individuals placed in the same situation. Experienced examiners eventually develop internal norms. They have an idea of how most subjects react to a certain task or situation and can

TABLE 12-1
Individual Versus Group Tests

Individual tests	Group tests
One subject is tested at a time.	Many subjects are tested at a time.
Examiner records responses.	Subjects record own responses.
Scoring requires considerable skill.	Scoring is straightforward and objective.
Examiner flexibility can elicit maximum performance if permitted by standardization.	There are no safeguards.

easily identify unusual reactions. The opportunity to observe behavior in a standard situation can be invaluable to an examiner who is trying to understand the unique attributes of a person and interpret the meaning of a test score.

By providing the opportunity to observe behavior under standardized conditions, individual tests add a whole new dimension to the information that one can obtain from an interview. Some subjects will not talk; some cannot talk. How can the examiner gain an understanding of such individuals? Information provided by friends or relatives cannot be relied on because they are rarely objective and usually are not trained in observing human behavior. Simply observing the person in a natural setting may provide some useful information, but then the examiner has nothing with which to compare these observations. Thus, by allowing observations of behavior under standard conditions, individual tests provide an invaluable opportunity for the examiner to get information beyond what he or she can obtain in an interview.

Advantages of Group Tests

Group tests also offer unique advantages. Group tests are cost-efficient because they minimize the time needed for administration and scoring; they also involve less expensive materials and usually require less examiner skill and training than do individual tests. Scoring for group tests is more objective and hence typically more reliable than the subjective scoring of many individual tests. Group tests can be used with large numbers of individuals. When combined with data from other sources, group test results can yield information that is as useful and meaningful as that obtained from individual tests.

Whereas individual tests find their greatest application in the assessment and diagnosis of psychological or medical problems, the application of group tests is far broader. Group tests are used in schools at every level. The military, industry, and researchers also use them extensively. Group test results can be used for screening and selection purposes; to assess mental, vocational, or special abilities; to assess learning in a particular discipline or subject area; and to assess interests and aptitudes for specific occupations or job duties.

If the examiner's purpose does not require the benefits of individual tests, or if many individuals must be tested in a limited time with limited personnel, then carefully administered and interpreted group tests can be extremely valuable tools. Table 12-2 summarizes the advantages of individual and group tests.

TABLE 12-2

Unique Advantages of Individual and Group Tests

Individual tests	Group tests
Provide information beyond the test score	Are cost-efficient
Allow the examiner to observe behavior in a standard setting	Minimize professional time for administration and scoring
Allow individualized interpretation of test scores	Require less examiner skill and training
	Have more-objective and more-reliable scoring procedures
	Have especially broad application

Overview of Group Tests

Characteristics of Group Tests

In general, group tests can be characterized as paper-and-pencil or booklet-and-pencil tests because the only materials required are a printed booklet of test items, a test manual, a scoring key, an answer sheet, and a pencil. However, computerized group testing is becoming more popular, and certain tests such as the GRE are administered exclusively by computer (Bennett, 2003; Goldberg & Pedulla, 2002). Most group tests are multiple-choice, but some require a free response such as completing a sentence or design, or writing an essay (Educational Testing Service, 2002).

Group tests by far outnumber individual tests. Like the latter, group tests vary among themselves in many respects. One major difference is whether the test is primarily verbal (thus requiring reading or language skills), primarily nonverbal, or a combination.

Some group tests group items by type (for example, all verbal analogy problems are in the same section, with items arranged in order of increasing difficulty). A test of this kind is ideally suited for producing a variety of scores such as those obtained from the Wechsler scales. Other group tests present different tasks arranged in no particular or systematic order. A test of this kind typically produces a single score related to general ability.

Group test scores can be converted to a variety of units. Most produce percentiles or some type of standard score, but a few produce ratio or deviation IQs.

Selecting Group Tests

Because there are a sufficient number of psychometrically adequate group tests for most purposes, the test user need never settle for anything but well-documented and psychometrically sound tests. This is especially true for ability tests used in the schools.

In view of the large number of psychometrically sound instruments, this chapter will not discuss poorly standardized or marginally reliable tests. However, tests excluded from this discussion are not necessarily psychometrically unsound. We gave highest priority to established, highly used tests that continue to generate interest among researchers and practitioners. We also include tests that illustrate concepts or meet specific needs. Finally, we include a few recent tests as well as tests of historical value.

Using Group Tests

Overall, the tests included in our discussion are about as reliable and well standardized as the best individual tests. However, as for some individual tests, validity data for some group tests are weak, meager, or contradictory—or all three. Therefore, all users of group tests must carefully interpret and make use of test scores. These tests should not be seen as a simple way of making decisions but as a tool to be used in conjunction with other data.

Test use is an especially important issue for group tests because the results from these procedures are used by more people than are the results from individual tests. All routine users of these tests—thousands of teachers, educators, school administrators, personnel staff, counselors, and so forth—as well as the many consumers of group test information can benefit from the following suggestions.

Use results with caution. Never consider scores in isolation or as absolutes. Try to include the test score as only one bit of data, tentatively accepted unless not confirmed by other data. Be especially careful in using these tests for prediction, except for predicting relatively limited factors over a brief time. Avoid overinterpreting test scores or attributing more to test scores than their limitations warrant.

Be especially suspicious of low scores. Users of group tests must assume that subjects understand the purpose of testing, want to do well, and are equally rested and free of emotional problems. Many group tests also require reading ability as well as an interest in solving test problems. Failing to fulfill any of these assumptions and requirements can produce an artificially low score.

Consider wide discrepancies a warning signal. When an individual exhibits wide discrepancies either among test scores or between a test score and other data, all may not be well with the individual (assuming no clerical errors). The discrepancy may reflect emotional problems or severe stress. For example, a child with high test scores may obtain poor grades because of emotional upset. Or a child with good grades may obtain a poor test score because of a crisis, such as a death in the family.

When in doubt, refer. With low scores, wide discrepancies, or sufficient reason to doubt the validity or fairness of a test result, the safest course is to refer the subject for individual testing. Given the reasons for the referral, a professional who is trained in individual test use can generally ascertain the cause of the problem and provide the unique interpretation called for in such cases. It is often dangerous as well as reckless to take on a responsibility meant only for a trained specialist.

Group Tests in the Schools: Kindergarten Through 12th Grade

The purpose of these tests is to measure educational achievement in schoolchildren. Before proceeding to a discussion of the specific tests, this section reviews the nature of achievement tests and how they differ from aptitude tests.

Achievement Tests Versus Aptitude Tests

Achievement tests attempt to assess what a person has learned following a specific course of instruction. As you saw in Chapter 1, the first achievement tests used in the schools were essay tests. These were rapidly replaced in the 1930s by standardized achievement tests such as the Stanford Achievement Test, which is still in use today. These tests were more cost-effective than their essay counterparts, and scoring was far more objective and reliable. However, like their predecessors, standardized achievement tests had as their goal the end-point evaluation of a student's knowledge after a standard course of training. In such tests, validity is determined primarily by content-related evidence. In other words, these tests are considered valid if they adequately sample the domain of the construct (e.g., math, science, or history) being assessed.

On the other hand, aptitude tests attempt to evaluate a student's potential for learning rather than how much a student has already learned. Unlike achievement tests, aptitude tests evaluate a wide range of experiences obtained in a variety of ways. They evaluate the effects of unknown and uncontrolled experiences. The validity of an aptitude test is judged primarily on its ability to predict future performance. Thus, such tests rely heavily on criterion-oriented evidence for validity. Table 12-3 summarizes the differences between achievement and aptitude tests.

As you know, the intelligence test measures general ability. Like aptitude tests, intelligence tests attempt to predict future performance. However, such tests predict generally and broadly, as opposed to aptitude tests, which typically predict potential in a specific area such as math, science, or music.

TABLE 12-3
Achievement Tests Versus Aptitude Tests

Achievement tests	Aptitude tests
1. Evaluate the effects of a known or controlled set of experiences	1. Evaluate the effects of an unknown, uncontrolled set of experiences
2. Evaluate the product of a course of training	2. Evaluate the potential to profit from a course of training
3. Rely heavily on content validation procedures	3. Rely heavily on predictive criterion validation procedures

Clearly, achievement, aptitude, and intelligence are highly interrelated. For example, an algebra achievement test might be used to predict success (aptitude) in a geometry course. The following discussion examines all three types, beginning with achievement tests. Then we consider group intelligence tests used in the school system. Finally, we examine tests used to measure scholastic aptitude.

Group Achievement Tests

As previously indicated, the Stanford Achievement Test (SAT) is one of the oldest of the standardized achievement tests widely used in the school system (Gardner, Rudman, Karlsen, & Merwin, 1982). Published by the Psychological Corporation, this test is well normed and criterion-referenced, with exemplary psychometric documentation. It evaluates achievement in the first through ninth grades in the following areas: spelling, reading comprehension, word study and skills, language arts, social studies, science, mathematics, and listening comprehension. Figure 12-1 shows an example of the scoring output for the Stanford Achievement Test. Two related tests, the Stanford Early School Achievement Tests–Second Edition (SESAT) and the Stanford Test for Academic Skills–Second Edition (TASK), are used to extend the grade range to kindergarten through 12th. Together, all three tests are referred to as the Stanford Achievement Series.

Another well-standardized and psychometrically sound group measure of achievement is the Metropolitan Achievement Test (MAT), which measures achievement in reading by evaluating vocabulary, word recognition, and reading comprehension. The MAT was renormed in 2000, and alternate versions of the test including Braille, large print, and audio formats we made available for use with children having visual limitations (Harcourt Educational Measurement, 2000). An example of a reading item follows:

Jennifer _____ to play house.

Pick the word that best completes the sentence.

A. wood   **B.** book   **C.** likes   **D.** hopes

The MAT also measures mathematics by evaluating number concepts (e.g., measurement, decimals, factors, time, money), problem solving (e.g., word problems), and computation (addition, subtraction, multiplication, division). For example, a child might be presented with this item:

Jason had four candy bars. He gave one to Mary and one to Bill. Which number sentence below shows how many candy bars he had left?

A. $4 - 2 =$ **B.** $4 + 2 =$ **C.** $2 + 2 =$ **D.** $2 - 2 =$

FIGURE 12-1

Example of a score report for the Stanford Achievement Test.

(Reproduced by permission from the Score Report for the Stanford Achievement Test, 8th Edition. Copyright © 1991 by Harcourt Brace Jovanovich, Inc. All Rights Reserved.)

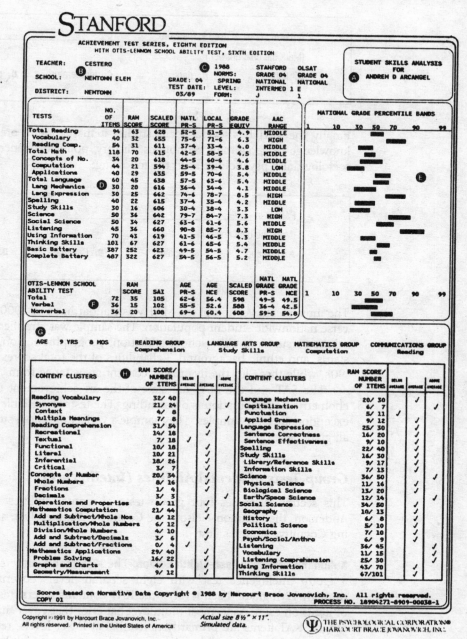

Spelling is evaluated on the MAT in a normal spelling test format in which the student is asked to spell an orally dictated word presented in a sentence. Language skills are evaluated with a grammar test as well as a measure of alphabetizing skills. Science knowledge is evaluated in items such as the following:

A thermometer is used to measure _____.

(Mark the best answer.)

A. light   **B.** dark   **C.** temperature   **D.** planets

Finally, the MAT has several social studies items. Students are tested on their knowledge of geography, economics, history, political science, anthropology, sociology, and psychology, as in the following:

Paris is in _____.

(Mark the best answer.)

A. England   **B.** Spain   **C.** Canada   **D.** France

The most recent version of the MAT was standardized in 2000, reflecting a diverse nationwide student population. The sample was stratified by school size, public versus nonpublic school affiliation, geographic region, socioeconomic status, and ethnic background. Reliabilities of the total scores run in the high .90's, while those for the five major content areas range from .90 to .96.

The SAT and the MAT are state-of-the-art achievement tests. Their psychometric documentation is outstanding. The tests are reliable and normed on exceptionally large samples. They sample a variety of school subjects and cover all grade levels.

Group Tests of Mental Abilities (Intelligence)

This section discusses four group tests of mental abilities: the Kuhlmann-Anderson, the Henmon-Nelson, the Cognitive Abilities Test, and the Developing Cognitive Abilities Test.

Kuhlmann-Anderson Test–Eighth Edition. The Kuhlmann-Anderson Test (KAT) is a group intelligence test with eight separate levels covering kindergarten through 12th grade. Each level of the KAT contains several tests with a variety of items on each. As in most multilevel batteries that cover many age or grade ranges, KAT items are primarily nonverbal at lower levels, requiring minimal reading and language ability. However, whereas most multilevel batteries become increasingly verbal with increasing age or grade level, the KAT remains primarily nonverbal throughout. Thus, the KAT is suited not only to young children but also to those who might be handicapped in following verbal procedures. It might even be suitable for adaptation for non–English-speaking populations, assuming proper norming.

The results of the most recent (eighth) edition of the KAT can be expressed in verbal, quantitative, and total scores. At some levels, total scores can be expressed as deviation IQs. Scores at other levels can be expressed as percentile bands. A **percentile band** is like a confidence interval. It provides the range of percentiles that most likely represent a subject's true score. One creates it by forming an interval one standard error of measurement above and below the obtained score and then converting the resulting values to percentiles.

An overwhelming majority of reviews have praised the KAT for its construction, standardization, and other excellent psychometric qualities. Normative data have been continually improved and are based on more than 10,000 subjects. Reliability coefficients are quite good, with split-half coefficients running in the low .90's and test–retest coefficients ranging from the low .80's to the low .90's. Validity is also well documented. The KAT correlates highly with a variety of ability and IQ tests. In sum, the KAT is an extremely sound, sophisticated group test. Its nonverbal items make it particularly useful for special purposes. Its impressive validity and reliability also make it one of the most popular group ability tests for all grade levels. Its potential for use and adaptation for non–English-speaking individuals or even non–English-speaking countries needs to be explored.

Henmon-Nelson Test. A second well-standardized, highly used, and carefully constructed test for all grade levels is the Henmon-Nelson Test (H-NT) of mental abilities. Although it produces only a single score that is believed to reflect general intelligence, two sets of norms are available. One set is based on raw score distributions by age, the other on raw score distributions by grade. Raw scores can be converted into deviation IQs as well as percentiles. The availability of only a single score has continued to spur controversy. However, a single score is consistent with the purpose of the test, which is to obtain a relatively quick measure of general intelligence (it takes approximately 30 minutes to complete the 90 items).

As in the other tests for school-age individuals, most of the reported reliability coefficients, both split-half and test–retest, run in the .90's. Furthermore, the H-NT correlates well with a variety of intelligence tests (median .76, range .50–.84) and achievement test scores (median .79, range .64–.85). Correlations with grades, though not as high, are impressive, with a median coefficient of .60, which would account for 36% of the variability.

In sum, the H-NT is an extremely sound instrument. It can help predict future academic success quickly. However, the H-NT has some important limitations when used as the sole screening instrument for selecting giftedness or identifying learning disabilities in minority, culturally diverse, and economically disadvantaged children.

By providing only a single score related to Spearman's g factor, the H-NT does not consider multiple intelligences. When the test was being developed, no special effort was made to check for content bias, either by judges or by statistical analysis. The manual presents no data pertaining to the norms for special racial, ethnic, or socioeconomic groups, nor was the test designed to be used for culturally diverse children. Indeed, the manual pointedly calls for caution when using the H-NT for individuals from an educationally disadvantaged subculture. It also advises caution when extreme scores (below 80 or above 130) are obtained. Consistent with these cautions, research suggests that the HNT tends to underestimate Wechsler full-scale IQ scores by 10 to 15 points for certain populations (Watson & Klett, 1975). A major problem with the H-NT is its relatively low ceiling. For example, to achieve an IQ of 130, a ninth-grade child would have to answer approximately 85 of the items correctly. This leaves only five items to discriminate all those above 130.

Cognitive Abilities Test. In terms of its reliability and validity, the Cognitive Abilities Test (COGAT) is comparable to the H-NT. Unlike the H-NT, however, the COGAT provides three separate scores: verbal, quantitative, and nonverbal. Reliabilities (KR_{20}) for the verbal score are in the high .90's; for the quantitative, the low .90's; and for the nonverbal, the high .90's.

The COGAT's item selection is superior to that of the H-NT in terms of selecting minority, culturally diverse, and economically disadvantaged children. Unlike the H-NT, the COGAT was specifically designed for poor readers, poorly educated people, and people for whom English is a second language. As with the KAT, it can potentially be adopted for use outside of the United States.

The test authors of the COGAT took special steps to eliminate irrelevant sources of test difficulty, especially those pertaining to cultural bias. All items were scrutinized for content that might be biased for or against any particular group. Statistical tests were then performed to eliminate items that might predict differentially for white and minority students. To eliminate the effect of test-taking skills, the test administration includes extensive practice exercises.

The COGAT offers advantages over the H-NT in evaluating minority, culturally diverse, and economically disadvantaged children. Moreover, research has revealed that the COGAT is a sensitive discriminator for giftedness (Chong, 2000; Harty, Adkins, & Sherwood, 1984) and a good predictor of future performance (Henry & Bardo, 1990; Luo, Thompson, & Detterman, 2003). It also is a good measure of verbal underachievement (Langdon, Rosenblatt, & Mellanby, 1998).

On the negative side, each of the three subtests of the COGAT requires 32 to 34 minutes of actual working time, which the manual recommends be spread out over two or three days. The manual claims that the tests are primarily "power tests" but provides no data to support this claim. Despite the apparent strength of the norms, uncertainty remains as to whether they are, in fact, representative. For example, when a selected community declined to participate in the norming process, a second, third, fourth, or, in some cases, fifth choice was needed to find a replacement. No data are provided regarding the frequency and magnitude of this type of sampling bias. A more serious potential drawback can be found in the information presented in the manual regarding ethnic group means. The standard age scores (SAS-normalized standard scores with a mean of 100 and standard deviation of 16) averaged some 15 or more points lower for African American students (versus whites) on the verbal battery and quantitative batteries. This negative aspect of the COGAT has been confirmed by independent research (McKay & Doverspike, 2001). Latino and Latina students also tended to score lower than white students across the test batteries and grade levels. Therefore, great care should be taken when scores on the COGAT are used for minority populations.

Summary of K–12 group tests. The SAT, MAT, KAT, H-NT, and COGAT are all sound, viable instruments. The SAT and MAT provide outstanding measures of achievement. A particular strength of the KAT in evaluating intelligence is its set of nonverbal items. The H-NT provides a quick estimate of g (general intelligence) for most children but is not as valid as the COGAT for assessing minority or culturally diverse children. Each test should be used only by those who know its particular properties, strengths, and limitations.

College Entrance Tests

Three of the most widely used and well-known entrance tests are the Scholastic Assessment Test (formally known as the Scholastic Aptitude Test), the Cooperative School and College Ability Tests, and the American College Test.

The Scholastic Assessment Test

Up until March 1995, the Scholastic Assessment Test (SAT-I) was known as the Scholastic Aptitude Test (SAT). The SAT-I remains the most widely used of the college entrance tests. In the 2000–2001 test year, more than 2.1 million students took the SAT-I: Reasoning Test as part of the admissions process for more than 1000 private and public institutions of higher education (Lawrence, Rigol, Van Essen, & Jackson, 2002).

In continuous use since 1926, the SAT was given on an annual basis to some 1.5 million students at 5000 test centers around the country. From 1941 through April 1995, norms for the SAT were based on a sample of 10,000 students who took the test in 1941. When compared with these original norms, modern users tended to score approximately 20 to 80 points lower for each of the two main sections of the test, the SAT-V (Verbal) and the SAT-M (Math). With the original mean at 500 for each of the two sections, national averages in the 1980s and early 1990s tended to run 420 for the SAT-V and 480 for the SAT-M. Numerous explanations were advanced to explain the decline, which became somewhat of a national embarrassment (Hanford, 1986).

In June 1994, the test developers announced that they would restore the national average to the 500-point level of 1941. They accomplished this by renorming the test on 1.8 million students and converting raw scores to standard scores with a mean of 500 and a standard deviation of 100. The new norms pushed up national SAT averages approximately 75 points on the Verbal and 20 points on the Math. In 2002, the average scores on the SAT were 504 for the verbal section and 516 for the math section.

The renorming of the SAT did not alter the standing of test takers relative to one another in terms of percentile rank. However, some confusion exists in comparing scores from individuals who took the SAT before April 1995 and those who have since taken the SAT. To help matters, the College Entrance Examination Board provides a "score converter" for colleges.

The revised SAT showed many changes that the College Board believed reflected educational reform movements of the 1980s and 1990s. The SAT Verbal and Math sections were renamed the SAT-I: Reasoning Tests. In the Verbal sections of the SAT-I, reasoning tests included an increased emphasis on critical reading—for example, two passages that differed only in point of view. Antonyms were removed, but several new questions that measure vocabulary in context were included. The Math section of the SAT-I now offers questions that require students to produce their own responses (as opposed to selecting from a set of given answers). Students are encouraged to bring calculators. In addition, emphasis on interpretation of data and applied mathematics has increased. The College Board provides a well-written guide for taking the SAT-I. This guide includes tips on how to prepare, simple test-taking strategies, sample questions with explanations, and a practice test. College counselors can read reports and other literature that explain the revision.[1] Figures 12-2 and 12-3 illustrate differences in the content for the Verbal and Math sections, respectively.

Along with the SAT-I: Reasoning Tests, the College Board released the SAT-II: Subject Tests. The SAT-II includes a direct writing test, new tests in Asian languages, and a new English-as-a-Second-Language Proficiency Test.

Most of the published research in the last half of the 1990s and early 2000s pertained to the original SAT (Lawlor, Richman, & Richman, 1997; Roznowski & Reith, 1999). However, SAT-I will most likely inherit many of the strengths as well as the weaknesses of the original.

A major weakness of the original SAT as well as other major college entrance tests is relatively poor predictive power regarding the grades of students who score in the middle ranges. It is not uncommon for a student at the mean on the SAT to have a higher college grade point average than a student who scores a standard deviation above the mean on both sections, perhaps because factors such as motivation, determination, personality, emotional stability, and home and social life also influence first-year grades. In other words, test scores and high-school performance records do not alone determine college success. Furthermore, the number of English or math units a student has does not correlate significantly with his or her SAT-V or SAT-M score (Sinha, 1986). This may result from the effects of coaching—that is, training courses that expose students to questions like those on the actual test and that promote good test-

---

[1]Such reports can be easily obtained by writing to the College Entrance Examination Board, P.O. Box 6200, Princeton, NJ 08514-6200.

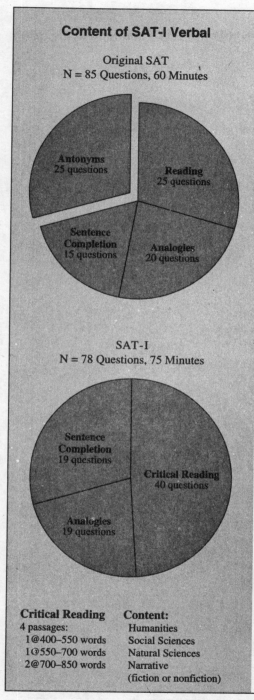

Content of SAT-I Verbal

Original SAT
N = 85 Questions, 60 Minutes

Antonyms
25 questions

Reading
25 questions

Sentence
Completion
15 questions

Analogies
20 questions

SAT-I
N = 78 Questions, 75 Minutes

Sentence
Completion
19 questions

Critical Reading
40 questions

Analogies
19 questions

Critical Reading
4 passages:
1@400–550 words
1@550–700 words
2@700–850 words

Content:
Humanities
Social Sciences
Natural Sciences
Narrative
(fiction or nonfiction)

SAT-I: Reasoning tests reflect what students experience in today's classrooms.

Consisting of two parts–Verbal Reasoning and Mathematical Reasoning–SAT-I will require three hours of testing time. Exact time limits will be determined after further research, but will approximate:

- **Verbal Reasoning:** 75 minutes
- **Mathematical Reasoning:** 75 minutes
- **Equating or Pretesting:** 30 minutes

Verbal Reasoning puts the emphasis on critical reading.

Much of the content of the SAT-I Verbal Test will remain the same, although antonyms will no longer appear. The test will include questions and reading passages that reflect both what colleges expect of today's students and current instructional theory.

The Verbal section of SAT-I will focus even more than the current test on students' ability to read critically. The SAT-I Verbal Test will include the following new features:

- Approximately half of the questions will be based on reading passages;
- Longer reading passages;
- Reading material that is more accessible and engaging;
- A pair of reading passages on the same or related topics. One of the passages will oppose, support, or in some way complement the point of view expressed in the other;
- Introductory information to give students a context for each reading passage;
- Questions that test students' verbal reasoning skills and knowledge of vocabulary in context.

FIGURE 12-2 *Verbal content of revised SAT (SAT-I) compared with the original.*

SAT-I: Mathematical Reasoning focuses on problem-solving skills important to success in college.

The content of the SAT-I Mathematical Reasoning Test will also remain fundamentally the same as the current SAT Mathematical Test, but with increased emphasis on a student's ability to apply mathematical concepts and interpret data. The current multiple-choice and quantitative comparisons will continue to appear on the test.

Two significant new features also will be introduced:

■ Questions that require students to produce and "grid-in" their own answers–not just select one from a set of multiple-choice alternatives, and
■ It is recommended that students bring calculators.

The introduction of calculator use will parallel the changes occurring nationally in the use of calculators in mathematics instruction.

The policies that govern the use of calculators on SAT-I are supported by the recommendations and standards of the:

■ National Council of Teachers of Mathematics
■ National Council of Supervisors of Mathematics
■ Mathematical Sciences Education Board
■ Mathematical Association of America
■ American Mathematical Society

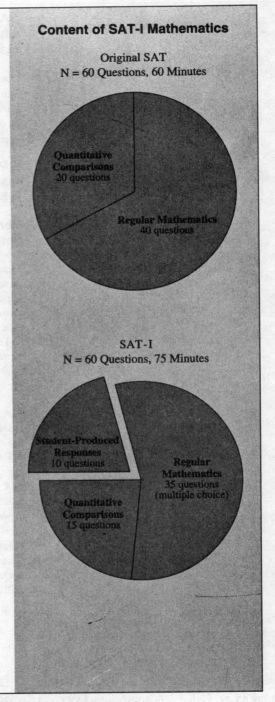

Content of SAT-I Mathematics

Original SAT
N = 60 Questions, 60 Minutes

Quantitative Comparisons
20 questions

Regular Mathematics
40 questions

SAT-I
N = 60 Questions, 75 Minutes

Student-Produced Responses
10 questions

Regular Mathematics
35 questions
(multiple choice)

Quantitative Comparisons
15 questions

FIGURE 12-3 *Math content of revised SAT (SAT-I) compared with the original.*
(*Copyright © 1992 by the College Entrance Examination Board. All Rights Reserved.*)

taking skills. However, research has generally shown that coaching accounts for minimal improvement in SAT score.

In 1998, Powers and Rock indicated that, when controlling for variables such as ethnicity, English proficiency, household income, educational and vocational aspirations, and parental education, verbal scores could be increased by an average of 6 to 8 points and math scores by an average of 13 to 18 points. Because social and cultural variables have a large effect on *who* elects to receive coaching services, studies that do not control for these variables are suspect. A meta-analysis (Powers, 1999) suggested that while uncontrolled, single group studies of the effects of coaching yielded average increases of 40.6 (standard error 10.1) on verbal and 53.8 (standard error 2.6) on math, studies that utilized randomized or matched groups yielded average increases of 10.1 (standard error 3.5) on verbal and 9.8 (standard error 3.8) on math. What actually tend to correlate with SAT scores are the characteristics of elementary, middle, and high schools the test takers have attended such as the schools' socioeconomic status and urbanicity (Stricker, Rock, Pollack, & Wenglinsky, 2002). Surprisingly, this same study suggested a greater association between school characteristics and SAT scores than school characteristics and high school GPA, suggesting that the SAT might be succeeding at measuring cognitive variance while grades may reflect motivational variance (see also Willingham, Pollack, & Lewis, 2000).

There is little doubt that the SAT predicts first-year college GPA (Bridges, 2001). Validity coefficients vary depending on the sample, with a median of approximately .4, which means that SAT scores account for some 16% of the variation in first-year GPA. The predictive validity of the SAT is about as good for Latino and Latina (Fuertes & Sedlacek, 1994) and African American (Lawlor et al., 1997) students as it is for whites. However, studies with the old SAT have shown that African American and Latino and Latina students tend to obtain lower scores on the average, sometimes by as much as 80 points lower on the average (Lawlor et al., 1997). In addition, although women tend to achieve higher grades in college, they tend to score lower than men on the SAT (Mau & Lynn, 2001). Results with the SAT are entirely consistent with those from all modern standardized tests: African Americans and Latinos and Latinas score significantly lower on average compared to whites, and women score lower than men. Critics have asked whether the newer SAT-I will show similar selection biases.

When used together with cumulative GPAs, the SAT has been proven as an important predictor of success in college (Camara & Echternacht, 2000). A major project conducted by the University of California evaluated the predictive quality and inequities in outcome according to race and socioeconomic status of the SAT-I and SAT-II (Geiser & Studley, 2001). Because the University of California requires prospective students to take both tests, they had a large pool of more than 78,000 SAT-I and SAT-II results from entering freshman from the years 1996–1999. They also had access to information concerning the academic success of these students. They found that the SAT-I accounted for 13.3% of the variance in University of California GPA (indicating a correlation of 3.65), while the SAT-II accounted for 16% (correlation = .4), and the undergraduate GPA accounted for 15.4% (correlation = 3.65). Although not used as an entrance requirement in most universities, it appears that the SAT-II has greater predictability than the SAT-I. Researchers also found that the validities of both the SAT-I and SAT-II were affected by socioeconomic status and race. Specifically, African Americans scored significantly lower on both the SAT-I and SAT-II, as did American Indians and Chicano or Latino students. These results are disappointing and again reveal the current situation in standardized tests: Their use will always result in a selection bias against certain groups. In support of the SAT-I, Williams and Ceci (1997) found evidence of a growing convergence in test scores across racial and socioeconomic segments in U.S. society. Similarly, Neisser (1998) has found that the gap in school achievement between white and African American children has closed substantially in recent years. Such evidence hints that the SAT-I may have the highest possible psychometric adequacy of any such test that has been achievable to date. There is little doubt that the SAT-I will play a role in college entrance decisions in the 21st century, but the need to study and understand selection bias in standardized tests persists.

Cooperative School and College Ability Tests

Second to the SAT in terms of use is the Cooperative School and College Ability Tests (SCAT), which was developed in 1955. In addition to the college level, the SCAT covers three precollege levels beginning at the fourth grade. The SCAT purports to measure school-learned abilities as well as an individual's potential to undertake additional schooling.

Although the SCAT is well designed and constructed, H. L. Butcher (1972) questioned the representativeness of its standardization sample. Psychometric documentation of the SCAT, furthermore, is neither as strong nor as extensive as that of the SAT. Another problem is that little empirical data support its major assumption—that previous success in acquiring school-learned abilities can predict future success in acquiring such abilities. Even if this assumption were accurate—and it probably is—grades provide about as much information about future performance as does the SCAT, especially at the college level. In view of these considerations, we concur with Butcher that additional evidence on the SCAT would be highly desirable. Also, despite its reasonably good correlation with the SAT, we see little advantage of the SCAT over the SAT for predicting college success.

The American College Test

The American College Test (ACT) is another popular and widely used college entrance (aptitude) test. In some states (e.g., Alabama), most students take it. The ACT produces specific content scores and a composite. The content scores are in English, mathematical usage, social studies reading, and natural science

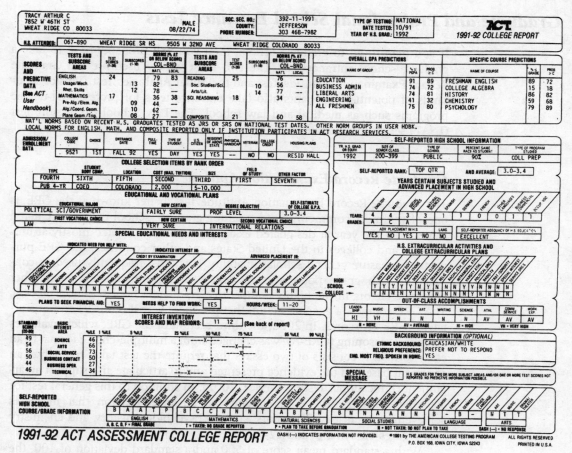

FIGURE 12–4 *A sample student profile from the ACT.*

(Copyright 1991 by the American College Testing Program. All Rights Reserved. Reproduced with permission.)

reading. In expressing results, the ACT makes use of the Iowa Test of Educational Development (ITED) scale. Scores on this scale can vary between 1 and 36, with a standard deviation of 5 and a mean of 16 for high-school students and a mean of 19 for college aspirants. Figure 12-4 shows a sample profile report from the ACT.

The ACT compares with the SAT in terms of predicting college GPA alone or in conjunction with high-school GPA (Stumpf & Stanley, 2002). In fact, the correlation between the two tests is quite high—in the high .80's (Pugh, 1968). However, internal consistency coefficients are not as strong in the ACT, with coefficients in the mid .90's for the composite and in the high .70's to high .80's for the four content scores.

Graduate and Professional School Entrance Tests

If you plan to go to graduate school, then you will probably have to take a graduate-school entrance test. The two most widely used are the Graduate Record Examination Aptitude Test and the Miller Analogies Test. Tens of thousands of potential applicants also take entrance tests for professional-degree programs such as medical and law school. The Law School Admission Test (LSAT) serves to illustrate such tests.

Graduate Record Examination Aptitude Test

The Graduate Record Examination Aptitude Test, better known as the GRE, is one of the most commonly used tests for graduate-school entrance. Offered throughout the year at designated examination centers located mostly at universities and colleges in the United States and other countries, the GRE purports to measure general scholastic ability. It is most frequently used in conjunction with grade point average, letters of recommendation, and other academic factors in the highly competitive graduate-school selection process. The GRE contains a general section that produces verbal (GRE-V) and quantitative (GRE-Q) scores. In 2002, the third section of the GRE, which evaluates analytical reasoning (GRE-A), was changed from a multiple-choice format to an essay format. It consists of two essays that require the test taker to analyze an argument based on the evidence presented and to articulate and support an argument (Educational Testing Service, 2002). In addition to this general test for all college majors, the GRE contains an advanced section that measures achievement in at least 20 majors, such as psychology, history, and chemistry (see Figures 12-5, 12-6, and 12-7).

With a standard mean score of 500 and a standard deviation of 100, the verbal section covers reasoning, identification of opposites, use of analogies, and paragraph comprehension. The quantitative section covers arithmetic reasoning, algebra, and geometry. However, the normative sample for the GRE is relatively small. The psychometric adequacy of the GRE is also less spectacular than that of the SAT, both in the reported coefficients of validity and reliability and in the extensiveness of documentation. Nevertheless, the GRE is a relatively sound instrument.

The stability of the GRE based on Kuder-Richardson and odd–even reliability is adequate, with coefficients only slightly lower than those of the SAT. However, the predictive validity of the GRE is far from convincing.

Independent studies of the GRE vary from those that find moderate correlations between the GRE and grade point average to those that find no or even a negative relationship between the two. House and Johnson (1998), for example, reported correlations ranging from .22 to .33 between GRE scores and various graduate-school courses, which would account for 4.84% to 10.89% of the variance. In 1999, House found that higher GRE scores were significantly correlated with higher grades in specific courses. Using regression analysis, Ji

FIGURE 12-5

GRE verbal ability sample items.

(GRE materials selected from GRE Practice General Test 2003–2004, 2003. Reprinted by permission of Educational Testing Service, the copyright owner. Permission to reprint GRE materials does not constitute review or Endorsement by Educational Testing Service of this publication as a whole or of any other testing information it may contain.)

Directions*

In each of the following questions, a related pair of words or phrases is followed by five lettered pairs of words or phrases. Select the lettered pair that best expresses a relationship similar to that expressed in the original pair.

Sample Question

COLOR : SPECTRUM :
(A) tone : scale
(B) sound : waves
(C) verse : poem
(D) dimension : space
(E) cell : organism

Strategies for Answering

- Establish a relationship between the given pair before reading the answer choices.
- Consider relationships of kind, size, spatial contiguity, or degree.
- Read all of the options. If more than one seems correct, try to state the relationship more precisely.
- Check to see that you haven't overlooked a possible second meaning for one of the words.
- *Never* decide on the best answer without reading all of the answer choices.

Answer

The relationship between *color* and *spectrum* is not merely that of part to whole, in which case (E) or even (C) might be defended as correct. A *spectrum* is made up of a progressive, graduated series of *colors*, as a *scale* is of a progressive, graduated sequence of *tones*. Thus, (A) is the correct answer choice. In this instance, the best answer must be selected from a group of fairly close choices.

Sentence Completions

Sentence completions measure your ability to recognize words or phrases that both logically and stylistically complete the meaning of a sentence.

Directions*

Each sentence below has one or two blanks, each blank indicating that something has been omitted. Beneath the sentence are five lettered words or sets of words. Choose the word or set of words for each blank that *best* fits the meaning of the sentence as a whole.

---

* The directions are presented as they appear on the actual test.

Sample Question

Early _____ of hearing loss is _____ by the fact that the other senses are able to compensate for moderate amounts of loss, so that people frequently do not know that their hearing is imperfect.
(A) discovery . . indicated
(B) development . . prevented
(C) detection . . complicated
(D) treatment . . facilitated
(E) incidence . . corrected

Strategies for Answering

- Read the incomplete sentence carefully.
- Look for key words or phrases.
- Complete the blank(s) with your own words; see if any options are like yours.
- Pay attention to grammatical cues.
- If there are two blanks, be sure that both parts of your answer choice fit logically and stylistically into the sentence.
- After choosing an answer, read the sentence through again to see if it makes sense.

Answer

The statement that the other senses compensate for partial loss of hearing indicates that the hearing loss is not *prevented* or *corrected*; therefore, choices (B) and (E) can be eliminated. Furthermore, the ability to compensate for hearing loss certainly does not facilitate the early *treatment* (D) or the early *discovery* (A) of hearing loss. It is reasonable, however, that early *detection* of hearing loss is *complicated* by the ability to compensate for it. The best answer is (C).

Reading Comprehension Questions

Reading comprehension questions measure your ability to
- read with understanding, insight, and discrimination
- analyze a written passage from several perspectives

Passages are taken from the humanities, social sciences, and natural sciences.

Directions*

The passage is followed by questions based on its content. After reading the passage, choose the best answer to each question. Answer all questions following the passage on the basis of what is *stated* or *implied* in the passage.

7

(1998) reported that GRE scores account for 16% to 6% of the variance in graduate GPA, indicating a correlation from .4 to approximately .25. In another study, House (1997) found that even though GRE scores were significantly correlated with students' degree completion, they were not significant predictors of grades for a group of Native American students. Moreover, false negative rates are high, which means that students whose GRE scores would not predict

FIGURE 12-6

GRE quantitative ability sample items.

(GRE materials selected from GRE Practice Test 2003–2004, 2003. Reprinted by permission of Educational Testing Service, the copyright owner. Permission to reprint GRE materials does not constitute review or Endorsement by Educational Testing Service of this publication as a whole or of any other testing information it may contain.)

the answer choices given.

Sample Question

When walking, a certain person takes 16 complete steps in 10 seconds. At this rate, how many complete steps does the person take in 72 seconds?

(A) 45
(B) 78
(C) 86
(D) 90
(E) 115

Strategies for Answering

- Determine what is given and what is being asked.
- Scan all answer choices before answering a question.
- When approximation is required, scan answer choices to determine the degree of approximation.
- Avoid long computations. Use reasoning instead, when possible.

Answer

72 seconds represents 7 ten-second intervals plus 2/10 of such an interval. Therefore, the person who takes 16 steps in 10 seconds will take (7.2)(16) steps in 72 seconds.

$$(7.2)(16) = (7)(16) + (0.2)(16)$$
$$= 112 + 3.2$$
$$= 115.2$$

Since the question asks for the number of complete steps, the best answer choice is (E).

Problem Solving – Data Interpretation Questions

Data interpretation questions measure your ability

- to synthesize information and select appropriate data for answering a question
- to determine that sufficient information for answering a question is not provided

The data interpretation questions usually appear in sets and are based on data presented in tables, graphs, or other diagrams.

Directions*

Each of the following questions has five answer

choices. For each of these questions, select the best of the answer choices given.

Sample Question

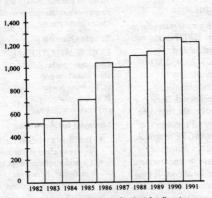

Number of Graduate Student Applicants at University X, 1982–1991

In which of the following years did the number of graduate student applicants increase the most from that of the previous year?

(A) 1985
(B) 1986
(C) 1988
(D) 1990
(E) 1991

Strategies for Answering

- Scan the set of data to see what it is about.
- Try to make visual comparisons and estimate products and quotients rather than perform computations.
- Answer questions only on the basis of data given.

Answer

This question can be answered directly by visually comparing the heights of the bars in the graph. The greatest increase in height between two adjacent bars occurs for the years 1985 and 1986. The best answer

---

* The directions are presented as they appear on the actual test.

11

success in graduate school succeed at high rates (Holmes & Beishline, 1996). In addition, the GRE overpredicts the achievement of younger students while underpredicting the performance of older students (House, 1998).

At this point, those who aspire to enter graduate school might be asking, "With its limitations, why is it that the GRE has such a critical effect on my chances for going to graduate school and on my future career?" One answer is

FIGURE 12-7

*GRE analytical
ability sample
items.*

*(Copyright © 1991
Education Testing
Service. Reprinted by
permission.)*

Directions: Each question or group of questions is based on a passage or set of conditions. In answering some of the questions, it may be useful to draw a rough diagram. For each question, select the best answer choice given.

Questions 1–3
(1) There are five people standing on a flight of six steps, with no more than one person to a step.
(2) R is two steps lower than J.
(3) L is one step lower than M.
(4) J is as far above R as L is below.
(5) P is one step above R.

1. The order of the people from top to bottom is

   (A) PRJLM   (B) JPRML   (C) LMJPR   (D) MPRJL   (E) MJRPL

2. Where is the empty step?

   (A) It could only be the top step.
   (B) It is between P and J.
   (C) It is between R and J.
   (D) It could be either the top or the bottom step.
   (E) It could be anywhere on the flight of steps.

3. Which condition by itself repeats all the information given by one of the other statements?

   (A) (2)   (B) (3)   (C) (4)   (D) (5)   (E) None of the above

that many schools have developed their own norms and psychometric documentation and can use the GRE, either independently or with other sources of data, to predict success in their programs. Furthermore, many graduate selection committees use the GRE broadly, as in requiring a minimum cutoff score to apply. Because more qualified students apply for graduate school than the available resources can train and job markets can absorb, the difficult job of selection must begin somewhere.

Finally, by looking at a GRE score in conjunction with GPA, graduate success can be predicted with greater accuracy than without the GRE (Morrison & Morrison, 1995). A 2001 meta-analysis of the GRE's predictive validity indicated that the GRE and undergraduate grade point average can be valid predictors of graduate grade point average, comprehensive examination scores, number of publications authored, and ratings by faculty (Kuncel, Hezlett, & Ones, 2001). That same year, a regression analysis conducted by Fenster, Markus, Wiedemann, Brackett, and Fernandez (2001) indicated that a linear combination of the verbal and quantitative sections of the GRE and undergraduate grade point average correlated .63 with the grade point average achieved in graduate school. As Melchert (1998) has noted, high achievement in any profession relies on a "confluence" of factors. Therefore, any single predictor such as the GRE will necessarily correlate only modestly with success in a profession.

Graduate schools also frequently complain that grades no longer predict scholastic ability well because of *grade inflation*—the phenomenon of rising average college grades despite declines in average SAT scores (Kuh & Hu, 1999). Thus, many people claim that a B today is equivalent to a C 15 or 20 years ago, and that an A today is equivalent to a B then. This grade inflation has led to a corresponding restriction in the range of grades. Thus, the median grade point average for applicants to clinical psychology Ph.D. programs can exceed 3.5. Another reason for reliance on GRE scores is that the Freedom of Information Act grants students the right to examine their files, including letters of recommendation. Schools argue that professors and others cannot be candid while knowing the student may someday read the letter. Thus, as the validity of grades and letters of recommendation becomes more questionable, reliance on test scores increases, fair or not. However, students with relatively poor GRE scores can take heart in the knowledge that their score does not necessarily predict performance in graduate school.

Miller Analogies Test

A second major graduate-school entrance test is the Miller Analogies Test (MAT). Like the GRE, the MAT is designed to measure scholastic aptitudes for graduate studies. However, unlike the GRE, the MAT is strictly verbal. In 50 minutes, the student must discern logical relationships for 100 varied analogy problems, including the most difficult items found on any test (see Figure 12-9). Knowledge of specific content and a wide vocabulary are extremely useful in this endeavor. However, the most important factors appear to be the ability to see relationships and a knowledge of the various ways analogies can be formed (by sound, number, similarities, differences, and so forth). Used in a variety of specializations, the MAT offers special norms for various fields.

FIGURE 12-9

MAT sample items.

(From the Miller Analogies Test. Copyright © 1988 by Harcourt Assessment, Inc. Reproduced by permission. All rights reserved.)

Look at the first sample analogy below. **Pain** is the right answer because **pain** is related to PLEASURE as DARK is related to LIGHT. On the **Answer Sheet** mark **c** for the first sample to show that choice **c. pain** is the right answer. The diagram at the right shows you how to mark on your **Answer Sheet.**

SAMPLES

1. LIGHT : DARK :: PLEASURE : (*a.* picnic, *b.* day, *c.* pain, *d.* night)
2. LEAVE : DEPART :: (*a.* stay, *b.* go, *c.* home, *d.* come) : REMAIN
3. STAPLE : (*a.* clamp, *b.* paper, *c.* glue, *d.* food) :: NAIL : WOOD
4. (*a.* 4, *b.* 5, *c.* 7, *d.* 6) : 12 :: 12 : 24

How to Mark on Answer Sheet

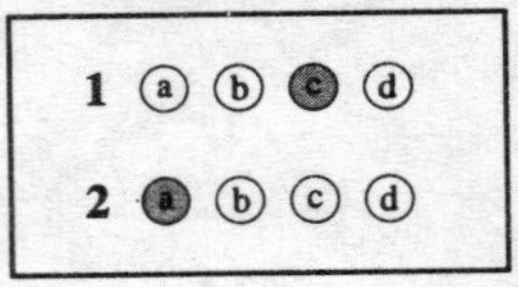

```
1  (a)  (b)  ●c  (d)
2  ●a   (b)  (c)  (d)
```

Choose the proper word in the **parentheses** in Sample 2 and mark the corresponding letter in the proper place on **your Answer Sheet.** Do the same thing in the third and fourth samples.

Odd–even reliability data for the MAT are adequate, with coefficients in the high .80's reported in the manual. Unfortunately, as with the GRE, the MAT lacks predictive validity support. Despite a substantial correlation with the GRE (coefficients run in the low .80's), validity coefficients reported in the manual for grades vary considerably from sample to sample and are only modest (median in the high .30's).

Like the GRE, the MAT has an age bias. MAT scores overpredicted the GPAs of a 25–34 year group and underpredicted the GPAs of a 35–44 year old group. However, it also overpredicted achievement for a 45+ year group (House & Keeley, 1996). According to House and Keeley (1996), motivation for academic achievement may be highest in the middle adult years, causing these students to obtain grades that were higher than predicted by their test scores. These same investigators have found that the MAT underpredicts the GPAs of women and overpredicts those of men (House & Keeley, 1995).

Generally, the psychometric adequacy of the MAT is reasonable when compared with ability tests in general, but GRE scores and grade point average remain its primary correlates. Furthermore, the MAT does not predict research ability, creativity, and other factors important to graduate-school and professional performance. However, as an aid in discriminating among graduate-school applications and adults at the highest level of verbal ability, the MAT is an excellent device as long as one keeps in mind its possible biases.

The Law School Admission Test

The Law School Admission Test (LSAT) provides a good example of tests for professional-degree programs. LSAT problems require almost no specific knowledge. Students of any major can take it without facing bias. As with the MAT, some of the problems on the LSAT are among the most difficult that one can encounter on a standardization test. The LSAT is taken under extreme time pressure. Few test takers are able to finish all sections.

The LSAT contains three types of problems: reading comprehension, logical reasoning, and analytical reasoning. Reading comprehension problems are similar to those found on the GRE. The student is given four 450-word passages followed by approximately seven questions per passage. The content of the passages may be drawn from just about any subject—history, the humanities, the women's movement, African American literature, science, and so forth. Each passage is purposefully chosen to be complicated and densely packed with information. The questions that follow may be long and complicated. Students may be asked what was not covered as well as to draw inferences about what was covered. All of this must be done in 35 minutes.

Approximately half of the problems on the LSAT are logical-reasoning problems. These provide a test stimulus as short as four lines or as long as half a page and ask for some type of logical deduction. Here is an example of a logical-reasoning question, as provided by law services:

"Electrons orbit around the nucleus of an atom the way the earth orbits around the sun. It is well known that gravity is a major force that determines the orbit of the earth. We may therefore, expect that gravity is the main force that determines the orbit of an electron."

The argument attempts to prove its case by:

(A) applying well-known general laws to a specific case

(B) appealing to well-known specific cases to prove a general law about them

(C) testing the conclusion by a definite experiment

(D) appealing to an apparently similar case

(E) stating its conclusions without giving any kind of reason to think that it might be true

Source: LAST/LSDAS Registration and Information Handbook, 1994–1995, p. 42. Copyright 1994 Law School Admission Council. Reprinted by permission.

According to Law Services, this question is a "middle difficulty" item. Approximately 60% of test takers answered correctly (D). Approximately 25% chose A. A student has some 35 minutes to complete 25 problems such as this.

Applying for law school is a little less mystical than applying to graduate school. Unlike graduate schools, the weight given to the LSAT score is openly published for each school approved by the American Bar Association. Although many law schools consider special factors such as overcoming hardship, entrance into most approved schools is based heavily on a weighted sum of GPA and LSAT scores.

The publishers of the LSAT have made available every single previously administered test since the format changed in 1991. With little variation from year to year, one can know what to expect by examining old tests. For each administration, scores are adjusted according to test difficulty; one can then compare scores from one test to the next. Law Services also provides booklets that analyze questions from past tests and explain various test-taking strategies.

The LSAT is psychometrically sound, with reliability coefficients in the .90's. It predicts first-year GPA in law school. Its content validity is exceptional in that the skills tested on the LSAT resemble the ones needed for success in the first year of law school. Although women tend to obtain lower scores than do men, this does not prevent women from applying to prestigious schools. Moreover, a large-scale study found no evidence of bias in the law-school admission process (Wrightsman, 1998).

Controversy over the bias issue continues, however. Jay Rosner, executive director of the Princeton Review Foundation, concludes that every question chosen to appear on every LSAT and SAT in the past 10 years has favored whites over blacks (Rosner, 2003). In his view, if a test item is more likely to be answered correctly by nonminorities than by minorities, then it is a biased item. He found this to be true for every question on the LSAT. In addition, it is clear that women and minorities tend to score slightly lower on the LSAT; by some standards, this differential result also defines test bias ("Black Issues in

Higher Education," 2001), and has led the Law School Admissions Council to create a $10 million initiative to increase diversity in American law schools.

However, there is evidence that may tend to nullify the arguments based on differential test results. If bias is defined not on the basis of differential item or test results but by how well these test results predict actual success in law school for each group, then the conclusions are much different. Using this second definition, if there is bias, it is in favor of minorities and women (Klein, 2002). Specifically, Klein found that even though females and minorities tend to score lower on the LSAT, the LSAT and undergraduate grade point average index scores tend to overpredict their success in the first year of law school. Conversely, nonminority males tend to earn a slightly higher first-year grade point average than would be predicted by their index scores. The same is generally true of the GRE and other standardized tests. It is a puzzling paradox in testing that has yet to be solved.

Nonverbal Group Ability Tests

As we have noted, nonverbal tests are needed for evaluating certain individuals. Like their individual-test counterparts, nonverbal group tests may be performance tests that require the subject to do something (draw, solve maze problems), or they may be paper-and-pencil tests that provide printed nonverbal items and instruct the subject to select the best of two or more multiple choice responses. Some nonverbal group tests can be administered without the use of language.

Raven Progressive Matrices

The Raven Progressive Matrices (RPM) test is one of the best known and most popular nonverbal group tests. Although used primarily in educational settings, the Raven is a suitable test anytime one needs an estimate of an individual's general intelligence. Only the SAT, Wechsler, and Binet tests are referenced more in the *Mental Measurements Yearbook*. One may administer the RPM to groups or individuals, from 5-year-olds to elderly adults. Instructions are simple and, if necessary, the RPM can be administered without the use of language. In fact, the test is used throughout the modern world. The RPM consists exclusively of one of the most common types of stimuli in nonverbal tests of any kind—matrices (see Figures 12-10 and 12-11). The 60 matrices of the Raven Plus are graded in difficulty (Raven, Raven, & Court, 1998). Each contains a logical pattern or design with a missing part. The subject must select the appropriate design from as many as eight choices. The test can be used with or without a time limit.

The original RPM also has 60 items, which were believed to be of increasing difficulty. However, item response and other analyses demonstrated that there were three items in the middle that were of roughly comparable difficulty.

FIGURE 12-10
Sample Progressive Matrices items.

(Reprinted by permission of J. C. Raven, Ltd.)

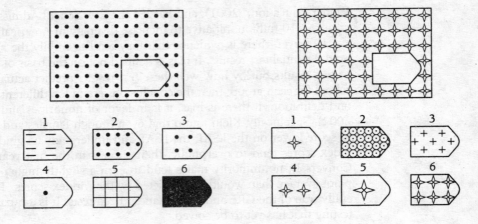

FIGURE 12-11
An advanced problem from the alternate Raven by N. E. Johnson et al., 1993.

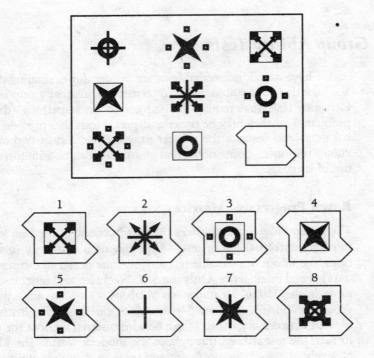

This resulted in an overestimation of the IQs of those individuals who were at the level of these items, because if they got one, they tended to get the other two. The newer 1998 Raven Plus corrects this problem (Raven et al., 1998).

Research supports the RPM as a measure of general intelligence, or Spearman's g (see Raven et al., 1998, for an extensive review; see also Colom, Flores-Mendoza, & Rebello, 2003). In fact, the Raven may be the best single measure of g available, as shown by a multidimensional scaling by Marshalek, Lohman, and Snow (1983) (see Figure 12-12). Because of the Raven's ability to measure general fluid intelligence, it was used in a recent brain-imaging study that eval-

FIGURE 12-12
*Marshalek,
Lohman, and
Snow's radix
analysis of the
Raven.*
(Courtesy of Richard
Snow.)

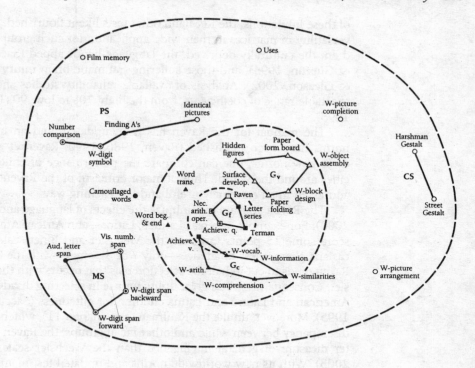

uated how the differences in ability to reason and solve problems translate into differences in the firing of neurons in the brain (Gray, 2003). By conducting magnetic resonance imaging (MRI) while participants completed the matrices, brain activity involved with the task was observed. The study revealed that variations in test performances were reflected in brain activity in the lateral pre-frontal cortex. In addition, participants who scored highly on the Raven showed an increased amount of brain activity in the anterior cingulated cortex and the cerebellum. As well as providing insight concerning the function of different areas of the brain, the study confirmed that standard intelligence tests such as Raven's Progressive Matrices are measuring the workings of essential and specific brain activities.

Figure 12-10 is the only illustration of an RPM problem that the test publisher allows to be reproduced. Recently, Johnson, Saccuzzo, Larson, Guertin, Christianson, and Longley (1993) developed a parallel research form for the RPM. Initial studies with the parallel form have revealed an alternate form reliability coefficient of .90 with comparable internal reliability coefficients between the two versions of the test (.94). Figure 12-11 illustrates one of the more difficult items from the parallel form. More recently, the publishers of the RPM have released their own parallel version (Raven et al., 1998).

A product of England, the RPM was originally designed to assess military recruits independently of educational factors. For years, the lack of adequate norms for the RPM and weaknesses in the manual received criticism. In spite of these limitations, the RPM and other tests like it flourished. One can see the versatility of matrices in their wide application for such groups as young children, the culturally deprived, the language-handicapped (Saccuzzo, Johnson, & Guertin, 1994), and those suffering traumatic brain injury (Hiscock, Inch, & Gleason, 2002). Analysis of available reliability studies shows a rather respectable range of coefficients, from the high .70's to low .90's (see Raven et al., 1998).

The manual for the Raven has been updated, and an impressive set of norms have been published (Raven, 1986, 1990; Raven et al., 1998). With these new norms, one can compare the performance of children from major cities around the world. Thus, a major criticism of the Raven has finally been addressed in an extremely useful and far-reaching way.

The Raven appears to minimize the effects of language and culture (Raven, 2000). For example, whereas Latinos, Latinas, and African Americans typically score some 15 points lower on the Wechsler and Binet scales than do Caucasians, there is less difference—only 7 or 8 points—with the Raven. Thus, the Raven tends to cut in half the selection bias that occurs with the Binet or Wechsler. Consequently, it has great utility for use in selecting disadvantaged African American and Latino and Latina children for giftedness (Saccuzzo & Johnson, 1995). Moreover, unlike the Kaufman (see Chapter 11), which also has a lower discrepancy between white and other racial groups, the Raven is actually a better measure of general intelligence than the Wechsler scales (Colom et al., 2003). With its new worldwide norms and updated test manual, as well as its successful computer administered version, the Raven holds promise as one of the major players in the testing field in the 21st century.

Goodenough-Harris Drawing Test

A remarkable nonverbal intelligence test that can be either group or individually administered is the Goodenough-Harris Drawing Test (G-HDT). Although not a standardized test in the strictest sense, the G-HDT is one of the quickest, easiest, and least expensive to administer of all ability tests. Therefore, it is widely used in educational and other settings, including clinical. A pencil and white unlined paper are the only materials needed. The subject is instructed to draw a picture of a whole man and to do the best job possible. The G-HDT was standardized by determining those characteristics of human-figure drawings that differentiated subjects in various age groups. Subjects get credit for each item included in their drawings. As a rule, each detail is given one point, with 70 points possible. For example, if only a head is included with no facial features, then the subject receives only 1 point. Points are added for additional details such as facial features and clothing.

The G-HDT was originally standardized in 1926 and restandardized in 1963 (Harris, 1963). Scoring of the G-HDT follows the principle of age differentiation—older children tend to get more points because of the greater accuracy and detail of their drawings. Thus, one can determine mental ages by comparing scores with those of the normative sample. Raw scores can be converted to standard scores with a mean of 100 and a standard deviation of 15. Split-half, test–retest, and interscorer reliability coefficients are good, with ranges in the high .60's to the low .90's for both old and revised forms (Dunn, 1972). Scores begin leveling off at age 14 or 15, so the use of the G-HDT is restricted primarily to children and works best with younger children (Scott, 1981). Despite the relatively outdated norms, scores on the G-HDT remain significantly related to Wechsler IQ scores (Abell, Horkheimer, & Nguyen, 1998; Alexopoulos, Haritos-Fatouros, Sakkas, Skaltsas, & Vlachos, 2000).

Because of their ease of administration and short administration time, the G-HDT and other human-figure drawing tests are used extensively in test batteries. The test allows an examiner to obtain a quick but rough estimate of a child's intelligence. The G-HDT is most appropriately used in conjunction with other sources of information in a battery of tests; results based on G-HDT data alone can be quite misleading (Abell et al., 1998).

IPAT Culture Fair Intelligence Test

All cultures tend to reinforce certain skills and activities at the expense of others. One purpose of nonverbal and performance tests is to remove factors related to cultural influences so that one can measure pure intelligence independently of learning, culture, and the like. Experience and empirical research have shown that such a test has yet to be developed. Indeed, many doubt whether such an accomplishment is even possible, although the Raven probably comes close to this goal.

The IPAT Culture Fair Intelligence Test was designed to provide an estimate of intelligence relatively free of cultural and language influences. Although this test succeeds no more in this regard than any other such attempt, the popularity of the Culture Fair Intelligence Test reflects the strong desire among users for a test that reduces cultural factors as much as possible (Tan & Tan, 1998).

Constructed under the direction of R. B. Cattell, the Culture Fair Intelligence Test is a paper-and-pencil procedure that covers three levels (ages 4–8 and mentally disabled adults, ages 8–12 and randomly selected adults, and high-school age and above-average adults). Two parallel forms are available.

Standardization varies according to age level. Kuder-Richardson reliabilities are only in the .70's, with substantially lower test–retest coefficients. The test has been correlated with a wide variety of other tests with mixed results. Correlations with the Wechsler and Binet tests are quite good, with a range of .56 to .85. Also, normative data from Western European countries, the United States, and Australia are comparable. Thus, if one wishes to estimate intelligence in a Western European or Australian individual, the Culture Fair Intelligence Test is probably the instrument of choice. The Culture Fair Test is viewed as an acceptable measure of fluid intelligence (Colom & Garcia-Lopez, 2002; Rammsayer & Brandler, 2002), although the norms are becoming outdated, and more work is needed if the Culture Fair Test is to compete with the Raven.

Standardized Tests Used in the U.S. Civil Service System

The number and variety of group ability tests for measuring aptitude for various occupations are staggering. The General Aptitude Test Battery (GATB), for example, is a reading ability test that purportedly measures aptitude for a variety of occupations.

The U.S. Employment Service developed the GATB for use in making employment decisions in government agencies. It attempts to measure a wide range of aptitudes from general intelligence (g) to manual dexterity. The GATB also produces scores for motor coordination, form perception (awareness of relevant details and ability to compare and discriminate various shapes), and clerical perception (for example, the ability to proofread). Scores are also available for verbal, numerical, and spatial aptitudes.

The GATB was originally standardized in 1952 on a sample of 4000 people believed to represent the working population of the United States in 1940. Stratified according to gender, education, occupation, and geographic location, the sample ranged in age from 18 to 54. The mean educational level of the sample, 11.0 years, reveals that the GATB is most appropriate for those who have not graduated from college. Moreover, with rapidly changing times and the advent of high technology, the GATB may be out of date (see, for example, Avolio & Waidman, 1990; Vandevijer & Harsveld, 1994).

The GATB has engendered considerable controversy because it used within-group norming prior to the passage of the Civil Rights Act of 1991. In within-group norming, individuals are compared with others within a specific subgroup. For example, women may be compared only with other women; African Americans only with other African Americans. Such norming practices were justified on the basis of fairness. If men consistently outperform women on a particular test, then, given an equal number of men and women applying for a job, more men will be selected. However, the Civil Rights Act of 1991 outlawed within-group norming, arguing that such norming was reverse discrimination (see Brown, 1994). Today, any kind of score adjustments through within-group norming in employment practices are strictly forbidden by law. (For more on these issues, see Chapter 21.)

Standardized Tests in the U.S. Military: The Armed Services Vocational Aptitude Battery

Designed for the Department of Defense, the Armed Services Vocational Aptitude Battery (ASVAB) is administered to more than 1.3 million individuals each year. A multiple aptitude battery, the ASVAB was designed for students in grades 11 and 12 and in postsecondary schools. The test yields scores used in both educational and military settings. In the latter, ASVAB results can help identify students who potentially qualify for entry into the military and can recommend assignment to various military occupational training programs.

The ASVAB consists of 10 subtests: general science, arithmetic reasoning, word knowledge, paragraph comprehension, numeral operations, coding speed, auto and shop information, mathematics knowledge, mechanical comprehension, and electronics information. These subtests are grouped into various composites, including three academic composites—academic ability, verbal, and math; four occupational composites—mechanical and crafts, business and clerical, electronics and electrical, and health and social; and an overall composite that reflects general ability.

The psychometric characteristics of the ASVAB are excellent (Ree & Carretta, 1994, 1995). The most recent form of the test was normed on a nationally representative group of nearly 12,000 men and women between the ages of 16 and 23 who took the ASVAB-8a between July and October 1980. African Americans, Latinos and Latinas, and economically disadvantaged whites were oversampled and then weighted to represent the national population distribution for all groups. Reliability coefficients for composite scores based on the Kuder-Richardson formula are excellent, ranging from .84 to .92 for women and .88 to .95 for men. The test manual and supporting documents strongly support the ASVAB as a valid predictor of performance during training for a variety of military and civilian occupations.

Recently, the military has been involved in presenting the ASVAB via microcomputer rather than in the traditional paper-and-pencil format (Moreno, Segall, & Hetter, 1997). Through this new computerized format, subjects can be tested *adaptively,* meaning that the questions given each person can be based on his or her unique ability. Briefly, adaptive testing of ability involves presenting an item of a known level of difficulty and then presenting either a more difficult or a less difficult item, depending on whether the subject is correct. The procedure cuts testing time almost in half and is far less fatiguing than the complete test. (We discuss computer adaptive testing in depth in Chapter 15.) After many political battles, the adaptive version of the ASVAB was finally put into use in the late 1990s (Sands, Waters, & McBride, 1997). By 2010, this format may become a normal part of the military testing procedure. However, as we go to press with this edition, the military is embarking on a large-scale effort to improve and expand the ASVAB, and one of us (D. P. Saccuzzo) has been invited on a committee toward that end.

SUMMARY

Standardized ability tests are available for just about any purpose. There appears to be no end to the construction of this type of test. Relative ease in scoring and administration gives group ability tests a major advantage over individual tests. In many cases, the results from group tests are as stable and valid as those from individual tests. However, low scores, wide discrepancies between two group test results, or wide discrepancies between a group test result and some other indicator such as grades are reasons for exercising caution in interpreting results. When in doubt, users of group ability tests should refer the problem to a competent professional who can administer an individual ability test. The public school system makes the most extensive use of group ability tests. Indeed, many sound tests exist for all levels from kindergarten through

12th grade. Achievement tests for this age include the Stanford Achievement Test (SAT-I, SAT-II) and the Metropolitan Achievement Test (MAT).

College and graduate-school entrance tests also account for a large proportion of the group ability tests used in the United States. The most popular college entrance tests include the Scholastic Assessment Test (SAT-I), the Cooperative School and College Ability Tests (SCAT), and the American College Test (ACT). Students looking toward postgraduate work may have to take the Graduate Record Examination Aptitude Test (GRE), the Miller Analogies Test (MAT), or a more specialized test such as the Law School Admission Test (LSAT).

Several nonverbal group ability tests have proven helpful for determining intelligence in certain populations. The Raven Progressive Matrices (RPM) and the Goodenough-Harris Drawing Test (G-HDT) can provide helpful data on intelligence; the latest edition of the former has norms that allow worldwide comparisons. The IPAT Culture Fair Intelligence Test also provides good data on intelligence; however, it may soon be obsolete without further revisions.

Other group ability tests can help vocational counselors assess ability for certain occupations; the General Aptitude Test Battery (GATB) is one. Still other group ability tests measure aptitude for advanced or professional training. Developed for the military, the Armed Services Vocational Aptitude Battery (ASVAB) provides helpful data for both military and civilian applications.

In viewing group ability tests, one gets the impression that there is almost no limit to the scope and applicability of psychological tests.

WEB ACTIVITY   For interesting and relevant Web sites, check the following:

http://edrev.asu.edu/reviews/rev27.htm
A national review of scholastic achievement in general education: How are we doing and why should we care?

http://cresst96.cse.ucla.edu/products/reports_set.htm
To search for reports such as "Will National Tests Improve Student Learning?" by Lorrie Shepard; and "Assessment and Education: Access and Achievement," by Robert Glaser (Technical Report No. 435, 1997)

www. gre.org/splash.html
Graduate Record Examination (GRE)

www.gre.org/
GRE online

http://www.netpsychology.com/health/neuropsych.htm
Pediatric clinical neuropsychology

http://www.ucs.umn.edu/mstp/mstpcogat.html
Cognitive Abilities Test (COGAT)

CHAPTER 13

Applications in Clinical and Counseling Settings

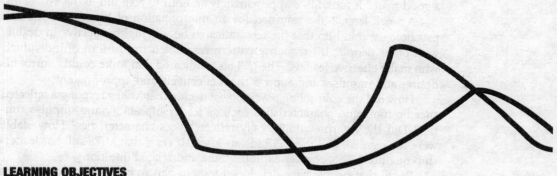

LEARNING OBJECTIVES

When you have completed this chapter, you should be able to:

☐ Identify the major characteristics of a structured personality test

☐ Identify the underlying assumption of the first structured personality test (the Woodworth Personal Data Sheet)

☐ Identify the assumptions of early structured personality tests based on the logical-content strategy

☐ Briefly discuss the strategy used in construction of the MMPI and MMPI-2

☐ Describe the K and F scales on the MMPI and MMPI-2

☐ Identify strengths and weaknesses of the MMPI and MMPI-2

☐ Explain how one uses factor analysis to build structured personality tests

☐ Explain the approach to test construction used in the NEO Personality Inventory

☐ Briefly describe the EPPS and explain the meaning of an ipsative score

*I*n his junior year in college, Mike went to the university counseling center for help in finding a direction in life. To aid him in his quest, a psychologist suggested that he respond to a long list of items known as the California Psychological Inventory (CPI). The CPI is a structured personality test used in counseling settings that provides a list of statements and asks the subject to respond "True" or "False" to each. It is widely used as a tool in career assessment (Gough, 1995). The statements went something like these: "I like to read mystery stories." "I am usually alert to my environment." "I would rather follow others than be the leader." "I like to solve difficult problems." "My father is a good man." It took Mike approximately an hour to respond to the 462 items.

A week later, Mike returned for an interpretation of his test scores. The psychologist told him that the test indicated he was highly effective in dealing with other people; his response pattern resembled the pattern of individuals who make effective leaders. The CPI also indicated that Mike could control his desires and impulses and express them effectively and appropriately.

How did the counseling psychologist decide that Mike's responses reflected specific traits and characteristics such as leadership ability and impulse control? Did the interpretations really reflect Mike's characteristics? How stable were the results? Will the CPI indicate after 10 years that Mike still has leadership qualities? This chapter explores these and related questions.

Recall that people have developed tests in part to help solve the problems that face modern societies. Tests of mental ability were created to distinguish those with subnormal mental abilities from those with normal abilities in order to enhance the education of both groups. However, there is far more to being human than having normal or subnormal mental capabilities. It is not enough to know that a person is high or low in such factors as speed of calculation, memory, range of knowledge, and abstract thinking. To make full use of information about a person's mental abilities, one must also know how that person uses those abilities. All the mental abilities in the world remain inert in someone who sits in the corner of a room all day. But even modest mental abilities can go far in a high-energy individual who relates well to others and is organized, persistent, determined, and motivated. These nonintellective aspects of human behavior, typically distinguished from mental abilities, are called *personality characteristics*. Such characteristics are of vital concern in clinical and counseling settings.

One can define *personality* as the relatively stable and distinctive patterns of behavior that characterize an individual and his or her reactions to the environment. Structured personality tests attempt to evaluate personality traits, personality types, personality states, and other aspects of personality, such as self-concept. *Personality traits* refer to relatively enduring dispositions—tendencies to act, think, or feel in a certain manner in any given circumstance and that distinguish one person from another. *Personality types* refer to general descriptions of people; for example, avoiding types have low social interest and low activity and cope by avoiding social situations. *Personality states* refer to emotional reactions that vary from one situation to another. Finally, *self-concept* refers to a person's self-definition or, according to C. R. Rogers (1959a), an organized and relatively consistent set of assumptions that a person has about him- or herself. This chapter focuses on the measurement of personality traits, with some discussion of personality types and self-concept.

Before the first Binet scale was developed, Alfred Binet hypothesized that a person's pattern of intellectual functioning might reveal information about personality factors (Binet & Henri, 1895, 1896). Subsequent investigators agreed with Binet's hypothesis (Hart & Spearman, 1912; Terman, 1916; Thorndike, 1921), and this hypothesis continues to find support (Groth-Marnat, 1999; Kossowska, 2002). However, specific tests of human personality were not developed until World War I. This created a need to distinguish people on the basis of emotional well-being.

Like pioneers in the measurement of mental ability, the early developers of personality tests traveled in uncharted territory. Imagine yourself faced with the task of measuring some aspect of human behavior. How would you begin? You could observe and record a person's behavior. However, this approach did not work for early investigators because their task was to identify emotionally unstable military recruits; the volume of applicants for military service in the United States during World War I was so great that it became impossible to use the one available method of the time—the psychiatric interview. Psychologists needed a measure of emotional functioning so they could evaluate large numbers of people and screen out those who were unfit for military service. To meet this need, psychologists used **self-report questionnaires** that provided a list of statements and required subjects to respond in some way to each, such as marking "True" or "False" to indicate whether the statement applied to them.

The general procedure in which the subject is asked to respond to a written statement is known as the *structured*, or objective, method of personality assessment, as distinguished from the *projective* method (see Chapter 14). As their name implies, structured measures of personality, also known as "objective" measures, are characterized by structure and lack of ambiguity. A clear and definite stimulus is provided, and the requirements of the subject are evident and specific. An example of a structured personality-test item is "Respond 'yes' or 'no' to the statement 'I am happy.'" In contrast, a projective test item may provide a picture of an inkblot and ask, "What might this be?" In a projective personality test, the stimulus is ambiguous and the subject has few guidelines about what type of response is required.

Strategies of Structured Personality-Test Construction

Like measures of mental ability, personality measures evolved through several phases. New features appeared as problems with older approaches became evident. In the realm of structured personality testing, many approaches or strategies have been tried. Psychologists disagree on how these strategies should be classified, what they should be called, and even how many distinctly different

FIGURE 13-1
Overview of strategies for structured personality-test construction.

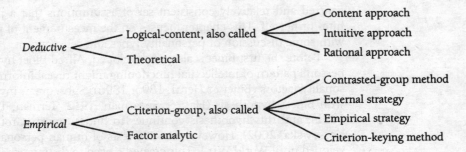

strategies exist (Ben-Porath & Butcher, 1991; Butcher, 2000; Waller, 1999). At the broadest level, the strategies are deductive and empirical. One can in turn divide each of these strategies as follows. Deductive strategies comprise the logical-content and the theoretical approach. Empirical strategies comprise the criterion-group and the factor analysis method. (See Figure 13-1.) Some procedures combine two or more of these strategies.

Deductive Strategies

Deductive strategies use reason and deductive logic to determine the meaning of a test response. The logical-content method has test designers select items on the basis of simple face validity; in the theoretical approach, test construction is guided by a particular psychological theory.

Logical-content strategy. The logical-content strategy, as its name implies, uses reason and deductive logic in the development of personality measures. In the most general use of this strategy, the test designer tries to logically deduce the type of content that should measure the characteristic to be assessed. For example, if one wants to measure eating behavior, it makes sense to include statements such as "I frequently eat between meals." Statements that have no direct logical relevance to eating behavior, such as "I enjoy solving complex puzzles," would not be included in tests that use the logical-content strategy. The principal distinguishing characteristic of this strategy is that it assumes that the test item describes the subject's personality and behavior. If a person marks "True" for the statement "I am outgoing," then testers assume that he or she is outgoing. Initial efforts to measure personality used the logical-content approach as the primary strategy.

Theoretical strategy. As its name implies, the theoretical strategy begins with a theory about the nature of the particular characteristic to be measured. As in the logical-content approach, an attempt is then made to deduce items. In the theoretical approach, however, items must be consistent with the theory. If the theory hypothesizes that personality can be broken down into six major areas, then developers strive to create items that tap each of these six areas. In addition, theoretical strategies demand that every item in a scale be related to the characteristic being measured. Thus, the theoretical approach attempts to create a homogeneous scale and, toward this end, may use statistical procedures such as item analysis.

Empirical Strategies

Empirical strategies rely on data collection and statistical analyses to determine the meaning of a test response or the nature of personality and psychopathology. These strategies retain the self-report features of the deductive strategies in that subjects are asked to respond to items that describe their own views, opinions, and feelings. However, empirical strategies attempt to use experimental research to determine empirically the meaning of a test response, the major dimensions of personality, or both. In the criterion-group approach, test designers choose items to distinguish a group of individuals with certain characteristics, the *criterion group,* from a control group; the factor analytic approach uses the statistical technique of factor analysis to determine the meaning of test items.

Criterion-group strategy. The criterion-group strategy begins with a criterion group, or a collection of individuals who share a characteristic such as leadership or schizophrenia. Test constructors select and administer a group of items to all the people in this criterion group as well as to a control group that represents the general population. Constructors then attempt to locate items that distinguish the criterion and control groups, or how the two groups *contrast.*

Suppose that a group of aggressive individuals mark "True" to items such as "I am not aggressive," "I like to attend concerts," and "I would rather read than write" significantly more often than did individuals in a control group. These items could then be included on an aggression scale. When new subjects endorse a large proportion of items on the aggression scale, one may hypothesize that they are aggressive because they endorsed the same items that distinguished aggressive individuals from control individuals. The content of the items is of little consequence. What matters is that aggressive individuals marked "True" to these items, thereby discriminating the aggressive individuals from the control group. As J. S. Wiggins (1973, p. 394) noted, depressed individuals respond "False" significantly more than controls do to the statement "I sometimes tease animals." There is no logical or rational reason for this response. The actual content or face validity of an item in the criterion-group strategy is of little importance. Instead, the approach attempts to determine which items discriminate the criterion and control groups.

Once distinguishing items have been determined for one sample of subjects to represent the criterion group, the next step is to *cross-validate* the scale by checking how well it distinguishes an independent criterion sample—individuals also known to possess the characteristics to be measured—from a control group. If the scale significantly distinguishes the two groups, then it is said to have been cross-validated. Once a scale has been developed, data from the normal controls can be used to obtain standard scores. One can then determine how far above or below the mean of the normal group each new subject scores in standardized units. Thus, a subject's score on each scale can be converted to percentiles (see Chapter 2).

After a scale has been constructed and cross-validated, the third step in the criterion approach is to conduct additional research to ascertain empirically what it means when subjects endorse a large number of items on a particular scale. An independent group of people who score two standard deviations above the mean on an aggression scale, for example, may be studied intensely to determine how they describe themselves, how others describe them, the characteristics of their family backgrounds, and so on.

Factor analytic strategy. The factor analytic strategy uses factor analysis to derive empirically the basic dimensions of personality. Recall from Chapter 3 that factor analysis boils down or reduces data to a small number of descriptive units or dimensions. A test, for example, may have two scales that correlate highly, such as hostility and aggression. This correlation means that the two overlap in what they measure; that is, they share common variance. Both, for example, may be related to paranoid personality, a problem characterized in part by aggression and hostility. The same test may also have two other scales, suspicion and defensiveness, variables also associated with the paranoid personality. These two scales may correlate not only with each other but also with the hostility and aggression scales. Thus, all four scales may share common variance. If one can show that a substantial proportion of the variability in all four scales is related to some common factor, then a factor analyst could argue that the test actually has only one scale that is related to the paranoid personality.

Factor analysts begin with an empirical database consisting of the intercorrelation of a large number of items or tests. They then factor analyze these intercorrelations, typically to find the minimum number of factors that account for as much of the variability in the data as possible. They then attempt to label these factors by ascertaining what the items related to a particular factor have in common.

Criteria Used in Selecting Tests for Discussion

There are far too many structured personality tests to discuss them all adequately in a book devoted exclusively to the subject, let alone in a single chapter. (We prefer the term *tests* for general purposes, although for specific procedures other terms such as *inventories, techniques, scales,* and *assessment procedures* are often preferred.) However, all available structured personality tests can be classified according to whether they use one or some combination of the four strategies just discussed: logical-content, theoretical, criterion-group, and factor analytic. The tests in the discussion that follows have been chosen because (1) they illustrate each of the major strategies; (2) they are widely used, as indicated by surveys of psychological test usage in the United

States (Lubin, Larson, & Matarazzo, 1984; Watkins, Campbell, Nieberding, & Hallmark, 1995); (3) they interest the research community, as determined by publication in major journals; and (4) they show historical value, as determined by the introduction of new concepts in structured personality testing.

The Logical-Content Strategy

We begin our discussion with the first personality test ever developed—the Woodworth Personal Data Sheet. We then present other examples of tests based on the logical-content approach.

Woodworth Personal Data Sheet

The first personality inventory ever, the Woodworth Personal Data Sheet, was developed during World War I and published in its final form after the war (Woodworth, 1920). Its purpose was to identify military recruits who would be likely to break down in combat. The final form of the Woodworth contained 116 questions to which the individual responded "Yes" or "No." The items were selected from lists of known symptoms of emotional disorders and from the questions asked by psychiatrists in their screening interviews. In effect, the scale was a paper-and-pencil psychiatric interview. The Woodworth consisted of questions similar to these: "Do you drink a fifth of whiskey a day?" "Do you wet the bed at night?" "Do you frequently daydream?" "Do you usually feel in good health?" "Do you usually sleep soundly at night?" The Woodworth yielded a single score, providing a global measure of functioning. Only those recruits who reported many symptoms received an interview. In this way, the military could concentrate its efforts on the most likely candidates for rejection.

Although its items were selected through the logical-content approach, the Woodworth had two additional features. First, items endorsed by 25% or more of a normal sample in the scored direction were excluded from the test. This technique tended to reduce the number of *false positives*—that is, subjects identified by the test as risks but who would most likely be cleared in an actual interview. Second, only those symptoms that occurred twice as often in a previously diagnosed neurotic group as in normals were included in the first version of the test.

The success of the Woodworth in solving the problem of mass screening stimulated the development of a host of structured tests aimed at measuring personality characteristics. These tests borrowed items from each other, particularly the Woodworth, and used a variety of methods for clustering and scoring items. However, all of them assumed that test responses had items that could be taken at face value; that is, they assumed the face validity of a test response. If someone marked "No" to "I wet the bed," for example, it was assumed that he or she had not wet the bed.

Early Multidimensional Logical-Content Scales

Two of the best-known early tests developed with the logical-content strategy were the Bell Adjustment Inventory and the Bernreuter Personality Inventory. The Bell attempted to evaluate the subject's adjustment in a variety of areas such as home life, social life, and emotional functioning. The Bernreuter could be used for subjects as young as age 13 and included items related to six personality traits such as introversion, confidence, and sociability. Each was first published in the 1930s and, in contrast to the Woodworth, produced more than one score. These multidimensional procedures laid a foundation for the many modern tests that yield multiple scores rather than a single overall index.

Mooney Problem Checklist

Few modern tests rely extensively on the logical-content method of test construction. One of the few such tests still in use, the Mooney Problem Checklist, was published in 1950. The Mooney contains a list of problems that recurred in clinical case history data and in the written statements of problems submitted by approximately 4000 high-school students. It resembles the Woodworth in that subjects who check an excessive number of items are considered to have difficulties. The main interpretive procedure is to assume the face validity of a test response. Thus, if a subject checks an item related to finances, then testers assume that the person is having financial difficulties.

Criticisms of the Logical-Content Approach

Psychologists involved in the development of the Woodworth and the plethora of subsequent tests satisfied an important need. These tests proved extremely useful as screening devices and methods of obtaining information about a person without an extensive interview. Before long, however, the weaknesses of the logical-content strategy became evident.

In assuming that one can interpret test items at face value, the logical content strategy also assumes that the subject takes a normal approach to the test, complies with the instructions, reads each item, and answers as honestly as possible. Even if this were all so, subjects might not be able to evaluate their own behavior objectively in the area covered by the test item (for example, "I never drink too much alcohol"). And even if subjects can provide accurate self-evaluation, they still may not interpret the test item in the same way as the test constructor or test user, which is also an implicit assumption of the logical content strategy. For example, what does "wet the bed" really mean?

None of these assumptions is necessarily true, and assuming that they are true is certain to produce errors. Indeed, structured personality tests based on the logic of face validity were so sharply criticized that the entire structured approach to personality was all but discarded (Ellis, 1946; Landis, 1936; Landis, Zubin, & Katz, 1935; McNemar & Landis, 1935). It was finally rescued by the introduction of a new conceptualization in personality testing, the empirical criterion-group strategy.

The Criterion-Group Strategy

Just when the development of an adequate structured personality test seemed nothing more than a pipe dream, the Minnesota Multiphasic Personality Inventory (MMPI) introduced several innovations in the construction of structured personality tests. Though not entirely new, the main idea—assume nothing about the meaning of a subject's response to a test item—was the only way of meeting objections to face validity. Because making assumptions had been the downfall of the logical-content approach, developers of the MMPI argued that the meaning of a test response could be determined only through empirical research. This section discusses the MMPI as well as its most recent offspring, the MMPI-2.

Minnesota Multiphasic Personality Inventory

The Minnesota Multiphasic Personality Inventory (MMPI and MMPI-2) is a true–false self-report questionnaire. Statements are typically of the self-reference type such as "I like good food" and "I never have trouble falling asleep." Subjects mark "True" or "False" for each statement as it applies to themselves. The heart of the test consists of its validity, clinical, and content scales. The validity scales provide information about the person's approach to testing, such as whether an attempt was made either to "fake bad" by endorsing more items of pathological content than any person's actual problems could justify or to "fake good" by avoiding pathological items. The clinical scales were designed to identify psychological disorders such as depression and schizophrenia. Today, clinicians use formulas, the pattern of scores, codebooks that provide extensive research summaries on the meaning of test scores, and clinical judgment to assess the meaning of the clinical scales. The content scales consist of groups of items that are empirically related to a specific content area. For example, the anger scale contains references to irritability, hotheadedness, and other symptoms of anger or control problems. Subjects obtain a raw score on each scale based on the number of items they have marked in the scored direction. Raw scores are then converted to *T* scores, with a mean of 50 and a standard deviation of 10 (see Figure 13-2).

Purpose. Like the Woodworth, the purpose of the MMPI and MMPI-2 is to assist in distinguishing normal from abnormal groups. Specifically, the test was designed to aid in the diagnosis or assessment of the major psychiatric or psychological disorders. For the most part, it is still used for this purpose. The MMPI requires at least a sixth-grade reading ability; the MMPI-2 requires an eighth-grade reading ability. Administrators must take great care to make sure the individual can read at the appropriate level and has an IQ within normal limits (see Focused Example 13-1).

Original development of the scales. Beginning with a pool of 1000 items selected from a wide variety of sources, including case histories, psychological reports, textbooks, and existing tests, the original authors of the MMPI, S. R. Hathaway,

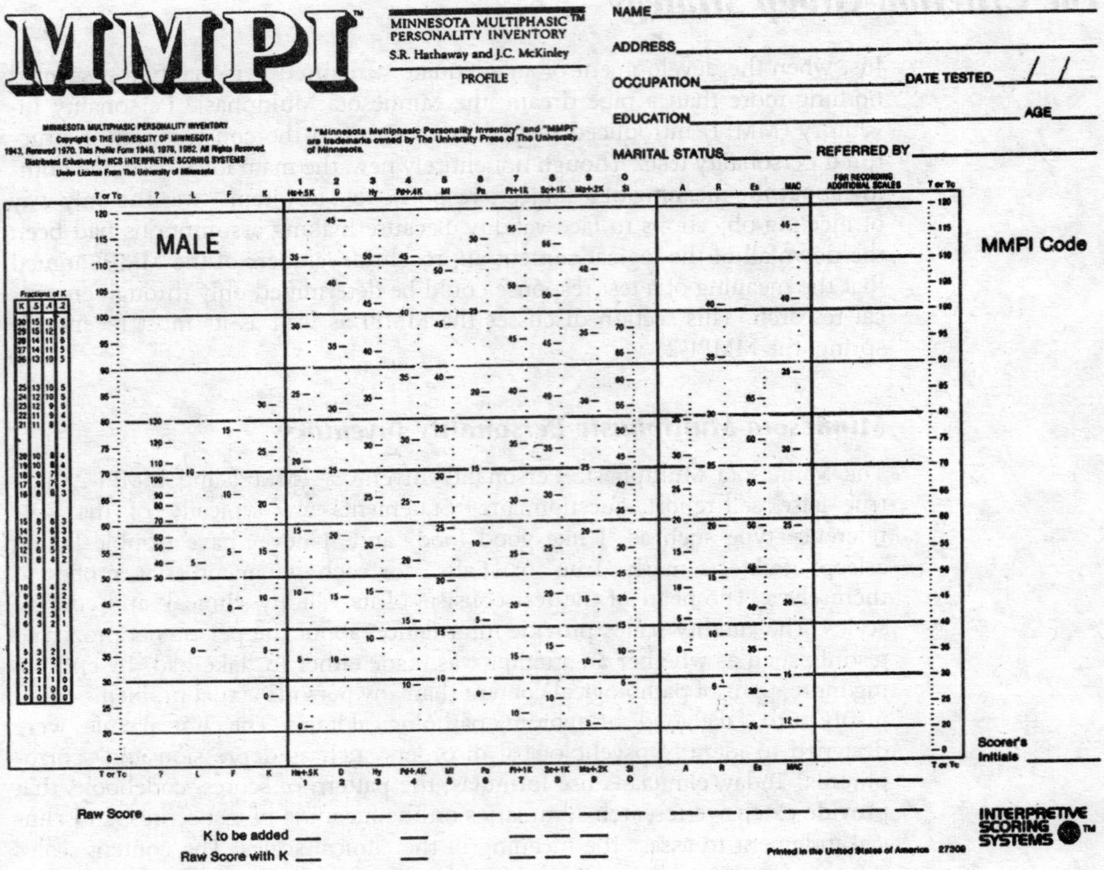

FIGURE 13-2   *An MMPI profile sheet.*
(*Reproduced by permission of University of Minnesota Press.*)

a psychologist, and J. C. McKinley, a physician, selected 504 items judged to be relatively independent of one another. The scales were then determined empirically by presenting the items to criterion and control groups.

The criterion groups used to develop the original MMPI consisted of psychiatric inpatients at the University of Minnesota Hospital. These psychiatric patients were divided into eight groups according to their psychiatric diagnoses. Though the original pool of patients had 800 people, this number was substantially reduced in order to find homogeneous groupings with sufficient agreement on diagnoses. The final eight criterion groups each consisted of approximately 50 patients:

- *hypochondriacs*—individuals preoccupied with the body and fears of illness;

- depressed patients;

- *hysterics*—primarily individuals who showed a physical problem with no physical cause, such as physical pain without cause;

- *psychopathic deviates*—delinquent, criminal, or antisocial individuals;

- *paranoids*—individuals who showed symptoms such as poor reality testing (for example, delusions in which they falsely believed that people were plotting against them);

- *psychasthenics*—individuals with a disorder characterized by excessive doubts and unreasonable fears;

- *schizophrenics*—individuals with a psychotic disorder involving dramatic symptoms (such as hallucinations) and thinking problems (such as illogical reasoning); and

- *hypomanics*—individuals with a disorder characterized by hyperactivity and irritability (see Table 13-1).

Those in the criterion groups were then compared with some 700 controls consisting primarily of relatives and visitors of the patients, excluding mental patients, in the University of Minnesota Hospital. The use of this control group was perhaps the original MMPI's greatest source of criticism. There is little basis for saying that the relatives of patients in a large city university hospital are representative of the general population, although the control group was augmented by other subjects such as a group of recent high-school graduates. The MMPI-2, by contrast, has a large and relatively good representative control sample.

Despite its weakness, the original control group did provide a reference sample. After an item analysis was conducted, items that separated the criterion from the control group were included on one or more of the eight scales.

TABLE 13-1		
Original Criterion Groups for the MMPI	Hypochondriacs	Patients who suffer from overconcern of bodily symptoms, express conflicts through bodily (somatic) symptoms
	Depressives	Patients with depressed mood, loss of appetite, loss of interest, suicidal thoughts, and other depressive symptoms
	Hysterics	Immature individuals who overdramatize their plight and may exhibit physical symptoms for which no physical cause exists
	Psychopathic deviates	Individuals who are antisocial and rebellious and exploit others without remorse or anxiety
	Paranoids	Individuals who show extreme suspicions, hypersensitivity, and delusions
	Psychasthenics	Individuals plagued by excessive self-doubts, obsessive thoughts, anxiety, and low energy
	Schizophrenics	Disorganized, highly disturbed individuals out of contact with reality and having difficulties with communication, interpersonal relations, sensory abnormalities (e.g., hallucinations), or motor abnormalities (e.g., catatonia)
	Hypomanics	Individuals in a high-energy, agitated state with poor impulse control, inability to sleep, and poor judgment

Focused Example 13-1

READING THE MMPI

 In one interesting case, a 16-year-old girl was detained by the juvenile court. Her mother had reported her to the police, stating she could not be controlled. A few hours before the girl's preliminary hearing, the judge requested psychological testing to aid in the assessment process. A psychology intern was the only professional staff member available. Though relatively inexperienced with the MMPI, he tried to carry out the judge's orders by administering the test. The intern warned the girl of the validity scales, stating that he could tell if she tried to fake. When presented with the test booklet, the girl groaned and stated, "This test is too hard." The intern assured her not to worry, that there were no right or wrong answers. "Oh, I hope I pass," the girl said. "I'm not good at tests."

Rather than the usual 1 to 2 hours, she took more than 3 hours to complete the MMPI, finishing moments before her court hearing began. The intern immediately scored it and found that she had marked nearly half of the 64 items in the scored direction on the F scale, one of the validity scales containing highly pathological content. Because the average for the general population on this scale is 4 items in the scored direction, with an average of 8

items in the scored direction for adolescents, the girl's endorsement of 30 items indicated she had not taken a normal approach to testing and suggested to the intern that she had "faked bad" by deliberately endorsing pathological items.

In court, the judge asked the intern what the results showed. "I can't tell," said the intern, "because she tried to fake." "Did you fake?" asked the judge. "No sir," said the girl, "I swear I didn't." The judge told her to go back and take the test again.

Irate, the intern again warned the girl not to fake. "Oh, I hope I pass," she moaned. "Just answer truthfully and you'll pass," said the intern. She completed the test, and the intern immediately scored it. The results were almost identical to those for the previous testing. The intern rushed into the testing room and scolded the girl for faking again. "I knew I'd flunk that test," she said. "It was too hard for me." Finally, it dawned on the intern to ask whether she could read the test. A reading test revealed that she could read at only the fourth-grade level. Most of the items were therefore incomprehensible to her. The embarrassed intern was forced to go back into court and explain what had happened. No doubt he never again administered the MMPI without checking the subject's reading level.

To cross-validate the scales, independent samples of the criterion and control groups were administered the items. To qualify as cross-validated, a scale had to distinguish the criterion group from the control group at the .05 level of significance (i.e., the probability of obtaining differences by chance is less than 5 out of 100).

In addition to the eight scales just described, two content scales were added: the masculinity–femininity (MF) scale, which contained items differentially endorsed by men and women, and the social-introversion (Si) scale, which measures introversion and extroversion (L. C. Ward & Perry, 1998). These two scales plus the eight scales already described constitute the original 10 clinical scales of the MMPI.

Because the logical-content approach had been criticized for its many assumptions, Hathaway and McKinley developed special scales called *validity*

TABLE 13-2

Original Validity Scales of the MMPI

Lie scale (L)	Fifteen rationally derived items included in both the MMPI and MMPI-2 designed to evaluate a naive attempt to present oneself in a favorable light. The items reflect personal weaknesses such as "I never lose control of myself when I drive." Most people are willing to admit to these weaknesses. People who score high on this scale are unwilling to acknowledge minor flaws.
Infrequency scale (F)	Of the original 64 items from the MMPI developed to detect deviant response patterns, 60 were retained for the MMPI-2. These are items that are scored infrequently (less than 10%) by the normal population. The F scale contains items such as "I am aware of a special presence that others cannot perceive." High scores on the F scale invalidate the profile.
K scale	Thirty items included on both the MMPI and MMPI-2 that detect attempts to deny problems and present oneself in a favorable light. People who score high on this scale are attempting to project an image of self-control and personal effectiveness. Extremely high scores on this scale invalidate the profile.

scales to measure test-taking attitude and to assess whether the subject took a normal, honest approach to the test (see Table 13-2). The L, or lie, scale was designed to detect individuals who attempted to present themselves in an overly favorable way.

The K scale served the same purpose but was empirically constructed. In deriving the K scale, Hathaway and McKinley compared the MMPI scores of nondisturbed individuals showing normal patterns with the MMPI scores of disturbed individuals who produced normal MMPI patterns—that is, they showed no scales that deviated significantly from the mean. The K scale thus attempts to locate those items that distinguished normal from abnormal groups when both groups produced a normal test pattern. It was assumed that pathological groups would produce normal patterns because of defensiveness, a tendency to hide or deny psychological problems, and that this defensiveness could be determined by comparing these individuals to nondisturbed normals.

The F or infrequency scale, which is designed to detect individuals who attempt to fake bad, consists of those items endorsed by less than 10% of the control group. Of the 64 items on the F scale, most of which contain pathological content such as "Odd odors come to me at times," the average number of items endorsed in the scored direction is four. Anyone who marks a lot of these items is taking an unusual approach to the test. Thus, high F scores bring the validity of the whole profile into question (Shores & Carstairs, 1998).

Finally, although it is referred to as a validity scale, the "cannot say" scale consists simply of the items to which the subject failed to respond either "True" or "False." If as few as 10% of the items are omitted, then the entire profile is invalid.

Initial interpretations. For all of the scales, the control group provided the reference for which standard scores were determined. McCall's *T*, with a mean of 50 and a standard deviation of 10, was used to compute standard scores. Subjects with *T* scores of 50 were thus at the mean of the control sample for any given scale. *T* scores of 70, two standard deviations above the mean, were considered significantly elevated for the MMPI. With the new norms for the MMPI-2, *T* scores of 65 are now considered significant.

The original approach taken to interpret the MMPI was simple and straightforward. Because the scales significantly discriminated the criterion groups from control groups and withstood the test of cross-validation, most users assumed that individuals with characteristics similar to those of a criterion group would have significant elevation on the appropriate scale. Schizophrenics, for example, would show significant elevation on the schizophrenia scale, hysterics would show elevation on the hysteria scale, and so on. Unfortunately, this assumption turned out to be false. Experience with the MMPI rapidly revealed that only a relatively small number of disturbed subjects showed elevation on only a single scale. More often, elevation was found in two, three, four, or even all of the scales. Thus, a problem had arisen: What did the test mean when someone showed elevation on the hysteria, psychopathic deviate, schizophrenia, and hypomania scales? There is no such thing as a hysterical psychopathic hypomanic schizophrenic!

To deal with multiple-scale elevations, clinicians made use of pattern (configural) analysis, which the test authors had originally suggested (Hathaway & McKinley, 1943). This change led to an avalanche of studies and proposals for identifying clinical groups on the basis of patterns of MMPI scores (e.g., Meehl & Dahlstrom, 1960). However, early investigations soon revealed the futility of this approach (Garfield & Sineps, 1959; Loy, 1959; Meikle & Gerritse, 1970). Either the rules were so complex that only an extremely small portion of the profiles met the criteria, such as the Gilberstadt and Duker (1965) rules, or the rules led to diagnoses that were no more accurate than those made by untrained nonprofessionals (Meehl, 1954, 1956, 1957; Meehl & Rosen, 1955). Led by Meehl, clinicians began to look at the two highest scales.

Meehl's extension of the empirical approach. Pointing to the possible advantages of analyzing the two highest scales, or *two-point code,* Meehl (1951) emphasized the importance of conducting research on individuals who showed specific two-point codes and other configural patterns. This way, developers could empirically determine the meaning of MMPI elevations. Thus, the validity of the MMPI was extended by finding homogeneous profile patterns and determining the characteristics of individuals who show these patterns. In other words, new criterion groups were established of individuals grouped on the basis of similarities in their MMPI profiles. In this approach, the characteristics of a criterion group, consisting of subjects who showed elevation on two scales (for example, the psychopathic deviate and hypomania scales), could be empirically determined. The difference in approach meant that MMPI configural patterns, rather than psychiatric diagnosis, became the criterion for the selection of homogeneous criterion groups.

Because the original idea of the contrasted-group method was extended by the use of criterion groups, we use the term *criterion-group strategy* rather than *contrasted-group strategy* to describe the MMPI and related tests. The most recent approach does not attempt to distinguish the criterion group from a control group. Instead, the characteristics of the criterion groups are evaluated through empirical means such as peer ratings, physician ratings, and demographic characteristics. The upshot has been numerous studies that describe the characteristics of individuals who show specific MMPI patterns (Demir, Batur, Mercan, & Ulug, 2002; Heinze & Purisch, 2001; McGrath, Sweeney, O'Malley, & Carlton, 1998).

Along with an empirical approach, Meehl and others began to advocate a change in the names of the clinical scales. Because elevation on the schizophrenia scale did not necessarily mean the person was schizophrenic, the use of such a name was awkward as well as confusing. Meehl and others therefore suggested that the scales be identified by number rather than by name. Table 13-3 lists the scales by their number. The validity scales retained their original names.

At this point, MMPI patterns could have a numerical code. For each of the two most commonly used coding systems, the clinical scales are listed in rank order from highest T score to lowest. A symbol indicates the level of elevation. In Welsh's (1948) well-established system, for example, T scores of 90 (four standard deviations above the mean) and greater are designated by *; T scores between 80 and 89 are designated by "; T scores between 70 and 79, by '; T scores between 60 and 69, by −; and so on for each 10-point interval down to # placed to the right of T scores below 29. For example, the code 13* 2" 7'

TABLE 13-3
Original MMPI Scales

Symbol currently in use	Old name	Number of items in scale*	Common interpretation of elevation
Validity Scales			
L	Lie scale	13	Naive attempt to fake good
K	K scale	30	Defensiveness
F	F scale	64	Attempt to fake bad
Clinical Scales			
1	Hypochondriasis	33	Physical complaints
2	Depression	60	Depression
3	Hysteria	60	Immaturity
4	Psychopathic deviate	50	Authority conflict
5	Masculinity–femininity	60	Masculine or feminine interests
6	Paranoia	40	Suspicion, hostility
7	Psychasthenia	48	Anxiety
8	Schizophrenia	78	Alienation, withdrawal
9	Hypomania	46	Elated mood, high energy
0	Social introversion	70	Introversion, shyness

*Because of item overlap, the total number of items here is 654.
Note: The validity scales (L, K, and F) determine the individual's approach to testing (normal or honest, fake bad, or fake good). Of the 10 clinical scales, two were developed rationally (5 and 0). The remaining eight scales were developed through the criterion-group method. Numerous interpretive hypotheses can be associated with each MMPI scale; however, the meaning of any MMPI scale depends on the characteristics of the subject (age, race, sex, socioeconomic status, education, IQ, and so forth).

456890— means that Scales 1 and 3 have *T* scores above 90, Scale 2 above 80, Scale 7 above 70, and the remaining scales between 60 and 69. This pattern is referred to as a one–three 2-point pattern or, more simply, a *13 code*, based on the two highest scales.

The restandardization: MMPI-2. Beginning in 1982, a major effort was made to update and restandardize the MMPI. The result was the MMPI-2 (Butcher, Graham, Dahlstrom, Tellegen, & Kaernmer, 1989). The purpose of the revision was to update and expand the norms; revise items that were out of date, awkward, sexist, or problematic; and broaden the item pool to extend the range of constructs that one could evaluate. At the same time, developers strove to retain all the features of the original MMPI, including the original validity and clinical scales. Finally, they wanted to develop a separate form for adolescents. Each of these goals was well accomplished (see Figure 13-3).

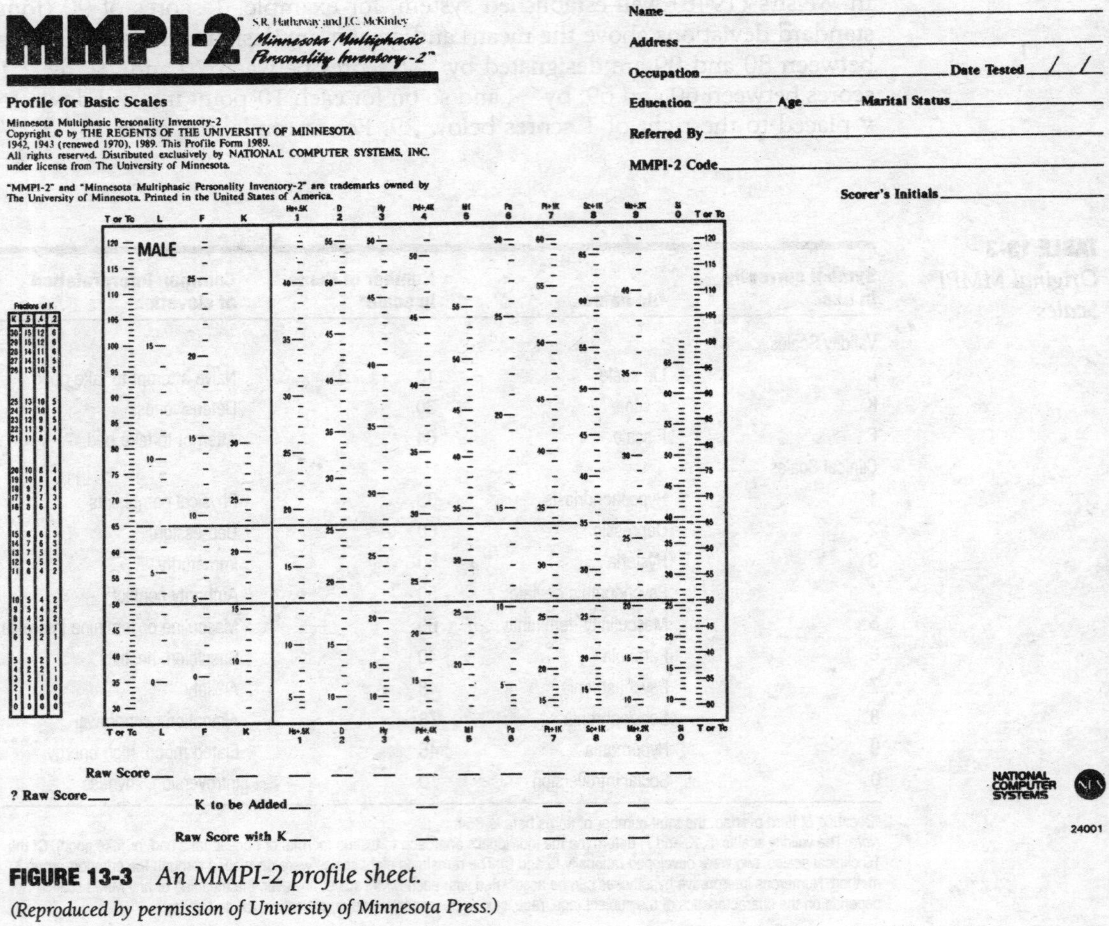

FIGURE 13-3   *An MMPI-2 profile sheet.*

(Reproduced by permission of University of Minnesota Press.)

The original MMPI contained 550 items, with 16 items repeated on the back of the scoring sheets for convenience of scoring, for a total of 566 items. The MMPI-2 has 567 items. Changes included dropping the 16 repeated items, dropping 13 items from the clinical scales, and dropping 77 items from the range 399 and 550, leaving 460 items from the original test. Then 81 items were added for the new content scales, two items were added to pick up severe pathology (critical items), and 24 unscored items were added for experimental purposes, for a total of 567. An additional 68 items were rewritten with no change in meaning (Ben-Porath & Butcher, 1989). Reasons for rewriting items included outdated language (24), sexist language (11), awkward language (6), and minor changes or simplifications (33).

Interpretation of the clinical scales remained the same because not more than four items were dropped from any scale, and the scales were renormed and scores transformed to uniform *T* scores. On the original MMPI, more people were scoring above a *T* score of 70 than a normal distribution would predict, and the scales were not uniform. To maintain consistency with previous research and interpretation, the cutting score was lowered to 65. With uniform *T* scores, the distribution is the same on all scores, with 8% scoring above 65, and 4% above 70.

In developing new norms, the MMPI project committee (James Butcher of the University of Minnesota, Grant Dahlstrom of the University of North Carolina, Jack Graham of Kent State University, and Auke Tellegen of the University of Minnesota) selected 2900 subjects from seven geographic areas of the United States: California, Minnesota, North Carolina, Ohio, Pennsylvania, Virginia, and Washington. Of these, 300 were eliminated because of incomplete or invalid profiles, resulting in a final sample of 2600 men and women. Potential subjects for the restandardization were initially identified by telephone and then contacted by letter. Testing centers were set up in major cities to make personal contact and arrange for the testing. The goal was to obtain a sample that reflected the demographics of the 1980 census. However, because participation was completely voluntary, the final sample was more educated and had greater economic means than the general population.

A major feature of the MMPI-2 is the inclusion of additional validity scales. On the original MMPI, all of the F items are in the first 370 items and appear on the front of the answer sheet. The MMPI-2 expanded the F scale to the back of the scoring sheet as well. The FB (Back F) score provides a check on validity and cooperation throughout the test and permits a confirmation of F scores obtained in the first half of the test. Two additional validity scales, the Variable Response Inconsistency Scale (VRIN) and the True Response Inconsistency Scale (TRIN), are included to evaluate response styles (see Baer & Sekirnjak, 1997). The VRIN attempts to evaluate random responding. The scale consists of matched pairs of items that have similar content. Each time the pairs are marked in opposite directions, a point is scored on the scale. The TRIN attempts to measure **acquiescence**—the tendency to agree or mark "True" regardless of content. This scale consists of matched pairs of items with opposite content. For example, to receive a point on the TRIN Scale, the person might mark "True" to both "I feel good" and "I feel bad."

There are 154 items on the MMPI-2 that permit the evaluation of various content areas (Arita & Baer, 1998; Strassberg, 1997). The MMPI-2 contains 15 content scales, including HEA (health concerns) and TPA, which evaluates for the hard-driving, irritable, impatient Type A personality. Other MMPI-2 content scales include FAM (family problems), which evaluates family disorders and possible child abuse, and WRK (work interference), which examines behaviors or attitudes likely to interfere with work performance.

Psychometric properties. The psychometric properties of the MMPI and MMPI-2 are comparable (Gaston, Nelson, Hart, Quatman, et al., 1994); the newer version maintains strong continuity with the original. For example, the factor structures of the new and original versions are quite similar.

Median split-half reliability coefficients for both the original MMPI and the MMPI-2 run in the .70's, with some coefficients as high as .96 but others much lower. Median test–retest coefficients range from the low .50's to the low .90's (median .80's). Although these coefficients are not as solid as those for the major ability tests such as the Binet and Wechsler, they are as high as or better than those reported in comparable tests. Moreover, when one looks at the basic higher-order factor structure, the MMPI and MMPI-2 are extremely reliable, with coefficients running in the high .90's.

Although the reliability of the MMPI is generally adequate, developers have not yet dealt with some notable problems. For example, because of the way scales were originally constructed, many items are on more than one scale, with some items on as many as six. Scale 8, which has more items than any other scale, contains only 16 unique items. This problem of item overlap was not confronted in the MMPI-2 revision because the goal was to retain all the original scales.

Perhaps as a result of item overlap, intercorrelations among the clinical scales are extremely high. For example, Scales 7 and 8 correlate between .64 and .87, depending on the sample studied (Butcher et al., 1989; Dahlstrom & Welsh, 1960). This high intercorrelation among the scales has led to several factor analytic studies (Johnson, Null, Butcher, & Johnson, 1984), which consistently show that two factors account for most of the variance in the original MMPI scales. These factors have been variously labeled throughout the literature (for instance, as negative or positive affectivity). Because of the high intercorrelations among the scales and the results of factor analytic studies, the validity of pattern analysis has often been questioned (Nichols & Greene, 1997).

Another problem with the MMPI and MMPI-2 is the imbalance in the way items are keyed. Many individuals approach structured tests with a **response style,** or bias, which is a tendency to mark an item in a certain way regardless of content. One of these tendencies, as you have seen, is acquiescence. Given the possibility of response tendencies, one would expect an equal number of items keyed true and keyed false. Not so; all of the items on the L scale and 29 of the 30 items on the K scale are keyed false. Scales 7, 8, and 9 are keyed on a 3:1 true–false ratio. The VRIN and TRIN scales of the MMPI-2 allow the examiner to evaluate response tendencies and represent a clear positive step toward overcoming this imbalance.

Major works devoted to the MMPI and MMPI-2 strongly emphasize the importance of taking into account the subject's demographic characteristics when interpreting profiles (Butcher, 1990; Butcher, Graham, Williams, & Ben-Porath, 1990; Nelson, Novy, Averill, & Berry, 1996). This advice is indeed warranted in that most of the studies have shown that age (Butcher, Aidwin, Levenson, & Ben-Porath, 1991; Osberg & Poland, 2002), gender (Butcher et al., 1989), race (Butcher, 1990), place of residence (Erdberg, 1969), and other demographic factors such as intelligence, education, and socioeconomic status (Butcher, 1990) are all related to the MMPI and MMPI-2 scales. This overwhelming evidence supporting the covariation between demographic factors and the meaning of MMPI and MMPI-2 scores clearly shows that two exact profile patterns can have quite different meanings, depending on the demographic characteristics of each subject. Despite these differences in interpretation, some evidence suggests that the MMPI-2 predicts equally well for at least whites and African Americans (Arbisi, Ben-Porath, & McNulty, 2002; Timbrook & Graham, 1994).

The major source of validity for the MMPI and MMPI-2 comes from the many research studies that describe the characteristics of particular profile patterns. Tens of thousands of studies have been conducted, with the number of new studies increasing every year (Groth-Marnat, 1999). In fact, our survey of the relevant literature between 1999 and 2004 revealed more citations for the MMPI and MMPI-2 than for any other personality test. This body of research provides ample evidence for the construct validity of the MMPI and MMPI-2.

Many studies, for example, have related MMPI response patterns to alcoholism and substance abuse (Gallucci, 1997; Guan, Tang, Xue, & Zhou, 2002; McMahon, Davidson, Gersh, & Flynn, 1991). For instance, evidence indicates that the MMPI and MMPI-2 might help detect individuals who might later become alcoholics (Hoffman, Loper, & Kammeier, 1974; Kammeier, Hoffman, & Loper, 1973; Malinchoc, Oxford, Colligan, & Morse, 1994). The items of the original MMPI were administered to a group of men while they were still in college. The response patterns of those individuals who later became alcoholics were compared with those of a control group who did not become alcoholics. Results showed that the subjects who eventually became alcoholics had significantly higher scores on one validity scale (F) and two clinical scales (4 and 9). Thus, these scales may be related to characteristics that contribute to alcoholism in men. Interestingly, the response pattern of those in the alcoholic group was the same as their retest pattern after they had become alcoholics.

Indeed, the range of problems that the MMPI and MMPI-2 can help with spans everything from eating disorders (Gleaves, May, & Eberenz, 1996; Strassberg, Ross, & Todt, 1995), soldiers' reaction in battle (Leach, 2002), posttraumatic stress syndrome (Gaston, Brunet, Koszychi, & Bradwejn, 1996; Glenn, Beckham, Sampson, Feldman, Hertzberg, & Moore, 2002; Munley, Bains, Bloem, & Busby, 1995), the detection of sexual abuse in children (Holifield,

Nelson, & Hart, 2002), risk factors of female criminals (Lui et al., 2002), the effects of acculturation (Kwon, 2002), differentiating criminal types (Glaser, Calhoun, & Petrocelli, 2002), and prediction of delinquent behavior (Pena, Megargee, & Brody, 1996) to prediction of neurological disorders (Cripe, Maxwell, & Hill, 1995) and psychosis-prone college students (Cadenhead, Kumar, & Braff, 1996). Of course, not all MMPI studies report positive results (Levenson, Olkin, Herzoff, & DeLancy, 1986), but the vast majority attest to its utility and versatility (Harkness, McNulty, & Ben-Porath, 1995; Iverson, Franzen, & Hammond, 1995). This large database and sound construction explain in part why the MMPI is accepted as evidence in the judicial system (Saccuzzo, 1999).

Current status. The restandardization of the MMPI has eliminated the most serious drawback of the original version: the inadequate control group. With its already widespread use and acceptance, the future of the MMPI appears extremely bright. A new set of clinical scales (MMPI-2 Restructured Clinical Scales) was introduced in 2003 and includes contemporary norms, additional content domains, and a revision of items that eliminates sexist content and dated references (Tellegen, 2003). The addition of new items is sure to generate many new applications. Furthermore, the newer items can be added to the original scales when appropriate to increase their reliability as well as their predictive validity. Indeed, the MMPI and MMPI-2 are without question the leading personality test of the 21st century.

California Psychological Inventory–Third Edition

The California Psychological Inventory (CPI) (Gough, 1987) is a second example of a structured personality test constructed primarily by the criterion-group strategy. For three of the 36 CPI scales in the most recent revision, criterion groups (for example, men versus women; homosexual men versus heterosexual men) were contrasted to produce measures of personality categorized as (1) introversion–extroversion, (2) conventional versus unconventional in following norms, and (3) self-realization and sense of integration.

In contrast to the MMPI and MMPI-2, the CPI attempts to evaluate personality in normally adjusted individuals and thus finds more use in counseling settings. The test contains 20 scales, each of which is grouped into one of four classes. Class I scales measure poise, self-assurance, and interpersonal effectiveness. Individuals who score high on these scales tend to be active, resourceful, competitive, outgoing, spontaneous, and self-confident. They are also at ease in interpersonal situations. Individuals who score high on Class II scales, which evaluate socialization, maturity, and responsibility, tend to be conscientious, honest, dependable, calm, practical, cooperative, and alert to ethical and moral issues. Class III scales measure achievement potential and intellectual efficiency. High scores in this class tend to indicate organized, efficient, sincere, mature, forceful, capable, and well-informed people. Class IV scales examine interest modes. High scorers tend to respond well to the inner needs of others and adapt well socially.

In addition, the CPI also includes 13 scales that are designed for special purposes such as managerial potential, tough-mindedness, and creativity as well as several experimental scales evaluating dimensions of operating style (Gough, 1996).

More than a third of the 434 items are almost identical to items in the original MMPI, and many others resemble them. However, the test does more than share items with the MMPI. Like the MMPI, the CPI shows considerable intercorrelation among its scales. Factor analytic studies have shown that only two factors in the CPI, associated with internal controls (Class II scales) and interpersonal effectiveness (Class I scales), account for a large part of the variance (Megargee, 1972). Also like the MMPI, true–false scale keying is often extremely unbalanced. Reliability coefficients are similar to those reported for the MMPI. Short-term test–retest coefficients range from .49 to .90, depending on the sample; long-term coefficients range from .38 to .77. However, the method used to establish some of the criterion groups for the CPI has been questioned. For example, for some of the scales, subjects were placed in criterion groups on the basis of ratings by friends. Nevertheless, one must consider the psychometric properties of the CPI adequate by today's standards because they are comparable to those of most widely used personality tests.

The CPI is commonly used in research settings to examine everything from typologies of sexual offenders (Worling, 2001) to career choices (Gough, 1995, 1996). The advantage of the CPI is that it can be used with normal subjects. The MMPI and MMPI-2 generally do not apply to normal subjects, and the meaning of nonelevated profiles is not well established. Therefore, if one intends to assess normal individuals for interpersonal effectiveness and internal controls, then the CPI is a good candidate for the measure. Furthermore, as with the MMPI and MMPI-2, a considerable body of literature has focused on the CPI. Each new piece of literature extends the utility of the test and adds to its construct validity. Therefore, the future of the CPI as a measure of normal personalities has good potential despite its limitations (Bolton, 1992; Groth-Marnat, 1999).

The Factor Analytic Strategy

Structured personality tests, as they exist today, share one common set of assumptions. These assumptions, simply stated, are that humans possess characteristics or traits that are stable, vary from individual to individual, and can be measured. Nowhere are these assumptions better illustrated than in the factor analytic strategy of test construction.

Recall that factor analysis is a statistical procedure for reducing the redundancy in a set of intercorrelated scores. For example, one major technique of factor analysis, the principal-components method (Hotelling, 1933), finds the minimum number of common factors that can account for an interrelated set of scores. As noted in the previous section, two factors can account for most of the variance in both the CPI and the MMPI, which suggests that these tests are actually measuring only two unique components and that all scales are related to these two components.

The advantages of factor analysis are quite evident. However, before computers, even simple factor analyses required several weeks or even months of tedious arithmetic operations on a hand calculator. Therefore, the development of the factor analytic strategy awaited computer technology. R. B. Cattell has particularly distinguished himself in using the factor analytic strategy of structured personality assessment; this section focuses largely on his work.

Guilford's Pioneer Efforts

One usual strategy in validating a new test is to correlate the scores on the new test with the scores on other tests that purport to measure the same entity. J. R. Guilford's approach was related to this procedure. However, instead of comparing one test at a time to a series of other tests, Guilford and his associates determined the interrelationship (intercorrelation) of a wide variety of tests and then factor analyzed the results in an effort to find the main dimensions underlying all personality tests. If the results from existing personality tests could be reduced to a few factors, then items that correlated highly with these factors could be used in a new test, which would therefore capture the major dimensions of personality.

The result of the initial attempt to apply this strategy was a series of inventories that Guilford and his associates published in the 1940s and which were ultimately collapsed into a single scale—the Guilford-Zimmerman Temperament Survey (Guilford & Zimmerman, 1956).

This survey reduces personality to 10 dimensions, each of which is measured by 30 different items. The 10 dimensions are general activity, restraint, ascendance (leadership), sociability, emotional stability, objectivity, friendliness, thoughtfulness, personal relations, and masculinity. The test presents a list of statements, most of which are self-statements as in the MMPI and MMPI-2. The subject must indicate "Yes" or "No" for each statement. Three verification keys are included to detect falsification and to evaluate the validity of the profile. However, this first major factor analytic structured personality test failed to catch on, perhaps because it was overshadowed by the MMPI and because of its arbitrary, subjective way of naming factors. Today, the Guilford-Zimmerman Temperament Survey primarily serves only historical interests.

Cattell's Contribution

Rather than attempting to uncover the major dimensions of personality by intercorrelating personality tests, R. B. Cattell began with all the adjectives applicable to human beings so he could empirically determine and measure the essence of personality. Beginning with a monumental catalog of all the adjectives (trait names) in an unabridged dictionary that apply to humans, Allport and Odbert (1936) reduced their list to 4504 "real" traits. Adding to the list traits found in the psychological and psychiatric literature, Cattell then reduced the list to 171 items that he believed accounted for the meaning of all items on the original list. College students then rated their friends on these 171 terms, and the results were intercorrelated and factor analyzed. The 171 terms were reduced to 36 dimensions, called *surface traits*. Subsequent investigation by factor analysis finally produced 16 distinct factors that accounted for all the variables. Thus, Cattell had reduced personality to 16 basic dimensions, which he called *source traits* (see Table 13-4).

The product of Cattell's marathon task was the Sixteen Personality Factor Questionnaire, better known as the 16PF (Schuerger, 1995), which was subsequently revised following continued factor analysis. Consistent with the factor analytic strategy, items that correlated highly with each of the 16 major factors, or source traits, were included, and those with relatively low correlations were excluded.

Developers took great care in standardizing the 16PF. Separate norms were provided for men alone, women alone, and men and women combined for each of three U.S. groups: adults, college students, and high-school seniors. Thus, nine sets of norms are available. To deal further with the covariation of structured personality-test data and demographic variables that plagues the MMPI, the 16PF provides age corrections for those scales that change significantly with age. Six forms of the test are available: two parallel forms for each of three levels of vocabulary proficiency, ranging from newspaper-literate adults through the educationally disadvantaged. For the latter, a tape-recorded (oral) form is also available. Norms for the various forms are based on more than 15,000 subjects representative of geographic area, population density, age, family income, and race according to figures provided by the U.S. census. Unlike the MMPI and CPI, the 16PF contains no item overlap, and keying is balanced among the various alternative responses. Short-term test–retest correlation coefficients for the 16 source traits are impressive, with a range of .65 to .93 and a median coefficient of .83. Long-term test–retest coefficients, however, are not so impressive (.21 to .64), and most such coefficients reported in the literature are lower than those reported for the MMPI and MMPI-2 (Schuerger, Tait, & Tavernelli, 1982). Also a bit disappointing are the correlations between the various forms, which range from a low of .16 to a high of .79, with median coefficients in the .50's and .60's, depending on which forms are correlated. Moreover, despite the method used for deriving the factors, the 16 source traits of the 16PF do intercorrelate, with some correlations as high as .75 (R. B. Cattell, Eber, & Tatsuoka, 1970). To deal with this overlap, the 16 factors themselves were factor analyzed, resulting in four second-order factors, for which one can obtain scores.

Other important features of the test are its provision of a parallel inventory for ages 12 to 18, the Junior Senior High School Personality Questionnaire, and still another parallel extension for use with ages 8 to 12, the Children's Personality Questionnaire. Cross-cultural studies have been conducted in Western Europe, Eastern Europe, the Middle East, Australia, Canada (Schuerger, 1995), and Korea (Sohn, 2002). To extend the test to the assessment of clinical populations, items related to psychological disorders have

TABLE 13-4

The Primary Source Traits Covered by the 16PF Test

Factor	Low Sten score description (1–3)	High Sten score description (8–10)
A	*Cool, reserved, impersonal, detached, formal, aloof* Sizothymia*	*Warm, outgoing, kindly, easygoing, participating, likes people* Affectothymia
B	*Concrete-thinking, less intelligent* Lower scholastic mental capacity	*Abstract-thinking, more intelligent, bright* Higher scholastic mental capacity
C	*Affected by feelings, emotionally less stable, easily annoyed* Lower ego strength	*Emotionally stable, mature, faces reality, calm* Higher ego strength
E	*Submissive, humble, mild, easily led, accommodating* Submissiveness	*Dominant, assertive, aggressive, stubborn, competitive, bossy* Dominance
F	*Sober, restrained, prudent, taciturn, serious* Desurgency	*Enthusiastic, spontaneous, heedless, expressive, cheerful* Surgency
G	*Expedient, disregards rules, self-indulgent* Weaker superego strength	*Conscientious, conforming, moralistic, staid, rule-bound* Stronger superego strength
H	*Shy, threat-sensitive, timid, hesitant, intimidated* Threctia	*Bold, venturesome, uninhibited, can take stress* Parmia
I	*Tough-minded, self-reliant, no-nonsense, rough, realistic* Harria	*Tender-minded, sensitive, overprotected, intuitive, refined* Premsia
L	*Trusting, accepting conditions, easy to get on with* Alaxia	*Suspicious, hard to fool, distrustful, skeptical* Protension
M	*Practical, concerned with "down-to-earth" issues, steady* Praxernia	*Imaginative, absent-minded, absorbed in thought, impractical* Autia
N	*Forthright, unpretentious, open, genuine, artless* Artlessness	*Shrewd, polished, socially aware, diplomatic, calculating* Shrewdness
O	*Self-assured, secure, feels free of guilt, untroubled, self-satisfied* Untroubled adequacy	*Apprehensive, self-blaming, guilt-prone, insecure, worrying* Guilt proneness
Q1	*Conservative, respecting traditional ideas* Conservatism of temperament	*Experimenting, liberal, critical, open to change* Radicalism
Q2	*Group-oriented, a "joiner" and sound follower, listens to others* Group adherence	*Self-sufficient, resourceful, prefers own decisions* Self-sufficiency
Q3	*Undisciplined self-conflict, lax, careless of social rules* Low integration	*Following self-image, socially precise, compulsive* High self-concept control
Q4	*Relaxed, tranquil, composed, has low drive, unfrustrated* Low ergic tension	*Tense, frustrated, overwrought, has high drive* High ergic tension

*Titles in roman type are the technical names for the factors and are explained more fully in the *Handbook*.
From the *Administrator's Manual for the Sixteen Personality Factor Questionnaire*. Copyright © 1972, 1979, 1986 by the Institute for Personality and Ability Testing, Inc. Reproduced by permission.

been factor analyzed, resulting in 12 new factors in addition to the 16 needed to measure normal personalities. These new factors were then used to construct a clinical instrument, the Clinical Analysis Questionnaire (CAQ) (Delhees & Cattell, 1971).

Despite the care that has gone into the 16PF, its research base and use pale when compared with those of the MMPI and MMPI-2. The fact is, neither clinicians nor researchers have found the 16PF to be as useful as the MMPI. Moreover, the claims of the 16PF to have identified the basic source traits of the personality are simply not true. However, various research investigations have supported the validity of Cattell's personality test (see Meyer, 1993).

Factor analysis is one of many ways of constructing tests. It will identify only those traits about which questions are asked, however, and it has no more claim to uniqueness than any other method. Even so, the 16PF remains an exemplary illustration of the factor analytic approach to structured personality testing.

Problems with the Factor Analytic Strategy

One major criticism of factor analytic approaches centers on the subjective nature of naming factors. To understand this problem, one must understand that each score on any given set of tests or variables can be broken down into three components: common variance, unique variance, and error variance. *Common variance* is the amount of variance a particular variable holds in common with other variables. It results from the overlap of what two or more variables are measuring. *Unique variance* refers to factors uniquely measured by the variable. In other words, it refers to some construct measured *only* by the variable in question. *Error variance* is variance attributable to error.

Factor analytic procedures generally identify sources of common variance at the expense of unique variance. Thus, important factors may be overlooked when the data are categorized solely on the basis of blind groupings by computers. Furthermore, all the computer can do is identify the groupings. The factor analyst must determine which factors these groupings measure, but no definite criteria or rules exist for naming factors. If five items such as *daring, outgoing, determined, excitable,* and *fearless* load high on a factor, then what should one call this factor? In factor analysis, one name for this factor has about as much validity as any other.

The Theoretical Strategy

To avoid the potential disagreement and biases that stem from factor analytic approaches, developers have proposed using theory as a way to guide the construction of structured personality tests. In this approach, items are selected to measure the variables or constructs specified by a major theory of personality. After the items have been selected and grouped into scales, construct-related evidence for validity is sought. In other words, predictions are made about the nature of the scale; if the predictions hold up, then the scale is supported.

Edwards Personal Preference Schedule

One of the best-known and earliest examples of a theoretically derived structured personality test is the Edwards Personal Preference Schedule (EPPS) (Edwards, 1954, 1959). According to Edwards, the EPPS is not actually a test in the strictest sense of the word because there are no right or wrong answers. At one time, the EPPS was used widely in counseling centers (Lubin, Wallis, & Paine, 1971). It has also been widely researched (Nittono, 1997; Thorson & Powell, 1996). Today, the test is not used extensively. However, in addition to illustrating the theoretical strategy, the EPPS elucidates some interesting concepts in personality-test construction, such as the concept of ipsative scores, which we shall discuss later.

The theoretical basis for the EPPS is the need system proposed by Murray (1938), probably the most influential theory in personality-test construction to date. The human needs proposed by Murray include the need to accomplish (achievement), the need to conform (deference), and the need for attention (exhibition). In developing the EPPS, Edwards selected 15 needs from Murray's list and constructed items with content validity for each (see Table 13-5).

Having selected items based on theory, Edwards could avoid the blind, subjective, and atheoretical approaches of other strategies. However, he still faced the perpetual problems of response styles and biases, which the MMPI had dealt with by including special scales to detect faking or unusual test-taking approaches. Edwards was especially concerned about faking and social desirability, the tendency to say good things about yourself or to mark items that you believe will be approved by the examiner, regardless of accuracy.

To deal with these sources of bias, Edwards attempted to rate each of his items on social desirability. He then formed pairs of items roughly comparable in social desirability and required subjects to select the item in the pair that was more characteristic of their likes or feelings. Subjects cannot simply provide the socially desirable or expected response because both items in the pair are presumably equal on social desirability. There is also not much point in faking—that is, selecting the less characteristic item. In addition, no problem of balancing scored items arises, as it does from the true–false imbalance of the MMPI.

As a further check on the validity of EPPS results, Edwards included a consistency scale with 15 pairs of statements repeated in identical form. In other words, of the 210 pairs of statements, only 195 are unique. The 15 that occur twice are presented more or less randomly throughout the test. With this format, the number of times a subject makes the identical choice can be converted to a percentile based on normative data. The approach provided the precursor to the VRIN and TRIN scales of the MMPI-2. The EPPS also permits an analysis of within-subject consistency, which consists of the correlation of odd and even scores in the 15 scales.

Norms for the EPPS were based on more than 1500 college men and women and approximately 9000 adults from the general population selected from urban and rural areas in 48 states. Separate normative data are available for each of these two groups and high-school students as well. For a given raw

TABLE 13-5

List and Description of Murray's Psychogenic Needs

Need	Description
Abasement	To submit passively to external force. To accept injury, blame, criticism, punishment. To surrender. To become resigned to fate. To admit inferiority, error, wrong-doing, or defeat. To confess and atone. To blame, belittle, or mutilate the self. To seek and enjoy pain, punishment, illness, and misfortune.
Achievement	To accomplish something difficult. To master, manipulate, or organize physical objects, human beings, or ideas. To do this as rapidly and as independently as possible. To overcome obstacles and attain a high standard. To excel one's self. To rival and surpass others. To increase self-regard by the successful exercise of talent.
Affiliation	To form friendships and associations. To greet, join, and live with others. To cooperate and converse sociably with others. To love. To join groups.
Aggression	To overcome opposition forcefully. To fight. To revenge an injury. To attack, injure, or kill another. To oppose forcefully or punish another.
Autonomy	To get free, shake off restraint, break out of confinement. To resist coercion and restriction. To avoid or quit activities prescribed by domineering authorities. To be independent and free to act according to impulse. To be unattached, unconditioned, irresponsible. To defy convention.
Blamavoidance	To avoid blame, ostracism, or punishment by inhibiting asocial or unconventional impulses. To be well-behaved and obey the law.
Counteraction	Proudly to refuse admission of defeat by restriving and retaliating. To select the hardest tasks. To defend one's honor in action.
Defendance	To defend oneself against blame or belittlement. To justify one's actions. To offer extenuations, explanations, and excuses. To resist "probing."
Deference	To admire and support a superior other. To praise, honor, or eulogize. To yield eagerly to the influence of an allied other. To emulate an exemplar. To conform to custom.
Dominance	To influence or control others. To persuade, prohibit, dictate. To lead and direct. To restrain. To organize the behavior of a group.
Exhibition	To make an impression. To be seen and heard. To excite, amaze, fascinate, entertain, shock, intrigue, amuse, or entice others.
Harmavoidance	To avoid pain, physical injury, illness, and death. To escape from a dangerous situation. To take precautionary measures.
Infavoidance	To avoid humiliation. To quit embarrassing situations or to avoid conditions that may lead to belittlement; the scorn, decision, or indifference of others. To refrain from action because of the fear of failure.
Nurturance	To nourish, aid, or protect a helpless other. To express sympathy. To "mother" a child.
Order	To put things in order. To achieve cleanliness, arrangement, organization, balance, neatness, tidiness, and precision.
Play	To relax, amuse oneself, seek diversion and entertainment. To "have fun," to play games. To laugh, joke, and be merry. To avoid serious tension.
Rejection	To snub, ignore, or exclude another. To remain aloof and indifferent. To be discriminating.
Sentience	To seek and enjoy sensuous impressions.
Sex	To form and further an erotic relationship. To have sexual intercourse.
Succorance	To seek aid, protection, or sympathy. To cry for help. To plead for mercy. To adhere to an affectionate, nurturant parent. To be dependent.
Understanding	To analyze experience, to abstract, to discriminate among concepts, to define relations, to synthesize ideas.

From *Explorations in Personality* by Henry A. Murray, copyright 1938, renewed 1966 by Henry A. Murray. Used by permission of Oxford University Press, Inc.

score on each of the 15 scales, a percentile can be obtained immediately from the profile sheet.

In constructing the EPPS, Edwards listed items for each of the scales and then paired them with items from the other 14 scales. When subjects make a choice, they select between one of two needs. In other words, in each choice, a subject selects one need at the expense of another. With this procedure, one can express the selection of items on one scale relative to the selection of items on another, thereby producing an **ipsative score.** Ipsative scores present results in relative terms rather than as absolute totals. Thus, two individuals with identical relative, or ipsative, scores may differ markedly in the absolute strength of a particular need. Ipsative scores compare the individual against himself or herself and produce data that reflect the relative strength of each need for that person; each person thus provides his or her own frame of reference (Popper, 1997).

Although the manual presents only short-term (one-week) test–retest reliability figures, the coefficients, which range from .74 to .88, are quite respectable for personality-test data. Though not as impressive, split-half reliabilities, which range from .60 to .87 as reported in the manual, are generally satisfactory. Furthermore, intercorrelations among the scales are lower than those for either the MMPI or 16PF, ranging between −.34 and .46. The lower intercorrelation is good because it supports the possibility of pattern analysis.

The EPPS has several interesting features. Its forced-choice method, which requires subjects to select one of two items rather than to respond "True" or "False" ("yes" or "no") to a single item, is an interesting solution to the problem of faking and other sources of bias. Because each subject provides his or her own frame of reference, testers can determine the relative strength of needs as well as the internal consistency of each individual subject. Item content follows established theoretical lines. The 15 identical pairs help researchers evaluate the profile's validity. Norms are based on large samples and are available for adults from the general population as well as for high-school and college students. Ipsative scores based on these norms can be converted to percentiles. Reliability data generally are adequate for the short term, and the 15 scales of the EPPS have lower intercorrelations than do the scales of the major tests developed by using factor analytic and criterion-group strategies. Last, but not least, the test is among the most researched of the personality inventories and is used widely in applied settings.

Despite its impressive features and the widespread interest and use it has engendered, the EPPS has not been well received by reviewers (e.g., Heilbrun 1972). Studies have shown that, like other structured personality tests, the EPPS can be faked in spite of its forced-choice procedure. Other data raise questions about the test's ability to control social-desirability effects (Steward, Gimenez, & Jackson, 1995). The appropriateness of converting ipsative scores, which are relative, to normative percentiles is also questionable.

Since the first attempts at test construction, tests have followed a trend of gradual improvement following criticism and the identification of problems. The EPPS seems to have originated in this spirit, but efforts are not being made to improve it. Many more validity studies are needed (Baburajan, 1998), and new norms are long overdue (Cooper, 1990).

Personality Research Form and Jackson Personality Inventory

Other attempts to use the theoretical strategy in constructing a structured personality test are the Personality Research Form (PRF) (Jackson, 1967) and the Jackson Personality Inventory (JPI) (Jackson, 1976a, 1976b, 1997). Like the EPPS, the PRF and JPI were based on Murray's (1938) theory of needs. However, unlike Edwards, the constructors of these tests developed specific definitions of each need. In this way, items for each scale could be as independent as possible, an important consideration in creating homogeneous scales. To further increase the homogeneity of scales, more than 100 items were tentatively written for each scale and administered to more than 1000 college students. Biserial correlational analysis then located the items that correlated highest with the proposed scale while showing relatively low correlations with other scales, particularly social desirability. In other words, strict definitional standards and statistical procedures were used in conjunction with the theoretical approach. This use of a combination of procedures is the latest trend in personality-test construction.

To help assess validity, a scale analogous to the F scale of the MMPI was constructed. Like the F scale, the PRF and JPI infrequency scales consist of items with low endorsement rates in a standard sample. Thus, high rates of endorsement on this scale throw doubt on the validity of the results. A social-desirability scale similar to the K scale of the MMPI is also included in the PRF. Two sets of parallel forms (four forms in all) as well as a form based on the best items from other forms were developed for the PRF. The latest revision of the JPI (JPI-R) has one form consisting of 300 true–false items and 15 scales for use with high-school students through college students and adults. These 15 scales have been organized in terms of five higher-order dimensions termed analytical, extroverted, emotional, opportunistic, and dependable. College norms have been updated and new norms for blue- and white-collar workers are now included. The PRF, as its name implies, is intended primarily for research purposes (Paunonen & Ashton, 1998; Randolph, Smart, & Nelson, 1997). The JPI is intended for use on normal individuals to assess various aspects of personality including interpersonal, cognitive, and value orientations (Ashton, 1998; Mikulay & Goffin, 1998). Figure 13-4 shows a profile sheet from the Jackson Personality Inventory.

Items for the PRF and JPI are balanced in true–false keying. Unlike the scales of the MMPI, the PRF and JPI scales have no item overlap. Furthermore, the scales are relatively independent, with most intercorrelation coefficients at ±30 (see Table 13-6).

By combining theory with rigorous statistical procedures, these tests appear to have established a new trend in the construction of structured personality tests. As with other structured personality tests, however, the PRF has yet to challenge the MMPI and MMPI-2 in terms of use (both clinical and research) and status.

Self-Concept

Many personality tests have evolved from a theoretical strategy to evaluate *self-concept*—the set of assumptions a person has about himself or herself. Pre-

Jackson Personality Inventory

PROFILE SHEET: MALE

Name _____ Age _____ Form Administered _____

Date Tested _____ Other Information _____

NOTES

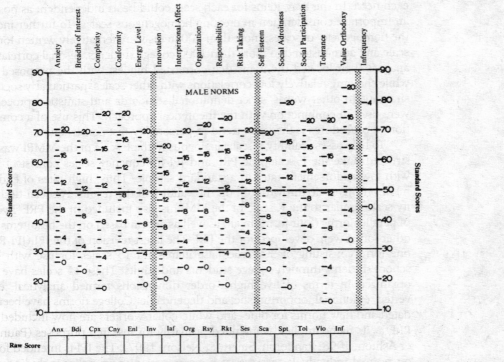

FIGURE 13-4 *Jackson Personality Inventory profile sheet.*
(Reprinted with permission of Sigma Assessment Systems, Inc., P.O. Box 610984, Port Huron, MI 48061-0984, copyright 1976.)

sumably, what you believe to be true about yourself will strongly affect your behavior. If you believe you are honest, then you will tend to act in conformity with this belief. If you believe you are effective with others, then you will more likely assume a leadership role than you would if you believed you were ineffective. The extent to which you use your leadership skills or other abilities is influenced by your self-concept.

Several adjective checklists have been developed to evaluate self-concept. In these, a list of adjectives is presented and subjects are asked to indicate which apply to them. Gough's Adjective Checklist, for instance, contains 300

TABLE 13-6

Trait Descriptions for the Jackson Personality Inventory

Scale trait	
Anxiety	Tendency to worry over minor matters
Breadth of interest	Curiosity; inquisitiveness
Complexity	Preference for abstract versus concrete thought
Conformity	Compliance; cooperativeness
Energy level	Energy; enthusiasm
Innovation	Originality; imagination
Interpersonal affect	Ability to identify with others
Organization	Planfulness; systematic versus disorganized
Responsibility	Responsibility; dependability
Risk taking	Reckless and bold versus cautious and hesitant
Self-esteem	Self-assured versus self-conscious
Social adroitness	Skill in persuading others
Social participation	Sociable and gregarious versus withdrawn and a loner
Tolerance	Broad-minded and open versus intolerant and uncompromising
Value orthodoxy	Moralistic and conventional versus modern and liberal
Infrequency	Validity of profile

adjectives in alphabetical order (Gough & Heilbrun, 1980). The Piers-Harris Children's Self-Concept Scale–Second Edition contains 80 self-statements (e.g., "I like my looks") and requires a "Yes" or "No" response (Piers, Harris, & Herzberg, 1999). Beyond checklists, the Tennessee Self-Concept Scale–Second Edition is a formal paper-and-pencil test that is designed to measure self-concept data (Fitts & Warren, 1996).

A novel approach to the assessment of self-concept is based on Carl Rogers's theory of the self. According to Rogers, the self is organized to remain consistent. New experiences that are consistent with a person's self-concept are easily integrated; experiences that are inconsistent with the self-concept tend to be denied or distorted. For example, if you view yourself as honest and moral and find yourself looking at another student's exam during the pressure of a difficult test, then you might try to distort the experience by thinking your classmate purposefully flashed her paper in front of your eyes.

To evaluate self-concept, Rogers uses a *Q-Sort technique*, in which a person receives a set of cards with appropriate self-statements such as "I am a good person." The individual then sorts the cards in piles from least to most personally descriptive. The person is asked to make two sorts of the cards. The first describes who the person really is (real self). The second describes what the person believes he or she should be (ideal self). Rogers's theory predicts that large discrepancies between the real and ideal selves reflect poor adjustment and low self-esteem (Rogers, 1961).

Combination Strategies

Clearly, the modern trend is to use a mix of strategies for developing structured personality tests. Indeed, almost all of the tests we have examined use factor analytic methods regardless of their main strategy. In this final section, we briefly discuss a test of positive personality characteristics that relies on a combination of strategies in scale development: the NEO Personality Inventories.

Positive Personality Measurement and the NEO-PI-R

The early history of personality measurement focused on negative characteristics such as anxiety, depression, and other manifestations of psychopathology. Although the reasons to assess negative affect and psychopathology are numerous and compelling, research suggests that it may be advantageous to evaluate individuals' positive characteristics in an attempt to understand the resources that an individual is endowed with and how this endowment affects behavior and well-being. Early research (Kobasa, 1979) suggested that stressful situations can be better endured by people high on the trait of "hardiness," defined as a way of characterizing stressful situations as meaningful, changeable, and challenging. Similarly, Bandura (1986) has espoused the view that individuals with a strong sense of "self-efficacy" or strong belief in their ability to organize resources and manage situations, are better able to persevere in the face of hardships. Assuming these authors are correct, the ability to live a satisfying life even in the midst of stress and hardship depends on positive personal characteristics rather than only on the *absence* of psychopathology or negative affect.

Although relatively little is known about the structure of positive human characteristics, their measurement, or their effects in mitigating adversity, there has been a recent surge of interest in positive personality (Diener, Sapyta, & Suh, 1998; Fredrickson & Joiner, 2002; Gaudreau, Blondin, & Lapierre, 2002; La Guardia, 2002; Pettit, Kline, Gencoz, Gencoz, & Joiner, 2002). Currently, several such measures of positive characteristics exist that evaluate traits such as conscientiousness, hope, optimism, and self-efficacy (Jerusalem & Schwarzer, 1992; Scheier, Carver, & Bridges, 1994; Viet & Ware 1989).

The NEO Personality Inventory (NEO-PI-R)

Forefront in the evaluation of positive personality characteristics has been the NEO Personality Inventory–Revised (Costa & McCrae, 1985, 1995; Costa, McCrae, & Jonsson, 2002; Costa, McCrae, & Kay, 1995; McCrae & Costa, 2003). The developers of this test used both factor analysis and theory in item development and scale construction. Quite ambitious, the NEO-PI-R attempts to provide a multipurpose inventory for predicting interests, health and illness behavior, psychological well-being, and characteristic coping styles. Of the personality tests, the NEO-PI-R has been among the most heavily researched during the last decade (e.g., Caprara, Barbaranelli, & Comrey, 1995; Huprich, 2003; Piedmont, 1998; Sherry, Henson, & Lewis, 2003).

Based on their review of extensive factor analytic studies and personality theory, the authors of the NEO-PI-R identified three broad domains: neuroticism (N), extroversion (E), and openness (O)—thus the name NEO. Each domain has six specific facets. Neuroticism (N) is defined primarily by anxiety and depression. The six facets of this domain are anxiety, hostility, depression, self-consciousness, impulsiveness, and vulnerability (describing people who do not feel safe). Extraversion (E) refers to the degree of sociability or withdrawal a person tends to exhibit. Its six facets are warmth, gregariousness, assertiveness, activity, excitement seeking, and positive emotions. Finally, openness (O) refers to the breadth of experience to which a person is amenable. Its six facets are fantasy, esthetics, feelings (openness to feelings of self and others), actions (willingness to try new activities), ideas (intellectual curiosity), and values. Figure 13-5 is a profile from the original NEO Personality Inventory.

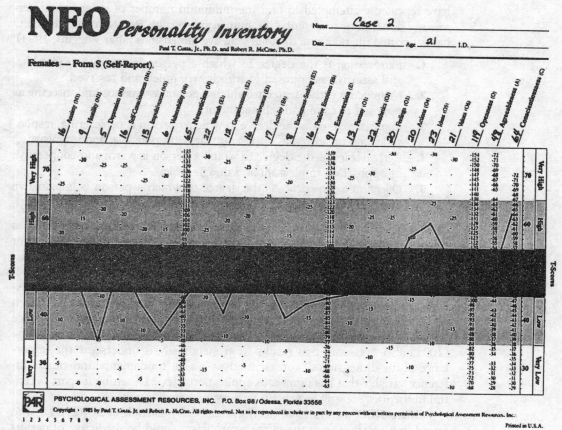

FIGURE 13-5   *NEO Personality Inventory profile sheet.*

(Reprinted by permission of Psychological Assessment Resources, Inc.)

Guided by personality theory and factor analytic findings, the authors of the NEO-PI-R took a rational approach in constructing items. For each of the 18 facets, 14 items were written. Seven were positively worded and seven negatively worded to create a balance. Subjects respond on a 5-point Likert format ranging from "strongly disagree" to "strongly agree." Initial items were then refined using a variety of statistical procedures.

Data in the manual and from a variety of research reports support the NEO-PI-R and its earlier version, the NEO. Factor analytic studies support the grouping of three major areas and associated facets. Reliabilities for the three domains are in the high .80's to the low .90's for both internal consistency and test–retest reliability. As is true of all major personality tests, reliabilities of the individual facets are lower. Predictive and concurrent validity studies are encouraging, with coefficients ranging into the .80's.

The NEO-PI-R has supported what is perhaps becoming one of the most accepted notions in personality and personality assessment—the *five-factor model* of personality (Costa et al., 2002). Recall that through factor analysis, researchers have repeatedly attempted to find the minimum number of independent personality dimensions to describe the human personality. Research with the NEO has supported the notion of the following five dimensions (after Wiggins, 1994):

1. *Extroversion* is the degree to which a person is sociable, leader-like, and assertive as opposed to withdrawn, quiet, and reserved.
2. *Neuroticism* is the degree to which a person is anxious and insecure as opposed to calm and self-confident.
3. *Conscientiousness* is the degree to which a person is persevering, responsible, and organized as opposed to lazy, irresponsible, and impulsive.
4. *Agreeableness* is the degree to which a person is warm and cooperative as opposed to unpleasant and disagreeable.
5. *Openness to experience* is the degree to which a person is imaginative and curious as opposed to concrete-minded and narrow in thinking.

Among positive characteristics, conscientiousness as identified on the NEO has been of particular interest. Conscientiousness is constructed of two major facets: achievement and dependability (Judge & Bono, 2000). Conscientiousness has been found to be valid as a positive predictor of performance in all occupations studied (Barrick et al., 2001; Barrick & Mount, 1991) and to be positively correlated with effective styles of coping with stressful situations (Haren & Mitchell, 2003; Hu et al., 2002) and with the Satisfaction with Life Scale (Hayes & Joseph, 2003), which is discussed below. Barrick, Mount, and Judge (2001) also suggested that results from meta-analysis underscore the importance of the dimension of conscientiousness as a "fundamental individual difference variable that has numerous applications" (p. 21), setting it apart as central in theories seeking to explain positive personality traits.

Other NEO factors have been evaluated by Barrick et al. (2001), who found that an absence of the factor neuroticism could be predictive of performance, though to a lesser degree than was conscientiousness, and with a less consistent relationship to specific performance criteria. Neuroticism was also negatively correlated with effective styles of coping with stressful situations (Hu et al., 2002). In addition, high neuroticism predicted lower scores on the Satisfaction with Life Scale (Hayes & Joseph, 2003).

The trait openness correlated significantly with crystallized intelligence (Bates & Sheiles, 2003), and the traits of openness, agreeableness, and extraversion were found to be beneficial in predicting success in specific job settings. In addition, Judge and Bono (2000) found that extraversion and agreeableness were effective in predicting transformational leadership.

Two converging areas of research with the NEO and NEO-PI-R discuss whether the five-factor model is actually the best way to categorize the minimum dimensions of human personality, and, if so, whether these dimensions hold up across cultures. Some researchers, including the authors of the Jackson Personality Inventory, have found support for an alternative model with a six-factor solution (Jackson, Paunonen, Fraboni, & Goffin, 1996; Rolland, Parker, & Stumpf, 1998). When six factors are found, five tend to parallel the "big five" of NEOPI- R (Detwiler & Ramanaiah, 1996). As of 2004, evidence for the six-factor model is weak and inconclusive (Heuchert, Parker, Stumpf, & Heinrich, 2000; Piedmont, 1998), and the amount of research attempting to confirm this alternative model has been subsiding.

In a related line of research, investigators have attempted to determine whether the five factors can be applied across cultures. Testing of this hypothesis is possible because the NEO-PI-R has been translated into numerous languages. The taxonomic structure of the NEO has become widely accepted because its five factors of personality have remained robust across cultures and measures (Egger, DeMay, Derksen, & van der Staak, 2003).

Finding that data from Filipino (Katigbak, Church, Guanzon-Lapena, Carlota, & del Pilar, 2002) and French translations tend to parallel U.S. data in support of the five-factor solution, some researchers have made the bold claim that the five-factor model is a "biologically based human universal" (McCrae, Costa, Del Pilar, Rolland, & Parker, 1998). This work is further supported by research on a Korean version of the NEO-PI-R (Spirrison & Choi, 1998; Yoon, Schmidt, & Ilies, 2002). However, Huang, Church, and Katigbak (1997) reported that even though the factor structure may be similar for Filipino populations, the mean scores tended to differ across populations. And in a study of approximately 3500 university students and employees in Kuwait, El-Ansarey (1997) reported that the NEO is not a valid or reliable inventory to assess personality in Kuwait society. Finally, a study of father–offspring and mother–offspring correlations indicated significant but "weak" family resemblances for the five personality dimensions (Bratko & Marusic, 1997).

Given its general amenability to cross-cultural and international studies, along with the potential significance of biologically based universal human traits, the NEO-PI-R is likely to engender considerable research for some time. Moreover, the NEO-PI-R reflects modern trends in personality-test construction by its reliance on theory, logic, and the liberal use of factor analysis and statistical approaches in test construction. It appears to be exceptionally promising for measuring a wide range of characteristics in the world community.

Frequently Used Measures of Positive Personality Traits

Rosenberg Self-Esteem Scale

The Rosenberg Self-Esteem Scale (Rosenberg, 1965) is widely used today in the United States (Heatherton & Wyland, 2003) and in various countries worldwide such as Germany (Gudjonsson & Sigurdsson, 2003), the United Kingdom (Schaefer, Koeter, Wouters, Emmelkamp, & Schene, 2003), and Turkey (Kugu, Akyuez, Dogan, Ersan, & Izgic, 2002). This scale measures global feelings of self-worth using 10 simple and straightforward statements that examinees rate on a 4-point Likert scale. The Rosenberg scale was created for use with adult populations. The scale has strong psychometric properties with considerable evidence of concurrent, known-groups, predictive, and construct validity. Internal reliability is .92, and test–retest reliability shows correlations of .85 and .88 over a 2-week period. One of the measure's greatest strengths is the amount of research conducted using a wide range of populations such as adolescents (Whiteside-Mansell & Corwyn, 2003; Yarcheski, Mahon, & Yarcheski, 2003) and individuals with eating disorders (Chen et al., 2003; Beato, Cano, & Belmonte, 2003) and hearing loss (Crowe, 2003).

General Self-Efficacy Scale

The General Self-Efficacy Scale (GSE) (Jerusalem & Schwarzer, 1992) was developed to measure an individual's belief in his or her ability to organize resources and manage situations, to persist in the face of barriers, and to recover from setbacks. The scale consists of 10 items and takes only 4 minutes to complete. Internal reliabilities for the GSE range from .76 to .90. Research from 25 countries indicates that the GSE is configurally equivalent across cultures and that the underlying construct of self-efficacy is global (Scholz, Dona, Sud, & Schwarzer, 2002). The GSE has been found to be positively correlated with favorable emotions, dispositional optimism, self-esteem, and work satisfaction. Negative correlations have been found with depression, anxiety, stress, burnout and health complaints.

Ego Resiliency Scale

This measure of ego resiliency or emotional intelligence was developed by Block and Kremen in 1996. The Ego Resiliency Scale (ER89) consists of 14 items, each answered using a 4-point Likert scale to rate statements such as "I am regarded as a very energetic person," "I get over my anger at someone reasonably quickly," and "Most of the people I meet are likeable." ER89 scores correlated highly with ratings for being sympathetic, considerate, dependable, responsible, cheerful, warm, assertive, socially adaptive, and not hostile. Fredrickson (2001) provided evidence of the scale's validity. The scales have been translated to into several languages, including French (Callahan et al.,

2001) and Korean (Min, Kim, Hwang, & Jahng, 1998), and are widely used in psychological research.

Dispositional Resilience Scale

The Dispositional Resilience Scale (DRS) was developed by Bartone, Wright, Ingraham, and Ursano (1989) to measure "hardiness," which is defined as the ability to view stressful situations as meaningful, changeable, and challenging. The coefficient alpha for the short version of the DRS, referred to as the Short Hardiness Scale, is .70., and the 3-week test–retest reliability coefficient is .78. In a study by Bartone (1995) using the Short Hardiness Scale, hardiness emerged as a significant predictor of grades among West Point cadets. Furthermore, research has indicated that those who measure high in hardiness have lower levels of worry (Hanton, Evans, & Neil, 2003); others have suggested that Hardiness, as measured by the DRS, can function as an index of mental health (Ramanaiah, Sharp, & Byravan, 1999).

Hope Scale

Snyder et al. (1991) proposed a cognitive model that characterizes hope as goal-driven energy (agency) in combination with the capacity to construct systems to meet goals (pathways) (Tennen, Affleck, & Tennen, 2002). The Hope Scale, developed by Snyder et al. (1991) measures the components of this cognitive model. The scale consists of 12 items that are rated on an 8-point Likert scale ranging from "definitely false" to "definitely true." Of the 12 items, four measure pathways, four measure agency, and four are distracters that are not scored. Snyder et al. (1991) have reported adequate internal reliability (alphas ranging from .74 to .84) and test–retest reliability (ranging from .76 to .82 over 10 weeks), and it appears that the Hope scale is particularly invulnerable to faking (Terrill, Friedman, Gottschalk, & Haaga, 2002). High scores on the scale have been shown to be predictive of college graduation (Snyder, Shorey, Cheavens, Pulvers, Adams, & Wiklund, 2002), healthy psychological adjustment, high achievement, good problem-solving skills, and positive health-related outcomes (Snyder, Sympson, Michael, & Cheavens, 2001). The Hope Scale takes 2 to 5 minutes to complete and is useful for examinees who read at the seventh-grade level or higher. Snyder and colleagues (1991) report that scores on the Hope Scale are positively correlated with measures of dispositional optimism and positive affect, and negatively correlated with hopelessness and depression. Magalette and Oliver (1999) indicate that the Hope Scale predicts variance independent of measures of self-efficacy and optimism, suggesting it measures a related, but not identical, construct.

Life Orientation Test–Revised (LOT-R)

The Life Orientation Test–Revised (LOT-R) is the most widely used self-report measure of dispositional optimism; which is defined as an individual's tendency to view the world and the future in positive ways. The LOT-R consists of 10 items developed to assess individual differences in generalized optimism versus pessimism. Items are answered on a 5-point response scale ranging from "strongly disagree" to "strongly agree." Cronbach's alpha is estimated at .82. Test–retest reliability for the LOT-R appears adequate ($r = .79$ over 4 weeks, as reported by Smith, Pope, Rhodewalt, and Poulton, 1989). The LOT-R and its predecessor, the LOT, have been used extensively in studies of stress and coping (Chico-Libran, 2002). Dispositional optimism scores correlate highly with self-esteem (.54), neuroticism (−.50), and trait anxiety (−.59) (Scheier, Carver, & Bridges, 1994). Scheier and Carver (1985) found that the LOT correlates negatively with depression (−.49), perceived stress (−.55), and hopelessness (−.47). A more recent study by Creed, Patton, and Bartrum replicate these findings (2002). In addition, the LOT-R is strongly positively correlated with active coping strategies (Chico-Libran, 2002) and with emotional regulation strategies (Scheier, Weintraub, & Carver, 1986). Although the Lot-R is widely used and has been shown to be a psychometrically sound instrument, it is notable that studies have suggested the LOT-R is more susceptible to faking good than are other tests of optimism (Terrill, Friedman, Gottschalk, & Haaga, 2002).

Satisfaction with Life Scale

The five-item Satisfaction with Life Scale (SWLS) (Diener, Emmons, Larsen, & Griffin, 1985) was developed as a multi-item scale for the overall assessment of life satisfaction as a cognitive–judgmental process, rather than for the measurement of specific satisfaction domains. This simple and flexible instrument is one of the most widely used measures of life-satisfaction or global well-being (Lucas, Deiner, & Larson, 2003). As an extremely popular research tool, the SWLS has been used to assess life satisfaction in many groups such as minorities (Constantine & Watt, 2002), cancer patients (Ferrario, Zotti, Massara, & Nuvolone, 2003), the elderly (Richeson & Thorson, 2002), immigrants (Neto, 2002), university students (Matheny et al., 2002), those suffering from traumatic injury (Corrigan, Bogner, Mysiw, Clinchot, & Fugate, 2001), and psychiatric patients (Arrindell, van Nieuwenhuizen, & Lutejin, 2001). Pons, Atienza, Balaguer, and Garcia-Merita (2002) report adequate internal reliability, and Diener et al. (1985) report satisfactory test–retest stability for a two-month period ($r = .82$). Others have shown that life satisfaction as measured by the SWLS can be relatively stable between years (Corrigan et al., 2001). Deiner et al. (1985) note that the inventory is designed to assess both fluctuations in life satisfaction and global ratings of this construct. A 6th- to 10th-grade reading level is necessary in order to complete the inventory accurately, and it takes only a minute or two to complete. The SWLS has been found to be positively correlated with healthy psychological and social functioning and negatively associated with measures of psychological distress (Arrindell et al., 2001).

Positive and Negative Affect Schedule

The Positive and Negative Affect Schedule (PANAS) was developed by Watson, Clark, and Tellegen (1988) to measure two orthogonal dimensions of affect. One of the most widely used measures of affect (Schmukle, Egloff, & Burns, 2002), the instrument has two scales—one for positive affect (PA) and one for negative affect (NA). Each scale consists of 10 adjectives such as *distressed, interested, guilty, afraid,* and *nervous.* The respondents are asked to rate the extent to which their moods have mirrored the feelings described by each adjective during a specified period of time. Watson et al. (1988) have presented extensive evidence demonstrating that the PANAS scales are internally consistent with coefficient alphas ranging from .84 to .90, and that they are largely uncorrelated with each other and stable over a 2-month period. Watson et al. (1988) have also presented evidence showing that the PANAS scales are valid measures of the underlying NA and PA constructs, with moderately high correlations between the NA scale of the PANAS and other measures of psychological distress. In addition, there is some evidence that the PANAS can be successfully translated into other languages and used across cultures and ethnic groups (Terraciano, McCrae, & Costa, 2003).

Coping Intervention for Stressful Situations

Active behavioral and cognitive coping strategies have been shown to be associated with measures of positive affect, and the strategy of coping by avoidance has been shown to be associated with high levels of negative affect (Pernas et al., 2001). Understanding individuals' styles of coping is key to understanding components of their personality. Endler and Parker (1990) created the Coping Intervention for Stressful Situations (CISS) as a 48-item questionnaire that measures coping styles by asking subjects how they would respond to a variety of stressful situations. Using a 5-point Likert scale with choices ranging from "not at all" to "very much," this inventory assesses individuals according to three basic coping styles: task-oriented coping, emotion-oriented coping, and avoidance-oriented coping.

Core Self-Evaluations

The widespread use of the NEO and other popular tests of positive characteristics has led to a deeper understanding of the fundamentals of personality. It has been suggested that measures of personality, to some extent, are all tapping into a single core construct (Judge, Erez, Bono, & Thoresen, 2002). Core Self-Evaluations is a framework for understanding and evaluating this core (Judge & Larsen, 2001). This broad-based personality construct is composed of four specific traits: self-esteem, generalized self-efficacy, neuroticism, and locus of control. The construct is not simply a descriptive system but explanatory of the dispositional source of life satisfaction and performance. In other words, the system not only describes the positive traits of individuals but also suggests ways in which these positive traits affect emotions and behaviors. Judge, Locke, Durham, and Kluger (1998) showed consistent effects of core evaluations on job satisfaction, with self-esteem and self-efficacy contributing most to the core self-evaluation conception. Heller, Judge, and Watson (2002) suggest that life satisfaction is largely the result of dispositional factors explained through core self-evaluations. Moreover, factor analytic evaluations of the core self-evaluation construct, though limited, have resulted in evidence of its validity for motivation, life satisfaction, and performance (Erez & Judge, 2001).

In light of all evidence to date, the core self-evaluation construct remains a better predictor of job performance than do individual traits and should give direction to further evaluation (Erez & Judge, 2001). When focusing on life or job satisfaction, a combination of the personality characteristics neuroticism and extroversion as well as measures of positive and negative affect appear to be best suited for prediction. Nevertheless, the interrelatedness among the various measures of positive characteristics remains largely unexplored and has provoked many questions.

Future of Positive Personality Research

Among the questions raised in the area of positive personality research is whether the various measures are capturing a series of unique and independent traits or are more generally related to a single underlying construct. There also is debate about whether positive characteristics are independent constructs or merely represent the absence of negative traits. The question also has been raised whether the presence of positive characteristics mitigate detrimental effects of negative characteristics, and, if so, to what extent.

In an attempt to answer these questions, Saccuzzo, Kewley, Johnson, Larson and colleagues (2003) analyzed the results of 15 separate tests of positive personality completed by 313 college-age students. The findings were clear in demonstrating that the various measures of positive affect, from hope through resiliency, are best conceptualized as a single construct or dimension. These measures shared considerable common variance, with no evidence at all for independence. Thus, regardless of what they are called, measures of positive affect measure just that and at varying levels of success. It appears to be feasible to create a robust single measure by locating those items with the highest correlation with the general factor. Furthermore, given the consistency among the measures, it would appear as though positive affect can be reliably and validly measured with relative economy in terms of number of items.

The data likewise indicated that measures of negative affect constitute a single dimension. Although there may be some utility from a clinical perspective in distinguishing among constructs such as anxiety and depression, negative affect can best be thought of as tapping into a broader, more general construct. This negative affect construct, however, has a strong and negative relationship with its positive affect counterpart.

There was strong empirical support to indicate that measures of positive and negative affect fall along a continuum ranging from the highest measures of positive affect through the highest measures of negative affect. In general, individuals who are high on positive are low on negative. Conversely, individuals who are high on negative are not high on positive. Thus, when measures of both positive and negative affect were evaluated in a single factor analysis, positive measures consistently loaded positively, while negative measures loaded negatively.

In effect, scoring high on measures of positive affect has the same meaning as scoring low on measures of negative affect. Conversely, scoring high on negative affect has the same meaning as scoring low on measures of positive affect. However, there are notable exceptions.

Despite the clear relationship between measures of positive and negative affect, there was also strong support for the existence of subgroups that do not conform to the general pattern. In particular, there is a subgroup that, although high on negative affect, also scores high on measures of positive affect. Such individuals are clearly distinguishable from individuals who fit the general pattern.

Differences between participants high on negative affect who either score high or low on positive affect suggest that the presence of positive affect might mitigate or negate the deleterious effects of negative affect. For example, individuals in the mixed group who scored high on negative and relatively high on positive affect scores showed more effective coping strategies, less neuroticism, and greater degrees of conscientiousness.

These findings confirm other research that suggests the understanding of personal characteristics is improved by considering both the positive and negative affect dimensions. At the simplest level, individuals who score high on positive and low on negative represent those best able to function. Conversely, those high on negative affect and low on positive will tend to have a diminished capacity to deal with stressful situations. However, within the negative affect group there may be a significant number of individuals whose scores in the positive dimension have a counterbalancing effect. Obviously, individuals in the mixed category should be further studied in order to confirm the findings of this study. Clearly, positive personality characteristics and their measurement are only beginning to be understood, and the decades ahead should prove interesting to those following the progress of this research.

SUMMARY   Structured personality tests are self-report procedures that provide statements to which the subject must either respond "True" or "False" ("Yes" or "No") or choose the most characteristic of two or more alternatives. These tests are highly structured and provide a definite, unambiguous stimulus for the subject. Scoring is straightforward and usually involves summing the number of items marked in a scored direction.

The original pressure to develop personality tests came from the demands created by the military in World War I for a screening instrument to identify emotionally unstable recruits who might break down under the pressures of combat. The first structured personality instrument, the Woodworth Personal Data Sheet, was based on a logical-content strategy in which items were interpreted in terms of face validity.

Not long after, tests based on the logical-content strategy fell into disrepute. The problem with these tests was the numerous assumptions underlying them, including the following: the subject complies with the instructions and provides an honest response; the subject understands the items and is an accurate observer capable of evaluating his or her own behavior and responding in a nondefensive manner; and the subject, test constructor, and test interpreter all define the questions in the same way. A wide body of research seriously questioned all of these assumptions.

The first major advance in structured personality assessment came with the MMPI, which used a strategy involving criterion groups. In this criterion-group strategy, groups with known characteristics were contrasted with a control population. Items that distinguished the criterion group were included in a scale that was then cross-validated on an independent sample of criterion and control subjects. The MMPI revitalized structured personality tests. Rather than making assumptions about the meaning of a subject's response to a test item, it attempted to discern empirically the response's meaning. In the criterion-group strategy, the content of the item is irrelevant. If a subject marks "True" to the statement "I hear loud voices when I'm alone," testers do not assume that he or she really does hear loud voices when alone.

In addition to its advantages over logical-content tests in avoiding assumptions, the MMPI featured validity scales. The two most important MMPI validity scales are the K scale, which measures social desirability, and the F scale, which consists of 64 infrequently endorsed items to pick out subjects who take an unusual or unconventional approach to testing. Theoretically, excessively high scores on the validity scales can identify biased results, thus avoiding the problems of faking and social desirability inherent in the logical-content approach.

Despite its extensive use, researchers' widespread interest in it, and its recent restandardization (the MMPI-2), the MMPI has its problems, including item overlap among the scales, an imbalance in true–false keying, high intercorrelation among the scales, and a lack of generalizability across demographic variables.

The factor analytic strategy of test construction attempts to overcome some of the problems inherent in the criterion strategy. Factor analytic strategies try to find areas of common variance in order to locate the minimum number of variables or factors that account for a set of intercorrelated data. R. B. Cattell has been the most important representative of this approach.

Using the factor analytic approach to find the common variance of all trait-descriptive terms in the dictionary, Cattell reduced an original pool of more than 4000 items to 16 and created the 16PF. Great care was taken to provide adequate norms. Nine separate normative samples based on demographic variables, plus an age-correction scale, are available. Also available are three sets of parallel forms that accommodate different levels of subjects' vocabulary proficiency.

The EPPS has found its primary use in counseling centers. It employs a forced-choice strategy that requires subjects to choose the more applicable of two statements. Ipsative scores, which use the subject as his or her own frame of reference, express results in terms of the relative strength of a need.

Several tests have been developed with the theoretical strategy. Among these are the Q-sort technique, which measures self-concept.

The modern trend is to use a combination of strategies in scale construction. This approach is used in the NEO Personality Inventory–Revised (NEO-PI-R), which is the most commonly used measure of positive personality characteristics. Of the structured personality tests, the NEO, along with the MMPI-2, promise to be the dominant tests of the 21st century.

WEB ACTIVITY

For interesting and relevant Web sites, check the following:

http://assessments.ncs.com/assessments/tests/mcmi_2.htm
Millon Clinical Multiaxial Inventory-II (MCMI-II)

http://assessments.ncs.com/assessments/tests/mmpi_2.htm
Minnesota Multiphasic Personality Inventory-2 (MMPI-2)

www.mmpi-info.com/welcome.html
MMPI, MMPI-2, and MMPI-A information site

www.personalitytest.net/ipip/ipipneo120.htm
A broad-bandwidth, public-domain, personality inventory measuring the lower-level facets of several five-factor models

www.lib.umich.edu/taubman/info/testsandmeasurement.htm
Tests and measurements

www.gsu.edu/~dschjb/wwwmbti.html
GSU Master Teacher Program: On learning styles

www.cps.nova.edu/~cpphelp/CPI.html
The California Psychological Inventory

www.paris95.k12.il.us/mayo/invent.html
Career Interest inventories

www.cps.nova.edu/~cpphelp/CPS.html
Carlson Psychological Survey (CPS)

http://choo.fis.utoronto.ca/DB/tsld010.htm
Myers-Briggs Type Indicator

www.personalitypage.com/
Myers-Briggs test online

CHAPTER 14

Projective Personality Tests

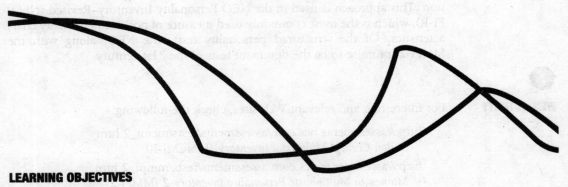

LEARNING OBJECTIVES

When you have completed this chapter, you should be able to:

☐ Define the projective hypothesis

☐ Identify five individuals who played a dominant role·in the development of the Rorschach

☐ Describe the Rorschach stimuli

☐ Briefly describe Rorschach administration and scoring

☐ List the pros and cons of the Rorschach

☐ Describe the Holtzman

☐ Describe the TAT stimuli

☐ Briefly describe TAT administration

☐ Identify the factors that should be considered in evaluating the TAT

☐ List some of the major similarities and differences between the Rorschach and the TAT

A few years ago, the wife of an army sergeant sued him for divorce after 14 years of marriage. She claimed that her husband was "mentally unstable and deranged." She accused him of beating her for no apparent reason. The sergeant went to a psychologist to "prove" his sanity. In addition to an interview, an ability test (the WAIS-III), and an objective personality test (the MMPI-2), the psychologist administered the Rorschach inkblot test. The Rorschach is one of the best known as well as the most controversial of the projective personality tests. According to the psychologist's evaluation, the Rorschach indicated that the sergeant was free of unusual or bizarre thought processes. The psychologist concluded that, based on the Rorschach and other test results, the sergeant was mentally stable, contrary to his wife's claims.

When the matter went to court, the psychologist was called to the witness stand. The cross-examination by the wife's attorney proceeded as follows:

Attorney: Based on the Rorschach and other tests, you concluded that this man is mentally stable.

Psychologist: I did.

Attorney: What is the Rorschach?

Psychologist: The Rorschach is a projective psychological test that contains 10 cards with inkblots on them. Five of the inkblots are black and gray; two are black, gray, and red; and the remaining three are composed of a variety of pastel colors of various shades.

Attorney: How do you administer a Rorschach?

Psychologist: The subject—that is, the person taking the test—is shown each of the cards, one at a time. The subject is required to state what the inkblot might be.

Attorney: You mean to say that you can tell whether a person is sane or insane by the way he or she interprets 10 black, gray, and variously colored inkblots?

Psychologist: That is correct.

Attorney: Your honor, this is ridiculous. For 14 years, a man beats his wife for no apparent reason, but the psychologist says he's normal because he passed an inkblot test!

Projective personality tests such as the Rorschach are among the most controversial and most misunderstood psychological tests (Aronow, Reznikoff, & Moreland, 1995; Blatt, 1990; Lilienfeld, Wood, & Garb, 2000). The Rorschach has been vigorously attacked on a variety of scientific and statistical grounds (Dawes, 1999; Hunsley & Bailey, 1999; Wood, Nezworski, & Stejskal, 1996; Wood, Lilienfeld, Nezworski, & Garb, 2003), yet surveys of psychological test usage in the United States consistently find that the Rorschach continues to be one of the most widely used tests in clinical settings (see Groth-Marnat, 1999; Wood et al., 2003). In addition, it was found that five projective techniques (two of which were the Rorschach and the TAT), were among the 10 testing instruments most frequently used in clinical settings (Watkins, Campbell, Nieberding, & Hallmark, 1995). The Rorschach is used extensively by psychologists and widely taught in doctoral training programs for clinical psychologists (Meloy & Singer, 1991; Piotrowski, 1984; Piotrowski, Sherry, & Keller, 1985; Ritzler & Alter, 1986; Hunsley & DiGiulio, 2001; Weiner, 2003). Moreover, our survey of the testing literature revealed that between 1996 and 2003 the Rorschach was by far the most-referenced projective personality test and continued to rank third only to the MMPI/MMPI-2 and the NEO in number of research citations.

Feelings against the Rorschach run so high that reviewers of this book have threatened that they would not use it if it includes a discussion of the Rorschach! Why is there such a widespread acceptance of projective tests such as the Rorschach, in spite of severe attacks from prominent researchers and psychometricians? And what among clinicians is the true story? To answer these questions, we need to begin with a look at the rationale for and the nature of projective tests.

The Projective Hypothesis

Numerous definitions have been advanced for the primary rationale underlying projective tests, known as the **projective hypothesis,** with credit for the most complete analysis usually given to L. K. Frank (1939). Simply stated, this hypothesis proposes that when people attempt to understand an ambiguous or vague stimulus, their interpretation of that stimulus reflects their needs, feelings, experiences, prior conditioning, thought processes, and so forth. When a frightened little boy looks into a dark room and sees a huge shadow that he interprets as a monster, he is projecting his fear onto the shadow. The shadow itself is neutral—neither good nor bad, neither fearsome nor pretty. What the child really sees is a reflection of the inner workings of his mind.

The concept of projection is not new. Exner (1993) notes, for example, that Leonardo da Vinci used ambiguous figures to evaluate young art students. The artist presented potential students with an ambiguous figure and presumably evaluated their imaginations according to the quality of the artistic forms the students created from it. The concept of projection is also reflected in Shakespeare's "Nothing is either good or bad, but thinking makes it so."

Although what the subject finally sees in a stimulus is assumed to be a reflection of personal qualities or characteristics, some responses may be more revealing than others. If, for example, you say that a round figure is a ball, you provide a relatively straightforward interpretation of the stimulus. The stimulus itself has little ambiguity; it is round and shaped like a ball. In viewing this stimulus, a high percentage of people probably see, though not necessarily report, a ball. Theoretically, even this simple response, however, can reveal a lot about you. For example, your response may indicate that you accurately perceive simple objects in the external environment and are willing to provide a conventional response. Suppose, however, you said that this same stimulus looked like a square peg in a round hole. Assuming the stimulus is actually round and contains no lines or shapes resembling a square peg, your perception of the stimulus does not conform to its actual property (roundness). Thus, your perceptions in general may not be accurate. Your response may also indicate that you are unwilling to provide the obvious, conventional response. Or it may indicate that you feel out of place, like a square peg in a round hole. If any or none of these interpretations have validity, then the Rorschach has a problem because there would be no clear way to interpret it.

Of course, examiners can never draw absolute, definite conclusions from any single response to an ambiguous stimulus. They can only hypothesize what a test response means. Even the same response to the same stimulus may have several possible meanings, depending on the characteristics of the people who make the response. A problem with all projective tests is that many factors can influence one's response to them. For example, a response may reflect a recent experience or an early experience one has forgotten. It may reflect something one has witnessed (a bloody murder) or something one imagines (flunking out of college) rather than something one has actually experienced directly. It may reflect day-to-day problems, such as an argument with a boyfriend or girlfriend. With all of these possible factors influencing a response, it is no wonder that the validity of projective tests has been seriously questioned. Arguably, the interpretation of projective tests requires highly trained, experienced practitioners, but even an expert can easily draw the wrong conclusions. Further, even the most experienced experts often disagree among themselves (Exner, 1995; Nezworski & Wood, 1995). As in the example at the beginning of the chapter, Rorschach users claim that they can use projective tests to draw valid conclusions. Researchers, however, remain firmly unconvinced (Sechrest, Stickle, & Stewart, 1998; Wood et al., 1996; Wood et al., 2003). As you will see, the researchers have the better argument.

The Rorschach Inkblot Test

As an example of a psychological test based on the projective hypothesis, the Rorschach has few peers. Indeed, no general discussion of psychological tests is complete without reference to the Rorschach, despite its scientific inadequacies. The Rorschach has been called everything from a psychological X-ray (Piotrowski, 1980) and "perhaps the most powerful psychometric instrument ever envisioned" (Board of Professional Affairs, 1998, p. 392) to an instrument that "bears a charming resemblance to a party game" (Wood et al., 2003, p.1) and should be "banned in clinical and forensic settings" (Garb, 1999, p. 316). Strangely, the Rorschach is both revered and reviled.

Historical Antecedents

Like most concepts, the notion of using inkblots to study human functioning did not simply appear out of thin air. More than 25 years before the birth of Herman Rorschach, the originator of the test that bears his name, J.

Kerner (1857) noted that individuals frequently report idiosyncratic or unique personal meanings when viewing inkblot stimuli. The wide variety of possible responses to inkblots does provide a rationale for using them to study individuals. Indeed, Binet proposed the idea of using inkblots to assess personality functioning (Binet & Henri, 1896) when Rorschach was only 10 years old. Several historic investigators then supported Binet's position concerning the potential value of inkblots for investigating human personality (Dearborn, 1897; Kirkpatrick, 1900). Their support led to the publication of the first set of standardized inkblots by Whipple (1910). Rorschach, however, receives credit for finding an original and important use for inkblots: identifying psychological disorders. His investigation of inkblots began in 1911 and culminated in 1921 with the publication of his famous book *Psychodiagnostik*. A year later, he suddenly and unexpectedly died of a serious illness at age 37.

Rorschach's work was viewed with suspicion and even disdain right from the outset. Not even the sole psychiatric journal of Switzerland, Rorschach's homeland, reviewed *Psychodiagnostik* (Allison, Blatt, & Zimet, 1968). In fact, only a few foreign reviews of the book appeared, and these tended to be critical. When David Levy first brought Rorschach's test to the United States from Europe, he found a cold, unenthusiastic response. U.S. psychologists judged the test to be scientifically unsound, and psychiatrists found little use for it. Nevertheless, the use of the test gradually increased, and eventually it became quite popular.

Five individuals have played dominant roles in the use and investigation of the Rorschach. One of these, Samuel J. Beck, was a student of Levy's. Beck was especially interested in studying certain patterns or, as he called them, "configurational tendencies" in Rorschach responses (Beck, 1933). Beck, who died in 1980, eventually wrote several books on the Rorschach and influenced generations of Rorschach practitioners (Beck, 1944, 1945, 1952). Like Beck, Marguerite Hertz stimulated considerable research on the Rorschach during the years when the test first established its foothold in the United States (Hertz, 1937, 1938). Bruno Klopfer, who immigrated to the United States from Germany, published several key Rorschach books and articles and played an important role in the early development of the test (Klopfer & Davidson, 1944; Klopfer & Kelley, 1942). Zygmunt Piotrowski (1947, 1964) and David Rapaport (Rapaport, Gill, & Schafer 1945–1946) came somewhat later than Beck, Hertz, and Klopfer, but like them continues to exert an influence on clinical practitioners who use the Rorschach in spite of overwhelming contrary evidence. The development of the Rorschach can be attributed primarily to the efforts of these five individuals. Like most experts, however, the five often disagreed. Their disagreements are the source of many of the current problems with the Rorschach (Hunsley & Bailey, 1999). Each expert developed a unique system of administration, scoring, and interpretation; they all found disciples who were willing to accept their biases and use their systems.

Stimuli, Administration, and Interpretation

Rorschach constructed each stimulus card by dropping ink onto a piece of paper and folding it. The result was a unique, bilaterally symmetrical form on a white background. After experimenting with thousands of such blots, Rorschach selected 20. However, the test publisher would only pay for 10. Of the 10 finally selected, five were black and gray, two contained black, gray, and red, and three contained pastel colors of various shades. An example of a Rorschach card is shown in Figure 14-1.

The Rorschach is an individual test. In the administration procedure, each of the 10 cards is presented to the subject with minimum structure. After preliminary remarks concerning the purpose of testing, the examiner hands the first card to the subject and asks something like, "What might this be?" No restriction is placed on the type of response permitted, and no clues are given concerning what is expected. If the subject asks for guidance or clarification, the examiner gives little information. If, for example, the subject asks, "Do I use the whole thing or just part of it?" the examiner replies, "As you like" or "Whatever you choose." Anxious subjects or individuals who are made uncomfortable by unstructured situations frequently ask questions, attempting to find out as much as possible before committing themselves. The examiner, however, must not give any cues that might reveal the nature of the expected response. Furthermore, in view of the finding that the examiner may inadvertently reveal information or reinforce certain types of responses through facial expressions and other forms of nonverbal communication (E. Lord, 1950; Wood, Lilienfeld, Garb, & Nezworski, 2000a), Exner (1993) advocated an administration procedure in which the examiner sits next to the subject rather than face-to-face as in Rapaport's system (Blais, Norman, Quintar, & Herzog, 1995).

Notice that the examiner is nonspecific and largely vague. This lack of clear structure or direction with regard to demands and expectations is a primary feature of all projective tests. The idea is to provide as much ambiguity as pos-

FIGURE 14-1

A Rorschach-type image is created by dropping ink onto a piece of paper and folding it. This is a reproduction of an actual card from the Rorschach.

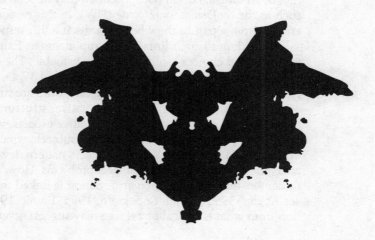

sible so that the subject's response reflects only the subject. If the examiner inadvertently provides too many guidelines, the response may simply reflect the subject's tendency to perform as expected or to provide a socially desirable response, as discussed in Chapter 13. Therefore, an administration that provides too much structure is antithetical to the main idea behind projective tests.

Each card is administered twice. During the *free-association* phase of the test, the examiner presents the cards one at a time. If the subject gives only one response to the first card, then the examiner may say, "Some people see more than one thing here." The examiner usually makes this remark only once. If the subject rejects the card—that is, states that he or she sees nothing—then the examiner may reply, "Most people do see something here, just take your time." The examiner records every word and even every sound made by the subject verbatim. In addition, the examiner records how long it takes a subject to respond to a card (reaction time) and the position of the card when the response is made (upside down, sideways).

In the second phase, the *inquiry,* the examiner shows the cards again and scores the subject's responses. Responses are scored according to at least five dimensions, including location (where the perception was seen), determinant (what determined the response), form quality (to what extent the response matched the stimulus properties of the inkblot), content (what the perception was), and frequency of occurrence (to what extent the response was popular or original; popular responses occur once in every three protocols on average). A complete discussion of these special scoring categories is beyond the scope of this text. For more information on scoring and interpretation, see Exner's (1993) Rorschach textbook.

In scoring for location, the examiner must determine where the subject's perception is located on the inkblot. To facilitate determining this location, a small picture of each card, known as the *location chart,* is provided. If necessary, on rare occasions, an examiner may give a subject a pencil and ask the subject to outline the perception on the location chart. In scoring for location, the examiner notes whether the subject used the whole blot (W), a common detail (D), or an unusual detail (Dd). Location may be scored for other factors as well, such as the *confabulatory response* (DW). In this response, the subject overgeneralizes from a part to the whole. We discuss this response in detail later.

According to such Rorschach proponents as Exner, a summary of a subject's location choices can be extremely valuable. The examiner may, for example, determine the number and percentage of W, D, and Dd responses. This type of information, in which scoring categories are summarized as a frequency or percentage, is known as the quantitative, structural, or statistical aspect of the Rorschach as opposed to the qualitative aspects, which pertain to the content and sequence of responses. Normal subjects typically produce a balance of W, D, and Dd responses. When a subject's pattern deviates from the typical balance, the examiner begins to suspect problems. However, no one has been able to demonstrate that a particular deviation is linked to a specific problem (e.g., see Acklin, 1995; Bartell & Solanto, 1995; Frank, 1995). A substantial deviation from what is typical or average may suggest several possibilities. The protocol may be invalid. The subject may be original or unconventional and thus fail to respond according to the typical pattern. Or the subject may have a perceptual problem associated with certain types of brain damage or severe emotional problems. The relative proportion of W, D, and Dd location choices varies with maturational development. Ames, Metraux, and Walker (1971), for example, noted that W responses occur most frequently in the 3- to 4-year-old group. As the child grows older, the frequency of W responses gradually decreases until young adulthood. Theoretically, adult protocols with a preponderance of W responses suggest immaturity or low mental age.

Like other quantitative aspects of the Rorschach, location patterns and frequencies have been studied in experimental investigations. Presumably, these investigations provide information about the meaning of various response patterns and thus contribute to the construct validity of the Rorschach. Unfortunately, many of the results of the studies conflict with the opinions of experts. Furthermore, many studies that support the validity of the Rorschach have been denounced as unreplicated, methodologically unsound, and inconsistent (Wood et al., 2003).

Having ascertained the location of a response, the examiner must then determine what it was about the inkblot that led the subject to see that particular percept. This factor is known as the *determinant*. One or more of at least four properties of an inkblot may determine or lead to a response: its form or shape, its perceived movement, its color, and its shading. If the subject uses only the form of the blot to determine a response, then the response is scored F and is called a *pure form response*. Responses are scored for form when the subject justifies or elaborates a response by statements such as "it looks like one," "It is shaped like one," or "Here are the head, legs, feet, ears, and wings." In all of these examples, the response is determined exclusively on the basis of shape. In addition to form, a perception may be based on movement, color, shading, or some combination of these factors. These other determinants can be further subdivided. Movement may be human (M), such as two people hugging; animal (FM), such as two elephants playing; or inanimate (m), such as sparks flying. As you can see, the scoring can become quite complex.

As with location, several attempts have been made to link the presence (or absence) of each determinant as well as the relative proportion of the various determinants to various hypotheses and empirical findings (Exner, 1999; Perry, Sprock, Schaible, & McDougall, 1995). Consider the movement response. Most Rorschach practitioners agree that whether and how a subject uses movement can be revealing. Like most Rorschach indicators, however, the meaning of movement is unclear because of disagreements among experts and contradictory or unclear experimental findings. Many experts believe that the movement response is related to motor activity and impulses. Numerous movement responses, for example, may suggest high motor activity or strong impulses. The ratio of M (human movement) to FM (animal movement) responses has been linked by some experts to a person's control and expression of internal impulses.

A special type of movement response is called *cooperative movement*. Such responses involve positive interaction between two or more humans or animals

(Exner, 1999). Exner and colleagues believe that such responses provide information about a subject's attitude concerning how people interact. One study, for example, reported that individuals who give more than two such responses tended to be rated by others as fun to be with, easy to be around, and trustworthy (Exner & Farber, 1983). The conclusion seemed to be that such responses were positive. Subsequent research, however, could not confirm the initial findings (Shaffer & Erdberg, 1996). In a study of 20 individuals who had committed sexual homicide, 14 gave cooperative-movement responses. Clearly, there is no simple or clear-cut approach to Rorschach interpretation (Gacano & Meloy, 1994). As such, critics have analogized Rorschach interpretations to reading tea leaves.

As you think about the inferences that can be drawn from the Rorschach, keep in mind that they are at best hypotheses. An examiner who blindly accepts one interpretation of a particular quantitative aspect must be making a big mistake. Certainly, one who blindly accepts a particular interpretation of a Rorschach pattern is ignoring the available literature. Focused Example 14-1 explains some of the ways that highly trained experts use the Rorschach to make clinically useful inferences.

Identifying the determinant is the most difficult aspect of Rorschach administration. Because of the difficulties of conducting an adequate inquiry and the current lack of standardized administration procedures, examiners vary widely in the conduct of their inquiries (Blais et al., 1995). It has been known for years that examiner differences influence the subject's response (Gibby, Miller, & Walker, 1953; Hartman, 2001). As a result of this problem, much of the Rorschach literature is confounded by differences in administration and scoring alone, let alone interpretation. This is one reason why reliable experimental investigations of the Rorschach are rare (Lewandowski & Saccuzzo, 1976).

On the other hand, scoring content is relatively simple. Most authorities list content categories such as human (H), animal (A), and nature (N). An inquiry is generally not necessary to determine content.

Similarly, most experts generally agree on the so-called populars, those responses frequently given for each card. Exner's (1993, 2003) Comprehensive System, which includes as populars only those responses that occur once in three protocols on the average, provides a standardized method for scoring populars.

Form quality is the extent to which the percept (what the subject says the inkblot is) matches the stimulus properties of the inkblot. Scoring form quality is difficult. Some experts argue that if the examiner can also see the percept, then the response has adequate form quality, but if the examiner cannot see it, then the response has poor form quality and is scored F−. Obviously, such a subjective system is grossly inadequate because scoring depends on the intelligence, imagination, skill, and psychological state of the examiner. Exner's (1993) comprehensive system, which uses the usual frequency of the occurrence of various responses in evaluating form quality, is more objective and thus more scientifically acceptable than the subjective method.

Focused Example 14-1

EXPERT INTERPRETATION OF THE RORSCHACH

 Rorschach experts resolutely maintain that, if properly used, the Rorschach can be an invaluable tool. Modern scientists are completely unconvinced. At best, Rorschach interpretations should be viewed only as tentative hypotheses. Hypotheses that are confirmed by other sources of data usually have more validity than do those that cannot be confirmed. When the Rorschach is rigidly or blindly interpreted, scientific skepticism is justified. When the Rorschach is interpreted cautiously and in conjunction with other sources of data, however, a highly trained expert may surprise even the most critical scientist.

When Dennis Saccuzzo had a predoctoral internship at a Veterans Administration hospital, Marguerite Hertz, one of the five original Rorschach experts, was a consultant there. Every second Thursday of the month, Hertz would interpret an actual Rorschach protocol presented by interns or staff members. Her interpretations were so detailed and exact that Saccuzzo, who was inexperienced with the Rorschach, doubted their validity. When other interns or staff agreed with everything Hertz said, he became even more skeptical. He thought they were merely awed by Hertz's reputation and were afraid to challenge this spirited woman.

When Saccuzzo's turn came to present a Rorschach, he used the protocol of a patient he had been seeing in psychotherapy for several months. He knew this patient well and fully expected Hertz to make errors in her interpretation. He was surprised, however, when Hertz was able to describe this patient after reading only the first four or five responses and examining the quantitative summary of the various scoring categories and ratios. Within 25 minutes, Hertz told him not only what he already knew but also things he had not seen but were obviously true once pointed out. This experience was most unsettling. Having started with a strong bias against the Rorschach, and still doubting its scientific underpinnings, he could not dismiss what Hertz had done.

Later, he came to believe that Hertz's secret was her experience. She had given or studied so many Rorschachs that she had great insight into the meaning of each pattern. After having seen the Rorschach patterns of dozens, if not hundreds, of disturbed individuals, she could identify a problem. Indeed, her knowledge and experience were so broad that she could even distinguish specific types of disturbances based on the Rorschach.

However, until the experts can specify the exact processes underlying correct interpretations from the Rorschach, the criticism from scientists will continue, as Hertz herself (1986), who has repeatedly called for innovation and rigorous research, has acknowledged.

Table 14-1 summarizes our discussion of Rorschach scoring. Though the discussion has been incomplete, we hope it has shown how a projective test can be scored to yield quantitative data. These quantitative data, in turn, permit the accumulation of norms for particular groups. If subjects deviate from the typical or expected performance, then the examiner must determine the reason underlying the deviation. Proponents argue that this process can lead to valuable information about individuals (Acklin, 1995; Groth-Marnat, 1999; Hilsenroth, Fowler, & Padawer, 1998).

Rorschach scoring is obviously difficult and complex. Use of the Rorschach requires advanced graduate training. You should not attempt to score or use a

TABLE 14-1
Summary of Rorschach Scoring

I. Location

Definition:	Where on the blot was the percept seen (located)?
*Types:**	1. Whole (W). The whole inkblot was used.
	2. Common detail (D). A common or well-defined part of the inkblot was used.
	3. Unusual detail (Dd). An unusual or poorly defined part of the inkblot was used.

II. Determinant

Definition:	What feature of the inkblot determined the response?
*Types:**	1. Form (F). The shape or outline of the blot determined the response ("because the inkblot looked like one").
	2. Movement (M, FM, m). Movement was seen ("two animals walking up a hill").
	3. Color (C). Color played a role in determining the response ("a brown bear," "pink clouds").
	4. Shading (T). Texture or shading features played a role in determining the response ("a furry bear because of the shading").

III. Form quality

Definition:	To what extent did the percept match the stimulus properties of the inkblot?
*Types:**	1. F+ or +. Percept matched stimulus properties of the inkblot in an exceptionally good way.
	2. F. Percept matched stimulus properties of the inkblot.
	3. F− or −. Percept matched the stimulus properties of the inkblot poorly.

IV. Content

Definition:	What was the percept?
*Types:**	1. Human (H).
	2. Animal (A).
	3. Nature (N).

V. Popular-original

Definition:	How frequently is the percept seen in normative samples? (Popular responses are seen in about one of every three protocols.)

*This list is incomplete and does not cover the entire range of possibilities. The information given is designed to illustrate quantitative scoring of a projective test.

Rorschach without formal and didactic graduate instruction and supervised experience. Without this detailed training, you might make serious errors because the procedure is so complex.

Rorschach protocols may be evaluated not only for its quantitative data but also for qualitative features, including specific content (Moreland, Reznikoff, & Aronow, 1995) and sequence of responses (Exner, 1999). One important aspect of a qualitative interpretation is an evaluation of content reported frequently by emotionally disturbed, mentally retarded, or brain-damaged individuals but infrequently by the normal population. Such responses have been used to discriminate normal from disordered conditions (Moreland et al., 1995).

Confabulatory responses also illustrate the idea behind qualitative interpretations. In this type of response, the subject overgeneralizes from a part to a whole: "It looked like my mother because of the eyes. My mother has large piercing eyes just like these." Here the subject sees a detail—"large piercing eyes"—and overgeneralizes so that the entire inkblot looks like his or her mother. Although one such response has no clear or specific meaning, experts believe that the more confabulatory responses a subject makes, the more likely that she or he is in a disordered state.

Psychometric Properties

Clinical validation. The mystique and popularity of the Rorschach became widespread in the 1940s and 1950s. This popularity was widely based on clinical evidence gathered from a select group of Rorschach virtuosos who had the ability to dazzle with blind analysis, a process by which a clinician conducts a Rorschach analysis of a patient with no former knowledge of the patient's history or diagnosis and then validates the results of the Rorschach evaluation by checking other sources (Klopfer & Davidson, 1962). For those who were interested in forming an opinion about the validity of the Rorschach, the impact of one stunning display of insightful blind analysis was far greater than the impact of vast collections of empirical evidence that disproved the Rorschach's scientific validity, and these displays were responsible for much of the wide and unquestioning acceptance of the Rorschach as a sound diagnostic tool (Zubin, 1954).

However, in the early 1960s, research began a long trend that has lasted to the present and has revealed that the Rorschach was less than miraculous. With the application of scientific methods of evaluation, there continue to be clear indications that even the Rorschach elite did not possess the ability to divine true diagnoses (Holtzman & Sells, 1954; Little & Schneidman, 1959). The astounding successes in clinical validation became an enigma that has been explained in several ways. First, it has been suggested that the great successes in blind analysis were the product of a few simple tricks (Wood et al., 2003). One of these tricks, labeled the Barnum effect by Bertram Forer, is illustrated by a demonstration he used with his introductory psychology class (Forer, 1949). Forer prepared a personality profile for each of his new students based on a questionnaire he had administered. He then requested that each of his students rate their personal profile for accuracy, 0 being inaccurate and 5 being perfect. Forer's students gave an average rating of 4.2 (highly accurate), and more than 40% of the students said their profiles were a perfect description of their personality. The catch is that Forer had given each of the students the exact same profile, which he had compiled from a book of horoscopes. Forer had selected statements that seemed precise but that actually fit most people. He demonstrated the degree to which people overestimate the uniqueness and precision of general statements concerning their personality. Wood et al. (2003) suggest that much of the overwhelming acceptance of diagnosis based on blind analysis resulted from the Barnum effect and not from stunning accuracy.

It has also been suggested that the extraordinary early success of blind analysis could be attributed to the evaluator giving several different, or even contradictory, analyses for an individual client. When the information from other psychological tests and interviews was then revealed, the accuracy of many results of the blind reading could be supported by some of the statements, and the reading appeared to be a success (Wittenborn & Sarason, 1949). Lastly, it has been suggested that many Rorschach virtuosos of the 1940s and 1950s actually gave their impressive interpretations after they had learned facts about the individuals being tested.

Others have explained the early successes not by trickery, but by the level of genius of the Rorschach virtuosos and by their ability to succeed in blind analysis because of their vast experience with the Rorschach (Klopfer & Kelly, 1946). But these explanations fall short when considering that the same virtuosos who stunned others with their success in clinical settings were able to perform no better than chance when tested in controlled studies (Holtzman & Sells, 1954). In addition, it has also been shown that experience with the Rorschach does not lend itself to a greater degree of accuracy in diagnosis (Turner, 1966).

Regardless of the means by which early success of blind analysis and clinical proof of the validity of the Rorschach was obtained, scientists contend that clinical validation is unreliable, subject to self-deception (Meehl, 1997), and unscientific (Zubin, 1954). Confirmation bias, the tendency to seek out and focus on information that confirms ardent beliefs and to disregard information that tends to contradict those beliefs, can mislead even the most honest and well-meaning clinicians. Consider a clinician who hopes to prove the validity of the Rorschach. The clinician makes an evaluation based on the patient's responses to the inkblots and is then presented with a myriad of details about the patient gleaned from different psychological tests, interviews, and the client's background. From that myriad of information, the data that support the diagnosis based on the Rorschach would tend to be automatically focused on and retained; information not supporting the Rorschach's findings could be easily passed over.

In response to several studies in the late 1950s and early 1960s that served to debunk the greatness of Rorschach, Exner, as indicated, began to develop a system to remedy many of the problems with which the Rorschach was plagued. Exner attempted to address these problems with his creation of the Comprehensive System for scoring. Because the Comprehensive System for scoring the Rorschach is widely taught and the most largely accepted method in use today (Guarnaccia, Dill, Sabatino, & Southwick, 2001), research concerning the reliability of this system is valuable when discussing the Rorschach. Many scientifically minded evaluators of the Rorschach are in agreement that the Comprehensive System has failed to remedy the inadequacies of the Rorschach. In their 2003 book entitled *What's Wrong with the Rorschach?* Wood and colleagues outlined several facets of the Rorschach that bring serious doubt about its use in situations, such as forensic and clinical settings, which require a high degree of diagnostic accuracy. The following summarizes their contentions.

Norms. As we have emphasized throughout the book, unless the scores of a client can be compared to the scores of a reference group, they are of no use. Although it has been estimated that the Rorschach is administered yearly to more than 6 million people worldwide (Sutherland, 1992), it has never been adequately normed (Wood et al., 2003). Attempts to create representative national norms have failed on several levels. Today, most clinicians who use the Rorschach depend on the norming carried out by Exner. By 1986, Exner, had established norms for average adult Americans; by 1990, Exner's books were filled with normative tables that included norms for practically every Rorschach variable. Although Exner was given credit for establishing the Rorschach's first reliable, nationally representative norms, Wood and colleagues (2003) contend that his attempt was significantly flawed because of a computational error created by using the same 221 cases twice in his sample. In other words, his sample of what was reported to be 700 individuals consisted of 479 individuals, 221 of whom were entered twice. Many clinicians now use Exner's revised norms, which he constructed by retaining the 479 unduplicated cases and adding 121 new cases. Although this revision is a positive step, it cannot undo the decade of inaccurate diagnoses that may have resulted because of faulty norms. Also, the revised norms have been criticized as being seriously flawed and differing significantly from those of other researchers. Furthermore, a review of the results from 32 separate studies concluded that the norms used in the Comprehensive System are inaccurate and tend to overidentify psychological disorders in nonpatient populations (Wood, Nezworski, Garb, & Lilienfeld, 2001b), a problem discussed in depth in the next section.

Overpathologizing. Research has suggested that diagnoses from the Rorschach, whether using the older system for scoring or Exner's Comprehensive System, wrongly identifies more than half of normal individuals as emotionally disturbed. The problem of overpathologizing has been seen not only in the diagnosis of healthy adults (Shaffer, Erdberg, & Haroian, 1999) but also in children (Hamel, 2000). Hamel found that slightly above-average children were labeled as suffering from significant social and cognitive impairments when evaluated with the Rorschach. The possible harm from mislabeling individuals as sick when they are not is immeasurable. Consider the consequences of wrongly diagnosing an individual in the family court setting, where a faulty finding could lead to a parent losing custody of a child. Equally devastating repercussions could result from mislabeling in clinical and forensic settings. Also, consider the life-altering consequences of mislabeling a child as psychologically unwell, such as the stigma and differential treatment associated with mental or emotional illness and the implementation of costly and time-consuming treatment plans.

Unreliable scoring. The traditional belief, especially among opponents of the Rorschach, is that the Rorschach is unreliable. Indeed, when one views individual studies in isolation, especially those published before 1985, the results appear confusing.

For every study that has reported internal consistency coefficients in the .80's and .90's, one can find another with coefficients of .10 or even .01. Psychologists who hope to shed light on this picture through meta-analysis, however have found themselves in the midst of controversy.

Meta-analysis is a statistical procedure in which the results of numerous studies are averaged in a single, overall investigation. In an early meta-analysis of Rorschach reliability and validity, K. Parker (1983) reported an overall internal reliability coefficient of .83 based on 530 statistics from 39 papers published between 1971 and 1980 in the *Journal of Personality Assessment,* the main outlet for research on projective techniques.

Meta-analyses conducted by Parker and others were subsequently criticized as flawed on the grounds that results on validity were not analyzed separately from results on reliability (Garb, Florio, & Grove, 1998, p. 402). Exner (1999) has countered, finding it "reasonable" to argue for test–retest coefficients in the .70's. Moreover, the lack of separate results on reliability and validity should affect only the assessment of the validity of the Rorschach, not its reliability.

Furthermore, when one uses the Kuder-Richardson formula (which examines all possible ways of splitting the test in two) to calculate internal consistency coefficients rather than the more traditionally used odd–even procedure, Rorschach reliability coefficients are markedly increased. In one study, E. E. Wagner and co-workers (1986) compared the split-half coefficients using the odd–even and the Kuder-Richardson techniques for 12 scoring categories.

With the odd–even technique, coefficients ranged between −.075 and +.785, which reflects the general findings in the literature through the 1990s (see Exner, 1999; Groth-Marnat, 1999; Meyer, 1999; Viglione, 1999). However, with the Kuder-Richardson, the coefficients ranged from .55 to .88, with a mean of .77. Thus, results from both meta-analysis and application of Kuder-Richardson techniques reveal a higher level of Rorschach reliability than has generally been attributed to the test.

Although there is a significant amount of research reporting that the test–retest reliability of the Comprehensive System for the Rorschach is quite high (Exner, 1993; Exner, Armbruster, & Viglione, 1978; Haller & Exner, 1985), all of this research repeatedly indicates test–retest reliability for the same 40 variables. Because the Comprehensive System consists of 125 or more variables, the test–retest coefficients for 85 variables remain unreported. Specifically, there are no figures about what experts characterize as key variables such as the Depression Index, the Coping Deficit Index, and the Schizophrenia Index (Wood & Lilienfeld, 1999). Although there is marginal support for the reliability of various Comprehensive System variables, and some proponents of the system consider scoring reliability of .61 to .74 to be adequate, experts have suggested that scoring reliability in forensic and clinical settings should range from .80 to .90. Applying this higher standard would eliminate the use of the Rorschach for a substantial number of variables, including some frequently used variable such as the Schizophrenia Index, the Coping Deficit Index, and the Suicidal Constellation.

Lack of relationship to psychological diagnosis. Although a few Rorschach scores accurately evaluate some conditions characterized by thought disorder and anxiety, there is a notable absence of proven relationships between the

Rorschach and psychological disorders and symptoms. Several classic studies examined the Rorschach's ability as a psychodiagnostic test and were disappointing to those who hoped to prove its accuracy (Holtzman & Sells, 1954; Newton, 1954; Little & Schneidman, 1959). More recently, Nezworski and Garb (2001) contend that Comprehensive System scores do not demonstrate a relationship to psychopathy, conduct disorder, or antisocial personality disorder, and the original and revised versions of the Depression Index have little relationship to depression diagnosis. Wood, Lilienfeld, Garb, and Nezworski (2000) reviewed hundreds of studies examining the diagnostic abilities of the Rorschach and found these studies did not support it as a diagnostic tool for such disorders as major depressive disorder, posttraumatic stress disorder, dissociative identity disorder, conduct disorder, psychopathy, anxiety disorders, or dependant, narcissistic, or antisocial personality disorders. Although even proponents of the Rorschach often agree that it is not a valid diagnostic tool, the Rorschach continues to be used in both clinical and forensic settings for the purpose of diagnosis hundreds of thousands of times each year in the United States alone (Wood et al., 2003).

Lack of incremental validity. Not only has it been shown that adding results obtained with the Rorschach to biographical information and MMPI results does not improve diagnoses or evaluation, but also some studies have determined that the addition of the Rorschach results in *less* accurate findings (Sines, 1959). Although a few studies support the incremental validity of the Rorschach when used with the MMPI (Meehl, 1956), the amount of incremental validity contributed by the Rorschach has been trivial (Lilienfeld et al., 2000).

The Problem of "R." Those who are being evaluated with the Rorschach are free to give as many responses ("R") to each inkblot as they wish. As early as 1950, it was determined that this aspect unduly influenced scores (Fiske & Baughman,1953). As the number of responses goes up, so do other scores on the test. This causes several problems. If a person is generally more cooperative or intellectual, then they are more likely to give more responses. Those who are more likely to give more responses are also more likely to give what are labeled *space responses* (responding to the white space within or around the inkblot instead of responding to the inkblot). More space responses are interpreted by clinicians as indicating oppositional and stubborn characteristics in the test taker. Thus, those who are most cooperative with the test are more likely to be falsely labeled as oppositional. This is just one example of how "R" can negatively effect Rorschach scores. (See also Focused Example 14-2.) Although the problem with "R" was determined in the early 1950s and continues to be demonstrated (Meyer, 1992), clinicians who use the Rorschach generally ignore the problem.

In sum, evaluating the Rorschach on classical psychometric properties (standardization, norms, reliability, validity) has proven exceptionally difficult. Indeed, this attempt to document or refute the adequacy of the Rorschach has

Focused Example 14-2

THE DANGER OF BASING RORSCHACH INTERPRETATIONS ON INSUFFICIENT EVIDENCE

We had the opportunity to become involved in a forensic case in which an individual claimed that the negligence of a large company in sealing pipes together caused a gas leak that resulted in brain damage. This individual consulted an attorney, who sent him to a psychologist. The psychologist administered a Rorschach test. Based on her findings, the psychologist concluded that the person was brain damaged and thus had a legitimate case. The company called us and asked whether the Rorschach could be used to diagnose or identify brain damage. We replied that there is absolutely no support for the idea that one can prove a person is brain damaged simply on the basis of Rorschach results.

Lawyers for the company brought in the psychologist's report and a copy of the Rorschach protocol. The person suspected of brain damage provided only six responses, far fewer than the 22 to 32 responses typically found for the 10 Rorschach cards. The protocol was as follows:

	Free Association	Inquiry	Scoring
Card 1	A bat.	Here are the wings; there is the head.	W F A P

Discussion

The W indicates the whole inkblot was used in the percept. The F indicates that only the form or shape (not color, movement, or shading) determined the response. The A stands for animal content. The P indicates this response is a popular (that is, one that is commonly given).

Card 2	I don't know.	No, I still don't.	Rejection

Discussion

When the subject fails to provide a response, this is known as a *rejection*. Some examiners present the card again in the inquiry and ask, "Now do you see anything?" A rejection could have several meanings. The typical or classical interpretation of a rejection is guardedness or defensiveness.

Card 3	I don't know. (Q) No, I don't see anything.	I said I don't know.	Rejection

Discussion

The (Q) indicates the examiner questioned the subject further, thus attempting to elicit a response. Notice the defensive quality in the subject's response during the inquiry.

Card 4	A gorilla.	All of it; big feet, head, body.	W F A
Card 5	A moth.	Whole thing; wings, feelers, head.	W F A P
Card 6	I don't know.	No, nothing.	Rejection
Card 7	A bird without a head.	Wings, but no head. (Q) All of it.	W F−A

Discussion

The F– indicates a poor correspondence between the response, bird, and the stimulus properties of the inkblot. *Bird* is an unusual response to this inkblot.

	Free Association	Inquiry	Scoring
Card 8	Animals, maybe rats trying to steal something.	Just two animals on the sides.	D F A P

Discussion

The two animals were formed from two common details (D). It was scored P because this response is a popular (that is, frequently occurring).

Card 9	I don't know.	No, it doesn't look like anything to me.	Rejection
Card 10	Nothing, wait, looks like a bug here.	Just a bug, legs, pinchers, head.	D F Insect

In our judgment, the psychologist who conducted this Rorschach administration more than stretched the interpretation when she claimed this person was brain damaged. In fact, her conduct may be viewed as unethical. The argument presented was that a small number of responses, a preponderance of W responses, a lack of determinants other than form, and misperception (the poor form quality response to Card 7) were all consistent with brain damage. Because the protocol contained qualities commonly found in the protocols of brain-damaged individuals, the psychologist argued that she had found evidence for brain damage.

We looked at this Rorschach protocol and concluded that its information alone could in no way be considered sufficient evidence for brain damage. First, a small number of responses in itself cannot be attributed to any single factor (Exner, 1999). A small number of responses can be found in retarded, depressed, and extremely defensive individuals as well as in those who are brain-damaged. Second, the small number of responses led to an imbalance in the proportion of W to D responses. Data on the typical ratio of W to D responses are based on protocols with 20 to 30 responses. With only six responses, all bets are off. No one can say anything about the balance with so few responses. In any case, there is no clear evidence that brain-damaged people give a preponderance of W responses. Third, the one F– response proves nothing. Furthermore, the subject gave three popular responses, indicating he was capable of accurate perceptions. Fourth, the lack of determinants other than form can have several possible interpretations. The significance of the exclusive use of form in this protocol is dubious, however, in view of the small number of responses. A protocol with 30 responses, all determined exclusively by form, would have quite a different meaning. Notice how the total number of responses can influence or alter the meaning of Rorschach data. As indicated, the Rorschach places no limit on the number of possible responses.

We suggested that other tests be used to evaluate brain damage in this individual. Taking a conservative approach, we did not deny that this person was brain-damaged. We simply stated that the Rorschach in no way documented the presence of brain damage. The person in question, however, dropped his suit after our analysis was communicated to his attorney and psychologist.

produced one of the greatest divisions of opinion within psychology. Time and again, psychologists have evaluated the available empirical data and concluded that the Rorschach is inadequate when judged by scientific standards. Despite these negative evaluations, the Rorschach has flourished in clinical settings.

In evaluating the Rorschach, keep in mind that there is no universally accepted method of administration. Some examiners provide lengthy introductions and explanations; others provide almost none. Most of the experts state that the length, content, and flavor of administrative instructions should depend on the subject. Empirical evidence, however, indicates that the method of providing instructions and the content of the instructions influence a subject's response to the Rorschach (Blais et al., 1995; Hartman, 2001). Given the lack of standardized instructions, which has no scientifically legitimate excuse, comparisons of the protocols of two different examiners are tenuous at best (see Wood et al., 1996).

Suppose, for example, one hypothesizes that the total number of responses to a Rorschach is related to the level of defensiveness. Even with an adequate criterion measure of defensiveness, if examiner instructions influence the number of responses, then one examiner might obtain an average of 32 responses whereas a second might obtain 22, independent of defensiveness. If protocols from both examiners are averaged in a group, then any direct relationship between number of responses and defensiveness can easily be masked or distorted.

Like administration, Rorschach scoring procedures are not adequately standardized. One system scores for human movement whenever a human is seen, whereas another has elaborate and stringent rules for scoring human movement. The former system obviously finds much more human movement than does the latter, even when the same test protocols are evaluated. Without standardized scoring, determining the frequency, consistency, and meaning of a particular Rorschach response is extremely difficult.

One result of unstandardized Rorschach administration and scoring procedures is that reliability investigations have produced varied and inconsistent results. Even when reliability is shown, validity is questionable. Moreover, scoring as well as interpretation procedures do not show criterion-related evidence for validity and are not linked to any theory, which limits construct-related evidence for validity. Researchers must also share in the responsibility for the contradictory and inconclusive findings that permeate the Rorschach literature. Many research investigations of tests such as the Rorschach have failed to control important variables, including race, sex, age, socioeconomic status, and intelligence. If race, for example, influences test results as research indicates (see Saccuzzo, Johnson, & Guertin, 1995; Wood, 1999; Garb, Wood, Nezworski, Grove, & Stejskal, 2001), then studies that fail to control for race may lead to false conclusions. Other problems that are attributable to the research rather than to psychometric properties include lack of relevant training experience in those who score the protocols, poor statistical models, and poor validating criteria (Frank, 1995; Meloy & Singer, 1991).

Whether the problem is lack of standardization, poorly controlled experiments, or both, there continues to be disagreement regarding the scientific sta-

TABLE 14-2
Summary of Arguments Against and in Favor of the Rorschach

Against	In favor
1. Lacks a universally accepted standard of administration, scoring, and interpretation.	1. Lack of standardized procedures is a historical accident that can be corrected.
2. Evaluations of data are subjective.	2. Test interpretation is an art, not a science; all test interpretation involves a subjective component.
3. Results are unstable over time.	3. A new look at the data reveals that the Rorschach is much more stable than is widely believed.
4. Is unscientific.	4. Has a large empirical base.
5. Is inadequate by all traditional standards.	5. Available evidence is biased and poorly controlled and has therefore failed to provide a fair evaluation.

tus of the Rorschach (Exner, 1995; Nezworski & Wood, 1995; Wood et al., 1996; Garfield, 2000; Wood et al., 2003; Hunsley, 2001; Viglione & Hilsenroth, 2001). As Buros (1970) noted, "This vast amount of writing and research has produced astonishingly little, if any, agreement among psychologists regarding the specific validities of the Rorschach" (p. xxvi). In brief, the meaning of the thousands of published Rorschach studies is still debatable. For every supportive study, there appears to be a negative or damaging one (see Table 14-2).

Clearly, the final word on the Rorschach has yet to be spoken. Far more research is needed, but unless practitioners can agree on a standard method of administration and scoring, the researchers' hands will be tied.

In the first edition of this book, published in 1982, we predicted that the 21st century would see the Rorschach elevated to a position of scientific respectability because of the advent of Exner's Comprehensive System. Over the years, we backed away from this position. Now, more than 20 years later, we must acknowledge that we were mistaken. The science has all but overwhelmingly put the Rorschach into serious question. Perhaps one day die-hard proponents will look objectively at the findings and act accordingly.

An Alternative Inkblot Test: The Holtzman

Among the prime problems of the Rorschach, from a psychometric viewpoint, are its variable number of responses from one subject to another, lack of standard procedures, and lack of an alternative form. The Holtzman Inkblot Test was created to meet these difficulties while maintaining the advantages of the inkblot methodology (Holtzman, Thorpe, Swartz, & Herron, 1961). In this test, the subject is permitted to give only one response per card. Administration and scoring procedures are standardized and carefully described. An alternate form is available that correlates well with the original test stimuli. Interscorer as well as split-half reliabilities are comparable to those found for objective personality tests.

Both forms, A and B, of the Holtzman contain 45 cards. Each response may be scored on 22 dimensions. Many of these dimensions resemble those found in the Rorschach and include location, determinant, and content. Responses may also be scored for such factors as anxiety and hostility. For each scoring category or variable, well-established norms are presented for several samples ranging from 5-year-olds through adults (Hill, 1972). Given the psychometric advantages of the Holtzman, it is interesting that the test hasn't even begun to challenge the Rorschach's popularity (Reisman, 1976).

There are several factors that contributed to the relative unpopularity of the Holtzman, the most significant of which may have been Holtzman's refusal to exaggerate claims of the test's greatness and his strict adherence to scientifically founded evidence of its utility (Wood et al., 2003). The main difficulty with the Holtzman as a psychometric instrument is its validity (Gamble, 1972; Zubin, 1972). Modern studies are rare and unimpressive. Those studies that show a positive relationship between the Holtzman and various criterion measures are based on qualitative rather than quantitative features. Thus, the available supportive evidence is highly subjective, depending on examiner skill rather than formal interpretive standards. In short, one cannot currently consider the Holtzman any more useful than the Rorschach, despite the former's superior psychometric features. Perhaps the best that can be said is that it is still too early to judge its clinical utility compared with the Rorschach (Leichsenring, 1990, 1991).

The Thematic Apperception Test

The Thematic Apperception Test (TAT) was introduced in 1935 by Christina Morgan and Henry Murray of Harvard University. It is comparable to the Rorschach in many ways, including its importance and psychometric problems. As with the Rorschach, use of the TAT grew rapidly after its introduction; with the exception of the Rorschach, the TAT is used more than any other projective test (Wood et al., 2003). Though its psychometric adequacy was (and still is) vigorously debated (Alvarado, 1994; Keiser & Prather, 1990; Lilienfeld et al., 2000), unlike the Rorschach, the TAT has been relatively well received by the scientific community. Also, the TAT is based on Murray's (1938) theory of needs (see Chapter 13), whereas the Rorschach is basically atheoretical. The TAT and the Rorschach differ in other respects as well. The TAT authors were conservative in their evaluation of the TAT and scientific in their outlook. The TAT was not oversold as was the Rorschach, and no extravagant claims were made. Unlike the Rorschach, the TAT was not billed as a diagnostic instrument—that is, a test of disordered emotional states. Instead, the TAT was presented as an instrument for evaluating human personality characteristics (see Table 14-3). This test also differs from the Rorschach because the TAT's nonclinical uses are just as important as its clinical ones. Indeed, the TAT is one of the most important techniques used in personality research (Abrams, 1999; Bellak, 1999; Cramer & Blatt, 1990; McClelland, 1999).

As stated, the TAT is based on Murray's (1938) theory, which distinguishes 28 human needs, including the needs for sex, affiliation, and dominance. Many of these needs have been extensively researched through use of the TAT

TABLE 14-3

A Comparison of the Rorschach and the TAT

Rorschach	TAT
Rejected by scientific community	Well received by scientific community
Atheoretical	Based on Murray's (1938) theory of needs
Oversold by extravagant claims	Conservative claims
Purported diagnostic instrument	Not purported as diagnostic
Primarily clinical use	Clinical and nonclinical uses

(McClelland, 1999). The theoretical need for achievement—"the desire or tendency to do things as rapidly and/or as well as possible" (Murray, 1938, p. 164)—alone has generated a very large number of studies involving the TAT (McClelland, 1999; Spangler, 1992). The TAT measure of the achievement need has been related to factors such as parental perceptions, parental expectations, and parental attitudes toward offspring. Need achievement is also related to the standards that you as a student set for yourself (for example, academic standards). The higher your need for achievement, the more likely you are to study and ultimately achieve a high economic and social position in society. Studies such as those on the achievement motive have provided construct-related evidence for validity and have increased the scientific respectability of the TAT.

Stimuli, Administration, and Interpretation

The TAT is more structured and less ambiguous than the Rorschach. TAT stimuli consist of pictures that depict a variety of scenes. There are 30 pictures and one blank card. Specific cards are designed for male subjects, others for female. Some of the cards are appropriate for older people, others for young ones. A few of the cards are appropriate for all subjects, such as Card 1. This card shows a boy, neatly dressed and groomed, sitting at a table on which lies a violin. In his description of Card 1, Murray stated that the boy is "contemplating" the violin. According to experts such as Bellak (1986), Card 1 of the TAT tends to reveal a person's relationship toward parental figures.

Other TAT cards tend to elicit other kinds of information. Card 4 is a picture of a woman "clutching the shoulders of a man whose face and body are averted as if he were trying to pull away from her" (Bellak, 1975, p. 51). This card elicits information concerning male–female relationships. Bellak (1986, 1996) and others provide a description of the TAT cards along with the information that each card tends to elicit. This knowledge is essential in TAT interpretation. Figure 14-2 shows Card 12F, which sometimes elicits conflicting emotions about the self. Other feelings may also be elicited.

Standardization of the administration and especially the scoring procedures of the TAT are about as poor as, if not worse than, those of the Rorschach. Most examiners typically state something like, "I am going to show you some pictures. I want you to tell me a story about each picture. Tell me what led up to the story, what is happening, what the characters are thinking

FIGURE 14-2 *Card 12F from the Thematic Apperception Test. This card often gives the subject a chance to express attitudes toward a mother or daughter figure. Sometimes attitudes toward marriage and aging also emerge.*

(Reprinted by permission of the publishers from Henry A. Murray, Thematic Apperception Test, Cambridge, MA: Harvard University Press. Copyright © 1943 by the President and Fellows of Harvard College. © 1971 by Henry A. Murray.)

and feeling, and what the outcome will be." In the original design of the test, 20 cards were to be administered to each subject, 10 cards in each of two separate 1-hour sessions. In actual practice, however, only 10 or 12 cards are typically used (Bellak, 1996) and administration of the entire test typically takes place during one session (Lilienfeld et al., 2000). As with the Rorschach and almost all other individually administered tests, the examiner records the subject's responses verbatim. The examiner also records the *reaction time*—the time interval between the initial presentation of a card and the subject's first response. By recording reaction time, the examiner can determine whether the subject has difficulty with a particular card. Because each card is designed to elicit its own themes, needs, and conflicts, an abnormally long reaction time may indicate a specific problem. If, for example, the reaction time substantially increases for all cards involving heterosexual relationships, then the examiner may hypothesize that the subject is experiencing difficulty in this area.

There are by far more interpretive and scoring systems for the TAT than for the Rorschach. In his comprehensive review of the TAT literature, Murstein (1963, p. 23) states, "There would seem to be as many thematic scoring systems as there were hairs in the beard of Rasputin." Murstein summarizes most of the major methods of interpretation for the TAT, grouping them into quantitative and nonquantitative methods. Unlike the quantitative aspects of the Rorschach, which most examiners consider extremely important, the quantitative methods of TAT interpretation are unpopular (Alvarado, 1994; Groth-Marnat, 1999). Most TAT examiners find the available scoring systems to be overly elaborate, complex, and time-consuming. They therefore tend to use only nonquantitative methods of interpretation. In a survey of more than 100 psychologists who practiced in juvenile and family courts in North America, most clinicians (97%) reported that they did not use any scoring system at all, but relied on their clinical judgment and intuition to interpret and score the TAT (Lilienfeld et al., 2000).

Almost all methods of TAT interpretation take into account the *hero, needs, press, themes,* and *outcomes.* The *hero* is the character in each picture with whom the subject seems to identify (Bellak, 1996). In most cases, the story revolves around one easily recognizable character. If more than one character seems to be important, then the character most like the storyteller is selected as the hero. Of particular importance are the motives and *needs* of the hero. Most systems, including Murray's original, consider the intensity, duration, and frequency of each need to indicate the importance and relevance of that need. In TAT interpretation, *press* refers to the environmental forces that interfere with or facilitate satisfaction of the various needs. Again, factors such as frequency, intensity, and duration are used to judge the relative importance of these factors. The frequency of various *themes* (for example, depression) and *outcomes* (for example, failures) also indicates their importance.

To understand the potential value of the TAT in evaluating personality characteristics, you should realize that different individuals offer quite different responses to the same card. For example, given Card 1, in which a boy is contemplating a violin, one subject may say, "This boy's mother has just reminded him to practice the violin. The boy hates the violin and is wondering what he can do to make his practice session less boring. As he daydreams, his mother scolds him, so he picks up the violin and plays, resenting every minute." Another subject may respond, "The boy has just come home from school and is getting ready to practice the violin. He hopes to become a great violin player someday but realizes he's just an average, ordinary person. He picks up the violin and plays, dreaming about success." A third story may go as follows: "It's violin practice again and the boy is fed up. Do this, do that; his parents are always trying to live his life. This time he fixes them. He picks up the violin, smashes it, and goes out to play baseball."

Think about these three stories. Because the stimulus was the same in each case, differences in the stories must in some way reflect differences in the storytellers. The primary issue is exactly what is revealed in these stories. Many years ago, Lindzey (1952) analyzed several assumptions underlying the TAT. Table 14-4 lists these major assumptions. Although there were problems with many of the studies cited by Lindzey, positive evidence was found to support these assumptions, the validity of which holds to this day (Johnson, 1994; Bellak, 1996). By understanding these assumptions, you can get an idea of the complexity of TAT interpretation.

Although Lindzey's analysis was conducted some time ago, many TAT practitioners are guided by the assumptions listed in Table 14-4. The primary

TABLE 14-4
*Lindzey's
Assumptions
for TAT
Interpretation*

Primary assumption

In completing an incomplete or unstructured situation, the individual may reveal his or her own characteristics (strivings, dispositions, conflicts).

Other assumptions

1. The storyteller ordinarily identifies with one person in the drama. The characteristics (wishes, strivings, conflicts) of this imaginary person may reflect those of the storyteller.

2. The storyteller's characteristics may be represented indirectly or symbolically.

3 All stories are not of equal importance.

4. Themes directly related to stimulus material are less likely to be significant than those unrelated to stimulus material.

5. Recurrent themes (those that show up in three or four different stories) are particularly likely to mirror the characteristics of the storyteller.

6. The stories may reflect momentary characteristics of the storyteller (those aroused by temporary environmental factors) as well as enduring characteristics.

7. Stories may reflect events from the past that the storyteller has only observed or witnessed. However, the selection of these stories suggests that the events may still reflect the storyteller's own characteristics.

8. The stories may also reflect group membership or sociocultural factors.

9. Dispositions and conflicts inferred from the storyteller's creations may be unconscious and thus may not always be reflected directly in overt behavior or consciousness.

Adapted from Lindzey (1952).

assumption—in completing an incomplete or unstructured situation, the individual may reveal his or her own strivings, dispositions, and conflicts—provides a rationale and support for projective tests in general. Most of the other assumptions, however, pertain specifically to the TAT. As these assumptions indicate, although a story reflects the storyteller, many other factors may influence the story. Therefore, all TAT experts agree that a complete interview and a case history must accompany any attempt to interpret the TAT. No matter how careful and thorough such an interview, however, final conclusions and interpretations are still based on many factors, including the skill and experience of the examiner.

Psychometric Properties

Many experts consider the TAT to be psychometrically unsound (see Karp, 1999; Lilienfeld et al., 2000). Given the TAT's unstandardized procedures for administration, scoring, and interpretation, one can easily understand why psychometric evaluations have produced inconsistent, unclear, and conflicting findings. As with the Rorschach, divisions of opinion run deep. Subjectivity affects not only the interpretation of the TAT, but also analysis of the TAT literature. In other words, as with the Rorschach, two experts can look at the same research data and draw different or even opposite conclusions. It should be no surprise, then, that for almost every positive empirical finding there is a negative counterpart.

Even so, an analysis of existing results reveals that the study of specific variables, such as the achievement need, produces respectably high reliability figures (Exner, 1976; Murstein, 1963). Test–retest reliabilities appear to fluctuate, however, and to diminish as the interval between the two testing sessions increases. The median test–retest correlation across studies is only approximately .30 (Kraiger, Hakel, & Cornelius, 1984; Winter & Stewart, 1977). However, J. W. Atkinson (1981) has argued that the validity of the TAT does not depend on test–retest reliability. Split-half reliabilities have been consistently poor. Many TAT proponents, though, do not consider the split-half method appropriate because each card is designed to produce its own theme and content (Cramer, 1999). What is needed is a study using Kuder-Richardson reliabilities, as has recently been done with the Rorschach.

Validity studies of the TAT have produced even murkier findings. Most experts agree that there is content-related validity evidence for using the TAT to evaluate human personality; however, criterion-related evidence for validity has been difficult to document. In an early but often cited study, Harrison (1940a, 1940b) found that his own inferences based on TAT stories correlated at .78 with hospital records for specific variables. He reported that he was 75% correct in diagnosing patients into major categories, such as psychotic versus neurotic, using TAT data. Little and Shneidman (1959) found, however, that when 12 specialists for each of four tests (TAT, Make-a-Picture Story, Rorschach, MMPI) were asked to match the judgments of a group of criterion judges who had conducted extensive interviews with each of the subjects, not only was there little agreement between the test judges and the criterion judges, but also the TAT had the lowest reliability and the poorest predictive validity of the four tests. Newer studies also report discouraging reliability coefficients (Singh, 1986). A more recent meta-analysis by Spangler (1992) found average correlations between the TAT and various criteria to run between .19 and .22, which is hardly impressive.

In short, like the Rorschach, the TAT has several significant problems. In spite of these problems, however, the TAT continues to find widespread application in clinical as well as research settings. As with the Rorschach, the most pressing need appears to be establishing standardized administration and scoring procedures. Until such standardization is achieved, the TAT will continue to fare poorly according to traditional psychometric standards.

Alternative Apperception Procedures

An alternative thematic apperception test (Ritzler, Sharkey, & Chudy, 1980; Sharkey & Ritzler, 1985) has been constructed with pictures from the *Family of Man* photo-essay collection (Museum of Modern Art, 1955). According to these authors, the relatively new procedure can be scored quantitatively. It provides a balance of positive and negative stories and a variety of action and energy levels for the main character. In comparison, the TAT elicits predominantly negative and low-energy stories (Ritzler et al., 1980). Preliminary results with this new procedure, known as the Southern Mississippi TAT (or SM-TAT), have been encouraging. These results indicate that the SM-TAT preserves many of the advantages of the TAT while providing a more rigorous and modern methodology. Naturally, more research is needed, but this attempt to modernize the TAT is to be applauded.

The versatility and usefulness of the TAT approach are illustrated not only by attempts such as those of Ritzler et al. (1980) to update the test but also by the availability of special forms of the TAT for children and others for the elderly. The Children's Apperception Test (CAT) was created to meet the special needs of children ages 3 through 10 (Bellak, 1975). The CAT stimuli contain animal rather than human figures as in the TAT.

A special children's apperception test has been developed specifically for Latino and Latina children (Malgady, Constantino, & Rogler, 1984). The Tell Me a Story Test (TEMAS) is a TAT technique that consists of 23 chromatic pictures depicting minority and nonminority characters in urban and familial settings (Constantino, Malgady, Colon-Malgady, & Bailey, 1992). Initial research has shown the promise of the TEMAS as a multicultural projective test for use with minority children (Constantino & Malgady, 1999).

The Gerontological Apperception Test uses stimuli in which one or more elderly individuals are involved in a scene with a theme relevant to the concerns of the elderly, such as loneliness and family conflicts (Wolk & Wolk, 1971). The Senior Apperception Technique is an alternative to the Gerontological Apperception Test and is parallel in content (Bellak, 1975; Bellak & Bellak, 1973).

All of these alternative perception tests hold promise as clinical tools (Mark, 1993).

Nonpictorial Projective Procedures

Projective tests need not involve the use of a pictorial stimulus. Words or phrases sometimes provide the stimulus, as in the Word Association Test and incomplete sentence tasks. Or a subject can be asked to create or draw something, as in the Draw-a-Man Test. This final section briefly describes each of these procedures.

Word Association Test

Imagine yourself comfortably seated in a psychologist's examining office. Your task is simple, or at least it seems so. The psychologist says a word and you say the first word that comes to mind. The test begins. The first word is *hat*. You reply *coat*, the most common response of college students according to Rapaport, Gill, and Schafer (1968). The test goes on as follows:

Lamp

Love

Father
Paper
Masturbation
Chair
Breast
Car
Penis
Suicide

Do some of these words arouse any feelings in you? Words such as *love, father, breast,* and *masturbation* do in many people. The purpose of word association tests is to infer possible disturbances and areas of conflict from an individual's response to specific words.

The use of word association tests dates back to Galton (1879) and was first used on a clinical basis by Jung (1910) and G. H. Kent and Rosanoff (1910). In the first to attempt to standardize word association procedures, Kent and Rosanoff developed a list of 100 standard words and presented them to a sample of 1000 normal adults who were partially stratified by geographic location, education, occupation, age, and intelligence. An objective scoring system was developed, and the Kent-Rosanoff word association test enjoyed moderate popularity in the 1920s and 1930s.

Rapaport et al. (1968) subsequently developed a 60-item word association test. The range of words covered familial, household, oral, anal, aggressive, and phobic content. Responses were quantified by collecting norms on college students and schizophrenics, although interpretations were clearly psychoanalytic in nature.

Interest in word association techniques dropped considerably after Rapaport et al. (1968) concluded that the procedures did not live up to their clinical promise. Although the techniques are still in use (deGroot, 1988; Merten, 1995; Pons, 1989), they play only a limited role in clinical and counseling settings.

Sentence Completion Tasks

Another family of projective techniques involving words is incomplete sentence tasks. These tasks provide a stem that the subject is asked to complete. For example:

1. I am_____
2. I enjoy_____
3. What annoys me_____
4. It pains me to _____
5. Men_____
6. Dancing_____
7. Sports _____

As with all projective techniques, the individual's response is believed to reflect that person's needs, conflicts, values, and thought processes. In clinical use, these tasks also give a person the opportunity to provide information that may have been too embarrassing to present in a face-to-face verbal interview. Clinicians look for recurring themes of conflict and pathological content.

Many incomplete sentence tasks have scoring procedures. Among the most widely used of these tasks is the Rotter Incomplete Sentence Blank (Rotter & Rafferty, 1950). The Rotter provides 40 stems, each of which is scored on a 7-point system. In general, short sentences with some humor and positive content get the highest scores—for example, "Men have their advantages and disadvantages." Long, complex sentences with negative or depressed content receive the lowest scores—for example, "Men who I can't stand and would like to sometimes kill and do away with really know how to make a person feel crazy all the time."

Sentence completion procedures are used widely in clinical as well as in research settings. A relatively recent addition to this family is the Incomplete Sentences Task of Lanyon and Lanyon (1980). Sentences are scored on a 3-point scale (0, 1, 2), and norms are available as a function of age and gender. The reviews of Lanyon and Lanyon's incomplete sentence task have been positive and encouraging (Cundick, 1985; Dush, 1985).

Quite possibly the most psychometrically impressive projective test (Manners & Derkin, 2001), the Washington University Sentence Completion Test (WUSCT), measures ego development, or degrees of autonomy, acceptance of self, and awareness of personal faults (Loevinger, 1998). The test consists of 36 incomplete sentences asking individuals to complete sentences similar to "I most regret that . . . ." and "When people don't get along . . . ." (Wood et al., 2003). Although there is evidence substantiating the validity of the WUSCT (Manners & Derkin, 2001), it is rarely used in clinical settings (Holaday, Smith, & Sherry, 2000). This is disappointing, considering the plethora of popular, psychometrically challenged projective tests that are commonly used by clinicians.

Figure Drawing Tests

Another set of projective tests uses expressive techniques, in which the subject is asked to create something, usually a drawing. In the Draw-a-Person Test (Machover, 1949), the subject, most often a child, is asked to draw the picture of a person. Later the child is asked to tell a story about the person. A similar technique is the House-Tree-Person Test (Buck, 1948), in which the subject draws a picture of a house, tree, and person and then makes up a story about it. In the Kinetic Family Drawing Test (Burns & Kaufman, 1970, 1972), the subject draws a picture of his or her family.

Projective drawing tests are scored on several dimensions, including absolute size, relative size, omissions, and disproportions. For example, in drawing her family, a young child may omit herself. Interpreters might then assume that the child feels alienated from her family. In drawing a house-tree-person, the child might draw himself in the house looking out, perhaps reflecting a feeling of being isolated or trapped.

If there is a tendency to overinterpret projective test data without sufficient empirical foundation, then projective drawing tests are among the worst offenders. Although one can draw interpretative hypotheses from such data (see Groth-Marnat, 1999), people tend to go too far. For instance, in the Draw-a-Person Test, a clinician is advised to interpret a large head as indicating an overconcern with matters of intellectual functioning; one system even suggests that it means brain damage (Machover, 1949). One projective drawing test that has been proven valid and useful in clinical settings is the Goodenough Draw-a-Man Test (Wood et al., 2003), which we first discussed in Chapter 12. The Goodenough-Harris Drawing Test (G-HDT) has acceptable correlations (.50 and higher) with intelligence tests such as the Stanford-Binet (Anastasi, 1988). Its benefits include its simplicity and practicality, especially in the evaluation of children who may struggle with the tedious task of completing less child-friendly tests and is useful, especially when used in conjunction with other tests. (See Chapter 12 for a more detailed description of the G-HDT.) Although figure drawing tests have a place in a test battery, great caution is called for in their use until rigorous research can document the valid inferences one can make from them (see Riethmiller & Handler, 1997).

SUMMARY

According to the *projective hypothesis,* interpretations of an ambiguous or vague stimulus reflect the subject's own needs, feelings, experiences, prior conditioning, thought processes, and so forth.

The Rorschach is the preeminent projective test. Five individuals played a dominant role in its development: Beck, Hertz, Klopfer, Piotrowski, and Rapaport. Rorschach stimuli consist of 10 inkblots with the colors black, gray, red, and various pastels. These stimuli were formed by dropping ink onto a piece of paper and folding the paper.

Rorschach administration involves two phases: free-association and inquiry. During the first phase, the examiner presents each card with a minimum of structure. During the second phase, the examiner presents each card again to obtain sufficient information for scoring purposes. The five major Rorschach scoring categories are *location* (where), *determinant* (why), *content* (what), *frequency of occurrence* (popular-original), and *form quality* (correspondence of percept to stimulus properties of the inkblot).

The Rorschach is extremely controversial. On the negative side, it has been attacked for its lack of standardized methods for administration, scoring, and interpretation. It has also been criticized because interpretations are subjective and results are unstable over time. With the exception of recent reliability studies, scientific evidence has strongly weighed against it.

The Holtzman is an alternative to the Rorschach. Though it overcomes much of the scientific criticism of the Rorschach, the value and importance of this procedure have not yet been determined.

Another projective test, the TAT, enjoys wide research as well as clinical use. The TAT stimuli consist of 30 pictures, of various scenes, and one blank card. Card 1, for example, shows a scene in which a boy, neatly dressed and groomed, sits at a table on which rests a violin. Specific cards are suited for adults, children, men, and women. In administering the TAT, the examiner asks the subject to make up a story; he or she looks for the events that led up to the scene, what the characters are thinking and feeling, and the outcome. Almost all methods of TAT interpretation take into account the *hero, needs, press, themes,* and *outcomes.*

Like the Rorschach, the TAT has strong supporters but has also been attacked on a variety of scientific grounds. Though not psychometrically sound by traditional standards, the TAT is in widespread use. Like the Rorschach, it can provide a wealth of information about an individual.

Some of the similarities between the TAT and Rorschach are as follows: They are both individual projective tests for measuring human functioning and personality characteristics. Both are poorly standardized for administration, scoring, and interpretation. Reliability coefficients for both tests vary widely. Both are highly criticized, yet both are used extensively and adopted enthusiastically by practitioners. Both provide a rich source of information about a single individual. Some of the differences between the TAT and Rorschach are as follows: The Rorschach stimuli are inkblots; the TAT stimuli depict scenes. Thus, TAT stimuli are more meaningful than Rorschach stimuli. The TAT is based on Murray's (1938) theory of needs; the Rorschach is atheoretical. Formal scoring and quantitative features, important in the Rorschach, are of little significance in the TAT. The TAT finds extensive use in research as well as in clinical settings; the Rorschach is primarily a clinical tool. TAT interpretation is guided by a variety of assumptions, which were listed and explored by Lindzey (1952). Rorschach interpretation still depends on the opinion of experts and on research surveys such as those described in Exner's (1993) Rorschach textbook.

Several nonpictorial projective tests are available, including word association tests and incomplete sentence tests. Expressive techniques require a person to make something, such as draw a picture of a person or of his or her family.

WEB ACTIVITY   For interesting and relevant Web sites, check the following:

http://web.utk.edu/~wmorgan/tat/tattxt.htm
TAT research

Schatz.sju.edu/introlec/rorschach/history.html
Historical development of inkblot technique

www.phil.gu.se/fu/ro.html
Devoted to the promotion of the Rorschach

www.rorschach.com/
International Rorschach Society

http://web.lemoyne.edu/~hevern/nr-clin.html
Topics in narrative psychology

www.healthatoz.com/healthatoz/Atoz/ency/thematic_apperception_test.html

and http://web.utk.edu/~wmorgan/tat/tattxt.htm
For more on the TAT

CHAPTER 15

Tests Based on Psychological Science and the New Age of Computers

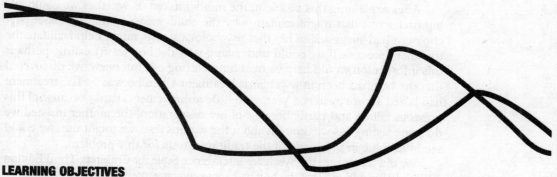

LEARNING OBJECTIVES

When you have completed this chapter, you should be able to:

☐ Identify the differences between cognitive-behavioral assessment and traditional assessment procedures

☐ Identify the difference between the beliefs underlying traditional tests and the beliefs underlying behavioral tests

☐ Briefly describe cognitive-behavioral assessment based on operant conditioning

☐ Identify the main difference between cognitive-behavioral self-report techniques and traditional self-report techniques

☐ List four types of behavioral self-report techniques

☐ Briefly describe the functional, or behavior-analytic, approach to behavioral assessment

☐ Describe a cognitive-functional analysis

☐ Briefly describe psychophysical assessment

☐ Discuss the role of computers in modern psychological testing

A high-school teacher once contacted us regarding her 7-year-old son. At the age of 4, the boy had suffered from an illness in which he could not eat solid food for 25 days because it made him gag. If he managed to swallow, he became extremely nauseous. Ever since he had recovered from the illness, he was reluctant to eat all but a few select foods. His usual menu was cold cereal for breakfast, a peanut butter sandwich for lunch, and plain spaghetti for dinner. He refused to eat meat or vegetables of any kind. His parents tried everything, but nothing worked. The mother was concerned that the boy was not developing properly. She had taken him to a pediatrician who told her that unless something could be done to get the boy to eat, he would have to be hospitalized. The physician suggested psychiatric intervention and gave the boy 1 month to improve.

After explaining this problem, the mother asked us whether we could administer a test that might explain why the child wasn't eating. A school psychologist had suggested to her that psychological tests might help facilitate the treatment process. If we could understand why the boy wasn't eating, perhaps this information would help us treat him. During our interview, we discovered that the boy had been in psychiatric treatment when he was 5. The treatment had lasted approximately 1 year, with little improvement. Partly because of this previous failure and partly because of her desperation, the mother insisted we do some testing. As we thought about the various tests we might use, we could see little value in using any of the traditional tests for this problem.

We did administer the Wechsler Intelligence Scale for Children, Third Edition (WISC-III) and found that the boy had above-average intelligence (full-scale IQ = 115). In achievement, the boy was functioning about half a grade level above his current grade placement in both reading and arithmetic. Thus, intellectual and achievement factors could not account for the problem. Unfortunately, personality tests were not much more useful than the ability tests had been. After administering the Children's Apperception Test and conducting extensive interviewing and observation (see Chapter 14), our interpretation confirmed our suspicion that the boy's eating problem originated with the trauma he had suffered when he could not eat solid foods. In simple terms, the boy had a fear of eating.

Knowing why the boy wasn't eating certainly wasn't much help. One of the weaknesses of the original model of testing as reflected in traditional tests is that they provide little information concerning possible treatment approaches. When we explained the situation to the mother, she pleaded, "Isn't there any other type of test you can give him? Isn't there a test that might also indicate what type of treatment would be most effective?" Thanks to advances within scientific psychology, we could answer, "Yes."

We told the mother that numerous alternatives to traditional tests had been developed by psychologists in the specialty based on learning principles known as *behavior modification*, or *behavior therapy*. Collectively, these testing techniques are known as *cognitive-behavioral assessment*. "Please try these procedures," she said. "If they might help, by all means use them."

In the hands of highly trained experts, traditional psychological tests may be extremely valuable, but they still fall short on several grounds. The tradi-

TABLE 15-1

Varieties of Alternatives to Traditional Testing Procedures

Operant conditioning techniques
Self-report techniques
Kanfer and Saslow's behavior-analytic approach
Cognitive techniques
Psychophysiological techniques
Psychophysiological and signal detection procedures

tional tests discussed thus far in this book offer little information concerning treatment approaches. As a rule, these traditional procedures also provide little information about how a person might behave in a particular situation. Even if these traditional procedures do explain the reason behind a particular symptom, this information usually offers little to the overall treatment process. The result of such shortcomings in traditional tests has been an explosion of alternative approaches based on principles of human learning and cognition, and more recently the advent of personal computers.

Behavioral assessment can be divided into several categories. These include procedures based on operant conditioning techniques, self-report techniques, Kanfer and Saslow's behavior-analytic approach, a variety of cognitive techniques, psychophysiological techniques, and signal-detection procedures. Each of these is discussed in turn (see Table 15-1).

Cognitive-Behavioral Assessment Procedures

The Rationale for Cognitive-Behavioral Assessment

Traditional testing procedures are based on a medical model. According to this model, the overt manifestations of a disordered psychological condition (for example, overeating or undereating) are only symptoms—surface expressions of an underlying cause. Disordered behavior is believed to be caused by some underlying characteristic such as an early traumatic experience. In the example at the beginning of this chapter, the boy's avoidance of food was, in a sense, caused by the trauma of an illness in which solid food made him nauseous. Treatment in the medical model is based on the idea that unless the cause of a symptom is removed, a new symptom may develop. Thus, one major function of traditional psychological tests is to ascertain the possible underlying causes of disordered behaviors.

In cognitive-behavioral assessment, by contrast, the behaviors, thought processes, or physiological responses that define a disordered condition are considered the real problem. If the person eats too much, then the problem is simply overeating and not some underlying cause. The overeating may, in fact, have been caused by some early experience, just as in the 7-year-old boy. However, in cognitive-behavioral assessment, the eating behavior becomes the direct target of treatment. Therefore, the testing procedure in this case would evaluate eating behavior.

This is not to say that cognitive-behavioral assessment denies, ignores, or negates the causes of psychological disorders. On the contrary, certain techniques of cognitive-behavioral assessment include an evaluation of the factors that precede, coexist with, and follow (maintain) disordered behavior (Haynes, 1990, 1991). These may be environmental factors (such as working conditions, home situation), thought processes (such as internal dialogue), or both. Thus, cognitive-behavioral assessment often includes an evaluation of the internal and external factors that lead to and maintain disordered behavior as well as an evaluation of the behavior itself (Groth-Marnat, 1999).

Cognitive-behavioral assessment is more direct than traditional psychological tests. It is characterized by fewer inferential assumptions and remains closer to observable phenomena (Haynes, 1991). Through cognitive-behavioral assessment, one might find that, just before eating, the 7-year-old boy in our example says to himself, "I don't want to eat; it will make me sick." Subsequently, the boy refuses to eat. As he leaves the dinner table, his mother says, "That's OK, honey, you don't have to eat." The boy's statement, "I don't want to eat," precedes the disordered behavior. His avoidance of food is the core of the disorder. His mother's comment, plus the boy's relief that he doesn't have to eat, reinforces or maintains the disorder. In cognitive-behavioral assessment, psychologists analyze preceding and subsequent factors and focus on a direct change in overt behavior, thoughts, or physiological processes. The treatment process thus involves an attempt to alter the disordered behavior (for example, increasing the frequency of eating). Treatment may also involve modifying the internal dialogue before and after the boy eats and modifying the mother's behavior so that she no longer reinforces avoidance of food but instead reinforces eating.

In traditional procedures, the boy's failure to eat would be viewed as only a symptom. Testing would be aimed at determining the cause of this symptom (the early trauma of the illness he had when he was 4), and treatment would be directed at the cause rather than at the behavior itself. Presumably, by giving the boy insight into the causes of his behavior, a psychologist could get the boy to understand why he wasn't eating. When he achieved this understanding, he would no longer need to avoid eating. Table 15-2 compares traditional and cognitive-behavioral assessment.

It is beyond the scope of this text to debate the pros and cons of the cognitive-behavioral and medical models. Our goal is to help you understand the differences between the two. Suffice it to say that cognitive-behavioral testing procedures, based on psychology's scientific base, have added a whole new dimension to the field of psychological testing.

Procedures Based on Operant Conditioning

In operant conditioning, psychologists observe the behaviors of an individual. After the individual has made a response, they can do something to the individual to alter the probability of the recurrence of the response. They may pre-

TABLE 15-2

Traditional Versus Behavioral Assessment

	Traditional assessment	**Cognitive-behavioral assessment**
Target	Underlying cause	Disordered behavior
Symptoms	Superficial	Focus of treatment
Assessment	Indirect; not related to treatment	Direct; related to treatment
Theory	Medical model	Behavioral model
Goal	Determine cause of symptoms	Analyze disordered behavior

sent something positive or remove something negative following the response, which should increase the rate of recurrence, or else they may present something aversive or remove something positive preceding the response, which should reduce the rate of recurrence.

In cognitive-behavioral assessment based on operant conditioning, one must first identify the critical response or responses involved in the disorder. One can then evaluate these critical responses for frequency, intensity, or duration. This evaluation establishes the baseline (usual rate of occurrence) for the particular behavior. According to an early system developed by Kanfer and Saslow (1969), if the behaviors occur too frequently, then they are called *behavioral excesses*. If they occur too infrequently, they are called *behavioral deficits*. Obviously, with a behavioral excess, treatment centers on reducing the frequency, intensity, or duration of the behavior in question. With a behavioral deficit, treatment focuses on increasing the behavior. Table 15-3 outlines the steps in cognitive-behavioral assessment based on operant conditioning.

After attempting to increase or decrease the behavior (treatment intervention), psychologists observe the effect of the intervention on the behavior in question relative to the baseline. If the goal was to decrease the behavior, then there should be a decrease relative to the baseline. If the critical behavior remains at or above baseline levels, then the intervention has failed.

In the example at the beginning of this chapter, we decided to use cognitive-behavioral assessment based on operant conditioning. The critical behavior was obvious: frequency of eating. Furthermore, the critical behavior was a deficit; that is, the boy wasn't eating enough. To evaluate the critical behavior (Step 3), we asked the boy's mother to record the amount and kind of food that the boy ate each day. Using standard calorie references, we converted the amount of food the boy ate into calories. The baseline looked something like the graph in Figure 15-1. The boy was eating an average of approximately

TABLE 15-3

Steps in a Cognitive-Behavioral Assessment

Step 1:	Identify critical behaviors.
Step 2:	Determine whether critical behaviors are excesses or deficits.
Step 3:	Evaluate critical behaviors for frequency, duration, or intensity (that is, obtain a baseline).
Step 4:	If excesses, attempt to decrease frequency, duration, or intensity of behaviors; if deficits, attempt to increase behaviors.

FIGURE 15-1
Baseline in eating-difficulty example.

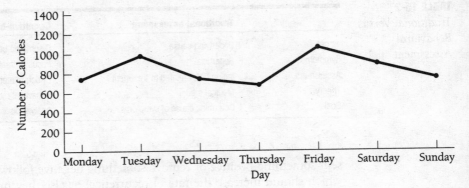

800 calories a day, with a range of 600 to 1000 calories on any given day. This number of calories is too few to prevent a small, gradual weight loss.

Because the behavior was a deficit, we tried to increase the boy's frequency of eating. For our intervention, we used a reward system based on points. The boy received points for everything he ate. The more he ate, the more points he got. Following each meal, his mother recorded the number of points that he received as well as the cumulative total. She posted this record on a bulletin board in the boy's room so he could observe his own progress. She also posted a chart that we had worked out with the two of them. The chart listed toys and other rewards that he could trade for points. For example, he could exchange 10 points for a package of baseball cards any time he wanted. He could also save his points for bigger prizes. For 350 points, he could get a computer game he had been wanting, and so on. In the treatment procedure, his mother recorded exactly what he ate each day just as she had during the pretreatment assessment in which the baseline was obtained. This record was then converted into calories, and each week we made a graph of his day-to-day calorie intake.

The intervention proved highly effective. Within 1 week, the boy had earned some 200 points and was well on the way to securing his computer game. The graph for this first week of treatment is shown in Figure 15-2. As the graph indicates, the boy doubled his average intake of calories to some 1600 (range 1400 to 1800). Thus, his intake of calories was far above baseline following the intervention. Assessment continued throughout the treatment and also provided feedback about the effects of the treatment. In the second week, the boy's consumption of calories fell below the dramatic increases of the first week, but it never fell below baseline levels. In 6 weeks, the boy gained approximately eight pounds. He had earned just about every toy he had ever wanted. At this point, his mother became concerned that he might gain too much weight or that she might go broke paying for rewards. After consultation with us, she terminated the point system. Following termination, there was a substantial drop in his eating behavior for 3 or 4 days, but then it increased to about a normal level for his age.

FIGURE 15-2
Eating behavior during the first week of intervention.

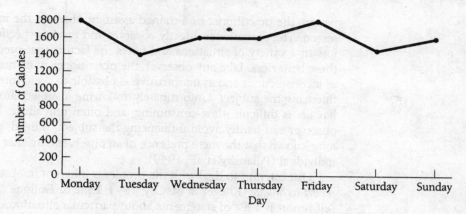

Over the course of treatment, the boy's parents had developed a different attitude about his eating behavior. So had the boy. Everybody concerned now knew that the boy could eat without negative consequences. The parents refused to permit the boy to get away without eating, and the boy no longer had an excuse not to eat. Although the therapy never attempted to get at an original or hypothetical underlying cause of the behavior, the boy was in every sense cured. He wasn't hospitalized, and his eating behavior was adequate 6 months following treatment. His mother complained that he was still a finicky eater, but his weight was within normal limits.

Practitioners can use the operant approach to solve a variety of problems, including smoking (Morgan, Davies, & Willner, 1999), poor study habits (Zimmerman, Greenberg, & Weinstein, 1994), coping with chronic pain (Vlaeyen, de Jong, Onghena, Kerckhoffs-Hanssen, & Kole-Snijders, 2002), and poor diet (Douglas, 2002). In each case, one first calculates a baseline. Then one implements an intervention. Finally, one observes the effects of this intervention on the baseline. If you feel you don't study enough, for instance, you can try the approach yourself. To assess your study behavior, record the number of minutes you study each day for 1 week. This is your baseline. Then decide on a reward for yourself. Every day record how long you study. Give yourself the reward whenever you study longer than 25% above the average time for your baseline. See whether this procedure doesn't increase the time you spend studying.

Self-Report Techniques

In our example, the frequency of the 7-year-old boy's disordered eating behavior was recorded by his mother because the assessment process required that someone observe the boy. Not all problems, however, can be so easily and readily observed. Further, when a parent or other relative of the subject does the observing and recording, the practitioner must depend on the skill, accuracy, and honesty of the well-meaning but untrained relative. Thus, in the ideal situation, the practitioner or a trained assistant observes the individual to be assessed. The practitioner directly observes and records specific problem behaviors in a variety of situations and notes the factors that precede and maintain these behaviors. Like any observer, the practitioner must make him- or herself as inconspicuous and as unobtrusive as possible to avoid interfering with or influencing the subject. Unfortunately, following a subject around to record behaviors is difficult, time-consuming, and often unrealistic. In most cases, the observer can hardly avoid influencing the subject. Indeed, psychologists have long known that the mere presence of an observer may alter the behavior of an individual (Polansky et al., 1949).

One attempt to deal with the problems inherent in observation is the *self-report technique* (Klieger & McCoy, 1994; Lane & Gullone, 1999). The typical self-report is a list of statements about particular situations. The subject's task may be either to respond "True" or "False" to each statement or to circle a number (1 to 5, for example) to indicate the importance or relevance of the statement. Table 15-4 gives examples of the types of statements used. Self-report techniques assume that the person's responses reflect individual differences and measure some other observable behavior. If, for example, one person circles 5 for fear of snakes and another person circles 1, then psychologists assume that direct observation of these two individuals in the presence

TABLE 15-4

Examples of a Behavioral Self-Report

Circle	1 if the item elicits no fear 2 if the item elicits some fear 3 if the item elicits a little fear 4 if the item elicits a lot of fear 5 if the item elicits extreme fear				
Worms	1	2	3	4	5
Bats	1	2	3	4	5
Psychological tests	1	2	3	4	5
Dogs	1	2	3	4	5
Snakes	1	2	3	4	5
Highways	1	2	3	4	5
Men	1	2	3	4	5

Circle true or false as the item applies to you.

I like to talk when in a group.	True	False
I relate easily to persons of the opposite sex.	True	False
I like to walk in dark places.	True	False
I like to give speeches to large groups.	True	False
I feel most comfortable with strangers.	True	False
I feel most comfortable with family.	True	False
I feel most comfortable with friends.	True	False
I like to be the leader in a group.	True	False
I would rather follow than lead in a group.	True	False

of snakes would reveal different, measurable responses. The person who circled 5 might scream and run. The person who circled 1 might simply ignore the snakes. In place of direct observation, the practitioner accepts the face validity of the subject's responses.

That cognitive-behavioral assessment has concentrated on phenomena such as fear illustrates the major distinction between cognitive-behavioral and traditional self-report procedures. Cognitive-behavioral procedures focus on situations that lead to particular response patterns; that is, situations are the primary determinant of behavior. Traditional self-report procedures focus on relatively enduring internal characteristics of the individual (personality traits) that lead to particular response patterns. In the cognitive-behavioral approach, one sees situations as the primary determinant of behavior. In the traditional approach, one sees characteristics that the person brings to a situation (for example, traits) as the primary determinant of behavior. Thus, in the cognitive-behavioral approach, a person is not simply fearful and therefore fearful no matter what the situation; a person is fearful only in certain circumstances or situations because these circumstances elicit fear in that person.

The Fear Survey Schedule. The Fear Survey Schedule (FSS) is the oldest and most researched of the cognitive-behavioral self-report procedures. In clinical and experimental use since the 1950s, it continues to be used for a variety of purposes (Beck, Carmin, & Henninger, 1998; Harris, Robinson, & Menzies, 2001). Since the FSS was introduced into the literature by Akutagawa (1956) as a 50-item test, it has undergone a variety of changes, and various versions have from 50 to 122 items, with ratings of fear on either 5-point or 7-point scales. It has been adapted for use with children (Muris, Merckelbach, Mayer, & Meesters, 1998; Shore & Rapport, 1998) and adolescents (Gullone & King, 1992) as well as adults (Klieger & Franklin, 1993). One adaptation of the FSS was created for measuring specific phobias (Antony, 2001). From its worldwide use (Abdelkhalek, 1994; Svensson & Oest, 1999), numerous cross-cultural studies are available (e.g., Ingman, Ollendick, & Akande, 1999; Milgrom, Jie, Yang, & Tay, 1994; Owen, 1998).

Items are typically related to situations that involve fear and avoidance behaviors, such as fear of open places, fear of snakes, fear of dead animals. Subjects rate each item according to the degree to which they experience that particular fear. Developers have derived items on the FSS from clinical observation of actual cases (Wolpe & Lang, 1964) and from experimental investigations in laboratory settings (Geer, 1965). The FSS attempts to identify those situations that elicit fear and thus avoidance. Once psychologists have identified these situations, they can aim treatment at helping people deal with these situations, thus reducing fear.

Assertiveness. Some individuals have difficulty speaking up for themselves. When they finally do speak up, they are often aggressive. Suppose someone cuts in front of you in a long line to see a popular movie. Assertiveness experts might suggest that you calmly and firmly inform this person of the location of the end of the line. If you encounter resistance, you calmly explain that everyone has been waiting in line and that the only polite and appropriate thing for the intruder to do is to go to the end of the line. Many people have difficulty acting appropriately in this type of situation. They may stew inside or go to the other extreme and display aggression, such as striking the intruder or throwing a temper tantrum.

Clinical practitioners have constructed various measures of assertiveness. Table 15-5 illustrates the type of item found in a self-report questionnaire for assertiveness, such as the Assertive Behavior Survey Schedule (ABSS). If you were taking the ABSS, you would indicate the responses you would make in specific situations that call for assertiveness. You would also be asked to speculate on the consequences of assertiveness for you. Thus, the ABSS can help determine whether you can be assertive if necessary, situations in which you might have difficulty being assertive, and your personal attitude toward assertiveness.

Self-report battery. Cautela and Upper (1976) have proposed the use of a self-report battery that incorporates many of the commonly used self-report techniques, such as a variety of behavioral self-rating checklists and the FSS. The battery contains three types of scales. Primary scales request general information, such as historical data, and assess general needs. Secondary scales yield information about the need for specific techniques such as relaxation or as-

---

TABLE 15-5

Sample Questions from a Behavioral Assertiveness Questionnaire

I. Suppose you were in the following situations. How would you respond? Indicate by circling number 1, 2, or 3.

   A. You have ordered filet mignon for you and your date at an expensive restaurant. You wanted yours cooked rare. The waiter brings it well done. What would you do?

     1. Tell the waiter to bring you another, cooked the way you wanted it.

     2. Complain to the waiter, but eat what he had brought for you anyway.

     3   Say nothing.

   B. You are at a bank. You've been waiting in line for nearly 10 minutes. Finally, you reach the head of the line. A man with a large briefcase comes from the outside and steps right in front of you. What would you do?

     1. Tell him to go to the end of the line.

     2. Tell him there is a long line, but let him go in front of you anyway.

     3. Say nothing.

II. In those situations in which you say nothing, what are you afraid of? (Check the best answer.)

   A. Being yelled at ( )

   B. Being beat up ( )

   C. Being embarrassed ( )

   D. Being rejected ( )

   E. Violating a personal or religious belief ( )

   F. Expending excessive energy ( )

Adapted from Cautela and Upper (1976, pp. 97–98).

sertiveness training. Requiring a highly specific response, tertiary scales yield information about specific problems such as alcohol and drug abuse, overeating, and inappropriate sexual behavior (Cameron & Evers, 1990).

Evaluation of self-report procedures. Obviously, any practitioner with a problem to assess can simply devise and publish a self-report device. Indeed, there appears to be no shortage of such practitioners. Unfortunately, little psychometric data, if any, are ever presented to help evaluate these devices. The little information presented is usually based on poorly controlled correlational studies with highly variable results (Maisto, McKay, & Connors, 1990).

In their use of self-report techniques, some psychologists "reinvent the wheel." For example, Cautela and Upper (1976) do not hesitate to admit that the prototypes of current self-report techniques are tests such as the Woodworth Personal Data Sheet (see Chapter 15). Early paper-and-pencil structured personality tests, finally abandoned in the 1930s, are indeed difficult to distinguish from many modern self-report procedures. Both implicitly assume that test responses have face validity. Thus, all of the problems associated with face validity—subject capacity and willingness to be truthful, response bias, poor reliability, poor validity, lack of norms—usually plague cognitive-behavioral self-report techniques. Unfortunately, only one of these self-report techniques, the FSS, has been subjected to anything close to an adequate psychometric analysis, with nearly 500 published research articles through 2004.

Practitioners have a long way to go before they can offer cognitive-behavioral self-report procedures as established clinical tools. However, when used in conjunction with other sources of data, such as psychophysiological recordings and direct observation, self-report data can provide useful information in clinical as well as research settings. Indeed, this is the modern trend (Angrilli, Sarlo, Palomba, & Schincaglia, 1997; Grana-Gomez, Andreu, Rogers, & Arango-Lasprilla, 2003; Haynes, 1991, 1992; Matias & Turner, 1986; Tucker, Slifer, & Dahlquist, 2001).

Kanfer and Saslow's Functional Approach

In the discussion of operant conditioning, we mentioned Kanfer and Saslow's (1969) original concepts of behavioral deficits and excesses. Now we shall discuss this approach in detail, particularly as it goes beyond the principles of operant conditioning.

Kanfer and Saslow (1969) are among the most important pioneers in the field of cognitive-behavioral assessment. Their method of cognitive-behavioral assessment provides an alternative to the traditional diagnostic labeling of the medical model (neurotic, psychotic, and so forth). These authors propose what they call a *functional (behavior-analytic) approach* to assessment. Rather than labeling people as schizophrenic or neurotic, the psychologist would focus on behavioral excesses and deficits. As previously indicated, a *behavioral excess* is any behavior or class of behaviors described as problematic by an individual because of its inappropriateness or because of excesses in its frequency, intensity, or duration. The functional approach adheres to the assumptions of the learning approach (to the study of disordered behavior); that is, the functional approach assumes that both normal and disordered behaviors develop according to the same laws and differ only in extremes. Taking a shower, for example, is a normal behavior. What about taking two showers a day? Clearly, the laws that govern the acquisition of the behaviors involved in taking one shower are the same as those for taking two showers. What about eight showers a day? Consider three hour-long showers a day, or a 2-hour-long shower taken within minutes after company arrives for an unexpected visit. This sort of behavior is abnormal only because it is excessive. Similarly, most of us blow off steam by yelling every now and then. However, if a person yells intensely every half an hour for 30 seconds at a time every time she goes to the library, then yelling behavior is clearly extreme and maladaptive.

Behavioral deficits are classes of behaviors described as problematic because they fail to occur with sufficient frequency, with adequate intensity, in appropriate form, or under socially expected conditions (Kanfer & Saslow, 1969; Ferro & Madureira, 2002). For example, one may view lack of assertiveness as a behavioral deficit.

Again, the behavior, or lack of it, is not by itself a disorder. If, for example, a gang of high-school dropouts drive their motorcycles into the parking spot you were prepared to pull into, then it may not be too wise to say, "That's my spot; there's another around the block." Finding another parking spot yourself is probably a far more adaptive behavior.

Besides isolating behavioral excesses and deficits, a functional analysis involves other procedures, including clarifying the problem and making suggestions for treatment. In the traditional approaches, knowing a person has a particular disorder or conflict does little to suggest treatment strategies. However, when behavioral excesses are identified, the psychologist can make efforts to reduce the behaviors' intensity, frequency, and so forth. When behavioral deficits are identified, the psychologist can make efforts to provide new behaviors or increase the frequency of existing behaviors.

The Dysfunctional Attitude Scale

A major pillar of cognitive-behavioral assessment that focuses primarily on thinking patterns rather than overt behavior is A. T. Beck's (1967, 1976, 2002) Cognitive Model of Psychopathology. The model is based on *schemas,* which are cognitive frameworks or organizing principles of thought. For example, in your first impression of an individual, you create a schema of that person. In your subsequent interactions with that person, you add to or subtract from that original schema. Moreover, the original schema influences your subsequent perceptions. For instance, if you originally pegged the person as a nerd, then you will likely label subsequent behavior accordingly. According to Beck, schemas serve to organize prior experience, guide the interpretations of new experiences, and shape expectancies and predictions. Beck's theory holds that dysfunctional schemas predispose an individual to develop pathological behaviors (Beck, Brown, Steer, & Weissman, 1991; Newman, Leahy, Beck, Reilly-Harrington, & Gyulia, 2003).

To evaluate negative schemas, Beck and colleagues have developed the Dysfunctional Attitude Scale (DAS) (Weissman, 1979; Weissman & Beck, 1978). The DAS has two parallel forms (Power, Katz, McGuffin, & Duggan, 1994). It identifies beliefs that might interact with a stressor to produce psychopathology. For instance, a person may believe that he cannot find happiness without being loved by another or that turning to someone else for advice or help is an admission of weakness. The subject is provided with a list of statements such as "Others can care for me even if they know all my weaknesses" and is asked to respond on a 7-point Likert scale ranging from "totally agree" to "totally disagree." The validity of the scale is supported by a variety of factor analytic data (Beck et al., 1991; Cane, Olinger, Gotlib, & Kuiper, 1986; Carro, Bernal, & Vea, 1998).

Irrational Beliefs Test

According to the cognitive viewpoint, human behavior is often determined by beliefs and expectations rather than reality. If, for example, your instructor announces that there will be an exam in the third week of classes, you will do most of your studying for it the day or two before it if you are like most students. Suppose, however, you miss the class just before the announced exam. And suppose that a "friend" of yours plays a trick on you: He telephones and tells you the exam has been canceled. If you believe him and therefore expect that there will be no exam, will you study as hard as you would have before (if at all)? It's unlikely. The exam will still be given (reality), but your behavior will have changed because of your belief that the exam has been canceled. In view of the influence of beliefs and expectations, several cognitive-behavioral tests have been developed to measure them. R. A. Jones (1968), for example, developed a 100-item Irrational Beliefs Test (IBT) to measure irrational beliefs (for example, the belief that you must always succeed to be worthwhile).

The IBT has found widespread use in clinical as well as research settings and has received considerable attention (Deffenbacher, Swerner, Whisman, Hill, & Sloan, 1986; T. E. Ellis, 1985; Bridges & Sanderman, 2002). The IBT requires subjects to indicate their level of agreement or disagreement with each of the 100 items on a 5-point scale (for example, "I frequently worry about things over which I have no control"). Half of the items indicate the presence of a particular irrational belief; the other half, its absence.

The reliability of the IBT appears to be similar to that of structured personality tests, with test–retest coefficients for short intervals (2 weeks or less) ranging from .48 to .90 for individual scales and .88 for the full scale. The validity documentation of the IBT is weak (Smith & Zurawski, 1983), although the IBT does appear to be related to both anxiety and depression (Cook & Peterson, 1986; Deffenbacher et al., 1986).

Cognitive Functional Analysis

What people say to themselves also influences behavior. If you tell yourself that you can't learn statistics, then you will likely avoid statistics. Furthermore, when confronted with a difficult statistics problem, you will tend to give up quickly. If you tell yourself you like statistics, you will probably confront difficult statistics problems by taking your time and systematically figuring out the answers. Self-statements have been shown to influence behaviors as diverse as coping behavior in cardiac patients (Kendall, Williams, Pechacek, Graham, Shisslak, & Herzoff, 1979), assertiveness (Schwartz & Gottman, 1976), and athletic performance (Perkos, Theodorakis, & Chroni, 2002). Interestingly, positive and negative self-statements do not function in the same way. Apparently, negative self-statements do far more harm than positive self-statements do good. Thus, treatment generally involves identifying and then eliminating negative self-statements rather than increasing positive self-statements. Try to become aware of your own self-statements for a moment. What do you say to yourself as you go about your daily activities? Odds are, if you make a lot of negative self-statements, you are hindering your personal efficiency and ability to cope.

One of the most important examples of cognitive-behavioral assessment is called *cognitive-functional analysis* (Meichenbaum, 1976, 2003). The premise underlying a cognitive-functional analysis is that what a person says to himself or herself plays a critical role in behavior. The cognitive-functional analyst is thus interested in internal dialogue such as self-appraisals and expectations. Again, what do you say to yourself about yourself as you go about your daily activities? Do you constantly criticize or belittle yourself? Or do you always reassure yourself of your capabilities? Research clearly indicates these self-statements influence your behavior and even your feelings (Meichenbaum, 1976, 1999; Martin & Swinson, 2000).

Cognitive-functional analysis is concerned with ascertaining the environmental factors that precede behavior (environmental antecedents) as well as those that maintain behavior (environmental consequences). In addition, however, a cognitive-functional analysis attempts to ascertain the internal or cognitive antecedents and consequences for the behavioral sequence (the internal dialogue). What does the person say to him- or herself before, during, and following the behavior? What is said before the behavior may influence what is done. What is said during the behavior may influence the way the behavior manifests itself. What is said following the behavior may influence its probability of recurrence.

If thoughts influence overt behavior, then modifying one's thoughts can lead to modifications in one's actions. In other words, to the extent that thoughts play a role in eliciting or maintaining one's actions, modification of the thoughts underlying the actions should lead to behavioral changes. For example, if the thought "I must have a cigarette" is consistently associated with the behavioral sequence involved in smoking, then changing that thought to "My lungs are clean, I feel healthy, and I have no desire to smoke" could help to modify the person's pattern of smoking behavior.

Parallel to Meichenbaum's technique of cognitive-functional analysis are procedures and devices that allow a person to test him- or herself, or *self monitoring devices*. Because cognitive-behavioral practitioners value the role and responsibility of the individual in the therapeutic process, they have developed a wide variety of these devices. In the simplest case, an individual must record the frequency of a particular behavior—that is, to monitor it so that he or she becomes aware of the behavior. To monitor your smoking behavior, simply count the number of cigarettes you smoke each day. To monitor your weight, weigh yourself each morning and record the number of pounds.

Some self-monitoring procedures are quite sophisticated. For example, a mechanical counter, marketed to the general public, can be attached to the jaw to count the number of bites a person takes when eating. The idea is to take fewer bites each day, even if only one less than the day before. Presumably, this procedure will ultimately result in a lower intake of food and eventually weight loss. Similarly, timing devices and procedures allow people to assess how long they engage in an activity. In one method, the subject plugs in a clock every time she studies, thus recording total study time. The goal is to increase this length of time, either by increasing the length of individual study sessions or by increasing the total study time within a specific period. These self-monitoring assessment tools are limited only by the imagination of the practitioner. Azrin and Powell (1968) developed an electronic device that counts the number of times a cigarette case is opened. Treatment is aimed at opening the case fewer times each day. Naturally, one can easily cheat with these devices, but to think of this possibility is to miss the point of these procedures. These devices help people help themselves by increasing awareness through feedback. You test yourself. If you cheat, you cheat yourself. Later in this chapter in our section about computerized psychological tests and measurement, we will discuss the latest computer equipment used to analyze thoughts and behaviors regarding everything from social regulation of emotion (Perrez, Wilhelm, Schoebi, & Horner, 2001) to fear responses (Newman, Kenardy, Herman, & Taylor, 1997).

Psychophysiological Procedures

Seen as a variant of cognitive-behavioral assessment by some and as an independent category by others, psychophysiological methods of assessment use such indicators as heart rate, blood pressure, galvanic skin response (GSR), and skin temperature to assess psychological problems (Iacono, 1991; Morales, 1994). In essence, psychophysiological assessment procedures attempt to quantify physiological responses (Roscoe, 1993). This quantification is then translated into psychological factors (Steptoe & Johnston, 1991). Thus, physiological data are used to draw inferences about the psychological state of the individual (Fredrikson, 1991). As Haynes (1991) stated, "A fundamental tenet of [psychophysiological assessment] is that social, behavioral, cognitive, and emotional phenomena are often a function of, and are often reflected in, physiological processes" (p. 307).

Physiological Variables with Treatment Implications

The feasibility of psychophysiological assessment received support in an early study conducted by Ax (1953). Ax demonstrated that the fear response was related to specific physiological changes such as increases in blood pressure and skin conductance levels. He found that he could distinguish fear and anger based on physiological data. Ax's early work, which has subsequently been supported (see Ekman, Levenson, & Friesen, 1983; Turpin, 1991), had interesting implications. For instance, it suggested the possibility of assessing abnormally chronic and intense anger or fear through strictly physiological methods.

This type of assessment represents a quantum leap from traditional procedures, which depend on voluntary responses from subjects. In addition, as with other methods of behavioral assessment, psychophysiological assessment has direct implications for treatment (Haynes, 1992).

The polygraph and related devices that measure blood pressure, heart rate, and GSR have been the primary tools of the psychophysiological assessment specialist. However, imaginative researchers continue to develop tools for special purposes. For example, psychophysiologists have been particularly interested in measuring adult sexual responses (Janssen, Everaerd, Vanlunsen, & Oerlemans, 1994; Morales, 1994). Measures of sexual arousal make use of the fact that it is directly related to the flow of blood into the penis in men and into the vagina in women (Masters & Johnson, 1966; Janssen, 2002). Using this knowledge, researchers have developed measures of human sexual arousal. For example, penile erection can be measured by the penile transducer, a device that encircles the penis (Baxter, Barbaree, & Marshall, 1986; Zuckerman, 1971). As erection occurs, an electrical signal is generated, and this signal can then be recorded. The procedure can be used to determine the type of stimuli (pictures, fantasies, men, women, and so forth) that lead to arousal in men as well as the strength of the male sexual response. The penile transducer and related devices are much more objective than traditional tools.

Evaluation of Psychophysiological Techniques

Support for psychophysiological assessment has come from investigations that have revealed a systematic covariation between measurable physiological processes and cognitive processes (Iacono, 1991; Jennings, 1986; Jacobson, Bondi, & Salmon, 2002). For example, Ahern and Beatty (1979) found that more-intelligent subjects show smaller task-evoked pupillary dilations than do less-intelligent subjects (as evaluated by their scores on the SAT). These results reveal physiological differences in individuals with differing mental abilities. In other studies, Beatty and colleagues (for example, Geiselman, Woodward, & Beatty, 1982) used measures of heart-rate variability and skin conductance to evaluate *processing intensity,* the amount of effort or energy devoted to a cognitive task. Presumably, brighter individuals expend less of their total available processing resources in solving a difficult problem, either because they have greater resources or because they make more efficient use of them.

Psychophysiological hardware seems to hold considerable promise for raising the scientific respectability of psychological testing. Problems still remain, however, and considerably more research and development are needed. One of the most serious problems in psychophysiological assessment concerns artifacts. For instance, movement by a subject may result in the recording of a physiological response that did not occur. In many cases, furthermore, direct measurement is difficult if not impossible. To measure brain-wave patterns, for example, one places electrodes on the head, whereas the electrical current measured actually comes from the brain. Thus, the skull distorts the electrical impulse measured by the recording device. There are other problems as well, including the long-known effect of initial values (Wilder, 1950), by which the strength of a response is influenced by the absolute prestimulus strength. Which is the stronger response: an increase in heart rate from 60 to 85 beats per minute or an increase from 110 to 125 beats per minute? Obviously, one must take initial values into account in evaluating the strength, intensity, and significance of a physiological response. Another problem, which you have seen throughout this book, is that demographic factors such as age, gender, and ethnicity influence psychophysiological responses (Anderson & Mc-Neilly, 1991). Thus, one must always consider cultural, ethnic, economic, gender, and other variables in making any kind of assessment. In spite of these problems, psychophysiological procedures appear to hold great promise for the future of psychological testing.

Computers and Psychological Testing

The application and use of computers in testing has been a major development in the field (Mills, 2002; Clauser, 2002; Wainer, 2000). For testing, one can use computers in two basic ways: (1) to administer, score, and even interpret traditional tests; and (2) to create new tasks and perhaps measure abilities that traditional procedures cannot tap. We will briefly look at the history and development of computers and psychological testing and recent applications of computers to the testing field, particularly to cognitive-behavioral assessment. In the last section, we briefly discuss signal-detection procedures.

In 1966, a Rogerian therapist named Eliza marked the beginning of a new phase in psychological testing and assessment (Epstein & Klinkenberg, 2001). With a great amount of empathy, Eliza encouraged her clients to talk about their experiences and how these experiences made them feel. Clients responded warmly and enjoyed the sense of empathy resulting from their interaction. The warmth and connection between Eliza and her clients came as a big surprise to researcher Dr. Joseph Weizenbaum. Eliza was his creation, a computer program developed to emulate the behavior of a psychotherapist. Weizenbaum had produced the program in an attempt to show that human–computer interaction was superficial and ineffective for therapy. Dr. Weizenbaum discovered that sessions with Eliza engendered positive emotions in the clients who had actually enjoyed the interaction and attributed human characteristics to the program. The research by Weizenbaum gave credence to the theory that human–computer interaction may be beneficial and opened the door for further study.

As Fowler (1985) has noted, computers began to be applied to psychological testing almost as soon as they were available. Early on, progress in the use of computer–human interaction in the field of psychology took a decided turn away from psychotherapy and to the area of interview and assessment. Currently, there are numerous programs for administering, scoring, and even interpreting a host of tests.

Computer-Assisted Interview

As it became apparent that the computer could be an effective means of gathering information from individuals, psychological computer testing began to encompass the presentation of interviews and assessments traditionally completed in paper-and-pencil form. The computer-assisted interview has been used for everything from comprehensive behavioral psychological assessment and diagnostics (Erdman, Klein, & Greist, 1985) to special topic evaluations such as screenings for suicide (Greist, Gustafson, Stauss, Rowse, Laughren, & Chiles, 1973), HIV risk (Williams, Freeman, Bowen, & Saunders, 1998), depression (Carr, Ancill, Ghosh, & Margo, 1981), and phobias (Carr & Ghosh, 1983).

Although there has been some controversy as to the equivalence of computer-based interviewing and paper-and-pencil forms, much of the research has indicated that the validity of computer-administered interviews is equal to or better than that of paper-and-pencil forms (Choca & Morris, 1992; Bressani & Downs, 2001). In part, this equivalence can be attributed to the fact that in creating computer-administered versions, it has been the goal to make these tests as similar to the original versions as possible (Epstein & Klinkenberg, 2001).

The explanation for computer versions that produce more accurate assessment is slightly more complicated and often debated. Computer interview success may exceed the interview accomplishments of some clinicians because the computer programs ask more standardized questions, covering areas that a clinician may neglect (Hugh, 1981). It has also been noted by Hugh that computer administration ensures that crucial facts are recorded more systematically.

More important, computer-administered interviews appear to reduce the likelihood of clients skewing their responses in an attempt to appear socially acceptable to the clinician. It has been shown that participants are more likely to share sensitive information about personal subjects when computer-assisted interviewing is used. This has been the case for the evaluation of children when assessing family problems and potentially embarrassing conditions such as enuresis and encopresis (Sawyer, Sarris, & Baghurst, 1992). When assessing adults, the computer-based versions of psychological interviews make individuals more at ease and willing to disclose information concerning their sexual behavior (Cooley, Rogers, Turner, Al-Tayyib, Willis, & Ganapathii, 2001; Hewitt, 2002), drug usage (Lessler, Caspar, Penne, & Barker, 2000), HIV risk

(Williams et al., 1998), and emotional problems (Slack & Slack, 1977). Although some studies show the effects of social desirability may be reducing over time (Dwight & Feigelson, 2000), a 1999 meta-analytic study of distortion caused by social desirability supports the idea that social desirability has less of an impact with computer-assisted interviewing than with traditional administration (Richman, Keisler, Weisband, & Fritz, 1999)

It is interesting to note that as computers become more sophisticated and begin to more closely emulate human characteristics, prompting clients to respond as if they are responding to a human, the likelihood of responding to sensitive personal questions in socially desirable ways does not increase (Tourangeau, Couper, & Steiger, 2003). In fact, people are sometimes more frank and candid in response to a computer then to a skilled therapist.

Computer-Administered Tests

Traditional assessments other than computer-assisted interviews have also been made available as computer-based tests. As with computer-assisted interviews, there has been much discussion about the equivalence of the paper-and-pencil forms and the computer-administered versions. A preponderance of the research suggests that, in general, tests such as the MMPI (Honaker, Harrell, & Buffaloe, 1988; Pinsoneault, 1996), the Category Test (Choca & Morris, 1992) and the Ansell-Casey Life Skills Assessment (Bressani & Downs, 2001) result in similar evaluations when administered by computer or by paper and pencil. The same is true for other types of traditional tests administered by computer such as the Strong-Campbell Interest Inventory (Vansickle, Kimmel, & Kapes, 1989), the Multidimensional Aptitude Battery (Harrell, Honaker, Hetu, & Oberwager, 1987), and other tests that measure anxiety, depression, and psychological reactance (Lukin, Dowd, Plake, & Kraft, 1985).

A small number of psychological tests that measure negative affect tend to produce different results than their paper-and-pencil forms (Clay, Lankford, & Wilson, 1992). Negative affect scores are particularly elevated when testing computer-anxious individuals and using the Beck Depression Inventory and Spielberger's State-Trait Anxiety Inventory. Computer anxiety also has an effect on educational testing and appears to be most pronounced when evaluating math skills (Shermis & Lombard, 1998).

Although questions remain about the impact of computer anxiety on test takers (Shermis, Mzumara, & Bublitz, 2001; Brosnan, 1998; Tseng, Tiplady, Macleod, & Wright, 1998), research suggests the benefits of computer administration outweigh the benefits of paper-and-pencil administration in several ways. Computer administration is generally less time-consuming for both the individual being tested and the test administrator (Carr & Ghosh, 1983), more cost-effective (Space, 1981), better accepted by test takers who are adults (Weber et al., 2003) or children (Powell, Wilson, & Hastya, 2002), and often more accurate (Richman et al., 1999).

Computer-administered psychological testing is not without drawbacks. The finer subtleties of human communication cannot be read by a computer program. Body language that may suggest hesitation or distortion of the truth to a human would not be captured by computer (Space, 1981). The use of subtle techniques by the clinician also cannot be emulated by a computer. To gather sensitive information, a clinician's line of questioning must be flexible and selective based on the client's responses (Erdman et al., 1985). Although some programs are becoming sophisticated to the extent that they can sense emotion and adjust responses accordingly (Picard & Klein, 2002), they have yet to match the clinician's ability to detect subtle emotional cues.

Computer Diagnosis, Scoring, and Reporting of Results

From educational testing to tests that evaluate personality and psychopathology, computers are taking a prominent role in the scoring of tests, reporting of results, and diagnosis of clients (Frase et al., 2003; Warzecha, 1991).

The effectiveness of computer scoring, computer-generated diagnosis, and narrative reports has been the issue of controversy since their inception (Tallent, 1987). From neuropsychological assessments such as the Halstead-Reitan Battery (Russell, 2000), to personnel screening tests, the scoring and report generation of certain tests seem to be straightforward, efficient, and accurate (Vale, Keller, & Bentz, 1986). Since early in the history of computers in psychological testing, there has been evidence suggesting computer diagnosis provides reliability comparable to that of psychiatrists (Sletten, Ulett, Altman, & Sundland, 1970).

Computer software that has been developed using criteria for diagnosis taken from the DSM-IV is being developed to screen for psychopathology (Krol, DeBruyn, van Aarle, & van der Bercken, 2001). When the usefulness of this program was examined, it appeared to serve as a supportive function in the process of diagnosis. Others have shown that severity of depression (Carr et al., 1981), suicidal ideation (Greist et al., 1973), and certain phobias (Carr & Ghosh, 1983) can be effectively diagnosed by computer.

Projective tests have also been successfully scored by computer. When examining the computer-scoring version of the Holtzman Inkblot Test, validity was confirmed by acceptable correlations between the computer-scoring methods and traditional methods of scoring (Gorham, Moseley, & Holtzman, 1968). Evaluation of the online version of the Rorschach determined that the computer can provide a report similar to that of a clinician (Harris, Robinson, & Menzies, 1981). Similarly, the Rotter Incomplete Sentence Blank showed only small differences between administration types that were not significant once attitudes toward computers were adjusted for (Rasulis, Schuldberg, & Murtagh, 1996).

In the field of educational testing, sophisticated computer programs have been designed to score essays. The oldest system of computerized writing analysis, Project Essay Grade (PEG), was developed in 1966 by E. Page (Rudner & Gagne, 2001). This system analyses the quality of a writing sample by measuring writing traits such as average word length, use of rare words, and the number of semicolons used. For more than 30 years, this system of analysis has consistently shown correlations with human scores as high as .87. A modern version of a PEG is the Expository Text Analysis Tool (ETAT). The ETAT is software designed to analyze text rapidly and objectively (Vidal-Abarca, Reyes, Gilabert, Calpe, Soria, & Graesser, 2002). ETAT accomplishes this task by a symbolic representation system that segments text into nodes, classifies the unidentified nodes, and links them with relational arcs.

The next generation of computerized essay scoring is the Intelligent Essay Assessor (IEA), which was introduced by T. Landauer and P. Foltz (Rudner & Gagne, 2001). The IEA was created in 1989 to index information from documents to allow for simple retrieval of facts. The IEA is used to evaluate essays according to content. This is done by listing every relevant content term used by the writer. Relevant terms are weighted, and a score is derived by a tally of the terms included. As with PEG, IEA scores are highly correlated with human scores.

A newer instrument dubbed "E-rater" (the Educational Testing Services Essay Rater) is a hybrid of PEG and IEA. E-rater analyzes the structure of the essay in the same fashion as PEG and measures the content of the essay as does the IEA. In addition, E-rater measures syntactic variety by counting the number of modal verbs and subordinate, infinitive, complimentary, and relative clauses. Analysis of assessment scores generated by E-rater revealed significant correlations between automated essay scoring and nontest indicators of proficiency such as academic success with writing (Powers, Burstein, Chodorow, Fowles, & Kukich, 2000) and returns grades that are highly correlated with grades given by human scorers (Rudner & Gagne, 2001).

Although, as of 2003, E-rater was put into use to score the General Management Aptitude Test (GMAT), there are some questions concerning E-rater use for the assessment of essays written as part of high-stakes tests. Powers and colleagues (2002) succeeded in stumping E-rater into assigning scores that were too high. Because E-rater uses a natural language-processing technique, detailed information about this approach to scoring may aid a test taker who is unskilled as a writer in producing an essay that is scored high. In the defense of E-rater's ability, these inflated scores could only be achieved when the essay writers were given specific information about E-rater's scoring system that is not available to the general population.

Caution is still in order, however. The fact that computer scoring of essays correlates well with human scoring may not be that impressive. The use of essays as components of tests has sometimes been rejected, in part because human scoring of written work tends to be highly subjective, and correlations between human scorers are generally between .70 and .75 (Rudner & Gagne, 2001). In other words, the proficiency of computers to score essays consistently has barely risen to a standard that is rather low and especially problematic when considering the importance of some high-stakes tests.

For every study that confirms the reliability of computer-generated scores, diagnoses, and reports, there is one that suggests caution is in order. Even the most popular tests such as the MMPI have been criticized for including scoring errors (Pope, Butcher, & Seelen, 2000) and generating reports that are markedly less accurate than those of clinicians (Epstein & Rotunda, 2000).

Allard and Faust (2000) also detected scoring errors when evaluating the MMPI, the Beck Depression Inventory, and the Spielberger State-Trait Anxiety inventory. The overall message gathered from decades of research concludes that computers are a tool, and interpretations of the scores, reports, and diagnoses they produce are appendages to clinical judgment (Butcher, Perry, & Atlis, 2000) that require the assessment and expertise of clinicians (Russell, 2000).

Internet Usage for Psychological Testing

The advent of computers and the Internet have revolutionized testing and played a major role in the proliferation of modern techniques. In the early 1990s, the Internet began to thrive, and its growth, development, and diversity of use have exploded since 1995 (Crespin & Austin, 2002). Today the Internet is inundated with a wide variety of psychological tests: from personality tests that are neither reliable nor valid and meant only for entertainment to tests used in the selection of qualified employees and massive scientifically complex research projects that use the Internet as a source of large numbers of participants and data collection. The Internet has already shown itself to be useful to the science of psychological testing and measurement.

Any interested person can easily find free psychological tests on the World Wide Web. Brain.com, for example, offers seven types of free IQ tests; another site offers more than 200 free tests about relationships, health, career, IQ, and personality. These tests are touted as statistically sound. Because individuals are often interested in evaluations about themselves, by offering free psychological test, sites can gather massive amounts of useful data for research purposes.

Although some researchers doubt the quality of data gathered online, the use of the Web to gather data has generally been shown to be adequate (McGraw, Tew, & Williams, 2000). Problems concerning the inability to standardize testing conditions when participants are testing at different locations, using different types of computers, and with different amounts of distraction in their environments may be compensated for by the massive sample sizes available to Web-based laboratories. Davis (1999) has shown that results gathered from Web-based participants in different environments did not covary. A study that compared Web-based assessment, traditional paper-and-pencil assessment, and Web-based assessment in a disruptive environment found no significant differences between assessment techniques and resulted in significantly high test–retest reliability coefficients for all three types of administration (Miller et al., 2002). Traditional tests conducted via the Internet are found to have similar results to their paper-and-pencil versions (Buchanan & Smith, 1999; Cronk & West, 2002) and to include less error in data collection (Pettit, 2002; Miller et al., 2002). It is also becoming evident that Web-based samples can more closely match the intended sample (McCabe, Boyd, Couper, Crawford, & D'Arcy, 2002), especially when methods that are used to publicize the project target specific interests (Epstein & Klinkenberg, 2002). And, once again, some evidence suggests that, as with the use of the computer alone, Web-based testing facilitates more thorough self-disclosure from participants (Davis, 1999).

The ease at which participants can be recruited to participate in online testing, the ease of data collection, and the reduction of error make Web-based data collection appealing to researchers (Pettit, 2002) and ensure its use in the future.

The Computerization of Cognitive-Behavioral Assessment

Farrell (1992) has identified seven major applications of computers to cognitive-behavioral assessment: (1) collecting self-report data, (2) coding observational data, (3) directly recording behavior, (4) training, (5) organizing and synthesizing behavioral assessment data, (6) analyzing behavioral assessment data, and (7) supporting decision making. As Farrell notes, the computerization of cognitive-behavioral self-report tests, such as those discussed earlier in the chapter, would be a relatively simple endeavor. Once computerized, such questionnaires could be easily administered and immediately scored by the computer, thus saving valuable professional time.

According to Farrell (1991), several factors have impeded the widespread use of computers in cognitive-behavioral assessment. Perhaps first among these is lack of acceptance by some practitioners. Another obstacle to this use of computers involves evaluation of software (Farrell, 1992). Apparently, vendors are reluctant to make their products available for review; consequently, potential users do not have sufficient information to evaluate the quality of the software. Despite such obstacles, it seems inevitable that the future will see a greater use of computers in all areas of assessment.

As with other computer-based psychological assessments, computer-based cognitive-behavioral evaluations appear to have equivalent results as their paper-and-pencil counterparts (Franceschina, Dorz, & Bari, 2001).

In addition to success in computer-based evaluation, computer-based cognitive-behavioral treatments have been found effective for reducing stuttering (Blood, 1995) and treating anxiety disorders (Heimberg & Coles, 1999), including generalized anxiety disorder (Newman, 1999; Newman, Consoli, & Taylor, 1997), panic disorder (Newman et al., 1997), and social phobia (Heimberg, 2001). They have also been found useful for evaluating body image disturbance in individuals with eating disorders (Shibata, 2002), levels of conflict and cooperation in individuals' social interactions (Aidman & Shmelyov, 2002), and different aspects of individuals' natural social, linguistic, and psychological lives (Mehl, Pennebaker, Crow, Dabbs, & Price, 2001).

One example of the use of a computer in cognitive-behavioral treatment is a palmtop computer program that has been developed for use in evaluating and treating symptoms of generalized anxiety disorder. The program includes a mobile self-monitoring component that is ever-present with the client and thus increases the reliability of client self-report. Treatment is delivered via three therapeutic modules (relaxation, cognitive restructuring, and imaginal exposure) that can be accessed by the client when needed (Newman, 1999). There is evidence that this particular computer-based treatment program may increase the effectiveness of cognitive-behavioral treatment.

Similarly, evaluations of a palmtop computer-based treatment for panic disorder has been shown to be effective (Newman et al., 1997). Comparisons were made between panic disorder symptom improvement by a group using 12 sessions of cognitive-behavioral treatment without the aid of a computer, and a group using only four sessions of cognitive-behavioral treatment with the aid of a computer. The computer-based treatment group carried palmtop computers with a cognitive-behavioral treatment program that they were told to use whenever they felt anxious or wanted to practice techniques. Although the computer-based treatment group did not show any greater improvement than the traditionally treated group at the time of follow-up, it is noteworthy that the computer-based group only required four sessions for an equivalent level of improvement.

The use of computers in cognitive-behavioral therapy substantially improves the quality and effectiveness of traditional techniques. The ability for a client to instantly record a target behavior and to access a tool to help deal with the behavior as it occurs is efficient and reduces the length of time needed to alter a pattern of behavior.

Computer programs can also generate schedules of reinforcement including fixed ratio, variable ratio, fixed interval, and variable interval schedules (Wolach & McHale, 2002). A cumulative recording of subjects' responses can then be documented, simplifying the evaluation concerning the effectiveness of the type of schedule used.

Tests Possible Only by Computer

In addition to tests that are merely computer-friendly versions of their traditional paper-and-pencil forms and tests conducted over the Internet, there are developments in psychological testing made possible only with the use of computers.

The use of computer-generated virtual reality programs for psychological testing and treatment of phobias has grown rapidly in the past decade. Virtual reality technology is ideal for safely and efficiently exposing clients to the objects of their phobias while evaluating physiological responses (Wiederhold, Jang, Kim, & Wiederhold, 2002), systematically recording those responses, and evaluating patient improvement (Kirkby, 1996). Equipment that measures heart rate, skin resistance, and skin temperature informs clinicians of the level of distress caused by a phobia and levels of improvement as treatment continues.

Virtual reality environments that mimic an airplane ride, an encounter with a spider, social situations, and being in front of an audience have all been found to engender the same reactions as the actual environment, only to a lesser degree and with the added confidence of the client being in control of the program. Studies that have measured physiological responses have found that controlled exposure to virtual environments can desensitize individuals to the object of their fear (Wiederhold et al., 2002). When using virtual reality to treat and measure fear responses associated with spider phobia, Garcia-Palacios and colleagues (2002) found that 83% of those being treated showed clinical signs of improvement. There have also been studies boasting success rates of 65 to 80% when treating fear of flying (Maltby, Kirsch, Mayers, & Allen, 2002; Wiederhold, Gervirtz, & Spira, 2001), and great improvements have been seen when treating clients with claustrophobia (Botella, Villa, Banos, Perpina, & Garcia-Palacios, 1999), fear of public speaking (Lee et al., 2002), fear of driving (Wald & Taylor, 2000), and fear of heights (North, North, & Coble, 1997).

Because of the relative safety of facing one's fear in a virtual environment, because virtual reality reduces the possibility of embarrassment to clients (North et al., 1997), and because virtual reality requires less time and money to conduct than does in vivo desensitization, it is seen as ideal for the treatment and measurement of phobic responses. These positive attributes of virtual reality also make individuals with phobias more likely to seek and complete treatment (Garcia-Palacios, Hoffman, See, Tsai, & Botella, 2001). The success of virtual reality in the treatment of phobias has spawned interest in those who are looking for improved ways to evaluate and treat those with schizophrenia, attention deficit and hyperactivity disorder, autism (Costa, De Carvalho, Drummond, Wauke, & De Sa Guimaraes, 2002), posttraumatic stress disorder, obsessive compulsive disorder, body image disorders (North, North, & Coble, 2002), and sexual dysfunction (Vincelli & Riva, 2000; Optale, Munari, Nasta, Pianon, Verde, & Viggiano, 1998). Interesting concepts, including the use of interactive computer games with embedded recording and assessment facilities that measure responses to virtual situations, are beginning to be used in the assessment of personality and psychopathology (Aidman & Shmelyov, 2002). Interactive virtual reality programs are also being appraised as a tool for educational assessment (Byers, 2001). As computer technology advances, computer-generated virtual reality will play a major role in several areas of psychological testing and measurement in the coming decades.

Computer-Adaptive Testing

Although to a smaller extent traditional tests allow for some adaptation according to the test taker's responses, advancements in computer technology have allowed for the construction of tests that adapt and metamorphize according to each response given. After each response, the computer updates the estimation of the test taker's ability. That estimation is then used to select the next item on the test. The selection of only items necessary for the evaluation of the test taker limits the number of items needed for an exact evaluation. Computer-adaptive tests have been found to be more precise and efficient than fixed-item tests (Vispoel, Rocklin, & Tianyou, 1994). Over the past two decades, computer-adaptive tests have been used for classroom testing (Signer, 1991), for evaluating general intelligence (Angoff, 1988), in the selection process for remedial instruction (Tatsuoka & Tatsuoka, 1997), to assess military personnel (Orlansky, Grafton, Martin, & Alley, 1990) and employees (Overton, Harms, Taylor, & Zickar, 1997), for college and graduate student placement, to assess health-related quality of life (Revicki & Cella, 1997), and in nursing licensure (Schmidt, 2000).

There are several practical benefits of computer-adaptive testing (Rudner, 1998). One benefit that is enjoyed by test takers is the decrease in time needed for test taking. In addition, efficiency is increased as scores are immediately recorded and made available. Expenses are reduced because no highly trained test administrators are needed because the computer acts as administrator. Finally, computer-adaptive tests are self-paced and provide accurate scores for test takers whose abilities range from gifted to impaired.

However, there are limitations to computer-adaptive tests. There may be some difficulty in presenting long reading passages, intricate graphs, or artwork. Computer-adaptive tests may not be suitable for all test subjects or skills. They may not calibrate with paper-and-pencil versions. Administrator facility with a large number of computers is required for group testing. The computer literacy levels of test takers may significantly affect performance. Finally, examinees' often question the equity of computer-adaptive tests as each test taker answers a different set of questions.

One of the most frequently debated drawbacks of computer-adaptive testing is the inability of test takers to go back and change previously answered questions (Wise, Finney, Enders, Freeman, & Severance, 1999). If allowed to do so, a test taker could purposefully answer the initial items incorrectly. The computer would then generate a simpler test for which the examinee is overqualified. After answering the simpler questions correctly, the examinee could then go back to the initial questions and change them to the right answer. Although some feel that this strategy would not be attractive to test takers (Wise et al., 1999), caution is still in order when considering item review.

In addition, there is concern that a test taker who is reviewing a completed test may be able to distinguish easier items from difficult items. The examinee would then be aware of which items were answered incorrectly and change the incorrect answers according to that feedback. Although this argument against item review in computer-adaptive testing appears to be sound, Wise and colleagues (1999) and others (Green, 1983) have found that test takers do not discriminate well between easy and difficult questions and therefore would not be informed of which items were answered incorrectly.

Regardless of the drawbacks, computer-adaptive testing is highly effective and frequently used. Of the Educational Testing Service's 11 million test administrations worldwide each year, some of its most frequently used tests (GREs, GMAT, and TOEFL) are computer-adaptive.

Psychophysical and Signal-Detection Procedures

An early impetus for using computers to generate tasks that one cannot present through traditional methods came from the application of psychophysical and signal-detection procedures. In these procedures, a signal is presented and the subject is required to report whether he or she saw it. Many variations in presenting a signal are possible. The examiner can vary the strength of the signal, use more than one signal and require the subject to guess which one has been presented, or follow the signal with noise or another signal to determine the effects of one signal on another.

Saccuzzo and colleagues suggest that one can use psychophysical methods to evaluate psychological disorders and perhaps detect them in their early stages (Saccuzzo, 1977, 1981; Saccuzzo & Braff, 1981, 1986; Saccuzzo, Kerr, Marcus, & Brown, 1979; Saccuzzo & Miller, 1977; Saccuzzo & Schubert, 1981). In a series of studies, beginning with Saccuzzo, Hirt, and Spencer (1974), Saccuzzo provided considerable evidence that schizophrenia may be related to the speed with which information is transferred throughout the nervous system (Saccuzzo, 1993). If schizophrenia does in fact develop because of slow processing by the individual, then it seems sensible to use a direct measure of processing speed to assess schizophrenia rather than indirect procedures such as the Rorschach.

Indeed, one can assess information-processing speed by flashing two stimuli in brief succession on a microcomputer screen or a tachistoscope. If a stimulus, such as the letter *T*, is presented and then terminated, the information is first registered by the nervous system. After the information is registered, it theoretically enters a brief perceptual memory system, which Neisser (1967) calls *iconic storage*. The person does not become consciously aware of the stimulus until it is transferred to the higher brain centers, where it is compared with previous learning. The rate of this transfer of information is the speed of information processing (Saccuzzo et al., 1974).

If a stimulus that has been presented and terminated is then followed by a second, noninformational stimulus such as a random pattern, the second and first stimuli may become integrated together in the visual system. Only this unidentifiable composite will then be transferred to the higher brain centers. Obviously, if this occurs, the individual will not able to identify the originally presented *T*. However, if the *T* is transferred to the higher centers before the noninformational stimulus is presented, then the person can identify the letter. By finding the minimum interval between presentation of the letter and presentation of the noninformational stimulus at which the noninformational stimulus no longer interferes with processing of the letter, one can estimate how long it took the letter to reach the higher centers (Saccuzzo & Miller, 1977). Thus, the speed of information processing can be determined by finding this minimum interval (see Figure 15-3). Furthermore, one can often use this information for diagnostic purposes. For example, Saccuzzo and colleagues have shown that schizophrenic people can be distinguished from normal people and others (for example, neurotic people) on the basis of information-processing speed (see Alain, Bernstein, He, Cortese, & Zipursky, 2002; Li, 2002; Saccuzzo, Cadenhead, & Braff, 1996). Normal people require a much shorter interval (150 milliseconds) to avoid the effects of the noninformational stimulus than do schizophrenics (300 milliseconds) (Saccuzzo et al., 1974).

Psychophysical and signal-detection procedures have also been applied to ability testing (Jensen, 1982; Nettelbeck, 1982). Reaction time and backward masking tasks (in which a briefly presented informational target stimulus is followed by a noninformational noise stimulus known as a *mask*) are used to measure the speed, capacity, or efficiency of information processing (Saccuzzo, Larson, & Rimland, 1986). The general idea is that variations among individuals

Target: T   or   A

                                 X
Mask: X X
                                 X

FIGURE 15-3 *Target and mask in signal detection. In signal-detection experiments, the target and mask are presented to the same visual area in close temporal succession. The minimum interval between presentation of the target and presentation of the mask at which the mask no longer interferes with processing of the target is used to evaluate the information-processing speed.*

who differ in psychometric intelligence reflect different information-processing capabilities (Hunt, 1980; Jensen, 1986; Mervis & Robinson, 2003).

Support for a relationship between information-processing capabilities and individual differences in intelligence has come from studies in which the individual must make a rapid response to two or more choices (Jensen, 1979; Jensen & Munro, 1979; Lunneborg, 1978; Smith & Stanley, 1983). When one uses parameters such as median reaction time, slope of reaction time as a function of the number of choices, and intraindividual standard deviations of reaction-time performance, large differences emerge between groups with mental retardation and those with normal IQs as well as between groups of vocational college students and university students (Jensen, 1980, 1982). However, results differ across samples (Lunneborg, 1978). Although the correlations vary widely, with estimates ranging from the high .60's to the low .20's, the correlations are almost always in the expected direction (Jensen, 1982).

The visual paradigm for studying the relationship between information processing and intelligence, in which the subject must respond to a visual stimulus, parallels the backward masking approach used by Saccuzzo and colleagues to study schizophrenia. The subject is required to discriminate between two briefly exposed target stimuli, such as identifying which of two lines presented to the right and left of central fixation is longer (see Figure 15-4). The targets are then followed by a spatially overlapping, noninformational mask (for example, two uniform lines that completely superimpose the lines of the target stimulus). Extensive literature indicates that the mask limits the time the informational impulse is available for processing in the nervous system (Felsten & Wasserman, 1980). Speed of processing, or inspection time (Vickers, Nettelbeck, & Wilson, 1972), can be evaluated by systematically varying the exposure duration of the target and estimating the minimum duration needed for accuracy (Brand, 1981; Lally & Nettelbeck, 1977; Nettelbeck & Lally, 1976) or by keeping the stimulus duration constant and varying the interval between target and mask (Saccuzzo et al., 1979; Saccuzzo & Marcus, 1983).

Numerous studies have reported a statistically significant (nonchance) difference between mentally retarded and nonretarded (average IQ) individuals in their speed of visual information processing as evaluated in a backward masking paradigm (Saccuzzo et al., 1979; Saccuzzo & Michael, 1984). Such differ-

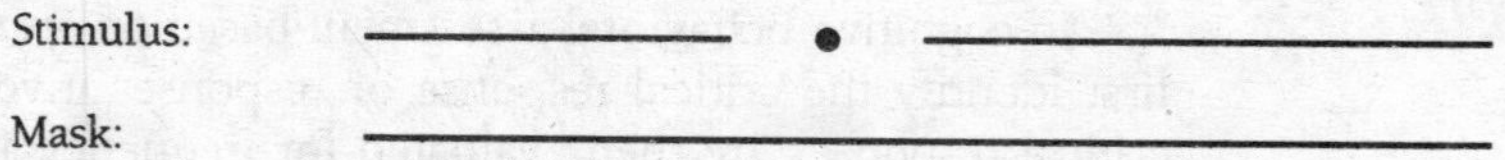

Stimulus: ——————————   •   ——————————

Mask: ———————————————————————

FIGURE 15-4 *Stimuli used in signal-detection studies of intelligence. The stimulus and mask are presented in close temporal succession. The subject must estimate which line is longer.*

ences occur in spite of wide variations in the nature of the stimuli, method of stimulus presentation, and technique used to estimate visual processing speed (Saccuzzo & Michael, 1984). In addition, there are clear-cut developmental differences, with a direct relationship between chronological or mental age and performance (Blake, 1974; Liss & Haith, 1970; Saccuzzo et al., 1979). Gifted children have a greater speed of processing than do nongifted children (Saccuzzo, Johnson, & Guertin, 1994). Finally, the evidence supports a significant relationship between degrees of normal intelligence and visual information processing. As in reaction-time studies, however, correlations vary widely, and the magnitude of the relationship remains highly controversial (Mackintosh, 1981; Nettelbeck, 1982).

The signal-detection approach, as yet in its infancy, offers many advantages over other procedures. Scoring can be simplified, administration can be easily standardized, and the effects of the examiner can be minimized. Developers have adapted the reaction time and backward masking tasks for presentation by personal computers (see Brand, 1981; Saccuzzo & Larson, 1987; Saccuzzo et al., 1986). With standard software, independent investigators can readily verify results from psychophysical and signal-detection procedures. Thus far, the findings seem to indicate a clear but modest relationship between information-processing capabilities and intelligence (Saccuzzo et al., 1994). In addition, there appears to be an interesting relationship between perceptual sensitivity and response bias and "big five" personality factors (Rose, Murphy, Byard, & Nikzad, 2002). In their current state of development, however, such information-processing tests cannot replace more standard procedures. If they eventually prove to be a valid substitute, however, the objectivity of assessment may be markedly enhanced.

SUMMARY

Cognitive-behavioral procedures differ from traditional tests in that they are more direct, have fewer inferential assumptions, and remain closer to observable phenomena. Traditional tests are based on the medical model, which views the overt manifestations of psychological disorders merely as symptoms of some underlying cause. This underlying cause is the target of the traditional procedures. Cognitive-behavioral tests are based on the belief that the overt manifestations of psychological disorders are more than mere symptoms. Although possibly caused by some other factor, the behaviors themselves—including actions, thoughts, and physiological processes—are the targets of behavioral tests.

In cognitive-behavioral assessment based on *operant conditioning*, one must first identify the critical response or responses involved in a disorder. These critical responses are then evaluated for frequency, intensity, or duration. The resulting data provide the baseline for the particular behaviors. Once a baseline is obtained, an intervention is introduced. The effect of this intervention on the baseline is then observed.

Self-report techniques focus on situations that lead to particular response patterns, whereas traditional procedures focus on determining the internal characteristics of the individual that lead to particular response patterns. Furthermore, the cognitive-behavioral procedures purport to be more related to observable phenomena than are traditional procedures.

Kanfer and Saslow developed the *functional,* or *behavior-analytic, approach* to cognitive-behavioral assessment. Rather than labeling people as schizophrenic or neurotic, this approach focuses on behavioral deficits and excesses. A behavioral excess is any behavior described as problematic because of excesses in its frequency, intensity, duration, or because of its inappropriateness; a behavioral deficit is the opposite (occurs too infrequently, etc.).

One of the most important examples of the cognitive-behavioral assessment approach is Meichenbaum's technique, *cognitive-functional analysis.* The premise underlying cognitive-functional analysis is that what a person says to him- or herself plays a critical role in determining behavior. A cognitive-functional analysis ascertains the environmental factors that precede behavior as well as those that maintain it. In addition, this kind of analysis attempts to ascertain the internal or cognitive antecedents and consequences of a behavioral sequence.

An important recent development is the application of computers to testing. In the psychophysical and signal-detection approaches, computers present tasks that cannot be given by traditional means. For example, the subject is required to make a visual discrimination or to respond rapidly to a stimulus in an effort to measure information-processing capabilities. Computers are also used more and more frequently for testing in all its phases, from administration to analysis; however, care must be taken in using computers wisely. Farrel (1992) has identified seven applications of computers in the field of cognitive-behavioral assessment: (1) collecting self-report data, (2) coding observational data, (3) directly recording behavior, (4) training, (5) organizing and synthesizing behavioral assessment data, (6) analyzing behavioral assessment data, and (7) supporting decision making.

WEB ACTIVITY   For interesting and relevant Web sites, check the following:

www.air-dc.org/cecp/resources/problembehavior/indivinterv.htm
Addressing student problem behavior: An IEP team's introduction to functional behavioral assessment and behavior intervention plans

www.ed.gov/databases/ERIC_Digests/ed388883.html
Mental health counseling assessment: Broadening one's understanding of the client and the client's presenting concerns.

www.nuts.cc/links/ed/gen/comp_mh.html
Mental Health Resource Centre

www.mayfieldpub.com/psychtesting/profiles/beck.htm
Aaron T. Beck, MD

www2.psy.uq.edu.au/~landcp/PY269/sorck/sorck4.html
The SORCK analysis

CHAPTER 16

Testing in Counseling Psychology

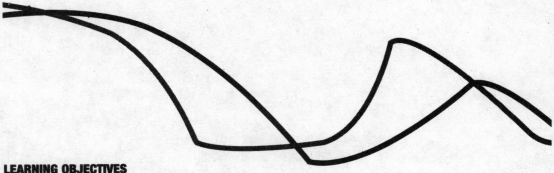

LEARNING OBJECTIVES

When you have completed this chapter, you should be able to:

☐ Describe the use of the criterion-keying method in the development of the SVIB

☐ List some of the criticisms of the SVIB

☐ Describe how the SCII and the CISS improved on the SVIB

☐ Describe how the KOIS differs from the SVIB, the SCII, and the CISS

☐ Outline some of the controversial issues in interest measurement

☐ Compare the approaches to career placement taken by Osipow, Super, and Roe

☐ Describe the template-matching method of assessment

At age 35, Harry found himself faced with a dilemma. He had studied hard for many years to become a dentist, but what he had suspected for many years was becoming obvious: He really did not like dentistry. Although Harry had chosen this occupation, he had not considered dentistry in detail before making a commitment to the field.

Harry could trace his interest in becoming a dentist to an experience he had during his childhood. As a young boy, he liked to play golf. While on the course one day, Harry met a dentist who explained that the practice of dentistry was lucrative but still allowed practitioners enough time to play golf and engage in other activities. Harry was a good student, and the encounter with the golfer-dentist made him think that dentistry would afford him the ideal lifestyle. Harry liked his science classes when he entered college, and he continued to be an outstanding student. After four years at a state university, he was accepted by a good dental school.

In dental school, Harry began to question his career choice. Two things were apparent by the end of his third year. First, he did not really enjoy doing dental work. He found himself uneasy when his patients fussed in the chair, and he disliked subjecting people to the discomfort associated with some dental procedures. Second, Harry discovered that he did not share many interests with other people in the field of dentistry.

After completing dental school, Harry did a brief tour of duty in the Air Force as a dentist. When he left the service, he decided he wanted to get away from dentistry for a while and enrolled in art school. However, despite his dislike for dentistry, he returned to the practice because of the large personal and financial investment he had already made in the profession. Dentistry paid well, and retraining in a field of more interest to him would be difficult and costly. During the 10 years following dental school, Harry quit and reentered his dental practice on three separate occasions. Throughout the entire experience, he remained unhappy with his choice of profession.

This true story recounts the lives of many people who feel they have made the wrong career choice. Some of the misery that talented people like Harry experience could be avoided with proper career counseling and guidance (Walsh, 2003; Watkins & Campbell, 2000). In this chapter, we examine the contribution of psychological tests to the selection of and preparation for a career.

The term *career* connotes "adventure" to many people. As a noun it means "swift course," and as a verb it means "to go swiftly or wildly." The Latin root is *carrus*, "chariot." Thus, the term for today's rat race has its roots in the exciting Roman races (Super & Hall, 1978). Careers can indeed be exciting and the essence of life if they are properly selected. They can also lead to misery if not carefully chosen. Psychological tests can help people select the right career. The first step in the identification of an appropriate career path is the evaluation of interests.

Measuring Interests

If you want to enter an appropriate career, you must identify your interests. Some people need little help finding work that interests them; others can benefit from the guidance given by a psychological test. In the more than 85 years since the introduction of interest inventories, millions of people have received feedback about their own interests to help them make wise career choices.

The first interest inventory, introduced in 1921, was called the Carnegie Interest Inventory. When the *Mental Measurements Yearbook* was first published in 1939, it discussed 15 different interest measures (Datta, 1975). The two most widely used interest tests were introduced relatively early: the Strong Vocational Interest Blank in 1927 and the Kuder Preference Survey in 1939.

Today there are more than 80 interest inventories in use; however, the Strong (which has now evolved into the Campbell Interest and Skill Survey) remains the most widely used test in research and practice.

The Strong Vocational Interest Blank

Shortly after World War I, E. K. Strong, Jr., and some of his colleagues began to examine the activities that members of different professions liked and disliked. They came to realize that people in different professional groups had different patterns of interests. To some extent, one might expect this, because people tend to choose lines of work that interest them. One might expect carpenters to like woodworking, and painting might interest an artist more than a salesperson. However, Strong and his colleagues also found that people in the same line of work had similar hobbies, liked the same types of entertainment, and read the same sorts of books and magazines.

With this research as a base, Strong set out to develop a test that would match the interests of a subject to the interests and values of a criterion group of people who were happy in the careers they had chosen. This procedure is called criterion keying, or the *criterion-group approach* (see Chapter 15). The test they created with this method was the Strong Vocational Interest Blank (SVIB).

In preliminary studies of the test, groups of individuals from many professions and occupations responded to approximately 400 items dealing with likes and dislikes related to these occupations and to leisure activities. The criterion keying then determined how the interests of new subjects resembled those of the criterion groups.

In the revised 1966 version of the SVIB, the 399 items were related to 54 occupations for men. A separate form presented 32 different occupations for women. Items in the SVIB were weighted according to how frequently an interest occurred in a particular occupational group as opposed to how frequently it occurred in the general population. Raw scores were converted to standard scores, with a mean of 50 and a standard deviation of 10. Each criterion group used in the construction of the SVIB contained approximately 300 people, a good normative sample. Numerous reliability studies produced impressive results, with odd–even and short-term test–retest figures generally running between the low .80's and the low .90's. Long-term (20-year) test–retest coefficients ran in the respectable .60's. Validity data indicated that the SVIB predicted job satisfaction well (for example, Strong & Campbell, 1966).

One of the most interesting findings to emerge from the hundreds of published studies using the SVIB is that patterns of interest remain relatively stable over time. Strong made a practice of asking a group of Stanford University students who took the test in the 1930s to take the test again as they grew older. These studies showed that interests remain relatively stable for as long as 22 years. Of course, most people did modify their interests slightly over this period, and a few people made complete turnabouts; nevertheless, the great majority remained consistent.

Studies also showed that interest patterns are fairly well established by age 17. For example, Stanford premed students who eventually became physicians scored high on the physician scale of the SVIB. When recontacted throughout life, they tended to remain high on that scale (Tyler & Walsh, 1979). Other studies showed some instability of interests during adolescence, with the patterns becoming stable by the senior year of high school (Hansen & Campbell, 1985).

Despite the widespread acceptance and use of the SVIB, disenchantment with the test began to mount in the late 1960s and early 1970s. Critics cited a gender bias in the scales because different tests were used for men and women. Others complained about the lack of theory associated with the test.

The Strong-Campbell Interest Inventory

In 1974, D. P. Campbell published a new version of the SVIB, which he called the Strong-Campbell Interest Inventory (SCII). The SCII was Campbell's (1974) response to the shortcomings of the SVIB. Items from both the men's and women's forms of the SVIB were merged into a single form that included scales devoid of gender bias. For example, the scales for waiter and waitress were merged, and items that referred to gender (for example, salesman) were appropriately modified.

In developing the SVIB, Strong had shied away from providing a theoretical explanation for why certain types of individuals liked some fields and disliked others. However, Campbell became interested in J. L. Holland's (1975) theory of vocational choice. After many years of study, Holland had postulated that interests express personality and that people can be classified into one or more of six categories according to their interests (see Table 16-1). These factors were quite similar to the patterns of interest that emerged from many years of research with the SVIB. In addition, the factors postulated by Holland could be used for either men or women. When Campbell incorporated Holland's theory and his six personality factors into the SCII (Tyler & Walsh, 1979), he provided a theoretical basis for a new test that the SVIB had lacked.

Over the years, research has generally supported Holland's ideas (Carless, 1999). For example, one detailed study that used all 437 occupational titles from the Bureau of the Census demonstrated that Holland's system can better describe work activities, general training requirements, and occupational rewards than can a variety of competing vocational classification systems (Gottfredson, 1980). Holland (1999) has summarized 50 years of research supporting the claim that occupational interests reflect personality.

TABLE 16-1

Holland's Six Personality Factors

Factor	Interest pattern
Realistic	Enjoys technical material and outdoor activities
Investigative	Is interested in science and the process of investigation
Artistic	Enjoys self-expression and being dramatic
Social	Is interested in helping others and in activities involving other people
Enterprising	Is interested in power and political strength
Conventional	Likes to be well organized and has clerical interests

Adapted from J. L. Holland (1985).

The SCII in its current form is divided into seven parts as summarized in Table 16-2. The test, which still retains the core of the SVIB, now has 325 items, to which a person responds "like," "dislike," or "indifferent" (Hansen, 2000).

Various agencies provide automated scoring services for the SCII, and most of them summarize several scores for each profile. The first score is a summary of general themes based on Holland's six personality types (see Table 16-1). For example, the profile might provide information about the general types of activities the person enjoys, the kinds of people the person might work well with, and the most suitable general occupational environment.

The second score summary given in a report is for the administrative indexes. Of less personal importance to the test taker, these are needed to ensure that errors were not made in the administration, scoring, or processing of the test.

The third set of scores provides a summary of a person's basic interests. For example, they suggest whether a person scored high, low, or about average in preference for science, mechanical activities, and athletics. This information is reported in standardized T scores (see Chapter 2). Remember that T scores have a mean of 50 and a standard deviation of 10. Thus, a T score of 60 would be one standard deviation above the mean or in approximately the 84th percentile (Hansen, 2000).

The final set of summary scores given in the SCII profile is for the occupational scales. These scales occupy most of the space on the SCII profile. The profile shows the person's score for each of 124 occupations, which are broken into six general occupational themes. The scoring for the occupational scales differs from that for the general theme and basic interest scales because the occupational scale compares the test taker's score with the scores of people working in the various professions. The general theme and basic interest scales compare the test taker's score with those of people in general. If you took the SCII, for each scale you would be assigned a score indicating the degree of similarity—very dissimilar, dissimilar, average, similar, or very similar—between your interests and the interests of people happy in their chosen occupations. Many of the occupations are divided so that different criterion groups are provided for men and women. For example, if you scored in the "very similar" category for the occupation social worker (for female), then this finding would suggest that your interests were close to those of women who had been employed as social workers and enjoyed the profession (Hansen, 2000).

TABLE 16-2

Summary of the Seven Parts of the Strong-Campbell Interest Inventory

Section	Name	Number of Items	Examples of Items
1	Occupations	131	Actor/actress, criminal lawyer, freelance writer, office clerk, x-ray technician
2	School subjects	36	Algebra, art, economics, literature, zoology
3	Activities	51	Cooking, taping a sprained ankle, watching an open-heart operation
4	Amusements	39	Fishing, boxing, listening to religious music, skiing, attending lectures
5	Types of people	24	Military officers, ballet dancers, very old people
6	Preference between two activities	30	Being an airline pilot or being an airline ticket agent, taking a chance or playing it safe, reading a book or watching TV
7	Your characteristics	14	Wins friends easily, can prepare successful advertisements, has patience when teaching others

Adapted from Hansen and Campbell (1985).

Evidence suggests that the interests measured by these tests are stable. For example, we tested a 39-year-old woman college professor named Jean A. on the SCII. The test was given twice, separated by 11 years. At the first testing, Jean was a 28-year-old psychology graduate student who had not started her professional career. Table 16-3 compares her SCII profiles at ages 28 and 39. During this 11-year interval, Jean completed her Ph.D., held three different jobs, and had two children. As the table shows, her interests remained remarkably stable.

The last version of the SCII was released in spring 1985. Although the test booklets and answer sheets did not change, the SCII profile was expanded to include 207 occupational scales, 144 of which have been developed since 1977. The 1985 revision has a national sample that represents every occupational criterion group. In addition, special precautions were taken to rule out potential difficulties in interpretation. For example, one criticism of the SCII has been that members of the criterion groups were older than those who would be just entering the workforce. In the revised SCII, younger and older members of each criterion group were compared to determine whether the interests and values of the recent entrants into the workforce differed from those of workers who had been on the job for many years (Hansen & Campbell, 1985).

The Campbell Interest and Skill Survey

The Strong scales have had an interesting and turbulent recent history. David Campbell began working on the Strong Vocational Interest Blank in 1960 when he was a graduate student at the University of Minnesota (Campbell, 2002). When Strong died in 1963, Campbell, then an assistant professor at the University of Minnesota, became the primary representative of the SVIB. Later versions were published under the authorship of Strong and Campbell. The first version of the Strong-Campbell Interest Inventory was published in 1974. Be-

TABLE 16-3
*SCII Results for
Jean A.*

Theme	Age 28	Age 39
Investigative	58	58
Artistic	51	51
Social	45	46
Enterprising	42	37
Conventional	37	44
Realistic	36	36

Similarity Scores	Age 28	Age 39
High similarity		
Physician	58	53
Optometrist	52	47
Psychologist	50	47
College professor	49	50
Low similarity		
Librarian	32	27
Beautician	28	31
Flight attendant	27	31
Army officer	27	25

cause Strong had been a professor at Stanford University, Stanford and the University of Minnesota became engaged in a legal dispute over ownership. In an out-of-court settlement in 1988, Stanford received the rights to publish the Strong Interest Inventory while Campbell received the rights to most of the cumulative work. In 1992, Campbell published the Campbell Interest and Skill Survey (CISS) (Campbell, 2002; Campbell, Hyne, & Nilsen, 1992).

The CISS asks respondents to assess their degree of interest in 200 academic and occupational topics. Further, it assesses the degree of skill in 120 specific occupations. The system produces an 11-page profile and a 2-page report summary (see Focused Example 16-1; Campbell, 1995). The CISS ultimately yields a variety of different types of scales. These are summarized in Table 16-4. For each of these scales, an interest level and a skill score are offered.

In addition to these specific scales, the CISS offers an academic focus scale that helps test takers understand how comfortable or successful they may be in an academic setting, and an extroversion scale that helps guide them to occupations with the appropriate amount and intensity of interpersonal relations. Recently, Campbell teamed up with *US News & World Report* to offer the CISS over the Internet (see www.usnews.com/usnews/edu/careers/ccciss.htm). For $17.95 plus tax, you can gain access to the 320-question survey The fee will cover a report that compares your results to the responses of people who are successfully employed in 60 occupations. The personalized report also in-

Focused Example 16-1

CAMPBELL INTEREST AND SKILL SURVEY INDIVIDUAL PROFILE

Orientations and Basic Scales

DATE SCORED: 7/31/95

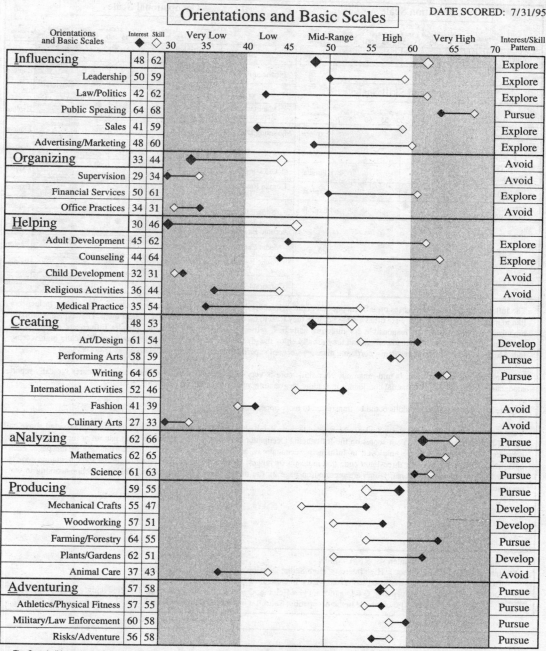

Orientations and Basic Scales	Interest ◆	Skill ◇	Interest/Skill Pattern
Influencing	48	62	Explore
Leadership	50	59	Explore
Law/Politics	42	62	Explore
Public Speaking	64	68	Pursue
Sales	41	59	Explore
Advertising/Marketing	48	60	Explore
Organizing	33	44	Avoid
Supervision	29	34	Avoid
Financial Services	50	61	Explore
Office Practices	34	31	Avoid
Helping	30	46	
Adult Development	45	62	Explore
Counseling	44	64	Explore
Child Development	32	31	Avoid
Religious Activities	36	44	Avoid
Medical Practice	35	54	
Creating	48	53	
Art/Design	61	54	Develop
Performing Arts	58	59	Pursue
Writing	64	65	Pursue
International Activities	52	46	
Fashion	41	39	Avoid
Culinary Arts	27	33	Avoid
aNalyzing	62	66	Pursue
Mathematics	62	65	Pursue
Science	61	63	Pursue
Producing	59	55	Pursue
Mechanical Crafts	55	47	Develop
Woodworking	57	51	Develop
Farming/Forestry	64	55	Pursue
Plants/Gardens	62	51	Develop
Animal Care	37	43	Avoid
Adventuring	57	58	Pursue
Athletics/Physical Fitness	57	55	Pursue
Military/Law Enforcement	60	58	Pursue
Risks/Adventure	56	58	Pursue

Chart scale columns: Very Low (30, 35), Low (40, 45), Mid-Range (50, 55), High (55, 60), Very High (65, 70)

From *The Campbell Interest and Skills Survey.* Paper presented at the annual meeting of the American Psychological Association, New York, August 1995. Reprinted by permission of David P. Campbell.

Continued

CAMPBELL INTEREST AND SKILL SURVEY INDIVIDUAL PROFILE

Influencing Orientation

Orientation Scale

	Standard Scores	Very Low 30 35	Low 40 45	Mid-Range 50 55	High 60 65	Very High 70	Interest/Skill Pattern
Influencing	I 48 / S 62			◆	◇		Explore

Basic Interest and Skill Scales

	Standard Scores	Very Low 30 35	Low 40 45	Mid-Range 50 55	High 60 65	Very High 70	Interest/Skill Pattern
Leadership	I 50 / S 59		◆	◇			Explore
Law/Politics	I 42 / S 62	◆		◇	◆		Explore
Public Speaking	I 64 / S 68			◇	◆		Pursue
Sales	I 41 / S 59	◆		◇			Explore
Advertising/Marketing	I 48 / S 60		◆	◇			Explore

Occupational Scales

	Orientation Code	Standard Scores	25 30 35	40 45	50 55	High 60 65	Very High 70 75	Interest/Skill Pattern
Attorney	I	I 48 / S 65		◆		◇		Explore
Financial Planner	IO	I 50 / S 66			◆	◇		Explore
Hotel Manager	IO	I 26 / S 52	◆		◇			Explore
Manufacturer's Representative	IO	I 54 / S 60			◆	◇		Explore
Marketing Director	IO	I 48 / S 71			◆	◇		Explore
Realtor	IO	I 36 / S 69		◆		◇		Explore
CEO/President	IOA	I 54 / S 64			◆	◇		Explore
Human Resources Director	IOH	I 53 / S 69			◆	◇		Explore
School Superintendent	IOH	I 26 / S 62	◆			◇		Explore
Advertising Account Executive	IC	I 46 / S 63			◆	◇		Explore
Media Executive	IC	I 42 / S 69		◆		◇		Explore
Public Relations Director	IC	I 49 / S 63			◆	◇		Explore
Corporate Trainer	ICH	I 66 / S 73				◆	◇	Pursue

The Influencing Orientation focuses on influencing others through leadership, politics, public speaking, sales, and marketing. Influencers like to make things happen. They are often visible because they tend to take charge of activities that interest them. They typically work in organizations where they are responsible for directing activities, setting policies, and motivating people. Influencers are generally confident of their ability to persuade others and they usually enjoy the give-and-take of debating and negotiating. Typically high-scoring individuals include company presidents, corporate managers, school superintendents, sales representatives, and attorneys.

Your Influencing interest score is mid-range but your skill score is very high. People who have this pattern of scores typically report moderate interest but very substantial confidence in leading, negotiating, marketing, selling, and public speaking.

Explore how your Influencing skills could be transferred to more appealing areas.

Your scores on the Influencing Basic Scales, which provide more detail about your interests and skills in this area, are reported above on the left-hand side of the page. Your scores on the Influencing Occupational Scales, which show how your pattern of interests and skills compares with those of people employed in Influencing occupations, are reported above on the right-hand side of the page. Each occupation has a one-, two-, or three-letter code that indicates its highest Orientation score(s). The more similar the Orientation code is to your highest Orientation scores (which are reported on page 2), the more likely it is that you will find satisfaction working in that occupation.

---

* Standard Scores: I (◆) = Interests; S (◇) = Skills
** Interest/Skill Pattern: Pursue = High Interests, High Skills; Develop = High Interest, Lower Skills;
   Explore = High Skills, Lower Interests; Avoid = Low Interest, Low Skills
*** Orientation Code: I = Influencing; O = Organizing; H = Helping; C = Creating; N = aNalyzing; P = Producing; A = Adventuring
   ▬▬▬ Range of middle 50% of people in the occupation: Solid Bar = Interests; Hollow Bar = Skills

460

CAMPBELL INTEREST AND SKILL SURVEY INDIVIDUAL PROFILE

Special Scales

DATE SCORED: 7/31/95

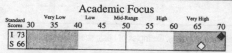

Academic Focus

	Very Low	Low	Mid-Range		High	Very High	
Standard Scores	30	35	40	45	50	55	60	65	70
I 73								
S 66								

The Academic Focus Scales reflect your feelings toward the academic world. High scores do not necessarily lead to academic success, nor low scores to failure, but your pattern of scores reflects your degree of comfort in educational settings and can help you plan your educational strategy. High scorers are attracted to intellectual ideas, academic pursuits, and scientific research. Typical high-scoring individuals include university professors, research scientists, technical writers, and other scholars. People who score low usually see themselves as more action-oriented and practical. Business people, especially those in sales and marketing, tend to score low on the Academic Focus Scales.

Your Academic Focus interest and skill scores are both very high. People who have scores as high as yours typically report very strong interest and very substantial confidence in academic activities, such as studying, conducting research, and writing scientific papers. Your scores suggest that earning an advanced degree would be a rewarding experience for you.

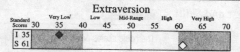

Extraversion

	Very Low	Low	Mid-Range		High	Very High	
Standard Scores	30	35	40	45	50	55	60	65	70
I 35								
S 61								

The Extraversion Scales indicate level of interest and confidence working with all types of people in many different occupational settings. High scores reflect an attraction to a wide range of people-oriented activities. Lower scores may suggest a narrower focus, such as an interest in working with children but not adults, or confidence in counseling others but not selling. Low scores may indicate a preference for less contact with people on the job.

Occupational Extraverts (such as guidance counselors, hotel managers, corporate trainers, and realtors) are energized by frequent social contact and enjoy working closely with others. People who score low on the Extraversion Scales may prefer more independent work assignments and the opportunity for private time and space. Low-scoring individuals include scientists, skilled craftsworkers, and veterinarians.

Your Extraversion interest score is very low but your skill score is very high. People who have this pattern of scores typically report almost no interest but very substantial confidence in work situations requiring a great deal of personal contact with others. You may want to explore the factors leading to your lower interest in people-oriented activities or perhaps discover new outlets for your Extraversion skills.

Procedural Checks

The Procedural Checks are designed to detect possible problems in the administration, completion, or processing of answer sheets. See the CISS manual for details.

All Procedural Checks are VALID

Interest Items

Response Percentage Check - Valid

Topic	STRONGLY LIKE	Like	slightly like	slightly dislike	Dislike	STRONGLY DISLIKE
Occupations	13	26	14	9	15	22
School Subjects	12	33	23	9	12	12
Varied Activities	7	21	11	8	17	36
Overall Percentage	11	26	15	9	15	25

Inconsistency Check - Valid	
# Inconsistent Pairs	0

Omitted Items Check - Valid	
# Omitted Items	0

Skill Items

Response Percentage Check - Valid

	EXPERT	Good	above average	below average	Poor	NONE
Varied Activities	16	19	31	11	16	8

Inconsistency Check - Valid	
# Inconsistent Pairs	0

Omitted Items Check - Valid	
# Omitted Items	0

TABLE 16-4
Summary of the Components of the Campbell Interest and Skill Survey

Orientation scales

Seven scales describe the test taker's occupational orientation: influencing, organizing, helping, creating, analyzing, producing, and adventuring.

Basic scales

The basic scales provide an overview for categories of occupations. Examples of basic scales include law/politics, counseling, and mathematics.

Occupational scales

Sixty occupational scales describe matches with particular occupations, including attorney, engineer, guidance counselor, and math teacher.

Source: D. P. Campbell (1995).

cludes a comprehensive career planner and a guide to help you interpret the results.

To a large extent, the CISS is a continuation of the research on the SVIB and the SCII. The CISS is now shorter and more efficient than the older SCII. The scales are standardized with means of 50 and standard deviations of 10. As with the earlier versions, the CISS uses the theoretical structure of John Holland. The manual provides extensive evidence for validity and reliability (Campbell, 1995).

The Kuder Occupational Interest Survey

Although the SCII is probably the most widely used interest inventory today, it competes with many other interest inventories. The Kuder Occupational Interest Survey (KOIS) ranks second in popularity. It is one of several interest scales that grew out of the original Kuder Preference Survey published in 1939. Throughout the years, the Kuder has offered a unique alternative to the SVIB-SCII- CISS.

The KOIS presents the test taker with 100 triads (sets of three) of alternative activities. For each triad, the test taker selects the most preferred and the least preferred alternatives. Scoring of the KOIS scales gives the same information yielded by the earlier Kuder Preference Surveys—data on 10 general occupational interests (for example, outdoor interests versus social service interests). However, in its current form (Kuder, 1979), the KOIS examines the similarity between a test taker's interests and those of people employed in various occupations in a manner much like that of the SCII and CISS. Furthermore, the KOIS has developed separate norms for men and women. The KOIS also has a separate set of scales for college majors. Thus, in addition to suggesting which occupational group might work best with a test taker's interests, the KOIS may also help students choose a major (Diamond & Zytowski, 2000).

To emphasize nontraditional occupations for men and women, a series of new scales has been added to the KOIS. Examples of these new scales are architect (female norms), journalist (female norms), and film and television producer or director (male norms) (Zytowski, 1985).

Although each test taker is evaluated with regard to the norms for many occupational and college major groups, the KOIS provides a summary of an individual's highest scores by signaling them with an asterisk.

In 1999, the National Career Assessment Service became the international distributor for the KOIS. An example of one of their reports is shown in Table 16-5. The report is divided into four sections. The first summarizes the dependability of the results. An analysis of answer patterns considers consistency. The report shown in the table suggests that the results appear to be dependable for this particular test taker. The second section rank orders interest patterns in comparison to the normative sample of men and women. In this example, the person taking the test has exceptionally high interests in literary and outdoor areas in comparison to both men and women. The female test taker had low interests in comparison to other women in the mechanical, social service, and persuasive areas.

The core of the KOIS report is shown in the third section. This section ranks the test taker in relation to men and women who are employed in different occupations and are satisfied with their career choices. The report shows that the woman who completed the measure has a pattern of interests that best matches those of journalists who are satisfied with their work. The pattern also shows good correspondence with interests of lawyers, personnel managers, and physicians. The pattern matches most poorly with bank clerk, beautician, and department store sales. The fourth section of the report matches patterns of interests to those of students who have selected different college majors. The woman whose results are shown in this example matches interest patterns most closely with women who are majoring in history, English, or political science. Her interests match most poorly with women majoring in physical education, nursing, and art.

Studies show that the psychometric properties of the KOIS are very good. Short-term reliabilities tend to be high (between .80 and .95), and increasing evidence indicates that scores remain stable for as long as 30 years (Zytowski, 1996). One study on the predictive validity of the KOIS showed that half of one group of adults who had taken an early version of the KOIS while they were high-school students were working in fields that the high-school KOIS suggested they enter. Predictive validity for the college major scales was even better. There was closer correspondence between interests and the occupation a person was working in for those who had completed college than for those who had not. A college degree thus provides more freedom than a high-school diploma does in finding personally desirable work (Zytowski, 1976).

In other studies, high-school students reported greater confidence in their knowledge of themselves when they received KOIS results than when they did not. But knowing the results of the KOIS did not make the high-school students more confident or more satisfied with their career plans, except when the students expressed a special interest in learning about the test results (Zytowski, 1977). Other studies have considered self-efficacy for the specific occupational tasks in the KOIS. *Self-efficacy* represents a person's expectation that he or she could perform the tasks in the occupational groups. The research

TABLE 16-5

Kuder Occupational Interest Survey Report Form

(*From National Career Assessment Sciences, Inc.™, Report of Scores, Kuder Occupational Survey, Form DD, copyright © 1965, 1968, 1970, 1979 National Career Assessment Services, Inc. Reprinted by permission.*)

Kuder Occupational Interest Survey Report Form

Name

Sex FEMALE   **Date**

Numeric Grid No.   **SRA No.**

1 **Dependability:** How much confidence can you place in your results? In scoring your responses several checks were made on your answer patterns to be sure that you understood the directions and that your results were complete and dependable. According to these:

YOUR RESULTS APPEAR
TO BE DEPENDABLE.

2 **Vocational Interest Estimates:** Vocational interests can be divided into different types and the level of your attraction to each type can be measured. You may feel that you know what interests you have already — what you may not know is how strong they are compared with other people's interests. This section shows the relative rank of your preferences for ten different kinds of vocational activities. Each is explained on the back of this report form. Your preferences in these activities, as compared with other people's interests, are as follows:

Compared with men		Compared with women	
HIGH		HIGH	
LITERARY	95	LITERARY	94
OUTDOOR	81	OUTDOOR	87
AVERAGE		AVERAGE	
ARTISTIC	51	SCIENTIFIC	58
SCIENTIFIC	49	MUSICAL	37
MUSICAL	33	ARTISTIC	33
CLERICAL	33	COMPUTATIONAL	28
LOW		CLERICAL	27
SOCIAL SERVICE	19	LOW	
COMPUTATIONAL	19	MECHANICAL	10
PERSUASIVE	04	SOCIAL SERVICE	06
MECHANICAL	02	PERSUASIVE	06

3 **Occupations:** The KOIS has been given to groups of persons who are experienced and satisfied in many different occupations. Their patterns of interests have been compared with yours and placed in order of their similarity with you. The following occupational groups have interest patterns *most* similar to yours:

Compared with men		Compared with women	
LIBRARIAN	.68	JOURNALIST	.72
LAWYER	.64	LAWYER	.67
FILM/TV PROD/DIR	.62	PERSONNEL MGR	.67
		PHYSICIAN	.67
THESE ARE NEXT		FILM/TV PROD/DIR	.66
MOST SIMILAR:			
		THESE ARE NEXT	
AUDIOL/SP PATHOL	.61	MOST SIMILAR:	
STATISTICIAN	.61		
MATHEMATICIAN	.57	AUDIOL/SP PATHOL	.65
ELEM SCH TEACHER	.56	PHARMACIST	.65
PSYCHOLOGIST	.56	ACCT, CERT PUB	.65

Compared with men
MOST SIMILAR, CONT.

BOOKSTORE MGR	.56

THE REST ARE
LISTED IN ORDER
OF SIMILARITY:

JOURNALIST	.55
CHEMIST	.54
OPTOMETRIST	.53
PHYSICIAN	.53
COMPUTER PRGRMR	.53
SOCIAL WORKER	.53
NURSE	.53
COUNSELOR, HS	.52
INTERIOR DECOR	.52
ACCT, CERT PUB	.52
ARCHITECT	.51
TRAVEL AGENT	.50
PODIATRIST	.49
MINISTER	.48
METEOROLOGIST	.48
SCHOOL SUPT	.48
PLANT NURSRY WKR	.47
PHOTOGRAPHER	.47
SCIENCE TCHR, HS	.47
RADIO STATON MGR	.46
PERSONNEL MGR	.46
PHYS THERAPIST	.45
DENTIST	.44
FORESTER	.42
ENGINEER	.42
CLOTHIER, RETAIL	.42
MATH TCHR, HS	.42
REAL ESTATE AGT	.42
VETERINARIAN	.41
X-RAY TECHNICIAN	.41
BUYER	.40
EXTENSION AGENT	.39
PHARMACEUT SALES	.39
PHARMACIST	.39
FLORIST	.38
PRINTER	.38
BANKER	.35
INSURANCE AGENT	.34
BOOKKEEPER	.33
AUTO SALESPERSON	.32
TV REPAIRER	.32
POSTAL CLERK	.31
POLICE OFFICER	.28
FARMER	.28
BLDG CONTRACTOR	.27
SUPERVSR, INDUST	.27
BRICKLAYER	.23
PLUMBING CONTRAC	.22
PAINTER, HOUSE	.21
MACHINIST	.19
WELDER	.19

Compared with women	Compared with men	Compared with women
MOST SIMILAR, CONT.	REST, CONT.	

Compared with women		Compared with men	
DENTIST	.64	ELECTRICIAN	.19
POLICE OFFICER	.62	TRUCK DRIVER	.18
PSYCHOLOGIST	.62	CARPENTER	.17
VETERINARIAN	.62	PLUMBER	.16
ENGINEER	.61	AUTO MECHANIC	.16
COMPUTR PRGRMR	.60		
INSURANCE AGENT	.60		
LIBRARIAN	.60		

THE REST ARE
LISTED IN ORDER
OF SIMILARITY:

4 *College Majors:* Just as for occupations, the **KOIS** has been given to many persons in different college majors. The following college major groups have interest patterns *most* similar to yours:

Compared with women		Compared with men		Compared with women	
BOOKSTORE MGR	.59	FOREIGN LANGUAGE	.64	HISTORY	.62
ARCHITECT	.59	ENGLISH	.62	ENGLISH	.61
BANKER	.59	HISTORY	.61	POLITICAL SCI	.61
MINISTER	.58			FOREIGN LANGUAGE	.60
SOCIAL WORKER	.58	THESE ARE NEXT			
NUTRITIONIST	.58	MOST SIMILAR:		THESE ARE NEXT	
COL STU PERS WKR	.57			MOST SIMILAR:	
DIETITIAN	.56	POLITICAL SCI	.57		
COUNSELOR, HS	.55	BIOLOGICAL SCI	.54	BIOLOGICAL SCI	.55
PHYS THERAPIST	.53	PSYCHOLOGY	.52	HOME ECON EDUC	.55
REAL ESTATE AGT	.53	SOCIOLOGY	.52	ELEMENTARY EDUC	.55
INTERIOR DECOR	.52			PSYCHOLOGY	.55
SCIENCE TCHR, HS	.52	THE REST ARE		DRAMA	.53
SECRETARY	.50	LISTED IN ORDER		MUSIC & MUSIC ED	.53
ELEM SCH TEACHER	.49	OF SIMILARITY:		MATHEMATICS	.52
EXTENSION AGENT	.48			ENGINEERING	.52
FLORIST	.47	MUSIC & MUSIC ED	.51	BUSINESS ADMIN	.51
OCCUPA THERAPIST	.46	ELEMENTARY EDUC	.51		
MATH TEACHER, HS	.46	PHYSICAL SCIENCE	.49	THE REST ARE	
RELIGIOUS ED DIR	.45	MATHEMATICS	.49	LISTED IN ORDER	
X-RAY TECHNICIAN	.44	ECONOMICS	.48	OF SIMILARITY:	
NURSE	.43	PREMED/PHAR/DENT	.47		
DENTAL ASSISTANT	.43	ART & ART EDUC	.44	HEALTH PROFESS	.49
BOOKKEEPER	.42	BUSINESS ADMIN	.44	SOCIOLOGY	.47
OFFICE CLERK	.41	FORESTRY	.43	PHYSICAL EDUC	.46
BANK CLERK	.39	ARCHITECTURE	.42	NURSING	.46
BEAUTICIAN	.37	SERV ACAD CADET	.42	ART & ART EDUC	.41
DEPT STORE-SALES	.31	PHYSICAL EDUC	.41		
		ANIMAL SCIENCE	.40		
		ENGINEERING	.40		
		AGRICULTURE	.40		

Experimental Scales.

V-SCORE 54

M	.40	MBI	.32	W	.54	WBI	.32
S	.36	F	.40	D	.46	MO	.49

7-3881

suggests that, in comparison to women, men have higher expectations that they will succeed in mechanical and physical work, and women have greater expectations that they will succeed when working with people than do men (Lucas, Wanberg, & Zytowski, 1997). Even though the KOIS has been less thoroughly studied than the SVIB-SCII, a growing amount of evidence indicates that it may be quite useful for guidance decisions for high-school and college students. Refinements published in 1985 reflect continuing development of this measure (Zytowski, 1992). You can get more information about the KOIS at www.dantes.doded.mil/dantes_web/distribution/guide4-text.htm.

The Jackson Vocational Interest Survey

The Jackson Vocational Interest Survey (JVIS), revised in 1995 and copyrighted in 1999, is used for the career education and counseling of high-school and college students. It can also be used to plan careers for adults, including those who want to make midlife career changes. Douglas Jackson, the developer of the measure, was strongly influenced by the psychometric pioneers from the Educational Testing Service (Jackson, 2002). The JVIS consists of 289 statements describing job-related activities. It takes 45 minutes to complete, and the scoring yields 34 basic interest scales. The test construction carefully avoided gender bias. The scale employs forced-choice formats in which the respondent must indicate a preference between two equally popular interests.

Studies suggest that the reliability for 10 general occupational themes is approximately .89 and that the test–retest stability of the 44 basic interest scales ranges from .84 to .88. Validity studies suggest that the JVIS predicts university and academic majors more accurately than do most other interest inventories. Available in both hand-scored and machine-scored forms, the JVIS offers computer software to administer and score the measure (Jackson & Livesley, 1995).

The Minnesota Vocational Interest Inventory

Some researchers criticize the SCII, CISS, and the KOIS because they emphasize professions that require college and professional training. Although an increasing number of people in the United States eventually obtain a college degree, most workers still do not graduate from college. The Minnesota Vocational Interest Inventory (MVII) is designed for men who are not oriented toward college and emphasizes skilled and semiskilled trades (Clark, 1961; Clark & Campbell, 1965). Modeled after the SVIB scales, the MVII has nine basic interest areas, including mechanical interests, electronics, and food service, as well as 21 specific occupational scales, including those for plumber, carpenter, and truck driver. The MVII has been used extensively by the military and by guidance programs for individuals who do not go to college.

The Career Assessment Inventory

A more modern interest inventory for nonprofessionally oriented adults than the MVII is the Career Assessment Inventory (CAI). Developed by Charles B. Johansson, the CAI is written at the sixth-grade reading level and is designed for the 80% of U.S. citizens who have fewer than four years of postsecondary education. The CAI provides information similar to that yielded by the SCII and CISS. Each test taker is evaluated on Holland's six occupational theme scales: realistic, investigative, artistic, social, enterprising, and conventional. The second portion of the CAI report describes basic interests. Each test taker is evaluated in 22 specific areas, including carpentry, business, and food service. The third section of the report is a series of occupational scales. Scores for the 89 occupational scales on the CAI were obtained by using a criterion-keying method. The interests of the test takers are matched to the interests of truck drivers, secretaries, waitpersons, and so forth.

Validity and reliability studies reported in the test manual suggest that the CAI has desirable psychometric properties. Scores tend to be quite stable, and people who find employment in occupations for which they have expressed strong interest tend to remain at their jobs and find more satisfaction with work than do those with low scores for those occupations. The test developer also took special pains to make the CAI culturally fair and eliminate gender bias. In many ways, the CAI has become the working person's CISS (Johannson, 1976; Johannson & Johansson, 1978).

The Self-Directed Search

Most interest inventories require professional or computer-automated scoring. In addition, they typically require interpretation by a trained counselor. J. L. Holland developed the Self-Directed Search (SDS) to be a self-administered, self-scored, and self-interpreted vocational interest inventory (Spokane & Catalano, 2000). The SDS attempts to simulate the counseling process by allowing respondents to list occupational aspirations, indicate occupational preferences in six areas, and rate abilities and skills in these areas (Srsic, Stimac, & Walsh, 2001). Then the test takers can score their own inventory and calculate six summary scores, which they can use to obtain codes that reflect the highest areas of interest. Using the SDS, test takers can develop a meaningful personal career theory. The personal theory goes beyond interests and includes readiness for career decision making and readiness to obtain guidance (Reardon & Lenz, 1999). The SDS is linked to an occupational finder. In the 1994 edition of the system, the individual can locate more than 1300 occupations and match his or her own interest codes to corresponding occupational choices.

The SDS includes 228 items. Six scales with 11 items each describe activities. Another 66 items assess competencies, with six scales of 11 items each. Occupations are evaluated in six scales of 14 items each. Self-estimates are obtained in two sets of six ratings. Studies have demonstrated that respondents accurately score their own tests. Validity studies reflect a moderate, but not high, association between SDS categories and stated vocational aspirations (Holland, 1985).

Another approach similar to the self-directed search is to allow subjects to interact with a computer-assisted guidance system (Spokane & Catalano,

2000). One study analyzed "dialogue" used in interactions with the computer. The SDS is now available online, and users appear to be more satisfied than those who respond to the paper-and-pencil version (Barak & Cohen, 2002). The analysis suggests that most people do not perform comprehensive searches but instead seek information on only some alternatives. The larger the number of choices, the smaller the number explored. This is not unexpected, because most people need to simplify information and gather it selectively (Gati & Tikotzki, 1989).

Despite the common and enthusiastic use of interest inventories, several problems have repeatedly surfaced, including faking, sex bias, and mismatches between abilities and interests.

Eliminating Gender Bias in Interest Measurement

Not all members of society have found the use and development of interest inventories acceptable. In particular, advocates of women's rights justifiably pointed out that the early interest inventories discriminated against women (Birk, 1974; Campbell, 1995; Diamond, 1979; Peoples, 1975; Tittle, 1983). The Association for Evaluation in Guidance appointed the Commission on Sex Bias in Measurement, which concluded that interest inventories contributed to the policy of guiding young men and women into gender-typed careers. The interest inventories tended to direct women into their traditional work roles, such as nursing, clerical service, and elementary-school teaching. The SVIB, the main interest inventory at the time of the commission report, had separate forms for men and for women. Careers on the women's form, it was noted, tended to be lower in status and to command lower salaries (Harmon, Cole, Wysong, & Zytowski, 1973).

In response to these criticisms, the SCII began using the same forms for both men and women. However, in the 1977 SCII manual, Campbell noted that if Strong were alive, he may have felt that using the same norming tables for both men and women would have harmed the validity of the test. A unisex interest inventory, according to Strong, ignores the social and statistical reality that men and women have different interests. In other words, knowing the sex of the test taker tells us a lot about his or her interests. Nevertheless, the SCII made major efforts to reduce gender bias, and newer measures, such as the CISS (Campbell, 1995), have gone even further.

Most measures have reduced but not eliminated gender bias. Contemporary studies show that many items in the Strong Interest Inventory function differently for men and for women. Furthermore, these differences have been observed in cultures as different as the United States and Iceland (Einarsdottir, 2002). Interest inventory developers have worked hard to address these concerns. Although the basic interest and general theme portions of the SCII and CISS compare a respondent's responses with those from a combined male and female reference group, the occupational scales are normed separately for men and women. Furthermore, the interpretive comments that are provided by most scoring services are geared toward the test taker's gender (Minton &

Schneider, 1980). We expect that using the same or different norms for men and women will continue to engender controversy and debate. The current versions of both the CISS and the KOIS reflect the growing concern about gender bias (Campbell, 1995; Hansen & Campbell, 1987). Because career choices for many women are complex, interest inventories alone may be inadequate and more comprehensive approaches are needed (McLennan & Arthur, 1999).

Aptitudes and Interests

Extensive research on interest inventories reinforces an important but often overlooked point: Interest inventories measure interests; they do not measure the chances that people will succeed in the jobs they find interesting.

The norm groups for the Strong inventories consist of people successful enough in various fields to remain working in them for defined periods. However, *degree* of success is not defined. If you obtain a high score for a particular occupation, then it means that you have interests similar to those of people in that field. Self-rated satisfaction with chosen careers does appear to be higher for people whose interests match those of others working in the field, but repeated studies have emphasized that the chances of succeeding in that job depend on aptitudes and abilities.

Measuring Personal Characteristics for Job Placement

Interests are just one of the many factors to be considered in career planning and placement. Career choices also depend on matches between skills and jobs. Employers want to find the right person for the job, and job hunters continually seek that one position that perfectly suits their personal skills and interests. Thus, psychologists and vocational guidance specialists look at job placement from many different perspectives. Some focus on the person and his or her characteristics, others attend the work environment, while still others concentrate on unique combinations of people and situations. To begin, let's look at some of the theories and measurement methods that focus on the person.

Trait Factor Approach: Osipow's Vocational Dimensions

Samuel Osipow has been a leading figure in the field of counseling psychology for many years. Like Holland's method of trait assessment, Osipow's (1983) approach to career guidance is to give extensive tests covering personality, abilities, interests, and personal values to learn as much about a person's traits as possible. Osipow's work is consistent with Holland's theory of personality and occupation interest (Osipow, 1999). This approach involves the administration of an extensive battery of tests, including many we have already covered, such as the SCII and the KOIS. Other tests given include the Purdue pegboard

(Fleishman & Quaintance, 1984) and the Seashore Measure of Musical Talents (Lezak, 1983). The results of this large battery of tests were factor analyzed (see Chapter 3) to find common factors or traits that characterize different occupational groups. People who require guidance take the battery of tests to learn about their traits. Then the counselor matches their traits to those that characterize the different occupations.

Used extensively in research and practice, Osipow's approach has undoubtedly helped many people find their occupational niches. However, the approach has also come under fire for overemphasizing the person and paying too little attention to the work environment. Furthermore, some critics suggest that Osipow's system focuses too much on a single point in time and does not attend sufficiently to the process of reaching a career decision (Tyler & Walsh, 1979).

The Career Maturity Inventory: Super's Development Theory

Many theories of career choice draw on stage theories from life-span developmental psychology, or the study of personal development throughout the life cycle (Osipow, 1987). Super (1953) proposed that individuals go through five developmental stages that are relevant to their career choices and aspirations (see Table 16-6). Super believed that people enter careers in order to express themselves; activities in the world of work are expressions of the worker's self-concept. Furthermore, the developmental stages define what vocational behavior is expected of an individual at each stage. The correlation between actual and expected vocational behavior is called *vocational maturity*.

Several tests measure vocational maturity. The best known and most widely used of these is the Vocational Maturity Inventory (VMI), which later became the Career Maturity Inventory (CMI) (Crites, 1973). This test provides scores for vocational maturity, attitude, self-knowledge or vocational competence, choosing a job, problem solving, occupational information, and looking ahead. Most of the psychometric data on the CMI are impressive. In particular, the vocational competence portion is well constructed, and data obtained with it seem to demonstrate the expected properties. For example, high-school students show an expected year-to-year increase in scores on the vocational competence scale. One would expect this result as the students become more vocationally mature (Crites, 1974). Unfortunately, some problems with the CMI

TABLE 16-6

Stages in Super's Developmental Vocational Maturity Model

Stage	Age Range
Crystallization	14–18
Specification	18–21
Implementation	21–24
Stabilization	25–35
Consolidation	35 and up

still remain; for example, scores suggest that 12th graders are less vocationally mature than 11th graders, which is inconsistent with the notion that students should become more vocationally mature with age (Crites, 1973).

The California Occupational Preference Survey: Roe's Career-Choice Theory

In her theory, Roe claims that career choice results from the type of relationship a person has had with his or her family during childhood. After extensive research on the personalities of scientists who had entered different fields of study, Roe concluded that some people are interested primarily in other people, whereas other people are not. Children reared in a warm and accepting environment, according to Roe, become people-oriented adults, whereas those exposed to a cold and aloof environment at home become more interested in things than in people (Roe & Klos, 1969; Roe & Siegelman, 1964).

Roe's theory identifies person or nonperson orientation as the main factor in career choice. Those who are people-oriented seek careers in which they will have contact with others, in such fields as service, the arts, or entertainment. Individuals who are not person-oriented may prefer occupations that minimize interpersonal relationships, such as those in science or technology or those involving outdoor activities. In an elaboration of the theory, Roe and Klos (1969) classified occupational roles according to two independent continua. The first continuum had "orientation to purposeful communication" at one extreme and "orientation to resource utilization" at the other. The second had "orientation to interpersonal relations" at one extreme and "orientation to natural phenomena" at the other. Table 16-7 summarizes the vocations that fall within these continua.

To measure the characteristics described in Roe's theory, Knapp and associates developed the California Occupational Preference Survey (COPS). This test requires respondents to indicate on a 4-point scale the degree to which they like or dislike 168 different occupational activities. The COPS gives scores in six fields: aesthetic, business, linguistic, scientific, service, and technical. Scores are also given for professional versus skilled orientation as well as for outdoor versus clerical orientation. (The COPS has been expanded to become the California Preference System Inventory, which includes nine occupational

TABLE 16-7

Examples of Career Fields for Individuals Rated on Roe's Continua

	High on orientation to purposeful communication	High on orientation to resource utilization
High on Orientation to Interpersonal Relations	Arts and entertainment; uses tastes	Business contacts; uses persuasive techniques
High on Orientation to Natural Phenomena	Science; uses "laws"	Technology; uses mechanics

Adapted from Roe and Klos, 1969.

clusters.) Reliabilities for the COPS have been reported to be in the .90's. Normative data have been reported for 512 high-school boys and 589 high-school girls (Knapp-Lee, 2000).

Despite the availability of many interest inventories, old-fashioned clinical skill remains an important asset in career counseling. Placement in a particular job within a field depends on an individual's ability and training. Counselors do not necessarily need to administer ability tests to all clients. Self-estimates of ability are often quite valuable (Prediger, 1999). Clinicians sometimes find other methods, such as simple card-sorting methods, for learning about career preferences (Hartung, 1999). Most of the interest assessment methods assume that interests and personality traits are stable over time. In the next section, we review evidence on the stability of personality traits.

Are There Stable Personality Traits?

Imagine that you are responsible for hiring employees for a large business, and you want to do everything you can to convince your supervisors that you are doing a good job. You need to make decisions about the personalities of the people you interview, and you need to communicate this information to the people who will supervise them. For example, you might ask whether interviewees have the traits of kindness, honesty, trustworthiness, reliability, and dedication. People often believe that knowledge of such personality traits provides them with a convenient way of organizing information about others—for describing how they have behaved in the past and for predicting how they will act in the future (Bradbury & Fincham, 1990; Higgins & Bargh, 1987; Jones & Nisbett, 1971; Kelly, 1967).

Indeed, all of the approaches to occupational interest assessment that we have presented in this chapter assume that interests are relatively stable personality characteristics. Much of the study of personality has been devoted to creating categories of traits, developing methods for measuring them, and finding out how groups of traits cluster. Indeed, the very concept of personality assumes that the characteristics of a person are stable over time. If Richard is "hardworking," then we expect him to work hard in many different situations. Although we commonly use trait names in this way to describe other people, the evidence that personality characteristics are stable is a little shaky. For example, Mischel (1984) showed that personality traits are simply not good predictors of how people will behave in particular situations. In a classic, well-argued attack on trait theorists, Mischel (1968) demonstrated that knowing how someone scores on measures of psychological traits sometimes gives little better than chance insight into how the person will act in a given situation. Thus, trait theorists were forced to rethink their assumptions.

Attribution theory. Another problem for traditional trait theories arises from research on *attribution theory*. Originally, attribution theory considered only how people make judgments about others; however, research in this area now covers all aspects of how people attempt to understand the causes of events in their lives.

First presented by Heider (1944, 1958), the ideas behind attribution theory became popular in the late 1960s. Attribution theorists suggested that events in a person's environment can be caused by one of three sources: persons, entities (things or some aspect of the environment), and times (situations) (Kelly, 1967). To determine which of these (or which combination) has caused an event, an observer uses three criteria: distinctiveness, consensus, and consistency. For example, if we want to explain why John is unhappy with his job today, we need to ask whether it has to do with something that happened on the job this particular day (distinctiveness), whether others in the same situation also dislike the job (consensus), or whether John is unhappy on all workdays (consistency).

Attribution theory is thus less concerned with predicting behavior than with studying how individuals make judgments about the causes of behavior. Some researchers have suggested that selecting an explanation for behavior depends on the role played by the person offering the judgment. The person making the judgment acts like a scientist in using all data to come to the best conclusion (Weiner, 1991). When we observe others and make judgments about them, we tend to use dispositional, or trait, explanations; however, we do not use trait explanations for our own behavior (Forsterling, 1988). When we are the actors in a situation, we see our own behavior in terms of the situation. In other words, we describe others in terms of traits, but we explain our own behavior in terms of situations. Why is there a difference between the attributions of actors and observers? E. E. Jones and Nisbett (1971) suggested that we know more about ourselves than about others. By searching our memory, we can remember behaving in many different situations. However, when we make judgments about others, we do not have as much information about how situations caused them to act differently. Yet we may be able to identify with others when they tell us that situations have influenced their behavior. For example, juries may be forgiving of a criminal defendant who claims to have been influenced by a situation and makes a confession (Weiner, Graham, Peter, & Zmuidinas, 1991).

To summarize, Mischel and the attribution theorists feel that psychologists have devoted too much attention to personality traits and not enough attention to situations. Thus, they recommend attention to the effect of situations on behavior.

SUMMARY

The beginning of this chapter presented the real-life case of Harry, a dentist who felt he had made the wrong career choice. Harry's problem might have been avoided through proper interest testing and career counseling. Several methods for assessing vocational interests are available. The best known of these is the SVIB, an empirically keyed test that matches the interests of male and female test takers with those of people satisfied with their career choices. Although one of the most widely used tests in the history of psychology, the SVIB has been harshly criticized for its sexist and atheoretical orientation.

Newer versions, such as the SCII and the CISS, respond to these criticisms by including male and female keys in the same form and by embracing Holland's theory of occupational themes.

The KOIS is the next most frequently used interest test. In contrast to earlier versions, the present KOIS provides occupational scores similar to those given by the SVIB. A unique feature of the KOIS is that it provides scores for college majors. Other occupational interest measures are also available, including the MVII and the CAI, both designed for use with non–college-oriented individuals.

Several prominent counseling psychologists have proposed that career placement be guided by personality traits. Osipow used multivariate statistics to identify clusters of interests and abilities that characterize people in different occupations. Super and Crites favored a developmental perspective, suggesting that career satisfaction is related to vocational maturity. Roe believed that different approaches to child rearing produced some individuals who were people-oriented and others who were thing-oriented. People-oriented individuals find their way into people-oriented careers, and individuals not oriented toward people gain more satisfaction from work that involves less contact with people. Readers who are interested in a more detailed discussion of the complex issues of career interest assessment and counseling can consult some excellent recent references (Holland, 1999; Osipow, 1999; Savickas, 1999).

In 1968, Mischel demonstrated that personality measures do not always accurately predict behavior in particular situations. At about the same time, many attribution theorists began demonstrating that people explain the behavior of others by using personality traits; however, when asked about their own behavior, they tend to attribute cause to the situation. These ideas gave rise to the development of measures to assess the characteristics of social environments and work settings.

WEB ACTIVITY   For interesting and relevant Web sites, check the following:

luna.cas.usf.edu/~mbrannic/files/tnm/svib.htm
Overview of the Strong-Campbell Interest Inventory

www.pearsonassessments.com/tests/ciss.htm
Overview of the Campbell Interest and Skills Survey

www.kuder.com/custom/user_manual/
Manual for the Kuder Career Search

CHAPTER 17

Testing in Health Psychology and Health Care

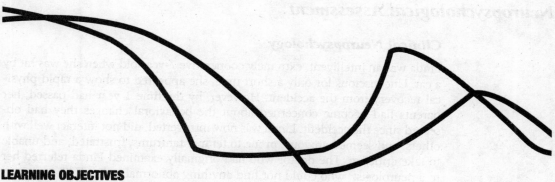

LEARNING OBJECTIVES

When you have completed this chapter, you should be able to

☐ Describe at least three important health-care situations in which psychological tests are used

☐ Define *clinical neuropsychology*

☐ Discuss the use of neuropsychological instruments in both childhood and adulthood

☐ Describe the Halstead-Reitan test battery

☐ Describe the Luria-Nebraska test battery

☐ Discuss the advantages of the California Verbal Learning Test

☐ Discuss some of the theoretical orientations that underlie anxiety measures

☐ Describe the strengths and weaknesses of two different approaches for the assessment of life stress

☐ Discuss the relationship among measures of coping, measures of life stress, and measures of social support

☐ Differentiate psychometric and decision theory approaches to quality-of-life measurement

☐ Describe the SF-36

☐ Discuss the concept of a quality-adjusted life-year

Today, more than 5% of all psychologists are directly employed by hospitals, medical centers, and clinics, and this figure is increasing. One of the main functions of psychologists in these settings is to use and interpret measurement instruments (Retzlaff & Gibertini, 2000). Although this chapter cannot discuss all of the measures used in medical settings, it focuses on three areas that have experienced rapid development in the last few years: neuropsychological assessment, anxiety and stress assessment, and quality-of-life assessment. Unlike other chapters, this chapter covers three separate topics—that is, the topics are not directly related to one another, except that each describes a common approach to assessment in contemporary health care.

Neuropsychological Assessment

Clinical Neuropsychology

Linda was an intelligent, extremely cooperative 7-year-old when she was hit by a car. Unconscious for only a short time, she appeared to show a rapid physical recovery from the accident. However, by the time 1 year had passed, her parents had become concerned about the behavioral changes they had observed since the accident. Linda was now introverted, did not interact well with others, and seemed anxious, prone to temper tantrums, frustrated, and unable to take criticism. The doctor who had originally examined Linda referred her to a neurologist, who could not find anything abnormal in her CAT scans and EEG tests. Unable to determine the source of her difficulties, the neurologist referred Linda to a specialized psychologist trained in neuropsychological assessment. The psychologist discovered that Linda's visual functioning and her ability to talk were superior; however, she had difficulties in hearing and in writing down phonemes she had heard. Furthermore, tests showed that she did quite well on things she had learned before the accident but that she had lost the ability to discriminate among the sounds of letters closely related to one another. This in turn generated a great deal of strain and caused her to believe that she was stupid and unable to keep up with other children. The test that helped identify Linda's specific problem is called the Luria-Nebraska Neuropsychological Battery. After discovering that Linda's problem was highly specific, her teachers designed a special education program that used a visual approach and avoided auditory presentations. Her parents could also adapt to their child's problem once they realized its nature. Given this support and the reduced pressure, Linda's introversion, sensitivity to criticism, and frustration decreased. As her injuries healed, she returned to normal (Golden, 1981).

Linda's case shows the importance of a rapidly expanding new field known as *clinical neuropsychology*. This field is a scientific discipline that focuses on psychological impairments of the central nervous system and their remediation (Broks, 2003). *Clinical neuropsychology* is defined as the scientific discipline that studies the relationship between behavior and brain functioning in the realms of cognitive, motor, sensory, and emotional functioning (Swanda, Haaland, &

LaRue, 2000). The activities of neuropsychologists include the identification, description, multivariate quantification, and treatment of diseases of the brain and spinal cord.

A multidisciplinary endeavor, clinical neuropsychology overlaps neurology, psychiatry, and psychometric testing in the following ways: Neuropsychology and neurology both focus on sensations and perceptions and on motor movements. Neuropsychology and psychiatry both study mood and adaptations to psychosocial situations (Fogel, Schiffer, & Rao, 2000; Kido, Sheline, & Reeve, 2000). Finally, neuropsychology and psychometrics both use psychological tests. Neuropsychology differs from these other clinical disciplines because it is finely specialized, focusing on attention, memory, learning, language and communication, spatial integration, and cognitive flexibility. In summary, neuropsychology is a field of study that actively attempts to relate brain dysfunction and damage to observable and measurable behavioral problems (Crockett, Clark, & Klonoff, 1981; Grant & Adams, 1996).

The practice of clinical neuropsychology has benefited from remarkable advances in neuro-imaging. New methods have made it possible to see diseases in the brain among living people. A few short years ago, the only way to learn about these problems was to study the brains of people who had already died. However, despite these major advances in imaging of the brain, neuropsychology is able to detect problems that are often missed even with the latest neuro-imaging devices. Furthermore, neuropsychological testing can detect Alzheimer's disease and other clinical problems in their earliest stages. It remains the primary method to diagnose the effects of minor traumatic injury (Bigler, 2003; Ewing-Cobbs, Barnes, et al., 2004; Hanten, Dennis, et al., 2004). It is unclear how much we will ever be able to understand about human memory and thought on the basis of physiology alone. Beyond physiologic findings, motivation or desire to perform well can profoundly affect performance (Green, 2003).

The roots of clinical neuropsychology can be traced to studies by Pierre Broca and Carl Wernicke in the 19th century. These early investigators recognized that functions such as the recognition of speech were localized in the left hemisphere of the brain. By the first decade of the 20th century, Brodmann had developed the first functional map of the cerebral cortex. A variety of investigators including Benton, Tuber, and Geschwind developed methods for associating function with different areas of the brain. Early neuropsychologists, including Luria and Reitan, used psychological tests to estimate areas of brain damage. However, major advances in brain imaging reduced the need for these types of services. Magnetic resonance imaging (MRI) and CAT scanning now allow clinicians to examine the brains of living people.

Clinical neuropsychology has developed rapidly over the last few decades. In 1970, neuropsychology was viewed as a new field characterized by rapid growth (Parsons, 1970). During the 1970s and early 1980s, research in neuropsychology exploded, and a practice specialty rapidly developed. Currently, neuropsychology has formally joined the ranks of other neurosciences. Using powerful measurement techniques, neuropsychologists have developed many procedures for identifying the relationship between brain problems and behavioral problems (Butters, Delis, & Lucas, 1995). The activities of neuropsychologists are extremely varied and require complex technology. An exploration of this important new discipline in any depth would require a review of neuroanatomy and other topics in neuroscience that we cannot discuss here. Instead, we describe some current activities of active neuropsychological research and practice. The interested reader should consult Baddeley, Wilson, and Watts (1995), Grant and Adams (1996), Hooper and March (1995), Lezak (1995), and Mapou and Spector (1986).

Neuropsychologists are quite specialized. Some focus on brain dysfunction in children (Fletcher, Taylor, Levin, & Satz, 1995; Hooper & March, 1995), whereas others work with adults (Heaton & Pendleton, 1981) or older adults (Kasdniak & Christenson, 1994; Welsh, Butters, Hughes, Mobs, & Hayman, 1991). Neuropsychologists focus mainly on brain dysfunction, but some are actively developing interventions for those who suffer brain injuries or related problems (Dikmen & Machamer, 1995). Neuropsychologists also study how cognitive processes are affected by mental illness (McKenna, Clare, & Baddeley, 1995) as well as alcohol abuse (Dawson & Grant, 2000) or serious diseases such as AIDS (Grant & Heaton, 1990). Some specialize in the evaluation of older adults (Koltai & Welsh-Bohmer, 2000; Lichtenberg & MacNeill, 2000). Some neuropsychologists prefer to use batteries of psychological tests, whereas others prefer specific tasks derived from experimental psychology (Delis, Filoteo, Massman, Kaplan, & Kramer, 1994; Satz & Fletcher, 1981).

Neuropsychological assessment has been used to evaluate specific problems in memory. Clearly, memory is a heterogeneous phenomenon; scientists make distinctions among memory systems such as short- and long-term memory. Short-term memory occurs when one recollects or produces material immediately after it has been presented. The capacity for short-term memory is probably limited; without repetition one can hold information only a few minutes. Conversely, long-term memory may be stored for a long time (more than a few days), and the capacity for long-term memory is quite large.

Examiners use a variety of clinical techniques to measure memory dysfunction, including the Wechsler Memory Scale–Revised (WMS-R), the Memory Assessment Scales (MAS), the RANDT Memory Test (RMT), and the Luria-Nebraska battery. Short-term memory is best assessed using verbal tests. These include the immediate recall span, the digit span, and several word tests (Butters et al., 1995). The techniques used to assess short-term memory include tests that evaluate memory for specific stories or memory for lists of unrelated words.

Significant progress has been made in linking performance on neuropsychological tests to specific clinical problems (Rao, 2000). For example, alcoholic dementia, which is caused by long-term chronic alcoholism, is characterized by dysfunction in visuospatial skills. Patients with Huntington's disease perform much better on recognition than do patients with Alzheimer's disease; however, the former may have retrograde amnesia with equally deficient recall of events from all decades, while the latter have more severe difficulties with recall for recent events and less for long-term memories (Butters et al., 1995).

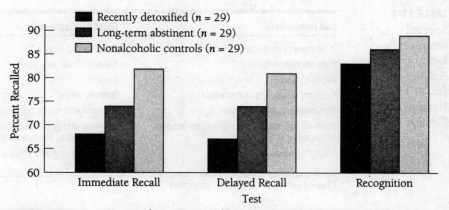

FIGURE 17-1 *Learning and memory performance by recently detoxified alcoholics (abstinent 2 weeks), long-term abstinent alcoholics (abstinent 18 months), and non-alcoholic controls.*
(Adapted from data in Dawson & Grant, 2000.)

Another example of a study that used neuropsychological evaluations compared recently detoxified alcoholics with nonalcoholic controls who were the same age and with recovering alcoholics who had been abstinent for at least 18 months. The groups were comparable in education, age, and IQ. However, comparisons on learning and retention of new information differed. Figure 17-1 shows some of these differences. Recently detoxified alcoholics scored lower on measures of immediate recall, 20-minute delayed recall, and recognition than did comparable subjects who had been off alcohol for 18 months. Both groups of former alcoholics performed more poorly that did the nonalcoholic controls. These findings suggest that there may be some recovery of learning and memory when alcoholics are abstinent for 18 months or more. However, chronic alcohol use may permanently affect some neuropsychological functioning (Dawson & Grant, 2000.)

New research also challenges the idea that functional problems are related to specific locations within the brain. New evidence suggests that complex cognitive, perceptual, and motor functioning are determined by neural systems rather than specific single structures. There are complicated circuits and dense interconnections between different locations in the brain. Neuropsychological evaluation estimates localized problems as well as problems with the brain's complex interconnections.

One of the most studied areas of neuropsychology is the identification of deficits in the left or right hemisphere of the brain. Evidence for left hemisphere control of language in right-handed individuals comes from studies on brain damage, studies of brain stimulation during surgery for patients with epilepsy, and from evaluation of people who have suffered a stroke on one side of the brain. However, approximately two-thirds of left-handed peo-

TABLE 11-1
Selected Neuropsychological Deficits Associated with Left or Right Hemisphere Damage

Left hemisphere	Right hemisphere
Word memory problems	Visual-spatial deficits
Right-left disorientation	Impaired visual perception
Finger agnosia	Neglect
Problems recognizing written words	Difficulty writing
Problems performing calculations	Problems with spatial calculations
Problems with detailed voluntary motor activities, not explained by paralysis	Problems with gross coordinated voluntary motor not explained by paralysis activities
Problems dressing	Inability to recognize a physical deficit (e.g., denial of a paralyzed limb)

Adapted from Swanda, Haaland, and LaRue (2000).

ple have language organized on the left side of the brain, approximately 20% have language organized in the right hemisphere, and the remainder appear to have language represented on both sides. Table 17-1 summarizes some of the problems associated with left or right hemisphere damage (Swanda et al., 2000).

Trained neuropsychologists can identify specific problems. For example, Wernicke's aphasia is characterized by impaired verbal comprehension and ability to repeat information. People with this pattern of impairment have damage to Wernicke's area of the brain (the superior temporal gyrus), problems monitoring their language output, and often have difficulty with the syntax of their spoken sentences. Sometimes people affected by Wernicke's aphasia utter unintelligible strings of words that can be confused with schizophrenic symptoms.

Neuropsychological tests can also be used to diagnose motor problems. For example, right-handed people who have damage to their right hemisphere often develop spatial disorders such as the inability to copy or draw objects or difficulties assembling certain objects. Some individuals may develop specific problems associated with right hemisphere damage, such as dressing apraxia. People with this condition have difficulty identifying the top or the bottom of a garment, and sometimes the left or the right side as well. Although these individuals may function well in other aspects of their lives, they have a great deal of difficulty dressing.

Neuropsychologists are also skilled at identifying which aspects of the information-processing systems may be damaged. For example, information retrieval and storage are related but different functions. Some people have problems in recall or retrieval of information. Tests can be used to determine whether the problem is in recognition or actual retrieval of information. Recognition might be evaluated using multiple-choice format items. Patients who have difficulty recognizing information may have deficiencies in storage, which is associated with the medial temporal lobes or the diencephalic system. Impaired retrieval of information may be associated with problems in the frontal lobes, for example. (See Focused Example 17-1.)

Focused Example 17-1

CASE STUDY: NEUROPSYCHOLOGICAL CONSEQUENCES OF LONG-TERM ALCOHOL ABUSE

Neuropsychological evaluation uses a variety of approaches to identify problems with brain functioning. One task that is often informative is to have the patient draw a clock. Damage to the right hemisphere of the brain is sometimes reflected in inaccurate global features of the drawing. Left hemisphere damage is associated with the reproduction of small features and details.

A case study helps illustrate the value of the clock-drawing task. The patient in this study had been admitted to the hospital after he had called 911 and stated he was suicidal. He was intoxicated at the time of admission and had a significant history of alcohol abuse. The same patient had received neurological evaluations on several previous occasions. The patient was well educated and had completed college. He had good verbal skills, with a WAIS verbal IQ of 103. However, some of his WAIS subscores were lower. For example, the digit span subtest was in the 25th percentile, and his performance on the memory domain was in the first percentile.

Figure 17-2 shows the subject's performance on the Draw-a-Clock task from the Boston Diagnostic Aphasia Examination. The task asks the patient, "Draw a clock, put in all of the numbers, and set the hands for ten after 11." The left-hand portion of the figure shows the clock drawn in 1996. The center section shows the clock drawn in 1998, while the third panel shows the clock drawn during the hospital admission in 1999.

The pattern of performance suggests a deterioration in parietal lobe functioning indicated by poor visuospatial functioning. It is likely that long-term alcohol abuse contributed to these problems.

FIGURE 17-2
*Results from the
Draw-a-Clock
task.*
(Dean Delis, Ph.D.
provided this example.)

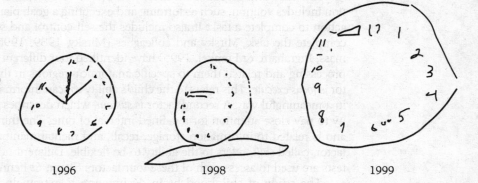

1996   1998   1999

Developmental Neuropsychology

Testing is typically done as part of a complex evaluation. When children are not performing well in school, a medical, educational, and psychological evaluation might be ordered. Sometimes, neuropsychological testing is done to provide a baseline. For example, a child who is undergoing intense medical therapy or a child with a serious medical illness such as epilepsy may face neurological changes over time. Repeated neuropsychological evaluations can help identify such changes (Baron & Fennell, 2000).

Neuropsychological assessment of children presents unique challenges. For example, a young child with a brain injury may adapt well to most situations, but she may later have problems with, say, her geometry class, which would require more complex visual–perceptual functioning than she had encountered before. Earlier brain injury may be missed until children reach the age where they are challenged with new types of problems.

Another challenge in evaluating children is brain plasticity. The human brain is remarkable in its potential to reorganize in response to injury. Although recovery is often impressive, it usually is not complete, and these problems are often hard to evaluate using neuropsychological tests.

Neuropsychological tests for children differ widely. One category of measures tests general development and adaptive functioning. Examples include the Child Development Inventory, Child Behavior Checklist, Reynolds Depression Scale, and Children's State-Trait Anxiety Scale.

A second group of measures estimates attention and executive function. These tests typically evaluate functioning related to several different aspects of information processing. The Trail Making Tests, for example, scatter sequential numbers (e.g., 1, 2, 3, 4) around different locations on a sheet of paper. The child is asked to draw lines to connect the numbers in sequence. Part B of the test adds scattered sequential letters, and the child must, for example, start at 1, go to *A*, then go to 2, then *B*, and so on. The test evaluates several cognitive skills including attention, sequencing, and thought processing.

Attention and executive function are believed to be separate. Executive function includes volition, such as forming and executing a goal, planning, and taking action to complete a task. It also includes the self-control and self-monitoring to complete the task. Mirsky and colleagues (Mirsky, 1989, 1996; Mirsky, Kugelmass, Ingraham, & Frenkel, 1995) have identified four different factors of mental processing and related them to specific anatomical regions in the brain. One factor is *focus execute*. This refers to the child's ability to scan information and respond in a meaningful way. A second factor is *sustain,* which describes the child's capacity to pay close attention for a defined interval of time. The third factor is *encode* and is related to information storage, recall, and mental manipulation. The final factor, called *shift,* refers to the ability to be flexible. Different neuropsychological tests are used to assess each of these four factors (Baron & Fennell, 2000).

The study of childhood brain dysfunction is extremely important. Neuropsychological problems appear in speech and reading disorders known generally as *learning disabilities,* which account for problems in significant numbers of young children. **Dyslexia** is a specific reading disorder characterized by difficulties in decoding single words. The problem may have a genetic base and may result from difficulties in processing phonemes. Unfortunately, it is difficult to estimate the exact number of children who are affected by dyslexia because different studies apply different definitions. The problem likely affects approximately 4% of school-age children and approximately 80% of children identified as having a learning disability.

Federal law now requires that children with specific disabilities receive individualized instructional programs and special attention. Thus, the identification of a disability means that considerable attention will be devoted to the child at enormous public expense. In other words, learning disabilities represent major public health problems. As such, considerable effort has been devoted to defining subcategories of learning disabilities, developing procedures to identify them, and instituting methods for helping children overcome these problems (Leong & Joshi, 1995; Pennington & Welsh, 1995; Shaywitz, Fletcher, & Shaywitz, 1995).

In addition to identification of brain injury, neuropsychological evaluations have been used for a variety of other purposes. For example, neuropsychological testing has been used to determine if people are faking illness. One application is the detection of malingering for adults who have traumatic brain injury. In one study, 65 patients who had previous brain injury were referred for a neuropsychological evaluation. Twenty-eight of these patients had been identified as having exaggerated their cognitive dysfunction in order to gain greater benefits or to escape reassignment to work. All subjects completed the WAIS (See Chapter 10). Using discriminate function analysis, which is a specialized method for identifying the linear combination of variables that separate groups, the researchers developed an equation that successfully separated malingerers from those who were not exaggerating their brain injury (Greve, Bianchini, Mathias, & Houston, 2003).

Another application of neuropsychological testing is to determine the seriousness of concussions among athletes (Erlanger, Kaushik, Cantu, Barth, Broshek, Freeman, et al., 2003). Head injury for athletes is common, particularly in sports such as boxing and football. An injured athlete often wants to return to play promptly. Returning the athlete to the playing field too soon might put him or her at serious risk. One application of clinical neuropsychology is the development of a concussion resolution index (CRI) to track the recovery following a sports-related concussion. CRI is made up of six subtests including reaction time, visual recognition, and speed of information processing. Validity studies show that the CRI is associated with other neuropsychological tests. For example, it correlates with the grooved pegboard test. Studies using athletes who have been injured demonstrated that this computer-based test can identify ongoing neuropsychological difficulties in cases where symptom reports and clinical examinations are normal. Ongoing problems in psychomotor speed and speed of information processing may put athletes at risk for future injury. Use of these new methods could be exceptionally helpful for determining when it is safe for athletes to return to the playing field (Erlanger, Feldman, Kutner, Kaushik, Kroger, et al., 2003)

Other clinical neuropsychologists have been busy identifying the cognitive consequences of early brain lesions. For example, studies have shown that high-risk infants show poor performance on tests of verbal ability, coordination, visual–spatial ability, and the like by the time they are 31.2 years old (Francis-Williams, 1974). Other studies focus on recovery from accidents and trauma. For example, a few years after children have been in accidents involving head injuries, neurological tests often show no remaining problems. Nevertheless, neuropsychological tests of intellectual abilities often show that these functions remain somewhat impaired (Butters et al., 1995). In summary, developmental neuropsychologists actively work toward understanding brain–behavior relationships in children. They have created extensive diagnostic procedures for identifying learning disabilities such as articulation disorders, speech disorders, and dyslexia. Furthermore, they have attempted to link specific medical problems such as birth complications and prematurity to later intellectual function. Finally, they have attempted to identify the cognitive consequences of early brain disease and injury.

Developmental neuropsychology is a difficult field because it requires several levels of assessment. Figure 17-3 shows a seven-step model that is used by neuropsychologists in the development of rehabilitation plans. The first step requires the application of formal tests to determine the nature of the problem. The second step calls for an assessment of the environment, such as the demands of the school environment and other academic expectations. The third and fourth steps require the formulation of treatment plans, which involve a prediction of the short- and long-term consequences of the brain problem and the chances that intervention will make a difference. The fifth step concerns the availability of resources. For example, is there a family member who can assist in treatment? Are there facilities and therapists in the community? The sixth step calls for the development of a realistic treatment plan that considers the information gained in Steps 1–5. Even if the neuropsychologist does not deliver the treatment, he or she may remain involved in the seventh step, evaluating progress made in the course of clinical care. When treatment is not achieving its objectives, modifications may be suggested (Fletcher et al., 1995).

As suggested by Figure 17-3, the neuropsychologist has many complex and important tasks that require the administration and interpretation of assessment devices.

Adult Neuropsychology

There are many different approaches to identifying the consequences of brain injury in adults. Perhaps the two best-known approaches involve administration of the Halstead-Reitan and Luria-Nebraska test batteries.

Halstead-Reitan Neuropsychological Battery. In 1935, Ward Halstead opened a laboratory to study the impact of impairments of brain function on a wide range of human abilities. Some of Halstead's observations were formal, while others involved observations in work and social settings. The formal observations were obtained through modifications of existing psychological tests. Over time, Halstead realized that determining inadequacy in brain function required a wide range of tests that measured characteristics and abilities beyond those targeted by existing psychological tests. In 1944, Halstead was joined in his neuropsychological laboratory by his first graduate student, Ralph M. Reitan. Halstead and Reitan worked together until 1950, when Reitan received his

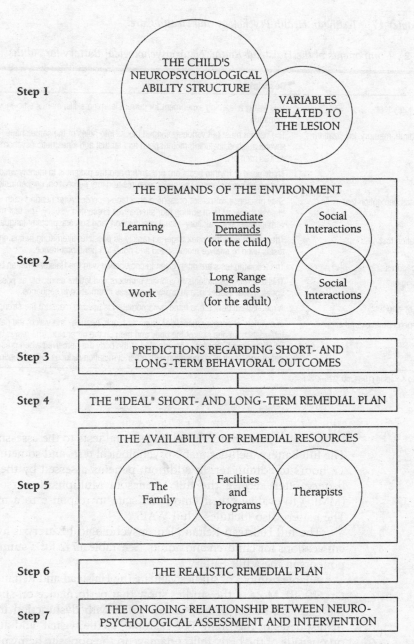

FIGURE 17-3 *The process of habilitation requires at least seven steps: (1) assessment of the child, (2) assessment of the environment, (3) predictions about short- and long-term outcomes, (4) development of an ideal plan, (5) assessment of resources, (6) development of a realistic intervention plan, and (7) ongoing assessment.*
(From J. M. Fletcher et al., 1995, p. 585. Reprinted by permission of Lippincott, Williams & Wilkins.)

TABLE 17-2 *Components of the Halstead-Reitan Neuropsychological Battery for Adults*

Test	Description
Halstead category test	This test is a learning experiment for current learning skills, mental efficiency, and abstract concept formation.
Tactual test (time, memory, localization)	The patient must put variously shaped blocks into holes of the same shape. The test assesses several abilities, including motor speed and tactual and kinesthetic psychomotor performance, as well as memory.
Rhythm test	Thirty pairs of rhythm beats are presented, and the patient is to identify which pairs are the same and which are different. The task measures auditory perception, concentration, and attention.
Speech-sounds perception test	Sixty nonsense words are presented on a tape recorder. After hearing each word, the patient must choose the word from among four alternatives presented visually. The test measures auditory–verbal perception, auditory–visual coordination, and some aspects of language and concentration.
Finger oscillation test	The patient taps the index finger as rapidly as possible, alternating hands on consecutive trials. The test is used to analyze motor speed and right–left hand preference.
Related Procedures	The following tests are often given in conjunction with the Halstead-Reitan battery.
Trail-making test	This test requires patients to connect numbers and letters as rapidly as possible. The test measures speed, visual scanning, and ability to process information in sequence.
Strength-of-grip test	A mechanical device (the hand dynamometer) is used to measure the strength of grip in each hand.
Sensory–perceptual examination	In a variety of sensory modalities, such as touch, hearing, and vision, the patient receives information on one side of the body and then on the other side. The test is used to determine whether stimuli presented on one side of the body are perceived when presented alone and also to determine whether competition with other stimulation reduces the perception of the stimulus.

From Saccuzzo & Kaplan (1984, pp. 226–227).

Ph.D. Reitan contributed by adding several tests to the assessment procedures. The full battery includes many psychological tests and sometimes requires 8 to 12 hours to administer. In addition, patients assessed by the Halstead-Reitan battery often receive the full Minnesota Multiphasic Personality Inventory (MMPI) to evaluate their emotional state in response to a medical situation. The battery also includes a full WAIS.

The full Halstead-Reitan Neuropsychological Battery is available in different versions for children and adults. See Table 17-2 for a summary of the components in the adult battery.

A large number of studies validate the Halstead and Reitan procedures (Reitan, 1968). Most of the studies show that performance on specific subtasks of the Halstead-Reitan battery is associated with dysfunction in one of the two hemispheres of the brain. For example, tactile, visual, and auditory problems on one side of the body reflect damage in the opposite hemisphere of the brain. Difficulty on the right side of the body indicates a problem in the left side of the brain (Wheeler & Reitan, 1962). Later studies by Reitan (1968) demonstrated that the battery can locate tumors or lesions in the right or left hemisphere of the brain and in the front or back portion of the brain in a significant number of cases. By studying performance in a systematic way, neuropsychologists have been able to provide important information about the location and the impact of brain problems (Reitan & Wolfson, 1997, 1999).

Critics of the Halstead-Reitan battery point out that the major advantage of the test may not be worth the effort in applying the measures. The battery can assist in localizing injury in either the left or right hemisphere of the brain. However, this advantage may be meager in relation to the many hours it takes to complete the test. New methods of brain imaging (MRI and CAT scan) may be more efficient for locating injury (Swanda et al., 2000).

Luria-Nebraska Neuropsychological Battery. A different approach to neuropsychological assessment is found in the work of Luria, who was recognized for many years as an expert on the functions of the human brain (Luria, 1966, 1973). While other researchers such as Halstead and Reitan attempted to find specific areas within the brain that correspond to particular behaviors, Luria did not acknowledge that any single area was solely responsible for any particular behavior. Instead, Luria saw the brain as a functional system, with a limited number of brain areas involved in each behavior. Each area in the functional system might be considered a necessary link in a chain. If any link is injured, the total system will break down.

Luria also introduced the concept of *pluripotentiality*—that any one center in the brain can be involved in several different functional systems (Golden, 1981). For example, one center in the brain may be involved in both visual and tactile senses. Luria also felt that multiple systems might be responsible for the same behavior. Thus, if a child's injury affects one system, another system may take over. Many clinical examples show the value of Luria's methods, particularly for severely disabled patients who may have multiple health problems and cannot complete traditional psychological tests (Guedalia, Finkelstein, Drukker, & Frishberg, 2000).

In practice, Luria applied his theory clinically to make intuitive judgments about deficits in functional systems. Because he did not use a standardized procedure, the amount of time he spent testing individuals varied greatly. In addition, it was difficult for others to repeat the exact steps Luria had used to reach conclusions about particular patients. Reitan (1976) criticized him on the grounds that Luria's opinion was the only known evidence for the validity of the tests.

Although Luria's procedures were widely regarded as important, they did not meet the psychometric standards of many U.S. psychologists. To face these criticisms, Golden (1981) developed a standardized version of Luria's procedures. Because Golden worked at the University of Nebraska, the test has become known as the Luria-Nebraska Neuropsychological Battery. The battery includes 269 items that can be administered in approximately 24 hours. The items are divided into 11 subsections; these are listed in Table 17-3. A similar test for children has also been developed (Plaisted, Gustavson, Wilkening, & Golden, 1983).

The inventory is scored by finding a standardized performance level for each of the 11 subtests. In addition, three more scores are reported. First, a pathognomonic scale consists of 32 items found in previous studies to be highly sensitive to brain dysfunction. The other two scores indicate whether

TABLE 17-3 *Subsections of Luria-Nebraska Neuropsychological Battery*

Test	Description
Motor functions	Examines basic and complex motor skills. Some items ask patients to perform fine tasks with the right and left hand and with the eyes open or closed. Other items involve mouth, tongue, and speech movements.
Rhythm	Evaluates rhythm and pitch skills. Patients must reproduce melodic sounds such as those from the song "Home on the Range." They are also to identify soft and loud sounds and musical patterns.
Tactile	Evaluates a variety of kinesthetic (movement) and tactile (touch) abilities. Patients are blindfolded and asked to identify where they have been touched. Then they must identify a variety of shapes and letters written on the back of the patients' hands. In addition, patients must identify common objects such as quarters, keys, paper clips, and so on.
Visual	Investigates visual and spatial skills. Patients are asked to identify objects through pictures and through progressively more difficult items. They are asked to put pieces together or identify objects in overlapping sketches.
Receptive speech	Tests ability to understand the spoken language. Items range from simple phonemes to comprehension of complex sentences.
Expressive speech	Estimates ability to express speech orally. The word sounds range from "see" to "Massachusetts" to "episcopal." Writing identifies basic writing skills including simple spelling, copying letters and words, and writing names.
Reading	Similar to writing section. It tests whether patients can identify individual letters and read symbols, words, sentences, and stories.
Arithmetic skills	Tests a variety of simple numeric and algebraic abilities.
Memory	Assesses verbal and nonverbal memory skills. Items range from simple recall to complex memorization tasks.
Intellectual processes	Evaluates intellectual level using items similar to those on traditional intelligence tests.

From Saccuzzo & Kaplan (1984, p. 230).

dysfunction is in the right or the left hemisphere of the brain. They are taken from the sections of the battery that independently test the function of the right or left side of the body.

A variety of studies (summarized by Golden, 1981) have demonstrated that the Luria-Nebraska battery can make fine distinctions in neuropsychological functions. Many of these studies used the battery to estimate the area of the brain damaged by a tumor or lesion. In many of these studies, confirmation of localization is made by surgery, angiogram, or CAT scan. In one study, the Luria-Nebraska battery localized problems in 22 of 24 right hemisphere and 29 of 36 left hemisphere cases (Golden, 1981). Some evaluations of the Luria-Nebraska battery are highly encouraging, whereas others show that these tests give little more information than do IQ tests (Carr, Sweet, & Rossini, 1986). Statistical methods for interpreting results are continually improving (Moses, Pritchard, & Faustman, 1994; Reynolds, 1982; Webster & Dostrow, 1982); nevertheless, the approach still has serious critics (Spiers, 1982).

An example of a profile from a patient tested with the Luria-Nebraska battery is shown in Figure 17-4. The two dark horizontal lines in the figure represent the normal ranges for performance on the various subtests. Scores above the top dark line indicate significant problem areas. As the figure shows, the patient demonstrates significant impairment in both expressive and receptive language, as well as problems in arithmetic and writing. Neuropsychologists have learned that memory problems are often associated with damage in the

FIGURE 17-4

Profile of a patient tested with the Luria-Nebraska battery.

(From Golden, 1981. Copyright © 1981 by John Wiley & Sons, Inc. Reprinted by permission of John Wiley & Sons, Inc.)

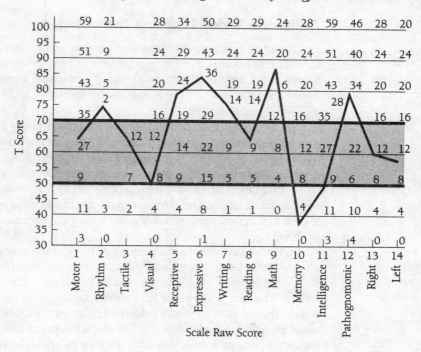

temporal lobe of the brain. Thus, the good performance on memory rules out a temporal lobe problem. Receptive and expressive language abilities seem to be localized more in the left than the right side of the brain. Comparing the profile with information acquired in other studies, the neuropsychologists estimated that there was damage in the left side of the brain in the parietal-occipital area (toward the back of the left side). A neurological report confirmed that a stroke had damaged this very area.

Using information from neuropsychological test batteries, clinicians can evaluate damage and suggest programs for rehabilitation. Despite important improvements in the Luria-Nebraska battery, several methodological questions still remain. After a detailed review of the test and the standardization procedures, Lezak (1995) argued that it is important to interpret results of these tests with great caution. Some neuropsychologists prefer to use specific experimental tasks in addition to test batteries. One of the ongoing debates among neuropsychologists concerns the value of qualitative versus quantitative approaches. The Halstead-Reitan is an example of a fixed quantitative battery. Psychologists using this approach simply follow a set of standardized procedures. Qualitative approaches allow greater flexibility in the assessment process. Often the measures are designed to identify a specific information-processing problem and the psychologist can choose the components that may address specific clinical problems (Baron & Fennell, 2000). The California Verbal Learning Test is an example of this more recent approach.

California Verbal Learning Test

For decades, psychologists have known that people can get a wrong response for different reasons. For example, Werner (1937) objected to the use of global scores based only on the number of right or wrong items. Instead, Werner favored tests that assess how problems are solved in addition to assessing overall level of achievement.

Modern cognitive psychology has identified many levels of human information processing (Squire & Butters, 1984). Contemporary cognitive psychology suggests that many factors determine performance on any given task. It is not enough to know that there is an impairment in cognitive functioning. Instead, one needs to know which aspects of the human information-processing system are defective and which aspects are functioning well. This information is essential in designing rehabilitation strategies for patients who have selective problems.

The California Verbal Learning Test (CVLT) is a relatively new approach to clinical neuropsychology that builds on research in psychological testing, cognitive psychology, and computer science (Delis, Kramer, Kaplan, & Ober, 1987). The test determines how errors are made in learning tasks. In other words, the intent is to identify different strategies, processes, and errors that are associated with specific deficits. The test attempts to link memory deficits with impaired performance on specific tasks for people who have known neurological problems. The CVLT assesses various variables, including levels of recall and recognition, semantic and serial strategies, serial position effects, learning rates across trials, consistency of item recall across trials, degree of vulnerability to proactive and retroactive interference, retention of information over short and long delays, and learning errors in recall and recognition.

In one component of the CVLT, the subject is asked to imagine that he or she is going to go shopping. Then the subject receives a list of items to buy. The examiner lists 16 items orally at a pace of approximately one word per second. The respondent is asked to repeat the list. This process is repeated through a series of five trials.

Performance on these tasks is analyzed in many ways. For example, learning across trials gives the test taker considerable information. Those who are highly anxious may perform poorly on the first trial but improve as the task is repeated (Lezak, 1995). However, adults with limited learning capacity may do relatively well on early trials but reach a plateau where repeated trials do not reflect improved performance. Adults with limited learning capacity may also have inconsistent recall across trials. This can happen when they abandon one strategy and adopt another. Studies have demonstrated that inconsistent recall across trials characterizes patients with amnesia caused by frontal lobe pathology.

The CVLT also includes other features derived from experimental cognitive psychology. For example, after five trials of exposure to the 16-word lists, a second interference list of 16 words is given. Subjects are tested immediately, and again after 20 minutes, for free recall, cued recall, and recognition of the first list.

Another unique feature of the CVLT is that one can administer it either in a paper-and-pencil form or with a microcomputer. Versions for both the PCs and the Macintosh are available. The computer does not replace test administrators but instead assists them. In the computer-assisted form of the test, the examiner can enter responses directly into the computer using a single key or a light pen to touch the words on a monitor screen. This greatly facilitates and speeds up the scoring process.

Several studies have evaluated the CVLT's validity. For example, the test correlates with other measures such as the Wechsler memory scale (Delis et al., 1987). In addition, factor analysis studies of the CVLT suggest independent factors for learning strategy, acquisition rate, serial position, discriminability, and learning performance. These constructs correspond to empirical findings from modern cognitive psychology. The diversity of deficits identified by the CVLT could not be identified using more-traditional psychometric tests (Delis et al., 1987).

The CVLT has been used to compare patients with Alzheimer's disease, Korsakoff's syndrome, and Huntington's disease. Alzheimer's disease is a serious neurological disorder that causes the inability to form short-term memories. Korsakoff's syndrome is an organic brain disorder often associated with long-term alcohol use that also results in the loss of short-term memory. Finally, Huntington's disease is an inherited disorder emerging in adulthood and associated with memory loss. Although all three organic brain problems are associated with memory loss, the nature of the deficit may be different. For example, patients with Alzheimer's and Huntington's may score about the same on measures of recall and memory tests but may differ in measures of forgetting (Bondi, Houston, Salmon, Corey-Bloom, Katzman, Thal, et al., 2003). Studies of brain pathology show that these two diseases affect different parts of the brain. An advantage of the CVLT is that it allows a more precise evaluation of the nature of the problems than do other tests.

When representative groups of patients from these three diagnostic groups are compared on the CVLT, those with Alzheimer's disease and with Korsakoff's syndrome appear quite similar, with comparable scores for recall, learning and forgetting, semantic clustering, and several other cognitive factors. However, each of these groups performed at a lower level than did patients with Huntington's disease on measures of retention, intrusion errors, and recognition (Delis, Magsman, Butters, Salmon, Cermak, & Kramer, 1991).

Studies of patients with Huntington's disease, Alzheimer's disease, and other neuropsychological impairments can help us understand properties of the tests. In one experiment, for example, normal patients, those with Huntington's disease, and those with Alzheimer's disease completed the CVLT. The patients were tested on immediate recall and long-delay free recall. As expected, the controls did significantly better than those with either Alzheimer's disease or Huntington's disease (see Figure 17-5). However, the correlation between the two tests were not the same for the different groups. Immediate recall and long-delayed recall were highly correlated (above $r = .80$) for normal patients and for patients with Huntington's disease. However, the two variables

FIGURE 17-5

Long-delay recall on CVLT in three patient groups.

(Adapted from Delis et al., 1991.)

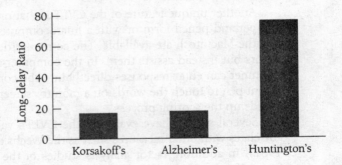

were correlated only 0.36 for patients with Alzheimer's disease. These findings are critically important because we often assume that the correlations between variables are the same for all patient groups. These findings suggest that the very nature of the association between variables is different for different patient populations. This challenges the idea that measures have the same validity for different patient groups (Delis, Jacobson, et al., 2003).

Figure 17-5 compares CVLT scores for immediate and for long-delay savings for the two patient groups in comparison to a control group. *Long-delay savings* require that subjects learn a list of words. Then, after a long delay, they are given a free-recall test. The results are reported as the average number of correct responses. The figure shows that Huntington's patients have significantly higher recall than do those with Alzheimer's disease but fewer correct responses than controls. These results are consistent with the neuroanatomy of the illnesses. Huntington's disease is a subcortical dementia, while Alzheimer's disease is associated with cortical lesions. The CVLT may be helpful in identifying the location of the organic problem.

In 1994, Delis and colleagues released a children's version of the CVLT, the CVLT-C. Appropriate for children aged 5–16, this individually administered test can be used to evaluate mild to severe learning disabilities, attention deficit disorder (ADD), mental retardation, and other neurological disorders. In addition, the CVLT-C provides information for the diagnosis of psychiatric disorders. Like the adult version, the CVLT-C assesses both recall and recognition of words. In a typical testing session, the child may receive a list of 15 words on Monday and an interference list of 15 words on Tuesday. After the interference list, the child is tested on the Monday list. After a 20-minute delay, a nonverbal test is administered, followed by tests of long-delay free recall and long-delay cued recall, then a test designed to assess recognition of the words that were administered the day before. These procedures produce several different scores including total recall, learning strategy, serial position effect, learning rate, consistency of item recall, proactive and retroactive interference, and retention over long and short delays.

The test was standardized on a large national sample. Internal consistency and alpha reliabilities for the test are generally high (usually above .80 for all age levels). Validity studies consistently show that the test is moderately correlated (between .32 and .40) with the WISC-R vocabulary subtest (Delis, Kramer, et al., 2004). In contrast to other tests, however, the CVLT-C provides substantially more diagnostic information (Delis et al., 1994). It is beginning to find a variety of clinical uses. For example, recent studies suggest that the CVLT can be used to detect whether patients are faking head injury in order to gain benefits (Sweet et al., 2000).

In summary, clinical neuropsychology is an emerging and important area in psychological testing. It is linked closely to basic research in both neuroscience and cognitive psychology. We expect this field to continue its rapid development over the next few decades.

Anxiety and Stress Assessment

It is the day of your final exam. You have studied hard and have every reason to expect an A. As you enter the classroom, the back of your neck feels stiff. Your hands sweat as you get out your pencil. Instead of concentrating on the task of test taking, you worry about not doing well, or you think about running out of time. When it is all over, you feel cheated. You knew the material well, but your grade on the exam did not reflect your knowledge.

If this story describes a situation you have experienced, then you have company. Test anxiety is a common problem among college students and a major factor in diminishing the validity of tests.

Test anxiety is also an important and active area in psychological research. Many theories about the relationship of anxiety to performance have led to the development of specific test-anxiety scales and measures (Endler, Kantor, & Parker, 1994; Flett & Blankstein, 1994; Sapp, 1999; Sarason & Sarason, 1999; Williams, 1994). In this section, we review the general concepts of anxiety and stress, and then we review in some detail the theory and measurement of the same.

Stress and Anxiety

Stress is a response to situations that involve demands, constraints, or opportunities (Sarason & Sarason, 1999). We all experience psychological stress at some point in our lives. For some people, stress is a debilitating problem that interferes with virtually every aspect of their lives. For others, stress causes problems in particular situations. Stress helps still others to accomplish important goals. The study of psychological stress has gained an increasingly central position within the psychological and biomedical sciences (Wainwright & Calnan, 2002). Psychological stress can interfere with performance on mental and academic tests (Oostdam & Meijer, 2003; Sapp, 1999), and some medical investigators now believe that stress is involved in 50% to 80% of all illnesses.

Psychological stress has three components: frustration, conflict, and pressure. *Frustration* occurs when the attainment of a goal is blocked. Though frustration takes different forms, the principle remains the same. A fourth-year premed student will likely become frustrated if she is rejected by every major medical school. Or if someone wants to get into a concert and is refused entrance, he may become frustrated. In each case, something or someone has blocked the attainment of a goal. *Conflict* is a type of stress that occurs when we must make a choice between two or more important goals, such as deciding between going to law school and going to graduate school in psychology. The final type of stress is *pressure* to speed up activities. External pressure occurs when your professor assigns a lot of extra reading right before the midterm exam; internal pressure occurs when no such reading is assigned but you take it on yourself because it fits your style and aspirations. Test anxiety does respond to treatment, particularly interventions that combine skills for test taking with cognitive and behavioral modification (Ergene, 2003).

Exposure to stressful situations can cause an observable reaction known as **anxiety,** an emotional state marked by worry, apprehension, and tension. When you are anxious, your autonomic nervous system becomes activated: Your heart beats fast, your pulse rate goes up, your hands tend to sweat. The amount of anxiety you experience depends in part on the intensity of the stress-producing stimulus as you perceive it, or your evaluation of a situation (Flett, Endler, & Fairlie, 1999; Spielberger & Sydeman, 1994; Stein, Hollander, & ebrary Inc., 2002; Trotter & Endler, 1999). How potentially harmful is the situation for you?

The State-Trait Anxiety Inventory

Actually, there are two types of anxiety. *State anxiety* is an emotional reaction that varies from one situation to another. *Trait anxiety* is a personality characteristic. Interest in these two types of anxiety led Charles D. Spielberger to develop the state-trait anxiety theory, which in turn led to the development of the State-Trait Anxiety Inventory (STAI). The STAI provides two separate scores: one for state anxiety (A-State) and another for trait anxiety (A-Trait). The STAI A-Trait scale consists of 20 items. On a 4-point scale, subjects indicate how they generally feel about each item. A similar set of items is used to evaluate the A-State.

Good evidence exists for the validity and the reliability of the STAI. Test–retest reliabilities range from .73 to .86 for the trait scale. The state scale, which is supposed to be inconsistent over time, indeed has low test–retest reliability (.16 to .54). Validity studies show that the STAI can be used to make several important and useful generalizations. For example, concurrent validity studies have shown that the STAI trait scale correlates well with other measures of trait anxiety. The STAI trait scale has been correlated with the Taylor Manifest Anxiety Scale (see Spielberger & Sydeman, 1994); it was also associated with another trait-anxiety scale known as the IPAT Anxiety Scale (Cattell & Scheier, 1961) for the same groups of college students and psychiatric patients. The correlations with the Taylor and the IPAT ranged from .75 to .85, which are quite impressive and suggest that these three scales measure much of the same psychological dimension. Other scales that attempt to measure trait anxiety do not do so well. One example is the Affect Adjective Checklist developed by Zuckerman (1960), which correlated only moderately with other tests designed to measure trait anxiety. In this case, the concurrent validity correlations ranged from .41 to .57 (Spielberger, Gorsuch, & Lushene, 1970). Overall, the STAI seems to measure the same thing as other scales that purport to assess trait anxiety.

To give a test a positive recommendation, we must also find discriminant evidence for construct validity (see Chapter 5). In one validity study for the STAI (Spielberger, Auerbach, Wadsworth, Dun, & Taulbee, 1975), patients scheduled to undergo surgery took the STAI before and after the medical procedure. Patients who had undergone major surgery showed less state anxiety after they had been told they were recovering well than they had before the operation. This finding demonstrates that state anxiety fluctuates with the situation—just as the test constructors said it would. Trait anxiety was not affected by the situation; it remained the same before and after surgery. People high in trait anxiety continued to respond in an anxious way, even in situations that evoked little or no anxiety among people low in trait anxiety (Trotter & Endler, 1999). Each component of the STAI thus appears to measure what it is supposed to measure, and the two components clearly assess different aspects of anxiety. The STAI is useful because behavior is influenced by both situations and personality traits. Studies using the STAI to evaluate tobacco use showed that smoking is influenced by situations, such as enjoyment and stimulation, and that it managed emotions among those with high levels of trait anxiety (Spielberger, Foreyt, Reheiser, & Poston, 1998).

Over the course of several decades, studies have continually supported the value of the STAI. Evidence suggests that the STAI is reliable and that most items perform well, even when the test takers are in extremely stressful situations (Roy & Deb, 1999). Recent factor analysis studies have continued to show the two-factor structure. For example, a study that involved 205 patients with panic disorder confirmed that state and trait anxiety are two different dimensions, even among people with fairly serious emotional problems (Oei, Evans, & Crook, 1990). The factor structure also seems to hold in studies of Japanese workers (Iwata et al., 1998). The STAI has been translated into many different languages and is available in both adult and children's versions. There are good psychometric evaluations of many of these forms. For example, the psychometric properties of the French-Canadian STAI for children have been reported (Turgeon & Chartrand, 2003). There are also comparisons showing modest evidence for the validity of parent reports of their children's anxiety (Turgeon & Chartrand, 2003).

Measures of Test Anxiety

For more than 50 years, much theoretical research within psychology has been centered on test anxiety. A lot of this research was stimulated by a theory of test anxiety proposed by Mandler and Sarason (1952), who described test anxiety as a drive, or motivational state, that could become manifest in two different types of responding—task relevant and task irrelevant. *Task-relevant responses* are directed toward accomplishing the task at hand. They direct the energy associated with the test situation toward the goal of achieving a good grade. These responses may actually reduce anxiety. Students with test anxiety suffer the most from *task-irrelevant responses*. In a test-taking situation, these students begin to respond in a way that interferes with their performance. Usually, they begin thinking in self-oriented ways; they entertain thoughts such as "I am going to fail." Because they focus on these thoughts at the expense of attention to the items on the test, they often do a poor job.

Because Mandler and Sarason concluded that general measures of anxiety were too general to assess test anxiety, they decided to develop a specific measure of test anxiety, the Test Anxiety Questionnaire. Over the years, people have discovered some inadequacies with this questionnaire and have transformed it into other measures such as the Test Anxiety Scale (Sarason, 1958), the Liebert-Morris Emotionality and Worry Scales (Liebert & Morris, 1967), and the Test Anxiety Inventory (Spielberger, Anton, & Bedell, 1976). Others have used different sources of items to construct tests such as the Achievement Anxiety Test (Alpert & Haber, 1960) and the Suinn Test Anxiety Behavior Scale (Suinn, 1969).

The Test Anxiety Questionnaire. The grandparent of all test-anxiety measures, the Test Anxiety Questionnaire (TAQ) was the outgrowth of the Mandler and Sarason (1952) test-anxiety theory. The theory distinguishes between two different drives, or motivational states, that operate in test-taking situations. One is the learned task drive, which is the motivation to emit responses relevant to the task at hand. The other is the learned anxiety drive, made up of task-relevant responses and task-irrelevant responses. Mandler and Sarason developed a 37-item questionnaire (the TAQ) that assesses a person's predisposition to think or act in a way that interferes with the completion of a task. In other words, they attempted to build a measure to assess task-irrelevant responses. Some of the items from the TAQ are presented in Table 17-4. You might check the items to see whether they describe the way you feel during testing situations. Responses to the TAQ items are obtained on a 15-centimeter graphic scale. On the scale, the endpoints and the midpoint are identified. For example, a student is asked whether he or she avoids intelligence tests more or less than other students avoid them. The endpoints of the scale are "More often than other students" and "Less often than other students." The midpoint is simply labeled "Midpoint."

The reliability of the TAQ is high. Early studies using a group of 100 Yale students demonstrated that the split-half reliability was .99, and a coefficient of .82 was obtained in a test–retest study over a six-week period. Some validity evidence showed that students who were high in test anxiety actually did more poorly on intellectual tasks than did students low in test anxiety (Mandler & Sarason, 1952).

TABLE 17-4

*Some of the
Questions Used in
the Test Anxiety
Questionnaire*

---

4. If you know that you are going to take a group intelligence test, how do you feel beforehand?

I . . . . .I. I

Feel very confident   Midpoint   Feel very unconfident

9. While taking a group intelligence test, to what extent do you perspire?

I . . . . .I. I

Perspire not at all   Midpoint   Perspire a lot

17. Before taking an individual intelligence test, to what extent are you (or would you be) aware of an "uneasy feeling"?

I . . . . .I. I

Am not aware of it at all   Midpoint   Am very much aware of it

24. In comparison to other students, how often do you (would you) think of ways of avoiding an individual intelligence test?

I . . . . .I. I

More often than other students   Midpoint   Less often than other students

26. When you are taking a course examination, to what extent do you feel that your emotional reactions interfere with or lower your performance?

I . . . . .I. I

Do not interfere with it at all   Midpoint   Interfere a great deal

---

From Mandler & Sarason (1952). Copyright 1952 by the American Psychological Association.

The Test Anxiety Scale. One early criticism of the TAQ was that it dealt with state anxiety rather than trait anxiety. The first revision of the TAQ began to consider individual or personality differences in test anxiety. In 1958, Irwin Sarason, the brother of Seymour Sarason (the original codeveloper of test-anxiety theory), rewrote the TAQ items in a true–false format to create the 21-item Test Anxiety Scale (TAS). Irwin Sarason agreed with the earlier theory that test anxiety produced interfering responses during test-taking situations, but he also recognized that there were personality differences between people high and those low in test anxiety. He believed that less test-anxious people respond to test-taking situations by increasing their effort and attention toward the problem they are working on. Highly test-anxious people react to the threatening situation by making self-oriented and personalized responses, often criticizing themselves rather than working on the test problems.

As you can see, the focus on the test-anxiety problem shifts from the situation in the TAQ to the person in the TAS. Although the two measures are quite similar and are indeed highly correlated, one measure assesses anxiety associated with situations, whereas the other determines which people are highly test anxious.

Since the introduction of the TAS, Sarason has accumulated convincing evidence of a meaningful distinction between more and less test-anxious individuals. For example, they respond differently to instructions. In some experiments, the experimenter intentionally gives instructions that produce stress, for example, by telling the students that they must finish in a limited time or by telling them that the test they are taking correlates well with measures of intelligence. For subjects who score low on the TAS, these instructions may actually help. Usually, less test-anxious students score better under stress-producing conditions than they would with less environmental stress. The opposite seems to be true for the more test-anxious group. These individuals tend to do better when the instructions are neutral or reassuring rather than stress-producing (Oostdam & Meijer, 2003; Paul & Eriksen, 1964; Sarason, 1958, 1959, 1961, 1975).

These studies show that the TAS does make meaningful distinctions among people; they also suggest that school performance may be associated with personality characteristics other than intelligence. Further, the research gives specific hints about the nature of test anxiety. Only the more test-anxious say negative things to themselves instead of thinking about the problems on the test. This interference with thought is most severe for test-anxious people while they are working on difficult tasks (Sarason & Palola, 1960).

Some studies demonstrate that students who score high and low on the TAS also use information in different ways. Those with low scores on the TAS tend to increase their efforts when they are told they have not done well. Given the same feedback, test-anxious people plunge into themselves instead of plunging themselves into the task (Mandler & Sarason, 1952; Marlett & Watson, 1968; Sarason, 1975). Similarly, after receiving neutral feedback, students who score high on the TAS tend to respond as though they had just been given bad news, and they do not have much faith in their future success. Those who score low on the TAS tend to be optimistic about their future performance after they have been given neutral feedback (Meunier & Rule, 1967).

When test-anxious individuals are placed in situations in which they will be evaluated (like describing themselves orally for half an hour), they attend most to negative references to themselves. They probably do not expect others to evaluate them well, and they actively search their environment for information to prove to themselves that this is true. For example, if someone leaves the room during a test, a test-anxious subject may interpret the behavior as an indication that he or she is not working fast enough (Sarason, 1975).

An extensive array of the literature supports the validity of the TAS as a measure of personality. The TAS shows that a combination of high trait anxiety and high environmental anxiety produce the most test anxiety.

Many physical effects are associated with test anxiety, such as increased heart rate, dry mouth, and upset stomach. Some researchers have proposed that anxiety is composed of emotional responses associated with such symptoms and that such responses should be measured separately.

Other measures of test anxiety. Several other measures of test anxiety are commonly used in research and practice. Liebert and Morris (1967) suggested that test anxiety has two components: emotionality and worry. *Emotionality,* the physical response to test-taking situations, is associated with conditions such as accelerated heart rate and muscle stiffness. *Worry* is the mental preoccupation with failing and with the personal consequences of doing poorly. The Liebert-Morris Emotionality and Worry Scales tap these components separately.

Spielberger, Anton, and Bedell (1976) also created a test-anxiety scale that has both factors. Spielberger's 20-item Test Anxiety Inventory conceptualizes test anxiety in terms of state and trait. According to Spielberger, *worry* is a trait that is more consistent over the course of time. Each person worries about tests to a characteristic degree. *Emotionality* is the manner in which arousal is expressed in particular situations. Thus, this theory proposes that the emotional component is a state, or situational, aspect. Systematic studies have confirmed that emotionality and worry are independent dimensions of test anxiety. Furthermore, these two dimensions have been observed in both male and female subjects. The latter score significantly higher than the former on the emotionality components but not on the worry components (Everson, Millsap, & Rodriguez, 1991; Zeidner, 1990). More recently, a 5-item version of the TAI has been developed. This short version retains many of the reliability and validity properties of the longer scale (Taylor & Deane, 2002).

Another approach to the measurement of test anxiety was proposed by Alpert and Haber (1960). Their Achievement Anxiety Test (AAT) is an 18-item scale that gives scores for two different components of anxiety: facilitating and debilitating. *Debilitating anxiety* resembles the anxiety that all of the other scales attempt to measure, or the extent to which anxiety interferes with performance on tests. The novel component of the AAT is *facilitating anxiety,* a state that can motivate performance. This type of anxiety gets one worried enough to study hard. If one is not anxious at all, one may not be motivated enough to gear up for the exam. Thus, facilitating anxiety is helpful, and debilitating anxiety is harmful.

In short, test anxiety affects many people. The many measures of test anxiety have shown the complexity of this problem and have helped lead to ways of reducing this sort of anxiety.

Measures of Coping

As we just saw in the case of test anxiety, different people confronted with the same stressful situation may respond quite differently. For instance, Feifel, Strack, and Nagy (1987) compared the coping styles of two different patient groups. Some of the patients had life-threatening illnesses such as cancer or heart attacks. The comparison group had non–life-threatening illnesses such as skin problems or arthritis. The coping styles of the two groups differed. In particular, those with life-threatening illnesses used confrontation more frequently. Interestingly, neither group used acceptance and resignation often.

Several measures have been developed to assess the ways in which people cope with stress (Dupue & Monroe, 1986; Folkman & Lazarus, 1980). One of these measures, the Ways of Coping Scale (Lazarus, 1995; Lazarus & Folkman, 1984), is a 68-item checklist. Individuals choose those thoughts and actions that they use to deal with stressful situations. The scale includes seven subscales for problem solving, growth, wishful thinking, advice seeking, minimizing threat, seeking support, and self-blame. Studies have suggested that the seven subscales can be divided into problem-focused and emotion-focused strategies for dealing with stressful situations. Problem-focused strategies involve cognitive and behavioral attempts to change the course of the stress; these are active methods of coping. Emotion-focused strategies do not attempt to alter the stressor but instead focus on ways of dealing with the emotional responses to stress (Cohen & Lazarus, 1994). The Ways of Coping questionnaire is one of the most widely used measures in health psychology. However, some researchers have offered criticism. For example, some studies have failed to replicate the basic factor structure (Parker, Endler, & Bagby, 1993).

A related measure is the Coping Inventory (Horowitz & Wilner, 1980), a 33-item measure derived from clinical interview data. Of three categories of items, the first describes activities and attitudes that people use to avoid stress. The second involves items that characterize strategies for working through stressful events. The third category considers socialization responses, or how each strategy would help the respondent cope with a specific stressful event. These measures and related tests, such as the Coping Resources Inventory (Hammer & Marting, 1985), have been useful in research on both adults and adolescents. For example, one study demonstrated that having good coping capabilities is important whether or not you are under stress (Zeidner & Hammer, 1990).

Ecological Momentary Assessment

Most psychological tests are designed to evaluate traits, which are constant over the course of time. Even measures of state anxiety are presumed to be reliable. However, levels of stress vary over the course of time. Measuring today's stress may tell us little about stress experienced next week. If we ask today about experiences last week, then the measurements may be inaccurate because memory fades over time. Recall affects virtually all autobiographical information.

New technical developments have made it possible to obtain information on an ongoing basis (Stone, Shiffman, & DeVries, 1999). One can obtain information repeatedly and average the results to get an overall impression of stress. Or one can assess information with reference to a particular event. For example, one might determine if levels of perceived stress coincide with particular stressors. Ecological Momentary Assessment (EMA) uses computers to collect information on a continuing basis. The equipment might measure blood pressure or hormonal state at specific points in time. Furthermore, a subject might be prompted to record information about mood, symptoms, or fatigue.

Most information in clinical studies is collected in clinics, offices, or laboratories—not necessarily the situations in which people ordinarily experience life events. One of the advantages of EMA is that the information is collected in the subject's natural environment. The EMA method usually involves a substantial number of repeated observations and shows variability within the subject over time (Stone & Shiffman, 1994).

One study of the co-use of alcohol and tobacco provides an example of EMA. Traditional studies of alcohol consumption might actually miss much of the information about drinking because the assessment is typically done during the day, whereas alcohol consumption often occurs in the evening. EMA allows the continual assessment of these behaviors in the subject's own environment. In one study, 57 subjects were given minicomputers that randomly prompted them to record their behaviors. The study showed that drinking was likely to occur between 8 P.M. and midnight. Smoking was more than twice as likely when subjects had been drinking as when they had not. In other words, smoking and drinking were linked (Shiffman, Fischer, Paty, Gnys, et al., 1995). Some investigators use the latest technologies, including cell phones to collect information in natural environments (Collins, Kashdan, & Gollnisch, 2003).

Other studies have used daily assessments to evaluate life stress (Todd, 2004). In one study, 74 patients with arthritis rated stress, mood, and pain for 75 days. Those who had experienced major stresses were more likely to experience pain on the day after a stressful event than on other days. This suggests that life stress may amplify the relationship between life events and pain (Affleck et al., 1994). Further technical developments such as the EMA should significantly improve the assessment of variable behaviors, pain, and emotions (Gendreau, Hufford, & Stone, 2003; Stone, Broderick, et al., 2004; Stone, Broderick, Schwartz, Shiffman, Litcher-Kelly, & Calvanese, 2003; Stone, Shiffman, Schwartz, Broderick, & Hufford, 2003).

Measures of Social Support

In recent years, health psychologists have devoted considerable effort to the study of social support. Research suggests that social resources and support serve as significant buffers for stressful life events and as moderators of psychological and physical well-being (Devine, Parker, Fouladi, & Cohen, 2003; Kahn, Hessling, & Russell, 2003; McCabe, Yeh, Lau, Garland, & Hough, 2003; Pomaki & Anagnostopoulou, 2003).

Although definitions vary, most measures of social support include both tangible (financial assistance and physical aid) and intangible (encouragement and guidance) support. Social support has been shown to help mediate stressful life events, speed recovery from illness, and increase the likelihood that a person will follow the advice of his or her doctor. However, there are many inconsistent findings in the literature, and it is difficult to resolve discrepancies because measures of social support vary widely from study to study. When Heitzmann and Kaplan (1988) reviewed 26 measures for evaluating social support, they looked for documented validity and reliability coefficients greater than .80. Correlations between various social support and criterion measures were simulated in order to demonstrate the consequences of choosing a measure with low reliability (see also Kaplan, 1994a). According to the review, few social support measures offered adequate documentation of reliability. In addition, documentation of validity was available for only some measures. Discriminant evidence for validity was almost never presented.

Perhaps the best example of a social support measure has been presented by I. G. Sarason and co-workers (1983). The Social Support Questionnaire (SSQ) includes 27 items, each with two parts. For each item the respondent must (1) list the people he or she can count on for support in given circumstances and (2) indicate the overall level of satisfaction with these supports. The SSQ yields two scores: the number (N) score for each item is the number of supports the person lists. The satisfaction (S) score ranges from 1 for very dissatisfied to 6 for very satisfied for each of these items. The number of people someone can count on is averaged from the 27 items to get a mean N score, and the satisfaction ratings are also averaged to get a mean S score.

Sarason and colleagues (1983) conducted a series of studies to determine the reliability and validity of their measure. Based on a normative sample of 602 undergraduate college students, coefficient alpha for satisfaction (S) was .94 and for number (N) was .97. Test–retest correlations over a four-week period were .90 for N and .83 for S. These results indicate that the SSQ is a highly stable instrument with high internal consistency. Validity data were based on comparisons between the SSQ and other measurement techniques. A sample of 277 undergraduate students were given the SSQ, the Multiple Affect Adjective Check List (MAACL), and the Lack of Protection scale (LP). There were significant negative correlations between the SSQ-N and SSQ-S and measures of emotional discomfort as tapped by the MAACL. Similarly, items on the LP that deal with recollections of separation anxiety in childhood also correlated negatively with the SSQ.

Studies continue to show that social support is a useful construct. One study, for example, used measures of social support to predict how high-school students would react to being placed as exchange students in a foreign country. A group of 242 students completed the measures before being placed with a family in Japan and then again after they had been in Japan for 6 months. Those who perceived most support at home and were closest to their families were the most vulnerable to emotional distress when they were in an environment where the support system was not available (Furukawa, Sarason, & Sarason, 1998).

Quality-of-Life Assessment

Have you ever thought about what you value most in life? Most people say that their health is more important than anything else. In fact, studies on the preference for different states of being sometimes exclude ratings of health because people show so little variability in their attitudes toward it. The actual definition of health status, however, has remained ambiguous.

Among the many definitions of health, we find two common themes. First, everyone agrees that premature mortality is undesirable, so one aspect of health is the avoidance of death. The health status of nations is often evaluated in terms of mortality rates or infant mortality rates (the number of children who die before 1 year of age per 1000 live births). Second, quality of life is important. In other words, disease and disability are of concern because they affect either life expectancy or life quality. For example, cancer and heart disease are the two major causes of premature death in the United States. A person with heart disease may face restrictions on daily living activities and may be unable to work or participate in social activities. Even relatively minor diseases and disabilities affect quality of life. Think about how a common cold interferes with your ability to attend school or to concentrate. Then think about how a serious problem, such as traumatic brain injury, affects quality of life (Tulsky & Rosenthal, 2003).

Within the last few years, medical scientists have come to realize the importance of quality-of-life measurement (Barofsky, 2003; Bottomley, Efficace, Thomas, Vanvoorden, & Ahmedzai, 2003; Dijkers, 2003; Naughton & Shumaker, 2003; Unruh, Miskulin, et al., 2004). Many major as well as minor diseases are evaluated in terms of the degree to which they affect life quality and life expectancy (Kaplan, 2002, 2004). One can also evaluate treatments by the amount of improvement they produce in quality of life. The Food and Drug Administration now considers quality-of-life data in its evaluations of new products, and nearly all major clinical trials in medicine use quality-of-life assessment measures. In the remainder of this chapter, we review several approaches to quality-of-life measurement.

What Is Health-Related Quality of Life?

Numerous quality-of-life measurement systems have evolved during the last 30 years and represent various traditions in measurement. Recent articles have presented at least two different conceptual approaches. One grows out of the tradition of health status measurement. In the late 1960s and early 1970s, the National Center for Health Services Research funded several major projects to develop general measures of health status. All of the projects were guided by the World Health Organization's (WHO) definition of health status: "Health is a complete state of physical, mental, and social well-being and not merely absence of disease" (WHO, 1948). The projects resulted in a variety of assessment tools, including the Sickness Impact Profile (Bergner, Babbitt, Carter, & Gilson, 1981), the Quality of Well-Being Scale (Kaplan & Anderson, 1990), the Mc-Master Health Index Questionnaire (Chambers, 1996), the SF-36 (Ware, Kosinski, Bayliss, McHorney, Rogers, & Raczek, 1995), and the Nottingham Health Profile (McEwen, 1992). Many of the measures examine the effect of disease or disability on performance of social role, ability to interact in the community, and physical functioning. Some of the systems have separate components for the measurement of social and mental health. The measures also differ in the extent to which they consider subjective aspects of life quality (Naughton & Shumaker, 2003).

There are two major approaches to quality-of-life assessment: psychometric and decision theory. The psychometric approach attempts to provide separate measures for the many different dimensions of quality of life. Perhaps the best-known example of the psychometric tradition is the Sickness Impact Profile (SIP). The SIP is a 136-item measure that yields 12 different scores displayed in a format similar to an MMPI profile.

The decision theory approach attempts to weight the different dimensions of health in order to provide a single expression of health status. Supporters of this approach argue that psychometric methods fail to consider that different health problems are not of equal concern. One hundred runny noses are not the same as 100 missing legs (Bush, 1984). In an experimental trial using the psychometric approach, one will often find that some aspects of quality of life improve while others get worse. For example, a medication might reduce high blood pressure but also produce headaches and impotence. Many argue that the quality-of-life notion is the subjective evaluation of observable or objective health states. The decision theory approach attempts to provide an overall measure of quality of life that integrates subjective function states, preferences for these states, morbidity, and mortality.

Common Methods for Measuring Quality of Life

This chapter presents some of the most widely used methods for measuring quality of life. Readers who are interested in more detailed reviews should consult Shumaker and Berzon (1995), Walker and Rosser (1993), or McDowell and Newell (1996).

SF-36. Perhaps the most commonly used outcome measure in the world today is the Medical Outcome Study Short Form-36 (SF-36). The SF-36 grew out of work by the RAND Corporation and the Medical Outcomes Study (MOS) (Ware & Gandek, 1998). The MOS attempted to develop a short, 20-item instrument known as the Short Form-20 or SF-20. However, the SF-20 did not have appropriate reliability for some dimensions. The SF-36 includes eight health concepts: physical functioning, role-physical, bodily pain, general health perceptions, vitality, social functioning, role-emotional, and mental health (Kosinski, Keller, Ware, Hatoum, & Kong, 1999). The SF-36 can be either administered by a trained interviewer or self-administered.

It has many advantages. For example, it is brief, and there is substantial evidence for its reliability and validity. The SF-36 can be machine-scored and has been evaluated in large population studies. The reliability and validity of the SF-36 are well documented (Keller, Ware, Hatoum, & Kong, 1999; Ware, 2000; Ware & Kosinski, 2001).

The SF-36 also presents some disadvantages. For example, it does not have age-specific questions, and one cannot clearly determine whether it is equally appropriate across age levels (Stewart & Ware, 1992). Nevertheless, the SF-36 has become the most commonly used behavioral measure in contemporary medicine (Ware, 2003).

Nottingham Health Profile. Another major approach, the Nottingham Health Profile (NHP), has particularly influenced the European community (Hagell, Whalley, McKenna, & Lindvall, 2003; Hinz, Klaiberg, Schumacher, & Brahler, 2003; Sivas, Ercin, Tanyolac, Barca, Aydog, & Ozoran, 2003; Uutela, Hakala, & Kautiainen, 2003). The NHP has two parts. The first includes 38 items divided into six categories: sleep, physical mobility, energy, pain, emotional reactions, and social isolation. Items within each section are rated in terms of relative importance. Items are rescaled in order to allow them to vary between 0 and 100 within each section.

The second part of the NHP includes seven statements related to the areas of life most affected by health: employment, household activities, social life, home life, sex life, hobbies and interests, and holidays. The respondent indicates whether or not a health condition has affected his or her life in these areas. Used in a substantial number of studies, the NHP has considerable evidence for its reliability and validity.

The NHP is consumer-based and arises from definitions of health offered by individuals in the community. Furthermore, this scale uses language that is easily interpreted by people in the community and conforms to minimum reading requirements. Substantial testing has been performed on the NHP; however, the NHP does not provide relative-importance weightings across dimensions. As a result, it is difficult to compare the dimensions directly with one another (Bureau-Chalot, Novella, Jolly, Ankri, Guillemin, & Blanchard, 2002).

Decision theory approaches. Within the last few years, interest has grown in using quality-of-life data to help evaluate the cost/utility or cost-effectiveness of health-care programs. Cost studies have gained in popularity because health-care costs have rapidly grown in recent years. All health-care interventions do not return equal benefit for the expended dollar. Cost studies might guide policymakers toward an optimal and equitable distribution of scarce resources. A cost-effectiveness analysis typically quantifies the benefits of a health-care intervention in terms of years of life, or quality-adjusted life-years (QALYs). Cost/utility is a special use of cost-effectiveness that weights observable health states by preferences or utility judgments of quality (Kaplan & Groessl, 2002). In cost/utility analysis, the benefits of medical care, behavioral interventions, or preventive programs are expressed in terms of well-years (Kaplan, 2002).

If a man dies of heart disease at age 50 and we expected him to live to age 75, then we might conclude that the disease precipitated 25 lost life-years. If 100 men died at age 50 (and also had a life expectancy of 75 years), then we might conclude that 2500 life-years (100 men $\times$ 25 years) had been lost. Death is not the only relevant outcome of heart disease. Many adults suffer myocardial infarctions that leave them disabled for a long time and suffering diminished quality of life. Quality-adjusted life-years take into consideration such consequences. For example, a disease that reduces quality of life by one-half will take away .5 QALY over the course of each year. If the disease affects two people, then it will take away 1 year (2 $\times$ .5) over each year. A medical treatment that improves quality of life by .2 for each of five individuals will result in the equivalent of 1 QALY if the benefit persists for 1 year. This system has the advantage of considering both benefits and side effects of programs in terms of the common QALY units.

The need to integrate mortality and quality-of-life information is clear in studies of heart disease. Consider hypertension. People with high blood pressure may live shorter lives if untreated, longer if treated. Thus, one benefit of treatment is to add years to life. However, for most patients, high blood pressure does not produce symptoms for many years. Conversely, the treatment for high blood pressure may cause negative side effects. If one evaluates a treatment only in terms of changes in life expectancy, then the benefits of the program will be overestimated because one has not taken side effects into consideration. On the other hand, considering only current quality of life will underestimate the treatment benefits because information on mortality is excluded. In fact, considering only current function might make the treatment look harmful because the side effects of the treatment might be worse than the symptoms of hypertension. A comprehensive measurement system takes into consideration side effects and benefits and provides an overall estimate of the benefit of treatment (Russell, 1986).

Most approaches for obtaining quality-adjusted life-years are similar (Kaplan, 2002). The approach that we prefer involves several steps. First, patients are classified according to objective levels of functioning. These levels are represented by the scales of mobility, physical activity, and social activity. Next, once observable behavioral levels of functioning have been classified, each individual is placed on the 0 to 1.0 scale of wellness, which describes where a person lies on the continuum between optimum function and death.

Most traditional measures used in medicine and public health consider only whether a person is dead or alive. In other words, all living people get the same score. Yet we know that there are different levels of wellness, and a need to score these levels exists. To accomplish this, the observable health states are weighted by quality ratings for the desirability of these conditions. Human value studies have been conducted to place the observable states onto a preference continuum, with an anchor of 0 for death and 1.0 for completely well (Kaplan, Feeny, & Revicki, 1999). Studies have shown that the weights are highly stable over a 1-year period and consistent across diverse groups of raters (Kaplan, 1994b). Finally, one must consider the duration of stay in various health states. Having a cough or a headache for 1 day is not the same as having the problem for 1 year.

This system has been used to evaluate many different health-care programs (Kaplan, 2003; Kaplan & Groessl, 2002). For example, it was used to demonstrate that a new medication for patients with arthritis produced an average of .023 QALY per year, whereas a new medication for AIDS produced nearly .46 of these units per year. However, the benefit of the arthritis medication may last as long as 20 years, ultimately producing .023 × 20 years = .46 year. The AIDS treatment produced a benefit for only 1 year, so its total effect was .46 × 1 year = .46 year. In other words, the general system allows the full potential benefits of these two completely different treatments to be compared (Kaplan et al., 1995).

SUMMARY

In this chapter, we considered three broad areas relevant to testing in health-care settings. First, we reviewed clinical neuropsychology. This remarkable new area of investigation has generated new research and clinical opportunities for psychologists. Neuropsychology involves the application of tests to evaluate the status of the central nervous system. Some of the more common approaches are the Halstead-Reitan and the Luria-Nebraska batteries. Each of these approaches is based on different principles of cognitive psychology. A newer approach, the California Verbal Learning Test, attempts to evaluate brain function by considering not only errors but also how people make errors.

Second, we reviewed some of the existing research on the theory and measurement of anxiety and stress. Research on test anxiety grew from general theories of learning. Early studies by J. Taylor identified anxiety as a motivational state that one could measure with a short scale. Using the scale, she could relate anxiety to a general theory that had previously depended primarily on evidence from animal studies. Later developments divided anxiety into state and trait components. The State-Trait Anxiety Inventory (STAI) provides two separate scores: one for state anxiety (A-State) and another for trait anxiety (A-Trait).

Many scales were devised to measure test-anxiety problems. Different theories emphasized test anxiety as a general motivational state, a personality trait, or both. In other words, there are many different theories of test anxiety and many different ways of measuring it. For example, the Test Anxiety Questionnaire (TAQ) is concerned with the learned task drive, which is the motivation to emit responses relevant to the task at hand, and the learned anxiety drive, which is made up of task-relevant responses and task-irrelevant responses. The Test Anxiety Scale (TAS) built on the TAQ but also measured differences due to trait anxiety.

A variety of measures quantify adaptation to stressful situations. These include measures of coping and measures of social support. Not all individuals faced with the same stresses have the same reactions. Measures of social support and coping help explain why some people can better adapt to stressful situations than can others. The Ways of Coping Scale, the Coping Inventory, and the Social Support Questionnaire (SSQ) are three such measures.

The third area for the application of tests in health-care settings involves health status and quality of life assessment. Health-care practitioners try to help people live longer and to live higher-quality lives than they might without health care. The quantification of life quality, however, is difficult. Two approaches to this type of assessment are psychometric methods and decision theory methods. Psychometric methods include the MOS Short Form-36 and the Nottingham Health Profile. Decision theory approaches include methods for estimating the value of the equivalent of a life-year (QALY). We expect the fields of psychological measurement and health-outcome measurement to continue to merge over the next few decades.

WEB ACTIVITY

For interesting and relevant Web sites, check the following:

cps.nova.edu/~cpphelp/HRNTB.html
Overview of the Halstead-Reitan Battery

www.div40.org/
Web site for the American Psychological Association Division of Clinical Neuropsychology

www.isoqol.org/newsletter.html
> *Provides Access to monthly Newsletter from the International Society for Quality of Life Research*

www.sf-36.org
> *Official Web site for the SF-36*

medicine.ucsd.edu/fpm/hoap/qwb.htm
> *Offers an overview of the Quality of Well-Being Scale*

CHAPTER 18

Testing in Industrial and Business Settings

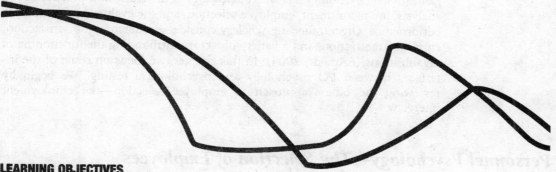

LEARNING OBJECTIVES

When you have completed this chapter, you should be able to:

- Discuss the application of tests in employee selection
- Identify the first consideration in determining whether it is worthwhile to administer a test
- Explain the meaning of base rates in personnel selection
- Identify three methods for estimating the amount of information a test gives beyond what is known by chance
- Define incremental validity
- Discuss the significance of utility and decision theory
- Explain some problems with utility theory equations
- Describe the characteristics of the MBTI and the WPI
- List the components of job analysis
- Explain the person-situation interaction
- Describe the advantages and disadvantages of employment interview

O ne of the fastest-growing fields of psychology involves the application of psychological principles to the workplace. This specialized field of psychology is known as *industrial/organizational* (I/O) *psychology*. This field is quite similar to the human resource management that is often taught in schools of business. However, I/O psychologists establish themselves by the methods they apply. One of the most important differences is I/O's emphasis on structured psychological testing (Berry, 2003). I/O psychologists rely extensively on research, quantitative methods, and testing procedures (AAmodt, 2004). Two major areas of I/O psychology are personnel psychology and organizational psychology. *Personnel psychology* is the study and practice of job analysis, job recruitment, employee selection, and the evaluation of employee performance. *Organizational psychology* considers leadership, job satisfaction, employee motivation, and a variety of factors surrounding the functioning of organizations (AAmodt, 2004). In this chapter, we focus on some of the interfaces between I/O psychology and psychological testing. We begin by reviewing the oldest approach to employee selection—the employment interview.

Personnel Psychology—The Selection of Employees

Employment Interview

The employment interview helps people make selection and promotion decisions in business and industry. The first extensive review of the employment interview was provided by R. Wagner (1949), who reviewed close to 100 studies. He severely criticized most of the studies, however, emphasizing that much of the literature consisted of contradicting opinions and how-to formulas. Following Wagner's call for more and better studies, E. C. Webster (1964) presented a series of important experimental investigations into the nature of the employment interview. Two independent reviews of the literature on the employment interview were subsequently published in the mid-1960s (Mayfield, 1964; Ulrich & Trumbo, 1965). Both reviews began where Wagner (1949) had left off. O. R. Wright (1969) then reviewed the literature between 1964 and 1969. Subsequent literature has been examined by Schmitt (1976), Arvey and Campion (1982), and Zedeck, Tziner, and Middlestadt (1983) (see also Dougherty, Ebert, & Callender, 1986). The most recent review of the literature (Posthuma, Morgeson, & Campion, 2002) was a comprehensive review of interview research conducted in the previous 10 years. More recent interview approaches have emphasized the importance of combining interview data with other sources of information (Dalessio & Silverhart, 1994); using simple procedures to enhance recall accuracy, such as note taking during the interview (Middendorf & Macan, 2002); and the influence of personal characteristics such as age (Delery & Kacmar, 1998; Kager, 2000), disability status (Nordstrom, Huffaker, & Williams, 1998; Miceli, Harvey, & Buckley, 2001), gender (Chapman & Rowe, 2001), and race (Huffcutt & Roth, 1998; Frazer & Wiersma, 2001).

These studies have revealed extremely valuable information about interviews in general and the employment interview in particular. The reviewers almost unanimously recommended a structured format for the employment interview. Several studies clearly pointed to the superiority of structured interviews for enabling interviewers to reach agreement on their employment decisions. Thus, the loss of flexibility in structured interviews can be balanced by increases in reliability. Meta-analytic investigations of the literature have found that structured interviews produced mean validity coefficients twice as high as did unstructured interviews (Wiesner & Cronshaw, 1988; Williamson, Campion, Malos, Roehling, & Campion,1997).

Later we shall discuss sources of error in the interview, which studies have found to affect many employment interviews (Cesare, 1996; Schuler, 1993). For now, we briefly touch on what interviewers look for in employment interviews and on methods of presenting oneself in an interview.

It has long been known that the employment interview often involves a search for negative or unfavorable rather than favorable evidence about a person. If negative evidence is found, the person will probably not be hired unless there is a high demand for workers and few individuals available to fill open positions. A classic study by E. C. Webster (1964) noted that as few as one unfavorable impression was followed by final rejection in 90% of the cases. This rejection rate, however, dropped to 25% when early impressions were favorable. Webster and others caution employment interviewers against forming an early bias that might result in rejecting a competent individual. Despite widespread knowledge of Webster's cautions, interviewers continue to make basic errors when formulating personnel decisions (Cesare, 1996).

Negative factors that commonly·lead to the rejection of candidates include poor communication skills, lack of confidence or poise, low enthusiasm, nervousness, and failure to make eye contact (Kager, 2000; Nykodym & Ruud, 1985; Nykodym & Simonetti, 1981; Posthuma et al., 2002). Positive factors include the ability to express oneself, self-confidence and poise, enthusiasm, the ability to sell oneself, and aggressiveness (Baehr, 1987).

Can you increase your chances of presenting yourself favorably in a job interview? As Heimberg, Keller, and Peca-Baker (1986) noted, competent performance in job interviews is widely regarded as one of the most important factors in obtaining employment. As such, several prospective employees who wish to tip the balance in their favor can choose any of several recommendations (Baron, 1986; Delery & Kacmar, 1998; Larkin & Pines, 1994).

A good first impression is one of the most important factors in a successful job interview (Dougherty, Turban, & Callender, 1994; Howard & Ferris, 1996). To make a good first impression, one needs to wear professional attire and show good grooming (Cash, 1985; Kennedy, 1994), project an aura of competence and expertise (Baron, 1986; Price & Garland, 1983), and give an impression of friendliness or personal warmth through nonverbal cues (Higgins, 2001; Imada & Hakel, 1977). But going too far with these tactics can sometimes backfire.

R. A. Baron (1986) had female confederates pose as applicants for an entry-level management position. Some wore perfume, others did not. In addition, some attempted to convey friendliness through nonverbal behaviors including a high level of eye contact with the interviewer, an informal friendly posture (such as leaning forward at predetermined points), and frequent smiling.

Interviewees in the neutral-cue condition refrained from these nonverbal behaviors. The results revealed that when used alone, either perfume or positive nonverbal behaviors produced enhanced ratings for the applicants. When used together, however, these tactics produced negative reactions among interviewers, probably because they caused the applicant to be perceived as manipulative (Baron, 1986). Thus, while putting one's best foot forward in an interview is important, one must be careful not to overdo it.

Interviews remain the primary tool for selecting employees. However, personnel psychology places a strong emphasis on formal quantitative models and the use of tests for employee selection.

For many industrial applications, other factors also must be considered, such as the amount of information a selection strategy gives beyond what would be known without it. This can be derived from an analysis of base rates and hit rates.

Base Rates and Hit Rates

Tests must be evaluated in terms of how much they contribute beyond what would be known without them. Often, tests are used to place individuals into one of two categories. For example, on the basis of an employment test, a candidate can be deemed acceptable or unacceptable. In a medical setting, a test may determine whether or not a person has a tumor in a certain area of the brain. Because tests vary in their accuracy, test administrators must examine the possibility of erroneously assigning someone to a category.

If a test is used to make a dichotomous (two-choice) decision, then a cutoff score usually is used. Values above this score might go into the plus category, and values below it into the minus category. The plus category might indicate that the person is suitable for the job (or, in medical testing, that he or she has the tumor). The score marking the point of decision is called the *cutting score*. Those at or above the cutting score might be selected for employment, while those below the score might be turned away. Establishing a cutting score does not ensure correct decisions. For example, suppose that a person scores above the cutting score for an employment test but later fails on the job. This suggests that the test has not done its job.

Tests can be evaluated by how well they sort people into the right categories. For example, in a test that determines which people to hire for a particular job, those who score above the cutting score might be labeled "acceptable" and those below it "unacceptable." In addition to the scores on the test, the employer must have some data on how people really do on the job. To do this, he or she must define some criterion for deciding whether job performance has been acceptable or unacceptable. Using these two sets of categories, the employer can construct a chart such as the one shown in Table 18-1. There

TABLE 18-1

Hits and Misses for Predicting a Dichotomous Outcome Using a Cutting Score

	Decision on the basis of cutting score	
Performance on the job	Acceptable	Unacceptable
Success	Hit	Miss
Failure	Miss	Hit

are four cells in this table. Two of the four cells are labeled "Hit" because the test has made the correct prediction. Hits occur when (1) the test predicts that the person will be unacceptable and he or she does fail, or (2) the test indicates that the person is acceptable and he or she does succeed. Misses occur when the test makes an inaccurate prediction. The **hit rate** is the percentage of cases in which a test accurately predicts success or failure.

Often, a test does not need a good hit rate, because the rate of predicting success on the job is high without the test. For example, admissions officers might predict who will do well in law school on the basis of information other than scores on the Law School Admissions Test (LSAT). They might use college grades. Success on the criterion in this case might be passing the bar examination on the first attempt. The pass rate without using the LSAT would be called the **base rate.** The real value of a test comes from a comparison of the hit rate with the base rate. In other words, the hit rate must tell us how much information a test contributes to the prediction of success beyond what we would know by just examining the proportion of people who succeed.

For example, suppose the LSAT has a hit rate of 76% for predicting who will pass the bar examination in a certain state. However, 85% of the people who take the test for the first time in that state pass. The LSAT in this case tells us less than does the available information. In other cases, you could imagine a low hit rate and an even lower base rate. For example, suppose you need to select people for a position that will involve world-class competition. Under the circumstances, very few people could be expected to do well—say only 3% would be expected to succeed. If a test could be developed that had a 10% hit rate, it might be considered valuable.

Another problem to consider with regard to hit and miss rates is relative cost. Medical situations provide good examples of costly misses. Consider the cost of concluding on the basis of a test that a tumor is benign (not cancerous) when it is really malignant (cancerous). The cost of this sort of miss is that the life of the patient is seriously endangered. In a psychological application, concluding that someone is not suicidal because he or she is below the cutoff score when, in fact, he or she is suicidal may allow a preventable suicide. These cases are examples of **false negatives.** If the cost of a false negative is high, then a test developer might lower the cutting score. With a lower cutting score, the test will make more but safer errors.

The other type of miss is the **false positive.** For example, say someone is selected for a job on the basis of a test. Once on the job, the person does poorly and

TABLE 18-2

Hypothetical Example of Hits and Misses, with 83% Accuracy and 80% Detection*

		Test result		
		Brain damage	**Normal**	**Total**
Actual	Brain damage	A 8	B 2	10
	Normal	C 15	D 75	90
	Total	23	77	100

A = hit

B = false negative
C = false positive
D = hit
A/(A + B) = detection rate (sensitivity)
D/(C + D) = specificity base rate
(A + D)/(A + B + C + D) = accuracy rate

A + B = base rate

*We are grateful to Dr. Frank M. Rosekrans, Eastern Washington University, for suggesting this example.

gets fired. High costs sometimes accompany this type of error. For instance, time and money might be invested to train a person who cannot really do the job. In addition, job failure can hurt the person's self-esteem and self-confidence. If the costs of a false positive are high, then you may want to raise the cutting score.

A few examples may help clarify the concepts of hits and misses for different base rates. Although this chapter is about employment testing, out students often find medical examples best illustrate these concepts. Table 18-2 presents a medical example in which a test indicates whether or not a patient has brain damage. In a validation study, an expensive radiological procedure is used to confirm whether the patient actually has brain damage. The radiological test suggests that 23 of 100 patients have brain damage, while the other 77 are normal. The table also shows the actual number of patients who have brain damage or are normal. In reality, 10 of the 100 have damage, while 90 are normal.

There are two types of hits in Table 18-2. For the 10 patients who actually have brain damage, eight are detected by the tests. In other words, the test has a detection rate of 80%. In addition, the test says that 75 individuals are normal who, it is confirmed, are actually normal. Both of these cases are hits because the test produces the correct result. There are 83 cases in 100 when the test produces an accurate conclusion; that is, the test has 83% accuracy.

There are also two types of misses. In two cases, the test suggests that a person is normal when he or she actually has brain damage. Those are false negatives. In addition, there are 15 false positives, or cases in which the test suggests that a person has a problem when in fact he or she is normal.

The cells in Table 18-2 are labeled A, B, C, and D. Cells A and D are hit cells. The sum of these cells divided by the sum of all cells (A + B + C + D) is the accuracy rate. Cell B is a false negative, Cell C a false positive. Cell A divided by the sum of A and B is the *detection rate*.

TABLE 18-3
Hypothetical Example of Hits and Misses, with 40% Accuracy and 44% Detection*

		Test result		
		Brain damage	**Normal**	**Total**
	Brain damage	A 40	B 50	90
Actual	Normal	C 10	D 0	10
	Total	50	50	100

A = hit
B = false negative
C = false positive
D = hit
A/(A + B) = detection rate (sensitivity)
D/(C + D) = specificity base rate
(A + D)/(A + B + C + D) = accuracy rate

A + B = base rate

*We are grateful to Dr. Frank M. Rosekrans, Eastern Washington University, for suggesting this example.

The example in Table 18-2 suggests that the test is relatively good at detecting brain damage. One of the reasons the test works well in this situation is that the base rate for brain damage is relatively low. In actuality, only 10% of the patients have this problem, and the test detects 80% of the cases.

Now consider the example in Table 18-3. In this case, a test is used on a population with a quite high base rate for brain damage (90%). The test suggests that 50 of 100 people have brain damage when, in fact, 90 of 100 people have the problem. The test is accurate in 44% (40/90 = .44) of the cases. In this example, there are only 10 false positives. The test, however, has a high false negative rate. Finally, the table suggests that the test never concludes that someone is normal when he or she does not have a problem.

False negatives and false positives may have different meanings, depending on their context. For example, a variety of methods have been developed to predict antisocial behavior in children. Childhood aggression is a good predictor of later aggressive behavior (Dishion, Andrews, & Crosby, 1995). However, measures of childhood aggression identify some children as potentially dangerous who turn out not to be aggressive when they are older (O'Donnell, Hawkins, & Abbott, 1995). These are false positives. In fact, as many as half the cases may be false positives (Lochman, 1995). A program that identifies and treats high-risk youth may subject many to unnecessary treatment. On one extreme, some people believe high-risk youth should be under police surveillance. Among adults, many people can be identified as potentially dangerous, but the number of people who commit serious violent crimes remains low (Steadman et al., 1998). Because of false positives, these programs would unjustly deprive some youth of their rights. Many controversies in health care are affected by the hit and miss rates of testing (see Focused Example 18-1).

Focused Example 18-1

THE MAMMOGRAPHY CONTROVERSY

 Medical tests resemble psychological tests in that they both have validity and reliability and can be assessed in relation to their hit rates and miss rates. One interesting controversy involves the use of mammography to screen women for breast cancer. Mammography has clearly been shown to be a valuable medical test for women age 50 and older. Some controversy, however, surrounds its use for younger women. The reason for this controversy is related to the base rates and the rates of false positives and false negatives.

Breast cancer is strongly related to age. Although the American Cancer Society (ACS) argues that 1 in 9 women will develop breast cancer, these tumors are much more common among older women than among younger ones (see Figure 18-1). For women in their 20s, breast cancer is an extremely rare disease. In fact, 100,000 mammograms would have to be performed to find one such woman with breast cancer. This suggests that for younger women the base rate for breast cancer is extremely low (1 in 100,000). This has become somewhat of a controversy because the popular media have launched a campaign to increase the use of mammography for all women. If we pay for mammography from public funds and the cost of a mammogram is $100, then it would cost about $10 million to detect one case. Of course, any investment would be valuable if

it saved lives. However, analyses of studies of breast cancer suggest that the rare case of breast cancer detected in young women results in no better chance of survival than does a case left undetected. Even so, this remains a matter of considerable debate in the medical community.

The related concern for performing mammography in younger women is that breast tissue in young women is denser than it is in older women. As a result, there is a significant number of false positives in younger women. One younger woman in three who gets repeated mammograms will have a false positive that requires further medical tests or biopsies (Miller, 1991).

The issue remains controversial. Early in the Clinton administration, the age initiating mammography was set at 50. As a result of this decision, Clinton was attacked for being against preventive medicine (Kaplan, 2000; Kaplan et al., 1996). However, the public health benefit from promoting screening mammography for women 40 to 50 years old may be somewhat limited. All clinical trials and meta-analyses have failed to show a population benefit from screening (Fletcher, 1997; Kerlikowske, Grady, Rubin, Sandrock, & Ernster, 1995).

In January 1997, a panel convened by the National Institutes of Health recommended that women aged 40 to 50 years old need not have routine screening mammograms unless the women are

---

Using cutting scores to find hits and misses involves criterion validity (see Chapter 5). Many years ago, H. C. Taylor and J. T. Russell (1939) demonstrated how to relate validity coefficients to accuracy rates in selection.

Taylor-Russell Tables

The decision to use a test must depend on what the test offers. In Chapter 5, we showed that tests with significant predictive or concurrent validity coefficients did better than chance in forecasting performance on a criterion. However, knowing that a test is better than chance is not good enough for making

FIGURE 18-1

Relationship of age to breast cancer.

(Data from National Cancer Institute, Cancer Statistics Review 1973–1988 (Bethesda, MD: July 1991, Table II-40.)

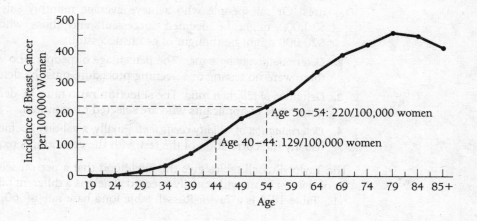

in a high-risk group or have felt a lump. The panel review shocked the ACS, an organization that had worked hard to promote screening of younger women. The headline of *USA Today* (January 24, 1997) read "Mammogram Panel Only Adds to Furor." Commentators on morning talk shows were outraged by the committee's decision. Richard Klausner, the Director of the National Cancer Institute, decided to disregard the report of his own expert panel. Shortly thereafter, the ACS appointed a panel of experts chosen because each already believed that screening was valuable for women aged 40 to 50. To no one's surprise, this ACS panel recommended that 40- to 50-year-old women should be screened (Fletcher, 1997). Following the ACS panel recommendation, the use of mammography

increased substantially. In 1999, the Centers for Disease Control studied mammography use in more than 50,000 women living in 38 states. The data were obtained from large cross-sectional surveys in 1989 and again in 1997. In 1997, 84.8% of women reported having had a mammogram. This was a substantial increase from the 63.9% observed in 1989.

What does this tell us? Clearly, mammography has been shown to be a valuable medical test for older women. For women in their 20s and early 30s, routine screening does not seem to help. For women aged 40–50, the jury is still out. Of course, women with risk factors for breast cancer, such as a strong family history of the condition, may still benefit from routine screening.

choices about whether it will serve in some applications. In other words, a worthwhile test must provide more information than do the base rates alone.

In 1939, Taylor and Russell developed a method for evaluating the validity of a test in relation to the amount of information it contributes beyond the base rates. This method is neatly summarized in a series of tables known as the **Taylor-Russell tables.** To use them, you must have the following information:

   1. *Definition of success.* For each situation in which the test is to be used, success on the outcome must be defined. This could be that the patient lived, that the person succeeded on the job, or that the student did well in col-

lege. One must define success clearly by dichotomizing some outcome variable. For example, first-year grade point averages above 2.3 might be defined as success in college, and those below 2.3 might be defined as failures. Or salespeople who achieve average monthly sales of more than $20,000 might be deemed successful, and those who sell less than $20,000 might be thought of as unsuccessful.

2. *Determination of base rate.* The percentage of people who would succeed if there were no testing or screening procedure must be determined.

3. *Definition of selection ratio.* The **selection ratio** must be defined. This is the percentage of applicants who are selected or admitted.

4. *Determination of validity coefficient.* Finally, a validity coefficient for the test, usually the correlation of the test with the criterion, is required.

The Taylor-Russell tables give the likelihood that a person selected on the basis of the test score will actually succeed. There is a different table for each base rate. Table 18-4 is a Taylor-Russell table for a base rate of .60.

TABLE 18-4 *Taylor-Russell Table for a Base Rate of .60*

Validity (ρ_{xy})	Selection Ratio										
	.05	.10	.20	.30	.40	.50	.60	.70	.80	.90	.95
.00	.60	.60	.60	.60	.60	.60	.60	.60	.60	.60	.60
.05	.64	.63	.63	.62	.62	.62	.61	.61	.61	.60	.60
.10	.68	.67	.65	.64	.64	.63	.63	.62	.61	.61	.60
.15	.71	.70	.68	.67	.66	.65	.64	.63	.62	.61	.61
.20	.75	.73	.71	.69	.67	.66	.65	.64	.63	.62	.61
.25	.78	.76	.73	.71	.69	.68	.66	.65	.63	.62	.61
.30	.82	.79	.76	.73	.71	.69	.68	.66	.64	.62	.61
.35	.85	.82	.78	.75	.73	.71	.69	.67	.65	.63	.62
.40	.88	.85	.81	.78	.75	.73	.70	.68	.66	.63	.62
.45	.90	.87	.83	.80	.77	.74	.72	.69	.66	.64	.62
.50	.93	.90	.86	.82	.79	.76	.73	.70	.67	.64	.62
.55	.95	.92	.88	.84	.81	.78	.75	.71	.68	.64	.62
.60	.96	.94	.90	.87	.83	.80	.76	.73	.69	.65	.63
.65	.98	.96	.92	.89	.85	.82	.78	.74	.70	.65	.63
.70	.99	.97	.94	.91	.87	.84	.80	.75	.71	.66	.63
.75	.99	.99	.96	.93	.90	.86	.81	.77	.71	.66	.63
.80	1.00	.99	.98	.95	.92	.88	.83	.78	.72	.66	.63
.85	1.00	1.00	.99	.97	.95	.91	.86	.80	.73	.66	.63
.90	1.00	1.00	1.00	.99	.97	.94	.88	.82	.74	.67	.63
.95	1.00	1.00	1.00	1.00	.99	.97	.92	.84	.75	.67	.63
1.00	1.00	1.00	1.00	1.00	1.00	1.00	1.00	.86	.75	.67	.63

From "The Relationship of Validity Coefficients to the Practical Effectiveness of Tests in Selection: Discussion and Tables" by H. C. Taylor and J. T. Russell. *Journal of Applied Psychology*, 1939, *23*, 565–578. Copyright 1939 by the American Psychological Association.

To use the table, find the row that represents the validity of the test that would be used for selection. Then find the column that is associated with the proportion of people who can be selected. The number in the body of the table that is associated with a particular row and a particular column gives an estimate of the percentage of people who could be expected to succeed when selected on the basis of the test.

For example, suppose that you are put in charge of deciding who will be admitted to a program to train secondary-education teachers. The first thing you must do is decide on a definition of success. After meeting with a committee, you may decide that success will be defined as completing the program and obtaining a satisfactory performance evaluation in student teaching. By studying records, you determine that when no selection procedure was used, 60% of the applicants to the program succeeded on this task. Thus, the base rate would be 60%, and the Taylor-Russell table for a base rate of .60 would be used. You then consider using the Graduate Record Examination (GRE) to select people for your program because you can accept only 70% of the applicants. A study is done and determines that the correlation between GRE scores and success (completing the program and obtaining a satisfactory evaluation in student teaching) is .30. This is the validity of the test for predicting the criterion.

Now you must estimate how many people would be expected to succeed if they were selected on the basis of GRE scores. Using the Taylor-Russell table (Table 18-4) for a base rate of .60, find the row associated with the .30 validity and move across the table until you are in the column for a selection ratio of .70 (the percentage of applicants you can admit to your program). You should arrive at the number .66, which is the proportion of applicants you would expect to be successful if the selection was based on the GRE. This analysis tells you that 66% of those selected on the basis of GRE scores can be expected to be successful, compared with a success rate of 60% for those selected at random. Should the GRE be required for admittance to your program? To answer this question, you must decide whether the increment of 6% associated with the use of the test is worth the extra effort and expense of requiring it.

Try to work through a real-life example using the data from the Yale Ph.D. program in psychology.[1] The correlation between the GRE quantitative score and GPA was approximately 0.10, rounded up (Sternberg & Williams, 1997). Assume that Yale is selective and admits only some 10% of its applicants and that the base rate for success is 60%. Using the Taylor-Russell table, you should find that 67% of the applicants would be successful if selected on the basis of the Graduate Record Exam's quantitative component (GRE-Q), while 60% would be successful if selected by chance. This 67% figure comes from the third row (validity = 0.10) and second column (selection ratio = 0.10) of Table 18-4.

---

[1] One problem with the Yale study is that it is based on students admitted to the program, not all who apply. If data on all applicants were available, it is possible that the validity of the GRE may have been higher because there would have been a greater range of scores.

Looking at Table 18-4, you can see that tests will be more valuable in some situations than in others. For example, a test is most useful when the validity of the test is high and the selection ratio is low, as the lower left-hand portion of Table 18-4 shows. Conversely, when the validity is low and the selection ratio is high (the upper right-hand portion of the table), the test will be of little value. When the test has no validity (the first row of the table), using the test will be no better than selecting applicants by chance. Similarly, when nearly everyone is selected (last column), there is little reason to use a test.

Whenever a selection procedure is used, always remember that some qualified applicants will be turned away. The use of rational selection procedures should help make the system more fair by decreasing the number of qualified applicants not selected. One way to evaluate the selection procedure is to show the ratio of people selected by the test who then succeed and the ratio of those who would have succeeded but were not selected.

Suppose that you are the personnel manager for a company and that you can choose 30 of 100 applicants for a job. To make this decision, you have the results of a test with a validity of .70. You also know that the base rate for success on the job is .60. Using the Taylor-Russell table for a base rate of .60, you find that 91% of those selected on the basis of the test would be expected to succeed on the job. Because you can select 30 people, the table implies that approximately 27 of them will succeed and three will fail (91% of 30 = 27.3).

When you decide to hire 30 of the applicants, you also are deciding not to hire 70 people. It is important to realize that not all of the 70 people would fail if they were selected. In fact, many of them are capable people whom the testing procedure has "misdiagnosed." To justify your use of the test, it would be your responsibility to explain why your selection procedure is worthwhile even though it turns down some people who would succeed and selects some who fail.

Table 18-5 shows what would happen to all of the applicants. Of 100, 30 would be accepted and 70 rejected (the selection ratio equals .30). However, because the base rate for success is .60, 60 of the 100 applicants would have succeeded on the job and 40 would have failed. As you have seen, the Taylor-Russell table shows that 91% of those selected on the basis of the test will succeed, or 27 of the 30 selected (.9 × 30 = 27.3), while only 3 of the 30 will likely fail.

Among the 60 people who would have succeeded, only 27 could be selected. This means that 33 people who would have been good choices were rejected. However, among the 40 people who would have failed, an estimated 37 would be in the rejected group. Using Table 18-5, we also can calculate the proportion of those rejected on the basis of the test who would be expected to succeed: 33/70 = .47. Although the procedure leads to the rejection of many capable applicants, it can be defended as rational because the proportion of those who succeed is much higher among those who are selected by the procedure than among those who are rejected.

A common argument is that increased minority hiring will result in lower average job performance because some applicants with lower test scores will be

TABLE 18-5

What Would Happen to 100 Applicants if 30 People Were Selected on the Basis of a Test with a Validity of .70 for a Job with a 60% Base Success Rate?

Performance	Decision		
	Select	**Reject**	**Total**
Success*	27	33	60
Failure	3	37	40
Total	30	70	100

*Success ratio given selection = 27/30 = .90 (actually .91 without rounding; see Table 7-6). Success ratio given rejection = 33/70 = .47.

hired. However, systematic study of this issue has not always supported these arguments. For example, increased minority hiring in some industries has resulted in only a small loss in job performance. There may be circumstances in which average job performance declines with an overselection of low-scoring job applicants, but the data from these studies are typically complex (Silva & Jacobs, 1993).

The Taylor-Russell tables also help reveal the futility of certain types of assessment procedures. For example, McDaniel (1989) suggested that routine background information may be useful in predicting employee success. In his study, McDaniel used information on school suspension, drug use, quitting school, participation in social clubs, school grades, contacts with the legal system, and socioeconomic status to predict success in the military service. The criterion for success was keeping from being discharged for being unsuitable. The study demonstrated that though most of the background variables predicted unsuitability discharges, the validity coefficients were extremely low, with the highest being approximately .15. Let us assume that the selection ratio for the armed services is .9. In other words, 9 out of every 10 applicants are admitted to the military service. Let us also assume the base rate of success of 60%. (In the McDaniel study, the base rate was approximately 85%, but assuming 60% allows us to do this exercise with Table 18-4.) When we use the Taylor-Russell table for a validity of .15 and a selection ratio of .90, we find that the proportion who succeed in military service goes to .61. Using only base-rate information, we would have predicted that 60% succeed. The information on dropping out of school improves this prediction by only 1%! The low validity for the background information is the reason for this negligible improvement. Although background information may be useful, it may provide only a minimum of information about future success.

Utility Theory and Decision Analysis

The use of Taylor-Russell tables requires that the criterion be a dichotomous variable. However, success usually is measured on a more refined numerical scale. By considering success only in terms of a dichotomous variable, one ignores much of the information available to the analyst. For example, it seems more reasonable to use a continuum of job performance as the criterion than to consider merely whether or not someone failed on a job. Since the publication of the Taylor-Russell tables, researchers have attempted to define levels besides success and failure. These formulations are based on utility theory (Boudreau & Ramstad, 2003; Brennan, 1994; Broaden, 1946, 1949; Cronbach & Gleser, 1965; Schmidt & Rothstein, 1994; Smith & George, 1994).

Although the use of decision and utility theory greatly serves the industrial psychologist, the equations used to calculate the value of test data are quite complex (Boudreau & Ramstad, 2003). Furthermore, the equations require certain information that is hard to estimate. For example, to use the equations, you must estimate the dollar value that is associated with different levels of performance on the job, an estimation that is difficult for most jobs (Dunnette & Borman, 1979). Schmidt and Hunter (1983) presented mathematical arguments showing that 40% of the average salary produces a reasonable estimate of the standard deviation of the output.

Several other approaches have been suggested to solve the problems of utility analysis, although progress has been slow (Cascio, 1998; Cascio & Ramos, 1986; Eaton, Wing, & Mitchell, 1985). For example, Raju and co-workers (1993) developed a new approach to utility assessment that does not require an estimate of the dollar value for performance. They proposed that the value of each individual can be estimated from the total value of his or her compensation package. This approach simplifies the calculations and produces results similar to those of other methods; however, the Raju method may shift the subjective judgment of the standard deviation of the criterion to estimating the coefficient of variation of the criterion. In other words, the estimation problem has not been solved (Judiesch, Schmidt, & Hunter, 1993). Other industrial psychologists believe that utility analysis may actually make managers less likely to use data in personnel selection. They suggest that there is a "futility of utility" (Latham & Whyte, 1994; Whyte & Latham, 1997). Some have argued that managers perceive the use of utility information as an attempt to manipulate them to invest in a personnel intervention (Latham & Whyte 1994; Kataoka, Latham, & Whyte, 1997; Whyte & Latham, 1997).

Clearly, the utility methods hold great promise for making rational personnel decisions, yet the difficulty in applying utility formulations has prevented their widespread use. Even so, studies do demonstrate financial advantages for companies that select employees on the basis of these formal models (Burke & Doran, 1989; Cascio, 1998). Furthermore, the methodology for utility analysis continues to improve (Schmidt, Law, Hunter, Rothstein, et al., 1993). See Focused Example 18-2 for an example of utility calculation.

Although utility theory is used only occasionally in personnel selection, it is beginning to find applications in other fields, including education (Sackett, 1998) and medicine (Lurie & Sox, 1999; Ridenour, Treloar, & Dean, 2003). In education, the placement decisions may have serious consequences. With tests being considered for tracking, promotion, and graduation, any decisions based on poor information may cause personal and financial harm (Heubert & Hauser, 1999). Medical researchers have long been aware that tests have false positive and false negative results. For some problems, such as the screening

Focused Example 18-2

HOW MUCH MONEY CAN BE SAVED THROUGH VALID SELECTION?

 A major issue in business and industrial psychology is how to get the most productivity out of employees. Employers often use tests to select employees who have the greatest chance of being productive. Some industrial psychologists, however, may have failed to realize just how much economic value can be gained from effective selection procedures. Although Cronbach and Gleser (1965) developed methods for evaluating the cost-effectiveness of testing many years ago, their technique was not frequently used because it required estimating the standard deviation of the dollar value of employee performance. However, newer methods developed to estimate this quantity allow one to determine how much money one saves by using a valid selection procedure.

In one study, a group of personnel psychologists evaluated measures for the selection of bus drivers. They reasoned that some bus drivers who demonstrated safer driving behaviors should be selected to work more hours. This selection procedure should make the transit companies more efficient. To select the bus drivers, researchers developed several different measures that were administered to 864 bus drivers at nine locations. After a detailed analysis of the skills required for bus drivers, it was concluded that being a good bus operator required the three "Be's": "Be there, be safe, and be courteous." Analysis also showed that supervisor's ratings could be successfully predicted, as could the absence of accidents. Furthermore, a utility analysis of the composite predictor variable demonstrated that use of the selection procedure could reduce overall operating expenses for the bus agencies by more than $500,000 per year (Jacobs, Conte, Day, Silva, et al., 1996).

---

test for prostate cancer in younger men, there are many false positives for each true positive. Each false positive has financial and personal ramifications: In addition to costing money, a false positive may lead to other painful and unnecessary medical procedures. Analysts often consider such consequences when they interpret test data. The growing interest in utility analysis for medical decisions has led to the formation of the Society for Medical Decision Making and publication of a specialized journal entitled *Medical Decision Making*.

Incremental Validity

Validity defines the inferences that one can make on the basis of a score or measure (see Chapter 5). Evidence that a test is valid for particular inferences does not necessarily mean that the test is valuable. Though a test may be reliable and valid, the decision to use it depends on additional considerations. For example, does the test give you more information than you could find if it were not used? If so, how much more information does it give? The unique information gained through using the test is known as *incremental validity*.

In the discussions of base and hit rates and Taylor-Russell tables, we presented methods for evaluating what a test contributed beyond what was known from base rates. This kind of evaluation provides evidence for incremental validity. However, the assessment of incremental validity is not necessarily limited to comparisons with base rates. A particularly important form of evidence for incremental validity is the determination of how much information a test contributes beyond some simpler method for making the same prediction.

Most of the examples given in the preceding sections concerned tests used for selection purposes. However, the same rules and methods apply to tests used for the evaluation of personality or in the practice of clinical psychology.

Recent research on the prediction of behavior in particular situations has yielded some simple but startling results. Although it is difficult to predict behavior on the basis of reports by trained clinical psychologists (Meehl, 1995), people are remarkably good at predicting their own behavior (Bandura, 1994; Funder, Parke, Tomhnson-Keasey, & Widaman, 1993). We can learn a lot simply by asking someone whether he or she will be able to perform a particular behavior.

Frequently, expensive and time-consuming psychological tests are given in order to predict future behavior. Before exerting this effort, one should ask what the tests might reveal beyond information obtained in some simpler manner. For example, for predicting functioning and life expectancy for lung patients, a simple self-rating of health serves about as well as a complex set of medical tests. Detailed interviews and tests give little information beyond the simple patient self-report (Kaplan, Ries, Prewitt, & Eakin, 1994). Through a variety of tests and self-ratings, other studies have attempted to determine how a person will be rated by peers. The results often demonstrate that, in predicting peer ratings, simple self-ratings are as good as complex personality tests that make inferences about underlying traits (Hase & Goldberg, 1967).

Alternatively, work supervisors are known to be inaccurate raters. One variable that may affect ratings is the supervisor's own level of security. For example, studies have demonstrated that supervisors who have conflict over their own roles give relatively higher ratings of the performance of their subordinates (Fried & Tiegs, 1995). Self-predictions are also not always accurate. Even so, they no less accurately predict, for instance, who will go under a hypnotic trance than do complex hypnotizability scales (Melei & Hilgard, 1964). Further, they are at times more accurate than expensive tests. For example, personality tests have been of little value in predicting whether snake phobics will learn to approach a snake after therapy; however, self-predictions have been found to be highly accurate (Bandura, 1994).

A variety of investigations have considered the validity of employment interviews. The most comprehensive summary of these studies, reported by McDaniel and associates (1994), combined results from a variety of other investigations involving a combined total of 86,331 individuals. The analysis suggested that the validity of interview information depends on many variables. Situational interviews had higher validity than did job-related interviews. Psychologically based interviews had the lowest validity of all the categories studied. Structured interviews had higher validity than did unstructured ones. Other studies have demonstrated that biographical information used for employment decisions is often unreliable (Schmidt & Rothstein, 1994). There is some hope for improving ratings. Studies have shown that rating accuracy can improve with specific cognitive training (Day & Sulsky, 1995).

Often, the predictive validity of selection tests is modest. For example, one investigation attempted to predict who would be the best support people for insurance agencies. A battery of tests involving cognitive ability, personality, and biographical data was administered to 357 subjects. Among these, 337 were eventually hired and rated by their immediate supervisor for job performance. The range of the validity coefficients was .17 to .28. In other words, the extensive testing battery explains only about 4% to 9% of the variance in job performance (Bosshardt, Carter, Gialluca, Dunnette, et al., 1992). Another study evaluated applicants for eight telecommunications companies. Using structural behavioral interviews to estimate job performance yielded criterion validity estimates of approximately .22 (Motowidlo, Carter, Dunnette, Tippins, et al., 1992).

We do not offer these examples to convince you that personality tests are meaningless. As you will see in Chapters 15–18, personality measures make many important contributions. However, test users always should ask themselves whether they can gain the same information with a simpler or less expensive method or with one that will cause the subject less strain. Tests should be used when they provide significantly more information than simpler methods would obtain. To ensure that testing is a worthwhile use of time and resources, one must carefully select the testing materials to be used.

Personnel Psychology from the Employee's Perspective: Fitting People to Jobs

One challenge in personnel psychology is to find the best matches between characteristics of people and characteristics of jobs. Temperament may be a critical component of job satisfaction. In this section, we review the Myers-Briggs Type Indicator, which is perhaps the most widely used measure of temperament in I/O psychology.

The Myers-Briggs Type Indicator

The Myers-Briggs Type Indicator (MBTI), developed by I. B. Myers and K. C. Briggs, is a theoretically constructed test based on Carl Jung's theory of psychology types (Quenk, 2000). Jung theorized that there are four main ways in which we experience or come to know the world:

- *sensing,* or knowing through sight, hearing, touch, and so on;
- *intuition,* inferring what underlies sensory inputs;
- *feeling,* focusing on the emotional aspect of experience; and
- *thinking,* reasoning or thinking abstractly.

Jung argued that although we must strive for balance in the four modes, each person tends to emphasize one way of experiencing the world over the others. In addition, Jung believed that one could distinguish all individuals in terms of introversion versus extroversion.

The purpose of the Myers-Briggs test is to determine where people fall on the introversion–extroversion dimension and on which of the four modes they most rely (Quenk, 2000). In line with Jung's theory, the underlying assumption of the MBTI is that we all have specific preferences in the way we construe our experiences, and these preferences underlie our interests, needs, values, and motivation.

The MBTI is widely used and has been extensively researched (Wyman, 1998). It has been used to study such issues as communication styles (Loffredo & Opt, 1998), career choices (McCaulley & Martin, 1995), emotional perception (Martin, Berry, Dobranski, Horne, et al., 1996), leadership (Fitzgerald, 1997), and self-efficacy (Tuel & Betz, 1998). The MBTI has even been used to study the relationship between personality and financial success (Mabon, 1998) and sensitivity and purpose in life (Doerries & Ridley, 1998). In fact, our review of studies published between 1996 and 2000 revealed literally hundreds of studies that have used the MBTI in creative ways to study human personality and its correlates (see Quenk, 2000).

Tests for Use in Industry: Wonderlic Personnel Test

Business and industry make extensive use of tests, especially as an aid in making decisions about employment, placement, and promotion. One such test widely used is the Wonderlic Personnel Test (WPT) (Bell, 2002). Based on another popular instrument, the Otis Self-Administering Tests of Mental Ability, the WPT is a quick (12-minute) test of mental ability in adults. Normative data are available on more than 50,000 adults 20 to 65 years old. Five forms, whose intercorrelations range from .82 to .94, are available. Odd–even reliability coefficients are also excellent, with a range of .88 to .94 reported in the manual. The main drawback of the WPT is its validity documentation, although available studies tend to support it (Dodrill & Warner, 1988; Rosenstein & Glickman, 1994).

In short, the WPT is a quick and stable paper-and-pencil intelligence test with extensive norms. Widely used for employee-related decisions in industry, it has its greatest value when local validity data are available (Saltzman, Strauss, Hunter, & Spellacy, 1998). In the absence of local data, test scores must be interpreted with some caution. Figure 18-2 shows a sample question from the Wonderlic.

To measure potential ability (aptitude) for specific vocations, one can choose from several fine tests. The Differential Aptitude Test (DAT) is especially useful in assessing clerical competence, such as speed, accuracy, and grammar. The Bennett Mechanical Comprehension Test and the Revised Minnesota Paper Form Board Tests are two popular measures of mechanical ability. The Accounting Orientation Test has shown some promise in measuring accounting

FIGURE 18-2

*Sample questions
from the
Wonderlic.*

(Copyright ©
Wonderlic Personnel
Test, Inc. Reprinted by
permission.)

Sample Questions

Look at the row of numbers below. What number should
come next?

8   4   2   1   1/2   1/4   ?

Assume the first 2 statements are true. Is the final one: (1)
true, (2) false, (3) not certain?
The boy plays baseball. All baseball players wear hats. The
boy wears a hat.

One of the numbered figures in the following drawing is
most different from the others. What is the number in that
figure?

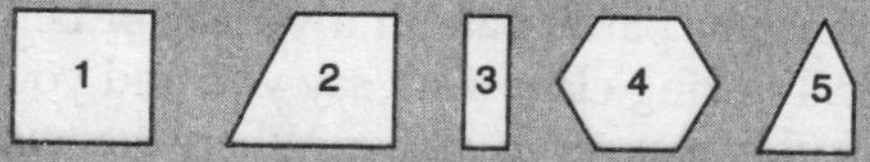

A train travels 20 feet in 1/5 second. At this same speed,
how many feet will it travel in three seconds?

How many of the six pairs of items listed below are exact
duplicates?

3421	1243
21212	21212
558956	558956
10120210	10120210
612986896	612986896
356471201	356571201

The hours of daylight and darkness in SEPTEMBER are
nearest equal to the hours of daylight and darkness in
(1) June   (2) March   (3) May   (4) November

skills. To assess business skills and readiness for graduate study in business,
one can use the Admission Test for Graduate Study in Business. Special ability
tests also exist for advanced study in dentistry (for example, the Dental Admission Testing Program) and medicine (for example, the Medical College Admission Test, or MCAT).

Measuring Characteristics of the Work Setting

To study the influence of situations, we need methods to describe and measure
them. This section describes these methods.

The Social-Ecology Approach

Ecology is the branch of biology that studies the relationship between living organisms and their environments. Organisms must adapt to the physical environment to survive. Similarly, environments can affect the social lives of their inhabitants. Thus, psychologists have come to recognize the importance of studying people in their natural environments and of analyzing the effects of physical environments on social behavior (Wicker, 1979). As Stokols states, "At a time when environmentalists and economists are proclaiming that 'small is beautiful,' the research literature on human behavior in relation to its environmental settings continues to expand at a staggering rate" (1978, p. 253). This field of study is called *environmental psychology*. A similar area, *ecological psychology,* focuses on events that occur in a behavioral setting. We refer to these topics of study together as **social ecology** (Stokols, 2000). One of the most important areas in social ecology is the study of behavioral settings.

Each day, you participate in a variety of behavioral settings, such as your psychological-testing class. Let's say you and your classmates are talking while you wait for the lecturer to arrive. When she enters the room, everyone grows quiet. As the presentation begins, you and your classmates focus your attention on the speaker. Why does this chain of events occur? It does, in part, because the room is set up to facilitate this kind of social interaction. For example, the chairs face the front of the room, where a chalkboard hangs. What would happen if the chairs were facing the other way? What if there were no chairs?

Barker has made the study of behavioral settings his life's work. For many years, he and his colleagues described the publicly available behavioral settings in two small towns: Oskaloosa, Kansas, and Leyburn, England. Both towns included many behavioral settings such as card games, court sessions, and special businesses. Barker's work involved documenting each setting by describing how long the observed interactions lasted, who participated, the gender of the people in the setting, and so on (Barker, 1979; Barker & Schoggen, 1973; Schoggen, 1979; Wicker, 1979).

The study of behavioral settings reveals a great deal about the social rules of the environment. For example, in both Oskaloosa and Leyburn, women spent less time in public behavioral settings than did men. The studies also confirmed what many feminists have been saying all along—that women are limited to certain settings. For example, women in both towns were observed most often in such settings as churches and schools. In other words, they were more often found in settings that favored social talking than in business and government settings.

Behavioral settings are truly self-regulating ecologies. When a component of the system is missing, the activities in the program are changed to correct the imbalance. For example, if there were no chairs in your psychological testing class, then students would probably go out looking for them in order to bring the situation into balance. If someone in the class made too much noise, then social forces would attempt to eliminate the disruption (Wicker, 1979). Thus, to avoid social condemnation, people must act according to the rules for a given behavioral setting. A catcall during psychology class might bring you strange and rejecting looks. In a rock concert, it is perfectly appropriate. Social adjustment requires that one know and follow the rules of many social behavioral settings.

The study of behavioral settings also involves examining the relationship between work satisfaction and the requirements of the job. Wicker and Kirmeyer (1976) used this approach in a study of coping behavior among park rangers in Yosemite National Park. During the summer, as the workload for the rangers increased, they felt more challenged on the job and used more coping strategies. By the end of the summer, when the workload peaked, the challenge of heavy crowds was no longer associated with job satisfaction. Instead, the rangers were less able to cope and felt physically and emotionally drained. To understand the relationship between work setting and satisfaction, one must consider many aspects of the ecology, including the workload, coping strategies, and the duration of work overload. One must also make a precise description of the work environment. When employees perceive that there is support for creativity at work, they report greater job satisfaction, better social climate, and less stress (Stokols, Clitheroe, & Zmuidzinas, 2002).

There are many applications of the social-ecology approach in clinical and health psychology. For example, restructuring the environment may modify health-damaging behaviors such as smoking and lack of exercise (Johansson, Johnson, & Hall, 1991). Considerable work has gone into characterizing family environments and the interaction between spouses. Like the workplace, the social environment may affect cigarette smoking, diet, and other health behaviors (Cohen & Lichtenstein, 1990; Ewart, 1991).

Classifying Environments

How do different environments affect our behavior? Can we work better when the sun is out? Or do we get more tired and irritable on hot days? Most of social psychology is based on the premise that situations influence behavior (Moos, 2003). Some of the earliest work in the field of environmental psychology involved building elaborate systems to classify the characteristics of environments that had been shown to affect individual or group behavior (Holahan, 1986). (This was similar to the work done by many early personality psychologists who built elaborate systems to classify personality types.)

Table 18-6 shows a classification system created by Moos (1973). It includes six characteristics of environments and gives examples. Many studies demonstrate that the characteristics of the people in one's environment affect one's behavior. The likelihood that a high-school girl will begin to smoke, for example, can be greatly influenced by how many girls she knows who already smoke or who approve of smoking (Gilpin & Pierce, 2003). Over the years, Moos and his colleagues have developed many different measures to evaluate the characteristics of environments (Moos, 2003). A summary of these scales is shown in Table 18-7.

Moos's work on measuring the characteristics of environments demonstrates the ways in which personal characteristics of the work environment af-

TABLE 18-6
Six Characteristics of Environments

Characteristics	Examples
Ecological dimensions	Architectural design, geographic location, weather conditions
Behavioral settings	Office, home, store
Organizational structure	Percentage of women in the student body, number of people per household, average age of group
Characteristics of inhabitants	Proportion of students who date, drink, or vote
Psychosocial and organizational climate	Work pressure, encouragement of participation, orientation toward helping with personal problems
Functional or reinforcing properties	Is aggression reinforced on the football field? Is it reinforced at home?

Adapted from Moos (1973).

TABLE 18-7
Summary of Scales Used to Evaluate Different Environments

Type of environment	Scale	Reference
Treatment	Ward Atmosphere Scale	Moos (1987e)
	Community-Oriented Programs Environment Scale	Moos (1987a)
Institutional	Correctional Institutions Environment Scale	Moos (1987b)
Educational	University Residence Environment Scale	Moos (1987d)
	Classroom Environment Scale	Moos and Truckett (1986)
Community	Work Environment Scale	Moos (1986b)
	Group Environment Scale	Moos (1986a)
	Family Environment Scale	Moos and Moos (1986)

fect job choice and worker satisfaction (Schaefer & Moos, 1996). For example, workers are more satisfied with work environments that promote quality interactions between workers and supervisors than they are with environments that keep these relationships more distant. The quality of the relationship between workers and supervisors also enhances productivity (Moos, 1987c). Some evidence indicates that workers in supportive work environments are less likely to develop disabilities caused by stress on the job than are workers in nonsupportive environments (Holahan & Moos, 1986). A pleasant work environment is also good for business. Bank customers who perceive employees as friendly and supportive tend to stay at their bank more than do customers who dislike the bank's social environment (Moos, 1986b).

Lemke and Moos (1986) have expanded this work by creating a *multiphasic environmental assessment procedure* (MEAP). There are many ways to apply this procedure. For example, we can use it to describe sheltered-care settings, including nursing homes and other housing situations for older adults. This complex approach includes evaluating the settings according to physical and architectural features, policy and program information, resident and staff information, attractiveness and other physical characteristics, and a general environ-

FIGURE 18-3
Physical and architectural resources profile for two nursing homes.
(Moos & Lemke, 1984, p. 22.)

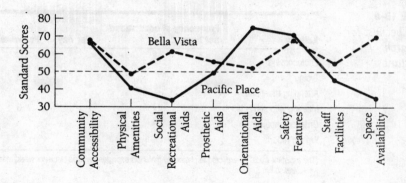

ment scale. Each feature has many subscales. For example, policy and program information includes how selective the home is in admitting new patients, how clearly its policies are specified, how much control residents have over policies, and so on. The resident and staff information includes the ratio of staff members to residents, the resident activity level, and the functional abilities of the residents. Figure 18-3 describes the physical and architectural resources of two nursing homes: Pacific Place and Bella Vista. As the figure shows, the homes are quite similar on some variables such as community accessibility and safety features. However, Bella Vista receives a much better score for social recreational activities, whereas Pacific Place receives a better score for orientational aids. Using this sort of information, one can quantitatively measure the characteristics of a work or home environment (Moos & Lemke, 1984).

In sum, behavioral settings and social environments are coming to be recognized as important factors in job and personal satisfaction. The study of work environments is a relatively new area that we expect to blossom in the coming decade.

Job Analysis

In addition to classifying work environments, the industrial psychologist must describe and measure characteristics of the job. Employers often want to detail the activities of their workplace to determine what type of personnel is needed or why some employees are unhappy working in the setting. Zedeck and Blood (1974) summarize five basic methods for doing so: checklists, critical incidents, observations, interviews, and questionnaires.

Checklists are used by job analysts to describe the activities and working conditions usually associated with a job title. An example of a checklist for a research assistant in behavioral research is shown in Table 18-8. The first column of the checklist shows the activities associated with the job title, while the other columns list the frequency of occurrence of these activities. The job analyst must simply record how frequently each activity occurs for people in this job classification.

TABLE 18-8
*Job Checklist for
Research
Assistant**

Activity	Frequency of occurrence per hour	Per day	Per week	Per month	Per year
Photocopying		1			
Typing			2		
Attending meetings				1	
Meeting with subjects			3		
Ordering supplies				1	
Writing reports					1

*The assistant would be expected to photocopy materials once per day, type twice per week, meet with subjects three times per week, and so on.

One of the concerns about job analysis is whether ratings are reliable. Dierdorff and Wilson (2003) reviewed 46 studies involving more than 299 estimates of reliability of job analysis. Ratings of tasks produce the highest estimates of interrater reliability than did generalized ratings of jobs.

In addition to evaluating jobs, employers must evaluate job performance. This is a complex field that is beyond the scope of this text. However, there are excellent summaries of performance evaluation. Suffice it to say that problems in performance evaluation are challenging. For example, there is controversy over whether there is racial bias in the evaluation of job performance. Some researchers still argue that there are important differences in performance across racial groups. For example, Roth and colleagues summarized studies on differences in job performance (Roth, Huffcutt, & Bobko, 2003). They compared differences between African American and white employees on subjective measures such as supervisor ratings versus objective measures based on more formal evaluations. Their analysis suggested that the objective measures showed even larger differences between African American and white employees than the subjective measures for measures of work quality, quantity, and absenteeism. Differences between Hispanic and white employees were not as large as those between African American and white employees.

Some researchers criticize checklists for providing neither an integrated picture of the job situation nor information about specific behaviors. There are methodological problems with checklists because it is sometimes difficult to determine if unchecked items were intentionally omitted or if the form was left incomplete (Clark & Watson, 1998). In contrast to Moos's environment scales, checklists do not predict well whether someone will like a particular job environment.

Critical incidents are observable behaviors that differentiate successful from unsuccessful employees. The critical-incident method was developed by J. C. Flanagan (1954). By acquiring specific descriptions of the behaviors of successful employees and their unsuccessful counterparts, one can learn something about the differences between the two groups. For example, a critical incident that might describe a successful employee is "always arrives at meetings on time." A critical incident that describes an unsuccessful employee might be "leaves work area disorganized."

Observation is another method for learning about the nature of the job. As we discussed in Chapter 8, information gathered through observational methods can sometimes be biased because people change their behavior when they know they are being watched. To avoid this problem, the participant-observation method is sometimes used. A participant-observer is someone who participates in the job and functions as though he or she were one of the workers.

Interviews can also be used to find out about a job. However, some workers may give an interviewer information that differs from what they would give another employee because they are uncomfortable or fear that what they say will be held against them. Another problem is that an interviewer unfamiliar with the job may not ask the right questions.

Questionnaires are commonly used to find out about job situations, but their use calls for special precautions. Many employers favor questionnaires because they are inexpensive. However, the employer may never know whether the respondent understood the questions. Furthermore, the type of information gained is limited to the specific questions. A more serious problem concerns the selective return rate in questionnaire studies. Those employees who feel highly favorable or highly unfavorable toward the company are the most likely to complete the questionnaire and return it.

Another approach to job description is the Occupational Information Network (O*NET) (Peterson, Mumford, Levin, Green, & Waksberg, 1999). The network was developed because traditional job descriptions in the U.S. Department of Labor's *Dictionary of Occupational Titles* did not provide enough information about how tasks and skills generalized across occupations. Job content can be described by both job-oriented and work-oriented tasks. The system includes three categories: (1) worker requirements, such as skills, knowledge, and abilities; (2) experience requirements, including training and licensure; and (3) job requirements, such as work activities, work context, and characteristics of the organization (Hanson, Borman, Kubisiak, & Sager, 1999). Using O*NET, one can understand divergent occupations in relation to tasks and skills that generalize across occupational categories (Jeanneret, Borman, Kubisiak, & Hanson, 1999).

The task of constructing methods of job analysis is extremely difficult (Hakel, 1986). Fleishman and Quaintance (1984) reviewed the methodological issues in developing taxonomies for job analysis and found that developers often do a poor job of characterizing jobs. Job analysis faces many of the same challenges as creating alternative tests and performance instruments.

Measuring the Person–Situation Interaction

In this chapter, we have presented two different perspectives. First, we reviewed research and methods from counseling psychology that emphasized the importance of people's characteristics or traits in their career satisfaction

(Campbell, 2000). Then we discussed how the characteristics of work environments and job requirements affect people.

To a growing number of psychologists, whether traits or situations are more important in determining behavior is a "pseudoquestion" (Anastasi & Urbina, 1997; McFall & McDonell, 1986; Sarason, Sarason, & Pierce, 1990; Trotter & Endler, 1999). It is meaningless to ask whether traits or situations are more important in explaining behavior, because behavior is clearly a joint function of both, or *person–situation interaction* (Endler, 1973; Endler & Hunt, 1968; Endler & Magnusson, 1976; Funder, 2001; Magnusson & Endler, 1977). To illustrate this, Focused Example 14-2 shows how a particular situation can have more impact on some people than on others (Flett, Endler, & Fairlie, 1999).

The interactionists support their position by reporting the proportion of variance in behavior explained by person, by situation, and by the interaction between person and situation. You might think of this as a pie divided to represent all the different influences on human behavior, including unknown causes (see Figure 18-4). Unique combinations of traits and situations cause this interaction. The beginning of Chapter 16 featured the case of Harry, a man who suffered throughout his life because he had made a bad career choice to become a dentist. For example, an interaction might describe how Harry reacts to being a dentist. This cause is different from the characteristics of Harry (in all situations) or the effects of anyone performing the role of a dentist. Careful studies that apply a statistical method known as *analysis of variance* have separated the proportion of variance attributable to each of these factors. As shown in Figure 18-4, the interaction accounts for a larger portion of the variance in behavior than does either the person or the situation (Endler, Parker, Bagby, & Cox 1991).

Focused Example 18-3

PERSON–SITUATION INTERACTION AND THE QUEBEC SEPARATIST MOVEMENT

 One example of person–situation interaction was demonstrated by reactions to the separation of Quebec from Canada. In 1996, the Province of Quebec held a referendum election to decide whether it would separate from Canada. The citizens of the province were almost equally divided on the issue, and many experienced considerable anxiety. Three hours before the vote and again 1 week later, college students were asked to complete measures of anxiety and were interviewed about their perception of the situation. Students who scored high on anxiety in their interviews showed higher anxiety about the vote and felt that the referendum was more threatening than did students who scored low on anxiety (Flett et al., 1999). So, it seems, the referendum affected anxious students differently than it did other students.

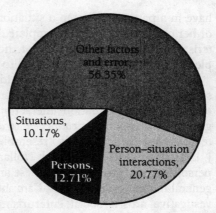

FIGURE 18-4   *Factors influencing behavior. A pie is divided according to the proportion of variation in behavior accounted for by trait, situation, and the interaction between trait and situation. The interaction is greater than either of the other two sources of influence. However, unexplained or error variance is much greater than any other factor.*
(*Adapted from data in Bowers, 1973.*)

As you can see, the interaction position explains only some of the people some of the time (Bem & Allen, 1974). As Figure 18-4 shows, the largest slice of the pie represents *error variance,* the proportion of the total not explained by the three sources of influence. After reviewing many studies on the influences of person and situation, I. G. Sarason, Smith, and Diener (1975) concluded that none of the three sources account for an impressive share of the variation when compared with the amount of variation left unexplained. Although the interaction is a better predictor than either trait or situation, it is only slightly better.

To help predict more of the people more of the time, Bem and Funder (1978) introduced the *template-matching technique,* a system that takes advantage of people's ability to predict their own behavior in particular situations. The system attempts to match personality to a specific template of behavior. For example, consider how to answer the question "Should Tom become an insurance salesperson?" Assuming you know nothing about Tom, perhaps the best way to guide him would be to describe how several hypothetical people might react to working in this job. You might say that shy people may have difficulty approaching new customers or that people with families may not like insurance sales because of the irregular work hours. Tom could then predict his own reaction to the job by matching his characteristics with the set of templates you have provided for him.

Along the same lines, Bem and Funder proposed that "situations be characterized as sets of template-behavior pairs, each template being a personality description of an idealized type of person expected to behave in a specified way in that setting" (1978, p. 486). The probability that a particular person will behave in a particular way in a situation is a function of the match between his or her characteristics and a template. For example, if Tom's personality characteristics matched the template for those who hated being insurance salespeople, then he might be best advised to avoid that career.

Because the template-matching idea arose from research in personality and social psychology, it is not often discussed in other areas of psychology. However, the person–situation interaction resembles what educational psychologists call the *aptitude-treatment interaction* (Rodger, 2002; Snow, 1991). The template-matching idea also resembles a popular theory of career choice that J. L. Holland (1997) proposed. Holland suggested that there are six clusters of personality and interest traits; these are the same clusters represented as the six general themes on the Strong-Campbell Interest Inventory (SCII) (realistic, investigative, artistic, social, enterprising, and conventional). Holland contended that six vocational environments correspond to these traits and that people will be happiest if they can match their traits to the characteristics of the work environment (Holland, 1975; Holland & Gottfredson, 1976). For example, an investigative individual will be most content if he or she can work in an investigative field such as science.

The idea of matching traits to situations is intuitively appealing. The concept of "different strokes for different folks" seems like a good way to structure one's search for the right job, the right apartment, or the right psychotherapist. However, this approach has some problems. First, there are an enormous number of combinations of persons and situations. For example, predicting how 10 personality types will perform in 20 different work environments produces $10 \times 20 = 200$ unique combinations. Most real-life decisions require many more factors. Second, research has not yet supported specific examples of matching traits and situations. Psychotherapists, for example, often account for lack of effectiveness by arguing that weak results should be expected because therapies must be tailored to the specific personalities of clients. In other words, some people will do well in behavior therapy, whereas others will have better success with a more cognitive approach. However, research has typically failed to correlate personalities with treatments. When these interactions are found, other studies tend not to replicate them (Smith & Sechrest, 1991). As a result, researchers must go back to the theoretical drawing board for new insights into the selection of treatment.

One finding that has been supported by research is that people often predict their own behavior better than do experts. However, some people tend to be overly positive in self-evaluations. This enhancement can be evaluated by comparing self-ratings with those provided by friends and professionals (Funder, 1993; Funder & West, 1993). Longitudinal studies show that self-enhancers tend to have poor social skills and poor psychological adjustment. Positive mental health may be associated with accurate self-appraisal (Colvin, Block, & Funder, 1995).

In general, career satisfaction depends on an appropriate match between person and job. The developing technology for finding job–person matches holds great promise for the field of career counseling and guidance testing

(Nystul, 1999). Counseling interventions must be tailored to individual needs (Savickas, 2000). Trying to use the same approach with every client might be like a shoe store attempting to sell the same size of shoe to each customer (Weigel, 1999).

SUMMARY

Making a selection among the many published tests has become a technical skill. One of your first considerations should always be whether it is worthwhile to administer a given test. How much information does the test promise beyond what can be learned without the test? Interviews remain the most common method for employee selection. However, the traditional interview has significant limitations. Modern personnel psychology makes extensive use of systematic selection procedures, often based on tests, performance samples, and job analysis. In personnel selection, the *base rate* is the probability of succeeding without any selection procedure. A variety of methods have been developed to estimate the amount of information a test gives beyond what is known by chance. This estimate depends on the validity of the test, the percentage of people being selected, and the proportion of people who can be expected to succeed if no selection test is used. *Taylor-Russell tables* can be used for outcomes defined in terms of success and failure. You can use utility and decision theories for some outcomes involving more than these two levels. However, the application of the utility theory equations is fairly difficult in most circumstances. To enhance productivity in business and industry, personnel psychologists study characteristics of people, work environments, and the interactions between people and the places they may work. Learning about the interface between people and work environments may hold the key to finding the best methods for employee selection.

WEB ACTIVITY

For interesting and relevant Web sites, check the following:

www.apa.org/about/division/div14.html
Official Web page for the American Psychological Association Division of Industrial and Organization Psychology

www.myersbriggs.org
Offers detailed information about the Myers-Briggs Type Indicator (MBTI)

luna.cas.usf.edu/~mbrannic/files/pmet/taylor1.htm
Discusses the application of Taylor-Russell tables

www.employment-testing.com
A commercial site that offers information on pre-employment testing

CHAPTER 19

Test Bias

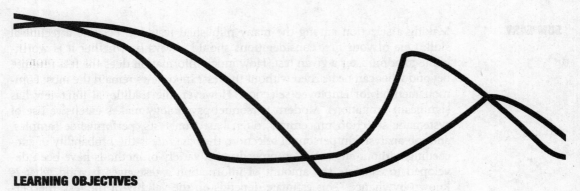

LEARNING OBJECTIVES

When you have completed this chapter, you should be able to:

☐ Discuss some of the current controversies surrounding the use of intelligence tests

☐ Give arguments for and against the belief that the content of standardized tests is biased in favor of white, middle-class children

☐ Explain how criterion-related validity studies, which review the slopes and intercepts of regression lines, are used in the study of test bias

☐ Discuss some of the problems with popular tests such as the Chitling Test and the BITCH

☐ List the components of the SOMPA and some of its advantages and disadvantages

☐ Describe how different social, political, and ethical viewpoints are represented by different definitions of test fairness

☐ Discuss some of the opportunities for developing improved predictors for minority group members

☐ Describe some of the problems with the criteria commonly used to evaluate standardized tests

☐ Describe how one can use differences in test scores to justify efforts to change the social environment

☐ Using the information from this chapter and from other sources, write an essay for or against the use of standardized tests for minority children

ince the early 1970s, serious emotional debates have flourished about the meaning of tests for the placement and classification of individuals. This chapter reviews test bias, an issue so controversial that it has inspired court evaluations of the meaning of tests for minority group members.

Although test bias is an unmistakably important issue (Betz, 2000), it was not the first controversy surrounding mental testing. Mental testing has faced serious questions since test reports began in 1905, and psychologists and others have debated the issues since the 1920s (Cronbach, 1975; Haney, 1981).

Why Is Test Bias Controversial?

That all persons are created equal is the cornerstone of political and social thought in U.S. society, yet all individuals are not treated equally. The history of social action is replete with attempts to remedy this situation. However, psychological tests are designed to measure differences among people, often in terms of desirable personal characteristics such as intelligence and aptitude. Test scores that demonstrate differences among people may suggest to some that people are not created with the same basic abilities.

The most difficult problem is that certain ethnic groups obtain lower average scores on some psychological tests. The most controversial case concerns intelligence tests. On average, African Americans score 15 points lower than white Americans on standardized IQ tests. (See Chapter 11 for the meaning of IQ scores.) This difference equates to approximately one standard deviation. Nobody disagrees that the two distributions overlap greatly and that some African Americans score as high as the highest whites. Similarly, some whites score as low as the lowest African Americans. Yet only some 15% to 20% of the African American population score above the average white score, and only approximately 15% to 20% of the white population score below the average African American score. Figure 19-1 shows the overlap between African American, white, and Asian American college-bound seniors on the SAT-I Math section. All distributions significantly overlap, but Asian American students obtained the highest average scores, followed by white and African American students.

This is not a debatable issue. If you were to administer the Stanford-Binet or the Wechsler scale (see Chapter 11) to large random samples of African Americans and white Americans, you would most likely get the same results. The dispute has not been over *whether* these differences exist but over *why* they do. Many have argued that the differences result from environmental factors (Kamin, 1974; Rosenthal & Jacobson, 1968; Turkheimer, 1991; Zuckerman, 1990), while others have suggested that the differences are biological (Eysenck, 1991; Jensen, 1969, 1972; Munsinger, 1975; Rushton, 1991) and related to the general (g) factor measured by IQ tests (Nyborg & Jensen, 2000). This debate lies beyond our concerns here, which center on the problems inherent in tests apart from environmental and biological factors. For now, see Focused Example 19-1 for a brief look at the issue of genes and IQ. Then see Focused Ex-

FIGURE 19-1

SAT-I Math score distributions for African American, white, and Asian American college-bound seniors, 1999.

(Source: Data provided by the College Board.)

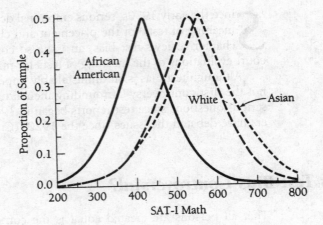

ample 19-2 for a possible environmental source of differences in test results. Finally, Focused Example 19-3 examines the very idea of race.

Beyond the other issues relevant to race and ethnicity, an increasing number of people no longer report their race when asked. Each year the College Board releases a report that summarizes SAT scores. In 2003, the report showed that overall SAT scores had improved slightly as had scores for minority students. However, the gap between African American and Hispanic students and Asian and non-Hispanic white peers was not closing. One of the difficulties in evaluating the report is that 1 in 4 test takers did not disclose their ethnicity. As a result, it is difficult to determine why the performance gap is not narrowing. Previous studies have shown that students who did not report ethnicity tended to get lower scores on the SAT. More recent studies indicate that the test performance of the nonresponder group is comparable to the rest of the SAT takers. It is not clear why so many students failed to report their racial identity. Steele believes that African American students perform more poorly on tests when they reveal their race (Steele & Aronson, 2004). Whittington (2004) reports that many white students decline to report their race because they feel there is discrimination in favor of ethnic minorities and that their majority status puts them at a disadvantage. The College Board believes that the reason for the increase in nonreporting ethnicity results from a poorly designed online questionnaire. The questionnaire has been redesigned to force respondents to click a box that reads, "I choose not to respond." It is still too early to determine whether the change on the online questionnaire will affect the rate of ethnic nonreporting.

Test Fairness and the Law

The U.S. government has attempted to establish clear standards for the use of psychological tests. Regulation of tests comes in many forms, including executive orders, laws, and court actions. The most important legal development was

Focused Example 19-1

GENES AND IMPROVING IQ

If intelligence were really determined genetically, then we would expect average IQ scores for different groups to be relatively constant over time. However, performance on intelligence tests has improved rather dramatically for some groups over the last 60 years. Figure 19-2 shows gains in IQ as estimated from the progressive matrix tests. These changes have been observed in a variety of Western countries including Great Britain, the Netherlands, and Israel. Jensen has argued that environment may affect IQ, suggesting that equalizing environments would reduce the 15-point gap between African Americans and their white counterparts by approximately 10 points. Indeed, in recent years African Americans have gained more in IQ than have whites. Since 1945, it appears that African Americans have increased average IQ by 16 points. By 1995, African Americans were performing on IQ tests at about the same level as whites in 1945 (Flynn, 1999). Because genetic change takes several generations, only an environmental hypothesis can explain these results. Many features of contemporary society have been used to explain these gains. One interesting suggestion is that heavy use of interactive video games may contribute the IQ gains (Greenfield, 1998).

FIGURE 19-2

Gains in average IQ over time in five countries.

(From J.R. Flynn, *Searching for Justice: The Discovery of IQ Gains Over Time, American Psychologist, Jan V 54 (n1), 1999, 5-20. Copyright © 1999 American Psychological Association. Reprinted by permission.)*

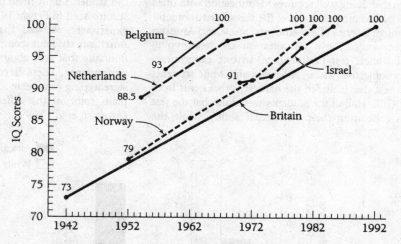

Note: Every nation is normed on its own samples. Therefore, although nations can be roughly compared in terms of different rates of IQ gain, they cannot be compared in terms of IQ scores. That is, the fact that the mean IQ of one nation appears higher than another at a given time is purely an artifact.

the passage of the 1964 Civil Rights Act. Title VII of this act created the Equal Employment Opportunity Commission (EEOC). In 1970, **EEOC guidelines** were published for employee-selection procedures. In 1978, the EEOC released *Uniform Guidelines on Employee Selection Procedures,* which are the major guidelines for the use of psychological tests in education and in industry.

Focused Example 19-2

CAN STEREOTYPING AFFECT TEST PERFORMANCE?

 Some research suggests that being a member of a group that is negatively stereotyped may adversely affect performance on standardized tests (Mayer & Hanges, 2003). As noted in this chapter, large studies consistently show that standardized tests (such as the SAT-I) overpredict college performance for African American, Latino, Latina, and Native American students. The overprediction occurs because many students from underrepresented groups do not get high grades in college. Steele argues that stereotyping adversely affects the victims' college grades, performance on standardized tests, and employment testing (Steele & Davies, 2003). In particular, he argues that doing well requires identification with one's school and other features of the school environment. Through a series of experiments, Steele and Aronson demonstrated how victimization by stereotyping could affect test performance. In one experiment, they subjected African American and white students to a test that included the hardest verbal items from the GRE. Half of the students were told that the test was measuring their intellectual ability, while the others were told that the test was about problem solving unrelated to ability. They hypothesized that informing subjects that they are going to take an ability test makes people who have been victims of stereotyping worry about their performance. This threatening experience, in turn, interferes with actual test performance (Aronson, Lustina, Good, Keough, Steele, & Brown, 1999; Steele & Aronson, 1998).

When told they were taking a test of intellectual abilities, white students scored significantly higher than African American students. However, some subjects were randomly assigned to take the same test but under conditions where there was no threat. Without a threat present, white and African American students performed equivalently. The results are summarized in Figure 19-3 (Steele, 1997). A related experiment showed that simply having African American students complete a demographic questionnaire that asks about their race also suppresses performance. These clever experiments suggest that stereotyping can create self-doubts that, in turn, explain some of the difference in test performance (Aronson et al., 1999).

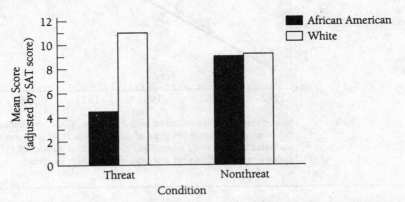

FIGURE 19-3 *Effects of stereotyping upon test performance. When told they were taking a test of intellectual abilities, white students scored significantly higher than African American students. However, some students were randomly assigned to take the same test but under conditions where there was no threat. Without a threat present, white and African American students performed equivalently.*

(Adapted from Steele, 1997, p. 621.)

Focused Example 19-3

IS RACE A MEANINGFUL CONCEPT?

 Race is one of the most commonly reported variables in social science. However, a growing literature argues that human races are highly similar to one another and that the construct of race has no biological meaning (Swallen, 2003). The evidence comes from studies in population genetics, the human genome, and physical anthropology (Freeman & Payne, 2000). Significant investigation has shown that the populations of the world are significantly intermingled—that is, humans have common genetic roots and the races of the world are not independent. The biological similarities among peoples of the world greatly outnumber the few differences. Nevertheless, race has remained an important variable in demography. Brawley and Freeman (1999) point out

that "race medicine" dominated the last few centuries. Race medicine was based on the belief that diseases behave differently in different races and was promoted by prominent 18th-century scientists whose opinions were used as the justification for slavery. However, medical research consistently shows that diseases function equivalently in people of different racial backgrounds (Freeman & Payne, 2000). Furthermore, equivalent treatment produces equivalent benefit for those of different racial backgrounds. Nevertheless, there are substantial disparities in the amount and quality of care that is available to those of different racial groups. This discrimination in access to health care may be the best explanation for the disparity in health outcomes among people of different races (Brawley & Freeman, 1999).

Regarding allowable uses of psychological test scores, the 1978 guidelines are stricter, more condensed, and less ambiguous than the 1970 guidelines. The original act clearly prohibited discrimination in employment on the basis of race, color, religion, gender, or national origin. However, the 1978 guidelines made clear that the government will view any screening procedure, including the use of psychological tests, as having an **adverse impact** if it systematically rejects substantially higher proportions of minority than nonminority applicants. When any selection procedure does so, the employer must demonstrate that the procedure has validity for the inferences the employer wants to make. These criteria for the validity of a selection procedure are similar to those discussed in Chapter 5. In particular, the guidelines detail the acceptable criteria for using a test; we review these criteria in detail in Chapter 20.

These guidelines have been adopted by several federal agencies, including the Civil Service Commission, the Department of Justice, the Department of Labor, and the Department of the Treasury. The Office of Federal Contract Compliance has the direct power to cancel government contracts held by employers who do not comply with these guidelines.

The guidelines became the focus of several political controversies in 1991. For example, when Clarence Thomas was nominated for a position on the U.S. Supreme Court, he was challenged because of his enforcement of the guidelines while he was the head of the EEOC. Also, former president George H. W. Bush had planned to relax these guidelines in the 1991 Civil Rights Bill, but

Focused Example 19-4

QUOTAS IN THE CIVIL RIGHTS ACT OF 1991

The difference between unqualified individualism and quota systems became a central issue in the passage of the 1991 Civil Rights Act. The bill never mentioned the word quota; however, the structure of the bill emphasized selection systems that would support affirmative action and increase the percentage of minority group members in federal jobs. President George H. W. Bush initially refused to support the bill and accused the Democratic Congress of pushing discriminatory quotas. Bush favored an unqualified individualism position and emphasized that many prominent minority group members had achieved success without special programs. During the 1980s, President Ronald Reagan had appointed a director of the EEOC who had, in effect, also supported unqualified individualism over quota systems. During that era, the EEOC failed to act on a substantial number of adverse selection cases. In the fall of 1991, newspapers reported that President Bush would add language to the bill that would halt the use of quota selection systems. However, last-minute lobbying by civil rights groups persuaded the president to leave the federal policies encouraging affirmative action undisturbed. (For more details, see Chapter 20.)

last-minute political pressure successfully encouraged Bush to leave them unchanged (see Focused Example 19-4). The standards have remained in place since then.

The Traditional Defense of Testing

This chapter focuses on a central issue: Are standardized tests as valid for African Americans and other minority groups as they are for whites? All of the types of evidence for validity we discussed in Chapter 5 come into play when the issue of test bias is considered (Cole, 1981). Some psychologists argue that the tests are differentially valid for African Americans and whites. Because **differential validity** is so controversial and emotional, it has forced psychologists to think carefully about many issues in test validation. Differences among ethnic groups on test performance do not necessarily indicate test bias. The question is whether the test has different meanings for different groups. In psychometrics, validity defines the meaning of a test. Some researchers still argue that there are important differences in performance across racial groups. For example, Roth and colleagues summarized studies on differences in job performance. They compared differences between black and white employees on subjective measures such as supervisor ratings versus objective measures based on more formal evaluations. Their analysis suggested that the objective measures showed even larger differences between African American and white employees than the subjective evaluations for measures of work quality, quantity, and absenteeism. Differences between Hispanic and white employees were not as large as those between African American and white employees (Roth, Huffcutt, & Bobko, 2003).

Content-Related Evidence for Validity

Articles have been published in the popular media on cultural fairness in testing. A *Newsweek* article listed several items from the general information portion of the Stanford-Binet scale that people with disadvantaged backgrounds might find problematic. Test constructors and users were accused of being biased because some children never have the opportunity to learn about some of the items; furthermore, members of ethnic groups might answer some items differently but still correctly.

Many researchers also argued that scores on intelligence tests are affected by language skills inculcated as part of a white, middle-class upbringing but foreign to inner-city children (Castenell & Castenell, 1988; Kagan, Moss, & Siegel, 1963; Lesser, Fifer, & Clark, 1965; Mercer, 1971; Pettigrew, 1964; Waldman, Weinberg, & Scarr, 1994). Children who are unfamiliar with the language have no chance of doing well on standardized IQ tests. For example, an American child does not usually know what a *shilling* is, but a British child probably does. Similarly, the American child would not know where one puts the *petrol;* a British child would. Some psychologists argue that asking an inner-city child about *opera* is just as unfair as asking an American child about *petrol.* In each case, the term is not familiar to the child (Hardy, Welcher, Mellits, & Kagan, 1976).

In response to this focus on the language and content of individual test items, Flaugher (1978) concluded that many perceived test bias problems are based on misunderstandings about the way tests are usually interpreted. Many people feel that a fair test asks questions they can answer. By contrast, a biased test does not ask about things a test taker knows. Flaugher argued that the purpose of aptitude and achievement tests is to measure performance on items sampled from a wide range of information. Not particularly concerned about individual items, test developers focus on test performance, making judgments about it based on correlations between the tests and external criteria. Many test critics, though, focus attention on specific items. For example, D. Owen (1985) reported that several intelligent and well-educated people had difficulty with specific items on the SAT and LSAT examinations. He also asserted that some items on standardized tests are familiar only to those with a middle-class background. Test developers are indifferent to the opportunities people have to learn the information on the tests. Again, the meaning they eventually assign to the tests comes from correlations of test scores with other variables.

Furthermore, some evidence suggests that the linguistic bias in standardized tests does not cause the observed differences (Scheuneman, 1987). Quay (1971) administered the Stanford-Binet test to 100 children in an inner-city Head Start program. Half of the children took a version of the test that used African American dialect, while the others took the standard version. The results demonstrated that the advantage produced by having the test in African American dialect translates into less than a 1-point increase in test scores. This finding is consistent with other research findings demonstrating that African American children can comprehend standard English about as well as they can comprehend African American dialect (Clarizio, 1979a; Copple & Succi, 1974). This finding does not hold for white children, who seem to comprehend only the standard dialect.

Systematic studies have failed to demonstrate that biased items in well-known standardized tests account for the differences in scores among ethnic groups (Flaugher, 1978). In one approach, developers ask experts to judge the unfairness of particular items. Without these unfair items, the test should be less biased. Unexpectedly, the many attempts to "purify" tests using this approach have not yielded positive results. In one study, 16% of the items in an elementary reading test were eliminated after experts reviewed them and labeled them as potentially biased toward the majority group. However, when the "purged" version of the test was used, the differences between the majority and the minority school populations were no smaller than they had been originally (Bianchini, 1976).

Another approach to the same problem is to find those classes of items that are most likely to be missed by members of a particular minority group. If a test is biased against that group, then significant differences between minority and nonminority groups should appear in certain categories of items. These studies are particularly important; if they identify certain *types* of items that discriminate among groups, then these types of items can be avoided on future tests. Again, the results have not been encouraging; studies have not clearly identified such categories of items (Wild, McPeek, Koffler, Braun, & Cowell, 1989). The studies show that groups differ for certain items but not whether these are real or chance differences.

Differential item functioning (DIF) analysis. Another approach to the analysis of test bias has been developed by the Educational Testing Service (Elder, McNamara, & Congdon, 2003; Educational Testing Service, 1991). The ETS creates and administers a variety of aptitude tests, including the Graduate Record Examination (GRE), the Scholastic Assessment Test (SAT-I), and the Law School Admissions Test (LSAT). In each of these programs, the performance of white test takers differs significantly from the performances of other racial and ethnic groups on verbal and analysis measures. On quantitative measures, Asian Americans tend to have the highest scores. On the GRE, men and women score equivalently on verbal and analytic measures. Men, however, obtain higher scores on the quantitative measures.

Differential item functioning (DIF) analysis attempts to identify items that are specifically biased against any ethnic, racial, or gender group (Borsboom, Mellenbergh, & van Heerden, 2002). The analysis first equates groups on the basis of overall score. For example, it would find subgroups of test takers who obtain equivalent scores. These might be groups of men and women who obtain scores of approximately 500 on the verbal portion of the GRE. Using these groups, it evaluates differences in performance between men and women on particular items. Items that differ significantly between the groups are thrown out and the entire test is rescored.

Similarly, items that show differences among racial and ethnic groups can be eliminated and the test rescored. In one study, 27 items from the original SAT were eliminated because ethnic groups consistently answered them differently. Then the test was rescored for everyone. Although it seems this procedure should have eliminated the differences between the two groups, it actually had only slight effects because the items that differentiated the groups tended to be the easiest items in the set. When these items were eliminated, the test was harder for everyone (Flaugher & Schrader, 1978).

There is at least some evidence that test items that depict people do not accurately portray the distribution of genders and races in the population. Zores and Williams (1980) reviewed the WAIS, WISC-R, Stanford-Binet, and Slosson Intelligence test items for race and gender characterization and found that white male characterization occurred with disproportionate frequency. Nevertheless, no one has yet established that the frequency of different groups appearing in items affects the outcome of tests. Studies have failed to demonstrate serious bias in item content. Most critics argue that the verbal content of test items is most objectionable because it is unfamiliar to minority groups. However, Scheuneman (1981) reviewed the problem and concluded that the verbal material reflected the life experiences of African Americans more closely than did the nonverbal material. In a related example, studies that manipulate gender bias by creating neutral, male, and female items demonstrate little effect on the performance differences between male and female test takers (McCarty, Noble, & Huntley, 1989).

Other statistical models have been used to evaluate item fairness. In these studies, which use a variety of populations and methods of analysis, little evidence has been produced of bias in test items (Gotkin & Reynolds, 1981). However, different models may identify different items in the same test as biased. In one comparison, Ironson and Sebkovial (1979) applied four different methods to analyze item bias in the National Longitudinal Study test battery. Three differential statistical methods identified many of the same items as biased in evaluating 1691 African American high-school seniors in contrast to 1794 white 12th graders. However, there was little agreement among these item evaluations and the bias items selected by a method proposed by D. R. Green and Draper (1972).

How do biased test items affect the differential validity of a test? In one theoretical example, 25% of the items on a test were presumed to be so biased that minority test takers would be expected to perform at chance level. Despite random performance, there would be only slight and perhaps undetectable differences in validity coefficients for minority and majority group members (Drasgow, 1982). However, this result may be artificial and depend on an unusual use of the phrase *test bias* (Dobko & Kehoe, 1983). Using a relatively general definition of test bias and biased items, they suggested that failure to find differences in validity coefficients is consistent with the belief that the tests are equally valid for members of different ethnic and racial groups.

In spite of the many studies about item bias, its role remains poorly understood. For example, those students who have taken the most tests may be best able to answer questions that are irrelevant to the knowledge base being assessed. Because such test-wise students tend to get these items correct, item analysis may incorrectly identify the irrelevant items as useful. These problems magnify the differences between high-achieving and low-achieving students (Masters, 1988).

In summary, studies have not supported the popular belief that items have different meanings for different groups; however, people must continue to scrutinize the content of tests. On some occasions, careful reviews of tests have turned up questionable items. Many tests are carelessly constructed, and every effort should be taken to purge items that have the potential for being biased.

Criterion-Related Sources of Bias

Each night on the evening news, the weatherperson forecasts the conditions for the next day. If such forecasts are consistently accurate, we come to depend on them. In evaluating the weather report, we make a subjective assessment of validity. Similarly, we evaluate tests by asking whether they forecast future performance accurately. Standardized tests such as the SAT-I have been found to satisfactorily predict performance during the first year of college. These tests clearly do not give us all of the information needed for perfect prediction, but they give enough information to make us pay attention to them.

College administrators who use the test scores face difficult problems. On the average, minority applicants have lower test scores than do nonminority applicants. At the same time, most universities and colleges are attempting to increase their minority enrollments. Because minority applicants are considered as a separate category, we should ask whether the tests have differential predictive power for the two groups of applicants.

As we mentioned in Chapter 5, we assess the criterion-related evidence for validity of a test by the coefficient of correlation between the test and some criterion. The higher the correlation, the more confident we can feel about making predictions. If college grades are the criterion (the variable we are trying to forecast), then the validity of a test such as the SAT-I is represented by the correlation between the SAT-I score and first-year college grades. If students who score well on the SAT-I do well in college and students who score poorly on it get lower grades, then the test might be considered valid for helping administrators decide which college students to admit.

In Chapter 3, we reviewed the interpretation of regression plots as they relate to the validity of psychological tests. Showing plots like the one in Figure 19-4, we explained how to obtain a predicted criterion score from a test score. First, you find the test score on the horizontal axis of the graph and draw a line directly upward until it hits the regression line. Then you draw a line directly left until it comes to the vertical axis. This gives the predicted criterion score. The only difference between Figure 19-4 and Figure 3-8 is that we have added

FIGURE 19-4

A sample regression plot. The slope of the line shows the relationship between a test and a criterion. The steeper the slope of the line, the better the prediction of the criterion score.

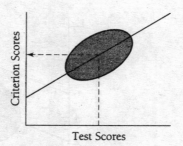

FIGURE 19-5

A single regression slope predicts performance equally well for two groups. However, the means of the groups differ.

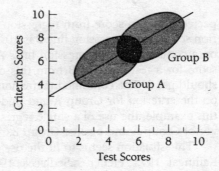

an ellipse, called an **isodensity curve**, around the regression line. This ellipse is used to encircle a specified portion of the cases that constitute a particular group.

   Figure 19-5 shows a regression line that represents two groups equally well. Group A appears to be performing less well than Group B on both the test (predictor) and the criterion scores. You can demonstrate this for yourself by selecting some points from the test scores for Group A and finding the expected scores on the criterion. By repeating this exercise for a few points in Group B, you will find that Group A is expected to do poorly on the criterion because it did more poorly on the test. However, for both Group A and Group B, the relationship between the test score and performance on the criterion is the same. Thus, Figure 19-5 shows there is little evidence for test bias.

   Figure 19-6 represents a different situation—a separate regression line for each group. Because their slopes are the same, the lines are parallel. However, the intercepts, or the points where the regression lines cross the vertical axis, differ. If you pick a particular test score, you get one expected criterion score if you use regression line A and another if you use B. For a test score of 8, the ex-

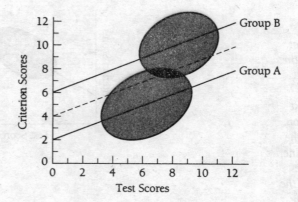

pected criterion score from regression line A is 6, whereas the expected criterion score from regression line B is 10. The broken line in Figure 19-6 is based
on a combination of regression lines A and B. Now try finding the predicted
score for a test score of 8 from this combined (broken) regression line. You
should get 8. The combined regression line actually overpredicts performance
on the criterion for Group A and underpredicts it for Group B. According to
this example, the use of a single regression line produces discrimination in favor of Group A and against Group B.

This situation seems to fit the use of the SAT (Cleary, 1968; Jensen, 1984;
Kallingal, 1971; Pfeifer & Sedlacek, 1971; Reynolds, 1986; Schneider & Briel,
1990; Temp, 1971). Each of these studies showed that the relationship between college performance and SAT scores was best described by two separate
regression equations. The commonly used combined regression equation overpredicts how well minority students will do in college and underpredicts the
performance of majority group students. In other words, it appears that the
SAT used with a single regression line yields biased predictions in favor of minority groups and against majority groups.

The equal slopes of the lines in Figure 19-6 suggest equal predictive evidence for validity. Most standardized intelligence, aptitude, and achievement tests in fact do confirm the relationships shown in the figure (Reschly
& Sabers, 1979; Reynolds, 1980; Reynolds & Nigl, 1981). Thus, there is little evidence that tests such as the SAT-I predict college performance differently for different groups or that IQ tests have different correlations with
achievement tests for African American, white, or Latino and Latina children. This finding has been reported for the original SAT (Temp, 1971),
preschool tests (Reynolds, 1980), and IQ tests such as the WISC-R (Reschly
& Sabers, 1979). Whether separate or combined regression lines are used
depends on different definitions of bias. (We shall return to this issue later
in the chapter. As you will see, the interpretation of tests for assessing different groups can be strongly influenced by personal and moral convic-
tions.) The situation shown in Figure 19-6 is independent of differences in

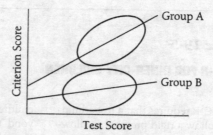

FIGURE 19-7 *Regression lines with different slopes suggest that a test has different meanings for different groups. This is the most clear-cut example of test bias.*

mean scores, which are equal to the differences between the two regression lines.

Some studies have shown that these problems are not specific to U.S. culture. Psychometric aptitude tests are currently used by all Israeli universities. A wide variety of cultural and ethnic groups makes up Israeli society. As in the United States, there is interest in determining whether or not aptitude tests include biases against specific ethnic or cultural groups. In a study of 1538 Israeli college candidates of varying ethnic backgrounds, the predictive test-criterion relationship was the same across groups in spite of mean differences among the groups (Zeidner, 1987).

A third situation outlined by Cleary and co-workers (1975) is shown in Figure 19-7. The two regression lines are not parallel; the coefficient of one group differs from that of the other. In the situation presented in Figure 19-6, each group was best represented by its own regression line. Using a common regression line causes error in predicting the scores for each group. However, the situation depicted in Figure 19-6 is not hopeless, and indeed some psychologists feel that this situation is useful because it may help increase the accuracy of predictions (Cleary, 1968). In Figure 19-7, however, the test is differentially valid for the two groups, meaning that the test has an entirely different meaning for each group. Although empirical studies have rarely turned up such a case, there are some known examples of differential slopes (Mercer, 1979). For example, a test that is designed to predict performance in a mechanical training program would show differential validity if it predicted performance much better for men than for women. Women might tend to score poorly on the test because women have traditionally had less previous experience with mechanical concepts than men. However, when taking the course, many women would easily acquire this information and perform well. Thus, the test would provide relatively little information about how these women would perform in the program, but it would tend to predict how men would perform. An extensive discussion of differential validity is presented by Bartlett and O'Leary (1989). Focused Example 19-5 illustrates the application of both content- and criterion-related evidence of validity.

Focused Example 19-5

SCORING THE WISC-R FOR INNER-CITY CHILDREN

The WISC-R requires that a test administrator follow a rigid protocol in allowing credit for certain types of responses. Over the years, many people have questioned whether these scoring procedures should be so stringent. In particular, they have suggested that some children may be giving an appropriate response for the subculture they are familiar with but it may not be given credit. The Johns Hopkins Child Development Study favors this conclusion (Hardy et al., 1976).

As part of the Johns Hopkins study, 200 children from the inner city of Baltimore received selected questions from the WISC-R. For this study, however, the standard WISC-R scoring instructions were abandoned, and an attempt was made to understand the reasoning behind the children's answers. For example, this WISC-R question was given: "What would you do if you were sent to buy a loaf of bread, and the grocer said he did not have any more?" The WISC-R scoring instructions state that the correct answer is "Go to another store." Among the 200 children in the study, 61 gave an incorrect response. However, when the examiners probed the children about their responses, they discovered that many of the children had given replies that were reasonable considering their circumstances. For instance, the rigid WISC-R scoring procedures do not allow credit for the response "Go home." Yet many of the inner-city children explained that there were no other stores near their homes and they were not allowed to go away from home without permission. Others reported that they used family credit to shop and would need to go home to get money if they had to go to another store. In each of these cases, the researchers suggested that the children had given correct and reasonable responses to the question (Hardy et al., 1976).

Other psychologists, however, emphasize the need for strict scoring procedures if intelligence tests are to be reliable. Standardization implies that all children take the test with the same set of rules. Beyond this objection, Sattler (1979b) carefully reviewed the study and found a variety of methodological problems. In particular, there was no control group of children not from the inner city. Thus, one cannot determine whether children in general would have benefited from a more liberal interpretation of the criteria for a correct answer. Abundant evidence suggests that permitting a tester to exercise judgment about the reasonableness of a response results in higher scores for children from many different walks of life. Under most circumstances, this procedure does not result in greater validity for the test (Sattler, 1988).

Another of Sattler's objections is that the study may have had serious rater bias. Quite likely, the psychologists who tested the inner-city children knew that the study was on test bias, and their interpretations of a reasonable response were thus influenced by a subjective predisposition.

Ultimately, a test is evaluated using criterion-related evidence for validity. How well does it do its job in predicting performance on some criterion of interest? Some researchers have argued that any scoring procedure is valid if it enhances the relationship between a test and a criterion (Barrett & Dupinet, 1991). In the Johns Hopkins study, there was not evidence that the liberal scoring system enhanced the criterion-related validity of the test (Hardy et al., 1976). Thus, different scoring procedures may make the scores of inner-city children higher, but whether the revised procedures would make the tests more meaningful remains to be seen (Sattler, 1979b). Most studies on the validity of IQ tests identify few meaningful differences between the test and outcome criteria for different groups of children (Barrett & Dupinet, 1991; Hall, Huppertz, & Levi, 1977; Hartigan & Wigdor, 1989; Hartlage & Steele, 1977; Henderson, Fay, Lindemann, & Clarkson, 1973; Lamp & Traxler, 1973; Lunemann, 1974; Palmer, 1970; Valencia & Lopez, 1992).

Other Approaches to Testing
Minority Group Members

To many U.S. psychologists, the defense of psychological tests has not been totally satisfactory. Although some consider the defense of the tests strong enough, others emphasize that developers must try to find selection procedures that will end all discriminatory practices and protect the interests of minority group members. Those who do not think that the tests are fair suggest one of two alternatives: Outlaw the use of psychological tests for minority students (Williams, 1974) or develop psychological assessment strategies that suit minority children. Advocates of the first alternative have launched a legal battle to restrict the use of tests. (This battle is discussed in detail in Chapter 20.) In this section, we review various approaches to the second alternative. In particular, we look at three different assessment approaches: the Chitling Test, the Black Intelligence Test of Cultural Homogeneity, and the System of Multicultural Pluralistic Assessment. Though each approach differs, they are all based on one common assumption: Minority children have not had the opportunity to learn how to answer items on tests that reflect traditional, white, middle-class values.

Ignorance Versus Stupidity

In a California trial about the use of testing in public schools, *Larry P. v. Wilson Riles*, the judge made an abrasive but insightful comment. Both sides in the case agreed that minority children perform more poorly than white children on standardized tests. The main issue debated was the meaning of the scores. One side argued that the scores reflect the underlying trait of intelligence. In other words, the tests allegedly measure how smart a child is. Witnesses for the other side suggested that the tests measure only whether the child has learned the appropriate responses needed to perform well on the test. This position claims that the tests do not measure how smart the child is but only whether the child has been exposed to the information on the test. Studies do show that it is possible to teach people to perform better on IQ tests (Perkins & Grotzer, 1997). After hearing the testimony for the different points of view, the judge commented that the issue was really one of ignorance versus stupidity. Although this comment appears insensitive and racist, it deserves reflection. There are two potential explanations for why some children do more poorly on standardized tests than do other children. One explanation is that they are less intelligent—the "stupidity" explanation. The other is that some children do more poorly because they are ignorant of the right responses for a particular test. If ignorance is the explanation, then differences in IQ scores are of less concern because they can be changed. The stupidity explanation is more damning because it implies that the lower test scores obtained by African American students are a product of some deficit that cannot be changed.

Ignorance implies that differences can be abolished. It also implies that IQ test performance is relative to content for whites as well as for minorities. Just as some minority children have not learned how to answer items that might predict success in white, middle-class culture, so many white, middle-class children have not learned how to succeed in the inner city. This proposition is illustrated by the Chitling Test.

The Chitling Test

Many years ago, animal psychologists talked about higher and lower animals. The higher animals were considered to be intelligent because they could do some of the same things humans could do, and the lower animals were considered to be unintelligent because they could not perform like humans. However, in 1969 Hodos and Campbell argued that all animals are equally intelligent for the environments in which they live. We cannot compare the intelligence of a rat with that of a cat, because a rat is adapted to a rat's environment and a cat to a cat's environment.

This insight seems not to have permeated the world of human affairs. Because of poverty and discrimination, minority and nonminority children grow up in different environments. To succeed in each requires different skills and knowledge. A psychological test may consider survival in only one of these environments, usually the white, middle-class one. Thus, using one of these tests for impoverished children is analogous to testing a cat on a task designed to determine how well a rat is adapted to a rat's environment.

Originally named the Dove Counterbalance General Intelligence Test, the Chitling Test was developed to demonstrate that there is a body of information about which the white middle class is ignorant (Dove, 1968). A major aim in developing this was to show that African Americans and whites are just not talking the same language.

Some of the items from the Chitling Test are listed in Table 19-1. If you do not know many of the answers, it may be because you have not been exposed to African American culture of the mid-1960s. People who have grown up in a ghetto in this era should clearly outperform you. On this test, a white, middle-class student would probably score as culturally deprived.

The Chitling Test may be a valid test for inferring how streetwise someone is, but this has not been demonstrated in studies. Currently, no more than face validity has been established for this test. No body of evidence demonstrates that the test successfully predicts performance on any important criterion. If we want to predict which students will do well in college, the Chitling Test will not help us. In fact, standardized tests predict performance for both minority and nonminority students, but the Chitling Test predicts performance for neither group. We must await validity evidence before we can make any generalizations. Dove described his efforts to develop an intelligence test as "half serious." But we have seen that the test does identify an area of content in which the races differ and African Americans outperform whites.

TABLE 19-1 *Selected Items from the Dove Counterbalance General Intelligence Test (the Chitling Test)*

1. A "handkerchief head" is: (a) a cool cat, (b) a porter, (c) an Uncle Tom, (d) a hoddi, (e) a preacher.
2. Which word is most out of place here? (a) splib, (b) blood, (c) gray, (d) spook, (e) African-American.
3. A "gas head" is a person who has a: (a) fast-moving car, (b) stable of "lace," (c) "process," (d) habit of stealing cars, (e) long jail record for arson.
4. "Bo Diddley" is a: (a) game for children, (b) down-home cheap wine, (c) down-home singer, (d) new dance, (e) Moejoe call.
5. If a pimp is uptight with a woman who gets state aid, what does he mean when he talks about "Mother's Day"? (a) second Sunday in May, (b) third Sunday in June, (c) first of every month, (d) none of these, (e) first and fifteenth of every month.
6. If a man is called a "blood," then he is a: (a) fighter, (b) Mexican-American, (c) Negro, (d) hungry hemophile, (e) Redman or Indian.
7. What are the "Dixie Hummingbirds"? (a) part of the KKK, (b) a swamp disease, (c) a modern gospel group, (d) a Mississippi Negro paramilitary group, (e) deacons.
8. T'Bone Walker got famous for playing what? (a) trombone, (b) piano, (c) "T-flute," (d) guitar, (e) "hambone."

From Dove (1968).

The Black Intelligence Test of Cultural Homogeneity

Some psychologists regard most achievement and intelligence tests as instruments of racism. Most racist actions are felt to be illogical and emotional. However, the use of intelligence tests is seen as a subtle and thus more dangerous racist move because the tests are supported by scientific validity studies (Garcia, 1981). R. L. Williams (1974) has labeled this phenomenon *scientific racism*. He views IQ and standardized achievement tests as "nothing but updated versions of the old signs down South that read 'For Whites Only' " (1974, p. 34).

Of particular interest to Williams and his colleagues is the assessment of the ability to survive in the African American community. Indeed, they feel that assessment of survival potential with a survival quotient (SQ) is more important than assessment of IQ, which indicates only the likelihood of succeeding in the white community. As a beginning, Williams developed the Black Intelligence Test of Cultural Homogeneity (BITCH), which asks respondents to define 100 vocabulary words relevant to African American culture. The words came from the *Afro-American Slang Dictionary* and from Williams's personal experience interacting with African Americans. African-American people obtain higher scores than do their white counterparts on the BITCH. When Williams administered the BITCH to 100 16- to 18-year-olds from each group, the average score for African American subjects was 87.07 (out of 100). The mean score for the whites was significantly lower (51.07). Williams argues that traditional IQ and achievement tests are nothing more than culture-specific tests that assess how much white children know about white culture. The BITCH is also a culture-specific test, but one on which African American subjects outperform whites.

Although the BITCH does tell us a lot about the cultural loading in intelligence and achievement tests, it has received mixed reviews. The reliability data reported by Williams show that the BITCH is quite reliable for African American test takers (standard error less than 3 points on the 100-point scale) and acceptably reliable for white test takers (standard error approximately 6). Conventional tests have similar reliabilities for both groups (Oakland & Feigenbaum, 1979). However, little convincing validity data on the BITCH are available. Although the test manual does report some studies, the samples are small and do not represent any clearly defined population (Cronbach, 1978). The difficulty is that one cannot determine whether the BITCH predicts how well a person will survive on the streets or how well he or she will do in school, in life, or in anything else. To support the conclusion that the BITCH is an intelligence test, one must have some evidence. Though the test does assess word association, it gives no information on reasoning abilities.

More studies are needed to determine whether the BITCH does what it is supposed to do. One of the rationales for the test is that it will identify children who have been unfairly assigned to classes for the educable mentally retarded (EMR) on the basis of IQ scores. In one study, Long and Anthony (1974) attempted to determine how many African American EMR children would be reclassified if they were retested with the BITCH. Among a small and limited sample of 30 African American EMR high-school students from Gainesville, Florida, all the students who performed poorly on the WISC also performed below the first percentile on the BITCH. Using the BITCH served to reclassify none of the students. However, this was just one small and nonrepresentative study. In its present state, the BITCH can be a valuable tool for measuring white familiarity with the African American community. When white teachers or administrators are sent to schools that have predominantly African American enrollments, the BITCH can help determine how much they know about the culture. Furthermore, the BITCH can help assess the extent to which an African American is in touch with his or her own community. As Cronbach (1978) has noted, people with good abstract reasoning skills may function poorly if they are unfamiliar with the community in which they live. Similarly, people with poor reasoning skills may get along just fine in a familiar community.

The System of Multicultural Pluralistic Assessment

No assessment technique covered in this book challenges traditional beliefs about testing as much as the System of Multicultural Pluralistic Assessment (SOMPA) (Mercer, 1979). This system has been adopted by several states.

Like many tests, the SOMPA is based on the values of its developers. Mercer asserted that people's beliefs about what is fair and what knowledge exists are related to the social structure. She agreed with Mannheim (1936) that members of the politically dominant group provide the interpretation of events within a society and that they do so from their own perspective. The traditional psychometric literature on IQ tests provides a scientific rationale for the dominant group to keep minority group members in their place by demonstrating that such members do not have the language and knowledge skills to perform well in a white cultural setting. The feedback given to the minority groups is not that they are ignorant about the rules for success in another culture (just as the dominant group would be in a minority culture) but that they are stupid and unlikely to succeed. Mercer emphasized that one must take into consideration that people work from different bases of knowledge.

We cannot give a complete description of the SOMPA here. The system is complex, and many technical issues have been raised about its validity and its applicability (Brown, 1979a, 1979b; Clarizio, 1979a, 1979b; Goodman, 1977, 1979; Mercer, 1979; Oakland, 1979; Oakland & Parmelee, 1985; Taylor, Sternberg, & Partenio, 1986).

One important philosophical assumption underlies the development of the SOMPA—that all cultural groups have the same average potential. Any differences among cultural groups are assumed to be caused by differences in access to cultural experiences. Those who do not perform well on the tests are not well informed about the criteria for success usually set forth by the dominant group. Within groups that have had the same cultural experiences, however, not all individuals are expected to be the same, and assessment of these differences is a better measure of ability than is assessment of differences among cultural groups.

Mercer (1972) was concerned about the consequences of labeling a child mentally retarded. She has convincingly argued that many children are incorrectly identified as retarded and that they suffer severely as a result. In particular, she was distressed that classes for EMR students have disproportionate numbers of minority children. Mercer maintained that some minority students score low on the traditional tests because they are ignorant about the ways of the dominant culture, and they are not in any way mentally retarded. Because misclassification may also stem from medical problems, a fair system of evaluation must include medical assessment. It must also include the assessment of children relative to other children who have had similar life experiences. The basic point of divergence between the SOMPA and earlier approaches to assessment is that the SOMPA attempts to integrate three different approaches to assessment: medical, social, and pluralistic.

One of the most consistent findings in the field of public health is that members of low-income groups have more health problems than those who are economically better off. The medical component of the SOMPA system asks, "Is the child an intact organism?" (Mercer, 1979, p. 92). The rationale for this portion is that medical problems can interfere with a child's performance on mental measures and in school.

The social-system component attempts to determine whether a child is functioning at a level that would be expected by social norms. For example, does the child do what is expected by family members, peer groups, and the community? Mercer felt that test users and developers typically adopt only a social-system orientation. For example, if a test predicts who will do well in school, it forecasts behavior expected by the dominant social system. Mercer has emphasized that the social-system approach is narrow because only the dominant group in society defines the criteria for success (Reschly, 1981).

The pluralistic component of the SOMPA recognizes that different subcultures are associated with different life experiences. Only within these subgroups do individuals have common experiences. Thus, tests should assess individuals against others in the same subculture. One must recognize the distinction between the criteria for defining deviance in the pluralistic model and those in the social-system model. The latter uses the norms of society as the criteria, whereas the former uses the norms within a particular group.

The SOMPA attempts to assess children relative to each of these models. The medical portion of the SOMPA includes physical measures such as tests of vision, hearing, and motor functioning. The social-system portion resembles most assessment procedures in that the entire WISC-R is given and evaluated according to the regular criteria. Finally, the pluralistic portion evaluates WISC-R scores against those for groups that have similar social and cultural backgrounds. In other words, the WISC-R scores are adjusted for socioeconomic background. These adjusted scores are known as **estimated learning potentials (ELPs).** An example of a SOMPA profile is shown in Figure 19-8.

The main dispute between Mercer and her many critics centered on the validity of the SOMPA. Mercer (1979) pointed out that validity applies not to tests themselves but to inferences made on the basis of test scores. She insisted that test users cannot validate ELPs in the same way that they can validate other test scores. In other words, validating a test by predicting who will do well in school is appropriate only for the social-system model. The appropriate validity criterion for ELPs should be the percentage of variance in WISC-R scores that is accounted for by sociocultural variables. Even so, many SOMPA critics (Brown, 1979a; Clarizio, 1979b; Goodman, 1979; Oakland, 1979) felt that one should always validate a test by demonstrating that it predicts performance. The correlation between ELPs and school achievement is approximately .40, whereas the correlation between the WISC-R and school achievement is near .60 (Oakland, 1979). Thus, ELPs are a poorer predictor of school success than are WISC-R scores. Mercer refuted these critics by arguing that the test is not designed to identify which children will do well in school but to determine which children are mentally retarded. One can do this only by comparing children with others who have had the same life experiences.

The potential effects of Mercer's work included a quota system for EMR classes and making the proportions of ethnic groups in EMR classes more representative. By identifying far fewer minority children as EMR students, it could save tax dollars. Yet researchers still do not know whether children no longer considered EMR students will benefit. Mercer's (1972) work suggested that a big part of the battle is just getting more children labeled as normal. Her critics retaliated by claiming that the effects of labeling are weak and inconsequential. They argued that no matter what these children are called, they will need some special help in school. The critics may have won the argument. Over the years since its introduction, the use of the SOMPA has decreased sig-

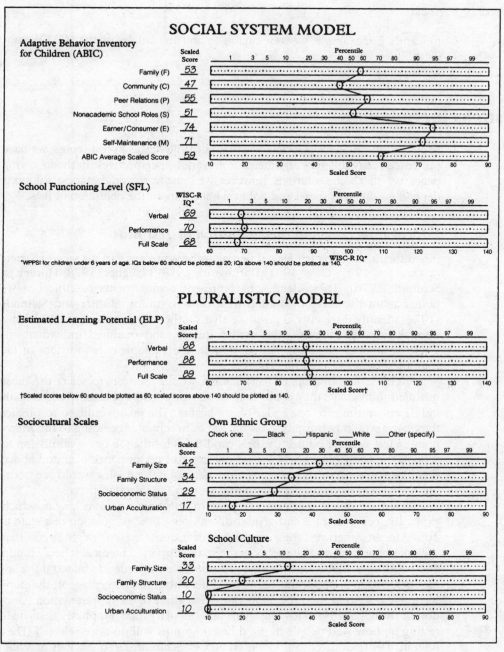

FIGURE 19-8 *Sample SOMPA profile.*

(From the System of Multicultural Pluralistic Assessment by June Lewis and Jane Mercer. Copyright © 1978 by The Psychological Corporation. Reproduced by permission of the authors. All rights reserved.)

nificantly. For example, we were unable to find any articles on the SOMPA published after 1989.

Suggestions for Solutions

Focusing on problems associated with ethnic differences in test scores, we have presented many different arguments from various perspectives. In the following pages, we offer some solutions; however, we must warn you that these solutions depend on different social and political beliefs about the definition of bias.

Ethical Concerns and the Definition of Test Bias

It is difficult to define *test bias;* different authors present various views (Barrett & Dupinet, 1991; Cole, 1981; Darlington, 1978; Flaugher, 1978; Hunter & Schmidt, 1976). These definitions represent commitments to ethical viewpoints about the way one should treat certain groups. Hunter and Schmidt (1976) identify three ethical positions that set the tone for much of the debate: unqualified individualism, the use of quotas, and qualified individualism. These positions focus on the use of tests to select people either for jobs or for training programs (including college).

Supporters of *unqualified individualism* would use tests to select the most qualified individuals they could find. In this case, users of tests would remain indifferent to the race or gender of applicants. The goal would be to predict those who would perform best on the job or in school. According to this viewpoint, a test is fair if it finds the best candidates for the job or for admission to school. If race or gender was a valid predictor of performance over and above the information in the test, then the unqualified individualist would see nothing wrong with considering this information in the selection process.

In a quite different ethical approach to selection, one uses *quotas,* which explicitly recognize race and gender differences. If the population of a state is 20% African American, then supporters of a quota system might argue that 20% of the new medical students in the state-supported medical school should also be African American. Selection procedures are regarded as biased if the actual percentage of applicants admitted differs from the percentage in the population; each group should demonstrate a fair share of the representation (Gordon & Terrell, 1981). This fair-share process places less emphasis than does testing on how well people in the different groups will do once selected (Darlington, 1971; Gottfredson, 1994; Hunter & Schmidt, 1976; Sackett & Wilk, 1994; Thorndike, 1971).

The final moral position considered by Hunter and Schmidt might be viewed as a compromise between unqualified individualism and a quota system. Like unqualified individualism, *qualified individualism* embraces the notion that one should select the best-qualified people. But unqualified individualists also take information about race, gender, and religion into consideration if it helps to predict performance on the criterion—that is, if not to do so results in underprediction of performance for one group and overprediction for another. Qualified individualists, however, recognize that although failing to include group characteristics (race, gender, and religion) may lead to differential accuracy in prediction, this differential prediction may counteract known effects of discrimination. It may, for example, lead to underprediction of performance for the majority group and overprediction for the minority group. The qualified individualist may choose not to include information about personal characteristics in selection because ignoring this information may serve the interests of minority group members. Many people have argued that increased minority hiring will result in lower average job performance because some applicants with lower test scores will be hired. However, systematic study of this issue has not always supported these arguments. For example, increased minority hiring in some industries has resulted in only a small loss in job performance. There may be circumstances in which average job performance drops with the overselection of low-scoring job applicants, but the data from these studies typically are complex (Silva & Jacobs, 1993).

One can relate each of these ethical positions to a particular statistical definition of test bias. Table 19-2 shows several different models of test bias, based on different definitions of fairness. All these models are based on regression lines. These models also apply to tests used for selection purposes, such as job placement and college, or for advanced degree programs.

The regression model described in this table (see also Cleary, 1968) represents unqualified individualism. The result of this approach is that a large number of majority group members may be selected. This approach maintains that an employer or a school should be absolutely color- and gender-blind. The reason for considering ethnicity or gender is to improve the prediction of future performance. This approach has been favored by business because it ensures the highest employee productivity.

At the other extreme is the quota system. To achieve fair-share representation, separate selection procedures are developed. One procedure, for example, is used to select the best available African American applicants, and another to select the best available non–African American applicants. If a community has 42% African American residents, then the first procedure would be used to select 42% of the employees, the other procedure to select the other 58%.

The quota system may lead to greater rates of failure among some groups. Suppose that a test devised to select telephone operators did indeed predict who would succeed on the job, but it selected 70% women and 30% men. The quota system would encourage the use of separate cutoff scores so that the proportion of men selected would approach 50%. But because the women scored higher on the average, they would perform better on the job, resulting in a higher rate of failure among the men. Thus, although quota systems often increase the selection of underrepresented groups, they also make it likely that the underrepresented groups will experience failure.

Table 19-2 shows two other models (Cole, 1973; Darlington, 1971; Thorndike, 1971), which represent compromises between the quota and the

TABLE 19-2   *Different Models of Test Fairness*

Model	Reference	Use of regression	Rationale	Effect on minority selection	Effect on average criterion performance
Regression	Cleary (1968)	Separate regression lines are used for different groups. Those with predicted criterion scores are selected.	This is fair because those with the highest estimated level of success are selected.	Few minority group members selected	Good performance on criteria
Constant ratio	Thorndike (1971)	Points equal to approximately half of the average difference between the groups are added to the test scores of the group with the lower score. Then a single regression line is used, and those with the highest predicted scores are selected.	This is fair because it best reflects the potential of the lower-scoring group.	Some increase in the number of minority group members selected	Somewhat lower
Cole/ Darlington	Cole (1973), Darlington (1971, 1978)	Separate regression equations are used for each group, and points are added to the scores of those from the lower group to ensure that those with the same criterion score have the same predictor score.	This is fair because it selects more potentially successful people from the lower group.	Larger increase in the number of minority group members selected	Lower
Quota	Dunnette and Borman (1979)	The proportion of people to be selected from each group is predetermined. Separate regression equations are used to select those from each group who are expected to perform highest on the criterion.	This is fair because members of different subgroups are selected based on their proportions in the community.	Best representation of minority groups	About the same as for the Cole/ Darlington model

Based on Dunnette & Borman (1979).

unqualified individualism points of view. Each of these cases reflects an attempt to select the most qualified people, yet there is some adjustment for minority-group members. When people from two different groups have the same test score, these procedures give a slight edge to those from the lower group and put those from the higher group at a slight disadvantage.

Although these approaches have been attacked for faulty logic (Hunter & Schmidt, 1976, 1978), plausible defenses have been offered. These procedures increase the number of people selected from underrepresented groups. However, these procedures also reduce the average performance score on the criterion. We cannot tell you which of these approaches is right and which wrong. That decision depends on your own values and judgment about what is fair.

Despite the many problems and controversies surrounding psychological testing, surveys show that psychologists and educational specialists generally have positive attitudes about intelligence and aptitude tests. In one survey, 1020 experts agreed that there were some sociocultural biases in the tests (Snyderman & Rothman, 1987). However, these experts also generally agreed that the tests were valid for predictive purposes. Their main concerns concerned the interpretation and application of test results by elementary and secondary schools. In general, industrial and organizational psychologists tend to feel that ability testing does not discriminate by race. In one study of 703 members of the Society of Industrial and Organizational Psychology, there appeared to be consensus that cognitive ability tests are valid and fair. However, the I/O psychologists also felt that tests provide an incomplete picture of human abilities and that job selection should consider tests as only one component.

Perhaps the most controversial defense of testing was presented in a 1994 book entitled *The Bell Curve*. This book is reviewed in Focused Example 19-6.

Thinking Differently: Finding New Interpretations of Data

Clearly, the observed differences between minority and nonminority groups on standardized tests pose a problem. Sometimes a problem stimulates us to think differently; in the words of the famous entrepreneur Henry Kaiser, "A problem is an opportunity in work clothes." The opportunity for test developers and users is to see test results in new ways.

For example, instead of indicating genetic variations or social handicaps, differences in test scores may reflect patterns of problem solving that characterize different subcultures. Knowing how groups differ in their approaches to problem solving can be helpful for two reasons. First, it can teach us important things about the relationship between socialization and problem-solving approaches. This information can guide the development of pluralistic educational programs (Castaneda & Ramirez, 1974). Second, knowing more about the ways different groups approach problems can lead to the development of improved predictors of success for minority groups (Goldman, 1973; Sternberg, 1991).

Along these lines, R. D. Goldman (1973) has proposed the *differential process theory*, which maintains that different strategies may lead to effective solutions for many types of tasks. According to this theory, strategies—ways people go about solving problems—mediate abilities and performance (Frederiksen, 1969; Sternberg, 1985).

For example, African American college students tend to score higher on the verbal subtest of the SAT-I on average than they do on the quantitative subtest. White students on average score about the same on both subtests. As the result of their socialization, African American students possibly structure the task of getting through school differently; they develop their verbal skills rather than their quantitative abilities. This result may also reflect differences in the

Focused Example 19-6

THE BELL CURVE

In 1994 Richard Herrnstein, a noted Harvard psychologist, and Charles Murray, a professional writer, published a controversial book entitled *The Bell Curve: Intelligence and Class Structure in American Life*. The controversial book provoked an immediate reaction from the mass media and serious scholars alike. In contrast to the many testing professionals who question the value of intelligence tests, Herrnstein and Murray argued that, indeed, intelligence tests are the primary correlates of success in American life. Consistent with Spearman, they argued that the g factor is essential to a variety of different skills and abilities.

The Bell Curve used data from the National Longitudinal Study of Youth, which had begun in 1979. The study has involved a representative sample of 12,686 youths who were between 14 and 21 years old in 1979 and who have been restudied each year. The book used data collected through 1990. For the analysis, testers used the Armed Services Vocational Aptitude Battery (ASVAB). Various analyses showed that IQ scores are related to a wide variety of indexes of success in life ranging from completion of a college degree through the attainment of substantial income. Some researchers argued that IQ tests predict who will fill the important leadership roles in society. According to the book, those with low IQs are likely to become involved in crime and delinquency, to end up on welfare, and to have illegitimate children.

Herrnstein and Murray were unusually optimistic about the relationship between job performance and IQ. From their data, they suggested that the correlation is .53 between IQ and job-performance rating, .22 between education and job performance, and .11 between college grades and performance. They even argued that the Supreme Court case of *Griggs v. Duke Power Company* (see Chapter 20), which restricted the use of IQ testing for job selection, has cost U.S. companies billions of dollars because it prevented the most-qualified individuals from being selected for various jobs. They attributed most social problems—such as school dropout rates, unemployment, and work-related injury and crime—to low intelligence. Further-

more, they suggested that the differences in economic attainment for various ethnic groups probably reflect differences in IQ. They concluded by arguing that the United States must face up to differences in intelligence. Finally, they suggested that we must recognize that not all people are created equal and that traditional approaches to these problems will simply not work.

Upon publication, *The Bell Curve* was robustly attacked for a variety of reasons. First, many complained about its arrogant writing style. For example, Herrnstein and Murray described themselves as classicists who favor the traditional view of g intelligence. They discussed alternative views of intelligence proposed by "revisionists" and "radicals." They then wrote off these theories as approaches that scholars do not take seriously, even though scholars do seriously consider them. Critics of the book's statistical methods focused on the simplified analyses. For example, many of the correlations between IQ and outcome depend highly on those in the lowest decimal of intelligence. Indeed, it may be that those with low IQs under 80 may have difficulty in various aspects of their lives. However, removing the bottom decile from the analyses would significantly reduce the relationship between IQ and several of the outcome variables.

Others have attacked *The Bell Curve* for not using measures of intelligence but measures of developed ability as captured by the ASVAB. Leman (1995) claimed that people from higher social classes would be expected to do better on the ASVAB because the test better reflects their culture. Finally, there is concern that comparisons on the basis of race have little meaning because race is not clearly defined. Gould (1996) argued persuasively that it is inappropriate to compare racial groups in countries such as the United States. In the biological sciences, races are considered to be biological subspecies defined by well-identified genetic markers. Today, there are few individuals who represent biologically distinct subgroups. To some extent, all human races are intermingled; we are all genetically linked. We tend to use racial terms in a social rather than a biological sense (Suzuki & Valencia, 1997).

opportunity to learn proper quantitative skills. In any case, African American students tend to choose college majors that emphasize their verbal abilities. It may thus be appropriate to build specific tests that predict how well these students will do in the majors they choose. These tests could deemphasize quantitative skills if shown to be unrelated to success for these particular majors. In other words, the test would be validated for the specific majors chosen by African American students.

A variety of studies have shown differences in information processing for different groups. For example, Native American and Hispanic groups tend to do better on visual-reasoning than verbal-reasoning subtasks (Suzuki & Valencia, 1997). In one quantitative review of the literature, Native American groups obtained average performance IQ scores of 100 while their average scores on verbal IQ tests were just 83 (Vraniak, 1997). One study used high-school grade point average to predict performance for 22,105 freshman in the University of California system. For white students, GPA and SAT-V scores were the best predictors of freshman success. SAT-M added little, once GPA and SAT-V were in the prediction equation. However, for Asian American students, GPA and SAT-M predicted success, with SAT-V adding minimal information (Sue, 1999).

In a related argument, H. Gardner (1993; Gardner, Krechevsky, Sternberg, & Okagaki, 1994) suggested seven distinct types of intelligence: linguistic, musical, logical-mathematical, spatial, bodily-kinesthetic, and two different forms of personal intelligence. Gardner sees no reason to call logical thinking "intelligence" and musical ability a "talent." Instead, he believes that these abilities are equal. Groups that perform best on tests of general intelligence do not necessarily excel in all of Gardner's talent domains.

Developing Different Criteria

Criterion-related evidence for validity is the correlation between the test and the criterion. But what are the criteria used to validate the tests for assessing the potential of children? Most of these tests are simply valid predictors of how well children will do on other standardized tests. In other words, most standardized tests are evaluated against other standardized tests. However, the criterion simply may be the test dressed in different clothes. For example, one may evaluate an intelligence test to determine how well it predicts performance on a standardized achievement test. This means that the intelligence test really measures achievement, not native ability. Differences in scores on this test between minority and nonminority groups are therefore the result of the opportunity to learn rather than the ability to learn. This is recognized by the Educational Testing Service, which requests special care in interpreting SAT-I and GRE scores for students who have had "an educational and cultural experience somewhat different from that of the traditional majority" (*GRE Guide*, 2003). These concerns forced the Educational Testing Service to change their tests. Beginning in 2005, the test will focus more on writing skills and less on analogies and traditional work problems.

If we do not accept standardized tests as a validity criterion for other tests, then how can we determine the meaning of the tests? A considerable debate concerns whether classroom grades should serve as this criterion. Supporters of the use of classroom grades claim that these grades are the only independent measure of how well the child is doing. It is no surprise, they maintain, that a correlation exists between IQ tests and scores on standardized achievement tests because both measure similar content. However, they argue that because they do not predict classroom grades for minority children, IQ tests are not valid for such youngsters. The support for this position comes from studies like one by R. D. Goldman and Hartig (1976). This study found scores on the WISC to be unrelated to teacher ratings of classroom performance for minority children. For the nonminority children, it found a significant relationship between IQ and teacher ratings. If the criterion becomes classroom grades rather than another standardized test, the IQ test appears valid for nonminority but not for minority children.

Supporters of the use of the tests give three reasons not to use grades as the criterion. First, teacher-assigned grades are unstandardized and open to subjective bias (Sattler, 1979a). For example, teachers sometimes reward effort more than ability (Weiner, 1994). Second, few available studies have used grades as the criterion. Third, the most frequently cited study (Goldman & Hartig, 1976) is open to other explanations. In this study, the teachers rated the classroom performance of nearly all of the minority children as poor. These low ratings resulted in little variance on the criterion measure. As we saw in Chapter 3, any variable for which there is no variability cannot correlate well with other variables.

The problem with criterion measures becomes even more apparent in relation to measures used with adults. For example, the Medical College Admissions Test (MCAT) predicts success in medical school. Yet, as Focused Example 19-7 demonstrates, it does not predict who will be a successful doctor. Similarly, the Law School Admission Test (LSAT) predicts performance in law school, yet there is little evidence that it predicts who will be a good attorney. The professional school admission tests may thus be eliminating people who are potentially better doctors and lawyers than those who are admitted. Imagine, for example, that an Anglo and a Latina doctor, trained equally well in the science of medical care, both practice in a public hospital in a Latino neighborhood. The Latina doctor will more likely be effective because she understands the culture and the language of the patients and thus can better understand specific complaints and symptoms. The Anglo doctor may do a poorer job at diagnosing the problems. The MCAT would have done its job poorly by focusing on the short-term criterion of medical school grades. More work is needed to develop measures that are good predictors of the long-range goal of clinical success (Altmaier, Smith, O'Halloran, & Franken, 1992). See Focused Example 19-7 for more on the prediction of medical school success.

A related problem is that many tests are not normed for different cultural groups. For example, cross-cultural norms are not available for most neuropsychological tests (Nell, 2000).

Focused Example 19-7

EVALUATING THE MEDICAL COLLEGE ADMISSIONS TEST

The ultimate goal in medical practice is the successful diagnosis and treatment of patients. Thus, the selection of medical students should proceed with this objective in mind. However, the MCAT is designed to predict only how well students will do in medical school. Although studies show that the MCAT adequately predicts medical school grades and performance on some other tests (Basco, Way, Gilbert, & Hudson, 2002), how meaningful are such grades?

Much debate has focused on the importance of medical school grades. For example, one study that considered measures of physician success in practice found that grades were not associated with measures of real-life performance (Loughmiller, Ellison, Tavlor, & Price, 1970). In another study of 217 physicians practicing in Utah, 76 measures of doctor performance were taken. Among more than 1000 correlations between grades and performance on these measures, 97% were nearly 0. On the basis of these results, the criteria for admission to medical school were seriously questioned (Taylor, Price, Richards, & Jacobsen, 1965). Although tests may predict medical school grades, it is unclear whether grades or the tests offer much information about who will be a successful doctor.

After students graduate from medical school, they must enter medical residency programs to obtain training in their specialty areas. To select the best residents, specialty training programs have typically used test scores and personal interviews. These interviews and tests determine where a physician will get training and which physicians will gain entry into the most prestigious programs. Studies have suggested that programs increasingly rely on academic test performance as selection criteria. In addition, most residency programs require interviews. During the interview process, prospective specialists are evaluated on their personality charac-

teristics, professional maturity, enthusiasm and energy, and rapport. Detailed studies have evaluated the relationship between these cognitive (test performance) and noncognitive (interview) predictors of success in the residency program. The studies have produced consistent results: Traditional tests and interviews are terrible predictors of success as a physician (Altmaier, McGuinnes, Wood, Ross, Bartley, & Smith, 1990; Altmaier et al., 1992; Wood, Smith, Altmaier, Tarico, & Franken, 1990). The MCAT also includes a writing sample. However, research has not been able to show that the writing sample predicts performance on the National Medical Licensing Board Exam (Gilbert, Basco, Blue, & O'Sullivan, 2002).

Why are these predictors inadequate? One explanation is that the practice of medicine is extremely complicated. Physicians need more than knowledge that can be tested. The tests often evaluate the physicians' understanding of the basic biological constructs but rarely tap into their motivation, ability to interact with people, or judgment. Although interviews are designed to capture some of these characteristics, personal interviews are notoriously poor at identifying the appropriate information (see Chapter 9). To target some of these abilities, newer approaches use techniques of job analysis and analysis of specific skills that are appropriate to the practice of medicine. Studies have identified specific behavioral skills related to lack of confidence, conscientiousness, interpersonal skills, curiosity, and a variety of other behaviors. Each of these was linked to specific behavioral incidents that could be self-reported. The early analysis has suggested that these techniques successfully predict performance in the residency programs as evaluated by senior physicians and patients (Wood et al., 1990). In the future, we expect more use of behavioral-based measures for the selection of medical residents.

Changing the Social Environment

It is not hard to determine that majority and minority children grow up in different social environments. You can learn this by reading any sociology textbook or by getting in your car and driving around awhile. Given this disparity in environment, it is not surprising that tests favor the majority. Many critics of tests, though, seem to hold the tests responsible for inequality of opportunity (Flaugher, 1978).

Another view claims that test scores accurately reflect the effects of social and economic inequality (Green, 1978). We know, for instance, that family income is one of the best predictors of performance on standardized tests. Figure 19-9 shows the relationship between family income and performance on the SAT-Verbal and Math components. The graph summarizes performance for all students who completed the test in 1999.

To understand these arguments, one must consider the purpose of testing. In educational settings, tests such as the SAT-I and the GRE or even IQ tests are usually considered to be tests of aptitude: They measure some inborn trait that is unlikely to change with environment. But most experts now agree that tests measure not just inborn potential but also the effects of cumulative experience. The University of California decided in 2001 to drop the aptitude focused SAT-I in favor of the SAT-2, which is more clearly an achievement test. The impact of this decision is discussed in Focused Example 19-8. With proper nurturing, a student can change his or her score. Verbal and numerical abilities are acquired through experience. Thus, low test scores should not be viewed as insurmountable problems; they can improve.

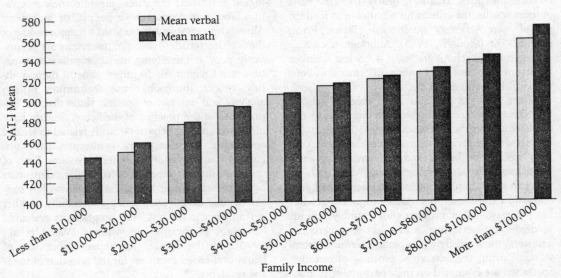

FIGURE 19-9   *Relation between family income and performance on SAT-Verbal and SAT-Math for college-bound seniors in 1999.*
(Data from College Board, 1999.)

Focused Example 19-8

CONSEQUENCES OF THE UNIVERSITY OF CALIFORNIA DECISION TO DROP THE SAT-I

 In Chapter 5 (Focused Example 5-4, page 142), we discussed the University of California's decision to reject the SAT-I. The University of California decision underscores many of the issues that challenge testing today. For example, the decision raised the important distinction between aptitude and achievement tests. When Carl Brigham from Princeton University stimulated the earliest work on the SAT, his intention was to develop an IQ-like test. Brigham and other early leaders eventually turned against the idea that aptitude tests were precise enough to select college students. Later in his life, Alfred Binet rejected the idea that IQ tests could be used to provide reliable distinctions between individuals at the higher end of the IQ continuum. The SAT-I has always been considered an aptitude test, whereas the SAT-II was designed as an achievement test. As we reported in Chapter 5, a large study of 78,000 University of California freshmen demonstrated that the SAT-II was a better predictor of college grades than the SAT-I. In addition, statistically controlling for socioeconomic background did not affect the predicted value of the SAT-II but had a significant effect on the predictive value of the SAT-I. Once the SAT-II and high-school grades are in a statistical equation, adding the SAT-I contributes essentially no new information. Thus, the achievement-oriented SAT-II was less influenced by social background than the aptitude-focused SAT-I.

The decision by the University of California to drop the SAT-I was interpreted by many people as a rejection of college admissions testing. In fact, the University of California will retain its policy of requiring the SAT-II. Furthermore, the decision stimulated the College Board to rethink the content of the SAT-I. In particular, the University of California decision emphasized the need for tests to include both a writing sample and higher levels of mathematics.

It took little time for the decision to have a significant impact. The University of California decision was announced in 2001. One year later, the College Board acknowledged that it would create a new SAT that included writing samples and higher-level mathematics. The new test will be used nationally in 2006. Plans to change the SAT may result in changes in high-school curricula because high schools recognize the need to prepare students for the SAT. In fact, by 2004, it was becoming apparent that high schools were requiring students to write more and were encouraging students to continue with their mathematics education. Framers of the test can help improve curricula and the quality of public education (Atkinson, 2004).

Much in this chapter is consistent with the view that tests do point out differences between minority and nonminority students. Furthermore, systematic attempts to show that the tests have created this problem have not been convincing. Many minority students do well on the tests, which accurately predict that these students will do well on the criterion. An African American student and a white student who both achieve a score of 1100 on the SAT-I are predicted to do equally well in college, and studies show that indeed they do perform at about the same level. However, the test is a relatively weak predictor for both white and African American studies.

There is little question that wealthy students have greater access to programs that might enhance their test scores. Although the value of special test preparation courses has been debated (see Focused Example 19-9), it appears

Focused Example 19-9

COACHING AND BIAS IN APTITUDE TESTS

 One criticism of standardized achievement tests is that coaching may improve performance. If coaching works, it could have adverse impact on low-income test takers who are unable to afford expensive test-preparation courses. So widespread is this belief that SAT, LSAT, and GRE preparatory schools have become a big business. If coaching does improve performance on these tests, then they are not really aptitude tests but achievement tests. Those who believe that coaching works have accused the ETS of bias and fraud because its tests do not measure pure aptitude.

One major problem with studies on coaching is that few of them include a proper control group. Thus, when students improve after coaching classes, it is not clear whether this was due to the coaching, their commitment to improve performance (as evidenced by enrollment in the course), or some other personality characteristic associated with taking a coaching course. The few studies with proper control groups show a small but significant gain in performance as a function of obtaining coaching, but is the small gain worth the effort?

Systematic reviews of the coaching literature suggest that the more time spent in preparation for the test, the greater the increase in score. Controlled studies in Israel suggest that test preparation increases performance by approximately one-quarter of one standard deviation. For a test such as the SAT, preparation classes would have an expected benefit of approximately 25 points (Allalouf & Ben-Shakhar, 1998). However, the relationship is non-

linear. Small increases in preparation time result in some improvement in test performance, but as preparation time increases, lesser returns in performance are realized. According to Messick and Jungeblut (1981, p. 191), "the student contact time required to achieve average score increases much greater than 20 to 30 points (on a 200- to 800-point scale) for both the SAT-V and the SAT-M rapidly approaches that of full-time schooling." The College Board Web page considers the question, "Do commercial coaching courses make a big difference in admission decisions?" The answer is simple: "No" (see http://www.collegeboard.org). Thus, according to ETS, expensive coaching classes do not create an advantage for the rich, because they do not work.

Despite these studies, ETS critics still maintain that coaching is useful. Owen (1985), for example, suggested that coaching schools can improve scores by teaching skills in multiple-choice test taking. He cited one test-preparation course that has achieved success by teaching students to analyze answer choices. In some cases, students can improve their scores without even studying alternative choices and without referring to the questions. Rebuffing the ETS claim that coaching makes little difference, Owen pointed out that ETS itself sells (at a handsome price) its own version of coaching booklets. Web pages for the Kaplan and the Princeton Review Course "guarantee" significant benefits from their coaching services. Besides the cost, the courses do no harm, and it seems likely that they offer some advantage to those who can afford them.

that coaching does provide some benefit. Blaming the tests for observed differences between groups may be a convenient way to avoid a much larger problem. No one has suggested that the tuberculin test is unfair because it demonstrates that poor people have the disease more often than wealthy people. Public health officials have correctly concluded that some people live in environments that predispose them to the disease. Getting rid of scales that identify underweight children will not cure malnutrition (Flaugher, 1978). Al-

TABLE 19-3   *For and Against the Use of Tests*

Against	For
The Stanford-Binet was standardized on only 1000 children and 400 adults. None of these people were African American (Guthrie, 1976).	Although not standardized on minority group members, tests appear to have the same validity for minority students as they do for majority students. Therefore, neglecting to include minorities in the original validation studies was not relevant (Barrett & Dupinet, 1991; Herrnstein & Murray, 1994).
The use of intelligence tests can have a damaging social impact. For example, the IQ scores of ethnic groups were used to limit immigration of certain groups into the United States during the early years of the 20th century (Kamin, 1974).	Examination of the *Congressional Record* covering the debates about the 1924 Immigration Act failed to uncover discussion of intelligence test data or claims that the mean IQ of Americans would decline if the immigration of certain groups was allowed (DuBois, 1972).
If a teacher just thinks some children have higher IQs, the actual test scores of those children will improve (Rosenthal & Jacobson, 1968).	Studies that document the effects of self-fulfilling prophecies and teacher expectations overinterpreted their original data, contained some results that are statistically impossible, and cannot be depended on (Elashoff & Snow, 1971; Snow, 1969; Thorndike, 1968).
Minority children can only be damaged by the continued use of psychological tests.	Psychological tests can be used to identify the most capable members of each group. Without the tests, people will be selected on the basis of personal judgment, which might be more racist than the tests (Ones, Chockalingam, & Schmidt, 1995).
The validity of IQ tests was documented using other standardized tests as the criterion rather than measures of classroom performance (Mercer, 1988).	The objective tests are better validity criteria than classroom performance, which is more subjective. Teachers may grade on the basis of effort rather than ability (Sattler, 2002).
Most test administrators are white; the scores of African American children would improve if they were tested by African American examiners (Forrester & Klaus, 1964; Pasamanick & Knobloch, 1955).	Some studies do indeed show that the race of the examiner is an important factor. However, most studies do not. Among 28 different studies on the effects of the examiner's race, 24 fail to show that the race of the examiner significantly affects scores (Sattler, 2002).

though measuring intelligence may not be the same as testing for tuberculosis or measuring weight, the analogy may be worth considering.

  If unequal access to adequate education and to stimulating experiences results in differences in test scores, it would be more useful to change the social environment than to bicker continuously about the tests. The tests may merely be the bearers of bad news. By documenting the problem's severity, the tests may be telling us that overcoming this problem will be expensive, difficult, and time-consuming. Blaming the tests for a problem that they did not cause seems to be shortsighted and nonproductive (Elliot, 1988).

SUMMARY

In this chapter, we examined two sides of the issue of test bias. Table 19-3 offers a summary of some of the arguments for and against the use of tests. As the table shows, there are strong differences of opinion about the value of intelligence and aptitude tests for minority group members. As a result of the challenge to traditional tests, new approaches such as the Chitling Test, the BITCH, and the SOMPA have been developed. Among these, the SOMPA is clearly the most sophisticated. All of these approaches are based on the assumption that social groups do not differ in their average potential. These approaches have been challenged because they do not have the same sort of validity evidence that traditional tests have.

Part of the debate about test bias results from different moral views about what is fair. Some have argued that a testing and selection program is fair if it selects the best-suited people, regardless of their social group. This approach is called *unqualified individualism.* It may lead to overrepresentation of one group. Another moral position supports *quotas,* or the selection of members from different racial and ethnic groups according to their proportions in the general population. A third moral position, *qualified individualism,* is a compromise between the other two.

Although test bias will surely remain an area of considerable controversy, some positive potential solutions have come to light. For example, differences in test scores may reflect patterns of problem solving that characterize different subcultures; this is supported by R. D. Goldman's (1973) *differential process theory.* Also, one might evaluate tests against outcome criteria relevant to minority groups.

A current controversy rages on about the nature of differences in test performance. One group believes the differences are biological in origin (Herrnstein, 1982; Rushton, 1991; Vandenburg & Vogler, 1985), while another believes the differences result from the influence of social environment (Kamin, 1974; Olmedo, 1981; Zuckerman, 1990). Some people believe there is evidence for both genetic and environmental explanations (Turkheimer, 1991). The social environment explanation (Gould, 1981) seems to be the most popular. If people accept this view, then differences in test performance might suggest that people need to escalate their efforts to wipe out inequality. If one endorses the genetic position, then one acknowledges that little can be done to equalize performance among different groups.

WEB ACTIVITY   For interesting and relevant Web sites, check the following:

http://epaa.asu.edu/epaa/v12n12/
  Link to study on gap in reporting ethnicity among SAT test takers

http://luna.cas.usf.edu/~mbrannic/files/tnm/tstbias.htm
  An overview of the issues and concepts of test bias

http://topics.practical.org/browse/Test bias
  Connections to a variety of books on test bias

CHAPTER 20

Testing in Forensic Settings

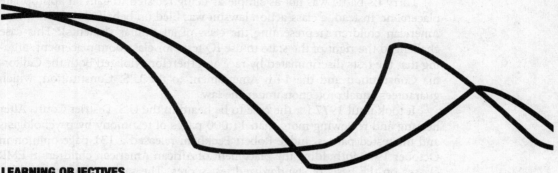

LEARNING OBJECTIVES

When you have completed this chapter, you should be able to:

☐ Describe the basis on which the federal government can regulate the use of psychological tests

☐ Describe the EEOC guidelines and their importance

☐ Describe how the New York Truth in Testing Law affects the use of psychological tests

☐ Discuss the impact of PL 94-142

☐ Discuss the importance of *Hobson v. Hansen*

☐ Describe the issue in *Diana v. State Board of Education* and how it differs from the major issue in *Larry P. v. Wilson Riles*

☐ Compare and contrast the decisions in *Larry P. v. Wilson Riles* and *Parents in Action on Special Education v. Hannon*

☐ Discuss the importance of *Regents of the University of California v. Bakke*

☐ Describe how the courts are involved in the use of personnel tests

☐ Discuss the events that led to the Civil Rights Act of 1991

☐ Review the issues in the University of Michigan Affirmative Action cases *Grutter v. Bollinger* and *Gratz v. Bollinger*

*I*n 1969, the California Department of Education began requiring the use of standardized IQ tests to diagnose retardation. Students who scored below 85 on the WISC or the Stanford-Binet were sent to special classes for the educable mentally retarded (EMR). Larry P. was one of approximately 6000 African American children assigned to EMR classes on the basis of the tests. However, a few years later, Larry P. and five of his African American school-mates were retested by African American psychologists, who reported higher IQ scores. On the basis of these new, higher test scores, Larry and the others were placed back in the regular school track.

Larry P.'s battle was not as simple as being retested to gain an appropriate placement. Instead, a class-action lawsuit was filed on behalf of the six African American children (representing the class of all similar students). This case challenged the right of the state to use IQ tests for classroom placement, arguing that the tests discriminated by race and therefore violated both the California Constitution and the 14th Amendment to the U.S. Constitution, which guarantees equal protection under the law.

It took until 1977 for the case to be heard in the U.S. District Court. After hearing and reviewing more than 11,000 pages of testimony by psychologists and interested parties, Judge Robert Peckham released a 131-page opinion in October 1979 forbidding the placement of African American children in EMR classes on the basis of standardized test scores. The same judge reversed his own decision in a 1992 opinion. Thus, the ultimate decision about the use of psychological tests was made not by trained psychologists, professional educators, or interested citizens, but by the courts.

The same year that the decision in Larry P.'s case was released, the state of New York passed its Truth in Testing Law, and a similar bill was introduced in the U.S. House of Representatives. In addition, a Florida judge ruled that African American students who did not receive all their education in integrated schools could not be denied a high-school credential on the basis of a minimum compe-tence test. By the end of the 1970s, the use of psychological tests had become a major legal issue. In the 1980s and early 1990s, the focus broadened to employ-ment testing. These courtroom and legislative battles over the appropriate use of psychological tests set the stage for the many current conflicts over testing.

In this chapter, we present major legal issues concerning the use of psy-chological tests. We begin by covering some of the basic laws that regulate the use of tests, and then we examine how the courts have interpreted some of these laws. Focused Example 20-1 discusses the meaning of the word *law*.

Laws Governing the Use of Tests

Federal Authorities

Many people believe that the federal government has unlimited authority to regulate almost any activity. Actually, the circumstances under which the fed-eral government can regulate are limited. Until fairly recently, the most com-monly used authority for regulation was interstate commerce.

Focused Example 20-1

WHAT IS A LAW?

As common as it is to refer to laws, many people are confused about what exactly constitutes the law. Most people think of law only as statutes, or the rules written by legislative bodies at any level of government. Before proposed statutes become law, they are called *bills* or *propositions*.

In addition to statutes, constitutions have the force of law. In the United States, there is a federal Constitution, and each state has its own constitution. In lawsuits (or litigation), lawyers frequently argue that a policy violates a constitutional rule or principle. The U.S. Constitution is considered the supreme law of the land; any federal, state, or local law is invalid if judged to conflict with it. State or local laws inconsistent with a state constitution can also be declared invalid.

Statutes and constitutions are typically worded in general terms. Often, they give authority to a specific agency to write regulations. These regulations

are also laws. For example, the Civil Rights Act of 1964 (a statute) created the Equal Employment Opportunity Commission (EEOC), which wrote guidelines for fair employment practices; these guidelines are regulations. Although not created by any elected officials, they are laws that one must follow.

The final form of law is judicial opinion. Statutes, constitutions, and regulations must be applied to specific facts. Thus, courts of law are frequently called on to interpret the law in view of a given situation. In doing so, the courts offer opinions that consider specific cases against the background of statutes, constitutions, and regulations. Once a court offers an opinion on a specific case, the opinion becomes law (Wing, 1976). For example, in the case of *Larry P. v. Wilson Riles,* a judge rendered the opinion that IQ tests could not be used to place African American children in EMR classes. This opinion was law in California until it was reversed in 1992.

Interstate commerce. The U.S. Constitution gives most of the ruling power to the states. Each state has its own constitution, which defines the general relationship between the state and its citizens. The states must make policies for the other administrative units, such as cities and counties, that exist within them. The U.S. Constitution does not directly recognize cities, counties, or school districts. The only restriction on the states' authority to pass laws is that no state can pass or enforce a law that is inconsistent with the U.S. Constitution.

Because each state has only that authority necessary to attend to its own affairs, the federal government regulates interstate commerce, or any business activity involving two or more states. For example, a test developed by a New Jersey company and shipped to Kansas to be administered for profit clearly involves interstate commerce. Some legal authorities now believe that interstate commerce involves almost all activities. The federal government can regulate many activities under this umbrella.

The regulation of interstate commerce is clear and direct. Federal agencies such as the Federal Trade Commission create policies to regulate specific products and activities. Congress also devotes much of its energy to creating laws that regulate specific business activities. These extensive and well-documented policies represent direct regulation. The other form of government regulation—the power to control spending—is indirect.

Control of spending. The U.S. government is a big spender—so big, in fact, that virtually all major U.S. business institutions depend to some extent on federal revenues. This spending gives the federal government considerable leverage. It can withhold money whenever federal authorities consider it just to do so. In effect, the government has the right to say, "Do it our way or we will not pay."

This policy is straightforward when the government is a customer. For example, when the federal government is paying for the development of a test, it has the right to withhold payment unless the work is done according to government standards. However, this power is frequently exercised indirectly. For example, the government can withhold grant money, saying in effect, "Conform to our employment guidelines or we will not pay you to develop a test."

Most school districts are happy to receive federal funds to implement certain programs; however, they may not be enthusiastic about implementing government policies. For example, a district may have a lunch program for underprivileged children. What happens if the government asks the district to build ramps for handicapped children? If the district does not follow through, there is no criminal penalty for deciding not to build the ramps; however, the government has the authority to withhold the funds for the lunch program until the district agrees to the ramps.

Virtually all public and most major private institutions can be regulated this way because of their dependence on federal contracts and grants. Institutions in the private sector that do not depend as heavily on federal funds can be regulated through interstate commerce. Government regulation is thus difficult to escape.

Guidelines of the Equal Employment Opportunity Commission. The government exercises its power to regulate testing in large part through interpretations of the 14th Amendment to the Constitution. This amendment guarantees all citizens due process and equal protection under the law. Over time, the way in which these principles are implemented has been carefully refined. The clearest statement to date from the federal government concerns employee testing and personnel procedures.

During the presidency of Lyndon Johnson, Congress enacted the Civil Rights Act of 1964, one of this century's most important pieces of legislation. Title VII of the act and its subsequent amendments created an Equal Employment Opportunity Commission (EEOC). In 1970, the EEOC released a set of guidelines that defined fair employee-selection procedures. In 1978, the guidelines were revised and simplified, published as the *Uniform Guidelines on Employee Selection Procedures,* and jointly adopted by the EEOC, the Civil Service Commission, and the Departments of Justice, Labor, and the Treasury. These guidelines thus affect most public employment and institutions that receive government funds (Novick, 1981).

The guidelines clearly state that an employer cannot discriminate on the basis of race, color, gender, national origin, or religion. Selection procedures that might have adverse impact receive particular attention. *Adverse impact* is interpreted according to one of the most controversial components of the guidelines, the **four-fifths rule**:

> A selection rate of any race, sex, or ethnic group which is less than four-fifths (4/5) (or 80%) of the rate for the group with the highest rate will generally be regarded by the federal enforcement agencies as evidence of adverse impact, while a greater than four-fifths rate will generally not be regarded by federal enforcement agencies as evidence of adverse impact.

In applying the four-fifths rule, employers place applicants in different categories, such as white women, African American women, and Latinas. If an employer hires 90% of the white female applicants and only 20% of African American female applicants, then the selection procedure violates the four-fifths rule. The employer then has to demonstrate that extenuating circumstances make the standard unreasonable. Suppose that an employer hires 60% of the applicants from the white female pool. Using the four-fifths rule, the employer must hire $4/5 \times 60\% = 48\%$ of the applicants from any other group. If there were 1000 white female applicants and 60% were hired, then there would be 600 new white female workers. Suppose that only 50 Latinas applied (and became members of the applicant pool). According to the four-fifths rule, the employer would need to hire 24 Latinas. This is calculated as:

$$\frac{4}{5} \times 60\% = 48\%$$

$$48\% \times 50 \text{ Latina applicants} = 24 \text{ Latinas selected}$$

Interestingly, by actively recruiting members of many minority groups, an employer can hire a smaller percentage of each group and still maintain the four-fifths rule. Thus, this rule, which was designed to protect minorities, may actually discourage the aggressive recruiting of these groups. The EEOC acknowledges these problems and has developed exceptions for particular circumstances. The authorization of these exceptions for specific individual cases is left up to the EEOC and in many cases has been left to the courts (McCormick & Ilgen, 1980).

The guidelines include many careful definitions of terms such as *validity*. Whenever using a psychological test or other selection device results in adverse impact (or overselection in one group), the employer must present extensive evidence for the validity of the selection procedure. Much of the text of the EEOC guidelines is devoted to a discussion of the minimum requirements for the validity of a selection procedure. These guidelines parallel the discussion presented in Chapter 5. Technical Box 20-1 gives the EEOC requirements for criterion validity.

If prospective employees feel they have been treated unfairly, they can file complaints with the commission. The EEOC's regional and district offices

TECHNICAL BOX 20-1

EEOC Guidelines for Criterion Validity

Technical standards for criterion-related validity studies—(1) Technical feasibility. Users choosing to validate a selection procedure by a criterion-related validity strategy should determine whether it is technically feasible (as defined in section 16) to conduct such a study in the particular employment context. The determination of the number of persons necessary to permit the conduct of a meaningful criterion-related study should be made by the user on the basis of all relevant information concerning the selection procedure, the potential sample, and the employment situation. Where appropriate, jobs with substantially the same major work behaviors may be grouped together for validity studies, in order to obtain an adequate sample. These guidelines do not require a user to hire or promote persons for the purpose of making it possible to conduct a criterion-related study.

(2) Analysis of the job. There should be a review of job information to determine measures of work behavior(s) or performance that are relevant to the job or group of jobs in question. These measures or criteria are relevant to the extent that they represent critical or important job duties, work behaviors, or work outcomes as developed from the review of job information. The possibility of bias should be considered both in selection of the criterion measures and their application. In view of the possibility of bias in subjective evaluations, supervisory rating techniques and instructions to raters should be carefully developed. All criterion measures and the methods for gathering data need to be examined for freedom from factors which would unfairly alter scores of members of any group. The relevance of criteria and their freedom from bias are of particular concern when there are significant differences in measures of job performance for different groups.

(3) *Criterion measures*. Proper safeguards should be taken to ensure that scores on selection procedures do not enter into any judgments of employee adequacy that are to be used as criterion measures. Whatever criteria are used should represent important or critical work behavior(s) or work outcomes. Certain criteria may be used without a full job analysis if the user can show the importance of the criteria to the particular employment context. These criteria include but are not limited to production rate, error rate, tardiness, absenteeism, and length of service. A standardized rating of overall work performance may be used where a study of the job shows that it is an appropriate criterion. Where performance in training is used as a criterion, success in training should be properly measured and the relevance of the training should be shown either through a comparison of the content of the training program with the critical or important work behavior(s) of the job(s) or through a demonstration of the relationship between measures of performance in training and measures of job performance. Measures of relative success in training include but are not limited to instructor evaluations, performance samples, or tests. Criterion measures consisting of paper-and-pencil tests will be closely reviewed for job relevance.

(4) *Representativeness of the sample*. Whether the study is predictive or concurrent, the sample subjects should insofar as feasible be representative of the candidates normally available in the relevant labor market for the job or group of jobs in question,

and should insofar as feasible include the races, sexes, and ethnic groups normally available in the relevant job market. In determining the representativeness of the sample in a concurrent validity study, the user should take into account the extent to which the specific knowledges or skills which are the primary focus of the test are those which employees learn on the job.

Where samples are combined or compared, attention should be given to see that such samples are comparable in terms of the actual job they perform, the length of time on the job where time on the job is likely to affect performance, and other relevant factors likely to affect validity differences; or that these factors are included in the design of the study and their effects identified.

(5) *Statistical relationships.* The degree of relationship between selection procedure scores and criterion measures should be examined and computed, using professionally acceptable statistical procedures. Generally, a selection procedure is considered related to the criterion, for the purposes of these guidelines, when the relationship between performance on the procedure and performance on the criterion measure is statistically significant at the .05 level of significance, which means that it is sufficiently high as to have a probability of no more than one (1) in twenty (20) to have occurred by chance. Absence of a statistically significant relationship between a selection procedure and job performance should not necessarily discourage other investigations of the validity of that selection procedure.

(6) *Operational use of selection procedures.* Users should evaluate each selection procedure to assure that it is appropriate for operational use, including establishment of cutoff scores or rank ordering. Generally, if other factors remain the same, the greater the magnitude of the relationship (e.g., correlation coefficient) between performance on a selection procedure and one or more criteria of performance on the job and the greater the importance and number of aspects of job performance covered by the criteria, the more likely it is that the procedure will be appropriate for use. Reliance upon a selection procedure which is significantly related to a criterion measure but which is based upon a study involving a large number of subjects and has a low correlation coefficient will be subject to close review if it has a large adverse impact. Sole reliance upon a single selection instrument which is related to only one of many job duties or aspects of job performance will also be subject to close review. The appropriateness of a selection procedure is best evaluated in each particular situation and there are no minimum correlation coefficients applicable to all employment situations. In determining whether a selection procedure is appropriate for operational use, the following considerations should also be taken into account: the degree of adverse impact of the procedure, the availability of other selection procedures of greater or substantially equal validity.

(7) *Overstatement of validity findings.* Users should avoid reliance upon techniques which tend to overestimate validity findings as a result of capitalization on chance unless an appropriate safeguard is taken. Reliance upon a few selection procedures or criteria of successful job performance when many selection procedures or criteria of performance have been studied, or the use of optimal statistical weights for selection procedures computed in one sample, are techniques which tend to inflate validity estimates as a result of chance. Use of a large sample is one safeguard; cross validation is another.

Continued

Continued

(8) *Fairness.* This section generally calls for studies of unfairness where technically feasible. The concept of fairness or unfairness of selection procedures is a developing concept. In addition, fairness studies generally require substantial numbers of employees in the job or group of jobs being studied. For these reasons, the federal enforcement agencies recognize that the obligation to conduct studies of fairness imposed by the guidelines generally will be upon users or groups of users with a large number of persons in a job class, or test developers; and that small users utilizing their own selection procedures will generally not be obligated to conduct such studies because it will be technically infeasible for them to do so.

(a) *Unfairness defined.* When members of one race, sex, or ethnic group characteristically obtain lower scores on a selection procedure than members of another group and the differences in scores are not reflected in differences in a measure of job performance, use of the selection procedure may unfairly deny opportunities to members of the group that obtains the lower scores.

(b) *Investigation of fairness.* Where a selection procedure results in an adverse impact on a race, sex, or ethnic group identified in accordance with the classifications set forth in section 4 above and that group is a significant factor in the relevant lab or market, the user generally should investigate the possible existence of unfairness for that group if it is technically feasible to do so. The greater the severity of the adverse impact on a group, the greater the need to investigate the possible existence of unfairness. Where the weight of evidence from other studies shows that the selection procedure predicts fairly for the group in question and for the same or similar jobs, such evidence may be relied on in connection with the selection procedure at issue.

(c) *General considerations in fairness investigations.* Users conducting a study of fairness should review the A.P.A. Standards regarding investigation of possible bias in testing.

An investigation of fairness of a selection procedure depends on both evidence of validity and the manner in which the selection procedure is to be used in a particular employment context. Fairness of a selection procedure cannot necessarily be specified in advance without investigating these factors. Investigation of fairness of a selection procedure in samples where the range of scores on selection procedures or criterion measures is severely restricted for any subgroup sample (as compared to other subgroup samples) may produce misleading evidence of unfairness. That factor should accordingly be taken into account in conducting such studies and before reliance is placed on the results.

(d) *When unfairness is shown.* If unfairness is demonstrated through a showing that members of a particular group perform better or poorer on the job than their scores on the selection procedure would indicate through comparison with how members of other groups perform, the user may either revise or replace the selection instrument in accordance with these guidelines, or may continue to use the selection instrument operationally with appropriate revisions in its use to ensure compatibility between the probability of successful job performance and the probability of being selected.

(e) *Technical feasibility of fairness studies.* In addition to the general conditions needed for technical feasibility for the conduct of a criterion-related study, an investigation of fairness requires the following.

(i) An adequate sample of persons in each group available for the study to achieve findings of statistical significance. Guidelines do not require a user to hire or promote persons on the basis of group classifications for the purpose of making it possible to conduct a study of fairness, but the user has the obligation otherwise to comply with these guidelines.

(ii) The samples for each group should be comparable in terms of the actual job they perform, length of time on the job where time on the job is likely to affect performance, and other relevant factors likely to affect validity differences; or such factors should be included in the design of the study and their effects identified.

(f) *Continued use of selection procedures when fairness studies not feasible.* If a study of fairness should otherwise be performed, but is not technically feasible, a selection procedure may be used which has otherwise met the validity standards of these guidelines, unless the technical infeasibility resulted from discriminatory employment practices which are demonstrated by facts other than past failure to conform with requirements for validation of selection procedures. However, when it becomes technically feasible for the user to perform a study of fairness and such a study is otherwise called for, the user should conduct the study of fairness.

From "EEOC Guidelines," Equal Employment Opportunity Commission (1978).

handle approximately 70,000 complaints each year. The EEOC also gathers information. Any organization with more than 100 employees must complete a form each year that describes the number of women and members of four different minority groups employed in nine different job categories within the organization. The specific minority groups are African American, Hispanic (Cuban, Spanish, Puerto Rican, or Mexican), Asian, and American Indian. After collecting these forms from 260,000 organizations, the EEOC can estimate broad patterns of discrimination. Each year, the EEOC is involved in hundreds of lawsuits concerning discrimination.

Although the validity requirements apply specifically to psychological tests, they also apply to other selection devices such as employment forms and interviews, as well as job requirements, including education and work experience (see Focused Example 20-2). In summary, the EEOC guidelines provide clear, unambiguous regulations for the use of any assessment device in the selection of employees.

As you might expect, many employers were furious when the EEOC guidelines first came out. They saw them as government interference in their business and as a barrier to hiring the best person for a job. Although one can easily sympathize with their concern about bureaucratic red tape, historical evidence supports the implementation of the guidelines. The basic rationale for the EEOC guidelines was provided by the equal protection clause in the 14th Amendment. Though ratified in the post–Civil War era, this clause did not strongly affect public policy for nearly 100 years—until the court battles over

Focused Example 20-2

CONTENT VALIDITY AND SEXUAL HARASSMENT DURING A PARAMEDIC EXAM

 The EEOC guidelines make it clear that questions asked on employment tests and during employment interviews must relate to performance on the job. However, not all agencies are in full compliance with this regulation, particularly in regard to job interviews. This noncompliance irritated Sandra Buchanan when she appeared before the Los Angeles City Fire Department to interview for a paramedic job. During the interview, she was asked as much about her sex life as she was about her four years of paramedic training and experience. For example, she was asked: "Have you ever had semipublic sex?" "Have you had sex on the beach?" "Have you had sex in a parked car?" "Have you ever exposed yourself indecently?" "Have you molested any children?" "Do you have any homosexual contacts?"

Buchanan was so disturbed by these questions that she filed a complaint with the Civil Service Commission. In the ensuing investigation, the fire department was asked to show how the questions about sex related to the paramedic job.

Its response was that the questions create stress and therefore give the department a chance to observe how a person handles him- or herself in stressful situations. The department also argued that it needed to delve deeply into the backgrounds of applicants because paramedics are entrusted with important responsibilities. One member of the fire department argued that the question on indecent exposure was necessary because "they have a dormitory situation that is quite different from other jobs; the nature of this job makes some of the questions job related that would not be related in other jobs."

The commission decided that the department had to review the questions and eliminate those that were not job related, then reinterview Buchanan. It appeared that the commission agreed with Buchanan's attorney, who argued, "It is time that the city of Los Angeles stop asking "How's your sex life" and get back to the business of finding the most qualified person for the job of Los Angeles paramedic" (*Los Angeles Times,* June 29, 1979).

school desegregation and the activities of the civil rights movement led to the passage of the 1964 Civil Rights Act. Even then, many employers did not follow fair employment practices. The specific EEOC guidelines were therefore necessary to enforce the law. Before these specific guidelines, more than 100 years had passed without employers recognizing the legal requirements of equal protection.

In 1980, the EEOC added specific guidelines on sexual harassment in the workplace. *Sexual harassment* was defined as unsolicited sexual advances, requests for sexual favors, or any other implicit or explicit conduct that might be interpreted as a condition of an individual's employment. The EEOC ruled that a company is always liable for sexual harassment by supervisors even when company officials are unaware of the problem, but the Supreme Court overturned this policy in a 1986 decision. Nevertheless, the Supreme Court affirmed that sexual harassment is sexual discrimination and underscored the need for employers to eliminate any form of sexual harassment (Wermiel & Trost, 1986). When traveling abroad, some Americans are

Focused Example 20-3

SEXISM IN OTHER COUNTRIES

The fairness in employment policies that characterizes some Western countries is not observed throughout the world. Consider this advertisement that appeared in a 1985 Hong Kong newspaper:

> **Obedient Young Secretary.** Very obedient young woman required by American Director of position as Secretary/Personal Assistant. Must be attractive and eager to submit to authority, have good typing and filing skills, and be free to travel. Knowledge of Mandarin an advantage. Most important, she should enjoy following orders without question and cheerfully accept directions. Send handwritten resume on unlined paper and recent photo to G.P.O. Box 6132, Hong Kong.

From Cascio (1987, p. 29).

---

surprised by evidence of sexual discrimination and the sexist standards apparent in job-selection procedures. Consider the advertisement in Focused Example 20-3.

In November 1991, the 1991 Civil Rights Bill became law. The bill essentially reaffirmed the EEOC guidelines. However, it was a reaction to a trend that had eroded the impact of these guidelines during the 1980s and early 1990s. We shall return to this bill later in the chapter.

Specific Laws

Other regulatory schemes attempt to control the use of tests. An example is the New York Truth in Testing Law of 1979.

Truth in testing laws. One of the most controversial measures in the testing field, the New York Truth in Testing Law sprang from an extensive investigation of the Educational Testing Service (ETS) by the New York Public Interest Research Group (NYPIRG). Though it affects other testing companies, the New York law was written specifically for the ETS.

In 1948, the ETS was created by the College Entrance Examination Board, the American Council on Education, and the Carnegie Foundation. Its original and best-known mission was to create and administer aptitude tests such as the SAT. ETS is responsible for more than 300 testing programs, including the Graduate Management Admission Test (GMAT), the Graduate Record Examination (GRE), the Multi-State Bar Exam, and the Law School Admission Test (LSAT). The assets and income of the company are substantial.

Though apparently upset by the wealth and success of ETS, NYPIRG objected even more to the power ETS wielded. Even now, each year several million people take tests designed and administered by ETS, and the results of these tests profoundly affect their lives (Orfield & Kornhaber, 2001). Many educational programs take the scores seriously. Students who score poorly on the LSAT, for example, may be denied entrance to law school. Higher scores might have brought them higher income, occupational status, and self-esteem. A Web site maintained by the Association for Supervision and Curriculum Development includes a book authored by W. James Popham (see www.ascd.org). The book, entitled *The Truth About Testing: An Educator's Call to Action*, offers an excellent contemporary review of the issues.

In its investigation, NYPIRG became dissatisfied with the available information on test validity, the calculation of test scores, and the financial accounting of the ETS. The Truth in Testing Law addresses these objections by requiring testing companies to (1) disclose all studies on the validity of a test, (2) provide a complete disclosure to students about what scores mean and how they were calculated, and (3) on request by a student, provide a copy of the test questions, the correct answers, and the student's answers.

The first two portions are relatively noncontroversial. The test developers argue that they already disclose all pertinent information on validity and release many public documents that highlight the strengths and weaknesses of their tests. Furthermore, the ETS strongly encourages institutions that use its tests to perform local validity studies. Any of these studies can be published in scholarly journals (found in most college libraries) with no interference from the ETS. However, the NYPIRG provided some evidence that the ETS and other testing companies have files of secret data that they do not make public because these data may reflect poorly on the product. The second aspect of the law was included because the ETS sometimes reports index scores to schools without telling students how the index was calculated and the exact index value being reported.

The controversial third portion of the law may seriously decrease the value of testing programs. Requiring that the test questions be returned to students means that the same questions cannot be used in future versions of the test. Several problems have resulted from this policy. First, it decreases the validity of the test. With the items constantly changing, the test essentially becomes a new test each time the items change. As a result, it is impossible to accumulate a record of construct validity. Second, new items make it difficult to equate scores across years. For example, a graduate school must often consider students who took the GRE in different years. Because the test itself differs each year, comparing the scores of students who took the test at different times is difficult. Although the bill eventually adopted in New York did allow testing companies to keep some of the items secret for equating purposes, this practice falls short of a satisfactory solution. Equating can be accomplished, but only at the risk of increasing the chances of error. Third, and most serious, the disclosure of test items increases costs, which the ETS passes on to the consumer.

The ETS does make booklets available to the public that present information on the scoring system, validity, reliability, and standard error of measurement for each of their tests. After completing this testing course, you will have little difficulty interpreting the manuals, but it has taken you a long term of hard study to get to this point. People with no background in testing will probably not comprehend all of this information. The authors of the bills fail to recognize that the proper use of tests and test results requires technical training in advanced courses such as psychological testing. After all, we do not expect people to be able to practice medicine without medical school training. Testing experts tend to agree that primary and secondary schools misuse test scores. Those who do not understand the limitations of tests may rely too much on test scores (Snyderman & Rothman, 1987).

Consider the ultimate impact of the truth-in-testing legislation. One side argues that the laws have made for a fairer and more honest testing industry. The other argues that students now have to pay a higher price for a poorer product. As a result of these laws, other tests are given on only a limited number of occasions, and test items are not reused. With the distribution of test items, tests are not as thoroughly validated before their use as they were 20 years ago. This may cause greater error in selecting students. In addition, continuing the development of the tests has increased expense. Ultimately, students may need to pay more to take a lower-quality test. In response to these concerns, the ETS argues that that the concurrent validity of the tests is still significant (www.collegeboard.com).

Major Lawsuits That Have Affected Psychological Testing

Legislation is not the only way to change policy. One option used with increasing frequency is litigation, usually considered a last resort for resolving conflicts. For example, if you feel you have been wronged but cannot persuade those who have offended you through other legal means, then you may file a lawsuit. In doing so, you trust the court to make a fair judgment about your case.

There have already been many lawsuits concerning the use of psychological tests, and we expect the number to increase. We shall now discuss some of the most important of these. Keep in mind that each of these complex cases involved considerably more evidence than we can cite here.

Early Desegregation Cases

The 14th Amendment requires that all citizens be granted equal protection under the law. At the end of the 19th century, some people argued that segregated schools did not offer such protection. In the famous 1896 case of *Plessy v. Ferguson,* the Supreme Court ruled that schools could remain segregated but that the quality of the schools must be equal. This was the famous separate-but-equal ruling.

Perhaps the most influential ruling in the history of American public school education came in the case of *Brown v. Board of Education* in 1954. In this case, the Supreme Court overturned the *Plessy v. Ferguson* decision by ruling that the schools must provide nonsegregated facilities for African American and white students. In this opinion, the Court raised several issues that would eventually affect the use of psychological tests.

The most important pronouncement of *Brown* was that segregation denied equal protection. In coming to its decision, the Court made extensive use of testimony by psychologists that suggested that African American children could be made to feel inferior if the school system kept the two races separate.

The story of the *Brown* case is well known, but what is less often discussed is the ugly history that followed. Many school districts did not want to desegregate, and the battle over busing and other mechanisms for desegregation continues even today. Many of the current arguments against desegregation are based on fears of children leaving their own neighborhoods or the stress on children who must endure long bus rides. The early resistance to the *Brown* decision was more clearly linked to the racist belief in African American inferiority.

Brown v. Board of Education is regarded as one of the most important civil rights decisions in American history. Although the decision had a revolutionary impact in some dimensions, severe problems in equal access to quality education remain. May 2004 marked the 50th anniversary of the *Brown* decision. At that time, many looked back critically at the progress made during that half century. The *Plessy v. Ferguson* decision of 1896 argued that schools could be racially separate but emphasized that the quality of the separate schools must be equal. The decision stood for more than half a century until the Supreme Court ruled on the *Brown* case in 1954. Fifty years following the *Brown* decision and more than 100 years following *Plessy v. Ferguson,* many people believe that today's public schools are often still separate and that they remain unequal. Have we made significant progress toward resolving the issue during the last century? In 2004, it was reported that 38% of African American students and 42% of Hispanic students were in extremely segregated schools with more than 90% minority enrollment.

An important 2004 study by the California-based Center for the Future of Teaching and Learning raised some disturbing issues. The state of California, responding to a teacher shortage, significantly increased the number of classroom teachers. In the 2002–2003 academic year, nearly 310,000 people were employed as public school teachers in California. In response to the demand for teachers, school districts had hired about 37,000 (12% of the workforce) that had not completed formal teacher training or were teaching a subject in which they had no formal training. These teachers were described as "underprepared." Many of these teachers did not even have a preliminary teaching credential. The problem is that the underprepared teachers tend to end up in schools with high percentages of minority students. For example, some schools still have 90% or more minority students while other schools have 30% or less minority students. In the schools with high concentrations of minority students, 20% of the teachers were underprepared, while in schools with low minority populations, only 4% of the teachers were underprepared. In other words, schools with large minority-student populations were more than five times as likely to have underprepared teachers as those with low percentages of minority students. Further, students in poverty area schools were about three times as likely to have teachers that were underprepared as students in low-poverty areas.

It might be argued that schools that have poor academic performance are the ones that need the best-prepared teachers. Poorly performing students need more help. Yet in 2002–2003, schools scoring low on California's Academic Performance Index (API) had students who were 4.5 times more likely to be taught by someone who was underprepared than schools in the top quartile of academic performance.

Fifty years following the landmark *Brown* decision and more than a century after the *Plessy* decision, our schools remain only partially desegregated, and the quality of the educational experience for many disadvantaged youths remains substandard.

Stell v. Savannah-Chatham County Board of Education

The most significant reactionary court case occurred when legal action was taken to desegregate the school system of Savannah, Georgia, on behalf of a group of African American children. The conflict began when the attorneys for two white children intervened. They argued that they were not opposed to desegregating on the basis of race but that African American children did not have the ability to be in the same classrooms as whites. Testimony from psychologists indicated that the median IQ score for African American children was 81, whereas that for white children was 101. Because there was such a large difference in this trait (assumed to be genetic), the attorneys argued that it could be to the mutual disadvantage of both groups to teach them in the same schools. Doing so might create even greater feelings of inferiority among African American children and might create frustration that would eventually result in antisocial behavior.

The court essentially agreed with this testimony and ruled that the district should not desegregate. The judge's opinion reflected his view of the best interest of all the children. Later, this decision was reversed. In doing so, the Supreme Court used the precedent set forth by *Brown* as the reason for requiring the Savannah district to desegregate. It is important to note that the validity of the test scores—the primary evidence—was never discussed (Bersoff, 1979, 1981).

Hobson v. Hansen

Stell was just one of many cases that attempted to resist the order set forth in the *Brown* desegregation case. Like *Stell,* many of these cases introduced test scores as evidence that African American children were genetically incapable of learning or being educated in the same classrooms as white children. The courts routinely accepted this evidence. Given the current controversy over the use of psychological tests, it is remarkable that several years passed before the validity of the test scores became an issue.

The first major case to examine the validity of psychological tests was *Hobson v. Hansen.* This case is relevant to many current lawsuits. Unlike the early desegregation cases, it did not deal with sending African American and white children to different schools. Instead, it concerned the placement of children once they arrived at a school. Although the courts had consistently required schools to desegregate, they tended to take a hands-off approach toward placement within schools.

The *Hobson* case contested the use of group standardized ability tests to place students in different learning tracks. Julius W. Hobson was the father of two African American children placed in a basic track by the District of Columbia School District. Carl F. Hansen was its superintendent. Within the district, children were placed in honors, regular, general, and basic tracks on the basis of group ability tests. The honors track was designed to prepare children for college, while the basic track focused on preparation for blue-collar jobs. Placement in the basic track made it essentially impossible to prepare for a high-income, high-prestige profession.

In *Hobson*, lawyers argued that the tracking system segregated groups by placing African American children in the basic track and white children in the other tracks. Psychological tests were the primary mechanism used to justify this separation.

The *Hobson* case was decided in 1967. Just two years before the decision, the Supreme Court had ruled that a group is not denied equal protection by "mere classification" (Bersoff, 1979). Nevertheless, Judge Skelly Wright ruled against classification based on group ability tests. After extensive expert testimony on the validity of the tests for minority children, the judge concluded that the tests discriminated against them. An interesting aspect of the opinion was that it claimed that grouping would be permissible if based on innate ability. The judge asserted that ability test scores were influenced by cultural experiences, and that the dominant cultural group had an unfair advantage on the tests and thereby gained admission to the tracks that provided the best preparation for high-income, high-prestige jobs. The Hobson case was unique because the court suggested that the tracking of students constituted intentional racial segregation. There has been only one similar decision (*People Who Care v. Rockford Board of Education*, 1997), but it was reversed by an appellate court.

Diana v. State Board of Education

The decision in *Hobson v. Hansen* opened the door for a thorough examination of the use of standardized tests for the placement of students in EMR tracks. The case of *Diana* has particular implications for the use of standardized tests for bilingual children. Diana was one of nine Mexican American elementary school children placed in EMR classes on the basis of scores on the WISC or Stanford-Binet test. Representing bilingual children, these nine students brought a class-action suit against the California State Board of Education, contending that the use of standardized IQ tests for placement in EMR classes denied equal protection, because the tests were standardized only for whites and had been administered by a non–Spanish-speaking psychometrist. Although only 18% of the children in Diana's school district had Spanish surnames, this group made up nearly one-third of the enrollment in EMR classes.

When tested in English, Diana had achieved an IQ score of only 30. However, when retested in Spanish and English, her IQ bounced to 79, high enough to keep her out of EMR classes. Seven of the other eight plaintiffs also achieved high enough scores on the retest to be taken out of the EMR classes.

Faced with this evidence, the California State Board of Education decided not to take the case to court. Instead, it adopted special provisions for testing Mexican American and Chinese American children, including the following:

1. The children would be tested in their primary language.
2. Questions based on vocabulary and information that the children could not be expected to know would be eliminated.
3. The Mexican American and Chinese American children already assigned to EMR classes would be reevaluated with tests that used their primary language and nonverbal items.
4. New tests would be developed by the state that reflected Mexican American culture and that were normed for Mexican American children (Bersoff, 1979).

Later studies confirmed that bilingual children do score higher when tested in their primary language (Bergan & Parra, 1979).

The combination of the judgment in *Hobson* and the change in policy brought about by *Diana* forced many people to question seriously the use of IQ tests for the assignment of children to EMR classes. However, these decisions were quite specific to the circumstances in each case. *Hobson* dealt with group tests but not individual ones, even though individual tests are used more often than group tests to make final decisions for EMR placement. The ruling in *Diana* was limited strictly to bilingual children. These two cases thus did not apply to African American children placed in EMR classes on the basis of individual IQ tests. This specific area was left for the most important court battle of them all—*Larry P. v. Wilson Riles*.

Larry P. v. Wilson Riles

In October 1979, Judge Robert Peckham of the Federal District Court for the Northern District of California handed down an opinion that declared that "the use of IQ tests which had a disproportionate effect on Black children violated the Rehabilitation Act, the Education for All Handicapped Children Act, Title VII, and the 14th Amendment when used to place children in EMR classes." Attorneys for Larry P., one of six African American elementary-school students assigned to EMR classes on the basis of IQ test results, had argued that the use of standardized IQ tests to place African American children in EMR classes violated both the California constitution and the equal protection clause of the 14th Amendment (Opton, 1979), as well as the laws mentioned.

During the trial, both sides geared up for a particularly intense battle. Wilson Riles, an African American, was the superintendent of public instruction in California; he had instituted many significant reforms that benefited minority children. Thus, it was particularly awkward to have a nationally recognized spokesperson for progressive programs named as the defendant for an allegedly racist scheme.

In defense of the use of tests, Riles and the state called many nationally recognized experts on IQ tests, including Lloyd Humphreys, Jerome Sattler, Robert Thorridike, Nadine Lambert, and Robert Gordon. These witnesses presented extensive evidence that IQ tests, particularly the Stanford-Binet and the WISC (used to test Larry and the others), were not biased against African Americans. Although the tests had not originally been normed for African American populations, studies had demonstrated that they were equally valid for African American and white children. (Many of the arguments that support the use of tests for all races are summarized in Chapter 19.) If the tests were not biased, then why did Larry and the others receive higher scores when they were retested by African American psychologists? The defense argued that the African American psychologists did not follow standard testing procedures and that IQ test scores are not changed when standardized procedures are followed.

Statements from special education teachers were also presented. The teachers argued that the children involved in the case could not cope with the standard curriculum and that they required the special tutoring available in the EMR classes. The children had not been learning in regular classes, and the schools investigated classes in which there was doubt about the placement. For all of these children, the assignment to EMR classes was deemed appropriate (Sattler, 1979a).

The Larry P. side of the case also had its share of distinguished experts, including George Albee, Leon Kamin, and Jane Mercer. The arguments for Larry varied widely. His lawyers argued that all humans are born with equal capacity and that any test that assigns disproportionate numbers of children from one race to an EMR category is racist and discriminatory. The witnesses testified that, throughout history, dominant social groups had used devices such as IQ tests to discriminate against less powerful social groups and that the school district had intentionally discriminated against African American children by using unvalidated IQ tests. Specifically, the tests were used to keep African Americans in dead-end classes for the mentally retarded in which they would not get the training they needed to move up in the social strata. Furthermore, the plaintiffs suggested that labeling someone as EMR has devastating social consequences. Children labeled as EMR lose confidence and self-esteem (Mercer, 1973); eventually, the label becomes a self-fulfilling prophecy (Rosenthal & Jacobson, 1968). In other words, labeling a child as mentally retarded may cause the child to behave as though he or she really is mentally retarded.

Clearly persuaded by the plaintiffs, the judge declared that the tests "are racially and culturally biased, have a discriminatory impact on African-American children, and have not been validated for the purpose of (consigning) African-American children into educationally dead-end, isolated, and stigmatizing classes." Furthermore, the judge stated that the Department of Education had "desired to perpetuate the segregation of minorities in inferior, dead-end, and stigmatizing classes for the retarded."

The effect of the ruling was a permanent discontinuance of IQ testing to place African-American children in EMR classes. The decision immediately affected all African American California schoolchildren who had been labeled as EMR. More than 6000 of these children had to be reassessed in some other manner.

There are strong differences of opinion about the meaning of the *Larry P.* decision. Harold Dent, one of the African American psychologists who had retested Larry P. and the other children, hailed the decision as a victory for African American children:

For more than 60 years, psychologists had used tests primarily to justify the majority's desire to "track" minorities into inferior education and dead-end jobs. The message of *Larry P.* was that psychologists must involve themselves in the task mandated in the last sentence of the court's opinion: "This will clear the way for more constructive educational reform." (Quoted in Opton, 1979)

Others did not share the belief that the *Larry P.* decision was a social victory. Nadine Lambert, an expert witness for the state, felt it was a terrible decision: "I think the people who will be most hurt by it are the African-American children" (quoted in Opton, 1979). Banning the use of IQ tests opens the door to completely subjective judgments, perhaps even more racist than the test results. Opponents of the *Larry P.* decision cite many instances in which gifted African American children were assumed to be average by their teachers but were recognized as highly intelligent because of IQ test scores.

The *Larry P.* decision has been frequently cited in subsequent cases, some of which are actually remote from the issues in that case. For example, in *Ana Maria R. v. California Department of Education,* parental rights were terminated on the grounds that the mother was mentally retarded. However, the mother was Spanish-speaking, and *Larry P.* was cited as precedent that tests used for classification of mental retardation discriminate against African Americans and Hispanics. In contrast to the case of *Ana Maria R.,* the factual situation in an Illinois case strongly resembled that of *Larry P.,* as you will see in the following section.

Parents in Action on Special Education v. Hannon

Just as *Larry P.* was making headlines in California, a similar case came to trial in Illinois: a class-action lawsuit filed on behalf of two African American children who had been placed in special classes for the educable mentally handicapped (EMH) on the basis of IQ test scores. Attorneys for the two student plaintiffs argued that the children were inappropriately placed in EMH classes because of racial bias in the IQ tests. They suggested that the use of IQ tests for African American children violates the equal protection clause of the Constitution and many federal statutes.

In their presentation to the court, the plaintiffs relied heavily on the *Larry P.* decision, which held that the WISC, the WISC-R, and the Stanford-Binet IQ tests are biased and inappropriate for testing minority children. However, Judge John Grady came to exactly the opposite conclusion that Judge Robert Peckham had in *Larry P.* Judge Grady found evidence for racial bias in the three major IQ tests to be unconvincing. In his opinion, he noted that the objectionable items comprised only a fraction of the entire test. For example, witnesses for the plaintiffs never mentioned whole subtests on the WISC and WISC-R such as arithmetic, digit span, block design, mazes, coding, and object assembly. The judge noted that these subtests were not biased in favor of

Focused Example 20-4

DIFFERENT OPINIONS FROM DIFFERENT JUDGES

 People often think that two judges looking at the same evidence will come to the same conclusion. However, judges often differ sharply in this regard. When confronted with different opinions from Judges Peckham (*Larry P. v. Wilson Riles*) and Grady (*Parents in Action on Special Education v. Hannon*), Sattler (1980) juxtaposed quotes from the two judges on selected issues in the cases. Below are some of the statements demonstrating how differently the judges viewed the issues.

What are the functions of special classes for the educable mentally retarded or educable mentally handicapped?

Judge Robert Peckham	Judge John Grady
"EMR classes are designed to separate out children who are incapable of learning in the regular classes. . . . Further, the curriculum was not and is not designed to help students learn the skills necessary to return to the regular instructional program. . . . Finally, consistent with the first two aspects of EMR classes, the classes are conceived of as 'dead-end classes.' Children are placed there, generally at about eight to ten years of age, because they are thought to be incapable of learning the skills inculcated by the regular curriculum. They are provided with instruction that deemphasizes academic skills in favor of adjustment, and naturally they will tend to fall farther and farther behind the children in the regular classes."	"The EMH curriculum is designed for the child who cannot benefit from the regular curriculum. It is designed for children who learn slowly, who have short attention spans, slow reaction time, and difficulty retaining material in both the short term and the long term. The curriculum also recognizes the difficulty an EMH child has in seeing similarities and differences, in learning by implication, in generalizing and in thinking abstractly. The curriculum thus involves much repetition and concrete teaching. Subjects are taught for short periods of time, in recognition of the children's short attention spans."

How much emphasis is given to the IQ in placing children in mentally retarded or educable mentally handicapped classes?

"The available data suggest very strongly that, even if in some districts the IQ scores were not always determinative, they were pervasive in the placement process. . . . Retardation is defined in terms of the IQ tests, and a low score in effect establishes a prima facie case of retardation."	"The IQ score is not the sole determinant of whether a child is placed in an EMH class. First, the score itself is evaluated by the psychologist who administers the test. The child's responses are recorded verbatim, and the significance of his numerical score is a matter involving judgment and interpretation. . . . The examiner who knows the milieu of the child can correct for cultural bias by asking the questions in a sensitive and intelligent way. . . . Finally, the IQ test and the psychologist's evaluation of the child in the light of that test are only one component of several which form the basis for an EMH referral."

To what extent do socioeconomic factors account for the findings that Black children score lower than White children on intelligence tests?

"It is clear that socioeconomic status by itself cannot explain fully the undisputed disparities in IQ test scores and in EMR placements. . . . The insufficiency of the above explanation leads us to question the cultural bias of IQ tests. The first important inferential evidence is that the tests were never designed to eliminate cultural biases against Black children, it was assumed in effect that Black children were less 'intelligent' than Whites."

"It is uncontradicted that most of the children in the EMH classes do in fact come from the poverty pockets of the city. This tends to suggest that what is involved is not simply race but something associated with poverty. It is also significant that many Black children who take the tests score at levels high enough to preclude EMH placement. Plaintiffs have not explained why the alleged cultural bias of the tests did not result in EMH-level scores for these children. Plaintiffs' theory of cultural bias simply ignores the fact that some Black children perform better than most Whites. Nationally, 15 to 20 percent of the Blacks who take the tests score above the White mean of 100."

To what extent does Black children's use of nonstandard English affect their performance on intelligence tests?

"At the outset, it is undeniable that to the extent Black children speak other than standard English, they will be handicapped in at least the verbal component of the tests. . . . Dr. [Asa] Hilliard and other witnesses pointed out that Black children are more likely to be exposed to nonstandard English, and that exposure will be reflected in IQ scores."

"The evidence does not establish how the use of nonstandard English would interfere with performance on the Wechsler and Stanford-Binet tests. . . . Dr. [Robert J.] Williams testified that a Black child might say, 'John go to town' instead of 'John is going to town,' or 'John book' instead of 'John's book'. . . . What is unclear is how the use of such nonstandard English would handicap a child either in understanding the test items or in responding to them. . . . Moreover, responding to a test item in nonstandard English should not affect a child's score on the item, since the examiners are specifically instructed by the test manuals to disregard the form of the answer so long as the substance is correct. . . . But there are no vocabulary items on the IQ tests, so far as I can tell, which are peculiar to White culture."

Was the issue of test validity important in the trial?

"If defendants could somehow have demonstrated that the intelligence tests had been 'validated' for the purpose of EMR placement of Black children, those tests could have been utilized despite their disproportionate impact. . . . However, defendants did not make these showings."

"We do not address the broader questions of whether these IQ tests are generally valid as measures of intelligence, whether individual items are appropriate for that purpose, or whether the tests could be improved. Those questions are not involved in this case."

Continued

To what extent do differences between Black culture and White culture affect Black children's performance on intelligence tests?

"To the extent that a 'Black culture'—admittedly a vague term—exists and translates the phenomenon of intelligence into skills and knowledge untested by the standardized intelligence tests, those tests cannot measure the capabilities of Black children. . . . On the basis of their different cultural background, which results particularly in lower scores on IQ tests, Black children are subjected to discrimination analogous to that borne by many San Francisco Chinese, who, because of their cultural background, could not communicate effectively in English. Certainly many Chinese Americans would succeed in those schools even without remedial English. Nevertheless, the failure to provide English-language teaching foreclosed substantial numbers of students from any meaningful educational opportunity. This same result occurs from the use of IQ tests and a biased placement process."

"Dr. Williams did not explain how he relates the other characteristics of Black culture to performance on the tests. It is not clear, for instance, how the extended family as opposed to the nuclear family would pertain to performance on the tests. Like Dr. [Leon] Kamin's description of the racist attitudes of Goddard, Yerkes and Terman, Dr. Williams's description of African-American culture has not been connected to the specific issue in this case. . . . Dr. Kamin's argument that the Black child does not obtain the same 'information,' and Dr. [George] Albee's argument that the Black child does not share in the dominant White culture, seem inapplicable to most items on all three of the tests in question. As already noted, many of the categories of test items have no precise counterpart in the experience of any children, of whatever race. Others have almost precise counterparts in the everyday experience of American children of all races. Any number of test items could be cited to illustrate this point."

Generally, to what extent are intelligence tests racially biased?

"The answer, as should be clear from the earlier discussion of the history and biases of IQ tests, is that validation has been assumed, not established, for Blacks. The tests were developed and standardized in the United States on White, essentially middle-class groups."

"All but a few of the items on their face appear racially neutral. . . . I conclude that the possibility of the few biased items on these tests causing an EMH placement that would not otherwise occur is practically nonexistent."

Does the use of intelligence tests violate some provisions of Public Law 94-142 (Education for All Handicapped)?

"Defendants have failed to take the steps necessary to assure the tests' validity. They have committed a serious error that Title VII regulations warn against in the employment situation: 'Under no circumstances will the general reputation of a test, its author, or its publisher, or casual reports of test utility be accepted in lieu of evidence of validity.' Whether or not the tests in fact do what they are supposed to do, the law is that defendants must come forward and show that they have been validated for each minority group with which they are used. This minimal burden has not been met for diagnosing the kind of mental retardation justifying EMR placement."

"The requirement that 'materials and procedures' used for assessment be nondiscriminatory, and that no single procedure be the sole criterion for assessment, seems to me to contemplate that the process as a whole be nondiscriminatory. It does not require that any single procedure, standing alone, be affirmatively shown to be free of bias. The very requirement of multiple procedures implies recognition that one procedure, standing alone, could well result in bias and that a system of cross-checking is necessary."

From Sattler (1980).

either African American or white children because most youngsters of both groups would never have confronted problems of this type before. The items for which there were legitimate objections were too few to affect test scores.

Thus, less than one year after the historic *Larry P.* case, another court concluded, "Evidence of racial bias in standardized IQ tests is not sufficient to render their use as part of classification procedures to place African-American children in 'educable mentally handicapped' classes violative of statutes prohibiting discrimination in federal funded programs." Focused Example 20-4 presents further conflicting statements from the two judges in these cases.

Crawford et al. v. Honig et al.

In 1986, the court modified the *Larry P.* court order to expand the intelligence testing ban to all African American children. The California Department of Education and the public interest lawyers who represented Larry P. gained an order from Judge Peckham to ban the use of standardized intelligence tests for African American children for assignment to special education programs. However, African American children could take intelligence tests to be considered for the state-supported gifted and talented education program (GATE).

After the 1986 strengthening of the *Larry P.* decision, several new problems arose. One of them is represented by the case of *Crawford v. Honig.* Some children do have special needs and may benefit from special education programs. Indeed, such programs were developed to identify learning problems and to provide special assistance. Under the 1986 modification of the *Larry P.* decision, one can evaluate white, Latino, Latina, Asian American, and Native American students with intelligence tests for placement in special education. However, these tests cannot be used for African American children. In fact, these tests cannot be given to African American children even if the families request them. Crawford's mother was African American, but her father was not. Recognizing that the child was struggling in school, the mother requested testing.

Citing *Larry P.,* the school denied the request because the child had been identified as African American. However, the mother was told that if she changed the child's racial identification to match the father's, testing would be permitted. The lawsuit that followed claimed that California Superintendent of Public Education Bill Honig and the California Board of Education violated Crawford's civil rights by denying a public service on the basis of race. The arguments in court suggested that a race-conscious testing policy promoted inequities and indignities. Eventually, the case was heard by Judge Peckham, the same judge who had issued the *Larry P.* ruling and the 1986 modification strengthening the original judgment. Crawford's case was vigorously opposed by the California Department of Education. However, since this 1991 case was not a class-action suit, it was uncertain whether or not the ruling would apply to all children. The plaintiffs petitioned the court to extend the judgment to all similar African American children (Bredemeier, 1991). In September 1992, Judge Peckham issued an order reversing the earlier ban on IQ tests for African American students.

Marchall v. Georgia

One of the first major decisions that had opposed the 1979 *Larry P.* judgment was *Marchall et al. v. Georgia*. This class-action suit was filed in 1981 on behalf of a group of African American students. Allegedly, students had received unfair treatment by being disproportionately placed in EMR classes and underrepresented in classes for learning disabilities (LD). The defendants in the case were 13 school districts, most in the state of Georgia. The key witness for the plaintiff was Robert Calfee, an educational psychologist from Stanford University. Calfee noted that racial differences accounted for differential performance in school more than did socioeconomic status. Through a series of complex analyses, Calfee concluded that the school experience itself was actually creating differences between groups. Thus, the practice of assigning students to groups was damaging. As a remedy, Calfee suggested that students be assigned to classrooms on a random basis.

The defense argued that placement into certain classrooms did provide benefits for students, and the court ultimately agreed. Further, the court allowed the use of tests to separate students because these procedures ultimately resulted in better outcomes. The critical result of the decision was that the focus shifted from possible test bias to the ultimate benefit to students. An important issue in the case was the focus on curriculum-based assessment rather than IQ testing. Perhaps the most important difference between the *Marchall* decision and previous court cases was the judge's belief that test information could be used to structure interventions that would help the children (*Marchall et al. v. Georgia*, 1984, 1985; Reschly, Kicklighter, & McKee, 1988; Reschly & Ward, 1991).

Debra P. v. Turlington

Some people feel that a test is biased if it contains questions that particular test takers cannot answer. One 1979 lawsuit in Florida involved 10 African American students, including Debra P., who had failed in their first attempt to pass Florida's minimum competence test, the State Student Assessment Test. In Hillsborough County, where the suit was filed, approximately 19% of the students in the public school system were African American; however, African American students constituted 64% of those who failed the test.

More than 30 states have adopted minimum competence tests similar to the one used in Florida, and 19 states require the exam for graduation. If they meet other requirements, students who do not pass the exam receive a certificate of completion, which acknowledges that they attended high school but does not carry the same status as a high-school diploma. Examples of items from a minimum competence test are shown in Table 20-1.

The Florida suit charged that the test should not be used for those minority students taught primarily in segregated schools. The dispute was therefore over whether the same test should be used for students with unequal opportunities to learn in school. Attorneys for the students argued that their clients had attended inferior schools and had suffered continued discrimination; thus,

TABLE 20-1

Examples of Items from a Minimum Competence Test

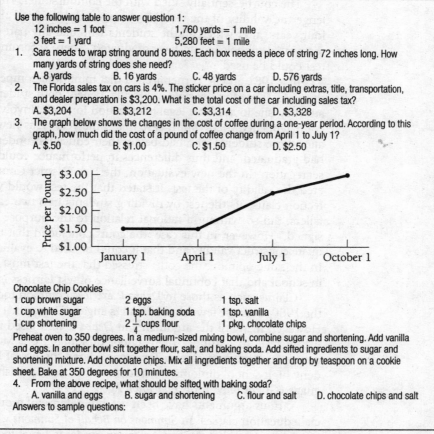

Use the following table to answer question 1:

| 12 inches = 1 foot | 1,760 yards = 1 mile |
| 3 feet = 1 yard | 5,280 feet = 1 mile |

1. Sara needs to wrap string around 8 boxes. Each box needs a piece of string 72 inches long. How many yards of string does she need?
    A. 8 yards   B. 16 yards   C. 48 yards   D. 576 yards
2. The Florida sales tax on cars is 4%. The sticker price on a car including extras, title, transportation, and dealer preparation is $3,200. What is the total cost of the car including sales tax?
    A. $3,204   B. $3,212   C. $3,314   D. $3,328
3. The graph below shows the changes in the cost of coffee during a one-year period. According to this graph, how much did the cost of a pound of coffee change from April 1 to July 1?
    A. $.50   B. $1.00   C. $1.50   D. $2.50

Chocolate Chip Cookies

1 cup brown sugar	2 eggs	1 tsp. salt
1 cup white sugar	1 tsp. baking soda	1 tsp. vanilla
1 cup shortening	2 $\frac{1}{4}$ cups flour	1 pkg. chocolate chips

Preheat oven to 350 degrees. In a medium-sized mixing bowl, combine sugar and shortening. Add vanilla and eggs. In another bowl sift together flour, salt, and baking soda. Add sifted ingredients to sugar and shortening mixture. Add chocolate chips. Mix all ingredients together and drop by teaspoon on a cookie sheet. Bake at 350 degrees for 10 minutes.

4. From the above recipe, what should be sifted with baking soda?
    A. vanilla and eggs   B. sugar and shortening   C. flour and salt   D. chocolate chips and salt
    Answers to sample questions:

From *State Student Assesment Test. Part II: Answers to your Questions.* Reprinted with permission of the State of Florida, Department of Education.

they should not be held to the standards for majority students, who had received better opportunities.

Ralph D. Turlington was the commissioner of education and one of the defendants in the case. He argued that basic minimum standards must be applied to certify that students have enough information to survive in situations that require a high-school education. These standards, he argued, must be absolute. Either students know the basic information or they do not. According to the commissioner, "To demand that a 12th-grade student with a 3rd-grade reading level be given a diploma is silly." The Florida case illustrates the kind of lawsuit we might expect in the future. It pits two sides with reasonable arguments against each other. One side argues that minority children have worked hard in school under great disadvantage and cannot be expected to have learned the things majority children know. In recognition of their work, they deserve a diploma. The other side argues that there should be an absolute standard for basic information (Seligmann, Coppola, Howard, & Lee, 1979).

The court essentially sided with the commissioner. The judge did not challenge the validity of the test. However, he did suspend the use of the test for four years, after which all the students who had any part of their education in segregated schools would have graduated. Then, according to the opinion, the test could be used.

In a 1981 article, Lerner argued that minimum competence exams, such as the SSAT II used in the state of Florida, benefit both students and society. As an attorney, she found little legal justification for court involvement. However, the court reopened the *Debra P.* case that same year. This new consideration came after those students who had begun their education under a segregated system had graduated, and thus differences in performance could not be attributed to segregation. In the new evaluation, the U.S. District Court of Appeals considered the validity of the test. It stated that the test would violate the equal protection clause if "the test by dividing students into two categories, passers and failers, did so without a rational relation to the purpose for which it was designed." However, in this case, the court concluded that the test did have adequate construct validity and that it could be used to evaluate functional literacy. In the same opinion, the court stressed that the test must reflect what is taught in school and that continual surveillance of test fairness is warranted.

Claims such as those in *Debra P.* are less common today than they were in the 1980s because few school districts engaged in explicit racial discrimination. However, many of the arguments in *Debra P.* were used in cases involving the use of tests to withhold high-school diplomas from Mexican American students. An important case in Texas considered the use of English-based tests to deny high-school diplomas to students who used Spanish as their primary language (*GI Forum v. Texas Education Agency,* 1997).

Various arguments have been used in defense of grouping students in special education classes. In *Simmons on Behalf of Simmons v. Hooks* (1994), school officials argued that African American students benefited from being grouped in a slower educational track. The court rejected their arguments.

Regents of the University of California v. Bakke

Alan Bakke was an engineer in his 30s who decided to apply to medical school at the University of California–Davis, in the early 1970s. Although Bakke had a high grade point average and good MCAT scores, he was denied admission. Bakke decided to investigate the matter. He discovered that his test scores were higher than those of minority students who had gained admission to the medical school under a special affirmative action program. Bakke eventually sued the university on the grounds that he had been discriminated against because he was not a minority group member. The suit ended in the Supreme Court.

A major argument in *Bakke* concerned the use of test scores. Under the affirmative action program, the cutoff value for MCAT scores was higher for nonminority than for minority students. The defense argued that the tests were not meaningful (valid) for minority students. However, evidence was also presented that the tests were equally meaningful for both groups.

The Supreme Court ruling did not specifically address the use of tests, but it ruled that the university had to admit Bakke and that it had denied him due process in the original consideration of the case. It also implied that the use of different cutoff scores was not appropriate. However, the court did acknowledge that race could be taken into consideration in selection decisions. The EEOC interpreted this acknowledgement as a green light for affirmative action programs based on numerical quotas (Norton, 1978). However, the *Bakke* case signified a change in attitude about affirmative action programs.

Then-President Ronald Reagan openly opposed selection goals and affirmative action and made a political issue out of "racial quotas." He appointed several people to key positions who agreed with his beliefs. For example, his assistant attorney general for civil rights, Bradford Reynolds, became an advocate for unqualified individualism (see Chapter 19). He argued for "color blind" equal opportunity in which skin color is not considered in selection decisions. According to Reynolds, selecting African Americans with lower test scores to remediate past discrimination would be "borrowing the tools of the racist." He emphasized that government must "never support the use of quotas or any other numerical formulas" (Bareak & Lauter, 1991, p. A18). In 1996, California voters passed Proposition 209 which made affirmative action illegal. However, in 2004, the courts were hearing continuing legal challenges.

Golden Rule Insurance Company et al. v. Washburn et al.

In 1976, the Golden Rule Insurance Company of Lawrenceville, Illinois, sued ETS and the Illinois Department of Insurance over "cultural bias" in the Illinois Insurance Licensing Examination, created by the ETS for the state of Illinois. A 1978 study showed that 77% of white applicants passed the exam, while only 52% of African Americans passed. The case was settled out of court. ETS made no admission of guilt but did agree to change the test, mainly in the way items are selected for the test. An expert committee of insurance officials and testing experts now oversee the selection of the items on the criterion that the proportions of correct answers for white and African American test takers differ by no more than .15.

When the *Golden Rule* case was settled in 1984, civil rights experts predicted that there would be a major revision in the way insurance tests were administered in 22 other states. Approximately 200,000 applicants for insurance licenses take these tests every year ("Insurance License Exams Will Be Revised," 1984, p. 5). In 1985, a related case, *Allen v. Alabama State Board of Education,* followed similar lines of reasoning. However, in *Allen* a much more stringent rule was used. The Alabama State Board of Education agreed to use items for which the African American to white proportion of correct answers differed by no more than .05. The *Golden Rule* case is important because it sets a new precedent within the testing industry. Although ETS admitted no guilt, it clearly agreed to revise its method of operation.

Adarand Constructors, Inc. v. Pena, Secretary of Transportation et al.

In 1995, the U.S. Supreme Court weakened the legal basis for affirmative action. The case involved Adarand Constructors, which was competing for a subcontract from the federal government. Before 1995, most federal contracts had included a compensation clause that gave the primary contractor a financial incentive to hire as subcontractors small businesses controlled by socially and economically disadvantaged individuals. This particular case involved a contract from the U.S. Department of Transportation. After submitting the low bid to complete construction work, Adarand Constructors was denied the job in favor of a small business controlled by minority group members. The Supreme Court, by a vote of 5–4, suggested that giving business to firms owned by minority group members violated the equal protection component of the 14th Amendment. This policy, the court argued, denied Adarand and other contractors their due process. The decision had an immediate impact. Hundreds of millions of dollars in federal grants had been awarded under special preference programs, and these practices were ended. The ultimate impact of the decision on affirmative action programs will be determined by future policies and decisions.

Affirmative Action in Higher Education

In addition to *Adarand*, recent cases concerning higher education have weakened affirmative action. For example, the early 1990s saw the beginning of a new type of lawsuit that held that affirmative action programs did not necessarily benefit all minority groups. For example, Asian students have historically done especially well on college admissions tests such as the SAT. Some people have argued that affirmative action programs systematically discriminate against both minority and majority students. In 1991, a California congressman requested an investigation of the University of California in San Diego (UCSD). The university admits approximately 60% of its first-year class according to grade point average and SAT scores. Admission to the university is extremely competitive. Those who are admitted often have a nearly perfect grade point average and high SAT scores. However, in the early 1990s, 40% of the spots were reserved for students admitted under special considerations, including special achievements in fields such as music, athletics, or student government. In addition, the supplemental criteria can include race and ethnicity. Students admitted under these criteria were often from traditionally underrepresented groups such as Latinos, Latinas, and African Americans. The USCD case was initiated by a Filipino student denied admission under both standard and supplemental criteria. However, if all students had been admitted under the standard criteria, this student would probably have been admitted, because both his grade point average and SAT scores were high. The congressman argued that Asian Americans had been systematically denied admission because of their race. They did not receive extra consideration under the supplemental criteria, because they were not underrepresented in the first 60% of students selected. On the other hand, their test scores and grade point averages were higher than other minority-group members who were selected under the special admissions policies.

Similar complaints were filed at other University of California campuses. The university's defense was that it does not discriminate on the basis of race. Selection criteria are not ironclad. In other words, the university reserves the right to have some flexibility in its decision to select students. Ethnic diversity, they argued, is an appropriate goal for a public university. In 1995, the Regents of the University of California voted to give up all affirmative action programs (see Focused Example 20-5). The decision had a dramatic effect on admissions to professional schools within the University of California system.

Grutter v. Bollinger and Gratz v. Bollinger

The question of affirmative action reached the U.S. Supreme Court once again in June 2003. Two law suits challenged the University of Michigan admissions policy. The first case involved Barbara Grutter (*Grutter v. Bollinger*), who was de-

---

Focused Example 20-5

THE TWISTS AND TURNS OF UNIVERSITY AFFIRMATIVE ACTION POLICIES

 Federal regulation of college admissions policies has taken many interesting twists and turns. Initially, affirmative action policies were designed to guarantee that institutions of higher learning would be ethnically diverse. Indeed, most disciplinary actions have been taken because universities had not successfully attracted an ethnically diverse student body. However, some institutions have been thoroughly successful. For example, Boalt Hall, the School of Law at the University of California–Berkeley, has made aggressive efforts to attract an ethnically diverse student body. In the class of 1996 (made up of students admitted in 1992), 39% of the students were from minority groups.

In September 1992, Boalt Hall's admissions policies came under scrutiny. The U.S. Department of Education's Office of Civil Rights argued that the university had engaged in policies inconsistent with Title VII of the 1964 Civil Rights Act in that the law school had allowed discrimination on the basis of race, color, or national origin. Because Boalt Hall set aside a portion of its entering class positions for minority students and used separate decision processes for minority and nonminority students, it was argued that discrimination was taking place against Asians and to some extent Caucasians.

When faced with the complaint, the university agreed to alter its admissions policies. It was required to report by 1994 the number of applicants in each racial and ethnic category and to list how many of these applicants were admitted. By the time the 1994 report was completed, the university faced several similar lawsuits. In 1995 the regents of the university decided to end their affirmative action programs. In 1996, California voters passed an initiative restricting affirmative action programs. The result has been a dramatic decline in the number of African American and Hispanic students. However, a 2003 California initiative that would have forbidden the collection of any information about race, was rejected by the voters.

nied admission to the law school in 1996. Grutter discovered that the university had given extra points to underrepresented students, and this created a bias against white students. The Court ruled by a margin of 5-4 in favor of the law school admission policy, ruling that it benefited the university by enriching the campus with racial diversity and helping to improve cross-racial understanding. The law school policy allowed membership in an underrepresented racial or ethnic group as a positive factor among the many factors that are considered in the admissions process. The second decision (*Gratz v. Bollinger*) by a vote of 6–3 reversed the university's undergraduate policy that allowed race to be considered but still allowed consideration of race among other factors in admission decisions. The Court argued that the policy did not provide for flexibility when considering applicants with various backgrounds. However, the Court agreed that race could be considered but not specifically quantified. These cases raised several important issues. For example, the decisions noted the need for incorporating time limits into admissions policies and for considering race-neutral alternatives. The Court also took into consideration extra burdens on non-minority students imposed by consideration of racial and economic background (Holden, 2003; "A victory for affirmative action," 2003).

Some believe that the Michigan decisions ushered in a new era of appreciation for civil rights. However, the decision also had opponents. For example, Ward Connerly, a noted African American conservative activist, cited the U.S. Constitution proclamation that "all men are created equal" and the equal protection clause of the Fourth Amendment, which states, "nor shall any state deprive any person of life, liberty, or property, without due process of law; nor deny any person within its jurisdiction to equal protection of the law." Connerly believes that the Michigan decision violated the law by allowing race to be considered in law school acceptance decisions. In contrast, Mary Sue Coleman, the University of Michigan president, stated, "I believe these rulings in support of affirmative action will go down in history as among the great landmark decisions of the Supreme Court." Dr. Coleman also argued, "The court has provided two important signals. The first is a green light to pursue diversity in the college classroom. The second is a road map to get us there. We will modify our undergraduate system to comply with today's ruling, but make no mistake; we will find the root that continues our commitment to a richly diverse student body." See Focused Example 20-6.

Personnel Cases

Several important lawsuits have dealt with testing in employment settings. Through a series of Supreme Court decisions, specific restrictions have been placed on the use of tests for the selection of employees. The most important of these cases are *Griggs v. Duke Power Company, Albemarle Paper Company v. Moody,* and *Washington v. Davis.* In effect, these decisions have forced employers to define the measure of job performance as well as how it relates to test scores. However, none of the decisions denies that tests are valuable tools in the personnel field and that the use of tests can continue.

Focused Example 20-6

CONTRASTING VIEWS ON AFFIRMATIVE ACTION

 Crosby and colleagues provided a detailed review of affirmative action and social policy. Several initiatives have made the issue more controversial (Crosby, Iyer, Clayton, & Downing, 2003). In 1996, California voters passed Proposition 209 and Washington voters passed Initiative 200 in 1998. Both of these ballot measures made the preferential treatment based on demographic characteristics illegal. Despite an enormous debate on the issue, we still do not have definitive evidence that supports some of the arguments. For example, Crosby and colleagues suggested that affirmative action has driven a wedge into the African American community by separating those who are lucky enough to gain entrance into universities and those who are not. However, examination of income evidence does not show larger difference between African American and white citizens in recent years. Furthermore, there is growing evidence that successful members of ethnic minority groups are generous in giving money back to their communities.

There is strongly compelling evidence that affirmative action policies do undermine self-confidence.

Many years of research have documented that white men question the skills of women and of minority group members who have been chosen under affirmative action policies (Crosby et al., 2003). Some research shows that stigmatization toward African Americans can be reduced if people think employees or school applicants are being evaluated on merit. In one study, 178 students and 168 corporate employees evaluated descriptions of African American and white employees who were working under different conditions. In one case, the employees were described as being selected by an illegal policy that favored minority candidates. In a second case, the subjects were told that the employees were selected by a legal policy that had the same effect as the illegal policy. In the third case, subjects were told that the employees were selected under an equal opportunity policy. When the subjects believed that the employees were selected by an illegal policy, they rated achievement-related traits for African American employees lower than those for white employees. However, the same effect did not occur when the judges were told that the employees were selected by a fair and legal process (Evans, 2003).

In Chapter 5, we mentioned *Griggs v. Duke Power Company*. The case involved 14 African American employees of the Duke Steam Plant in North Carolina who were concerned about their lack of opportunity. In the steam plant, few employees, either African American or white, had graduated from high school. In 1966, the most an African American employee could earn was $1.65 per hour, while whites started at $1.81. Furthermore, white men generally rose through the ranks of the company and became managers or supervisors, with comfortable offices and bathrooms down the hall. Though assigned to clean the toilets in those bathrooms, African American men were not allowed to use them. Instead, the company built a "colored" bathroom and placed it across the railroad tracks behind the coal pile. The leader of the African American employees, Willie Boyd, had learned about the EEOC and become acquainted with a civil rights leader who persuaded Boyd and his co-workers to file a complaint. When they presented their complaint to the company, they were told that education and training were necessary for advancement. However, only 15 white employees had finished high school. The company reacted by creating a test and telling the African American employees that they needed to pass it in order to gain advancement. The test included 50 items such as this:

> In printing an article of 24,000 words, a printer decides to use two sizes of type. With the larger type, a printed page contains 900 words. With the smaller type, a page contains 1200 words. The article is allotted 21 full pages in the magazine. How many pages must be in small type?

None of the African-American employees passed this difficult test. Neither did any of the white employees. The validity of the test became the central issue in the lawsuit that followed. Specifically, evidence was required on the relationship between the test and the job duties. Although Boyd led the group, the lawsuit was filed under the name of Willie Griggs, the youngest of the group with the least seniority and the least to lose. After 5 years, the case worked its way to the U.S. Supreme Court, which ruled that employment tests must be valid and reliable. The *Griggs* case set the tone for the next two decades of civil rights action in the United States (Bareak & Lauter, 1991; Crosby et al., 2003).

In the 1988 Supreme Court case, *Watson v. Fort Worth Bank and Trust,* it was argued that any procedure that appears to discriminate because of the ratio of minorities selected violates the law. The case involved Clara Watson, an African American employee of the Fort Worth Bank and Trust. After being passed over for promotion to a supervisory position, Watson filed suit. She argued that African Americans made up 13% of the bank's workforce and 10% of Fort Worth's population. However, the bank had only one African American supervisor. Thus, there was a misrepresentation in selection for higher jobs. The lower courts had rejected Watson's petition, arguing that statistical evidence for bias applied only to objective selection devices, such as psychological tests, and that subjective judgments could be defended when there was evidence of "business necessity." The Supreme Court disagreed, suggesting that employers could protect themselves from discrimination suits by adding just one subjective item to objective tests. The court affirmed that statistical selection ratios are sufficient evidence of adverse impact.

Wards Cove and the 1991 Civil Rights Act. Sometimes trends in one direction spur reactions in another. Legislation like California's Proposition 209 reacted to earlier affirmative action developments by emphasizing the "color blind" selection of employees. *Watson* was one of the first important civil rights cases decided by a conservative group of Supreme Court justices. The next major case that came to the court was *Wards Cove Packing Company v. Antonio.* The case concerned salmon canneries in Alaska. Most of the workers were unskilled Filipinos and Eskimos who sliced up the fish during fishing season. Because these jobs were unsteady and dirty, they were the worst in the company. The employees claimed that the company was biased against them and kept them out of the better-paying skilled jobs such as machinery repair. The nine Supreme Court justices decided not to hear the case, returning it to the lower courts.

This decision reversed a central theme of the *Griggs* decision. In refusing to hear the case, the Court noted that the burden of proof should be shifted from the employer to the employee. In other words, instead of requiring the employer to show that a psychological test is valid and reliable, the burden fell to the employee to demonstrate that it did not have these properties. This may seem like a minor point, but in practice it could have had an enormous impact. Employers know how to interpret their own tests, financial records, and selection procedures. Requiring the plaintiff to discredit these procedures gives him or her an almost impossible task. Even the most skilled lawyers felt that the long fight for equal employment opportunity had been lost (Bareak & Lauter, 1991).

The *Wards Cove Packing Company v. Antonio* decision upset the Democratic-controlled 1991 Congress. In response to court actions, it proposed new and stronger legislation that culminated in the 1991 Civil Rights Act. Here are the purposes of the act:

1. Provide appropriate redress for intentional discrimination and unlawful harassment in the workplace.
2. Overrule proof burdens and the meaning of business necessity in *Wards Cove Packing Company v. Antonio* and codify the proof burdens and the meaning of business necessity used in *Griggs v. Duke Power Company.*
3. Confirm the basic aspects of the 1964 Civil Rights Act.
4. Provide a clear response to the Supreme Court decision.

In short, the act placed the burden of proof back on the employer.

One provision of the 1991 Civil Rights Act deals specifically with test scores. Section 9, "Prohibition Against Discriminatory Use of Test Scores," states,

> It shall be an unlawful employment practice for a respondent in connection with the selection or referral of applicants or candidates for employment or promotion to adjust the scores of, use different cutoff scores, or otherwise alter the results of employment related tests on the basis of race, color, religion, sex, or natural origin.

This part of the bill appears to outlaw the use of differential cutoff scores by race, gender, or ethnic backgrounds. Thus, it may cause a shift away from the use of quotas. See Focused Example 20-7 to see how African Americans and whites see these issues differently.

Test administration and validity. The courts have sometimes been asked to decide on issues of test administration. For example, because of a low test score, an employee of the Detroit Edison Company was not promoted. In his defense, his union suggested that the low score might have been an error and requested a copy of the test to check the scoring. Detroit Edison did not want to release the test because it feared that the union would distribute the items to other employees. By a 5–4 vote, the Supreme Court ruled on the side of Detroit Edison

Focused Example 20-7

DIFFERENT VIEWS OF AFFIRMATIVE ACTION

African Americans and whites differ in their views of affirmative action. For example, a 1991 poll conducted by the *Los Angeles Times* suggested that nearly two-thirds of whites felt that affirmative action was either adequate or had gone too far. One-third thought that it had not gone far enough. Among African-American respondents, 60% felt that it had not gone far enough.

On average, African Americans have less desirable jobs, income, and housing than do whites. Sixty-five percent of African American respondents said that discrimination was the cause of this problem, while only 33% of whites came to the same conclusion. These data, shown in the accompanying bar graphs, suggest important attitudinal differences between African Americans and whites that we must address to resolve these problems.

Percent stating affirmative action programs had gone too far, 1991

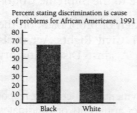

Percent stating discrimination is cause of problems for African Americans, 1991

In addition to differences of opinion about whether affirmative action is fair, opinion differs about how effective these programs have been. Most observers believe that the programs have effectively increased the number of African American and other underrepresented groups in various jobs. The increase in African Americans in professional jobs over the last few decades is undeniable. However, some believe that the trend was established before affirmative action programs were put into place. For example, there was a sharp increase in the percentage of African Americans in professional and technical jobs prior to the 1964 Civil Rights Act. Since then, the slope of the trend in technical and professional jobs has been less steep and appears unaffected by the *Griggs* decision and the EEOC guidelines (see line graph) (Herrnstein & Murray, 1994). However, one cannot assume that the *Griggs* decision and the Civil Rights Act did not affect the hiring of African Americans. It is possible that the number of African Americans in professional jobs would have reverted back to the 1960s level had these programs not helped.

Sources: Bureau of Labor Statistics 1983, 1989; U.S. Department of Labor 1991. Figures before 1973 reported for "blacks and others" are adjusted pro rata to the black-only population.

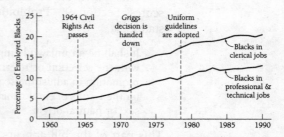

Sources: Bureau of Labor Statistics 1983, 1989; U.S. Department of Labor 1991. Figures prior to 1973, reported for "blacks and others," are adjusted pro-rata to the black-only population.

in *Detroit Edison Co. v. N.L.R.B.* It is interesting that in a major decision such as this, a single vote can make a difference in policy (Cronbach, 1980).

A 1982 Supreme Court decision, *Connecticut v. Teal,* considered the issue of discrimination against an individual when there has been no adverse impact. In this case, a written test unrelated to any specific job was used as an initial screening device. This screening device significantly reduced the number of

African Americans in the application pool. However, at the next step in the screening process, African Americans who had passed the test had a better chance of being hired than did whites. In short, the total number of African Americans hired did not reflect an adverse impact.

On review of the situation, the U.S. Supreme Court ruled that Title VII protects individuals, not just the groups to which they belong. Thus, it ruled that African American applicants had been discriminated against by the use of a test that did not have validity for the particular job. The Court suggested that these individuals were not compensated just because other members of their minority group received favorable treatment if they could pass the initial test. In other words, one cannot defensibly argue that a particular result justifies discrimination against individuals. In more recent decisions, the Court has upheld hiring goals that favor formerly underrepresented groups as interim relief for past discrimination while new and more valid selection procedures are being established (*United States v. City of Buffalo,* 1985).

On the other hand, the courts have allowed testing that excludes some groups when the tests are well constructed. For example, a class-action suit in California demonstrated that a teacher certification test had a higher failure rate for Mexican American teachers than for non-Hispanic Caucasian teachers. However, the court ruled that the test could still be used. The decision was based on three arguments. First, teacher educators and content experts had agreed to the items on the test before the measure was administered. Second, content-analysis and job-analysis studies had been conducted and questionable items had been eliminated. Third, the cutoff scores for failure had been established using acceptable methods (*Association of Mexican-American Educators v. California,* 1996).

In one summary article, Hogan and Quigley (1986) reviewed all of the cases that involved physical standards used in employment decisions. Physical tests, including height, weight, and physical strength, must be subjected to the same validity criteria as psychological tests. We expect many future lawsuits to arise concerning these issues.

A major issue that has plagued job discrimination cases is the evidence that one can use to prove bias. Proof of discrimination has often been difficult. In blue-collar jobs, employers have defended their hiring practices on the basis of the validity of aptitude tests. Challenges were typically based on the test criterion validity and the ratio of minority applicants that the test selected. In contrast, decisions about the selection and advancement of people in white-collar jobs have been based on subjective impressions of job performance and interviews. This promotes a double standard. White-collar employees have promoted the use of tests even though tests are not used for white-collar evaluations.

Cases Relevant to the Americans with Disabilities Act

One of the major challenges in test administration was created by the passage of the Americans with Disabilities Act (ADA) in 1991. The major focus of the ADA is the removal of physical barriers that make it difficult for people with disabilities to gain employment and education. However, according to some interpretations of the act, people with learning or other disabilities may request accommodations including substantially more time, rest breaks, or testing over multiple days.

The ADA, in effect, made private entities responsible for the same requirements that public agencies had addressed under Section 504 of the 1973 Rehabilitation Act. Section 504 creates a specific conflict with regard to testing:

> A recipient (of federal funds) shall make reasonable accommodations to the known physical or mental limitations of an otherwise qualified handicapped applicant or employee unless the recipient can demonstrate that the accommodation would impose an undue hardship on the operation of its program.

This passage has been interpreted to mean that those with disabilities should be afforded extra time or other accommodations in the completion of psychological or achievement tests. This policy contrasts with the *APA Standards for Educational and Psychological Tests.*

In typical applications, test administrators should follow carefully the standardized procedures for administration and scoring specified by the test publisher. Specifications regarding instructions to test takers, time limits, a form of item presentation or response, and test materials or equipment should be strictly observed. Exceptions should be made only on the basis of carefully considered professional judgment, primarily in clinical applications (P-83). (Geisinger, 1994)

The Americans with Disability Act defines reasonable accommodation as modifications in the job-application process, work environment, or benefits and privileges of employment that enable the disabled person to be considered for, perform the essential job functions, or enjoy the benefits of employment of similarly situated employees without disabilities (U.S. Equal Employment Opportunity Commission, 2003; see www.eeoc.gov). There are a variety of ways in which employees can be accommodated. For example, shifting responsibility to other employees for some job task that the employee cannot perform is a form of accommodation. Employers can also restructure a job to allow a person with a disability to perform it. For example, a department store salesperson who has arthritis of the hands and cannot wrap packages might be relieved of this responsibility while still being able to perform sales activities. Some accommodations are not considered reasonable. For example, the ADA does not require an employer to change the supervisor of a disabled person. However, they may ask that the supervisor's behavior, such as their method of communicating assignments, be changed.

The Americans with Disabilities Act has provoked a variety of lawsuits. One of the earliest cases, *Brookhart v. Illinois State Board of Education* (1983), concerned minimum competency tests. Because they failed a minimum competency test, several disabled students were denied high-school diplomas. They filed a lawsuit arguing that they had completed individualized educational programs and therefore qualified for a diploma. The test, they argued, denied them due process. In particular, the disabled students, including those with learning disabilities, may have had difficulty completing the test within the required time. In their decision, the federal court suggested that schools must provide accommodations for disabled students. However, the court argued that the test administrator did not have to modify the test substantially. Further, the court noted that the test need not be modified to ensure a passing grade for a person unable to learn because of a disability. On the other hand, the court left unanswered many decisions about the degree of accommodation required of test administrators.

In another case, the Hawaii Department of Education refused to allow a reader to assist a learning-disabled boy in a statewide graduation test. Because the student did not have impaired vision, the court decided that the use of a reader for the reading portions of the test would be inappropriate; that is, the decision by the Hawaii Department of Education was not discriminatory. However, the court also concluded that readers could be provided for aspects of the test that did not measure reading competency. Furthermore, the ruling suggested that denying a reader for these portions of the test did constitute unlawful discrimination against those with disabilities (Phillips, 1994).

A Critical Look at Lawsuits

As surely as the sun rises, court battles over the use of psychological tests will continue to develop. The problems that psychologists cannot resolve themselves will eventually be turned over to someone else for a binding opinion. This move, though, may not be in the best interest of the field of psychology or of the people whom the profession serves.

Inconsistencies in court decisions are commonplace. Even worse, judges who make important decisions about the use of tests often have little background in psychology or testing. On completing this course, you should be better able to evaluate most of the evidence than can some judges. Often, judges obtain their entire education about testing during the course of a trial.

In the near future, society must grapple with many difficult issues. For example, many current social problems seem related to the differential distribution of resources among the races in the United States. Changing the income distribution seems to be one of the only ways to effect social change. To accomplish this redistribution, society must get minority children in appropriate educational tracks, into professional schools, and into high-income positions. The courts have ruled that psychological tests are blocking this progress.

Psychologists themselves are not of one mind regarding the use of psychological tests. Though some researchers do not agree with the predominant court opinion, the courts have the power, and their judgment is law.

SUMMARY   With increasing frequency, tests are coming under legal regulation. Created by the Civil Rights Act of 1964, the EEOC has issued strict guidelines for the use of tests. The guidelines clearly spell out the minimum criteria for validity and reliability of psychological measures. The role of the EEOC became the focus of considerable debate in the 1980s, and the power of the commission was questioned by two court decisions at the end of that decade. However, the 1991 Civil Rights Bill breathed new life into affirmative action programs.

Tests have also come to be regulated by statute. The states of California and New York were among the first to pass truth-in-testing laws that place many requirements on commercial testing companies. These laws have required testing companies to disclose actual test items to test takers. In the past, test items were protected by copyright. Items on tests affected by these laws must now be rewritten frequently, and this procedure may damage the reliability and the validity of the tests. In 1975, Congress passed PL 94-142, which outlined standards for the assessment of potential among handicapped children. This law continues to affect the use of tests in the educational system.

Many lawsuits have also affected the use of tests. In *Stell v. Savannah-Chatham County Board of Education,* the court ruled that differences between African Americans and whites in IQ scores could not justify segregation. In *Hobson v. Hansen,* group tests were found to be inappropriate for the assignment of African American children to EMR classes. The concern over IQ tests was extended in *Diana v. State Board of Education.* Settled out of court, this case established that IQ tests could not be used with bilingual children, and it stimulated the development of new methods of assessment for these children. The impact of each of these decisions was magnified in *Larry P. v. Wilson Riles,* in which tests were banned as a means of assigning African American children to EMR classes. In 1980, a court apparently reversed this decision in the case of *Parents in Action on Special Education v. Hannon.* In *Debra P. v. Turlington,* a court ruled that a minimum competence test could be used only when the students had received their entire education in integrated schools. The courts have created new challenges in the *Adarand* case, which eliminated affirmative action. In 2003, the U.S. Supreme Court made two important rulings relevant to affirmative action. Both decisions allowed race and ethnicity to be considered as one factor in admissions decisions.

The regulation of testing through statute (laws passed by legislators), regulation (rules created by agencies), and litigation (lawsuits) has only recently become common. The passage of the Americans with Disabilities Act is one example of a set of laws likely to affect the testing industry. One can expect more interactions between testing and the law.

WEB ACTIVITY For interesting and relevant Web sites, check the following:

www.law.cornell.edu/ny/ctap/087_0384.htm
Reference to a case in which the ETS refused to release a test score for a student who had shown exceptional improvement when retaking the SAT

http://caselaw.lp.findlaw.com/cgi-bin/getcase.pl?court=5th&navby=case&no=9830425cv0
Description of a case in which a student had an exceptional improvement on the SAT. When forced to take the test again, his performance was similar to the first occasion.

www.psychtesting.org.uk/hotissues.asp?id=83
Summary of a case from England in which two psychologists were alleged to have failed to diagnose a case of dyslexia.

CHAPTER 21

Ethics and the Future of Psychological Testing

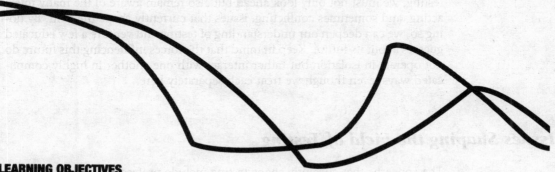

LEARNING OBJECTIVES

When you have completed this chapter, you should be able to:

☐ Explain why the question of whether people possess stable traits is an issue in the testing field

☐ Explain the issue of actuarial versus clinical prediction

☐ Identify human rights as they pertain to testing

☐ Explain the problem of labeling

☐ Explain the issue of divided loyalties

☐ Identify some important responsibilities of test users and constructors

☐ Identify four important current trends in the testing field

☐ Describe the future prospects of testing

*I*n a special issue of *Psychological Assessment,* specialists in psychological testing received a glimpse of the field's future (Haynes, 1995). This future involves the assimilation of new concepts such as chaos theory, nonlinear dynamical models, and mathematical models, which have been recently applied to fields such as economics, ecology, biology, and physics (Haynes, Blaine, & Meyer, 1995; Heiby, 1995a, 1995b). Indeed, the future of testing depends on the application of ultramodern theoretical notions and technologies (Embretson & Hershberger, 1999; Pedersen, 2002), especially computers and the Internet (Frase et al., 2003; Saccuzzo & Johnson, 2000). To discuss the future of testing, we must not only look ahead but also remain aware of the many interacting, and sometimes conflicting, issues that currently shape the field. By doing so, we can deepen our understanding of testing and venture a few educated guesses about its future. Keep in mind that the forces influencing this future do not operate in isolation but rather interact with one another in highly complicated ways, even though we treat each separately here.

Issues Shaping the Field of Testing

The concerns that currently shape testing include professional, moral, and social issues. Ethical issues underlie each of these concerns.

Professional Issues

Three major professional issues play an especially important role in the current status and the future of psychological testing: theoretical concerns, the adequacy of tests, and actuarial versus clinical prediction (see Figure 21-1).

Theoretical concerns. One of the most important considerations underlying tests is the dependability (reliability) of test results (Thomas & Selthon, 2003; Tryon & Bernstein, 2003). Reliability places an upper limit on validity. According to the *Standards for Educational and Psychological Testing* of the American Education Research Association, the American Psychological Association, and the National Council on Measurement in Education, a test that is totally unreliable (unstable) has no meaning. There may be exceptions to this rule, but current practice generally demands that tests possess some form of stability. As a corollary, whatever is being measured must itself have stability. Saying that a test has reliability implies that test results are attributable to a systematic source of variance, which is stable itself. In other words, the test is presumed to measure a stable entity. There are various types of reliability, depending on the different purposes of the tests. Each test must possess the type of reliability that is appropriate to the test's uses (AERA , APA, & NCME, 1999; APA, 2002).

Most existing tests measure a presumably stable entity—either the individual as he or she currently functions or some temporally stable characteristic of the individual. In describing current functioning, psychologists imply

FIGURE 21-1
Schematic summary of professional issues.

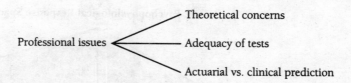

that the person functions this way in a fairly stable, though perhaps short-term, manner that is independent of the situation or environment. In other words, they assume that they can describe the person in absolute terms, as if in a vacuum. They may say something like, "The person is emotionally unstable" or "The person is out of contact with reality" or else provide a diagnostic label such as "schizophrenic" or "neurotic." Similarly, and even more strikingly, psychologists purport to measure enduring qualities that will manifest themselves over time regardless of immediate or long-term external (situational, environmental, and so forth) factors. Again, they assume that what they are measuring exists in absolute terms.

Whether measuring current functioning or a temporally stable characteristic, testers always assume that the systematic source of variance measured by the test results entirely from the person rather than some other factor. When we try to measure a stable characteristic of an individual and finds less than perfect temporal reliability, we assume that the imperfections proceed from test-related inadequacies, such as measurement error, or from minor fluctuating subject variables, such as fatigue. Presumably, then, the characteristic or variable being measured is stable, it exists, and only the test instrument limits one's ability to measure it. Therefore, the more accurate a test, the more stable the results should be.

In simple terms, testers assume that people possess stable characteristics (for example, intelligence) and stable response tendencies (for example, traits) that hold up across situations and exist independently of the environment. However, many empirical investigations (Cacioppo, Berntson, & Anderson, 1991) show that even the best tests have yet to achieve such temporal stability. In other words, testers cannot readily attribute differences over time solely to measurement error or fluctuating subject variables. Hence, this primary assumption underlying tests is not entirely correct. Moreover, the social environment affects behavior (Corrigan, Bogner, Mysiw, Clinchot, & Fugate, 2001), as illustrated in a model by Cacioppo and colleagues (1991), which shows the relationship between the psychological and the physiological domain (see Figure 21-2).

The trait question applies to psychology as a whole and to personality psychology in particular. Early formulations of human personality tended to view personality as comprising stable and lasting traits (behavioral dispositions). Freud and many of his followers, for example, believed that early experiences, memories, traumas, and anxieties often resulted in behavioral dispositions that persisted throughout life. Views such as Freud's, however, were challenged by those who saw human personality as changing rather than fixed and stationary

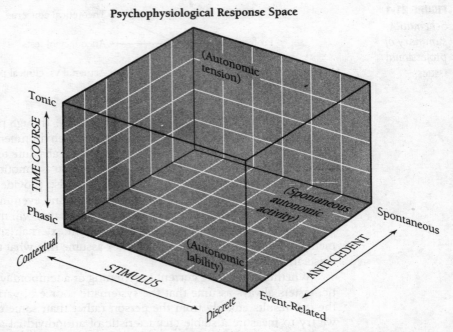

FIGURE 21-2 *Dimensions of psychophysiological response space. One dimension represents the antecedent of the physiological event (event-related/spontaneous), a second dimension represents the nature of the stimulus (discrete/contextual), and a third represents the time course of the physiological event (tonic/phasic). Each of the pairs of terms in this figure represents·endpoints on a continuum rather than narrowly and absolutely defined categories of activity.*

(From Cacioppo, Berntson, and Anderson, 1991. Copyright 1991 by the American Psychological Association. Reprinted by permission of the author.)

as well as by those who saw that situations and external factors influence behavior.

Most of the tests discussed in this text are based on the assumption that one can measure human characteristics independently of the context in which these characteristics occur, a theory not only disputable but also without significant support (Bandura, 1986; Mischel, 1968; Ziskin, 1995). Psychological tests can be no better than the science of psychology that underlies them. As the science clarifies basic theoretical issues, testing conforms to the available knowledge. In the meantime, perhaps the single most important theoretical assumption of tests—that human characteristics are stable and can be measured independently of the environment—is debatable.

Human behavior may be the result of long-term stable behavioral tendencies (traits); the external or internal environments that precede, coexist with, and follow behavior; or some other factor such as the interaction between traits and environments. Either tests have a long way to go before they will be able to measure the precise determinants of human behavior or current conceptualizations and underlying assumptions of tests are not precise enough to make accurate predictions.

After reviewing the psychometric qualities and the limits of mental ability and personality tests, we have concluded that, although people exhibit a core of stability, they continually change. Certainly, one explanation for the relatively poor long-term reliability of personality tests is that as the individual adjusts to the environment, he or she changes. Indeed, most definitions of intelligence include the ability to adapt or change according to circumstances.

A theory that is consistent with the available data would postulate that all normal people possess the ability to adapt to changing circumstances (Garlick, 2002; Sternberg, 2001; Zautra, 2003). This ability in turn involves a combination of factors that change. We refer to these combined factors as the individual's *index of competency,* which we believe is correlated with scores on major ability tests in use today. An individual with a high index of competency can adapt more readily and perhaps find more effective solutions to environmental pressures than can those with a low index. However, reacting to the environment may change not only behavioral tendencies but also the index of competency. Repeated failures or consistent success, for example, may increase rigidity, which in turn can lower the index of competency. However, an extremely demanding environment, such as one that forces an individual to call on latent reserves, may increase the index. In this theory, ability and personality are always changing and can be measured only within the context in which they occur.

The point here is that all psychological tests are based on theories of human functioning. Unfortunately, the validity of these theories and their underlying assumptions is far from proven. Furthermore, there is no consensus concerning either a definition of human intelligence or the essence of human personality, normal or abnormal. A revolution in psychological theory, therefore, could revolutionize psychological tests. In any case, today's tests are no better than the theories and assumptions that underlie them.

The adequacy of tests. A second professional issue in testing with strong overtones concerns the adequacy of existing tests. This entire book has been aimed at providing you with the knowledge you need to evaluate tests. To this end, the book is filled with statements about standardization, norms, scoring, interpretation, test design, reliability, and validity. Thus far, however, we have evaluated tests relative to traditionally accepted psychometric standards rather than absolute external criteria. Many psychologists and others have questioned whether even the best existing tests possess sufficiently sound psychometric qualities to warrant their use (Greene, 2000; Wood, Nezworski, Lilienfeld, & Garb, 2003; Ziskin, 1995).

As we have noted, the real issue in testing is how tests are used. One could argue that no test at all is better than a test that often leads to an incorrect conclusion. No doubt, there are situations in which all concerned would be better off without test results than with them.

We do not think all tests should be eliminated until better ones are developed, but we do believe that people should view the adequacy of tests from all possible perspectives. Some tests, such as certain ability tests, are generally adequate in reliability. However, just about any test could benefit from greater validity documentation. Clearly, people should consider absolute standards, not just relative ones, when evaluating current and future trends in testing.

In the end, how tests are used may be determined by law or by the threat of litigation. Tests that lead to selection biases are suspect. If the SAT consistently underselects African Americans, Latinos, and Latinas for college, then we have to ask how accurate the SAT is, how much it adds to prediction, and whether loss of diversity is justified by increased prediction (Geiser & Studley, 2001; Rosner, 2003). In the end, it may be the U.S. Supreme Court or Congress that tells us whether the use of a test is justified.

Actuarial versus clinical prediction. A third issue concerns the accuracy of predictions made by test users. Throughout this book we have argued that tests provide a standard setting in which practitioners can observe behavior. Further, they can use this situation in conjunction with experience and local norms to gain accuracy in their observations and decisions. Certainly, users of psychological tests must feel this way or they simply would not waste their time with tests. However, test users rarely, if ever, receive feedback on the accuracy of their predictions and decisions based on tests. Do tests, then, truly enhance assessment, or are practitioners fooling themselves, repeating their errors, and teaching them to students?

One can examine this question from all sides (see Campbell, 2003; Monahan, 2003; Ogloff & Douglas, 2003). The early work of Meehl (Meehl, 1954; Meehl & Rosen, 1955) and Little and Shneidman (1959) drew attention to the limits of test data even in the hands of trained practitioners. In subsequent analyses, Sawyer (1966) and Sines (1970) reviewed studies that compared an actuarial approach, in which test results were interpreted by using a set of rules, with a clinical approach, in which trained professionals interpreted test results. These reviews indicated that the set of rules was more accurate than the trained professional practitioners, even when the practitioners knew the rules. This research confirmed Meehl's (1954) earlier finding that trained practitioners could not surpass predictions based on statistical formulas. Most recently, Ziskin (1995) and Dawes (1999) have argued that simple tables of actuarial data, such as number of prior arrests and severity of crime, predict recidivism better than do tests or clinical judgments. Do we really need trained clinicians and sophisticated tests to make decisions? Other studies and analyses indicate that the trained practitioner is a better predictor than actuarial formulas are, especially when practitioners use data from a variety of sources such as a test battery, an interview, and a case history (for example, Matarazzo, 1990; see also Garb, 1998; Wood et al., 2003). In this argument, we again find professional disagreement at the most basic levels.

The issue of actuarial versus clinical prediction has recently reemerged with the proliferation of computerized test interpretations. As discussed in

FIGURE 21-3
Schematic summary of moral issues.

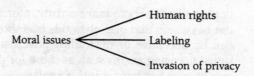

Chapter 15, computers are taking a prominent role in the scoring of tests, reporting of results, and diagnosis of clients (Frase et al., 2003). Can a computer accurately interpret a psychological test? The many problems inherent in such interpretations have fostered much debate about the computer's potential as a diagnostician (Saccuzzo, 1994). As Hartman (1986) noted, several potential abuses accompany the use of computer software to interpret psychological tests, including trivialization of assessment, use of software inappropriate to the client, and inadequate contribution of the clinician to the assessment process. Further, the question remains as to whether the computer's interpretations can ever be as good as, let alone better than, those of the clinician. Regardless of whether clinicians rely on a computer-generated diagnosis, a testing service, or on their own interpretation of results, the APA guidelines entitled *Ethical Principles of Psychologists and Code of Conduct* specify that it is the clinician who retains responsibility for the appropriateness of the analysis (APA, 2002).

Moral Issues

Professional issues alone will not determine the future of testing. The field is also being shaped by moral issues—human rights, labeling, and invasion of privacy (see Figure 21-3). Two other important ethical issues are divided loyalties and the responsibilities of test users and test constructors .

Human rights. Several different kinds of human rights are relevant to psychological testing, including the right not to be tested. Individuals who do not want to subject themselves to testing should not, and ethically cannot, be forced to do so. Nevertheless, exceptions to this directive are noted in the 2002 APA guidelines. Specifically, informed consent to testing is not required when "testing is mandated by law or government," when "informed consent is implied because testing is conducted as a routine educational, institutional, or organizational activity," or when "the purpose of the testing is to evaluate decisional capacity" (p. 13). Clearly, these exceptions negate the right not to be tested in an inestimable number of situations.

Another right due test takers is their right to know their test scores and interpretations as well as the bases of any decisions that affect their lives. In the past, guarding the security of tests was of paramount importance. Today, one must still take all precautions to protect test security, but not at the expense of an individual's right to know the basis of detrimental or adverse decisions. Test publishers who hide behind the veil of U.S. copyright laws and special rules protecting secure tests have a responsibility to make public sufficient information to allow users to make a truly informed decision of their adequacy. If the test has a selection bias, then this bias should be openly identified and not hidden by deceptive or misleading advertising. This is especially true of professional licensing exams such as those for physicians and attorneys, as these exams are the last barrier into a profession and would be suspect of bias if they underselected a disproportionate number of women and minorities.

Other human rights, some of which are only now being widely accepted, are the right to know who will have access to test data and the right to confidentiality of test results. The current frequent use of Internet and computer-based services has induced the APA to add a requirement for clinicians to warn clients of the risk to privacy and limits of confidentiality resulting from electronic transmission of information (APA, 2002).

Test interpreters have an ethical obligation to protect human rights. Potential test takers are responsible for knowing and demanding their rights. The increasing awareness among test users and the public of human rights is an important influence on the testing field.

Labeling. In standard medical practice, a person's disease or disorder is first identified (diagnosed). Once diagnosed, the disease can be labeled and standard medical intervention procedures implemented. It is no embarrassment to be diagnosed as having gall bladder or kidney disease. However, labeling people with certain medical diseases, such as AIDS, and psychiatric disorders can be extremely damaging. The public has little understanding of the label schizophrenia, for example. Therefore, those who receive this label are often stigmatized, perhaps for life (Shibre et al., 2003). Labels may also affect one's access to help. Chronic schizophrenia, for example, has no cure. Labeling someone a chronic schizophrenic may be a self-fulfilling prophecy (McReynolds, Ward, & Singer, 2002). Because the disorder is incurable, nothing can be done. Because nothing can be done, why should one bother to help? Because no help is given, the person is a chronic case.

Still another problem with labels, which people unfortunately often justify with psychological tests, is theoretical. As Szasz (1961) originally noted, a medical label such as schizophrenia implies that a person is ill or diseased. Because no one can be blamed for becoming ill, a medical or psychiatric label implies that the person is not responsible for the condition. However, it may well be that those who are labeled as psychiatrically disturbed must take responsibility for their lives if they are to get better.

When we take responsibility for our lives, we believe that we can exercise some degree of control over our fates (after all, what is intelligence?) rather than simply being the victims of uncontrollable external forces. Individuals who feel a sense of control or responsibility for themselves should be able to tolerate more stress, frustration, and pain than do those who feel like passive victims. Certainly, a person who feels responsible or in control has more incentive to alter negative conditions than one who does not.

Labels that imply a person is not responsible may increase the risk that the person so labeled will feel passive. Thus, the labeling process may not only stigmatize the person but also lower tolerance for stress and make treatment more difficult. In view of the potentially negative effects of labels, a person should have the right not to be labeled. When testing is necessary, a test such as the Rorschach, which has been shown to overpathologize test takers (Hamel, Shaffer, & Erdberg, 2000; Shaffer, Erdberg, & Haroaian, 1999), should not be relied on to determine pathology.

Invasion of privacy. When people respond to psychological tests, they have little idea what is being revealed, but they often feel that their privacy has been invaded in a way not justified by the test's benefits. Public concern over this issue once became so strong that tests were investigated by the Senate Subcommittee on Constitutional Rights and the House Subcommittee on invasion of privacy. Neither found evidence of deliberate and widespread misuse of tests (see Brayfield, 1965).

There are two sides to the issue. Dahlstrom (1969b) argued that the issue of invasion of privacy is based on serious misunderstandings. He states that because tests have been oversold, the public doesn't realize their limitations. Psychological tests are so limited that they *cannot* invade one's privacy. Another issue, according to Dahlstrom (1969b), is the ambiguity of the notion of invasion of privacy. It isn't necessarily wrong, evil, or detrimental to find out about a person. The person's privacy is invaded when such information is used inappropriately. Psychologists are ethically and often legally bound to maintain confidentiality and do not have to reveal any more information about a person than is necessary to accomplish the purpose for which testing was initiated. Furthermore, psychologists must inform subjects of the limits of confidentiality. As Dahlstrom (1969b) noted, subjects must cooperate in order to be tested. If the subjects do not like what they hear, they can simply refuse to be tested.

The ethical code of the APA (1992, 2002) includes confidentiality. Guaranteed by law in most states that have laws governing the practice of psychology, this principle means that, as a general rule, personal information obtained by the psychologist from any source is communicated only with the person's consent. Exceptions include circumstances in which withholding information causes danger to the person or society, as well as cases that require subpoenaed records. Therefore, people have the right to know the limits of confidentiality and to know that test data can be subpoenaed and used as evidence in court (Benjamin & Gollan, 2003) or in employment decisions (Ones et al., 1995).

Divided loyalties. Jackson and Messick (1967, Chap. 69) argued long ago that no one has formulated a coherent set of ethical principles that govern all legitimate uses of testing. Today, this is still true. The core of the problem lies in divided loyalties—the often conflicting commitments of the psychologist who uses tests. Despite the almost 40 years that have elapsed since Jackson and Messick first articulated the problem, the issue of divided loyalties remains a central dilemma to all psychologists who use tests in clinics, schools, business, industry, government, the military, and so forth. The question is, who is the client—the individual or the institution that ordered the test?

A conflict arises when the individual's welfare is at odds with that of the institution that employs the psychologist. For example, a psychologist working for an industrial firm to identify individuals who might break down under stress has a responsibility to the institution to identify such individuals as well as a responsibility to protect the rights and welfare of clients who are seeking employment with the firm. Thus, the psychologist's loyalty is divided. Similarly, the psychologist must not only maintain test security but also not violate the client's right to know the basis for an adverse decision. However, if the basis for an adverse decision is explained to one client, this information may leak out, and others with the same problem might then outsmart the test. Again, the test user is trapped between two opposing forces and principles.

The conflict is currently being resolved as follows. Ethically, psychologists must inform all concerned where their loyalty lies. They must tell clients or subjects in advance how tests are to be used and describe the limits of confidentiality. To the institution, they provide only the minimum information needed, such as "This subject has a low probability of breaking down under stress, and the probability that this conclusion is accurate is 68/100." Unnecessary or irrelevant personal information remains confidential.

In addition, the person's right to know the basis of an adverse decision may override issues of test security. Either the results are explained to the client or they are given to a representative of the client who is qualified to explain them (AERA, APA, & NCME, 1999; APA, 2002).

Responsibilities of test users and test constructors. A second ethical issue in testing concerns the responsibilities of test users. Because even the best test can be misused, the testing profession has become increasingly stringent and precise in outlining the ethics of responsible test use. According to the APA (2002), almost any test can be useful in the right circumstances, but even the best test, when used inappropriately, can hurt the subject. Of particular concern is the use of tests with different populations. A test that is valid and reliable for one group may not be valid and reliable for another. In light of this issue, the 2002 version of the APA Code of Ethics has added two subsections that direct psychologists who administer tests to "use assessment instruments whose validity and reliability have been established for use with members of the population being tested" and to "use assessment methods that are appropriate to an individual's language preference and competence." In addition, when interpreting test results, psychologists are instructed to take into account "characteristics of the person being assessed, such as situational, personal, linguistic, and cultural differences that might affect psychologists' judgments or reduce the accuracy of their interpretations" (p. 13). To aid clinicians in the process of choosing the correct type of test for individuals who are members of different populations, several guidebooks are available (Dana, 2000; Merrell, 2003; Naar-King, Ellis, & Frey, 2003). To reduce potential damage, the APA (1974, 2002) makes users of tests responsible for knowing the reason for using the test, the consequences of using the test, and the procedures necessary to maximize the test's effectiveness and to minimize unfairness. Test users must thus possess sufficient knowledge to understand the principles underlying the construction and supporting research of any test they administer. They must also know the psychometric qualities of the test being used as well as the literature relevant to the test. In addition, they are to ensure that interpretations based on the test are justified and that the test is properly used. A test user cannot claim ignorance: "I didn't realize normative data were not representative." The test user is responsible for finding out all pertinent information before using any test (APA, 1992, 2002).

The test developer is responsible for providing the necessary information (Franklin, 2003). Current standards for test use state that test constructors must provide a test manual with sufficient data to permit appropriate use of the test, including adequate validity and reliability data, clearly specified scoring and administration standards, and a clear description of the normative sample (AERA, APA, & NCME, 1999; APA 2002). It is not unusual for a researcher to receive requests from test designers to investigate a newly developed test. These designers hope that others will conduct the necessary research to provide adequate psychometric documentation. The standards also state that the test manual should warn against possible misinterpretation and identify necessary qualifications for responsible test use. Despite these guidelines, tests that do not meet specified standards continue to be published (Wood et al., 2003).

A test user has no excuse for employing an inadequately documented instrument that has damaging consequences (Embretson & Hershberger, 1999). The test user must know enough to tell the difference between a test that meets present standards and one that does not. Jackson and Messick (1967, Chap. 69) wisely suggested that the test user ask two questions whenever a test is proposed for a particular use. First, "Is the test any good as a measure of the characteristics it purports to measure?" The answer lies in the psychometric qualities of the test, such as reliability and validity documentation. Second, "Should the test be used for this purpose?" The answer to this question rests on the ethical and social values of the test user, who must think about the test's effect on the person and his or her human rights. Thus, though test constructors bear some responsibility for a poorly designed test or an inadequate manual, the responsibility for the ethical use of tests ultimately rests on the test user.

Social Issues

In addition to professional and moral issues, social issues play an important role in the testing field. We discuss three of these issues: dehumanization, the usefulness of tests, and access to psychological testing sources (see Figure 21-4).

Dehumanization. One social issue in the testing field concerns the dehumanizing tendencies that lurk in the testing process. For example, some corporations provide computerized analyses of the MMPI-2 and other test results. Such technology tends to minimize individual freedom and uniqueness. With high-speed computers and centralized data banks, the risk that machines will someday make important decisions about our lives is always increasing. Thus, society must weigh the risks against the benefits of the growing application of

FIGURE 21-4
*Schematic
summary of social
issues.*

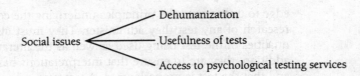

modern technology to the testing field. People must make this evaluation now
before an undesirable but unalterable situation develops. As psychologists and
the public allow test results to be stored and analyzed by computers, it may become extremely difficult to reverse this trend. U.S. society is founded on principles of individual rights and freedom. Anything that might threaten these
principles—such as computerized test interpretations—must be evaluated.
Only when the benefits far outweigh the risks and the risks are minimized can
the decision be socially acceptable.

Usefulness of tests. Tests need not be perfect in all ways. Society often finds uses
for initially crude tools that become precise with research and development.
One can discriminate between the useful and the true or correct. For example,
when Western society believed the sun revolved around the earth, the available
formulas and principles were useful in that they led to some accurate predictions, even though the underlying theories were incorrect. Similarly, the assumptions underlying today's tests may be fundamentally incorrect and the resulting test instruments far from perfect. However, the tests may still be useful
as long as they provide information that leads to better predictions and understanding than can otherwise be obtained. A test may be useful to society even
if all of the principles that underlie it are totally incorrect.

Thus, the crucial social issue in testing is not whether tests are perfect
but whether they are useful to society. Obviously, the answer to this question
to date has been a strong but disputed and controversial "Yes" (see Camara &
Schneider, 1994; Meyer et al., 2003; Ones, Chockalingam, & Schmidt,
1995). However, as new knowledge is gained, society must continually weigh
the risks of tests against the benefits. The risks, of course, include the possible misuse of tests, which in turn may adversely affect the life of an individual or may discriminate systematically against a specific cultural group (see
Fish, 2002; Henry, Bryson, & Henry, 1990). The benefits include the potential for increased precision and fairness in the decision-making process. Obviously, the resolution of this recurring issue will profoundly affect the field
of testing.

Society has used modern tests on a wide scale. First the military, then the
schools and psychiatric facilities, and finally business and industry have found
important uses for psychological tests. Indeed, there appears to be no end to
the proliferation of tests, despite criticism and heated debate. If the pervasive-
ness of tests indicates society's opinion of their usefulness, then certainly society has found them useful. As long as tests continue to serve a function, they
will most likely be used.

Access to psychological testing services. Who will have access to psychological testing services? Being tested can be expensive. A practitioner in a large metropolitan area often commands a fee of $5000 or more to administer a full battery of individual tests, score and interpret the findings, and produce a written report. In fact, the average cost of a custody evaluation in Southern California is $10,000, and can run as high as more than $20,000. Fees for extensive neurological testing, particularly in a legal battle, can be even higher. Moreover, the cost of test materials continues to skyrocket. A WAIS-R kit cost $98 in 1983. In 2003, the WAIS-III cost more than $775 with further price increases no doubt in the works. As with many other commodities, this price tag places testing beyond the reach of many. However, if a person's well-being depends on information from a psychological test battery, then how will the decision be made about who will have access to testing and who will not?

As it stands now, the expensive test batteries for neurological and psychiatric assessment are available to those who can afford them and to those who have enough insurance. For example, anyone with a developmental disability in California may be eligible to receive Medi-Cal, which provides free medical care, including the services of a psychologist. The individual may also be eligible for federal assistance such as Medicare and SSI, which provide cash benefits. Further, in California, developmentally disabled people (for example, the mentally retarded) or those with suspected developmental disabilities have access to psychological testing services at regional centers throughout the state. Unless California laws are changed, anyone suspected of having a handicap that originated during the developmental years can request (or have someone request on his or her behalf) an evaluation that may include a medical examination and psychological testing. The service is free, and if a team of specialists finds the person developmentally disabled, then additional services are available. Thus, current California and federal laws and policies help ensure that certain disabled people will have access to psychological testing services. However, such guarantees are not available in all states, and only certain people are covered.

National laws are in place to protect the rights of disabled children and their access to tests. The Individuals with Disabilities Education Act, or IDEA (20 U.S.C. §§ 1400, et seq.), requires school districts all over the country to seek to identify children whose disabilities may interfere with their education. The IDEA guarantees all schoolchildren access to a free and appropriate public education. To ascertain a child's needs, tests are typically needed. If parents are unhappy with a school's assessment of their child, then they have a right under the IDEA to request an independent assessment at the school's expense. This right is usually enough to force the school to provide adequate testing. However, this protection is limited to schoolchildren with disabilities or suspected disabilities.

Some in our society have offered national health insurance as a way to provide adequate medical care to everyone. As of this writing, no program of national health insurance has been implemented. One of the controversies in proposals for such programs concerns the extent of mental health coverage and whether psychological testing services will be included. If they are, then anyone who needs such services will have access to them. If not, then the availability of testing services may become substantially limited. In a sense, society will be judging the value of tests in deciding whether or not to include them in health insurance programs. Because resources are limited, testing services may preclude some other needed service, or vice versa.

Current Trends

Professional, moral, social, and even legal issues have interacted to produce today's trends in testing. These trends can be placed into four main categories: the proliferation of new tests; higher standards, improved technology, and increased objectivity; greater public awareness and influence; and computer and Internet applications.

The Proliferation of New Tests

New tests keep coming out all the time, with no end in sight. If we count revised and updated tests, we find hundreds of new tests being published each year. The impetus for developing these new tests comes from professional disagreement over the best strategies for measuring human characteristics, over the nature of these characteristics, and over theories about the causes of human behavior. (For an example, see the discussion of the K-ABC in Chapter 11.) The impetus also stems from public and professional pressure to use only fair, accurate, and unbiased instruments. Finally, if tests are used, then the authors and publishers of tests stand to profit financially. As long as someone can make a profit publishing tests, then new tests will be developed and marketed.

An examination of major reference books on tests indicates that the majority of new tests are based on the same principles and underlying theories as the more established tests. Indeed, most newly developed tests are justified on the grounds that they are either psychometrically superior to the existing tests or more specific and thus more appropriate for particular problems. However, as you saw in Chapter 15, some of the newer tests are based on models, theories, and concepts that fundamentally differ from those that underlie traditional tests. These nontraditional tests stem from modern concepts and theories from learning, social, physiological, and experimental psychology. Most of these newer tests are rooted in empirically derived data (Iacono, 1991).

The proliferation of nontraditional tests is related to two other trends in testing. First, it reflects the increasing role of the science of psychology in testing (Haynes, 1991, 1995; Wood et al., 2003). Even critics of testing must admit that a responsiveness to criticism and an honest and persistent effort to improve the quality of tests have characterized testing. The application of insights and empirical findings from psychological laboratories currently reflects this responsiveness.

Second, efforts are being made to integrate tests with other aspects of applied psychology (Aidman & Shmelyov, 2002; Wiederhold, Jang, Kim, & Wiederhold, 2002). Many psychologists, especially the behaviorally oriented, have long regretted the poor relationship among clinical assessment, traditional tests, and subsequent treatment interventions. They prefer test results that not only have a direct relationship to treatment but also can be used to assess the effectiveness of treatment. Because psychologists continually try to devise such procedures, their products add to the list of the many new tests published each year (Chabanne, Peruch, & Thinus-Blanc, 2003; Garcia-Palacios, Hoffman, Carlin, Furness, & Botella, 2002; Mehl, Pennebaker, Crow, Dabbs, & Price, 2001).

Higher Standards, Improved Technology, and Increasing Objectivity

Various pressures and issues have led to another current trend. The minimum acceptable standards for tests are becoming higher. Before the APA (1974) clearly and specifically defined their responsibilities, test constructors had neither a uniform nor a widely accepted set of guidelines. As a result, the quality of newly published tests varied greatly. With published standards, test constructors no longer have to work in the dark. An increasing percentage of new tests provides the information necessary for test users to make a fully informed choice in test selection, thus maximizing the chance of proper test use.

Higher standards of test construction have encouraged better use of tests (Clauser, 2002). The 1999 standards have helped considerably by reemphasizing the critical importance of proper test use and by articulating the responsibilities of test users (AERA, APA, & NCME, 1999; APA 2002). In addition, a working group of the Joint Committee on Testing Practices sponsored by the American Association for Counseling and Development, the American Educational Research Association, the American Psychological Association, the American Speech-Language-Hearing Association, and the National Council on Measurement in Education has published a thorough document that delineates the qualifications of test users (Eyde, Moreland, & Robertson, 1988). This comprehensive guide clearly specifies the competencies needed to use various types of tests and will provide a beacon for some time to come. Moreover, as we indicated earlier, the ethics of testing have been modified to encourage the proper use of tests and to avoid misuse (APA, 1992, 2002). Now that test users have a published set of standards, they have no excuse for misusing a test. Naturally, misuse and even abuse will never be entirely eliminated, but the trend toward better use of existing tests is most desirable.

Related to higher standards, improved technology has greatly benefited the testing field (Farrell, 1991, 1992; Haynes, 1992; Lowman, 1991; Matarazzo, 1990; Wilson, De Boeck, Moss, & Draney, 2003). Primarily because of advances in computer technology, statistical procedures such as factor analysis and item analysis can be performed with great ease. This technology thus contributes to the current trend toward better tests.

Also related to high standards is the trend toward increasing objectivity in test interpretation. As of this writing, attacks on the Rorschach have become devastating and merciless (see Hunsley & Bailey, 1999; Wood et al., 2003). As a result, practitioners tend to rely heavily on objective data such as that provided by the MMPI-2. One can readily see this trend in how the relative proportion of references devoted to the Rorschach and the MMPI in the *Mental Measurements Yearbook* and other sources has changed (for example, Archer, Maruish, Imhof, & Piotrowski, 1991).

The continuing research interest in testing also reflects the trend toward objectivity in the field. In view of the tens of thousands, if not hundreds of thousands, of published studies directly or indirectly related to psychological tests, a casual observer might conclude that little remains to be done. This conclusion is far from correct. Despite more than 10,000 articles already devoted to the MMPI and MMPI-2, for example, hundreds more creative and scientifically rigorous articles are published each year on these tests, not to mention the hundreds of other tests listed in the *Mental Measurements Yearbook* and other resource books. As long as tests are anything but perfect, and in this regard they have a long way to go, psychological researchers will no doubt keep conducting investigations to facilitate the objective use of tests.

Greater Public Awareness and Influence

Greater public awareness of the nature and use of psychological tests has led to increasing external influence on testing. At one time, the public knew little about psychological tests; psychologists played an almost exclusive role in governing how tests were used. With the public's greater assertiveness during the 1990s, the days when psychologists alone called the shots are gone forever (Saccuzzo, 1994). We believe this trend has affected the field positively.

Public awareness has led to an increased demand for psychological services, including testing services. This demand is balanced by the tendency toward restrictive legislative and judicial regulations and policies such as the judicial decision that restricts the use of standard intelligence tests in diagnosing mental retardation. These restrictions originate in real and imagined public fears. In short, the public seems to be ambivalent about psychological testing, simultaneously desiring the benefits yet fearing the power they attribute to tests.

Perhaps the greatest benefit of increased public awareness of tests has been the extra focus on safeguarding human rights. As more individuals share the responsibility of encouraging the proper use of tests by becoming informed of their rights and insisting on receiving them, the probability of misuse and abuse of tests will be reduced. The commitment of the field of psychology to high ethical standards can be easily seen in the published guidelines, position papers, and debates that have evolved during the relatively short period beginning in 1947 with the development of formal standards for training in clinical psychology (Shakow, Hilgard, Kelly, Sanford, & Shaffer, 1947). Practitioners of psychology, their instructors, and their supervisors show a deep concern for social values and the dignity of the individual human being. However, the pressure of public interest in psychological tests has led practitioners to an even greater awareness about safeguarding the rights and dignity of the individual.

Interrelated with all of these issues is the trend toward greater protection for the public. Nearly every state has laws that govern the use of psychological tests. Several factors give the public significant protection against the inherent risks of testing: limiting testing to reduce the chance that unqualified people will use psychological tests, sensitivity among practitioners to the rights of the individual, relevant court decisions, and a clearly articulated set of ethical guidelines and published standards for proper test use.

The Computerization of Tests

Throughout this book we have discussed how computers are being applied to testing on a rapid and widespread basis. The computerization of tests is a major trend, and computers, as you saw in Chapter 15, are being used in many different ways.

In adaptive computerized testing, different sets of test questions are administered via computer to different individuals, depending on each individual's status on the trait being measured (Mills, Potenza, Fremer, & Ward, 2002; Weiss, 1983, 1985). In ability testing, for example, the computer adjusts the level of item difficulty according to the subject's response. If the subject's answer is incorrect, then an easier item is given; if correct, then a more difficult item appears next. Such an approach individualizes a test and reduces total testing time. Research conducted in the 1980s and 1990s has finally led to the conversion of the Armed Services Vocational Aptitude Battery, given to millions, to an adaptive computerized format (see Chapter 18). In addition, by the year 2010 most students will probably be taking tests such as the SAT, GRE, and LSAT through adaptive computer programs.

Computers are also being used to administer, score, and even interpret psychological tests. In addition, computers are being used to generate tasks that cannot be presented by traditional methods (see Chapter 15) (Costa, De Carvalho, Drummond, Wauke, & De Sa Guimaraes, 2002). Through computer technology, one might be able to tap a whole new range of abilities heretofore beyond the scope of traditional tests (Saccuzzo, Johnson, & Guertin, 1994). Objective personality tests such as the MMPI-2 can be processed by a computer that generates a typed report. Each year, developers create more programs that score tests and produce written reports (Frase et al., 2003; Prince & Guastello, 1990). The use of the computer extends to all types of tests, including behavioral assessment (Farrell, 1991, 1992).

Testing on the Internet

According to Crespin and Austin (2002), one of the most important future applications of psychological testing is through its use on the Internet. Imagine the possibility of taking a test on the Internet and having the results immediately sent to your doctor. As mentioned in Chapter 15, the Internet company

Brain.com offers Internet-based testing for intelligence, memory, and levels of depression. The company recently asked us to evaluate the psychometric characteristics of one of its Internet tests, a 5-minute IQ test. Though the company does not advertise, more than 1 million people have logged on to this site and taken the test. Our initial evaluation of this test was based on more than 850,000 valid cases (Saccuzzo & Johnson, 2000). Such numbers are unprecedented in psychological test research. We found an encouraging coefficient alpha of more than .84. Thus, it seems that future testing on the Internet is inevitable.

Future Trends

Having analyzed the major relevant issues and forces in testing and identified current trends, we are now ready to venture a few guesses about what the future holds for the field. Certainly, we are reasonably safe in stating that the current trends will continue and become established in the field. However, our predictions for the future are educated guesses based on limited knowledge.

Future Prospects for Testing Are Promising

We believe that testing has a promising future. We base our optimism on the integral role that testing has played in the development and recognition of psychology. On a less lofty note, testing is a multibillion-dollar industry, and even relatively small testing companies can gross millions of dollars per year. With so much at stake, testing is probably here to stay. The field gained its first real status from its role in the development of screening tests for the military in World War I. Later, psychologists' creativity and skill in the testing field during World War II no doubt numbered among the factors that ultimately led to government funding through the Veterans Administration to encourage the development of professional psychology. Indeed, this federal funding, first earmarked for psychology in 1945, played an important role in the birth of clinical psychology and formal training standards.

As indicated, the central role played by testing in the development and recognition of psychology does not alone ensure an important future role for testing. Despite division within psychology about the role and value of testing, it remains one of the few unique functions of the professional psychologist. When one sees psychological testing as encompassing not only traditional but also new and innovative uses—as in cognitive-behavioral assessment, psychophysiology, evaluation research, organizational assessment, community assessment, and investigations into the nature of human functioning—one can understand just how important tests are to psychologists.

Thus, with this fundamental tie to testing, psychologists remain the undisputed leaders in the field. It is unlikely that attacks on and dissatisfaction with traditional psychological tests will suddenly compel psychologists to abandon tests. Instead, psychologists will likely continue to take the lead in this field to produce better and better tests, and such a direction will benefit psychologists, the field, and society. Even if this doesn't happen, testing corporations that publish and sell widely used high-stakes standardized tests will no doubt continue to market their products aggressively.

Moreover, tests are used in most institutions—schools, colleges, hospitals, industry, business, the government, and so forth—and new applications and creative uses continue to emerge in response to their demands. Tests will not suddenly disappear with nothing to replace them. If anything, current tests will continue to be used until they are replaced by still better tests, which of course may be based on totally new ideas. Though current tests may gradually fade from the scene, we believe psychological testing will not simply survive but will flourish through the 21st century.

The Proliferation of New and Improved Tests Will Continue

The future will likely see the development of many more tests. Chapters 9, 10, and 11 presented our belief that currently available intelligence tests are far from perfect and have a long way to go. Further, we believe that the dominant role of the Stanford-Binet and Wechsler tests is far from secure. These two major intelligence scales are probably about as technically adequate as they will ever be. They can, of course, be improved through minor revisions to update test stimuli and to provide larger and even more representative normative samples with special norms for particular groups and through additional research to extend and support validity documentation. However, despite the changes in the modern Binet and the WAIS-III, the fundamental characteristics and underlying concepts resemble those of the original scales.

During the next few decades, we shall be surprised if these two major intelligence scales are not challenged at least once or twice by similar tests with superior standardization and normative data or with less bias against certain minorities. However, if history indicates what is to be, then a true challenge can come only from a test based on original concepts and a more comprehensive theoretical rationale than that of the present scales. The Kaufman Assessment Battery for Children may be one such contender in its age range. We believe that the development of such a test is only a question of time. Should a compelling need for such an instrument arise, then we shall see it sooner rather than later.

In structured personality testing, the MMPI-2 appears destined to be the premier test of the 21st century. This favorable prediction for the MMPI-2 is a turnabout from the 1982 prediction made in the first edition of this book. We had not anticipated the innovative approach of Butcher and colleagues in dealing with the original MMPI's inadequate normative sample. Thus, future prospects for the MMPI-2 are indeed bright.

As indicated in our discussion of projective tests, we believe that use of the Rorschach will diminish greatly as clinicians come to grips with the realities of the scientific debate. The Rorschach is based on the early theories of Freud. Its psychometric properties are under continual attack (Wood et al., 2003). There is serious doubt whether the Rorschach provides clinically useful information (Hunsley & Bailey, 1999). Some say the Rorschach is no better than reading tea leaves. Although we would not go this far, it is clear that proponents of the Rorschach are fighting an uphill battle (Exner, 1999; Weiner, 2003). Again, this prediction is a turnabout from earlier versions of this book. We had thought that Exner's comprehensive system would provide the scoring reliability and standardized administration needed to support the Rorschach. As of 2004, this promise has not been fulfilled.

The future of the TAT is more difficult to predict. Affixed to some of the main arteries of psychological theory, the TAT has an incredibly extensive research base and is a prominent clinical tool. Unfortunately, the TAT stimuli are outdated. In a projective test, outdated stimuli are not a devastating weakness because projective stimuli are by nature ambiguous. Nevertheless, because the TAT stimuli have been revised (Ritzler, Sharkey, & Chudy, 1980) the TAT may enjoy increased respectability as more data are acquired on the more recent versions.

Revolutionary Changes: "Perestroika" in School Testing?

Years ago, we attended a meeting on testing in Washington, D.C. Speaker after speaker, including the U.S. Secretary of Education, predicted changes in testing in schools. Whereas some speakers emphasized national standardized tests, others rejected the idea. According to one speaker, there would soon be a "perestroika" in the field of testing in the schools. Performance tests would replace standardized multiple-choice tests by the year 2000.

Panic is indeed raging in Washington, D.C., because of the poor performance of U.S. schoolchildren compared with that of children from other industrialized nations including Japan, Korea, Canada, and the European Community. At the heart of this panic is how we evaluate school performance and measure progress.

A report of the National Commission on Testing and Public Policy (1990) made the following points:

1. "America must revamp the way it develops and utilizes human talent, and to do that, educational and employment testing must be restructured" (p. ix).

2. "Current testing, predominantly multiple choice in format, is overrelied upon, lacks adequate public accountability, sometimes leads to unfairness in the allocation of opportunities, and far too often undermines vital social policies" (p. ix).

3. "To help promote greater development of the talents of all our people, alternative forms of assessment must be developed and more critically judged and used, so that testing and assessment open gates of opportunity rather than close them off" (p. ix).

TABLE 21-1
Performance Testing

Purchasing an automobile

You are considering two used cars: a 1988 Ford Taurus priced at $3,800 and a 1988 Honda Accord priced at $4,100. How would you go about determining which is the best decision for you? Your task is to design and carry out a study to answer this question.

Grade level:	12th
Curriculum topics:	Computational skills: ability to work with money, ability to make relative judgments and comparisons, ability to analyze and write conclusions in a clear narrative form
Suggested length of time:	1–2 weeks
In class:	2 periods
Out of class:	4 periods

Based on the Connecticut Common Core of Learning Performance Assessment Project sponsored by the National Science Foundation.

The "new" assessment currently being called for by the National Education Association and others is performance testing. As you have seen, such testing requires a subject to do something rather than to provide a verbal response or fill in a blank (Harris, 2002). In performance testing in the schools, students would write essays, provide written responses to specified problems, or solve open-ended math problems (see Table 21-1).

Performance testing includes such varied procedures as observing a foreign-language student having a conversation in the foreign language, requiring science students to conduct a real experiment, asking students to work together as a group and observing the interaction, and giving problems that have no answer or more than one correct answer and observing a student's approach. A related idea is the *portfolio,* a collection of samples of the student's work.

We currently see two contrary positions, each purporting to solve the problems in the U.S. school system: national standardized testing versus performance testing and portfolios. This battle is not new. As you saw in Chapter 1, performance tests were replaced by standardized achievement tests in the 1930s because the latter were seen as more objective. Now, more than 70 years later, certain educators are calling for a return to the older method. As of this writing, we have not seen the promised "perestroika" in testing. Indeed, reliance on standardized testing has increased, and the stakes have become higher for individual educators and school districts to increase scores on standardized tests. The broadest survey ever conducted on this issue (Pedulla et al., 2003) indicated that teachers, in order to increase scores, diverted valuable class time to the instruction of specific knowledge to be tested and adjusted their curriculum in such a way that test results might appear favorable. The level of adjustment increased as the stakes increased. Although favorable results on standardized tests have been achieved in this manner, many teachers feel that the actual educational success of their students has been sacrificed. Forty percent of teachers believed that scores could be raised without any real improvements in learning, and 75% believed that the benefits of standardized testing programs were not worth the time and money they required. Even more disheartening, almost one-third of teachers in states where standardized testing stakes were the highest agreed that standardized testing was causing many students to drop out of high school or be held back a grade. Regardless of the apparent failures connected with the expansion of standardized testing, performance tests are still not being used on a widespread basis, and may soon be as obsolete as the old Soviet Union and record albums.

Controversy, Disagreement, and Change Will Continue

It doesn't matter whether the topic is testing or animal learning—disagreement and controversy are second nature to psychologists. Disagreement brings with it new data that may ultimately produce some clarification along with brand new contradictions and battle lines. Psychologists will probably never agree that any one test is perfect, and change will be a constant characteristic of the field. We continue to be optimistic because we see the change as ultimately resulting in more empirical data, better theories, continuing innovations and advances, and higher standards.

The Integration of Cognitive Science and Computer Science Will Lead to Several Innovations in Testing

As you saw in Chapter 15, concepts from basic psychological sciences have worked their way into the field: learning theory in the 1970s and 1980s, and psychophysiological and psychophysical concepts in the 1980s and 1990s. Today, the integration of concepts from experimental cognitive psychology, computer science, and psychometrics are rapidly shaping the field.

Multimedia computerized tests form the most recent cutting edge in the new generation of assessment instruments. The test taker sits in front of a computer that presents realistically animated situations with full color and sound. The program is both interactive and adaptive. The computer screen freezes and asks the test taker to provide a response. If the response is good, then a more difficult item is presented. For example, in research programs now being developed at companies such as IBM, the computer may show a scene involving sexual harassment. The screen freezes just after an employee has made an inappropriate joke. The test taker, who is applying for a manager's job, is given four choices to deal with the situation. If an effective choice is made, the computer moves on to an even more difficult situation, such as a threat from the offensive employee.

The computer offers test developers unlimited scope in developing new technologies: from interactive virtual reality games that measure and record minute responses to social conflict within a digital world to virtual environments that are suitable for measuring physiological responses while offering safe and effective systematic desensitization experiences to individuals with phobias. As we noted at the outset, the computer holds one of the major keys to the future of psychological testing.

SUMMARY

The future of psychological testing depends on many issues and developments. Professional issues include theoretical concerns, such as the usefulness of the trait concept as opposed to index of adjustment; the adequacy of tests; and actuarial versus clinical prediction. Moral issues include human rights such as the right to refuse testing, the right not to be labeled, and the right to privacy. Another ethical issue that concerns test users and developers is the divided loyalty that can result from administering a test to an individual for an institution: Whose rights come first? Also, professionals have an ethical duty to provide and understand the information needed to use a test properly. Finally, social issues such as dehumanization, the usefulness of tests, and access to testing services also inform the field of testing today.

Current trends include the proliferation of new tests, higher standards, improved technology, increasing objectivity, greater public awareness and influence, the computerization of tests, and testing on the Internet.

As for the future, anything is possible, especially in a field as controversial as testing. Psychology is now better equipped in technique, methodology, empirical data, and experience than ever before, and the members of this new and expanding field, as a group, are relatively young. Therefore, it does not seem unrealistic or overly optimistic to expect that the next 50 years will see advances equal to those of the last 50. On the other hand, psychology has come so far in the last 50 years that a comparable advance in the next 50 could easily produce results unimaginable today. What happens to testing in the future will depend on the goals and objectives chosen by those in the field and by their persistence and creativity in accomplishing their goals.

WEB ACTIVITY

For interesting and relevant Web sites, check the following:

www.pearsonassessments.com/assessments/resources/vipreview.htm
VIP Validity Indicator Profile: Review of a new instrument to assess response style

www.cspp.edu/news/forensic.htm
Forensic psychologists: Modern pioneers bridging the divide between psychology and the law

www.ucm.es/info/Psyap/iaap/pslaw.htm
24th International Congress of Applied Psychology (law and psychology)

www.dennisfox.net/psylaw/index.html
Psychology, law, and justice

www.law.ua.edu/lawpsychology/
The Law & Psychology Review

Appendix 1

Areas of a Standard Normal Distribution

Z	% Rank	Z	% Rank
−3.0	.13	0	50.00
−2.9	.19	.1	53.98
−2.8	.26	.2	57.93
−2.7	.35	.3	61.79
−2.6	.47	.4	66.54
−2.5	.62	.5	69.15
−2.4	.82	.6	72.57
−2.3	1.07	.7	75.80
−2.2	1.39	.8	78.81
−2.1	1.79	.9	81.59
−2.0	2.28	1.0	84.13
−1.9	2.87	1.1	86.43
−1.8	3.59	1.2	88.49
−1.7	4.46	1.3	90.32
−1.6	5.48	1.4	91.92
−1.5	6.68	1.5	93.32
−1.4	8.08	1.6	94.52
−1.3	9.68	1.7	95.54
−1.2	11.51	1.8	96.41
−1.1	13.57	1.9	97.13
−1.0	15.87	2.0	97.72
− .9	18.41	2.1	98.21
− .8	21.19	2.2	98.61
− .7	24.20	2.3	98.93
− .6	27.43	2.4	99.18
− .5	30.58	2.5	99.38
− .4	34.46	2.6	99.53
− .3	38.21	2.7	99.65
− .2	42.07	2.8	99.74
− .1	46.02	2.9	99.81
0	50.00	3.0	99.87

PART II

Areas Between Mean and Various Z Scores

Z	.00	.01	.02	.03	.04	.05	.06	.07	.08	.09
.0	.0000	.0040	.0080	.0120	.0160	.0199	.0239	.0279	.0319	.0359
.1	.0398	.0438	.0478	.0517	.0557	.0596	.0636	.0675	.0714	.0753
.2	.0793	.0832	.0871	.0910	.0948	.0987	.1026	.1064	.1103	.1141
.3	.1179	.1217	.1255	.1293	.1331	.1368	.1406	.1443	.1480	.1517
.4	.1554	.1591	.1628	.1664	.1700	.1736	.1772	.1808	.1844	.1879
.5	.1915	.1950	.1985	.2019	.2054	.2088	.2123	.2157	.2190	.2224
.6	.2257	.2291	.2324	.2357	.2389	.2422	.2454	.2486	.2517	.2549
.7	.2580	.2611	.2642	.2673	.2704	.2734	.2764	.2794	.2823	.2852
.8	.2881	.2910	.2939	.2967	.2995	.3023	.3051	.3078	.3106	.3133
.9	.3195	.3186	.3212	.3238	.3264	.3289	.3315	.3340	.3365	.3389
1.0	.3413	.3438	.3461	.3485	.3508	.3531	.3554	.3577	.3599	.3621
1.1	.3643	.3665	.3686	.3708	.3729	.3749	.3770	.3790	.3810	.3830
1.2	.3849	.3869	.3888	.3907	.3925	.3944	.3962	.3980	.3997	.4015
1.3	.4032	.4049	.4066	.4082	.4099	.4115	.4131	.4147	.4162	.4177
1.4	.4192	.4207	.4222	.4236	.4251	.4265	.4279	.4292	.4306	.4319
1.5	.4332	.4345	.4357	.4370	.4382	.4394	.4406	.4418	.4429	.4441
1.6	.4452	.4463	.4474	.4484	.4495	.4505	.4515	.4525	.4535	.4545
1.7	.4554	.4564	.4573	.4582	.4591	.4599	.4608	.4616	.4625	.4633
1.8	.4641	.4649	.4656	.4664	.4671	.4678	.4686	.4693	.4699	.4706
1.9	.4713	.4719	.4726	.4732	.4738	.4744	.4750	.4756	.4761	.4767
2.0	.4772	.4778	.4783	.4788	.4793	.4798	.4803	.4808	.4812	.4817
2.1	.4821	.4826	.4830	.4834	.4838	.4842	.4846	.4850	.4854	.4857
2.2	.4861	.4864	.4868	.4871	.4875	.4878	.4881	.4884	.4887	.4890
2.3	.4893	.4896	.4898	.4901	.4904	.4906	.4909	.4911	.4913	.4916
2.4	.4918	.4920	.4922	.4925	.4927	.4929	.4931	.4932	.4934	.4936
2.5	.4938	.4940	.4941	.4943	.4945	.4946	.4948	.4949	.4951	.4952
2.6	.4953	.4955	.4956	.4957	.4959	.4960	.4961	.4962	.4963	.4964
2.7	.4965	.4966	.4967	.4968	.4969	.4970	.4971	.4972	.4973	.4974
2.8	.4974	.4975	.4976	.4977	.4977	.4978	.4979	.4979	.4980	.4981
2.9	.4981	.4982	.4982	.4983	.4984	.4984	.4985	.4985	.4986	.4986
3.0	.4987	.4987	.4987	.4988	.4988	.4989	.4989	.4989	.4900	.4990.

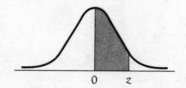

0   z

Standard score values are listed in the column headed "Z." To find the proportion of the total area occurring between the mean and any given Z score, locate the entry indicated by the Z score. For example, a Z score of +1.85 is located by reading across to the column for .05 from the value of 1.8 in the "Z" column. The value in the table is .4678. Since the total area above the mean is equal to .5000, this means that only .0322 of the area is beyond the Z score of +1.85.

Appendix 2

Publishers of Major Tests

Listed are the names and addresses of the publishers of major tests mentioned in this book.

Bayley Scale of Infant Development
The Psychological Corporation
555 Academic Court
San Antonio, TX 78204-2498
www.hbtpc.com/

Clinical Analysis Questionnaire
Institute for Personality and Ability Testing
P.O. Box 1188
Champaign, IL 61824
www.ipat.com/

Bender Visual Motor Gestalt Test
Riverside Publishing
425 Spring Lake Drive
Itasca, IL 60143-2079
www.riverpub.com/

Cognitive Abilities Test
Riverside Publishing
425 Spring Lake Drive
Itasca, IL 60143-2079
www.riverpub.com/

Bennett Mechanical Comprehension Test
The Psychological Corporation
555 Academic Court
San Antonio, TX 78204-2498
www.hbtpc.com/

Columbia Mental Maturity Scale
The Psychological Corporation
555 Academic Court
San Antonio, TX 78204-2498
www.hbtpc.com/

Benton Visual Retention Test–Fifth Edition
The Psychological Corporation
555 Academic Court
San Antonio, TX 78204-2498
www.hbtpc.com/

Cooperative School and College Ability
Test-Series II
Out of print—no longer available

Beta Examination III
The Psychological Corporation
555 Academic Court
San Antonio, TX 78204-2498
www.hbtpc.com/

Culture Fair Intelligence Test
Institute for Personality and Ability Testing
P.O. Box 1188
Champaign, IL 61824, USA
www.ipat.com/

California Psychological Inventory
CPP, Inc. and Davies-Black Publishing
3803 East Bayshore Road
P.O. Box 10096
Palo Alto, CA 94303
www.cpp.com/

Dental Admission Testing Program
Division of Educational Measurements
Council of Dental Education
American Dental Association
211 East Chicago Avenue, Suite 1846
Chicago, IL 60611
www.ada.org/prof/ed/testing/dat.asp

Cattell Infant Intelligence Scale
The Psychological Corporation
555 Academic Court
San Antonio, TX 78204-2498
www.hbtpc.com/

Differential Aptitude Test
The Psychological Corporation
555 Academic Court
San Antonio, TX 78204-2498
www.hbtpc.com/

Children's Apperception Test
C.P.S., Inc.
P.O. Box 83
Larchmont, NY 10538
914-833-1633

Edwards Personal Preference Schedule
The Psychological Corporation
555 Academic Court
San Antonio, TX 78204-2498
www.hbtpc.com/

Children's Personality Questionnaire
Institute for Personality and Ability Testing,
P.O. Box 1188
Champaign, IL 61824
www.ipat.com/

Fear Survey Schedule
Educational and Industrial Testing Service
P.O. Box 7234
San Diego, CA 92167
www.edits.net/

Goodenough-Harris Drawing Test
The Psychological Corporation
555 Academic Court
San Antonio, TX 78204-2498
www.hbtpc.com/

Memory-for-Designs Test
Psychological Tests Specialists
P.O. Box 9229
Missoula, MT 59807

Graduate Record Examination
Aptitude Test
Educational Testing Service
P.O. Box 6736
Princeton, NJ 08540-6736
www.gre.org/splash.html

Meyers-Briggs
CPP, Inc. and Davies-Black Publishing
3803 East Bayshore Road
P.O. Box 10096
Palo Alto, CA 94303
www.cpp.com/

Guilford-Zimmerman Temperament Survey
Pearson Education Technologies
27042 Towne Centre Drive, Suite 100
Foothill Ranch, CA 92610-2810
assessments.ncspearson.com/assessments/tests/gzts.htm

Miller Analogies Test
Psychological Corporation
555 Academic Court
San Antonio, TX 78204-2498
www.hbtpc.com/

Henmon-Nelson Test of Mental Ability
Riverside Publishing
425 Spring Lake Drive
Itasca, IL 60143-2079
www.riverpub.com/index.html

MMPI-Pearson Assessments
Order Processing
5601 Green Valley Drive
Bloomington, MN 55437
www.pearsonassessments.com/

Holtzman Inkblot Test
The Psychological Corporation
555 Academic Court
San Antonio, TX 78204-2498
www.hbtpc.com/

Minnesota Multiphasic Personality Questionnaire
University of Minnesota Press
Mill Place, Suite 290
111 Third Avenue South
Minneapolis MN 55401-2520
http://assessments.ncspearson.com/

Illinois Test of Psycholinguistic Abilities
Out of print—no longer available

Minnesota Paper Form Board Test
Psychological Corporation
555 Academic Court
San Antonio, TX 78204-2498
www.hbtpc.com/

Junior Senior High School Ability Questionnaire
Institute for Personality and Ability Testing
(Test Services Division)
P.O. Box 1188
Champaign, IL 61824-1188
www.ipat.com/

Mooney Problem Checklist
Psychological Corporation
555 Academic Court
San Antonio, TX 78204-2498
www.hbtpc.com/

Kuder Occupational Interest Survey
National Career Assessment Services, Inc.,
P.O. Box 277
Adel, IA 50003
www.ncasi.com

Otis Lennon Test of School Ability
Psychological Corporation
555 Academic Court
San Antonio, TX 78204-2498
www.hbtpc.com/

Kuhlmann-Anderson Test (eighth edition)
Scholastic Testing Service Inc.,
480 Meyer Road
Bensenville, IL 60106-1617
www.ststesting.com

Peabody Picture Vocabulary
American Guidance Services Publishing
4201 Woodland Road
Circle Pines, MN 55014-1796
www.agsnet.com/

Law School Admission Test
Law Services
661 Penn Street
Newton, PA 18940
www.lsac.org/

Pictorial Test of Intelligence
Out of print—no longer available

Leiter International Performance Scale
Stoelting Company
620 Wheat Lane
Woodale, IL 60191
www.stoeltingco.com/

Porteus Maze Test
Psychological Corporation
555 Academic Court
San Antonio, TX 78204-2498
www.hbtpc.com/

McCarthy Scales of Children's Abilities
Psychological Corporation
555 Academic Court
San Antonio, TX 78204-2498
www.hbtpc.com/

Quick Neurological Screening Test
Psychological Corporation
555 Academic Court
San Antonio, TX 78204-2498
www.hbtpc.com/

Raven Standard Progressive Matrices
Psychological Corporation
555 Academic Court
San Antonio, TX 78204-2498
www.hbtpc.com/

Rorschach Inkblot Test
Psychological Corporation
555 Academic Court
San Antonio, TX 78204-2498
www.hbtpc.com/

Scholastic Achievement Test
Educational Testing Service
P.O. Box 6736
Princeton, NJ 08540-6736
www.ets.org/

Thematic Apperception Test
Harvard University Press
79 Garden Street
Cambridge, MA 02138
www.hup.harvard.edu/

Senior Apperception Technique
C.P.S., Inc.
P.O. Box 83
Larchmont, NY 10538
914-833-1633

Torrance Tests of Creative Thinking
Scholastic Testing Service Inc.,
480 Meyer Road
Bensenville, IL 60106-1617
www.ststesting.com

Sixteen Personality Factor Questionnaire
Institute for Personality and Ability Testing
(Test Services Division)
P.O. Box 1188
Champaign, IL 61824-1188
www.ipat.com/

Wechsler Adult Intelligence Scale
Psychological Corporation
555 Academic Court
San Antonio, TX 78204-2498
www.hbtpc.com/

State-Trait Anxiety Inventory
CPP, Inc. and Davies-Black Publishing
3803 East Bayshore Road
P.O. Box 10096
Palo Alto, CA 94303
www.cpp.com/

Wechsler Intelligence Scale for Children–Revised
Psychological Corporation
555 Academic Court
San Antonio, TX 78204-2498
www.hbtpc.com/

Strong Interest Inventory
CPP, Inc. and Davies-Black Publishing
3803 East Bayshore Road
P.O. Box 10096
Palo Alto, CA 94303
www.cpp.com/

Wechsler Preschool and Primary Scale of Intelligence
Psychological Corporation
555 Academic Court
San Antonio, TX 78204-2498
www.hbtpc.com/

System of Multicultural Pluralistic
Psychological Corporation
555 Academic Court
San Antonio, TX 78204-2498
www.hbtpc.com/

Wide Range Achievement Test III
Psychological Corporation
555 Academic Court
San Antonio, TX 78204-2498
www.hbtpc.com/

Wonderlic Personnel Test
Psychological Corporation
555 Academic Court
San Antonio, TX 78204-2498
www.hbtpc.com/
Online Testing
www.agribiz.com/fbFiles/philo/mindlinks.htm

Appendix 3

Critical Values of *r* for α = .05 and α = .01 (*Two-Tailed Test*)

df*	α = .05	α = .01	df*	α = .05	α = .01
1	.99692	.999877	17	.456	.575
2	.9500	.99000	18	.444	.561
3	.878	.9587	19	.433	.549
4	.811	.9172	20	.423	.537
5	.754	.875	25	.381	.487
6	.707	.834	30	.349	.449
7	.666	.798	35	.325	.418
8	.632	.765	40	.304	.393
9	.602	.735	45	.288	.372
10	.576	.708	50	.273	.354
11	.553	.684	60	.250	.325
12	.532	.661	70	.232	.302
13	.514	.641	80	.217	.283
14	.497	.623	90	.205	.267
15	.482	.606	100	.195	.254
16	.468	.590			

*df are equal to $N - 2$, where N is the number of paired observations.

Reprinted with permission from Table IX-1. Percentage Points. Distribution of the Correlation Coefficient. When $p = 0$, *CRC Handbook of Tables for Probability and Statistics* (2nd ed.). Copyright 1968, CRC Press, Inc., Boca Raton, Florida.

Appendix 4

Critical Values of *t**

For any given *df*, the table shows the values of *t* corresponding to various levels of probability. Obtained *t* is significant at a given level if it is equal to or greater than the value shown in the table.

*Appendix 4 is taken from Table III of R. A. Fisher and R. Yates, 1967, *Statistical Tables for Biological, Agricultural and Medical Research* (6th ed.), New York: Hafner. With permission of the authors and publishers.

	Level of significance for one-tailed test					
	.10	.05	.025	.01	.005	.0005
	Level of significance for two-tailed test					
df	.20	.10	.05	.02	.01	.001
1	3.078	6.314	12.706	31.821	63.657	636.619
2	1.886	2.920	4.303	6.965	9.925	31.598
3	1.638	2.353	3.182	4.541	5.841	12.941
4	1.533	2.132	2.776	3.747	4.604	8.610
5	1.476	2.015	2.571	3.365	4.032	6.859
6	1.440	1.943	2.447	3.143	3.707	5.959
7	1.415	1.895	2.365	2.998	3.499	5.405
8	1.397	1.860	2.306	2.896	3.355	5.041
9	1.383	1.833	2.262	2.821	3.250	4.781
10	1.372	1.812	2.228	2.764	3.169	4.587
11	1.363	1.796	2.201	2.718	3.106	4.437
12	1.356	1.782	2.179	2.681	3.055	4.318
13	1.350	1.771	2.160	2.650	3.012	4.221
14	1.345	1.761	2.145	2.624	2.977	4.140
15	1.341	1.753	2.131	2.602	2.947	4.073
16	1.337	1.746	2.120	2.583	2.921	4.015
17	1.333	1.740	2.110	2.567	2.898	3.965
18	1.330	1.734	2.101	2.552	2.878	3.922
19	1.328	1.729	2.093	2.539	2.861	3.883
20	1.325	1.725	2.086	2.528	2.845	3.850
21	1.323	1.721	2.080	2.518	2.831	3.819
22	1.321	1.717	2.074	2.508	2.819	3.792
23	1.319	1.714	2.069	2.500	2.807	3.767
24	1.318	1.711	2.064	2.492	2.797	3.745
25	1.316	1.708	2.060	2.485	2.787	3.725
26	1.315	1.706	2.056	2.479	2.779	3.707
27	1.314	1.703	2.052	2.473	2.771	3.690
28	1.313	1.701	2.048	2.467	2.763	3.674
29	1.311	1.699	2.045	2.462	2.756	3.659
30	1.310	1.697	2.042	2.457	2.750	3.646
40	1.303	1.684	2.021	2.423	2.704	3.551
60	1.296	1.671	2.000	2.390	2.660	3.460
120	1.289	1.658	1.980	2.358	2.617	3.373
∞	1.282	1.645	1.960	2.326	2.576	3.291

Code of Fair Testing Practices in Education

Prepared by the Joint Committee
on Testing Practices

The Code of Fair Testing Practices in Education states the major obligations to test takers or professionals who develop or use educational tests. The Code is meant to apply broadly to the use of tests in education (admissions, educational assessment, educational diagnosis, and student placement). The Code is not designed to cover employment testing, licensure or certification testing, or other types of testing. Although the Code has relevance to many types of educational tests, it is directed primarily at professionally developed tests such as those sold by commercial test publishers or used in formally administered testing programs. The Code is not intended to cover tests made by individual teachers for use in their own classrooms.

The Code addresses the roles of test developers and test users separately. Test users are people who select tests, commission test development services, or make decisions on the basis of test scores. Test developers are people who actually construct tests as well as those who set policies for particular testing programs. The roles may, of course, overlap as when a state education agency commissions test development services, sets policies that control the test development process, and makes decisions on the basis of the test scores.

The Code has been developed by the Joint Committee on Testing Practices, a cooperative effort of several professional organizations, that has as its aim the advancement, in the public interest, of the quality of testing practices. The Joint Committee was initiated by the American Educational Research Association, the American Psychological Association, and the National Council on Measurement in Education. In addition to these three groups, the American Association for Counseling and Development/Association for Measurement and Evaluation in Counseling and Development and the American Speech-Language-Hearing Association are now also sponsors of the Joint Committee.

This is not copyrighted material. Reproduction and dissemination are encouraged. Please cite this document as follows:
Code of Fair Testing Practices in Education. (1988) Washington, D.C. Joint Committee on Testing Practices. (Mailing Address: Joint Committee on Testing Practices, American Psychological Association, 1200 17th Street, NW, Washington, D.C. 20036.)

The Code presents standards for educational test developers and users in four areas:

A. Developing/Selecting Tests
B. Interpreting Scores
C. Striving for Fairness
D. Informing Test Takers

Organizations, institutions, and individual professionals who endorse the Code commit themselves to safeguarding the rights of test takers by following the principles listed. The Code is intended to be consistent with the relevant parts of the *Standards for Educational and Psychological Testing* (AERA, APA, NCME, 1985). However, the Code differs from the Standards in both audience and purpose. The Code is meant to be understood by the general public, it is limited to educational tests, and the primary focus is on those issues that affect the proper use of tests. The Code is not meant to add new principles over and above those in the Standards or to change the meaning of the Standards. The goal is rather to represent the spirit of a selected portion of the Standards in a way that is meaningful to test takers and/or their parents or guardians. It is the hope of the Joint Committee that the Code will also be judged to be consistent with existing codes of conduct and standards of other professional groups who use educational tests.

*Developing/Selecting Appropriate Tests**

Test developers should provide the information that test users need to select appropriate tests.

Test users should select tests that meet the purpose for which they are to be used and that are appropriate for the intended test-taking populations.

Test Developers Should:

1. Define what each test measures and what the test should be used for. Describe the population(s) for which the test is appropriate.

2. Accurately represent the characteristics, usefulness, and limitations of tests for their intended purposes.

3. Explain relevant measurement concepts as necessary for clarity at the level of detail that is appropriate for the intended audience(s).

Test Users Should:

1. First define the purpose for testing and the population to be tested. Then, select a test for that purpose and that population based on a thorough review of the available information.

2. Investigate potentially useful sources of information, in addition to test scores, to corroborate the information provided by tests.

3. Read the materials provided by test developers and avoid using tests for which unclear or incomplete information is provided.

---

*Many of the statements in the Code refer to the selection of existing tests. However, in customized testing programs test developers are engaged to construct new tests. In those situations, the test development process should be designed to help ensure that the completed tests will be in compliance with the Code.

4. Describe the process of test development. Explain how the content and skills to be tested were selected.

5. Provide evidence that the test meets its intended purpose(s).

6. Provide either representative samples or complete copies of test questions, directions, answer sheets, manuals, and score reports to qualified users.

7. Indicate the nature of the evidence obtained concerning the appropriateness of each test for groups of different racial, ethnic, or linguistic backgrounds who are likely to be tested.

8. Identify and publish any specialized skills needed to administer each test and to interpret scores correctly.

4. Become familiar with how and when the test was developed and tried out.

5. Read independent evaluations of a test and of possible alternative measures. Look for evidence required to support the claims of test developers.

6. Examine specimen sets, disclosed tests or samples of questions, directions, answer sheets, manuals, and score reports before selecting a test.

7. Ascertain whether the test content and norms group(s) or comparison group(s) are appropriate for the intended test takers.

8. Select and use only those tests for which the skills needed to administer the test and interpret scores correctly are available.

Interpreting Scores

Test developers should help users interpret scores correctly.

Test users should interpret scores correctly.

Test Developers Should:

9. Provide timely and easily understood score reports that describe test performance clearly and accurately. Also explain the meaning and limitations of reported scores.

10. Describe the population(s) represented by any norms or comparison group(s), the dates the data were gathered, and the process used to select the samples of test takers.

11. Warn users to avoid specific, reasonably anticipated misuses of test scores.

12. Provide information that will help users follow reasonable procedures for setting passing scores when it is appropriate to use such scores with the test.

Test Users Should:

9. Obtain information about the scale used for reporting scores, the characteristics of any norms or comparison group(s), and the limitations of the scores.

10. Interpret scores taking into account any major differences between the norms or comparison groups and the actual test takers. Also take into account any differences in test administration practices or familiarity with the specific questions in the test.

11. Avoid using tests for purposes not specifically recommended by the test developer unless evidence is obtained to support the intended use.

12. Explain how any passing scores were set and gather evidence to support the appropriateness of the scores.

13. Provide information that will help users gather evidence to show that the test is meeting its intended purpose(s).

13. Obtain evidence to help show that the test is meeting its intended purpose(s).

Striving for Fairness

Test developers should strive to make tests that are as fair as possible for test takers of different races, gender, ethnic backgrounds, or handicapping conditions.

Test users should select tests that have been developed in ways that attempt to make them as fair as possible for test takers of different races, gender, ethnic backgrounds, or handicapping conditions.

Test Developers Should:

14. Review and revise test questions and related materials to avoid potentially insensitive content or language.

15. Investigate the performance of test takers of different races, gender, and ethnic backgrounds when samples of sufficient size are available. Enact procedures that help to ensure that differences in performance are related primarily to the skills under assessment rather than to irrelevant factors.

16. When feasible, make appropriately modified forms of tests or administration procedures available for test takers with handicapping conditions. Warn test users of potential problems in using standard norms with modified tests or administration procedures that result in noncomparable scores.

Test Users Should:

14. Evaluate the procedures used by test developers to avoid potentially insensitive content or language.

15. Review the performance of test takers of different races, gender, and ethnic backgrounds when samples of sufficient size are available. Evaluate the extent to which performance differences may have been caused by inappropriate characteristics of the test.

16. When necessary and feasible, use appropriately modified forms of tests or administration procedures for test takers with handicapping conditions. Interpret standard norms with care in the light of the modifications that were made.

Informing Test Takers

Under some circumstances, test developers have direct communication with test takers. Under other circumstances, test users communicate directly with test takers. Whichever group communicates directly with test takers should provide the information described below.

Under some circumstances, test developers have direct control of tests and test scores. Under other circumstances, test users have such control. Whichever group has direct control of tests and test scores should take the steps described below.

Test Developers or Test Users Should:

17. When a test is optional, provide test takers or their parents/guardians with information to help them judge whether the test should be taken, or if an available alternative to the test should be used.

Test Developers or Test Users Should:

19. Provide test takers or their parents/ guardians with information about rights test takers may have to obtain copies of tests and completed answer sheets, retake tests, have tests rescored, or cancel scores.

18. Provide test takers the information they need to be familiar with the coverage of the test, the types of question formats, the directions, and appropriate test-taking strategies. Strive to make such information equally available to all test takers.

20. Tell test takers or their parents/guardians how long scores will be kept on file and indicate to whom and under what circumstances test scores will or will not be released.

21. Describe the procedures that test takers or their parents/guardians may use to register complaints and have problems resolved.

Note: The membership of the Working Group that developed the Code of Fair Testing Practices in Education and of the Joint Committee on Testing Practices that guided the Working Group was as follows:

Theodore P. Bartell
John R. Bergan
Esther E. Diamond
Richard P. Duran
Lorraine D. Eyde
Raymond D. Fowler
John J. Fremer
   (Co-chair, JCTP and
   Chair, Code Working
   Group)

Edmund W. Gordon
Jo-Ida C. Hansen
James B. Lingwall
George F. Madaus
   (Co-chair, JCTP)
Kevin L. Moreland
Jo-Ellen V. Perez
Robert J. Solomon
John T. Stewart

Carol Kehr Tittle
   (Co-chair, JCTP)
Nicholas A. Vacc
Michael J. Zieky
Debra Boltas and Wayne
   Camara of the American Psychological Association served as staff liaisons.

Glossary

achievement Previous learning.

acquiescence The tendency to agree or to endorse a test item as true.

adverse impact The effect of any test used for selection purposes if it systematically rejects substantially higher proportions of minority than majority job applicants.

age differentiation Discrimination based on the fact that older children have greater capabilities than do younger children.

age scale A test in which items are grouped according to age level. (The Binet scale, for example, grouped into one age level items that two-thirds to three-quarters of a representative group of children at a specific age could successfully pass.)

anxiety An unpleasant emotional state marked by worry, apprehension, and tension.

aptitude Potential for learning a specific skill (for example, musical aptitude).

assessment A procedure used to evaluate an individual so that one can describe the person in terms of current functioning and also so that one can predict future functioning. Tests are used in the assessment process.

basal The level at which a minimum criterion number of correct responses is obtained.

basal age In the Stanford-Binet scale, the highest year level at which the subject successfully passes all tests.

base rate In decision analysis, the proportion of people expected to succeed on a criterion if they are chosen at random.

biserial correlation An index used to express the relationship between a continuous variable and an artificially dichotomous variable.

category format A rating-scale format that often uses the categories 1 to 10.

ceiling A certain number of incorrect responses that indicate the items are too difficult.

class interval The unit for the horizontal axis in a frequency distribution.

closed-ended question In interviewing, a question that can be answered specifically (for example, "yes" or "no"). Such questions generally require the interviewee to recall something.

coefficient alpha A generalized method for estimating reliability. Alpha is similar to the KR_{20} formula, except that it allows items to take on values other than 0 and 1.

coefficient of alienation In correlation and regression analysis, the index of nonassociation between two variables.

coefficient of determination The correlation coefficient squared; gives an estimate of the percentage of variation in Y that is known as a function of knowing X (and vice versa).

concurrent validity evidence Evidence for criterion validity in which the test and the criterion are administered at the same point in time.

confrontation A statement that points out a discrepancy or inconsistency.

construct validity evidence A process used to established the meaning of a test through a series of studies. To evaluate evidence for construct validity, a researcher simultaneously defines some construct and develops the instrumentation to measure it. In the studies, observed correlations between the test and other measures provide evidence for the meaning of the test. See also *convergent evidence* and *discriminant evidence.*

content validity evidence The evidence that the content of a test represents the conceptual domain it is designed to cover.

convergent evidence Evidence obtained to demonstrate that a test measures the same attribute as do other measures that purport to measure the same thing. A form of construct validity evidence.

correction for attenuation Correction of the reduction, caused by low reliability, in the estimated correlation between a test and another measure. The correction for attenuation formula is used to estimate what the correlation would have been if the variables had been perfectly reliable.

correlation coefficient A mathematical index used to describe the direction and the magnitude of a relationship between two variables. The correlation coefficient ranges between -1.0 and 1.0.

criterion-referenced test A test that describes the specific types of skills, tasks, or knowledge of an individual relative to a well-defined mastery criterion. The content of criterion-referenced tests is limited to certain well-defined objectives.

criterion validity evidence The evidence that a test score corresponds to an accurate measure of interest. The measure of interest is called the *criterion*.

cross validation The process of evaluating a test or a regression equation for a sample other than the one used for the original studies.

deciles Points that divide the frequency distribution into equal tenths.

descriptive statistics Methods used to provide a concise description of a collection of quantitative information.

developmental quotient (DQ) In the Gesell Developmental Schedules, a test score that is obtained by assessing the presence or absence of behaviors associated with maturation.

dichotomous format A test item format in which there are two alternatives for each item.

differential validity The extent to which a test has different meanings for different groups of people. For example, a test may be a valid predictor of college success for white but not for black students.

discriminability In item analysis, how well an item performs in relation to some criterion. For example, items may be compared according to how well they separate groups who score high and low on the test. The index of discrimination would then be the correlation between performance on an item and performance on the whole test.

discriminability analysis See *discriminability*.

discriminant analysis A multivariate data analysis method for finding the linear combination of variables that best describes the classification of groups into discrete categories.

discriminant evidence Evidence obtained to demonstrate that a test measures something different from what other available tests measure. A form of construct validity evidence.

distractors Alternatives on a multiple-choice exam that are not correct or for which no credit is given.

drift The tendency for observers in behavioral studies to stray from the definitions they learned during training and to develop their own idiosyncratic definitions of behaviors.

dyslexia A specific reading disorder characterized by reading backwardness.

EEOC guidelines A set of procedures created by the Equal Employment Opportunity Commission (EEOC) to ensure fairness in employment practices. The EEOC guidelines discuss the minimum requirements for the validity and reliability of the psychological tests used for employee selection.

estimated learning potentials (ELPs) In the SOMPA system, WISC-R scores adjusted for the socioeconomic background of the children. ELPs take the place of IQ scores.

evaluative statement A statement in interviewing that judges or evaluates.

expectancy effects The tendency for results to be influenced by what experimenters or test administrators expect to find (also known as the **Rosenthal effect**, after the psychologist who has studied this problem intensively).

face validity The extent to which items on a test appear to be meaningful and relevant. Actually not evidence for validity because face validity is not a basis for inference.

factor analysis A set of multivariate data analysis methods for reducing large matrixes of correlations to fewer variables. The variables are linear combinations of the variables that were in the original correlation matrix.

false negative In test-decision theory, a case in which the test suggests a negative classification, yet the correct classification is positive.

false positive In test-decision analysis, a case in which the test suggests a positive classification, yet the correct classification is negative.

four-fifths rule A rule used by federal agencies in deciding whether there is equal employment opportunity. Any procedure that results in a selection rate for any race, gender, or ethnic group that is less than four-fifths (80%) of the selection rate for the group with the highest rate is regarded as having an adverse impact.

frequency distribution The systematic arrangement of scores on a measure to reflect how frequently each value on the measure occurred.

general cognitive index (GCI) In the McCarthy Scales of Children's Abilities, a standard score with a mean of 100 and standard deviation of 16.

group test A test that a single test administrator can give to more than one person at a time.

hit rate In test-decision analysis, the proportion of cases in which a test accurately predicts success or failure.

hostile statement In interviewing, a statement that reflects anger.

human ability Behaviors that reflect either what a person has learned or the person's capacity to emit a specific behavior; includes *achievement*, *aptitude*, and *intelligence*.

individual tests Tests that can be given to only one person at a time.

inferences Logical deductions (from evidence) about something that one cannot observe directly.

inferential statistics Methods used to make inferences from a small group of observations, called a *sample*. These inferences are then applied to a larger group of individuals, known as a *population*. Typically, the researcher wants to make statements about the larger group but cannot make all of the necessary observations.

intelligence General potential independent of previous learning.

intelligence quotient (IQ) A unit for expressing the results of intelligence tests. The intelligence quotient is based on the ratio of the individual's mental age (MA) (as determined by the test) to actual or chronological age (CA): IQ = MA/CA × 100.

intercept On a two-dimensional graph, the point on the Y axis where X equals 0. In regression, this is the point at which the regression line intersects the Y axis.

interquartile range The interval of scores bounded by the 25th and the 75th percentiles.

interval scale A scale that one can use to rank order objects and on which the units reflect equivalent magnitudes of the property being measured.

interview A method of gathering information by talk, discussion, or direct questions.

ipsative score A test result presented in relative rather than absolute terms. Ipsative scores compare the individual against him- or herself. Each person thus provides his or her own frame of reference.

isodensity curve An ellipse on a scatterplot (or two-dimensional scatter diagram) that encircles a specified proportion of the cases constituting particular groups.

item A specific stimulus to which a person responds overtly and that can be scored or evaluated.

item analysis A set of methods used to evaluate test items. The most common techniques involve assessment of item difficulty and item discriminability.

item characteristic curve A graph prepared as part of the process of item analysis. One graph is prepared for each test item and shows the total test score on the X axis and the proportion of test takers passing the item on the Y axis.

item difficulty A form of item analysis used to assess how difficult items are. The most common index of difficulty is the percentage of test takers who respond with the correct choice.

item discriminability See *discriminability*.

Kuder-Richardson 20 A formula for estimating the internal consistency of a test. The KR_{20} (or KR_{20}) method is equivalent to the average split-half correlation obtained from all possible splits of the items. For the KR_{20} formula to be applied, all items must be scored either 0 or 1.

Likert format A format for attitude scale items in which subjects indicate their degree of agreement to statements using these categories: strongly disagree, disagree, neither disagree nor agree, agree, strongly agree.

McCall's T A standardized score system with a mean of 50 and a standard deviation of 10. McCall's T can be obtained from a simple linear transformation of Z scores ($T = 10Z + 50$).

mean The arithmetic average of a set of scores on a variable.

measurement error The component of an observed test score that is neither the true score nor the quality you wish to measure.

median The point on a frequency distribution marking the 50th percentile.

mental age A unit for expressing the results of intelligence tests. This unit is based on comparing the individual's performance on the test with the average performance of individuals in a specific chronological age group.

multiple regression A multivariate data analysis method that considers the relationship between a continuous outcome variable and the linear combination of two or more predictor variables.

multivariate analysis A set of methods for data analysis that considers the relationships between combinations of three or more variables.

nominal scales Systems that arbitrarily assign numbers to objects. Mathematical manipulation of numbers from a nominal scale is not justified. For example, numbers on the backs of football players' uniforms are a nominal scale.

normative sample A comparison group consisting of individuals who have been administered a test under standard conditions—that is, with the instructions, format, and general procedures outlined in the test manual for administering the test (also called a *standardization sample*).

norm-referenced test A test that evaluates each individual relative to a normative group.

norms A summary of the performance of a group of individuals on which a test was standardized. The norms usually include the mean and the standard deviation for the reference group and information on how to translate a raw score into a percentile rank.

one-tailed test A directional test of the null hypothesis. With a one-tailed test, the experimenter states the specific end of the null distribution that should be used for the region of rejection of the null hypothesis. For example, an experimenter studying weight loss may state that group B should lose more weight than group A. Thus, the null hypothesis would be rejected only if it was statistically improbable that the amount of weight group B lost was greater than group A. If group A lost more weight than group B, the null hypothesis would not be rejected.

open-ended question In interviewing, a question that usually cannot be answered specifically. Such questions require the interviewee to produce something spontaneously.

ordinal scale A scale that one can use to rank order objects or individuals.

parallel forms reliability The method of reliability assessment used to evaluate the error associated with the use of a particular set of items. Equivalent forms of a test are developed by generating two forms using the same rules. The correlation between the two forms is the estimate of parallel forms reliability.

Pearson product moment correlation An index of correlation between two continuous variables.

percentile band The range of percentiles that are likely to represent a subject's true score. It is created by forming an interval one standard error of measurement above and below the obtained score and converting the resulting values to percentiles.

percentile rank The proportion of scores that fall below a particular score.

performance scale A test that consists of tasks that require a subject to do something rather than to answer questions.

personality tests Tests that measures overt and covert dispositions of individuals (the tendency that individuals will show a particular behavior or response in any given situation). Personality tests measure typical human behavior.

point scale A test in which points (0, 1, or 2, for example) are assigned to each item. In a point scale, all items with a particular content can be grouped together.

polytomous format A format for objective tests in which three or more alternative responses are given for each item. This format is popular for multiple-choice exams. Also called *polychotomous format.*

predictive validity evidence The evidence that a test forecasts scores on the criterion at some future time.

probing statement A statement in interviewing that demands more information than the interviewee has been willing to provide of his or her own accord.

projective hypothesis The proposal that when a person attempts to understand an ambiguous or vague stimulus, his or her interpretation reflects needs, feelings, experiences, prior conditioning, thought processes, and so forth.

projective personality tests Tests in which the stimulus or the required response or both are ambiguous. The general idea behind projective tests is that a person's interpretation of an ambiguous stimulus reflects his or her unique characteristics.

prophecy formula A formula developed by Spearman and Brown that one can use to correct for the loss of reliability that occurs when the split-half method is used and each half of the test is one-half as long as the whole test. The method can also be used to estimate how much the test length must be increased to bring the test to a desired level of reliability.

psychological test A device for measuring characteristics of human beings that pertain to overt (observable) and covert (intraindividual) behavior. A psychological test measures past, present, or future human behavior.

psychological testing The use of psychological tests. Psychological testing refers to all of the possible uses, applications, and underlying concepts of psychological tests.

quartiles Points that divide the frequency distribution into equal fourths.

randomly parallel tests Tests created by successive random sampling of items from a domain or universe of items.

ratio scale An interval scale with an absolute zero, or point at which there is none of the property being measured.

reactivity The phenomenon that causes the reliability of a scale in behavior studies to be higher when an observer knows that his or her work is being monitored.

reassuring statement In interviewing, a statement intended to comfort or support.

receptive vocabulary In the Peabody Picture Vocabulary Test, a nonverbal estimate of verbal intelligence; in general, the ability to understand language.

regression line The best-fitting straight line through a set of points in a scatter diagram.

reliability The extent to which a score or measure is free of measurement error. Theoretically, reliability is the ratio of true score variance to observed score variance. This ratio can be estimated using a variety of correlational methods, including *coefficient alpha, Kuder-Richardson 20, test–retest,* and *parallel forms.*

representative sample A sample (group) composed of individuals with characteristics similar to those for whom the test is to be used.

residual The difference between predicted and observed values from a regression equation.

response style The tendency to mark a test item in a certain way irrespective of content.

restricted range In correlation and regression, variability on one measure is used to forecast variability on a second measure. If the variability is restricted on either measure, the observed correlation is likely to be low. For example, the correlation between the GRE and performance among students in an elite graduate program is likely to be low because GRE scores among students admitted to the program might have very little variability. The true correlation considering all students at all universities may be higher.

Rosenthal effect See *expectancy effect.*

scaled score On the Wechsler tests, a standard score with a mean of 10 and a standard deviation of 3.

scales Tools that relate raw scores on test items to some defined theoretical or empirical distribution.

scatter diagram A picture of the relationship between two variables. For each individual, a pair of observations is obtained, and the values are plotted in a two-dimensional space created by variables X and Y.

selection ratio In test decision analysis, the proportion of selected applicants to unselected ones.

self-report questionnaire A questionnaire that provides a list of statements about an individual and requires him or her to respond in some way to each, such as "True" or "False."

shrinkage Many times a regression equation is created for one group and used to predict the performance of another group of subjects. This procedure tends to overestimate the magnitude of the relationship for the second group. The amount of decrease in the strength of the relationship from the original sample to the sample with which the equation is used is known as *shrinkage.*

social ecology A relatively new field of study that deals with the relationship between environments and behavior, the description of behavioral settings, and other related topics.

social facilitation Tendency of people to behave like the models around them.

Spearman's rho A method for finding the correlation between two sets of ranks.

split-half reliability A method for evaluating reliability in which a test is split into halves. The correlation between the halves of the test, corrected for the shortened length of the halves, is used as an estimate of reliability.

standard administration The procedures outlined in the test manual for administering a test.

standard deviation The square root of the average squared deviation around the mean (or the variance). It is used as a measure of variability in a distribution of scores.

standard error of estimate An index of the accuracy of a regression equation. It is equivalent to the standard deviation of the residuals from a regression analysis. Prediction is most accurate when the standard error of estimate is small.

standard error of measurement An index of the amount of error in a test or measure. The standard error of measurement is a standard deviation of a set of observations for the same test.

standardization sample A comparison group consisting of individuals who have been administered a test under standard conditions—that is, with the instructions, format, and general procedures outlined in the test manual for administering the test (also called a *normative sample*).

standardized interview An interview conducted under standard conditions that are well defined in a manual or procedure book.

stanine system A system for assigning the numbers 1 through 9 to a test score. The system was developed by the U.S. Air Force. The standardized stanine distribution has a mean of 5 and a standard deviation of approximately 2.

state anxiety An emotional reaction to a situation. State anxiety varies from one situation to the next.

stress A response to situations that pose demands, place constraints, or give opportunities.

structured personality tests Tests that provide a statement, usually of the self-report variety ("I like rock and roll music"), and require the subject to choose between two or more alternative responses ("True" or "False," for example). Sometimes called *objective personality tests.*

subtest scatter On the Wechsler tests, the degree of subtest variability.

Taylor-Russell tables A series of tables one can use to evaluate the validity of a test in relation to the amount of information it contributes beyond what would be known by chance.

test A measurement device that quantifies behavior.

test administration The act of giving a test.

test administrator Person giving a test.

test anxiety Anxiety that occurs in test-taking situations.

test battery A collections of tests, the scores of which are used together in appraising an individual.

test–retest reliability A method for estimating how much measurement error is caused by time sampling, or administering the test at two different points in time. Test–retest reliability is usually estimated from the correlation between performances on two different administrations of the test.

third variable A variable that may account for the observed relationship between two other variables.

tracking The tendency to stay at about the same level of growth or performance relative to peers who are the same age.

trait anxiety A personality characteristic reflecting the differences among people in the intensity of their reaction to stressful situations.

traits Enduring or persistent characteristics of an individual that are independent of situations.

T score On the MMPI, a standard score with a mean of 50 and a standard deviation of 10. (See also *McCall's T.*)

true score The score that would be obtained on a test or measure if there were no measurement error. In practice, the true score can be estimated but not directly observed.

two-tailed test A non-directional test of the null hypothesis. In contrast to a one-tailed test which states a specific direction, the two-tailed test is used to evaluate whether observations are significantly different from chance in either the upper or lower end of the sampling distribution.

understanding response In interviewing, a statement that communicates understanding (also called an *empathy response*).

unstructured interview An interview conducted without any specific or particular questions or sequences of questions.

validity The extent to which a test measures the quality it purports to measure. Types of validity evidence include *content validity, criterion validity,* and *construct validity evidence.*

variance The average squared deviation around the mean; the standard deviation squared.

References

AAmodt, M. G. (2004). *Applied industrial/orgnaizational psychology* (4th ed.). Belmont, CA: Wadsworth.

Abbott, R. D., Amtmann, D., & Munson, J. (2003). Exploratory and confirmatory methods in learning disabilities research. In H. L. Swanson & K. R. Harris (Eds.), *Handbook of learning disabilities* (pp. 471–482). New York: Guilford Press.

Abdelkhalek, A. M. (1994). Normative results on the Arabic Fear Survey Schedule 3. *Journal of Behavior Therapy and Experimental Psychiatry, 25*(1), 61–67.

Abell, S. C., Horkheimer, R., & Nguyen, S. E. (1998). Intellectual evaluations of adolescents via human figure drawings: An empirical comparison of two methods. *Journal of Clinical Psychology, 54,* 811–815.

Abrams, D. M. (1999). Six decades of the Bellak Scoring System. In L. Gieser & M. I. Stein (Eds.), *Evocative images: The Thematic Apperception Test and the art of projection.* Washington: American Psychological Assocation.

Abramson, L. Y., Alloy, L. B., & Metalsky, G. I. (1995). Hopelessness depression: Explanatory style. In G. M. Buchanan & E. P. Seligman (Eds.), *Explanatory style* (pp. 113–134). Hillsdale, NJ: Erlbaum.

Abramson, T. (1969). The influence of examiner race on first-grade and kindergarten subjects' Peabody Picture Vocabulary Test scores. *Journal of Educational Measurement, 6,* 241–246.

Acklin, M. W. (1995). Rorschach assessment of the borderline child. *Journal of Clinical Psychology, 51*(2), 294–302.

Adarand Constructors, Inc. v. Pena, Secretary of Transportation et al. (1995). 115 U. S. 2097

Affleck, G., Termen, H., Urrows S., & Higgins, P. (1994). Person and contextual features of daily stress reactivity: Individual differences in relations of undesirable daily events with mood disturbance and chronic pain intensity. *Journal of Personality and Social Psychology, 66*(2), 329–340.

Ahern, S., & Beatty, J. (1979). Pupillary responses vary during information processing with scholastic aptitude test score. *Science, 205,* 1289–1292.

Aidman, E. V., & Shmelyov, A. G. (2002). Mimics: A symbolic conflict/cooperation simulation program, with embedded protocol recording and automatic psychometric assessment. *Behavior Research Methods, Instruments, and Computers, 34*(1) 83–89.

Aiken, L. R. (1987). *Assessment of intellectual functioning.* Newton, MA: Allyn & Bacon.

Akehurst, L., & Vrij, A. (1999). Creating suspects in police interviews. *Journal of Applied Social Psychology, 29,* 192–210.

Akutagawa, D. A. (1956). *A study in construct validity of the psychoanalytic concept of latent anxiety and a test of projection distance hypothesis.* Unpublished doctoral dissertation, University of Pittsburgh, PA.

Alain, C., Bernstein, L. J., He, Y., Cortese, F., & Zipursky, R. B. (2002). Visual feature conjunction in patients with schizophrenia: An event-related brain potential study. *Schizophrenia Research, 57*(1) 69–80.

Albemarle Paper Company v. Moody. (1975). 442 U.S. 405.

Alexander, G. E., Prohovnik, I., Stem, Y., & Mayeux, R. (1994). WAIS-R subtest profile and cortical perfusion in Alzheimer's disease. *Brain and Cognition, 24*(l), 24–43.

Alexopoulos, D., Haritos-Fatouros, M., Sakkas, D., Skaltsas, A., & Vlachos, O. (2000). Reliability and validity of the WISC-R for the age range 6 to 11 years in Greece. *Psychology: Journal of the Hellenic Psychological Society, 7*(1), 35–45.

Alfonso, V. C., & Flanagan, D. P. (1999). Assessment of cognitive functioning in preschoolers. In E. V. Nuttall, I. Romero, et al. (Eds.), *Assessing and screening preschoolers: Psychological and educational dimensions* (2nd ed.) (pp. 186–217). Boston: Allyn & Bacon.

Allalouf, A., & Ben-Shakhar, G. (1998). The effect of coaching on the predictive validity of scholastic aptitude tests. *Journal of Educational Measurement, 35*(1), 31–47.

Allard, G., & Faust, D. (2000). Errors in scoring objective personality tests. *Assessment, 7*(2), 119–129.

Allen, F. (1994). The diagnostic interview for genetic studies. *Archives of General Psychiatry, 51*(11), 863–864.

Allen, J. G., & Smith, W. H. (1993). Diagnosing dissociative disorders. *Bulletin of the Menninger Clinic, 57*(3), 328–343.

Allen, M. J., & Yen, W. M. (1979). *Introduction to measurement theory.* Pacific Grove, CA: Brooks/Cole.

Allen v. Alabama State Board of Education. (1985). 612 F. Supp. 1046.

Allison, J., Blatt, S. J., & Zimet, C. N. (1968). *The interpretation of psychological tests.* New York: Harper & Row.

Allport, G. W., & Odbert, H. S. (1936). Trait-names, a psycholexical study. *Psychological Monographs, 47*(1).

Alpert, R., & Haber, R. N. (1960). Anxiety in academic achievement situations. *Journal of Abnormal and Social Psychology, 61,* 207–215.

Altmaier, E. M., McGuinnes, S. G., Wood, P., Ross, R. R., Bartley, J., & Smith, W. L. (1990). Defining successful performance among pediatric residents. *Pediatrics, 85,* 139–143.

Altmaier, E. M., Smith, W. L., O'Halloran, C. M., & Franken, E. A., Jr. (1992). The predictive utility of behavior-based interviewing compared with traditional interviewing in the selection of radiology residents. *Investigative Radiology, 27* (5), 385–389.

Alvarado, N. (1994). Empirical validity of the Thematic Apperception Test. *Journal of Personality Assessment, 63*(1), 59–79

American Educational Research Association (AERA), American Psychological Association (APA), & National Council on Measurement in Education (NCME) (1999). *Standards for educational and psychological testing.* Washington, DC: AERA.

American Psychiatric Association. (1980). *Diagnostic and statistical manual of mental disorders* (3rd ed.). Washington, DC: American Psychiatric Association.

American Psychiatric Association. (1995). *Diagnostic and statistical manual of mental disorders* (4th ed.). Washington, DC: American Psychiatric Association.

American Psychological Association (APA). (1954). *Psychology and its relations with other professions.* Washington, DC: American Psychological Association.

American Psychological Association (APA). (1974). *Standards for educational and psychological tests.* Washington, DC: American Psychological Association.

American Psychological Association (APA). (1992). *APA code of conduct.* Washington, DC: American Psychological Association.

American Psychological Association (2002). *The Ethical Principles of Psychologists and Code of Conduct.* Available at www. apa. org/ethics/code2002. html.

American Psychological Association (APA), American Educational Research Association (AERA), & National Council on Measurement in Education (NCME). (1999). *Standards for educational and psychological testing.* Washington, DC: AERA.

Ames, L. B., Metraux, R. W., & Walker, R. N. (1971). *Adolescent Rorschach responses.* New York: Brunner/Mazel.

Ana Maria R. v. California Department of Education. (1976). 96 U.S. 2040(c).

Anastasi, A. (1984). The K-ABC in historical and contemporary perspective. *Journal of Special Education, 78*(3), 357–366.

Anastasi, A. (1988). *Psychological testing* (6th ed.) New York: Macmillan.

Anastasi, A. (1993). A century of psychological testing: Origins, problems, and progress. In T. K. Fagan & G. R. VandenBos (Eds.), *Exploring applied psychology: Origins and critical analyses* (pp. 13–36). Washington, DC: American Psychological Association.

Anastasi, A. (1995). Psychology evolving: Linkages, hierarchies, and dimensions. In F. Kessel (Ed.), *Psychology, science, and human affairs: Essays in honor of William Bevan* (pp. 245–260). Boulder, CO: Westview.

Anastasi, A., & Urbina, S. (1997). *Psychological testing* (7th ed.). Upper Saddle River, NJ: Prentice-Hall.

Anderson, M. (2001). Conceptions of intelligence. *Journal of Child Psychology and Psychiatry and Allied Disciplines, 42*(2) 287–298.

Anderson, N. B., & McNeilly, M. (1991). Age, gender, and ethnicity as variables in psychophysiological assessment: Sociodemographics in context. *Psychological Assessment: A Journal of Consulting and Clinical Psychology, 3,* 376–384.

Anderson, N. H. (1991). *Contributions to information integration theory.* Hillsdale, NJ: Erlbaum.

Andersson, H. W. (1996). The Fagan Test of Infant Intelligence: Predictive validity in a random sample. *Psychological Reports, 78,* 1015–1026.

Andrews, J. J. W., Saklofske, D. H., & Janzen, H. L. (2001). *Handbook of psychoeducational assessment: Ability, achievement, and behavior in children.* San Diego: Academic Press.

Angoff, W. H. (1988). Promising areas for psychometric research. *Applied Measurement in Education, 1*(3) 203–206.

Angrilli, A., Sarlo, M., Palomba, D., & Schincaglia, M. (1997). Respiratory sinus arrhythmia in blood phobic subjects. *Perceptual and Motor Skills, 84,* 505–506.

Antony, M. M. (2001). Measures for specific phobia. In M. M. Antony & S. M. Orsillo (Eds.), *Practitioner's guide to empirically based measures of anxiety. AABT clinical assessment series* (pp. 133–158). New York: Klumer Academic/Plenum.

Arbisi, P. A., Ben-Porath, Y. S., & McNulty, J. (2002). A comparison of MMPI-2 validity in African American and Caucasian psychiatric inpatients. *Psychological Assessment, 14*(1), 3–15.

Archer, R. P., Maruish, M., Imhof, E. A., & Piotrowski, C. (1991). Psychological test usage with adolescent clients: 1990 survey. *Professional Psychology: Research and Practice, 22,* 247–252.

Arita, A. A., & Baer, R. A. (1998). Validity of selected MMPI-A content scales. *Psychological Assessment, 10,* 59–63.

Arkes, H. R. (1991). Costs and benefits from judgment errors: Implications for debiasing. *Psychological Bulletin, 110,* 486–489.

Aron, A., & Aron, E. (2003). *Statistics for psychology* (3rd ed.). Upper Saddle River, NJ: Prentice-Hall.

Aronow, E., Reznikoff, M., & Moreland, K. L. (1995). The Rorschach: Projective technique or psychometric test? *Journal of Personality Assessment, 64*(3), 213–228.

Aronson, J., Lustina, M. J., Good, C., Keough, K., Steele, C. M., & Brown, J. (1999). When white men can't do math: Necessary and sufficient factors in stereotype threat. *Journal of Experimental Social Psychology, 35*(1), 29–46.

Arrindell, W. A., van Nieuwenhuizen, C., & Lutejin, F. (2001). Chronic psychiatric status and satisfaction with life. *Personality and Individual Differences, 31*(2), 145–155.

Arthur, G. (1930). *Arthur point scale of performance tests.* Chicago: Stoelting.

Arvey, R. D., & Campion, J. E.

(1982). The employment interview: A summary and review of recent research. *Personnel Psychology, 35,* 281–322.

Asher, J. J., & Sciarrino, J. A. (1974). Realistic work sample tests: A review. *Personnel Psychology, 27,* 519–533.

Ashton, M. C. (1998). Personality and job performance: The importance of narrow traits. *Journal of Organizational Behavior, 19,* 289–303.

Association of Mexican-American Educators v. California. (1996). 836 F. Supp. 1534.

Atkinson, J. W. (1981). Studying personality in the context of an advanced motivational psychology. *American Psychologist, 36,* 117–128.

Atkinson, L. (1990). Reliability and validity of ratio developmental quotients from the Cattell Infant Intelligence Scale. *American Journal of Mental Retardation, 95,* 215–219.

Atkinson, R. C. (2004, April 28). *College admissions and the SAT.* University of California Center for the Humanities Public Lecture.

Avolio, B. J., & Waidman, D. A. (1990). An examination of age and cognitive test performance across job complexity and occupational types. *Journal of Applied Psychology, 75,* 43–50.

Ax, A. F. (1953). The physiological differentiation between fear and anger in humans. *Psychosomatic Medicine, 15,* 433–442.

Azrin, N. H., Holz, W., Ulrich, R., & Goldiamond, I. (1961). The control of the content of conversation through reinforcement. *Journal of the Experimental Analysis of Behavior, 4,* 25–30.

Azrin, N. H., & Powell, J. (1968). Behavioral engineering: The reduction of smoking behavior by a conditioning apparatus and procedure. *Journal of Applied Behavior Analysis, 1,* 193–200.

Baburajan, P. K. (1998). Psychosocial factors associated with contraceptive initiation: A multivariate analysis. *Psychological Studies, 43,* 37–43.

Baddeley, A. D., Wilson, B. A., & Watts, F. N. (1995). *Handbook of memory disorders.* Chichester, England: Wiley.

Baehr, M. (1987). A review of employee evaluation procedures and a description of "high potential" executives and professionals. *Journal of Business and Psychology, 1,* 172–202.

Baer, R. A., & Sekirnjak, G. (1997). Detection of underreporting on the MMPI-2 in a clinical population: Effects of information about validity scales. *Journal of Personality Assessment, 69,* 555–567.

Baily, K. J. (2001). Social competence of children with autism classified as best-outcome following behavior analytic treatment. *Dissertation Abstracts International, 61,* 12B. (UMI No. 9997891)

Bandura, A. (1986a). The explanatory and predictive scope of self-efficacy theory. *Journal of Social & Clinical Psychology, 4,* 359–373.

Bandura, A. (1986b). *Social foundations of thought and action: A social cognitive theory.* Englewood Cliffs, NJ: Prentice-Hall.

Bandura, A. (1994). Regulative function of perceived self-efficacy. In M. G. Rumsey, C. B. Walker, & J. H. Harris (Eds.), *Personnel selection and classification* (pp. 261–271). Hillsdale, NJ: Erlbaum.

Banerji, M. (1992a). Factor structure of the Gessell-School Readiness Screening Test. *Journal of Psychoeducational Assessment, 10*(4), 342–354.

Banerji, M. (1992b). An integrated study of the predictive properties of the Gessell School Readiness Screening Test. *Journal of Psychoeducational Assessment, 10*(3), 240–256.

Banerji, M., & Ferron, J. (1998). Construct validity of scores on a developmental assessment with mathematical patterns tasks. *Educational and Psychological Measurement, 58,* 634–660.

Barak, A. (1999). Psychological applications on the Internet: A disci-

pline on the threshold of a new millenium. *Applied and Preventive Psychology, 8,* 231–245.

Barak, A., & Cohen, L. (2002). Empirical examination of an online version of the Self-Directed Search. Thousand Oaks, CA: Sage.

Barber, T. X., & Silver, M. J. (1968). Fact, fiction, and the experimenter bias effect. *Psychological Bulletin Monograph Supplement, 70,* 1–29.

Bareak, B., & Lauter, D. (1991, November 5). 1991 rights bill a return to earlier path of bias redress. *Los Angeles Times,* pp. A1, A18.

Barenbaum, N. B., & Winter, D. G. (2003). Personality. In D. K. Freedheim (Ed.), *Handbook of psychology: History of psychology* (Vol. 1, pp. 177–203). New York: Wiley & Sons.

Barker, R. G. (1979). Settings of a professional lifetime. *Journal of Personality and Social Psychology, 37,* 2137–2157.

Barker, R. G., & Schoggen, P. (1973). *Qualities of community life.* San Francisco: Jossey-Bass.

Barofsky, I. (2003). Cognitive approaches to summary measurement: Its application to the measurement of diversity in health-related quality of life assessments. *Quality of Life Research, 12*(3), 251–260.

Baron, I. S., & Fennell, E. B. (2000). Neuropsychological and intellectual assessment of children. In B. J. Sadock & V. A. Sadock (Eds.), *Comprehensive textbook of psychiatry* (7th ed.) (Vol. 1, pp. 722–732). Philadelphia: Lippincott, Williams & Wilkins.

Baron, R. A. (1986). Self-presentation in job interviews: When there can be "too much" of a good thing. *Journal of Applied Social Psychology, 16,* 16–28.

Barrett, G. V., & Dupinet, R. L. (1991). A reconsideration of testing for confidence rather than for intelligence. *American Psychologist, 46,* 1012–1024.

Barrick, M. R., & Mount, M. K. (1991). The Big Five Personality

Dimensions and job performance: A meta-analysis. *Personnel Psychology, 44,* 1–26.

Barrick, M. R., Mount, M. K., & Judge, T. A. (2001). Personality and performance at the beginning of the new millennium: What do we know and where do we go next? *Personality and Performance, 9*(1–2), 9–30.

Bartell, S. S., & Solanto, M. V. (1995). Usefulness of the Rorschach Inkblot Test in assessment of attention deficit hyperactivity disorder. *Perceptual and Motor Skills, 80*(2), 531–541.

Bartholomew, D. J., & Knott, M. (1999). *Latent variable models and factor analysis.* New York: Oxford University Press.

Bartlett, C. J., & O'Leary, B. S. (1989). A differential prediction model to moderate the effects of heterogeneous groups in personnel selection and classification. *Personnel Psychology, 22,* 117.

Bartone, P. T. (1995). *A short hardiness scale.* Paper presented at the Annual Convention of the American Psychological Society, New York.

Bartone, P. T., Wright, K. M., Ingraham, L. H., & Ursano, R. J. (1989). The impact of a military air disaster on the health of assistance workers. *Journal of Nervous and Mental Disease, 177,* 317–328.

Basco, W. T., Jr., Way, D. P., Gilbert, G. E., & Hudson, A. (2002). Undergraduate institutional MCAT scores as predictors of USMLE step 1 performance. *Academy of Medicine, 77*(10 Suppl.), S13–16.

Bates, T. C., & Shieles, A. (2003). Crystallized intelligence as product of speed and drive for experience: The relationship of inspection time and openness to g and Gc. *Intelligence, 31*(3), 275–287.

Baxter, D. J., Barbaree, H. E., & Marshall, W. L. (1986). Sexual responses to consenting and forced sex in a large sample of rapists and nonrapists. *Behaviour Research and Therapy, 24,* 513–520.

Bay, M. (1998). An exploratory factor analysis of the Leiter-R. *Dissertation Abstracts International: Section B. The Physical Sciences and Engineering, 58,* 4513.

Bayles, K. A. (1990). Language and Parkinson disease. *Alzheimer's Disease and Associated Disorders, 4,* 171–180.

Bayley, N. (1969). *Manual: Bayley Scales of Infant Development.* New York: Psychological Corporation.

Beal, J. A. (1991). Methodological issues in conducting research on parent-infant attachment. *Journal of Pediatric Nursing, 6,* 11–15.

Beato, L., Cano, T. R., & Belmonte, A. (2003). Relationship of dissociative experiences to body shape concerns in eating disorders. *European Eating Disorders Review, 11*(1), 38–45.

Beck, A. T. (1967). *Depression: Clinical, experimental, and theoretical aspects.* New York: Harper & Row.

Beck, A. T. (1976). *Cognitive therapy and the emotional disorders.* New York: International Universities Press.

Beck, A. T., Brown, G., Steer, R. A., & Weissman, A. N. (1991). Factor analysis of the Dysfunctional Attitude Scale in a clinical population. *Psychological Assessment: Journal of Consulting and Clinical Psychology, 3,* 478–583.

Beck, A. T., & Rector, N. A. (2002). Delusions: A cognitive perspective. *Journal of Cognitive Psychotherapy, 16*(4) 455–468.

Beck, J. G., Carmin, C. H., & Henninger, N. J. (1998). The utility of the Fear Survey Schedule—III: An extended replication. *Journal of Anxiety Disorders, 12,* 177–182.

Beck, S. J. (1933). Configurational tendencies in Rorschach responses. *American Journal of Psychology, 45,* 433–443.

Beck, S. J. (1944). *Rorschach's test: Vol. 3. Basic processes.* New York: Grune & Stratton.

Beck, S. J. (1945). *Rorschach's test: Vol. 2. A variety of personality pictures.* New York: Grune & Stratton.

Beck, S. J. (1952). *Rorschach's test: Vol. 3. Advances in interpretation.* New York: Grune & Stratton.

Becker, B. J. (2003). Introduction to the Special Section on Metric in Meta-Analysis. *Psychological Methods, 8*(4), 403–405.

Beel-Bates, C. A. (2001). Visuospatial function in ambulatory aged women with probable Alzheimer's disease: A multiple case study. *Dissertation Abstracts International, 62,* 1B. (UMI No. 3000920)

Bell, N. L., Lassiter, K. S., Matthews, T. D., & Hutchinson, M. B. (2001). Comparison of the Peabody Picture Vocabulary Test–Third Edition and Wechsler Adult Intelligence Scale–Third Edition with university students. *Journal of Clinical Psychology, 57*(3), 417–422.

Bell, N. L., Matthews, T. D., Lassiter, K. S., & Leverett, J. (2002). Validity of the Wonderlic Personnel Test as a measure of fluid or crystallized intelligence: Implications for career assessment. *North American Journal of Psychology, 4*(1), 113–120.

Bell, T. K. (1990). Rapid sequential processing in dyslexic and ordinary readers. *Perceptual and Motor Skills, 71,* 1155–1159.

Bellack, A. S. (Ed.). (1998). *Behavioral assessment: A practical handbook* (4th ed.). Needham Heights, MA: Allyn & Bacon.

Bellack, A. S., & Hersen, M. (1988). *Behavioral assessment: A practical handbook* (3rd ed.). New York: Pergamon Press.

Bellak, L. (1975). The *TAT, CAT, and SAT in clinical use* (3rd ed.). New York: Grune & Stratton.

Bellak, L. (1986). The *TAT, CAT, and SAT in clinical use* (4th ed.) New York: Grune & Stratton.

Bellak, L. (1996). The *TAT, CAT, and SAT in clinical use* (6th ed.). New York: Grune & Stratton.

Bellak, L. (1999). My perceptions of the Thematic Apperception Test in psychodiagnosis and psychotherapy. In L. G. Gieser & M. I. Stein (Eds.), *Evocative images: The Thematic Apperception Test and the art of projection*. Washington, DC: American Psychological Association.

Bellak, L., & Bellak, S. S. (1973). *Manual: Senior Apperception Technique*. Larchmont, NY: CPS.

Bem, D. J., & Allen, A. (1974). On predicting some of the people some of the time: The search for cross-situational consistencies in behavior. *Psychological Review, 81*, 506–520.

Bem, D. J., & Funder, D. C. (1978). Predicting more of the people more of the time: Assessing the personality of situations. *Psychological Review, 85*, 485–501.

Bender, L. (1962). *Bender-Gestalt Test*. Los Angeles, CA: Western Psychological Services.

Benjamin, G. A., & Gollan, J. K. (2003). Evidentiary standards and rules of evidence. In G. A. Benjamin & J. K. Gollan (Eds.), *Family evaluation in custody litigation: Reducing risks of ethical infractions and malpractice. Forensic practice guidebook* (pp. 17–28). Washington, DC: American Psychological Association.

Bennett, R. E. (2003). An electronic infrastructure for a future generation of tests. In H. F. O'Neil & R. S. Perez (Eds.), *Technology applications in education: A learning view* (pp. 267–281). Mahwah, NJ: Erlbaum.

Ben-Porath, Y. S., & Butcher, J. N. (1989). The comparability of MMPI and MMPI-2 scales and profiles. *Psychological Assessment: Journal of Consulting and Clinical Psychology, 1*, 1–3.

Ben-Porath, Y. S., & Butcher, J. N. (1991). The historical development of personality assessment. In C. E. Walker (Ed.), *Clinical psychology: Historical and research foundations*. New York: Plenum.

Bentler, P. M. (1990). Comparative fit indexes in structural models. *Psychological Bulletin, 107*(2), 238–246.

Bentler, P. M. (1991). Modeling of intervention effects. *Nida Research Monograph, 107*, 159–182.

Bentler, P. M. (1994). On the quality of test statistics in covariance structure analysis: Caveat emptor. In C. R. Reynolds (Ed.), *Cognitive assessment: A multidisciplinary perspective. Perspectives on Individual differences* (pp. 237–260). New York: Plenum.

Bereby-Meyer, Y., Meyer, J., & Flascher, O. M. (2002). *Prospect theory analysis of guessing in multiple choice tests*. New York: Wiley.

Bergan, A., McManis, D. L., & Melchert, P. A. (1971). Effects of social and token reinforcement on WISC block design performance. *Perceptual and Motor Skills, 32*, 871–880.

Bergan, J. R., & Parra, E. B. (1979). Variations in IQ testing and instruction and the letter learning and achievement of Anglo and bilingual Mexican-American children. *Journal of Educational Psychology, 71*, 819–826.

Bergner, M., Babbitt, R. A., Carter, W. B., & Gilson, B. S. (1981). The Sickness Impact Profile: Development and final revision of a health status measure. *Medical Care, 19*, 787–788.

Bergstrom, B. A., & Lunz, M. E. (1999). CAT for certification and licensure. In E. Fritz Drasgow, E. Julie, B. Olson-Buchanan, et al. (Eds.), *Innovations in computerized assessment* (pp. 67–91). Mahwah, NJ: Erlbaum.

Bernheimer, L. P., & Keogh, B. K. (1988). Stability of cognitive performance of children with developmental delays. *American Journal of Mental Retardation, 92*, 539–542.

Berry, L. M. (2003). *Employee selection*. Belmont, CA: Wadsworth.

Bersoff, D. N. (1979). Regarding psychologists testily: Legal regulation of psychological assessment in the public schools. In B. Sales & M. Novick (Eds.), *Perspectives in law and psychology: Testing and evaluation* (Vol. 3). New York: Plenum.

Bersoff, D. N. (1981). Testing and the law. *American Psychologist, 36*, 1047–1057.

Betz, N. E. (2000). Contemporary is-

sues in testing use. In E. C. Edward Watkins, Jr., E. Vicki, L. Campbell, et al. (Eds.), *Testing and assessment in counseling practice* (2nd ed.) (pp. 481–516). Mahwah, NJ: Erlbaum.

Beutler, L. E. & Berren, M. R. (Eds.). (1995). *Integrative assessment of adult personality*. New York: Guilford Press.

Bianchini, J. C. (1976, May). *Achievement tests and differentiated norms*. Paper presented at the U. S. Office of Education invitational conference on achievement testing of disadvantaged and minority students for educational program evaluation, Reston, VA.

Bigler, E. D. (2003). Neurobiology and neuropathology underlie the neuropsychological deficits associated with traumatic brain injury. *Archives of Clinical Neuropsychology, 18*(6), 595–621, 623–627.

Binet, A. (1890a). Perceptions d'enfants. *La Revue Philosophique, 30*, 582–611.

Binet, A. (1890b). Recherches sur les mouvements de quelques jeunes enfants. *La Revue Philosophique, 29*, 297–309.

Binet, A., & Henri, V. (1895). La psychologie individuelle. *L'Annee Psychologique, 2*, 411–463.

Binet, A., & Henri, V. (1896). La psychologie individuelle. *L'Annee Psychologique, 3*, 296–332.

Binet, A., & Simon, T. (1905). Methodes nouvelles pour le diagnostic du niveau intellectuel des anormaux. *L'Annee Psychologique, 11*, 191–244.

Birk, J. M. (1974). Interest inventories: A mixed blessing. *Vocational Guidance Quarterly, 22*, 280–286.

Black, S. (2003). Distance learning. *Nursing Standards, 17*(19), 18–19.

Black, T. R. (1999). *Doing quantitative research in the social sciences: An integrated approach to research design, measurement and statistics*. London: Sage.

Black issues in higher education. (2001). *Black Issues in Higher Education, 17*(24), p. 14.

Blair, J. (2000). OCR issues revised guidance on high-stakes testing. *Education Week, 19*(17), 25.

Blais, M. A., Norman, D. K., Quintar, B., & Herzog, D. B. (1995). The effect of the administration method: A comparison of the Rapaport and Exner Rorschach systems. *Journal of Clinical Psychology, 51*(1),119–121.

Blake, J. (1974). Developmental changes in visual information processing under backyard masking. *Journal of Experimental Child Psychology, 17,* 133–146.

Blatt, S. J. (1990). The Rorschach: A test of perception or an evaluation of representation? *Journal of Personality Assessment, 55,* 394–416.

Block, J. (1961). *The Q-sort method in personality assessment and psychiatric research.* Springfield, IL: Thomas.

Block, J., & Kremen, A. (1996). IQ and ego-resiliency: Conceptual and empirical connections and separateness. *Journal of Personality and Social Psychology, 70,* 349–361.

Blood, G. W. (1995). A behavioral-cognitive therapy program for adults who stutter: Computers and counseling. *Journal of Communication Disorders, 28*(2) 165–180.

Blumberg, T. A. (1995). A practitioner's view of the WISC-III. *Journal of School Psychology, 33*(1), 95–97.

Board of Education v. Rowley. (1982). 458 U.S. 176; 102 S. Ct. 3034; 73 L. Ed. 2d 690.

Board of Professional Affairs, American Psychological Association. (1998). Awards for distinguished professional contributions: John Exner. *American Psychologist, 53,* 391–392.

Bobic, J., Pavicevic, L., & Gomzi, M. (2000). Cognitive functional inefficiency in alcoholics. *Studia Psychologa, 42*(1–2), 105–110.

Boegels, S. M., van der Vleuten, C. P. M., Blok, G., & Kreutzkamp, R. (1996). Assessment and validation of diagnostic interviewing skills for mental health professionals. *Journal of Psychopathology and Behavioral Assessment, 17,* 217–230.

Boerum, L. J. (2000). Developing portfolios with disabled students. *Reading and Writing Quarterly, 16*(3), 211–238.

Bolen, L. M., Hewett, J. B., Hall, C. W., & Mitchell, C. C. (1992). Expanded Koppitz Scoring System of the Bender Gestalt Visual-Motor Test for adolescents: A pilot study. *Psychology in the Schools, 29*(2), 113–115.

Bolt, D. (2003). Essays on item response theory. *Psychometrika, 68*(1) 155–158.

Bolton, B. (1992). Review of the California Psychogical Inventory, Revised Edition. In J. J. Framer & J. C. Conely (Eds.), *Eleventh mental measurements yearbook* (pp. 558–562). Lincoln, NE: Buros Institute of Mental Measurements.

Bombardier, C., Ware, J., Russell, I. J., et al. (1986). Auranofin therapy in quality of life for patients with rheumatoid arthritis: Results of a multicenter trial. *American Journal of Medicine, 81,* 565–578.

Bondi, M. W., Houston, W. S., Salmon, D. P., Corey-Bloom, J., Katzman, R., Thal, L. J., et al. (2003). Neuropsychological deficits associated with Alzheimer's disease in the very old: Discrepancies in raw vs. standardized scores. *Journal of the International Neuropsychology Society, 9*(5), 783–795.

Borman, W. C., & Hallman, G. L. (1991). Observational accuracy for assessors of work-sample performance: Consistency across task and individual differences correlate. *Journal of Applied Psychology, 76,* 11–18.

Bornstein, M. H., Hahn, C., Suwalsky, J. T. D., and Haynes, O. M. (2003). Socioeconomic status, parenting, and child development: The Hollingshead Four-Factor Index of Social Status and the Socioeconomic Index of Occupations. In M. H. Bornstein, & R. H. Bradley (Eds.), *Socioeconomic status, parenting, and child development: Mono-graphs in parenting series* (pp. 29–82). Mahwah, NJ: Erlbaum.

Borsboom, D., Mellenbergh, G. J., & van Heerden, J. (2002). Different kinds of DIF: A distinction between absolute and relative forms of measurement invariance and bias. Thousand Oaks, CA: Sage.

Bos, J. S. (1996). Factor structure of the field edition of the Leiter International Performance Scale—Revised. *Dissertation Abstracts International: Section B. The Physical Sciences and Engineering, 57,* 1494.

Bosshardt, M. J., Carter, G. W., Gialluca, K. A., Dunnette, M. D., et al. (1992). Predictive validation of an insurance agent support person selection battery [Special Issue: Test validity yearbook I]. *Journal of Business and Psychology, 7,* 213–224.

Botella, C., Villa, H., Banos, R., Perpina, C., & Garcia-Palacios, A. (1999). The treatment of claustrophobia with virtual reality: Changes in other phobic behaviors not specifically treated. *Cyberpsychology and Behavior, 2*(2) 135–141.

Botet, F., de Caceres, M. L., Rosales, S., & Costas, C. (1996). Behavior assessment of newborns from diabetic mothers. *Behavioral Neurology, 9*(1), 1–4.

Bottomley, A., Efficace, F., Thomas, R., Vanvoorden, V., & Ahmedzai, S. H. (2003). Health-related quality of life in non-small-cell lung cancer: Methodologic issues in randomized controlled trials. *Journal of Clinical Oncology, 21*(15), 2982–2992.

Boudreau, J. W., & Ramstad, P. M. (2003). Strategic industrial and organizational psychology and the role of utility analysis models. New York: Wiley.

Bourmenskaya, G. V. (2002). A study of individual differences by means of stage-by-stage formation of mental actions and notions. *Voprosky Psikhologii, 5,* 89–103.

Bowers, K. S. (1973). Situationalism in psychology: An analysis and critique. *Psychological Review, 80,* 307–336.

Bracken, B. A. (1985). A critical review of the Kaufman Assessment Battery for Children (K-ABC). *School Psychology Review, 14,* 21–35.

Bracken, B. A., & Walker, K. C. (1997). The utility of intelligence tests for preschool children. In D. P. Flanagan, J. L. Genshaft, et al. (Eds.), *Contemporary intellectual assessment: Theories, tests, and issues* (pp. 484–502). New York: Guilford.

Bradbury, T. N., & Fincham, F. D. (1990). Attributions in marriage: Review and critique. *Psychological Bulletin, 1070,* 333.

Bradley-Johnson, S. (2001). Cognitive assessment for the youngest children: A critical review of tests. *Journal of Psychoeducational Assessment, 19*(2), 19–44.

Brand, C. R. (1981). General intelligence and mental speed: Their relationship and development. In M. P. Friedman, J. P. Das, & N. O'Conner (Eds.), *Intelligence and teaming.* New York: Plenum.

Bratko, D., & Marusic, I. (1997). Family study of the big five personality dimensions. *Personality and Individual Differences, 23,* 365–369.

Brawley, O. W., & Freeman, H. P. (1999). Race and outcomes: Is this the end of the beginning for minority health research? [editorial; comment]. *Journal of the National Cancer Institute, 91*(22), 1908–1909.

Brayfield, A. H. (Ed.). (1965). Testing and public policy. *American Psychologist, 20,* 857–1005.

Brazelton, T. B. (1973). *Neonatal behavioral assessment scale.* Philadelphia: Lippincott.

Brazelton, T. B. (1984, November–December). *Neonatal behavioral assessment scale* (2nd ed.). Philadelphia: Lippincott.

Brazelton, T. B. (1993). Why children and parents must play while they eat: An interview with T. Berry Brazelton, MD [interview by Nancy I. Hahn]. *Journal of the American Dietetic Association, 93*(12), 1385–1387.

Bredemeier, M. (1991, November–December). IQ test ban for blacks called unconstitutional. *California Associations of School Psychologists Today,* pp. 22–23.

Breggin, P. R. (2002). Empathetic self-transformation in therapy. In P. R. Breggin, G. Breggin, & F. Bemak (Eds.), *Dimensions of empathetic therapy* (pp. 177–189). New York: Springer.

Breggin, R., Breggin, G., & Bemak, F. (Eds.). (2002). *Dimensions of empathetic therapy.* New York: Springer.

Brennan, R. L. (1994). Variance components in generalizability theory. In C. R. Reynolds (Ed.), *Cognitive assessment: A multidisciplinary perspective* (pp. 175–207). New York: Plenum.

Bressani, R. V., & Downs, C. (2002). Youth independent living assessment: Testing the equivalence of web and paper/pencil versions of the Ansell-Casey Life Skills Assessment. *Computers in Human Behavior, 18*(4), 543–464.

Bridgeman, B., & A. Schmitt (1997). Fairness issues in test development and administration. In E. Warren W. Willingham, E. Nancy, S. Cole, et al. (Eds.), *Gender and fair assessment* (pp. 185–226). Mahwah, NJ: Erlbaum.

Bridges, K. R. (2001). Using attributional style to predict academic performance: How does it compare to traditional methods? *Personality and Individual Differences, 31*(5), 723–730.

Bridges, K. R., & Sanderman, R. (2002). The irrational beliefs inventory: Cross cultural comparisons between American and Dutch samples. *Journal of Rational-Emotive and Cognitive Behavior Therapy, 20*(1) 65–71.

Brill, S. (1973). The secrecy behind the college boards. *New York Magazine.* (Reprinted by the NYG Corporation.)

Brillinger, D. R. (Ed.). (1994). *The collected works of John W. Tukey.* Belmont, CA: Wadsworth.

Britt, G. C., & Myers, B. J. (1994a).

The effects of the Brazelton Intervention: A review. *Infant Mental Health Journal, 15*(3), 278–292.

Britt, G. C., & Myers, B. J. (1994b). Testing the effectiveness of BNAS intervention with a substance-using population. *Infant Mental Health Journal, 15,* 293–304.

Britton, B. K., & Tidwell, P. (1995). Cognitive structure testing: A computer system for diagnosis of expert-novice differences. In P. D. Nichols, S. F. Chipman, & R. L. Brennan (Eds.), *Cognitively diagnostic assessment* (pp. 251–278). Hillsdale, NJ: Erlbaum.

Broaden, H. E. (1946). On the interpretation of the correlation coefficient as a measure of predictive efficiency. *Journal of Educational Psychology, 37,* 65–76.

Broaden, H. E. (1949). When tests pay off. *Personnel Psychology, 2,* 171–183.

Broks, P. (2003). *Into the silent land: Travels in neuropsychology.* New York: Atlantic Monthly Press.

Brookhart v. Illinois State Board of Education. (1983). 697 F. 2d. 179. 7th Cir.

Brosnan, M. J. (1998). The impact of computer anxiety and self-efficacy upon performance. *Journal of Computer Assisted Learning, 14*(3), 223–234.

Brown, D. C. (1994). Subgroup norming: Legitimate testing practice or reverse discrimination? *American Psychologist, 49*(11), 927–928.

Brown, F. G. (1979a). The algebra works—but what does it mean? *School Psychology Digest, 80,* 213–218.

Brown, F. G. (1979b). The SOMPA: A system of measuring potential abilities? *School Psychology Digest, 8,* 37–46.

Brown, J. S., & Burton, R. B. (1978). Diagnostic models for procedural bugs in basic mathematical skills. *Cognitive Science, 2,* 155–192.

Brown, M., Gordon, W. A., and Haddad, L. (2000). Models for predicting subjective quality of life in individuals with traumatic brain injury. *Brain Injury, 14*(1), 5–19.

Brown v. Board of Education. (1955). 347 U.S. 483 (1954), 349 U.S. 294.

Bryant, F. B. & Yarnold, P. R. (1995). Principal-components analysis and exploratory and confirmatory factor analysis. In L. G. Grimm & P. R. Yarnold (Eds.), *Reading and understanding multivariate statistics* (p. 9). Washington, DC: American Psychological Association.

Bryson, G., Greig, T., Lysaker, P., & Bell, M. (2003). Longitudinal Wisconsin Card Sorting performance in schizophrenia patients in rehabilitation. *Applied Neuropsychology, 9*(4), 203–209.

Buchanan, T., & Smith, J. L. (1999). Using the Internet for psychological research: Personality testing on the World Wide Web. *British Journal of Psychology, 90*(1), 125–144.

Buck, J. N. (1948). The H-T-P technique as a qualitative and quantitative scoring manual. *Journal of Clinical Psychology, 4,* 317–396.

Bureau-Chalot, F., Novella, J. L., Jolly, D., Ankri, J., Guillemin, F., & Blanchard, F. (2002). Feasibility, acceptability and internal consistency reliability of the nottingham health profile in dementia patients. *Gerontology, 48*(4), 220–225.

Burke, M. J., & Doran, L. I. (1989). A note on the economic utility of generalized validity coefficients. *Journal of Applied Psychology, 73,* 171–175.

Burns, R. C., & Kaufman, S. H. (1970). *Kinetic Family Drawings (K-F-D): An introduction to understanding through kinetic drawings.* New York: Brunner/Mazel.

Burns, R. C., & Kaufman, S. H. (1972). *Actions, styles, and symbols in Kinetic Family Drawings (K-F-D).* New York: Brunner/Mazel.

Buros, O. K. (Ed.). (1970). *Personality tests and reviews.* Highland Park, NJ: Gryphon Press.

Buros, O. K. (Ed.). (1978). *The eighth mental measurements yearbook* (2

vols.). Highland Park, NJ: Gryphon Press.

Burton, D. B., Sepehri, A., Hecht, F., VandenBroek, A., Ryan, J. R., & Drabman, R. (2001). A confirmatory factor analysis of the WISC-III in a clinical sample with cross-validation in the standardized sample. *Child Neuropsychology, 7*(2), 104–116.

Burtt, H. E. (1926). *Principles of employment psychology.* Boston: Houghton Mifflin.

Bush, J. W. (1984). Relative preferences versus relative frequencies in health-related quality of life evaluations. In N. K. Wenger, M. E. Mattson, C. D. Furberg, & J. Elinson (Eds.), *Assessment of quality of life in clinical trials of cardiovascular therapies.* New York: LaJacq.

Butcher, H. L. (1972). Review of cooperative school and college ability tests: Series 2. In O. K. Buros (Ed.), *The seventh mental measurements yearbook* (Vol. 1). Highland Park, NJ: Gryphon Press.

Butcher, J. N. (1989). *MMPI-2 users' guide.* Minneapolis, MN: Natural Computer Systems.

Butcher, J. N. (1990). *MMPI-2 in psychological treatment.* New York: Oxford University Press.

Butcher, J. N., (2000). Dynamics of personality responses: The empiricist's manifesto revisited. *Journal of Clinical Psychology, 56*(3), 375–386.

Butcher, J. N., Aidwin, C. M., Levenson, M. R., & Ben-Porath, Y. S. (1991). Personality and aging: A study of the MMPI-2 among older men. *Psychology and Aging, 6,* 361–370.

Butcher, J. N., Graham, J. R., Dahlstrom, W. G., Tellegen, A. M., & Kaernmer, B. (1989). *MMPI-2 manual for administrators and scoring.* Minneapolis: University of Minnesota Press.

Butcher, J. N., Graham, J. R., Williams, C. L., & Ben-Porath, Y. S. (1990). *Development and use of the MMPI-2 Content Scales.* Minneapolis: University of Minnesota Press.

Butcher, J. N., Perry, J. N., & Atlis, M. M. (2000). Validity and utility of computer-based test interpretation. *Psychological Assessments, 12*(1) 6–18.

Butters, N., Delis, D. C., & Lucas, J. A. (1995). Clinical assessment of memory disorders in amnesia and dementia. *Annual Review of Psychology, 46,* 493–523.

Byers, C. (2001). Interactive assessment: An approach to enhance teaching and learning. *Journal of Interactive Learning Research, 12*(4), 359–374.

Cacioppo, J. T., Berntson, G. G., & Anderson, B. L. (1991). Physiological approaches to the evaluation of psychotherapeutic process and outcome, 1991: Contributions from social psychophysiology. *Psychological Assessment: Journal of Consulting and Clinical Psychology, 3,* 321–336.

Cadenhead, K., Kumar, C., & Braff, D. (1996). Clinical and experimental characteristics of "hypothetically psychosis prone" college students. *Journal of Psychiatric Research, 30,* 331–340.

Cahan, S., & Noyman, A. (2001). The Kaufman Ability Battery for Children Mental Processing Scale: A valid measure of "pure" intelligence? *Educational and Psychological Measurement, 61*(5), 827–840.

Caldwell, M. B., & Knight, D. (1970). The effects of Negro and white examiners on Negro intelligence test performance. *Journal of Negro Education, 39,* 177–179.

Callahan, S., Roge, B., Cardenal, M., Cayrou, S., & Sztulman, H. (2001). Ego control and ego resiliency: French translation of a scale measuring these concepts and initial reliability and validity status. *Journal de Therapie Comportementale et Cognitive, 11*(4) 144–150.

Callender, J. C., & Dougherty, T. W. (1983). *Effects of interviewer training on interview information, interviewer behavior, and interview* ratings: A field investigation. Proceedings of the Southwest Division of the Academy of Management, Houston, TX.

Callinan, M., & Robertson, I. T. (2000). Work sample testing. London, United Kingdom: Blackwell.

Camaioni, L., Ercolani, A. P., Penge, R., Riccio, M., & Bernabei, P. (2001). Typical and atypical profiles of referential communication ability: A comparison of normal Ss and Ss with a specific learning disorder. Psicologia Clinica Dello Sviluppo, 5(1), 77–94.

Camara, W., & Echternacht, G. (2000). The SAT-I and high school grades: Utility in predicting success in college. (College Board Report No. RN-10). New York: College Entrance Examination Board.

Camara, W. J., & Schneider, D. L. (1994). Integrity tests: Facts and unresolved issues. American Psychologist, 49(2), 112–119.

Cameron, R., & Evers, S. E. (1990). Self-report issues in obesity and weight management: State of the art and future directions. Behavioral Assessment, 12, 91–106.

Camilli, G. (1999). Measurement error, multidimensionality, and scale shrinkage: A reply to Yen and Burket. Journal of Educational Measurement, 36, 73–78.

Camilli, G., Cizek, G. J., & Lugg, C. A. (2001). Psychometric theory and the validation of performance standards: History and future perspectives. Mahwah, NJ: Erlbaum.

Campbell, D. (2002). The history and development of the Campbell Interest and Skill Survey. Thousand Oaks, CA: Sage.

Campbell, D. P. (1974). Manual for the SVIB-SCII Strong-Campbell Interest Inventory (2nd ed.). Stanford, CA: Stanford University Press.

Campbell, D. P. (1977). Manual for the Strong-Campbell Interest Inventory. Stanford, CA: Stanford University Press.

Campbell, D. P. (1995, August). The Campbell Interest and Skills Survey (SCII). Paper presented at the an-

nual meeting of the American Psychological Association, New York.

Campbell, D. P., Hyne, S. A., & Nilsen, D. (1992). Manual for the Campbell Interest and Skill Survey. Minneapolis, MN: National Computer Systems.

Campbell, D. T., & Fiske, D. W. (1959). Convergent and discriminant validation by the multitrait-multimethod matrix. Psychological Bulletin, 56, 81–105.

Campbell, J. M., Bell, S. K., & Keith, L. K. (2001). Concurrent validity of the Peabody Picture Vocabulary Test–Third Edition as an intelligence and achievement screener for low SES African American children. Assessment, 8(1), 85–94.

Campbell, K. A., Rohlman, D. S., Storzbach, D., & Binder, L. M. (1999). Test–retest reliability of psychological and neurobehavioral tests self-administered by computer. Assessment, 6(1), 21–32.

Campbell, T. W. (2003). Sex offenders and actuarial risk assessment: Ethical considerations. Behavioral Science and the Law, 21(2), 269–279.

Campbell, V. L. (2000). A framework for using tests in counseling. In E. C. Edward Watkins, Jr., E. Vicki, L. Campbell, et al. (Eds.), Testing and assessment in counseling practice (2nd ed.) (pp. 3–11). Mahwah, NJ: Erlbaum.

Campion, J. E. (1972). Work sampling for personnel selection. Journal of Applied Psychology, 56, 40–44.

Cane, D. B., Olinger, L. J., Gotlib, I. N., & Kuiper, N. A. (1986). Factor structure of the Dysfunctional Attitude Scale in a student population. Journal of Clinical Psychology, 42, 307–309.

Cannell, C. F., & Henson, R. (1974). Incentives, motives, and response bias. Annals of Economic and Social Measurement, 3, 307–317.

Caprara, G. V., Barbaranelli, C., & Comrey, A. L. (1995). Factor analysis of the NEO-PI Inventory and Comprey Personality Scales in an

Italian sample. Personality and Individual Differences, 18(2), 193–200.

Carkhuff, R. R. (1969). Helping and human relations: I. Selection and training; II. Practice and research. New York: Holt, Rinehart & Winston.

Carkhuff, R. R., & Berenson, B. C. (1967). Beyond counseling and therapy. New York: Holt, Rinehart & Winston.

Carless, S. A. (1999). Career assessment: Holland's vocational interests, personality characteristics, and abilities. Journal of Career Assessment, 7(2), 125–144.

Carlin, J. B., & Rubin, D. B. (1991). Summarizing multiple-choice tests using three information statistics. Psychological Bulletin, 110, 338–349.

Carlson, R. E., Thayer, P. W., Mayfield, E. C., & Peterson, D. A. (1971). Improvements in the selection interview. Personnel Journal, 50, 268–275.

Carr, A. C., Ancill, R. J., Ghosh, A., & Margo, A. (1981). Direct assessment of depression by microcomputer: A feasibility study. Acta Psychiatrica Scandinavica, 64(5), 415–422.

Carr, A. C., & Ghosh, A. (1983). Accuracy of behavioral assessment by computer. British Journal of Psychiatry, 142, 66–70.

Carr, M. A., Sweet, J. J., & Rossini, E. (1986). Diagnostic validity of the Luria-Nebraska Neuropsychological Battery—Children's revision. Journal of Consulting and Clinical Psychology, 54, 354–358.

Carro, I. L., Bernal,I. L., & Vea, H. B. (1998). Depression in Cuba: Validation of Beck Depression Inventory (BDI) and the Dysfunctional Attitudes Scale (DAS-A) with Cuban population. Avances en Psicologia Clinica Latinoamericana, 16, 111–120.

Carvajal, H., Hardy, K., Harmon, K., Sellers, T. A., & Holmes, C. B. (1987). Relationships among scores on the Stanford-Binet IV, Peabody Picture Vocabulary

Test–Revised, and Columbia Mental Maturity Scale. *Bulletin of the Psychonomic Society, 25* (4), 275–276.

Carvajal, H., Karr, S. K., Hardy, K. M., & Palmer, B. L. (1988). Relationships between scores on Stanford-Binet IV and scores on McCarthy Scales of Children's Abilities. *Bulletin of the Psychonomic Society, 26*(4), 349.

Cascio, W. F. (1987). *Applied psychology in personnel management* (3rd ed.). Englewood Cliffs, NJ: Prentice-Hall.

Cascio, W. F. (1998). *Applied psychology in human resource management.* Englewood Cliffs, NJ: Prentice-Hall.

Cascio, W. F., & Ramos, R. A. (1986). Development and application of a new method for assessing job performance in behavioral economic terms. *Journal of Applied Psychology, 71,* 20–28.

Cash, T. F. (1985). The impact of grooming style on the evaluation of women in management. In M. Solomon (Ed.), *The psychology of fashion.* New York: Lexington Press.

Castaneda, A., & Ramirez, M. (1974). *Cultural democracy, bicognitive development, and education.* New York: Academic Press.

Castenell, L. A., & Castenell, N. E. (1988). Norm-referenced testing in low-income blacks. *Journal of Counseling and Development, 67,* 205–206.

Cattell, J. M. (1890). Mental tests and measurements. *Mind, 15,* 373–380.

Cattell, R. B., Eber, H. W., & Tatsuoka, M. M. (1970). *Handbook for the Sixteen Personality Factor Questionnaire (16 PF).* Champaign, IL: Institute for Personality and Ability Testing.

Cattell, R. B., & Scheier, I. H. (1961). *The meaning and measurement of neuroticism and anxiety.* New York: Ronald Press.

Cautela, J. R., & Upper, D. (1976). The behavioral inventory battery: The use of self-report measures in behavioral analyses and therapy. In

M. Hersen & A. S. Bellack (Eds.), *Behavioral assessment.* New York: Pergamon Press.

Cesare, S. J. (1996). Subjective judgment and the selection interview: A methodological review. *Public Personnel Management, 25,* 291–306.

Chabanne, V., Peruch, P., & Thinus-Blanc, C. (2003). Virtual to real transfer of spatial learning in a complex environment: The role of path network and additional features. *Spatial Cognition and Computation, 31*(1), 43–59.

Chambers, L. W. (1996). The McMaster Health Index Questionnaire. In B. F. Spilker (Ed.), *Quality of life and Pharmcoeconomics in clinical trials* (2nd ed.) (pp. 267–279). New York: Raven.

Champney, H., & Marshall, H. (1939). Optimal refinement of the rating scale. *Journal of Applied Psychology, 23,* 323–331.

Chan, D. W. (2000). Identifying gifted and talented students in Hong Kong. *Roeper Review, 22*(2), 88–93.

Chan, K. -Y., Drasgow, F., & Sawin, L. L. (1999). What is the shelf life of a test? The effect of time on the psychometrics of a cognitive ability test battery. *Journal of Applied Psychology 84*(4), 610–619.

Chapman, D. S., & Rowe, P. M. (2001). The impact of videoconference technology, interview structure, and interviewer gender on interviewer evaluations in the employment interview: A field experiment. *Journal of Occupational and Organizational Psychology, 74*(3), 279–298.

Chasnoff, I. J., Burns, K. A., & Burns, W. J. (1987). Cocaine use in pregnancy: Perinatal morbidity and mortality. *Neurotoxicology and Teratology, 9,* 291–293.

Chattin, S. H., & Bracken, B. A. (1989). School psychologists' evaluation of the K-ABC, McCarthy Scales, Stanford-Binet IV, and WISC-R. *Journal of Psychoeducational Assessment, 7,* 112–130.

Chen, E., Touyz, S. W., Beumont, P. J. V., Fairburn, C. G., Griffiths, R.,

Butow, P., Russell, J., Schotte, D. E., Gertler, R., & Basten, C. (2003). Comparison of group and individual cognitive-behavioral therapy for patients with bulimia nervosa. *International Journal of Eating Disorders, 33*(3), 241–254.

Chen, T. -Y. (2002). A Monte Carlo study of three new nonparametric tests for equivalence. *Dissertation Abstracts International: Section A. The Humanities and Social Sciences, 62,* 7A.

Chico-Libran, E. (2002). Dispositional optimism as a predictor of strategies coping. *Psicothema, 14*(3), 544–550.

Choca, J. & Morris, J. (1992). Administering the Category Test by computer: Equivalence of results. *Clinical Neuropsychologist, 6*(1), 9–15.

Chong, B. H. (2000). Early childhood gifted education: Relationship of screening tests with measured intelligence. *Dissertation Abstracts International: Section A. The Humanities and Social Scienes, 61,* 5A.

Chun, K., & Campbell, J. B. (1974). Dimensionality of the Rotter Interpersonal Trust Scale. *Psychological Reports, 35,* 1059–1070.

Cicchetti, D. V. (1994). Guidelines, criteria, and rules of thumb for evaluating normed and standardized assessment instruments in psychology. *Psychological Assessment, 60,* 284–290.

Clapham, M. M. (1998). Structure of Figural Forms A and B of the Torrance Tests of Creative Thinking. *Educational and Psychological Measurement, 58,* 275–283.

Clarizio, H. F. (1979a). In defense of the IQ test. *School Psychology Digest, 8*(1), 79–88.

Clarizio, H. F. (1979b). SOMPA: A symposium continued: Commentaries. *School Psychology Digest, 8*(2), 207–209.

Clark, K. E. (1961). *The vocational interests of nonprofessional men.* Minneapolis: University of Minnesota Press.

Clark, K. E., & Campbell, D. P. (1965). *Manual for the Minnesota*

Vocational Interest Inventory. New York: Psychological Corporation.

Clark, L. A., & Watson, D. (1998). Assessment. In E. Alan, E. Kazdin, et al. (Eds.), *Methodological issues and strategies in clinical research* (2nd ed.) (pp. 193–281). Washington, DC: American Psychological Association.

Clauser, B. E. (2002). Advances in computerized scoring of complex item formats. *Applied Measurement in Education, 1*(4), 1–104.

Clay, E. J., Lankford, J. S., & Wilson, S. E. (1992). The effects of computerized versus paper-and-pencil administration on measures of negative affect. *Computers in Human Behavior, 8*(2–3), 203–209.

Cleary, T. A. (1968). Test bias: Prediction of grades of Negro and white students in integrated colleges. *Journal of Educational Measurement, 5,* 115–124.

Cleary, T. A., Humphreys, L. G., Kendrick, S. A., & Wesman, A. (1975). Educational uses of tests with disadvantaged populations. *American Psychologist, 30,* 15–41.

Cliff, N. (1987). *Analyzing multivariate data*. San Diego: Harcourt, Brace, Jovanovich.

Coakes, S. J., & Steed, L. G. (1999). *SPSS: Analysis without anguish. Versions 7. 0, 7. 5, 8. 0 for Windows*. Brisbane, Australia: Wiley.

Cohen, F., & Lazarus, R. S. (1994). Active coping processes, coping dispositions, and recovery from surgery. In A. Steptoe & J. Wardle (Eds.), *Psychosocial processes and health: A reader* (pp. 348–368). Cambridge, England: Cambridge University Press.

Cohen, J. (1960). A coefficient of agreement for nominal scales. *Educational and Psychological Measurement, 20,* 37–46.

Cohen, B. H., & Lea, R. B. (2004). *Essentials of statistics for the social and behavioral sciences*. Hoboken, NJ: Wiley.

Cohen, S., & Lichtenstein, E. (1990). Partner behaviors that support quitting smoking. *Journal of Consulting and Clinical Psychology, 58,* 304–309.

Cole, N. S. (1973). Bias in selection. *Journal of Educational Measurement, 10,* 237–255.

Cole, N. S. (1981). Bias in testing. *American Psychologist, 36,* 1067–1077.

Coleman, J. C. (1973). Life stress and maladaptive behavior. *American Journal of Occupational Therapy, 27,* 169–180.

Coles, C. D., Smith, I. E., & Falek, A. (1987). Prenatal alcohol exposure and infant behavior: Immediate effects and implications for later development. *Advances in Alcohol and Substance Abuse, 6,* 87–104.

College Board. (1999). *1999 college-bound seniors, national report*. Available at www. collegeboard. org/sat/cbsenior/yr1999/NAT/natbk499. html#income.

Collett, D. (2003). *Modeling binary data* (2nd ed.). Boca Raton, FL: Chapman & Hall/CRC.

Collins, R. L., Kashdan, T. B., & Gollnisch, G. (2003). The feasibility of using cellular phones to collect ecological momentary assessment data: Application to alcohol consumption. *Experimental Clinical Psychopharmacology, 11*(1), 73–78.

Colom, R., Flores-Mendoza, C., & Rebello, I. (2003). Working memory and intelligence. *Personality and Individual Differences, 34*(1), 33–39.

Colom, R., & Garcia-Lopez, O. (2002). Sex differences in fluid intelligence among high school graduates. *Personality and Individual Differences, 32*(3), 445–451.

Colvin, C. R., Block, J., & Funder, D. C. (1995). Overly positive self-evaluations and personality: Negative implications for mental health. *Journal of Personality and Social Psychology, 68,* 1152–1162.

Connecticut v. Teal. (1982). 102 S. Ct. 2525.

Constantine, M. G., & Watt, S. K. (2002). Cultural congruity, womanist identity attitudes, and life satisfaction among African American college women attending historically Black and predominately White institutions. *Journal of College Student Development, 43*(2) 184–194.

Constantino, G., & Malgady, R. G. (1999). The Tell-Me-A-Story Test: A multicultural offspring of the Thematic Apperception Test. In L. G. Gieser & M. I. Stein (Eds.). *Evocative images: The Thematic Apperception Test and the art of projection*. Washington, DC: American Psychological Association.

Constantino, G., Malgady, R. G., Colon-Malgady, G., & Bailey, J. (1992). Clinical utility of the TEMAS with nonminority children. *Journal of Personality Assessment, 59*(3), 433–438.

Cook, M. L., & Peterson, C. (1986). Depressive irrationality. *Cognitive Therapy and Research, 10,* 293–298.

Cooley, P. C., Rogers, S. M., Turner, C. F., Al-Tayyib, A. A., Willis, G., & Ganapathii, L. (2001). Using touch screen audio-CASI to obtain data on sensitive topics. *Computers in Human Behavior, 17*(3), 285–293.

Cooper, D. (1990). Factor structure of the Edwards Personal Preference Schedule in a vocational rehabilitation sample. *Journal of Clinical Psychology, 46,* 421–425.

Copple, C. E., & Succi, G. J. (1974). The comparative ease of processing standard English and black nonstandard English by lower-class black children. *Child Development, 45,* 1048–1053.

Cordes, A. K. (1994). The reliability of observational data: I. Theories and methods for speech-language pathology. *Journal of Speech and Hearing Research, 37*(2), 264–278.

Corrigan, J. D., Bogner, J. A., Mysiw, W. J., Clinchot, D., & Fugate, L. (2001). Life satisfaction after traumatic brain injury. *Journal of Head Trauma Rehabilitation, 16*(6), 543–555.

Cortadellas, Angel, M. (1995). Analysis of difficulties of the McCarthy Scale items for different ages and socioeconomic status [Spanish]. *Psicothema, 7,* 61–73.

Costa, P. T., Jr., & McCrae, R. R. (1985). *The NEO Personality Inventory: Manual.* New York: Psychological Assessment Resources.

Costa, P. T., & McCrae, R. R. (1992). *Revised NEO Personality Inventory (NEO-PI-R) and the NEO Five-Factor Inventory (NEO-FFI): Professional manual.* Odessa, FL: Psychological Assessment Resources.

Costa, P. T., Jr., & McCrae, R. R. (1995). Domains and facets: Hierarchical personality assessment using the revised NEO Personality Inventory. *Journal of Personality Assessment, 64*(1), 21–50.

Costa, P. T., McRae, R. R., & Jonsson, F. H. (2002). Validity and utility of the revised NEO personality inventory: Examples from Europe. In B. de Raad (Ed.), *Big five assessment* (2nd ed.) (pp. 61–72). Ashland, OH: Hogrefe & Huber.

Costa, P. T., McCrae, R. R., & Kay, G. G. (1995). Persons, places, and personality: Career assessment using the revised NEO Personality Inventory. *Journal of Career Assessment, 76*(2), 123–139.

Costa, R. M. E., De Carvalho, L. A. V., Drummond, R., Wauke, A. P. T., & De Sa Guimaraes, M. (2002). The UFRJ-UERJ group: Interdisciplinary virtual reality experiments in neuropsychiatry. *Cyberpsychology and Behavior, 5*(5) 423–431.

Costello, H., Moss, S., Prosser, H. & Hatton, C. (1997). Reliability of the ICD 10 version of the Psychiatric Assessment Schedule for adults with developmental disabilities (PAS-ADD). *Social Psychiatry and Psychiatric Epidemiology, 32*, 339–343.

Costello, J., & Dickie, J. (1970). Leiter and Stanford-Binet IQ's of preschool disadvantaged children. *Developmental Psychology, 2*, 314.

Craig, R. J. (2003). Assessing personality and psychopathology with interviews. In J. R. Graham & J. A. Naglieri (Eds.), *Handbook of psychology: Assessment psychology* (Vol. 10) (pp. 487–508). New York: Wiley.

Craig, R. J., & Olson, R. E. (1995). MCMI-II profiles and typologies for the patients seen in marital therapy. *Psychological Reports, 76*(1), 163–170.

Craig, R. J. & Olson, R. E. (2001). Adjective descriptions of personality disorders: A convergent validity study of the MCMI-III. *Journal of Personality Assessment, 77*(2), 259–271.

Cramer, P. (1999). Future directions for the Thematic Apperception Test. *Journal of Personality Assessment, 72*, 74–92.

Cramer, P., & Blatt, S. J. (1990). Use of the TAT to measure change in defense mechanisms following intensive psychotherapy. *Journal of Personality Assessment, 54*, 236–251.

Crawford et al. v. Honig et al. (1994). 37 F. 3d 485, 487.

Creed, P. A., Patton, W., Bartrum, D. (2002). Multidimensional properties of the LOT-R: Effects of optimism and pessimism on career and well-being related variables in adolescents. *Journal of Career Assessment, 10*, 42–61.

Crespin, T. R., & Austin, J. T. (2002). Computer technology applications in industrial and organizational psychology. *Cyber Psychology and Behavior, 5*(4) 279–303.

Cripe, L. I., Maxwell, J. K., & Hill, E. (1995). Multivariate discrimination function analysis of neurologic, pain, and psychiatric patients with the MMPI. *Journal of Clinical Psychology, 51*(2), 258–268.

Crisco, J. J., Dobbs, J. M., & Mulhern, R. K. (1988). Cognitive processing of children with Williams syndrome. *Developmental Medicine and Child Neurology, 30*, 650–656.

Crites, J. O. (1973). *Career Maturity Inventory: Theory and research handbook and administration and use manual.* Monterey, CA: CTB/McGraw-Hill.

Crites, J. O. (1974). The Career Maturity Inventory. In D. E. Super (Ed.), *Measuring vocational maturity for counseling and evaluation.* Washington, DC: National Vocational Guidance Association.

Crocker, L. M., & Algina, J. (1986). *Introduction to classical and modern test theory.* New York: Holt, Rinehart & Winston.

Crockett, D., Clark, C., & Klonoff, H. (1981). Introduction-overview of neuropsychology. In F. E. Filskov & T. J. Boll (Eds.), *Handbook of clinical neuropsychology.* New York: Wiley.

Cronbach, L. J. (1951). Coefficient alpha and the internal structure of tests. *Psychometrika, 16*, 297–334.

Cronbach, L. J. (1975). Five decades of public controversy over mental testing. *American Psychologist, 30*, 1–14.

Cronbach, L. J. (1978). Black Intelligence Test of Cultural Homogeneity: A review. In O. K. Buros (Ed.), *The eighth mental measurements yearbook* (Vol. 1). Highland Park, NJ: Gryphon Press.

Cronbach, L. J. (1980). Validity on parole: How can we go straight? *New Directions for Testing and Measurement, 5*, 99–108.

Cronbach, L. J. (1989). Construct validation after thirty years. In R. Linn (Ed.), *Intelligence: Measurement, theory, and public policy.* Urbana: University of Illinois Press.

Cronbach, L. J. (1995). Giving method variance its due. In P. E. Shrout & S. T. Fiske (Eds.), *Personality research, methods, and theory: A festschrift honoring Donald W. Fiske* (pp. 145–157). Hillsdale, NJ: Erlbaum.

Cronbach, L. J., & Furby, L. (1970). How we should measure "change"—or should we? *Psychological Bulletin, 74*, 68–80.

Cronbach, L. J., & Gleser, G. C. (1965). *Psychological tests and personnel decisions.* Urbana: University of Illinois Press.

Cronbach, L. J., & Meehl, P. E. (1955). Construct validity in psychological tests. *Psychological Bulletin, 52*, 281–302.

Cronk, B. C. & West, J. L. (2002). Personality research on the Internet: A comparison of Web-based and traditional instruments in take-home and in-class settings. *Behavior Research Methods, Instruments, and Computers, 34*(2) 177–180.

Crosby, F. J., Iyer, A., Clayton, S., & Downing, R. A. (2003). Affirmative action. Psychological data and the policy debates. *American Psychologist, 58*(2), 93–115.

Crowe, S. F., Benedict, T., Enrico, J., Mancuso, N., Matthews, C., & Wallace, J. (1999). Cognitive determinants of performance on the Digit-Symbol-coding test, the Symbol Search Test of the WAIS-III, and the Symbol Digit Modalities Test: An analysis in a healthy sample. *Australian Psychologist, 34*(3), 204–210.

Crowe, T. V. (2003). Self-esteem scores among deaf college students: An examination of gender and parents' hearing status and signing ability. *Journal of Deaf Studies and Deaf Education, 8*(2), 199–206.

Cundick, B. P. (1985). Review of Incomplete Sentences Task. In J. V. Mitchell (Ed.), *Ninth mental measurements yearbook* (Vol. 1) (pp. 681–682). Highland Park, NJ: Gryphon Press.

Cureton, E. E., Cronbach, L. J., Meehl, P. E., Ebel, R. L., et al. (1996). *Validity.* Lanham, MD: University Press of America.

Cyranowski, J. M., Shear, M. K., Rucci, P., Fagiolini, A., Frank, E., Grochocinski, V. J., Kupfer, D. J., Banti, S., Armani, A., & Cassano, G. (2002). Adult separation anxiety: Psychometric properties of a new structure clinical interview. *Journal of Psychiatric Research, 36*(2), 77–86.

Dahlstrom, W. G. (1969a). Invasion of privacy: How legitimate is the current concern over this issue? In J. N. Butcher (Ed.), *MMPI: Research developments and clinical applications.* New York: McGraw-Hill.

Dahlstrom, W. G. (1969b). Recurrent issues in the development of the MMPI. In J. N. Butcher (Ed.), *MMPI: Research developments and clinical applications.* New York: McGraw-Hill.

Dahlstrom, W. G., & Welsh, G. S. (1960). *An MMPI handbook. A guide to use in clinical practice and research.* Minneapolis: University of Minnesota Press.

Dalessio, A. T., & Silverhart, T. A. (1994). Combining biodata test and interview information: Predicting decisions and performance criteria. *Personnel Psychology, 47*(2), 303–315.

Damarin, F. (1978b). Review of Cattell Infant Intelligence Scale. In O. K. Buros (Ed.), *The eighth mental measurements yearbook* (Vol. 1). Highland Park, NJ: Gryphon Press.

Dana, R. H. (2000). *Handbook of cross-cultural and multicultural personality assessment.* Mahwah, NJ: Erlbaum.

Dangel, H. L. (1970). *The biasing effect of pretest information on the MSC scores of mentally retarded children.* (Doctoral dissertation, Pennsylvania State University). (University Microfilms No. 7116,588)

Daniel, W. W. (1990). *Applied nonparametric statistics* (2nd ed.). Boston: PWS-Kent.

Darlington, R. B. (1971). Another look at "cultural fairness. " *Journal of Educational Measurement, 8,* 71–82.

Darlington, R. B. (1978). Cultural test bias: Comment on Hunter and Schmidt. *Psychological Bulletin, 85,* 673–674.

Das, J. P. (1973). Cultural deprivation and cognitive competence. In N. R. Ellis (Ed.), *International review of research in mental retardation* (Vol. 6). New York: Academic Press.

Das, J. P. (1987). Simultaneous and successive processes and K-ABC. *Journal of Special Education, 18,* 229–238.

Datta, L. (1975). Foreword. In E. E. Diamond (Ed.), *Issues of sex bias and sex fairness in career interest measurement.* Washington, DC: National Institutes of Education.

Dattilo, J., Hoge, G., & Malley, S. M. (1996). Interviewing people with mental and physical complaints: The validity of the HY Scale and associated MMPI signs. *Journal of Clinical Psychology, 42,* 754–760.

Daub, D., & Colarusso, R. P. (1996). The validity of the WJ-R, PIAT-R, and DAB-2 reading subtests with students with learning disabilities. *Learning Disabilities Research and Practice, 11,* 90–95.

Davis, R. B. (1979). *Error analysis in high school mathematics, conceived as information processing pathology.* Paper presented at the annual meeting of the American Educational Research Association, San Francisco.

Davis, R. N. (1999). Web-based administration of a personality questionnaire: Comparison with traditional methods. *Behavior Research Methods, Instruments and Computers, 31*(4), 572–577.

Dawes, R. M. (1999). Two methods for studying the incremental validity of a Rorschach variable. *Psychological Assessment, 11,* 297–302.

Dawson, J. K., & Grant, I. (2000). Alcoholics' initial organization and problem-solving skills predict learning and memory performance on the Rey-Osterrieth complex figure. *Journal of the International Neuropsychological Society, 6*(1), 12–19.

Day, D. V., & Sulsky, L. M. (1995). Effects of frame-of-reference training and information configuration on memory organization and rating accuracy. *Journal of Applied Psychology, 80,* 158–167

Dearborn, G. (1897). Blots of ink in experimental psychology. *Psychological Review, 4,* 390–391.

Debra P. v. Turlington. (1979). 474 F. Supp. 244, 260 (M.D. Fla.)

Deffenbacher, J. L., Swerner, W. A., Whisman, M. A., Hill, R. A., & Sloan, R. D. (1986). Irrational beliefs and anxiety. *Cognitive Therapy and Research, 10,* 281–292.

deGroot, A. M. (1988). Word association norms with reaction times. *Nederlands-Tiydschriftvoor-de-Psychologie-haar-Grensqebieden, 43,* 280–296.

Delery, J. E., & Kacmar, K. M. (1998). The influence of applicant and interviewer characteristics on use of impression management. *Journal of Applied Social Psychology, 28,* 1649–1669.

Delhees, K. H., & Cattell, R. B. (1971). *Manual for the Clinical Analysis Questionnaire (CAQ).* Champaign, IL: Institute for Personality and Ability Testing.

Delis, D. C., Filoteo, J. V., Massman, P. J., Kaplan, E., & Kramer, J. H. (1994). The clinical assessment of memory disorders. In E. Laird, S. Cermak, et al. (Eds.), *Neuropsychological explorations of memory and cognition: Essays in honor of Nelson Butters* (pp. 223–239). New York: Plenum.

Delis, D. C., Jacobson, M., et al. (2003). The myth of testing construct validity using factor analysis or correlations with normal or mixed clinical populations: Lessons from memory assessment. *Journal of the International Neuropsychological Society, 9*(6), 936–946.

Delis, D. C., Kramer, J. H., et al. (2004). Reliability and validity of the Delis-Kaplan Executive Function System: An update. *Journal of the International Neuropsychological Society, 10*(2): 301–303.

Delis, D. C., Kramer, J. H., Kaplan, E., & Ober, B. A. (1987). The *California Verbal Learning Test* (Research ed.). San Diego: Harcourt Brace Jovanovich.

Delis, D. C., Magsman, P. J., Butters, N., Salmon, D. P., Cermak, L. S., & Kramer, J. H. (1991). Profiles of demented and amnesic patients on the California Verbal Learning Test: Implications for the assessment of memory disorders. *Psychological Assessment: A Journal of Consulting and Clinical Psychology, 3,* 19–26.

Demir, B., Batur, S., Mercan, S., & Ulug, B. (2002). Executive functions and personality profiles in early and late onset alcoholism. *Turk Psikoloju Dergisi, 17*(49) 63–76.

DeRosa, A., & Patalano, F. (1991). Effects of familiar proctor on fifth and sixth grade students' test anxiety. *Psychological Reports, 68,* 103–113.

Detroit Edison Co. v. N. L. R. B. (1979). 99 S. Ct. 1123.

Detwiler, F. R., & Ramanaiah, N. V. (1996). Structure of the Jackson Personality Inventory from the perspective of the five-factor model. *Psychological Reports, 79,* 411–416.

Devanand, D. P., Pelton, G. H., Marston, K., Camacho, Y., Roose, S. P., Stern, Y., & Sackheim, H. A. (2003). Sertraline treatment of elderly patients with depression and cognitive impairment. *International Journal of Geriatric Psychiatry, 18*(2), 123–130.

DeVellis, R. F. (1991). *Scale development: Theory and applications.* Newbury Park, CA: Sage.

Devine, D., Parker, P. A., Fouladi, R. T., & Cohen, L. (2003). The association between social support, intrusive thoughts, avoidance, and adjustment following an experimental cancer treatment. *Psycho-Oncology, 12*(5), 453–462.

Devoe, E. R., & Faller, K. C. (2002). Question strategies in interviews with children who may have been sexually abused. *Child Welfare, 81*(1), 5–31.

DeWitt, M. B., Schreck, K. A., & Mulick, J. A. (1998). Use of Bayley Scales in individuals with profound mental retardation: Comparison of the first and second editions. *Journal of Developmental and Physical Disabilities, 10,* 307–313.

Diamond, E. E. (1979). Sex equality and measurement practices. *New Directions for Test and Measurement, 3,* 61–78.

Diamond, E. E., & Zytowski, D. G. (2000). The Kuder Occupational Interest Survey. In E. C. Edward Watkins, Jr., E. Vicki, L. Campbell, et al. (Eds.), *Testing and assessment in counseling practice* (2nd ed.) (pp. 263–294). Mahwah, NJ: Erlbaum.

Diana v. State Board of Education.

(1970). C. A. No. C-70 37 RFP (N. D. Cal., filed Feb. 3, 1970).

DiBello, L. V., Stout, W. F., & Roussos, L. A. (1995). Unified cognitive/psychometric diagnostic assessment likelihood-based classification techniques. In P. D. Nichols, S. F. Chipman, & R. L. Brennan (Eds.), *Cognitively diagnostic assessment* (pp. 361–389). Hillsdale, NJ: Erlbaum.

Diener, E., Emmons, R. A., Larsen, R. J., & Griffin, S. (1985). The Satisfaction with Life Scale. *Journal of Personality Assessment, 49,* 71–75.

Diener, E., Sapyta, J. J., Suh, E. (1998). Subjective well-being is essential to well-being. *Psychological Inquiry, 9*(1), 33–37.

Dierdorff, E. C., & Wilson, M. A. (2003). A meta-analysis of job analysis reliability. *Journal of Applied Psychology, 88*(4), 635–646.

Dijkers, M. P. (2003). Individualization in quality of life measurement: instruments and approaches. *Archives of Physical Medicine and Rehabilitation, 84*(4 Suppl. 2), S3–S14.

Dikmen, S., & Machamer, J. E. (1995). Neurobehavioral outcomes and their determinants. *Journal of Head Trauma Rehabilitation, 10,* 74–78.

Dillard, J. P., & Marshall, L. J. (2003). Persuasion as a social skill. In J. O. Greene & B. R. Burleson, (Eds.), *Handbook of communication and social interaction skills,* (pp. 479–513). Mahwah, NJ: Erlbaum.

Dishion, T. J., Andrews, D. W., & Crosby, L. (1995). Antisocial boys and their friends in early adolescence: Relationship characteristics, quality, and interactional process. *Child Development, 66,* 139–151.

Dixon, J. L. (1998). Concurrent validity of the Koppitz BenderGestalt Emotional Indicators among women with mental retardation. *Perceptual and Motor Skills, 86,* 195–197.

Dobko, P., & Kehoe, J. F. (1983). On the fair use of bias: A comment on Drasgow. *Psychological Bulletin, 93,* 604–608.

Doctor, R. (1972). Review of the Porteus Maze Test. In O. K. Buros (Ed.), *The seventh mental measurements yearbook* (Vol. 1). Highland Park, NJ: Gryphon Press.

Dodrill, C. B., & Warner, M. H. (1988). Further studies of the Wonderlic Personnel Test as a brief measure of intelligence. *Journal of Consulting and Clinical Psychology, 59,* 145–147.

Doerries, L. E., & Ridley, D. R. (1998). Time sensitivity and purpose in life: Contrasting theoretical perspectives of Myers-Briggs and Victor Frankl. *Psychological Reports, 83,* 67–71.

Donahue, D., & Sattler, J. M. (1971). Personality variables affecting WAIS scores. *Journal of Consulting and Clinical Psychology, 36,* 441.

Dorans, N. J., & Drasgow, F. (1980). A note on cross-validating prediction equations. *Journal of Applied Psychology, 65,* 728–730.

Dougherty, T. W., Ebert, R. J., & Callender, J. C. (1986). Policy capturing in the employment interview. *Journal of Applied Psychology, 71,* 9–15.

Dougherty, T. W., Turban, D. B., & Callender, J. C. (1994). Confirming first impressions in the employment interview: A field study of interviewer behavior. *Journal of Applied Psychology, 79*(5), 659–665.

Douglas, J. (2002). Psychological treatment of food refusal in young children. *Child and Adolescent Mental Health, 7*(4), 173–180.

Dove, A. (1968). Taking the Chitling Test. *Newsweek, 72,* 51–52.

Downey, J., Elkin, E. J., Ehrhardt, A. A., Meyer-Bahlburg, H. F., Bell, J. J., & Morishima, A. (1991). Cognitive ability and everyday functioning in women with Turner Syndrome. *Journal of Learning Disabilities, 24,* 3239.

Drasgow, F. (1982). Biased test items and differential validity. *Psychological Bulletin, 92,* 526–531.

Drasgow, F., & Olson-Buchanan, J. (1999). *Innovations in computerized assessment.* Mahwah, NJ: Erlbaum.

Dreher, G. F., Ash, R. A., & Hancock, P. (1988). The role of the tradi-

tional research design in understanding the validity of the employment interview. *Personnel Psychology, 41,* 315–327.

Duan, C., & Kivlighan, D. M., Jr. (2002). Relationship among therapist pre-session mood, therapist empathy, and session evaluation. *Psychotherapy Research, 21*(1), 23–37.

DuBois, P. H. (1966). A test-dominated society: China 115 B.C. –1905 A.D. In A. Anastasi (Ed.), *Testing problems in perspective.* Washington, DC: American Council on Education.

DuBois, P. H. (1970). A history of psychological testing. Boston: Allyn & Bacon.

DuBois, P. H. (1972). Increase in educational opportunity through measurement. *Proceedings of the 1971 Invitational Conference on Testing Problems.* Princeton, NJ: Educational Testing Service.

Dunn, J. A. (1972). Review of the Goodenough-Harris Drawing Test. In O. K. Buros (Ed.), *The seventh mental measurements yearbook* (Vol. 1). Highland Park, NJ: Gryphon Press.

Dunn, L. M., & Dunn, I. M. (1981). *Peabody Picture Vocabulary Test–Revised.* Circle Pines, MN: American Guidance Service.

Dunnette, M. D. (1967). The assessment of managerial talent. In F. R. Wickert & D. E. McFarland (Eds.), *Measuring executive effectiveness.* New York: Appleton-Century-Crofts.

Dunnette, M. D. (1972). *Validity study results for jobs relevant to the petroleum refining industry.* Washington, DC: American Petroleum Institute.

Dunnette, M. D., & Borman, W. C. (1979). Personnel selection and classification systems. *Annual Review of Psychology, 30,* 477–525.

Dupue, R. A., & Monroe, S. M. (1986). Conceptualization and measurement of human disorder in life stress research: The problem of chronic disturbance. *Psychological Bulletin, 99,* 36–51.

Dush, D. M. (1985). Review of In-

complete Sentences Task. In J. V. Mitchell (Ed.), *The ninth mental measurements yearbook* (Vol. 1) (pp. 682–683). Highland Park, NJ: Gryphon Press.

Dvir, T., Eden, D., & Banjo, M. (1995). Self-fulfilling prophecy and gender: Can women be Pygmalion and Galatea? *Journal of Applied Psychology, 80,* 253–270.

Dwight, S. A., & Feigelson, M. E. (2000). A quantitative review of the effect of computerized testing on the measurement of social desirability. *Educational and Psychological Measurement, 60*(3), 340–360.

Eaton, N. K., Wing, H., & Mitchell, K. J. (1985). Alternative methods of estimating the dollar value of performance. *Personnel Psychology, 38,* 27–40.

Ebel, R. L. (1977). Comments on some problems of employment testing. *Personnel Psychology, 30,* 55–63.

Edelstein, B. & Kalish, K. (1999). Clinical assessment of older adults. In E. John, C. Cavanaugh, E. Susan Krauss Whitbourne, et al. (Eds.), *Gerontology: An interdisciplinary perspective* (pp. 269–304). New York: Wiley.

Educational Testing Service. (1991). *Sex, race, ethnicity, and performance on the GRE General Test.* Princeton, NJ: Educational Testing Service.

Educational Testing Service. (2002). *GRE for educators: Interpreting scores on the GRE Analytical writing measure.* Princeton, NJ: Educational Testing Service.

Educational Testing Service. (2002). *GRE for test takers.* Princeton, NJ: Educational Testing Service.

Edwards, A. L. (1954). Manual *for the Edwards Personal Preference Schedule.* New York: Psychological Corporation.

Edwards, A. L. (1959). *Edwards Personal Preference Schedule.* New York: Psychological Corporation.

Egger, J. I., De May, H. R., Hubert, R. A., Dersen, J. J. L., van der Staak, C. P. F. (2003). Cross-cultural replication of the five-factor model and comparison of the NEO-PI-R and MMPI-2 PSY-5 scales in a Dutch psychiatric sample. *Psychological Assessment, 15*(1) 81–88.

Eggly, S. (2002). Physician-patient co-construction of illness narratives in the medical interview. *Health Communication, 14*(3), 339–360.

Einarsdottir, S. (2002). Structural equivalence of vocational interests across culture and gender: Differential item functioning in the Strong Interest Inventory (Iceland). *Dissertation Abstracts International: Section B. The Physical Sciences and Engineering, 62,* 8B.

Eisenberger, R., & Cameron, J. (1998). Reward, intrinsic interest, and creativity: New findings. *American Psychologist, 53*(6), 676–679.

Ekman, P. (2003). *Emotions revealed: Recognizing faces and feelings to improve communication and emotional life.* New York: Times Books/Holt.

Ekman, P., Levenson, R. W., & Friesen, W. V. (1983). Autonomic nervous system activity distinguishes among emotions. *Science, 221,* 1208–1210.

Ekman, P., & O'Sullivan, M. (1991). Who can catch a liar? *American Psychologists, 46,* 913–920.

Ekren, U. W. (1962). *The effect of experimenter knowledge of subjects' scholastic standing on the performance of a task.* Unpublished master's thesis, Marquette University, WI.

El-Ansarey, B. M. (1997). The psychometric properties of NEO Five-Factor Inventory (NEO-FFI-S) based on the Kuwaiti society [Arabic]. *Derasat Nafseyah, 7,* 277–310.

Elashoff, J., & Snow, R. E. (Eds.). (1971). *Pygmalion revisited.* Worthington, OH: C. A. Jones.

Elder, C., McNamara, T., & Congdon, P. (2003). Rasch techniques for detecting bias in performance assessments: an example comparing the performance of native and non-native speakers on a test of academic English. *Journal of Applied Measurement, 4*(2), 181–197.

Elliott, C. D. (1990). *Differential abil-ity scales.* San Antonio, TX: Psychological Corporation.

Elliot, R. (1988). Tests, abilities, race, and conflict. *Intelligence, 12,* 333–350.

Ellis, A. (1946). The validity of personality questionnaires. *Psychological Bulletin, 43,* 385–440.

Ellis, T. E. (1985). The hopelessness scale and social desirability: More data and a contribution from the Irrational Beliefs Test. *Journal of Clinical Psychology, 41,* 634–639.

Embretson, S. E., & Hershberger, S. L. (1999). *The new rules of measurement: What every psychologist and educator should know.* Mahwah, NJ: Erlbaum.

Emory, E. K., Tynan, W. D., & Dave, R. (1989). Neurobehavioral anomalies in neonates with seizures. *Journal of Clinical and Experimental Neuropsychology, 11,* 231–240.

Endler, N. S. (1973). The person versus the situation: A pseudo issue? A response to Alker. *Journal of Personality, 41,* 287–303.

Endler, N. S., & Hunt, J. McV. (1968). S-R inventories of hostility and comparisons of the proportions of variance from persons, responses, and situations for hostility and anxiousness. *Journal of Personality and Social Psychology, 9,* 309–315.

Endler, N. S., Kantor, L., & Parker, J. D. A. (1994). State-trait coping, state-trait anxiety and academic performance. *Personality and Individual Differences, 16* (5), 663–670.

Endler, N. S., & Magnusson, D. (1976). *Interactional psychology and personality.* Washington, DC: Hemisphere.

Endler, N. S. & Parker, J. D. A. (1990). *Coping Intervention for Stressful Situations.* Towanda, NY: Mulit-Health Systems Inc.

Endler, N. S., Parker, J. D. A., Bagby, R. M., & Cox B. J. (1991). Multidimensionality of state and trait anxiety: Factor structure of the Endler multidimensional anxiety scales. *Journal of Personality and Social Psychology, 60,* 919–926.

Epstein, J., & Klinkenberg, W. D.

(2001). From Eliza to internet: a brief history of computerized assessment. *Computers in Human Behavior, 17*(3), 295–314.

Epstein, J., & Klinkenberg, W. D. (2002). Collecting data via the Internet: The development and deployment of a Web-based survey. *Journal of Technology in Human Services, 19*(2–3) 33–47.

Epstein, J., & Rotunda, R. J. (2000). The utility of computer versus clinician-authored assessments in aiding the prediction of patient symptomatolgy. *Computers in Human Behavior, 16*(5) 519–536.

Erdberg, S. P. (1969). *AIMPI differences associated with sex, race, and residence in a Southern sample.* Unpublished doctoral dissertation, University of Alabama, Birmingham.

Erdman, H. P., Klein, M. H., & Greist, J. H. (1985). Direct patient computer interviewing. *Journal of Consulting and Clinical Psychology, 53*(6) 760–773.

Erez, A., & Judge, T. A. (2001). Relationship of core self-evaluations to goal setting, motivation, and performance. *Journal of Applied Psychology, 86*(6) 1270–1279.

Ergene, T. (2003). Effective interventions on test anxiety reduction: A meta-analysis. *School Psychology International, 24*(3), 313–328.

Erlanger, D., Feldman, D., Kutner, K., Kaushik, T., Kroger, H., & et al. (2003). Development and validation of a Web-based neuropsychological test protocol for sports-related return to play decision making. *Archives of Clinical Neuropsychology, 18*(3), 293–316.

Erlanger, D., Kaushik, T., Cantu, R., Barth, J. T., Broshek, D. K., Freeman, J. R., et al. (2003). Symptom-based assessment of the severity of a concussion. *J Neurosurg, 98*(3), 477–484.

Esquivel, G. B., & Lopez, E. (1988). Correlations among measures of cognitive ability, creativity, and academic achievement for gifted minority children. *Perceptual and Motor Skills, 67,* 395–398.

ETAT: Expository text analysis tool. *Behavior Research Methods, Instruments, & Computers, 34*(1) 93–107.

Evans, D. C. (2003). A comparison of the other-directed stigmatization produced by legal and illegal forms of affirmative action. *Journal of Applied Psychology, 88*(1), 121–130.

Evans, J. H., Carlsen, R. N., & McGrew, K. S. (1993). Classification of exceptional students with the Woodcock-Johnson PsychoEducational Battery–Revised. In B. A. Bracken & R. S. McCallum (Eds.), Woodcock-Johnson PsychoEducational Battery—Revised [Monograph]. *Journal of Psychoeducational Assessment,* pp. 6–19.

Evans, J. J., Floyd, R. G., McGrew, K. S., & Leforgee, M. H. (2003). The relations between measures of Cattell-Horn-Carroll (CHC) cognitive abilities and reading achievement during childhood and adolescence. *School Psychology Review, 31*(2), 246–262.

Everson, H. T., Millsap, R. E., & Rodriguez, C. M. (1991). Isolating gender differences in test anxiety: A confirmatory factor analysis of the test anxiety inventory. *Educational and Psychological Measurement, 51,* 243–251.

Ewart, C. K. (1991). Social action theory for a public health psychology. *American Psychologist, 46,* 931–946.

Ewing-Cobbs, L., Barnes, M., et al. (2004). Modeling of longitudinal academic achievement scores after pediatric traumatic brain injury. *Developments in Neuropsychology, 25*(1–2), 107–133.

Exner, J. E. (1976). Projective techniques. In I. B. Weiner (Ed.), *Clinical methods in psychology.* New York: Wiley.

Exner, J. E. (1993). *The Rorschach: A comprehensive system: Vol. 1. Basic foundation* (3rd ed.). New York: Wiley.

Exner, J. E. (1995). Narcissism in the comprehensive system for the Rorschach—Comment. *Clinical Psychology—Science and Practice, 2*(2), 200–206.

Exner, J. E. (1999). The Rorschach: Measurement concepts and issues of validity. In S. E. Embretson & S. L. Hershberger (Eds.), *The new rules of measurement.* Mahwah, NJ: Erlbaum.

Exner, J. E. (2003). *The Rorschach: A comprehensive system* (4th ed.). New York: Wiley.

Exner, J. E., Armbruster, G. L., & Viglione, D. (1978) The temporal stability of some Rorschach features. *Journal of Personality Assessment, 42,* 474–482.

Exner, J. E., & Farber, J. G. (1983). Peer nominations among female college students living in a dormitory setting. In *Workshops study 290* [unpublished]. Bayville, NY: Rorschach Workshops.

Eyde, L. D., Moreland, K. L., & Robertson, G. J. (with Primoff, E. S., & Most, R. B.). (1988, December). *Test user qualifications: A data-based approach to promoting good test use.* Washington, DC: American Psychological Association.

Eysenck, H. J. (1991). Raising IQ through vitamin and mineral supplementation: An introduction. *Personality and Individual Differences, 12,* 329–333.

Fagan, J. F. (1985). A new look at infant intelligence. In D. K. Detterman (Ed.), *Current topics in human intelligence: Research methodology* (Vol. 1) (pp. 223–246). Norwood, NJ: Ablex.

Fagundes, D. D., Haynes, W. O., Haak, N. J., and Moran, M. J. (1998). Task variability effects on the language test performance of Southern lower socioeconomic class African American and Caucasian five-year-olds. *Language, Speech, and Hearing Services in Schools, 29*(3), 148–157.

Fairburn, C. G., & Harrison, P. J. (2003). Eating disorders. *Lancet, 361*(9355), 407–416.

Fan, X., Willson, V. T., & Reynolds, C. R. (1995). Assessing the similarity of the factor structure of the K-ABC for African-American and white children. *Journal of Psychoeducational Assessment, 13,* 120–131.

Farrell, A. D. (1989). The impact of computers on professional practice: A survey of current practices and attitudes. *Professional Psychology: Research and Practice, 20,* 172–178.

Farrell, A. D. (1991). Computers and behavioral assessment: Current applications, future possibilities, and obstacles to routine use. *Behavioral Assessment, 13,* 159–179.

Farrell, A. D. (1992). Behavioral assessment with adults. In R. T. Ammerman & M. Hersen (Eds.), *Handbook of behavior therapy with children and adults: A developmental and longitudinal perspective.* New York: Pergamon Press.

Farrell, M. M. (2001). A comparison between the UNIT and the Leiter-R with children having language impairment. *Dissertation Abstracts International 62,* 4A. (UMI No. 3010817)

Feifel, H., Strack, S., & Nagy, V. T. (1987). Degree of lifethreat and differential use of coping modes. *Journal of Psychosomatic Research, 31,* 91–99.

Feinstein, A. R., & Cicchetti, D. V. (1990). High agreement but low kappa: I. The problem of two paradoxes. *Journal of Clinical Epidemiology, 43,* 543–549.

Feldman, S. E., & Sullivan, D. S. (1960). Factors mediating the effects of enhanced rapport on children's performances. *Journal of Consulting and Clinical Psychology, 36,* 302.

Felsten, G., & Wasserman, G. S. (1980). Visual masking: Mechanisms and theories. *Psychological Bulletin, 88,* 329–353.

Fenster A., Markus, K. A., Wiedemann, C. F., Brackett, M. A. & Fernandez, J. (2001). Selecting tomorrow's forensic psychologists: A fresh look at familiar predictors. *Educational and Psychological Measurement, 61*(2), 336–348.

Ferrando, P. J. (1999). Likert scaling using continuous, censored, and graded response models: Effects on criterion-rated validity. *Applied Psychological Measurement, 23*(2), 161–175.

Ferrario, S. R., Zotti, A. M., Massara, G., & Nuvolone, G. (2003). A comparative assessment of psychological and psychosocial characteristics of cancer patients and their caregivers. *Psycho-Oncology, 12*(1) 1–7.

Ferro, J. M., & Madureira, S. (2002). Recovery from cognitive and behavioral deficits. In J. Bogousslavsky (Ed.), *Long-term effects of stroke* (pp. 149–181). New York: Marcel Dekker.

Feuer, M. J., National Research Council (U.S.) Committee on Equivalency and Linkage of Educational Tests, National Research Council (U.S.) Commission on Behavioral and Social Sciences and Education, & Board on Testing and Assessment. (1999). *Uncommon measures: Equivalence and linkage among educational tests.* Washington, DC: National Academy Press.

Field, T. M. (1993). [Review of the book *Touch: The foundation of experience*]. *Contemporary Psychology, 38*(7), 735–736.

Field, T., Diego, M. A., Dieter, J., Hernandez-Reif, M., Schanberg, S., Kuhn, C., Yando, R., & Bendell, D. (2001). Depressed withdrawn and intrusive mothers' effects on their fetuses and neonates. *Infant Behavior and Development, 24*(1), 27–39.

Field, T., Diego, M., Hernandez-Reif, M., Schanberg, S., & Kuhn, C. (2002). Relative right versus left frontal EEG in neonates. *Developmental Psychobiology, 41*(2), 147–155.

Fielding-Barnsley, R., & Purdie, N. (2003). Early intervention in the home for children at risk of reading failure. *Support for Learning, 18*(2), 77–82.

Fish, D. D. (2001). The mechanisms of homogeneity: Individual and social structure influences on selection outcomes. *Dissertation Abstracts International, 61,* 9B.

Fish, J. M. (2002). *Race and Intelligence: Separating science from myth.* Mahwah, NJ: Erlbaum.

Fiske, D. W., & Baughman, E. E. (1953). Relationships between Rorschach scoring categories and the total number of responses. *Journal of Abnormal and Social Psychology, 48,* 25–32.

Fitts, W. H., & Warren, W. L. (1996). *Tennessee Self-Concept Scale* (2nd ed.). Los Angeles: Western Psychological Services.

Fitzgerald, C. (1997). The MBTI and leadership development: Personality and leadership reconsidered in changing times. In C. Fitzgerald, L. K. Kirby, et al. (Eds.), *Developing leaders: Research and applications in psychological type and leadership development: Integrating reality and vision, mind and heart* (pp. 33–59). Palo Alto, CA: Davies-Black.

Flanagan, D. P., & Alfonso, V. C. (1995). A critical review of the technical characteristics of new and recently revised intelligence tests for preschool children. *Journal of Psychoeducational Assessment, 13,* 66–90.

Flanagan, D. P., & McGrew, K. S. (1998). Interpreting intelligence tests from contemporary *Gf-Gc* theory: Joint confirmatory factor analysis of the WJ-R and KAIT in a non-white sample. *Journal of School Psychology, 36,* 151–182.

Flanagan, D. P., McGrew, K. S., & Ortiz, S. O. (2000). *The Wechsler Intelligence Scale and Gf-Gc theory: A contemporary approach to interpretation.* Needham Heights, MA: Allyn & Bacon.

Flanagan, J. C. (1954). The critical incident technique. *Psychological Bulletin, 51,* 327–358.

Flanagan, R. (1995). The utility of the Kaufman Assessment Battery for Children (K-ABC) and the Wechsler Intelligence Scales for Linguistically Different Children: Clinical considerations. *Psychology in the Schools, 32*(1), 5–11.

Flaugher, R. L. (1978). The many definitions of test bias. *American Psychologist, 33,* 671–679.

Flaugher, R. L., & Schrader, W. B. (1978). *Eliminating differentially difficult items as an approach to test bias* (RB-78-4). Princeton, NJ: Educational Testing Service.

Fleishman, E. A., & Quaintance, M. K. (1984). *Taxonomies of human performance: The description of human tasks.* Orlando, FL: Academic Press.

Fleiss, J. L. (1971). Measuring nominal scale agreement among many raters. *Psychological Bulletin, 76,* 378–382.

Fleiss, J. (1981). *Statistical methods for rates and proportions.* New York: Wiley.

Fletcher, J. M., Taylor, H. G., Levin, H., & Satz, P. (1995). Neuropsychological and intellectual assessment of children. In H. I. Kaplan & B. J. Saddock (Eds.), *Comprehensive textbook of psychiatry* (6th ed.) (pp. 581–601). Baltimore: Williams & Wilkens.

Fletcher, S. W. (1997). Whither scientific deliberation in health policy recommendations? Alice in the Wonderland of breast-cancer screening. *New England Journal of Medicine, 336*(16), 1180–1183.

Flett, G. L., & Blankstein, K. R. (1994). Worry as a component of test anxiety: A multidimensional analysis. In G. C. L. Davey & Frank Tallis (Eds.), *Worrying: Perspectives on theory, assessment and treatment* (pp. 219–239). Chichester, England: Wiley.

Flett, G. L., Endler, N. S., and Fairlie, P. (1999). The interaction model of anxiety and the threat of Quebec's separation from Canada. *Journal of Personality and Social Psychology, 76*(1), 143–150.

Floyd, R. G., Evans, J. J., & McGrew, K. S. (2003). Relations between measures of Cattell-Horn-Carroll (CHC) cognitive abilities and mathematics achievement across the school-age years. *Psychology in the Schools, 40*(2), 155–171.

Flynn, D., Schaik, P., & van Wersch, A. (2004). A comparison of multi-item Likert and visual analogue scales for the assessment of transactionally defined coping function. *European Journal of Psychological Assessment, 20*(1), 49–58.

Flynn, J. R. (1999). Searching for justice: The discovery of IQ gains over time. *American Psychologist, 54*(1), 5–20.

Fogel, B. S., Schiffer, R. B., & Rao, S. M. (Eds.). (2000). *Synopsis of neuropsychiatry*: Philadelphia: Lippincott.

Foley, K. L., Reed, P. S., Mutran, E. J., & DeVellis, R. F. (2002). *Measurement adequacy of the CES-D among a sample of older African-Americans*. London, United Kingdom: Elsevier Science.

Folkman, S., & Lazarus, R. S. (1980). An analysis of coping in a middle aged community sample. *Journal of Health and Social Behavior, 21*, 219–239.

Ford &. Ford v. Long Beach Unified School Dist., 291 F.3d 1086 (9th Cir. 2002).

Forer, B. R. (1949). The fallacy of personal validation: A classroom demonstration of gullibility. *Journal of Abnormal and Social Psychology, 44*, 118–123.

Forrester, B. J., & Klaus, R. A. (1964). The effect of race of the examiner on intelligence test scores of Negro kindergarten children. *Peabody Papers in Human Development, 2*, 1–7.

Forsterling, F. (1988). *Attribution theory in clinical psychology*. New York: Wiley.

Forsyth, R. A. (1991). Do NAEP scales yield valid criterion-referenced interpretations? *Educational Measurement: Issues and Practice, 10*, 16.

Fowler, R. D. (1985). Landmarks in computer-assisted psychological assessment. *Journal of Consulting and Clinical Psychology, 53*, 748–759.

Fox, H. R. (1999). APA urges postponement of OCR resource guide on *High-stakes testing. Psychological Science Agenda, 12*, 13.

Franceschina, E., Dorz, S., & Bari, M. (2001). Computer and traditional administration of the Cognitive Behavioral Assessment 2. 0. *Bollettino di Psicologia Applicata, 235*(48) 57–62.

Francis-Williams, J. (1974). *Children with specific learning disabilities* (2nd ed.). Oxford, England: Pergamon Press.

Frank, G. (1995). On the assessment of self representations and object representations from the Rorschach: A review of the research and commentary. *Psychological Reports, 76*(2), 659–671.

Frank, L. K. (1939). Projective methods for the study of personality. *Journal of Psychology, 8*, 343–389.

Franklin, R. D. (2003). *Prediction in forensic and neuropsychology: Sound statistical practices*. Mahwah, NJ: Erlbaum.

Frase, L. T., Almond, R. G., Burstein, J., Kukich, K., Sheehan, K. M., Steinberg, L. S., Mislevy, R. J., Singley, K., & Chodorow, M. (2003). Technology and assessment. In H. F. O'Neil & R. S. Perez (Eds.), *Technology applications in education: A learning view (213–244)*. Mahwah, NJ: Erlbaum.

Frazer, R. A., & Wiersma, U. J. (2001). Prejudice versus discrimination in the employment interview: We may hire equally, but our memories harbor prejudice. *Human Relations, 54*(2), 173–191.

Frederiksen, C. (1969). Abilities transfer and information retrieval in verbal learning. *Multivariate Behavioral Research Monographs, 69*, 1–82.

Fredrickson, B. L. (2001). The role of positive emotions in positive psychology: The broaden-and-build theory of positive emotions. *American Psychologist, 56*, 218–226.

Fredrickson, B. L., & Joiner, T. (2002). Positive emotions trigger upward spirals toward emotional well-being. *Psychological Science, 13*(2), 172–175.

Fredrikson, M. (1991). Physiological responses to stressors: Implications for clinical assessment. *Psychological Assessment: A Journal of Consulting and Clinical Psychology, 3*, 350–355.

Freeman, F. S. (1955). *Theory and practice of psychological testing*. New York: Holt.

Freeman, H. P., & Payne, R. (2000). Racial injustice in health care [editorial; comment]. *New England Journal of Medicine, 342*(14), 1045–1047.

Freeman, L., & Miller, A. (2001). *Norm-referenced, criterion-referenced, and dynamic assessment: What exactly is the point?* United Kingdom: Pitman Publishing.

Fried, Y., & Tiegs, R. B. (1995). Supervisors' role conflict and role ambiguity differential relations with performance ratings of subordinates and the moderating effect of screening ability. *Journal of Applied Psychology, 80*, 282–296.

Frisby, C. L. (1998). Culture and cultural differences. In E. Jonathan, H. Sandoval, E. Craig, L. Frisby, et al. (Eds.), *Test interpretation and diversity: Achieving equity in assessment* (pp. 51–73). Washington, DC: American Psychological Association.

Frumkin, R. M. (1997). Significant neglected sociocultural and physical factors affecting intelligence. *American Psychologist 52*(1), 76–77.

Fuchs, D., & Fuchs, L. S. (1986). Test procedure bias: A metaanalysis of examiner familiarity effects. *Review of Educational Research, 56*, 243–262.

Fuertes, J. N., & Sedlacek, W. E. (1994). Predicting the academic success of Hispanic college students using SAT scores. *College Student Journal, 28*, 350–352.

Fuller, G. B., & Vance, B. (1995). Interscorer reliability of the Modified Version of the Bender-Gestalt Test for Preschool and Primary School Children. *Psychology in the Schools, 32*, 264–266.

Funder, D. C. (1993). Judgments as data for personality and developmental psychology: Error versus accuracy. In D. C. Funder, R. D. Parke, C. Tomlinson-Keasey, & K. Widaman (Eds.), *Studying lives through time: Personality and development*. APA science volumes (pp. 121–146). Washington, DC: American Psychological Association.

Funder, D. C. (2001). Accuracy in personality judgment: Research and theory concerning an obvious, question. Washington, DC: American Psychological Association.

Funder, D. C., Parke, R. D., Tomhnson-Keasey, C., & Widaman, K. (Eds.). (1993). *Studying lives through time: Personality and development*. Washington, DC: American Psychological Association.

Funder, D. C., & West, S. G. (1993). Consensus, self-other agreement, and accuracy in personality judgment: An introduction. *Journal of Personality, 61*, 457–476.

Furnham, A., & Petrides, K. V. (2003). Trait emotional intelligence and happiness. *Social Behavior and Personality, 31*(8), 815–824.

Furukawa, T., Sarason, I. G., & Sarason, B. R. (1998). Social support and adjustment to a novel social environment. *International Journal of Social Psychiatry, 44* (1), 56–70.

Gacano, C. B., & Meloy, J. R. (1994). *The Rorschach assessment of aggressive and psychopathic personalities*. Hillsdale, NJ: Erlbaum.

Gaffner, D. C. & Hazler, R. J. (2002). Factors related to indecisiveness and career indecision in undecided college students. *Journal of College Student Development, 43*(3), 317–326.

Gallucci, N. T. (1997). Correlates of MMPI-A substance abuse scales. *Assessment, 4*, 87–94.

Galton, F. (1869). *Hereditary genius: An inquiry into its laws and consequences*. London: Collins.

Galton, F. (1879). Psychometric experiments. *Brain, 2*, 149–162.

Galton, F. (1883). *Inquiries into human faculty and its development*. London: Macmillan.

Gamble, K. R. (1972). The Holtzman Inkblot Technique: A review. *Psychological Bulletin, 77*, 172–194.

Garb, H. N., Florio C. M., & Grove, W. M. (1998). The validity of the Rorschach and the Minnesota Multiphasic Personality Inventory: Results from meta-analyses. *Psychological Science, 9*, 402–404.

Garb, H. N., (1998). *Studying the clinician: Judgment research and psychological assessment*. Washington, DC: American Psychological Association.

Garb, H. N. (1999). Call for a moratorium on the use of the Rorschach Inkblot in clinical and forensic settings. *Assessment, 6*, 313–315.

Garb, H. N., Wood, J. M., Nezworski, M. T., Grove, W. M., & Stejskal, W. J. (2001). Towards a resolution of the Rorschach controversy. *Psychological Assessment, 13*, 433–448.

Garcia, J. (1981). The logic and limits of mental aptitude testing. *American Psychologist, 36*, 1172–1180.

Garcia, N., & Fleming, J. (1998). Are standardized tests fair to African Americans? *Journal of Higher Education, 69*, 471.

Garcia-Esteve, L., Ascaso, C., Ojuel, J., & Navarro, P. (2003). Validation of the Edinburgh Postnatal Depression Scale (EPDS) in Spanish mothers. *Journal of Affective Disorders. 75*(1) 71–76.

Garcia-Palacios, A., Hoffman, H., Carlin, A., Furness, T. A., & Botella, C. (2002). Virtual reality in the treatment of spider phobia: A controlled study. *Behavior & Research Therapy, 40*(9) 983–993.

Garcia-Palacios, A., Hoffman, H. G., See, S. K., Tsai, A., & Botella, C. (2001). Redefining therapeutic success with virtual reality exposure therapy. *Cyberpsychology and Behavior, 4*(3) 341–348.

Gardner, E. F., Rudman, H. C., Karlsen, B., & Merwin, J. C. (1982). *The Stanford Achievement Test: Seventh edition*. New York: Harcourt Brace Jovanovich.

Gardner, H. (1983). *Frames of mind: The theory of multiple intelligences*. New York: Basic Books.

Gardner, H. (1993). The relationship between early giftedness and later achievement. In *The origins and development of high ability* (pp. 175–186). Ciba Foundation Symposium: Vol. 178. Chichester, England: Wiley.

Gardner, H., Krechevsky, M., Sternberg, R. J., & Okagaki, L. (1994). Intelligence in context: Enhancing students' practical intelligence for school. In K. McGilly (Ed.), *Classroom lessons: Integrating cognitive theory and classroom practice* (pp. 105–127). Cambridge, MA: MIT Press.

Garfield, S. L. (2000). The Rorschach test in clinical diagnosis: A brief commentary. *Journal of Clinical Psychology, 56*, 431–434.

Garfield, S. L., & Sineps, J. (1959). An appraisal of Taulbee and Sisson's "Configurational analysis of MMPI profiles of psychiatric groups. " *Journal of Consulting Psychology, 23*, 333–335.

Garlick, D. (2002). Understanding the nature of the general factor of intelligence: The role of individual differences in neural plasticity as an explanatory mechanism. *Psychological Review, 109*(1), 116–136.

Gaston, L., Brunet, A., Koszychi, D., & Bradwejn, J. (1996). MMPI profiles of acute and chronic PTSD in a civilian sample. *Journal of Traumatic Stress, 9*, 817–832.

Gaston, M. F., Nelson, W. M., Hart, K. J., Quatman, G., & others. (1994). The equivalence of the MMPI and MMPI-2. *Assessment, 1*, 415–418.

Gati, I., & Tikotzki, Y. (1989). Strategies for collection and processing of occupational information in making career decisions. *Journal of Counseling Psychology, 36*, 430–439.

Gaudreau, P., Blondin, J. P., Lapierre, A. M. (2002). Athlete's coping during a competition: Relationship of coping strategies with positive affect, negative affect, and performance–goal discrepancy. *Psychology of Sport and Exercise, 3*(2), 125–150.

Gauvain, M. (1994). [Review of the book *The cultural context of infancy: Vol. 2: Multicultural and interdisciplinary approaches to parent-infant relations*]. *Merrill Palmer Quarterly Journal of Developmental Psychology, 40*(4), 568–572.

Geer, J. H. (1965). The development of a scale to measure fear. *Behaviour Research and Therapy, 3,* 45–53.

Geiselman, R. E., Woodward, J. A., & Beatty, J. (1982). Individual differences in verbal memory performance: A test of alternative information-processing models. *Journal of Experimental Psychology: General, 111,* 109–134.

Geiser, S., & Studley, R. (2001). *UC and the SAT: Predictive validity and differential impact of the SAT I and SAT II at the University of California.* Available from www.ucop.edu/sas/research/researchandplanning/pdf/sat_study. pdf.

Geisinger, K. F. (1994). Crosscultural normative assessment: Translation and adaption issues influencing the normative interpretation of assessment instruments. *Psychological Assessment, 6*(4), 304–312.

Geisinger, K. F. (2003). Testing and assessment in cross-cultural psychology. In J. R Graham & J. A. Naglieri (Eds.), *Handbook of psychology: Assessment psychology* (pp. 95–117). New York: Wiley.

Gendreau, M., Hufford, M. R., & Stone, A. A. (2003). Measuring clinical pain in chronic widespread pain: Selected methodological issues. *Best Practices and Research in Clinical Rheumatology, 17*(4), 575–592.

Georgas, J., Weiss, L. G., van de Vijver, F. J., & Sakloske, D. H. (2003). *Culture and children's intelligence.* New York: Academic Press.

Gerken, K. C., Eliason, M. J., & Arthur, C. R. (1994). The assessment of at-risk infants and toddlers with the Mental Scale and the Batelle Developmental Inventory: Beyond the data. *Psychology in the Schools, 31*(3), 181–187.

Gesell, A. (1925). Monthly increments of development in infancy. *Journal of Genetic Psychology, 32,* 203–208.

Gesell, A., Halverson, H. M., Thompson, H., Ilg, F. L., Castner, B. M., Ames, L. B., & Amatruda, C. S. (1940). *The first five years of life: A guide to the study of the preschool child.* New York: Harper & Row.

GI Forum et al. v. Texas Education Agency et al. (1997). CA No. SA-97-CA1278EP.

Gibby, R. G., Miller, D. R., & Walker, E. L. (1953). The examiner's influence on the Rorschach protocol. *Journal of Consulting Psychology, 17,* 425–428.

Gilberstadt, H., & Duker, J. (1965). *A handbook for clinical and actuarial MMPI interpretation.* Philadelphia: Saunders.

Gilbert, G. E., Basco, W. T., Jr., Blue, A. V., & O'Sullivan, P. S. (2002). Predictive validity of the Medical College Admissions Test Writing Sample for the United States medical licensing examination steps 1 and 2. *Advances in Health Science Education Theory and Practices, 7*(3), 191–200.

Gillingham, W. H. (1970). An investigation of examiner influence on Wechsler Intelligence Scale for Children scores. *Dissertation Abstracts International, 31,* 2178. (University Microfilms No. 70-20,458)

Gilpin, E. A., & Pierce, J. P. (2003). Concurrent use of tobacco products by California adolescents. *Preventive Medicine, 36*(5), 575–584.

Girotto, V., & Gonzalez, M. (2000). Strategies and models in statistical reasoning. In E. Walter Schaeken, E. Gino De Vooght, et al. (Eds.), *Deductive reasoning and strategies.* (pp. 267–285). Mahwah, NJ: Erlbaum.

Glas, C. A. W., & Meijer, R. R. (2003). A Bayesian approach to person fit analysis in item response theory models. *Applied Psychological Measurement, 27*(3) 217–233.

Glaser, B. A., Calhoun, G. B., & Petrocelli, J. V. (2002). Personality characteristics of male juvenile offenders by adjudicated offenses as indicated by the MMPI-A. *Criminal Justice & Behavior, 29*(2), 183–201.

Gleaves, D. H., May, M. C., & Eberenz, K. P. (1996). Measuring and discriminating dissociative and borderline symptomatology among women with eating disorders. *Dissociation: Progress in the Dissociative Disorders, 9,* 110–117.

Glenn, D. M., Beckham, J. C., Sampson, W. S., Feldman, M. E., Hertzberg, M. A., & Moore, S. D. (2002). MMPI-2 profiles of Gulf and Vietnam combat veterans with chronic posttraumatic stress disorder. *Journal of Clinical Psychology, 58*(4), 371–381.

Glutting, J. J. (1989). Introduction to the structure and application of the Stanford-Binet Intelligence Scale–Fourth Edition. *Journal of School Psychology, 27,* 69–80.

Goldberg, A. L., & Pedulla, J. J. (2002). Performance differences according to test mode and computer familiarity on a practice Graduate Record Exam. *Educational and Psychological Measurement, 62*(6), 1053–1067.

Goldberg, L. R. (1974). Objective personality tests and measures. *Annual Review of Psychology, 25,* 343–366.

Golden, C. J. (1981). A standardized version of Luria's neuropsychological tests: Quantitative and qualitative approach in neuropsychological evaluation. In F. E. Filskov & T. J. Boll (Eds.), *Handbook of clinical neuropsychology.* New York: Wiley.

Goldman, B. A., & Osbourne, W. (1985). *Unpublished experimental mental measures* (Vol. 4). New York: Human Sciences Press.

Goldman, R. D. (1973). Hidden opportunities in the prediction of college grades for different subgroups. *Journal of Educational Measurement, 10*(3), 205–210.

Goldman, R. D., & Hartig, L. (1976). The WISC may not be a valid predictor of school performance for primary-grade minority children.

American Journal of Mental Deficiency, 80, 583–587.

Goldstein, D. J., Fogle, E. E., Wieber, J. L., & O'Shea, T. M. (1995). Comparison of the Bayley Scales of Infant Development–Second Edition and the Bayley Scales of Infant Development with premature infants. *Journal of Psychoeducational Assessment, 13*, 391–396.

Goldstein, G., Minshew, N. J., Allen, D. N., & Seaton, B. E. (2002). High-functioning autism and schizophrenia: A comparison of an early and late onset neurodevelopmental disorder. *Archives of Clinical Neuropsychology, 17*(5), 461–475.

Goldstein, L. H., Canavan, A. G., & Polkey, C. E. (1988). Verbal and abstract designs paired associate learning after unilateral temporal lobectomy. *Cortex, 24*, 41–52.

Golomb, B. A. (1998). Dietary fats and heart disease: Dogma challenged? *Journal of Clinical Epidemiology, 51*(6), 461–464.

Golomb, B. A., Stattin, H., & Mednick, S. (2000). *Low cholesterol and violent crime.* United Kingdom: Elsevier Science.

Gonzalez, K. (2002, June 28). *GRE general test to change format in October 2002.* Retrieved July, 28, 2003 from www. ets. org/textonly/news/01062801. html.

Goodman, J. (1977). The diagnostic fallacy: A critique of Jane Mercer's concept of mental retardation. *Journal of School Psychology, 15*, 197–206.

Goodman, J. (1979). "Ignorance" versus "stupidity"—the basic disagreement. *School Psychology Digest, 8*(2), 218–223.

Gordon, E. W., & Terrell, M. D. (1981). The changed social context of testing. *American Psychologist, 36*, 1167–1171.

Gorham, D. R., Moseley, E. C., & Holtzman, W. H. (1968). Norms for the computer-scored Holtzman Inkblot Technique. *Perceptual and Motor Skills, 26*(3) 1279–1305.

Gotkin, T. D., & Reynolds, C. R. (1981). Factorial similarity of the WISC-R white and black children from the standardization sample. *Journal of Educational Psychology, 73*, 227–231

Gottfredson, L. S. (1980). Construct validity of Holland's occupational typology in terms of prestige, census, Department of Labor, and other classification systems. *Journal of Applied Psychology, 65*, 697–714.

Gottfredson, L. S. (1994). The science and politics of race-norming. *American Psychologist, 49, 955–963.*

Gottlib, I. H., & Cine, D. B. (1989). Self-report assessment of depression and anxiety. In P. C. Kendill & D. Watson (Eds.), *Anxiety and depression: Distinctive and overlapping features* (pp. 131–169). San Diego: Academic Press.

Gough, H. G. (1960). The adjective checklist as a personality assessment research technique. *Psychological Reports, 6*, 107–122,

Gough, H. G. (1987). *California Psychological Inventory, revised manual.* Palo Alto, CA: Consulting Psychologists Press.

Gough, H. G. (1995). Career assessment and the California Psychological Inventory. *Journal of Career Assessments, 30*, 101–122.

Gough, H. G. (1996). *California Psychological Inventory.* Retrieved February 2, 2003 from www. stevejudah. com/DescCalifornia. htm.

Gough, H. G., & Heilbrun, A. B., Jr. (1980). *The Adjective Checklist manual (revised).* Palo Alto, CA: Consulting Psychologists Press.

Gould, S. J. (1981). The *mismeasure of man.* New York: Norton.

Gould, S. J. (1996). The *mismeasure of man* (rev. ed.). New York: Norton.

Graham, F. K., & Kendall, B. S. (1960). Memory-for-Designs test: Revised general manual. *Perceptual Motor Skills, 11*, 147–190.

Grana-Gomez, J. L., Andreu, J. M., Rogers, H. L., & Arango-Lasprilla, J. C. (2003). Structural dimensions of the social representation of aggression. *Social Behavior & Personality, 31*(3) 223–236.

Grant, I., & Adams, K. M. (Eds.). (1996). *Neuropsychological assessment of neuropsychiatric disorders* (2nd ed.). New York: Oxford University Press.

Grant, I., & Heaton, R. K. (1990). Human immunodeficiency virustype I (HIV-1) and the brain. *Journal of Consulting and Clinical Psychology, 58*, 27–30.

Gray, J. R. (2003). Neural mechanisms of general fluid intelligence. *Nature Neuroscience, 6*, 316–322.

GRE Guide. (1990). Princeton, NJ: Educational Testing Service.

GRE Guide. (1991). Princeton, NJ: Educational Testing Service.

GRE Guide. (2003). Princeton, NJ: Educational Testing Service.

Greaud, V. A., & Green, B. F. (1986). Equivalence of conventional and computer presentation of speeded tests. *Applied Psychological Measurement, 10*, 23–34.

Green, B. F. (1978). In defense of measurement. *American Psychologist, 33*, 664–670.

Green, B. L., & Kenrick, D. T. (1994). The attractiveness of gender-typed traits at different relationship levels: Androgynous characteristics may be desirable after all. *Personality and Social Psychology Bulletin, 20*(3), 244–253.

Green, D. F., Jr., & Wing, H. (1988). *Analysis of job performance measurement data: Report of a workshop.* Washington, DC: National Academy Press.

Green, D. R., & Draper, J. F. (1972, September). *Exploratory studies of bias and achievement.* Paper presented at the meeting of the American Psychological Association, Honolulu, HI.

Green, K. E. (1983). Subjective judgment of multiple choice item characteristics. *Educational & Psychological Measurement, 43*, 563–570.

Green, P. (2003). Welcoming a paradigm shift in neuropsychology. *Archives of Clinical Neuropsychology, 18*(6), 625–627.

Greene, R. L. (2000). *The MMPI-2: An*

interpretive manual. Boston: Allyn & Bacon.

Greenfield, P. M. (1998). The cultural evolution of IQ. In E. Ulric Neisser et al. (Eds.), *The rising curve: Longterm gains in IQ and related measures* (pp. 81–123). Washington, DC: American Psychological Association.

Gregory, R. J. (1999). *Foundations of intellectual assessment*. Boston: Allyn & Bacon.

Greisinger, K. F. (2003). Testing and assessment in cross-cultural psychology. In J. R. Graham & J. A. Naglieri (Eds.), *Handbook of psychology: Assessment psychology* (Vol. 10) (pp. 95–117). New York: Wiley.

Greist, J. H. Gustafson, D. H., Stauss, F. F., Rowse, G. L., Laughren, T. P., & Chiles, J. A. (1973). A computer interview for suicide-risk prediction. *American Journal of Psychiatry, 12*, 1327–1332.

Gresham, F. M., McIntyre, L. L., Olson-Tinker, H., Dolstra, L., McLaughlin, V., & Van, M. (2004). Relevance of functional behavioral assessment research for school-based interventions and positive behavioral support. *Research in Developmental Disabilities, 25*(1), 19–37.

Greve, K. W., Bianchini, K. J., Mathias, C. W., & Houston, R. J. (2003). Detecting malingering performance on the Wechsler Adult Intelligence Scale. *Archives of Clinical Neuropsychology, 18*, 245–260.

Griggs v. Duke Power Company. (1971). 401 U.S. 424(a).

Grillis, A. E., & Ollendick, T. H. (2002). Issues in parent-child agreement: The case of structured diagnostic interviews. *Clinical Child & Family Psychology Review, 5*(1), 57–83.

Grim, L. G., & Yarnold, P. R. (Eds.). (1995). *Reading and understanding multivariate statistics*. Washington, DC: American Psychological Association.

Groenweg, G., Conway, D. G., & Stan, E. A. (1986). Performance of adults with developmental handi-caps on alternate forms of the Peabody Picture Vocabulary Test. *Journal of Speech and Hearing Disorders, 51*, 259–263.

Groessl, E. J., Kaplan, R. M., & Cronan, T. A. (2003). Quality of well-being in older people with osteoarthritis. *Arthritis and Rheumatology, 49*(1), 23–28.

Grossman, L. S., & Craig, R. J. (1995). Comparisons of the MCMI-II and 16 PF validity scales. *Journal of Personality Assessment, 64*(2), 384–389.

Groth-Marnat, G. (1999). *Handbook of psychological assessment* (3rd ed.). New York: Wiley.

Groth-Marnat, G. (2003). *Handbook of psychological assessment* (4th ed.). New York, NY: Wiley.

Groth-Marnat, G., & Shumaker, J. (1989). Computer-based psychological testing: Issues and guidelines. *American Journal of Orthopsychiatry, 59*, 257–263.

Guan, G., Tang, J., Xue, J., & Zhou, H. (2002). MMPI results of 105 patients with alcohol dependence. *Chinese Mental Health Journal, 16*(2), 116–120.

Guarnaccia, V., Dill, C. A., Sabatino, S., & Southwick, S. (2001). Scoring accuracy using the Comprehensive System for the Rorschach. *Journal of Personality Assessment, 77*, 464–474.

Gudjonsson, G. H., & Sigurdsson, J. F. (2003). The relationship of compliance with coping strategies and self-esteem. *European Journal of Psychological Assessment, 19*(2) 117–123.

Guedalia, J., Finkelstein, Y., Drukker, A., & Frishberg, Y. (2000). The use of Luria's method for the neurobehavioral assessment of encephalopathy in an adolescent: Application in a rehabilitation setting. *Archives of Clinical Neuropsychology, 15*(2), 177–184.

Guilford, J. P., & Zimmerman, W. S. (1956). Fourteen dimensions of temperament. *Psychological Monographs, 70*(10).

Guion, R. M., & Ironson, G. H.

(1983). Latent trait theory for organizational research. *Organizational Behavior and Human Performance, 31*, 54–87.

Gullone, E., & King, N. J. (1992). Psychometric evaluation of a Revised Fear Survey Schedule for children and adolescents. *Journal of Child Psychology and Psychiatry and Allied Disciplines, 33*(6), 987–998.

Guthrie, R. V. (1976). *Even the rat was white: A historical view of psychology*. New York: Harper & Row.

Gutloff, K. (1999). Is high-stakes testing fair? *NEA Today, 17*, 6.

Guttman, L. (1950). Relation of scalogram analysis to other techniques. In S. A. Stouffer et al. (Eds.), *Measurement and prediction*. Princeton, NJ: Princeton University Press.

Gyurke, J. S., Stone, B. J., & Beyer, M. (1990). A confirmatory factor analysis of the WPPSI-R. *Journal of Psychoeducational Assessment, 8*, 15–21.

Hagell, P., Whalley, D., McKenna, S. P., & Lindvall, O. (2003). Health status measurement in Parkinson's disease: Validity of the PDQ-39 and Nottingham Health Profile. *Movement Disorders, 18*(7), 773–783.

Hakel, M. D. (1986). Personnel selection and placement. *Annual Review of Psychology, 37*, 351–380.

Hale, J. B., Hoeppner, J. B., & Fiorello, C. A. (2002). Analyzing digit span components for assessment of attention processes. *Journal of Psychoeducational Assessment, 20*(2), 128–143.

Hall, V. C., Huppertz, J. W., & Levi, A. (1977). Attention and achievement exhibited by middle- and lower-class black and white elementary school boys. *Journal of Educational Psychology, 69*, 115–120.

Haller, N., & Exner, J. E. (1985). The reliability of Rorschach variables for inpatients presenting symptoms of depression and/or helplessness. *Journal of Personality Assessment, 49*, 516–521.

Hambleton, R. K. (1994). The rise and fall of criterion-referenced measurement? *Educational Measurement: Issues and Practice, 13,* 21–26.

Hamel, M., Shaffer, T. W., & Erdberg, P. (2000). A study of nonpatient preadolescent Rorschach protocols. *Journal of Personality Assessments, 75,* 280–294.

Hammer, A. L., & Marting, M. S. (1985). *Manual for the Coping Resources Inventory.* Palo Alto, CA: Consulting Psychologists Press.

Hampson, E., & Kimura D. (1988). Reciprocal effects of hormonal fluctuations on human motor and perceptual-spatial skills. *Behavioral Neuroscience, 102,* 456–459.

Handel, R. W., Ben-Porath, Y. S., & Matt, M. (1999). Computerized adaptive assessment with the MMPI-2 in a clinical setting. *Psychological Assessment, 11*(3), 369–380.

Haney, W. (1981). Validity, vaudeville, and values: A short history of social concerns over standardized testing. *American Psychologist, 36,* 1021–1034.

Hanford, G. H. (1986). The SAT and statewide assessment: The distinction between measurement and evaluation. *Vital Speeches of the Day, 52*(24), 765–768.

Hansen, B. M., Dinesen, J., Hoff, B., & Greisen, G. (2002). Intelligence in preterm children at four years of age as a predictor of school function: A longitudinal controlled study. *Developmental Medicine and Child Neurology, 44*(8), 517–521.

Hansen, J. –I. C. (2000). Interpretation of the Strong Interest Inventory. In E. C. Edward Watkins, Jr., E. Vicki, L. Campbell, et al. (Eds.), *Testing and assessment in counseling practice* (2nd ed.) (pp. 227–262). Mahwah, NJ: Erlbaum.

Hansen, J. C., & Campbell, D. P. (1985). *Manual for the SVIB-SCII* (4th ed.). Stanford, CA: Stanford University Press.

Hanson, M. A., Borman, W. C., Kubisiak, U. C., & Sager, C. E. (1999). Cross-domain analyses. In E. Norman, G. Peterson, E. Michael, D. Mumford, et al. (Eds.), *An occupational information system for the 21st century: The development of O*NET* (pp. 247–258). Washington, DC: American Psychological Association.

Hanson, M. A., Borman, W. C., Mogilka, H. J., Manning, C., & Hedge, J. W. (1999). Computerized assessment of skill for a highly technical job. In E. Fritz Drasgow, E. Julie B. OlsonBuchanan, et al. (Eds.), *Innovations in computerized assessment* (pp. 197–220). Mahwah, NJ: Erlbaum.

Hanten, G., Dennis, M., et al. (2004). Childhood head injury and metacognitive processes in language and memory. *Developments in Neuropsychology, 25*(1–2), 85–106.

Hanton, S., Evans, L., & Neil, R. (2003). Hardiness and the competitive trait anxiety response. *Anxiety, Stress, & Coping, 16*(2) 167–184.

Harasym, P. H., Woloschuk, W., Mandin, H., & Brundin-Mather, R. (1996). Reliability and validity of interviewer's judgments of medical school candidates. *Academic Medicine, 71,* 540–542.

Harcourt Educational Measurement. (2002). *The Metropolitan Achievement Tests* (8th ed.). San Antonio, TX: Author.

Hardy, J. B., Welcher, D. W., Mellits, E. D., & Kagan, J. (1976). Pitfalls in the measurement of intelligence: Are standardized intelligence tests valid for measuring the intellectual potential of urban children? *Journal of Psychology, 94,* 43–51.

Haren, E. G. & Mitchell, C. W. (2003). Relationship between the Five-Factor Personality Model and coping styles. *Psychology and Education: An Interdisciplinary Journal, 40*(1) 38–49.

Harkness, A. R., McNulty, J. L., & Ben-Porath, Y. S. (1995). The personality psychopathology—5 (Psy5): Construct and MMPI-2 scales. *Psychological Assessment, 7*(1), 104–114.

Harlow, G., Boulmetis, J., Clark, P. G., Willis, G. H. (2003). Computer-assisted life stories. *Computers in Human Behavior, 19*(4) 391–406.

Harmon, L. W., Cole, N., Wysong, E., & Zytowski, D. G. (1973). AMEG commission report on sex bias in interest measurement. *Measurement and Evaluation in Guidance, 6,* 171–177.

Harrell, T. H., Honaker, L. M., Hetu, M., & Oberwager, J. (1987). Computerized versus traditional administration of the multidimensional aptitude battery-verbal scale: An examination of reliability and validity. *Computers in Human Behavior, 3*(2) 129–137.

Harris, D. B. (1963). *Children's drawings as measures of intellectual maturity: A revision and extension of the Goodenough Draw-a-Man Test.* New York: Harcourt, Brace, & World.

Harris, D. H. (2002). Human performance testing. In S. G. Charlton & T. G. O'Brien (Eds.), *Handbook of human factors testing and evaluation* (2nd ed.) (pp. 79–96). Mahwah, NJ: Erlbaum.

Harris, F. C., & Lahey, B. B. (1982). Subject reactivity in direct observational assessment: A review and critical analysis. *Clinical Psychology Review, 2,* 523–538.

Harris, L. M., Robinson, J., & Menzies, R. G. (2001). Predictors of panic symptoms during magnetic resonance imaging scans. *International Journal of Behavioral Medicine, 8*(1) 80–87.

Harris, M. M. (1989). Reconsidering the employment interview: A review of recent literature and suggestions for future research. *Personnel Psychology, 42,* 691–726.

Harris, W. G., Neider, D., Feldman, C., Fink, A., & Johnson, J. H. (1981). An online interpretive Rorschach approach: Using Exner's comprehensive system. *Behavior Research Methods and Instrumentation, 13*(4) 588–591.

Harrison, R. (1940a). Studies in the use and validity of the Thematic

Apperception Test with mentally disordered patients: II. A quantitative validity study. *Character and Personality, 9,* 192–133.

Harrison, R. (1940b). Studies in the use and validity of the Thematic Apperception Test with mentally disordered patients: III. Validation by blind analysis. *Character and Personality, 9,* 134–138.

Hart, B., & Spearman, C. (1912). General ability, its existence and nature. *British Journal of Psychology, 5,* 51–84.

Hartigan, J., & Wigdor, A. (1989). Fairness in employment testing. *Science, 245,* 14.

Hartlage, L. C., & Steele, C. T. (1977). WISC and WISC-R correlates of academic achievement. *Psychology in the Schools, 14,* 15–18.

Hartman, D. E. (1986). On the use of clinical psychology software: Practical, legal, and ethical concerns. *Professional Psychology: Research and Practice, 17,* 473–475.

Hartman, E. (2001). Rorschach administration: A comparison of the effect of two instructions. *Journal of Personality Assessment, 76*(3), 461–471.

Hartman, J. G., & Looney, M., Jr. (2003). *Norm-referenced and criterion-referenced reliability and validity of the Back-Saver Sit-and-Reach.* Mahwah, NJ: Erlbaum.

Hartung, P. J. (1999). Interest assessment using card sorts. In E. Mark, L. Savickas, E. Arnold, R. Spokane, et al. (Eds.), *Vocational interests: Meaning, measurement, and counseling use* (pp. 235–252). Palo Alto, CA: Consulting Psychologists Press.

Harty, H., Adkins, D. M., & Sherwood, R. D. (1984). Predictability of giftedness identification indices for two recognized approaches to elementary school gifted education. *Journal of Educational Research, 77,* 337–342.

Harwell, M. (1999). Evaluating the validity of educational rating data. *Educational and Psychological Measurement, 59,* 25–37.

Hase, H. D., & Goldberg, L. R. (1967). Comparative validity of different strategies of constructing personality inventory scales. *Psychological Bulletin, 67,* 231–248.

Hathaway, S. R., & McKinley, J. C. (1943). *Manual for the Minnesota Multiphasic Personality Inventory.* New York: Psychological Corporation.

Hattie, J. (1980). Should creativity tests be administered under testlike conditions? An empirical study of three alternative conditions. *Journal of Educational Psychology, 72,* 87–98.

Hayes, F. B., & Martin, R. P. (1986). Effectiveness of the PPVT-R in the screening of young gifted children. *Journal of Psychoeducational Assessment, 4,* 27–33.

Hayes, J. S. (1997). Reliability and validity of the HOME preschool inventory in Jamaica. *Early Child Development and Care, 136,* 45–55.

Hayes, N., & Joseph, S. (2003). Big 5 correlates of three measures of subjective well-being. *Personality and Individual Differences, 34*(4) 723–727.

Hayes, R. D., Morales, L. S., & Reise, S. P. (2000). Item response theory and health outcomes measurement in the 21st century. *Med Care, 38* (9 Suppl), II28–42.

Haynes, S. N. (1990). Behavioral assessment of adults. In A. Goldstein & M. Hersen (Eds.), *Handbook of psychological assessment* (2nd ed.) (pp. 423–467). New York: Pergamon Press.

Haynes, S. N. (1991). Clinical application of psychophysiological assessment: An introduction. *Psychological Assessment: A Journal of Consulting and Clinical Psychology, 3,* 307–308.

Haynes, S. N. (1992). Behavioral assessment. In M. Hersen, A. Kazdin, & A. Bellack (Eds.), *The clinical psychology handbook* (2nd ed.) (pp. 430–446). New York: Pergamon Press.

Haynes, S. N. (1995). Introduction to the special section on chaos theory and psychological assessment. *Psychological Assessment, 7*(1),3–4.

Haynes, S. N., Blaine, D., & Meyer, K. (1995). Dynamical models for psychological assessment: Phase space functions. *Psychological Assessment,* 7(l), 17–24.

Hays, P. A. (2001). Putting culture to the test: Considerations with standardized testing. In P. A. Hays (Ed.), *Addressing cultural complexities in practice: A framework for clinicians and counselors* (pp. 111–127). Washington, DC: American Psychological Association.

Healy, W., & Fernald, G. M. (1911). Tests for practical mental classification. *Psychological Monographs, 13*(2).

Hearst, E. (1979). One hundred years: Themes and perspectives. In E. Hearst (Ed.), *The first century of experimental psychology.* Hillsdale, NJ: Erlbaum.

Heatherton, T. F., & Wyland, C. L. (2003). Assessing self-esteem. In S. J. Lopez & C. R. Snyder (Eds.), *Positive psychological assessment: A handbook of models and measures* (pp. 219–233). Washington DC: American Psychological Association.

Heaton, R. K., & Pendleton, M. G. (1981). Use of neuropsychological tests to predict adult patients' everyday functioning. *Journal of Consulting and Clinical Psychology, 49,* 807–821.

Heiby, E. M. (1995a). Assessment of behavioral chaos with a focus on transitions in depression. *Psychological Assessment, 7*(l), 10–16.

Heiby, E. M. (1995b). Chaos theory, nonlinear dynamical models, and psychological assessment. *Psychological Assessment, 7*(l), 5–9.

Heider, F. (1944). Social perception and phenomenal causation. *Psychological Review, 51,* 358–374.

Heider, F. (1958). *The psychology of interpersonal relations.* New York: Wiley.

Heilbrun, A. B., Jr. (1972). Edwards Personal Preference Schedule. In O. K. Buros (Ed.), *The seventh mental measurements yearbook* (Vol. 1).

Highland Park, NJ: Gryphon Press.

Heimberg, R. C., Keller, K. E., & Peca-Baker, T. (1986). Cognitive assessment of social-evaluative anxiety in the job interview: Job Interview Self-Statement Schedule. *Journal of Counseling Psychogy, 33,* 190–195.

Heimberg, R. G. (2001). Current status of psychotherapeutic interventions for social phobia. *Journal of Clinical Psychiatry, 62*(1) 36–42.

Heimberg, R. G., & Coles, M. E. (1999). Reflections on innovations in cognitive behavioral treatments of anxiety disorders. *Cognitive and Behavioral Practice, 6*(3) 248–263.

Heinze, M. C., & Purisch, A. D. (2001). Beneath the mask: Use of psychological tests to detect and subtype malingering in criminal defendants. *Journal of Forensic Psychology, 1*(4) 23–52.

Heitzmann, C. A., & Kaplan, R. M. (1988). Assessment of measures for measuring social support. *Health Psychology, 7,* 75–109.

Heller, D., Judge, T. A., & Watson, D. (2002). The confounding role of personality and trait affectivity in the relationship between job and life satisfaction. *Journal of Organizational Behavior, 23*(7) 815–835.

Heller, K. (1971). Laboratory interview research as an analogue to treatment. In A. E. Bergin & S. L. Garfield (Eds.), *Handbook of psychotherapy and behavior change.* New York: Wiley.

Henderson, N. B., Fay, W. H., Lindemann, S. J., & Clarkson, Q. D. (1973). Will the IQ test ban decrease the effectiveness of reading prediction? *Journal of Educational Psychology, 65,* 345–355.

Henricksson, W. (1994). Meta-analysis as a method for integrating results of studies about effects of practice and coaching on test scores. *British Journal of Educational Psychology, 64,* 319–329.

Henry, P., & Bardo, H. R. (1990). Relationship between scores on de-veloping cognitive abilities test and scores on medical college admissions test for nontraditional pre-medical students. *Psychological Reports, 67,* 55–63.

Henry, P., Bryson, S., & Henry, C. A. (1990). Black student attitudes toward standardized tests. *College Student Journal, 23,* 346–354.

Hensley, W. (1994). Height as a basis for physical attraction. *Adolescence, 29*(114), 469–474.

Herbert, W. (1982). Intelligence tests: Sizing up a newcomer. *Science News, 122,* 280–281.

Hernstein, R. J. (1981). Try again, Dr. Albee. *American Psychologist, 36,* 424–425.

Hernstein, R. J. (1982, August). IQ testing and the media. *Atlantic Monthly,* pp. 68–74.

Herrnstein, R. J., & Murray, C. A. (1994). *The bell curve: Intelligence and class structure in American life.* New York: Free Press.

Hersen, M., Kazdin, A. E., & Bellack, A. S. (1991). *The clinical psychology handbook* (2nd ed.). New York: Pergamon Press.

Hersh, J. B. (1971). Effects of referral information on testers. *Journal of Consulting and Clinical Psychology, 37,* 116–122.

Hershkowitz, I. (2002). The role of facilitative prompts in interviews of alleged sex and abuse victims. *Legal and Criminological Psychology, 7*(1), 63–71.

Hertz, M. R. (1937). Discussion on "Some recent Rorschach problems." *Rorschach Research Exchange, 2,* 53–65.

Hertz, M. R. (1938). Scoring the Rorschach Inkblot Test. *Journal of Genetic Psychology, 52,* 16–64.

Hertz, M. R. (1986). Rorschach bound: A 50-year memory. *Journal of Personality Assessment, 50,* 396–416.

Heubert, J. P., & Hauser, R. M. (1999). *High stakes: Testing for tracking, promotion and graduation.* Washington, DC: National Academy Press.

Heuchert, J. W. P., Parker, W. D., Stumpf, H., & Myburgh, C. P. H. (2000). The five-factor model of personality in South African college students. *American Behavioral Scientist, 44*(1) 112–125.

Hewitt, M. (2002). Attitudes toward interview mode and comparability of reporting sexual behavior by personal interview and audio computer-assisted self-interviewing: Analysis of the 1995 National Survey of Family Growth. *Sociological Methods and Research, 31*(1), 3–26.

Higgins, C. A. (2001). The effect of applicant influence tactics on recruiter perceptions of fit. *Dissertation Abstracts International 61,* 9A.

Higgins, E. T., & Bargh, J. A. (1987). Social cognition and social perception. *Annual Review of Psychology, 38,* 369–425.

Hill, E. F. (1972). *The Hoitzman inkblot technique.* San Francisco: Jossey-Bass.

Hiller, J. B., Rosenthal, R. Bornstein, R. F., Berry, D. T. R., & Brunell-Neuleib, S. (1999). A comparative meta-analysis of Rorschach and MMPI validity. *Psychological Assessment, 11.* 278–296.

Hilsenroth, M. J., Fowler, J. C., & Padawer, J. R. (1998). The Rorschach Schizoprenia Index (SCZI): An examination of reliability, validity, and diagnostic efficiency. *Journal of Personality Assessment, 70,* 514–534.

Hinz, A., Klaiberg, A., Schumacher, J., & Brahler, E. (2003). The psychometric quality of the Nottingham Health Profile (NHP) in the general population. *Psychotherapy and Psychosomatic Medical Psychology, 53*(8), 353–358.

Hiscock, M., Inch, R., & Gleason, A. (2002). Raven's Progressive Matrices performance in adults with traumatic brain injury. *Applied Neuropsychology, 9*(3), 129–138.

Hobson v. Hansen. (1967). 269 F. Supp. 401 (D. D. C. 1967).

Hodapp, A. F., & Hass, J. K. (1997). Correlations between Wechsler Intelligence Scale for Children–III and Peabody Picture Vocabulary

Test–Revised. *Psychological Reports, 80,* 491–495.

Hodges, K. (1994). Structured interviews for assessing children. *Journal of Child Psychology and Psychiatry and Allied Disciplines, 34* (1), 49–68.

Hofer, P. J., & Green, B. I. (1985). The challenge of competence and creativity in computerized psychological testing. *Journal of Consulting and Clinical Psychology, 53,* 826–838.

Hoffman, H., Loper, R. G., & Kammeier, M. L. (1974). Identifying future alcoholics with MMPI alcoholism scales. *Quarterly Journal of Studies on Alcohol, 35,* 490–498.

Hogan, J., & Quigley, A. M. (1986). Physical standards for employment and the courts. *American Psychologist, 41,* 1193–1217.

Holaday, M., Smith, D. A., & Sherry, A. (2000). Sentence completion test: A review of the literature and results of a survey of members of the Society for Personality Assessment. *Journal of Personality Assessment, 74,* 371–385.

Holahan, C. J. (1986). Environmental psychology. *Annual Review of Psychology, 37,* 381–407.

Holahan, C. J., & Moos, R. H. (1986). Personality, coping, and family support in stress resistance: A longitudinal analysis. *Journal of Personality and Social Psychology, 51,* 389–395.

Holden, C. (2003). Affirmative action. Careful use of race is OK, high court tells colleges. *Science, 300*(5628), 2012.

Holifield, J. E., Nelson, W. M., III, & Hart, K. J. (2002). MMPI profiles of sexually abused and nonabused outpatient adolescents. *Journal of Adolescent Research, 17*(2), 188–195.

Holland, J. L. (1975). *Manual for the Vocational Preference Inventory.* Palo Alto, CA: Consulting Psychologists Press.

Holland, J. L. (1985). *The Self-Directed Search: Professional manual.* Odessa, FL: Psychological Assessment Resources.

Holland, J. L. (1997). *Making vocational choices: A theory of vocational personalities and work environments* (3rd ed.). Odessa, FL: Psychological Assessment Resources.

Holland, J. L. (1999). Why interest inventories are also personality inventories. In E. Mark, L. Savickas, E. Arnold, R. Spokane, et al. (Eds.), *Vocational interests: Meaning, measurement, and counseling use.* (pp. 87–101). Palo Alto, CA: American Psychological Association.

Holland, J. L., & Gottfredson, G. D. (1976). Using a typology of persons and environments to explain careers: Some extensions and clarifications. *Counseling Psychologist, 6,* 20–29.

Holland, P. W., & Hoskens, M. (2003). *Classical test theory as a first-order item response theory: Application to true-score prediction from a possibly nonparallel test.* Washington, DC: Psychometric Society.

Holland, P. W., & Wainer, H. (1993). *Differential item functioning.* Hillsdale, NJ: Erlbaum.

Hollingworth, H. L. (1922). *Judging human character.* New York: Appleton-Century-Crofts.

Holmes, C. B., & Beishline, M. J. (1996). Correct classification, false positives, and false negatives in predicting completion of the Ph. D. from GRE scores. *Psychological Reports, 79,* 939–945.

Holt, R. R. (1967). Diagnostic testing: Present status and future prospects. *Journal of Nervous and Mental Disease, 141,* 444–464.

Holtzman, W. H., & Sells, S. B. (1954). Prediction of flying success by clinical analysis of test protocols. *Journal of Abnormal and Social Psychology, 49,* 485–490.

Holtzman, W. H., Thorpe, J. S., Swartz, J. D., & Herron, E. W. (1961). *Inkblot perception and personality.* Austin: University of Texas Press.

Honaker, L. M., Harrell, T. H., & Buffaloe, J. D. (1988). Equivalency of Microtest computer MMPI administration for standard and special scales. *Computers in Human Behavior, 4*(4) 323–337.

Hooper, S. R., Conner, R. E., & Umansky, W. (1986). The Cattell Infant Intelligence Scale: A review of the literature. *Developmental Review, 6,* 146–164.

Hooper, S. R., & March, J. S. (1995). Neuropsychology. In J. S. March (Ed.), *Anxiety disorders in children and adolescents* (pp. 35–60), New York: Guilford Press.

Horley, J. (2000). Measuring health: A review of "Quality of life measurement scales" (1997) (English) by A. Bowling. *Social Indicators Research, 49*(1), 115–120.

Horn, J. L. (1994). Theory of fluid and crystallized intelligence. In R. J. Sternberg (Ed.), *Encyclopedia of human intelligence* (pp. 443– 451). New York: Macmillan.

Horn, J. L., & Cattell, R. B. (1966). Refinement and test of the theory of fluid and crystallized intelligence. *Journal of Educational Psychology, 57,* 253–276.

Horn, J. L., & Noll, J. (1997). Human cognitive capabilities: *Gf-Gc* theory. In D. P. Flanagan, J. L. Genshaft, & P. L. Harrison (Eds.), *Contemporary intellectual assessment: Theories, tests, and issues.* (pp. 53–91). New York: Guilford Press.

Horowitz, M. J., & Wilner, N. (1980). Life events, stress, and coping. In L. Poon (Ed.), *Aging in the eighties.* Washington, DC: American Psychological Association.

Hotelling, H. (1933). Analysis of a complex statistical variable into principal components. *Journal of Educational Psychology, 24,* 417–441, 498–520.

Houldin, A. D., & Forbes, E. J. (1990). Nursing students' personalities as measured by the California Psychological Inventory: Participants vs. nonparticipants in a program of research. *Psychological Reports, 67,* 1119–1122.

House, J. D. (1997). Predictive validity of Graduate Record Examination scores for outcomes of American Indian/Alaska Native students. *Psychological Reports, 81,* 337–338.

House, J. D. (1998). Age differences in prediction of student achievement from Graduate Record Examination scores. *Journal of Genetic Psychology, 159,* 379–382.

House, J. D. (1999). Predictive validity of the Graduate Record Examination for grades in graduate chemistry courses. *Psychological Reports, 85*(1), 41–44.

House, J. D., & Johnson, J. J. (1998). Predictive validity of the graduate record examination for grade performance in graduate psychology courses. *Psychological Reports, 82,* 1235–1238.

House, J. D., & Keeley, E. J. (1995). Gender bias in prediction of graduate grade performance from Miller Analogies Test scores. *Journal of Psychology, 129,* 353–355.

House, J. D., & Keeley, E. J. (1996). Differential prediction of adult student performance from Miller Analogies Test scores. *Journal of Genetic Psychology, 157,* 501–503.

Howard, J. L., & Ferris, G. R. (1996). The employment interview context: Social and situational influences on interviewer decisions. *Journal of Applied Social Psychology, 26,* 112–136.

Hu, C., Cui, Z., Dai, X., Chen, X., Gao, B., Hou, Y., & Guan, Y. (2002). Coping style, mental health status, and personality of policemen. *Chinese Mental Health Journal, 16*(9) 642–643.

Huang, C. D., Church, A. T., & Katigbak, M. S. (1997). Identifying cultural differences in items and traits: Differential item functioning in the NEO Personality Inventory. *Journal of Cross-Cultural Psychology, 28,* 192–218.

Hubbs-Tait, L., Culp, A. M., Culp, R. E., & Miller, C. E. (2002). Relation of maternal cognitive stimulation, emotional support, and intrusive behavior during Head Start to children's kindergarten cognitive abilities. *Child Development, 73*(1), 110–131.

Huffcutt, A. I., Conway, J. M., Roth, P. L., & Stone, N. (2001). Identification and meta-analytic assessment of psychological constructs measured in employment interviews. *Journal of Applied Psychology, 86*(5), 897–913.

Huffcutt, A. I., & Roth, P. L. (1998). Racial group differences in employment interview evaluations. *Journal of Applied Psychology, 83,* 179–189.

Huffcutt, A. I., Roth, P. L., & McDaniel, M. A. (1996). A meta-analytic investigation of cognitive ability in employment interview evaluations: Moderating characteristics and implications for incremental validity. *Journal of Applied Psychology, 81,* 459–473.

Hugh, H. V. (1981). The interviewing computer: A technology for gathering comprehensive treatment information. *Behavior Research Methods and Instrumentation. 13*(4), 607–612.

Huibregtse, I., Admiraal, W., & Meara, P. (2002). *Scores on a yes-no vocabulary test: Correction for guessing and response style.* London, United Kingdom: Hodder Arnold.

Hunsley, J., & Bailey, J. M. (1999). The clinical utility of the Rorschach: Unfulfilled promises and an uncertain future. *Psychological Assessment, 11,* 266–277.

Hunsley, J. & Bailey, J. M. (2001). Whither the Rorschach? An analysis of the evidence. *Psychological Assessment, 13,* 472–485.

Hunsley, J., & DiGiulio, G. (2001). Norms, norming, and clinical assessment. *Clinical Psychology: Science and Practice, 8,* 378–382.

Hunt, E. (1980). Intelligence as an information-processing concept. *British Journal of Psychology, 71,* 449–474.

Hunt, T. V. (1978). Review of McCarthy Scales of Children's Abilities. In O. K. Buros (Ed.), *The eighth mental measurements yearbook* (Vol. 1). Highland Park, NJ: Gryphon Press.

Hunter, J. E., & Schmidt, F. L. (1976).

Critical analysis of statistical and ethical implications of various definitions of test bias. *Psychological Bulletin, 83,* 1053–1071.

Hunter, J. E., & Schmidt, F. L. (1978). Bias in defining test bias: Reply to Darlington. *Psychological Bulletin, 85,* 675–676.

Huprich, S. K. (2003). Evaluating the NEO Personality Inventory-Revised profiles in veterans with personality disorders. *Journal of Personality Disorders, 17*(1) 33–44.

Hurlburt, R. T. (2003). *Comprehending behavioral statistics* (3rd ed.). Belmont, CA: Wadsworth.

Hurt, S. W., Reznikoff, M., & Clarkin, J. F. (1995). The Rorschach. In L. E. Beutler & M. R. Berren (Eds.), *Integrative assessment of adult personality* (pp. 187–205). New York: Guilford Press.

Iacono, W. G. (1991). Psychophysiological assessment of psychopathology. *Psychological Assessment: Journal of Consulting and Clinical Psychology, 3,* 309–320.

Imada, A. S., & Hakel, M. D. (1977). Influences of nonverbal communication and rater proximity on impressions and decisions in simulated employment interviews. *Journal of Applied Psychology, 62,* 295–300.

Impara, J. C., Plake, B. S., & Murphy, L. L. (1998). *The thirteenth mental measurements yearbook.* Lincoln, NE: Buros Institute of Mental Measurements.

Ingman, K. A., Ollendick, T. H., & Akande, A. (1999). Cross-cultural aspects of fears in African children and adolescents. *Behaviour Research and Therapy, 37,* 337–345.

Ingram, F., Caroselli, J., Robinson, H., Hetzel, R. D., Reed, K., & Masel, B. E. (1998). The PPVT-R: Validity as a quick screen of intelligence in a postacute rehabilitation setting for brain-injured adults. *Journal of Clinical Psychology, 54,* 877–884.

Ingram, R. E. (1980). *The GREs: Are we weighing them too heavily in grad-*

uate psychology admissions? Unpublished manuscript, University of Kansas, Lawrence.

Institute for Applied Psychometrics. (2003). Current research projects. Retrieved July 31, 2003, from iapsych.com.

Insurance license exams will be revised. (1984, November 29). *Los Angeles Times*, Part 1, p. 5.

Ironson, G. H., & Sebkovial, N. J. (1979). A comparison of several methods for assessing item bias. *Journal of Educational Measurement, 16,* 209–225.

Iverson, G. L., Franzen, M. D., & Hammond, J. A. (1995). Examination of inmates' ability to malinger on the MMPI-2. *Psychological Assessment, 7*(1), 118–121.

Iwata, N., Mishima, N., Shimizu, T., Mizoue, T., Fukuhara, M., Hidano, T., & Spielberger, C. D. (1998). Positive and negative affect in the factor structure of the state-trait anxiety inventory for Japanese workers. *Psychological Reports, 82*(2), 651–656.

Jaccard, J., & Wan, C. K. (1995). Measurement error in the analysis of interaction effects between continuous predictors using multiple regression: Multiple indicator and structural equation approaches. *Psychological Bulletin, 117*(2), 348–357.

Jackson, D. N. (1967). *Personality Research Form Manual.* Goshen, NY: Research Psychologists Press.

Jackson, D. N. (1976a). *Jackson Personality Inventory.* Goshen, NY: Research Psychologists Press.

Jackson, D. N. (1976b). *Manual for the Jackson Personality Inventory.* Goshen, NY: Research Psychologists Press.

Jackson, D. N. (1997). *Jackson Personality Inventory–Revised.* London Ontario: Sigma Assessment Systems.

Jackson, D. N. (2002). *The constructs in people's heads.* Mahwah, NJ: Erlbaum.

Jackson, D. N., & Livesley, W. J.

(1995). Possible contributions from personality assessment to the classification of personality disorders. In W. J. Livesley (Ed.), *The DSM-IV personality disorders: Diagnosis and treatment of mental disorders* (pp. 459–481). New York: Guilford Press.

Jackson, D. N., & Messick, S. (Eds.). (1967). *Problems in human assessment.* New York: McGraw-Hill.

Jackson, D. N., Paunonen, S. V., Fraboni, M., & Goffin, R. D. (1996). A five-factor versus six-factor model of personality structure. *Personality and Individual Differences, 20,* 33–45.

Jackson, E. W. (1980). Identification of gifted performance in young children. In W. C. Roedell, N. E. Jackson, & H. B. Robinson (Eds.), *Gifted young children.* New York: Teachers College Press.

Jacob, B. A. (2001). Getting tough, the impact of high school graduation exams. *Educational Evaluation, 23*(2), 99–121.

Jacobs, R. R., Conte, J. M., Day, D. V., Silva, J. M., et al. (1996). Selecting bus drivers: Multiple predictors, multiple perspectives on validity, and multiple estimates of utility. *Human Performance 9*(3), 199–217.

Jacobson, M. W., Bondi, M. W., & Salmon, D. P. (2002). Do neuropsychological tests detect preclinical Alzheimer's disease: Individual test versus cognitive discrepancy score analysis. *Neuropsychology, 16*(2).

Jacobson, M. W., Delis, D. C., & Bondi, M. W. (2002). Do neuropsychological tests detect preclinical Alzheimer's disease: Individual-test versus cognitive score analyses. *Neuropsychology, 16*(2), 132–139.

Janowsky, D. S., Morte, S., & Hong, L. (2002). Relationship of Myers-Briggs type indicator personality characteristics to suicidality in affective disorder patients. *Journal of Psychiatric Research, 36*(1), 33–39.

Janssen, E. (2002). Psychophysiologi-

cal measurement of sexual arousal. In M. W. Wiederman & B. E. Whitley, Jr. (Eds.), *Handbook for conducting research on human sexuality* (139–171). Mahwah, NJ: Erlbaum.

Janssen, E., Everaerd, W., Vanlunsen, R. H. W., & Oerlemans, S. (1994). Validation of a psychophysiological Waking Erectile Assessment (WEA) for the diagnosis of Male Erectile Disorder. *Urology, 43*(5), 686–695.

Jeanneret, P. R., Borman, W. C., Kubisiak, U. C., & Hanson, M. A. (1999). Generalized work activities. In E. Norman, G. Peterson, E. Michael, D. Mumford, et al. (Eds.), *An occupational information system for the 21st century: The development of O*NET* (pp. 105–125). Washington, DC: American Psychological Association.

Jennings, J. R. (1986). Bodily changes during attention. In M. G. H. Coles, E. Donchin, & S. W. Porges (Eds.), *Psychophysiology: Systems, processes, and applications.* New York: Guilford Press.

Jensen, A. R. (1969). How much can we boost IQ and scholastic achievement? *Harvard Educational Review, 39,* 1–23.

Jensen, A. R. (1972). *Genetics and education.* New York: Harper & Row.

Jensen, A. R. (1979). g—Outmoded theory or unconquered frontier? *Creative Science and Technology, 2,* 16–29.

Jensen, A. R. (1980). *Bias in mental testing.* New York: Free Press.

Jensen, A. R. (1982). Reaction time and psychometric "g. " In H. J. Eysenck (Ed.), *A model for intelligence.* New York: Springer-Verlag.

Jensen, A. R. (1984). The black-white difference on the K-ABC: Implication for future tests. *Journal of Special Education, 18,* 377–408.

Jensen, A. R. (1985). The nature of black-white differences on various psychometric tests: Spearman's hypothesis. *Behavioral and Brain Sciences, 8,* 193–263.

Jensen, A. R. (1986). The "g" beyond factor analysis. In J. C. Conoley, J. A. Glover, & R. R. Ronnings

(Eds.), *The influence of cognitive psychology on testing and measurement.* Hillsdale, NJ: Erlbaum.

Jensen, A. R., & Munro, E. (1979). Reaction time, movement time, and intelligence. *Intelligence, 3,* 121–126.

Jerusalem, M., & Schwarzer, R. (1992). *Self-efficacy: Thought control of action.* Washington, DC: Hemisphere.

Ji, C. C. (1998). Predictive validity of the Graduate Record Examination in education. *Psychological Reports, 82,* 899–904.

Jing, G., Deqing, T., & Longhui, L. (2001). Visual-motor deficits in children with learning disabilities. *Chinese Mental Health Journal, 15(6),* 388–390.

Johansson, C. B. (1976). *Manual for the Career Assessment Inventory.* Minneapolis, MN: National Computer Systems.

Johansson, C. B., & Johansson, J. C. (1978). *Manual supplement for the Career Assessment Inventory.* Minneapolis, MN: National Computer Systems.

Johansson, G., Johnson, J. V., & Hall, E. M. (1991). Smoking and sedentary behavior as related to work organization. *Social Science and Medicine, 32(7),* 837–846.

Johnson, J. H., Null, C., Butcher, J. N., & Johnson, K. N. (1984). Replicated items level factor analysis of the full MMPI. *Journal of Personality and Social Psychology, 47,* 105–114.

Johnson, J. L. (1994). The Thematic Apperception Test and Alzheimer's Disease. *Journal of Personality Assessment, 62(2),* 314–319.

Johnson, N. E., Saccuzzo, D. P., Larson, G. E., Guertin, T. L., Christianson, L., & Longley, S. (1993). *The San Diego Test of Reasoning Ability (S. A. N. T. R. A.).* [Available from N. E. Johnson, Ph. D., & D. P. Saccuzzo, Ph. D., 6363 Alvarado Court, Suite 103; San Diego, CA 92120–4913]

Johnstone, B., Holland, D., & Larimore, C. (2000). Language and academic abilities. In G. Groth-Marnat (Ed.), *Neuropsychological assessment in clinical practice: A guide to test interpretation and integration* (pp. 335–354). New York: Wiley.

Jones, E. E., & Nisbett, R. E. (1971). *The actor and observer: Divergent perceptions of the causes of behavior.* Morristown, NJ: General Learning Press.

Jones, P. W., & Kaplan, R. M. (2003). Methodological issues in evaluating measures of health as outcomes for COPD. *European Respiration Journal Supplement, 41,* 13s–18s.

Jones, R. A. (1968). *A factored measure of Ellis' irrational belief system with personality and maladjustment correlates.* Unpublished doctoral dissertation, Texas Technological College, Lubbock.

Jones, R. N. (2003). Racial bias in the assessment of cognitive functioning of older adults. *Aging and Mental Health, 7(2)* 83–102.

Judge, T. A., & Bono, J. E. (2000). Five factor model of personality and transformational leadership. *Journal of Applied Psychology, 85(5)* 751–765.

Judge, T. A., & Bono, J. E. (2001). Relationship to core self-evaluations traits—Self-esteem, generalized self-efficacy, locus of control, and emotional stability—With job satisfaction and job performance: A meta-analysis. *Journal of Applied Psychology, 86(1),* 80–92.

Judge, T. A., Erez, A., Bono, J. E., & Thoresen, C. J. (2002). Are measures of self-esteem, neuroticism, locus of control, and generalized self-efficacy indicators of a common core construct? *Journal of Personality and Social Psychology, 83(3),* 693–710.

Judge, T. A., & Larsen, R. J. (2001). Dispositional affect and job satisfaction: A review and theoretical extension. *Organizational Behavior and Human Decision Processes, 86* (1), 67–98.

Judge, T. A., Locke, E. A., Durham, C. C., & Kluger, A. N. (1998). Dispositional effects on job and life satisfaction: The role of core evaluations. *Journal of Applied Psychology, 83(1)* 17–34.

Judiesch, M. K., Schmidt, F. L., & Hunter, J. E. (1993). Has the problem of judgment in utility analysis been solved? *Journal of Applied Psychology, 78,* 903–911.

Jung, C. G. (1910). The association method. *American Journal of Psychology, 21,* 219–269.

Kagan, J., Moss, H. A., & Siegel, I. E. (1963). Psychological significance of styles of conceptualization. *Monographs of the Society for Research in Child Development, 28(2,* Serial No. 86), 73–124.

Kager, M. B. (2000). Factors that affect hiring: A study of age discrimination and hiring. *Dissertation Abstracts International, 60,* 11A.

Kahn, J. H., Hessling, R. M., & Russell, D. W. (2003). Social support, health, and well-being among the elderly: What is the role of negative affectivity? *Personality and Individual Differences, 35(1),* 5–17.

Kallingal, A. (1971). The prediction of grades for black and white students at Michigan State University. *Journal of Educational Measurement, 8,* 263–265.

Kamhi, A. G., Minor, J. S., & Mauer, D. (1990). Content analysis and intratest performance profiles on the Columbia and the TONI. *Journal of Speech and Hearing Research, 33,* 375–379.

Kamin, L. J. (1974). *The science and politics of IQ.* Hillsdale, NJ: Eribaum.

Kammeier, M. L., Hoffman, H., & Loper, R. G. (1973). Personality characteristics of alcoholics as college freshmen and at time of treatment. *Quarterly Journal of Studies on Alcohol, 34,* 390–399.

Kane, M. J., & Engle, R. W. (2002). *The role of prefrontal cortex in working-memory capacity, executive attention, and general fluid intelligence: An individual-differences perspective.* US: Psychonomic Society, [URL: http://www.psychonomic.org].

Kanfer, F. H., & Saslow, G. (1969).

Behavioral diagnosis. In C. M. Franks (Ed.), *Behavior therapy: Appraisal and status.* New York: Mc-Graw-Hill.

Kaplan, C. (1993). Reliability and validity of test-session behavior observations: Putting the horse before the cart. *Journal of Psychoeducational Assessment, 11*(4), 314–322.

Kaplan, R. M. (1973). Components of trust: Note on use of Rotter's scale. *Psychological Reports, 33,* 13–14.

Kaplan, R. M. (1982). Nader's raid on the Educational Testing Service: Is it in the best interest of the consumer? *American Psychologist, 37,*15–23.

Kaplan, R. M. (1985). The controversy related to the use of psychological tests. In B. B. Wolman (Ed.), *Handbook of Intelligence: Theories, measurements, and applications.* New York: Wiley.

Kaplan, R. M. (1987). Basic statistics for the behavioral sciences. Newton, MA: Allyn & Bacon.

Kaplan, R. M. (1990). Behavior as the central outcome in health care. *American Psychologist, 45,* 1211–1220.

Kaplan, R. M. (1993). *The hippocratic predicament.* San Diego, CA: Academic Press.

Kaplan, R. M. (1994a). Measures of health outcome in social support research. In S. A. Schumaker & S. M. Czajkowski (Eds.), *Social support and cardiovascular disease: Plenum series in behavioral psychophysiology and medicine* (pp. 65–94). New York: Plenum.

Kaplan, R. M. (1994b). Value judgment in the Oregon Medicaid experiment. *Medical Care, 32*(10), 975–988.

Kaplan, R. M. (1999). Health-related quality of life in mental health services evaluation. In E. Nancy, E. Miller, E. Kathryn, M. Magruder, et al. (Eds.), *Cost-effectiveness of psychotherapy: A guide for practitioners, researchers, and policymakers* (pp. 160–173). New York: Springer.

Kaplan, R. M. (2000). Two pathways to prevention. *American Psychologist, 55*(4), 382–396.

Kaplan, R. M. (2002). *Quality of life and chronic illness.* Malden, MA: Blackwell.

Kaplan, R. M. (2003). The significance of quality of life in health care. *Quality of Life Research, 12*(Suppl. 1), 3–16.

Kaplan, R. M. (2004). Achievements of the Veterans Health Study. *Journal of Ambulatory Care Management, 27*(1), 66–67.

Kaplan, R. M., & Anderson, J. P. (1990). The general health policy model: An integrated approach. In B. Spilker (Ed.), *Quality of life assessments in clinical trials* (pp. 131–149). New York: Raven Press.

Kaplan, R. M., Anderson, J. P., Patterson, T. L., McCutchan, J. A., Weinrich, J. D., Heaton, R. K., Atkinson, J. H., Thal, L., Chandler, J., & Grant, I. (1995). Validity of the Quality of Well-Being Scale for persons with human immunodeficiency virus infection. HNRC Group. HIV Neurobehavioral Research Center. *Psychosomatic Medicine, 57,* 138–147.

Kaplan, R. M., Criqui, M. H., Denenberg, J. O., Bergan, J., & Fronek, A. (2003). Quality of life in patients with chronic venous disease: San Diego population study. *Journal of Vascular Surgery, 37*(5), 1047–1053.

Kaplan, R. M., & Ernst, J. (1983). Do category rating scales produce biased preference weights for a health index? *Medical Care, 21,* 193–207.

Kaplan, R. M., Feeny, D., and Revicki, D. A. (1999). Methods for assessing relative importance in preference based outcome measures. In E. C. R. B. Joyce, E. Hannah, M. McGee, et al. (Eds.), *Individual quality of life: Approaches to conceptualisation and assessment* (pp. 135–149). Amsterdam, Netherlands: Klewer.

Kaplan, R. M., Ganiats, T. G., Sieber, W. J., & Anderson, J. P. (1998). The Quality of Well-Being Scale:

Critical similarities and differences with SF-36. *International Journal for Quality in Health Care, 10*(6), 509–520.

Kaplan, R. M., & Golomb, B. A. (2001). *Cost-effectiveness of statin medications.* Washington, DC: American Psychological Association.

Kaplan, R. M., & Grant, I. (2000). Statistics and experimental design. In B. J. Sadcock & V. A. Sadock (Eds.), *Comprehensive Textbook of Psychiatry* (7th ed.). Baltimore: Williams & Wilkins.

Kaplan, R. M., & Groessl, E. J. (2002). Applications of cost-effectiveness methodologies in behavioral medicine. *Journal of Consulting Clinical Psychology, 70*(3), 482–493.

Kaplan, R. M., Navarro, A. M., Castro, F. G., Elder, J. P., Mishra, S. I., Hubbell, A., Chrvala, C., Flores, E., Ramirez, A., Fernandezesquer, M. E., & Ruiz, E. (1996). Increased use of mammography among Hispanic women: Baseline results from the NCI cooperative group on cancer prevention in Hispanic communities. *American Journal of Preventive Medicine, 12*(6), 467–471.

Kaplan, R. M., & Ries, A. L. (1996), Cognitive-behavioral interventions and the quality of life of patients with chronic obstructive pulmonary disease. In J. Bach (Ed.), *Pulmonary rehabilitation: The obstructive and paralytic conditions* (pp. 133–144). Philadelphia: Hanley & Delfus.

Kaplan, R. M., Ries, A. L., Prewitt, L. M., & Eakin, E. (1994). Self-efficacy expectations predict survival for patients with chronic obstructive pulmonary disease. *Health Psychology, 13,* 366–368.

Kaplan, R. M., Sieber, W. J., and Ganiats, T. G. (1997). The Quality of Well-Being Scale: Comparison of the interviewer-administered version with a self-administered questionnaire. *Psychology and Health, 12*(6), 783–791.

Kaplan, R. M., & Toshima, M. T. (1992). Does a reduced fat diet cause retardation in child growth? *Preventive Medicine, 21,* 33–52.

Kaplan, S. L., & Alfonso, V. C. (1997). Confirmatory factor analysis of the Stanford-Binet Intelligence Scale: Fourth edition with preschoolers with developmental delays. *Journal of Psychoeducational Assessment, 15,* 226–236.

Kappelman, M. M. (1993). [Review of the book *Touchpoints: The essential reference: Your Child's Emotional and Behavioral Development*]. *Journal of Developmental and Behavioral Pediatrics, 14*(5), 350–351.

Kareken, D. A., Gur, R. C., & Saykin, A. J. (1995). Reading on the Wide-Range Achievement Test—Revised and parental education as predictors of IQ: Comparisons with the Barona formula. *Archives of Clinical Neuropsychology, 10*(2), 147–157.

Karp, S. A. (Ed.). (1999). *Studies of objective/projective personality tests.* Brook/Andville, MD: Tests, Inc.

Kaszniak, A. W., & Christenson, G. (1994). Differential diagnosis of dementia and depression. In M. Storandt & G. R. VandenBos (Eds.), *Neuropsychological assessment of dementia and depression in older adults: A clinician's guide* (pp. 81–117). Washington, DC: American Psychological Association.

Kataoka, H. C., Latham, G. P., & Whyte, G. (1997). The relative resistance of the situational, patterned behavior, and conventional structured interviews to anchoring effects. *Human Performance, 10*(1), 47–63.

Katigbak, M. S., Church, A. T., Guanzon-Lapena, M. A., Carlota, A. J., & del Pilar, G. H. (2002). Are indigenous personality dimensions culture specific? Philipinne inventories and the five-factor model. *Journal of Personality & Social Psychology, 82*(1), 89–101.

Kaufman, A. S. (1978). Review of Columbia Mental Maturity Scale. In O. K. Buros (Ed.), *The eighth mental measurements yearbook* (Vol. 1). Highland Park, NJ: Gryphon Press.

Kaufman, A. S. (1984). K-ABC and controversy. *Journal of Special Education, 18*(3), 409–444.

Kaufman, A. S. (1990). *Assessment of adolescent and adult intelligence.* Boston: Allyn & Bacon.

Kaufman, A. S., & Kaufman, N. L. (1983a). *K-ABC administration and scoring manual.* Circle Pines, MN: American Guidance Service.

Kaufman, A. S., & Kaufman, N. L. (1983b). *K-ABC interpretive manual.* Circle Pines, MN: American Guidance Service.

Kaufman, A. S., & Kaufman, N. L. (1993). *The Kaufman Adolescent and Adult Intelligence Test.* Circle Pines, MN: American Guidance Service.

Kaufman, A., & Kaufman, N. (2004a). *KABC-II manual.* Circle Pines, MN: American Guidance Service.

Kaufman, A., & Kaufman, N. (2004b). *KTEA-II comprehensive interpretation manual.* Circle Pines, MN: American Guidance Service.

Kaufman, A. S., Kaufman, R. W., & Kaufman, N. L. (1985). The Kaufman Assessment Battery for Children (K-ABC). In C. S. Newmark (Ed.), *Major psychological assessment instruments.* Newton, MA: Allyn & Bacon.

Kazdin, A. E. (1977). Artifact, bias, and complexity of assessment: The ABC's of reliability. *Journal of Applied Behavior Analysis, 10,* 141–150.

Kazdin, A. E. (2004). *Research design in clinical psychology* (4th ed.). Needham Heights, MA: Allyn & Bacon.

Kefyalew, F. (1996). The reality of child participation in research: Experience from a capacity-building program. *Childhood, 3,* 203–213.

Keiser, R. E., & Prather, E. N. (1990). What is the TAT? A review of ten years of research. *Journal of Personality Assessment, 55,* 800–803.

Keller, S. D., Ware, J. E., Jr., Hatoum, H. T., & Kong, S. X. (1999). The SF-36 Arthritis-Specific Health Index (ASHI): II. Tests of validity in four clinical trials. *Medical Care, 37*(5 Suppl.), MS51–60.

Kellogg, R. T. (2003). *Cognitive psychology* (2nd ed.). Thousand Oaks, CA: Sage.

Kelly, H. H. (1967). Attribution theory in social psychology. In D. Levine (Ed.), *Nebraska Symposium on Motivation.* Lincoln: University of Nebraska Press.

Kendall, P. C., Williams, S., Pechacek, T. F., Graham, L. G., Shisslak, C. S., & Herzoff, N. (1979). Cognitive-behavioral and patient education interventions in cardiac catheterization procedures: The Palo Alto medical psychology project. *Journal of Consulting and Clinical Psychology, 47,* 49–58.

Kennedy, R. B. (1994). The employment interview. *Journal of Employment Counseling, 31,* 110–114.

Kennedy, W. A., Van de Riet, V., & White, J. C., Jr. (1963). A normative sample of intelligence and achievement of Negro elementary school children in the Southeast United States. *Monographs of the Society for Research in Child Development, 28*(6, Serial No. 90).

Kent, G. H., & Rosanoff, A. J. (1910). A study of association in insanity. *American Journal of Insanity, 67,* 37–96, 317–390.

Kent, R. N., Kanowitz, J., O'Leary, K. D., & Cheiken, M. (1977). Observer reliability as a function of circumstances of assessment. *Journal of Applied Behavior Analysis, 10,* 317–324.

Kent, R. N., O'Leary, K. D., Diament, C., & Dietz, A. (1974). Expectation biases in observational evaluation of therapeutic change. *Journal of Consulting and Clinical Psychology, 42,* 774–780.

Kerlikowske, K., Grady, D., Rubin, S. M., Sandrock, C., & Ernster, V. L. (1995). Efficacy of screening mammography: A meta-analysis. *Journal of the American Medical Association, 273*(2), 149–154.

Kerner, D. N., Patterson, T. L., Grant, I., & Kaplan, R. M. (1998). Validity of the Quality of Well-Being Scale for patients with Alzheimer's disease. *Journal of Aging and Health, 10*(1) 44–61,

Kerner, J. (1857). Klexographien (Pt. VI). In R. Pissin (Ed.), *Kerners Werke*. Berlin, Germany: Bong.

Kido, D. K., Sheline, Y. I., & Reeve, A. (2000). Diagnostic testing. In E. Barry, S. Fogel, E. Randolph, B. Schiffer, et al. (Eds.), *Synopsis of neuropsychiatry* (pp. 27–52). Philadelphia: Lippincott.

Kiersh, E. (1979, January 15). Testing is the name, power is the game. *The Village Voice*.

Kimble, G. A., & Wertheimer, M. (Eds.). (2003). *Portraits of pioneers in psychology* (Vol. 5). Mahwah, NJ: Erlbaum.

Kimura, D. (1999). *Sex and cognition*. Cambridge, MA: MIT Press.

Kirkby, K. C. (1996). Computer-assisted treatment of phobias. *Psychiatric Services, 47*(2) 139–140.

Kirkpatrick, E. A. (1900). Individual tests of school children. *Psychological Review, 7,* 274–280.

Kirsch, I., Ed. (1999). *How expectancies shape experience*. Washington, DC: American Psychological Association.

Klausen, O., Moller, P., Holmeford, A., Reiseaeeter, S., & Asbjornsen, A. (2000). Lasting effects of orbitis media with effusion on language skills and listening performance. *Acta Oto-Laryngoloca, 120*(Suppl. 543), 73–76.

Kleberg, A., Westrup, B., Stjernqvist, K., & Lagercrantz, H. (2002). Indications of improved cognitive development at one year of age among infants born very prematurely who receive care based on the Newborn Individualized Developmental Care and Assessment Program (NIDCAP). *Early Human Development, 68*(2), 83–91.

Klein, B. P., & Mervis, C. B. (1999). Contrasting patterns of cognitive abilties of 9- and 10-year-olds with Williams syndrome or Down syndrome. *Developmental Neuropsychology, 16*(2), 177–196.

Klein, S. P. (2002). Law school admissions, LSATs, and the bar. *Academic Questions, 15*(1), 33–39.

Klieger, D. M., & Franklin, M. E.

(1993). Validity of the Fear Survey Schedule in phobia research: A laboratory test. *Journal of Psychopathology and Behavioural Assessment, 15*(3), 207–217.

Klieger, D. M., & McCoy, M. L. (1994). Improving the concurrent validity of the Fear Survey Schedule—III. *Journal of Psychopathology and Behavioral Assessment, 16*(3), 201–220.

Kline, P. (1994). *An easy guide to factor analysis*. London: Routledge.

Kline, R. B. (1989). Is the Fourth Edition Stanford-Binet a four-factor test? Confirmatory factor analyses of alternative methods for ages 2 through 23. *Journal of Psychoeducational Assessment, 7,* 4–13.

Klopfer, B., & Davidson, H. H. (1944). Form level rating: A preliminary proposal for appraising mode and level of thinking as expressed in Rorschach records. *Rorschach Research Exchange, 8,* 164–177.

Klopfer, B., & Davidson, H. H. (1962). *The Rorschach technique: An introductory manual*. Orlando: Harcourt Brace.

Klopfer, B., & Kelley, D. (1942). *The Rorschach technique*. Yonkers, NY: World Book.

Klopfer, B., & Kelly, D. M. (1946). *The Rorschach technique* (2nd ed.). Yonkers-on-Hudson, NY: World Book.

Knapp-Lee, L. (2000). A complete career guidance program: The COP System. In E. C. Edward Watkins, Jr., E. Vicki, L. Campbell, et al. (Eds.), *Testing and assessment in counseling practice* (2nd ed.) (pp. 295–338). Mahwah, NJ: Erlbaum.

Knotek, P. C., Bayles, K. A., & Kaszniak, A. W. (1990). Response consistency on a semantic memory task in persons with dementia of the Alzheimer type. *Brain and Language, 38,* 465–475.

Knox, H. A. (1914). A scale based on the work at Ellis Island for estimating mental defect. *Journal of the American Medical Association, 62,* 741–747.

Kobasa, S. C. (1979). Stressful life events, personality and health: An inquiry into hardiness. *Journal of Personality and Social Psychology, 37,* 1–11.

Koen, W. J., & Penland, A. L. (2002, April). *Special education: The effects of gender, ethnicity, and attractiveness on placement*. Poster session presented at the annual conference of the Western Psychological Association, Irvine, CA.

Kohs, S. C. (1923). *Intelligence measurement: A psychological and statistical study based upon the block-design tests*. New York: Macmillan.

Kok, F. (1992). Differential item functioning. In L. Verhoeven & J. H. A. L. De Jong (Eds.), *The construct of language proficiency: Applications of psychological models to language assessment* (pp. 115–124). Amsterdam, Netherlands: John Benjamins.

Koloski, N. A., Talley, N. J., & Boyce, P. M. (2000). The impact of functional gastrointestinal disorders on quality of life. *American Journal of Gastroenterology, 95*(1), 67–71.

Koltai, D. C., & Welsh-Bohmer, K. A. (2000). Geriatric neuropsychological assessment. In E. Rodney, D. Vanderploeg, et al. (Eds.), *Clinician's guide to neuropsychological assessment* (pp. 383–415). Mahwah, NJ: Erlbaum.

Koppitz, E. M. (1964). *The Bender Gestalt test for young children*. New York: Grune & Stratton.

Kosinski, M., Keller, S. D., Ware, J. E., Jr., Hatoum, H. T., & Kong, S. X. (1999). The SF-36 Health Survey as a generic outcome measure in clinical trials of patients with osteoarthritis and rheumatoid arthritis: Relative validity of scales in relation to clinical measures of arthritis severity. *Medical Care, 37*(5, Suppl.), MS23–39.

Kossowska, M. (2002). Relationship between cognitive strategies, intelligence, and personality. *Polish Psychological Bulletin, 33*(2) 47–54.

Kraepelin, E. (1912). *Lehrbuch der psychiatric.* Leipzig: Barth.

Kraiger, K., Hakel, M. D., & Cornelius, E. T., III. (1984). Exploring fantasies of TAT reliability. *Journal of Personality Assessments, 48,* 365–370.

Kranzler, G., & Moursund, J. (1999). *Statistics for the terrified* (2nd ed.). Upper Saddle River, NJ: Prentice-Hall.

Kreiner, D. S., & Ryan, J. J. (2001). Memory and motor skill components of the WAIS-III Digit Symbol-Coding Subtest. *Clinical Neuropsychologist, 15*(1), 109–113.

Krikorian, R., & Bartok, J. A. (1998). Developmental data for the Porteus Maze Test. *Clinical Neuropsychologist, 12,* 305–310.

Krinsky, S. G. (1990). The feeling of knowing in deaf adolescents. *American Annals of the Deaf, 135,* 389–395.

Krol, N. P. C. M., De Bruyn, E. E. J., van Aarle, E. J. M., & van den Bercken, J. H. L. (2001). Computerized screening for DSM classifications using CBCL/YSR extended checklists: A clinical try-out. *Computers in Human Behavior, 17*(3) 315–337.

Kuder, G. F. (1979). *Manual, Kuder Occupational Interest Survey, 1979 revision.* Chicago: Science Research Associates.

Kuder, G. F., & Richardson, M. W. (1937). The theory of the estimation of reliability. *Psychometrika, 2,* 151–160.

Kugu, N., Akyuez, G. Dogan, O., Ersan, E., & Izgic, F. (2002). Prevalence of eating disorders in a university population and the investigation of its relation to self-esteem, family functions, childhood abuse and neglect. *Psikiyatri Psikoloji Psikofarmakoloji Dergisi, 10*(3) 255–266.

Kuh, G. D., & Hu, S. (1999). Unraveling the complexity of the increase in college grades from the mid-1980s to the mid-1990s. *Educational Evaluation and Policy Analysis, 21*(3), 297–320.

Kuncel, N. R., Hezlett, S. A., & Ones, D. S. (2001). A comprehensive meta-analysis of the predictive validity of the graduate record examination: Implications for graduate student selection and performance. *Psychological Bulletin, 127*(1), 162–181.

Kush, J. C., Watkins, M. W., Ward, T. J., Ward, S. B., Canivez, G. L., & Worrell, F. C. (2001). Construct validity for white and black students from the WISC-III standardization sample and for black students referred for psychological evaluation. *School Psychology Review, 30*(1), 70–85.

Kwon, P. (2002). Comment on "Effects of acculturation on the MMPI-2 scores of Asian American students." *Journal of Personality Assessment, 78*(1), 187–189.

La Guardia, J. G., (2002). Interpersonal compartmentalization: An examination of self-concept variation, need satisfaction, and psychological vitality. *Dissertation Abstracts International, 62,* 8B.

Lai, T. J., Guo, Y. I., Guo, N. W., & Hsu, C. C. (2001). Effects of prenatal exposure to polychlorinated biphenyls on cognitive development in children: A longitudinal study in Taiwan. *British Journal of Psychiatry, 178*(40), s49–s52.

Lally, M., & Nettelbeck, T. (1977). Intelligence, reaction time, and inspection time. *American Journal of Mental Deficiency, 82,* 273–281.

Lamp, R. E., & Krohn, E. J. (2001). A longitudinal predictive validity investigation of the SB: FE and K-ABC with at-risk children. *Journal of Psychoeducational Assessment, 19*(4), 334–349.

Lamp, R. E., & Traxler, A. J. (1973). The validity of the Slosson Intelligence Test for use with disadvantaged Head Start and first grade children. *Journal of Community Psychology, 1,* 27–30.

Landis, C. (1936). Questionnaires and the study of personality. *Journal of Nervous and Mental Disease, 83,* 125–134.

Landis, C., Zubin, J., & Katz, S. E. (1935). Empirical evaluation of three personality adjustment inventories. *Journal of Educational Psychology, 26,* 321–330.

Landy, F. J. (1986). Stamp collecting versus science: Validation as hypothesis testing. *American Psychologist, 41,* 183–192.

Landy, F. J. (2003). *Validity generalization: Then and now.* Mahwah, NJ: Erlbaum.

Landy, F. J., Farr, J. L., & Jacobs, R. (1982). Utility concepts in performance measurement. *Organizational Behavior and Human Performance, 30,* 15–40.

Landy, F. J., & Shankster, L. J. (1994). Personnel selection and placement. *Annual Review of Psychology, 45,* 261–296.

Landy, F. J., Vance, R. J., Barnes-Farrell, J. L., & Steele, J. W. (1980). Statistical control of halo error in performance ratings. *Journal of Applied Psychology, 65,* 501–506.

Lane, B., & Gullone, E. (1999). Common fears: A comparison of adolescents' self-generated and fear survey schedule generated fears. *Journal of Genetic Psychology, 160,* 194–204.

Langdon, D. W., Rosenblatt, N., & Mellanby, J. H. (1998). Discrepantly poor verbal skills in poor readers: A failure of learning or ability? *British Journal of Psychology, 89,* 177–190.

Langenbucher, J. W., Labouvie, E., Martin, C. S., Sanjuan, P. M., Bavly, L., Kirisci, L., et al. (2004). An application of item response theory analysis to alcohol, cannabis, and cocaine criteria in DSM-IV. *Journal of Abnormal Psychology, 113*(1), 72–80.

Lanyon, B. P., & Lanyon, R. I. (1980). *Incomplete Sentences Task: Manual.* Chicago: Stoelting.

Larkin, J. E., & Pines, H. A. (1994). Affective consequences of self-monitoring style in a job interview setting. *Basic and Applied Social Psychology, 15*(3), 297–310.

Larrabee, L. L., & Kleinsaser, L. D (1967). *The effect of experimenter bias on WISC performance.* Unpublished manuscript.

Larry P. v. Wilson Riles, 343 F. Supp. 1306 (N. D. Cal. 1972), affd 502 F. 2d 963 (9th Cir. 1979).

Larson, J. H., Parks, A. A., Harper, J. M., & Heath, V. A. (2001). A psychometric evaluation of the family rules from the past questionnaire. *Contemporary Family Therapy, 23*(1), 83–103.

Latham, G. P., & Whyte, G. (1994). The futility of utility analysis. *Personnel Psychology, 47*(1), 31–46.

Latham, V. M. (1987). Interviewee training: A review of some empirical literature. *Journal of Career Development, 14,* 96–107.

Laub, D. (2002). Testimonials in the treatment of genocidal trauma. *Journal of Applied Psychoanalytic Studies 4*(1), 63–87.

Laurent, J. (1997). Characteristics of the standard and supplemental batteries of the Woodcock-Johnson Tests of Cognitive Ability Revised with a college sample. *Journal of School Psychology, 35,* 403–416.

Lautenschlager, G. J., & Flaherty, V. L. (1990). Computer administration of questions: More desirable or more social desirability? *Journal of Applied Psychology, 75,* 310–314.

Lawlor, S., Richman, S., & Richman, C. L. (1997). The validity of using the SAT as a criterion for black and white students' admission to college. *College Student Journal, 31,* 507–515.

Lawrence, I., Rigol, G. W., Van Essen, T., & Jackson, C. A. (2002). *A historical perspective on the SAT: 1926–2001* (College Board Research Report No. 2002-7). New York: College Entrance Examination Board.

Law School Admissions Council (1994). *LSAT/LSDAS registration and information handbook, 1994–1995.* Newtown, Pennsylvania.

Lawshe, C. L. (1985). Inferences from personnel tests and their validities. *Journal of Applied Psychology, 70,* 237–238.

Lazarus, R. S. (1995). Psychosocial factors play a role in health, but we have to tackle them with more sophisticated research and thought. *Advances, 11*(2), 14–18.

Lazarus, R. S., & Folkman, S. (1984). *Stress, appraisal, and coping.* New York: Springer-Verlag.

Leach, J. (2002). Personality profiles of prisoners of war and evaders. *Military Psychology, 14*(1), 73–81.

Leahy, R. L., & Dowd, E. T. (Eds.). (2002). *Clinical advances in cognitive psychotherapy: Theory and application.* New York: Springer.

Lee, J. A., Moreno, K, E., & Sympson, J. B. (1986). The effects of mode of test administration on test performance. *Educational and Psychological Measurement, 46,* 467–473.

Lee, J. M., Ku, J. H., Jang, D. P., Kim, D. H., Choi, Y. H., Kim, I. Y., & Kim, S. I. (2002). Virtual reality system for treatment of the fear of public speaking using image-based rendering and moving pictures. *Cyberpsychology and Behavior, 5*(3) 191–195.

Leekam, S. R., Libby, S. J., Wing, L., Gould, J., & Taylor, C. (2002). The Diagnostic Interview for Social and Communication Disorders: Algorithms for ICD-10 childhood autism and Wing and Gould autistic spectrum disorder. *Journal of Child Psychology and Psychiatric and Allied Disciplines, 43*(3), 327–342.

Leichsenring, F. (1990). Discriminating borderline from neurotic patients: A study with the Holtzman Inkblot Technique. *Psychopathology, 23,* 21–26.

Leichsenring, F. (1991). Primary process thinking, primitive defensive operations and object relations in borderline and neurotic patients. *Psychopathology, 24,* 39–44.

Leman, N. (1995, September). The Great Sorting. *Atlantic Monthly,* pp. 84–100.

Lemke, S., & Moos, R. H. (1986).

Quality of residential settings of elderly adults. *Journal of Gerontology, 41,* 268–276.

Leong, C., & Joshi, R. (1995). *Developmental and acquired dyslexia: Neuropsychological and neurolinguistic perspectives.* Dordrecht, Netherlands: Kluwer Academic Publishers.

Lerner, B. (1979). Tests and standards today: Attacks, counterattacks, and responses. *New Directions in Testing and Measurement, 1*(3), 15–31.

Leslie, L. K., Gordon, J. N., Ganger, W., & Gist, K. (2002). Developmental delay in young children in child welfare by initial placement type. *Infant Mental Health Journal, 23*(5), 496–516.

Lesser, G. S., Fifer, G., & Clark, D. H. (1965). Mental abilities of children from different social-class and cultural groups. *Monographs of the Society for Research in Child Development, 30*(4, Serial No. 102).

Lessler, J. T., Caspar, R. A., Penne, M. A., & Barker, P. R. (2000). Developing computer assisted interviewing (CAI) for the National Household Survey on Drug Abuse. *Journal of Drug Issues, 30*(1), 9–34.

Levenson, H., Olkin, R., Herzoff, N., & DeLancy, M. (1986). MMPI evaluation of erectile dysfunction: Failure of organic vs. psychogenic decision rules. *Journal of Clinical Psychology, 42,* 752–754.

Levin, H. S., Song, J., Ewing-Cobbs, L.,& Roberson, G. (2001). Porteus Maze performance following traumatic brain injury in children. *Neuropsychology, 15*(4), 557–567.

Levine, D. W., Lewis, M. A., Bowen, D. J., Kripke, D. F., Kaplan, R. M., Naughton, M. J., et al. (2003). *Reliability and validity of Women's Health Initiative Insomnia Rating Scale.* Washington, DC: American Psychological Association.

Levitas, A. S., Hurley, A. D., & Pary, R. (2002). The mental status examination in patients with mental retardation and developmental disabilities. *Mental Health Aspects of*

Developmental Disabilities (2–16), 4 (1).

Levy, S. (1979). E. T. S. and the "coaching" cover-up. *New Jersey Monthly, 3*(5), 4–7.

Lewandowski, D. G., & Saccuzzo, D. P. (1976). The decline of psychological testing: Have traditional procedures been fairly evaluated? *Professional Psychology, 7,* 177–184.

Lewinsohn, P. N., & Teri, L. (1982). Selection of depressed and nondepressed subjects on the basis of self-report data. *Journal of Consulting and Clinical Psychology, 50,* 590–591.

Lewis, C. D., & Lorentz, S. (1994). Comparison of the Leiter International Performance Scale and the Wechsler Intelligence Scales. *Psychological Reports, 74*(2), 521–522.

Lezak, M. D. (1983). *Neuropsychological assessment* (2nd ed.). New York: Oxford University Press.

Lezak, M. D. (1995). *Neuropsychological assessment* (3rd ed.). New York: Oxford University Press.

Li, C. R. (2002). Impaired detection of visual motion in schizophrenia patients. *Progress in Neuro-Psychopharmacology & Biological Psychiatry, 26*(5) 929–934.

Li, F., Wang, E., & Zhang, F. (2002). The multitrait-multirater approach to analyzing rating biases. *Acta Psychologica Sinica, 34*(1), 98–96.

Lichtenberg, P. A., & MacNeill, S. E. (2000). Neuropsychological assessment in geriatric facilities. In E. Victor Molinari et al. (Eds.), *Professional psychology in long term care: A comprehensive guide* (pp. 29–49). New York: Wiley.

Lichtenberger, E. O., & Kaufman, A. S. (2003). *Essentials of WPSSI-III assessment.* New York: Wiley.

Liebert, R. M., & Morris, L. W. (1967). Cognitive and emotional components of test anxiety: A distinction and some initial data. *Psychological Reports, 20,* 975–978.

Likert, R. (1932). A technique for the measurement of attitudes. *Archives of Psychology,* No. 40.

Lilienfeld, S. O., Alliger, G., &

Mitchell, K. (1995). Why integrity testing remains controversial. *American Psychologist, 50*(6), 457–458.

Lilienfeld, S. O., Wood, J. M., & Garb, H. N. (2000). The scientific status of projective techniques. *Psychological Science in the Public Interest, 1,* 27–66.

Lincoln, R. K., Crosson, B., Bauer, R. M., & Cooper, P. V. (1994). Relationship between WAIS-R subtests and language measures after blunt head injury. *Clinical Neurospychologist, 80,* 140–152.

Lindsey, M. L. (1998). Culturally competent assessment of African American clients. *Journal of Personality Assessment, 70*(1), 43–53.

Lindzey, G. (1952). The Thematic Apperception Test: Interpretive assumptions and related empirical evidence. *Psychological Bulletin, 49,* 1–25.

Linn, R. L. (1980). Test design and analysis for measurement of educational achievement. *New Directions for Testing and Measurement, 5,* 81–92.

Linn, R. L. (1994a). *Criterion-referenced measurement: A valuable perspective clouded by surplus meaning.* Annual Meeting of the American Educational Research Association: Criterion-referenced measurement: A 30-year retrospective (1993, Atlanta, Georgia). *Educational Measurement: Issues and Practice, 13,* 12–14.

Linn, R. L. (1994b). Fair test use: Research and policy. In M. G. Rumsey, C. B. Walker, & J. H. Harris (Eds.), *Personnel selection and classification* (pp. 363–375). Hillsdale, NJ: Erlbaum.

Linn, R. L., & Burton, E. (1994). Performance-based assessment: Implications of task specificity. *Educational Measurement: Issues and Practice, 13,* 15.

Lipsitz, J. D., Dworkin, R. H., & Erlenmeyer-Kimling, L. (1993). Wechsler comprehension and picture arrangement subtests and so-

cial adjustment. *Psychological Assessment, 5*(4), 430–437.

Lipsitz, S. (1969). *Effect of the race of the examiner on results of intelligence test performance of Negro and white children.* Unpublished master's thesis, Long Island University, NY.

Liss, P. H., & Haith, M. M. (1970). The speed of visual processing in children and adults: Effects of backward and forward masking. *Perception and Psychophysics, 8,* 396–398.

Little, K. B., & Schneidman, E. S. (1959). Congruencies among interpretations of psychological test and anamnestic data. *Psychological Monographs, 73*(6).

Liu, K. K., Spicuzza, R., & Erickson, R. (1999). Focus-group research on Minnesota's implementation of graduation standards. *Journal of Educational Research, 92,* 312.

Llorente, A., Brouwers, P., Charurat, M., Magder, L., Malee, K., Mellins, C., Ware, J., Hittleman, J., Mofenson, L., Velez-Borras, J., & Adeniyi-Jones, S. (2003). Early neurodevelopmental markers predictive of mortality in infants infected with HIV-1. *Developmental Medicine and Child Neurology, 45*(2), 76–84.

LoBello, S. G., & Gulgoz, S. (1991). Factor analysis of the Wechsler Preschool and Primary Scale of Intelligence—Revised. *Psychological Assessment: A Journal of Consulting and Clinical Psychology, 3,* 130–132.

Lochman, J. E. (1995). Conduct Problems Prevention Research Group: Screening of child behavior problems for prevention programs at school entry [Special Section: Prediction and prevention of child and adolescent antisocial behavior]. *Journal of Consulting and Clinical Psychology, 63,* 549–559.

Locke, S. D. & Gilbert, B. O. (1995). Method of psychological assessment, self-disclosure, and experiential differences: A study of computer, questionnaire, and interview assessment formats. *Journal of Social Behavior and Personality, 10,* 255–263.

Loehlin, J. C. (1998). *Latent variable models: An introduction to factor, path, and structural analysis.* Mahwah, NJ: Erlbaum.

Loevinger, J. (1998). *Technical foundations for measuring ego development: The Washington University Sentence Completion Test.* Mahwah, NJ: Erlbaum.

Loffredo, D. A., & Opt, S. K. (1998). Relating the MBTI to communication apprehension, receiver apprehension, and argumentativeness. *Journal of Psychological Type, 47,* 21–27.

Long, P. A., & Anthony, J. J. (1974). The measurement of retardation by a culture-specific test. *Psychology in the Schools, 11,* 310–312.

Longford, N. T. (1997). Shrinkage estimation of linear combinations of true scores. *Psychometrika, 62,* 237–244.

Lord, E. (1950). Experimentally induced variations in Rorschach performance. *Psychological Monographs, 64*(10, Whole No. 316).

Lord, F. M. (1950). *Efficiency of prediction when a regression equation from one sample is used in a new sample* (Research Bulletin 50-40). Princeton, NJ: Educational Testing Service.

Lorenzo-Seva, U. (2003). A factor simplicity index. *Psychometrica, 68*(1), 49–60.

Loughmiller, G. C., Ellison, R. L., Tavlor, C. W., & Price, P. B. (1970). Predicting career performances of physicians using the biographical inventory approach. *Proceedings of the American Psychological Association, 5,* 153–154.

Lowman, R. L. (1991). *The clinical practice of career assessment.* Washington, DC: American Psychological Association.

Loy, D. L. (1959). The validity of the Taulbee-Sisson MMPI scale pairs in female psychiatric groups. *Journal of Clinical Psychology, 15,* 306–307.

Lubin, B., Larsen, R., & Matarazzo, J. (1984). Patterns of psychological test usage in the United States: 1935–1982. *American Psychologist, 39,* 451–454.

Lubin, B., & Sands, E. W. (1992). Bibliography of the psychometric properties of the Bender Visual-Motor Gestalt Test: 1970–1991. *Perceptual and Motor Skills, 75*(2), 385–386.

Lubin, B., Wallis, H. R., & Paine, C. (1971). Patterns of psychological test usage in the United States: 1935–1969. *Professional Psychology, 2,* 70–74.

Lucas, J. L., Wanberg, C. R., & Zytowski, D. G. (1997). Development of a career task self-efficacy scale: The Kuder Task Self-Efficacy Scale. *Journal of Vocational Behavior, 50*(3), 432–459.

Lucas, R. E., Diener, E., & Larsen, R. J. (2003). Measuring positive emotions. In S. J. Lopez & C. R. Snyder (Eds.), *Positive psychological assessment: A handbook of models and measures.* (pp. 201–218). Washington DC: American Psychological Association.

Ludgate, D. R. (2001). An examination of the relationship between personality variables and managerial behavior as measured by power and influence tactics in project planning. *Dissertation Abstracts International, 62,* 6A.

Lui, Z., Chen, X., Qin, S., Xue, J., Hao, W., Lu, X., Lui, B., Man, C., & Zhang, Z. (2002). Risk factors for female criminals. *Chinese Mental Health Journal, 16*(2), 106–108.

Lukin, M. E., Dowd, T., Plake, B. S., & Kraft, R. G. (1985). Comparing computerized versus traditional psychological assessment. *Computers in Human Behavior, 1*(1) 49–58.

Lundqvist, C., & Sabel, K. G. (2000). Brief report: The Brazelton Neonatal Assessment Scale detects differences among newborn infants of optimal health. *Journal of Pediatric Psychology, 25*(8), 577–582.

Lunemann, A. (1974). The correlational validity of I.Q. as a function of ethnicity and desegregation. *Journal of School Psychology, 12,* 263–268.

Lunneborg, C. (1978). Some information-processing correlates of measures of intelligence. *Multivariate Behavioral Research, 13,* 153–161.

Luo, D., Thompson, L. A., & Detterman, D. K. (2003). The causal factor underlying the correlation between psychometric g and scholastic performance. *Intelligence, 31*(1), 67–83.

Luria, A. R. (1966). *Higher cortical functions in man.* New York: Basic Books.

Luria, A. R. (1973). The *working brain.* New York: Basic Books.

Lurie, J. D., & Sox, H. C. (1999). Principles of medical decision making. *Spine, 24*(5), 493–498.

Lysaker, P. H., Clements, C. A., Wright, D. E., Evans, J., & Marks, K. A. (2001). Neurocognitive correlates of helplessness, hopelessness, and well-being in schizophrenia. *Journal of Nervous and Mental Disease, 189*(7), 457–462.

Mabon, H. (1998). Utility aspects of personality and performance. *Human Performance, 11,* 289–304.

Mabry, L. (1995). Review of the Wide Range Achievement Test–3. In *The 12th mental measurements yearbook* (pp. 1108–1110). Lincoln, NE: Buros Institute of Mental Measurements.

Machover, K. (1949). *Personality projection in the drawings of the human figure: A method of personality investigation.* Springfield, IL: Thomas.

Macias, M. M., Saylor, C. F., Greer, M. K., Charles, J. M., Bell, N., & Katikaneni, L. D. (1998). Infant screening: The usefulness of the Bayley Infant Neurodevelopment Screener and the Clinical Adaptive Test/Clinical Linguistic Auditory Milestone Scale. *Journal of Development and Behavioral Pediatrics, 19,* 155–161.

MacKinnon, R. A. (1980). Psychiatric interview. In H. I. Kaplan, A. M. Freedman, & B. J. Sadock (Eds.), *Comprehensive textbook for psychiatry* (Vol. 3). Baltimore: Williams & Wilkins.

Mackintosh, N. J. (1981). A new measure of intelligence. *Nature, 289*(5798), 529–530.

Magalette, P. R., & Oliver, J. M. (1999). The hope construct, will, and ways: Their relations with self-efficacy, optimism, and general well-being. *Journal of Clinical Psychology, 55*(5) 539–551.

Magnusson, D., & Endler, N. S. (1977). Interactional psychology: Present status and future prospects. In D. Magnusson & N. S. Endler (Eds.), *Personality at the crossroads: Current issues in interactional psychology.* Hillsdale, NJ: Erlbaum.

Maisto, S. A., McKay, J. R., & Connors, G. J. (1990). Self-report issues in substance abuse: State of the art and future directions. *Behavioral Assessment, 12,* 117–134.

Maj, M., Gaebel, W., Lopez-Ibor, J. J., & Sartorius, N. (Eds.). (2002). *Psychiatric diagnosis and classification.* New York: Wiley.

Majnemer, A., & Mazer, B. (1998). Neurologic evaluation of the newborn infant: Definition and psychometric properties. *Developmental Medicine and Child Neurology, 40,* 708–715.

Malgady, R. G., Constantino, G., & Rogler, L. H. (1984). Development of a Thematic Apperception Test (TEMAS) for urban Hispanic children. *Journal of Consulting and Clinical Psychology, 52*(6), 986–996.

Malgady, R., Barcher, P. R., Davis, J., & Towner, G. (1980). Validity of the vocational adaptation rating scale: Prediction of mentally retarded workers' placement in sheltered workshops. *American Journal of Mental Deficiency, 84,* 633–640.

Malinchoc, M., Oxford, K. P., Colligan, R. C., & Morse, R. M. (1994). The Common Alcohol Logistic–Revised Scale (CAL-R): A revised alcoholism scale for the MMPI and MMPI-2. *Journal of Clinical Psychology, 50*(3), 436–445.

Maloney, M. P., & Ward, M. P. (1976). *Psychological assessment: A conceptual approach.* New York: Oxford University Press.

Malreaux, J. (1999). A two-pronged attack on standardized tests is needed. *Black Issues in Higher Education, 73.*

Maltby, N., Kirsch, I., Mayers, M., & Allen, G. J. (2002). Virtual reality exposure therapy for the treatment of fear of flying: A controlled investigation. *Journal of Consulting & Clinical Psychology, 70*(5) 1112–1118.

Mandes, E., & Gessner, T. (1988). Differential effects on verbal performance achievement levels on the WAIS-R as a function of progressive error rate on the Memory for Designs Test (MFD). *Journal of Clinical Psychology, 44,* 795–798.

Mandler, G., & Sarason, S. B. (1952). A study of anxiety and learning. *Journal of Abnormal and Social Psychology, 47,* 166–173.

Manners, J. & Derkin, K. (2001). A critical review of the validity of ego development theory and its measurement. *Journal of Personality Assessment, 77,* 541–567.

Mannheim, K. (1936). *Ideology and utopia.* London: Kegan, Paul, Trench, Trubner.

Mapou, R. L., & Spector, J. (1995). *Clinical neuropsychological assessment: A cognitive approach.* New York: Plenum.

Marchall et al. v. Georgia. (1985). U.S. District Court for the Southern District of Georgia, CV482-233 (June 28, 1984), *aff'd,* 11th cir no 848771 (Oct. 29, 1985).

Marchman, V. A., Saccuman, C., & Wulfeck, B. (2004). Productive use of the English past tense in children with focal brain injury and specific language impairment. *Brain and Language, 88,* 202–214.

Mark, J. C. (1993). [Review of the book *The Thematic Apperception Test, the Children's Apperception Test, and the Senior Apperception Technique in clinical use,* 5th edition]. *Contemporary Psychology, 38*(9), 971–972.

Marlett, N. J., & Watson, D. (1968). Test anxiety and immediate or delayed feedback in a test-avoidance task. *Journal of Personality and Social Psychology, 8,* 200–203.

Marsh, H. W., & Bazeley, P. (1999). Multiple evaluations of grant proposals by independent assessors: Confirmatory factor analysis evaluations of reliability, validity, and structure. *Multivariate Behavioral Research 34*(1), 1–30.

Marshalek, B., Lohman, D. F., & Snow, R. E. (1983). The complexity continuum in the Radex and hierarchical models of intelligence. *Journal of Intelligence, 7,* 107–127.

Martin, A., & Swinson, R. P. (2000). Cognitive strategies. In A. Martin & R. P. Swinson (Eds.), *Phobic disorders and panic in adults: A guide to assessment and treatment* (pp. 239–254). Washington, DC: American Psychological Association.

Martin, P., Johnson, M., Poon, L. W., Clayton, G. M., et al. (1994). Group or individual testing: Does it make a difference? *Educational Gerontology, 20,* 171–176.

Martin, R., Sawrie, S., Gilliam, F., Mackey, M., Faught, E., Knowlton, R., & Kuzniekcy, R. (2002). Determining reliable cognitive change after epilepsy surgery: Development of reliable change indices and standardized regression-based change norms for the WMS-III and WASI-III. *Epilepsia, 43*(12), 1551–1558.

Martin, R. A., Berry, G. E., Dobranski, T., Horne, M., & others. (1996). Emotion perception threshold: Individual differences in emotional sensitivity. *Journal of Research in Personality, 30,* 290–305.

Masters, B. N. (1988). Item discrimination: One more is worse. *Journal of Educational Measurement 25,* 15–29.

Masters, W., & Johnson, V. (1966). *Human sexual response.* Boston: Little, Brown.

Matarazzo, J. D. (1986). Computerized clinical psychological test interpretations: Unvalidated plus all mean and no sigma. *American Psychologist, 41,* 14–24.

Matarazzo, J. D. (1990). Psychological assessment versus psychological testing: Validation from Binet to the school, clinic, and court room. *American Psychologist, 45,* 999–1017.

Matheny, K. B., Curlette, W. L., Aysan, F., Herrington, A., Gfroerer, C. A., Thompson, D., & Hamarat, E. (2002). Coping resources, perceived stress and life satisfaction among Turkish and American university students. *International Journal of Stress Management, 9*(2) 81–97.

Mather, N., & Schrank, F. A. (2001). *Use of the WJ III discrepancy procedures for learning disabilities identification and diagnosis* (Assessment bulletin no. 3). Itasca, IL: Riverside.

Matias, R., & Turner, S. M. (1986). Concordance and discordance in speech anxiety assessment: The effects of demand characteristics on the tripartite assessment method. *Behavior Research and Therapy, 24,* 537–545.

Mau, W., & Lynn, R. (2001). Gender differences on Scholastic Aptitude Test, the American College Test, and college grades. *Educational Psychology, 21*(2), 133–136.

Maurer, T. J., & Alexander, R. A. (1991). Contrast effects in behavioral measurement: An investigation of alternative process explanations. *Journal of Applied Psychology, 76,* 3–10.

Maurer, T. J., Solamon, J. M., Andrews, K. D., & Troxtel, D. D. (2001). Interviewee coaching, preparation strategies, and response strategies in relation to performance in situational employment interviews: An extension of Maurer, Solamon, and Troxtel (1998). *Journal of Applied Psychology, 86,* 709–717.

Mayer, D. M., & Hanges, P. J. (2003). Understanding the stereotype threat effect with "culture-free" tests: An examination of its mediators and measurement. *Human Performance, 16*(3), 207–230.

Mayfield, E. C. (1964). The selection interview: A re-evaluation of published research. *Personnel Psychology, 17,* 239–260.

McCabe, S. E., Boyd, C. J., Couper, M. P., Crawford, S., & D'Arcy, H. (2002). Mode effects for collecting alcohol and other drug use data: Web and U.S. mail. *Journal of Studies on Alcohol, 63*(6) 755–761.

McCabe, K. M., Yeh, M., Lau, A., Garland, A., & Hough, R. (2003). Racial/ethnic differences in caregiver strain and perceived social support among parents of youth with emotional and behavioral problems. *Mental Health Services Research, 5*(3), 137–147.

McCall, R. B. (1994). *Fundamental statistics for behavioral sciences* (6th ed.). Fort Worth, TX: Harcourt Brace.

McCall, R. B. (2001). *Fundamental statistics for behavioral sciences* (8th ed.). Belmont, CA: Wadsworth.

McCall, W. A. (1939). *Measurement.* New York: Macmillan.

McCallum, R. S. (1990). Determining the factor structure of the Stanford-Binet: Fourth Edition—The right choice. *Journal of Psychoeducational Assessment, 8,* 436–442.

McCallum, R. S., Karnes, F. A. & Oehler-Stinnett, J. (1985). Construct validity of the K-ABC for gifted children. *Psychology in the Schools, 22,* 254–259.

McCarty, J. R., Noble, A. C., & Huntley, R. M. (1989). Effects of item wording on sex bias. *Journal of Educational Measurement, 26,* 285–293.

McCaulley, M. H., & Martin, C. R. (1995). Career assessment and the Myers-Briggs Type Indicator. *Journal of Career Assessment, 3,* 219–239.

McClelland, D. C. (1994). The knowledge-testing-educational complex strikes back. *American Psychologist, 490,* 66–69.

McClelland, D. C. (1999). How the test lives on: Extensions of the Thematic Apperception Test approach. In L. G. Gieser & M. I. Stein (Eds.). *Evocative images: The Thematic Apperception Test and the art of projection.* Washington, DC: American Psychological Association.

McCormick, E. J., & Ilgen, D. (1980). *Industrial psychology* (7th ed.). Englewood Cliffs, NJ: Prentice-Hall.

McCrae, R. R., & Costa, P. T. (2003). *Personality in adulthood: A five factor theory perspective* (2nd ed.). New York: Guilford Press.

McCrae, R. R., Costa, P. T., Del Pilar, G. H., Rolland, J. P., & Parker, W. D. (1998). Cross-cultural assessment of the five-factor model: The Revised NEO Personality Inventory. *Journal of Cross-Cultural Psychology, 29,* 171–188.

McCrowell, K. L., & Nagle, R. J. (1994). Comparability of the WPPSI-R and the S-B: IV among preschool children. *Journal of Psychoeducational Assessment, 12* (2), 126–134.

McDaniel, M. A. (1989). Biographical constructs for predicting employee suitability. *Journal of Applied Psychology, 74,* 964–970.

McDaniel, M. A., Whetzel, D. L., Schmidt, F. L., & Maurer, S. D. (1994). The validity of employment interviews: A comprehensive review and meta-analysis. *Journal of Applied Psychology, 79,* 599–616.

McDonald, R. P. (1999). *Test theory: A unified treatment.* Mahwah, NJ: Erlbaum.

McDowell, I., & Newell, C. (1996). *Measuring health: A guide to rating scales and questionnaires* (2nd ed.). New York: Oxford University Press.

McEwen, J. (1992). The Nottingham Health Profile. In S. R. Walker & R. M. Rosser (Eds.), *Quality of life assessment: Key issues for the 1990s.* Dordreht, Netherlands: Kluwer Academic Publishers.

McFall, R. M., & McDonell, A. (1986). The continuous search for units of analysis in psychology: Beyond persons, situations, and their interactions. In R. O. Nelson & S. C. Hays (Eds.), *Conceptual foundations of behavioral assessment.* New York: Guilford Press.

McGhee, R. (1993). Fluid and crystallized intelligence: Confirmatory factor analyses of the Differential Abilities Scale, Detroit Tests of Learning Aptitude—3, and Woodcock-Johnson Psycho-Educational Battery—Revised. In B. A. Bracken & R. S. McCallum (Eds.), *Woodcock-Johnson PsychoEducational Battery–Revised* [Monograph]. *Journal of Psychoeducational Assessment,* pp. 20–38.

McGill-Evans, J., & Harrison, M. J. (2001). Parent-child interactions, parenting stress, and developmental outcomes at 4 years. *Children's Health Care, 30*(2), 135–140.

McGivern, R. F., Berka, C., Langlais, M. L., & Chapman, S. (1991). Detection of deficits in temporal pattern discrimination using the Seashore Rhythm Test in young children with reading impairments. *Journal of Learning Disabilities, 24,* 58–62.

McGrath, R. E., Sweeney, M., O'Malley, W. B., & Carlton, T. K. (1998). Identifying psychological contributions to chronic pain complaints with the MMPI-2: The role of the K scale. *Journal of Personality Assessment, 70,* 448–459.

McGraw, K. O., Tew, M. D., & Williams, J. E. (2000). The integrity of web-delivered experiments: Can you trust the data? *Psychological Science, 11*(6), 502–506.

McGrew, K. S. (1986). Investigation of the verbal/nonverbal structure of the Wookcock-Johnson: Implications for subtest interpretation and comparisons with the Wechsler scales. *Journal of Psychoeducational Assessment, 3*(1), 65–71.

McGrew, K. S., & Flanagan, D. P. (1998). *The intelligence test desk reference (ITDR).* Boston: Allyn & Bacon.

McGrew, K. S., & Murphy, S. (1995). Uniqueness and general factor characteristics of the Woodcock-Johnson Tests of Cognitive Ability—Revised. *Journal of School Psychology, 33,* 235–245.

McGrew, K. S., & Woodcock, R. W. (2001). *Technical manual. Woodcock-Johnson III.* Itasca. IL: Riverside.

McGrew, S. (1993). The relationship between the Woodcock-Johnson Psycho-Educational Battery—Revised *Gf-Gc* cognitive clusters and reading achievement across the lifespan. In B. A. Bracken & R. S. McCallum (Eds.), *Woodcock-Johnson Psycho-Educational Battery—Revised* [Monograph]. *Journal of Psychoeducational Assessment,* pp. 39–53.

McHorney, C. A. (1999). Health status assessment methods for adults: past accomplishments and future challenges. *Annual Review of Public Health, 20*(3), 309–335.

McIntire, S. A., & Miller, L. A. (2000). *Foundations of psychological testing.* Boston: McGraw-Hill.

McKay, P. F., & Doverspike, D. (2001). African Americans' test-taking attitudes and their effect on cognitive ability test performance: Implications for public personnel management selection practice. *Public Personnel Management, 30*(1), 67–75.

McKenna, P., Clare, L., & Baddeley, A. D. (1995). Schizophrenia. In A. D. Baddeley, B. A. Wilson, & F. N. Watts (Eds.), *Handbook of memory disorders* (pp. 271–292). Chichester, England: Wiley.

McLennan, N. A., & Arthur, N. (1999). Applying the Cognitive Information Processing approach to career problem solving and decision making to women's career development. *Journal of Employment Counseling, 36*(2), 82–96.

McMahon, R. C., Davidson, R. S., Gersh, D., & Flynn, P. (1991). A comparison of continuous and episodic drinkers using the MCMI, MMPI, and ALCEVAL-R. *Journal of Clinical Psychology, 47,* 148–159.

McMichael, A. J., Baghurst, P. A., Wigg, N. R., Vimpani, G. V., Robertson, E. F., & Roberts, R. J. (1988). Port Pirie Cohort Study: Environmental exposure to lead and children's abilities at the age of four years. *New England Journal of Medicine, 319,* 468–475.

McNemar, O. W., & Landis, C. (1935). Childhood disease and emotional maturity in the psychopathic woman. *Journal of Abnormal and Social Psychology, 30,* 314–319.

McNemar, Q. (1969). *Psychological statistics* (4th ed.). New York: Wiley.

McReynolds, C. J., Ward, D. M., & Singer, O. (2002). Stigma, discrimination, and invisibility: Factors affecting successful integration of individuals diagnosed with schizophrenia. *Journal of Applied Rehabilitation Counseling, 33*(4) 32–39.

Medoff-Cooper, B., McGrath, J. M., & Bilker, W. (2000). Nutritive sucking and neurobehavioral development in preterm infants from 34 weeks PCA to term. *American Journal of Maternal Child Nursing, 25*(2), 64–70.

Meehl, P. E. (1951). *Research results for counselors.* St. Paul, MN: State Department of Education.

Meehl, P. E. (1954). *Clinical versus statistical prediction: A theoretical analysis and a review of the evidence.* Minneapolis: University of Minnesota Press.

Meehl, P. E. (1956). Wanted—a good cookbook. *American Psychologist, 11,* 263–272.

Meehl, P. E. (1957). When shall we use our heads instead of the formula? *Journal of Counseling Psychology, 4,* 268–273.

Meehl, P. E. (1995). Utiles, hedons, and the mind-body problem, or, who's afraid of Vilfredo? In P. E. Shrout & S. T. Fiske (Eds.), *Personality research, methods, and theory: A festschrift honoring Donald W. Fiske* (pp. 45–66). Hillsdale, NJ: Erlbaum.

Meehl, P. E. (1997). Credentialed persons, credentialed knowledge. *Clinical Psychology: Science and Practice, 4,* 91–98.

Meehl, P. E., & Dahlstrom, W. G. (1960). Objective configural rules for discriminating psychotic from neurotic MMPI profiles. *Journal of Consulting Psychology, 24,* 375–387.

Meehl, P. E., & Rosen, A. (1955). Antecedent probability and the efficiency of psychometric signs, patterns or cutting scores. *Psychological Bulletin, 52,* 194–216.

Meesters, C., van Gastel, N., Ghys, A., & Merckelbach, H. (1998). Factor analyses of WISC-R and KABC in a Dutch sample of children referred for learning disabilities. *Journal of Clinical Psychology, 54,* 1053–1061.

Megargee, E. I. (1972). *The California Psychological Inventory Handbook.* San Francisco: Jossey-Bass.

Mehl, M. R., Pennebaker, J. W., Crow, D. M., Dabbs, J., & Price, J. H. (2001). The Electronically Activated Recorder (EAR) : A device for sampling naturalistic daily activities and conversations. *Behavior Research Methods, Instruments, and Computers, 13*(4) 517–523.

Mehrens, W. A. (2000). Defending a state graduation test: *GI Forum* v. *Texas Education Agency.* Measurement perspectives from an external evaluator. *Applied Measurement in Education, 13*(4), 387–401.

Meichenbaum, D. (1976). A cognitive-behavior modification approach to assessment. In M. Hersen & A. S. Bellack (Eds.), *Behavioral assessment.* New York: Pergamon Press.

Meichenbaum, D. (1999). Behandlung von Patienten mit posttraumatischen Belastungsstoerungen: Ein konstruktiv-narrativer Ansatz. [Treatment of patients with posttraumatic stress disorder: A constructive-narrative approach]. *Verhaltenstherapie, 9*(4) 186–189.

Meichenbaum, D. (2003). Cognitive behavior therapy: Folktales and the unexpurgated history. *Cognitive Therapy & Research, 27*(1) 125–129.

Meijer, R. R. (2003). Diagnosing item score patterns on a test using item response theory-based person-fit statistics. Washington, DC: American Psychological Association.

Meikle, S., & Gerritse, R. (1970). NIMPI cookbook pattern frequencies in a psychiatric unit. *Journal of Clinical Psychology, 26,* 82–84.

Meinhardt, M., Hibbett, C., Koller, J., & Busch, R. (1993). Comparison of the Woodcock-Johnson PsychoEducational Battery—Revised and the Wechsler Intelligence Scale for Children—Revised with incarcerated adolescents. In B. A. Bracken & R. S. McCallum (Eds.), *Woodcock-Johnson PsychoEducational Battery—Revised* [Monograph]. *Journal of Psychoeducational Assessment,* pp. 64–70.

Melchert, T. P. (1998). Support for the validity of the Graduate Record Examination. *American Psychologist, 53,* 573–574.

Melei, J. P., & Hilgard, E. R. (1964). Attitudes toward hypnosis, self predictions, and hypnotic susceptibility. *International Journal of Clinical and Experimental Hypnosis, 12,* 99–108.

Mellenbergh, G. J. (1999). A note on simple gain precision. *Applied Psychological Measurement, 23*(1), 87–89

Meloy, J. R., & Singer, J. (1991). A psychoanalytic view of the Rorschach Comprehensive System "Special Scores. " *Journal of Personality Assessment, 56,* 202–217.

Ment, L. R., Vohr, B., Allan, W., Katz, K. H., & Schneider, K. C., Westerveld, M., Duncan, C. C., & Makuch, R. W. (2003). Change in cognitive function over time in very low-birth-weight infants. *Journal of the American Medical Association, 289*(6), 705–711.

Mercer, J. R. (1971). Sociocultural factors in labeling mental retardates. *Peabody Journal of Education, 48,* 188–203.

Mercer, J. R. (1972, September). *Anticipated achievement: Computerizing the self-fulfilling prophecy.* Paper presented at the meeting of the American Psychological Association, Honolulu, HI.

Mercer, J. R. (1973). *Labeling the mentally retarded: Clinical and social sys-* *tem perspective on mental retardation.* Berkeley: University of California Press.

Mercer, J. R. (1979). In defense of racially and culturally nondiscriminatory assessment. *School Psychology Digest, 8*(1), 89–115.

Mercer, J. R. (1988). Ethnic differences in IQ scores: What do they mean? (A response to Lloyd Dunn) [Special Issue: Achievement testing: Science vs. ideology]. *Hispanic Journal of Behavioral Sciences, 10,* 199–218.

Merrell, K. W. (1999). *Behavioral, social, and emotional assessment of children and adolescents.* Mahwah, NJ: Erlbaum.

Merrell, K. W. (2003). *Behavioral, social, and emotional assessment of children and adolescents* (2nd ed.). Mahwah, NJ: Erlbaum.

Merten, T. (1995). Factors influencing word-association responses: A reanalysis. *Creativity Research Journal, 8,* 249–263.

Mervis, C. B., & Robinson, B. F. (2003). Methodological issues in cross-group comparisons of language and cognitive development. In Y. Levy & J. Schaeffer (Eds.), *Language competence across populations: Toward a definition of special language impairment* (pp. 233–258). Mahwah, NJ: Erlbaum.

Messick, S. (1994). Foundations of validity: Meaning and consequences in psychological assessment. Second Conference of the European Association of Psychological Assessment Keynote Address (1993, Groningen, Netherlands). *European Journal of Psychological Assessment, 10*(1), 1–9.

Messick, S. J. (1998a). Alternative modes of assessment, uniform standards of validity. In Milton D. Hakel (Ed.), *Beyond multiple choice: Evaluating alternatives to traditional testing for selection* (pp. 59–74). Mahwah, NJ: Erlbaum.

Messick, S. (1998b). Test validity: A matter of consequence. *Social Indicators Research, 45* (1–3), 35–44.

Messick, S. J. (Ed.). (1999). *Assessment in higher education: Issues of access, quality, student development, and public policy.* Mahwah, NJ: Erlbaum.

Messick, S., & Jungeblut, A. (1981). Time and method in coaching for the SAT. *Psychological Bulletin, 89,* 191–216.

Meunier, C., & Rule, B. G. (1967). Anxiety, confidence, and conformity. *Journal of Personality, 35,* 498–504.

Meyer, G. J. (1992). Response frequency problems in the Rorschach: Clinical and research implications with suggestions for the future. *Journal of Personality Assessment, 58,* 231–244.

Meyer, G. J. (1999). Introduction to the special series on the utility of the Rorschach for clinical assessment. *Psychological Assessment, 11,* 235–239.

Meyer, G. J., Finn, S. E., Eyde, L. D., Kay, G. G., Moreland, K. L., Dies, R. R., Eisman, E. J., Kubiszyn, T. W., & Reed, G. M. (2003). Psychological testing and psychological assessment: A review of evidence and issues. In A. E. (Ed.), *Methodological issues and strategies in clinical research* (3rd ed.) (pp. 265–345). Washington, DC: American Psychological Association.

Meyer, R. G. (1993). *The clinician's handbook: Integrated diagnostics, assessment, and intervention in adult and adolescent psychopathology* (3rd ed.). Boston: Allyn & Bacon.

Miceli, N. S., Harvey, M., & Buckley, M. R. (2001). Potential discrimination in structured employment interviews. *Employee Responsibilities & Rights Journal, 12* (1), 15–38.

Michell, J. (1999). *Measurement in psychology: Critical history of a methodological concept.* New York: Cambridge University Press.

Middendorf, C. H., & Macan, T. H. (2002). Note-taking in the employment interview: Effects on recall and judgements. *Journal of Applied Psychology, 87*(2), 293–303.

Miele, F. (2002). *Intelligence, race, and genetics: Conversations with Arthur R. Jensen.* Boulder, CO: Westview Press.

Mikulay, S. M., & Goffin, R. D. (1998). Measuring and predicting counterproductivity in the laboratory using integrity and personality testing. *Educational and Psychological Measurement, 58,* 768–790.

Milgrom, P., Jie, Z., Yang, Z., & Tay, K. M. (1994). Cross-cultural validity of a Parent's Version of the Dental Fear Survey Schedule for Children in Chinese. *Behaviour Research and Therapy, 32*(1), 131–135.

Miller, A. B. (1991). Is routine mammography screening appropriate for women 40–49 years of age? *American Journal of Preventive Medicine, 91,* 55–62.

Miller, E. T., Neal, D. J., Roberts, L. J., Baer, J. S., Cressler, S. O., Metrik, J., & Marlatt, G. A. (2002). Test-retest reliability of alcohol measures: Is there a difference between internet-based assessment and traditional methods? *Psychology of Addictive Behaviors, 16*(1) 56–63.

Miller, J. A. L., Scurfield, B. K., Drga, V., Galvin, S. J., & Whitmore, J. (2002). Nonparametric relationships between single-interval and two-interval forced-choice tasks in the theory of signal detectability. *Journal of Mathematical Psychology, 46*(4), 383–417.

Miller, J. M., Goodyear-Orwat, A., & Malott, R. W. (1996). The effects of intensive, extensive, structured study on GRE scores. *Journal of Behavioral Education, 6*(4), 369–379.

Miller, J. O., & Phillips, J. (1966). *A preliminary evaluation of the Head Start and other metropolitan Nashville kindergartens.* Unpublished manuscript, George Peabody College for Teachers, TN.

Millon, T. (1969). *Modern psychopathology: A biosocial approach to maladaptive learning and functioning.* Philadelphia: Saunders.

Millon, T. (1983). *Millon Clinical Multiaxial Inventory Manual* (2nd ed.). Minneapolis, MN: National Computer Systems.

Millon, T. (1985). The MCMI provides a good assessment of DSMI-II disorders: The MCMI-II will prove even better. *Journal of Personality Assessment, 49,* 379–391.

Millon T. (1987). *Millon Clinical Multiaxial Inventory—II (Manual).* Minneapolis, MN: National Computer Systems.

Mills, C. N., Potenza, M. T., Fremer, J. J., & Ward, W. C. (2002). *Computer based testing: Building the foundation for future assessments.* Mahwah, NJ: Erlbaum.

Min., K. H., Kim, J. H., Hwang, S. H. S., & Jahng, S. M. (1998). Variations in emotion response patterning across genders, generations, and personality types. *Korean Journal of Social & Personality Psychology, 12*(2) 119–140.

Minton, H. L., & Schneider, F. W. (1980). *Differential psychology.* Pacific Grove, CA: Brooks/Cole.

Mirsky, A. F. (1989). The neuropsychology of attention: Elements of a complex behavior. In E. Ellen Perecman et al. (Eds.), *Integrating theory and practice in clinical neuropsychology* (pp. 75–91). Hillsdale, NJ: Erlbaum.

Mirsky, A. F. (1996). Disorders of attention: A neuropsychological perspective. In G. Reid Lyon, E. Norman, A. Krasnegor, et al. (Eds.), *Attention, memory, and executive function* (pp. 71–95). Baltimore: Williams & Wilkins.

Mirsky, A. F., Kugelmass, S., Ingraham, L. J., & Frenkel, E. (1995). Overview and summary: Twenty-five-year followup of high-risk children. *Schizophrenia Bulletin, 21*(2), 227–239.

Mischel, W. (1968). *Personality and assessment.* New York: Wiley.

Mischel, W. (1984). Convergences and challenges in the search for consistency. *American Psychologist, 39,* 351–364.

Mislevy, R. J. (2002). *Psychometric principles in student assessment.* Los Angeles, CA: Center for the Study of Evaluation National Center for Research on Evaluation Standards and Student Testing Graduate School of Education & Information Studies University of California Los Angeles.

Moe, V. (2002). Foster placed and adopted children exposed to in utero opiates and other substances: Prediction and outcome at four and a half years. *Journal of Developmental and Behavioral Pediatrics, 23*(5), 330–339.

Molfese, V. J., Modglin, A., Molfese, D. L. (2003). The role of environment in the development of readings skills: A longitudinal study of preschool and school-age measures. *Journal of Learning Disabilities, 36*(1), 59–67.

Monahan, J. (2003). Violence risk assessment. In A. M. Goldstein (Ed.), *Handbook of psychology: Forensic psychology* (Vol. 11) (pp. 527–540), New York: Wiley.

Moos, R. H. (1973). Conceptualizations of human environment. *American Psychologist, 28*, 652–665.

Moos, R. H. (1986a). *Group Environment Scale* (2nd ed.). Palo Alto, CA: Consulting Psychologist Press.

Moos, R. H. (1986b). *Work Environment Scale* (2nd ed.). Palo Alto, CA: Consulting Psychologist Press.

Moos, R. H. (1987a). *Community-Oriented Programs Environment Scale manual* (2nd ed.). Palo Alto, CA: Consulting Psychologist Press.

Moos, R. H. (1987b). *Correctional Institutions Environment Scale manual* (2nd ed.). Palo Alto, CA: Consulting Psychologist Press.

Moos, R. H. (1987c). Person-environment congruence in work, school, and health care settings. *Journal of Vocational Behavior, 31*, 231–247.

Moos, R. H. (1987d). *University Residents Environment Scale* (2nd ed.). Palo Alto, CA: Consulting Psychologist Press.

Moos, R. H. (1987e). Ward *Atmosphere Scale Manual* (2nd ed.). Palo Alto, CA: Consulting Psychologist Press.

Moos, R. H. (2003). Social contexts: Transcending their power and their

fragility. Netherlands: Kluwer Academic Publishers.

Moos, R. H., & Lemke, S. (1994). *Group residences for older adults: Physical features, policies, and social climate.* New York: Oxford University Press.

Moos, R. H., & Moos, B. (1986). *Family Environment Scale Manual* (2nd ed.). Palo Alto, CA: Consulting Psychologist Press.

Moos, R. H., & Truckett, E. (1986). *Classroom Environment Scale* (2nd ed.). Palo Alto, CA: Consulting Psychologist Press.

Morales, A. (1994). Validation of a psychophysiological Waking Erectile Assessment (WEA) for the diagnosis of Male Erectile Disorder: Comment. *Urology, 43*(5), 695–696.

Moreland, K. L. (1985). Validation of computer-based test interpretations: Problems and prospects. *Jounral of Consulting and Clinical Psychology, 53*, 816–825.

Moreland, K. L., Reznikoff, M., & Aronow, E. (1995). Integrating Rorschach interpretation by carefully placing more of your eggs in the content basket. *Journal of Personality Assessment, 64*(2), 239–242.

Moreno, K. E., Segall, D. O., & Hetter, R. D. (1997). The use of computerized adaptive testing in the military. In R. F. Dillon et al. (Eds.), *Handbook on testing* (pp. 204–219). Westport, CT: Greenwood.

Morgan, M. J., Davies, G. M., & Willner, P. (1999). The questionnaire of smoking urges is sensitive to abstinence and exposure to smoking-related cues. *Behavioral Pharmacology, 10*(6–7) 619–626.

Morrison, T., & Morrison, M. (1995). A meta-analytic assessment of the predictive validity of the quantitative and verbal components of the Graduate Record Examination with graduate grade point average representing the criterion of graduate success. *Educational and Psychological Measurement, 55*(2), 309–316.

Morrow, C. E., Bandstra, E. S., Emmalee, S., Anthony, J. C., Ofir, A.

Y., Xue, L., & Reyes, M. L. (2001). Influence of prenatal cocaine exposure on full-term infant neurobehavioral functioning. *Neurotoxicology and Teratology, 23*(6), 533–544.

Moses, J. A., Pritchard, D. A., & Faustman, W. O. (1994). Modal profiles for the Luria-Nebraska Neuropsychological Battery. *Archives of Clinical Neuropsychology, 9*, 15–30.

Motowidlo, S. J., Carter, G. W., Dunnette, M. D., Tippins, N., & others. (1992). Studies of the structured behavioral interview. *Journal of Applied Psychology, 77*, 571–587.

Moun, T. (1998). Mode of administration and interviewer effects in self-reported symptoms of anxiety and depression. *Social Indicators Research, 45*(1–3), 279–318.

Muir, S. P., & Tracy, D. M. (1999). Collaborative essay testing. *College Teaching, 47*, 33.

Mulsant, B. H., Kastango, K. B., Rosen, J., Stone, R. A., Mazumdar, S., & Pollock, B. G. (2002). *Interrater reliability in clinical trials of depressive disorders.* Washington, DC: American Psychiatric Association.

Munley, P. H., Bains, D. S., Bloem, W. D., & Busby, R. M. (1995). Post-traumatic stress disorder and the MMPI-2. *Journal of Traumatic Stress, 8*(1), 171–178.

Munsinger, H. (1975). The adopted child's I.Q.: A critical review. *Psychological Bulletin, 82*, 623–659.

Muris, P., Merckelbach, H., Mayer, B., & Meesters, C. (1998). Common fears and their relationship to anxiety disorders symptomatology in normal children. *Personality and Individual Differences, 24*, 575–578.

Murphy, K. R. (2003a). *The logic of validity generalization.* Mahwah, NJ: Erlbaum.

Murphy, K. R. (Ed.). (2003b). *Validity generalization: A critical review.* Mahwah, NJ: Erlbaum.

Murphy, L. L., Impara, J. C., Plake, B. S., & Buros Institute of Mental Measurements. (1999). *Tests in print V: An index to tests, test reviews, and the literature on specific tests*. Lincoln, NE: Buros Institute of Mental Measurements.

Murray, H. A. (1938). *Explorations in personality*. New York: Oxford University Press.

Murray, H. A. (1943). *Thematic Apperception Test*. Cambridge, MA: Harvard University Press.

Murstein, B. I. (1963). *Theory and research in projective techniques*. New York: Wiley.

Museum of Modern Art. (1955). *The family of man*. New York: Maco Magazine Corporation.

Naar-King, S., Ellis, D. A., & Frey, M. A. (2003). *Assessing children's well being: A handbook of measures*. Mahwah, NJ: Erlbaum.

Naglieri, J. A. (1985). Review of the Gesell Preschool Test. In J. V. Mitchell (Ed.), *The ninth mental measurements yearbook* (Vol. 1). Highland Park, NJ: Gryphon Press.

Naglieri, J. A., & Ford, D. Y. (2003). Addressing underrepresentation of gifted minority children using the Naglieri Nonverbal Ability Test (NNAT). *Gifted Child Quarterly, 47*(2) 155–160.

Nathanson, B. H., Higgins, T. L., Giglio, R. J., Munshi, I. A., & Steingrub, J. S. (2003). An exploratory study using data envelopment analysis to assess neurotrauma patients in the intensive care unit. *Health Care Management Science, 6*(1), 43–55.

National Cancer Institute. (1991, July). *Cancer Statistics Review: 1973–1988*. Bethesda, MD: Unpublished government report.

National Center for Education Statistics. (1995). *The condition of education 1995/ Indicator 21: Graduate Record Examination (GRE) scores*. Washington, DC: U.S. Department of Education.

National Center for Education Statistic. (2000). *Table 315, Scores on Graduate Record Examination (GRE) and subject matter tests: 1965–1999*. Washington, DC: U.S. Department of Education.

National Center for Health Statistics,

Health Resources Administration, June 1976.

National Commission on Testing and Public Policy. (1990). From *gatekeeper to gateway: Transforming testing in America*. Chestnut Hill, MA: National Computer Systems, Boston College.

Naughton, M. J., & Shumaker, S. A. (2003). The case for domains of function in quality of life assessment. *Quality of Life Research, 12*(Suppl. 1), 73–80.

Neary, M. P., Cort, S., Bayliss, M. S., and Ware, J. E., Jr. (1999). Sustained virologic response is associated with improved health-related quality of life in relapsed chronic hepatitis C patients. *Seminars in Liver Disease, 19*(2 Suppl. 1), 77–85.

The neglected "R": The need for a writing revolution. (2003). Report of the National Commission on Writing in America's Schools and Colleges. Retrieved May 10, 2003 from www. writingcommission. org/prod_downloads/writingcom/n eglectedr. pdf

Neisser, U. A. (1967). *Cognitive psychology*. New York: Appleton-Century-Crofts.

Neisser, U. (1998). *The rising curve: Long-term gains in IQ and related measures*. Washington, DC: American Psychological Association.

Neisser, U., Boodoo, G., Bouchard, T. J., Jr., Boykin, A. W., Brody, N. Ceci, S. J., Halpern, D. F., Loehlin, J. C., Perloff, R., Sternberg, R. J., & Urbina, S. (1996). Intelligence: Knowns and unknowns. *American Psychologist, 51*, 77–101.

Nell, V. (2000). *Cross-cultural neuropsychological assessment: Theory and practice*: Mahwah, NJ: Erlbaum.

Nellis, L., & Gridley, B. E. (1994). Review of the Bayley Scales of Infant Development, Second Edition. *Journal of School Psychology, 32*(2), 201–209.

Nelson, D. V., Novy, D. M., Averill, P. M., & Berry, L. A. (1996). Ethnic comparability of the MMPI in pain

patients. *Journal of Clinical Psychology, 52*, 485–497.

Neto, F. (2002). Social adaptation difficulties of adolescents with immigrant backgrounds. *Social Behavior and Personality, 30*(4) 335–346.

Nettelbeck, T. (1982). Inspection time: An index for intelligence? *Quarterly Journal of Experimental Psychology, 34A*, 299–312.

Nettelbeck, T., & Lally, M. (1976). Inspection time and measured intelligence. *British Journal of Psychology, 67*, 17–22.

Nevo, B., & Jager, R. S. (Eds.). (1993). *Educational and psychological testing: The test taker's outlook*. Gottingen, Germany: Huber.

Newman, C., Leahy, R. L., Beck, A. T., Reilly-Harrington, N. A., & Gyulia, L., (2003). Bipolar disorder: A cognitive therapy approach. *Behavioral & Cognitive Psychotherapy, 31*(1) 113–114.

Newman, M. G. (1999). The clinical use of palmtop computers in the treatment of generalized anxiety disorder. *Cognitive & Behavioral Practice, 6*(3) 222–234.

Newman, M. G., Consoli, A., & Barr, T. C. (1997). Computers in assessment and cognitive behavioral treatment for clinical disorders: Anxiety as a case in point. *Behavior Therapy, 28*(2), 211–235.

Newman, M. G., Consoli, A., & Taylor, C. B. (1999). A palmtop computer program for the treatment of generalized anxiety disorder. *Behav Modif, 23*(4), 597–610.

Newman, M. G., Kenardy, J., Herman, S., & Taylor, C. B. (1997). Comparison of palm-top-computer-assisted brief cognitive-behavioral treatment to cognitive-behavioral treatment for panic disorder. *Journal of Consulting & Clinical Psychology, 65*(1), 178–183.

Newton, R. L. (1954). The clinician as judge: Total Rorschachs and clinical case material. *Journal of Consulting Psychology, 18*, 248–250.

Nezworski, M. T., & Wood, J. M. (1995). Narcissism in the comprehensive system for the Rorschach. *Clinical Psychology—Science and Practice, 2,* 179–199.

Niccols, A., & Lachman, A. (2002). Stability of the Bayley Mental Scale of Infant Development with high risk infants. *British Journal of Developmental Disabilities, 48*(94, Pt. 1), 3–13.

Nichols, D. S., & Greene, R. L. (1997). Dimensions of deception in personality assessment: The example of the MMPI-2. *Journal of Personality Assessment, 68,* 251–266.

Nittono, H. (1997). Personality needs and short-term memory. *Psychological Reports, 81,* 19–24.

Norcross, J. C., & Beutler, I. E. (1997). Determining the therapeutic relationship of choice in brief psychotherapy. In J. N. Butcher (Ed.), *Personality assessment in managed care: A practitioner's guide.* New York: Oxford University Press.

Nordstrom, C. R., Huffaker, B. J., & Williams, K. B. (1998). When physical disabilities are not liabilities: The role of applicant and interviewer characteristics on employment interview outcomes. *Journal of Applied Social Psychology, 28,* 283–306.

Norlin, J. W. (2003). *The special educator 2003 desk book.* Palm Beach Gardens, FL: LRP Publications.

Norman, G. (2003). Hi! How are you? Response shift, implicit theories and differing epistemologies. *Quality of Life Research, 12*(3), 239–249.

North, M. M., North, S. M., & Coble, J. R. (1997). Virtual reality therapy: An effective treatment for psychological disorders. In G. Riva (Ed.), *Virtual reality in neuro-psycho-physiology: Cognitive, clinical, and methodological issues in assessment and rehabilitation. Studies in Health Technology and Informatics, 58,* 112–119.

North, M. M., North, S. M., & Coble, J. R. (2002). Virtual reality therapy: An effective treatment for psychological disorders. In K. M. Stanney (Ed.), *Handbook of virtual environments: Design, implementation, and applications. Human factors and ergonomics* (1065–1078). Mahwah, NJ: Erlbaum.

Norton, E. H. (1978, July). *The Bakke decision and the future of affirmative action.* Statement of the Chair, U.S. Equal Employment Opportunity Commission, at the convention of the National Association for the Advancement of Colored People.

Novick, B. Z., & Arnold, M. M. (1995). *Why is my child having trouble at school? A parent's guide to learning disabilities.* New York: Putnam.

Novick, M. R. (1981). Federal guidelines and professional standards. *American Psychologist, 36,* 1035–1046.

Nugent, W. R. (2003). *A psychometric study of the Multi-Problem Screening Inventory depression subscale using item response and generalizability theories.* Thousand Oaks, CA: Sage.

Nunnally, J. C., & Bernstein, I. H. (1994). *Psychometric theory* (3rd ed.). New York: McGraw-Hill.

Nurius, P. S. (1990). A review of automated assessment. *Computers in human services, 6,* 265–281.

Nyborg, H., & Jensen, A. R. (2000). Black-white differences on various psychometric tests: Spearman's hypothesis tested on American armed services veterans. *Personality and Individual Differences, 28*(3), 593–599.

Nykodym, N., & Ruud, W. N. (1985). Intraview: Career development through business communication. *Journal of Employment Counseling, 22,* 161–165.

Nykodym, N., & Simonetti, J. L. (1981). *Communication: The key to business and organizational effectiveness.* Toledo, OH: Management Skills Books.

Nystul, M. S. (1999). *Introduction to counseling: An art and science perspective:* Boston, MA: Allyn & Bacon.

Oakland, T. (1979). Research on the ABIC and ELP: A revisit to an old topic. *School Psychology Digest, 8,* 209–213.

Oakland, T., & Feigenbaum, D. (1979). Multiple sources of test bias on the WISC-R and the Bender-Gestalt test. *Journal of Consulting and Clinical Psychology, 47,* 968–974.

Oakland, T., & Parmelee, R. (1985). Mental measurement of minority-group children. In B. B. Wolman (Ed.), *Handbook of intelligence: Theories, measurements, and applications.* New York: Wiley-Interscience.

O'Donnell, J., Hawkins, J. D., & Abbott, R. D. (1995). Predicting serious delinquency and substance use among agressive boys [Special Section: Prediction and prevention of child and adolescent antisocial behavior]. *Journal of Consulting and Clinical Psychology, 63,* 529–437.

Oei, T. P. S., Evans, I., & Crook, G. M. (1990). Utility and validity of the STAI with anxiety disorder patients. *British Journal of Clinical Psychology, 29,* 429–432.

Ogloff, J. R. P. & Douglas, K. S. (2003). Psychological assessment in forensic settings. In J. R. Graham & J. A. Naglieri (Eds.), *Handbook of psychology: Assessment psychology* (Vol. 10) (pp. 345–363). New York: Wiley.

Okazaki, S., & Sue, S. (2003). *Methodological issues in assessment research with ethnic minorities.* Washington, DC: American Psychological Association.

O'Leary, K. D., & Kent, R. N. (1973). Behavior modification for social action: Research tactics and problems. In L. A. Hamerlynck, P. O. Davidson, & L. E. Acker (Eds.), *Critical issues in research and practice.* Champaign, IL: Research Press.

O'Leary, K. D., Kent, R. N., & Kanowitz, J. (1975). Shaping data collection congruent with experimental hypotheses. *Journal of Applied Behavior Analysis, 8,* 43–51.

Olmedo, E. L. (1981). Testing linguistic minorities. *American Psychologist, 36,* 1078–1085.

Ones, D. S., Chockalingam, V., & Schmidt, F. L. (1995). Integrity tests: Overlooked facts, resolved issues, and remaining questions. *American Psychologist, 50*(6), 456–457.

Oostdam, R., & Meijer, J. (2003). *Influence of test anxiety on measurement of intelligence.* Washington, DC: Psychological Reports.

Optale, G., Munari, A., Nasta, A., Pianon, C., Verde, J. B., & Viggiano, G. (1998). Virtual environments in the treatment of impotence and premature ejaculation. *Cyberpsychology & Behavior, 1*(3) 213–223.

Opton, E. (1977, April). From California, two views. *APA Monitor,* pp. 5–18.

Opton, E. (1979, December). A psychologist takes a closer look at the recent landmark *Larry P.* opinion. *APA Monitor,* pp. 1–4.

Orfield, G., & Kornhaber, M. L. (2001). *Raising standards or raising barriers? Inequality and high-stakes testing in public education.* New York: Century Foundation Press.

Orlansky, J., Grafton, F., Martin, C. J., & Alley, W. (1990). *The current status of research and development on selection and classification of enlisted personnel.* Institute for Defense Analysis paper (IDA Document D-715, 72). Washington, DC: Institute for Defense Analysis.

Osberg, T. M., & Poland, D. L. (2002). Comparative accuracy of the MMPI-2 and the MMPI-A in the diagnosis of psychopathology in 18-year-olds. *Psychological Assessment, 14*(2), 164–169.

Osipow, S. H. (1983). *Theories of career development* (3rd ed.). Englewood Cliffs, NJ: Prentice-Hall.

Osipow, S. H. (1987). Counselling psychology: Theory, research, and practice in career counselling. *Annual Review of Psychology, 38,* 257–278.

Osipow, S. H. (1999). Assessing career indecision. *Journal of Vocational Behavior, 55*(1), 147–154.

Othmer, E. & Othmer, S. C. (2002). *The clinical interview using DSM-IV-TR: Vol. 2. The difficult patient.* Washington, D. C. : American Psychiatric Publishing.

Ottem, E. (2002a). Confirmatory factor analysis of ITPA models with language-impaired children. *Scandinavian Journal of Psychology, 43*(4), 299–305.

Ottem, E. (2002b). The complementary nature of ITPA and WISC-R results for language-impaired children. *Scandinavian Journal of Educational Research, 46*(2), 145–160.

Overton, R. C., Harms, H. J., Taylor, L. R., & Zickar, M. J. (1997). Adapting to adaptive testing. *Personnel Psychology, 50*(1) 171–185.

Owen, D. (1985). *None of the above: Behind the myth of scholastic aptitude.* Boston: Houghton Mifflin.

Owen, P. R. (1998). Fears of Hispanic and Anglo children: Real-world fears in the 1990s. *Hispanic Journal of Behavioral Sciences, 20,* 483–491.

Pagano, R. R. (2004). *Understanding statistics in the behavioral sciences* (7th ed.). Belmont, CA: Wadsworth.

Palaniappan, A. K., & Torrance, E. P. (2001). Comparison between regular and streamlined versions of scoring of Torrance Tests of Creative Thinking. *Korean Journal of Thinking and Problem Solving, 11*(2), 5–7.

Palmer, F. H. (1970). Socioeconomic status and intellectual performance among Negro preschool boys. *Developmental Psychology, 3,* 1–9.

Parducci, A. (1968). The relativism of absolute judgments. *Scientific American, 219*(6), 84–90.

Parducci, A. (1995). *Happiness, pleasure, and judgment: The contextual theory and its applications.* Mahwah, NJ: Erlbaum.

Parents in Action on Special Education v. Hannon. (1980). USDC N111 (J. Grady pub. July 7, 1980).

Parker, J. D., Endler, N. S., & Bagby, R. M. (1993). If it changes, it might be unstable: Examining the factor structure of the Ways of Coping Questionnaire. *Psychological Assessment, 5*(3), 361–368.

Parker, K. (1983). A meta-analysis of the reliability and validity of the Rorschach. *Journal of Personality Assessment, 42,* 227–231.

Parsons, O. A. (1970). Clinical neuropsychology. In C. D. Spielberger (Ed.), *Current topics in clinical and community psychology* (Vol. 2). New York: Academic Press.

Pasamanick, B. A., & Knobloch, H. (1955). Early language behavior in Negro children and the testing of intelligence. *Journal of Abnormal and Social Psychology, 50,* 401–402.

Patrick, D. L., & Chiang, Y. P. (2002). Measurement of health outcomes in treatment effectiveness evaluations: conceptual and methodological challenges. *Med Care, 33* (9 Suppl), II14–25.

Patrick, D. L., Bushnell, D. M., & Rothman, M. (2004). Performance of two self-report measures for evaluating obesity and weight loss. *Obesity Research, 12*(1), 48–57.

Patterson, M., Slate, J. R., Jones, C. H., & Steger, H. S. (1995). The effects of practice administrations in learning to administer and score the WAIS-R: A partial replication. *Educational and Psychological Measurement, 55*(1), 32–37.

Patterson, T. L., Kaplan, R. M., Grant, I., Semple, S. J., Moscona, S., Koch, W. L., et al. (1996). Quality of well-being in late-life psychosis. *Psychiatry Research, 63*(2–3), 169–181.

Patterson, T. L., Kaplan, R. M., & Jeste, D. V. (1999). Measuring the effect of treatment on quality of life in patients with schizophrenia: Focus on utility-based measures. *CNS Drugs, 12*(1), 49–64.

Pattishall, E. (1992). Smoking and body weight. *Health Psychology* (Suppl. 32), 3.

Paul, G. L., & Eriksen, C. W. (1964). Effects of test anxiety on "real life" examinations. *Journal of Personality, 32,* 480–494.

Paul, R., Cohen, R., Moser, D., Ott, B., Zawacki, T., & Gordon, N. (2001). Performance on the Hooper Visual Organizational Test in patients diagnosed with subcortical vascular dementia: Relation to naming performance. *Neuropsychiatry, Neuropsychology, and Behavioral Neurology, 14*(2), 93–97.

Paunonen, S. V., & Ashton, M. C. (1998). The structured assessment of personality across cultures. *Journal of Cross-Cultural Psychology, 29,* 150–170.

Pearson, K. (1901). *Mathematical contributions to the theory of evolution.* London: Dulau & Co.

Pedersen, N. L. (2002). Behavior genetics and the future of psychology. In C. von Hofsten & L. Baeckman (Eds.), *Psychology at the turn of the millennium. Vol. 2: Social, developmental, and clinical perspectives* (pp. 3–16). Florence, KY: Taylor & Frances/Routledge.

Pedhazur, E. J. (1991). *Measurement, design, and analysis: An integrated approach.* Hillsdale, NJ: Erlbaum.

Pedhazur, E. J. (1997). *Multiple regression in behavioral research: Explanation and prediction* (3rd ed.). Fort Worth, TX: Harcourt Brace.

Pedulla et al. (2003). *Perceived effects of state-mandated testing programs on teaching and learning: Findings from a national survey of teachers.* Boston: Boston College, National Board on Educational Testing and Public Policy, Lynch School of Education.

Pena, L. M., Megargee, E. I., & Brody, E. (1996). MMPI-A patterns of male juvenile delinquents. *Psychological Assessment, 8,* 388–397.

Penfield, R. D. (2003a). IRT-Lab: Software for research and pedagogy in item response theory. *Applied Psychological Measurement, 27*(4), 301–302.

Penfield, R. D. (2003b). A score method of constructing asymmetric confidence intervals for the mean of a rating scale item. *Psychological Methods, 8*(2), 149–163.

Pennington, B. F., & Welsh, M.

(1995). Neuropsychology and developmental psychopathology. In D. Cicchetti & D. J. Cohen (Eds.), *Developmental psychopathology* (Vol. 1) (pp. 254–290). New York: Wiley.

People Who Care v. Rockford Board of Education School District No. 205. (1997). 111 F. 3d 528 (7th Cir. 1997).

Peoples, V. Y. (1975). Measuring the vocational interest of women. In S. H. Osipow (Ed.), *Emerging women: Career analysis and outlooks.* Columbus, OH: Merrill.

Perkins, D. N., & Grotzer, T. A. (1997). Teaching intelligence. *American Psychologist, 52* (10), 1125–1133.

Perkins, E. L. (2002). Wise persons' personality temperaments: Differences and similarities found in the wise and compared with the general population. *Dissertation Abstracts International, 62,* 8B.

Perkos, S., Theodorakis, Y., & Chronni, S. (2002). Enhancing performance and skill acquisition in novice basketball players with instructional self-talk. *Sport Psychologist, 16*(4), 368–383.

Pernas, A., Iraurgi C. I., Bermejo, P., Basebe, N., Carou, M., Paez, D., & Cabarcos, A. (2001). Coping and affectivity in persona with HIV/AIDS. *Psiquis: Revista de Psiquiatria, Psicologia Medica y Psicosomatica, 22*(5), 30–35.

Perrez, M., Wilhelm, P., Schoebi, D., & Horner, M. (2001). Simultaneous computer-assisted assessment of causal attribution and social coping in families. In J. Fahrenberg & U. Freilberg (Eds.), *Progress in ambulatory assessment: Computer assisted psychological and psychophysiological methods in monitoring and field studies* (pp. 25–43). Kirkland, WA: Hogrefe & Huber.

Perry, W., Sprock, J., Schaible, D., & McDougall, A. (1995). Amphetamine on Rorschach measures in normal subjects. *Journal of Personality Assessment, 64*(3), 456–465.

Peterson, N. G., Mumford, M. D.,

Levin, K. Y., Green, J., & Waksberg, J. (1999). Research method: Development and field testing of the content model. In E. Norman, G. Peterson, E. Michael, D. Mumford, et al. (Eds.), *An occupational information system for the 21st century: The development of O*NET* (pp. 31–47). Washington, DC: American Psychological Association.

Pettigrew, T. F. (1964). *A profile of the American Negro.* New York: Van Nostrand Reinhold.

Pettit, F. A. (1999). Exploring the use of the World Wide Web as a psychology data collection tool. *Computers in Human Behavior, 15*(1) 67–71.

Pettit, F. A. (2002). A comparison of world-wide web and paper-and-pencil personality questionnaires. *Behavior Research Methods, Instruments, & Computers, 34*(1) 6–18.

Pettit, J. W., Kline, J. P., Gencoz, T., Gencoz, F., & Joiner, T. E. (2002). Are happy people healthier? The specific role of positive affect in predicting self-reported health symptoms. *Journal of Research in Personality, 35*(4) 521–536.

Pfeifer, C., & Sedlacek, W. (1971). The validity of academic predictors for black and white students at a predominantly white university. *Journal of Educational Measurement, 8,* 253–261.

Pfister, H. (1995). New technology for administering group tests. *Australian Psychologist, 30;* 24–26.

Phares, E. J., & Trull, T. J. (2000). *Clinical psychology* (6th ed.). Pacific Grove, CA: Brooks/Cole.

Phillips, S. E. (1994). High-stakes testing accommodations: Validity versus disabled rights. *Applied Measurement in Education, 7* (2), 93–120.

Phillips, S. E. (2002). Legal issues affecting special populations in large-scale testing programs. In G. Tindal & T. M. Haladyna (Eds.), *Large-scale assessment programs for all students: Validity, technical adequacy, and implementation* (pp. 109–148). Mahwah, NJ: Erlbaum.

Picard, R. W., & Klein, J. (2002). Computers that recognize and respond to user emotion: Theoretical and practical implications. *Interacting with Computer, 14*(2), 141–169.

Picone, L., Regine, A., & Ribaudo, F. (2001). Factorial validity of the McCarthy Scales of Children's Abilities by measuring cognitive ability in young children. *Bollettino di Psicologia Applicata, 234*(48), 21–31.

Piedmont, R. L. (1998). *The revised NEO Personality Inventory: Clinical and research applications: The Plenum series in social/clinical psychology.* New York: Plenum.

Pierce, J. P., Burns, D., Gilpen, E., Rosenberg, B., Johnson, M., & Bal, D. (1992). *California baseline tobacco survey.* Unpublished report. University of California, San Diego.

Piers, V. P., Harris, D. B., & Herzberg, D. S. (1999). *Piers Harris Children's Self-Concept Scale–second edition.* Los Angeles: Western Psychological Services.

Pinsoneault, T. B. (1999). Equivalency of computer assisted and paper-and-pencil administered versions of the Minnesota Multiphasic Personality Inventory-2. *Computers in Human Behavior, 12*(2) 291–300.

Piotrowski, Z. (1964). Digital computer interpretation of inkblot test data. *Psychiatric Quarterly, 38,* 1–26.

Piotrowski, C. (1984). The status of projective techniques: Or, "wishing won't make it go away." *Journal of Clinical Psychology, 40,* 1495–1499.

Piotrowski, C. (1995). A review of the clinical and research use of the Bender-Gestalt Test. *Perceptual and Motor Skills, 81,* 1272–1274.

Piotrowski, C. (1997). Use of the Millon Clinical Multiaxial Inventory in clinical practice. *Perceptual and Motor Skills, 84,* 1185–1186.

Piotrowski, C., Sherry, D., & Keller, J. W. (1985). Psychodiagnostic test usage: Survey of the Society for Personality Assessment. *Journal of Personality Assessment, 49,* 115–119.

Piotrowski, Z. (1947). Rorschach compendium. *Psychiatric Quarterly, 21,* 79–101.

Piotrowski, Z. A. (1980). CPR: The psychological X-ray in mental disorders. In J. B. Sidowski, J. H. Johnson, & T. A. Williams (Eds.), *Technology in mental health care delivery systems* (pp. 85–108). Norwood, NJ: Ablex.

Plaisted, J. R., Gustavson, J. L., Wilkening, G. N., & Golden, C. J. (1983). The Luria-Nebraska Neuropsychological Battery Children's revision: Theory and current research findings. *Journal of Clinical Child Psychology, 12,* 13–21.

Plessy v. Ferguson. (1896). 163 U.S. 537.

Polansky, N., Freeman, W., Horowitz, M., Irwin, L., Papanis, N., Rapaport, D., & Whaley, F. (1949). Problems of interpersonal relations in research on groups. *Human Relations, 2,* 281–291.

Pomaki, G., & Anagnostopoulou, T. (2003). A test and extension of the Demand/Control/Social support model: Prediction of wellness/health outcomes in Greek teachers. *Psychology and Health, 18*(4), 537–550.

Pomerlau, A., Leahey, L., & Malcuit, G. (1994). Evaluation of infant development during the first 12 months: Use of the Bayley Scales. *Canadian Journal of Behavioural Science—Revue Canadienne des sciences du Comportement, 26*(1), 85–103.

Pons, D., Atienza, F. L., Balaguer, I., & Garcia-Merita, M. (2002). Psychometric properties of Satisfaction with Life Scale in elderly. *Revista Iberoamericana de Diagnostico y Evaluacion Psicologica, 13*(1) 71–82.

Pons, L. (1989). Effects of age and sex upon availability of responses on a word-association test. *Perceptual and Motor Skills, 68,* 85–86.

Pope, K. S., Butcher, J. N., & Seelen, J. (2000). *The MMPI, MMPI-2, & MMPI-A in court: A practical guide for expert witnesses and attorneys* (2nd ed.). Washington, DC: American Psychological Association.

Popham, W. J. (1994). The instructional consequences of criterion-referenced clarity. *Educational Measurement: Issues and Practice, 13*(4), 15–18, 30.

Popper, S. E. (1997). Validity of using non-pilot subjects to represent pilots in a sustained acceleration environment. *Aviation Space and Environmental Medicine, 68,* 1081–1087.

Posthuma, R. A., Morgeson, F. P., & Campion, M. A. (2002). Beyond employment interview validity: A comprehensive narrative review of recent research and trends over time. *Personnel Psychology, 55*(1).

Potter, E. F. (1999). What should I put in my portfolio? Supporting young children's goals and evaluations. *Childhood Education, 75,* 210.

Powell, M. B., Wilson, J. C., & Hastya, M. K. (2002). Evaluation of the usefulness of 'Marvin'; a computerized assessment tool for investigative interviewers of children. *Computers in Human Behavior, 18*(5), 577–592.

Power, M. J., Katz, R., McGuffin, P., & Duggan, C. F. (1994). The Dysfunctional Attitude Scale (DAS): A comparison of Form A and Form B and proposals for a new subscaled version. *Journal of Research in Personality, 28*(3), 263–276.

Powers, D. E. (1999). *Coaching and the SAT I* (College Board Research Report No. RN-06, April 1999). New York: College Entrance Examination Board.

Powers, D. E., Burstein, J. C., Chodorow, M., Fowles, M. E., & Kukich, K. (2000). *Comparing validity of automated and human essay scoring.* Princeton, NJ: Educational Testing Service.

Powers, D. E., Burstein, J. C., Chodorow, M., Fowles, M. E., & Kukich, K. (2002). Stumping E-rater: Challenging the validity of automated essay scoring. *Computers in Human Behavior, 18*(2) 103–134.

Powers, D. E., & Rock, D. A. (1998). *Effects of coaching on SAT I: Reasoning scores* (College Board Research

Report No. 98-6). New York: College Entrance Examination Board.

Powers, D. E. (2001). *Validity of GRE General test scores for admission to colleges of veterinary medicine* (No. GRE Board 98-09R). Princeton, NJ: Educational Testing Service.

Prediger, D. J. (1999). Integrating interests and abilities for career exploration: General considerations. In M. L. Savickas & A. R. Spokane (Eds.), *Vocational interests: Meaning, measurement, and counseling use* (pp. 295–325). Palo Alto, CA: Davies-Black.

Prewett, P. N., & Farhney, M. R. (1994). The concurrent validity of the Matrix Analogies Test—Short Form with the Stanford Binet: Fourth Edition and KTEA-BF (academic achievement). *Psychology in the Schools, 31*(1), 20–25.

Prewett, P. N., & Matavich, M. A. (1994). A comparison of referred students' performance on the WISC-III and the Stanford Binet Intelligence Scale: Fourth Edition. *Journal of Psychoeducational Assessment, 12*(1), 42–48.

Price, K. H., & Garland, H. (1983). Compliance with a leader's suggestions as a function of perceived leader/member competence and potential reciprocity. *Journal of Applied Psychology, 66,* 329–336.

Primi, R. (2002). Complexity of geometric inductive reasoning tasks: Contribution to the understanding of fluid intelligence. *Intelligence, 30*(1), 41–70.

Prince, R. J., & Guastello, S. J. (1990). The Barnum effect in a computerized Rorschach interpretation system. *Journal of Psychology, 124,* 217–222.

Prinstein, M. J. (2004). The interview. In C. Williams-Nickelson (Ed.), *Internships in psychology: The APAGS workbook for writing successful applications and finding the right match* (pp. 79–92). Washington, DC: American Psychological Association.

Prout, H. T., & Sheldon, K. L. (1984). Classifying mental retardation in vocational rehabilitation: A study of diagnostic practices and their adherence to accepted guidelines. *Rehabilitation Counseling Bulletin, 28,* 125–128.

Pugh, R. C. (1968). Evidence for the validity of the behavioral dimensions of Teaching-Characteristics Schedule Scales. *Educational and Psychological Measurement, 28*(4), 1173–1179.

Pugliese, M. D., Lifshitz, F., Grad, G., Fort, P., & Marks-Katz, M. (1983). Fear of obesity: A cause of short stature and delayed puberty. *New England Journal of Medicine, 309,* 513–518.

Pyne, J. M., Sieber, W. J., David, K., Kaplan, R. M., Hyman Rapaport, M., & Keith Williams, D. (2003). Use of the quality of well-being self-administered version (QWB-SA) in assessing health-related quality of life in depressed patients. *Journal of Affect Disord, 76*(1–3), 237–247.

Quay, L. C. (1971). Language dialect, reinforcement, and the intelligence-test performance of Negro children. *Child Development, 42,* 5–15.

Quenk, N. L. (2000). *Essentials of Myers-Briggs Type Indicator Assessment.* New York: Wiley.

Raggio, D. J., Massingale, T. W., & Bass, J. D. (1994). Comparison of Vineland Adaptive Behavior Scales Survey Form age equivalent and standard score with the Bayley Mental Development Index. *Perceptual and Motor Skills, 79*(1), 203–206.

Raju, N. S., Burke, M. J., Normand, J., & Lezotte, D. V. (1993). What would be if what is wasn't? Rejoinder to Judiesch, Schmidt, and Hunter (1993). *Journal of Applied Psychology, 78,* 912–916.

Ralston, S. M. (1988). The effect of applicant race upon personnel selection decisions: A review with recommendations. *Employee Responsibilities and Rights Journal, 1,* 215–226.

Ramanaiah, N. V., Sharp, J. P., & Byravan, A. (1999). Hardiness and major personality factors. *Psychological Reports, 84*(2) 497–500.

Rammsayer, T. H., & Brandler, S. (2002). On the relationship between general fluid intelligence and psychophysical indicators of temporal resolution in the brain. *Journal of Research in Personality, 36*(5), 507–530.

Randolph, D. L., Smart, T. K., & Nelson, W. (1997). The Personality Research Form as a discriminator of attachment styles. *Journal of Social Behavior and Personality, 12,* 113–127.

Rao, S. M. (2000). Neuropsychological evaluation. In E. Barry, S. Fogel, E. Randolph, B. Schiffer, et al. (Eds.), *Synopsis of neuropsychiatry* (pp. 17–25). Philadelphia: Lippincott.

Rapaport, D., Gill, M. M., & Schafer, R. (1945–1946). *Diagnostic psychological testing* (2 vols.). Chicago: Yearbook Publishers.

Rapaport, D., Gill, M. M., & Schafer, R. (1968). *Diagnostic psychological testing* (Rev. ed., R. R. Holt, Ed.). New York: International Universities Press.

Rappaport, N. B., & McAnulty, D. P. (1985). The effect of accented speech on the scoring of ambiguous WISC-R responses by prejudiced and nonprejudiced raters. *Journal of Psychoeducational Assessment, 3,* 275–283.

Rasulis, R., Jr., Schuldberg, D., & Murtagh, M. (1996). Computer administered testing with the Rotter Incomplete Sentences Blank. *Computers in Human Behavior, 12*(4) 497–513.

Ratliff-Shaub, K., Hunt, C. E., Crowell, D., Golub, H., Smok-Pearsall, S., Palmer, P., Schafer, S., Bak, S., Cantey-Kiser, J., & O'Bell, R. (2001). Relationship between infant sleep position and motor development in preterm infants. *Journal of Developmental and Behavioral Pediatrics, 22*(5), 293–299.

Raven, J. (1986). *Manual for Raven's Progressive Matrices and Vocabulary*

Scales: Research supplement No. 3. London: H. K. Lewis.

Raven, J. (1990). *Raven manual research supplement 3: American and international norms.* London: Oxford Psychologist Press.

Raven, J. (2000). The Raven's Progressive Matrices: Change and stability over culture and time. *Cognitive Psychology, 41*(1), 1–48.

Raven, J., Raven, J. C., & Court, J. H. (1998). *Standard progressive matrices, 1998 edition.* Oxford, England: Oxford University Press.

Ray, W. J. (2000). *Methods: Toward a science of behavior and experience* (6th ed.). Belmont, CA: Wadsworth.

Reardon, R. C., & Lenz, J. G. (1999). Holland's theory and career assessment. *Journal of Vocational Behavior, 55*(1), 102–113.

Rebok, G., Brandt, J., & Folstein, M. (1990). Longitudinal cognitive decline in patients with Alzheimer's disease. *Journal of Geriatric Psychiatry and Neurology, 3,* 91–97.

Redden, S. C., Forness, S. R., Ramey, S. L., Ramey, C. T., Brezausek, C. M., & Kavale, K. A. (2001). Children at risk: Effects of a four-year head start transition program on special education identification. *Journal of Child and Family Studies, 10*(2), 255–270.

Redfield, J., & Paul, G. L. (1976). Bias in behavioral observation as a function of observer familiarity with subjects and typically of behavior. *Journal of Consulting and Clinical Psychology, 44,* 156.

Ree, M. J., & Carretta, T. R. (1994). Factor analysis of the ASVAB: Confirming a Vernon-like structure. *Educational and Psychological Measurement, 54*(2) 459–463.

Ree, M. J., & Carretta, T. R. (1995). Group differences in aptitude factor structure on the ASVAB. *Educational and Psychological Measurement, 55*(2), 268–277.

Reed, S. B. (2000). An investigation of the physical attractiveness stereotype. *Dissertation Abstracts International, 60,* 12B.

Regents of the University of California v. Bakke. (1978). 438 U.S. 265, 17 Fair Empl. Prac. Cas. (BNA) 1000.

Reid, J. B. (1970). Reliability assessment of observation data: A possible methodological problem. *Child Development, 41,* 1143–1150.

Reid, J. B., & DeMaster, B. (1972). The efficacy of the spotcheck procedure in maintaining the reliability of data collected by observers in quasinatural settings: Two pilot studies. *Oregon Research Institute Research Bulletin, 12.*

Reise, S. P., & Waller, N. G. (2003). How many IRT parameters does it take to model psychopathology items? *Psychological Methods, 8*(2), 164–184.

Reisman, J. M. (1976). *A history of clinical psychology.* New York: Irvington.

Reitan, R. M. (1968). Theoretical and methodological bases of the Halstead-Reitan Neuropsychological Test Battery. In I. Grant & K. N. Adams (Eds.), *Neuropsychological assessment of neuropsychiatric disorders.* New York: Oxford University Press.

Reitan, R. M. (1976). Neuropsychology: The vulgarization that Luria always wanted. *Contemporary Psychology, 21,* 737–738.

Reitan, R. M., & Wolfson, D. (1997). Consistency of neuropsychological test scores of head-injured subjects involved in litigation compared with head-injured subjects not involved in litigation: Development of the Retest Consistency index. *Clinical Neuropsychologist, 11*(1), 69–76.

Reitan, R. M., & Wolfson, D. (1999). The two faces of mild head injury. *Archives of Clinical Neuropsychology, 14*(2), 191–202.

Reschly, D. J. (1981). Psychological testing in educational classification and placement. *American Psychologist, 36,* 1094–1102.

Reschly, D. J., Kicklighter, R., & McKee, P. (1988). Recent placement of litigation part III: Analysis of differences in Larry P., Marshal and S-1, and implications for future practices. *School Psychology Review, 17,* 39–50.

Reschly, D. J., & Sabers, D. L. (1979). Analysis of test bias in four groups with the regression definition. *Journal of Educational Measurement, 16,* 1–9.

Reschly, D. J., & Ward, S. M. (1991). Use of adaptive behavior measures and overrepresentation of black students in programs for students with mild mental retardation. *American Journal on Mental Retardation, 96,* 257–268.

Resnick, S. M., Trotman, K. M., Kawas, C., & Zonderman, A. B. (1995). Age-associated changes in specific errors on the Benton Visual Retention Test. *Journals of Gerontology Series B—Psychological Sciences and Social Sciences, 50B,* 171–178.

Retzlaff, P. D., and Gibertini, M. (2000). Neuropsychometric issues and problems. In E. Rodney, D. Vanderploeg, et al. (Eds.), *Clinician's guide to neuropsychological assessment* (pp. 277–299). Mahwah, NJ: Erlbaum.

Revicki, D. A., & Cella, D. F. (1997). Health status assessment for the twenty-first century: Item response theory, item banking, and computer adaptive testing. *Quality of life Research, 6*(6) 595–600.

Reynolds, C. R. (1980). An examination of bias in a pre-school battery across race and sex. *Journal of Educational Measurement, 17,* 137–146.

Reynolds, C. R. (1982). Determining statistically reliable strengths and weaknesses in the performance of single individuals on the Luria Nebraska Neuropsychological Battery. *Journal of Consulting and Clinical Psychology, 50,* 525–529.

Reynolds, C. R. (1986). Wide Range Achievement Test (WRAT-R), 1984 edition. *Journal of Counseling and Development, 64,* 540–541.

Reynolds, C. R., & Gutkin, J. R. (Eds.). (1999). *The handbook of school psychology* (3rd. ed.). New York: Wiley.

Reynolds, C. R., & Kamphaus, R. W. (1997). The Kaufman Assessment Battery for Children: Development, structure, and applications in neuropsychology. In A. M. Horton, D. Wedding, et al. (Eds.), *The neuropsychology handbook: Vol. 1. Foundations and assessment* (2nd ed.) (pp. 290–330). New York: Springer.

Reynolds, C. R., & Nigl, A. J. (1981). A regression analysis of differential validity: An intellectual assessment for black and white inner-city children. *Journal of Clinical and Child Psychology, 10,* 176–179.

Reynolds, C. R., & Ramsay, M. C. (2003). Bias in psychological assessment: An empirical review and recommendations. In J. R. Graham & J. A. Naglieri (Eds.), *Handbook of psychology: Assessment psychology* (Vol. 10) (pp. 67–93). New York: Wiley.

Richeson, N. & Thorson, J. A. (2002). The effect of autobiographical writing on the subjective well-being of older adults. *North American Journal of Psychology, 4*(3), 395–404.

Richman, W. L., Kiesler, S., Weisband, S., & Fritz, D. (1999). A meta-analytic study of social desirability distortion in computer-administered questionnaires, traditional questionnaires, and interviews. *Journal of Applied Psychology, 84*(5), 754–775.

Ridenour, T. A., Treloar, J. H., & Dean, R. S. (2003). Utility analysis for clinical decision-making in small treatment settings. *International Journal of Neurosciences, 113*(3), 417–430.

Ridge, S., Campbell, W., & Martin, D. (2002). Striving towards an understanding of Conscious Identification: Its definition and its effects. *Counseling Psychology Quarterly, 15*(1), 91–105.

Rieke, M. L., & Guastello, S. J. (1995). Unresolved issues in honesty and integrity testing. *American Psychologist, 50,* 458–459.

Riethmiller, R. J., & Handler, L. (1997). The great figure drawing controversy: The integration of research and clinical practice. *Journal of Personality Assessment, 69,* 488–496.

Riggio, R. E., Murphy, S. E., Pirozzolo, F. J. (Eds.) (2002). *Multiple intelligences and leadership.* Mahwah, NJ: Erlbaum.

Righetti-Veltema, M., Bousquet, A., & Manzano, J. (2003). Impact of postpartum depressive symptoms on mother and her 18-month-old infant. *European Child and Adolescent Psychiatry, 12*(2), 75–83.

Ritzler, B. A., & Alter, B. (1986). Rorschach teaching in APA-approved clinical graduate programs: Ten years later. *Journal of Personality Assessment, 50,* 44–49.

Ritzler, B. A., Sharkey, K. J., & Chudy, J. F. (1980). A comprehensive projective alternative to the TAT. *Journal of Personality Assessment, 44,* 358–362.

Rizza, M. G., McIntosh, D. E., & McCunn, A. (2001). Profile analysis of the Woodcock-Johnson III Tests of Cognitive Abilities with gifted students. *Psychology in the Schools, 38*(5), 447–455.

Roberts, J. S., Laughlin, J. E., & Wendel, D. H. (1999). Validity issues in the Likert and Thurstone approaches to attitude measurement. *Educational and Psychological Measurement, 59*(2), 211–233.

Robins, R. W., Gosling, S. D., & Craik, K. H. (1999). An empirical analysis of trends in psychology. *American Psychologist, 54,* 117–128.

Roderiques, A. B. (2002). A comparison of ability-achievement discrepancy models for identifying learning disabilities. *Dissertation Abstracts International, 62,* 8A. (UMI No. 3022757)

Rodger, S. (1994). A survey of assessments used by paediatric occupational therapists. *Australian Occupational Therapy Journal, 41,* 137–142.

Rodger, S. C. (2002). Teacher clarity and student anxiety: An aptitude-treatment interaction experiment. *Dissertation Abstracts International: Section B. The Physical Sciences and Engineering, 63,* 4B.

Roe, A., & Klos, D. (1969). Occupational classification. *Counseling Psychologist, 1,* 84–92.

Roe, A., & Seigelman, M. (1964). The origin of interests. Washington, DC: American Personnel and Guidance Association.

Roeckelein, J. E. (2002). A demonstration of undergraduate students' first impression and their ratings of pathology. *Psychological Reports, 90*(2).

Rogers, C. R. (1961). *On becoming a person.* Boston: Houghton Mifflin.

Rogers, C. R. (1959a). A tentative scale for the measurement of process in psychotherapy. In E. A. Rubinstein & M. B. Parloff (Eds.), *Research in psychotherapy.* Washington, DC: American Psychological Association.

Rogers, C. R. (1959b). A theory of therapy, personality, and interpersonal relationships, as developed in the client-centered framework. In S. Koch (Ed.), *Psychology: A study of science* (Vol. 3). New York: McGraw-Hill.

Rogers, C. R. (1980). *A way of being.* Boston: Houghton Mifflin.

Roid, G. H. (2003a). *Stanford Binet Intelligence Scales* (5th ed.) Itasca, IL: Riverside.

Roid, G. H. (2003b). *Stanford Binet Intelligence Scales* (5th ed.), Examiners Manual. Itasca, IL: Riverside.

Roid, G. H. (2003c). *Stanford Binet Intelligence Scales* (5th ed.), Technical Manual. Itasca, IL: Riverside.

Rolland, J. P., Parker, W. D., & Stumpf, H. (1998). A psychometric examination of the French translations of the NEO-PI-R and NEO-FFI. *Journal of Personality Assessment, 71,* 269–291.

Rollnick, J. D., Borsutsky, M., Huber, T. J., Mogk, H., Seifert, J., Emrich, H. M., & Schneider, U. (2002). Short-term cognitive improvement in schizophrenics treated with typical and atypical neuroleptics. *Neuropsychobiology, 45*(2), 74–80.

Roscoe, A. H. (1993). Heart rate as a psychophysiological measure for in-flight workload assessment. *Ergonomics, 36*(9), 1055–1062.

Rose, C. L., Murphy, L. B., Byard, L., & Nikzad, K. (2002). The role of Big Five personality factors in vigilance performance and workload. *European Journal of Personality, 16*(3) 185–200.

Rosenberg, M. (1965). *Society and the adolescent self-image.* Princeton, New Jersey: Princeton University Press.

Rosenfeld, P., Doherty, L. M., Vicino, S. M., Kantor, J., et al. (1989). Attitude assessment in organizations: Testing three microcomputer-based survey systems. *Journal of General Psychology, 116*, 145–154.

Rosenstein, R., & Glickman, A. S. (1994). Type size and performance of the elderly on the Wonderlic Personnel Test. *Journal of Applied Gerontology, 13*(2), 185–192.

Rosenthal, R. (1966). *Experimenter effects in behavioral research.* New York: Appleton-Century-Crofts.

Rosenthal, R. (2002a). *Experimenter and clinician effects in scientific inquiry and clinical practice.* Washington, DC: American Psychological Assocation.

Rosenthal, R. (2002b). *The Pygmalion effect and its mediating mechanisms.* San Diego, CA: Academic Press.

Rosenthal, R., & Fode, K. L. (1963). The effects of experimenter bias on the performance of the albino rat. *Behavioral Science, 8*, 183–189.

Rosenthal, R., & Jacobson, L. (1968). *Pygmalion in the classroom.* New York: Holt, Rinehart & Winston.

Rosenthal, R., & Rosnow, R. L. (1991). *Essentials of behavioral research: Method and data analysis* (2nd ed.). New York: McGrawHill.

Rosenthal, R., Rosnow, R. L., & Rubin, D. B. (2000). *Contrasts and effect sizes in behavioral research: A correlational approach.* New York: Cambridge University Press.

Rosner, J. (2003). On white preferences. *The Nation*, April 14, 2003.

Ross, G., & Lawson, K. (1997). Using the Bayley-II: Unresolved issues in assessing the development of prematurely born children. *Journal of Developmental and Behavioral Pediatrics, 18*, 109–111.

Roth, P. L., Huffcutt, A. I., & Bobko, P. (2003). Ethnic group differences in measures of job performance: A new meta-analysis. *Journal of Applied Psychology, 88*(4), 694–706.

Rothstein, H. R. (2003). *Progress is our most important product: Contributions of validity generalization and meta-analysis to the development and communication of knowledge in I/O psychology.* Mahwah, NJ: Erlbaum.

Rotter, J. B. (1967). A new scale for the measurement of interpersonal trust. *Journal of Personality, 35*, 651–665.

Rotter, J. B., & Rafferty, J. E. (1950). *Manual: The Rotter Incomplete Sentences Blank.* San Antonio, TX: Psychological Corporation.

Roy, D. D., & Deb, N. C. (1999). Item-total-score correlations of state anxiety inventory across different months in Antarctic expedition. *Psychological Studies, 44*(1–2), 43–45.

Roznowski, M., & Reith, J. (1999). Examining the measurement quality of tests containing differentially functioning items: Do biased items result in poor measurement? *Educational and Psychological Measurement, 59*, 248–269.

Rubin, Z. (1970). Measurement of romantic love. *Journal of Personality and Social Psychology, 16*, 265–273.

Rubin, Z. (1973). *Liking and loving: An invitation to social psychology.* New York: Holt, Rinehart & Winston.

Rubin, Z. (1979, February 21). Los Angeles says it with love on a scale. *Los Angeles Times.*

Rubio, D. M., Berg-Weger, M., Tebb, S. S., Lee, E. S., & Rauch, S. (2003). Objectifying content validity: Conducting a content validity study in social work research. *Social Work Research, 27*(2), 94–104.

Rudner, L. & Gagne, P. (2001). *An overview of three approaches to scor-*

ing written essays by computer. (Report No. EDO-TM-01-09) College Park, MD: ERIC Clearinghouse on Assessment and Evaluation (ERIC Document Reproduction Service No. ED458290)

Rudner, L. M. (1998). Online, interactive, computer adaptive testing tutorial. ERIC Clearinghouse on Assessment and Evaluation. Retrieved April 9, 2003 from http://ericae. net/scripts/cat.

Ruisel, I. (2001). Dichotomy in intelligence. *Studia Psychologica, 34*(4), 255–273.

Rush, A. J. (2003). Toward an understanding of bipolar disorder and its origin. *Journal of Clinical Psychiatry, 64*(16) 4–8.

Rushton, J. P. (1991). Do r-K strategies underlie human race differences? *Canadian Psychology, 32*, 29–42.

Russell, E. W. (2000). The application of computerized scoring programs to neuropsychological assessment. In R. D. Vanderploeg (Ed.), *Clinician's guide to neuropsychological assessment* (pp. 483–515). Mahwah, NJ: Erlbaum.

Russell, L. B. (1986). *Is prevention better than cure?* Washington, DC: Brookings Institution.

Russo, A., & Warren, S. H. (1999). Collaborative test taking. *College Teaching, 47*, 18.

Rutter, M., Thorpe, K., Greenwood, R., Northstone, K., & Golding, J. (2003). Twins as a natural experiment to study the causes of mild language delay. *Journal of Child Psychology and Psychiatry and Allied Disciplines, 44*(3), 326–341.

Ryan, J. M., & DeMark, S. (2002). Variation in achievement scores related to gender, item format, and content area tested. In G. Tindal & T. M. Haladyna (Eds.), *Large-scale assessment programs for all students: Validity, technical adequacy, and implementation* (pp. 67–88). Mahwah, NJ: Erlbaum.

Ryan, J. J., Paolo, A. M., & Van Fleet, J. N. (1994). Neurodiagnostic implications of abnormal verbal-performance IQ discrepancies on the WAIS-R: A comparison with the standardization sample. *Archives of Clinical Neuropsychology, 9*(3), 251–258.

Ryan, J. J., Sattler, J. M., & Lopez, S. J. (2000). Age effects in Wechsler Adult Intelligence Scale-III subtests. *Archives of Clinical Neuropsychology, 15*(4), 311–317.

Saccuzzo, D. P. (1975). Canonical correlation as a method of assessing the correlates of good and bad therapy hours. *Psychotherapy: Theory, Research and Practice, 12,* 253–256.

Saccuzzo, D. P. (1977). The practice of psychotherapy in America: Issues and trends. *Professional Psychology, 8,* 297–306.

Saccuzzo, D. P. (1981). Input capability and speed of processing in mental retardation: A reply to Stanovich and Purcell. *Journal of Abnormal Psychology, 90,* 172–174.

Saccuzzo, D. P. (1993). Measuring individual differences in cognition in schizophrenia and other disordered states: Backward masking paradigm. In D. K. Detterman (Ed.), *Individual differences and cognition: Current topics in human intelligence* (Vol. 3) (pp. 219–237). Norwood, NJ: Ablex.

Saccuzzo, D. P. (1994, August). *Coping with complexities of contemporary psychological testing: Negotiating shifting sands.* Invited presentation for the G. Stanley Hall Lecture Series, American Psychological Association 102nd Annual Meeting, Los Angeles.

Saccuzzo, D. P. (1999). Still crazy after all these years: California's persistent use of the MMPI as character evidence in criminal cases. *University of San Francisco Law Review, 33,* 379–400.

Saccuzzo, D. P., & Braff, D. L. (1981). Early information processing deficits in schizophrenia: New findings using schizophrenic subgroups and manic controls. *Archives of General Psychiatry, 38,* 175–179.

Saccuzzo, D. P., & Braff, D. L. (1986). Information-processing abnormalities in schizophrenia and psychotic patients: Trait and state dependent components. *Schizophrenia Bulletin, 12,* 447–458.

Saccuzzo, D. P., Braff, D. L., Shine, A., & Lewandowski, D. G. (1981, April). *A differential WSC pattern in the retarded as a function of sex and race.* Paper presented at the meeting of the Western Psychological Association, Los Angeles.

Saccuzzo, D. P., Cadenhead, K., & Braff, D. L. (1996). Backward versus forward visual masking deficits in schizophrenia patients: Appear to be centrally not peripherally mediated. *American Journal of Psychiatry, 153,* 1564–1570.

Saccuzzo, D. P., Hirt, M., & Spencer, T. J. (1974). Backward masking as a measure of attention in schizophrenia. *Journal of Abnormal Psychology, 83,* 512–522.

Saccuzzo, D. P., & Johnson, N. E. (1995). Traditional psychometric test and proportionate representation: An intervention and program evaluation study. *Psychological Assessment, 7*(2), 183–194.

Saccuzzo, D. P., & Johnson, N. E. (2000). *The 5-minute IQ test: Item characteristics and reliability.* San Diego, CA: Applications of Psychology to Law.

Saccuzzo, D. P., Johnson, N. E., & Guertin, T. L. (1994). Information processing in gifted versus nongifted African-American, Latino, Filipino, and white children: Speeded versus nonspeeded paradigms. *Intelligence, 19,* 219–243.

Saccuzzo, D. P., Johnson, N. E., & Guertin, T. (1995). Traditional psychometric tests and proportionate representation: An intervention and program evaluation study. *Psychological Assessment, 7,* 183–194.

Saccuzzo, D. P., Johnson, N. E., & Russell, G. (1992). Verbal versus performance IQs for gifted African-American, Caucasian, Filipino, and Hispanic children. *Psychological Assessment, 4,* 239–244.

Saccuzzo, D. P., & Kaplan, R. M. (1984). *Clinical psychology.* Boston: Allyn & Bacon.

Saccuzzo, D. P., Kerr, M., Marcus, A., & Brown, R. (1979). Input capability and speed of information processing in mental retardation. *Journal of Abnormal Psychology, 88,* 312–317.

Saccuzzo, D., Kewley, & Johnson, N., et al. (2003). *An examination of positive affect measures.* (Naval Health Research Center Rep. No. TCN 02109/D. I. 0118).

Saccuzzo, D. P., & Larson, G. E. (1987, November). *Analysis of test-retest reliability for a battery of cognitive speed tests* (Technical Report 88-10). San Diego, CA: Navy Personnel Research and Development Center.

Saccuzzo, D. P., Larson, G. E., & Rimland, B. (1986). Visual, auditory and reaction time approaches to the measurement of speed of information-processing and individual differences in intelligence. *Personality and Individual Differences, 2,* 659–668.

Saccuzzo, D. P., & Lewandowski, D. G. (1976). The WISC as a diagnostic tool. *Journal of Clinical Psychology, 32,* 115–124.

Saccuzzo, D. P., & Marcus, A. (1983). *Speed of visual information-processing improves with practice in mental retardation.* Paper presented at the 91st Annual Convention of the American Psychological Association, Anaheim, CA.

Saccuzzo, D. P., & Michael, B. (1984). Speed of information processing and structural limitations in retarded and dual diagnosis retarded-schizophrenic persons. *American Journal of Mental Deficiency, 89,* 187–194.

Saccuzzo, D. P., & Miller, S. (1977). Critical interstimulus interval in delusional schizophrenics and normals. *Journal of Abnormal Psychology, 86,* 261–266.

Saccuzzo, D. P., & Schubert, D. (1981). Backward masking as a measure of slow processing in the schizophrenia spectrum of disorders. *Journal of Abnormal Psychology, 90,* 305–312.

Saccuzzo, D. P., & Schulte, R. (1978). The value of a master's degree for the Ph.D. pursuing student in psychology. *American Psychologist, 33,* 862–864.

Sackett, P. R. (1998). Performance assessment in education and professional certification: Lessons for personnel selection? In E. Milton, D. Hakel, et al. (Eds.), *Beyond multiple choice: Evaluating alternatives to traditional testing for selection* (pp. 113–129). Mahwah, NJ: Erlbaum.

Sackett, P. R. (2003). *The status of validity generalization research: Key issues in drawing inferences from cumulative research findings.* Mahwah, NJ: Erlbaum.

Sackett, P. R., & Wilk, S. L. (1994). Within-group norming and other forms of score adjustment in pre-employment testing. *American Psychologist, 49,* 929–954.

Saklofske, D. H., Schwean, V. L., Yackulic, R. A., & Quinn, D. (1994). WISC-III and SV: FE performance of children with attention deficit hyperactivity disorder. *Canadian Journal of School Psychology, 10*(2), 167–171.

Saltzman, J., Strauss, E., Hunter, M., & Spellacy, F. (1998). Validity of the Wonderlic Personnel Test as a brief measure of intelligence in individuals referred for evaluation of head injury. *Archives of Clinical Neuropsychology, 13,* 611–616.

Sanders, C. E. (1997). Assessment during the preschool years. In G. D. Phye et al. (Eds.), *Handbook of classroom assessment: Learning achievement and adjustment. Educational psychology series* (pp. 227–264). San Diego, CA: Academic Press.

Sands, W. A., Waters, B. K., & McBride, J. R. (1997). *Computerized adaptive testing: From inquiry to operation.* Washington, DC: American Psychological Association.

Sanford, K. (1998). Memories of feel-ing misunderstood, and a schema of partner empathic responding: New scales for marital research. *Journal of Social and Personal Relationships, 15,* 490–501.

Sangwan, S. (2001). Ecological factors as related to I.Q. of children. *Psycho-Lingua, 31*(2), 89–92.

Sapp, M. (1999). *Test anxiety: Applied research, assessment, and treatment interventions* (2nd ed.). Lanham, MD: University Press of America.

Sarason, B. R., & Sarason, I. G. (1994). Assessment of social support. In S. A. Shumaker & S. M. Czajkowski, (Eds.), *Social support and cardiovascular disease: Plenum series in behavioral psychophysiology and medicine* (pp. 41–63). New York: Plenum.

Sarason, I. G. (1958). Effects on verbal learning of anxiety, reassurance, and meaningfulness of material. *Journal of Experimental Psychology, 56,* 472–477.

Sarason, I. G. (1959). Intellectual and personality correlates of test anxiety. *Journal of Abnormal and Social Psychology, 59,* 272–275.

Sarason, I. G. (1961). The effects of anxiety and threat on solution of a difficult task. *Journal of Abnormal and Social Psychology, 62,* 165–168.

Sarason, I. G. (1975). Test anxiety, attention, and the general problem of anxiety. In C. D. Spielberger & I. G. Sarason (Eds.), *Stress and anxiety* (Vol. 1). New York: Halsted.

Sarason, I. G., Levine, H. M., Bashhnan, R. B., & Sarason, B. R. (1983). Assessing social support: The social support questionnaire. *Journal of Personality and Social Psychology, 44,* 127–139.

Sarason, I. G., & Palola, E. G. (1960). The relationship of test and general anxiety, difficulty of task, and experimental instructions to performance. *Journal of Experimental Psychology, 59,* 185–191.

Sarason, I. G., & Sarason, B. R. (1999). *Abnormal psychology: The problem of maladaptive behavior* (9th ed.). Upper Saddle River, NJ: Prentice-Hall.

Sarason, I. G., Sarason, B. R., & Pierce, G. R. (1990). *Social support: An interactional view.* New York: Wiley.

Sarason, I. G., Smith, R. E., & Diener, E. (1975). Personality research: Components of variance attributable to the person and the situation. *Journal of Personality and Social Psychology, 3,* 199–204.

Sarouphim, K. M. (2002). DISCOVER in high school. *Journal of Secondary Gifted Education, 14*(1), 30–38.

Sattler, J. M. (1970). Racial "experimenter effects" in experimentation, testing, interviewing, and psychotherapy. *Psychological Bulletin, 73,* 137–160.

Sattler, J. M. (1973a). Examiners' scoring style, accuracy, ability, and personality scores. *Journal of Clinical Psychology, 29,* 38–39.

Sattler, J. M. (1973b). Intelligence testing of ethnic minority-group and culturally disadvantaged children. In L. Mann & D. Sabatino (Eds.), *The first review of special education* (Vol. 2). Philadelphia: JSE Press.

Sattler, J. M. (1973c). Racial experimenter effects. In K. S. Miller & R. M. Dreger (Eds.), *Comparative studies of blacks and whites in the United States.* New York: Seminar Press.

Sattler, J. M. (1977). The effects of therapist-client racial similarity. In A. S. Gurman & A. M. Razin (Eds.), *Effective psychotherapy. A handbook of research* (pp. 252–290). Elmsford, NY: Pergamon Press.

Sattler, J. M. (1979a, April). *Intelligence tests on trial: Larry P. et al. v. Wilson Riles et al.* Paper presented at the meeting of the Western Psychological Association, San Diego, CA.

Sattler, J. M. (1979b). Standard intelligence tests are valid for measuring the intellectual potential of urban children: Comments on pitfalls in the measurement of intelligence. *Journal of Psychology, 102,* 107–112.

Sattler, J. M. (1980, November). Intelligence tests on trial: An interview with Judges Robert F. Peckham and John F. Grady. *APA Monitor*, pp. 7–8.

Sattler, J. M. (1982). *Assessment of children's intelligence and special abilities*. Boston: Allyn & Bacon.

Sattler, J. M. (1988). *Assessment of children* (3rd ed.). San Diego, CA: Sattler.

Sattler, J. M. (1992). *Assessment of children* (4th ed.). San Diego, CA: J. M. Sattler.

Sattler, J. M. (1998). *Clinical and forensic interviewing of children and families: Guidelines for the mental health, education, pediatric, and child maltreatment fields*: San Diego, CA: Author.

Sattler, J. M. (2002). *Assessment of children: Behavioral and clinical applications* (4th ed.). La Mesa, CA: Jerome M. Sattler.

Sattler, J. M. (2004). *Assessment of children: WISC-IV and WPPSI-III SUPPLEMENT*. La Mesa, CA: Jerome M. Sattler.

Sattler, J. M., & Gwynne, J. (1982). Ethnicity and Bender Visual Motor Test performance. *Journal of School Psychology, 20*, 69–71.

Sattler, J. M., Hillix, W. A., & Neher, L. A. (1970). Halo effect in examiner scoring of intelligence test responses. *Journal of Consulting and Clinical Psychology, 34*, 172–176.

Sattler, J. M., & Theye, F. (1967). Procedural, situational, and interpersonal variables in individual intelligence testing. *Psychological Bulletin, 68*, 347–360.

Sattler, J. M., & Winget, B. M. (1970). Intelligence testing procedures as affected by expectancy and IQ. *Journal of Clinical Psychology, 26*, 446–448.

Satz, P., & Fletcher, J. M. (1981). Emergent trends in neuropsychology: An overview. *Journal of Consulting and Clinical Psychology, 49*, 851–865.

Saunders, B. T., & Vitro, F. T. (1971). Examiner expectancy and bias as a function of the referral process in cognitive assessment. *Psychology in the Schools, 8*, 168–171.

Savickas, M. L. (1999). The psychology of interests. In E. Mark, L. Savickas, E. Arnold, R. Spokane et al. (Eds.), *Vocational interests: Meaning, measurement, and counseling use* (pp. 19–56). Palo Alto, CA: Davies-Black.

Savickas, M. L. (2000). Assessing career decision making. In E. C. Edward Watkins, Jr., E. Vicki, L. Campbell, et al. (Eds.), *Testing and assessment in counseling practice* (2nd ed.) (pp. 429–477). Mahwah, NJ: Erlbaum.

Sawyer, J. (1966). Measurement and prediction, clinical and statistical. *Psychological Bulletin, 66*, 178–200.

Sawyer, M. G., Sarris, A., & Baghurst, P. (1992). The effect of computer-assisted interviewing on the clinical assessment of children. *Australian & New Zealand Journal of Psychiatry, 26*(2), 223–231.

Sawyer, M. G., Sarris, A., Quigley, R., & Baghurst, P. (1991). The attitude of parents to the use of computer-assisted interviewing in a child psychiatry service. *British Journal of Psychiatry, 157*, 675–678.

Schaefer, B. A., Koeter, M. W. J., Wouters, L., Emmelkamp, P. M. G., & Schene, A. H. (2003). What patient characteristics make clinicians recommend brief treatment? *Acta Psychiatrica Scandinavica, 107*(3) 188–196.

Schaefer, J. A., & Moos, R. H. (1996). Effects of work stressors and work climate on long-term care staff's job morale and functioning. *Research in Nursing and Health, 19*(1), 63–73.

Scheier, M. F., & Carver, C. S. (1985). Optimism, coping, and health: Assessment and implications of generalized outcome expectancies. *Health Psychology, 4*, 219–247.

Scheier, M. F., Carver, C. S., & Bridges, M. W. (1994). Distinguishing optimism from neuroticism (and trait anxiety, self-master, and self-esteem): A re-evaluation of the Life Orientation Test. *Journal of Personality and Social Psychology, 67*, 1063–1078.

Scheier, M. F., Weintraub, J. K., &

Carver, C. S. (1986). Coping with stress: divergent strategies of optimists and pessimists. *J Pers Soc Psychol, 51*(6), 1257–1264.

Scheuneman, J. D. (1981). New look at bars and aptitude tests. *New Directions in Testing and Measurement, 12*, 5–25.

Scheuneman, J. D. (1987). An experimental, exploratory study of causes of bias in test items. *Journal of Educational Measurement, 24*, 97–118.

Schleicher, A. & Tamassia C. (2000). *Measuring student knowledge and skills: The PISA Assessment of Reading, Mathematical, and Scientific Literacy*. Retrieved April 16, 2003, from www. pisa. oecd. org/ knowledge/home/intro.htm.

Schmidt, A. E. (2000). An approximation of a hierarchical logistic regression model used to establish the predictive validity of scores on a nursing licensure exam. *Educational & Psychological Measurement. 60*(3) 463–478.

Schmidt, F., & Hunter, J. (2003). *History, development, evolution, and impact of validity generalization and meta-analysis methods, 1975–2001.* Mahwah, NJ: Erlbaum.

Schmidt, F. L., & Hunter, J. E. (1983). Individual differences in productivity: An empirical test of estimates derived from studies of selection procedure utility. *Journal of Applied Psychology, 68*, 407–414.

Schmidt, F. L., Law, K., Hunter, J. E., Rothstein, H. R., et al. (1993). Refinements in validity generalization methods: Implications for the situational specificity hypothesis. *Journal of Applied Psychology, 78*, 3–12.

Schmidt, F. L., & Rothstein, H. R. (1994). Application of validity generalization to biodata scales in employment selection. In G. S. Stokes, M. D. Mumford, & W. A. Owens (Eds.), *Biodata handbook: Theory, research, and use of biographical information in selection and performance prediction* (pp. 237–260). Palo Alto, CA: CPP Books.

Schmidt, K. M., & Embretson, S. E. (2003). *Item response theory and measuring abilities.* New York: Wiley.

Schmitt, N. (1976). Social and situational determinants of interview decisions: Implications for the employment interview. *Personnel Psychology, 29,* 79–101.

Schmukle, S. C., Egloff, B., & Burns, L. R. (2002). The relationship between positive and negative affect in the Positive and Negative Affect Schedule. *Journal of Research in Personality, 36*(5) 463–475.

Schneider, L. M., & Briel, J. B. (1990). *Validity of the GRE: 1988–1989 Summary Report.* Princeton, NJ: Educational Testing Service.

Schneider, R. J., Goff, M., Anderson, S., & Borman, W. C. (2003). Computerized adaptive rating scales for measuring managerial performance. *International Journal of Selection & Assessment, 11*(2–3), 237–246.

Schoggen, P. (1979). Roger G. Barker and behavioral settings: A commentary. *Journal of Personality and Social Psychology, 37,* 2158–2160.

Scholz, U., Dona, B. G., Sud, S., & Schwarzer, R. (2002). Is general self-efficacy a universal construct? Psychometric findings from 25 countries. *European Journal of Psychological Assessment, 18*(3), 242–251.

Schrank, F. A., Flanagan, D. P., Woodcock, R. W., & Mascolo, J. T. (2002). *Essentials of WJ III cognitive abilities assessment.* New York: Wiley.

Schrank, F. A., McGrew, K. S., & Woodcock, R. W. (2001). *Technical abstract (Assessment service bulletin no. 2).* Itasca, IL: Riverside.

Schroeder, H. E., & Kleinsaser, L. D. (1972). Examiner bias: A determinant of children's verbal behavior on the WISC. *Journal of Consulting and Clinical Psychology, 39,* 451–454.

Schuerger, J. M. (1995). Career assessment and the Sixteen Personality Factor Questionnaire. *Journal of Career Assessment, 3,* 157–175.

Schuerger, J. M., Tait, E., & Tavernelli, M. (1982). Temporal stability of personality by questionnaire. *Journal of Personality and Social Psychology, 43,* 176–182.

Schulenberg, S. E., & Yutrzenka, B. A. (1999). The equivalence of computerized and paper-and-pencil psychological instruments: Implications for measures of negative affect. *Behavior Research Methods, Instruments and Computers, 31*(2), 315–321.

Schuler, H. (1993). Is there a dilemma between validity and acceptance in the employment interview? In B. Nevo & R. S. Jager (Eds.), *Educational and psychological testing: The test taker's outlook* (pp. 239–250). Gottingen, Germany: Huber.

Schultz, C. B., & Sherman, R. H. (1976). Social class, development, and differences in reinforcer effectiveness. *Review of Educational Research, 46,* 25–59.

Schwab-Stone, M., Fallon, T., Briggs, M., & Crowther, B. (1994). Reliability of diagnostic reporting for children aged 6–11 years: A test-retest study of the Diagnostic Interview Schedule for Children-Revised. *American Journal of Psychiatry, 151*(7), 1048–1054.

Schwartz, R., & Gottman, J. (1976). Toward a task analysis of assertive behavior. *Journal of Consulting and Clinical Psychology, 44,* 910–920.

Scott, L. H. (1981). Measuring intelligence with the Goodenough-Harris Drawing Test. *Psychological Bulletin, 89,* 483–505.

Scott, P., Burton, R. V., & Yarrow, M. (1967). Social reinforcement under natural conditions. *Child Development, 38,* 53–63.

Scott-Lennox, J. A., Wu, A. W., Boyer, J. G., & Ware, J. E., Jr. (1999). Reliability and validity of French, German, Italian, Dutch, and UK English translations of the Medical Outcomes Study HIV Health Survey. *Medical Care, 37*(9), 908–925.

Sechrest, L., Stickle, T. R., & Stewart, M. (1998). The role of assessment in clinical psychology. In A. Bellack, M. Hersen (Series Ed.), & C.

R. Reynolds (Vol. Ed.), *Comprehensive clinical psychology* (Vol. 4, Chap. 1). New York: Pergamon Press.

Segal, D. L. (1997). Structured Interviewing and DSM classification. In S. M. Turner & M. Hersen (Eds.), *Adult psychopathology and diagnosis* (3rd ed.) (pp. 24–57). New York: Wiley.

Segal, H. G., Westen, D., Lohr, N. E., & Silk, K. R. (1993). Clinical assessment of object relations and social cognition using stories told to the Picture Arrangement subtest of the WAIS-R. *Journal of Personality Assessment, 61*(1), 58–80.

Seguin, E. (1907). *Idiocy: Its treatment by the physiological method.* New York: Bureau of Publications, Teachers College, Columbia University. (Original work published 1866)

Self, P. A., & Horowitz, F. D. (1979). The behavioral assessment of the neonate: An overview. In J. D. Osofsky (Ed.), *Handbook of infant development.* New York: Wiley.

Seligmann, J., Coppola, V., Howard, L., & Lee, E. D. (1979, May 28). A really final exam. *Newsweek,* pp. 97–98.

Senior, C., Phillips, M. L., Barns, J., & David, A. S. (1999). An investigation into the perception of dominance from schematic faces: A study using the World-Wide Web. *Behavior Research Methods, Instruments and Computers, 31*(2), 341–346.

Sexton, M., Fox, N. L., & Hebel, J. R. (1990). Prenatal exposure to tobacco: II. Effects on cognitive functioning at age three. *International Journal of Epidemiology, 19,* 72–77.

Shaffer, D. (1994). Structured interviews for assessing children. *Journal of Child Psychology and Psychiatry and Allied Disciplines, 35* (4), 783–784.

Shaffer, L. (1953). Of whose reality I cannot doubt. *American Psychologist, 8,* 608–623.

Shaffer, T. W., & Erdberg, P. (1996, July). *Cooperative movement in the*

Rorschach response: A qualitative approach. Paper presented at the 15th International Congress of Rorschach and Projective Methods, Boston, MA.

Shaffer, T. W., Erdberg, P., & Horaian, J. (1999). Current nonpatient data for the Rorschach, WAI$-R, and MMPI-2. *Journal of Personality Assessment, 73,* 305–316.

Shakow, D., Hilgard, E. R., Kelly, E. L., Sanford, R. N., & Shaffer, L. F. (1947). Recommended graduate training in clinical psychology. *American Psychologist, 2,* 539–558.

Shapiro, S. K., & Simpson, R. G. (1994). Patterns and predictors of performance on the Bender-Gestalt and the Developmental Test of Visual Motor Integration in a sample of behaviorally and emotionally disturbed adolescents. *Journal of Psychoeducational Assessment, 12*(3), 254–263.

Sharkey, K. J., & Ritzler, B. A. (1985). Comparing diagnostic validity of the TAT and a new Picture Projective Test. *Journal of Personality Assessment, 49,* 406–412.

Shavelson, R. J., & Ruiz-Primo, M. A. (2000). On the psychometrics of assessing science understanding. In E. Joel, J. Mintzes, E. James, H. Wandersee, et al. (Eds.), *Assessing science understanding: A human constructivist view* (pp. 303–341). San Diego, CA: Academic Press.

Shaywitz, B. A., Fletcher, J. M., & Shaywitz, S. E. (1995). Defining and classifying learning disabilities and attention-deficit/hyperactivity disorder. *Journal of Child Neurology, 10,* S50–S57

Shermis, M. D., & Lombard, D. (1998). Effects of computer-based test administrations on test anxiety and performance. *Computers in Human Behavior, 14*(1) 111–123.

Shermis,M. D., Mzumara, H. R., & Bublitz, S. T. (2001). On test and computer anxiety: Test performance under CAT and SAT conditions. *Journal of Educational Computing Research, 24*(1) 57–75.

Sherry, A., Henson, R. K., & Lewis,

J. G. (2003). Evaluating the appropriateness of college-age norms for use with adolescents on the NEO Personality Inventory-Revised. *Assessment, 10*(1) 71–78.

Shibata, S. (2002). A Macintosh and Windows program for assessing body-image disturbance using adjustable image distortion. *Behavior Research Methods, Instruments, and Computers, 34*(1), 90–92.

Shibre, T. Kebede, D. Alem, A. Negash, A. Deyassa, N., Fekada, A. Fekada, D. Jacobsson, L., & Kullgren, G. (2003). Schizophrenia: Illness impact on family members in a traditional society—Rural Ethiopia. *Social Psychiatry & Psychiatric Epidemiology, 38*(1), 27–34.

Shiffman, S., Fischer, L. A., Paty, J. A., Gnys, M., et al. (1995). Drinking and smoking: A field study of their association. *Annals of Behavioral Medicine, 16*(3), 203–209.

Shimmel, J., & Langer, P. (2001). Raising the graduation bar for the schools: Expectations vs outcomes. *Psychological Reports, 89*(2), 317–325.

Shore, G. N., & Rapport, M. D. (1998). The Fear Survey Schedule for Children—Revised (FSSC-HI): Ethnocultural variations in children's fearfulness. *Journal of Anxiety Disorder, 12,* 437–461.

Shores, E. A., & Carstairs, J. R. (1998). Accuracy of the MMPI-2 computerized Minnesota Report in identifying fake-good and fake-bad response sets. *Clinical Neuropsychologist, 12,* 101–106.

Shrout, P. E., Spitzer, R. L., & Fleiss, J. L. (1987). Quantification of agreement in psychiatric diagnosis revisited. *Archives of General Psychiatry, 44*(2), 172–177.

Shull-Senn, S., Weatherly, M., Morgan, S. K., & Bradley-Johnson, S. (1995). Stability reliability for elementary-age students on the Woodcock-Johnson Psychoeducational Battery—Revised (Achievement section) and the Kaufman Test of Educational Achievement. *Psychology in the Schools, 32,* 86–92.

Shumaker, S. A., & Berzon, R. (1995). *The international assessment of health-related quality of life: Theory, translation, measurement and analysis.* New York: Oxford University Press.

Sidick, J. T., Barrett, G. V., & Doverspike, D. (1994). Three alternative multiple choice tests: An attractive option. *Personnel Psychology, 47,* 829–835.

Signer, B. R. (1991). CAI and at-risk minority urban high school students. *Psychology & Marketing, 8*(4) 243–258.

Sijtsma, K., & Verweij, A. C. (1999). Knowledge of solution strategies and IRT modeling of items for transitive reasoning. *Applied Psychological Measurement, 23*(1), 55–68.

Silva, J. M., & Jacobs, R. R. (1993). Performance as a function of increased minority hiring. *Journal of Applied Psychology, 78,* 591–601.

Silver, H., & Shlomo, N. (2001). Perception of facial emotions in chronic schizophrenia does not correlate with negative symptoms but correlates with cognitive and motor dysfunction. *Schizophrenia Research, 52*(3), 265–273.

Silver, N. C., & Dunlap, W. P. (1987). Averaging correlation coefficients: Should Fisher's Z transformation be used? *Journal of Applied Psychology, 72,* 146–148.

Simmons v. Hooks. (1994). 843 F. Supp. 1296 (E. D. Ark. 1994).

Sines, L. K. (1959). The relative contribution of four kinds of data to accuracy in personality assessment. *Journal of Counseling Psychology, 23,* 483–492.

Sines, J. O. (1970). Actuarial versus clinical prediction in psychopathology. *British Journal of Psychiatry, 116,* 129–144.

Singh, L. (1986). Standardization of n-power measuring instrument (T. A. T.). *Journal of Psychological Researches, 28,* 14–20.

Sinha, D. K. (1986). Relationships of graduation requirements and course offerings to Scholastic Aptitude Test performance of seniors in high schools. *Journal of Educational Research, 80,* 5–9.

Sireci, S. G. (1998). The construct of content validity. *Social Indicators Research, 45*(1–3), 83–117.

Sivas, F., Ercin, O., Tanyolac, O., Barca, N., Aydog, S., & Ozoran, K. (2003). The Nottingham health profile in rheumatoid arthritis: correlation with other health status measurements and clinical variables. *Rheumatol Int.*

Slack, W. V. & Slack, C. W. (1977). Talking to a computer about emotional problems: A comparative study. *Psychotherapy: Theory, Research & Practice, 14*(2), 156–164.

Sletten, I. W., Ulett, G., Altman, H., & Sundland, D. (1970). The Missouri Standard System of Psychiatry (SSOP): Computer generated diagnosis. *Archives of General Psychiatry, 23*(1) 73–79.

Smith, A. E., & Knight-Jones, E. B. (1990). The abilities of very low-birthweight children and their classroom controls. *Developmental Medicine and Child Neurology, 32,* 590–601.

Smith, B., & Sechrest, L. (1991). Treatment of aptitude X treatment interactions. *Journal of Consulting and Clinical Psychology, 59,* 233–244.

Smith, E. V., Jr., Wakely, M. B., De Kruif, R. E. L., & Swartz, C. W. (2003). *Optimizing rating scales for self-efficacy (and other) research.* Thousand Oaks, CA: Sage.

Smith, G. A., & Stanley, G. (1983). Clocking "g": Relating intelligence and measures of timed performance. *Intelligence, 7,* 353–358.

Smith, M., & George, D. (1994). Selection methods. In E. Cary, L. Cooper, E. Ivan, T. Robertson, et al. (Eds.), *Key reviews in managerial psychology: Concepts and research for practice* (pp. 54–96). New York: Wiley.

Smith, T. W., Pope, M. K., Rhodewalt, F., & Poulton, J. L. (1989). Optimism, neuroticism, coping, and symptom reports: An alternative interpretation of the life orientation

test. *Journal of Personality and Social Psychology, 56,* 640–648.

Smith, T. W., & Zurawski, R. M. (1983). Assessment of irrational beliefs: The question of discriminant validity. *Journal of Clinical Psychology, 39,* 976–979.

Snelbaker, A. J., Wilkinson, G. S., Robertson, G. J., & Glutting, J. J. (2001). Wide Range Achievement Test 3 (WRAT-3). In W. I. Dorfman & M. Hersen (Eds.), *Understanding psychological assessment. Perspective on individual differences* (pp. 259–274). New York: Kluwer Academic/Plenum.

Snow, J. H. (1998). Clinical use of the Benton Visual Retention Test for children and adolescents with learning disabilities. *Archives of Clinical Neuropsychology, 13,* 629–636.

Snow, R. E. (1969). Review of Pygmalion in the Classroom by R. Rosenthal and L. Jacobson. *Contemporary Psychology, 14,* 197–199.

Snow, R. E. (1991). Aptitude treatment interaction as a framework for research on individual differences in psychotherapy. *Journal of Consulting and Clinical Psychology, 59,* 205–216.

Snyder, C. R., Harris, C., Anderson, J. R., Holleran, S. A., Irving, L. M., Sigmon, S. T., Yoshinobu, L., Gibb, J., Langelle, C., & Harney, P. (1991). The will and the ways: Development and validation of an individual difference measure of hope. *Journal of Personality and Social Psychology, 60,* 570–585.

Snyder, C. R., Shorey, H. S., Cheavens, J., Pulvers, K. M., Adams, V. G., & Wiklund, C. (2002). Hope and academic success in college. *Journal of Educational Psychology, 94*(4) 820–826.

Snyder, C. R., Sympson, S. C., Michael, S. T., & Cheavens, J. (2001). Optimism and hope constructs: Variants on a positive expectancy theme. In E. C. Chang (Ed.), *Optimism & pessimism: Implications for theory, research, and practice,* p. 101–125. 395p.

Snyderman, M., & Rothman, S. (1987). Survey of expert opinion in intelligence and aptitude testing. *American Psychologist, 42,* 137–144.

Sohn, W. J. (2002). Using differential item functioning (DIF) procedures for investigating the cross-cultural equivalence of personality test. *Dissertation Abstracts International, 62,* 8B.

Sostek, A. M. (1978). Review of the Brazelton Neonatal Assessment Scale. In O. K. Buros (Ed.), *The eighth mental measurements yearbook* (Vol. 1). Highland Park, NJ: Gryphon Press.

Sousa, D. A. (2001). *How the brain learns: A classroom teacher's guide* (2nd ed.). Thousand Oaks, CA: Corwin Press.

Space, L. G. (1981). The computer as psychometrician. *Behavior Research Methods and Instrumentation, 13*(4), 595–606.

Spangler, W. D. (1992). Validity of questionnaire and TAT measures of need for achievement: Two meta-analyses. *Psychological Bulletin, 112,* 140–154.

Spearman, C. E. (1904). General intelligence objectively determined and measured. *American Journal of Psychology, 15,* 201–293.

Spearman, C. E. (1923). The *nature of intelligence and the principles of cognition.* London: Macmillan.

Spearman, C. E. (1927). *The abilities of man.* New York: Macmillan.

Sperry, R. W. (1968). Hemisphere deconnection and unity in conscious awareness. *American Psychologist, 23,* 723–733.

Spielberger, C. D., Anton, W. B., & Bedell, J. (1976). The nature and treatment of test anxiety. In M. Zuckerman & C. D. Spielberger (Eds.), *Emotions and anxiety: New concepts, methods and applications.* Hillsdale, NJ: Erlbaum.

Spielberger, C. D., Auerbach, S. M., Wadsworth, A. P., Dun, T. M., & Taulbee, E. S. (1975). Emotional reactions to surgery. *Journal of Consulting and Clinical Psychology, 40,* 33–38.

Spielberger, C. D., Foreyt, J. P., Reheiser, E. C., & Poston, W. S. C. (1998). Motivational, emotional, and personality characteristics of smokeless tobacco users compared with cigarette smokers. *Personality and Individual Differences, 25*(5), 821–832.

Spielberger, C. D., Gorsuch, R. L., & Lushene, R. E. (1970). *Manual for the State-Trait Anxiety Inventory.* Palo Alto, CA: Consulting Psychologists Press.

Spielberger, C. D., & Sydeman, S. J. (1994). State-Trait Anxiety Inventory and State-Trait Anger Expression Inventory. In M. E. Maruish (Ed.), *The use of psychological testing for treatment planning and outcome assessment* (pp. 292–321). Hillsdale, NJ: Erlbaum.

Spiers, P. A. (1982). The Luria Nebraska Neuropsychological Battery revisited: A theory in practice or just practicing? *Journal of Consulting and Clinical Psychology, 50,* 301–306.

Spilker, B. (1990). *Quality of life assessment in clinical trials.* New York: Raven Press.

Spilker, B. (Ed.). (1996). *Quality of life and pharmacoeconomics in clinical trials* (2nd ed.). New York: Raven Press.

Spirrison, C. L., & Choi, S. (1998). Psychometric properties of a Korean version of the revised NeoPersonality Inventory. *Psychological Reports, 83,* 263–274.

Spitzer, R. L., & Wakefield, J. C. (1999). DSM-IV diagnostic criterion for clinical significance: Does it help solve the false positives problem? *American Journal of Psychiatry, 156*(12), 1856–1864.

Spitzer, R. L., Williams, J. B. W., Gibbon, M., & First, M. B. (1990a). *Structured clinical interview for DSM-III-R—patient edition* (SCIDP, 9/1/89 version). Washington DC: American Psychiatric Press.

Spitzer, R. L., Williams, J. B. W., Gibbon, M., & First, M. B. (1990b). *Structured clinical interview for DSM-III-R—personality disorders* (SCID-II, 9/1/89 version). Washington, DC: American Psychiatric Press.

Spitzer, R. L., Williams, J. B. W., Gibbon, M., & First, M. B. (1992). The structured clinical interview for DSM-III-R (SCID). I: History, rationale, and description. *Arch Gen Psychiatry, 49*(8), 624–629.

Spokane, A. R., & Catalano, M. (2000). The Self-Directed Search: A theory-driven array of self-guiding career interventions. In E. C. Edward Watkins, Jr., E. Vicki, L. Campbell, et al. (Eds.), *Testing and assessment in counseling practice* (2nd ed.) (pp. 339–370). Mahwah, NJ: Erlbaum.

Squire, L. R., & Butters, N. (1984). *The neurosychology of memory.* New York: Guilford Press.

Srsic, C. S., Stimac, A. P., & Walsh, W. B. (2001). Self-Directed Search. Dordrecht, Netherlands: Kluwer Academic Publishers.

Stallones, R. A., (1983). Ischemic heart disease and lipids in blood and diet. *Annual Review of Nutrition, 3,* 155–185.

Stankov, L. (2003). Complexity in human intelligence. In Sternberg, R. J., Lautrey, J., (Eds.), *Models of intelligence: International perspectives.* (27-42). Washington, DC: American Psychological Association.

Stanley, J. C. (1971). Reliability. In R. L. Thorndike (Ed.), *Educational measurement.* Washington, DC: American Council on Education.

Stannard, L., Wolfgang, C. H., Jones, I., & Phelps, P. (2001). A longitudinal study of the predictive relations among construction play and mathematical achievement. *Early Child Development and Care, 167,* 115–125.

Statistical Package for the Social Sciences. (1995). *Statistical Package for the Social Sciences reference guide.* Chicago: Author.

Steadman, H. J., Mulvey, E. P., Monahan, J., Robbins, P. C., Appelbaum, P. S., Grisso, T., Roth, L. H., & Silver, E. (1998). Violence by people discharged from acute psychiatric inpatient facilities and by others in the same neighborhoods. *Archives of General Psychiatry, 55*(5), 393–401.

Steele, C. M. (1997). A threat in the air: How stereotypes shape intellectual identity and performance. *American Psychologist, 52*(6), 613–629.

Steele, C. M., & Aronson, J. (1995). Stereotype threat and the intellectual test performance of African Americans. *Journal of Personality and Social Psychology, 69*(5), 797–811.

Steele, C. M., & Aronson, J. (1998). Stereotype threat and the test performance of academically successful African Americans. In E. C. Jencks, E. M. Phillips, et al. (Eds.), *The black-white test score gap* (pp. 401–427). Washington, DC: American Psychological Association.

Steele, C. M., & Aronson, J. A. (2004). Stereotype threat does not live by Steele and Aronson (1995) alone. *American Psychologist, 59*(1), 47–48.

Steele, C. M., & Davies, P. G. (2003). Stereotype threat and employment testing: A commentary. *Human Performance, 16*(3), 311–326.

Steinberg, L., & Thissen, D. (1995). Item response theory in personality research. In P. E. Shrout & S. T. Fiske (Eds.), *Personality research, methods, and theory: A festschrift honoring Donald W. Fiske.* Hillsdale, NJ: Erlbaum.

Stein, D. J., Hollander, E., & ebrary Inc. (2002). *Anxiety disorders comorbid with depression social anxiety disorder, post-traumatiac stress disorder, generalized anxiety disorder, and obsessive-compulsive disorder.* Florence, KY: Taylor & Francis.

Stell v. Savannah-Chatham County Board of Education. (1964). 210 F. Supp. 667, 668 (S.D. Ga. 1963), rev'd 333 F.2d 55 (5th Cir. 1964), cert denied, 379 U.S. 933 (1964).

Stephenson, W. (1953). *The study of behavior.* Chicago: University of Chicago Press.

Steptoe, A., & Johnston, D. (1991). Clinical applications of cardiovascular assessment. *Psychological Assessment: A Journal of Consulting and Clinical Psychology, 3,* 337–349.

Stern, W. (1912). *Die psychologische Methoden der Intelligenzprufung.* Leipzig, Germany: Barth.

Sternberg, R. J. (1984). The Kaufman Assessment Battery for Children: An information processing analysis and critique. *Journal of Special Education, 180,* 269–279.

Sternberg, R. J. (1985). *Beyond IQ: A triarchic theory of human intelligence.* New York: Cambridge University Press.

Sternberg, R. J. (1986). *Intelligence applied: Understanding and increasing your intellectual skills.* San Diego, CA: Harcourt Brace Jovanovich.

Sternberg, R. J. (1988). *The triarchic mind: A theory of human intelligence.* New York: Viking.

Sternberg, R. J. (1991). Death, taxes, and bad intelligence tests. *Intelligence, 15,* 257–269.

Sternberg, R. J. (2001). Successful intelligence: Understanding what Spearmann had rather than what he studied. In J. M. Collis & S. Messick (Eds.), *Intelligence and personality: Bridging the gap in theory and measurement* (pp. 347–373). Mahwah, NJ: Erlbaum.

Sternberg, R. J., & Gardner, M. K. (1982). A componential interpretation of the general factor in human intelligence. In H. J. Eysenck (Ed.), *A model for intelligence.* New York: Springer-Verlag.

Sternberg, R. J., & Williams, W. M. (1997). Does the Graduate Record Examination predict meaningful success in the graduate training of psychologists? *American Psychologist, 52,* 630–641.

Stevens, K. B., & Price, J. R. (1999). Adult reading assessment: Are we doing the best with what we have? *Applied Neuropsycholology, 6*(2), 68–78.

Stevens, M. C., Kaplan, R. F., & Hesselbrock, V. M. (2003). Executive-cognitive functioning in the development of antisocial personality disorder. *Addictive Behaviors, 28*(2), 285–300.

Stevens, S. S. (1966). A metric for the social consensus. *Science, 151,* 530–541.

Stevenson, J. D. (1986). Alternate form reliability and concurrent validity of the PPVT-R for referred rehabilitation agency adults. *Journal of Clinical Psychology, 42,* 650–653.

Steward, R. J., Gimenez, M. M., & Jackson, J. D. (1995). A study of personal preferences of successful university students as related to race/ethnicity, and sex: Implications and recommendations for training, practice, and future research. *Journal of College Student Development, 36,* 123–131.

Stewart, A. L., & Ware, J. E. (Eds.). (1992). *Measuring functioning and well-being: The medical outcomes study approach.* Durham, NC: Duke University Press.

Stinchfield, R. (2003). *Reliability, validity, and classification accuracy of a measure of DSM-IV diagnostic criteria for pathological gambling.* Washington, DC: American Psychiatric Association.

Stoelhorst, G. M. S. J., Rijken, M., Martens, S. E., van Zwieten, P. H. T., Feenstra, J., Zwinderman, A. H., Wit, J.-M., & Veen, S. (2003). Developmental outcome at 18 and 24 months of age in very preterm children: A cohort study from 1996-1997. *Early Human Development, 72*(2), 83–95.

Stokols, D. (1978). Environmental psychology. *Annual Review of Psychology, 29,* 253–295.

Stokols, D. (1992). Establishing and maintaining healthy environments: Toward a social ecology of health promotion. *American Psychologist, 47*(l), 6–22.

Stokols, D. (2000). *Theory development in environmental psychology: A prospective view.* Dordrecht, Netherlands: Kluwer Academic Publishers.

Stokols, D., Clitheroe, C., & Zmuidzinas, M. (2002). *Qualities of work environments that promote perceived support for creativity.* Mahwah, NJ: Erlbaum.

Stone, A. A. (1995). Measurement of affective response. In S. Cohen, R. C. Kessler, & L. U. Gordon (Eds.), *Measuring stress: A guide for health and social scientists* (pp. 148–171). New York: Oxford University Press.

Stone, A. A., Broderick, J. E., et al. (2004). Understanding recall of weekly pain from a momentary assessment perspective: Absolute agreement, between- and within-person consistency, and judged change in weekly pain. *Pain, 107*(1–2), 61–69.

Stone, A. A., Broderick, J. E., Schwartz, J. E., Shiffman, S., Litcher-Kelly, L., & Calvanese, P. (2003). Intensive momentary reporting of pain with an electronic diary: Reactivity, compliance, and patient satisfaction. *Pain, 104*(1–2), 343–351.

Stone, A. A., Kennedy-Moore, E., & Neale, J. M. (1995). Association between daily coping and end-of-day mood. *Health Psychology, 14*(4), 341–349.

Stone, A. A., & Shiffman, S. (1994). Ecological momentary assessment (EMA) in behavioral medicine. *Annals of Behavioral Medicine, 16*(3), 199–202.

Stone, A. A., Shiffman, S. S., & DeVries, M. W. (1999). Ecological momentary assessment. In E. D. Kahneman, E. E. Diener, et al. (Eds.), *Well-being: The foundations of hedonic psychology* (pp. 26– 39). New York: Russell Sage Foundation.

Stone, A. A., Shiffman, S., Schwartz, J. E., Broderick, J. E., & Hufford, M. R. (2003). Patient compliance with paper and electronic diaries. *Controlled Clinical Trials, 24*(2), 182–199.

Stone, V. E., Catania, J. A., & Binson, D. (1999). Measuring change in sexual behavior: Concordance between survey measures. *Journal of Sex Research, 36*(1), 102.

Stout, W. (2002). Psychometrics: From practice to theory and back:

15 years of nonparametric multidimensional IRT, DIF/test equity, and skills diagnostic assessment. *Psychometrika, 67*(4), 485–518.

Strack, S., Choca, J. P., & Gurtman, M. B. (2001). Circular structure of the MCMI-III personality disorder scales. *Journal of Personality Disorders, 15* (3), 263–274.

Strassberg, D. S. (1997). A cross-national validity study of four MMPI-2 content scales. *Journal of Personality Assessment, 69,* 596–606.

Strassberg, D. S., Ross, S., & Todt, E. H. (1995). MMPI performance among women with bulimia: A cluster-analytic study. *Addictive Behaviors, 20*(1), 137–140.

Strauss, M. E., & Brandt, J. (1990). Are there neuropsychologic manifestations of the gene for Huntington's disease in asymptomatic, at-risk individuals? *Archives of Neurology, 47,* 905–908.

Strauss, M., Lessen-Firestone, J., Starr, R., Jr., & Ostrea, E., Jr. (1975). Behavior of narcotics-addicted newborns. *Child Development, 46,* 887–893.

Strauss, S. G., Miles, J. A., & Levesque, L. L. (2001). The effects of videoconference, telephone, and face-to-face media on interviewer and applicant judgements in employment interviews. *Journal of Management, 27*(3), 363–381.

Stricker, L. J., Rock, D. A., Pollack, J. M., & Wenglinsky, H. H. (2002). *Measuring educational disadvantage of SAT candidates.* (College Board Research Report No. 2002-1). College Entrance Examination Board, New York.

Strong, E. K., Jr., & Campbell, D. P. (1966). *Manual for Strong Vocational Interest Blank.* Stanford, CA: Stanford University Press.

Stumpf, H., & Stanley, J. C. (2002). Group data on high school grade point average and scores on academic aptitude tests as predictors of institutional graduation rates. *Educational and Psychological Measurement, 62*(6), 1042–1052.

Sue, S. (1999). Science, ethnicity, and bias. *American Psychologist, 54*(12), 1070–1077.

Sue, S. (2003). *Science, ethnicity, and bias: Where have we gone wrong?* Washington, DC: American Psychological Association.

Suinn, R. M. (1969). The STABS, a measure of test anxiety for behavior therapy: Normative data. *Behaviour Research and Therapy, 7,* 335–339.

Summerfeldt, L. J., & Antony, M. M. (2002). Structured and semistructured diagnostic interviews. In M. M. Antony & D. H. Barlow (Eds.), *Handbook of assessment and treatment planning for psychological disorders* (pp. 3–37). New York: Guilford Press.

Super, D. E. (1953). A theory of vocational development. *American Psychologist, 8,* 185–190.

Super, D. E., & Hall, D. T. (1978). Career development: Exploitation and planning. *Annual Review of Psychology, 29,* 333–372.

Sutherland, S. (1992). *Irrationality: Why we don't think straight!* New Brunswick, NJ: Rutgers University Press.

Suzuki, L. A., & Valencia, R. R. (1997). Race-ethnicity and measured intelligence: Educational implications. *American Psychologist, 52,* 1103–1114.

Svensson, L., & Oest, L. G. (1999). Fears in Swedish children: A normative study of the Fear Survey Schedule for Children–Revised. *Scandinavian Journal of Behaviour Therapy, 28,* 23–36.

Swallen, K. C. (2003). Race and genomics. *N Engl J Med, 348*(25), 2581–2582.

Swanda, R. M., Haaland, K. Y., & LaRue, A. (2000). Clinical neuropsychology and intellectual assessment of adults. In B. J. Sadock & V. A. Sadock (Eds.), *Comprehensive Textbook of Psychiatry* (Vol. 1) (pp. 689–702). Philadelphia: Lippincott Williams & Wilkins.

Sweet, J. J., Wolfe, P., Sattlberger, E., Numan, B., Rosenfeld, J. P.,

Clingerman, S., & Nies, K. J. (2000). Further investigation of traumatic brain injury versus insufficient effort with the California Verbal Learning Test. *Archives of Clinical Neuropsychology, 15*(2), 105–113.

Sweet, R. C. (1970). Variations in the intelligence test performance of lower-class children as a function of feedback or monetary reinforcement. *Dissertation Abstracts International, 31*(2A), 648–649. (University Microfilms No. 70-37,21)

Sweet, S. A. (1999). *Data analysis with SPSS.* Boston: Allyn & Bacon.

Symonds, P. M. (1924). On the loss of reliability in ratings due to coarseness of the scale. *Journal of Experimental Psychology, 7,* 456–461.

Szasz, T. S. (1961). *The myth of mental illness.* New York: Harper & Row.

Tabachnick, B. G., & Fidell, L. S. (1989). *Using multivariate statistics* (2nd ed.). New York: Harper & Row.

Tabachnick, B. G., & Fidell, L. S. (1996). *Using multivariate statistics* (3rd ed.). New York: Harper-Collins.

Tallent, N. (1987). Computer-generated psychological reports: A look at the modern psychometrics machine. *Journal of Personality Assessment, 51*(1) 95–108.

Tan, U., & Tan, M. (1998). Curvilinear correlations between total testosterone levels and fluid intelligence in men and women. *International Journal of Neuroscience, 95,* 77–83.

Taplin, P. S., & Reid, J. B. (1973). Effects of instructional set and experimenter influence on observer reliability. *Child Development, 44,* 547–554.

Tatsuoka, K. K., & Tatsuoka, M. M. (1997). Computerized cognitive diagnostic adaptive testing: Effect on remedial instruction. *Journal of Educational Measurement, 34*(1) 3–21.

Taylor, C. W., Price, P. B., Richards, J. M., Jr., & Jacobsen, T. L. (1965).

An investigation of the criterion problem for a group of medical general practitioners. *Journal of Applied Psychology, 49*, 399–406.

Taylor, H. C., & Russell, J. T. (1939). The relationship of validity coefficients to the practical effectiveness of tests in selection: Discussion and tables. *Journal of Applied Psychology, 23*, 565–578.

Taylor, J., & Deane, F. P. (2002). *Development of a short form of the Test Anxiety Inventory (TAI)*. Washington, DC: Heldref.

Taylor, R. L., Sternberg, L., & Partenio, I. (1986). Performance of urban and rural children on the SOMPA: Preliminary investigation. *Perceptual and Motor Skills, 63*, 1219–1223.

Taylor, T. R. (1994). A review of three approaches to cognitive assessment, and a proposed integrated approach based on a unifying theoretical framework. *South African Journal of Psychology, 24*, 183–193.

Te'eni, D. R. (1998). Nomothetics and idiographics as antonyms: Two mutually exclusive purposes for using the Rorschach. *Journal of Personality Assessment, 70*, 232–247.

Tellegen, A. (2003). *Introducing the new MMPI-2 Restructured Clinical (RC) Scales—The first variant version of the clinical scales*. Minneapolis: University of Minnesota Press Test Division.

Temp, G. (1971). Test bias: Validity of the SAT for blacks and whites in thirteen integrated institutions. *Journal of Educational Measurement, 8*, 245–251.

Templer, D. I., Schmitz, S. P., & Corgiat, M. D. (1985). Comparison of the Stanford-Binet with the Wechsler Adult Intelligence Scale—Revised: Preliminary report. *Psychological Reports, 57*, 335–336.

Teng, E. L., Wimer, C., Roberts, E., Darnasio, A. R., Eslinger, P. J., Folstein, M. F., Tune, L. E., Whitehouse, P. J., Bardolph, E. L., & Chui, H. C. (1989). Alzheimer's dementia: Performance on parallel forms of the dementia assessment battery. *Journal of Clinical and Experimental Neuropsychology, 11*, 899–912.

Tennen, H., Affleck, G., & Tennen, R. (2002). Clipped feathers: The theory and measurement of hope. *Psychological Inquiry, 13*(4) 311–317.

Tenopyr, M. L. (1993). Construct validation needs in vocational behavior theories. *Journal of Vocational Behavior, 43*(1), 84–89.

Tenopyr, M. L. (1998). Measure me not: The test taker's new bill of rights. In M. D. Hakel (Ed.), *Beyond multiple choice: Evaluating alternatives to traditional testing for selection* (pp. 17–22). Mahwah, NJ: Erlbaum.

Teplin, L. A., & Schwartz, J. (1989). Screening for severe mental disorder in jails: The development of the Referral Decision Scale. *Law and Human Behavior, 13*, 118.

Terman, L. M. (1916). *The measurement of intelligence*. Boston: Houghton Mifflin.

Terraciano, A., McCrae, R. R., & Costa, P. T. (2003). Factorial and construct validity of the Italian Positive and Negative Affect Schedule (PANAS). *European Journal of Psychological Assessment, 19*(2), 131–141.

Terrell, F., Taylor, J., & Terrell, S. L. (1978). Effects of type of social reinforcement on the intelligence test performance of lower-class black children. *Journal of Consulting and Clinical Psychology, 46*, 1538–1539.

Terrill, D. R., Friedman, D. G., Gottschalk, L. A., & Haaga, D. A. F. (2002). Construct validity of the Life Orientation Test. *Journal of personality Assessment, 79*(3), 550–563.

Thayer, P. W. (1992). Construct validation: Do we understand our criteria? *Human Performance, 5*, 97–108.

Thayer, P. W., & Kalat, J. W. (1998). Questionable criteria. *American Psychologist, 53*, 566.

The Psychological Corporation (2001). *Wechsler Individual Achievement Test*®*—Second Edition*. Retrieved July, 28, 2003 from: http://www.harcourt.com/bu_info/tpc.html.

The Psychological Corporation. (2003). *Technical Reports*. Retrieved July, 28, 2003 from: http://www.harcourt.com/bu_info/tpc.html.

The Status of the Teaching Profession 2003. Research Findings and Policy. Available online at www.cftl.org.

Thomas, J. C. & Selthon, L. (2003). Planning data collection and performing analysis. In J. C. Thomas & M. Hersen (Eds.), *Understanding research in clinical and counseling psychology*. (pp. 319–339). Mahwah, NJ: Erlbaum.

Thompson, D. E., & Thompson, T. A. (1982). Court standards for job analysis in test validation. *Personnel Psychology, 35*, 865–874.

Thorndike, E. L. (1904). *An introduction to the theory of mental and social measurements*. New York: Science Press.

Thorndike, E. L. (1920). A constant error in psychological rating. *Journal of Applied Psychology, 4*, 25–29.

Thorndike, E. L. (1921). Intelligence and its measurement: A symposium. *Journal of Educational Psychology, 12*, 123–147, 195–216.

Thorndike, R. L. (1968). Review of *Pygmalion in the Classroom* by R. Rosenthal and L. Jacobson. *American Educational Research Journal, 5*, 708–711.

Thorndike, R. L. (1971). Concepts of culture-fairness. *Journal of Educational Measurement, 8*, 63–70.

Thorndike, R. L. (1973). *Stanford-Binet Intelligence Scale, Form L-M, 1972 norms tables*. Boston: Houghton Mifflin.

Thorndike, R. L., Hagen, E. P., & Sattler, J. M. (1986). *Technical manual: Stanford-Binet Intelligence Scale: Fourth Edition*. Chicago: Riverside.

Thorndike, R. M. (1990a). Origins of intelligence and its measurement. *Journal of Psychoeducational Assessment, 8*, 223–230.

Thorndike, R. M. (1990b). Would the

real factors of the Stanford-Binet Fourth Edition please come forward? *Journal of Psychoeducational Assessment, 8,* 412–435.

Thorson, J. A., & Powell, F. C. (1996). Women, aging, and sense of humor. *Humor: International Journal of Humor Research, 9,* 169–186.

Thurstone, L. L. (1938). Primary mental abilities. *Psychometric Monographs, 1.*

Timbrook, R. E., & Graham, J. R. (1994). Ethnic differences on the MMPI-2? *Psychological Assessment, 6*(3), 212–217.

Timmerman, M. E., & Kiers, H. A. L. (2003). Four simultaneous component models for the analysis of multivariate time series from more than one subject to model intraindividual and interindividual differences. *Psychometrica, 68*(1), 105–121.

Tittle, C. K. (1983). Studies of the effects of career interest inventories: Expanding outcome criteria to include women's experience. *Journal of Vocational Behavior, 22,* 148–158.

Todd, M., H. Tennen, et al. (2004). Do we know how we cope? Relating daily coping reports to global and time-limited retrospective assessments. *Journal of Personal and Social Psychology, 86*(2), 310–319.

Torrance, E. P. (1970). Broadening concepts of giftedness in the 70's. *Gifted Child Quarterly, 14,* 199–208.

Torrance, E. P. (1977). *Discovery and nurturance of giftedness in the culturally different.* Reston, VA: Council for Exceptional Children.

Torre, E., Zeppegno, P., Usai, C., Torre, E. M., Artioli, P., Guaiana, G. & Olgiati, P. (2001). Burn-out: Quantitative aspects and personality styles: A study. *Minerva Psichiatrica, 42*(2), 83–89.

Tourangeau, R., Couper, M. P., & Steiger, D. M. (2003). Humanizing self-administration surveys: Experiments on social presence in Web and IVR surveys. *Computers in Human Behavior, 19*(1) 1–24.

Triandis, H. C., Dunnette, M. D., &

Hough, L. M. (1994). *Handbook of industrial and organizational psychology* (Vol. 4, 2nd ed.). Palo Alto, CA: Consulting Psychologists Press.

Tronick, E. Z. (1987). The neonatal behavioral assessment scale as a biomarker of the effects of environmental agents on the newborn. *Environmental Health Perspectives, 74,* 185–189.

Tronick, E., & Brazelton, T. B. (1975). Clinical uses of the Brazelton Neonatal Behavioral Assessment. In B. Friedlander, G. Sterritt, & G. Kirk (Eds.), *Exceptional infant* (Vol. 3). New York: Brunner/Mazel.

Trotter, M. A., & Endler, N. S. (1999). An empirical test of the interaction model of anxiety in a competitive equestrian setting. *Personality and Individual Differences, 27*(5), 861–875.

Truax, C. B., & Carkhuff, R. R. (1967). *Toward effective counseling and psychotherapy: Training and practice.* Chicago: Aldine Atherton.

Truax, C. B., & Mitchell, K. M. (1971). Research on certain therapist interpersonal skills in relation to process and outcome. In A. E. Bergin & S. L. Garfield (Eds.), *Handbook of psychotherapy and behavior change.* New York: Wiley.

Tryon, W. W. (1991). *Activity measurement in psychology and medicine.* New York: Plenum.

Tryon, W. W., & Bernstein, D. (2003). Understanding measurement. In J. C. Thomas & M. Hersen (Eds.), *Understanding research in clinical and counseling psychology.* (pp. 27–68). Mahwah, NJ: Erlbaum.

Tsatsanis, K. D., Dartnall, N., Cicchetti, D., Sparrow, S. S., Klin, A., & Volkmar, F. R. (2003). Concurrent validity and classification accuracy of the Leiter and Leiter-R in low-functioning children with autism. *Journal of Autism and Developmental Disorders, 33*(1), 23–30.

Tseng H. M., Tiplady, B., Macleod, H. A., & Wright, P. (1998). Computer anxiety: A comparison of pen-based personal digital assis-

tants, conventional computer and paper assessments of mood and performance. *British Journal of Psychological Society, 89*(4) 599–610.

Tucker, C. L., Slifer, K. J., & Dahlquist, L. M. (2001). Reliability and validity of the Brief Behavioral Distress Scale: A measure of children's distress during invasive medical procedures. *Journal of Pediatric Psychology, 26*(8) 513–523.

Tuel, B. D., & Betz, N. E. (1998). Relationships of career self-efficacy expectations to the Myers-Briggs Type Indicator and the Personal Styles Scales. *Measurement and Evaluation in Counseling and Development, 31,* 150–163.

Tukey, J. W. (1977). *Exploratory data analysis.* Reading, MA: Addison-Wesley.

Tulsky, D. S., & Rosenthal, M. (2003). Measurement of quality of life in rehabilitation medicine: Emerging issues. *Archives of Physical and Medical Rehabilitation, 84*(4 Suppl. 2), S1–2.

Tulsky, D., Zhu, J., & Ledbetter, M. (1997). *WAIS-III WMS-III technical manual.* San Antonio, TX: Psychological Corporation.

Turgeon, L., & Chartrand, E. (2003). Psychometric properties of the French Canadian version of the State-Trait Anxiety Inventory for Children. Thousand Oaks, CA: Sage.

Turkheimer, E. (1991). Individual and group differences in adoption studies of IQ. *Psychological Bulletin, 110,* 392–405.

Turner, C. F., Ku, L., Rogers, S. M., Lindberg, L. D., & Pleck, J. H. (1998). Adolescent sexual behavior, drug use, and violence: Increased reporting with computer survey technology. *Science, 280,* 867–873.

Turner, D. R. (1966). Predictive efficiency as a function of amount of information and level of professional experience. *Journal of Projective Techniques and Personality Assessment, 30,* 4–11.

Turner, J. A., Herron, L., & Weiner, P. (1986). Utility of the MMPI Pain Assessment Index in predicting outcomes after lumbar surgery. *Journal of Clinical Psychology, 42,* 764–769.

Turner, R. J. (1981). Social support as a contingency in psychological well-being. *Journal of Health and Social Behavior, 22,* 357–367.

Turpin, G. (1991). The psychophysiological assessment of anxiety disorders: Three-systems measurement and beyond. *Psychological Assessment: A Journal of Consulting and Clinical Psychology, 3,* 366–375.

Tyler, L. E. (1969). *The work of the counselor* (3rd ed.). New York: Appleton-Century-Crofts.

Tyler, L. E., & Walsh, W. B. (1979). *Tests and measurements* (3rd ed.). Englewood Cliffs, NJ: Prentice-Hall.

Ulrich, L., & Trumbo, D. (1965). The selection interview since 1949. *Psychological Bulletin, 63,* 100–116.

United States v. City of Buffalo. (1985). 37 U.S. 628 (W.D. N.Y. 1985).

Unruh, M., Miskulin, D., et al. (2004). Racial differences in health-related quality of life among hemodialysis patients. *Kidney International, 65*(4), 1482–1491.

Uutela, T., Hakala, M., & Kautiainen, H. (2003). Validity of the Nottingham Health Profile in a Finnish out-patient population with rheumatoid arthritis. *Rheumatology* (Oxford), 42(7), 841–845.

Vale, C. D., Keller, L. S., & Bentz, V. J. (1986). Development and validation of a computerized interpretation system for personnel tests. *Personnel Psychology, 39*(3) 525–542.

Valencia, R. R. (1988). The McCarthy Scales and Hispanic children: A review of psychometric research. *Hispanic Journal of Behavioral Sciences, 10,* 81–104.

Valencia, R. R., & Lopez, R. (1992). Assessment of racial and ethnic minority students: Problems and prospects. In M. Zeidner & R. Most (Eds.), *Psychological testing: An inside view.* Palo Alto, CA: Consulting Psychologists Press.

Valencia, R. R., Rankin, R. J., & Livingston, R. (1995). K-ABC content bias: Comparisons between Mexican American and white children. *Psychology in the Schools, 32,* 153–169.

van Baar, A. (1990). Development of infants of drug dependent mothers. *Journal of Child Psychology and Psychiatry and Allied Disciplines, 31,* 911–920.

van der Linden, W. J., Scrams, D. J., & Schnipke, D. L. (1999). Using response-time constraints to control for differential speededness in computerized adaptive testing. *Applied Psychological Measurement, 23*(3), 195–210.

Vandenburg, S. G., & Vogler, G. P. (1985). Genetic determinants of intelligence. In B. B. Wolman (Ed.), *Handbook of intelligence.* New York: Wiley.

Vandevijer, F. J. R., & Harsveld, M. (1994). The incomplete equivalence of the paper-and-pencil and computerized versions of the General Aptitude Test Battery. *Journal of Applied Psychology, 79*(6), 852–859.

Van Scotter, J., Motowidlo, S. J., & Cross, T. C. (2000). *Effects of task performance and contextual performance on systemic rewards.* Washington, DC: American Psychological Association.

Vansickle, T. R., Kimmel, C., & Kapes, J. T. (1989). Test equivalency of the computer-based paper-pencil versions of the Strong-Campbell Interest Inventory. *Measurement and Evaluation in Counseling and Development, 22*(2) 89–93.

Verschuren, W. M., Jacobs, D. R., Bloemberg, B. P., Kromhout, D., Menotti, A., Aravanis, C., Blackburn, H., Buzina, R., Dontas, A. S., Fidanza, F., & others. (1995). Serum total cholesterol and long-term coronary heart disease mortality in different cultures: Twenty-five-year follow-up of the seven countries study. *Journal of the American Medical Association,* 274(2), 131–136.

Vickers, D., Nettelbeck, T., & Wilson, R. J. (1972). Perceptual indices of performance: The measurement of "inspection time" and "noise" in the visual system. *Perception, 1,* 263–295.

A victory for affirmative action. (2003). *Lancet, 362*(9377), 1.

Vidal-Abarca, E., Reyes, H., Gilabert, R., Calpe, J., Soria, E., Graesser, A. C. (2002). ETAT: Expository test analysis tool. *Behavior Research Methods, Instruments, & Computers, 34*(1) 93–107.

Viet, C. T., & Ware, J. E. (1989). An improved test of the disaggregation hypothesis of job and life satisfaction. *Journal of Occupational Psychology, 62,* 33–39.

Vigil-Colet, A., & Codorniu-Raga, M. J. (2002). How inspection time and paper and pencil measures of processing speed are related to intelligence. *Personality & Individual Differences, 33*(7) 1149-1161.

Viglione, D. (1999). A review of recent research addressing the utility of the Rorschach. *Psychological Assessment, 11,* 251–265.

Viglione, D. J., & Hilsenroth, M. K. (2001). The Rorschach: Facts, fictions, and future. *Psychological Assessment, 13*(4), 452–471.

Vincelli, F., & Riva, G. (2000). Immersive virtual reality in clinical psychology and psychotherapy. *Rivista di Psichiatria, 35*(4) 153–162.

Vispoel, W. P., Rocklin, T. R., & Tianyou, W. (1994). Individual differences and test administration procedures: A comparison of fixed-item, computer-adaptive, and self-adaptive testing. *Applied Measurement in Education, 7*(1) 53–80.

Vlaeyen, J. W. S., de Jong, J. R., Onghena, P., Kerckhoffs-Hanssen, M., & Kole-Snijders, A. M. J. (2002). Can pain-related fear be reduced? The application of cognitive-behavioural exposure in vivo. *Pain Research and Management, 7,* 144–153.

Vraniak, D. (1997). Mapping contexts for supporting American Indian families of youth with disabilities. *Families, Systems and Health, 15*(3), 283–302.

Wagner, E. E., Alexander, R. A., Roos, G., & Adair, H. (1986). Optimum split-half reliabilities for the Rorschach: Projective techniques are more reliable than we think. *Journal of Personality Assessment, 50*, 107–112.

Wagner, E. E., & Flamos, O. (1988). Optimized split-half reliability for the Bender Visual Motor Gestalt Test: Further evidence for the use of the maximization procedure. *Journal of Personality Assessment, 52*, 454–458.

Wagner, P. A. (1994). Adaptations for administering the Peabody Picture Vocabulary Test—Revised to individuals with severe communications and motor dysfunctions. *Mental Retardation, 32*(2), 107–112.

Wagner, R. (1949). The employment interview: A critical review. *Personnel Psychology, 2*, 17–46.

Wagner, R. K. (1997). Intelligence, training, and employment. *American Psychologist, 52*(10), 1059–1069.

Wainer, H. (2000). *Computerized adaptive testing: A primer* (2nd ed.). Mahwah, NJ: Erlbaum.

Wainwright, D., & Calnan, M. (2002). *Work stress: The making of a modern epidemic*. Phildelphia: Open University Press.

Wald, J. & Taylor, S. (2000). Efficacy of virtual reality exposure therapy to treat driving phobia: A case report. *Journal of Behavior Therapy and Experimental Psychology, 31*(3–4) 249–257.

Waldman, I. D., Weinberg, R. A., & Scarr, S. (1994). Racial-group differences in IQ in the Minnesota Transracial Adoption Study: A reply to Levin and Lynn. *Intelligence, 19*, 29–44.

Walker, A. M., Rablen, R. A., & Rogers, C. R. (1960). Development of a scale to measure process changes in psychotherapy. *Journal of Clinical Psychology, 16*, 79–85.

Walker, M. T. (2001). Practical applications of the Rogerian perspective in post-modern psychotherapy. *Journal of Systematic Therapies, 20*(2), 41–57.

Walker, S., & Rosser, R. (1992). *Quality of life assessment: Key issues for the 1990s*. Dordrect, Netherlands: Kluwer Press.

Waller, N. G. (1999). Searching for structure in the MMPI. In S. E. Embretson & S. L. Hershberger (Eds.), *The new rules of measurement*. Mahwah, NJ: Erlbaum.

Walsh, W. B. (2003). *Counseling psychology and optimal human functioning*. Mahwah, N. J. : Erlbaum.

Ward, L. C. (1995). Correspondence of the MMPI-2 and MCMI-II male substance abusers. *Journal of Personality Assessment, 64*(2), 390–393.

Ward, L. C., & Perry, M. S. (1998). Measurement of social introversion by the MMPI-2. *Journal of Personality Assessment, 70*, 171–182.

Ward, T. J., et al. (1989). The effect of computerized tests on the performance and attitudes of college students. *Journal of Educational Computing Research, 5*, 327–333.

Wards Cove Packing Company v. Antonio. (1989). 490, U.S. 642.

Ware, J. E., Jr. (2000). SF-36 health survey update. *Spine, 25*(24), 3130–3139.

Ware, J. E., Jr. (2003). Conceptualization and measurement of health-related quality of life: Comments on an evolving field. *Archives of Physical and Medical Rehabilitation, 84*(4 Suppl. 2), S43–51.

Ware, J. E., Jr., Bayliss, M. S., Mannocchia, M., & Davis, G. L. (1999). Health-related quality of life in chronic hepatitis C: Impact of disease and treatment response. *Hepatology, 30*(2), 550–555.

Ware, J. E., Jr., & Gandek, B. (1998). Overview of the SF-36 Health Survey and the International Quality of Life Assessment (IQOLA) Project. *Journal of Clinical Epidemiology, 51*(11), 903–912.

Ware, J. E., & Kosinski, M. (2001). Interpreting SF-36 summary health measures: A response. *Quality of Life Research, 10*(5), 405–413, 415–420.

Ware, J. E., Jr., Kosinski, M., Bayliss, M. S., McHorney, C. A., Rogers, W. H., & Raczek, A. (1995). Comparison of methods for the scoring and statistical analysis of SF-36 health profile and summary measures: Summary of results from the Medical Outcomes Study. *Medical Care, 33*, AS264–AS279.

Warner-Benson, D. M. (2001). The effect of a modified test administration procedure on the performance of male and female African American inner-city school children on a group administered intelligence test. *Dissertation Abstracts International Section A. The Humanities and Social Sciences, 61*, 10A.

Warzecha, G. (1991). The challenge to psychological assessment from modern computer technology. *European Review of Applied Psychology, 41*(3), 213–220.

Washington v. Davis. (1976). 96 U.S. 2040(c).

Washington, J. A., & Craig, H. K. (1999). Performance of at-risk African American Preschoolers on the Peabody Picture Vocabulary Test-III. *Language, Speech, and Hearing Services in Schools, 30*(1), 75–82.

Wasik, B. H., Ramey, C. T., Bryant, D. M., & Sparling, J. J. (1990). A longitudinal study of two early intervention strategies: Project CARE. *Child Development, 61*, 1682–1696.

Watkins, C. E., Jr., & Campbell, V. L. (Eds.). (2000). *Testing and assessment in counseling practice* (2nd ed.). Mahwah, NJ: Erlbaum.

Watkins, C. E., Jr., Campbell, V. L., Nieberding, R., & Hallmark, R. (1995). Contemporary practice of psychological assessment by clinical psychologists. *Professional Psychology: Research and Practice, 26*, 54–60.

Watson, C. W., & Klett, W. G. (1975). The Henmon-Nelson, Cardall-Miles, Slosson, and Quick Tests as predictors of NAIS IQ. *Journal of Clinical Psychology, 31,* 310–313.

Watson, D. (1988). The vicissitudes of mood measurement: Effects of varying descriptors, time frames, and response formats on measures of positive and negative affect. *Journal of Personality and Social Psychology, 55,* 128–141.

Watson, D., Clark, L. A., & Tellegen, A. (1988). Development and validation of brief measures of positive and negative affect: The PANAS scales. *Journal of Personality and Social Psychology, 54,* 1063–1070.

Watson v. Fort Worth Bank and Trust. (1988). 487 U.S. 977.

Weber, B., Schneider, B., Fritze, J., Gille, B., Hornung, S., Kuhner, T., & Maurer, K. (2003). Acceptance of computerized compared to paper-and-pencil assessment in psychiatric inpatients. *Computers in Human Behavior, 19*(1) 81–93.

Weber, C. P. (2001). The relationship of mental status and estrogen use on visual-motor and visual-spatial abilities. *Dissertation Abstracts International, 61,* 9B. (UMI No. 9986387)

Webster, E. C. (1964). *Decision making in the employment interview.* Montreal: Industrial Relations Center, McGill University.

Webster, J. S., & Dostrow, V. (1982). Efficacy of a decision-tree approach to the Luria-Nebraska Neuropsychological Battery. *Journal of Consulting and Clinical Psychology, 50,* 313–315.

Wechsler, D. (1939). *The measurement of adult intelligence.* Baltimore: Williams & Wilkins.

Wechsler, D. (1955). *Manual: Wechsler Adult Intelligence Scale.* New York: Psychological Corporation.

Wechsler, D. (1958). *The measurement and appraisal of adult intelligence* (4th ed.). Baltimore: Williams & Wilkins.

Wechsler, D. (1981). *Wechsler Adult Intelligence Scale—Revised.* New York: Psychological Corporation.

Wechsler, D. (1989). *Wechsler Preschool and Primary Scale of Intelligence–Revised (WPPSI-R).* San Antonio, TX: Psychological Corporation.

Wechsler, D. (1991a). *WISC-III manual.* San Antonio, TX: The Psychological Corporation.

Wechsler, D. (1991b). *Wechsler Intelligence Scales for Children–Third Edition.* San Antonio, TX: Psychological Corporation.

Wechsler, D. (2002). *WPPSI-III administration and scoring manual.* San Antonio: The Psychological Corporation.

Wechsler, D. (2003). *WISC-IV administration and scoring manual.* San Antonio: The Psychological Corporation.

Weeks, J. R., Morison, S. J., Millson, W. A., & Fettig, D. M. (1995). A comparison of Native, Metis, and Caucasian offender profiles on the MCMI. *Canadian Journal of Behavioural Science—Revue Canadienne des Sciences du Comportement, 27*(2), 187–198.

Weigel, R. G. (1999). One size does not fit all. *Consulting Psychology Journal: Practice and Research, 51*(1), 47–56.

Weiner, B. (1991). Metaphors in motivation and attribution. *American Psychologist, 46,* 921–930.

Weiner, B. (1994). Ability versus effort revisited: The moral determinants of achievement evaluation and achievement as a moral system. *Educational Psychologist, 29*(3), 163–172.

Weiner, B., Graham, S., Peter, O., & Zmuidinas, M. (1991). Public confession and forgiveness. *Journal of Personality, 59,* 281–312.

Weiner, I. B. (2003). *Principles of Rorschach interpretation* (2nd ed.) Mahwah, NJ: Erlbaum.

Weinstein, C. E., & Way, P. J. (2003) Educational psychology. In D. K. Freedheim (Ed.), *Handbook of psychology: History of psychology* (Vol. 1). New York: Wiley.

Weiss, D. J. (Ed.). (1983). *New horizons in testing.* New York: Academic Press.

Weiss, D. J. (1985). Adaptive testing by computer. *Journal of Consulting and Clinical Psychology, 53,* 774–789.

Weiss, D. J., & Yoes, M. E. (1991). Item response theory. In R. K. Hambleton & J. N. Zaal (Eds.), *Advances in educational and psychological testing: Theory and applications. Evaluation in education and human services series* (pp. 69–95). Boston, MA: Kluwer Academic Publishers.

Weissman, A. N. (1979). The Dysfunctional Attitude Scale: A validation study. *Dissertation Abstracts International, 40,* 1389A–1390B. (University Microfilms No. 7919,533)

Weissman, A. N., & Beck, A. T. (1978, November). *Development and validation of the Dysfunctional Attidude Scale: A preliminary investigation.* Paper presented at the meeting of the Association for the Advancement of Behavior Therapy, Chicago.

Weissman, M. M., Sholomskas, D., Pottenger, M., Prusoff, B. A., & Locke, B. Z. (1977). Assessing depressive symptoms in five psychiatric populations: A validation study. *American Journal of Epidemiology, 106,* 203–214.

Welch, H. G. (2004). *Should I be tested for cancer?* Berkeley: University of California Press.

Welsh, G. S. (1948). An extension of Hathaway's MMPI profile coding system. *Journal of Consulting Psychology, 12,* 343–344.

Welsh, K., Butters, N., Hughes, J., Mobs, R., & Hayman, A. (1991). Detection of abnormal memory decline in mad cases of Alzheimer's disease using CERAD Neuropsychological Measures. *Archives of Neurology, 48,* 278–281.

Wermiel, S., & Trost, C. (1986, June 20). Justices say hostile job environment due to sex harrassment violates rights. *Wall Street Journal,* p. 2.

Werner, H. (1937). Process and achievement: The basic problem of education and developmental psychology. *Hayward Educational Review, 7,* 353–368.

Wesman, A. G. (1971). Writing the test item. In R. L. Thorndike (Ed.), *Educational measurement* (2nd ed.). Washington, DC: American Council on Education.

Wheeler, L., & Reitan, R. M. (1962). A presence and alaterality of brain damage predicted from response to a short aphasia screening test. *Perceptual and Motor Skills, 15,* 783–799.

Whipple, C. M. (1910). *Manual of mental and physical tests.* Baltimore: Warwick & York.

Whiteside-Mansell, L., & Corwyn, R. F. (2003). Mean and covariance structures analysis: An examination of the Rosenberg Self-Esteem Scale among adolescents and adults. *Educational and Psychological Measurement, 63*(1) 163–173.

Whittington, D. (2004, April 5). The achievement gap: Should we rely on SAT scores to tell us anything about it? *Education Policy Analysis Archives, 12*(12).

Whyte, G., & Latham, G. (1997). The futility of utility analysis revisited: When even an expert fails. *Personnel Psychology, 50*(3), 601–610.

Wiberg, M. (2003). An optimal design approach to criterion-referenced computerized testing. *Journal of Educational and Behavioral Statistics, 28*(2), 97–110.

Wicker, A. W. (1979). Ecological psychology: Some recent and prospective developments. *American Psychologist, 34,* 755–765.

Wicker, A. W., & Kirmeyer, S. L. (1976). From church to laboratory to national park. In S. Wapner, S. B. Conen, & B. Kaplan (Eds.), *Experiencing the environment.* New York: Plenum.

Wickham, T. (1978). *WISC patterns in acting-out delinquents, poor readers, and normal controls.* Unpublished doctoral dissertation, United States International University, San Diego.

Wiederhold, B. K., Gervirtz, R. N., & Spira, J. L. (2001). Virtual reality exposure therapy vs. imagery desensitization therapy in the treatment of flying phobia. In G. Riva & C. Galimberti (Eds.), *Towards cyberpsychology: Mind, cognition and society in the internet age* (pp. 253–273). Washington, DC: IOS.

Wiederhold, B. K., Jang, D. P., Kim, S. I., Wiederhold, M. D. (2002). Physiological monitoring as an objective tool in virtual reality therapy. *Cyberpsychology and Behavior, 5*(1) 77–82.

Wiesner, W. H., & Cronshaw, S. F. (1988). A meta-analytic investigation of the impact of interview format and degree of structure on the validity of the employment interview. *Journal of Occupational Psychology, 61,* 275–290.

Wiggins, J. G. (1994). Would you want your child to be a psychologist? *American Psychologist, 49*(6), 485–492.

Wiggins, J. S. (1973). *Personality and prediction: Principles of personality assessment.* Reading, MA: Addison-Wesley.

Wild, C. L., McPeek, W. M., Koffler, S. L., Braun, H. I., & Cowell, W. (1989). Concurrent validity of verbal item types for ethnic and gender subgroups. *GRE Publication Report 84–1Op.* Princeton, NJ: Educational Testing Service.

Wilder, J. (1950). The law of initial values. *Psychosomatic Medicine, 12,* 392–401.

Wilkinson, L. (1999). Statistical methods in psychology journals: Guidelines and explanations. *American Psychologist, 54*(8), 594–604.

Williams, J. E. (1994). Anxiety measurement: Construct validity and test performance. *Measurement and Evaluation in Counseling and Development, 27,* 302–307.

Williams, J. M., Voelker, S., & Ricciardi, P. W. (1995). Predictive validity of the K-ABC for exceptional preschoolers. *Psychology in the Schools, 32,* 178–185.

Williams, M. L., Freeman, R. C., Bowen, A. M., & Saunders, L. (1998). The acceptability of a computer HIV/AIDS risk assessment to not-in-treatment drug users. *AIDS Care, 10*(6) 701–711.

Williams, R. L. (1974). Scientific racism and I.Q.: The silent mugging of the black community. *Psychology Today, 7,* 32–41.

Williams, W. M., & Ceci, S. J. (1997). Are Americans becoming more or less alike? Trends in race, class, and ability differences in intelligence. *American Psychologist, 52,* 1226–1235.

Williamson, L. G., Campion, J. E., Malos, S. B., Roehling, M. V., & Campion, M. (1997). Employment interview on trial: Linking interview structure with litigation outcomes. *Journal of Applied Psychology, 82,* 900–912.

Williamson, W. D., Wilson, G. S., Lifschitz, M. H., & Thurbers, S. A. (1990). Nonhandicapped very-low-birth-weight infants at one year of age developmental profile. *Pediatrics, 85,* 405–410.

Willingham, W. W., Pollack, J. M., & Lewis, C. (2000). *Grades and test scores: Accounting for observed differences* (ETS Research Report 00-15). Princeton, NJ: Educational Testing Service.

Wilson, M., De Boeck, P., Moss, P., & Draney, K. (2003). Measurement: Interdisciplinary research and perspectives. 1(1).

Wing, K. R. (1976). *The law and the public's health.* St. Louis, MO: Mosby.

Winkler, A. (2002, November). High-stakes testing: Division in the ranks—Standardized testing draws lines between new and veteran teachers. *Phi Delta Kappan.*

Winter, D. G., & Stewart, A. J. (1977). Power motive reliability, as a function of retest instructions. *Journal of Consulting and Clinical Psychology, 42,* 436–440.

Wise, S. L., Finney, S. J., Enders, C. K., Freeman, S. A., & Severance, D. D. (1999). Examinee judgments of changes in item difficulty: Implications for item review in computerized adaptive testing. *Applied Measurement in Education, 12*(2), 185–199.

Wissler, C. (1901). The correlation of mental and physical tests. *Psychological Review, 3* (Monograph Supp. 16).

Witmer, J. M., Bernstein, A. V., & Dunham, R. M. (1971). The effects of verbal approval and disapproval upon the performance of third and fourth grade children of four subtests of the Wechsler Intelligence Scale for Children. *Journal of School Psychology, 9,* 347–356.

Witt, J. C., & Gresham, F. M. (1985). Review of the Wechsler Intelligence Scale for Children—Revised. In J. V. Mitchell (Ed.), *The ninth mental measurements yearbook* (Vol. 1). Highland Park, NJ: Gryphon Press.

Wittenborn, J. R., & Sarason, S. B. (1949). Exceptions to certain Rorschach criteria of pathology. *Journal of Consulting Psychology, 13,* 21–27.

Wolach, A. H., & McHale, M. A. (2002). Computer program to generate operant schedules. *Behavior Research Methods, Instruments, and Computers, 34*(2), 245–249.

Wolber, G. J., Reynolds, B., Ehrmantraut, J. E., & Nelson, A. J. (1997). In search of a measure of intellectual functioning for an inpatient psychiatric population with low cognitive ability. *Psychiatric Rehabilitation Journal, 21,* 59–63.

Wolk, R. L., & Wolk, R. B. (1971). *Manual: Gerontological Apperception Test.* New York: Behavioral Publications.

Wolpe, J., & Lang, P. J. (1964). A fear survey schedule for use in behavior therapy. *Behaviour Research and Therapy, 2,* 27–30.

Wood, J. M., & Lilienfeld, S. O. (1999). The Rorschach Inkblot Test: A case of overstatement? *Assessment, 6,* 341–349.

Wood, J. M., Lilienfeld, S. O., Garb, H. N., & Nezworski, M. T. (2000). Limitations of the Rorschach as a diagnostic tool: A reply to Garfield (2000), Lerner (2000), and Weiner (2000). *Journal of Clinical Psychology, 56*(3), 441–448.

Wood, J. M., Lilienfeld, S. O., Nezworski, M. T., & Garb, H. N. (2001). Coming to grips with negative evidence for the comprehensive system for the Rorschach: A comment on Gacono, Loving, and Bodholdt; Ganellen; and Bornstein. *Journal of Personality Assessment. 77*(1) 48–70.

Wood, J. M., Nezworski, M. T., Garb, H. N., & Lilienfeld, S. O. (2001). The misperception of psychopathology: Problems with the norms of the Comprehensive System for the Rorschach. *Clinical Psychology: Science and Practice, 8,* 350–373.

Wood, J. M., Nezworski, M. T., Lilienfeld, S. O., & Garb, H. N. (2003). *What's wrong with the Rorschach? Science confronts the controversial inkblot test.* San Francisco: Jossey-Bass.

Wood, J. M., Nezworski, T., & Stejskal, W. J. (1996). The comprehensive system for the Rorschach: A critical examination. *Psychological Science, 7,* 3–10.

Wood, P. S., Smith, W. L., Altmaier, E. M., Tarico, V. S., & Franken, E. A. (1990). A prospective study of cognitive and non-cognitive selection criteria as predictors of resident performance. *Investigative Radiology, 25,* 855–859.

Woodcock. R. W., & Johnson, M. (1989). *Woodcock-Johnson Psycho-Educational Battery—Revised.* Chicago: Riverside.

Woodcock, R. W., McGrew, K. S., & Mather, N. (2001). *Woodcock-Johnson III battery.* Itasca, IL: Riverside.

Woodworth, R. S. (1920). *Personal data sheet.* Chicago: Stoelting.

World Health Organization (WHO). (1948). *Constitution of the World Health Organization.* Geneva, Switzerland: WHO Basic Documents.

Worling, J. A. (2001). Personality-based typology of adolescent male sexual offenders: Differences in recidivism rates, victim-selection characteristics, and personal victimization histories. *Sexual Abuse: Journal of Research and Treatment, 13*(3) 149–166.

Wright, O. R., Jr. (1969). Summary of research on the selection interview since-1964. *Personnel Psychology, 22,* 391–413.

Wright, T. L., & Tedeschi, R. G. (1975). Factor analysis of the interpersonal trust scale. *Journal of Consulting and Clinical Psychology, 43,* 470–477.

Wrightman, L. F. (1988). An examination of sex differences in WAT scores from the perspective of sound consequences. *Applied Measurement in Education, 11,* 255–277.

Wrightsman, L. F. (1998). *Psychology and the legal system* (4th ed.). Belmont, CA: Wadsworth.

Wyman, P. (1998). Integrating the MBTI and the Enneagram in psychotherapy: The core self and the defense system. *Journal of Psychological Type, 46,* 28–40.

Xu, F., Fu, G., & Zhang, T. (1996). A use of the Bender-Gestalt Test (BGT) in mentally retarded children [Chinese]. *Chinese Mental Health Journal, 10,* 208–209.

Yan, L., Yang, X., & Wang, H. (2001). Effects of gingo bilboa on cognition of patients at the early stage of Alzheimer's disease. *Chinese Mental Health Journal, 15*(1), 31–32.

Yanai, H. (2003). *New developments in psychometrics: Proceedings of the International Meeting of the Psychometric Society* (Tokyo). New York: Springer.

Yarcheski, T. J., Mahon, N. E., & Yarcheski, A. (2003). Social support, self-esteem, and positive health practices of early adolescents. *Psychological Reports, 92*(1) 99–103.

Yerkes, R. M. (Ed.). (1921). Psychological examining in the United States Army. *Memoirs of the National Academy of Sciences, 15.*

Yoon, K., Schmidt, F., & Ilies, R. (2002). Cross-cultural construct validity of the five-factor model of personality among Korean employees. *Journal of Cross-Cultural Psychology, 33*(3), 217–235.

Yurong, H., Dun, X., & Xiurong, X. (2001). Clinical analysis of 95 children with autistic disorder. *Chinese Mental Health Journal, 15*(6), 396–397.

Zautra, A. J. (2003). *Emotions, stress, and health.* London: Oxford University Press.

Zedeck, S., & Blood, M. R. (1974). *Foundations of behavioral science research in organizations.* Pacific Grove, CA: Brooks/Cole.

Zedeck, S., & Cascio, W. F. (1984). Psychological issues in personnel decisions. *Annual Review of Psychology, 35*, 461–518.

Zedeck, S., Tziner, A., & Middlestadt, S. E. (1983). Interviewer validity and reliability: An individual analysis approach. *Personnel Psychology, 36*, 355–370.

Zeidner, M. (1987). Test of the cultural bias hypothesis: Some Israeli findings. *Journal of Applied Psychology, 72*, 38–48.

Zeidner, M. (1990). Does test anxiety bias scholastic aptitude performance by gender and sociocultural group? *Journal of Personality Assessment, 55*, 145–160.

Zeidner, M., & Hammer, A. (1990). Life events and coping resources as predictors of stress symptoms in adolescents. *Personality and Individual Differences, 11*, 693–703.

Zimmerman, B. J., Greenberg, D., & Weinstein, C. E. (1994). Self-regulating academic study time: A strategy approach. In D. H. Schunk & B. J. Zimmerman (Eds.), *Self-regulation of learning and performance: Issues and educational applications* (pp. 181–199). Hillsdale, NJ: Erlbaum.

Zimmerman, M., & Coryell, W. (1987). The Inventory to Diagnose Depression (IDD): A self-report scale to diagnose major depressive disorders. *Journal of Consulting and Clinical Psychology, 55*, 55–59.

Ziskin, J. (1995). *Coping with psychiatric and psychological testimony* (5th ed.). Los Angeles: Law and Psychology Press.

Zores, L. S., & Williams, P. B. (1980). A look at the content bias in IQ tests. *Journal of Educational Measurement, 17*, 313–322.

Zubin, J. (1954). Failures of the Rorschach technique. *Journal of Projective Techniques, 18*, 303–315.

Zubin, J. (1972). Discussion of symposium on newer approaches to personality assessment. *Journal of Personality Assessment, 36*, 427–434.

Zuckerman, M. (1960). The development of an affect adjective check list measure of anxiety. *Journal of Consulting Psychology, 24*, 457–462.

Zuckerman, M. (1971). Physiological measures of sexual arousal in the human. *Psychological Bulletin, 75*, 297–329.

Zuckerman, M. (1990). Some dubious premises in research and theory on racial differences. *American Psychologist, 45*, 1297–1303.

Zumbo, B. D. (1998). Opening remarks to the special issue on validity theory and the methods used in validation: Perspectives from the social and behavioral sciences. *Social Indicators Research, 45*(1), 1–3.

Zytowski, D. G. (1976). Predictive validity of the Kuder Occupational Interest Survey: A 12–19 year follow-up. *Journal of Counseling Psychology, 23*, 921–233.

Zytowski, D. G. (1977). The effects of being interest inventoried. *Journal of Vocational Behavior, 11*, 153–158.

Zytowski, D. G. (1985). *Kuder Occupational Interest Survey Form DD manual supplement.* Chicago: Science Research Associates.

Zytowski, D. G. (1992). Three generations: The continuing evolution of Frederic Kuder's interest inventories. *Journal of Counseling and Development, 71*, 245–248.

Zytowski, D. G. (1996). Three decades of interest inventory results: A case study. *Career Development Quarterly, 45*(2), 141–148.

Name Index

Aamodt, M. J., 510
Aarita, A. A., 364
Abbott, R. D., 235
Abdelkhalek, A. M., 429
Abel, S. C., 343
Abrams, D. M., 410
Abramson, L. Y., 192
Abramson, T., 187
Acklin, M. W., 396, 399
Adams, K. M., 477, 478
Adams, V. G., 383
Adkins, D. M., 322
Admiraal, W., 162
Affleck, G., 383, 501
Ahern, S., 436
Ahmedzai, A. H., 503
Aidman, E. V., 443, 445, 625
Aidwin, C. M., 365
Aiken, L. R., 294
Akande, A., 429
Akehurst, L., 206
Akutagawa, D. A., 429
Akyuez, G., 382
Alain, C., 447
Albee, G., 590, 594
Alexander, G. E., 268
Alexander, R. A., 197
Alexopoulos, D., 343
Alfonso, V. C., 287, 288
Algina, J., 112
Allalouf, A., 570
Allard, G., 442
Allen, A., 535
Allen, D. N., 260
Allen, F., 218, 222
Allen, G. J., 445
Allen, J. G., 205
Allen, M. J., 104, 111, 168, 170
Alley, W., 445
Alliger, G., 199
Allison, J., 394
Alloy, L. B., 192
Allport, G. W., 368
Alpert, R., 496, 499
Al-Tayyib, A. A., 438
Alter, B., 392
Altmaier, E. M., 566, 567
Altman, H., 440
Alvarado, N., 410, 413
Ames, L. B., 397
Amtmann, D., 235
Anagnostopoulou, T., 501
Anastasi, A., 135, 153, 160, 294, 419, 534
Ancill, R. J., 438
Anderson, B. L., 613, 614
Anderson, J. P., 151, 503
Anderson, M., 231
Anderson, N. B., 437
Anderson, N. H., 166
Anderson, S., 178
Andersson, H. W., 300
Andreu, J. M., 431
Andrews, D. W., 515
Angoff, W. H., 445
Angrilli, A., 431
Ankri, J., 505
Anton, W. B., 496, 499
Antony, M. M., 217, 218, 429
Arango-Lasprilla, J. C., 431
Arbisi, P. A., 365

Archer, R. P., 626
Arkes, H. R., 190
Armbruster, G. L., 404
Arnold, M. M., 299
Aron, A., 27
Aron, E., 27
Aronow, E., 391, 400
Aronson, J. A., 540, 542
Arrindell, W. A., 384
Arthur, G., 262
Arthur, N., 469
Arvey, R. D., 226, 510
Asbjornsen, A., 300
Ascaso, C., 218
Ash, R. A., 227
Asher, J. J., 138
Ashton, M. C., 375
Atienza, F. L., 384
Atkinson, J. W., 108, 415
Atkinson, L., 289
Atkinson, R., 142
Atkinson, R. C., 569
Atlis, M. M., 442
Auerbach, S. M., 495
Austin, J. T., 442, 627
Averill, P. M., 365
Avolio, B. J., 344
Ax, A. F., 436
Aydog, S., 504
Azrin, N. H., 197, 435

Babbitt, R. A., 503
Baburajan, P. K., 374
Baddeley, A. D., 478
Baehr, M., 511
Baer, R. A., 353, 354
Bagby, R. M., 500, 534
Bailey, J., 416
Bailey, J. M., 391, 394, 626, 630
Bains, D. S., 365
Bakke, A., 598–599
Balaguer, I., 384
Bandura, A., 378, 524, 614
Banerji, M., 285
Banjo, M., 189
Banos, R., 445
Barak, A., 468
Barbaranelli, C., 378
Barbaree, H. E., 436
Barber, T. X., 189
Barca, N., 504
Bardo, H. R., 322
Bareak, B., 599, 604, 605
Barenbaum, N. B., 231
Bargh, J. A., 472
Bari, M., 443
Barker, P. R., 438
Barker, R. G., 528
Barnes, M., 477
Barnes-Farrell, J. L., 199
Barns, J., 194
Barofsky, I., 503
Baron, I. S., 482, 489
Baron, R. A., 511–512
Barrett, G. V., 161, 552, 560, 571
Barrick, M. R., 380
Bartell, S. S., 396
Barth, J. T., 483
Bartholomew, D. J., 92, 101, 126
Bartlett, C. J., 551

Bartley, J., 567
Bartok, J. A., 298
Bartone, P. T., 383
Bartrum, D., 384
Basco, W. T., Jr., 567
Bass, J. D., 288
Bates, T. C., 236, 381
Batur, S., 361
Bauer, R. M., 267
Baughman, E. E., 405
Baxter, D. J., 436
Bay, M., 298
Bayles, K. A., 296
Bayley, N., 287–288
Bayliss, M. S., 503
Bazeley, P., 189
Beal, J. A., 284
Beato, L., 382
Beatty, J., 436
Beck, A. T., 432–433
Beck, J. G., 429
Beck, S. J., 19, 394
Becker, B. J., 241
Beckham, J. C., 365
Bedell, J., 496, 499
Beishline, M. J., 332
Bell, J. J., 304
Bell, M., 258
Bell, N., 288
Bell, N. L., 297, 526
Bell, S. K., 297
Bell, T. K., 300
Bellack, A. S., 196
Bellak, L., 410, 411, 412, 413, 416
Bellak, S. S., 416
Belmonte, A., 382
Bem, D. J., 535–536
Bemak, F., 216
Bender, L., 304–305
Benedict, T., 264
Benjamin, G. A., 619
Bennett, R. E., 315
Ben-Porath, Y. S., 194, 350, 363, 365, 366
Ben-Shakhar, G., 570
Bentler, P. M., 101
Benton, 477
Bentz, V. J., 440
Bereby-Meyer, Y., 162
Berenson, B. C., 214–216
Bergan, A., 191
Bergan, J. R., 151, 589
Bergstrom, B. A., 185
Berg-Weger, M., 136
Bernabei, P., 296
Bernheimer, L. P., 285
Bernstein, A. V., 184
Bernstein, I. H., 100, 104, 124
Bernstein, L. J., 447
Berren, M. R., 199
Berry, G. E., 526
Berry, L. A., 365
Berry, L. M., 510
Bersoff, D. N., 587, 588, 589
Berstein, I. H., 27
Bertson, G. G., 613, 614
Berzon, R., 504
Betz, N. E., 526, 539

Beutler, L. E., 199, 216
Bianchini, J. C., 546
Bianchini, K. J., 483
Bigler, E. D., 477
Bilker, W., 284
Binder, L. M., 185
Binet, A., 14–15, 233, 236–239, 250, 349, 394
Binson, D., 119
Birk, J. M., 468
Black, S., 180
Blaine, D., 612
Blais, M. A., 395, 398, 408
Blake, J., 449
Blanchard, F., 505
Blankstein, K. R., 493
Blatt, S. J., 391, 394, 410
Block, J., 167, 382, 536
Bloem, W. D., 365
Blok, G., 223
Blondin, J. P., 378
Blood, G. W., 443
Blood, M. R., 531
Blue, A. V., 567
Bobic, J., 304
Bobko, P., 532, 545
Boegels, S. M., 223
Boerum, L. J., 17
Bogner, J. A., 384, 613
Bolen, L. M., 304
Bolt, D., 175, 234
Bolton, B., 367
Bombardier, C., 151
Bondi, M. W., 303, 436, 491
Bono, J. E., 380, 381, 385
Borman, W. C., 178, 185, 194, 199, 522, 533, 562
Bornstein, M. H., 232
Borsboom, D., 546
Bos, J. S., 298
Bosshardt, M. J., 525
Botella, C., 445, 625
Botet, F., 283
Bottomley, A., 503
Boudreau, J. W., 522
Boulmetis, J., 222
Bourmenskaya, G. V., 232
Bousquet, A., 288
Bowen, A. M., 438
Bowers, K. S., 535
Boyd, C. J., 442
Boyd, W., 603–604
Bracken, B. A., 294
Brackett, M. A., 333
Bradbury, T. N., 472
Bradley-Johnson, S., 298, 303
Bradwejn, J., 365
Braff, D. L., 269, 366, 447
Brahler, E., 504
Brand, C. R., 448, 449
Brandler, S., 343
Brandt, J., 305
Bratko, D., 381
Braun, H. I., 546
Brawley, O. W., 543
Brayfield, A. H., 619
Brazelton, T. B., 283–284
Bredemeier, M., 595
Breggin, G., 216
Breggin, P. R., 206
Breggin, R., 216

Brennan, R. L., 83, 522
Bressani, R. V., 439
Bridgeman, B., 187
Bridges, K. R., 327, 433
Bridges, M. W., 378, 384
Briel, J. B., 312, 550
Briggs, K. C., 525–526
Briggs, M., 227
Brigham, C., 569
Brij, A., 206
Britt, G. C., 284
Britton, B. K., 193
Broaden, H. E., 522
Broca, P., 477
Broderick, J. E., 501
Brody, E., 366
Broks, P., 476
Broshek, D. K., 483
Brosnan, M. J., 439
Brown, D. C., 55, 344
Brown, F. G., 557, 558
Brown, G., 433
Brown, J., 542
Brown, J. S., 181
Brown, R., 447
Browning, E. B., 148
Brundin-Mather, R., 227
Brunet, A., 365
Bryant, F. B., 92
Bryson, G., 258
Bryson, S., 622
Bublitz, S. T., 439
Buchanan, S., 582
Buchanan, T., 442
Buck, J. N., 418
Buckley, M. R., 510
Buffaloe, J. D., 439
Bureau-Chalot, F., 505
Burke, M. J., 522
Burns, L. R., 385
Burns, R. C., 418
Buros, O. K., 409
Burstein, J. C., 441
Burton, D. B., 274
Burton, R. B., 181
Burton, R. V., 197
Burtt, H. E., 225
Busby, R. M., 365
Bush, G. H. W., 543, 544
Bush, J. W., 504
Bushnell, D. M., 108
Butcher, H. L., 328
Butcher, J. N., 20, 350,
    362–363, 364, 365, 441,
    442
Butters, N., 478, 484, 490, 491
Byard, L., 449
Byers, C., 445
Byravan, A., 383

Cacioppo, J. T., 613, 614
Cadenhead, K., 366, 447
Cahan, S., 294
Caldwell, M. B., 185
Calfee, R., 596
Calhoun, G. B., 366
Callahan, S., 382–383
Callender, J. C., 202, 227, 510,
    511
Callinan, M., 139
Calnan, M., 493
Calpe, J., 441
Calvanese, P., 501
Camaioni, L., 296
Camara, W. J., 198, 327, 622
Cameron, J., 191, 192
Cameron, R., 431
Camilli, G., 27, 83

Campbell, D. P., 454–472, 466,
    468, 469
Campbell, D. T., 150
Campbell, J. M., 297
Campbell, J. P., 90
Campbell, K. A., 185
Campbell, T. W., 616
Campbell, V. L., 392, 453, 534
Campbell, W., 206
Campion, J. E., 138, 226, 510,
    511
Campion, M. A., 205, 223, 225,
    510, 511
Canavan, A. G., 305
Cane, D. B., 433
Cannell, C. F., 191
Cano, T. R., 382
Cantu, R., 483
Caprara, G. V., 378
Carkhuff, R. R., 214–216
Carless, S. A., 455
Carlin, A., 625
Carlin, J. B., 162
Carlota, A. J., 381
Carlson, R. E., 226
Carlton, T. E., 361
Carmin, C. H., 429
Caroselli, J., 297
Carr, A. C., 438, 439, 440
Carr, M. A., 488
Carretta, T. R., 345
Carro, I. L., 433
Carstairs, J. R., 359
Carter, G. W., 525
Carter, W. B., 503
Carver, C. S., 378, 384
Cascio, W. F., 522, 583
Cash, T. F., 511
Caspar, R. A., 438
Castaneda, A., 563
Castenell, L. A., 545
Castenell, N. E., 545
Catalano, M., 467
Cattell, J. M., 13, 14
Cattell, R. B., 20, 246, 343,
    368–371, 371, 388, 494
Cautela, J. R., 430, 431
Ceci, S. J., 328
Cella, D. F., 445
Cermak, L. S., 491
Cesare, S. J., 224, 511
Chabanne, V., 625
Chambers, L. S., 503
Champney, H., 166
Chan, D. W., 306
Chan, K.-Y., 159
Chapman, D. S., 510
Charles, J. M., 288
Chartrand, E., 495
Cheavens, J., 383
Cheiken, M., 196
Chen, E., 382
Chen, T. -Y, 29
Chico-Libran, E., 384
Chiles, J. A., 438
Choca, J., 438, 439
Chockalingam, V., 198, 571, 622
Chodorow, M., 441
Choi, S., 381
Chong, B. H., 322
Christenson, G., 478
Christianson, L., 341
Chronni, S., 434
Chudy, J. F., 415, 630
Chun, K., 90
Church, A. T., 381
Cicchetti, D. V., 118, 298
Cine, D. B., 138

Cizek, G. J., 27
Clapham, M. M., 306
Clare, L., 478
Clarizio, H. F., 546, 557, 558,
    586
Clark, C., 477
Clark, D. H., 545
Clark, K. E., 466
Clark, L. A., 163, 166, 167, 385,
    532
Clark, P. G., 222
Clarkin, J. F., 199
Clarkson, Q. D., 552
Clauser, B. E., 437, 625
Clay, E. J., 439
Clayton, G. M., 195
Clayton, S., 603
Cleary, T. A., 550, 551, 561
Clements, C. A., 263
Cliff, N., 87
Clinchot, D., 384, 613
Clinton, W. J., 141, 198
Clitheroe, C., 529
Coakes, S. J., 115
Coble, J. R., 445
Cohen, B. H., 26
Cohen, F., 500
Cohen, J., 118
Cohen, L., 468, 501
Cohen, R., 263
Cohen, S., 529
Cole, N. S., 468, 544, 560, 561
Coleman, M. S., 602
Coles, C. D., 284
Coles, M. E., 443
Collett, D., 26
Colligan, R. C., 365
Collins, R. L., 501
Colom, R., 340, 342, 343
Colon-Malgady, G., 416
Colvin, C. R., 536
Comrey, A. L., 378
Congdon, P., 546
Conner, R. E., 289
Connelly, W., 602
Connors, G. J., 431
Consoli, A., 443
Constantine, M. G., 384
Constantino, G., 416
Conte, J. M., 523
Conway, D. G., 297
Conway, J. M., 227
Cook, M. L., 433
Cooley, P. C., 438
Cooper, D., 374
Cooper, P. V., 267
Copple, C. E., 546
Coppola, V., 599
Cordes, A. K., 118
Cordorniu-Raga, M. J., 236
Corey-Bloom, J., 491
Cornelius, E. T., III, 415
Corrigan, J. D., 384, 613
Cortadellas, A. M., 292
Cortese, F., 447
Corwyn, R. F., 382
Coryell, W., 139
Costa, P. T., Jr., 378, 381, 385
Costa, R. M. E., 378, 445, 627
Costello, H., 217
Costello, J., 185
Couper, M. P., 439, 442
Court, J. H., 339
Cowell, W., 546
Cox, B. J., 534
Craig, H. K., 297
Craig, R. J., 217
Cramer, P., 410, 415

Crawford, S., 442
Creed, P. A., 384
Crespin, T. R., 442, 627
Cripe, L. I., 366
Criqui, M. H., 151
Crites, J. O., 470–471
Crocker, L. M., 112
Crockett, D., 477
Cronan, T. A., 151
Cronbach, L. J., 101, 110, 112,
    113, 115, 136, 150, 153,
    193, 384, 522, 523, 539,
    556, 606
Cronk, B. C., 442
Cronshaw, S. F., 511
Crook, G. M., 495
Crosby, F. J., 603, 604
Crosby, L., 515
Cross, T. C., 137
Crosson, B., 267
Crow, D. M., 443, 625
Crowe, S. F., 264
Crowe, T. V., 382
Crowther, B., 227
Culp, A. M., 292
Culp, R. E., 292
Cundick, B. P., 418
Cureton, E. E., 136
Cyranowski, J. M., 218

Dabbs, J., 443, 625
Dahlquist, L. M., 431
Dahlstrom, W. G., 20, 360, 362,
    363, 364, 619
Dalessio, A. T., 510
Dana, R. H., 620
Dangel, H. L., 190
D'Arcy, H., 442
Darlington, R. B., 560, 561
Dartnall, N., 298
Darwin, C., 12–13, 14
Das, J. P., 231
Datta, L., 454
Dattilo, J., 217
Dave, R., 284
Davidson, H. H., 394, 401
Davidson, R. S., 365
Davies, G. M., 427
Davies, P. G., 542
da Vinci, L., 392
Davis, A. S., 194
Davis, R. B., 180
Davis, R. N., 442
Dawes, R. M., 391, 616
Dawson, J. K., 478, 479
Day, D. V., 523, 525
Dean, R. S., 522
Deane, F. P., 499
Deb, N. C., 495
De Boeck, P., 625
De Bruyn, E. E. J., 440
De Carvalho, L. A. V., 445, 627
Deffenbacher, J. L., 433
deGroot, A. M., 417
de Jong, J. R., 427
De Kruif, R. E. L., 178
DeLancy, M., 366
Delery, J. E., 510, 511
Delhees, K. H., 371
Delis, D. C., 303, 478, 481, 490,
    491, 492, 493
del Pilar, G. H., 381
DeMark, S., 11
DeMaster, B., 197
DeMay, H. R., 381
Demir, B., 361
De Moivre, A., 101
Denenberg, J. O., 151

Dennis, M., 477
Dent, H., 591
Deqing, T., 304
Derkin, K., 418
DeRosa, A., 184
Dersen, J. J. L., 381
De Sa Guimaraes, M., 445, 627
Detterman, D. K., 322
Detwiler, F. R., 381
Devanand, D. P., 265
DeVellis, R. F., 158–159, 168
Devine, D., 501
Devoe, E. R., 208, 217
DeVries, M. W., 500
DeWitt, M. B., 288
Diamond, E. E., 462, 468
Dickie, J., 185
Diego, M. A., 284
Diener, E., 378, 384, 535
Dierdorff, E. C., 532
DiGiulio, G., 392
Dijkers, M. P., 503
Dikmen, S., 478
Dill, C. A., 402
Dillard, J. P., 207
Dinesen, J., 292
Dishion, T. J., 515
Dixon, J. L., 304
Dobko, P., 547
Dobranski, T., 526
Doctor, R., 298
Dodrill, C. B., 526
Doerries, L. E., 526
Dogan, O., 382
Doherty, L. M., 194
Dolstra, L., 196
Dona, B. G., 382
Donahue, D., 190
Doran, L. I., 522
Dorans, N. J., 145
Dorz, S., 443
Dostrow, V., 488
Dougherty, T. W., 202, 227, 510, 511
Douglas, J., 427
Dove, A., 554–555
Doverspike, D., 161, 323
Dowd, E. T., 11
Dowd, T., 439
Downey, J., 304
Downing, R. A., 603
Downs, C., 439
Drabman, R., 274
Draney, K., 625
Draper, J. F., 547
Drasgow, F., 101, 145, 159, 547
Dreher, G. F., 227
Drga, V., 29
Drukker, A., 487
Drummond, R., 445, 627
Duan, C., 207
DuBois, P. H., 12, 571
Duggan, C. F., 433
Duker, J., 360
Dun, T. M., 495
Dun, X., 285
Dunham, R. M., 184
Dunlap, W. P., 105
Dunn, I. M., 296, 297
Dunn, J. A., 343
Dunn, L. M., 296, 297
Dunnette, M. D., 137, 138, 142, 522, 525, 562
Dupinet, R. L., 552, 560, 571
Dupue, R. A., 499
Durham, C. C., 386
Dush, D. M., 418

Dvir, T., 189
Dwight, S. A., 439
Dworkin, R. H., 268

Eakin, E., 524
Earborn, G., 394
Eaton, N. K., 522
ebary Inc., 494
Ebel, R. L., 136
Eber, H. W., 369
Eberenz, K. P., 365
Ebert, R. J., 227, 510
Echternacht, G., 327
Edelstein, B., 193
Eden, D., 189
Edwards, A. L., 372–374
Efficace, F., 503
Egger, J. I., 381
Eggly, S., 205
Egloff, B., 385
Ehrhardt, A. A., 304
Einarsdottir, S., 468
Eisenberger, R., 191, 192
Ekman, P., 198, 436
Ekren, U. W., 190
El-Ansarey, B. M., 381
Elashoff, J., 189, 571
Elder, C., 546
Elkin, E. J., 304
Elliot, R., 571
Elliott, C. D., 303
Ellis, A., 354
Ellis, D. A., 620
Ellis, T. E., 433
Ellison, R. L., 567
Embretson, S. E., 175, 177, 612, 621
Emmelkamp, P. M. G., 382
Emmons, R. A., 384
Emory, E. K., 284
Enders, C. K., 446
Endler, N. S., 385, 493, 494, 495, 500, 534
Engle, R. W., 236
Enrico, J., 264
Epstein, J., 437, 438, 441, 442
Ercin, O., 504
Ercolani, A. P., 296
Erdberg, P., 398, 403, 619
Erdberg, S. P., 365
Erdman, H. P., 438, 440
Erez, A., 385, 386
Ergene, T., 494
Erickson, R., 3
Eriksen, C. W., 498
Erlanger, D., 483
Erlenmeyer-Kimling, L., 268
Ernst, J., 166
Ernster, V. L., 516
Ersan, E., 382
Evans, D. C., 603
Evans, I., 495
Evans, J., 263
Evans, J. J., 303
Evans, L., 383
Everaerd, W., 436
Evers, S. E., 431
Everson, H. T., 499
Ewart, C. K., 529
Ewing-Cobbs, L., 298, 477
Exner, J. E., 309, 392, 393, 395, 396, 397, 398, 400, 402, 403, 404, 407, 415, 420, 630
Eyde, L. D., 625
Eysenck, H. J., 538

Fagan, J. F., 284

Fagundes, D. D., 187
Fairburn, C. G., 222
Fairlie, P., 494
Falek, A., 284
Faller, K. C., 208, 217
Fallon, T., 227
Fan, X., 294
Farber, J. G., 398
Farr, J. L., 142
Farrell, A. D., 443, 450, 625, 627
Faust, D., 442
Faustman, W. O., 488
Fay, W. H., 552
Fechner, G. T., 14
Feeny, D., 506
Feifel, H., 499
Feigelson, M. E., 439
Feinstein, A. R., 118
Feldman, D., 483
Feldman, M. E., 365
Feldman, S. E., 184
Felsten, G., 448
Fennell, E. B., 482, 489
Fenster, A., 333
Fernandez, J., 333
Ferrando, P. J., 163
Ferrario, S. R., 384
Ferris, G. R., 225, 511
Ferro, J. M., 432
Feuer, M. J., 179
Fidell, L. S., 87, 126
Field, T. M., 284
Fielding-Barnsley, R., 296
Fifer, G., 545
Filoteo, J. V., 478
Fincham, F. D., 472
Finkelstein, Y., 487
Finney, S. J., 446
Fiorello, C. A., 259
First, M. B., 217, 218
Fischer, A. R., 501
Fish, D. D., 225
Fish, J. M., 622
Fiske, D. W., 150, 405
Fitts, W. H., 377
Fitzgerald, C., 526
Flaherty, V. L., 194
Flamos, O., 305
Flanagan, D. P., 232, 236, 263, 287, 288, 302, 303
Flanagan, J. C., 532–533
Flascher, O. M., 162
Flaugher, R. L., 545, 546, 547, 560, 568, 570
Fleishman, E. A., 470, 533
Fleiss, J. L., 118
Fleming, J., 15
Fletcher, J. M., 478, 483, 484, 485
Fletcher, S. W., 516, 517
Flett, G. L., 493, 494, 534
Flores-Mendoza, C., 340
Florio, C. M., 404
Floyd, R. G., 303
Flynn, D., 163–164
Flynn, J. R., 541
Flynn, P., 365
Fode, K. L., 189
Fogel, B. S., 477
Fogle, E. E., 288
Foley, K. L., 159
Folkman, S., 499–500
Foltz, P., 441
Ford, D. Y., 280
Forer, B. R., 401
Foreyt, J. P., 495
Forrester, B. J., 571
Forsterling, F., 473

Forsyth, R. A., 154
Fort, P., 58
Fouladi, R. T., 501
Fowler, J. C., 399
Fowler, R. D., 178, 438
Fowles, M. E., 441
Fox, H. R., 11
Fox, N. L., 292
Fraboni, M., 381
Franceschina, E., 443
Frank, G., 396, 408
Frank, L. K., 392
Franken, E. A., Jr., 566, 567
Franklin, M. E., 429
Franklin, R. D., 621
Franzen, M. D., 366
Frase, L. T., 440, 612, 627
Frazer, R. A., 510
Frederiksen, C., 563
Fredrickson, B. L., 378, 382
Fredrikson, M., 435
Freeman, F. S., 231
Freeman, H. P., 543
Freeman, J. R., 483
Freeman, L., 154
Freeman, R. C., 438
Freeman, S. A., 446
Fremer, J. J., 627
Frenkel, E., 482
Freud, S., 613–614, 629–630
Frey, M. A., 620
Fried, Y., 524
Friedman, D. G., 383, 384
Friesen, W. V., 436
Frisby, C. L., 187, 191
Frishberg, Y., 487
Fritz, D., 439
Fronek, A., 151
Frumkin, R. J., 191
Fu, G., 304
Fuchs, D., 184
Fuchs, L. S., 184
Fuertes, J. N., 327
Fugate, L., 384, 613
Fuller, G. B., 305
Funder, D. C., 524, 534, 535–536, 536
Furby, L., 115
Furness, T. A., 625
Furnham, A., 236
Furukawa, T., 502

Gacano, C. B., 398
Gaebel, W., 212
Gagne, P., 440, 441
Gallucci, N. T., 365
Galton, F., 13, 14, 71, 234, 417
Galvin, S. J., 29
Gamble, K. R., 410
Ganapathii, L., 438
Gandek, B., 504
Ganger, W., 288
Ganiats, T. G., 151
Garb, H. N., 20, 391, 393, 395, 403, 404, 405, 408, 616
Garb, H.N., 615
Garcia, J., 555
Garcia, N., 15
Garcia-Esteve, L., 218
Garcia-Lopez, O., 343
Garcia-Merita, M., 384
Garcia-Palacios, A., 444, 445, 625
Gardner, E. F., 318
Gardner, H., 231, 270, 565
Garfield, S. L., 360, 409
Garland, A., 501
Garland, H., 511
Garlick, D., 615

Gaston, L., 365
Gaston, M. F., 364
Gati, I., 468
Gaudreau, P., 378
Gauvain, M., 284
Geer, J. H., 429
Geiselman, R. E., 436
Geiser, S., 327, 616
Geisinger, K. F., 11, 608
Gencoz, F., 378
Gencoz, T., 378
Gendreau, M., 501
Georgas, J., 274
George, D., 522
Gerritse, R., 360
Gersh, D., 365
Gervitz, R. N., 445
Geschwind, D. H., 477
Gesell, A., 285–286
Gessner, T., 305
Ghosh, A., 438, 439, 440
Ghys, A., 293
Gialluca, K. A., 525
Gibbon, M., 217, 218
Gibby, R. G., 398
Gibertini, M., 476
Giglio, R. J., 26
Gilabert, R., 441
Gilberstadt, H., 360
Gilbert, B. O., 194
Gilbert, G. E., 567
Gill, M. M., 263, 394, 416–417
Gillingham, W. H., 190
Gilpin, E. A., 529
Gilson, B. S., 503
Gimenez, M. M., 374
Gist, K., 288
Glas, C. A. W., 234
Glaser, B. A., 366
Gleason, A., 342
Gleaves, D. H., 365
Glenn, D. M., 365
Gleser, G. C., 522, 523
Glickman, A. S., 526
Glutting, J. J., 307
Gnys, M., 501
Goff, M., 178
Goffin, R. D., 375, 381
Goldberg, A. L., 315
Goldberg, L. R., 524
Golden, C. J., 476, 487–488
Goldiamond, I., 197
Goldman, R. D., 563, 566, 572
Goldstein, D. J., 288
Goldstein, L. H., 260, 305
Gollan, J. K., 619
Gollnisch, G., 501
Golomb, B. A., 143, 506
Gomzi, M., 304
Gonzalez, K., 23
Good, C., 542
Goodman, J., 557, 558
Goodyear-Orwat, A., 335
Gordon, E. W., 560
Gordon, J. N., 288
Gordon, N., 263
Gordon, R., 590
Gorham, D. R., 440
Gorsuch, R. L., 495
Gotkin, T. D., 547
Gotlib, I. N., 433
Gottfredson, G. D., 536
Gottfredson, L. S., 55, 144, 455, 560
Gottlib, I. H., 138
Gottman, J., 434
Gottschalk, L. A., 383, 384
Gough, H. G., 166, 348, 366, 367, 377

Gould, J., 218
Gould, S. J., 232, 564, 572
Goulding, J., 292
Grad, G., 58
Grady, D., 516
Grady, J., 591, 592–594
Graesser, A. C., 441
Grafton, F., 445
Graham, F. K., 305
Graham, J. R., 362, 363, 365
Graham, L. G., 434
Graham, S., 473
Grana-Gomez, J. L., 431
Grant, I., 65, 151, 477, 478, 479
Gray, J. R., 341
Green, B. F., 568
Green, B. L., 207
Green, D. F., Jr., 196
Green, D. R., 547
Green, J., 533
Green, K. E., 446
Green, P., 477
Green, R. L., 364
Greenberg, D., 427
Greene, R. L., 615
Greenfield, P. M., 541
Greenwood, R., 292
Greer, M. K., 288
Gregory, R. J., 232, 259, 260, 261, 262, 263, 265, 266
Greisen, G., 292
Greisinger, K. F., 232
Greist, J. H., 438, 440
Greit, T., 258
Gresham, F. M., 196
Greve, K. W., 483
Gridley, B. E., 287
Griggs, W., 133, 604
Grillis, A. E., 217
Grim, L. G., 87
Groenweg, G., 297
Groessl, E. J., 151, 505
Groth-Marnat, G., 194, 195, 205, 349, 365, 367, 391, 399, 404, 419, 424
Grotzer, T. A., 553
Grove, W. M., 404, 408
Grutter, B., 601–602
Guan, G., 365
Guanzon-Lapena, M. A., 381
Guarnaccia, V., 402
Guastello, S. J., 198, 627
Gudjonsson, G. H., 382
Guedalia, J., 487
Guertin, T. L., 235, 264, 341, 342, 408, 449, 627
Guilford, J. R., 20, 368
Guillemin, F., 505
Guion, R. M., 176
Gullone, E., 428, 429
Guo, N. W., 288
Guo, Y. I., 288
Gur, R. C., 307
Gustafson, D. H., 438
Gustavson, J. L., 487
Guthrie, R. V., 571
Gutloff, K., 3
Guttman, L., 178
Gwynne, J., 186–187
Gyulia, L., 433

Haaga, D. A. F., 383, 384
Haak, N. J., 187
Haaland, K. Y., 476–477, 480
Haber, R. N., 496, 499
Hagell, P., 504
Hagen, E. P., 243, 303
Hahn, C., 232
Haith, M. M., 449

Hakala, M., 504
Hakel, M. D., 415, 511, 533
Hale, J. B., 259
Hall, C. W., 304
Hall, D. T., 453
Hall, E. M., 529
Hall, V. C., 552
Haller, N., 404
Hallman, G. L., 199
Hallmark, R., 392
Halstead, W., 484–487
Hambleton, R. K., 154
Hamel, M., 403, 619
Hammer, A. L., 500
Hammond, J. A., 366
Hampson, E., 195
Hancock, P., 227
Handel, R. W., 194
Handler, L., 419
Haney, W., 539
Hanford, G. H., 323
Hanges, P. J., 542
Hansen, B. M., 292
Hansen, C. F., 588
Hansen, J. C., 455–457, 469
Hanson, M. A., 185, 194, 533
Hanten, G., 477
Hanton, S., 383
Harasym, P. H., 227
Hardy, J. B., 545, 552
Haren, E. G., 380
Haritos-Fatouros, M., 343
Harkness, A. R., 366
Harlow, G., 222
Harmon, L. W., 468
Harms, H. J., 445
Haroaian, J., 619
Harper, J. M., 232
Harrell, T. H., 439
Harris, D. B., 342, 377
Harris, D. H., 17, 631
Harris, F. C., 196
Harris, L. M., 429, 440
Harris, M. M., 227
Harrison, M. J., 292
Harrison, P. J., 222
Harrison, R., 415
Harsveld, M., 344
Hart, B., 349
Hart, K. J., 364, 366
Hartig, L., 566
Hartigan, J., 55, 552
Hartlage, L. C., 552
Hartman, D. E., 194–195
Hartman, E., 398, 408
Hartman, J. G., 59
Hartung, P. J., 472
Harty, H., 322
Harvey, M., 510
Harwell, M., 119
Hase, H. D., 524
Hass, J. K., 297
Hastya, M. K., 439
Hathaway, S. R., 355–356, 358–359, 360
Hatoum, H. T., 504
Hattie, J., 306
Hatton, C., 217
Hauser, R. M., 105, 124, 141, 153, 522
Hayes, F. B., 297
Hayes, J. S., 292
Hayes, N., 380, 381
Hayes, R. D., 176, 178
Hayman, A., 478
Haynes, O. M., 232
Haynes, S. N., 424, 431, 435, 436, 612, 624, 625
Haynes, W. O., 187

Hays, P. A., 232
He, Y., 447
Hearst, E., 14
Heath, V. A., 232
Heatherton, T. F., 382
Heaton, R. K., 478
Hebell, J. R., 292
Hecht, F., 274
Hedge, J. W., 185
Heiby, E. M., 612
Heider, F., 473
Heilbrun, A. B., Jr., 374, 377
Heimberg, R. G., 443, 511
Heinrich, 381
Heinze, M. C., 361
Heitzmann, C. A., 501
Heller, D., 386
Heller, K., 206
Henderson, N. B., 552
Henninger, N. J., 429
Henri, V., 349, 394
Henry, C. A., 622
Henry, P., 322, 622
Hensley, W., 207
Henson, R., 191
Henson, R. K., 378
Herbart, J. E., 13, 14
Herbert, W., 294
Herman, S., 435
Hernandez-Reif, M., 284
Herrnstein, R. J., 144, 239, 564, 571, 572, 606
Herron, E. W., 409
Hersen, M., 196
Hersh, J. B., 190
Hershberger, S. L., 612, 621
Hershkowitz, I., 217
Hertz, M., 394, 399
Hertzberg, M. A., 365
Herzberg, D. S., 377
Herzoff, N., 366, 434
Herzog, D. B., 395
Hesselbrock, V. M., 298
Hessling, R. M., 501
Hetter, R. D., 345
Hetu, M., 439
Hetzel, R. D., 297
Heubert, J. P., 105, 124, 141, 153, 522
Heuchert, J. W. P., 381
Hewett, J. B., 304
Hewitt, M., 438
Hezlett, S. A., 333
Higgins, C. A., 511
Higgins, E. T., 472
Higgins, T. L., 26
Hilgard, E. R., 21, 524, 626
Hill, E., 366
Hill, E. F., 410
Hill, R. A., 433
Hilliard, A., 593
Hillix, W. A., 190
Hilsenroth, M. J., 399
Hilsenroth, M. K., 409
Hinz, M., 504
Hirt, M., 447
Hiscock, M., 342
Hobson, J. W., 588
Hodapp, A. F., 297
Hoeppner, J. B., 259
Hoff, B., 292
Hoffman, H., 365
Hoffman, H. G., 445, 625
Hogan, J., 607
Hoge, G., 217
Holaday, M., 418
Holahan, C. J., 530
Holden, C., 602
Holifield, J. E., 365–366

Holland, D., 307
Holland, J. L., 455–456, 462, 467, 469, 474, 536
Holland, P. W., 175
Hollander, E., 494
Hollingworth, H. L., 225
Holmeford, A., 300
Holmes, C. B., 332
Holt, R. R., 22
Holtzman, W. H., 401, 402, 405, 409–410, 440
Holz, W., 197
Honaker, L. M., 439
Honig, B., 595
Hooper, S. R., 289, 478
Horaian, J., 403
Horkheimer, R., 343
Horn, J. L., 236, 246
Horne, M., 526
Horner, M., 435
Horowitz, F. D., 288
Horowitz, M. J., 500
Hoskens, M., 175
Hotelling, H., 367
Hough, L. M., 137
Hough, R., 501
House, J. D., 330, 331, 332, 337
Houston, R. J., 483
Houston, W. S., 491
Howard, J. L., 225, 511
Howard, L., 597
Hsu, C. C., 288
Hu, C., 380, 381
Hu, S., 334
Huang, C. D., 381
Hubbs-Tait, L., 292
Hubert, R. A., 381
Hudson, A., 567
Huffaker, B. J., 510
Huffcutt, A. I., 225, 226, 227, 510, 532, 545
Hufford, M. R., 501
Hugh, H. V., 438
Hughes, J., 478
Huibregste, I., 162
Humphreys, L., 590
Hunsley, J. M., 391, 392, 394, 409, 626, 630
Hunt, E., 448
Hunt, J. McV., 534
Hunt, T. V., 292
Hunter, J. E., 153, 522, 560, 562
Hunter, M., 526
Huntley, R. M., 547
Huppertz, J. W., 552
Huprich, S. K., 378
Hurlburt, R. T., 27
Hurley, A. D., 223
Hurt, S. W., 199
Hutchinson, M. B., 297
Hwang, S. H. S., 383
Hyne, S. A., 458

Iacono, W. G., 435, 436
Ilgen, D., 577
Ilies, R., 381
Imada, A. S., 511
Imhof, E. A., 626
Inch, R., 342
Ingman, K. A., 429
Ingraham, L. H., 383
Ingraham, L. J., 482
Ingram, F., 297
Ingram, R. E., 145
Ironson, G. H., 176, 547
Iverson, G. L., 366
Iwata, N., 495
Iyer, A., 603
Izgic, F., 382

Jaccard, J., 83
Jackson, C. A., 323
Jackson, D. N., 375, 381, 466, 619, 621
Jackson, E. W., 232
Jackson, J. D., 374
Jacob, B. A., 3
Jacobs, R., 142
Jacobs, R. R., 521, 523, 561
Jacobsen, T. L., 567
Jacobson, L., 538, 571, 590
Jacobson, M. W., 303, 436, 492
Jager, R. S., 225
Jahng, S. M., 383
Jang, D. P., 444, 625
Janssen, E., 436
Jeanneret, P. R., 533
Jennings, J. R., 436
Jensen, A. R., 294, 447, 448, 538, 550
Jerusalem, M., 378, 382
Ji, C. C., 330–331
Jie, Z., 429
Jing, G., 304
Johansson, C. B., 466–467
Johansson, G., 529
Johansson, J. C., 467
Johnson, J. H., 364
Johnson, J. J., 330
Johnson, J. V., 529
Johnson, K. N., 364
Johnson, L. B., 576
Johnson, N. E., 235, 264, 265, 312, 341, 342, 386, 408, 449, 612, 627, 628
Johnson, V., 436
Johnston, D., 435
Johnstone, B., 307
Joiner, T. E., 378
Jolly, D., 505
Jones, C. H., 188
Jones, E. E., 472, 473
Jones, I., 292
Jones, P. W., 108
Jones, R. A., 433
Jones, R. N., 232
Jonsson, F. H., 378
Joseph, S., 380, 381
Joshi, R., 483
Judge, T. A., 380, 381, 385, 386
Judiesch, M. K., 522
Jung, C. G., 417, 525–526
Jungeblut, A., 570

Kacmar, K. M., 510, 511
Kaernmer, B., 362
Kagan, J., 545
Kager, M. B., 510, 511
Kahn, J. H., 501
Kaiser, H., 563
Kalat, J. W., 312
Kalish, K., 193
Kallingal, A., 550
Kamhi, A. G., 295
Kamin, L. J., 538, 571, 572, 590, 594
Kammeier, M. L., 365
Kamphaus, R. W., 293
Kamura, D., 195
Kane, M. J., 236
Kanfer, F. H., 425, 431–432, 450
Kanowitz, J., 196, 197
Kantor, J., 194
Kantor, L., 493
Kapes, J. T., 439
Kaplan, C., 118
Kaplan, E., 478, 490
Kaplan, R. F., 298

Kaplan, R. M., 22, 58, 62, 65, 69, 90, 108, 140–141, 143, 147, 151, 166, 195, 486, 488, 501, 503, 505–506, 516, 524
Kappelman, M. M., 284
Kareken, D. A., 307
Karlsen, B., 318
Karnes, F. A., 294
Karp, S. A., 414
Kashdan, T. B., 501
Kastanago, K. B., 197
Kaszniak, A. W., 478
Katania, J. A., 119
Katigbak, M. S., 381
Katikaneni, L. D., 288
Katz, R., 433
Katz, S. E., 354
Katzman, R., 491
Kaufman, A. S., 259, 260, 262, 263, 275, 292–295, 303, 342
Kaufman, N. L., 292–295, 303
Kaufman, S. H., 418
Kaushik, T., 483
Kautiainen, H., 504
Kawas, C., 304
Kay, G. G., 378
Kazdin, A. E., 196
Keeley, E. J., 337
Kefyalew, F., 222
Kehoe, J. F., 547
Keiser, R. E., 410
Keith, L. K., 297
Keller, J. W., 392
Keller, K. E., 511
Keller, L. S., 440
Keller, S. D., 504
Kelley, T. L., 16
Kellogg, R. T., 11
Kelly, D., 402
Kelly, E. L., 21, 626
Kelly, H. H., 472, 473
Kenardy, J., 435
Kendall, P. C., 434
Kendell, B. S., 305
Kennedy, R. B., 511
Kenrick, D. T., 207
Kent, G. H., 417
Kent, R. N., 196, 197
Keogh, B. K., 285
Keough, K., 542
Kerckhoffs-Hanssen, M., 427
Kerlikowske, K., 516
Kerner, D. N., 151
Kerner, J., 393–394
Kerr, M., 447
Kewley, S., 386
Kicklighter, R., 596
Kido, D. K., 477
Kiers, H. A. L., 235
Kiesler, S., 439
Kim, J. H., 383
Kim, S. I., 444, 625
Kimble, G. A., 287
Kimmel, C., 439
King, N. J., 429
Kirkby, K. C., 444
Kirkpatrick, E. A., 394
Kirmeyer, S. L., 529
Kirsch, I., 189, 445
Kivlighan, D. M., Jr., 207
Klaiaberg, A., 504
Klaus, R. A., 571
Klausen, O., 300
Kleberg, A., 288
Klein, B. P., 292
Klein, J., 440
Klein, M. H., 438

Klein, S. P., 339
Kleinsaser, L. D., 190
Klett, W. G., 322
Klieger, D. M., 428, 429
Klin, A., 298
Kline, J. P., 378
Kline, P., 92
Klinkenberg, W. D., 437, 438, 442
Klonoff, H., 477
Klopfer, B., 394, 401, 402
Klos, D., 471
Kluger, A. N., 386
Knapp-Lee, L., 471–472
Knight, D., 185
Knight-Jones, E. B., 292
Knobloch, H., 571
Knott, M., 92, 101, 126
Kobasa, S. C., 378
Koeter, M. W. J., 382
Koffler, S. L., 546
Kohs, S. C., 262
Kole-Snijders, A. J., 427
Koltai, D. C., 478
Kong, S. X., 504
Kornhaber, M. L., 584
Koppitz, E. M., 304
Kosinski, M., 503, 504
Kossowska, M., 349
Koszychi, D., 365
Kraepelin, E., 14
Kraft, R. G., 439
Kraiger, K., 415
Kramer, J. H., 478, 490, 491, 493
Krechevsky, M., 565
Kreiner, D. S., 262
Kremen, A., 382
Kreutzkamp, R., 223
Krikorian, R., 298
Krinsky, S. G., 296
Kroger, H., 483
Krohn, E. J., 294
Krol, N. P. C. M., 440
Ku, L., 222
Kubisiak, U. C., 533
Kuder, G. F., 101, 111–112, 462–466
Kugelmass, S., 482
Kugu, N., 382
Kuh, G. D., 334
Kuhn, C., 284
Kuiper, N. A., 433
Kukich, K., 441
Kumar, C., 366
Kuncel, N. R., 333
Kutner, K., 483
Kwon, P., 366

Lachman, A., 288
Lagercrantz, H., 288
La Guardia, J. G., 378
Lahey, B. B., 196
Lai, T. J., 288
Lally, M., 448
Lambert, N., 590
Lamp, R. E., 294, 552
Landauer, T., 441
Landis, C., 354
Landy, F. J., 136, 142, 143, 144, 153, 199
Lane, B., 428
Lang, P. J., 429
Langdon, D. W., 322
Langenbucher, J. W., 108
Langter, P., 3
Lankford, J. S., 439
Lanyon, B. P., 418
Lanyon, R. I., 418

Lapierre, A. M., 378
Larimore, C., 307
Larkin, J. E., 511
Larrabee, L. L., 190
Larsen, R., 353
Larsen, R. J., 384, 385
Larson, G. E., 341, 447, 449
Larson, J. H., 232
LaRue, A., 476–477, 480
Lassiter, K. S., 297
Latham, G. P., 522
Latham, V. M., 223
Lau, A., 501
Laub, D., 216
Laughlin, J. E., 163
Laughren, T. P., 438
Lautenschlager, G. J., 194
Lauter, D., 599, 604, 605
Law, K., 522
Lawlor, S., 324, 327
Lawrence, I., 323
Lawshe, C. L., 136
Lawson, K., 288
Lazarus, R. S., 499–500
Lea, R. B., 26
Leach, J., 365
Leahey, L., 287
Leahy, R. L., 11, 433
Ledbetter, M., 261
Lee, E. D., 597
Lee, E. S., 136
Lee, J. M., 445
Leekham, S. R., 218
Legorgee, M. H., 303
Leichsenring, F., 410
Leman, N., 564
Lemke, S., 530–531
Lenz, J. G., 467
Leong, C., 483
Lerner, B., 598
Leslie, L. K., 288
Lessen-Firestone, J., 284
Lesser, G. S., 545
Lessler, J. T., 438
Levenson, H., 366
Levenson, M. R., 365
Levenson, R. W., 436
Levesque, L. L., 225
Levi, A., 552
Levin, H., 478
Levin, H. S., 298
Levin, K. Y., 533
Levine, D. W., 152
Levitas, A. S., 223
Levy, D., 19, 394
Lewandowski, D. G., 22, 268,
   269, 398
Lewinsohn, P. N., 138
Lewis, C., 327
Lewis, C. D., 298
Lewis, J. G., 378
Lezak, M. D., 389, 470, 478,
   490
Li, F., 225
Libby, S. J., 218
Lichtenberg, P. A., 478
Lichtenberger, E. O., 275
Lichtenstein, E., 529
Liebert, R. M., 496, 498–499
Lifschitz, M. H., 285
Lifshitz, F., 58
Likert, R., 162–164
Lilienfeld, S. O., 20, 199, 391,
   395, 403, 404, 405, 410,
   412, 413, 414, 615
Lincoln, R. K., 267
Lindberg, L. D., 222
Lindemann, S. J., 552
Lindsey, M. L., 187, 191

Lindvall, O., 504
Lindzey, G., 413–414, 420
Linn, R. L., 178, 181
Lipsitz, J. D., 268
Lipsitz, S., 186–187
Liss, P. H., 449
Litcher-Kelly, L., 501
Little, K. B., 401, 405, 415, 616
Liu, K. K., 3
Livesley, W. J., 466
Livingston, R., 294
Llorente, A., 288
Lochman, J. E., 515
Locke, E. A., 386
Locke, S. D., 194
Loehlin, J. C., 92, 126
Loevinger, J., 418
Loffredo, D. A., 526
Lohman, D. F., 340–341
Lohr, N. E., 263
Lombard, D., 439
Longford, N. J., 83
Longhui, L., 304
Longley, S., 341
Looney, M., Jr., 59
Loper, R. G., 365
Lopez, R., 552
Lopez, S. J., 262
Lopez-Ibor, J. J., 212
Lord, E., 395
Lord, F. M., 83
Lorentz, S., 298
Lorenzo-Seva, U., 235
Loughmiller, G. C., 567
Lowman, R. L., 625
Loy, D. L., 360
Lubin, B., 305, 353, 372
Lucas, J. A., 478
Lucas, J. L., 466
Lucas, R. E., 384
Lugg, C. A., 27
Lui, Z., 366
Lukin, M. E., 439
Lundqvist, C., 284
Luneman, R., 552
Lunneborg, C., 448
Lunz, M. E., 185
Luo, D., 322
Luria, A. R., 293, 477, 487–489
Lurie, J. D., 522
Lushene, R. E., 495
Lustina, M. J., 542
Lutejin, F., 384
Lynn, R., 327
Lysaker, P., 258
Lysaker, P. H., 263

Mabon, H., 526
Mabry, L., 307
Macan, T. H., 510
Machamer, J. E., 478
Machover, K., 418, 419
Macias, M. M., 288
Mackintosh, N. J., 449
MacLeod, H. A., 439
MacNeill, S. E., 478
Madureira, S., 432
Magalette, P. R., 383
Magnusson, D., 534
Magsman, P. J., 491
Mahon, N. E., 382
Maistro, S. A., 431
Maj, M., 212
Majnemer, A., 284
Malcuit, G., 287
Malgady, R., 416
Malinchoc, M., 365
Malley, S. M., 217
Maloney, M. P., 216

Malos, S. B., 511
Malreaux, J., 15
Maltby, N., 445
Mancuso, N., 264
Mandes, E., 305
Mandin, H., 227
Mandler, G., 495–497, 498
Manners, J., 418
Mannheim, K., 556
Manning, C., 185
Manzano, J., 288
Mapou, R. L., 478
March, J. S., 478
Marchman, V. A., 296
Marcus, A., 447, 448
Margeson, F. P., 205
Margo, A., 438
Mark, J. C., 416
Marks, K. A., 263
Marks, N., 263
Marks-Katz, M., 58
Markus, K. A., 333
Marlett, N. J., 498
Marlott, R. W., 335
Marsh, H. W., 189
Marshalek, B., 340–341
Marshall, H., 166
Marshall, L. J., 207
Marshall, W. L., 436
Martin, A., 434
Martin, C. J., 445
Martin, C. R., 526
Martin, P., 195
Martin, R., 265
Martin, R. A., 526
Martin, R. P., 297
Marting, M. S., 500
Maruish, M., 626
Marusic, I., 381
Marvin, L., 148
Marvin, M. T., 148
Mascolo, J. T., 302
Masel, B. E., 297
Massara, G., 384
Massingale, T. W., 288
Massman, P. J., 478
Masters, B. N., 548
Masters, W., 436
Matarazzo, J. D., 194, 353, 616,
   625
Matheny, K. B., 384
Mather, N., 301, 302
Mathias, C. W., 483
Matias, R., 431
Matt, M., 194
Matthews, C., 264
Matthews, T. D., 297
Mau, W., 327
Mauer, D., 295
Maurer, T. J., 197, 224
Maxwell, J. K., 366
May, M. C., 365
Mayer, B., 429
Mayer, D. J., 542
Mayers, M., 445
Mayeux, R., 268
Mayfield, E. C., 226, 510
Mazer, B., 284
Mazumdar, S., 197
McAnulty, D. P., 190
McBride, J. R., 345
McCabe, K. M., 501
McCabe, S. E., 442
McCall, W. A., 27, 28, 50–51
McCallum, R. S., 294
McCarty, J. R., 547
McCauley, M. H., 526
McClelland, D. C., 108, 410,
   411
McCormick, E. J., 577

McCoy, M. L., 428
McCrae, R. R., 381, 385
McCunn, A., 303
McDaniel, M. A., 225, 226, 521,
   524
McDonald, R. P., 101
McDonnell, A., 534
McDougall, A., 397
McDowell, I., 504
McEwen, J., 503
McFall, R. M., 534
McGill-Evans, J., 292
McGrath, J. M., 284
McGrath, R. E., 361
McGraw, K. O., 442
McGrew, K. S., 232, 236, 263,
   301, 303
McGuffin, P., 433
McGuinness, S. G., 567
McHale, M. A., 444
McHorney, C. A., 185, 503
McIntosh, D. E., 303
McIntyre, L. L., 196
McKay, J. R., 431
McKay, P. F., 323
McKee, P., 596
McKenna, P., 478
McKenna, S. P., 504
McKinley, J. C., 356, 358–359,
   360
McLaughlin, V., 196
McLennan, N. A., 469
McMahon, R. C., 365
McManis, D. L., 191
McMichael, A. J., 292
McNamara, T., 546
McNeilly, M., 437
McNemar, O. W., 354
McNemar, Q., 83
McNulty, J. L., 365, 366
McPeek, W. M., 546
McRae, R. R., 378
McReynolds, C. J., 618
Meara, P., 162
Mednick, S., 143
Medoff-Cooper, B., 284
Meehl, P. E., 136, 150, 360–362,
   402, 405, 524, 616
Meesters, C., 293, 429
Megargee, E. I., 366, 367
Mehl, M. R., 443, 625
Mehrens, W. A., 3
Meichenbaum, D., 434–435,
   450
Meijer, J., 195, 493, 498
Meijer, R. R., 178, 234
Meikle, S., 360
Melchert, P. A., 191
Melchert, T. P., 334
Melei, J. P., 524
Mellanby, J. H., 322
Mellenbergh, G. J., 115, 546
Mellits, E. D., 545
Meloy, J. R., 392, 398, 408
Ment, L. R., 296
Menzies, R. G., 429, 440
Mercan, S., 361
Mercer, J. R., 545, 551,
   556–560, 571, 586, 590
Merckelbach, H., 293, 429
Merrell, K. W., 191, 620
Merten, T., 417
Mervis, C. B., 292, 448
Merwin, J. C., 318
Messick, S. J., 136, 153, 570,
   619, 621
Metalsky, G. I., 192
Metraux, R. W., 397
Meunier, C., 498

Meyer, G. J., 404, 405, 622
Meyer, J., 162
Meyer, K., 612
Meyer, R. G., 371
Meyer-Bahlburg, H. F., 304
Miceli, N. S., 510
Michael, B., 448, 449
Michael, S. T., 383
Michell, J., 101
Middendorf, C. H., 510
Middlestadt, S. E., 227, 510
Miele, F., 232
Mikulay, S. M., 375
Miles, J. A., 225
Milgrom, P., 429
Miller, A., 154
Miller, A. B., 516
Miller, C. E., 292
Miller, D. R., 398
Miller, E. T., 442
Miller, J. A. L., 29
Miller, J. M., 335
Miller, J. O., 185
Miller, S., 447
Mills, C. N., 437, 627
Millsap, R. E., 499
Min, K. H., 383
Minor, J. S., 295
Minshew, N. J., 260
Minton, H. L., 468–469
Mirsky, A. F., 482
Mischel, W., 472, 473, 474, 614
Miskulin, D., 503
Mislevy, R. J., 100
Mitchell, C. D., 304
Mitchell, C. W., 380
Mitchell, K., 199
Mitchell, K. J., 522
Mitchell, K. M., 216
Mobs, R., 478
Modglin, A., 232
Moe, V., 288
Mogilka, H. J., 185
Molfese, D. L., 232
Molfese, V. J., 232
Moller, P., 300
Monahan, J., 616
Monroe, S. M., 499
Moore, S. D., 365
Moos, R. H., 529–531
Morales, A., 435, 436
Moran, M. J., 187
Moreland, K. L., 391, 400, 625
Moreno, K. E., 345
Morgan, C., 19–20, 410
Morgan, M. J., 427
Morgan, S. K., 303
Morgeson, F. P., 223, 225, 510
Morishima, A., 304
Morris, J., 438, 439
Morris, L. W., 496, 498–499
Morrison, M., 333
Morrison, T., 333
Morrow, C. E., 284
Morse, R. M., 365
Moseley, E. C., 440
Moser, D., 263
Moses, J. A., 488
Moss, H. A., 545
Moss, P., 625
Moss, S., 217
Motgilka, H. J., 194
Motowidlo, S. J., 137, 525
Moun, T., 185, 186
Mount, M. K., 380
Muir, S. P., 17
Mulick, J. A., 288
Mulsant, B. H., 197

Mumford, M. D., 533
Munari, A., 445
Munley, P. H., 365
Munro, E., 448
Munshi, I. A., 26
Munsinger, H., 538
Munson, J., 235
Muris, P., 429
Murphy, K. R., 143, 144, 153
Murphy, L. B., 449
Murphy, S. E., 236
Murray, C. A., 144, 564, 571, 606
Murray, H. A., 19–20, 372, 373, 375, 410–411, 412, 420
Murstein, B. I., 412, 415
Murtagh, M., 440
Mutran, E. J., 159
Myers, B. J., 284
Myers, I. B., 525–526
Mysiw, W. J., 384, 613
Mzumara, H. R., 439

Naar-King, S., 620
Nader, R., 140–141
Naglieri, J. A., 280, 286
Nagy, V. T., 499
Nasta, A., 445
Nathanson, B. H., 26
Naughton, M. J., 503
Navarro, P., 218
Neher, L. A., 190
Neil, R., 383
Neisser, U., 293, 312, 328, 447
Nell, V., 566
Nellis, L., 287
Nelson, D. V., 365
Nelson, W. M., 364, 366, 375
Neto, F., 384
Nettelbeck, T., 447, 448, 449
Nevo, B., 225
Newell, C., 504
Newman, M. G., 433, 435, 443, 444
Newton, R. L., 405
Nezworski, M. T., 20, 391, 393, 395, 403, 405, 408, 409, 615
Nguyen, S. E., 343
Niccols, A., 288
Nichols, D. S., 364
Nieberding, R., 392
Nigl, A. J., 550
Nikzad, K., 449
Nilsen, D., 458
Nisbett, R. E., 472, 473
Nittono, H., 372
Noble, A. C., 547
Noll, J., 236, 246
Norcross, J. C., 216
Nordstrom, C. R., 510
Norlin, J. W., 279, 280
Norman, D. K., 395
Norman, G., 165
North, M. M., 445
North, S. M., 445
Northstone, K., 292
Norton, E. H., 599
Novella, J. L., 505
Novick, B. Z., 299
Novick, M. R., 576
Novy, D. M., 365
Noyman, A., 294
Nugent, W. R., 178
Null, C., 364
Nunnally, J. C., 27, 100, 104, 124
Nurius, P. S., 222

Nuvolone, G., 384
Nyborg, H., 538
Nykodym, N., 511
Nystul, M. S., 537

Oakland, T., 144, 557, 558
Ober, B. A., 490
Oberwager, J., 439
Odbert, H. S., 368
Oehler-Stinnett, J., 294
Oei, T. P. S., 495
Oerlemans, S., 436
Oest, L. G., 429
O'Halloran, C. M., 566
Ojuel, J., 218
Okagaki, L., 565
Okazaki, S., 188
O'Leary, B. S., 551
O'Leary, K. D., 196, 197
Olinger, L. J., 433
Oliver, J. M., 383
Olkin, R., 366
Ollendick, T. H., 217, 429
Olmedo, E. L., 572
Olson-Buchanan, J., 101
Olson-Tinker, H., 196
O'Malley, W. B., 361
Ones, D. S., 198, 333, 571, 619, 622
Onghena, P., 427
Oostdam, R., 195, 493, 498
Opt, S. K., 526
Optale, G., 445
Opton, E., 589, 591
Orfield, G., 584
Orlansky, J., 445
Ortiz, S. O., 263
Osberg, T. M., 365
O'Shea, T. M., 288
Osipow, S. H., 469–470, 474
Ostrea, E., Jr., 284
O'Sullivan, M., 198
O'Sullivan, P. S., 567
Othmer, E., 217
Othmer, S. C., 217
Ott, B., 263
Ottern, E., 300
Overton, R. C., 445
Owen, D., 232, 545, 570
Owen, P. R., 429
Oxford, K. P., 365
Ozoran, K., 504

Padawer, J. R., 399
Page, E., 440
Paine, C., 372
Palaniappan, A. K., 306
Palmer, F. H., 552
Palola, E. G., 498
Palomba, D., 431
Paolo, A. M., 267
Parducci, A., 164–165
Parke, R. D., 524
Parker, J. D. A., 385, 493, 500, 534
Parker, K., 404
Parker, P. A., 501
Parker, W. D., 381
Parks, A. A., 232
Parmelee, R., 144, 557
Parra, E. B., 589
Parsons, O. A., 477
Partenio, I., 557
Pary, R., 223
Pasamanick, B. A., 571
Patalano, F., 184
Patrick, D. L., 108
Patterson, M., 188

Patterson, T. L., 151
Pattishall, E., 108
Patton, W., 384
Paty, J. A., 501
Paul, G. L., 197, 498
Paul, R., 263
Paunonen, S. V., 375, 381
Pavicevic, L., 304
Payne, R., 543
Pearson, K., 71
Peca-Baker, T., 511
Pechacek, T. F., 434
Peckham, R., 574, 589–591, 592–594, 595
Pedersen, N. L., 612
Pedhazur, E. J., 65
Pedulla, J. J., 631
Pedulla, J. A., 315
Pena, L. M., 366
Pendleton, M. G., 478
Penfield, R. D., 166, 176
Penge, R., 296
Penne, M. A., 438
Pennebaker, J. W., 443, 625
Pennington, B. F., 483
Peoples, V. Y., 468
Perkins, D. N., 553
Perkos, S., 434
Pernas, A., 385
Perpina, C., 445
Perrez, M., 435
Perry, J. N., 442
Perry, M. S., 358
Perry, W., 397
Peruch, P., 625
Peter, O., 473
Peterson, C., 433
Peterson, D. A., 226
Peterson, N. G., 533
Petrides, K. V., 236
Petrocelli, J. V., 366
Pettigrew, T. F., 545
Pettit, F. A., 442
Pettit, J. W., 378
Pfeifer, C., 550
Pfister, H., 193
Phares, E. J., 261, 263, 264, 265
Phelps, P., 292
Phillips, J., 185
Phillips, M. L., 194
Phillips, S. E., 11, 609
Pianon, C., 445
Picard, R. W., 440
Picone, L., 291
Piedmont, R. L., 378, 381
Pierce, G. R., 534
Pierce, J. P., 529
Piers, V. P., 377
Pines, H. A., 511
Pinsoneault, T. B., 439
Piotrowski, C., 392, 626
Piotrowski, Z. A., 305, 393, 394
Pirozzolo, F. J., 236
Plaisted, J. R., 487
Plake, B. S., 439
Pleck, J. H., 222
Poland, D. L., 365
Polansky, N., 428
Polkey, C. E., 305
Pollack, J. M., 327
Pollock, B. G., 197
Pomaki, G., 501
Pomerlau, A., 287
Pons, D., 384
Pons, L., 417
Poon, L. W., 195
Pope, K. S., 441
Pope, M. K., 384

Popham, W. J., 154
Popper, S. E., 374
Posthuma, R. A., 205, 223, 225, 510, 511
Poston, W. S. C., 495
Potenza, M. T., 627
Potter, E. F., 17
Poulton, J. L., 384
Powell, F. C., 372
Powell, J., 435
Powell, M. B., 439
Power, M. J., 433
Powers, D. E., 146, 327, 441
Prather, E. N., 410
Prediger, D. J., 472
Prewitt, L. M., 524
Price, J. H., 443, 625
Price, K. H., 511
Price, P. B., 567
Primi, R., 236
Prince, R. J., 627
Prinstein, M. J., 223
Pritchard, D. A., 488
Prohovnik, I., 268
Prosser, H., 217
Prout, H. T., 297
Pugh, R. C., 329
Pugliese, M. D., 58, 59
Pulvers, K. M., 383
Purdie, N., 296
Purisch, A. D., 361
Pyne, J. M., 151

Quaintance, M. K., 470, 533
Quatman, G., 364
Quay, L. C., 545
Quenk, N. L., 525, 526
Quigley, A. M., 607
Quintar, B., 395

Rablen, R. A., 214
Raczek, A., 503
Rafferty, J. E., 418
Raggio, D. J., 288
Raju, N. S., 522
Ralston, S. M., 225–226
Ramanaiah, N. V., 381, 383
Ramirez, M., 563
Rammsayer, T. H., 343
Ramos, R. A., 522
Ramsay, M. C., 11, 232
Ramstad, P. M., 522
Randolph, D. L., 375
Rankin, R. J., 294
Rao, S. M., 477, 478
Rapaport, D., 263, 394, 416–417
Rappaport, N. B., 190
Rapport, M. D., 429
Rasulis, R., Jr., 440
Ratliffr-Shaub, K., 288
Rauch, S., 136
Raven, J., 339–342
Raven, J. C., 339–342
Reagan, R., 599
Reardon, R. C., 467
Rebello, I., 340
Redfield, J., 197
Ree, M. J., 345
Reed, K., 297
Reed, P. S., 159
Reed, S. B., 225
Reeve, A., 477
Regine, A., 291
Reheiser, E. C., 495
Reid, J. B., 196, 197
Reilly-Harrington, N. A., 433
Reise, S. P., 178
Reiseaeeter, S., 300

Reisman, J. M., 410
Reitan, R. M., 477, 484–487
Reith, J., 324
Reschly, D. J., 550, 558, 596
Resnick, S. M., 304
Retzlaff, P. D., 476
Revicki, D. A., 445, 506
Reyes, H., 441
Reynolds, B., 599
Reynolds, C. R., 11, 232, 293, 294, 488, 547, 550
Reznikoff, M., 199, 391, 400
Rhodewalt, F., 384
Ribaudo, F., 291
Ricciardi, P. W., 294
Riccio, M., 296
Richards, J. M., Jr., 567
Richardson, M. W., 101, 111–112
Richeson, N., 384
Richman, C. L., 324
Richman, S., 324
Richman, W. L., 439
Ridenour, T. A., 522
Ridge, S., 206
Ridley, D. R., 526
Rieke, M. L., 198
Ries, A. L., 151, 524
Riethmiller, R. J., 419
Riggio, R., 236
Righetti-Velterna, M., 288
Rigol, G. W., 323
Rimland, B., 447
Ritzler, B. A., 392, 415–416, 630
Riva, G., 445
Rizza, M. G., 303
Roberson, J., 298
Roberts, J. S., 163
Robertson, G. J., 307, 625
Robertson, I. T., 139
Robinson, B. F., 448
Robinson, H., 297
Robinson, J., 429, 440
Rock, D. A., 327
Rocklin, T. R., 445
Rodger, S., 285
Rodger, S. C., 536
Rodriguez, C. M., 499
Roe, A., 471
Roeckelein, J. E., 202
Roehling, M. V., 511
Rogers, C. R., 212, 214, 216, 348–349, 377
Rogers, H. L., 431
Rogers, S. M., 222, 438
Rogers, W. H., 503
Rogler, L. H., 416
Rohlman, D. S., 185
Roid, G. H., 231, 234, 236, 247, 250
Rolland, J. P., 381
Rollnick, J. D., 304
Rorschach, H., 19, 393–394
Rosales, S., 283
Rosanoff, A. J., 417
Roscoe, A. H., 435
Rose, C. L., 449
Rosekrans, F. M., 514, 515
Rosen, A., 360, 616
Rosen, J., 197
Rosenberg, M., 382
Rosenblatt, N., 322
Rosenfeld, P., 194
Rosenstein, R., 526
Rosenthal, M., 503
Rosenthal, R., 188–189, 190, 538, 571, 590
Rosner, J., 338, 616

Rosnow, R. L., 189
Ross, G., 288
Ross, R. R., 567
Ross, S., 365
Rosser, R., 504
Rossini, E., 488
Roth, P. L., 225, 226, 227, 510, 532, 545
Rothman, M., 108
Rothman, S., 232, 563
Rothstein, H. R., 153, 522, 525
Rotter, J. B., 90, 418
Rotunda, R. J., 441
Roussos, L. A., 193
Rowe, P. M., 510
Rowse, G. L., 438
Roy, D. D., 495
Roznowski, M., 324
Rubin, D. B., 162
Rubin, S. M., 516
Rubin, Z., 148–149
Rubio, D. M., 136
Ruch, G. M., 16
Rudman, H. C., 318
Rudner, L. M., 440, 441, 446
Ruisel, I., 232
Rule, B. G., 498
Rush, A. J., 222
Rushton, J. P., 538, 572
Russell, D. W., 501
Russell, E. W., 440, 442
Russell, G., 265
Russell, I. J., 151
Russell, J. T., 516–521
Russell, L. B., 506
Russo, A., 17
Rutter, M., 292
Ruud, W. N., 511
Ryan, J. J., 262, 267
Ryan, J. M., 11
Ryan, J. R., 274

Sabatino, S., 402
Sabel, K. J., 284
Sabers, D. L., 550
Saccuman, C., 296
Saccuzzo, D. P., 11, 22, 207, 235, 264, 265, 268, 269, 312, 335, 341, 342, 366, 386, 398, 399, 408, 447, 448–449, 486, 488, 612, 626, 627, 628
Sackett, P. R., 55, 143, 144, 150, 153, 522, 560
Sager, C. E., 533
Sakkas, D., 343
Sakloske, D. H., 274
Salmon, D. P., 436, 491
Saltzman, J., 526
Sampson, W. S., 365
Sanderman, R., 433
Sandrock, C., 516
Sands, E. W., 305
Sands, W. A., 345
Sanford, R. N., 21, 626
Sangwan, S., 232
Sapp, M., 195, 493
Sapyta, J. J., 378
Sarason, B. R., 493, 497–498, 502, 534
Sarason, I. G., 493, 497–498, 502, 534, 535
Sarason, S. B., 402, 495, 498
Sarlo, M., 431
Saroiu, K. M., 270
Sarris, A., 438
Sartorius, N., 212
Saslow, G., 425, 431–432, 450

Sattler, J. M., 144, 185, 186, 190, 192, 193, 197, 223, 225, 226, 243, 262, 263, 265, 301, 303, 552, 566, 571, 586, 590, 592–594
Satz, P., 478
Saunders, B. T., 190
Saunders, L., 438
Savickas, M. L., 474, 537
Sawin, L. L., 159
Sawyer, J., 616
Sawyer, M., 438
Saykin, A. J., 307
Saylor, C. F., 288
Scarr, S., 545
Schaefer, B. A., 382
Schaefer, J. A., 530
Schafer, R., 263, 394, 416–417
Schaible, D., 397
Schaik, P., 163–164
Schanberg, S., 284
Scheier, I. H., 494
Scheier, M. F., 378, 384
Schene, A. H., 382
Scheuneman, J. D., 545, 547
Schiffer, R. B., 477
Schincaglia, M., 431
Schleicher, A., 3
Schmidt, F. L., 153, 198, 381, 522, 525, 560, 562, 622
Schmidt, K. M., 175, 177
Schmitt, A., 187
Schmitt, N., 510
Schmukle, S. C., 385
Schneider, D. L., 198, 622
Schneider, F. W., 468–469
Schneider, L. M., 312, 550
Schneider, R. J., 178
Schneidman, E. S., 401, 405, 415, 616
Schnipke, D. L., 178
Schoebi, D., 435
Schoggen, P., 528
Scholz, U., 382
Schrader, W. B., 547
Schrank, F. A., 301–302, 303
Schreck, K. A., 288
Schroeder, H. E., 190
Schubert, D., 447
Schuerger, J. M., 369
Schuldberg, D., 440
Schulenberg, S. E., 194
Schuler, H., 224, 511
Schulte, R., 335
Schultz, C. B., 191
Schumacher, J., 504
Schwab-Stone, M., 227
Schwartz, J., 218
Schwartz, J. E., 501
Schwartz, R., 434
Schwarzer, R., 378, 382
Sciarrino, J. A., 138
Scott, L. H., 343
Scott, P., 197
Scrams, D. J., 178
Scurfield, B. K., 29
Seaton, B. E., 20
Sebkovial, N. J., 547
Sechrest, L., 393, 536
Sedlacek, W. E., 327, 550
See, S. K., 445
Seelen, J., 441
Segal, D. L., 217
Segal, H. G., 263
Segall, D. O., 345
Seguin, E., 14
Sekirnjak, G., 353
Self, P. A., 288

Seligman, M., 471
Seligmann, J., 597
Sells, S. B., 401, 402, 405
Selthon, L., 612
Senior, C., 194
Sepehri, A., 274
Serverance, D. D., 446
Sexton, M., 292
Shaffer, D., 205, 217
Shaffer, L. F., 21, 626
Shaffer, T. W., 398, 403, 619
Shakow, D., 21, 626
Shankster, L. J., 142
Shapiro, S. K., 304
Sharkey, K. J., 415, 630
Sharp, J. P., 383
Shaywitz, B. A., 483
Shaywitz, S. E., 483
Sheiles, A., 381
Sheldon, K. L., 297
Sheline, Y. I., 477
Sherman, R. H., 191
Shermis, M. D., 439
Sherry, A., 378, 418
Sherry, D., 392
Sherwood, R. D., 322
Shibata, S., 443
Shibre, T., 618
Shieles, A., 236
Shiffman, S. S., 500–501
Shimmel, J., 3
Shine, A., 269
Shisslak, C. S., 434
Shlomo, N., 304
Shmelyov, A. G., 443, 445, 625
Shore, G. N., 429
Shores, E. A., 359
Shorey, H. S., 383
Shrout, P. E., 118
Shull-Senn, S., 303
Shumaker, J., 194, 195
Shumaker, S. A., 503, 504
Sidick, J. T., 161
Sieber, W. J., 151
Siegel, I. E., 545
Signer, B. R., 445
Sigurdsson, J. F., 382
Sijtsma, K., 178
Silk, K. R., 263
Silva, J. M., 521, 523, 561
Silver, H., 304
Silver, M. J., 189
Silver, N. C., 105
Silverhart, T. A., 510
Simon, T., 14, 233, 236
Simonetti, J. L., 511
Simpson, R. G., 304
Sineps, J., 360
Sines, J. O., 616
Sines, L. K., 405
Singer, J., 392, 408
Singer, O., 618
Singh, L., 415
Sinha, D. K., 324
Sireci, S. G., 136
Sivas, F., 504
Skaltsas, A., 343
Slack, C. W., 439
Slack, W. V., 439
Slate, J. R., 188
Sletten, I. W., 440
Slifer, K. J., 431
Sloan, R. D., 433
Smart, T. K., 375
Smith, A. E., 292
Smith, B., 536
Smith, D. A., 418
Smith, E. V., Jr., 178

Smith, G. A., 448
Smith, I. E., 284
Smith, J. L., 442
Smith, M., 522
Smith, R. E., 535
Smith, T. W., 384, 433
Smith, W. H., 205
Smith, W. L., 566, 567
Snelbaker, A. J., 307
Snow, J. H., 304
Snow, R. E., 189, 340–341, 536, 571
Snyder, C. R., 383
Snyderman, M., 232, 563
Sohn, W. J., 369
Solamon, J. M., 224
Solanto, M. V., 396
Song, J., 298
Soria, E., 441
Sostek, A. M., 284
Sousa, D. A., 232
Southwick, S., 402
Sox, H. C., 522
Space, L. G., 439, 440
Spangler, W. D., 411, 415
Sparrow, S. S., 298
Spearman, C. E., 101, 231, 234–236, 250, 349
Spector, J., 478
Spellacy, F., 526
Spencer, T. J., 447
Sperry, R., 293
Spicuzza, R., 3
Spielberger, C. D., 494–495, 496, 499
Spiers, P. A., 488
Spilker, B., 195
Spira, J. L., 445
Spirrison, C. L., 381
Spitzer, R. L., 118, 188, 217, 218
Spokane, R. A., 467
Sprock, J., 397
Squire, L. R., 490
Srsic, C. S., 467
Stallones, R. A., 143
Stan, E. A., 297
Stankov, L., 236
Stanley, G., 448
Stanley, J. C., 101, 329
Stannard, L., 292
Starr, R., Jr., 284
Stattin, H., 143
Stauss, F. F., 438
Steadman, H. J., 515
Steed, L. G., 115
Steele, C. M., 540, 542
Steele, C. T., 552
Steele, J. W., 199
Steer, R. A., 433
Steger, H. S., 188
Steiger, D. M., 439
Stein, D. J., 494
Steingrub, J. S., 26
Stejskal, W. J., 391, 408
Stem, Y., 268
Stephenson, W., 167
Steptoe, A., 435
Sternberg, L., 557
Sternberg, R. J., 145–146, 231, 294, 312, 519, 563, 565, 615
Stevens, M. C., 298
Stevens, S. S., 165
Steward, R. J., 374
Stewart, A. J., 415
Stewart, A. L., 504
Stewart, M., 393

Stickle, T. R., 393
Stimac, A. P., 467
Stinchfield, R., 188
Stjernqvist, K., 288
Stoelhorst, G. M. S. J., 288
Stokols, D., 528, 529
Stone, A. A., 500–501
Stone, N., 227
Stone, R. A., 197
Stone, V. E., 119
Storzbach, D., 185
Stout, W. F., 29, 193
Strack, S., 499
Strassberg, D. S., 365
Strauss, E., 526
Strauss, M., 284
Strauss, M. E., 305
Strauss, S. G., 225
Stricker, G., 327
Strong, E. K., Jr., 454–457
Studley, R., 327, 616
Stumpf, H., 329, 381
Succi, G. J., 546
Sud, S., 382
Sue, S., 188, 565
Suh, E., 378
Suinn, R. M., 496
Sullivan, D. S., 184
Sulsky, L. M., 525
Summerfeldt, L. J., 217, 218
Sundland, D., 440
Super, D. E., 453
Sutherland, S., 403
Suwalsky, J. T. D., 232
Suzuki, L. A., 232, 564, 565
Svensson, L., 429
Swallen, K. C., 543
Swanda, R. M., 476–477, 480, 487
Swartz, C. W., 178
Swartz, J. D., 409
Sweeney, M., 361
Sweet, J. J., 488, 493
Sweet, R. C., 191
Sweet, S. A., 115
Swerner, W. A., 433
Swinson, R. P., 434
Sydeman, S. J., 494
Symonds, P. M., 166
Sympson, S. C., 383
Szasz, T. S., 618

Tabachnick, B. G., 87, 126
Tait, E., 369
Tallent, N., 440
Tamassia, C., 3
Tang, J., 365
Tanyolac, O., 504
Taplin, P. S., 196
Tarcher, 299
Tarico, V. S., 567
Tarsuoka, K. K., 445
Tatsuoka, M. M., 369, 445
Taulbee, E. S., 495
Tavernelli, M., 369
Tavlor, C. W., 567
Tay, K. M., 429
Taylor, C., 218
Taylor, C. B., 435
Taylor, C. W., 567
Taylor, H. C., 516–521
Taylor, H. G., 478
Taylor, J., 191, 499, 507
Taylor, L. R., 445
Taylor, R. L., 557
Taylor, S., 445
Taylor, T. R., 231
Tebb, S. S., 136

Tedeschi, R. G., 90
Tellegen, A. M., 362, 363, 366, 385
Temp, G., 550
Teng, E. L., 305
Tennen, H., 383
Tennen, R., 383
Tenopyr, M. L., 136, 141
Teplin, L. A., 218
Teri, L., 138
Terman, L. M., 15–16, 231, 239–244, 250, 349, 594
Terraciano, A., 385
Terrell, F., 191
Terrell, M. D., 560
Terrell, S. L., 191
Terrill, D. R., 383, 384
Tew, M. D., 442
Thal, L. J., 491
Thayer, P. W., 226, 312
Theodorakis, Y., 434
Theye, F., 190
Thinus-Blanc, C., 625
Thomas, C., 543
Thomas, J. C., 612
Thomas, R., 503
Thompson, D. E., 139
Thompson, L. A., 322
Thompson, T. A., 139
Thoresen, C. J., 385
Thorndike, E. L., 101, 225, 349
Thorndike, R. L., 189, 243, 244, 303, 560, 561, 571, 590
Thorpe, J. S., 409
Thorpe, K., 292
Thorson, J. A., 372, 384
Thurbers, S. A., 285
Thurstone, L. L., 14, 246
Tianyou, W., 445
Tidwell, P., 193
Tiegs, R. B., 524
Tikotzki, Y., 468
Timbrook, R. E., 365
Timmerman, M. E., 235
Tiplady, B., 439
Tippins, N., 525
Titchner, E. B., 14
Todd, M. H., 501
Todt, E. H., 365
Tomhnson-Keasey, C., 524
Torrance, E. P., 306
Toshima, M. T., 58
Tourangeau, R., 439
Tracy, D. M., 17
Traxler, A. J., 552
Treloar, J. H., 522
Triandis, H. C., 137
Tronick, E. Z., 284
Trost, C., 582
Trotman, K. M., 304
Trotter, M. A., 494, 495, 534
Troxtel, D. D., 224
Truax, C. B., 214, 216
Trull, T. J., 261, 263, 264, 265
Trumbo, D., 226, 227, 510
Tryon, W. W., 196
Tsai, A., 445
Tsatsanis, K. D., 298
Tseng, H. M., 439
Tuber, D. S., 477
Tucker, C. L., 431
Tuel, B. D., 526
Tukey, J. W., 26
Tulsky, D. S., 261, 262, 264, 265, 266, 268, 269, 503
Turban, D. B., 202, 511
Turgeon, L., 495
Turkheimer, E., 538, 572

Turlington, R. D., 596–598
Turner, C. F., 222, 438
Turner, S. M., 431
Turpin, G., 436
Tyler, L. E., 455, 470
Tynan, W. D., 284
Tziner, A., 227, 510

Ulett, G., 440
Ulrich, L., 226, 227, 510
Ulrich, R., 197
Ulug, B., 361
Umansky, W., 289
Unruh, M. D., 503
Upper, D., 430, 431
Urbina, S., 153, 160, 534
Ursano, R. J., 383
Uutela, T., 504

Vale, C. D., 440
Valencia, R. R., 232, 292, 294, 552, 564, 565
Van, M., 196
van Aarle, E. J. M., 440
Vance, B., 305
Vance, R. J., 199
van den Bercken, J. H. L., 440
VandenBroek, A., 274
Vandenburg, S. G., 572
van der Linden, W. J., 178
van der Staak, C. P. F., 381
van der Vleuten, C. P. M., 223
Vandevijer, F. J. R., 344
van de Vijver, F. J., 274
Van Essen, T., 323
Van Fleet, J. N., 267
van Gastel, N., 293
van Heerden, J., 546
VanLunsen, R. H. W., 436
van Nieuwenhuizen, C., 384
Van Scotter, J., 137
Vansickle, T. R., 439
Vanvoorden, V., 503
van Wersch, A., 163–164
Vea, H. B., 433
Verde, J. B., 445
Verweij, A. C., 178
Vicino, S. M., 194
Vickers, D., 448
Vidal-Abarca, E., 441
Viet, C. T., 378
Viggiano, G., 445
Vigil-Colet, A., 236
Viglione, D. J., 404, 409
Villa, H., 445
Vincelli, F., 445
Vispoel, W. P., 445
Vitro, S. T., 190
Vlachos, O., 343
Vlaeyen, J. W. S., 427
Voelker, S., 294
Vogler, G. P., 572
Volkmar, F. R., 298
Vraniak, D., 565

Wadsworth, A. P., 495
Wagner, E. E., 305, 404
Wagner, P. A., 296
Wagner, R., 226, 227, 510
Wagner, R. K., 196
Waidman, D. A., 344
Wainer, H., 437
Wainwright, D., 493
Wakely, M. B., 178
Waksberg, J., 533

Wald, J., 445
Waldman, I. D., 545
Walker, A. M., 214
Walker, E. L., 398
Walker, M. T., 212
Walker, R. N., 397
Walker, S., 504
Wallace, J., 264
Waller, N. G., 178, 350
Wallis, H. R., 372
Walsh, W. B., 453, 455, 467, 470
Wan, C. K., 83
Wanberg, C. R., 466
Wang, E., 225
Wang, H., 304
Ward, D. M., 618
Ward, L. C., 358
Ward, M. P., 216
Ward, S. M., 596
Ward, T. J., 194
Ward, W. C., 627
Ware, J. E., Jr., 151, 378, 503, 504
Warner, M. H., 526
Warner-Benson, D. M., 187
Warren, S. H., 17
Warren, W. L., 377
Warzecha, G., 440
Washington, J. A., 297
Wasik, B. H., 292
Wasserman, G. S., 448
Waters, B. K., 345
Watkins, C. E., Jr., 392, 453
Watson, C., 604
Watson, C. W., 322
Watson, D., 163, 166, 167, 385, 386, 498, 532
Watt, S. K., 384
Watts, F. N., 478
Wauke, A. P. T., 445, 627
Way, D. P., 567
Way, P. J., 11
Weatherly, M., 303
Weber, B., 439
Weber, E. H., 13–14, 14
Webster, E. C., 227, 510, 511
Webster, J. S., 488
Wechsler, D., 17, 253–254, 256–257, 266, 270, 271, 273, 274, 303
Weigel, R. G., 537
Weinberg, R. A., 545
Weiner, B., 473, 566
Weiner, I. B., 392
Weinstein, C. E., 11, 427
Weintraub, J. K., 384
Weisband, S., 439
Weiss, D. J., 177, 178
Weiss, L. G., 274
Weissman, A. N., 433
Weissman, M. M., 138
Weizenbaum, J., 437–438
Welch, H. G., 121
Welcher, D. W., 545
Welsh, G. S., 361, 364
Welsh, K., 478
Welsh, M., 483
Welsh-Bohmer, K. A., 478
Wendel, D. H., 163
Wenglinsky, H. H., 327
Wermiel, S., 582
Werner, H., 490
Wernicke, C., 477
Wertheimer, M., 287

Wesman, A. G., 168
West, J. L., 442
West, S. G., 536
Western, D., 263
Westrup, B., 288
Whalley, D., 504
Wheeler, L., 486
Whipple, C. M., 394
Whipple, G., 14
Whisman, M. A., 433
Whiteside-Mansell, L., 382
Whitmore, J., 29
Whittington, D., 540
Whyte, G., 522
Wiberg, M., 59
Wicker, A. W., 528, 529
Wickham, T., 268
Widaman, K., 524
Wieber, J. L., 288
Wiedemann, C. F., 333
Wiederhold, B. K., 444, 445, 625
Wiederhold, M. D., 444, 625
Wiersma, U. J., 510
Wiesner, W. H., 511
Wigdor, A., 55, 552
Wiggins, J. G., 380
Wiggins, J. S., 12, 351
Wiklund, C., 383
Wild, C. L., 546
Wilder, J., 437
Wilhelm, P., 435
Wilk, S. L., 55, 144, 560
Wilkening, G. N., 487
Wilkinson, G. S., 307
Wilkinson, L., 64
Williams, C. L., 365
Williams, J. B. W., 217, 218
Williams, J. E., 442, 493
Williams, J. M., 294
Williams, K. B., 510
Williams, M. L., 439
Williams, M. S., 438
Williams, P. B., 547
Williams, R. J., 593, 594
Williams, R. L., 553, 555
Williams, S., 434
Williams, W. M., 145–146, 312, 328, 519
Williamson, L. G., 511
Williamson, W. D., 285, 286
Willingham, W. W., 327
Willis, G., 438
Willis, G. H., 222
Willner, P., 427
Willson, V. T., 294
Wilner, N., 500
Wilson, B. A., 478
Wilson, G. S., 285
Wilson, J. C., 439
Wilson, M., 625
Wilson, M. A., 532
Wilson, R. J., 448
Wilson, S. E., 439
Wing, H., 196, 522
Wing, K. R., 575
Wing, L., 218
Winget, AB. M., 190
Winter, D. G., 231, 415
Wise, S. L., 446
Wissler, C., 233
Witmer, J. M., 184
Wittenborn, J. R., 402
Wolach, A. H., 444
Wolfgang, C. H., 292

Wolfson, D., 486
Wolk, R. B., 416
Wolk, R. L., 416
Woloschuk, W., 227
Wolpe, J., 429
Wood, J. M., 20, 391, 393, 395, 397, 401, 402, 403, 404, 405, 408, 409, 410, 418, 419, 615, 616, 621, 624, 626, 630
Wood, P., 567
Woodcock, R. W., 301, 302
Woodward, J. A., 436
Woodworth, R. S., 353
Worling, J. A., 367
Wouters, L., 382
Wright, D. E., 263
Wright, K. M., 383
Wright, O. R., 510
Wright, P., 439
Wright, T. L., 90
Wrightsman, L. S., 338
Wulfeck, B., 296
Wundt, W., 14
Wyland, C. L., 382
Wyman, P., 526
Wysong, E., 468

Xiurong, X., 285
Xu, F., 304
Xue, J., 365

Yan, L., 304
Yanai, H., 27, 108, 175
Yang, X., 304
Yang, Z., 429
Yarcheski, A., 382
Yarcheski, T. J., 382
Yarnold, P. R., 87, 92
Yarrow, M., 197
Yeh, M., 501
Yen, W. M., 104, 111, 168, 170
Yerkes, G., 594
Yerkes, R. M., 16
Yoon, K., 381
Yurong, H., 285
Yutrzenka, B. A., 194

Zautra, A. J., 615
Zawacki, T., 263
Zedeck, S., 227, 510, 531
Zeidner, M., 499, 500, 551
Zhang, F., 225
Zhang, T., 304
Zhou, H., 365
Zhu, J., 261
Zickar, M. J., 445
Zimet, C. N., 394
Zimmerman, B. J., 427
Zimmerman, M ., 139
Zimmerman, W. S., 368
Zipursky, R. B., 447
Ziskin, J., 614, 615, 616
Zmuidinas, M., 473
Zmuidzinas, M., 529
Zonderman, A. B., 304
Zores, L. S., 547
Zotti, A. M., 384
Zubin, J., 354, 401, 402, 410
Zuckerman, M., 436, 495, 538, 572
Zumbo, B. D., 136
Zurawski, R. M., 433
Zytowski, D. G., 462, 463, 466, 468

Subject Index

Ability tests, 7
Absolute 0 property, 28
Access to testing services, 623–624
Accounting Orientation Test, 526–527
Achievement Anxiety Test (AAT), 496, 499
Achievement tests, 8
  evolution of, 16–17
  group achievement tests, 318–320
  individual achievement tests, 307
  in schools, 317–320
Acquiescence
  response set, 158–159
  True Response Inconsistency Scale (TRIN)
    measuring, 363–364
ACT (American College Test), 140, 328–329
  linking test scores, 178
Active listening, 216
Actuarial v. clinical prediction, 616–617
Adaptive Behavior Assessment System, 275
Adarand Constructors, Inc. v. Pena, Secretary of
  Transportation et al., 600
Adequacy of tests, 615–616
ADHD (attention deficit hyperactive disorder)
  Stanford-Binet Intelligence Scale for,
    249
  virtual reality programs and, 445
Adjective checklists, 166–167
  Affect Adjective Checklist, 495
  Multiple Affect Adjective Check List
    (MAACL), 502
  for self-concept evaluations, 376–377
Admission Test for Graduate Study in
  Business, 527
Adolescents, Rosenberg Self-Esteem Scale
  and, 382
Adverse impact of tests, 543, 577
Affect Adjective Checklist, 495
Affirmative action, 599, 600–601
  contrasting views on, 603
  effectiveness, views on, 606
  in law schools, 601–602
  variety of policies on, 601
African Americans. See Race and ethnicity
Afro-American Slang Dictionary, 555
Age differentiation
  for Cognitive Abilities Test (COGAT),
    322–323
  and Goodenough-Harris Drawing Test (G-
    HDT), 342–343
  intelligence tests and, 233–234
Age-related norms, 54–59
  in Wechsler Adult Intelligence Scale, Third
    Edition (WAIS-III), 261
Age scale, 237
Aggression, 515
Agreeableness, 381
  NEO Personality Inventory (NEO-PI-R)
    and, 380
Agreement, studies of, 118–119
AIDS. See HIV/AIDS
Albemarle paper Company v. Moody, 602
Alcohol abuse
  case study of, 481
  Ecological Momentary Assessment (EMA)
    and, 501
  memory and, 479–480
  Minnesota Multiphasic Personality
    Inventory (MMPI) and, 365
  neuropsychological assessment and, 478
Allen v. Alabama State Board of Education, 599
Alzheimer's disease, 304

California Verbal Learning Test (CVLT)
  and, 491–492
  neuropsychological assessment and, 477
American Association for Counseling and
  Development, 625
American Bar Association, 338
American Cancer Society (ACS), 516–517
American Civil Service Commission, 12
American Educational Research Association
  (AERA), 612
  Joint Committee on Testing Practices, 625
  on reliability standards, 120, 122–123
  on validity, 134
American Psychological Association (APA),
  612
  on clinical psychology and testing, 21
  ethical principles, 198
  Ethical Principles of Psychologists and Code of
    Conduct, 617
  Joint Committee on Testing Practices, 625
  on reliability standards, 120, 122–123
  Task Force on Statistical Inference, 64
  on truth in testing laws, 585
  on validity, 134
American Speech-Language-Hearing
  Association, 625
Americans with Disabilities Act (ADA),
  607–609
Ana Maria R. v. California Department of
  Education, 591
Ansell-Casey Life Skills Assessment, 439
Antimodes, 180
Anxiety. See also Test anxiety
  assessment of, 493–502
  computer anxiety, 439
  computer-based treatments, 443
  confrontation inducing, 216–217
  State-Trait Anxiety Inventory (STAI),
    494–495
  test administration and, 186
Anxiety Disorders Interview Schedule for
  DSM-IV-IV, 218
Approval and responses, 191
Aptitudes
  interests and, 469
  potential ability, measuring, 526–527
  tests, 8, 317–319
  treatment interaction, 536
Armed Services Vocational Aptitude Battery
  (ASVAB), 159, 344–345, 564
  computerized format, 627
Army Alpha test, 16
Arthritis, quality-adjusted life-years (QALYs)
  and, 506
Artifacts, psychophysiological assessment
  and, 437
Artificially dichotomous variables, 79
Asian Americans. See Race and ethnicity
Assertive Behavior Survey Schedule (ABSS),
  430
Assertiveness
  behavioral deficits and, 432
  self-report techniques and, 429–430
Association for Evaluation in Guidance, 468
Association of Mexican-American Educators v.
  California, 607
Attention, 482
  mental status examination on, 223
Attenuation, reliability and, 126–127
Attitudes or interviewing, 207
Attribution theory, 472–473

Attrition, validity and, 144
Autism, virtual reality programs and, 445

Bar codes, use of, 193
Baseline intelligence, 258–259
Base rates, 513, 518
Bayley Scales of Infant Development-Second
  Edition (BSID-II), 286–288
Beck Depression Inventory, 139
  computer-scoring errors, 442
  computer tests, 439
Behavior. See also Coping behaviors
  attribution theory and, 473
  methodology for assessinsg, 195–199
  prediction of, 524
Behavioral deficits, 425, 432
Behavioral excesses, 425, 431–432
Behavioral observation studies
  kappa statistic, 118–119
  reliability in, 117–119
Behavioral settings, 528–529
Behavior modification, 422
Behavior therapy, 422
Bell Adjustment Inventory, 354
The Bell Curve (Herrnstein & Murray), 563,
  564
Bender Visual Motor Gestalt Test (BVMGT),
  304–305
Bennett Mechanical Comprehension Test, 526
Benton Visual Retention Test (BVRT), 303–304
Bernreuter Personality Inventory, 354
Best-fitting line, 68–70
Bias. See Gender bias; Test bias
Bilingual students, 588–589
Binet-Simon scale, 15–16. See also Stanford-
  Binet Intelligence Scale
  early scales, 236–239
  1905 scale, 236–237
  1908 scale, 237–239
  Wechsler Intelligence Scales compared,
    254–256
Biserial correlations, 80
Black Intelligence Test of Cultural
  Homogeneity (BITCH), 553, 555–556
Blood pressure indicators, 435
Boalt Hall, University of California, 601
Board of Education v. Rowley, 308
Brain.com, 442, 628
Brain damage
  Draw-a-Person Test and, 419
  Halstead-Reitan Neuropsychological
    Battery, 486–487
  neuropsychological assessment and, 478
  Rorschach inkblot test and, 406–407
Brain plasticity, 482
Brain tumors, 488
Branching algorithm, 223
Brazelton Neonatal Assessment Scale (BNAS),
  283–284
Breast cancer, 516–571
Brookhart v. Illinois State Board of Education,
  608
Brown v. Board of Education, 585–587
Business skills, assessing, 527

Calculation of, 93–96
California Occupational Preference Survey
  (COPS), 471–472
California Psychological Inventory (CPI), 21,
  348, 366–367
  formats for, 162

California Verbal Learning Test (CVLT), 489, 490–493
children's version, 492
Campbell Interest and Skill Survey (CISS), 454, 457–462
example of, 459–461
Cancer, 502–503
Career Assessment Inventory (CIA), 466–467
Career Maturity Inventory (CMI), 470–471
Careers. *See* Jobs and careers
Carnegie Interest Inventory, 14, 454
Carroll Depression Scale, 139
Carryover effect in test–retest method, 107
Case history interviews, 221–222
Case law on testing, 586–609
Category format for items, 164–166
Category Test, 439
Cattell Infant Intelligence Scale (CIIS), 288–289
Caution, 90–91
Celsius scale, 30
Center for Epidemiologic Studies Depression Scale (CES-D), 43–45
Change, ability for, 615
Change score reliability, 115
Checklists. *See also* Adjective checklists
Child Behavior Checklist, 482
items written as, 166–167
for job analysis, 531–532
Child Assessment Schedule (CAS), 218
Child Behavior Checklist, 482
Child Development Inventory, 482
Child psychology, 22
Children. *See also* Disabled persons; Intelligence tests; Wechsler Intelligence Scale for Children, Fourth Edition (WISC-IV)
California Verbal Learning Test (CVLT) version, 492
individual ability tests for, 289–295
item analysis and, 180–181
Kaufman Assessment Battery for Children, Second Edition (KABC-II), 292–295
potential, criterion for assessing, 565–566
tracking with growth charts, 54, 56–59
Children's Apperception Test (CAT), 416
Children's Personality Questionnaire, 369–370
Children's State-Trait Anxiety Scale, 482
China, testing in, 12
Chitling Test, 553, 554–555
Chronological age, IQ and, 239
CIA (Central Intelligence Agency), 198–199
Civil rights. *See also* Affirmative action; Race and ethnicity
personnel lawsuits, 602–607
Civil Rights Act of 1964, 541, 575, 576
Civil Rights Act of 1991, 55, 133, 344, 543–544, 583
quotas in, 544
Wards Cove Packing Company v. Antonio, 604–605
Civil Service Commission, 543, 576
Civil service tests, 12, 344
Clarification statements in interviews, 211–212
Class action suits. *See* Legal issues
Class intervals, 32
Claustrophobia, virtual reality programs and, 445
Clinical Analysis Questionnaire (CAQ), 371
Clinical neuropsychology, 476–477, 476–480. *See also* Neuropsychological assessment
Clinical psychology, 21
Closed-end questions, 209
Coaching and test bias, 570

Code of Fair Testing Practices in Education, 644–648
Coefficient alpha (a), 113–114
internal consistency and, 120
in split-half reliability, 110–111
split-half reliability, estimating, 129
Coefficient of alienation, 83
Coefficient of determination, 82–83
Cognitive Abilities Test (COGAT), 322–323
Cognitive-behavioral assessment, 422422
cognitive functional analysis, 434–435
computerization of, 443–444
Dysfunctional Attitude Scale (DAS), 432–433
functional approach to, 431–432
Irrational Beliefs Test (IBT), 433
operant conditioning, 424–427
procedures for, 423–435
self-report techniques, 427–431
Cognitive functional analysis, 434–435
Cognitive Model of Psychopathology, 432–433
Cognitive psychology, 11
California Verbal Learning Test (CVLT) and, 490
Cognitive science, 632
College Entrance Examination Board, 324
College entrance tests, 323–329. *See also* SAT (Scholastic Aptitude Test); SAT-II
Columbia Mental Maturity Scale-Third Edition (CMMS), 295–296
Commercial coaching programs, 570
Commission on Sex Bias in Measurement, 468
Common variance, 371
Comprehensive System for scoring Rorschach inkblot test, 402
Computers, 437–449. *See also* Internet
anxiety, 439
Armed Services Vocational Aptitude Battery (ASVB) and, 345
California Verbal Learning Test (CVLT) and, 491
case history interviews on, 222·
cognitive and computer science, 632
cognitive-behavioral assessment, computerization of, 443–444
computer-adaptive testing, 177–178, 445–446
current trends and, 627
diagnosis and, 440–442
Ecological Momentary Assessment (EMA) and, 500
games, 445
interviews, computer-assisted, 438–439
projective testing with, 440
psychophysical procedures, 446–449
reporting of results, 440–442
scoring, 440–442
signal-detection procedures, 446–449
test administration, computer-assisted, 193–195, 439–440
virtual reality programs, 444–445
Concurrent validity evidence, 137–139
Concussion resolution index (CRI), 483
Concussions, 483
Confabulatory response to Rorschach inkblot test, 396, 400–401
Confidence intervals
for rating scales, 166
standard errors of measurement and, 122
Confidentiality issues, 619
Confirmatory data analysis, 26–27
Conflict, 494
Conflict of interests issues, 619–620
Confrontation in evaluation interviews, 216–217
Connecticut v. Teal, 606–607

Conscientiousness, NEO Personality Inventory (NEO-PI-R) and, 380
Consistency scale for Edwards Personal Preference Schedule (EPPS), 372
Construct
defined, 148
-irrelevant variance, 136
underrepresentation, 136
Construct validity, 147–154
of Brazelton Neonatal Assessment Scale (BNAS), 284
convergent evidence, 150–151
discriminant evidence and, 152–153
insomnia rating scale, 152
love, meaning of, 148–149
for Woodcock-Johnson III, 303
Content validity, 135–137, 545–548
sexual harassment and, 581
Context, value ratings and, 164–165
Contrasted-group strategy, 360
Convergent evidence, 150–151
Cooperative movement in Rorschach inkblot test, 397–398
Cooperative School and College Ability Tests (SCAT), 328
Coping behaviors, 385, 404
measures of, 499–500
self-statements and, 434
work satisfaction and, 529
Coping Deficit Index, 404
Coping Intervention for Stressful Situations (CISS), 385
Coping Inventory, 500
Coping Resources Inventory, 500
Core Self-Evaluations, 385–386
Correction for attenuation, 126–127
Correlation-causation problem, 84, 85
Correlation coefficients, 65–66
averaging, 105
biserial correlations, 80
calculation of, 96–98
coefficient of alienation, 83
coefficient of determination, 82–83
Pearson product moment correlation coefficient, 70
reciprocal nature of, 71
Spearman's rho (p), 79–80
statistical significance, testing, 70, 73–75
Correlations, 65–66. *See also* Multivariate analysis; Regression
attenuation, correction for, 126–127
comparison of regression, 71–72
correlation-causation problem, 84, 85
example of, 74
reliability coefficients as, 106
residuals, 80, 82
restricted range problem, 84–86
theoretical discussion of, 71–73
Costs of testing, 623
Counseling
career counseling, 472
psychology, 21, 452–474
Covariance, 67, 72–73
KR_{20} formula and, 112
shrinkage and, 83
Covert behavior, 7
Crawford et al. v. Honig et al., 595
Creativity tests, 306–307
Criminality
false positives and negatives and, 515
Minnesota Multiphasic Personality Inventory (MMPI) and, 366
Criterion, 137. *See also* Validity coefficients
in construct validity evidence, 151
EEOC guidelines for measures, 578
potential of children, assessing, 565–566
predictors and, 145
reliability of, 144

Criterion (continued)
  restricted range on, 145–146
  test bias, criterion-related, 548–552
  validity of, 144
Criterion-group strategy, 351–352, 355–367.
  See also Minnesota Multiphasic
    Personality Inventory (MMPI)
  California Psychological Inventory (CPI),
    366–367
  Strong Vocational Interest Blank in, 454
Criterion-referenced tests, 59–60
  items for, 179–180
  validity studies for, 153–154
Criterion scores, 77
Criterion validity, 137–147
  differential prediction and, 147
  EEOC guidelines for, 578–581
  regression plots and, 75
Critical incidents, 532–533
Cross-validation, 84
  in criterion-group strategy, 351–352
  validity studies and, 144–145
Crystallized abilities, 244
Crystallized intelligence (gc), 236
Cultural considerations. See also Race and
    ethnicity; Test bias
  and Cognitive Abilities Test (COGAT), 322
  Henmon-Nelson Test (H-NT) and,
    321–322
  interview errors and, 226
  IPAT Culture Fair Intelligence Test, 343
  in Kaufman Assessment Battery for
    Children, Second Edition (KABC-II),
    294
  NEO Personality Inventory (NEO-PI-R)
    and, 381
  Raven Progressive Matrices (RPM) and,
    342
  reinforcing responses and, 191
  for 16 PF, 369, 371
  and Wechsler Intelligence Scale for
    Children, Fourth Edition (WISC-IV),
    274
  writing items and, 159
Culture Fair Intelligence Test, 343
Current trends, 22–23, 624–628
  computerization of tests, 627
  on Internet, 627–628
  public awareness, 626–627
Cutting scores, 180, 512

DEA (Drug Enforcement Agency), 198–199
Death
  decision theory approach and, 505
  premature mortality, 502–503
Debilitating anxiety, 499
Debra P. v. Turlington, 596–598
Deception, 198–199
Deciles, 51–53
Decision analysis, 521–523
Decision theory, 505–506
Deductive strategies, 350–351
Degrees of freedom (df), 73–75
Dehumanization issues, 621–622
Demographics, MMPI and, 365
Dental Admission Testing Program, 527
Depression, 404
  computer diagnosis, 440
  Minnesota Multiphasic Personality
    Inventory (MMPI) and, 357
  test administration and, 186
  validity of self-report on, 138–139
Depression Index, 404
Descriptive statistics, 27
Desegregation cases, 586–587
Detection rate, 514–515
Determinant in Rorschach inkblot test, 397,
    398

Detroit Edison Co. v. N.L.R.B., 605–606
Developmental neuropsychology, 481–484
Developmental quotient (DQ), 285–286
Deviation IQ, 243
Diagnosis. See also Diagnostic and Statistical
    Manual of Mental Disorders (DSM-IV)
  computer, 440–442
  Diagnostic Interview Schedule, 139, 218
Diagnostic and Statistical Manual of Mental,
    217
Diagnostic and Statistical Manual of Mental
    Disorders (DSM-IV), 217
  computer diagnosis and, 440
  on depression, 138
Diagnostic and Statistic Manual of Mental
    Disorders (DSM-IV-TR), 217
Diagnostic Interview Schedule, 139, 218
Diagnostic Interview Schedule for Children
    (DISC), 218
Dialects and test bias, 545–546
Diana v. State Board of Education, 588–589
Dichotomous format for items, 159–160
Dichotomous variables, 79–80
Difference score reliability, 114–115
Differential Abilities Scale (DAS), 303
Differential Aptitude Test (DAT), 526
Differential item function (DIF) analysis,
    546–548
Differential prediction, 147
Differential process theory, 563, 565
Differential validity, 544
Difficulty
  of items, 168–170
  KR_{21} formula and, 112
Directive interviews, 204
Direct questions, 217
Disabled persons. See also Individual with
    Disabilities Education Act (IDEA)
  Americans with Disabilities Act (ADA)
    cases, 607–609
  assessment of, 308–309
  due process for, 309
  Education for All Handicapped Children
    Act of 1975, 583, 585–586
  functional behavioral assessment (FBA) for,
    196
  individual ability tests for, 295–299
  legal issues and special education, 308–309
  minimum competency tests for, 608–609
  schools identifying, 308
  Stanford-Binet Intelligence Scale for, 249
Discriminability, 126
  item analysis and, 170–172
  Likert scales and, 163
  of social support measures, 501
Discriminant analysis, 88–89
Discriminant evidence, 152–153
Discriminant function analysis, 483
Discrimination. See also Gender bias; Race
    and ethnicity; Test bias
  EEOC guidelines and, 581
  minimum competence tests and, 596–598
  personnel lawsuits, 602–607
  reverse discrimination lawsuit, 598–599
  sexual harassment as, 582
Discrimination index, 170, 171
Distance learning, 180
Distractors, 160–161
Distributions. See Frequency distributions
Divergent validation, 153
Divided loyalties issues, 619–620
Documentation for tests, 621
Domain, defined, 104
Domain sampling model, 103–105
  coefficient alpha (a) and, 113
Double-barreled items, 158
Dove Counterbalance General Intelligence
    Test, 554–555

Draw-a-Person Test, 418, 419
Drift, 197
Drug usage, computer-assisted interviews on,
    438
Due process for disabled children, 309
Dysfunctional Attitude Scale (DAS), 432–433
Dyslexia, 482

Eating disorders
  computer-based treatments, 443
  failure to eat, 422–423, 424
  Minnesota Multiphasic Personality
    Inventory (MMPI) and, 365
  overeating, 423–424
  Rosenberg Self-Esteem Scale and, 382
Ecological Momentary Assessment (EMA),
    500–501
Ecology, 528
Edinburgh Postnatal Depression Scale
    (EPDS), 218
Educable mentally retarded (EMR), 556, 574
  Diana v. State Board of Education, 588–589
  Marchall et al. v. Georgia and, 596
  quota system for classes, 558, 560
Educational psychology, 21
Educational Testing Service (ETS), 23,
    140–141, 466
  differential item function (DIF) analysis,
    546–548
  New York Truth in testing Law, 583–585
Education for All Handicapped Children Act
    of 1975, 583, 585–586
Edwards Personal Preference Schedule
    (EPPS), 372–374
  ipsative scores, 374
EEOC guidelines. See Equal Employment
    Opportunity Commission (EEOC)
Ego Resiliency Scale (ER89), 382–383
Elderly persons
  Gerontological Apperception Test, 416
  Senior Apperception Technique, 416
Eligibility in Local Context (ELC) program,
    60
Emotionality, 498–499
Emotional problems, 439
Emotion-focused coping strategies, 500
Empathy in interviews, 212–213
Empirical strategies, 351–352
Employee Polygraph Protection Act, 198–199
Employment. See Jobs and careers
Employment interviews, 510–512
  validity of, 524–525
Encode factor, 482
Encopresis, 438
Endpoints, 166
  in Test Anxiety Questionnaire (TAQ), 496
English East India Company, 12
Enuresis, 438
Environment
  attribution theory and, 473
  classifying environments, 529–531
  cognitive functional analysis and, 434
  social ecology and, 528–529
  social environment, changing, 568–571
  virtual reality programs, 444–445
Environmental psychology, 528
Equal Employment Opportunity Commission
    (EEOC), 541, 575
  guidelines of, 576–581
Equal intervals property, 28
Equal protection clause, 581–582
Equivalent forms reliability, 106, 108–109
E-rater (Educational Testing Services Essay
    Rater), 441
Errors, 100
  in behavioral observation studies, 118
  in Bender Visual Motor Gestalt Test
    (BVMGT), 304–305

in Benton Visual Retention Test (BVRT), 304
conceptualization of, 100–101
in interviews, 224–227
KR_{20} formula, 111–112
rating error, 199
sources of, 106, 119–120
standard error of measurement, 103
test–retest method, 106, 107–108
test score theory, 101–103
Error variance, 371
person–situation interaction and, 535
Essays, computer scoring of, 441
Estimated learning potentials (ELPs), 558
Ethical Principles of Psychologists and Code of Conduct, 617
Ethics
conflict of interests issues, 619–620
moral issues, future of, 617–621
responsibilities of test users/constructors, 620–621
test bias and, 560–563
Ethnicity. *See* Race and ethnicity
Evaluation interviews, 216–217
Examiners, 7, 8. *See also* Interviews
actuarial v. clinical prediction, 616–617
drift in, 197
expectancies of, 185, 197
expectancy effects, 189–190
race of tester, effect of, 185–187
reactivity, 196–197
reinforcing responses and, 190–193
relationship of test taker and, 184–185
for Rorschach inkblot test, 395–396
of Thematic Apperception Test (TAT), 412
training of, 188
Executive functioning, 482
Expectancy effects, 188–190
Experimental psychology, 13–14
Exploratory data analysis, 26
Expository Text Analysis Tool (ETAT), 441
External criteria, 178
External validity of translated tests, 188
Extreme group method, 170, 171
Extroversion (E), 379, 380
Eye contact, 511, 512

Face validity, 134–135
of Inventory to Diagnose Depression (IDD), 139
Facilitating anxiety, 499
Factor analysis, 20, 89–92, 235
California Psychological Inventory (CPI) and, 367
coefficient alpha (a) and, 113–114
content validity evidence and, 136
Core Self-Evaluations and, 386
Likert format, responses to, 163
love, meaning of, 149
NEO Personality Inventory (NEO-PI-R) and, 380
in personality assessment, 20, 352, 367–371
reliability and, 126
for Torrance Tests of Creative Thinking (TTCT), 306
of Wechsler Intelligence Scale for Children, Fourth Edition (WISC-IV), 274
Factor loading, 91–92
Factors, 90, 235
of trust, 90–91
Fahrenheit scale, 30
Fairness. *See also* Test bias
EEOC guidelines for, 580–581
False negatives, 513–515
False positives, 513–515
in Woodworth Personal Data Sheet, 353
False reassurance in interviews, 208–209

Family of Man, 415–416
FBI (Federal Bureau of Investigation), 198–199
FDA (Food and Drug Administration), 503
Fear Survey Schedule (FSS), 429
Federal government
Education for All Handicapped Children Act of 1975, 583, 585–586
interstate commerce, regulation of, 575–576
role of, 574–583
spending, control of, 575
Feedback and responses, 190–193
Figure drawing tests, 418–419
First impressions, 202
in employment interviews, 511
Fisher's r to Z transformation, 105
Fixed quantitative batteries, 489
Fluid-analytic abilities, 244, 246
Fluid intelligence (gf), 236
Culture Fair Intelligence Test measuring, 343
Raven Progressive Matrices (RPM) measuring, 340–341
Focus execute factor, 482
Forced-choice tests, 163
Edwards Personal Preference Schedule (EPPS) as, 374
Ford and Ford v. Long Beach Unified School District, 279
Forensic psychology, 22
Four-choice rule, 577
Fourteenth Amendment, U.S. Constitution, 576
Free-association phase of Rorschach inkblot test, 396
Freedom of Information Act, 334
Frequency distributions, 31–34
mean, 39–40
of random errors, 102
standard deviation, 40–42
Frustration, 493–494
FTC (Federal Trade Commission), 575
Full-scale IQs (FSIQs), 264
Functional approach to assessment, 431–432
Functional behavioral assessment (FBA), 196
Future trends, 628–632

Gain-score information, 115
Galvanic skin response (TGSR) indicators, 435
Gender bias
and Career Assessment Inventory (CIA), 467
differential item function (DIF) analysis and, 547
in interest measurement, 468–469
LSAT (Law School Admission Test) issues, 339
General Aptitude Test Battery (GATB), 55, 344
General cognitive index (GCI), 291
General (g) factor, 539
Generalized anxiety disorder, 443
General mental ability, 234
implications of, 235–236
Spearman's model, 234–236
General Self-Efficacy Scale (GSE), 382
General standoutishness error, 225
Genes and intelligence, 541
Gerontological Apperception Test, 416
Gesell Development Schedules (GDS), 284–286
gf-gc theory of intelligence, 236, 244
GI Forum v. Texas Education Agency, 598
Gifted and talented education program (GATE), 595
Gifted persons

gifted and talented education program (GATE), 595
and Peabody Picture Vocabulary Test - Third Edition (PPVT-III), 297
Stanford-Binet Intelligence Scale for, 249
Global scores, 490
Glossary, 649–654
GMAT (Graduate Management Aptitude Test), 441, 583
as computer-adapted test, 446
Golden Rule Insurance Company et al. v. Washburn et al., 599
Goodenough-Harris Drawing Test (G-HDT), 342–343, 419
Gough's Adjective Checklist, 376–377
Government. *See* Federal government
GPA (grade point average)
ACT (American College Test) and, 329
GRE (Graduate Record Examination) and, 333–334
LSAT (Law School Admission Test) and, 338
SAT (Scholastic Aptitude Test) and, 324, 327–328
success in college and, 565
and Taylor-Russell tables, 519
Grades. *See also* GPA (grade point average)
drop case study, 266–267
inflation, 334
potential of children, assessing, 566
Graduate Record Examination (GRE). *See* GRE (Graduate Record Examination)
Graduate school entrance tests, 330–339. *See also* GRE (Graduate Record Examination); LSAT (Law School Admission Test)
Gratz v. Gollinger, 601–602
GRE (Graduate Record Examination), 3, 312, 330–336, 583
analytical ability sample items, 333
coaching and test bias, 570
as computer-adaptive test, 446
computerized format, 627
differential item function (DIF) analysis, 546
problems with, 145–146
score trends in, 324–325
studying for, 335–336
Taylor-Russell tables and, 519
testing industry and, 140–141
verbal ability sample items, 331
Griggs v. Duke Power Company, 133, 564, 602, 603–604
Group tests, 7
achievement tests, 318–320
advantages of, 314–315
characteristics of, 315
discrepancies, consideration of, 316–317
individual ability tests compared, 313–315
of mental abilities, 320–323
nonverbal ability tests, 339–345
in schools, 317–323
selecting, 315–316
using, 316–317
World War I and, 16
Growth charts, 54, 56–59
Grutter v. Bollinger, 601–602
Guessing, 161–162
formula correcting for, 161
threshold, 162
Guilford-Zimmerman Temperament Survey, 368
Guttman split-half method, 116

Halo effect, 199, 225
Halstead-Reitan Neuropsychological Battery, 486–487
computer scoring, 440

Hamilton Rating Scale for Depression, 139
Handicapped persons. *See* Disabled persons
Han Dynasty, China, 12
Hardiness, measurement of, 383
Health. *See also* Quality-of-life assessment
 index studies, 150–151
 insurance, 623–624
 low-income groups and, 557
Health psychology, 22
Hearing loss. *See also* Disabled persons
 Rosenberg Self-Esteem Scale and, 382
Heart disease, 502–503
 quality-of-life information and, 505–506
Heart rate indicators, 435
Henmon-Nelson Test (H-NT), 321–322
Heredity Genius: An Inquiry into Its Laws and Consequences (Galton), 13, 234
High blood pressure, 505–506
High school competency tests, 3
High Stakes: Testing for Tracking, Promotion, and Graduation, 141
Hispanic Americans. *See* Race and ethnicity
Histograms, 32–34
History
 of achievement tests, 16–17
 early developments, 12
 evolution of testing, 14–17
 of intelligence text, 14–16
 of personality tests, 17–20
 of reliability, 100–103
 World War I, testing movement and, 16
Hit rates, 513–514
 mammography and, 516
HIV/AIDS
 computer-assisted interviews on, 438
 neuropsychological assessment and, 478
 quality-adjusted life-years (QALYs) and, 506
Hobson v. Hansen, 587–588
Holtzman Inkblot Test, 409–410
Honesty
 detection of, 198–199
 structured interviews and, 221
Hope Scale, 383
House Subcommission Invasion of Privacy, 619
House-Tree-Person Test, 418
Human ability tests, 8
Human rights issues, 617–618
 public awareness and, 626–627
Human value studies, 506
Huntington's disease, 478
 California Verbal Learning Test (CVLT) and, 491–492
Hypochondriacs, 356
Hypomanics, 357
Hypotheses
 null hypothesis, 73
 in projective drawing tests, 418
 and Wechsler Adult Intelligence Scale, Third Edition (WAIS-III), 266–268
Hysterics, 357

IBM, 632
Iconic storage, 447
Idiot, defined, 237
Ignorance
 vs. stupidity, 553–554
 test user claiming, 621
Illinois Test of Psycholinguistic Abilities (ITPA), 300–301
Imbecile, defined, 237
Incentive scoreboard, 192
Incomplete Sentences Task, 418
Incremental validity, 523–525
Index in WAIS-III, 257–258, 264–265
Individual ability tests, 283–299
 advantages of, 313–314

creativity tests, 306–307
 for disabled persons, 295–299
 group tests compared, 313–315
 for infants, 283–289
 learning disabilities, testing, 299–307
 for young children, 289–295
Individual achievement tests, 307
Individual education program (IEP), 308, 309
Individuals with Disabilities Education Act (IDEA), 299, 623
 Amendments, 196
 enforcing rights under, 308–309
Individual tests, 7, 8
Industrial psychology, 21. *See also* Personnel psychology
 decision analysis and, 521–523
 utility theory and, 521–523
Infants
 neuropsychological assessment and, 483–484
 scales, 283–289
Inferential statistics, 26–27
Information, reliability and, 115
Information-processing speed, 447–448
 intelligence and, 232
 neuropsychological assessment and, 480
 schizophrenia and, 447
 Wechsler Adult Intelligence Scale, Third Edition (WAIS-III) and, 264
 for Wechsler Intelligence Scale for Children, Fourth Edition (WISC-IV), 271
Inkblot tests, 9. *See also* Rorschach inkblot test
 Holtzman Inkblot Test, 409–410
Inquiry phase of Rorschach inkblot test, 396
Insomnia rating scale, 152
Institutional trust, 90–91
Instructions for test administration, 192–193
Integrity tests, 198–199
Intelligence, 240–241. *See also* Intelligence tests
 definitions of, 231
 differential variability in, 243
 genes and, 541
 gf-gc theory, 236
 information-processing speed and, 448
 multiple intelligences, 236
 problems of defining, 231–233
 Spearman's model, 234
Intelligence tests, 8. *See also* Race and ethnicity; specific tests
 age differentiation, 233–234
 alternative tests, 279–282
 Binet's principles of construction, 233–234
 comparing alternative tests, 281–282
 computer-adaptive testing, 445–446
 criticisms of, 232
 evolution of, 14–17
 expectancy effects and, 190
 general mental ability, 234
 group tests, 320–323
 history of, 232–233
 infant scales, 283–289
 on Internet, 442
 norms for, 54
 potential of children, assessing, 566
 pros and cons for, 571
 Raven Progressive Matrices (RPM), 339–342
 socioeconomic background and, 232
 Spearman's model, 234–236
 for young children, 289–295
Intelligent Essay Assessor (IEA), 441
Interactive testing, 193–195
Intercept, 67–68
Interests. *See also* Occupational interests

measuring, 453–469
Interjudge reliability, 118
Internal consistency, 106, 120
Internal criteria, 178
Internal reliability of Rosenberg Self-Esteem Scale, 382
Internet
 Campbell Interest and Skill Survey (CISS) on, 458
 current trends with, 627–628
 distance learning, 180
 psychological testing and, 442
 Self-Directed Search (SDS) on, 468
Interobserver reliability, 118
Interpersonal attraction, interviews and, 207
Interpersonal influence, interviews and, 207
Interpretation, objective, 626
Interquartile range, 52
Interrater agreement, 121
Interrater reliability, 118
Interscorer reliability, 118
Interstate commerce, 575–576
Interval data, 31
Interval scales, 30
Interviews, 11. *See also* Examiners
 active listening in, 216
 attitudes for, 207
 avoidable responses, 207–208
 case history interviews, 221–222
 computer-assisted interviews, 438–439
 cultural distortions and, 226
 effective interviewing, 207–216
 effective responses in, 209–210
 empathetic responses in, 212–213
 employment interviews, 510–512
 errors, sources of, 224–227
 evaluation interviews, 216–217
 first impressions, 202
 flexibility in conducting, 210
 flow of interview, maintaining, 210–214
 generalizing and, 225
 hostile statements in, 208
 and job analysis, 533
 judgmental statements in, 208
 levels of responses in, 215–216
 mental status examinations, 222–223
 personal appearance and, 225
 probing statements in, 208
 reassuring statements in, 208–209
 reciprocal nature of, 206
 reliability of, 227
 skills development for, 223–224
 stress interviews, 207
 structured interviews, 204, 217–221
 reliability of, 227
 supervised practice for, 224
 as tests, 205–206
 transitional phrases in, 210–211
 types of, 216–224
 understanding
 measurement of, 214–216
 responses, 212–213
 unstructured interviews, 204
 reliability of, 227
 validity of, 224–226
Invasion of privacy, 619
Inventory to Diagnose Depression (IDD), 139
Iowa Test of Educational Development (ITED) scale, 329
IPAT Culture Fair Intelligence Test, 343
Ipsative scores, 374
IQ. *See* Intelligence; Intelligence tests
Irrational Beliefs Test (IBT), 433
Isodensity curve, 549
Item analysis, 168–181
 characteristic curves, 172–178
 difficulty of items, 168–170
 discriminability of items, 170–172

external criteria, 178
extreme group method, 170, 171
internal criteria, 178
item response theory (IRT), 175–178
limitations of, 180–181
linking uncommon measures, 178–179
point biserial method, 170–172
reliability and, 126
uncommon measures, linking, 178–179
Item characteristic curves, 172–178
categories of test performance for, 172–175
Item loading, 90–91
Item response theory (IRT), 101, 175–178, 234
Items. *See also* Item analysis
category format for, 164–166
checklists as, 166–167
for criterion-referenced tests, 179–180
defined, 6
dichotomous format, 159–160
differential item function (DIF) analysis, 546–548
formats for, 159
Likert formula for, 162–164
polytomous format, 160–162
Q-sorts as, 166–167, 168
in self-report tests, 9
writing items, 158–168
Item sampling, 108–109
as error source, 119

Jackson Personality Inventory (JPI), 375
profile sheet, 376
trait descriptions for, 377
Jackson Vocational Interest Survey (JVIS), 466
Jobs and careers, 453. *See also* Occupational interests; Personnel psychology
counseling, 472
interviews, 510–512
job analysis, 531–533
performance analysis, 532
personal characteristics for, 469–473
Johns Hopkins Child Development Study, 552
Joint Committee on Testing Practices, 625
Code of Fair Testing Practices in Education, 644–648
Judgmental statements in interviews, 208
Junior Senior High School Personality Questionnaire, 369–370
Justice Department, 543, 576

Kappa statistic, 118–119
Kaufman Assessment Battery for Children, Second Edition (KABC-II), 292–295
Kaufman Test of Educational Achievement, Second Edition (KTEA-II), 293
Kent-Rosanoff word association test, 417
Keyboard phobia, 193
Kinetic Family Drawing Test, 418
Korsakoff's syndrome, 491
KR_{20} formula, 111–112
internal consistency and, 120
reliability and, 129–131
KR_{21} formula, 112
K scale for MMPI, 359
Kuder Occupational Interest Survey (KOIS), 462–466
example of, 464–465
psychometric properties of, 463
Kuder Preference Survey, 454
Kuder-Richardson reliabilities
of Armed Services Vocational Aptitude Battery (ASVB), 345
for Culture Fair Intelligence Test, 343
GRE (Graduate Record Examination) and, 330

Rorschach inkblot test and, 404
of Thematic Apperception Test (TAT), 415
Kuhlmann-Anderson Test, Eighth Edition (KAT), 320–321

Labeling issues, 618–619
Labor Department, 543, 576
norming controversy, 55
Lack of Protection scale (LP), 502
Language
content-related validity and, 545
Luria-Nebraska Neuropsychological Battery and, 489
of test taker, 188
Larry P. v. Wilson Riles, 553, 574, 575, 589–591
Latinos. *See* Race and ethnicity
Laws. *See also* Legal issues
defined, 575
New York testing laws, 583
Law School Admissions Council, 339
Law School Admission Test (LSAT). *See* LSAT (Law School Admission Test)
Learned helplessness, 192
Learning disabilities
developmental neuropsychology and, 482–483
testing, 299–307
visiographic tests for, 303–306
Least squares, principle of, 66–67, 68–70
Left hemisphere of brain, 479–480
Legal issues
Americans with Disabilities Act (ADA) cases, 607–609
judges, different decisions by, 591, 592–594
personnel lawsuits, 602–607
psychological testing lawsuits, 586–609
in special education, 308–309
test administration lawsuits, 605–607
of test fairness, 540–544
use of tests, 574–586
Leiter International Performance Scale-Revised (LIPS-R), 256, 297–298
Liebert-Morris Emotionality and Worry Scales, 496, 499
Life expectancy, 503
Life Orientation Test-Revised (LOT-R), 383–384
Lifestyle information, 222
Likert scales, 162–164
Dysfunctional Attitude Scale (DAS), 433
example of, 163
in NEO Personality Inventory (NEO-PI-R), 380
Linear combination of variables, 87
Linguistic bias. *See* Test bias
Logical-content strategy, 350
criticisms of, 354
early multidimensional scales, 354
Mooney Problem Checklist, 354
Woodworth Personal Data Sheet, 353
Long-delay savings, 492
Lorge-Thorndike Intelligence Test, 186–187
Love, meaning of, 148–149
LSAT (Law School Admission Test), 23, 312, 337–339, 583
base rate in, 513
coaching and test bias, 570
computerized format, 627
differential item function (DIF) analysis, 546
hit rate in, 513
potential, assessment of, 566
questions, 2–3
Luria-Nebraska Neuropsychological Battery, 476, 478, 487–490
Lying, 198–199

Magnetic resonance imaging (MRI), 341
Magnitude, 27–28
Malingering, assessment of, 483
Mammography, 516–517
Manuals, providing, 621
Marchall et al. v. Georgia, 596
Masculinity-femininity (MF) scale, 358
Mask, 447–448
MCAT (Medical College Admissions Test), 3, 527
evaluation of, 567
potential, assessment of, 566
McCall's T, 50–51
for Minnesota Multiphasic Personality Inventory (MMPI), 359–360
McCarthy Scales of Children's Abilities (MSCA), 289–292
McMaster Health Index Questionnaire, 503
Mean, 39–40
areas between mean and Z scores, 635
grading and, 49–50
for intelligence tests, 54
summarizing mean of test, 162
symbol for, 40
of Z scores, 47
Measurement. *See also* Scales
defined, 27
Median
quartiles and, 52
for Stanford-Binet Intelligence Scale, 250
Medi-Cal, 623
Medical College Admissions Test. *See* MCAT (Medical College Admissions Test)
Medicare, 623
Memory. *See also* Short-term memory
California Verbal Learning Test (CVLT) and, 491
Luria-Nebraska Neuropsychological Battery and, 488–489
neuropsychological assessment and, 478
Memory Assessment Scales (MAS), 478
Mental age, 234
in Binet-Simon scale, 15
in Binet-Simon scale, 1908, 238–239
intelligence quotient (IQ) concept and, 239
Mental illness. *See also* specific illnesses
neuropsychological assessment and, 478
Mental Measurements Yearbook, 339, 454, 626
Mental retardation
Bayley Scales of Infant Development-Second Edition (BSID-II) predicting, 288
and Peabody Picture Vocabulary Test-Third Edition (PPVT-III), 297
Stanford-Binet Intelligence Scale for, 249
visual information processing and, 448–449
Mental status examinations, 222–223
Mental tests, 13
Meta-analysis
of employment interviews, 511
Rorschach inkblot test and, 404
Methods of rotation, 92
Metropolitan Achievement Test (MAT), 318–320
Midpoints in Test Anxiety Questionnaire (TAQ), 496
Military personnel, 344–345
Armed Services Vocational Aptitude Battery (ASVAB), 159, 344–345, 564, 627
computer-adaptive testing, 445–446
Raven Progressive Matrices (RPM) for, 341–342
Miller Analogies Test (MAT), 336–337
Ming Dynasty, China, 12
Minimum competency tests, 597
for disabled students, 608–609
Minnesota Multiphasic Personality Inventory-II (MMPI-2), 20, 362–364

Minnesota Multiphasic Personality Inventory
  (MMPI), 20, 21, 355–366, 626
  changes in, 629
  computer-assisted administration and, 194
  computer tests, 439
  current status of, 366
  formats for, 162
  initial interpretations of, 359–360
  Meehls, P. E. and, 360–362
  names of clinical states in, 361
  numerical codes for, 361–362
  original development of, 355–359
  profile sheet, 356
  psychometric properties, 364–366
  range of problems covered by, 365–366
  reading levels and, 358
  response style and, 364–365
  restandardization of, 362–364
  scoring errors, 441
  validity scales in, 358–359
Minnesota Vocational Interest Inventory
  (MVII), 466
Miss rates, 513–514
  mammography and, 516
Money-for-Designs (MFD) Test, 305–306
Mood, interviews and, 206
Mooney Problem Checklist, 354
Moral issues, 617–621
  conflict of interests issues, 619–620
  divided loyalties issues, 619–620
  human rights issues, 617–618
  invasion of privacy, 619
  labeling issues, 618–619
  responsibilities of test users/constructors,
    620–621
Moron, defined, 237
Motor problems, assessment of, 480
Motor skills, intelligence tests and, 282
Multidimensional Aptitude Battery, 439
Multimedia computerized tests, 632
Multiphasic environmental assessment
  procedure (MEAP), 530–531
Multiple Affect Adjective Check List
  (MAACL), 502
Multiple-choice examinations
  difficulty of items in, 169
  items for, 159
  polytomous format for, 160–162
  scoring of, 161
Multiple discriminant analysis, 88–89
Multiple intelligences, 236
Multiple regression, 87–88
Multi-State Bar Exam, 583
Multivariate analysis, 86–92
  multiple regression, 87–88
Myers-Briggs Type Indicator (MBTI), 525–526

National Academy of Sciences
  norming controversy, 55
  reliability, report on, 124
National Assessment of Educational Progress
  (NAEP) program, 179
National Career assessment Service, 463
National Center for Health Services Research,
  503
National Commission on Testing and Public
  Policy, 630
National Commission on Writing in America's
  Schools and Colleges, 334
National Council on Measurement in
  Education (NCME), 612
  Joint Committee on Testing Practices, 625
  on reliability standards, 120, 122–123
  on validity, 134
National health insurance, 623–624
National Longitudinal Study of Youth, 564
National Research Council, National
  Academy of Sciences, 179

National Security Agency, 198–199
National standardized testing, 631
A Nation at Risk, 334
Native Americans. See Race and ethnicity
Needs
  psychogenic needs, 372, 373
  Thematic Apperception Test (TAT) and,
    410
Negative affect, 386–387
Negative correlations, 65
Negatively worded items, 158–159
Negative self-statements, 434
Negative Z scores, 48
NEO Personality Inventory (NEO-PI-R),
  378–381
  five dimensions of, 380–381
  six factor model, 381
Neuro-imaging, 477
Neuropsychological assessment, 476–493
  adult neuropsychology, 484–493
  alcohol abuse and, 481
  California Verbal Learning Test (CVLT),
    489, 490–493
  developmental neuropsychology, 481–484
  specialization in field, 478
Neuropsychology, 22
Neuroticism (N), 379, 380–381
Newsweek magazine, 545
New York Public Interest Research Group
  (NYPIRG), 583–585
New York Truth in testing Law, 583–585
Nominal data, 31
Nominal scales, 20
Nondirective interviews, 204
Nontraditional tests, 624
Nonverbal group ability tests, 339–345
Normative, 76
Norm-referenced tests, 59–60
Norms, 53–60
  age-related norms, 54
  criterion-referenced tests, 59–60
  reference-group norms in WAIS-III, 262
  tracking with age-related norms, 54, 56–59
  university admissions, within-school norms
    for, 60
  within-group controversy, 55
Nottingham Health Profile (NHP), 503,
  504–505
Null hypothesis, 73

Objective interpretation, 626
Observation and job analysis, 533
Observed scores, 114
Observed values, 67
Observers. See Examiners
Obsolescence of tests, 159
Obtained score. See Raw scores
Occupational Information Network (O*NET),
  533
Occupational interests, 453–469
  aptitudes and, 469
  Campbell Interest and Skill Survey (CISS),
    457–462
  Career Assessment Inventory (CIA),
    466–467
  Jackson Vocational Interest Survey (JVIS),
    466
  Kuder Occupational Interest Survey
    (KOIS), 462–466
  Minnesota Vocational Interest Inventory
    (MVII), 466
  Strong-Campbell Interest Inventory,
    455–457
  Strong Vocational Interest Blank, 454–455
Odd–even reliabilities
  GRE (Graduate Record Examination) and,
    330
  for Miller Analogies Test (MAT), 337

of Rorschach inkblot test, 404
Odd–even system, 109
Office of Civil Rights, 601
Office of Federal Contract Compliance, 543
Office of Technology Assessment, 198–199
Omitted responses, 161
Open-ended questions
  effective responses in, 209–210
  in evaluation interviews, 216–217
Openness (O), 379, 380, 381
Operant conditioning, 424–427
  baseline, establishment of, 425, 427
Optimism, testing of, 18
Ordinal scales, 29–33
Organizational psychology, 510
Organization for Economic Co-operation and
  Development (OECD), 3–5
The Origin of Species (Darwin), 12–13
Osipow's vocational dimensions, 469–470
Otis-Lennon School Ability Test (OLSAT),
  187
Overeating, 423–424
Overselection, 55
Overt behavior, 7

Pain, operant conditioning and, 427
Panic disorder, computer-based treatments
  for, 444
Parallel forms reliability, 106, 108–109
Paranoids, 357
Paraphrasing statements, 211–212
Parents in Action on Special Education v.
  Hannon, 591, 595
Partial correlation, 199
Pattern analysis
  validity of, 268
  in Wechsler Adult Intelligence Scale, Third
    Edition (WAIS-III), 266
Peabody Picture Vocabulary Test-Third
  Edition (PPVT-III), 296–297
  race of examiner and, 185
Pearson product moment correlation
  coefficient, 70
  in parallel forms reliability, 109
People Who Care v. Rockford Board of Education,
  588
Percentile brands, 321
Percentile ranks, 34–38
  for negative Z scores, 48
  percentiles compared, 39
  and Z scores, 47–49
Percentiles, 38–39
  percentile ranks compared, 39
  to stanines, 52
Perception, interviews and, 207
Perceptual organization index, 265
Performance IQ (PIQ), 264
  verbal IQ compared, 265–266
Performance scale concept, 255–256
Performance testing, 631
Personal appearance, 225
Personality. See also Personality tests
  attribution theory, 472–473
  career placement and, 469–473
  characteristics, 348
  defined, 348
  occupational interests and, 455–456
  states, 348
  types, 348
Personality Research Form (PRF), 375
Personality tests, 8–9, 349. See also specific
  tests
  combination strategies, 378–381
  criterion-group strategy in, 351–352
  deductive strategies for, 350–351
  dichotomous format for, 159–160
  Edwards Personal Preference Schedule
    (EPPS), 372–374

empirical strategies, 351–352
factor analysis and, 20, 352, 367–371
Guilford-Zimmerman Temperament
  Survey, 368
history of, 17–20
Jackson Personality Inventory (JPI), 375
NEO Personality Inventory (NEO-PI-R),
  378–381
new approaches to, 20
Personality Research Form (PRF), 375
positive personality measurement, 378
projective personality tests, 390–420
Rorschach inkblot tests, 19
self-concept evaluations, 375–377
structured personality tests, 9, 18–19,
  349–353
theoretical strategy, 371–377
types of, 9
Woodworth Personal Data Sheet, 353
Personality traits, 7, 348. *See also* Positive
  personality traits
personality tests, 18
self-report procedures and, 429
source traits, 369
stable traits, 472–473
surface traits, 369
theoretical concerns and, 613–614
trait anxiety, 494
Personnel psychology, 510–512
classifying environments and, 529–531
decision analysis, 521–523
economic value of, 523
employment interviews, 510–512
hits and misses in, 513–514
job analysis, 531–533
multiphasic environmental assessment
  procedure (MEAP), 530–531
Myers-Briggs Type Indicator (MBTI),
  525–526
Occupational Information Network
  (O*NET), 533
person–situation interaction, 533–537
social-ecology approach, 528–529
Taylor-Russell tables and, 516–521
tests in, 512–525
utility theory, 521–523
Wonderlic Personnel Test, 526–527
work satisfaction, 529
Person–situation interaction, 533–537
Pessimism, testing of, 18
Phi coefficients, 80
formula for, 91
Phobias
computer diagnosis, 440
Fear Survey Schedule (FSS), 429
virtual reality programs, 445
Piers-Harris Children's Self-Concept Scale-
  Second Edition, 377
Plessy v. Ferguson, 585–587
Pluripotentiality, 487
Point biserial correlations, 80, 170–172
formula for, 91
Point scale concept, 254–255
Polychotomous format for items, 160
Polygraph devices, 436
Polytomous format for items, 160–162
Population, 27
for percentiles and percentile ranks, 39
symbols for, 42
validity coefficients and, 144
Porteus Maze Test (PMT), 298–299
Portfolios, 17
Positive affect, 386–387
Positive and Negative Affect Schedule
  (PANAS), 385
Positive correlations, 65
Positive manifold, 235
Positive personality traits

future research on, 386–387
measures of, 378, 382–386
Positive self-statements, 434
Positive skew, variables with, 32
Postively-worded items, 158–159
Post-traumatic stress syndrome, 366
Practice, carryover effect and, 107–108
Praise, test scores and, 191
Predicted values, 67
Prediction
of behavior, 524
standard error of estimate and, 82
Predictive validity, 137
of Brazelton Neonatal Assessment Scale
  (BNAS), 284
cholesterol test example, 143
of Kuder Occupational Interest Survey
  (KOIS), 463
for Miller Analogies Test (MAT), 337
Predictors
criterion and, 145
restricted range on, 145–146
Predictor variable, 137
Premorbid intelligence, 258–259
Preschool Language Assessment Instrument,
  187
Pressure, 494
Princeton Review, 140, 336
Princeton Review Foundation, 338
Principal components, 89–90
Principle of least squares, 66–67, 68–70
Principles of psychological testing, 10
Privacy issues, 619
Probing statements in interviews, 208
Problem-focused coping strategies, 500
Processing intensity, 436
Processing speed index. *See* Information-
  processing speed
Professional issues, 612–617
actuarial vs. clinical prediction, 616–617
adequacy of tests, 615–616
social issues, 621–624
theoretical issues, 612–615
Professional school entrance tests, 330–339.
  See also GMAT (Graduate Management
  Aptitude Test); LSAT (Law School
  Admission Test); MCAT (Medical
  College Admissions Test)
Programme for International Student
  Assessment (PISA), 3–5
Project Essay Grade (PEG), 440–441
Projective hypesthesias, 392–393
Projective personality tests, 9, 349, 390–420.
  See also Rorschach inkblot test
Children's Apperception Test (CAT), 416
Holtzman Inkblot Test, 409–410
nonpictorial projective procedures,
  416–419
projective hypesthesias, 392–393
Southern Mississippi TAT (SM-TAT), 416
Thematic Appercception Test (TAT),
  410–415
Proliferation of tests, 629–630
Prophecy formula, 125–126
Psychasthenics, 357
Psychodiagnostik (Rorschach), 394
Psychogenic needs, 372, 373
Psychological Assessment, 612
Psychological deficit, 303–304
Psychological services industry, 198–199
Psychological testing
applications of, 10–11
principles of, 9–10
Psychological tests, defined, 6–7
Psychometric analysis, 160–161
Psychometric g, 235
Psychopathic deviates, 357
Psychophysical measurement, 13–14

Psychophysiological procedures, 435–437
evaluation of, 436–437
Psychosis, MMPI and, 366
Public awareness, 626–627
Publishers of tests, list of, 637–640
Purdue pegboard, 469–470
Pure form response, 397

Q-Sort technique
items written as, 166–167, 168
for self-concept evaluation, 377
Qualified individualism, 560–561
Qualitative batteries, 489
Quality-adjusted life-years (QALYs), 505
Quality-of-life assessment, 502–506
decision theory and, 503–504, 505–506
psychometric approach to, 503
Quartiles, 51–53
Quebec Separatist Movement, 534
Questionnaires. *See also* specific
  questionnaires
and job analysis, 533
self-report questionnaires, 349
Quotas
and Civil Rights Act of 1991, 544
and educable mentally retarded (EMR),
  558, 560
test bias and, 560

r, critical values of, 641
Race and ethnicity. *See also* Legal issues; Test
  bias
alternatives to traditional tests, 553–560
Armed Services Vocational Aptitude Battery
  (ASVB) and, 345
Black Intelligence Test of Cultural
  Homogeneity (BITCH), 553, 555–556
Chitling Test, 554–555
desegregation cases, 586–587
differential item function (DIF) analysis,
  546–548
educable mentally retarded (EMR) issue,
  574
of examiners, 185–187
General Aptitude Test Battery (GATB) and,
  344
genes and intelligence, 541
intelligence tests and, 539
interview errors and, 225–226
IPAT Culture Fair Intelligence Test, 343
job performance analysis and, 532
in Kaufman Assessment Battery for
  Children, Second Edition (KABC-II),
  293–294
LSAT (Law School Admission Test) issues,
  338–339
norms and, 55
Raven Progressive Matrices (RPM) and,
  342
reporting of, 540
SAT (Scholastic Aptitude Test) and, 327,
  539–540
significance of concept, 543
in Stanford-Binet Revision and Deviation
  IQ (SB-LM), 1960, 243–244
stereotyping, 542
System of Multicultural Pluralistic
  Assessment (SOMPA), 553, 556–560
verbal-performance IQ comparisons and,
  265–266
writing items and, 159
Random error, 102–103
RANDT Memory Test (RMT), 478
Rating errors, 199
Ratio scales, 30–31
Raven Progressive Matrices (RPM),
  339–342
Raw regression coefficients (b's), 88

Raw scores
  on Bayley Scales of Infant Development-
    Second Edition (BSID-II), 287
  cross validation methodology and, 145
  and Goodenough-Harris Drawing Test (G-
    HDT), 342–343
  in Kaufman Assessment Battery for
    Children, Second Edition (KABC-II),
    293
  regression and, 71
  for standard deviation, 42
  to stanines, 52–53
  in Strong Vocational Interest Blank, 454
  symbol for, 40
  in Wechsler Adult Intelligence Scale, Third
    Edition (WAIS-III), 261–262
  for Wechsler Intelligence Scale for
    Children, Fourth Edition (WISC-IV),
    272
Reaction time
  signal-detection procedures, 447
  in Thematic Apperception Test (TAT), 412
Reactivity, 196–197
Reassuring statements in interviews, 208–209
Reference-group norms in WAIS-III, 262
Referral Decision Scale (RDS), 218
Regents of the University of California v. Bakke,
  598–599
Regression, 66–79
  best-fitting line, 68–70
  correlation compared, 71–72
  interpretation of, 75–79
  multiple regression, 87–88
  raw regression coefficients (b's), 88
  restricted range problem, 84–86
  standardized regression coefficients
    (B's/betas), 88
  statistical definition of, 72–73
  theoretical discussion of, 71–73
Regression coefficients, 67
  in multiple regression, 87–88
Regression equations, 67–68
  coefficient of alienation, 83
  cross validation, 84
  residuals, 80, 82
  shrinkage, 83–84
  standard error of estimate, 82
Regression lines, 66–68, 77
  standardized slopes with, 78
Regression plots, 75–79, 78
  isodensity curve, 549
  for test bias, 549–550
Rehabilitation process, 484, 485
Reliability, 10. See also Errors; specific types
  of Armed Services Vocational Aptitude
    Battery (ASVB), 345
  attenuation, correction for, 126–127
  in behavioral observation studies, 117–119
  of California Psychological Inventory
    (CPI), 367
  of Career Assessment Inventory (CIA), 467
  for Cattell Infant Intelligence Scale (CIIS),
    289
  change and, 615
  coefficient alpha (a), 113–114
  of computer-generated scores, 441–442
  of criterion, 144
  of difference scores, 114–115
  domain sampling model and, 103–105
  of Edwards Personal Preference Schedule
    (EPPS), 374
  of employment interviews, 511
  factor analysis and, 126
  Guttman split-half method, 116
  history of, 100–103
  and information, 115
  internal consistency method, 106
  of interviews, 227

  item analysis and, 126
  KR_{20} formula and, 111–112, 129–131
  of Kuhlmann-Anderson Test, Eighth
    Edition (KAT), 321
  low reliability, 124–127
  models of, 105–115
  number of items, increasing, 124–126
  parallel forms reliability, 106, 108–109
  prophecy formula and, 125–126
  of Rorschach inkblot test, 403–404
  of Rosenberg Self-Esteem Scale, 382
  satisfactory reliability, 123–124
  of social support measures, 501
  of Social Support Questionnaire (SSQ),
    502
  sources of error and assessment of,
    119–120
  of SP-36, 504
  Spearman-Brown formula, 109–111
  split-half reliability, 109–111
  Stanford-Binet Intelligence Scale, 249–250
  1937 scale, 242
  of State-Trait Anxiety Inventory (STAI),
    494
  of Strong Vocational Interest Blank, 454
  summarizing reliability of test, 162
  summary of guidelines for, 122–123
  of Test Anxiety Questionnaire (TAQ), 496
  test–retest method, 106, 107–108
  theoretical issues regarding, 612–615
  of translated tests, 188
  unbiased estimate of, 105
  using information on, 120–127
  validity, relationship to, 154–155
  of Wechsler Adult Intelligence Scale, Third
    Edition (WAIS-III), 269
  of Wechsler Intelligence Scale for Children,
    Fourth Edition (WISC-IV), 273–274
Representative sample, 15
Residuals, 80, 82
  standard error of estimate, 82
Response style, 364–365
Responsibilities of test users/constructors,
  620–621
Restatement in interviews, 211–212
Restricted range, 84, 85
  checking for, 145–146
Revised Minnesota Paper Form Board Tests,
  526
Rewards, operant conditioning and, 426
Reynolds Depression Scale, 482
Rho coefficient (p), 79–80
Right hemisphere of brain, 479–480
Roe's career-choice theory, 471
Rorschach inkblot test, 9, 19, 21, 391,
  393–409
  administration of, 395–401
  blind analysis and, 401–402
  clinical validation of, 401–402
  Comprehensive System for scoring, 402
  computer scoring, 440
  confabulatory response to, 396, 400–401
  determinant, identifying, 397, 398
  diagnosis, relationship to, 404–405
  diminished use of, 629–630
  evidence for interpretations, 406–407
  form quality, 398
  history of, 393–394
  incremental validity in, 405
  interpretation of, 395–401, 399
  labeling issues and, 619
  location choices, 396–397
  movement response in, 397–398
  norms in, 402–403
  objective interpretation and, 626
  overpathologizing with, 403
  psychometric properties of, 401–409
  "R" responses to, 405, 408

  scoring in, 398–401, 408
  space responses to, 405
  stimuli in, 395–401
  unreliability of, 403–404
Rosenberg Self-Esteem Scale, 382
Rosenthal effects, 188–190
Rotation, methods of, 92
Rotter Incomplete Sentence Blank, 418
  computer scoring, 440
Routing
  in Stanford-Binet Intelligence Scale,
    247–248
  in Wechsler Preschool and Primary Scale of
    Intelligence, Third Edition (WPPSI-III),
    275
Rubber yardsticks, 100
  standard error of measurement and, 103,
    120–123
  test score theory and, 102

Samples, 27
  domain sampling model and, 104
  EEOC guidelines for measures, 578–579
  increasing sample size and reliability,
    124–126
  symbols for, 42
Sample size
  shrinkage and, 83
  validity coefficients and, 144–145
Satisfaction with Life Scale (SWLS), 384
  neuroticism and, 381
SAT (Scholastic Aptitude Test), 23, 140,
  323–328
  affirmative actions and, 600
  cirterion-related bias, 548–550
  coaching and test bias, 570
  computerized format, 627
  differential item function (DIF) analysis,
    546
  linking test scores, 178
  mathematical content of, 326
  norms in, 53–54
  race and ethnicity and, 539–540
  renorming of, 324
  revisions in, 141
  social environment and, 568
  standardized scores in, 51
  success in college and, 565
  University of California and, 142, 569
  verbal content o4, 325
  weakness of, 324, 327
SAT-II, 324, 569
  scores, 142
  validity of, 328
Scaled scores
  in Wechsler Adult Intelligence Scale, Third
    Edition (WAIS-III), 261–262
  for Wechsler Intelligence Scale for
    Children, Fourth Edition (WISC-IV),
    272
Scales, 7, 27–31
  absolute 0 property, 28
  endpoints of, 166
  equal intervals property, 28
  magnitude property, 27–28
  permissible operations, 31
  properties of, 27–29
  10-point scales, 164–166
  types of, 29–31
  visual analogue scales, 166, 167
Scatter diagrams, 63–65
  regression line in, 70
  summarizing information in, 64–65
Schizophrenia, 357
  and Benton Visual Retention Test (BVRT),
    304
  information-processing speed and, 447
  labels, use of, 618

virtual reality programs and, 445
Wechsler Adult Intelligence Scale, Third Edition (WAIS-III) and, 266
Schizophrenia Index, 404
Scholastic Aptitude Test. See SAT (Scholastic Aptitude Test)
School psychology, 21
Scientific racism, 555
Scores. See also Frequency distributions; Raw scores; Z scores
of Career Assessment Inventory (CIA), 467
computer scoring, 440–442
cutting scores, 512
global scores, 490
GRE (Graduate Record Examination) score trends, 324–325
of Kuder Occupational Interest Survey (KOIS), 463
multiple-choice examinations, 161
regression and, 71
for Rorschach inkblot test, 398–401, 408
for sentence completion tests, 418
for Strong-Campbell Interest Inventory, 456
symbols for, 40
test score theory, 101–103
for Thematic Apperception Test (TAT), 412–413
in Wechsler-Bellvue Intelligence Scale (W-B), 17
Seashore Measure of Musical Talents, 470
Seguin Form Board Test, 14
Selection goals, 599
Selection ratio, 518
Self, Rogers' theory of, 377
Self-concept, 348–349
evaluations, 375–377
Self-Directed Search (SDS), 467–468
Self-efficacy, 378
General Self-Efficacy Scale (GSE), 382
and Kuder Occupational Interest Survey (KOIS), 463, 466
Self-monitoring procedures, 435
Self-predictions, 524
Self-ratings, 536
prediction of behavior and, 524
Self-reports, 427–431
assertiveness and, 429–430
battery, self-report, 430–431
evaluation of, 431
example of report, 428
Fear Survey Schedule (FSS), 429
items in tests, 9
questionnaires, 349
validation of self-report depression measure, 138–139
Self-statements, 434
Senate Subcommittee on Constitutional Rights, 619
Senior Apperception Technique, 416
Sensitive information, computers and, 194
Sentence completion tests, 417–418
Sequential processing, 293
Sequential-simultaneous distinction, 293
Sexism. See also Gender bias
in other countries, 583
Sexual harassment, 582
Sexual issues
computer-assisted interviews on, 438
Minnesota Multiphasic Personality Inventory (MMPI) and, 365–366
response measures, 436
SF-36, 503
Shakow, Hilgard, Kelly, Sanford, and Shaffer report, 21
Shift factor, 482
Short Hardiness Scale, 383

Short-term memory
assessment, 478
in Stanford-Binet Intelligence Scale, 246
Shrinkage, 83–84
Sickness Impact Profile (SIP), 503–504
Signal-detection procedures, 446–449
Simmons on Behalf of Simmons, v. Hooks, 598
Sincerity, 90–91
Situational interviews, 524–525
Sixteen Personality Factor Questionnaire (16PF), 20, 21, 369–371
primary source traits covered by, 370
Skills for interviewing, 223–224
Slopes, 67
of regression lines, 78
Slosson Intelligence Test, 547
Slow learner case study, 267–268
Smoking
cognitive functional analysis and, 434–435
Ecological Momentary Assessment (EMA) and, 501
operant conditioning and, 427
Social adjustment, 529
Social-desirability scale
and Edwards Personal Preference Schedule (EPPS), 374
for Jackson Personality Inventory (JPI), 375
for Personality research Form (PRF), 375
Social-ecology approach, 528–529
Social environment, changing, 568–571
Social facilitation, 206
Social-introversion (Si) scale, 358
Social issues, 621–624
access to testing services, 623–624
dehumanization issues, 621–622
usefulness of tests, 622
Social support measures, 501–502
Social Support Questionnaire (SSQ), 502
Society of Industrial and Organizational Psychology, 563
Socioeconomic considerations, 232, 557–558
Software. See Computers
Source traits, 369
Southern Mississippi TAT (SM-TAT), 416
SP-36, 504
Spearman-Brown formula, 109–111
length of test and reliability, 125
in SPSS program, 116
Spearman's g factor, 321–322
Spearman's rho, 91
Special education issues, 308–309
Special Educator 2003 Desk Book (Norlin), 279
Spelling achievement tests, 8
Spielberger's State-Trait Anxiety Inventory
computer-scoring errors, 442
computer tests, 439
Split-half reliability, 109–111
on Bayley Scales of Infant Development-Second Edition (BSID-II), 287
coefficient alpha (a) for estimating, 129
and Columbia Mental Maturity Scale-Third Edition (CMMS), 295
internal consistency and, 120
of Kuhlmann-Anderson Test, Eighth Edition (KAT), 321
for Money-for-Designs (MFD) Test, 305
for Peabody Picture Vocabulary Test-Third Edition (PPVT-III), 296
in SPSS program, 116
of Thematic Apperception Test (TAT), 415
for Wechsler Adult Intelligence Scale, Third Edition (WAIS-III), 269
for Woodcock-Johnson III, 302
Sports-related injuries, assessment of, 483
SPSS (Statistical Package for the Social Sciences) program, 115–117
SSI (Supplemental Security Income), 623, 623

Stability and reliability, 612–613
Standard conditions, 15
Standard deviation, 40–42
grading and, 49–50
for intelligence tests, 54
in McCall's T, 50–51
standard error of estimate, 82
standard error of measurement and, 103
symbols used for, 41–42
Z scores, 42–45
Standard error of estimate, 82
cross validation, 84
Standard error of measurement (SEM), 103
rubber yardsticks and, 120–123
usefulness of, 124
for Wechsler Adult Intelligence Scale, Third Edition (WAIS-III), 269
Standardization sample, 15
and Columbia Mental Maturity Scale-Third Edition (CMMS), 295
of Kuhlmann-Anderson Test, Eighth Edition (KAT), 321
for Porteus Maze Test (PMT), 298–299
for Woodcock-Johnson III, 302
Standardized regression coefficients (B's/betas), 88
Standardized slopes, 78
Standard normal deviation, 45–50
Standards, current trends in, 625–626
Standards for Educational and Psychological Testing, 134
Americans with Disabilities Act (ADA) and, 608
directions for administration, 192–193
on reliability, 612
on validity coefficients, 143–144
Stanford Achievement Test (SAT), 16, 317, 318–320
example of score report from, 319
Stanford-Binet Intelligence Scale, 15–16, 232, 303
age-related norms, 54–59
alternatives to, 279–282
basal level, 248
ceiling level, 248
changes in, 629
characteristics of 2003 edition, 247–249
cover page of, 245
Education for All Handicapped Children Act and, 586
median validity for 2003 edition, 250
model for modern scale, 244–246
modern Binet scale, 244–250
pros and cons for, 571
psychometric properties of 2003 edition, 249–250
race and ethnicity and, 539
race of examiner and, 185
reliability of, 249–250
reliability of 1937 scale, 242
routing tests in, 247–248
1916 scale, 239–240
1937 scale, 17, 241–242
1960 Stanford-Binet Revision and Deviation IQ (SB-LM), 243–244
1986 scale, 246
standard deviation in 2003 edition, 249
start point, 248
test bias in, 547, 590
Stanford-Binet Revision and Deviation IQ (SB-LM), 1960, 243–244
Stanford Early School Achievement Tests-Second Edition (SESAT), 318
Stanford Test for Academic Skills-Second Edition (TASK), 318
Stanford University, 458
Stanines, 52
Stanley Kaplan program, 140, 336

Start point in Stanford-Binet Intelligence Scale, 248
State anxiety, 494
State-Trait Anxiety Inventory (STAI), 494–495
Statistics
  for description, 26
  for distributions, 39
  for inferences, 26–27
  need for, 26–27
Stell v. Savannah-Chatham County Board of Education, 587
Stereotyping, 542
Stress
  assessment of, 493–502
  defined, 493
  Ecological Momentary Assessment (EMA), 500–501
  types of, 493–494
Strong-Campbell Interest Inventory (SCII), 455–457
  computer tests, 439
  personality clusters on, 536
  summary of, 457
Strong Vocational Interest Blank, 14, 454–455
Structured Clinical Interview for DSM-III-R Personality Disorders (SCID-II), 218
Structured Clinical Interview for DSM-IV (SCID), 188, 218
  example of, 219–221
  example of diagnosis with, 217–218
Structured Clinical Interview for Separation Anxiety Symptoms, 218
Structured interviews. *See* Interviews
Structured personality tests, 9, 18–19, 349–353
Stuttering, computer-based treatments for, 443
Subject variables, 195
Success and Taylor-Russell tables, 517–518
Suicide, computer diagnosis of, 440
Suinn Test Anxiety Behavior Scale, 496
Summarizing in interviews, 211–212
Summation sign, 40
Sum of squares, 67, 72
Surface traits, 369
Sustain factor, 482
Symbols
  meaning of, 40
  for populations, 42
  for samples, 42
  for standard deviation, 41–42
Symmetrical binomial probability distribution, 46
Systematic carryover, 107
System of Multicultural Pluralistic Assessment (SOMPA), 553, 556–560, 586
  sample profile, 559

Task-relevant responses, 496
Taylor Manifest Anxiety Scale, 494
Taylor-Russell tables, 516–521
T distribution, 73
  critical values of, 642–643
Teacher certification tests, 607
Teaching to the test, 181
Tell Me a Story Test (TEMAS), 416
Template-matching technique, 535–536
Tennessee Self-Concept Scale-Second Edition, 377
10-point scales, 164–166
Test administration, 10. *See also* Examiners
  anxiety reporting rates and, 186
  deception affecting, 198–199
  depression reporting rates and, 186
  expectancy effects, 189–190
  lawsuits involving, 605–607

reactivity, 196–197
  reinforcing responses and, 190–193
  text anxiety and, 195
Test anxiety, 195
  Liebert-Morris Emotionality and Worry Scales, 499
  measures of, 495–499
  Test Anxiety Questionnaire (TAQ), 496–498
  Test Anxiety Scale (TAS), 497–498
Test Anxiety Questionnaire (TAQ), 496–498
Test Anxiety Scale (TAS), 496–498
Test bias. *See also* Gender bias; Race and ethnicity
  alternatives to traditional tests, 553–560
  coaching and, 570
  content-related validity evidence, 545–548
  controversy of, 539–540
  criterion-related sources of, 548–552
  defense of testing, 544–552
  defined, 560
  differential item function (DIF) analysis, 546–548
  ethical considerations, 560–563
  interpretations of data, 563, 565
  Larry P. v. Wilson Riles and, 553, 574, 575, 589–591
  legal issues, 540–544
  in Miller Analogies Test (MAT), 337
  pros and cons for tests, 571
  regression plots for, 549–550
  selection bias, 618
  social environment, changing, 568–571
  stereotyping and, 542
  wealth of students and, 569–570
Testing industry, 140–141
Test linkages, 178–179
Test manuals, providing, 621
Test-preparation programs, 570
Test–retest reliability, 106, 107–108
  and Columbia Mental Maturity Scale-Third Edition (CMMS), 295
  for Internet testing, 442
  interval between tests, 108
  of Kuhlmann-Anderson Test, Eighth Edition (KAT), 321
  for Memory-for-Designs (MFD) Test, 305
  for Peabody Picture Vocabulary Test-Third Edition (PPVT-III), 296
  of Rorschach inkblot test, 404
  of Rosenberg Self-Esteem Scale, 382
  for 16PF, 369
  of Social Support Questionnaire (SSQ), 502
  of State-Trait Anxiety Inventory (STAI), 494
  of Thematic Apperception Test (TAT), 415
  for Wechsler Adult Intelligence Scale, Third Edition (WAIS-III), 269
Tests, defined, 6–7
Test score theory, 101–103
  domain sampling model and, 103–105
Tetrachoric correlations, 80
Thematic Apperception Test (TAT), 19–20, 21, 205, 410–415
  administration of, 411–414
  future of, 630
  interpretation of, 411–414
  psychometric properties of, 414–415
  reaction time in, 412
  scoring, 412–413
  stimuli in, 411–414
  stories, interpretation of, 413
Theoretical issues, 612–615
Theoretical strategy, 350–351, 371–377
Therapeutic interviews, 216
Third variable explanation, 84
Time sampling as error source, 119

TOEFL as computer-adapted test, 446
Torrance Tests of Creative Thinking (TTCT), 306–307
Tracking students, 58, 588
  with age-related norms, 54, 56–59
Trail Making Tests, 482
Trait anxiety, 494
Traits. *See* Personality traits
Translating tests, 188
Treasury Department, 543, 576
True dichotomous variables, 79
True-false examinations
  difficulty of items in, 168–169
  items for, 159
True Response Inconsistency Scale (TRIN), 363–364
True scores, 104
Trust, 90–91
Truth in testing laws, 583–585
T scores, 50–51, 355
  for Minnesota Multiphasic Personality Inventory (MMPI), 359–360
Two-point codes, MMPI and, 360
Two-tailed tests, 75, 641
Types of tests, 7–10

Unbiased estimate of reliability, 105
Understanding. *See also* Interviews
  for mental status examinations, 223
Unidimensional tests, 126
Uniform Guidelines on Employee Selection Procedures, 541, 576–581
Unique variance, 371
United States Constitution, 574
  Fourteenth Amendment, 576
United States Employment Service, 344
United States v. City of Buffalo, 607
University of California, 327–328
  affirmative action and, 600–601
  Boalt Hall diversity program, 601
  SAT (Scholastic Aptitude Test) and, 142, 569
University of Minnesota, 457, 458
Unqualified individualism, 560, 599
Unstructured interviews. *See* Interviews
US News & World Report, 458
Utility theory, 521–523

Validity, 10. *See also* Validity coefficients
  biased test items and, 547–548
  of California Verbal Learning Test (CVLT), 491, 492–493
  of Career Assessment Inventory (CIA), 467
  concurrent validity evidence, 137–139
  construct validity evidence, 147–154
  content-related validity evidence, 545–548
  content validity evidence, 135–137
  convergent evidence for, 150–151
  of criterion, 144
  of criterion-referenced tests, 153–154
  criterion validity evidence, 137–147
  defined, 134
  discriminant evidence, 152–153
  of Edwards Personal Preference Schedule (EPPS), 374
  EEOC guidelines and, 577
  face validity, 134–135
  incremental validity, 523–525
  of interviews, 224–226
  of Irrational Beliefs Test (IBT), 433
  in Kaufman Assessment Battery for Children, Second Edition (KABC-II), 293–294
  of pattern analysis, 268
  for Peabody Picture Vocabulary Test-Third Edition (PPVT-III), 296–297
  predictive validity evidence, 137
  reliability, relationship to, 154–155

of Rorschach inkblot test, 404
of SAT (Scholastic Aptitude Test), 327
of self-reports on depression, 138–139
self-report techniques and, 431
of Social Support Questionnaire (SSQ), 502
of SP-36, 504
of State-Trait Anxiety Inventory (STAI), 494
of System of Multicultural Pluralistic Assessment (SOMPA), 557
Taylor-Russell tables and, 517–521
of Thematic Apperception Test (TAT), 415
of translated tests, 188
variance and, 155
of Wechsler Adult Intelligence Scale, Third Edition (WAIS-III), 270
of Wechsler Intelligence Scale for Children, Fourth Edition (WISC-IV), 274
Validity coefficients, 140–147
criterion, reliability and validity of, 144
differential prediction and, 147
evaluating, 142–147
generalization and, 146–147
GRE and, 145–146
sample size, adequacy of, 144–145
Taylor-Russell tables and, 518
Validity scales
in MMPI, 358–359
in MMPI-2, 363–364
Value ratings, context and, 164–165
Variability
in intelligence quotient (IQ) scores, 243
standard deviation and, 41
Variable Response Inconsistency Scale (VRIN), 363
Variables. See also Multivariate analysis
coefficient of alienation, 83
defined, 39
dichotomous variables, 79–80
factor analysis, 89–92
linear combination of, 87
restricted range problem, 84–86
subject variables, 195
third variable explanation, 84
Variance, 41, 72
coefficient alpha (a) and, 113–114
covariance and, 73
factor analytic strategy and, 371
KR20 formula and, 112
person-situation interaction and, 534–535
positive personality research and, 386
reliability and, 106
shrinkage and, 83
sources of, 155
symbol for, 106
Verbal IQ (VIQ)
performance IQ compared, 265–266
in Wechsler Adult Intelligence Scale, Third Edition (WAIS-III), 261–262
for Wechsler Intelligence Scale for Children, Fourth Edition (WISC-IV), 271
Verbatim playback in interviews, 211–212
Veterans administration, 628
Virtual reality programs, 444–445

Visiographic tests, 303–306
Visual analogue scales, 166, 167
Vocational maturity, 470–471
Vocational Maturity Inventory (VMI), 470

Wards Cove Packing Company v. Antonio, 604–605
Washington University Sentence Completion Test (WUSCT), 418
Washington v. Davis, 602
Watson v. Fort Worth Bank and Trust, 604
Ways of Coping Scale, 499–500
Web-based assessment, 442–443
Wechsler Adult Intelligence Scale, Third Edition (WAIS-III), 253, 256
alternatives to, 279–282
arithmetic subtest, 259
block design subtest, 262–263
changes in, 629
comprehension subtest, 260
costs of, 623
digit span subtest, 259
digit symbol-coding subtest, 262
evaluation of, 270
full-scale IQs (FSIQs), 264
hypothetical case studies and, 266–268
index approach, 257–258
index scores in, 264–265
information subtest, 259–260
interpretive features of, 265–268
letter–number sequencing subtest, 260–261
matrix reasoning subtest, 263
object assembly subtest, 263–264
pattern analysis in, 266
performance IQs (PIQs) in, 264
performance subtests, 262–264
picture arrangement subtest, 263
picture completion subtest, 262
psychometric properties of, 268–270
race and ethnicity and, 539
raw scores, 261–262
reliability of, 269
scaled scores, 261–262
scales in, 256–265
similarities subtest, 259
subtests in, 257
symbol search subtest, 264
validity of, 270
verbal IQ and, 261–262
verbal-performance IQ comparisons, 265–266
verbal subtests, 258–261
vocabulary subtest, 258–259
Wechsler Adult Intelligence Scale–Revised (WAIS-R)
costs of, 623
test bias in, 547
training administrators of, 188
Wechsler-Bellvue Intelligence Scale (W-B), 17, 254–256
Wechsler Individual Achievement Test (WIAT-II), 272, 275
Wechsler Intelligence Scale for Children, Fourth Edition (WISC-IV), 184, 253–254, 257, 270–274, 303
alternatives to, 279–282

Education for All Handicapped Children Act and, 586
inner-city children, scoring for, 552
interpretation of, 273
item bias in, 272
race of examiners and, 187
raw scores, 272
reinforcing responses and, 191
reliability of, 273–274
scaled scores, 272
social-system phenomenon, 558
standardization sample for, 272, 273
test bias in, 547, 590
validity of, 274
Wechsler Memory Scale–Revised (WMS-R), 478, 491
Wechsler Preschool and Primary Scale of Intelligence, Third Edition (WPPSI-III), 254, 257, 271, 274–275, 303
Weight loss, self-monitoring procedures for, 435
Wernicke's area of brain, 480
What's Wrong with the Rorschach? (Wood, et al.), 402
Why Is My Child Having Trouble at School? (Novick & Arnold), 299
Wide Range Achievement Test-3 (WRAT-3), 307
Within-group norming, GATB using, 344
Women's Health Initiative Insomnia Rating Scale (WHIIRS), 152
Wonderlic Personnel Test, 526–527
Woodcock-Johnson III, 301–303
Woodworth Personal Data Sheet, 18, 21, 353
self-report techniques and, 431
Word association tests, 416–417
Working memory index
for Wechsler Adult Intelligence Scale, Third Edition (WAIS-III), 265
for Wechsler Intelligence Scale for Children, Fourth Edition (WISC-IV), 271
Work samples, 17, 196
Work satisfaction, 529
World Health Organization (WHO), 503
World War I, 16, 628
World War II, 17–18, 20–21, 628
Worry, test anxiety and, 498–499
Writing items, 158–168

Yale Tests of Child Development, 284–286

Z distribution, 73
Z scores, 42–45, 634
areas between mean and Z scores, 635
correlation and, 70
grades and, 49–50
in McCall's T, 50–51
mean of, 47
in multiple regression, 87–88
negative Z scores, 48
percentile ranks and, 47–49
for SAT (Scholastic Aptitude Test), 52
for standard normal deviation, 46–49
for stanines, 52